Lecture Notes in Computer Science 10322

Commenced Publication in 1973
Founding and Former Series Editors:
Gerhard Goos, Juris Hartmanis, and Jan van Leeuwen

Aggelos Kiayias (Ed.)

Financial Cryptography and Data Security

21st International Conference, FC 2017
Sliema, Malta, April 3–7, 2017
Revised Selected Papers

Springer

Editor
Aggelos Kiayias
University of Edinburgh
Edinburgh
UK

ISSN 0302-9743 ISSN 1611-3349 (electronic)
Lecture Notes in Computer Science
ISBN 978-3-319-70971-0 ISBN 978-3-319-70972-7 (eBook)
https://doi.org/10.1007/978-3-319-70972-7

Library of Congress Control Number: 2017959723

LNCS Sublibrary: SL4 – Security and Cryptology

Printed on acid-free paper

This Springer imprint is published by Springer Nature
The registered company is Springer International Publishing AG
The registered company address is: Gewerbestrasse 11, 6330 Cham, Switzerland

Preface

The 21st International Conference on Financial Cryptography and Data Security, FC 2017, was held during April 3–7, 2017, at the Palace Hotel in Malta.

We received 132 papers by the submission deadline for the conference which was November 14, 2016. Of these, seven were withdrawn and 35 were accepted – five as short papers and 30 as full papers – resulting in an acceptance rate of 26.5%. The present proceedings volume contains revised versions of all the papers presented at the conference.

The conference started with an invited talk by Silvio Micali, titled "ALGORAND: A New Public Ledger" and concluded with a panel titled "When Cash and Crypto Collide" with panelists Adam Back, Tiago Teles, and Tarah Wheeler, moderated by William Scannell.

The Program Committee consisted of 46 members spanning both industry and academia and covering all facets of financial cryptography. The review process took place over a period of two months and was double-blind. Each paper received at least three reviews; certain papers, including submissions by Program Committee members, received additional reviews. The Program Committee used the EasyChair system to organize the paper reviewing. The merits of each paper were discussed thoroughly and intensely in the online platform as we converged to the final decisions. In the end, a number of worthy papers still had to be rejected owing to the limited number of slots in the conference program. The Program Committee made a substantial effort in improving the quality of accepted papers in the post-notification stage: 11 of the papers were conditionally accepted; each one was assigned a shepherd from the Program Committee who guided the authors in the preparation of the conference version.

A number of grateful acknowledgments are due. First and foremost, I would like to thank the authors of all submissions for contributing their work for peer review by the Program Committee. Their support of FC 2017 was the most important factor for the success of the conference. Second, I would like to thank the members of the Program Committee for investing a significant amount of their time in the review and discussion of the submitted papers. In addition to the Program Committee, 89 external reviewers were invited to contribute to the review process and I also thank them for their efforts. In total, 416 reviews were submitted, 3.328 on average per submission, with 76% of the reviews prepared by the Program Committee and the remainder by the external reviewers.

The conference also featured a poster session. I am grateful to the presenters of the posters for submitting their work and presenting it at the conference. The abstracts of the posters are included in this proceedings volume.

The general chairs of the conference were Adam Back and Rafael Hirschfeld. I would like to especially thank Rafael for his continued and tireless efforts to make FC a success over the years. A special thanks also goes to the board of directors of the International Financial Cryptography Association for their support and guidance.

Finally, I would like to thank Joe Bonneau for handling a submission with which I had a conflict of interest (it was authored by two PhD students of mine) completely outside to the reviewing system. I also thank the board of directors for allowing this submission to be considered.

Finally, I would like to thank all our sponsors this year, whose generous support was crucial in making the conference a success. In particular our platinum sponsors Blockstream, IOHK, and Thales, our gold sponsor Rohde and Schwarz, our silver sponsor *Journal of Cybersecurity* and our sponsor in kind WorldPay. For student support, I specifically thank the Office of Naval Research.

August 2017   Aggelos Kiayias

Organization

Program Committee

Masa Abe	NTT Laboratories
Ross Anderson	Cambridge University, UK
Diego Aranha	Institute of Computing, University of Campinas, Brazil
Frederik Armknecht	Universität Mannheim, Germany
Giuseppe Ateniese	Stevens Institute of Technology, USA
Foteini Baldimtsi	George Mason University, USA
Alex Biryukov	University of Luxembourg, Luxembourg
Jeremiah Blocki	Purdue University, USA
Joe Bonneau	Stanford University, USA
Rainer Böhme	University of Innsbruck, Austria
Christian Cachin	IBM Research – Zurich, Switzerland
Jean Camp	Indiana University, USA
Srdjan Capkun	ETH Zurich, Switzerland
Jung Hee Cheon	Seoul National University, South Korea
Nicolas Christin	Carnegie Mellon University, USA
Jeremy Clark	Concordia University, Canada
Jean Paul Degabriele	RHUL
Dario Fiore	IMDEA Software Institute
Matt Green	Johns Hopkins, USA
Thomas Gross	University of Newcastle upon Tyne, UK
Jaap-Henk Hoepman	Radboud University Nijmegen, The Netherlands
Nicholas Hopper	University of Minnesota, USA
Kevin Huguenin	UNIL-HEC Lausanne, Switzerland
Stas Jarecki	University of California, Irvine, USA
Marc Joye	NXP Semiconductors
Stefan Katzenbeisser	TU Darmstadt, Germany
Aggelos Kiayias	University of Edinburgh, UK
Gäetan Leurent	Inria, France
Andrew Miller	University of Maryland, USA
Payman Mohassel	University of Calgary, Canada
Arvind Narayanan	Princeton, USA
Charalampos Papamanthou	University of Maryland, College Park, USA
Rafael Pass	Cornell University, USA
Bart Preneel	KU Leuven COSIC and iMinds, Belgium
Liz Quaglia	Royal Holloway, University of London, UK
Kazue Sako	NEC, Japan

Dominique Schröder	Friedrich-Alexander-Universität Erlangen-Nürnberg, Germany
Douglas Stebila	McMaster University, Canada
Qiang Tang	Cornell University, USA
Kami Vaniea	The University of Edinburgh, UK
Serge Vaudenay	EPFL, Switzerland
Eric Wustrow	University of Colorado Boulder, USA
Bingsheng Zhang	Lancaster University, UK
Zhenfeng Zhang	Chinese Academy of Sciences, China
Hong-Sheng Zhou	Virginia Commonwealth University, USA
Vasilis Zikas	ETH Zurich, Switzerland
Aviv Zohar	The Hebrew University of Jerusalem, Israel

Additional Reviewers

Abramova, Svetlana	Hils, Maximilian
Agrawal, Shashank	Hiromasa, Ryo
Alpar, Gergely	Humbert, Mathias
Balli, Fatih	Isshiki, Toshiyuki
Blazy, Olivier	Jeong, Jinhyuck
Bogos, Sonia	Karvelas, Nikolaos
Bos, Joppe	Khovratovich, Dmitry
Bünz, Benedikt	Kilinc, Handan
Carter, Henry	Kim, Duhyeong
Chaidos, Pyrros	Kim, Miran
Chepurnoy, Alex	Koide, Toshio
Cherubin, Giovanni	Kosba, Ahmed
Choi, Gwangbae	Kostiainen, Kari
Costello, Craig	Köhler, Olaf Markus
Davidson, Alex	Lacharité, Marie-Sarah
Duong, Tuyet	Laube, Stefan
Durak, F. Betül	Leontiadis, Iraklis
Eom, Jieun	Li, Shuai
Fan, Lei	Li, Xinyu
Fan, Xiong	Li, Zengpeng
Feher, Daniel	Liu, Jian
Frankel, Yair	Lu, Rongxing
Gervais, Arthur	Lu, Yun
Gordon, Dov	Luhn, Sebastian
Großschädl, Johann	Malavolta, Giulio
Han, Kyoohyung	Meyer, Maxime
Hansen, Torben	Mori, Kengo
Heilman, Ethan	Naehrig, Michael
Hhan, Minki	Ohkubo, Miyako

Olteanu, Alexandra-Mihaela
Pankova, Alisa
Peeters, Roel
Plût, Jérôme
Poettering, Bertram
Reinert, Manuel
Reuter, Christian A.
Riek, Markus
Ringers, Sietse
Ruffing, Tim
Schoettle, Pascal
Singelee, Dave
Son, Yongha
Teranishi, Isamu
Thyagarajan, Sri Aravinda Krishnan
Tikhomirov, Sergei

Tomida, Junichi
Udovenko, Aleksei
Vizár, Damian
Wang, Minqian
Wang, Qingju
Watson, Gaven
Weinstock, Avi
Woodage, Joanne
Yang, Kang
Young, Adam
Yu, Der-Yeuan
Zenner, Erik
Zhang, Lin
Zhang, Yupeng
Zindros, Dionysis

Contents

Privacy in Data Storage and Retrieval

Poster Papers

Privacy and Identity Management

An Efficient Self-blindable Attribute-Based Credential Scheme

Sietse Ringers$^{(\boxtimes)}$, Eric Verheul, and Jaap-Henk Hoepman

Radboud University, Nijmegen, The Netherlands
{sringers,e.verheul,jhh}@cs.ru.nl

Abstract. An attribute-based credential scheme allows a user, given a set of attributes, to prove ownership of these attributes to a verifier, voluntarily disclosing some of them while keeping the others secret. A number of such schemes exist, of which some additionally provide unlinkability: that is, when the same attributes were disclosed in two transactions, it is not possible to tell if one and the same or two different credentials were involved. Recently full-fledged implementations of such schemes on smart cards have emerged; however, these need to compromise the security level to achieve reasonable transaction speeds. In this paper we present a new unlinkable attribute-based credential scheme with a full security proof, using a known hardness assumption in the standard model. Defined on elliptic curves, the scheme involves bilinear pairings but only on the verifier's side, making it very efficient both in terms of speed and size on the user's side.

Keywords: Attribute-based credentials · Unlinkable · Self-blindable Elliptic curves · Bilinear pairings

1 Introduction

An attribute-based credential (ABC) scheme allows a user, given a set of attributes $k_1, \ldots, k_n$, to prove ownership of these attributes to a verifier, voluntarily disclosing some of them while keeping the others secret. A number of such credential schemes exist, of which some additionally provide *unlinkability*: that is, when reusing a credential the verifier cannot tell whether two transactions did or did not originate from the same user (assuming the same attributes with the same values were disclosed in both transactions). This allows for very flexible identity management schemes, that are simultaneously very secure and privacy-friendly.

Two well-known ABC schemes are Idemix [12,24] and U-Prove [10,29]. However, to date there is no provably secure scheme that is sufficiently efficient to allow truly secure implementations on smart cards, while also providing unlinkability of transactions. For example, since Idemix is based on the strong RSA-problem, one would want the keysize to be at least 2048 bits and preferably even 4096 bits; the IRMA project[1] has implemented Idemix on smart cards using 1024 bits. On the

---

[1] https://privacybydesign.foundation.

© International Financial Cryptography Association 2017
A. Kiayias (Ed.): FC 2017, LNCS 10322, pp. 3–20, 2017.
https://doi.org/10.1007/978-3-319-70972-7_1

other hand, U-Prove is more efficient but does not provide unlinkability; in addition, its security is not fully proven.

In this paper, we provide a new provably secure, efficient and unlinkable attribute-based credential scheme, that is based on the concept of *self-blindability* [33]: before showing the credential, it is randomly modified into a new one (containing the same attributes) that is still valid. This results in a showing protocol in which the verifier learns nothing at all about the credential besides the attributes that are disclosed (and the fact that the credential is valid). In fact, the showing protocol is a zero-knowledge proof of knowledge. The scheme does not rely on the random oracle model (although usage of this model can lead to a performance increase through the Fiat-Shamir heuristic [18]), and it uses elliptic curves and bilinear pairings, allowing the same security level as RSA-type groups at much smaller key sizes. Although computing a pairing is a much more expensive operation than performing exponentiations on an elliptic curve, all pairings occur on the verifier's side. In addition, the kinds of pairing that we use (Type 3) involves two distinct groups of which one is more expensive to do computations on. However, the user only needs to perform computations on the cheaper of the two. These two facts ensure that the amount of work that the user has to perform is minimal.

The unforgeability of our credential scheme will be implied by the LRSW assumption [13, 26, 27] introduced by Lysyanskaya et al., and used in many subsequent works (for example, [1, 11, 13, 35, 36]). Actually, for our purposes a weaker (in particular, non-interactive and thus falsifiable [28]) version of this assumption called the whLRSW assumption [36] will suffice. After having defined attribute-based credential schemes as well as unforgeability and unlinkability in the next section, we will discuss these assumptions in Sect. 3. In the same section we will introduce a signature scheme on the space of attributes, that will serve as the basis for our credential scheme. In Sect. 4 we turn to our credential scheme, defining issuing and showing protocols, and proving that these provide unlinkability and unforgeability for our scheme. This in turn implies the unforgeability of the signature scheme. In Sect. 5 we will discuss the performance of our scheme, by counting the amount of exponentiations that the user has to perform and by showing average runtimes of an implementation of our scheme. First, we briefly review and compare a number of other attribute-based credential schemes, in terms of features, efficiency and speed, and security.

1.1   Related Work

The Idemix credential scheme [12, 24] by Camenisch and Lysyanskaya is probably the most well-known unlinkable attribute-based credential scheme, relying on the difficulty of the strong RSA problem in the group of integers modulo an RSA modulus $n = pq$, of recommended size at least 2048 bits. Although this credential scheme has a lot of desirable properties (it is provably unlinkable and unforgeable, and the length of the signatures does not depend on the amount of attributes), the large size of the modulus means that, when implementing the user on smart cards, it is difficult to get acceptable running times for the protocols. For example, in [34] the Idemix showing protocol has been implemented with 4 attributes and n around 1024 bits (while n should really be at least 2048 bits); there the running time for the ShowCredential protocol ranged from 1 to 1.3 s, depending on the amount of disclosed attributes.

Another well-known credential scheme is U-Prove [10, 29] by Brands. Based on the difficulty of the discrete logarithm problem in a cyclic group, it can be implemented using elliptic curves, and additionally the showing protocol is much less complicated than that of Idemix, also resulting in more efficiency. However, in U-Prove two transactions executed with the same credential are always linkable, and the showing protocol is only honest-verifier zero-knowledge (i.e., there is no proof that dishonest verifiers cannot extract or learn information about the undisclosed attributes). Moreover, there is no unforgeability proof for U-Prove credentials, and it even seems that no such proof exists under standard intractability assumptions [4].

We also mention the "Anonymous Credentials Light" construction from [3], which can also be implemented on elliptic curves, but the credentials are not unlinkable; and [21], which runs in RSA groups like Idemix.

The credential scheme from [13], also by Camenisch and Lysyanskaya, is much closer to the scheme presented here: it is unlinkable, uses the (interactive) LRSW assumption, as well as elliptic curves and bilinear pairings (of the less efficient Type 1). In addition, how the signature scheme is used to obtain a credential scheme with a zero-knowledge disclosure protocol is similar to this work. The signature scheme that is used in [13] is, however, rather more complicated than ours: for example, when showing a credential the user has to compute an amount of pairings that is linear in the amount of disclosed attributes.

In [2] the BBS signature scheme [9] is modified into an unlinkable attribute-based credential scheme that, like the scheme from [13], requires the user to compute a number of (Type 2) pairings. However, the signatures in this scheme are short, and (like in Idemix but unlike our own scheme) its length does not depend on the amount of attributes.

More recently Fuchsbauer et al. [19] proposed a novel attribute-based credential scheme using structure-preserving signatures and a new commitment scheme, in which the undisclosed attributes are not hidden by knowledge proofs but rather by a partial opening to a commitment. As a result, like in Idemix the signature length does not depend on the amount of attributes. The scheme does, however, rely on a new variant of the strong Diffie-Hellman assumption that was newly introduced in the same paper.

In [5] an unlinkable scheme based on proofs of knowledge of Boneh-Boyen-like signature was proposed, achieving an efficient scheme with short signatures like Idemix and Fuchsbauer et al., and involving pairings only on the verifier's side.

In [23] we have examined a number of broken self-blindable credential schemes, and we posed a criterion which can indicate if a self-blindable credential scheme is linkable or forgeable. The scheme that we introduce in this paper is however not susceptible to this criterion, as it only holds for deterministic signature schemes while ours is non-deterministic.

Finally, a blindable version of U-Prove was recently proposed in [22]. Although an unlinkable credential scheme is aimed at, the paper contains no unlinkability proof. Moreover, we have found that the scheme is forgeable: if sufficiently many users collide then they can create new credentials containing any set of attributes of their choice, without any involvement of the issuer [32].

2   Attribute-Based Credential Schemes

First we fix some notation. We denote algorithms with calligraphic letters such as $\mathcal{A}$ and $\mathcal{B}$. By $y \leftarrow \mathcal{A}(x)$ we denote that y was obtained by running $\mathcal{A}$ on input x. If $\mathcal{A}$ is a deterministic algorithm then y is unique; if $\mathcal{A}$ is probabilistic then y is a random variable. We write $\mathcal{A}^O$ when algorithm $\mathcal{A}$ can make queries to oracle O. That is, A has an additional tape (read/write-once) on which it writes its queries; once it writes a special delimiter oracle O is invoked, and its answer appears on the query tape adjacent to the delimiter.

If $\mathcal{A}$ and $\mathcal{B}$ are interactive algorithms, we write $a \leftarrow \mathcal{A}(\cdot) \leftrightarrow \mathcal{B}(\cdot) \rightarrow b$ when $\mathcal{A}$ and $\mathcal{B}$ interact and afterwards output a and b, respectively. By $\mathcal{A} \overset{\blacksquare}{\rightarrow} \mathcal{B}$ we denote that algorithm $\mathcal{A}$ has black-box access to an interactive algorithm $\mathcal{B}$ – that is, $\mathcal{A}$ has oracle access to the next-message function $\mathcal{B}_{x,y,r}(m)$ which, on input x that is common to $\mathcal{A}$ and $\mathcal{B}$, auxiliary input y and random tape r, specifies the message that $\mathcal{B}$ would send after receiving messages m. Finally, $|x|$ denotes the length of x in bits. For example, if x is an integer then $|x| = \lceil \log_2 x \rceil$.

For zero-knowledge proofs we will use the Camenisch-Stadler notation [14]. For example, if K, P_1, P_2 are elements of some (multiplicatively written) group then

$$\mathrm{PK}\{(k_1, k_2) \colon K = P_1^{k_1} P_2^{k_2}\}$$

denotes a zero-knowledge proof of knowledge of the numbers k_1, k_2 that satisfy the relation $K = P_1^{k_1} P_2^{k_2}$. (Unlike Camenisch and Stadler, we do not use Greek letters for the unknowns; instead we will consistently write them on the right-hand side of the equation.) Such proofs are based on standard techniques and occur in many areas of cryptography. In our case the protocol from [15] could for example be used.

For the full definitions of bilinear pairings, zero-knowledge proofs, and the unforgeability game of signature schemes, we refer to the full version of this paper [30].

Definition 1. An attribute-based credential scheme consists of the following protocols. (We assume a single issuer, but this can easily be generalized to multiple issuers).

KeyGen$(1^\ell, n)$. This algorithm takes as input a security parameter ℓ and the number of attributes n that the credentials will contain, and outputs the issuer's private key s and public key σ, which must contain the number n, and a description of the attribute space M.

Issue. An interactive protocol between an issuer $\mathcal{I}$ and user $\mathcal{P}$ that results in a credential c:

$$\mathcal{I}(\sigma, s, (k_1, \ldots, k_n)) \leftrightarrow \mathcal{P}(\sigma, k_0, (k_1, \ldots, k_n)) \to c.$$

Here k_0 is the user's private key, that is to be chosen from the attribute space M by the user; the Issue protocol should prevent the issuer from learning it. We assume that before execution of this protocol, the issuer and user have reached agreement on the values of the attributes $k_1, \ldots, k_n$. The secret key and attributes $k_0, k_1, \ldots, k_n$ are contained in the credential c.

ShowCredential. An interactive protocol between a user $\mathcal{P}$ and verifier $\mathcal{V}$ which is such that, if c is a credential[2] issued using the Issue protocol over attributes $(k_1, \ldots, k_n)$ using private signing key s corresponding to public key σ, then for any disclosure set $\mathcal{D} \subset \{1, \ldots, n\}$ the user can make the verifier accept:

$$\mathcal{P}(\sigma, c, \mathcal{D}) \leftrightarrow \mathcal{V}(\sigma, \mathcal{D}, (k_i)_{i \in \mathcal{D}}) \to 1.$$

Thus, the user will have to notify the verifier in advance of the disclosure set $\mathcal{D}$ and disclosed attributes $(k_i)_{i \in \mathcal{D}}$.

We expect our attribute-based credential scheme to satisfy the following properties.

- *Unforgeability* (see Definition 14): no user can prove possession of attributes that were not issued to it by the issuer.
- *Multi-show unlinkability* (see Definition 15): If a verifier $\mathcal{V}$ participates in the ShowCredential protocol twice, in which the same credential was involved, it should be impossible for it to tell whether both executions originated from the same credential or from two different ones.
- *Issuer unlinkability*: If in a run of the ShowCredential protocol certain attributes were disclosed, then of all credentials that the issuer issued with those attributes, the issuer cannot tell which one was used.
- *Offline issuer*: The issuer is not involved in the verification of credentials.
- *Selective disclosure*: Any subset of attributes contained in a credential can be disclosed.

The unforgeability and both kinds of unlinkability of an attribute-based credential scheme are defined in terms of two games. We have included these games in Appendix A.

The notion of unlinkability captures the idea that it is impossible for the verifier to distinguish two credentials from each other in two executions of the ShowCredential protocol, as long as they disclosed the same attributes with the same values. We will achieve this for our scheme by proving that our ShowCredential protocol is *black-box zero-knowledge*, which essentially means that the verifier learns nothing at all besides the statement that the user proves. Since the verifier learns nothing that it can use to link transactions, unlinkability follows from this (see Theorem 12).

---

[2] As in Idemix and U-Prove, our ShowCredential protocol can easily be extended to simultaneously show multiple credentials that have the same secret key, and to proving that the hidden attributes satisfy arbitrary linear combinations [10].

3   Preliminaries

If $e\colon G_1 \times G_2 \to G_T$ is a bilinear pairing [20], we will always use uppercase letters for elements of G_1 or G_2, while lowercase letters (including Greek letters) will be numbers, i.e., elements of $\mathbb{Z}_p$. We will always use the index i for attributes, and in the unforgeability proofs below we will use the index j for multiple users or multiple credentials. For example, the number $k_{i,j}$ will refer to the i-th attribute of the credential of user j. If a, b are two natural numbers with $a < b$, then we will sometimes for brevity write $[a, b]$ for the set $\{a, \ldots, b\}$.

We write $\nu(\ell) < \mathrm{negl}(\ell)$ when the function $\nu\colon \mathbb{N} \to \mathbb{R}_{\geq 0}$ is negligible; that is, for any polynomial p there exists an ℓ' such that $\nu(\ell) < 1/p(\ell)$ for all $\ell > \ell'$.

3.1   Intractability Assumptions

The unforgeability of the credential and signature schemes defined in the paper will depend on the *whLRSW assumption* [36], which as we will show below, is implied by the LRSW assumption [26,27] introduced by Lysyanskaya, Rivest, Sahai, and Wolf. The latter assumption has been proven to hold in the generic group model [31], and has been used in a variety of schemes (for example, [1,11,13,35,36]). Although this assumption suffices to prove unforgeability of our scheme, it is stronger than we need. In particular, the LRSW assumption is an interactive assumption, in the sense that the adversary is given access to an oracle which it can use as it sees fit. We prefer to use the weaker whLRSW assumption, which is implied by the LRSW assumption but does not use such oracles. Consequentially, unlike the LRSW assumption itself, and like conventional hardness assumptions such as factoring and DDH, this assumption is falsifiable [28]. We describe both assumptions below; then we prove that the LRSW assumption implies the whLRSW assumption. After this we will exclusively use the latter assumption.

Let $e\colon G_1 \times G_2 \to G_T$ be a Type 3 pairing, where the order p of the three groups is ℓ bits, and let $a, z \in_R \mathbb{Z}_p^*$. If $(\kappa, K, S, T) \in \mathbb{Z}_p \times G_1^3$ is such that $K \neq 1$, $S = K^a$ and $T = K^{z + \kappa a z}$, then we call (κ, K, S, T) an *LRSW-instance*.

Definition 2 (LRSW assumption). Let e be as above, and let $O_{a,z}$ be an oracle that, when it gets $\kappa_j \in \mathbb{Z}_p$ as input on the j-th query, chooses a random $K_j \in_R G_1 \setminus \{1\}$ and outputs the LRSW-instance $(\kappa_j, K_j, K_j^a, K_j^{z + \kappa_j az})$. The *LRSW problem* is, when given $(p, e, G_1, G_2, G_T, Q, Q^a, Q^z)$ where $Q \in_R G_2 \setminus \{1\}$, along with oracle access to $O_{a,z}$, to output a new LRSW-instance $(\kappa, K, K^a, K^{z + \kappa az})$ where κ has never been queried to $O_{a,z}$. The *LRSW assumption* is that no probabilistic polynomial-time algorithm can solve the LRSW problem with non-negligible probability in ℓ. That is, for every probabilistic polynomial-time algorithm $\mathcal{A}$ we have

$$\Pr\Big[a, z \in_R \mathbb{Z}_p^*;\ Q \in_R G_2 \setminus \{1\};$$
$$\sigma \leftarrow (p, e, G_1, G_2, G_T, Q, Q^a, Q^z);\quad (\kappa, K, S, T) \leftarrow \mathcal{A}^{O_{a,z}}(\sigma):$$
$$K \in G_1 \setminus \{1\} \ \wedge\ \kappa \notin L \ \wedge\ S = K^a \ \wedge\ T = K^{z + \kappa az} \Big] < \mathrm{negl}(\ell),$$

where L is the list of oracle queries sent to $O_{a,z}$, and where the probability is over the choice of a, z, Q, and the randomness used by $\mathcal{A}$ and the oracle $O_{a,z}$.

Definition 3 (q-whLRSW assumption[36]). Let e be as above, and let $\{(\kappa_j, K_j, \ K_j^a, K_j^{z+\kappa_j az})\}_{j=1,\ldots,q}$ be a list of q LRSW-instances, where the κ_j and K_j are randomly distributed in $\mathbb{Z}_p$ and $G_1 \setminus \{1\}$, respectively. The *q-whLRSW problem* (for q-wholesale LRSW [36]) is, when given this list along with $(p, e, G_1, \ G_2, G_T, Q, Q^a, Q^z)$, to output a new LRSW-instance $(\kappa, K, K^a, K^{z+\kappa az})$ where $\kappa \notin \{\kappa_1, \ldots, \kappa_q\}$. The *$q$-whLRSW assumption* is that no probabilistic polynomial-time algorithm can solve the q-whLRSW problem with non-negligible probability in ℓ. That is, for every probabilistic polynomial-time algorithm $\mathcal{A}$ we have

$$\Pr\Big[a, z \in_R \mathbb{Z}_p^*; \ \kappa_1, \ldots, \kappa_q \in_R \mathbb{Z}_p; \ K_1, \ldots, K_q \in_R G_1 \setminus \{1\};$$
$$Q \in_R G_2 \setminus \{1\}; \ \sigma \leftarrow (p, e, G_1, G_2, G_T, Q, Q^a, Q^z);$$
$$(\kappa, K, S, T) \leftarrow \mathcal{A}(\sigma, \{\kappa_j, K_j, K_j^a, K_j^{z+\kappa_j az}\}_{j \in [1,q]}) :$$
$$K \in G_1 \setminus \{1\} \ \wedge \ \kappa \notin \{\kappa_1, \ldots, \kappa_q\}$$
$$\wedge \ S = K^a \ \wedge \ T = K^{z+\kappa az}\Big] < \mathrm{negl}(\ell), \tag{1}$$

where the probability is over the choice of $a, z, \kappa_1, \ldots, \kappa_q, K_1, \ldots, K_q, Q$, and the randomness used by $\mathcal{A}$.

Finally we define an unparameterized version of the assumption above by allowing q to be polynomial in ℓ, in the following standard way (e.g., [8]). Intuitively, the reason that this unparameterized assumption is implied by the LRSW assumption is simple: if there is no adversary that can create LRSW-instances when it can (using the oracle) control the κ's of the LRSW-instances that it gets as input, then an adversary that can create them *without* having control over the κ's also cannot exist.

Definition 4. Let e, p and $\ell = |p|$ be as above. The *whLRSW assumption* states that for all polynomials $q \colon \mathbb{N} \to \mathbb{N}$, the $q(\ell)$-whLRSW assumption holds.

Proposition 5. *The LRSW assumption implies the whLRSW assumption.*

We prove this in the full version of this paper [30]. Thus if we prove that our scheme is safe under the whLRSW assumption, then it is also safe under the LRSW assumption. Additionally, we have found that the whLRSW assumption can be proven by taking an extension [7] of the Known Exponent Assumption [16], so that unforgeability of our scheme can also be proven by using this assumption. However, because of space restrictions this proof could not be included here.

3.2 A Signature Scheme on the Space of Attributes

In this section we introduce a signature scheme on the space of attributes. This signature scheme will be the basis for our credential scheme, in the following sense: the Issue protocol that we present in Sect. 4 will enable issuing such signatures over a set of attributes to users, while the ShowCredential protocol allows the user to prove that it has a signature over any subset of its signed attributes.

Definition 6 (Signature scheme on attribute space). The signature scheme is as follows.

KeyGen$(1^\ell, n)$. The issuer generates a Type 3 pairing $e\colon G_1 \times G_2 \to G_T$, such that $|p| = \ell$ where p is the prime order of the three groups. Next it takes a generator $Q \in_R G_2$, and numbers $a, a_0, \ldots, a_n, z \in_R \mathbb{Z}_p^*$ and sets $A = Q^a, A_0 = Q^{a_0}, \ldots, A_n = Q^{a_n}$, and $Z = Q^z$. The public key is the tuple $\sigma = (p, e, Q, A, A_0, \ldots, A_n, Z)$ and the private key is the tuple $(a, a_0, \ldots, a_n, z)$.

Sign$(k_0, \ldots, k_n)$. The issuer chooses $\kappa \in_R \mathbb{Z}_p^*$ and $K \in_R G_1$, and sets $S = K^a, S_0 = K^{a_0}, \ldots, S_n = K^{a_n}$, and $T = (K S^\kappa \prod_{i=0}^n S_i^{k_i})^z$. The signature is $(\kappa, K, S, S_0, \ldots, S_n, T)$.

Verify$((k_0, \ldots, k_n), (\kappa, K, S, S_0, \ldots, S_n, T), \sigma)$. The signature is checked by setting $C = K S^\kappa \prod_{i=0}^n S_i^{k_i}$; verifying that $K, C \neq 1$; generating random numbers $r, r_0, \ldots, r_n \in_R \mathbb{Z}_p^*$ and verifying[3]

$$e(S^r S_0^{r_0} \cdots S_n^{r_n}, Q) \overset{?}{=} e(K, A^r A_0^{r_0} \cdots A_n^{r_n}), \quad e(T, Q) \overset{?}{=} e(C, Z). \tag{2}$$

The numbers $k_n \in \mathbb{Z}_p$ are the attributes. Although p may vary each time the KeyGen$(1^\ell, n)$ algorithm is invoked on a fixed security parameter ℓ, the attribute space $\mathbb{Z}_p$ will always contain $\{0, \ldots, 2^{\ell-1}\}$. In our credential scheme in Sect. 4, the zeroth attribute k_0 will serve as the user's secret key, but at this point it does not yet have a special role.

Notice that contrary to Idemix and the BBS+ scheme from [2], but like the scheme from [13], the length of a signature is not constant in the amount n of attributes, but $O(n)$.

Although the element $C = K S^\kappa \prod_{i=0}^n S_i^{k_i}$ is, strictly speaking, not part of the signature and therefore also not part of the credential (since it may be calculated from κ, the attributes $(k_0, \ldots, k_n)$ and the elements $(K, S, S_0, \ldots, S_n)$), we will often think of it as if it is. Finally, we call a message-signature pair, i.e., a tuple of the form $((k_0, \ldots, k_n), (\kappa, K, S, S_0, \ldots, S_n, T))$ where $(\kappa, K, S, S_0, \ldots, S_n, T)$ is a valid signature over $(k_0, \ldots, k_n)$, a *credential*.

Notice that if $(k_0, \ldots, k_n), (\kappa, K, S, S_0, \ldots, S_n, T)$ is a valid credential, then for any $\alpha \in \mathbb{Z}_p^*$,

$$(k_0, \ldots, k_n), (\kappa, K^\alpha, S^\alpha, S_0^\alpha, \ldots, S_n^\alpha, T^\alpha) \tag{3}$$

---

[3] Combining the verification of the elements S, S_i in this fashion achieves with overwhelming probability the same as separately verifying $e(S, Q) \overset{?}{=} e(K, A)$ and $e(S_i, Q) \overset{?}{=} e(K, A_i)$ [17], reducing the amount of necessary pairings from $n + 3$ to 2. In implementations it will probably suffice to choose these numers from $\{1, \ldots, 2^{\ell_r}\}$ (with, say, $\ell_r = 80$), resulting in a probability of 2^{ℓ_r} that the S, S_i are the correct powers a, a_i of K. We are very grateful to I. Goldberg for suggesting this improvement.

is another valid credential having the same attributes. That is, in the terminology of Verheul [33] our credentials are *self-blindable*. This self-blindability is what makes this signature scheme suitable for the purpose of creating an unlinkable ShowCredential protocol.

The number κ will play a critical role in the unforgeability proof of our signature and credential schemes (Theorem 10).[4]

Theorem 7. *Our credentials are existentially unforgeable under adaptively chosen message attacks, under the whLRSW assumption.*

This is proven in the full version of this paper [30].

4   The Credential Scheme

In this section we present our credential scheme. The strategy is as follows: having defined an unforgeable signature scheme on the set of attributes $\mathbb{Z}_p^n$ (Definition 6), we provide an issuing protocol, in which the issuer grants a credential to a user, and a showing protocol, which allows a user to give a zero-knowledge proof to a verifier that he possesses a credential, revealing some of the attributes contained in the credential while keeping the others secret. The Issue protocol is shown in Fig. 1,

---

Common information: Attributes $k_1, \ldots, k_n$, issuer's public key $\sigma = (p, e, Q, A, A_0, \ldots, A_n, Z)$

User	**Issuer**
knows secret key k_0	knows $a, a_0, \ldots, a_n, z$
	choose $\bar{K} \in_R G_1$
	$\longleftarrow$ send $\bar{S} = \bar{K}^a, \bar{S}_0 = \bar{K}^{a_0}$
choose $\alpha, \kappa' \in_R \mathbb{Z}_p^*$	
set $S = \bar{S}^\alpha, S_0 = \bar{S}_0^\alpha$	
send $S, S_0, R = S^{\kappa'} S_0^{k_0}$ $\longrightarrow$	
$\mathrm{PK}\{(\kappa', k_0) : R = S^{\kappa'} S_0^{k_0}\}$ $\longleftrightarrow$	
	set $K = S^{1/a}$
	verify $S \neq \bar{S}, K = S_0^{1/a_0}$
	choose $\kappa'' \in_R \mathbb{Z}_p$
	set $S_i = K^{a_i} \ \forall i \in [1, n]$
	set $T = \left(K S^{\kappa''} R \prod_{i=1}^n S_i^{k_i} \right)^z$
	$\longleftarrow$ send $\kappa'', K, S_1, \ldots, S_n, T$
set $\kappa = \kappa' + \kappa''$	
return $(k_0, \ldots, k_n), (\kappa, K, S, S_0, \ldots, S_n, T)$	

Fig. 1. The Issue protocol.

---

[4] We could have eased the notation somewhat by denoting the number κ as an extra attribute k_{n+1}, but because it plays a rather different role than the other attributes (it is part of the signature), we believe this would create more confusion than ease.

Common information: Issuer's public key $\sigma = (p, e, Q, A, A_0, \ldots, A_n, Z)$; disclosure set $\mathcal{D}$, undisclosed set $\mathcal{C} = \{1, \ldots, n\} \setminus \mathcal{D}$; disclosed attributes $(k_i)_{i \in \mathcal{D}}$

User	**Verifier**
knows $K, S, S_0, \ldots, S_n, \kappa, (k_i)_{i \in \mathcal{C}}, C, T$	

choose $\alpha, \beta \in_R \mathbb{Z}_p^*$
set $\bar{K} = K^\alpha$, $\bar{S} = S^\alpha$, $\bar{S}_i = S_i^\alpha \; \forall i \in [0, n]$
set $\tilde{C} = C^{-\alpha/\beta}$, $\tilde{T} = T^{-\alpha/\beta}$
send $\bar{K}, \bar{S}, (\bar{S}_i)_{i=0,\ldots,n}, \tilde{C}, \tilde{T} \longrightarrow$

set $D = \bar{K}^{-1} \prod_{i \in \mathcal{D}} \bar{S}_i^{-k_i}$ set $D = \bar{K}^{-1} \prod_{i \in \mathcal{D}} \bar{S}_i^{-k_i}$

$\mathrm{PK}\{(\beta, \kappa, k_0, k_i)_{i \in \mathcal{C}} : D = \tilde{C}^\beta \bar{S}^\kappa \bar{S}_0^{k_0} \prod_{i \in \mathcal{C}} \bar{S}_i^{k_i}\} \longleftrightarrow$

choose $r, r_0, \ldots, r_n \in_R \mathbb{Z}_p^*$
verify $e(\tilde{C}, Z) \overset{?}{=} e(\tilde{T}, Q)$
and $e(\bar{S}^r \bar{S}_0^{r_0} \cdots \bar{S}_n^{r_n}, Q)$
$\overset{?}{=} e(\bar{K}, A^r A_0^{r_0} \cdots A_n^{r_n})$

Fig. 2. The ShowCredential protocol. We assume that the user has the element $C = KS^\kappa S_0^{k_0} \cdots S_n^{k_n}$ stored so that it does not need to compute it every time the protocol is run (see Sect. 5 for more such optimizations).

and the ShowCredential protocol is shown in Fig. 2. Here and in the remainder of the paper, we will write $\mathcal{D} \subset \{1, \ldots, n\}$ for the index set of the disclosed attributes, and

$$\mathcal{C} = \{1, \ldots, n\} \setminus \mathcal{D}$$

for the index set of the undisclosed attributes. We do not consider the index 0 of the secret key k_0 to be part of this set, as it is always kept secret.

The Issue protocol is such that both parties contribute to κ and K with neither party being able to choose the outcome in advance (unlike the signing algorithm of the signature scheme from the previous section, where the signer chooses κ and K on its own). This ensures that these elements are randomly distributed even if one of the parties is dishonest. Additionally, the issuer is prevented from learning the values of κ and the secret key k_0.

As noted earlier, we assume that the user and issuer have agreed on the attributes $k_1, \ldots, k_n$ to be contained in the credential before executing this protocol. Similarly, we assume that the user sends the disclosure set $\mathcal{D}$ and disclosed attributes $(k_i)_{i \in \mathcal{D}}$ to the verifier prior to executing the ShowCredential protocol.

If the user wants to be sure at the end of the Issue protocol that the new credential is valid, he will need to compute the pairings from Eq. (2). Even if the user is implemented on resource-constrained devices such as smart cards this is not necessarily a problem; generally in ABC's the issue protocol is performed much less often than the disclosure protocol so that longer running times may be more acceptable. Alternatively, the user could perform the ShowCredential protocol in which it discloses none of its attributes with the issuer, or perhaps another party; if the credential was invalid then this will fail.

The ShowCredential credential can be seen to consist of two separate phases: first, the user blinds the elements K, S, S_i, C and T with the number α as in Eq. (3), resulting in a new signature over his attributes. Second, the user uses the blinded elements to prove possession of this fresh signature over his attributes. The elements $\bar{S}$ and $\bar{S}_i$ can be used for this proof of knowledge only if they have all been correctly blinded using the same number α, which the verifier checks using the pairings at the end of the protocol. Thus, since α is only used to create a new blinded signature in advance of the proof of knowledge of this new signature, the value of α need not be known to the verifier, which is why the user does not need to prove knowledge of it. The same holds for the number α that is used during issuance; as long as it is correctly applied (which the issuer here checks by directly using his secret key instead of having to compute pairings), the user can prove knowledge of κ' and his secret key k_0 without the issuer needing to know α.

Mathematically, we can formalize what the ShowCredential protocol should do as follows. The common knowledge of the user and verifier when running the ShowCredential protocol consists of elements of the following formal language:

$$L = \left\{ \left(\sigma, \mathcal{D}, (k_i)_{i \in \mathcal{D}}\right) \mid \mathcal{D} \subset \{1, \ldots, n\},\ k_i \in \mathbb{Z}_p\, \forall i \in \mathcal{D} \right\} \tag{4}$$

where σ ranges over the set of public keys of the credential scheme, and where n is the amount of attributes of σ. In addition, let the relation R be such that $R(x, w) = 1$ only if $x = (\sigma, \mathcal{D}, (k_i)_{i \in \mathcal{D}}) \in L$, and $w = ((k_0', \ldots, k_n'), s)$ is a valid credential with respect to σ, with $k_i' = k_i$ for $i \in \mathcal{D}$ (i.e., the disclosed attributes $(k_i)_{i \in \mathcal{D}}$ are contained in the credential w.) Thus the equation $R(x, w) = 1$ holds only if w is a valid credential having attributes $(k_i)_{i \in \mathcal{D}}$.

Theorem 8. *The showing protocol is complete with respect to the language L: if a user has a valid credential then it can make the verifier accept.*

Proof. If the user follows the ShowCredential protocol, then $e(\bar{K}, A) = e(K^\alpha, Q^a) = e(K^{\alpha a}, Q) = e(S^\alpha, Q) = e(\bar{S}, Q)$, so the first verification that the verifier does will pass. An almost identical calculation shows that the second and third verifications pass as well. As to the proof of knowledge, setting $\bar{C} = C^\alpha$ we have

$$\tilde{C}^\beta \bar{S}^\kappa \bar{S}_0^{k_0} \prod_{i \in \mathcal{C}} \bar{S}_i^{k_i} = \bar{C}^{-1} \bar{S}^\kappa \bar{S}_0^{k_0} \prod_{i \in \mathcal{C}} \bar{S}_i^{k_i} = \bar{K}^{-1} \prod_{i \in \mathcal{D}} \bar{S}_i^{-k_i} = D, \tag{5}$$

so the user can perform this proof without problem. $\square$

4.1 Unforgeability and Unlinkability

The proofs of the following theorems may be found in the full version of this paper [30].

Lemma 9. *With respect to the language L defined in (4), the ShowCredential protocol is black-box extractable.*

In the proofs of the unforgeability and unlinkability theorems, we will need a tuple $(\hat{K}, \hat{S}, \hat{S}_0, \ldots, \hat{S}_n, \hat{C}, \hat{T}) \in G_1^{n+5}$ such that $\hat{S} = \hat{K}^a$ and $\hat{S}_i = \hat{K}^{a_i}$ for all i, as well as $\hat{T} = \hat{C}^z$. For that reason we will henceforth assume that such a tuple is included in the issuer's public key. Note that one can view these elements as an extra credential of which the numbers $(\kappa, k_0, \ldots, k_n)$ are not known. Therefore the credential scheme remains unforgeable (the adversary can in fact already easily obtain such a tuple by performing an Issue query in the unforgeability game).[5]

Theorem 10. *Our credential scheme is unforgeable under the whLRSW assumption.*

Theorem 11. *The ShowCredential protocol is a black-box zero-knowledge proof of knowledge with respect to the language L.*

Theorem 12. *Let (KeyGen, Issue, ShowCredential) be an attribute-based credential scheme whose ShowCredential protocol is black-box zero-knowledge. Then the scheme is unlinkable.*

Theorem 13. *Our credential scheme is unlinkable.*

5   Performance

5.1   Exponentiation Count

Table 1 compares the amount of exponentiations in our scheme to those of [13], U-Prove and Idemix. However, note that exponentiations in RSA-like groups, on which Idemix depends, are significantly more expensive than exponentiations in elliptic curves. The scheme from [19] is slightly cheaper than ours for the prover, but relies on a newly introduced hardness assumption. Also, the U-Prove showing protocol offers no unlinkability. As to the scheme from [13], Camenisch and Lysyanskaya did not include a showing protocol that allows attributes to be disclosed (that is, it is assumed that all attributes are kept secret), but it is not very difficult to keep track of how much less the user has to do if he voluntarily discloses some attributes. We see that the amount of exponentiations that the user has to perform in the ShowCredential protocol of [13] is roughly 1.5 times as large as in our scheme. Since, additionally, computing pairings is significantly more expensive than exponentiating, we expect our credential scheme to be at least twice as efficient.

---

[5] Credential owners already have such a tuple; verifiers can obtain one simply by executing the ShowCredential protocol; and issuers can of course create such tuples by themselves. Therefore in practice, each party participating in the scheme will probably already have such a tuple, so that including it in the public key may not be necessary in implementations.

Table 1. Exponentiation and pairing count for the user of the ShowCredential protocol of several attribute-based credential schemes. The columns G_{EC}, G_T and G_{RSA} show the amount of exponentiations in elliptic curves, the target group of a bilinear pairing, and RSA groups respectively, while the column labeled e counts the amount of pairings the user has to compute. The number n denotes the amount of attributes, excluding the secret key, and the function $pk(n)$ denotes the amount of exponentiations necessary in order to perform a zero-knowledge proof of knowledge of n numbers (in the case of the Fiat-Shamir heuristic applied to the Schnorr Σ-protocol, which Idemix also uses, we have $pk(n) = n$).

	G_{EC}	G_T	e	G_{RSA}	Unlinkable
Our scheme	$n + pk(|\mathcal{C}| + 3) + 6$	0	0	0	Yes
[13]	$2n + 3$	$pk(|\mathcal{C}| + 2)$	$n + 3$	0	Yes
[19]	$|\mathcal{C}| + pk(2) + 5$	0	0	0	Yes
[5]	$pk(|\mathcal{C}| + 7) + 5$	0	0	0	Yes
Idemix	0	0	0	$|\mathcal{C}| + 3$	Yes
U-Prove	$|\mathcal{C}| + 1$	0	0	0	No

5.2 Implementation

In order to further examine the efficiency of our credential scheme we have written a preliminary implementation, using the high-speed 254-bit BN-curve and pairing implementation from [6]. The latter is written in C++ and assembly but also offers a Java API, and it uses the GMP library from the GNU project[6] for large integer arithmetic. Table 2 shows the running times of our implementation along with those from the Idemix implementation from the IRMA project.[7] We have tried to make the comparison as honest as possible by writing our implementation in Java, like the IRMA Idemix implementation, which we have modified to also use the GMP library for its large integer arithmetic. In addition, like IRMA we have used the Fiat-Shamir heuristic. However, the comparison can still only go so far, because the elliptic curve group that [6] offers is heavily optimized for fast computations, from which our scheme profits because it allows multiple issuers to use the same group. Such optimizations are not possible in Idemix because each Idemix public key necessarily involves its own group. Moreover, the IRMA Idemix implementation is 1024-bits, which according to [25] corresponds to a 144 bit curve (see also www.keylength.com), so that the two implementations do not offer the same level of security.

For these reasons we will go no further than draw qualitative conclusions from the data. Nevertheless, both remarks actually demonstrate the efficiency of our scheme: the first means that our scheme can be optimized further than Idemix could, and Table 2 shows that even though our implementation offers a much higher level of security, it is still significantly faster than the IRMA Idemix

---

[6] See gmplib.org.

[7] See privacybydesign.foundation and github.com/credentials.

Table 2. A comparison of the running times of various actions in the implementation of our credential scheme and the IRMA Idemix implementation, both of them using the Fiat-Shamir heuristic. The columns labeled "computing proof" and "verifying proof" show how long it takes to compute and to verify a disclosure proof, respectively, while the column labeled "verifying credential" shows how long it takes to verify the signature of a credential. $\ell_r = 80$ was used (see the Footnote 3). The left column shows the total number of attributes and, if applicable, the amount of disclosed attributes (this does not apply to the "verifying credential" column). The attributes were randomly chosen 253-bit integers, the same across all tests, and the computations were performed on a dual-core 2.7 GHz Intel Core i5. All running times are in milliseconds, and were obtained by computing the average running time of 1000 iterations.

# attributes total (discl.)	Computing proof		Verifying proof		Verifying credential	
	This work	Idemix	This work	Idemix	This work	Idemix
6 (1)	2.6	11.7	4.0	11.2	3.2	6.5
7 (1)	2.6	12.6	4.4	12.2	3.3	6.9
8 (1)	2.9	13.4	4.4	13.2	3.3	7.4
9 (1)	3.1	14.3	4.6	14.0	3.3	7.7
10 (1)	3.4	15.2	4.7	14.9	3.4	8.3
11 (1)	3.6	16.5	4.9	15.8	3.6	8.7
12 (1)	3.9	17.1	5.1	16.9	3.7	8.9
6 (5)	2.1	7.6	3.4	9.2		
7 (6)	2.1	7.5	3.6	9.7		
8 (7)	2.2	7.5	3.6	10.1		
9 (8)	2.2	7.4	3.7	10.7		
10 (9)	2.3	7.4	4.1	10.9		
11 (10)	2.5	7.5	4.2	11.4		
12 (11)	2.6	7.5	4.5	12.0		

implementation. We believe therefore that the conclusion that our scheme is or can be more efficient than Idemix – at least for the user in the ShowCredential protocol – is justified.

6   Conclusion

In this paper we have defined a new self-blindable attribute-based credential scheme, and given a full security proof by showing that it is unforgeable and unlinkable. Our scheme is based on a standard hardness assumption and does not need the random oracle model. Based on the fact that it uses elliptic curves and bilinear pairings (but the latter only on the verifier's side), on a comparison of exponentiation counts, and on a comparison of run times with the IRMA Idemix implementation, we have shown it to be more efficient than comparable schemes such as Idemix and the scheme from [13], achieving the same security goals at less cost.

Acknowledgments. We are very grateful to the anonymous referees for their helpful and constructive feedback, and to I. Goldberg for suggesting the method from [17] for reducing the verification pairing count.

A   Unforgeability and Unlinkability Games

Unforgeability of a credential scheme is defined using the following game (resembling the signature scheme unforgeability game).

Definition 14 (unforgeability game). The unforgeability game of an attribute-based credential scheme between a challenger and an adversary $\mathcal{A}$ is defined as follows.

Setup. For a given security parameter ℓ, the adversary decides on the number of attributes $n \geq 1$ that each credential will have, and sends n to the challenger. The challenger then runs the $\mathsf{KeyGen}(1^\ell, n)$ algorithm from the credential scheme and sends the resulting public key to the adversary.

Queries. The adversary $\mathcal{A}$ can make the following queries to the challenger.

Issue$(k_{1,j}, \ldots, k_{n,j})$. The challenger and adversary engage in the Issue protocol, with the adversary acting as the user and the challenger acting as the issuer, over the attributes $(k_{1,j}, \ldots, k_{n,j})$. It may choose these adaptively.

ShowCredential$(\mathcal{D}, k_1, \ldots, k_n)$. The challenger creates a credential with the specified attributes $k_1, \ldots, k_n$, and engages in the ShowCredential protocol with the adversary, acting as the user and taking $\mathcal{D}$ as disclosure set, while the adversary acts as the verifier.

Challenge. The challenger, now acting as the verifier, and the adversary, acting as the user, engage in the ShowCredential protocol. The adversary chooses a disclosure set $\mathcal{D}$, and if it manages to make the verifier accept then it wins if one of the following holds:

- If the adversary made no Issue queries then it wins regardless of the disclosure set (even if $\mathcal{D} = \emptyset$);
- Otherwise $\mathcal{D}$ must be nonempty, and if $(k_i)_{i \in \mathcal{D}}$ are the disclosed attributes, then there must be no j such that $k_i = k_{i,j}$ for all $i \in \mathcal{D}$ (i.e., there is no single credential issued in an Issue query containing all of the disclosed attributes $(k_i)_{i \in \mathcal{D}}$).

We say that the credential scheme is *unforgeable* if no probabilistic polynomial-time algorithm can win this game with non-negligible probability in the security parameter ℓ.

Next we turn to the unlinkability game.

Definition 15 (unlinkability game). The unlinkability game of an attribute-based credential scheme between a challenger and an adversary $\mathcal{A}$ is defined as follows.

Setup. For a given security parameter ℓ, the adversary decides on the number of attributes $n \geq 1$ that each credential will have, and sends n to the challenger. The adversary then runs the $\mathsf{KeyGen}(1^\ell, n)$ algorithm from the credential scheme and sends the resulting public key to the challenger.

Queries. The adversary $\mathcal{A}$ can make the following queries to the challenger.

$\mathsf{Issue}(k_{1,j}, \ldots, k_{n,j})$. The adversary chooses a set of attributes $(k_{1,j}, \ldots, k_{n,j})$, and sends these to the challenger. Then, acting as the issuer, the adversary engages in the Issue protocol with the challenger, issuing a credential j to the challenger having attributes $(k_{1,j}, \ldots, k_{n,j})$.

$\mathsf{ShowCredential}(j, \mathcal{D})$. The adversary and challenger engage in the showing protocol on credential j, the challenger acting as the user and the adversary as the verifier. Each time the adversary may choose the disclosure set $\mathcal{D}$.

$\mathsf{Corrupt}(j)$. The challenger sends the entire internal state, including the secret key k_0, of credential j to the adversary.

Challenge. The adversary chooses two uncorrupted credentials j_0, j_1 and a disclosure set $\mathcal{D} \subset \{1, \ldots, n\}$. These have to be such that the disclosed attributes from credential j_0 coincide with the ones from credential j_1, i.e., $k_{i,j_0} = k_{i,j_1}$ for each $i \in \mathcal{D}$. It sends the indices j_0, j_1 and $\mathcal{D}$ to the challenger, who checks that this holds; if it does not then the adversary loses.

Next, the challenger flips a bit $b \in_R \{0, 1\}$, and acting as the user, it engages in the ShowCredential with the adversary on credential j_b. All attributes whose index is in $\mathcal{D}$ are disclosed.

Output. The adversary outputs a bit b' and wins if $b = b'$.

We define the advantage of the adversary $\mathcal{A}$ as $\mathsf{Adv}_\mathcal{A} := |\Pr[b = b'] - 1/2|$. When no probabilistic polynomial-time algorithm can win this game with non-negligible advantage in the security parameter ℓ, then we say that the credential scheme is *unlinkable*.

References

1. Ateniese, G., Camenisch, J., de Medeiros, B.: Untraceable RFID tags via insubvertible encryption. In: Proceedings of the 12th ACM Conference on Computer and Communications Security (CCS 2005), pp. 92–101. ACM, New York (2005)
2. Au, M.H., Susilo, W., Mu, Y.: Constant-size dynamic k-TAA. In: De Prisco, R., Yung, M. (eds.) SCN 2006. LNCS, vol. 4116, pp. 111–125. Springer, Heidelberg (2006). https://doi.org/10.1007/11832072_8
3. Baldimtsi, F., Lysyanskaya, A.: Anonymous credentials light. In: Proceedings of the 2013 ACM SIGSAC Conference on Computer & Communications Security (CCS 2013), pp. 1087–1098. ACM, New York (2013)
4. Baldimtsi, F., Lysyanskaya, A.: On the security of one-witness blind signature schemes. In: Sako, K., Sarkar, P. (eds.) ASIACRYPT 2013. LNCS, vol. 8270, pp. 82–99. Springer, Heidelberg (2013). https://doi.org/10.1007/978-3-642-42045-0_5
5. Barki, A., Brunet, S., Desmoulins, N., Traoré, J.: Improved algebraic MACs and practical keyed-verification anonymous credentials. In: Avanzi, R., Heys, H. (eds.) SAC 2016. LNCS, vol. 10532, pp. 360–380. Springer, Cham (2016). https://doi.org/10.1007/978-3-319-69453-5_20

6. Beuchat, J.-L., González-Díaz, J.E., Mitsunari, S., Okamoto, E., Rodríguez-Henríquez, F., Teruya, T.: High-speed software implementation of the optimal ate pairing over Barreto–Naehrig curves. In: Joye, M., Miyaji, A., Otsuka, A. (eds.) Pairing 2010. LNCS, vol. 6487, pp. 21–39. Springer, Heidelberg (2010). https://doi.org/10.1007/978-3-642-17455-1_2

7. Bitansky, N., Canetti, R., Chiesa, A., Tromer, E.: From extractable collision resistance to succinct non-interactive arguments of knowledge, and back again. In: Proceedings of the 3rd Innovations in Theoretical Computer Science Conference (ITCS 2012), pp. 326–349. ACM, New York (2012)

8. Boneh, D., Boyen, X.: Short signatures without random oracles and the SDH assumption in bilinear groups. J. Cryptol. 21(2), 149–177 (2008)

9. Boneh, D., Boyen, X., Shacham, H.: Short group signatures. In: Franklin, M. (ed.) CRYPTO 2004. LNCS, vol. 3152, pp. 41–55. Springer, Heidelberg (2004). https://doi.org/10.1007/978-3-540-28628-8_3

10. Brands, S.: Rethinking Public Key Infrastructures and Digital Certificates: Building in Privacy. MIT Press, Cambridge (2000)

11. Camenisch, J., Hohenberger, S., Pedersen, M.Ø.: Batch verification of short signatures. In: Naor, M. (ed.) EUROCRYPT 2007. LNCS, vol. 4515, pp. 246–263. Springer, Heidelberg (2007). https://doi.org/10.1007/978-3-540-72540-4_14

12. Camenisch, J., Lysyanskaya, A.: An efficient system for non-transferable anonymous credentials with optional anonymity revocation. In: Pfitzmann, B. (ed.) EUROCRYPT 2001. LNCS, vol. 2045, pp. 93–118. Springer, Heidelberg (2001). https://doi.org/10.1007/3-540-44987-6_7

13. Camenisch, J., Lysyanskaya, A.: Signature schemes and anonymous credentials from bilinear maps. In: Franklin, M. (ed.) CRYPTO 2004. LNCS, vol. 3152, pp. 56–72. Springer, Heidelberg (2004). https://doi.org/10.1007/978-3-540-28628-8_4

14. Camenisch, J., Stadler, M.: Efficient group signature schemes for large groups. In: Kaliski, B.S. (ed.) CRYPTO 1997. LNCS, vol. 1294, pp. 410–424. Springer, Heidelberg (1997). https://doi.org/10.1007/BFb0052252

15. Cramer, R., Damgård, I., MacKenzie, P.: Efficient zero-knowledge proofs of knowledge without intractability assumptions. In: Imai, H., Zheng, Y. (eds.) PKC 2000. LNCS, vol. 1751, pp. 354–372. Springer, Heidelberg (2000). https://doi.org/10.1007/978-3-540-46588-1_24

16. Damgård, I.: Towards practical public key systems secure against chosen ciphertext attacks. In: Feigenbaum, J. (ed.) CRYPTO 1991. LNCS, vol. 576, pp. 445–456. Springer, Heidelberg (1992). https://doi.org/10.1007/3-540-46766-1_36

17. Ferrara, A.L., Green, M., Hohenberger, S., Pedersen, M.Ø.: Practical short signature batch verification. In: Fischlin, M. (ed.) CT-RSA 2009. LNCS, vol. 5473, pp. 309–324. Springer, Heidelberg (2009). https://doi.org/10.1007/978-3-642-00862-7_21

18. Fiat, A., Shamir, A.: How to prove yourself: practical solutions to identification and signature problems. In: Odlyzko, A.M. (ed.) CRYPTO 1986. LNCS, vol. 263, pp. 186–194. Springer, Heidelberg (1987). https://doi.org/10.1007/3-540-47721-7_12

19. Fuchsbauer, G., Hanser, C., Slamanig, D.: Structure-preserving signatures on equivalence classes and constant-size anonymous credentials. Cryptology ePrint Archive, Report 2014/944 (2014). https://eprint.iacr.org/2014/944

20. Galbraith, S.D., Paterson, K.G., Smart, N.P.: Pairings for cryptographers. Discrete Appl. Math. 156(16), 3113–3121 (2008)

21. Hajny, J., Malina, L.: Unlinkable attribute-based credentials with practical revocation on smart-cards. In: Mangard, S. (ed.) CARDIS 2012. LNCS, vol. 7771, pp. 62–76. Springer, Heidelberg (2013). https://doi.org/10.1007/978-3-642-37288-9_5

22. Hanzlik, L., Kluczniak, K.: A short paper on how to improve U-Prove using self-blindable certificates. In: Christin, N., Safavi-Naini, R. (eds.) FC 2014. LNCS, vol. 8437, pp. 273–282. Springer, Heidelberg (2014). https://doi.org/10.1007/978-3-662-45472-5_17

23. Hoepman, J.-H., Lueks, W., Ringers, S.: On linkability and malleability in self-blindable credentials. In: Akram, R.N., Jajodia, S. (eds.) WISTP 2015. LNCS, vol. 9311, pp. 203–218. Springer, Cham (2015). https://doi.org/10.1007/978-3-319-24018-3_13

24. IBM Research Zürich Security Team: Specification of the identity mixer cryptographic library, version 2.3.0. Technical report, IBM Research, Zürich, February 2012. https://tinyurl.com/idemix-spec

25. Lenstra, A.K., Verheul, E.R.: Selecting cryptographic key sizes. J. Cryptol. **14**(4), 255–293 (2001)

26. Lysyanskaya, A.: Pseudonym systems. Master's thesis, Massachusetts Institute of Technology (1999). https://groups.csail.mit.edu/cis/theses/anna-sm.pdf

27. Lysyanskaya, A., Rivest, R.L., Sahai, A., Wolf, S.: Pseudonym systems. In: Heys, H., Adams, C. (eds.) SAC 1999. LNCS, vol. 1758, pp. 184–199. Springer, Heidelberg (2000). https://doi.org/10.1007/3-540-46513-8_14

28. Naor, M.: On cryptographic assumptions and challenges. In: Boneh, D. (ed.) CRYPTO 2003. LNCS, vol. 2729, pp. 96–109. Springer, Heidelberg (2003). https://doi.org/10.1007/978-3-540-45146-4_6

29. Paquin, C., Zaverucha, G.: U-Prove cryptographic specification v1.1 (revision 3), December 2013. http://research.microsoft.com/apps/pubs/default.aspx?id=166969. Released under the Open Specification Promise

30. Ringers, S., Verheul, E., Hoepman, J.H.: An efficient self-blindable attribute-based credential scheme. Cryptology ePrint Archive, Report 2017/115 (2017). https://eprint.iacr.org/2017/115

31. Shoup, V.: Lower bounds for discrete logarithms and related problems. In: Fumy, W. (ed.) EUROCRYPT 1997. LNCS, vol. 1233, pp. 256–266. Springer, Heidelberg (1997). https://doi.org/10.1007/3-540-69053-0_18

32. Verheul, E., Ringers, S., Hoepman, J.-H.: The self-blindable U-Prove scheme from FC'14 is forgeable (short paper). In: Grossklags, J., Preneel, B. (eds.) FC 2016. LNCS, vol. 9603, pp. 339–345. Springer, Heidelberg (2017). https://doi.org/10.1007/978-3-662-54970-4_20

33. Verheul, E.R.: Self-blindable credential certificates from the weil pairing. In: Boyd, C. (ed.) ASIACRYPT 2001. LNCS, vol. 2248, pp. 533–551. Springer, Heidelberg (2001). https://doi.org/10.1007/3-540-45682-1_31

34. Vullers, P., Alpár, G.: Efficient selective disclosure on smart cards using Idemix. In: Fischer-Hübner, S., de Leeuw, E., Mitchell, C. (eds.) IDMAN 2013. IAICT, vol. 396, pp. 53–67. Springer, Heidelberg (2013). https://doi.org/10.1007/978-3-642-37282-7_5

35. Wachsmann, C., Chen, L., Dietrich, K., Löhr, H., Sadeghi, A.-R., Winter, J.: Lightweight anonymous authentication with TLS and DAA for embedded mobile devices. In: Burmester, M., Tsudik, G., Magliveras, S., Ilić, I. (eds.) ISC 2010. LNCS, vol. 6531, pp. 84–98. Springer, Heidelberg (2011). https://doi.org/10.1007/978-3-642-18178-8_8

36. Wei, V.K., Yuen, T.H.: More short signatures without random oracles. IACR Cryptology ePrint Archive 2005, 463 (2005). http://eprint.iacr.org/2005/463

Real Hidden Identity-Based Signatures

Sherman S. M. Chow[1(✉)], Haibin Zhang[2], and Tao Zhang[1]

[1] Chinese University of Hong Kong, Shatin, NT, Hong Kong
{sherman,zt112}@ie.cuhk.edu.hk
[2] University of Connecticut, Mansfield, CT 06269, USA
haibin.zhang@uconn.edu

Abstract. Group signature allows members to issue signatures on behalf of the group anonymously in normal circumstances. When the need arises, an opening authority (OA) can open a signature and reveal its true signer. Yet, many constructions require not only the secret key of the OA but also a member database (cf. a public-key repository) for this opening. This "secret members list" put the anonymity of members at risk as each of them is a potential signer.

To resolve this "anonymity catch-22" issue, Kiayias and Zhou proposed hidden identity-based signatures (Financial Crypt. 2007 and IET Information Security 2009), where the opening just takes in the secret key of the OA and directly outputs the signer identity. The membership list can be hidden from the OA since there is no membership list whatsoever. However, their constructions suffer from efficiency problem.

This paper aims to realize the vision of Kiayias and Zhou for real, that is, an efficient construction which achieves the distinctive feature of hidden identity-based signatures. Moreover, our construction is secure against concurrent attack, and easily extensible with linkability such that any double authentication can be publicly detected. Both features are especially desirable in Internet-based services which allow anonymous authentication with revocation to block any misbehaving user. We believe our work will improve the usability of group signature and its variant.

Keywords: Anonymous authentication · Group signature
Hidden identity-based signature

1 Introduction

Group signature, introduced by Chaum and van Heyst [1], is a useful tool in applications which expect anonymous authentication, where the signers typically remain anonymous, yet some authorities can identify any misbehaving user in case of abuse. To join a group, users first obtain their group signing keys from a group manager (GM). The joining protocol is often interactive. Once this registration is done, they can sign on behalf of the group with (conditional) anonymity using the signing keys. The verifiers only know that someone in the

© International Financial Cryptography Association 2017
A. Kiayias (Ed.): FC 2017, LNCS 10322, pp. 21–38, 2017.
https://doi.org/10.1007/978-3-319-70972-7_2

group signed the message, but cannot identify the specific signer. Whenever the GM deems appropriate, it can use a system trapdoor to "open" a group signature and reveal its true signer.

A later refinement by Camenisch and Michels [2] separates the power of opening from the GM, by introducing an opening authority (or opener). GM in this setting is in charge of user registration only, and the opening authority (OA) is in charge of opening signatures. However, to enable anonymity revocation in many realizations of group signature, the OA actually requires some help of the GM, specifically, for the membership database the GM holds. This design comes with some flaws—either the OA holds the member list, or the GM interacts with the OA each time an opening is needed, which means the GM should remains online for answering opening requests and it can possibly deny such a request of the OA. Note that the reason why group signatures are used is that the user wants to protect their anonymity. However, the existence of such secret membership list conflicts with this purpose. The members cannot sign in peace because the OA is too powerful with this membership list. This list is a very valuable asset attracting any adversary who aims to compromise user anonymity to attack the OA. However, since it is not a secret key by definition and secure storage for such a large list is relatively expensive, it may not be as well-protected as the opening trapdoor. We end up with a "no-win" no matters which of the above options to adopt.

Kiayias and Zhou [3,4] observed this inconvenient situation and put forth the notion of hidden identity-based signatures (HIBS). The *hidden feature* of HIBS is that not only the signer identity can be hidden from a regular verifier (like group signature), but the membership list is also hidden from the OA since there is no membership list whatsoever. In particular, anonymity revocation will not require such a list.

Realizing HIBS is not straightforward, even though many group signature schemes exist. In their first concrete construction [3], one needs to solve discrete logarithm problem to get the signer identity. Discrete logarithm problem cannot be efficiently solved by any probabilistic polynomial-time algorithm. This makes the hidden feature of their scheme rather artificial. Some existing group signature schemes before their work can (be extended easily to) support this "hidden-identity" feature if the opening requires solving discrete logarithm problem. In other words, one can consider this scheme not a *"real"* hidden identity-based signature scheme. Indeed, other scheme which opens to a group element embedding the identity as an exponent also exists [5]. Their second scheme [4] does not suffer from this problem, yet the efficiency is not that satisfactory. Specifically, it uses Paillier encryption and thus a more involved zero-knowledge proof. Not only the signature contains more group elements, but also each of those becomes larger since the composite order group should be large enough to withstand the best-known factorization attack. In other words, the price for this hidden-identity feature is the cost of the efficiency of all other algorithms of the signature scheme. Liu and Xu [6,7] proposed pairing-based HIBS schemes in the random oracle model which claimed to achieve concurrent security, CCA-anonymity, and exculpability, but their constructions still require solving the discrete logarithm problem for opening.

1.1 Our Contributions

We propose a generic construction for HIBS based on standard primitives: digital signature, encryption, and non-interactive zero-knowledge (NIZK) (or non-interactive witness-indistinguishable (NIWI)) proof. Though conceptually simple, it has impacts in multiple aspects.

- First, we show that the seemingly difficult goal of constructing HIBS can be *generally* achieved from various cryptographic assumptions in a *modular* manner, leading to efficient instantiations without random oracles.
- Beyond retaining the nice feature of supporting opening without requiring any membership list, our generic construction is secure even under concurrent joining, such that the GM can interact with multiple joining users in an arbitrarily interleaving manner. Concurrent joining is more practical than sequential joining for applications over the Internet such as anonymous communication (say, via Tor), which is the original scenario Kiayias and Zhou [3,4] brought up to motivate the concept of HIBS.
- We extend our generic construction of HIBS with linkability [8], where HIBS signatures generated by the same signer on the same message can be linked without revealing the identity of the signer. We call this extension linkable hidden identity-based signature (LHIBS). This extension disallows double-posting of the same user with respect to the same "call for contributions", may it be two responses to the same thread of discussion or two votes cast in the associated reputation systems. With our modular construction, advanced features such as escrowed linkability can be easily equipped [9].
- Finally, our generic construction and its instantiations are highly compatible with other privacy enhancing features such as (real) traceability [10,11] and uniqueness [12]. This echoes the work of Galindo, Herranz, and Kiltz [13], which obtains identity-based signature schemes with additional properties from standard signature with the corresponding properties. The details are shown in the full version.

1.2 Relation to Existing Notions

Note that a major difference of identity-based signature from the traditional signatures based on public-key infrastructure, is simply the removal of a huge list of public-key certificates. One can simply include a signature from the certificate authority in every signature, to realize an identity-based signature. However, every signature comes with this additional certificate, which also means an additional verification is needed in verifying any given signatures.

In hidden identity-based signatures, this certificate can be considered as hidden via an implicit encryption mechanism. As such, one may not agree that such construction should be named as identity-based. Yet, our notion does not suffer from the loss of efficiency as in the case for "certificate-based" identity-based signatures. This is exactly the purpose of this work to show that such construction of HIBS can be constructed in an efficient (and modular) manner. On the other hand, we stick with the original naming of Kiayias and Zhou [3]. Indeed, as acknowledged in their work, HIBS is essentially a group signature scheme, but just with a special care on the input requirement of the opening mechanism.

Galindo et al. [13] studied what additional properties of identity-based signatures (such as proxy, blind, undeniable, etc.) can be generically obtained from standard signature schemes with the same properties. Their work is also based on the above generic construction of identity-based signatures from standard signatures. Our modular construction here is also compatible with many additional properties in the world of group signatures [11,12,14].

2 Preliminaries

2.1 Notations

If S is a set, $s \xleftarrow{\$} S$ denotes the operation of selecting an element s from S uniformly at random. $\emptyset$ denotes an empty set. If $\mathcal{A}$ is a randomized algorithm, we write $z \xleftarrow{\$} \mathcal{A}(x, y, \cdots)$ to indicate the operation that runs $\mathcal{A}$ on inputs $x, y, \cdots$ (and uniformly selected internal randomness from an appropriate domain) which outputs z. A function $\epsilon(\lambda) \colon \mathbb{N} \to \mathbb{R}$ is *negligible* if, for any positive number d, there exists some constant $\lambda_0 \in \mathbb{N}$ such that $\epsilon(\lambda) < (1/\lambda)^d$ for any $\lambda > \lambda_0$.

2.2 Bilinear Map

Bilinear pairing is a powerful tool for cryptographers to construct a diversity of primitives. In a bilinear group $\mathcal{G} = (\mathbb{G}, \mathbb{H}, \mathbb{G}_T, p, e, g, h)$, $\mathbb{G}, \mathbb{H}$, and $\mathbb{G}_T$ are groups of prime order p. g and h are random generators for the groups $\mathbb{G}$ and $\mathbb{H}$ respectively. An efficient bilinear map $e : \mathbb{G} \times \mathbb{H} \to \mathbb{G}_T$ maps two group elements from $\mathbb{G}$ and $\mathbb{H}$ to one from the target group $\mathbb{G}_T$ with the following property.

- *Bilinearity.* For all $u \in \mathbb{G}$, $v \in \mathbb{H}$, $a, b \in \mathbb{Z}$, $e(u^a, v^b) = e(u, v)^{ab}$.
- *Non-degeneracy.* $e(g, h) \neq 1$.
- *Efficiency.* For all $(u, v) \in \mathbb{G} \times \mathbb{H}$, $e(u, v)$ is efficiently computable.

2.3 Assumptions

Assumption 1 (Decisional Diffie-Hellman (DDH)). *For a group $\mathbb{G}$ with a random generator g, given (g^a, g^b, g^c) where a, b, c are randomly chosen from $\mathbb{Z}_p$, it is hard for any probabilistic polynomial-time algorithm to decide whether $g^c = g^{ab}$ or not.*

Assumption 2 (SXDH). *For a bilinear group $\mathcal{G} = (\mathbb{G}, \mathbb{H}, \mathbb{G}_T, p, e, g, h)$ where $e : \mathbb{G} \times \mathbb{H} \to \mathbb{G}_T$, DDH assumption holds for both $\mathbb{G}$ and $\mathbb{H}$.*

Symmetric eXternal Diffie-Hellman (SXDH) assumption implies that there does not exist any efficient transformation from $\mathbb{G}$ to $\mathbb{H}$ or from $\mathbb{H}$ to $\mathbb{G}$.

Assumption 3 (Decisional Linear (DLIN)). *For a group* $\mathbb{G}$, *given the tuple* $(g_1, g_2, g_3, g_1^a, g_2^b, g_3^c) \in \mathbb{G}^6$ *where* $g_1, g_2, g_3 \in \mathbb{G}^*$ *and* $a, b, c \in \mathbb{Z}_p$, *it is hard for any probabilistic polynomial-time algorithm to decide whether* $g_3^c = g_3^{a+b}$ *or not.*

3 Hidden Identity-Based Signatures

We present the syntax and notions of security for HIBS. The contents of this section are strengthening and extending those proposed by Kiayias and Zhou [3, 4], adding useful functionalities, and establishing stronger notions of security.

3.1 Syntax of HIBS

We consider HIBS with separated *issuer* (or *group/identity manager*) and *opener* (or *opening authority*) [3,15]. An issuer is responsible for member enrollment, while an opener is responsible for recovering the identities hidden in the signatures given by the enrolled users, whenever need arises.

A *hidden identity-based signature* (HIBS) scheme $\mathcal{HIBS}$ is a set of nine algorithms (KGen, UKGen, Reg, RegCheck, Sign, Verify, Open, Judge, Dispute):

- KGen(1^λ) → (gpk, ik, ok): The *group key generation*[1] algorithm takes as input the security parameter λ and outputs the *group public key* gpk, the *issuer key* ik (for the issuer) and the *opening key* ok (for the opener).
- UKGen(1^λ, ID) → (upk$_{ID}$, usk$_{ID}$): The *user private key generation* algorithm takes as input the security parameter λ and a user identity ID, and outputs the *user personal public and private key pair* (upk$_{ID}$, usk$_{ID}$).
- Reg(gpk, ik, ID, upk$_{ID}$) → cert$_{ID}$: The *registration* algorithm takes as input the group public key gpk, the issuer key ik, a user identity ID, and a user personal public key upk$_{ID}$ to return a *user membership certificate* cert$_{ID}$.
- RegCheck(gpk, ID, upk$_{ID}$, cert$_{ID}$) → 0/1: The *registration checking* algorithm[2] takes as input the group public key gpk, a user identity ID, a user personal public key upk$_{ID}$, and a user membership certificate cert$_{ID}$ to return a single bit b. We say cert$_{ID}$ is a *valid* user membership certificate with respect to ID if RegCheck(gpk, ID, upk$_{ID}$, cert$_{ID}$) = 1.
- Sign(gpk, ID, cert$_{ID}$, usk$_{ID}$, m) → σ: The *HIBS signing* algorithm takes as input the group public key gpk, a user identity ID, the corresponding user membership certificate cert$_{ID}$, the user private key usk$_{ID}$, and a message m to return a signature σ.
- Verify(gpk, m, σ) → 0/1: The *HIBS verification* algorithm takes as input the group public key gpk, a message m, a signature σ on m, and returns a single bit b. We say that σ is a *valid* signature of m if Verify(gpk, m, σ) = 1.

---

[1] We put issuing key generation and opening key generation together for brevity. It is easy to separate them in our schemes such that the respective private keys of the issuer and the opener are generated independently except according to the same security parameter, and the corresponding public keys will be put together in gpk.

[2] This algorithm may be optional for some application scenarios.

- Open(gpk, ok, m, σ) $\rightarrow$ (ID, ω): The opener takes as input the group public key gpk, its opening key ok, a message m, and a valid signature σ for m, and outputs (ID, ω), where ω is a *proof* to support its claim that user ID indeed signed the message. It is possible that (ID, ω) = $\perp$ for a valid signature, in which case the opening procedure is foiled.

- Judge(gpk, (ID, ω), (m, σ)) $\rightarrow$ 0/1: The *judge* algorithm takes as input the group public key gpk, the opening (ID, ω), a message m, and a valid signature σ of m to verify that the opening of σ to ID is indeed correct. We say that the opening is *correct* if Judge(gpk, (ID, ω), (m, σ)) = 1.

- Dispute(gpk, upk$_{ID}$, cert$_{ID}$, (ID, ω)) $\rightarrow$ 0/1: The *dispute* algorithm is triggered if a registered user ID refuses to admit guilt after an opening (ID, ω) is published. It takes as input the group public key gpk, the user personal public key upk$_{ID}$, the user membership certificate cert$_{ID}$, which are both provided by the user, and the opening result (ID, ω) published by the opener, and returns a single bit b. The issuer is *guilty* with respect to ID if Dispute(gpk, upk$_{ID}$, cert$_{ID}$, (ID, ω)) = 1.

We note that the hidden-identity nature just applies on the opener. Obviously, the group manager is governing who can join the group, and hence it can store such a list after every Reg invocation. However, it is natural to assume that the group manager is not motivated to put its member at risk.

Following [15] and different from [3,4], we further equip our HIBS with a judge algorithm Judge() to protect against a fully corrupt opener. Compared to that of [15], the Join()/Issue() algorithm [15] is replaced with Reg() and RegCheck() algorithms for the sake of simplicity.

We now briefly consider the correctness notions for HIBS. Correctness includes *registration correctness* (with respect to Reg() and RegCheck() algorithms), *signing correctness* (with respect to Sign() and Verify() algorithms), *opening correctness* (with respect to Open() and Judge() algorithms), and *dispute correctness*. The first three can be easily adapted from those of [3,15], while the last one requires the Dispute() algorithm to function correctly when a suspected user was indeed framed.

3.2 Syntax of Linkable HIBS

We extend hidden identity-based signatures to the notion of linkable HIBS (LHIBS) which supports linking the signatures on the same message by the same (hidden) signer. This feature is implemented by the algorithm below.

- Link(gpk, m, σ_1, σ_2) $\rightarrow$ 0/1: This algorithm takes in the group public key and two signatures on the same message m. If σ_1 and σ_2 are two valid signatures (resulting in 1 from Verify()) generated by the same signer, this algorithm outputs 1; otherwise, it outputs 0.

This linking feature can identify double-posting without opening the identity of any signer.

3.3 Security Notions for HIBS

We strengthen the notions due to Kiayias and Zhou [3,4], and consider the "strongest" achievable notions (following [15]): anonymity, traceability, and non-frameability. The security notions in [3,4], namely, security against misidentification forgery and exculpability attacks (formally given in [4]), have been shown to be implied by traceability and non-frameability [16].

Similar to the study of Kiayias and Zhou [3,4], we do not have an explicit security definition to model the hidden identity nature of the scheme. It is more a functionality requirement that the opener does not need such a list for the proper operation. In principle, such opener can collect all signatures in the system, open each of them, with the goal of recovering the whole membership list. Hence, by the correct functionality of the scheme, we cannot afford to have a security definition which prevents an adversary with the opening secret key from outputting the identity of any member.

Notation. We use HU and CU (both initially empty) to denote a set of honest and corrupted users respectively, and use MSG_{ID} (initially empty) to denote the set of messages queried by the adversary to SignO oracle for ID. An adversary may have access of the following oracles in the security games to be described.

- RegO(ID): The adversary queries this oracle with a user identity ID. If ID $\in$ CU$\cup$HU, returns $\perp$. Otherwise, this oracle runs $(upk_{ID}, usk_{ID}) \leftarrow$ UKGen(1^λ, ID) and cert$_{ID}$ ← Reg(gpk, ik, ID, upk$_{ID}$), sets $MSG_{ID} \leftarrow \emptyset$, and sets HU ← HU $\cup$ {ID} and stores (ID, upk$_{ID}$, usk$_{ID}$, cert$_{ID}$) internally.
- SignO(ID, cert$_{ID}$, m): This oracle takes in an identity ID and a message m from the adversary, runs $\sigma \leftarrow$ Sign(gpk, ID, cert$_{ID}$, usk$_{ID}$, m) where cert$_{ID}$ is the certificate on ID generated by RegO, sets $MSG_{ID} \leftarrow MSG_{ID} \cup \{m\}$, and returns σ.
- CorruptO(ID): This oracle takes in an identity ID, sets CU ← CU $\cup$ {ID} and HU ← HU \ {ID}, and returns (upk$_{ID}$, usk$_{ID}$, cert$_{ID}$).
- OpenO(m, σ): If Verify() outputs 1 on (m, σ), this oracle returns (ID, ω) ← Open(gpk, ok, m, σ). Otherwise, outputs $\perp$.

Definition 1 (CCA-Anonymity). *An HIBS scheme $\mathcal{HIBS}$ is CCA-anonymous, if in the following experiment, $\mathbf{Adv}_{\mathcal{HIBS}}^{anon}(\mathcal{A})$ is negligible.*

> **Experiment Exp$_{\mathcal{HIBS}}^{\text{cca-anon}}(\mathcal{A})$**
>
> $(gpk, ik, ok) \xleftarrow{\$} $ KGen(1^λ); CU ← $\emptyset$; HU ← $\emptyset$;
>
> $(ID_0, ID_1, m, s) \xleftarrow{\$} \mathcal{A}^{\text{CorruptO}(\cdot), \text{RegO}(\cdot), \text{OpenO}(\cdot, \cdot)}(\text{'find'}, gpk, ik)$
>
> $b \xleftarrow{\$} \{0, 1\}; \sigma \xleftarrow{\$} $ Sign$(gpk, ID_b, \text{cert}_{ID_b}, usk_{ID_b}, m)$
>
> $b' \xleftarrow{\$} \mathcal{A}^{\text{CorruptO}(\cdot, \cdot), \text{RegO}(\cdot), \text{OpenO}(\cdot, \cdot)}(\text{'guess'}, \sigma, s)$
>
> if $b' \neq b$ then return 0
>
> return 1

where the adversary $\mathcal{A}$ must not have queried $\mathsf{OpenO}(\cdot, \cdot)$ with m and σ in guess phase. We define the advantage of $\mathcal{A}$ in the above experiment by

$$\mathbf{Adv}^{\mathrm{anon}}_{\mathcal{HIBS}}(\mathcal{A}) = \Pr[\mathbf{Exp}^{\mathrm{anon}}_{\mathcal{HIBS}}(\mathcal{A}) = 1] - 1/2.$$

The opening of a group signature corresponds to the chosen ciphertext attack (CCA) which features a decryption oracle to the adversary of public-key encryption. Naturally, one can also consider a variant anonymity notion, chosen-plaintext attack (CPA) anonymity, where the adversary is never given access to the opening oracle. It is known as CPA-anonymity.

Our anonymity notion *strengthens* that of Kiayias and Zhou [4] in the sense the adversary is given access to two more oracles $\mathsf{CorruptO}(\cdot, \cdot)$ and $\mathsf{RegO}(\cdot)$.

We also consider a weak CCA-anonymity for our extension with linkability. The definition is stated below.

Definition 2 (Weak CCA-Anonymity). *An HIBS scheme $\mathcal{HIBS}$ is weak CCA-anonymous, if in the following experiment, $\mathbf{Adv}^{\mathrm{anon}}_{\mathcal{HIBS}}(\mathcal{A})$ is negligible.*

> **Experiment $\mathbf{Exp}^{\mathrm{weak\text{-}anon}}_{\mathcal{HIBS}}(\mathcal{A})$**
>
> $(\mathsf{gpk}, \mathsf{ik}, \mathsf{ok}) \xleftarrow{\$} \mathsf{KGen}(1^{\lambda}); \mathsf{CU} \leftarrow \emptyset; \mathsf{HU} \leftarrow \emptyset;$
>
> $(\mathsf{ID}_0, \mathsf{ID}_1, m, \mathsf{s}) \xleftarrow{\$} \mathcal{A}^{\mathsf{CorruptO}(\cdot), \mathsf{RegO}(\cdot), \mathsf{OpenO}(\cdot, \cdot)}(\text{'find'}, \mathsf{gpk}, \mathsf{ik})$
>
> **if** $m \in \mathsf{MSG}_{\mathsf{ID}_0}$ **or** $m \in \mathsf{MSG}_{\mathsf{ID}_1}$ **then abort**
>
> $b \xleftarrow{\$} \{0, 1\}; \sigma \xleftarrow{\$} \mathsf{Sign}(\mathsf{gpk}, \mathsf{ID}_b, \mathsf{cert}_{\mathsf{ID}_b}, \mathsf{usk}_{\mathsf{ID}_b}, m)$
>
> $b' \xleftarrow{\$} \mathcal{A}^{\mathsf{CorruptO}(\cdot, \cdot), \mathsf{RegO}(\cdot), \mathsf{OpenO}(\cdot, \cdot)}(\text{'guess'}, \sigma, \mathsf{s})$
>
> **if** $b' \neq b$ **then return** 0
>
> **return** 1

where the adversary $\mathcal{A}$ must not have queried $\mathsf{OpenO}(\cdot, \cdot)$ with m and σ in guess phase. We define the advantage of $\mathcal{A}$ in the above experiment by

$$\mathbf{Adv}^{\mathrm{anon}}_{\mathcal{HIBS}}(\mathcal{A}) = \Pr[\mathbf{Exp}^{\mathrm{anon}}_{\mathcal{HIBS}}(\mathcal{A}) = 1] - 1/2.$$

One can formulate a CPA counterpart for this definition. For the linkable HIBS, the linking token is deterministic, and is decided by the combination of identity and message to be signed. Hence, in the weak CCA-anonymity game, the adversary is not allowed to submit challenge identity-message pairs which have appeared in the signing queries. Otherwise, the adversary will obtain a linking token on the challenge identity-message pair, and break anonymity of HIBS trivially.

Next, we present traceability and non-frameability, which together imply (and in fact stronger than) the security against misidentification forgery and exculpability attacks [4].

Definition 3 (Traceability). *An HIBS scheme $\mathcal{HIBS}$ is traceable, if in the following experiment, $\mathbf{Adv}^{trace}_{\mathcal{HIBS}}(\mathcal{A})$ is negligible.*

Experiment $\mathbf{Exp}^{\text{trace}}_{\mathcal{HIBS}}(\mathcal{A})$

$(\text{gpk}, \text{ik}, \text{ok}) \xleftarrow{\$} \text{KGen}(1^{\lambda});\ \text{CU} \leftarrow \emptyset;\ \text{HU} \leftarrow \emptyset;$

$(m, \sigma) \xleftarrow{\$} \mathcal{A}^{\text{CorruptO}(\cdot), \text{RegO}(\cdot, \cdot)}(\text{gpk}, \text{ok})$

if $\text{Verify}(\text{gpk}, m, \sigma) = 0$

    then return 0

$(\text{ID}, \omega) \leftarrow \text{Open}(\text{gpk}, \text{ok}, m, \sigma)$

if $(\text{ID}, \omega) = \bot$ **or** $\text{Judge}(\text{gpk}, \text{ID}, \omega, m, \sigma) = 0$

    then return 1

return 0

The advantage of $\mathcal{A}$ in the above experiment is defined by

$$\mathbf{Adv}^{\text{trace}}_{\mathcal{HIBS}}(\mathcal{A}) = \Pr[\mathbf{Exp}^{\text{trace}}_{\mathcal{HIBS}}(\mathcal{A}) = 1].$$

Definition 4 (Non-frameability). *The definition of non-frameability consists of two aspects:* ***signer-non-frameability*** *and* ***issuer-non-frameability***.

– An HIBS scheme $\mathcal{HIBS}$ is signer-non-frameable, if in the following experiment, $\mathbf{Adv}^{\text{signer-nf}}_{\mathcal{HIBS}}(\mathcal{A})$ is negligible.

Experiment $\mathbf{Exp}^{\text{signer-nf}}_{\mathcal{HIBS}}(\mathcal{A})$

$(\text{gpk}, \text{ik}, \text{ok}) \xleftarrow{\$} \text{KGen}(1^{\lambda});\ \text{CU} \leftarrow \emptyset;\ \text{HU} \leftarrow \emptyset;$

$(m, \sigma, \text{ID}, \omega) \xleftarrow{\$} \mathcal{A}^{\text{CorruptO}(\cdot), \text{SignO}(\cdot, \cdot), \text{RegO}(\cdot)}(\text{gpk}, \text{ik}, \text{ok})$

if $\text{Verify}(\text{gpk}, m, \sigma) = 0$

    then return 0

if $\text{ID} \in \text{HU}$ **and** $m \notin \text{MSG}_{\text{ID}}$ **and**

    $\text{Judge}(\text{gpk}, \text{ID}, \omega, m, \sigma) = 1$ **and**

    $\text{Dispute}(\text{gpk}, \text{cert}_{\text{ID}}, \text{upk}_{\text{ID}}, \text{ID}, \omega) = 0$

    then return 1

return 0

We define the advantage of $\mathcal{A}$ in the above experiment by

$$\mathbf{Adv}^{\text{signer-nf}}_{\mathcal{HIBS}}(\mathcal{A}) = \Pr[\mathbf{Exp}^{\text{signer-nf}}_{\mathcal{HIBS}}(\mathcal{A}) = 1].$$

– An HIBS scheme $\mathcal{HIBS}$ is issuer-non-frameable, if in the following experiment, $\mathbf{Adv}^{\text{issuer-nf}}_{\mathcal{HIBS}}(\mathcal{A})$ is negligible.

Experiment $\text{Exp}^{\text{issuer-nf}}_{\mathcal{HIBS}}(\mathcal{A})$

$(\text{gpk}, \text{ik}, \text{ok}) \xleftarrow{\$} \text{KGen}(1^\lambda); \text{CU} \leftarrow \emptyset; \text{HU} \leftarrow \emptyset;$

$(m, \sigma, \text{ID}, \omega) \xleftarrow{\$} \mathcal{A}^{\text{CorruptO}(\cdot), \text{SignO}(\cdot, \cdot), \text{RegO}(\cdot)}(\text{gpk}, \text{ok})$

if $\text{Verify}(\text{gpk}, m, \sigma) = 0$

   then return 0

if $\text{Judge}(\text{gpk}, \text{ID}, \omega, m, \sigma) = 1$ and

   $\text{Dispute}(\text{gpk}, \text{cert}_{\text{ID}}, \text{upk}_{\text{ID}}, \text{ID}, \omega) = 1$

   then return 1

return 0

We define the advantage of $\mathcal{A}$ in the above experiment by

$$\text{Adv}^{\text{issuer-nf}}_{\mathcal{HIBS}}(\mathcal{A}) = \Pr[\text{Exp}^{\text{issuer-nf}}_{\mathcal{HIBS}}(\mathcal{A}) = 1].$$

In the signer-non-frameability game, the issuer is considered honest, and any other parties, including the signers, are not guaranteed to be honest. This security game models the scenario that an adversary creates an HIBS forgery on an identity of an honest signer without the consent of the issuer.

On the other hand, the issuer-non-frameability game models the scenario that the adversary chooses an honest signer and creates forgery on behalf of this chosen signer without being caught.

The combination of signer-non-frameability and issuer-non-frameability implies unforgeability. Suppose an adversary can win the game of unforgeability against chosen message attack, it can trivially win both the signer-non-frameability game and the issuer-non-frameability game.

LHIBS and HIBS share the security requirements above, and LHIBS has one more security requirement called linkability.

Definition 5 (Linkability). *An HIBS scheme $\mathcal{LHIBS}$ is linkable, if in the following experiment, $\text{Adv}^{link}_{\mathcal{HIBS}}(\mathcal{A})$ is negligible.*

Experiment $\text{Exp}^{\text{link}}_{\mathcal{LHIBS}}(\mathcal{A})$

$(\text{gpk}, \text{ik}, \text{ok}) \xleftarrow{\$} \text{KGen}(1^\lambda); \text{CU} \leftarrow \emptyset; \text{HU} \leftarrow \emptyset;$

$(m, \text{ID}, \sigma_0, \sigma_1) \xleftarrow{\$} \mathcal{A}^{\text{CorruptO}(\cdot), \text{SignO}(\cdot, \cdot), \text{RegO}(\cdot)}(\text{gpk}, \text{ik}, \text{ok})$

$\text{ID}_i \leftarrow \text{Open}(\text{gpk}, \text{ok}, m, \sigma_i), \ i \in \{0, 1\}$

if $\exists i \in \{0, 1\}, \text{s.t. } \text{Verify}(\text{gpk}, m, \sigma_i) = 0$

   then return 0

if $\text{ID}_0 = \text{ID}_1$ and $\text{Link}(\text{gpk}, m, \sigma_0, \sigma_1) = 0$

   then return 1

if $\text{ID}_0 \neq \text{ID}_1$ and $\text{Link}(\text{gpk}, m, \sigma_0, \sigma_1) = 1$

   then return 1

return 0

We define the advantage of $\mathcal{A}$ in the above experiment by

$$\mathbf{Adv}^{\text{link}}_{\mathcal{LHIBS}}(\mathcal{A}) = \Pr[\mathbf{Exp}^{\text{link}}_{\mathcal{LHIBS}}(\mathcal{A}) = 1].$$

4   Generic Construction

This section presents a generic construction of HIBS built from standard signature schemes and an NIZK (or NIWI) proof system, then extends it to support linkability.

4.1   Generic HIBS

To design a generic construction of HIBS, we start from a generic construction of identity-based signature (IBS) from standard signature schemes—certificate-based approach to IBS, originally brought up by Shamir [17] and formally proven secure by Bellare, Neven, and Namprempre [18]. To construct our generic HIBS, we "hide" the whole signing process with an encryption and prove so in an NIZK (or NIWI) sense.[3]

When a signer joins the system, it generates a public-private key pair of a signature scheme, and sends the public key along with its identity to the GM for a certificate. The GM use its signing key to generate a signature on the identity and public key of the signer, and returns this signature to the signer as a certificate. To create an HIBS, the signer first uses its own signing key to create a signature on the message, then encrypts the certificate, the signature on the message, its identity, and its public key, and finally generates an NIZK proof on the certificate, the signature on the message, and the ciphertext. The ciphertext and the proof are output as the HIBS signature. The proof asserts three statements. First, the certificate is a valid signature generated by the GM. Second, the signature on the message is valid with respect to the public key from the certificate. Third, the identity, the public key, and the certificate encrypted in the ciphertext are the ones used to create the signature. The validity of the first two statements indicates that the signer is authentic. The validity of the third statement enforces the traceability of HIBS. The party with the decryption key can open the signature and obtain the identity of the signer.

Let $\mathcal{DS}_1 = (\text{SKG}, \text{SIG}, \text{VFY})$ and $\mathcal{DS}_2 = (\text{skg}, \text{sig}, \text{vfy})$ be two signature schemes. Let $\mathcal{OTS} = (\text{OKGen}, \text{OSig}, \text{OVerify})$ be a one-time signature scheme. Let $\mathcal{E} = (\text{EKGen}, \text{Enc}, \text{Dec})$ be a public key encryption scheme. Let (P, V) be an NIZK (or NIWI) proof system. We define an HIBS scheme $\mathcal{HIBS}$ in Fig. 1. In particular, the underlying language for the proof system (P, V) is defined as

$$\begin{aligned} \mathcal{L} :=\{&(m, \text{ovk}, \text{VK}, \text{ek}, C, T) | \exists (r, \sigma, \text{ID}, \text{upk}_{\text{ID}}, \text{cert}_{\text{ID}}) \\ &[\text{VFY}(\text{VK}, (\text{ID}, \text{upk}_{\text{ID}}), \text{cert}_{\text{ID}}) = 1 \wedge \text{vfy}(vk_{\text{ID}}, (m, \text{ovk}), \sigma) = 1 \\ &\wedge C = \text{Enc}(\text{ek}, r, (\sigma, \text{ID}, \text{upk}_{\text{ID}}, \text{cert}_{\text{ID}}))]\} \end{aligned}$$

---

[3] Or, we could directly use NIZK proof of knowledge (NIZKPoK), being notionally equivalent to CCA encryption.

where we write $\mathsf{Enc}(\mathsf{ek}, r, M)$ for the encryption of a message M under the public key ek using the randomness r.

In the proposed generic construction, when a user joins the system, the communication between the user and the GM just consists of one round (two message flows). Thus, even when multiple users are joining the system at the same time, the issuing process can still be conducted securely. The follow theorem establishes the security of $\mathcal{HIBS}$.

Theorem 1. *The proposed generic construction $\mathcal{HIBS}$ in Fig. 1 is CCA-anonymous (CPA-anonymous), traceable, signer-non-frameable, and issuer-non-frameable, if $\mathcal{DS}_1$ and $\mathcal{DS}_2$ are unforgeable against chosen message attacks, $\mathcal{OTS}$ is a one-time secure signature, $\mathcal{E}$ is IND-CCA-secure (IND-CPA-secure), and the proof system (P, V) is adaptively sound, adaptively zero-knowledge, and one-time simulation-sound.*

Alg $\mathsf{KGen}(1^\lambda)$
$R \xleftarrow{\$} \{0,1\}^{p(\lambda)}$
$(\mathsf{VK}, \mathsf{SK}) \xleftarrow{\$} \mathcal{DS}_1.\mathsf{SKG}(1^\lambda)$
$(\mathsf{ek}, \mathsf{dk}) \xleftarrow{\$} \mathcal{E}.\mathsf{EKGen}(1^\lambda)$
$\mathsf{gpk} \leftarrow (R, \mathsf{ek}, \mathsf{VK})$
$\mathsf{ik} \leftarrow \mathsf{SK}$
$\mathsf{ok} \leftarrow \mathsf{dk}$
return $(\mathsf{gpk}, \mathsf{ik}, \mathsf{ok})$

Alg $\mathsf{UKGen}(1^\lambda, \mathsf{ID})$
$(\mathsf{upk}_{\mathsf{ID}}, \mathsf{usk}_{\mathsf{ID}}) \xleftarrow{\$} \mathcal{DS}_2.\mathsf{skg}(1^\lambda)$
return $(\mathsf{upk}_{\mathsf{ID}}, \mathsf{usk}_{\mathsf{ID}})$

Alg $\mathsf{Reg}(\mathsf{gpk}, \mathsf{ik}, \mathsf{ID}, \mathsf{upk}_{\mathsf{ID}})$
$\mathsf{cert}_{\mathsf{ID}} \xleftarrow{\$} \mathsf{SIG}(\mathsf{SK}, (\mathsf{ID}, \mathsf{upk}_{\mathsf{ID}}))$
return $\mathsf{cert}_{\mathsf{ID}}$

Alg $\mathsf{RegCheck}(\mathsf{gpk}, \mathsf{ID}, \mathsf{upk}_{\mathsf{ID}}, \mathsf{cert}_{\mathsf{ID}})$
return $\mathsf{VFY}(\mathsf{VK}, (\mathsf{ID}, \mathsf{upk}_{\mathsf{ID}}), \mathsf{cert}_{\mathsf{ID}})$

Alg $\mathsf{Judge}(\mathsf{gpk}, (\mathsf{ID}, \omega), (m, \sigma))$
parse ω **as** $(\sigma', \mathsf{upk}_{\mathsf{ID}}, \mathsf{cert}_{\mathsf{ID}})$
return $\mathsf{VFY}(\mathsf{VK}, (\mathsf{ID}, \mathsf{upk}_{\mathsf{ID}}), \mathsf{cert}_{\mathsf{ID}})$
$\quad \wedge \mathsf{vfy}(\mathsf{upk}_{\mathsf{ID}}, m, \sigma')$

Alg $\mathsf{Sign}(\mathsf{gpk}, \mathsf{ID}, \mathsf{cert}_{\mathsf{ID}}, \mathsf{usk}_{\mathsf{ID}}, m)$
$\sigma' \leftarrow \mathsf{sig}(\mathsf{usk}_{\mathsf{ID}}, m)$
$C \leftarrow \mathsf{Enc}(\mathsf{ek}, r, (\sigma', \mathsf{ID}, \mathsf{upk}_{\mathsf{ID}}, \mathsf{cert}_{\mathsf{ID}}))$
$\pi \xleftarrow{\$} P(R, (m, \mathsf{VK}, \mathsf{ek}, C),$
$\quad\quad (r, \sigma', \mathsf{ID}, \mathsf{upk}_{\mathsf{ID}}, \mathsf{cert}_{\mathsf{ID}}))$
$\sigma \leftarrow (C, \pi)$
return (m, σ)

Alg $\mathsf{Verify}(\mathsf{gpk}, m, \sigma)$
return $V(R, (m, \mathsf{VK}, \mathsf{ek}, C), \pi)$

Alg $\mathsf{Open}(\mathsf{gpk}, \mathsf{ok}, m, \sigma)$
if $V(R, (m, \mathsf{VK}, \mathsf{ek}, \tau, C, \pi)) = 0$
$\quad$ **return** $\bot$
$(\sigma', \mathsf{ID}, \mathsf{upk}_{\mathsf{ID}}, \mathsf{cert}_{\mathsf{ID}}) \leftarrow \mathsf{Dec}(\mathsf{dk}, C)$
$\omega \leftarrow (\sigma', \mathsf{upk}_{\mathsf{ID}}, \mathsf{cert}_{\mathsf{ID}})$
return (ID, ω)

Alg $\mathsf{Dispute}(\mathsf{gpk}, \mathsf{upk}_{\mathsf{ID}}, \mathsf{cert}_{\mathsf{ID}}, (\mathsf{ID}, \omega))$
parse ω **as** $(\sigma', \mathsf{upk}'_{\mathsf{ID}}, \mathsf{cert}'_{\mathsf{ID}})$
if $\mathsf{VFY}(\mathsf{VK}, (\mathsf{ID}, \mathsf{upk}_{\mathsf{ID}}), \mathsf{cert}_{\mathsf{ID}}) = 0$
$\quad$ **then return** $\bot$
if $\mathsf{VFY}(\mathsf{VK}, (\mathsf{ID}, \mathsf{upk}'_{\mathsf{ID}}), \mathsf{cert}'_{\mathsf{ID}}) = 1$ **and**
$\quad \mathsf{upk}'_{\mathsf{ID}} \neq \mathsf{upk}_{\mathsf{ID}}$
$\quad$ **then return** 1
return 0

Fig. 1. A generic construction for hidden identity-based signature $\mathcal{HIBS} = (\mathsf{KGen}, \mathsf{UKGen}, \mathsf{Reg}, \mathsf{RegCheck}, \mathsf{Sign}, \mathsf{Verify}, \mathsf{Open}, \mathsf{Judge}, \mathsf{Dispute})$: R is the common reference string for the underlying proof system (P, V).

4.2   Extension with Linkability

Figure 2 shows how we extend the generic construction $\mathcal{HIBS} = (\mathsf{KGen}, \mathsf{UKGen}, \mathsf{Reg}, \mathsf{RegCheck}, \mathsf{Sign}, \mathsf{Verify}, \mathsf{Open}, \mathsf{Judge}, \mathsf{Dispute})$ to a linkable HIBS (LHIBS) scheme.

```
Alg KGen(1^λ)                              Alg Sign(gpk, ID, cert_ID, usk_ID, m)
  (gpk, ik, ok) ← HIBS.KGen(1^λ)             parse usk_ID as (sk, sk_F)
  return (gpk, ik, ok)                       (T, π_F) ← FProve(sk_F, (ID, m))
                                             σ' ← sig(sk, m)
Alg UKGen(1^λ, ID)                           C ← Enc(ek, r, (σ', ID, upk_ID, cert_ID))
  (vk, sk) ←$ HIBS.UKGen(1^λ, ID)            π ←$ P(R, (m, VK, ek, C, T),
  (pk_F, sk_F) ← FGen(1^λ)                       (r, σ', ID, upk_ID, cert_ID, π_F))
  upk_ID ← (vk, pk_F)                        σ ← (C, π, T)
  usk_ID ← (sk, sk_F)                        return (m, σ)
  return (upk_ID, usk_ID)
                                           Alg Verify(gpk, m, σ)
Alg Reg(gpk, ik, ID, upk_ID)                 return V(R, (m, VK, ek, C, T), π)
  cert_ID ←$ HIBS.Reg(gpk, ik, ID, upk_ID)
  return cert_ID                           Alg Dispute(gpk, upk_ID, cert_ID, (ID, ω))
                                             return HIBS.Dispute(gpk, upk_ID,
Alg RegCheck(gpk, ID, upk_ID, cert_ID)                    cert_ID, (ID, ω))
  return HIBS.RegCheck(gpk, ID,
                  upk_ID, cert_ID)         Alg Link(gpk, m, σ_1, σ_2)
                                             if Verify(gpk, m, σ_1) = 0
Alg Open(gpk, ok, m, σ)                      or Verify(gpk, m, σ_2) = 0
  return HIBS.Open(gpk, ok, m, σ)            then return ⊥
                                             parse σ_i as (C_i, π_i, T_i)
Alg Judge(gpk, (ID, ω), (m, σ))              if T_1 = T_2 then return 1;
  return HIBS.Judge(gpk, (ID, ω), (m, σ))    else return 0
```

Fig. 2. A generic construction for linkable hidden identity-based signature $\mathcal{LHIBS} =$ (KGen, UKGen, Reg, RegCheck, Sign, Verify, Open, Judge, Dispute, Link)

In this extension, $F - (\mathsf{FGen}, \mathsf{FProve}, \mathsf{FVerify})$ is a pseudorandom function. The verification of computation correctness of $\mathsf{FVerify}()$ is compatible with Groth-Sahai proof. The underlying language for the proof system (P, V) is defined as

$$\mathcal{L} := \{(m, \mathsf{VK}, \mathsf{ek}, C, T) | \exists (r, \sigma, \mathsf{ID}, \mathsf{upk_{ID}}, \mathsf{cert_{ID}}, \pi_F)$$
$$[\mathsf{VFY}(\mathsf{VK}, (\mathsf{ID}, \mathsf{upk_{ID}}), \mathsf{cert_{ID}}) = 1 \wedge \mathsf{vfy}(vk_{\mathsf{ID}}, m, \sigma) = 1$$
$$\wedge C = \mathsf{Enc}(\mathsf{ek}, r, (\sigma, \mathsf{ID}, \mathsf{upk_{ID}}, \mathsf{cert_{ID}}))$$
$$\wedge \mathsf{FProve}(\mathsf{pk}_F, (\mathsf{ID}, m), T, \pi_F) = 1]\}.$$

Theorem 2. $\mathcal{LHIBS}$ *in Fig. 2 is traceable, linkable, weak CCA-anonymous (weak CPA-anonymous), signer-non-frameable, and issuer-non-frameable, if* $\mathcal{DS}_1$ *and* $\mathcal{DS}_2$ *are unforgeable against chosen message attacks,* $\mathcal{OTS}$ *is a one-time secure signature,* $\mathcal{E}$ *is IND-CCA-secure (IND-CPA-secure), the proof system* (P, V) *is adaptively sound, adaptively zero-knowledge, and one-time simulation-sound, and* F *is a PRF.*

5 Efficient Instantiations

To instantiate our general paradigm without resorting to random oracles, we use Groth-Sahai proof [19]. To this end, we use the group elements representation for user identities such that they are compatible with Groth-Sahai proof system. In particular, we select a structure-preserving signature [20] as the first-level signature ($\mathcal{DS}_1$) to sign the second-level signature ($\mathcal{DS}_2$) public key and user identity, both of which are group elements. Moreover, the identities, being group elements, can be fully extracted from the Groth-Sahai commitments. This makes the Open algorithm to be purely based on identity, in particular, does not require any archived membership information obtained when the user joins the systems and gets the credential.

We present three instantiations here. All the proposed instantiations use Groth-Sahai proof system as the underlying proof system. The first two instantiations use the full Boneh and Boyen (BB) signature [21] as the second-level scheme (for $\mathcal{DS}_2$), while the third instantiation uses a signature scheme by Yuen et al. [22] which is based on a static assumption. The public-key of BB signature consists of 2 group elements $upk_{\mathsf{ID}} = (y_1, y_2) \in \mathbb{G}^2$. A signature for message $m \in \mathbb{Z}_q$ is of the form $(s, t) \in \mathbb{G} \times \mathbb{Z}_q^*$ which is verifiable by $e(s, y_1 g^m y_2^t) = e(g, g)$. We do not mention the above common designs and only describe the different part in the following instantiations.

Table 1 summarizes the previous HIBS construction (with exculpability) due to Kiayias and Zhou [4], our two instantiations of HIBS in our stronger model, Inst1 and Inst2, and the most efficient group signature scheme (as a baseline) that provides concurrent security, CCA-anonymity, and non-frameability [23]. The size in kilobytes (KB) of the group elements are measured on "MNT159" [24] curve.

Table 1. Summary of the properties among the Kiayias-Zhou HIBS construction (with exculpability), the most efficient group signatures that provides CCA-anonymity and non-frameability (as a baseline), and our two instantiations of HIBS in our stronger model: $[N]$, $[n]$, and $[q]$ respectively denote the size of an element in $\mathbb{Z}_N^*$, $\mathbb{Z}_n^*$, and $\mathbb{Z}_q$ (assuming that the group elements and scalars can be represented in a similar bit-size)

Scheme	RO	Hidden-ID	Non-frame.	Anon.	Concur.	Assumption	Sig. size	Length
KZ [4]	Yes	Yes	Yes	CCA	No	DCR; S-RSA	$\approx 3^{[N]} + 16^{[n]}$	7.33 KB
AHO [23]	No	No	Yes	CCA	Yes	q-SFP	$55 + 1^{[q]}$	1.09 KB
Inst1	No	Yes	Yes	CCA	Yes	q-SFP; q-SDH	$60 + 1^{[q]}$	1.15 KB
Inst2	No	Yes	Yes	CCA	Yes	DLIN; q-SDH	$176 + 1^{[q]}$	3.41 KB
Inst3	No	Yes	Yes	CCA	Yes	DLIN	$494 + 1^{[q]}$	9.58 KB

5.1   Instantiation 1

In our first instantiation Inst1, we select Groth-Sahai proof system instantiated basing on SXDH assumption as the underlying proof system (P, V). As we have discussed previously, this setting is suitable for ElGamal encryption. Furthermore, SXDH setting is the most efficient instantiation of Groth-Sahai proof system, and Type III bilinear group operates with higher efficiency than the other two types do.

This instantiation uses the signature scheme proposed by Abe et al. [23] to implement the first-level structure-preserving signature $\mathcal{DS}_1$. It consists of 7 group elements, 4 of which can be perfectly randomized. The message signed by the first-level signature consists of 3 group elements, including the user identity which is one group element. A proof for the first-level signature consists of 4 elements (since the corresponding two pairing product equations are linear) and a proof for the second-level signature takes 4 group elements. For the underlying encryption scheme $\mathcal{E}$, we selected DDH-based ElGamal [25], which fits with the SXDH setting. $\mathcal{OTS}$ can be instantiated with a weak BB signature [21] which is not one-time. Its public key consists of 1 group element, and its signature consists of 1 group element.

The resulting CPA-anonymous HIBS Inst1 consists of 45 group elements and 1 scalar value (in $\mathbb{Z}_q$). Following the existing approach [26], the proposed instantiation Inst1 can achieve CCA-anonymity with extra 15 group elements. Thus, the resulting CCA-anonymous HIBS Inst1 consists of 60 group elements and 1 scalar value (in $\mathbb{Z}_q$).

5.2   Instantiation 2

Our second HIBS instantiation Inst2 is proven secure basing on simple assumptions in the standard model. The first level signature $\mathcal{DS}_1$ can be proven secure basing on static assumptions in the standard model. If we replace the second level signature, BB signature, with another scheme basing on a static assumption, then the HIBS scheme is basing on static assumption which is more desirable than basing on a q-type assumption as Inst1. This instantiation raises the security level in the cost of losing efficiency.

The DLIN-based Groth-Sahai proof is chosen as the proof system. This DLIN setting is compatible with Camenisch et al.'s encryption scheme [27].

We select the signature scheme from [27] to instantiate $\mathcal{DS}_1$. It consists of 17 group elements, only 2 of which can be perfectly randomized. The proof (for two signatures) includes 10 pairing product equations (none of them are linear) and thus consists of 90 group elements.

Since we select a CCA-secure structure-preserving encryption scheme [28], there is no extra overhead (e.g., addition of the extra 15 group elements in Inst1) to achieve CCA-anonymity. However, it is instantiated with a Type I bilinear group which is not as efficient as a Type III bilinear group. $\mathcal{OTS}$ is instantiated with weaker BB signature. The CCA-anonymous HIBS Inst2 obtained therefore consists of 176 group elements and 1 scalar value.

5.3   Instantiation 3

Our third HIBS instantiation Inst3 replaces the second level signature, and the one-time signature with a dual form exponent inversion signature scheme proposed by Yuen et al. [22]. This signature is based on static assumptions, making the whole scheme constructed upon static assumptions.

The DLIN-based Groth-Sahai proof is chosen as the proof system.

Again, we use the signature scheme from [27] as $\mathcal{DS}_1$. It consists of 17 group elements, only 2 of which can be perfectly randomized. The proof for the first-level signature includes 9 pairing product equations (none of them are linear) and thus consists of 81 group elements. Although the proof for the second-level signature only include 1 pairing product equation, this scheme requires more elements in the prime order group since it is converted from a dual form signature constructed originally in composite order group. Suppose an n-dimensional space is used to simulate the composite order group in prime order setting. We need n elements in the prime order group to represent one composite order group element, and need n^2 target group elements to represent a target group element in the composite order setting. In this signature scheme, $n = 6$, hence, there are totally 405 elements in this proof. The CCA-anonymous HIBS Inst3, instantiated with a Type I bilinear group, consists of 489 group elements and 1 scalar value.

6   Concluding Remarks

The motivation of group signature is to protect the member's anonymity in issuing signatures on behalf of the group, with an opening mechanism to indirectly ensure well-behavior of signers (or supports anonymity revocation especially when the signing key is compromised by an adversary). Yet, many existing realizations require the existence of a member list for opening to work. The existence of such list simply put the anonymity of the members in danger. A refinement of the group signature without such a list is called *hidden identity-based signatures* (HIBS) in the literature, such that the identity of a real signer is hidden in normal circumstance (just like group signature), yet can be revealed directly via the opening procedure (which does not require any input such as membership database apart from the opening secret key). Moreover, until recent advance in Groth-Sahai proof and structure-preserving signatures (SPS), group signature does not support concurrent member joining efficiently, which makes it impractical for settings with many users joining everyday such as Internet-based applications. In this paper, we propose efficient realization of HIBS which supports concurrent join.

Group signature is a fundamental primitive in supporting anonymous online communication, and we have already witnessed many extensions of group signatures. With our generic design of HIBS based on SPS, we show how various extended notion of group signatures can be realized.

A future direction is to remove the opening authority altogether, as in black-listable anonymous credential without trusted third party (TTP). However, the newer schemes (e.g. [29] and its follow-up works) often require the verifier to be the issuer itself, and the user credential is updated after each authentication for the efficiency of the whole system. In other words, the concurrency issue in granting the credential becomes even more prominent. Proposing such a system with concurrent security and acceptable efficiency is another interesting question.

Acknowledgment. Sherman Chow is supported in part by the Early Career Scheme and the Early Career Award (CUHK 439713), and General Research Funds (CUHK 14201914) of the Research Grants Council, University Grant Committee of Hong Kong. Haibin acknowledges NSF grant CNS 1330599 and CNS 1413996, as well as the Office of Naval Research grant N00014-13-1-0048.

References

1. Chaum, D., van Heyst, E.: Group signatures. In: Davies, D.W. (ed.) EUROCRYPT 1991. LNCS, vol. 547, pp. 257–265. Springer, Heidelberg (1991). https://doi.org/10.1007/3-540-46416-6_22

2. Camenisch, J., Michels, M.: Separability and efficiency for generic group signature schemes. In: Wiener, M. (ed.) CRYPTO 1999. LNCS, vol. 1666, pp. 413–430. Springer, Heidelberg (1999). https://doi.org/10.1007/3-540-48405-1_27

3. Kiayias, A., Zhou, H.-S.: Hidden identity-based signatures. In: Dietrich, S., Dhamija, R. (eds.) FC 2007. LNCS, vol. 4886, pp. 134–147. Springer, Heidelberg (2007). https://doi.org/10.1007/978-3-540-77366-5_14

4. Kiayias, A., Zhou, H.: Hidden identity-based signatures. IET Inf. Secur. **3**(3), 119–127 (2009)

5. Boyen, X., Waters, B.: Full-domain subgroup hiding and constant-size group signatures. In: Okamoto, T., Wang, X. (eds.) PKC 2007. LNCS, vol. 4450, pp. 1–15. Springer, Heidelberg (2007). https://doi.org/10.1007/978-3-540-71677-8_1

6. Liu, X., Xu, Q.-L.: Improved hidden identity-based signature scheme. In: International Conference on Intelligent Computing and Intelligent Systems (ICIS) (2010)

7. Liu, X., Xu, Q.-L.: Practical hidden identity-based signature scheme from bilinear pairings. In: 3rd International Conference on Computer Science and Information Technology (ICCSIT) (2010)

8. Liu, J.K., Wei, V.K., Wong, D.S.: Linkable spontaneous anonymous group signature for ad hoc groups. In: Wang, H., Pieprzyk, J., Varadharajan, V. (eds.) ACISP 2004. LNCS, vol. 3108, pp. 325–335. Springer, Heidelberg (2004). https://doi.org/10.1007/978-3-540-27800-9_28

9. Chow, S.S.M., Susilo, W., Yuen, T.H.: Escrowed linkability of ring signatures and its applications. In: Nguyen, P.Q. (ed.) VIETCRYPT 2006. LNCS, vol. 4341, pp. 175–192. Springer, Heidelberg (2006). https://doi.org/10.1007/11958239_12

10. Kiayias, A., Yung, M.: Group signatures with efficient concurrent join. In: Cramer, R. (ed.) EUROCRYPT 2005. LNCS, vol. 3494, pp. 198–214. Springer, Heidelberg (2005). https://doi.org/10.1007/11426639_12

11. Chow, S.S.M.: Real traceable signatures. In: Jacobson, M.J., Rijmen, V., Safavi-Naini, R. (eds.) SAC 2009. LNCS, vol. 5867, pp. 92–107. Springer, Heidelberg (2009). https://doi.org/10.1007/978-3-642-05445-7_6

12. Franklin, M., Zhang, H.: Unique group signatures. In: Foresti, S., Yung, M., Martinelli, F. (eds.) ESORICS 2012. LNCS, vol. 7459, pp. 643–660. Springer, Heidelberg (2012). https://doi.org/10.1007/978-3-642-33167-1_37

13. Galindo, D., Herranz, J., Kiltz, E.: On the generic construction of identity-based signatures with additional properties. In: Lai, X., Chen, K. (eds.) ASIACRYPT 2006. LNCS, vol. 4284, pp. 178–193. Springer, Heidelberg (2006). https://doi.org/10.1007/11935230_12

14. Abe, M., Chow, S.S.M., Haralambiev, K., Ohkubo, M.: Double-trapdoor anonymous tags for traceable signatures. Int. J. Inf. Secur. **12**(1), 19–31 (2013)

15. Bellare, M., Shi, H., Zhang, C.: Foundations of group signatures: the case of dynamic groups. In: Menezes, A. (ed.) CT-RSA 2005. LNCS, vol. 3376, pp. 136–153. Springer, Heidelberg (2005). https://doi.org/10.1007/978-3-540-30574-3_11

16. Bootle, J., Cerulli, A., Chaidos, P., Ghadafi, E., Groth, J.: Foundations of fully dynamic group signatures. In: Manulis, M., Sadeghi, A.-R., Schneider, S. (eds.) ACNS 2016. LNCS, vol. 9696, pp. 117–136. Springer, Cham (2016). https://doi.org/10.1007/978-3-319-39555-5_7

17. Shamir, A.: Identity-based cryptosystems and signature schemes. In: Blakley, G.R., Chaum, D. (eds.) CRYPTO 1984. LNCS, vol. 196, pp. 47–53. Springer, Heidelberg (1985). https://doi.org/10.1007/3-540-39568-7_5

18. Bellare, M., Namprempre, C., Neven, G.: Security proofs for identity-based identification and signature schemes. In: Cachin, C., Camenisch, J.L. (eds.) EUROCRYPT 2004. LNCS, vol. 3027, pp. 268–286. Springer, Heidelberg (2004). https://doi.org/10.1007/978-3-540-24676-3_17

19. Groth, J., Sahai, A.: Efficient noninteractive proof systems for bilinear groups. SIAM J. Comput. **41**(5), 1193–1232 (2012)

20. Abe, M., Fuchsbauer, G., Groth, J., Haralambiev, K., Ohkubo, M.: Structure-preserving signatures and commitments to group elements. In: Rabin, T. (ed.) CRYPTO 2010. LNCS, vol. 6223, pp. 209–236. Springer, Heidelberg (2010). https://doi.org/10.1007/978-3-642-14623-7_12

21. Boneh, D., Boyen, X.: Short signatures without random oracles. In: Cachin, C., Camenisch, J.L. (eds.) EUROCRYPT 2004. LNCS, vol. 3027, pp. 56–73. Springer, Heidelberg (2004). https://doi.org/10.1007/978-3-540-24676-3_4

22. Yuen, T.H., Chow, S.S.M., Zhang, C., Yiu, S.: Exponent-inversion signatures and IBE under static assumptions. IACR Cryptology ePrint Archive, Report 2014/311 (2014)

23. Abe, M., Haralambiev, K., Ohkubo, M.: Signing on elements in bilinear groups for modular protocol design. IACR Cryptology ePrint Archive, Report 2010/133 (2010). http://eprint.iacr.org/2010/133

24. Miyaji, A., Nakabayashi, M., Takano, S.: New explicit conditions of elliptic curve traces for FR-reduction. IEICE Trans. Fund. **84**(5), 1234–1243 (2001)

25. ElGamal, T.: A public key cryptosystem and a signature scheme based on discrete logarithms. In: Blakley, G.R., Chaum, D. (eds.) CRYPTO 1984. LNCS, vol. 196, pp. 10–18. Springer, Heidelberg (1985). https://doi.org/10.1007/3-540-39568-7_2

26. Groth, J.: Fully anonymous group signatures without random oracles. In: Kurosawa, K. (ed.) ASIACRYPT 2007. LNCS, vol. 4833, pp. 164–180. Springer, Heidelberg (2007). https://doi.org/10.1007/978-3-540-76900-2_10

27. Abe, M., Chase, M., David, B., Kohlweiss, M., Nishimaki, R., Ohkubo, M.: Constant-size structure-preserving signatures: generic constructions and simple assumptions. In: Wang, X., Sako, K. (eds.) ASIACRYPT 2012. LNCS, vol. 7658, pp. 4–24. Springer, Heidelberg (2012). https://doi.org/10.1007/978-3-642-34961-4_3

28. Camenisch, J., Haralambiev, K., Kohlweiss, M., Lapon, J., Naessens, V.: Structure preserving CCA secure encryption and applications. In: Lee, D.H., Wang, X. (eds.) ASIACRYPT 2011. LNCS, vol. 7073, pp. 89–106. Springer, Heidelberg (2011). https://doi.org/10.1007/978-3-642-25385-0_5

29. Au, M.H., Tsang, P.P., Kapadia, A.: PEREA: practical TTP-free revocation of repeatedly misbehaving anonymous users. ACM Trans. Inf. Syst. Secur. **14**(4), 29 (2011)

BehavioCog: An Observation Resistant Authentication Scheme

Jagmohan Chauhan[1,2]($\boxtimes$), Benjamin Zi Hao Zhao[1], Hassan Jameel Asghar[2], Jonathan Chan[2], and Mohamed Ali Kaafar[2]

[1] UNSW, Sydney, Australia
{jagmohan.chauhan,ben.zhao}@data61.csiro.au
[2] Data61, CSIRO, Sydney, Australia
{hassan.asghar,jonathan.chan,dali.kaafar}@data61.csiro.au

Abstract. We propose that by integrating behavioural biometric gestures such as drawing figures on a touch screen with challenge-response based cognitive authentication schemes, we can benefit from the properties of both. On the one hand, we can improve the usability of existing cognitive schemes by significantly reducing the number of challenge-response rounds by (partially) relying on the hardness of mimicking carefully designed behavioural biometric gestures. On the other hand, the observation resistant property of cognitive schemes provides an extra layer of protection for behavioural biometrics; an attacker is unsure if a failed impersonation is due to a biometric failure or a wrong response to the challenge. We design and develop a prototype of such a "hybrid" scheme, named BehavioCog. To provide security close to a 4-digit PIN—one in 10,000 chance to impersonate—we only need two challenge-response rounds, which can be completed in less than 38 s on average (as estimated in our user study), with the advantage that unlike PINs or passwords, the scheme is secure under observation.

1 Introduction

In Eurocrypt 1991 [30], Matsumoto and Imai raised an intriguing question: Is it possible to authenticate a user when someone is observing? Clearly, passwords, PINs or graphical patterns are insecure under this threat model. Unfortunately, a secure observation resistant authentication scheme is still an open problem. Most proposed solutions are a form of shared-secret challenge-response authentication protocols relying on human cognitive abilities, henceforth referred to as cognitive schemes. To minimize cognitive load on humans, the size $|R|$ of the response space R needs to be small, typically ranging between 2 and 10 [5,20,26,39]. Since anyone can randomly guess the response to a challenge with probability $|R|^{-1}$, the number of challenges (or rounds) per authentication session needs to be increased, thereby increasing authentication time. For example, to achieve a security equivalent to (guessing) a six digit PIN, i.e., 10^{-6}, the cognitive authentication scheme (CAS) [39] requires 11 rounds resulting in 120 s to authenticate,

---

The full (more detailed) version is available as the conference version of this paper.

© International Financial Cryptography Association 2017
A. Kiayias (Ed.): FC 2017, LNCS 10322, pp. 39–58, 2017.
https://doi.org/10.1007/978-3-319-70972-7_3

while the Hopper and Blum (HB) scheme [20] requires 20 rounds and 660 s [41]. An authentication time between 10 to 30 s per round is perhaps acceptable if we could reduce the number of rounds, since cognitive schemes provide strong security under observation.

Our idea is to leverage gesture-based behavioural biometrics by mapping $|R|$ different gesture-based *symbols* (words or figures) to the $|R|$ different responses. Both the mapping and the symbols are public. The user renders symbols on the touch screen of a device, e.g., a smartphone. A classifier decides whether the rendering matches that of the target user. We could tune the classifier to achieve a true positive rate (TPR) close to 1, while giving it some leverage in the false positive rate (FPR), say 0.10. The attacker has to correctly guess the cognitive response and correctly mimic the target user's gesture. We now see how we can reduce the number of rounds of the cognitive scheme. Suppose $|R| = 4$ in the cognitive scheme. If the average FPR of rendering four symbols, (i.e., success rate of mimicking a target user's rendering of the four symbols), is 0.10, then the probability of randomly guessing the response to a challenge can be derived as FPR $\times |R|^{-1} = 0.10 \times 0.25 = 0.025$. Thus, only 4 rounds instead of 11 will make the guess probability lower than the security of a 6-digit PIN. Reducing the number of rounds minimizes the authentication time and reduces the cognitive load on the user. The idea also prevents a possible attack on standalone behavioural biometric based authentication. Standalone here mean schemes which only rely on behavioural based biometrics. Minus the cognitive scheme, an imposter can use the behavioural biometric system as an "oracle" by iteratively adapting its mimicking of the target user's gestures until it succeeds. Integrated with a cognitive scheme, the imposter is unsure whether a failed attempt is due to a biometric error or a cognitive error, or both.

Combining the two authentication approaches into a "hybrid" scheme is not easy, because: (a) to prevent observation attacks, the behavioural biometric gestures should be hard to mimic. Simple gestures (swipes) are susceptible to mimicry attacks [23], while more complex gestures [31,33] (free-hand drawings) only tackle shoulder-surfing attacks, and (b) the cognitive schemes proposed in the literature are either not secure [39] against known attacks or not usable due to high cognitive load (see Sect. 7). This leads to our other main contributions:

– We propose a new gesture based behavioural biometric scheme that employs a set of words constructed from certain letters of English alphabets (e.g., b, f, g, x, m). Since such letters are harder to write [22], we postulate that they might show more inter-user variation while being harder to mimic. Our results indicate plausibility of this claim; we achieve an average FPR of 0.05 under video based observation attacks.
– We propose a new cognitive authentication scheme inspired from the HB protocol [20] and the Foxtail protocol [1,26]. The scheme can be thought of as a contrived version of learning with noisy samples, where the noise is partially a function of the challenge. The generalized form of the resulting scheme is conjectured to resist around $|R| \times n$ challenge-response pairs against computationally efficient attacks; n being the size of the problem.

- We combine the above two into a hybrid authentication scheme called BehavioCog and implement it as an app on Android smartphones. The app is configurable; parameter sizes of both the cognitive (challenge size, secret size, etc.) and behavioural biometric (symbols, amount of training, etc.) components can be tuned at set up.
- We extensively analyze the usability, security and repeatability of our scheme with 41 users. The average authentication time for each round is as low as 19 s, and we achieve security comparable to a 4-digit and 6-digit PIN in just 2 and 3 rounds, respectively, even under observation attacks. Our user study assesses security against video-based observation by recording successful authentication sessions and then asking users to impersonate the target users. None of the video based observation attacks were successful (with two rounds in one authentication session). We show that by carefully designing the training module, the error rate in authentication can be as low as 14% even after a gap of one week, which can be further reduced by decreasing the secret size.

We do not claim that our idea completely solves the problem raised by Matsumoto and Imai, but believe it to be a step forward towards that goal, which could potentially revive interest in research on cognitive authentication schemes and their application as a separate factor in multi-factor authentication schemes.

2   Overview of BehavioCog

2.1   Preliminaries

Authentication Schemes: A *shared-secret challenge-response* authentication scheme consists of two protocols: *registration* and *authentication*, between the a user (prover) $\mathcal{U}$, and an authentication service (verifier) $\mathcal{S}$, who share a secret x from a secret space X during registration. The authentication phase is as follows: for γ rounds, $\mathcal{S}$ sends a challenge $c \in C$ to $\mathcal{U}$, who sends the response $r = f(x, c)$ back to $\mathcal{S}$. If all γ responses are correct $\mathcal{S}$ accepts $\mathcal{U}$. Here, C is the challenge space, and r belongs to a response space R. We refer to the function $f : X \times C \rightarrow R$ as the cognitive function. It has to be computed mentally by the user. The server also computes the response (as the user and the server share the same secret). Apart from the selected secret $x \in X$, everything else is public. A challenge and a response from the same round shall be referred to as a challenge-response pair. An authentication session, consists of γ challenge-response pairs. In practice, we assume $\mathcal{U}$ and $\mathcal{S}$ interact via the $\mathcal{U}$'s device, e.g., a smartphone.

Adversarial Model: We assume a passive adversary $\mathcal{A}$ who can observe one or more authentication sessions between $\mathcal{U}$ and $\mathcal{S}$. The goal of $\mathcal{A}$ is to impersonate $\mathcal{U}$ by initiating a new session with $\mathcal{S}$, either via its own device or via $\mathcal{U}$'s device, and making it accept $\mathcal{A}$ as $\mathcal{U}$. In practice, we assume that $\mathcal{A}$ can observe the screen of the device used by $\mathcal{U}$. This can be done either via shoulder-surfing (simply by looking over $\mathcal{U}$'s shoulder) or via a video recording using a spy camera.

The attacker is a human who is given an indefinite access to the video recordings of the user touch gestures and tries to mimic the user. Unlike the original threat model from Matsumoto and Imai, our threat model assumes that the device as well as the communication channel between the device and $\mathcal{S}$ are secure.

2.2 The BehavioCog Scheme

The main idea of BehavioCog hybrid authentication scheme is as follows. Instead of sending the response r to a challenge c from $\mathcal{S}$, $\mathcal{U}$ renders a *symbol* corresponding to r (on the touch screen of the device), and this rendered symbol is then sent to $\mathcal{S}$. More specifically, we assume a set of symbols denoted Ω, e.g., a set of words in English, where the number of symbols equals the number of responses $|R|$. Each response $r \in R$ is mapped to a symbol in Ω. The symbol corresponding to r shall be represented by sym(r). Upon receiving the rendering of sym(r), $\mathcal{S}$ first checks if the rendered symbol "matches" a previously stored rendering from $\mathcal{U}$ (called template) by using a classifier D and then checks if the response r is correct by computing f. If the answer to both is yes in each challenge-response round, $\mathcal{S}$ accepts $\mathcal{U}$.

The scheme consists of setup, registration and authentication protocols. We begin by detailing the cognitive scheme first. Assume a global pool of n objects (object is a generic term and can be instantiated by emojis, images or alphanumerics). We used pass-emojis in the paper. A secret $x \in X$ is a k-element subset of the global pool of objects. Thus, $|X| = \binom{n}{k}$. Each object of x is called a pass-object, and the remaining $n - k$ objects are called decoys. The challenge space C consists of pairs $c = (a, w)$, where a is an l-element sequence of objects from the global pool, and w is an l-element sequence of integers from $\mathbb{Z}_d$, where $d \geq 2$. Members of w shall be called weights. The ith weight in w is denoted w_i and corresponds to the ith element of a, i.e., a_i. The notation $c \in_U C$ means sampling a random l-element sequence of objects a and a random l-element sequence of weights w. The cognitive function f is defined as

$$f(x, c) = \begin{cases} \left(\sum_{i \mid a_i \in x} w_i\right) \bmod d, & \text{if } x \cap a \neq \emptyset \\ r \in_U \mathbb{Z}_d, & \text{if } x \cap a = \emptyset. \end{cases} \qquad (1)$$

That is, sum all the weights of the pass-objects in c and return the answer modulo d. If no pass-object is present then a random element from $\mathbb{Z}_d$ is returned. The notation $\in_U$ means sampling uniformly at random. It follows that the response space $R = \mathbb{Z}_d$ and $|R| = d$. Now, let Ω be a set of d symbols, e.g., the words zero, one, two, and so on. The mapping sym $: \mathbb{Z}_d \to \Omega$ is the straightforward lexicographic mapping and is public. We assume a $(d + 1)$-classifier D (see Sect. 4) which when given as input the templates of all symbols in Ω, and a rendering purported to be of some symbol from Ω, outputs the corresponding symbol in Ω if the rendering matches any of the symbol templates. If no match is found, D outputs "none." D needs a certain number of renderings of each symbol to build its templates, which we denote by t (e.g., $t = 3, 5$ or 10).

The setup phase consists of S publishing the parameters n, k, l and d (e.g., $n = 180$, $k = 14$, $l = 30$, $d = 5$), a pool of n objects (e.g., emojis), a set of d symbols Ω (e.g., words), the map sym from $\mathbb{Z}_d$ to Ω, the (untrained) classifier D, and t Fig. 1 describes the registration and authentication protocols. Since the registration protocol is straightforward, we only briefly describe the authentication protocol here. S initializes an *error* flag to 0 (Step 1). Then, for each of the γ rounds, S sends $c = (a, w) \in_U C$ to $\mathcal{U}$ (Step 3). $\mathcal{U}$ computes f according to Eq. 1, and obtains the response r (Step 4). $\mathcal{U}$ gets the symbol to be rendered through sym(r), and sends a rendering of the symbol to S (Step 5). Now, S runs the trained classifier D on the rendered symbol (Step 6). If the classifier outputs "none," S sets the error flag to 1 (Step 8). Otherwise, D outputs the symbol corresponding to the rendering. Through the inverse map, S gets the response r corresponding to the symbol (Step 10). Now, if $x \cap a = \emptyset$, i.e., none of the pass-objects are in the challenge, then any response $r \in \mathbb{Z}_d$ is valid, and therefore S moves to the next round. Otherwise, if $x \cap a \neq \emptyset$, S further checks if r is indeed the correct response by computing f (Step 11). If it is incorrect, S sets the error flag to 1 (Step 12). Otherwise, if the response is correct, S moves to the next round. If after the end of γ rounds, the error flag is 0, then S accepts $\mathcal{U}$, otherwise it rejects $\mathcal{U}$ (Step 13).

1: Registration.

1 $\mathcal{U}$ and S share a secret $x \in X$.
2 For each symbol in Ω, $\mathcal{U}$ sends t renderings to S.
3 For each symbol in Ω, S trains D on the t renderings to obtain $\mathcal{U}$'s template.
4 The secret consists of x and the d templates.

2: Authentication.

1 S sets err $= 0$.
2 **for** γ *rounds* **do**
3   S samples $c = (a, w) \in_U C$ and sends it to $\mathcal{U}$.
4     $\mathcal{U}$ computes $r = f(x, c)$.
5     $\mathcal{U}$ renders the symbol sym(r), and sends it to S.
6   S runs D on the rendering.
7   **if** D *outputs "none"* **then**
8   S sets err $= 1$.
9   **else**
10   S obtains r corresponding to the symbol output by D.
11   **if** $x \cap a \neq \emptyset$ *and* $r \neq f(x, c)$ **then**
12   S sets err $= 1$.
13 **If** err $= 1$, S rejects $\mathcal{U}$; otherwise it accepts $\mathcal{U}$.

Fig. 1. The registration and authentication protocols of BehavioCog.

3   The Cognitive Scheme

Our proposed cognitive scheme can be thought of as an amalgamation of the HB scheme based on the learning parity with noise (LPN) problem [20], and the Foxtail scheme (with window) [1,26]. Briefly, a round of the HB protocol consists of an n-element (random) challenge from $\mathbb{Z}_2^n$. The user computes the dot product modulo 2 of the challenge with a binary secret vector from $\mathbb{Z}_2^n$. With a predefined probability η, say 0.25, the user flips the response, thus adding noise. When the series of challenge-response pairs are written as a system of linear congruences, solving it is known as the LPN problem. The HB protocol can be generalized to a higher modulus d [20]. The Foxtail scheme consists of dot products modulo 4 of the secret vector with challenge vectors from $\mathbb{Z}_4^n$. If the result of the dot product is in $\{0,1\}$ the user sends 0 as the response, and 1 otherwise. The "window-based" version of Foxtail, consists of challenges that are of length $l < n$. More specifically, we use the idea of using an l-element challenge from the Foxtail with window scheme. However instead of using the Foxtail function, which maps the sum of integers modulo $d = 4$, to 0 if the sum is in $\{0,1\}$, and 1 otherwise, we output the sum itself as the answer. The reason for that is to reduce the number of rounds, i.e., γ, for a required security level (the success probability of random guess is $\frac{1}{2}$ in one round of the Foxtail scheme). Now if we allow the user to only output 0 in case none of its pass-objects are present in a challenge, the output of f is skewed towards 0, which makes the scheme susceptible to a statistical attack proposed by Yan et al. [41] outlined in Sect. 3.1. To prevent such attacks, we ask the user to output a random response from $\mathbb{Z}_d$ (not only zero) in such a case. Due to the random response, we can say that the resulting scheme adds noise to the samples (challenge-response pairs) collected by $\mathcal{A}$, somewhat similar in spirit to HB. The difference is that in our case, the noise is (partially) a function of the challenge, whereas in HB the noise is independently generated with a fixed probability and added to the sum. We remark that if we were to use the HB protocol with a restricted window (i.e., parameter l) and restricted Hamming weight (i.e., parameter k), the resulting scheme is not based on the standard LPN problem. We next discuss the security of our cognitive scheme.

3.1   Security Analysis

Due to space limitation we only discuss the general results here and leave their derivation and detailed explanation to Appendix A in our full paper. This analysis is based on well-known attacks on cognitive authentication schemes. We do not claim this analysis to be comprehensive, as new efficient attacks may be found in the future. Nevertheless, the analysis shown here sheds light on why the scheme was designed the way it is.

Random Guess Attack: The success probability p_{RG} of a random guess is conditioned on the event $a \cap x$ being *empty* or not. Since this event shall be frequently referred to in the text, we give it a special name: the *empty case*. The probability of the empty case is $\mathbb{P}\left[|a \cap x| = 0\right] \doteq p_0 = \binom{n-k}{l}/\binom{n}{l}$. We shall use the notation $\doteq$ when defining a variable. Thus, $p_{\mathrm{RG}} = p_0 + (1 - p_0)\frac{1}{d}$.

Brute Force Attack (BF) and Information Theoretic Bound. This attack outputs a unique candidate for the secret after $m \doteq m_{\mathrm{it}} = -\log_2 \binom{n}{k}/\log_2(p_0 + (1 - p_0)\frac{1}{d})$ challenge-response pairs have been observed. We call m_{it}, the information theoretic bound on m. The complexity of the brute force attack is $\binom{n}{k}$.

Meet-in-the-Middle Attack (MitM). This attack [20] works by dividing the search space in half by computing $\frac{k}{2}$-sized subsets of X, storing "intermediate" responses in a hash table, and then finding collisions. The time and space complexity of this attack is $\binom{n}{k/2}$. There could be variants of the meet-in-the-middle attack that could trade less space with time. For this analysis, we focus on the version that is most commonly quoted.

Frequency Analysis. Frequency analysis, proposed by Yan et al. [41],[3] could be done either independently or dependent on the response. In response-independent frequency analysis, a frequency table of δ-tuples of objects is created, where $1 \le \delta \le k$. If a δ-tuple is present in a challenge, its frequency is incremented by 1. After gathering enough challenge-response pairs, the tuples with the highest or lowest frequencies may contain the k secret objects if the challenges are constructed with a skewed distribution. In the response-dependent frequency analysis, the frequency table contains frequencies for each possible response in $\mathbb{Z}_d$, and the frequency of a δ-tuple is incremented by 1 in the column corresponding to the response (if present in the challenge). Our scheme is immune to both forms of frequency analysis (see Appendix A of the full paper).

Coskun and Herley Attack. Since only l objects are present in each challenge, the number of pass-objects present is also less than k with high probability. Let u denote the average number of bits of x used in responding to a challenge. The Coskun and Herley (CH) attack [14] states that if u is small, then candidates $y \in X, y \ne x$, that are close to x in terms of some distance metric, will output similar responses to x. If we sample a large enough subset from X, then with high probability there is a candidate for x that is a distance ξ from x. We can remove all those candidates whose responses are far away from the observed responses, and then iteratively move closer to x. The running time of the CH attack is at least $|X|/\binom{\log_2 |X|}{\xi}$ [14] where $|X| = \binom{n}{k}$, with the trade off that $m \approx \frac{1}{\epsilon^2}$ samples are needed for the attack to output x with high probability [2,7]. The parameter ϵ is the difference in probabilities that distance $\xi + 1$ and $\xi - 1$ candidates have the same response as x.

Linearization. Linearization works by translating the observed challenge-response pairs into a system of linear equations (or congruences). If this can be done, then Gaussian elimination can be used to uniquely obtain the secret. In Appendix A of our full paper, we show two different ways our proposed cognitive schemes can be translated into a system of linear equations with dn unknowns. This means that the adversary needs to observe dn challenge-response pairs to obtain a unique solution through Gaussian elimination. Note that if $\mathcal{U}$ were to respond with 0 in the empty case, then we could obtain a linear system of equations after n challenge-response pairs. The introduction of noise expands the number of required challenge-response pairs by a factor of d. Gaussian elimination is by far the most efficient attack on our scheme, and therefore this

---

[3] We borrow the term frequency analysis from [4].

constitutes a significant gain. We believe the problem of finding a polynomial time algorithm in (k, l, n) which uses $m < dn$ number of samples (say $(d-1)n$ samples) from the function described in Eq. 1 is an interesting open question.

3.2   Example Parameter Sizes

Table 1 (left) shows example list of parameter sizes for the cognitive scheme. These are obtained by fixing $d = 5$ and changing k, l and n such that p_{RG} is approximately 0.25. We suggest $d = 5$ as a balance between reducing the number of rounds required, i.e., γ, and ease of computing f. The column labelled m_{it} is the information theoretic bound to uniquely obtain the secret. Thus, the first two suggestions are only secure with $\leq m_{it}$ observed samples. The complexity shown for both the meet-in-the-middle attack (MitM) and Coskun and Herley (CH) attack represents time as well as space complexity. The last column is Gaussian elimination (GE), for which the required number of samples is calculated as dn. For other attacks, we show the minimum number of required samples m, such that $m \geq m_{it}$ and the complexity is as reported. We can think of the last two suggested sizes as secure against an adversary with time/memory resources $\approx 2^{70}/2^{40}$ (medium strength) and $\approx 2^{80}/2^{50}$ (high strength), respectively. The medium and high strength adversaries are defined in terms of the computational resources they possess. In general, there can be many levels of strength (by assigning limits of time/space resources an adversary can have). The strength levels are chosen to illustrate how parameter sizes can be chosen against adversarial resources. The parameter sizes are chosen such that the attack complexity vs the number of samples required are as given in Table 1.

Based on parameter sizes for the cognitive scheme and results from the user study, we recommend the parameters for BehavioCog shown in Table 1 (right). The columns labelled "Sessions" indicate whether the target is a medium-strength or high-strength adversary $\mathcal{A}$. Based on our experiments, CW (complex words) gave the best average FPR of 0.05 (see next section). The "Security" column shows $\mathcal{A}$'s probability in impersonating the user by random guess and mimicking the corresponding behavioural biometric symbol. By setting $p_{RG} = 0.25$ and multiplying it with FPR, we estimate the total impersonation probability of $\mathcal{A}$. For reference, the same probability for a 4-digit PIN is 1×10^{-4}, and for a 6-digit PIN is 1×10^{-6} (but with no security under observation).

4   The Behavioural Biometric Scheme

Our behavioural biometric authentication scheme is based on touch gestures. We first describe the set of symbols followed by the classifier D and finally the identified features. For each symbol in Ω, TPR of D is the rate when it correctly matches $\mathcal{U}$'s renderings of the symbol to $\mathcal{U}$'s template. FPR of D is the rate when it wrongly decides $\mathcal{A}$'s rendering of the symbol matches $\mathcal{U}$'s template.

Table 1. Example parameter sizes for cognitive scheme (left) and BehavioCog (right), where m_{it}: information theoretic bound, p_{RG}: random guess probability, BF: Brute Force, MitM: Meet in the Middle, CH: Coksun and Harley, GE: Gaussian Elimination.

(d, k, l, n)	m_{it}	p_{RG}	BF	MitM	CH	GE
$(5, 5, 24, 60)$	11	0.255	2^{22}	2^{12}	2^{11}	poly(n)
Samples required	-	0	11	11	23	300
$(5, 10, 30, 130)$	24	0.252	2^{48}	2^{28}	2^{33}	poly(n)
Samples required	-	0	24	24	24	650
$(5, 14, 30, 180)$	34	0.256	2^{68}	2^{40}	2^{40}	poly(n)
Samples required	-	0	34	34	94	900
$(5, 18, 30, 225)$	44	0.254	2^{87}	2^{51}	2^{51}	poly(n)
Samples required	-	0	44	44	168	1125

(d, k, l, n)	γ	Sessions (med. $\mathcal{A}$)	Sessions (high $\mathcal{A}$)	Ω	Security
$(5, 5, 24, 60)$	1	10	10	CW	1.3×10^{-2}
$(5, 5, 24, 60)$	2	5	5	CW	1.5×10^{-4}
$(5, 5, 24, 60)$	3	3	3	CW	2×10^{-6}
$(5, 10, 30, 130)$	1	24	24	CW	1.3×10^{-2}
$(5, 10, 30, 130)$	2	12	12	CW	1.5×10^{-4}
$(5, 10, 30, 130)$	3	8	8	CW	2×10^{-6}
$(5, 14, 30, 180)$	1	94	34	CW	1.3×10^{-2}
$(5, 14, 30, 180)$	2	47	17	CW	1.5×10^{-4}
$(5, 14, 30, 180)$	3	31	11	CW	2×10^{-6}
$(5, 18, 30, 225)$	1	511	168	CW	1.3×10^{-2}
$(5, 18, 30, 225)$	2	255	84	CW	1.5×10^{-4}
$(5, 18, 30, 225)$	3	170	56	CW	2×10^{-6}

4.1 Choice of Symbols

We require that symbols be: (a) rich enough to simulate multiple swipes, (b) hard for $\mathcal{A}$ to mimic even after observation, (c) easily repeatable by $\mathcal{U}$ between successive authentications, and (d) easily distinguishable from each other by D. Accordingly, we choose four different sets of symbols (see Table 2). We tried testing all the four sets of symbols in our first phase of the user study to see which one satisfies all the four aforementioned criteria. We used complex words in the implementation of our scheme as it was the best symbol set. The words or figures are used for behavioural biometrics while emojis are used for cognitive scheme.

Easy words: These are English words for the numbers, and serve as the base case.

Complex words: Since the letters $b, f, g, h, k, m, n, q, t, u, w, x, y, z$ are more difficult to write cursively than others as they contain more turns [22], we hypothesize that words constructed from them might also show more inter-user variation and be difficult to mimic. Our user study shows positive evidence, as complex words were the most resilient against observation attacks. We constructed five words of length 4 from these 14 letters since users find it hard to render higher length words on touchscreen. As it is difficult to construct meaningful words without vowels, we allowed one vowel in each word.

Easy figures: This set contains numbers written in blackboard bold shape. A user can render them by starting at the top left most point and traversing in a down and right manner without lifting the finger. This removes the high variability within user's drawings present in the next set of symbols.

Complex figures: These figures were constructed by following some principles (to make them harder to mimic): no dots or taps [13,24], contain sharp turns and angles [33], the users finger must move in all directions while drawing the symbol. To help the user associate responses in $\mathbb{Z}_5$ to complex words, mnemonic associations were used (Appendix D in the full paper).

Table 2. Mapping of responses ($d = 5$) to symbols.

response	0	1	2	3	4
easy words	zero	one	two	three	four
complex words	xman	bmwz	quak	hurt	fogy
easy figures					
complex figures					

4.2 Choice of Classifier

We picked dynamic time warping (DTW) [32] because: (a) all chosen symbols exhibit features that are a function of time, (b) it shows high accuracy with a small number of training samples (5–10) [17,31] (to minimize registration time). Given two time series, DTW finds the *optimal warped* path between the two time series to measure the similarity between them [32]. Assume there is a set Q of features, each of which is a time series. Let $\hat{Q}$ represent the set of templates of the features in Q, which are also time series. Given a test sample of these features (for authentication), also represented Q, the multi-dimensional DTW distance between $\hat{Q}$ and Q is defined as [34]: $\mathrm{DTW}(\hat{Q}, Q) = \sum_{i=1}^{|Q|} \mathrm{DTW}(\hat{q}_i, q_i)$, where $\hat{q}_i \in \hat{Q}$ and $q_i \in Q$, are time series corresponding to feature i.

4.3 Template Creation

For each user-symbol pair (each user drawing a particular symbol) we obtain t sample renderings, resulting in t time series for each feature. Fix each feature, we take one of the t time series at a time, compute its DTW distance with the $t-1$ remaining time series, and sum the distances. The time series with the minimum sum is chosen as the *optimal feature template*. The process is repeated for all features to create the template $\hat{Q}$. We created two sets of optimal templates: (1) $\hat{Q}_{\text{sym}}$ to check if $\mathcal{U}$ produced a valid rendering of a symbol from Ω (only using x, y coordinates) and (2) $\hat{Q}_{\text{user}}$ to check if the rendering comes from the target user $\mathcal{U}$ or an attacker. Basically, the first template set is used to check if the user rendered a symbol from the set of allowed symbols Ω or some random symbol not in Ω. After this has been ascertained, it is checked whether the symbol is close to the user's template from the other template set (check behavioural biometrics).

4.4 Classification Decision

Given a set of feature values Q from a sample, the decision is made based on whether $DTW(\hat{Q}, Q)$ lies below the threshold calculated as $\hbar \doteq \mu + z\sigma$. Here μ is the mean DTW distance between the user's optimal template $\hat{Q}$ and all of the user's t samples in the registration phase [27]. σ is the standard deviation, and $z \geq 0$ is a global parameter that is set according to data collected from all users and remains the same for all users. The thresholds $\hbar_{sym}$ and $\hbar_{user}$ correspond to $\hat{Q}_{sym}$ and $\hat{Q}_{user}$, respectively. The classification works as follows:

Step 1: If for a given challenge $c = (a, w)$, $x \cap a \neq \emptyset$ (non-empty case), $\mathcal{S}$ first gets the target symbol by computing f. Target symbol is the symbol corresponding to the correct response. Then, $\mathcal{S}$ rejects $\mathcal{U}$ if the DTW distance between $\hat{Q}_{sym}$ and the sample is $> \hbar_{sym}$. Otherwise, $\mathcal{S}$ moves to Step 2. In the empty case, $\mathcal{S}$ computes the DTW distance between the sample and $\hat{Q}_{sym}$ for each symbol and picks the symbol which gives the least distance. Next, the distance is compared with $\hbar_{sym}$ for that symbol, and $\mathcal{S}$ accordingly rejects or goes to Step 2.

Step 2: $\mathcal{S}$ computes the DTW distance between the sample and $\hat{Q}_{user}$ of the symbol. If the distance is $> \hbar_{user}$, the user is rejected, otherwise it is accepted.

4.5 Feature Identification and Selection

We identify 19 types of features from the literature [11,13,35,40] and obtain 40 features (Table 3), most of which are self explanatory. Explanation of curvature, slope angle and path angle is described in [35]. Device-interaction features were obtained using the inertial motion sensors: accelerometer and gyroscope of the smartphone. Our scheme can be used for any device equipped with a touch screen and inertial motion sensors. We perform a standard z-score normalization on each feature. As an example, Appendix B in the full paper illustrates the discriminatory power of a single feature (x). To select the most distinguishing features from the 40 features for each symbol, we created our own variation of sequential forward feature selection (SFS) [15]. See Algorithm 1 in Appendix C of our full paper. The algorithm takes as an input a list of features Q_{tot} and a symbol, and outputs a selected list of features Q for that symbol. The algorithm starts with an empty list and iteratively adds one feature at a time by keeping TPR = 1.0 and minimizing the FPR values (calculated based on user-adversary pairs, see Sect. 5) until all features in Q_{tot} are exhausted. At the end, we are left with multiple candidate subsets for Q from which we pick the one with TPR = 1.0 and the least FPR as the final set of features. The algorithm calls the Get z-List algorithm (Algorithm 2 in Appendix C of our full paper) as a subroutine (based on a similar procedure from [27]). This algorithm computes the z values that give TPR of 1 and the least FPR for each possible feature subset. The z values give the amount of deviation from the standard deviation.

Table 3. List of features.

Touch feature	Symbol	Stylometric feature	Symbol	Device-interaction feature	Symbol
Coordinates and change in coordinates	x, y, δx, δy	Top, bottom, left, right most point	TMP, BMP, LMP, RMP	Rotational position of device in space	R_x, R_y, R_z
Velocity along coordinates	$\dot{x}$, $\dot{y}$	Width: RMP − LMP, Height: TMP − BMP	width, height	Rate of rotation of device in space	G_x, G_y, G_z
Acceleration along coordinates	$\ddot{x}$, $\ddot{y}$	Rectangular area: width × height	area	3D acceleration force due to device's motion and gravity	A_x, A_y, A_z
Pressure and change in pressure	p, δp	Width to height ratio	WHR	3D acceleration force solely due to gravity	g_x, g_y, g_z
Size and change in size	s, δs	Slope angle	θ_{slope}	3D acceleration force solely due to device's motion	a_x, a_y, a_z
Force: p × s	F	Path angle	θ_{path}		
Action type: finger lifted up, down or on touchscreen	AT	Curvature	curve		

4.6   Implementation

We implemented BehavioCog for Android smartphones using a set of *twemojis* [37]. We used the parameters $(k, l, n) = (14, 30, 180)$ (corresponding to the medium strength adversary, see Sect. 3.2). FastDTW was used to implement DTW [32] with radius 20. More details are available in our full paper.

5   User Study

We did a three phase controlled experimental evaluation of our proposed scheme with 41 participants on a Nexus 5x smartphone after getting the ethics approval.

Phase 1: We collected touch biometric samples from 22 participants: 8 females and 14 males for different symbol sets in two sessions (a week apart) to select the best symbol set (in terms of repeatability and mimicking hardness). As some users contributed samples for multiple symbol sets, we had 40 logical users which were equally divided into four groups, one for each symbol set. Each user did 13 and 3 renderings of each symbol in the first and second session, respectively. The first session was video recorded. Each user acted as an attacker (to mimic a target user's symbol based on video recordings with unrestricted access) for a particular target user and vice versa from the same group.

Phase 2: This phase had a total of 30 participants (11 from Phase 1) and consisted of two sessions (a week apart) to assess the usability and security of BehavioCog. The first session involved cognitive and biometric registration and authentication (video recorded). Second session involved authentication, performing attacks against a target user, and filling a questionnaire. The 30 users were equally divided into three groups: Group 1, 2 and 3 according to the time they spent on registration. All the users chose

14 pass-emojis. 3, 8 and 10 biometric samples for each of the 5 complex words were collected from users in Group 1, Group 2 and Group 3, respectively. The registration for Group 2 and Group 3 users included an extended training game to help them recognize their pass-emojis for better authentication accuracy. The training game was divided into multiple steps in increasing order of difficulty (see Appendix D of our full paper). Users from Group 3 had to perform double the steps of Group 2 users. Additionally, during Session 2, we asked each user to (a) pick their 14 pass-emojis from the whole pool of emojis, and (b) pick 14 pass-emojis, which they believed belonged to their target (attacked) user.

Phase 3: To find the cause of high number of cognitive errors in Session 2 of Phase 2, we carried out Phase 3 across two sessions (a week apart) with users from Group 3, since they were most familiar with the authentication scheme. First session involved an extended cognitive training: each user was shown 14 pass-emojis one by one for 10 s followed by a 3 s cool off period (inspired by cognitive psychology literature [29,36]), followed by authentication attempts. Session 2 only involved authentication attempts. There are three possible reasons for high cognitive errors: (1) user confuses some of the decoys as pass-emojis since only a subset of pass-emojis are present in a challenge ($l = 30$), (2) user makes errors in computing f, and/or (3) number of pass-emojis is too high (14). To find the exact reason, we asked the user to do the following in order: (a) authenticate six times simply by *selecting* pass-emojis present in the challenge with no weights (to address reason 1); (b) authenticate a further six times, but this time the emojis had weights and the user had to compute f (to address reason 2), (c) select the 14 pass-emojis from the total pool of 180 (to address reason 3). Phase 3 did not involve any biometrics.

6 Results

Phase 1. We find the best symbol set in terms of repeatability and security by selecting features (Algorithm 1, Appendix C of the full paper) for two scenarios: *best case scenario* (secure against random attacks) and *worst case scenario* (secure against video based observation attacks, and repeatability). In both scenarios, first 10 biometric samples from a user (Session 1) are used for training. For the best case, three samples from the same user (Session 1) and three samples from an assigned attacker (Session 1) are used for testing. For the worst case, three samples from the same user (Session 2) and three attacker samples (video based observation attack) are used for testing. Table 4 shows the FPR and top features for each symbol set (TPR is one in all cases). Complex words yield the least FPR which was: 0.0, 0.06, 0.0, 0.2, and 0.0 for xman, bmwz, quak, hurt and fogy, respectively, in the worst case scenario. All symbol categories have an almost 0% FPR against random attacks. The majority of features providing repeatability and mimicking hardness across all symbol sets are touch and stylometric based. More analysis is in Appendix E.1 of our full paper.

Table 4. Results for best and worst case scenarios for different symbol sets.

Symbol set	Average FPR		Top features	
	Best case	Worst case	Best case	Worst case
Easy words	0.01	0.24	x, y, δx, δy, TMP, θ_{slope}, θ_{path}, R_x	TMP, height, WHR, θ_{slope}, θ_{path}
Complex words	0.00	0.05	y, δy, p, height, area, θ_{slope}, R_y	δx, height, θ_{path}
Easy figures	0.01	0.38	y, δx, δy, p, F, height, area, θ_{slope}, θ_{path}	y, δy, p, height
Complex figures	0.01	0.39	δx	x, TMP, BMP

Phase 2. The goal of Phase 2 was to test the full BehavioCog scheme. We only present selected results related to training and authentication time, errors and attacks. More results are in Appendix E of our full paper.

Registration Time: The average time to select 14 pass-emojis was around 2 min for all groups. The maximum training time was 12 min for Group 3, since it had the most amount of training, and the minimum was 4 min for Group 1. High training time is not a major hurdle, because it is a one time process and most of the users reported enjoying the process as it had a "game-like" feel to it (Appendix E.8 of our full paper). Detailed results regarding registration are shown in Appendix E.2 of our full paper.

Authentication Time: Table 5 shows the average authentication time (per round) taken by different user groups in the two sessions. Generally, the user spends 15–20 s in computing f and 6–8 s in entering the biometric response, which does not change drastically between the two sessions. Group 3 has the least login time (more training results in quicker recognition).

Table 5. Authentication statistics for different user groups.

Group & Session	Av. Cognitive Time (sec)	Av. Biometric Time (sec)	Av. Processing Time (sec)	Av. Total Time (sec)	Success Rate (%)	Cognitive Errors (%)	Biometric Errors (%)
Group 1 - Session 1 (Phase 2)	18.3	7.9	0.7	27.0	38.3	31.6	31.0
Group 2 - Session 1 (Phase 2)	19.8	6.4	0.7	27.0	50.0	18.3	36.0
Group 3 - Session 1 (Phase 2)	12.2	5.6	0.8	18.7	85.0	15.0	0.0
Group 1 - Session 2 (Phase 2)	18.5	7.5	0.7	26.8	26.6	55.0	18.3
Group 2 - Session 2 (Phase 2)	18.4	6.4	0.7	25.6	23.3	55.0	26.6
Group 3 - Session 2 (Phase 2)	15.8	5.4	0.9	22.0	50.0	41.6	8.3
Group 3 - Session 1 (Phase 3)	-	-	-	-	94.0	6.0	-
Group 3 - Session 2 (Phase 3)	-	-	-	-	86.0	14.0	-

Authentication Errors: Table 5 shows the percentage of successful authentication attempts along with the cognitive and biometric errors. There were a total of $v = 60$ authentication attempts (six per user) for each user group in each session. If users were randomly submitting a cognitive response, the probability that i out of v cognitive attempts would succeed is: $p \doteq \binom{v}{i} p_{\mathrm{RG}}^i (1 - p_{\mathrm{RG}})^{v-i}$. We consider $i \geq 20$ out of 60 attempts (<66% error rate) as statistically significant ($p < 0.05$). Since all groups had cognitive error rate less than 66%, it implies that users were not passing a cognitive challenge by mere chance. Cognitive training aids the user's short term memory, since Group 3 users authenticated successfully 85% of the time, whereas Group 1 users (without cognitive training) were only successful 36% of the time. Group 2 users (with some cognitive training), accrue 18% cognitive errors, similar to Group 3. For Group 2 users most failures originate from biometric errors (they had lesser number of biometric training samples than Group 3). By collecting more biometric data, performance of Group 2 can be made similar to Group 3 with less cognitive training. We see a drastic decrease in the successful authentication attempts in Session 2 from Session 1 especially for Group 3 (from 85% to 50%) and Group 2 (from 50% to 24%). Cognitive errors are predominantly responsible for the drastic decrease as they caused more than half of the authentication attempts to fail for Group 2 and 3, and 40% for Group 1. Phase 3 was done to find out the cause for a high number of cognitive errors.

Attack Statistics: We picked those 12 users (9 from Group 3, 2 from Group 2, 1 from Group 1) to be attacked who successfully authenticated 5 out of 6 times in Session 1. Each of the 30 users in the three groups attacked only one of the 12 target users by performing three random and three video based observation attacks totalling 90 attempts. The probability of a random attack can be approximated as $p_{\mathrm{tot}} = p_{\mathrm{RG}} \times \overline{\mathrm{FPR}} \approx 0.256 \times 0.05 \approx 0.013$. Thus i out of $v = 90$ correct guesses would be binomially distributed as $p \doteq \binom{v}{i} p_{\mathrm{tot}}^i (1 - p_{\mathrm{tot}})^{v-i}$. We consider $i \geq 4$ as statistically significant ($p < 0.05$). Only 3 attempts (3.33%) for both attacks were successful, and none of them were consecutive. In all six cases, the target user wrote the words using block letters (easier to mimic [8]).

Phase 3. This phase was carried out to find the main cause of cognitive errors and to improve our training to alleviate the issue. The users did 12 authentication attempts each in Sessions 1 and 2. The first 6 involved merely selecting the pass-emojis present whereas the second involved computing f as well. The results are shown in the last two rows of Table 5. The results show that our improved training module (more exposure to each individual pass-emojis followed by blank screens) drastically decreases the error rate. Even after a week's gap the success rate is 86%. We rule out the possibility that the errors in Phase 2 were due to the size of the secret, as the average number of pass-emojis recognized by the users in Sessions 1 and 2 were 13.6 and 13.5, respectively. We also counted the total number of errors made by the users in the first 6 authentication attempts, which turned up 13, and the last 6 authentication attempts, which turned up 11, adding results from both sessions. This shows no evidence that computing

f was causing errors. We, therefore, believe that the main cause of errors is due to the user confusing decoy emojis as its pass-emojis since only a subset of the k emojis are present in the challenge (due to l).

7   Related Work

We proposed a new cognitive scheme in our work because existing schemes did not possess all the attributes we desired. During actual login in CAS [39], the user has to compute a path on a panel of images from top-left corner to the bottom-edge corner or right side of the panel based on whether the image on the panel at any point belongs to the user portfolio. The row or column at the bottom or right side of the panel has labels. When the user finishes the path, they have to input the label in response. The CAS scheme [39] is susceptible to SAT solver based attacks [19]. CAS also uses parameter sizes of $n = 80$ and $k = 30$, and all n images need to be shown on the screen at once, which is hard to display on touch screens of smartphones. requires all $n = 80$ images to be shown at once similar to the APW scheme [5], which is impractical on small screens. The cognitive load of the scheme from Li and Teng [28] is very high as it requires the user to remember three different secrets and perform lexical-first matching on the challenge to obtain hidden sub-sequences. HB protocol [20] can be modified to use window based challenges, but it requires the user to add random responses with a skewed probability $\eta < \frac{1}{2}$, which can be hard for users. Foxtail protocol [26] reduces the response space to $\{0, 1\}$ at the expense of a high number of rounds for secure authentication. PAS [6] only resist a very small number of authentication sessions (<10) [25]. The CHC scheme asks the user to locate at least three pass-images in the challenge and click randomly within the imaginary convex hull of the pass-images. With the default parameter sizes $k = 5$ and $l = 82$ (on average), CHC is vulnerable to statistical attacks [3,41] and usability is impacted with larger parameter sizes. Blum et al. [10] propose simple cognitive schemes which are easily human computable but are information theoretically secure for only 6 to 10 observed sessions. The scheme from Blocki et al. [9] is provably secure against statistical adversaries and can resist a sizeable number of observed sessions. However, their scheme's require extensive training.

Various touch-based behavioural biometric schemes have been proposed for user authentication [18,24,40], which rely on simple gestures such as swipes. Simple gestures require a large number of samples to be collected to get good accuracy and are prone to observation attacks [23]. Sherman et al. [33] designed more complex (free-form) gestures, but which are only shown to resist human shoulder-surfing attacks. The closest work similar to ours is by Toan et al. [31]. Their scheme authenticates users on the basis of how they write their PINs on the smartphone touch screen using x, y coordinates. In comparison, we do a more detailed feature selection process to identify features, which are repeatable and resilient against observation attacks. Furthermore, they report an equal error rate (EER) of 6.7% and 9.9% against random and shoulder-surfing attacks, respectively. Since these are EER values, the TPR is much lower than 1.0.

To obtain a TPR close to 1.0, the FPR will need to be considerably increased. Thus, after observing one session, the observer has a non-negligible chance of getting in (since the PIN is no longer a secret). To achieve a low probability of random guess, the number of rounds in their scheme would need to be higher. Furthermore, after obtaining the PIN, the attacker may adaptively learn target user's writing by querying the authentication service. The use of a cognitive scheme removes this drawback. KinWrite [35], which asks the user to write their passwords in 3D space, and then authenticates them based on their writing patterns suffers from the same drawbacks. Pure graphical password schemes such as DéJà Vu [16] where the user has to click directly on pass-images or reproduce the same drawing on the screen, have the same vulnerability.

8   Discussion and Limitations

We show that a carefully designed training inspired by cognitive psychology helped users recognize their pass-emojis better. The potential of this needs to be further explored to see how large a set of images could be successfully recognized by users after longer gaps. A smaller number of pass-emojis is also possible in our scheme at the expense of withstanding less observations; it may still be impractical for an attacker to follow a mobile user to record enough observations over a sustained period. We also show that users make themes to pick their pass-emojis (Appendix E.5 in our full paper). Issues arising due to picking similar theme based images is left as a future research.

Behavioural biometrics tend to evolve over time and hence we see a slight increase in biometric errors after a week. A remedy is to frequently update the biometric template by replacing older samples [13]. On the flip side, we prefer behaviour biometrics over physiological biometrics due to this exact reason, since if stolen the consequences are less dire (user behaviour might evolve, words could be replaced, etc.). Additionally, the exact difficulty in mimicking cursively written words derived from certain English letters needs to be further explored (either experimentally or in theory). Also, the security of our proposed scheme is to be tested against a professional handwriting forger or a sophisticated robot who can be programmed to mimic gestures. Our cognitive scheme might be susceptible to timing attacks [38] (c.f. Table 5). One way to circumvent this is to not allow the user to proceed unless a fixed amount of time has elapsed based on the highest average-time taken Finally, to protect the user's secret (pass-emojis and biometric templates), the authentication service could keep it encrypted and decrypt it only during authentication. A better solution can use techniques such as fuzzy vaults [21] and functional encryption [12], and is left as a future work.

9   Conclusion

The promise offered by cognitive authentication schemes that they are resistant to observation has failed to crystallize in the form of a workable protocol. Many researchers speculate that such schemes may never be practical. We do not deny this, but instead argue that combining cognitive schemes with other behavioural biometric based authentication schemes may make the hybrid scheme practical and still resistant to observation. Our scheme is not the only possibility. In fact, in addition to touch based biometrics other behavioural biometric modalities can be explored. This way, several different constructions are conceivable.

References

1. Asghar, H.J., Steinfeld, R., Li, S., Kaafar, M.A., Pieprzyk, J.: On the linearization of human identification protocols: attacks based on linear algebra, coding theory, and lattices. IEEE TIFS **10**(8), 1643–1655 (2015)
2. Asghar, H.J., Kaafar, M.A.: When are identification protocols with sparse challenges safe? the case of the Coskun and Herley attack. IACR's Cryptology ePrint Archive: Report 2015/1231 (2015)
3. Asghar, H.J., Li, S., Pieprzyk, J., Wang, H.: Cryptanalysis of the convex hull click human identification protocol. Int. J. Inf. Secur. **12**(2), 83–96 (2013)
4. Asghar, H.J., Li, S., Steinfeld, R., Pieprzyk, J.: Does counting still count? revisiting the security of counting based user authentication protocols against statistical attacks. In: NDSS (2013)
5. Asghar, H.J., Pieprzyk, J., Wang, H.: A new human identification protocol and coppersmith's baby-step giant-step algorithm. In: Zhou, J., Yung, M. (eds.) ACNS 2010. LNCS, vol. 6123, pp. 349–366. Springer, Heidelberg (2010). https://doi.org/10.1007/978-3-642-13708-2_21
6. Bai, X., Gu, W., Chellappan, S., Wang, X., Xuan, D., Ma, B.: PAS: Predicate-based authentication services against powerful passive adversaries. In: ACSAC 2008, pp. 433–442 (2008)
7. Baignères, T., Junod, P., Vaudenay, S.: How far can we go beyond linear cryptanalysis? In: Lee, P.J. (ed.) ASIACRYPT 2004. LNCS, vol. 3329, pp. 432–450. Springer, Heidelberg (2004). https://doi.org/10.1007/978-3-540-30539-2_31
8. Ballard, L., Lopresti, D., Monrose, F.: Forgery quality and its implications for behavioral biometric security. IEEE Trans. Syst. Man Cybern. **37**(5), 1107–1118 (2007)
9. Blocki, J., Blum, M., Datta, A., Vempala, S.: Towards human computable passwords. In: ITCS (2017)
10. Blum, M., Vempala, S.S.: Publishable humanly usable secure password creation schemas. In: Third AAAI Conference on Human Computation and Crowdsourcing (2015)
11. Bo, C., Zhang, L., Li, X.Y., Huang, Q., Wang, Y.: SilentSense: silent user identification via touch and movement behavioral biometrics. In: MobiCom, pp. 187–190 (2013)
12. Boneh, D., Sahai, A., Waters, B.: Functional encryption: definitions and challenges. In: Ishai, Y. (ed.) TCC 2011. LNCS, vol. 6597, pp. 253–273. Springer, Heidelberg (2011). https://doi.org/10.1007/978-3-642-19571-6_16
13. Chauhan, J., Asghar, H.J., Mahanti, A., Kaafar, M.A.: Gesture-based continuous authentication for wearable devices: the smart glasses use case. In: Manulis, M., Sadeghi, A.-R., Schneider, S. (eds.) ACNS 2016. LNCS, vol. 9696, pp. 648–665. Springer, Cham (2016). https://doi.org/10.1007/978-3-319-39555-5_35
14. Coskun, B., Herley, C.: Can "something you know" be saved? In: Wu, T.-C., Lei, C.-L., Rijmen, V., Lee, D.-T. (eds.) ISC 2008. LNCS, vol. 5222, pp. 421–440. Springer, Heidelberg (2008). https://doi.org/10.1007/978-3-540-85886-7_29

15. Devijver, P.A., Kittler, J.: Pattern Recognition: A Statistical Approach. Prentice-Hall, Englewood Cliffs (1982)
16. Dhamija, R., Perrig, A.: DéJà Vu: a user study using images for authentication. In: USENIX Security, pp. 45–58 (2000)
17. Ding, H., Trajcevski, G., Scheuermann, P., Wang, X., Keogh, E.: Querying and mining of time series data: experimental comparison of representations and distance measures. Proc. VLDB Endow. 1(2), 1542–1552 (2008)
18. Frank, M., Biedert, R., Ma, E., Martinovic, I., Song, D.: Touchalytics: on the applicability of touchscreen input as a behavioral biometric for continuous authentication. IEEE TIFS 8(1), 136–148 (2013)
19. Golle, P., Wagner, D.: Cryptanalysis of a cognitive authentication scheme (extended abstract). In: SP, pp. 66–70 (2007)
20. Hopper, N.J., Blum, M.: Secure human identification protocols. In: Boyd, C. (ed.) ASIACRYPT 2001. LNCS, vol. 2248, pp. 52–66. Springer, Heidelberg (2001). https://doi.org/10.1007/3-540-45682-1_4
21. Juels, A., Sudan, M.: A fuzzy vault scheme. Des. Codes Crypt. 38(2), 237–257 (2006)
22. Kao, H.S., Shek, D.T., Lee, E.S.: Control modes and task complexity in tracing and handwriting performance. Acta Psychol. 54(1), 69–77 (1983)
23. Khan, H., Hengartner, U., Vogel, D.: Targeted mimicry attacks on touch input based implicit authentication schemes. In: MobiSys 2016, pp. 387–398 (2016)
24. Li, L., Zhao, X., Xue, G.: Unobservable re-authentication for Smartphones. In: NDSS (2013)
25. Li, S., Asghar, H.J., Pieprzyk, J., Sadeghi, A.R., Schmitz, R., Wang, H.: On the security of PAS (Predicate-Based Authentication Service). In: ACSAC, pp. 209–218 (2009)
26. Li, S., Shum, H.Y.: Secure Human-Computer Identification (Interface) Systems against Peeping Attacks: SecHCI. Cryptology ePrint Archive, Report 2005/268
27. Li, S., Ashok, A., Zhang, Y., Xu, C., Lindqvist, J., Gruteser, M.: Whose move is it anyway? authenticating smart wearable devices using unique head movement patterns. In: PerCom, pp. 1–9 (2016)
28. Li, X.Y., Teng, S.H.: Practical human-machine identification over insecure channels. J. Comb. Optim. 3(4), 347–361 (1999)
29. Mandler, J.M., Johnson, N.S.: Some of the thousand words a picture is worth. J. Exp. Psychol. Hum. Learn. Mem. 2(5), 529–540 (1976)
30. Matsumoto, T., Imai, H.: Human identification through insecure channel. In: Davies, D.W. (ed.) EUROCRYPT 1991. LNCS, vol. 547, pp. 409–421. Springer, Heidelberg (1991). https://doi.org/10.1007/3-540-46416-6_35
31. Nguyen, T.V., Sae-Bae, N., Memon, N.: Finger-drawn PIN authentication on touch devices. In: ICIP, pp. 5002–5006 (2014)
32. Sakoe, H., Chiba, S.: A dynamic programming approach to continuous speech recognition. In: Seventh International Congress on Acoustics, vol. 3, pp. 65–69 (1971)
33. Sherman, M., Clark, G., Yang, Y., Sugrim, S., Modig, A., Lindqvist, J., Oulasvirta, A., Roos, T.: User-generated free-form gestures for authentication: security and memorability. In: MobiSys, pp. 176–189 (2014)
34. Shokoohi-Yekta, M., Hu, B., Jin, H., Wang, J., Keogh, E.: Generalizing DTW to the multi-dimensional case requires an adaptive approach. Data Min. Knowl. Discov. 31, 1–31 (2016)
35. Tian, J., Qu, C., Xu, W., Wang, S.: KinWrite: handwriting-based authentication using kinect. In: NDSS (2013)

36. Tversky, B., Sherman, T.: Picture memory improves with longer on time and off time. J. Exp. Psychol. Hum. Learn. Mem. **1**(2), 114–118 (1975)
37. Twitter, I., et al.: https://github.com/twitter/twemoji
38. Čagalj, M., Perković, T.: Timing attacks on cognitive authentication schemes. IEEE TIFS **10**(3), 584–596 (2014)
39. Weinshall, D.: Cognitive authentication schemes safe against spyware (Short Paper). In: SP, pp. 295–300 (2006)
40. Xu, H., Zhou, Y., Lyu, M.R.: Towards continuous and passive authentication via touch biometrics: an experimental study on Smartphones. In: SOUPS, pp. 187–198 (2014)
41. Yan, Q., Han, J., Li, Y., Deng, R.H.: On limitations of designing leakage-resilient password systems: attacks, principles and usability. In: NDSS (2012)

Updatable Tokenization: Formal Definitions and Provably Secure Constructions

Christian Cachin[(⊠)], Jan Camenisch, Eduarda Freire-Stögbuchner, and Anja Lehmann

IBM Research, Zurich, Switzerland
{cca,jca,efr,anj}@zurich.ibm.com

Abstract. Tokenization is the process of consistently replacing sensitive elements, such as credit cards numbers, with non-sensitive surrogate values. As tokenization is mandated for any organization storing credit card data, many practical solutions have been introduced and are in commercial operation today. However, all existing solutions are static yet, i.e., they do not allow for efficient updates of the cryptographic keys while maintaining the consistency of the tokens. This lack of updatability is a burden for most practical deployments, as cryptographic keys must also be re-keyed periodically for ensuring continued security. This paper introduces a model for updatable tokenization with key evolution, in which a key exposure does not disclose relations among tokenized data in the past, and where the updates to the tokenized data set can be made by an untrusted entity and preserve the consistency of the data. We formally define the desired security properties guaranteeing unlinkability of tokens among different time epochs and one-wayness of the tokenization process. Moreover, we construct two highly efficient updatable tokenization schemes and prove them to achieve our security notions.

1 Introduction

Increasingly, organizations outsource copies of their databases to third parties, such as cloud providers. Legal constraints or security concerns thereby often dictate the de-sensitization or anonymization of the data before moving it across borders or into untrusted environments. The most common approach is so-called *tokenization* which replaces any identifying, sensitive element, such as a social security or credit card number, by a surrogate random value.

Government bodies and advisory groups in Europe [6] and in the United States [9] have explicitly recommended such methods. Many domain-specific industry regulations require this as well, e.g., HIPAA [13] for protecting patient

This work has been supported in part by the European Commission through the Horizon 2020 Framework Programme (H2020-ICT-2014-1) under grant agreement number 644371 WITDOM and through the Seventh Framework Programme under grant agreement number 321310 PERCY, and in part by the Swiss State Secretariat for Education, Research and Innovation (SERI) under contract number 15.0098.

A. Kiayias (Ed.): FC 2017, LNCS 10322, pp. 59–75, 2017.
https://doi.org/10.1007/978-3-319-70972-7_4

information or the Payment Card Industry Data Security Standard (PCI DSS) [10] for credit card data. PCI DSS is an industry-wide set of guidelines that must be met by any organization that handles credit card data and mandates that instead of the real credit card numbers only the non-sensitive tokens are stored.

For security, the tokenization process should be *one-way* in the sense that the token does not reveal information about the original data, even when the secret keys used for tokenization are disclosed. On the other hand, usability requires that a tokenized data set preserves *referential integrity*. That is, when the same value occurs multiple times in the input, it should be mapped consistently to the same token.

Many industrial white papers discuss solutions for tokenization [11,12,14], which rely on (keyed) hash functions, encryption schemes, and often also non-cryptographic methods such as random substitution tables. However, none of these methods guarantee the above requirements in a *provably secure* way, backed by a precise security model. Only recently an initial step towards formal security notions for tokenization has been made [5].

However, all tokenization schemes and models have been *static* so far, in the sense that the relation between a value and its tokenized form never changes and that the keys used for tokenization cannot be changed. Thus, *key updates* are a critical issue that has not yet been handled. In most practical deployments, all cryptographic keys must be re-keyed periodically for ensuring continued security. In fact, the aforementioned PCI DSS standard even mandates that keys (used for encryption) must be rotated at least annually. Similar to proactively secure cryptosystems [8], periodic updates reduce the risk of exposure when data leaks gradually over time. For tokenization, these key updates must be done in a consistent way so that already tokenized data maintains its referential integrity with fresh tokens that are generated under the updated key. None of the existing solutions allows for efficient key updates yet, as they would require to start from scratch and tokenize the complete data set with a fresh key. Given that the tokenized data sets are usually large, this is clearly not desirable for real-world applications. Instead the untrusted entity holding the tokenized data should be able to re-key an already tokenized representation of the data.

Our Contributions. As a solution for these problems, this paper introduces a model for *updatable tokenization (UTO)* with *key evolution*, distinguishes multiple security properties, and provides efficient cryptographic implementations. An updatable tokenization scheme considers a data *owner* producing data and tokenizing it, and an untrusted *host* storing tokenized data only. The scheme operates in *epochs*, where the owner generates a fresh tokenization key for every epoch and uses it to tokenize new values added to the data set. The owner also sends an *update tweak* to the host, which allows to "roll forward" the values tokenized for the previous epoch to the current epoch.

We present several formal security notions that refine the above security goals, by modeling the evolution of keys and taking into consideration adaptive corruptions of the owner, the host, or both, at different times. Due to the temporal dimension of UTO and the adaptive corruptions, the precise formal notions require careful modeling. We define the desired security properties in the form of *indistinguishability* games which require that the tokenized representations of two data values are indistinguishable to the adversary unless it trivially obtained them. An important property for achieving the desired strong indistinguishability notions is *unlinkability* and we clearly specify when (and when not) an untrusted entity may link two values tokenized in different epochs. A further notion, orthogonal to the indistinguishability-based ones, formalizes the desired one-wayness property in the case where the owner discloses its current key material. Here the adversary may guess an input by trying all possible values; the *one-wayness* notion ensures that this is also its best strategy to reverse the tokenization.

Finally, we present two efficient UTO constructions: the first solution (UTO$_{SE}$) is based on symmetric encryption and achieves one-wayness, and indistinguishability in the presence of a corrupt owner *or* a corrupt host. The second construction (UTO$_{DL}$) relies on a discrete-log assumption, and additionally satisfies our strongest indistinguishability notion that allows the adversary to (transiently) corrupt the owner *and* the host. Both constructions share the same core idea: First, the input value is hashed, and then the hash is encrypted under a key that changes every epoch.

We do not claim the cryptographic constructions are particularly novel. The focus of our work is to provide formal foundations for key-evolving and updatable tokenization, which is an important problem in real world applications. Providing clear and sound security models for practitioners is imperative for the relevance of our field. Given the public demands for data privacy and the corresponding interest in tokenization methods by the industry, especially in regulated and sensitive environments such as the financial industry, this work helps to understand the guarantees and limitations of efficient tokenization.

Related Work. A number of cryptographic schemes are related to our notion of updatable tokenization: key-homomorphic pseudorandom functions (PRF), oblivious PRFs, updatable encryption, and proxy re-encryption, for which we give a detailed comparison below.

A key-homomorphic PRF [3] enjoys the property that given $PRF_a(m)$ and $PRF_b(m)$ one can compute $PRF_{a+b}(m)$. This homomorphism does not immediately allow convenient data updates though: the data host would store values $PRF_a(m)$, and when the data owner wants to update his key from a to b, he must compute $\Delta_m = PRF_{b-a}(m)$ for each previously tokenized value m. Further, to allow the host to compute $PRF_b(m) = PRF_a(m) + \Delta_m$, the owner must provide some reference to which $PRF_a(m)$ each Δ_m belongs. This approach has several drawbacks: (1) the owner must store all previously outsourced values m and (2) computing the update tweak(s) and its length would depend on the amount of tokenized data. Our solution aims to overcome exactly these limitations. In fact, tolerating (1) + (2), the owner could simply use any standard PRF, re-compute all tokens and let the data host replace all data. This is clearly not efficient and undesirable in practice.

Boneh et al. [3] also briefly discuss how to use such a key-homomorphic PRF for updatable encryption or proxy re-encryption. Updatable encryption can be seen as an application of symmetric-key proxy re-encryption, where the proxy re-encrypts ciphertexts from the previous into the current key epoch. Roughly, a ciphertext in [3] is computed as $C = m + \mathsf{PRF}_a(N)$ for a nonce N, which is stored along with the ciphertext C. To rotate the key from a to b, the data owner pushes $\Delta = b - a$ to the data host which can use Δ to update *all* ciphertexts. For each ciphertext, the host then uses the stored nonce $'N$ to compute $\mathsf{PRF}_\Delta(N)$ and updates the ciphertext to $C' = C + \mathsf{PRF}_\Delta(N) = m + \mathsf{PRF}_b(N)$. However, the presence of the static nonce prevents the solution to be secure in our tokenization context. The tokenized data should be *unlinkable* across epochs for any adversary not knowing the update tweaks, and we even guarantee unlinkability in a forward-secure manner, i.e., a security breach at epoch e does not affect any data exposed before that time.

In the full version of their paper [4], Boneh et al. present a different solution for updatable encryption that achieves such unlinkability, but which suffers from similar efficiency issues as mentioned above: the data owner must retrieve and partially decrypt all of his ciphertexts, and then produce a dedicated update tweak for each ciphertext, which renders the solution unpractical for our purpose. Further, no formal security definition that models adaptive key corruptions for such updatable encryption is given in the paper.

The Pythia service proposed by Everspaugh et al. [7] mentions PRFs with key rotation which is closer to our goal, as it allows efficient updates of the outsourced PRF values whenever the key gets refreshed. The core idea of the Pythia scheme is very similar to our second, discrete-logarithm based construction. Unfortunately, the paper does not give any formal security definition that covers the possibility to update PRF values nor describes the exact properties of such a key-rotating PRF. As the main goal of Pythia is an *oblivious* and *verifiable* PRF service for password hashing, the overall construction is also more complex and aims at properties that are not needed here, and vice-versa, our unlinkability property does not seem necessary for the goal of Pythia.

While the aforementioned works share some relation with updatable tokenization, they have conceptually quite different security requirements. Starting with such an existing concept and extending its security notions and constructions to additionally satisfy the requirements of updatable tokenization, would reduce efficiency and practicality, for no clear advantage. Thus, we consider the approach of directly targeting the concrete real-world problem more suitable.

An initial study of security notions for tokenization was recently presented by Diaz-Santiago et al. [5]; they formally define tokenization systems and give several security notions and provably secure constructions. In a nutshell, their definitions closely resemble the conventional definitions for deterministic encryption and one-way functions adopted to the tokenization notation. However, they do not consider adaptive corruptions and neither address updatable tokens, which are the crucial aspects of this work.

2   Preliminaries

In this section, we recall the definitions of the building blocks and security notions needed in our constructions.

Deterministic Symmetric Encryption. A deterministic symmetric encryption scheme SE consists of a key space $\mathcal{K}$ and three polynomial-time algorithms SE.KeyGen, SE.Enc, SE.Dec satisfying the following conditions:

SE.KeyGen: The probabilistic key generation algorithm SE.KeyGen takes as input a security parameter λ and produces an encryption key $s \xleftarrow{r}$ SE.KeyGen(λ).

SE.Enc: The deterministic encryption algorithm takes a key $s \in \mathcal{K}$ and a message $m \in \mathcal{M}$ and returns a ciphertext $C \leftarrow$ SE.Enc(s, m).

SE.Dec: The deterministic decryption algorithm SE.Dec takes a key $s \in \mathcal{K}$ and a ciphertext C to return a message $m \leftarrow$ SE.Dec(s, C).

For correctness we require that for any key $s \in \mathcal{K}$, any message $m \in \mathcal{M}$ and any ciphertext $C \leftarrow$ SE.Enc(s, m), we have $m \leftarrow$ SE.Dec(s, C).

We now define a security notion of deterministic symmetric encryption schemes in the sense of indistinguishability against chosen-plaintext attacks, or IND-CPA security. This notion was informally presented by Bellare et al. in [1], and captures the scenario where an adversary that is given access to a left-or-right (LoR) encryption oracle is not able to distinguish between the encryption of two distinct messages of its choice with probability non-negligibly better than one half. Since the encryption scheme in question is deterministic, the adversary can only query the LoR oracle with *distinct* messages on the same side (left or right) to avoid trivial wins. That is, queries of the type $(m_0^i, m_1^i), (m_0^j, m_1^j)$ where $m_0^i = m_0^j$ or $m_1^i = m_1^j$ are forbidden. We do not grant the adversary an explicit encryption oracle, as it can obtain encryptions of messages of its choice by querying the oracle with a pair of identical messages.

Definition 1. *A deterministic symmetric encryption scheme* SE = (SE.KeyGen, SE.Enc, SE.Dec) *is called* IND-CPA *secure if for all polynomial-time adversaries* $\mathcal{A}$, *it holds that* $|\Pr[\text{Exp}_{\mathcal{A},\text{SE}}^{\text{ind-cpa}}(\lambda) = 1] - 1/2| \leq \epsilon(\lambda)$ *for some negligible function* ϵ.

Experiment $\text{Exp}_{\mathcal{A},\text{SE}}^{\text{ind-cpa}}(\lambda)$:
$s \xleftarrow{r}$ SE.KeyGen(λ)
$d \xleftarrow{r} \{0, 1\}$
$d' \xleftarrow{r} \mathcal{A}^{\mathcal{O}_{\text{enc}}(s, d, \cdot, \cdot)}(\lambda)$
   where $\mathcal{O}_{\text{enc}}$ on input two messages m_0, m_1 returns $C \leftarrow$ SE.Enc(s, m_d).
   return 1 if $d' = d$ and all values $m_0^1, \ldots, m_0^q$ and all values $m_1^1, \ldots, m_1^q$ are
   distinct, respectively, where q denotes the number of queries to $\mathcal{O}_{\text{enc}}$.

Hash Functions. A hash function $H : \mathcal{D} \to \mathcal{R}$ is a deterministic function that maps inputs from domain $\mathcal{D}$ to values in range $\mathcal{R}$. For our second and stronger construction we assume the hash function to behave like a random oracle.

In our first construction we use a *keyed* hash function, i.e., H gets a key $hk \xleftarrow{r} H.\mathsf{KeyGen}(\lambda)$ as additional input. We require the keyed hash function to be *pseudorandom* and *weakly collision-resistant* for any adversary not knowing the key hk. We also need H to be *one-way* when the adversary is privy of the key, i.e., H should remain hard to invert on random inputs.

Pseudorandomness: A hash function is called pseudorandom if no efficient adversary $\mathcal{A}$ can distinguish H from a uniformly random function $f : \mathcal{D} \to \mathcal{R}$ with non-negligible advantage. That is, $\left| \Pr[\mathcal{A}^{H(hk,\cdot)}(\lambda)] - \Pr[\mathcal{A}^{f(\cdot)}(\lambda)] \right|$ is negligible in λ, where the probability in the first case is over $\mathcal{A}$'s coin tosses and the choice of $hk \xleftarrow{r} H.\mathsf{KeyGen}(\lambda)$, and in the second case over $\mathcal{A}$'s coin tosses and the choice of the random function f.

Weak collision resistance: A hash function H is called weakly collision-resistant if for any efficient algorithm $\mathcal{A}$ the probability that for $hk \xleftarrow{r} H.\mathsf{KeyGen}(\lambda)$ and $(m, m') \xleftarrow{r} \mathcal{A}^{H(hk,\cdot)}(\lambda)$ the adversary returns $m \neq m'$, where $H(hk, m) = H(hk, m')$, is negligible (as a function of λ).

One-wayness: A hash function H is one-way if for any efficient algorithm $\mathcal{A}$ the probability that for $hk \xleftarrow{r} H.\mathsf{KeyGen}(\lambda)$, $m \xleftarrow{r} \mathcal{D}$ and $m' \xleftarrow{r} \mathcal{A}(hk, H(hk, m))$ returns m', where $H(hk, m) = H(hk, m')$, is negligible (as a function of λ).

Decisional Diffie-Hellman Assumption. Our second construction requires a group $(\mathbb{G}, g, p)$ as input where $\mathbb{G}$ denotes a cyclic group $\mathbb{G} = \langle g \rangle$ of order p in which the Decisional Diffie-Hellman (DDH) problem is hard w.r.t. λ, i.e., p is a λ-bit prime. More precisely, a group $(\mathbb{G}, g, p)$ satisfies the DDH assumption if for any efficient adversary $\mathcal{A}$ the probability $| \Pr[\mathcal{A}(\mathbb{G}, p, g, g^a, g^b, g^{ab})] - \Pr[\mathcal{A}(\mathbb{G}, p, g, g^a, g^b, g^c)]|$ is negligible in λ, where the probability is over the random choice of p, g, the random choices of $a, b, c \in \mathbb{Z}_p$, and $\mathcal{A}$'s coin tosses.

3   Formalizing Updatable Tokenization

An updatable tokenization scheme contains algorithms for a data *owner* and a *host*. The owner de-sensitizes data through tokenization operations and dynamically outsources the tokenized data to the host. For this purpose, the data owner first runs an algorithm setup to create a tokenization key. The tokenization key evolves with *epochs*, and the data is tokenized with respect to a specific epoch e, starting with $e = 0$. For a given epoch, algorithm token takes a data value and tokenizes it with the current key k_e. When moving from epoch e to epoch $e + 1$, the owner invokes an algorithm next to generate the key material k_{e+1} for the new epoch and an update tweak Δ_{e+1}. The owner then sends Δ_{e+1} to the host, deletes k_e and Δ_{e+1} immediately, and uses k_{e+1} for tokenization from now on. After receiving Δ_{e+1}, the host first deletes Δ_e and then uses an algorithm upd to update all previously received tokenized values from epoch e to $e+1$, using Δ_{e+1}. Hence, during some epoch e the update tweak from $e - 1$ to e is available at the host, but update tweaks from earlier epochs have been deleted.

Definition 2. *An updatable tokenization scheme* UTO *consists of a data space* $\mathcal{X}$, *a token space* $\mathcal{Y}$, *and a set of polynomial-time algorithms* UTO.setup, UTO.next, UTO.token, *and* UTO.upd *satisfying the following conditions:*

UTO.setup: The algorithm UTO.setup is a probabilistic algorithm run by the owner. On input a security parameter λ, this algorithm returns the tokenization key for the first epoch $k_0 \xleftarrow{\text{r}} \text{UTO.setup}(\lambda)$.

UTO.next: This probabilistic algorithm is also run by the owner. On input a tokenization key k_e for some epoch e, it outputs a tokenization key k_{e+1} and an update tweak Δ_{e+1} for epoch $e+1$. That is, $(k_{e+1}, \Delta_{e+1}) \xleftarrow{\text{r}} \text{UTO.next}(k_e)$.

UTO.token: This is a deterministic *injective* algorithm run by the owner. Given the secret key k_e and some input data $x \in \mathcal{X}$, the algorithm outputs a tokenized value $y_e \in \mathcal{Y}$. That is, $y_e \leftarrow \text{UTO.token}(k_e, x)$.

UTO.upd: This deterministic algorithm is run by the host and uses the update tweak. On input the update tweak Δ_{e+1} and some tokenized value y_e, UTO.upd updates y_e to y_{e+1}, that is, $y_{e+1} \leftarrow \text{UTO.upd}(\Delta_{e+1}, y_e)$.

The *correctness* condition of a UTO scheme ensures referential integrity inside the tokenized data set. A newly tokenized value from the owner in a particular epoch must be the same as the tokenized value produced by the host using update operations. More precisely, we require that for any $x \in \mathcal{X}$, for any $k_0 \xleftarrow{\text{r}} \text{UTO.setup}(\lambda)$, for any sequence of tokenization key/update tweak pairs $(k_1, \Delta_1), \ldots, (k_e, \Delta_e)$ generated as $(k_{j+1}, \Delta_{j+1}) \xleftarrow{\text{r}} \text{UTO.next}(k_j)$ for $j = 0, \ldots, e-1$ through repeated applications of the key evolution algorithm, and for any $y_e \leftarrow \text{UTO.token}(k_e, x)$, it holds that

$$\text{UTO.token}(k_{e+1}, x) = \text{UTO.upd}(\Delta_{e+1}, y_e).$$

3.1 Privacy of Updatable Tokenization Schemes

The main goal of UTO is to achieve *privacy* for data values, ensuring that an adversary cannot gain information about the tokenized values and cannot link them to input data tokenized in past epochs. We introduce three indistinguishability-based notions for the privacy of tokenized values, and one notion ruling out that an adversary may reverse the tokenization and recover the input value from a tokenized one. All security notions are defined through an experiment run between a challenger and an adversary $\mathcal{A}$. Depending on the notion, the adversary may issue queries to different oracles, defined in the next section.

At a high level, the four security notions for UTO are distinguished by the corruption capabilities of $\mathcal{A}$.

IND-HOCH: *Indistinguishability with Honest Owner and Corrupted Host:* This is the most basic security criterion, focusing on the updatable dynamic aspect of UTO. It considers the owner to be honest and permits corruption of the host during the interaction. The adversary gains access to the update tweaks for all epochs following the compromise and yet, it should (roughly speaking) not be able to distinguish values tokenized before the corruption.

IND-COHH: *Indistinguishability with Corrupted Owner and Honest Host:* Modeling a corruption of the owner at some point in time, the adversary learns the tokenization key of the compromised epoch and all secrets of the owner. Subsequently $\mathcal{A}$ may take control of the owner, but should not learn the correspondence between values tokenized before the corruption. The host is assumed to remain (mostly) honest.

IND-COTH: *Indistinguishability with Corrupted Owner and Transiently Corrupte Host:* As a refinement of the first two notions, $\mathcal{A}$ can transiently corrupt the host during multiple epochs according to its choice, and it may also permanently corrupt the owner. The adversary learns the update tweaks of the specific epochs where it corrupts the host, and learns the tokenization key of the epoch where it corrupts the owner. Data values tokenized prior to exposing the owner's secrets should remain unlinkable.

One-Wayness: This notion models the scenario where the owner is corrupted right at the first epoch and the adversary therefore learns all secrets. Yet, the tokenization operation should be one-way in the sense that observing a tokenized value does not give the adversary an advantage for guessing the corresponding input from $\mathcal{X}$.

3.2   Definition of Oracles

During the interaction with the challenger in the security definitions, the adversary may access oracles for *data tokenization*, for moving to the *next epoch*, for *corrupting the host*, and for *corrupting the owner*. In the following description, the oracles may access the state of the challenger during the experiment. The challenger initializes a UTO scheme with global state (k_0, Δ_0, e), where $k_0 \leftarrow$ UTO.setup(λ), $\Delta_0 \leftarrow \perp$, and $e \leftarrow 0$. Two auxiliary variables e_h^* and e_o^* record the epochs where the host and the owner were first corrupted, respectively. Initially $e_h^* \leftarrow \perp$ and $e_o^* \leftarrow \perp$.

$\mathcal{O}_{\text{token}}(x)$: On input a value $x \in \mathcal{X}$, return $y_e \leftarrow$ UTO.token(k_e, x) to the adversary, where k_e is the tokenization key of the current epoch.

$\mathcal{O}_{\text{next}}$: When triggered, compute the tokenization key and update tweak of the next epoch as $(k_{e+1}, \Delta_{e+1}) \leftarrow$ UTO.next(k_e) and update the global state to $(k_{e+1}, \Delta_{e+1}, e + 1)$.

$\mathcal{O}_{\text{corrupt-h}}$: When invoked, return Δ_e to the adversary. If called for the first time $(e_h^* = \perp)$, then set $e_h^* \leftarrow e$. This oracle models the corruption of the host and may be called multiple times.

$\mathcal{O}_{\text{corrupt-o}}$: When invoked for the first time $(e_o^* = \perp)$, then set $e_o^* \leftarrow e$ and return k_e to the adversary. This oracle models the corruption of the owner and can only be called once. After this call, the adversary no longer has access to $\mathcal{O}_{\text{token}}$ and $\mathcal{O}_{\text{next}}$.

Note that although corruption of the host at epoch e exposes the update tweak Δ_e, the adversary should not be able to compute update tweaks of future epochs from this value. To obtain those, $\mathcal{A}$ should call $\mathcal{O}_{\text{corrupt-h}}$ again in the corresponding epochs; this is used for IND-HOCH security and IND-COTH security, with different side-conditions. A different case arises when the owner is corrupted, since this exposes all *relevant* secrets of the challenger. From that point the adversary can generate tokenization keys and update tweaks for all subsequent epochs on its own. This justifies why the oracle $\mathcal{O}_{\text{corrupt-o}}$ can only be called once. For the same reason, it makes no sense for an adversary to query the $\mathcal{O}_{\text{token}}$ and $\mathcal{O}_{\text{next}}$ oracles after the corruption of the owner. Furthermore, observe that $\mathcal{O}_{\text{corrupt-o}}$ does not return Δ_e according to the assumption that the owner deletes this atomically with executing the next algorithm.

We are now ready to formally define the security notions for UTO in the remainder of this section.

3.3 IND-HOCH: Honest Owner and Corrupted Host

The IND-HOCH notion ensures that tokenized data does not reveal information about the corresponding original data when $\mathcal{A}$ compromises the host and obtains the update tweaks of the current and all future epochs. Tokenized values are also unlinkable across epochs, as long as the adversary does not know at least one update tweak in that timeline.

Definition 3 (IND-HOCH). *An updatable tokenization scheme* UTO *is said to be* IND-HOCH *secure if for all polynomial-time adversaries* $\mathcal{A}$ *it holds that* $|\Pr[\text{Exp}_{\mathcal{A},\text{UTO}}^{\text{IND-HOCH}}(\lambda) = 1] - 1/2| \leq \epsilon(\lambda)$ *for some negligible function* ϵ.

Experiment $\text{Exp}_{\mathcal{A},\text{UTO}}^{\text{IND-HOCH}}(\lambda)$:
$k_0 \xleftarrow{\text{r}} \text{UTO.setup}(\lambda)$
$e \leftarrow 0; \quad e_h^* \leftarrow \perp$ // *these variables are updated by the oracles*
$(\tilde{x}_0, \tilde{x}_1, state) \xleftarrow{\text{r}} \mathcal{A}^{\mathcal{O}_{\text{token}}, \mathcal{O}_{\text{next}}, \mathcal{O}_{\text{corrupt-h}}}(\lambda)$
$\tilde{e} \leftarrow e; \quad d \xleftarrow{\text{r}} \{0, 1\}$
$\tilde{y}_{d,\tilde{e}} \leftarrow \text{UTO.token}(k_{\tilde{e}}, \tilde{x}_d)$
$d' \xleftarrow{\text{r}} \mathcal{A}^{\mathcal{O}_{\text{token}}, \mathcal{O}_{\text{next}}, \mathcal{O}_{\text{corrupt-h}}}(\tilde{y}_{d,\tilde{e}}, state)$
return 1 if $d' = d$ and at least *one* of following conditions holds
    a) $(e_h^* \leq \tilde{e} + 1) \wedge \mathcal{A}$ has not queried $\mathcal{O}_{\text{token}}(\tilde{x}_0)$ or $\mathcal{O}_{\text{token}}(\tilde{x}_1)$ in epoch $e_h^* - 1$ or later
    b) $(e_h^* > \tilde{e} + 1 \vee e_h^* = \perp) \wedge \mathcal{A}$ has not queried $\mathcal{O}_{\text{token}}(\tilde{x}_0)$ or $\mathcal{O}_{\text{token}}(\tilde{x}_1)$ in epoch $\tilde{e}$

This experiment has two phases. In the first phase, $\mathcal{A}$ may query $\mathcal{O}_{\text{token}}$, $\mathcal{O}_{\text{next}}$ and $\mathcal{O}_{\text{corrupt-h}}$; it ends at an epoch $\tilde{e}$ when $\mathcal{A}$ outputs two challenge inputs $\tilde{x}_0$ and $\tilde{x}_1$. The challenger picks one at random (denoted by $\tilde{x}_d$), tokenizes it, obtains the challenge $\tilde{y}_{d,\tilde{e}}$ and starts the second phase by invoking $\mathcal{A}$ with $\tilde{y}_{d,\tilde{e}}$. The adversary may then further query $\mathcal{O}_{\text{token}}$, $\mathcal{O}_{\text{next}}$, and $\mathcal{O}_{\text{corrupt-h}}$ and eventually outputs its guess d' for which data value was tokenized. Note that only the first host corruption matters for our security notion, since we are assuming that once corrupted, the host is always corrupted. For simplicity, we therefore assume that $\mathcal{A}$ calls $\mathcal{O}_{\text{corrupt-h}}$ once in every epoch after e_h^*.

The adversary wins the experiment if it correctly guesses d while respecting two conditions that differ depending on whether the adversary corrupted the host (roughly) before or after the challenge epoch:

(a) If $e_h^* \leq \tilde{e} + 1$, then $\mathcal{A}$ first corrupts the host before, during, or immediately after the challenge epoch and may learn the update tweaks to epoch e_h^* and later ones. In this case, it must not query the tokenization oracle on the challenge inputs in epoch $e_h^* - 1$ or later.

In particular, if this restriction was not satisfied, when $e_h^* \leq \tilde{e}$, the adversary could tokenize data of its choice, including $\tilde{x}_0$ and $\tilde{x}_1$, during any epoch from $e_h^* - 1$ to $\tilde{e}$, subsequently update the tokenized value to epoch $\tilde{e}$, and compare it to the challenge $\tilde{y}_{d,\tilde{e}}$. This would allow $\mathcal{A}$ to trivially win the security experiment.

For the case $e_h^* = \tilde{e} + 1$, recall that according to the experiment, the update tweak Δ_e remains accessible until epoch $e + 1$ starts. Therefore, $\mathcal{A}$ learns the update tweak from $\tilde{e}$ to $\tilde{e} + 1$ and may update $\tilde{y}_{d,\tilde{e}}$ into epoch $\tilde{e} + 1$. Hence, from this time on it must not query $\mathcal{O}_{\text{token}}$ with the challenge inputs either.

(b) If $e_h^* > \tilde{e} + 1 \vee e_h^* = \bot$, i.e., the host was first corrupted after epoch $\tilde{e} + 1$ or not at all, then the only restriction is that $\mathcal{A}$ must not query the tokenization oracle on the challenge inputs during epoch $\tilde{e}$. This is an obvious restriction to exclude trivial wins, as tokenization is deterministic.

This condition is less restrictive than case (a), but it suffices since the adversary cannot update tokenized values from earlier epochs to $\tilde{e}$, nor from $\tilde{e}$ to a later epoch. The reason is that $\mathcal{A}$ only gets the update tweaks from epoch $\tilde{e} + 2$ onwards.

3.4   IND-COHH: Corrupted Owner and Honest Host

The IND-COHH notion models a compromise of the owner in a certain epoch, such that the adversary learns the tokenization key and may generate tokenization keys and update tweaks of all subsequent epochs by itself. Given that the tokenization key allows to derive the update tweak of the host, this implicitly models some form of host corruption as well. The property ensures that data tokenized before the corruption remains hidden, that is, the adversary does not learn any information about the original data, nor can it link such data with data tokenized in other epochs.

Definition 4 (IND-COHH). *An updatable tokenization scheme* UTO *is said to be* IND-COHH *secure if for all polynomial-time adversaries $\mathcal{A}$ it holds that* $|\Pr[\text{Exp}_{\mathcal{A},\text{UTO}}^{\text{IND-COHH}}(\lambda) = 1] - 1/2| \leq \epsilon(\lambda)$ *for some negligible function ϵ.*

Experiment $\mathsf{Exp}_{\mathcal{A},\mathsf{UTO}}^{\mathsf{IND\text{-}COHH}}(\lambda)$:

$k_0 \xleftarrow{r} \mathsf{UTO.setup}(\lambda)$

$e \leftarrow 0; \quad e_o^* \leftarrow \perp$ *// these variables are updated by the oracles*

$(\tilde{x}_0, \tilde{x}_1, state) \xleftarrow{r} \mathcal{A}^{\mathcal{O}_{\mathsf{token}}, \mathcal{O}_{\mathsf{next}}}(\lambda)$

$\tilde{e} \leftarrow e; \quad d \xleftarrow{r} \{0,1\}$

$\tilde{y}_{d,\tilde{e}} \leftarrow \mathsf{UTO.token}(k_{\tilde{e}}, \tilde{x}_d)$

$d' \xleftarrow{r} \mathcal{A}^{\mathcal{O}_{\mathsf{token}}, \mathcal{O}_{\mathsf{next}}, \mathcal{O}_{\mathsf{corrupt\text{-}o}}}(\tilde{y}_{d,\tilde{e}}, state)$

return 1 if $d' = d$ and all following conditions hold

    a) $e_o^* > \tilde{e} \vee e_o^* = \perp$

    b) $\mathcal{A}$ never queried $\mathcal{O}_{\mathsf{token}}(\tilde{x}_0)$ or $\mathcal{O}_{\mathsf{token}}(\tilde{x}_1)$ in epoch $\tilde{e}$

During the first phase of the IND-COHH experiment the adversary may query $\mathcal{O}_{\mathsf{token}}$ and $\mathcal{O}_{\mathsf{next}}$, but it may not corrupt the owner. At epoch $\tilde{e}$, the adversary produces two challenge inputs $\tilde{x}_0$ and $\tilde{x}_1$. Again, the challenger selects one at random and tokenizes it, resulting in the challenge $\tilde{y}_{d,\tilde{e}}$. Subsequently, $\mathcal{A}$ may further query $\mathcal{O}_{\mathsf{token}}$ and $\mathcal{O}_{\mathsf{next}}$, and now may also invoke $\mathcal{O}_{\mathsf{corrupt\text{-}o}}$. Once the owner is corrupted (during epoch e_o^*), $\mathcal{A}$ knows all key material of the owner and may generate tokenization keys and update tweaks of all subsequent epochs by itself. Thus, from this time on, we remove access to the $\mathcal{O}_{\mathsf{token}}$ or $\mathcal{O}_{\mathsf{next}}$ oracles for simplicity.

The adversary ends the experiment by guessing which input challenge was tokenized. It wins when the guess is correct and the following conditions are met:

(a) $\mathcal{A}$ must have corrupted the owner only after the challenge epoch ($e_o^* > \tilde{e}$) or not at all ($e_o^* = \perp$). This is necessary since corruption during epoch $\tilde{e}$ would leak the tokenization key $k_{\tilde{e}}$ to the adversary. (Note that corruption before $\tilde{e}$ is ruled out syntactically.)

(b) $\mathcal{A}$ must neither query the tokenization oracle with any challenge input ($\tilde{x}_0$ or $\tilde{x}_1$) during the challenge epoch $\tilde{e}$. This condition eliminates that $\mathcal{A}$ can trivially reveal the challenge input since the tokenization operation is deterministic.

On the (Im)possibility of Additional Host Corruption. As can be noted, the IND-COHH experiment does not consider the corruption of the host at all. The reason is that allowing host corruption in addition to owner corruption would either result in a non-achievable notion, or it would give the adversary no extra advantage. To see this, we first argue why additional host corruption capabilities at any epoch $e_h^* \leq \tilde{e} + 1$ is not allowed. Recall that such a corruption is possible in the IND-HOCH experiment if the adversary does not make any tokenization queries on the challenge values $\tilde{x}_0$ or $\tilde{x}_1$ at any epoch $e \geq e_h^* - 1$. This restriction is necessary in the IND-HOCH experiment to prevent the adversary from trivially linking the tokenized values of $\tilde{x}_0$ or $\tilde{x}_1$ to the challenge $\tilde{y}_{d,\tilde{e}}$. However, when the owner can also be corrupted, at epoch $e_o^* > \tilde{e}$, that restriction is useless. Note that upon calling $\mathcal{O}_{\mathsf{corrupt\text{-}o}}$ the adversary learns the owner's tokenization key and can simply tokenize $\tilde{x}_0$ and $\tilde{x}_1$ at epoch e_o^*. The results can be compared with an updated version of $\tilde{y}_{d,\tilde{e}}$ to trivially win the security experiment.

Now we discuss the additional corruption of the host at any epoch $e_h^* > \tilde{e}+1$. We note that corruption of the owner at epoch $e_o^* > \tilde{e}$ allows the adversary to obtain the tokenization key of epoch e_o^* and compute the tokenization keys and update tweaks of all epochs $e > e_o^*+1$. Thus, the adversary then trivially knows all tokenization keys from e_o^*+1 onward and modeling corruption of the host after the owner is not necessary. The only case left is to consider host-corruption before owner corruption, at an epoch e_h^* with $\tilde{e}+1 < e_h^* < e_o^*$. However, corrupting the host first would not have any impact on the winning condition. Hence, without loss of generality, we assume that the adversary always corrupts the owner first, which allows us to fully omit the $\mathcal{O}_{\text{corrupt-h}}$ oracle in our IND-COHH experiment.

We stress that the impossibility of host corruption at any epoch $e_h^* \leq \tilde{e}+1$ only holds if we consider *permanent* corruptions, i.e., the adversary, upon invocation of $\mathcal{O}_{\text{corrupt-h}}$ is assumed to fully control the host and to learn all future update tweaks. In the following security notion, IND-COTH, we bypass this impossibility by modeling *transient* corruption of the host.

3.5   IND-COTH: Corrupted Owner and Transiently Corrupted Host

Extending both of the above security properties, the IND-COTH notion considers corruption of the owner and repeated but transient corruptions of the host. It addresses situations where some of the update tweaks received by the host leak to $\mathcal{A}$ and the keys of the owner are also exposed at a later stage.

Definition 5 (IND-COTH). *An updatable tokenization scheme* UTO *is said to be* IND-COTH *secure if for all polynomial-time adversaries* $\mathcal{A}$ *it holds that* $|\Pr[\text{Exp}_{\mathcal{A},\text{UTO}}^{\text{IND-COTH}}(\lambda) = 1] - 1/2| \leq \epsilon(\lambda)$ *for some negligible function* ϵ.

Experiment $\text{Exp}_{\mathcal{A},\text{UTO}}^{\text{IND-COTH}}(\lambda)$:

$k_0 \xleftarrow{r} \text{UTO.setup}(\lambda)$

$e \leftarrow 0; \quad e_o^* \leftarrow \bot$ // these variables are updated by the oracles

$e_{\text{last}} \leftarrow \bot; \quad e_{\text{first}} \leftarrow \bot$

$(\tilde{x}_0, \tilde{x}_1, state) \xleftarrow{r} \mathcal{A}^{\mathcal{O}_{\text{token}}, \mathcal{O}_{\text{next}}, \mathcal{O}_{\text{corrupt-h}}}(\lambda)$

$\tilde{e} \leftarrow e; \quad d \xleftarrow{r} \{0,1\}$

$\tilde{y}_{d,\tilde{e}} \leftarrow \text{UTO.token}(k_{\tilde{e}}, \tilde{x}_d)$

$d' \xleftarrow{r} \mathcal{A}^{\mathcal{O}_{\text{token}}, \mathcal{O}_{\text{next}}, \mathcal{O}_{\text{corrupt-h}}, \mathcal{O}_{\text{corrupt-o}}}(\tilde{y}_{d,\tilde{e}}, state)$

$e_{\text{last}} \leftarrow$ last epoch before $\tilde{e}$ in which $\mathcal{A}$ queried $\mathcal{O}_{\text{token}}(\tilde{x}_0)$ or $\mathcal{O}_{\text{token}}(\tilde{x}_1)$

$e_{\text{first}} \leftarrow$ first epoch after $\tilde{e}$ in which $\mathcal{A}$ queried $\mathcal{O}_{\text{token}}(\tilde{x}_0)$ or $\mathcal{O}_{\text{token}}(\tilde{x}_1)$

return 1 if $d' = d$ and all following conditions hold

    a) $e_o^* > \tilde{e} \vee e_o^* = \bot$

    b) $\mathcal{A}$ never queried $\mathcal{O}_{\text{token}}(\tilde{x}_0)$ or $\mathcal{O}_{\text{token}}(\tilde{x}_1)$ in epoch $\tilde{e}$

    c) either $e_h^* = \bot$ or *all* following conditions hold

       i) $(e_{\text{last}} = \bot) \vee \exists\, e'$ with $e_{\text{last}} < e' \leq \tilde{e}$ where $\mathcal{A}$ has not queried $\mathcal{O}_{\text{corrupt-h}}$

       ii) $(e_{\text{first}} = \bot) \vee \exists\, e''$ with $\tilde{e} < e'' \leq e_{\text{first}}$ where $\mathcal{A}$ has not queried $\mathcal{O}_{\text{corrupt-h}}$

       iii) $(e_o^* = \bot) \vee \exists\, e'''$ with $\tilde{e} < e''' \leq e_o^*$ where $\mathcal{A}$ has not queried $\mathcal{O}_{\text{corrupt-h}}$

Observe that the owner can only be corrupted after the challenge epoch, just as in the IND-COHH experiment. As before, $\mathcal{A}$ then obtains all key material and, for simplicity, we remove access to the $\mathcal{O}_{\text{token}}$ or $\mathcal{O}_{\text{next}}$ oracles from this time on. The transient nature of the host corruption allows to grant $\mathcal{A}$ additional access to $\mathcal{O}_{\text{corrupt-h}}$ *before* the challenge, which would be impossible in the IND-COHH experiment if permanent host corruption was considered.

Compared to the IND-HOCH definition, here $\mathcal{A}$ may corrupt the host *and* ask for a challenge input to be tokenized after the corruption. Multiple host corruptions may occur before, during, and after the challenge epoch. But in order to win the experiment, $\mathcal{A}$ must leave out at least one epoch and miss an update tweak. Otherwise it could trivially guess the challenge by updating the challenge output or a challenge input tokenized in another epoch to the same stage. In the experiment this is captured through the conditions under (c). In particular:

(c-i) If $\mathcal{A}$ calls $\mathcal{O}_{\text{token}}$ with one of the challenge inputs $\tilde{x}_0$ or $\tilde{x}_1$ *before* triggering the challenge, it must not corrupt the host and miss the update tweak in at least one epoch from this point up to the challenge epoch. Thus, the *latest* epoch before the challenge epoch where $\mathcal{A}$ queries $\mathcal{O}_{\text{token}}(\tilde{x}_0)$ or $\mathcal{O}_{\text{token}}(\tilde{x}_1)$, denoted e_{last}, must be smaller than the last epoch before $\tilde{e}$ where the host is not corrupted.

(c-ii) Likewise if $\mathcal{A}$ queries $\mathcal{O}_{\text{token}}$ with a challenge input $\tilde{x}_0$ or $\tilde{x}_1$ *after* the challenge epoch, then it must not corrupt the host and miss the update tweak in at least one epoch after $\tilde{e}$. Otherwise, it could update the challenge $\tilde{y}_{d,\tilde{e}}$ to the epoch where it calls $\mathcal{O}_{\text{token}}$. The *first* epoch after the challenge epoch where $\mathcal{A}$ queries $\mathcal{O}_{\text{token}}(\tilde{x}_0)$ or $\mathcal{O}_{\text{token}}(\tilde{x}_1)$, denoted e_{first}, must be larger than or equal to the first epoch after $\tilde{e}$ where the host is not corrupted.

(c-iii) If $\mathcal{A}$ calls $\mathcal{O}_{\text{corrupt-o}}$, it must not obtain at least one update tweak after the challenge epoch and before, or during, the epoch of owner corruption e_o^*. Otherwise, $\mathcal{A}$ could tokenize $\tilde{x}_0$ and $\tilde{x}_1$ with the tokenization key of epoch e_o^*, exploit the exposed update tweaks to evolve the challenge value $\tilde{y}_{d,\tilde{e}}$ to that epoch, and compare the results.

PRF-style vs. IND-CPA-style Definitions. We have opted for definitions based on indistinguishability in our model. Given that the goal of tokenization is to output random looking tokens, a security notion in the spirit of pseudorandomness might seem like a more natural choice at first glance. However, a definition in the PRF-style does not cope well with *adaptive* attacks: in our security experiments the adversary is allowed to adaptively corrupt the data host and corrupt the data owner, upon which it gets the update tweaks or the secret tokenization key. Modeling this in a PRF vs. random function experiment would require the random function to contain a key and to be compatible with an update function that can be run by the adversary. Extending the random function with these "features" would lead to a PRF vs. PRF definition. The IND-CPA inspired approach used in this paper allows to cover the adaptive attacks and consistency features in a more natural way.

Relation Among the Security Notions. Our notion of IND-COTH security is the strongest of the three indistinguishability notions above, as it implies both IND-COHH and IND-HOCH security, but not vice-versa. That is, IND-COTH security is not implied by IND-COHH and IND-HOCH security. A distinguishing example is our UTO$_{SE}$ scheme. As we will see in Sect. 4.1, UTO$_{SE}$ is both IND-COHH and IND-HOCH secure, but not IND-COTH secure.

The proof of Theorem 1 below can be found in the full version of this paper.

Theorem 1 (IND-COTH $\Rightarrow$ IND-COHH + IND-HOCH). *If an updatable tokenization scheme* UTO *is* IND-COTH secure, *then it is also* IND-COHH secure *and* IND-HOCH secure.

3.6   One-Wayness

The one-wayness notion models the fact that a tokenization scheme should not be reversible even if an adversary is given the tokenization keys. In other words, an adversary who sees tokenized values and gets hold of the tokenization keys cannot obtain the original data. Because the keys allow one to reproduce the tokenization operation and to test whether the output matches a tokenized value, the resulting security level depends on the size of the input space and the adversary's uncertainty about the input. Thus, in practice, the level of security depends on the prior knowledge of the adversary about $\mathcal{X}$.

Our definition is similar to the standard notion of one-wayness, with the difference that we ask the adversary to output the exact preimage of a tokenized challenge value, as our tokenization algorithm is an injective function.

Definition 6 (One-Wayness). *An updatable tokenization scheme* UTO *is said to be* one-way *if for all polynomial-time adversaries* $\mathcal{A}$ *it holds that*

$$\Pr[\, x = \tilde{x} : x \leftarrow \mathcal{A}(\lambda, k_0, \tilde{y}),$$
$$\tilde{y} \leftarrow \mathsf{UTO.token}(k_0, \tilde{x}), \tilde{x} \xleftarrow{r} \mathcal{X}, k_0 \xleftarrow{r} \mathsf{UTO.setup}(\lambda)] \leq 1/|\mathcal{X}|.$$

4   UTO Constructions

In this section we present two efficient constructions of updatable tokenization schemes. The first solution (UTO$_{SE}$) is based on symmetric encryption and achieves one-wayness, IND-HOCH and IND-COHH security; the second construction (UTO$_{DL}$) relies on a discrete-log assumption, and additionally satisfies IND-COTH security. Both constructions share the same core idea: First, the input value is hashed, and then the hash is encrypted under a key that changes every epoch.

4.1   An UTO Scheme Based on Symmetric Encryption

We build a first updatable tokenization scheme $\mathsf{UTO_{SE}}$, that is based on a symmetric deterministic encryption scheme $\mathsf{SE} = (\mathsf{SE.KeyGen}, \mathsf{SE.Enc}, \mathsf{SE.Dec})$ with message space $\mathcal{M}$ and a keyed hash function $\mathsf{H} : \mathcal{K} \times \mathcal{X} \to \mathcal{M}$. In order to tokenize an input $x \in \mathcal{X}$, our scheme simply encrypts the hashed value of x. At each epoch e, a distinct random symmetric key s_e is used for encryption, while a fixed random hash key hk is used to hash x. Both keys are chosen by the data owner. To update the tokens, the host receives the encryption keys of the previous and current epoch and re-encrypts all hashed values to update them into the current epoch. More precisely, our $\mathsf{UTO_{SE}}$ scheme is defined as follows:

$\mathsf{UTO.setup}(\lambda)$: Generate keys $s_0 \xleftarrow{r} \mathsf{SE.KeyGen}(\lambda)$, $hk \xleftarrow{r} \mathsf{H.KeyGen}(\lambda)$ and output $k_0 \leftarrow (s_0, hk)$.

$\mathsf{UTO.next}(k_e)$: Parse k_e as (s_e, hk). Choose a new key $s_{e+1} \xleftarrow{r} \mathsf{SE.KeyGen}(\lambda)$ and set $k_{e+1} \leftarrow (s_{e+1}, hk)$ and $\Delta_{e+1} \leftarrow (s_e, s_{e+1})$. Output (k_{e+1}, Δ_{e+1}).

$\mathsf{UTO.token}(k_e, x)$: Parse k_e as (s_e, hk) and output $y_e \leftarrow \mathsf{SE.Enc}(s_e, \mathsf{H}(hk, x))$.

$\mathsf{UTO.upd}(\Delta_{e+1}, y_e)$: Parse Δ_{e+1} as (s_e, s_{e+1}) and output the updated value $y_{e+1} \leftarrow \mathsf{SE.Enc}(s_{e+1}, \mathsf{SE.Dec}(s_e, y_e))$.

This construction achieves IND-HOCH, IND-COHH, and one-wayness but not the stronger IND-COTH notion. The issue is that a transiently corrupted host can recover the static hash during the update procedure and thus can link tokenized values from different epochs, even without knowing all the update tweaks between them.

Theorem 2. *The $\mathsf{UTO_{SE}}$ as defined above satisfies the IND-HOCH, IND-COHH and one-wayness properties based on the following assumptions on the underlying encryption scheme SE and hash function H:*

$\mathsf{UTO_{SE}}$	SE	H
IND-COHH	IND-CPA	Weak collision resistance
IND-HOCH	IND-CPA	Pseudorandomness
One-wayness	–	One-wayness

The proof of Theorem 2 can be found in the full version of this paper.

4.2   An UTO Scheme Based on Discrete Logarithms

Our second construction $\mathsf{UTO_{DL}}$ overcomes the limitation of the first scheme by performing the update in a proxy re-encryption manner using the re-encryption idea first proposed by Blaze et al. [2]. That is, the hashed value is raised to an exponent that the owner randomly chooses at every new epoch. To update tokens, the host is not given the keys itself but only the quotient of the current and previous exponent. While this allows the host to consistently update his data, it does not reveal the inner hash anymore and guarantees unlinkability across epochs, thus satisfying also our strongest notion of IND-COTH security.

More precisely, the scheme makes use of a cyclic group $(\mathbb{G}, g, p)$ and a hash function $\mathsf{H} : \mathcal{X} \to \mathbb{G}$. We assume the hash function and the group description to be publicly available. The algorithms of our $\mathsf{UTO_{DL}}$ scheme are defined as follows:

$\mathsf{UTO.setup}(\lambda)$: Choose $k_0 \xleftarrow{r} \mathbb{Z}_p$ and output k_0.
$\mathsf{UTO.next}(k_e)$: Choose $k_{e+1} \xleftarrow{r} \mathbb{Z}_p$, set $\Delta_{e+1} \leftarrow k_{e+1}/k_e$, and output (k_{e+1}, Δ_{e+1}).
$\mathsf{UTO.token}(k_e, x)$: Compute $y_e \leftarrow \mathsf{H}(x)^{k_e}$, and output y_e.
$\mathsf{UTO.upd}(\Delta_{e+1}, y_e)$: Compute $y_{e+1} \leftarrow y_e^{\Delta_{e+1}}$, and output y_{e+1}.

Our $\mathsf{UTO_{DL}}$ scheme is one-way and satisfies our strongest notion of IND-COTH security, from which IND-HOCH and IND-COHH security follows (see Theorem 1). The proof of Theorem 3 below can be found in the full version of this paper.

Theorem 3. *The* $\mathsf{UTO_{DL}}$ *scheme as defined above is IND-COTH secure under the DDH assumption in the random oracle model, and one-way if* H *is one-way.*

Acknowledgements. We would like to thank our colleagues Michael Osborne, Tamas Visegrady and Axel Tanner for helpful discussions on tokenization.

References

1. Bellare, M., Boldyreva, A., O'Neill, A.: Deterministic and efficiently searchable encryption. In: Menezes, A. (ed.) CRYPTO 2007. LNCS, vol. 4622, pp. 535–552. Springer, Heidelberg (2007). https://doi.org/10.1007/978-3-540-74143-5_30
2. Blaze, M., Bleumer, G., Strauss, M.: Divertible protocols and atomic proxy cryptography. In: Nyberg, K. (ed.) EUROCRYPT 1998. LNCS, vol. 1403, pp. 127–144. Springer, Heidelberg (1998). https://doi.org/10.1007/BFb0054122
3. Boneh, D., Lewi, K., Montgomery, H., Raghunathan, A.: Key homomorphic PRFs and their applications. In: Canetti, R., Garay, J.A. (eds.) CRYPTO 2013. LNCS, vol. 8042, pp. 410–428. Springer, Heidelberg (2013). https://doi.org/10.1007/978-3-642-40041-4_23
4. Boneh, D., Lewi, K., Montgomery, H.W., Raghunathan, A.: Key homomorphic PRFs and their applications. IACR Cryptology ePrint Archive 2015, 220 (2015). http://eprint.iacr.org/2015/220
5. Diaz-Santiago, S., Rodríguez-Henríquez, L.M., Chakraborty, D.: A cryptographic study of tokenization systems. In: Obaidat, M.S., Holzinger, A., Samarati, P. (eds.) Proceedings of the 11th International Conference on Security and Cryptography (SECRYPT 2014), Vienna, 28–30 August 2014, pp. 393–398. SciTePress (2014). https://doi.org/10.5220/0005062803930398
6. European Commission, Article 29 Data Protection Working Party: Opinion 05/2014 on anonymisation techniques (2014). http://ec.europa.eu/justice/data-protection/article-29/documentation/opinion-recommendation/

7. Everspaugh, A., Chatterjee, R., Scott, S., Juels, A., Ristenpart, T.: The Pythia PRF service. In: Jung, J., Holz, T. (eds.) 24th USENIX Security Symposium, USENIX Security 2015, Washington, D.C., 12–14 August 2015, pp. 547–562. USENIX Association (2015). https://www.usenix.org/conference/usenixsecurity15/technical-sessions/presentation/everspaugh
8. Herzberg, A., Jakobsson, M., Jarecki, S., Krawczyk, H., Yung, M.: Proactive public key and signature systems. In: Proceedings of the 4th ACM Conference on Computer and Communications Security (CCS 1997), Zurich, 1–4 April 1997, pp. 100–110 (1997). https://doi.org/10.1145/266420.266442
9. McCallister, E., Grance, T., Scarfone, K.: Guide to protecting the confidentiality of personally identifiable information (PII). NIST special publication 800-122, National Institute of Standards and Technology (NIST) (2010). http://csrc.nist.gov/publications/PubsSPs.html
10. PCI Security Standards Council: PCI Data Security Standard (PCI DSS) (2015). https://www.pcisecuritystandards.org/document_library?document=pci_dss
11. Securosis: Tokenization guidance: How to reduce PCI compliance costs. https://securosis.com/assets/library/reports/TokenGuidance-Securosis-Final.pdf
12. Smart Card Alliance: Technologies for payment fraud prevention: EMV, encryption and tokenization. http://www.smartcardalliance.org/downloads/EMV-Tokenization-Encryption-WP-FINAL.pdf
13. United States Department of Health and Human Services: Summary of the HIPAA Privacy Rule. http://www.hhs.gov/sites/default/files/privacysummary.pdf
14. Voltage Security: Voltage secure stateless tokenization. https://www.voltage.com/wp-content/uploads/Voltage_White_Paper_SecureData_SST_Data_Protection_and_PCI_Scope_Reduction_for_Todays_Businesses.pdf

Privacy and Data Processing

SecGDB: Graph Encryption for Exact Shortest Distance Queries with Efficient Updates

Qian Wang[1,2]($\boxtimes$), Kui Ren[3], Minxin Du[1], Qi Li[4], and Aziz Mohaisen[3]

[1] School of CS, Wuhan University, Wuhan, China
{qianwang,duminxin}@whu.edu.cn
[2] Collaborative Innovation Center of Geospatial Technology, Wuhan University, Wuhan, China
[3] Department of CSE, University at Buffalo, SUNY, Buffalo, USA
{kuiren,mohaisen}@buffalo.edu
[4] Graduate School at Shenzhen, Tsinghua University, Shenzhen, China
qi.li@sz.tsinghua.edu.cn

Abstract. In the era of big data, graph databases have become increasingly important for NoSQL technologies, and many systems can be modeled as graphs for semantic queries. Meanwhile, with the advent of cloud computing, data owners are highly motivated to outsource and store their massive potentially-sensitive graph data on remote untrusted servers in an encrypted form, expecting to retain the ability to query over the encrypted graphs.

To allow effective and private queries over encrypted data, the most well-studied class of *structured encryption* schemes are searchable symmetric encryption (SSE) designs, which encrypt search structures (*e.g.*, inverted indexes) for retrieving data files. In this paper, we tackle the challenge of designing a Secure Graph DataBase encryption scheme (SecGDB) to encrypt graph structures and enforce private graph queries over the encrypted graph database. Specifically, our construction strategically makes use of efficient additively homomorphic encryption and garbled circuits to support the shortest distance queries with optimal time and storage complexities. To achieve better amortized time complexity over multiple queries, we further propose an auxiliary data structure called *query history* and store it on the remote server to act as a "caching" resource. We prove that our construction is adaptively semantically-secure in the random oracle model and finally implement and evaluate it on various representative real-world datasets, showing that our approach is practically efficient in terms of both storage and computation.

Keywords: Graph encryption · Shortest distance query
Homomorphic encryption · Garbled circuit

1 Introduction

Graphs are used in a wide range of application domains, including social networks, online knowledge discovery, computer networks, and the world-wide web, among

© International Financial Cryptography Association 2017
A. Kiayias (Ed.): FC 2017, LNCS 10322, pp. 79–97, 2017.
https://doi.org/10.1007/978-3-319-70972-7_5

others. For example, online social networks (OSN) such as Facebook and LinkedIn employ large social graphs with millions or even billions of vertices and edges in their operation. As a result, various systems have been recently proposed to handle massive graphs efficiently, where examples include GraphLab [22], Horton [29] and TurboGraph [9]. These database applications allow for querying, managing and analyzing large-scale graphs in an intuitive and expressive way.

With the increased popularity of cloud computing, data users, including both individuals and enterprises, are highly motivated to outsource their (potentially huge amount of sensitive) data that may be abstracted and modeled as large graphs to remote cloud servers to reduce the local storage and management costs [6,15,19–21,30,31]. However, database outsourcing also raises data confidentiality and privacy concerns due to data owners' loss of physical data control. Privacy-sensitive data therefore should be encrypted locally before outsourcing it to the untrusted cloud. Data encryption, however, hinders data utilization and computation, making it difficult to efficiently retrieve or query data of interest as opposed to the case with plaintext.

To address this challenge, the notion of *structured encryption* was first introduced by Chase and Kamara [3]. Roughly speaking, a structured encryption scheme encrypts structured data in such a way that it can be privately queried through the use of a specific token generated with knowledge of the secret key. Specifically, they presented approaches for encrypting (structured) graph data while allowing for efficient neighbor queries, adjacency queries and focused subgraph queries on labeled graphs.

Despite all of these important types of queries, finding the shortest distance between two vertices was not supported. The shortest distance queries are not only building blocks for various more complex algorithms, but also have applications of their own. Such applications include finding the shortest path for one person to meet another in an encrypted social network graph, seeking the shortest path with the minimum delay in an encrypted networking or telecommunications abstracted graph, or performing a privacy-preserving GPS guidance in which one party holds the encrypted map while the other knows his origin and destination.

Recently, Meng *et al.* [24] addressed the graph encryption problem by precomputing a data structure called the *distance oracle* from an original graph. They leveraged somewhat homomorphic encryption and standard private key encryption for their construction, thus answering shortest distance queries *approximately* over the encrypted distance oracle. Although their experimental results show that their schemes are practically efficient, the accuracy is sacrificed for using the *distance oracle* (*i.e.*, only the approximate distance or even the negative result is returned). On the one hand, the distance oracle based methods only provide an estimate on the length of the shortest path. On the other hand, the exact path itself could also be necessary and important in many of the aforementioned application scenarios. Furthermore, both of the previous solutions only deal with static graphs [3,24]: the outsourced encrypted graph structure cannot explicitly support efficient graph updates, since it requires to either re-encrypt the entire graph, or make use of generic and expensive dynamization techniques similar to [4].

To tackle the practical limitations of the state-of-the-art, we propose a new Secure Graph DataBase encryption scheme (SecGDB) that supports both exact shortest distance queries and efficient dynamic operations. Specifically, our construction addresses four major challenges. First, to seek the best tradeoff between accuracy and efficiency, we process the graph itself instantiated by adjacency lists instead of encrypting either the *distance oracle* pre-computed from the original graph or the adjacency matrix instantiation. Second, to compute the exact shortest path over the encrypted graph, we propose a hybrid approach that combines additively homomorphic encryption and garbled circuits to implement Dijkstra's algorithm [5] with the priority queue. Third, to enable dynamic updates of encrypted graphs, we carefully design an extra encrypted data structure to store the relevant information (*e.g.*, neighbor information of nodes in adjacency lists) which will be used to perform modifications homomorphically over the graph ciphertexts. Fourth, to further optimize the performance of the query phase, we introduce an auxiliary data structure called the *query history* by leveraging the previous queried results stored on the remote server as a "caching" resource; namely, the results for subsequent queries can be returned immediately without incurring further cost.

Our main contributions are summarized as follows.

- *Functionality and efficiency.* We propose SecGDB to support exact shortest distance queries with optimal time and storage complexity. We further obtain an improved amortized running time over multiple queries with the auxiliary data structure called *"query history"*.
- *Dynamics.* We design an additional encrypted data structure to facilitate efficient graph updates. Compared with the state-of-the-art [3,24], which consider only static data, SecGDB performs dynamic (*i.e.*, addition or removal of specified edges over the encrypted graph) operations with $O(1)$ time complexity.
- *Security, implementation and evaluation.* We formalize our security model using a simulation-based definition and prove the adaptive semantic security of SecGDB under the random oracle model with reasonable leakage. We implement and evaluate the performance of SecGDB on various representative real-world datasets to demonstrate its efficiency and practicality.

2 Preliminaries and Notations

We begin by outlining some notations. Given a graph $G = (V, E)$ which consists of a set of vertices V and edges E, we denote its total number of vertices as $n = |V|$ and its number of edges as $m = |E|$. G is either *undirected* or *directed*. If G is undirected, then each edge in E is an *unordered* pair of vertices, and we use len(u, v) to denote the length of edge (u, v), otherwise, each edge in E is an *ordered* pair of vertices. In an undirected graph, deg(v) is used to denote the number of vertices adjacent to the vertex v (*i.e.*, *degree*). For a directed graph, we use $\deg^-(v)$ and $\deg^+(v)$ to denote the number of edges directed to vertex v (*indegree*) and out of vertex v (*outdegree*), respectively. A shortest distance query $q = (s,t)$ asks for the length (along with the route) of the shortest path between s and t, which we denote by $\mathsf{dist}(s,t)$ or dist_q. $[n]$ denotes the set of positive integers less than or equal to n, *i.e.*, $[n] = \{1, 2, \ldots, n\}$. We write $x \xleftarrow{\$} X$ to represent an element x being uniformly sampled at random from a set X. The output x of a probabilistic algorithm $\mathcal{A}$ is denoted by $x \leftarrow \mathcal{A}$ and that of a deterministic algorithm $\mathcal{B}$ by $x := \mathcal{B}$. Given a sequence of elements $\mathbf{v}$, we refer to the ith element as $\mathbf{v}[i]$ or $\mathbf{v}_i$ and to the total number of elements in $\mathbf{v}$ by $|\mathbf{v}|$. If A is a set then $|A|$ refers to its cardinality, and if s is a string then $|s|$ refers to its bit length. We denote the concatenation of n strings $s_1, \ldots, s_n$ by $\langle s_1, \ldots, s_n \rangle$, and also denote the high-order $|s_2|$-bit of the string s_1 by $s_1^{|s_2|}$.

We also use various basic data structures including linked lists, arrays and dictionaries. Specifically, a dictionary T (also known as a map or associative array) is a data structure that stores key-value pairs (k, v). If the pair (k, v) is in T, then $\mathsf{T}[k]$ is the value v associated with k. An insertion operation of a new key-value pair (k, v) to the dictionary T is denoted by $\mathsf{T}[k] := v$. Similarly, a lookup operation takes a dictionary T and a specified key k as input, then returns the associated value v denoted by $v := \mathsf{T}[k]$.

2.1 Cryptographic Tools

Homomorphic encryption. Homomorphic encryption allows certain computations to be carried out on ciphertexts to generate an encrypted result which matches the result of operations performed on the plaintext after being decrypted. In this work, we only require the evaluation to efficiently support any number of additions, and there are many cryptosystems satisfying with this property. In particular, we use the Paillier cryptosystem [27] in our construction.

In the Paillier cryptosystem, the public (encryption) key is $pk_p = (n = pq, g)$, where $g \in \mathbb{Z}_{n^2}^*$, and p and q are two large prime numbers (of equivalent length) chosen randomly and independently. The private (decryption) key is $sk_p = (\varphi(n), \varphi(n)^{-1} \bmod n)$. Given a message a, we write the encryption of a as $[\![a]\!]_{pk}$, or simply $[\![a]\!]$, where pk is the public key. The encryption of a message $x \in \mathbb{Z}_n$ is $[\![x]\!] = g^x \cdot r^n \bmod n^2$, for some random $r \in \mathbb{Z}_n^*$. The decryption of the ciphertext is $x = L([\![x]\!]^{\varphi(n)} \bmod n^2) \cdot \varphi^{-1}(n) \bmod n$, where $L(u) = \frac{u-1}{n}$. The homomorphic property of the Paillier cryptosystem is given by $[\![x_1]\!] \cdot [\![x_2]\!] = (g^{x_1} \cdot r_1^n) \cdot (g^{x_2} \cdot r_2^n) = g^{x_1+x_2}(r_1 r_2)^n \bmod n^2 = [\![x_1 + x_2]\!]$.

Pseudo-random functions (PRFs) and permutations (PRPs). Let $F : \{0,1\}^\lambda \times \{0,1\}^* \to \{0,1\}^*$ be a PRF, which is a polynomial-time computable function that cannot be distinguished from random functions by any probabilistic polynomial-time adversary. A PRF is said to be a PRP when it is bijective. Readers can refer to [16] for the formal definition and security proof.

Oblivious transfer. Parallel 1-out-of-2 Oblivious Transfer (OT) of m l-bit strings [13,25], denoted as OT_l^m, is a two-party protocol run between a chooser

C and a sender S. For $i = 1, \ldots, m$, the sender S inputs a pair of l-bit strings $s_i^0, s_i^1 \in \{0,1\}^l$ and the chooser C inputs m choice bits $b_i \in \{0,1\}$. At the end of the protocol, C learns the chosen strings $s_i^{b_i}$ but nothing about the unchosen strings $s_i^{1-b_i}$, whereas S learns nothing about the choice b_i.

Garbled circuits. Garbled circuits were first proposed by Yao [32] for secure two-party computation and later proven practical by Malkhi *et al.* [23]. At a high level, garbled circuits allow two parties holding inputs x and y, respectively, to jointly evaluate an arbitrary function $f(x, y)$ represented as a boolean circuit without leaking any information about their inputs beyond what is implied by the function output.

Several optimization techniques have been proposed in the literature to construct the standard garbled circuits. Kolensikov *et al.* [18] introduced an efficient method for creating garbled circuits which allows "free" evaluation of XOR gates. Pinkas *et al.* [28] proposed an approach to reduce the size of garbled gates from four to three entries, thus saving 25% of the communication overhead.

2.2 Fibonacci Heap

Fibonacci heap [7] is a data structure for implementing priority queues, which consists of a collection of *trees* satisfying the *minimum-heap* property; that is, the key of a child is always greater than or equal to the key of the parent. This implies that the minimum key is always at the root of one of the trees. Generally, a heap data structure supports the following six operations: Make-Heap(), Insert(H, x), Minimum(H), Extract-MIN(H), Decrease-Key(H, x) and Delete(H, x).

Compared with many other priority queue data structures including the *Binary heap* and *Binomial heap*, the Fibonacci heap achieves a better amortized running time [7].

3 System Model and Definitions

In this work, we consider the problem of designing a structured encryption scheme that supports the shortest distance queries and dynamic operations over an encrypted graph stored on remote servers efficiently.

At a high level, as shown in Fig. 1, our construction contains three entities, namely the client C, the server S and the proxy P. In the initialization stage, the client C processes the original graph G to obtain its encrypted form Ω_G, outsources Ω_G to the server S and distributes partial secret key sk to the proxy P. The privacy holds as long as the server S and the proxy P do not collude, and this architecture of two non-colluding entities has been commonly used in the related literature [1,6,26]. Subsequently, to enable the shortest distance query over the encrypted graph Ω_G, the client generates a query token τ_q based on the query q and submits it to the cloud server S. Finally, the encrypted shortest distance along with the path are returned to the client C. In addition, the graph storage service in consideration is *dynamic*, such that the client C may add or remove edges to or from the

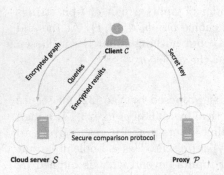

Fig. 1. System model   **Fig. 2.** The secure comparison circuit.

encrypted graph Ω_G as well as modify the length of the specified edge. To do so, the client generates an update token τ_u corresponding to the dynamic operations. Given τ_u, the server $\mathcal{S}$ can securely update the encrypted graph Ω_G.

Formally, the core functionalities of our system are listed as below.

Definition 1. *An encrypted graph database system supporting the shortest distance query and dynamic updates consists of the following five (possibly probabilistic) polynomial-time algorithms/protocols:*

$sk \leftarrow$ Gen(1^λ): *is a probabilistic key generation algorithm run by the client. It takes as input a security parameter λ and outputs the secret key sk.*

$\Omega_G \leftarrow$ Enc(sk, G): *is a probabilistic algorithm run by the client. It takes as input a secret key sk and a graph G, and outputs an encrypted graph Ω_G.*

dist$_q \leftarrow$ Dec(sk, c_q): *is a deterministic algorithm run by the client. It takes as input a secret key sk and an encrypted result c_q, and outputs dist$_q$ including the shortest distance as well as its corresponding path.*

$(c_q; \sigma') \leftarrow$ DistanceQuery($sk, q; \Omega_G, \sigma$): *is a (possibly interactive and probabilistic) protocol run between the client and the server[1]. The client takes as input a secret key sk and a shortest distance query q, while the server takes as input the encrypted graph Ω_G and the query history σ (which is empty in the beginning). During the protocol execution, a query token τ_q is generated by the client based on the query q and then sent to the server. Upon completion of the protocol, the client obtains an encrypted result c_q while the server gets a (possibly new) query history σ'.*

$(\perp; \Omega'_G, \sigma) \leftarrow$ UpdateQuery($sk, u; \Omega_G$): *is a (possibly interactive and probabilistic) protocol run between the client and the server. The client takes as input a secret key sk and an update object u (e.g., the edges to be updated), while the server takes as*

---

[1] A protocol P run between the client and the server is denoted by $(u; v) \leftarrow P(x; y)$, where x and y are the client's and the server's inputs, respectively, and u and v are the client's and the server's outputs, respectively.

input the encrypted graph Ω_G. During the protocol execution, an update token τ_u is generated by the client based on the object u and then sent to the server. Upon completion of the protocol, the client gets nothing while the server obtains an updated encrypted graph Ω'_G and a new empty query history σ.

3.1   Security Definitions

As in previous SSE systems [2, 4, 8, 14, 15] we also relax the security requirements appropriately by allowing some reasonable information leakage to the adversary in order to obtain higher efficiency. To capture this relaxation, we follow [3, 4, 8, 15] to parameterize the information by using a tuple of well-defined leakage functions (see Sect. 5). Besides, we assume that the server and the proxy are both semi-honest entities in our setting.

In the following definition, we adapt the notion of adaptive semantic security from [3, 4, 15] to our encrypted graph database system.

Definition 2. *(Adaptive semantic security) Let* (Gen,Enc,Dec,DistanceQuery, UpdateQuery) *be a dynamic encrypted graph database system and consider the following experiments with a stateful adversary $\mathcal{A}$, a stateful simulator $\mathcal{S}$ and three stateful leakage functions $\mathcal{L}_1$, $\mathcal{L}_2$ and $\mathcal{L}_3$:*

Real$_{\mathcal{A}}(\lambda)$: *The challenger runs* Gen(1^λ) *to generate the key sk. $\mathcal{A}$ outputs G and receives $\Omega_G \leftarrow$ Enc(sk, G) from the challenger. $\mathcal{A}$ then makes a polynomial number of adaptive shortest distance queries q or update queries u. For each q, the challenger acts as a client and runs* DistanceQuery *with $\mathcal{A}$ acting as a server. For each update query u, the challenger acts as a client and runs* UpdateQuery *with $\mathcal{A}$ acting as a server. Finally, $\mathcal{A}$ returns a bit b as the output of the experiment.*

Ideal$_{\mathcal{A},\mathcal{S}}(\lambda)$: *$\mathcal{A}$ outputs G. Given $\mathcal{L}_1(G)$, $\mathcal{S}$ generates and sends Ω_G to $\mathcal{A}$. $\mathcal{A}$ makes a polynomial number of adaptive shortest distance queries q or update queries u. For each q, $\mathcal{S}$ is given $\mathcal{L}_2(G, q)$, and simulates a client who runs* DistanceQuery *with $\mathcal{A}$ acting as a server. For each update query u, $\mathcal{S}$ is given $\mathcal{L}_3(G, u)$, and simulates a client who runs* UpdateQuery *with $\mathcal{A}$ acting as a server. Finally, $\mathcal{A}$ returns a bit b as the output of the experiment.*

We say such a queryable encrypted graphs database system is adaptively $(\mathcal{L}_1, \mathcal{L}_2, \mathcal{L}_3)$-semantically secure if for all probabilistic polynomial-time (PPT) adversaries $\mathcal{A}$, there exists a probabilistic polynomial-time simulator $\mathcal{S}$ such that

$$|\Pr[\mathbf{Real}_{\mathcal{A}}(\lambda) = 1] - \Pr[\mathbf{Ideal}_{\mathcal{A},\mathcal{S}}(\lambda) = 1]| \leq \mathsf{negl}(\lambda),$$

where $\mathsf{negl}(\cdot)$ is a negligible function.

4   Our Construction: SecGDB

In this section, we present our encrypted graph database system–SecGDB, which efficiently supports the shortest distance query and the update query (*i.e.*, to add, remove and modify a specified edge).

4.1   Overview

We assume that an original graph is instantiated by adjacency lists, and every node in each adjacency list contains a pair of the neighboring vertex and the length of the corresponding edge (*i.e.*, vertex and length pair).

Our construction is inspired by [15], and the key idea is as follows. During the initialization phase, we place every node of each adjacency list at a random location in the array while updating the pointers so that the "logical" integrity of the lists are preserved. We then use the Paillier cryptosystem to encrypt the length of the edge in each node, and use a "standard" private-key encryption scheme [16] to blind the entire node. In the shortest distance query phase, if the query has been submitted before or was a subpath of the *query history*, the result can be immediately returned to the client; otherwise, we implement the Dijkstra's algorithm with the aid of Fibonacci heap in a secure manner, and then query history is updated based on the results. To support efficient dynamic operations on the encrypted graph, we generate the relevant update token, which allows the server to add or remove the specified entry to and from the array. After finishing the updates, the query history is rebuilt for future use.

4.2   Initialization Phase

Intuitively, the initialization phase consists of Gen and Enc as presented in Definition 1. The scheme uses the Paillier cryptosystem, and three pseudo-random functions P, F and G, where P is defined as $\{0,1\}^\lambda \times \{0,1\}^* \to \{0,1\}^\lambda$, F is defined as $\{0,1\}^\lambda \times \{0,1\}^* \to \{0,1\}^*$ and G is defined as $\{0,1\}^\lambda \times \{0,1\}^* \to \{0,1\}^\lambda$. We also use a random oracle H which is defined as $\{0,1\}^* \to \{0,1\}^*$.

Gen(1^λ): Given a security parameter λ, generate the following keys uniformly at random from their respective domains: three PRF keys $k_1, k_2, k_3 \xleftarrow{\$} \{0,1\}^\lambda$ for $P_{k_1}(\cdot)$, $F_{k_2}(\cdot)$ and $G_{k_3}(\cdot)$, respectively, and (sk_p, pk_p) for the Paillier cryptosystem. The output is $sk = (k_1, k_2, k_3, sk_p, pk_p)$, where sk_p is sent to the proxy through a secure channel.

As shown in Algorithm 1, the setup procedures are done in the first five steps. From line 6 to 29, the length of the edge is encrypted under the Paillier cryptosystem and the entire node N_i is encrypted by XORing an output of the random oracle H. Meanwhile, the neighboring information of each node N_i (*i.e.*, the nodes following and previous to N_i in the original adjacency lists, and the corresponding positions in A_G) constitutes the dual node D_i, and the encrypted dual node will be stored in the dictionary T_D. Generally speaking, T_D stores the pointer to each edge, and it is used to support efficient delete updates on the

Algorithm 1. Graph Enc algorithm

Input: $G = (V, E), sk$
Output: Ω_G

1: Set $n = |V|, m = |E|$;
2: Initialize an array A_G of size $m + z$;
3: Initialize two dictionaries T_G, T_D of size $n+1$ and m;
4: Initialize a random permutation π over $[m + z]$;
5: Initialize a counter $\mathtt{ctr} = 1$;
6: **for** each vertex $u \in V$ **do**
7:     Generate $K_u := G_{k_3}(u)$;
8:     **for** $i = 1$ to $\deg^+(u)$ **do**
9:         Encrypt the length of the edge (u, v_i) under the Paillier cryptosystem $c_i \leftarrow [\![\mathsf{len}(u, v_i)]\!]_{n^{k}k_p}$
10:        **if** $i = 1$ and $i \neq \deg^+(u)$ **then**
11:            Set $\mathtt{N}_i := \langle P_{k_1}(v_i), F_{k_2}(v_i), c_i, \pi(\mathtt{ctr} +1)\rangle$;
12:            Set $\mathtt{D}_i := \langle \mathbf{0}, \mathbf{0}, \pi(\mathtt{ctr} + 1), P_{k_1}(\langle u, v_{i+1}\rangle)\rangle$;
13:        **else if** $i \neq 1$ and $i = \deg^+(u)$ **then**
14:            Set $\mathtt{N}_i := \langle P_{k_1}(v_i), F_{k_2}(v_i), c_i, \mathtt{NULL}\rangle$;
15:            Set $\mathtt{D}_i := \langle P_{k_1}(\langle u, v_{i-1}\rangle), \pi(\mathtt{ctr} - 1), \pi(\mathtt{ctr}), \mathbf{0}, \mathbf{0}\rangle$;
16:        **else if** $i = 1$ and $i = \deg^+(u)$ **then**
17:            Set $\mathtt{N}_i := \langle P_{k_1}(v_i), F_{k_2}(v_i), c_i, \mathtt{NULL}\rangle$;
18:            Set $\mathtt{D}_i := \langle \mathbf{0}, \mathbf{0}, \pi(\mathtt{ctr}), \mathbf{0}, \mathbf{0}\rangle$;
19:        **else**
20:            Set $\mathtt{N}_i := \langle P_{k_1}(v_i), F_{k_2}(v_i), c_i, \pi(\mathtt{ctr} +1)\rangle$;
21:            Set $\mathtt{D}_i := \langle P_{k_1}(\langle u, v_{i-1}\rangle), \pi(\mathtt{ctr} - 1), \pi(\mathtt{ctr}), \pi(\mathtt{ctr} + 1), P_{k_1}(\langle u, v_{i+1}\rangle)\rangle$;
22:        **end if**
23:        Sample $r_i \overset{\$}{\leftarrow} \{0,1\}^{\lambda}$;
24:        Store the encrypted $\mathtt{N}_i$ in the array $A_G[\pi(\mathtt{ctr})] := \langle \mathtt{N}_i \oplus H(K_u, r_i), r_i\rangle$;
25:        Store the encrypted $\mathtt{D}_i$ in the dictionary $T_D[P_{k_1}(\langle u, v_i\rangle)] := \mathtt{D}_i \oplus F_{k_2}(\langle u, v_i\rangle)$;
26:        Increase $\mathtt{ctr} = \mathtt{ctr} + 1$;
27:    **end for**
28:    Store a pointer to the head node of the adjacency list for u in the dictionary $T_G[P_{k_1}(u)] := \langle \mathsf{addr}(\mathtt{N}_1), F_{k_1}(\langle u, v_1\rangle), K_u\rangle \oplus F_{k_2}(u)$;
29: **end for**
30: **for** $i = 1$ to z **do**
31:    Set $\mathtt{F}_i := \langle \mathbf{0}, \pi(\mathtt{ctr}+1)\rangle$;
32:    **if** $i = z$ **then**
33:        Set $\mathtt{F}_i := \langle \mathbf{0}, \mathtt{NULL}\rangle$;
34:    **end if**
35:    Store the unencrypted $\mathtt{F}_i$ in the array $A_G[\pi(\mathtt{ctr})] := \mathtt{F}_i$;
36:    Increase $\mathtt{ctr} = \mathtt{ctr} + 1$;
37: **end for**
38: Store a pointer to the head node of the free list in the dictionary $T_G[\mathtt{free}] := \langle \mathsf{addr}(\mathtt{F}_1), \mathbf{0}\rangle$;
39: Output the encrypted graph $\Omega_G = (A_G, T_G, T_D)$;

encrypted graph. After the aforementioned operations are done, the address of each head node will be encrypted and stored in the dictionary T_G, namely, T_G stores the pointer to the head of each adjacency list. The remaining z cells in the array construct an unencrypted free list, which is used in the add updates. To ensure the size of all the entries in A_G, T_G and T_D is identical, we should pad by a string of 0's (*i.e.*, $\mathbf{0}$). Finally, we output the encrypted graph Ω_G.

Figure 3 gives an illustrative example to construct the encrypted graph from a directed graph with four vertices v_1, v_2, v_3 and v_4 as well as five edges. All the nodes contained in the original (three) adjacency lists are now stored at random locations in A_G, and the dictionaries T_G and T_D are also shown in Fig. 3. Note that in a real encrypted graph, there would be padding to hide partial structural information of the original graph (as will be discussed in Sect. 5); we omit this padding for simplicity in this example.

4.3 Shortest Distance Query Phase

In this section, we describe the process of performing the exact shortest distance query over the encrypted graph, as summarized in Algorithm 2.

First, the client generates the query token τ_q based on a query $q = (s, t)$, and then sends it to the server. If the token has been queried before or acts as a sub-path of the *query history* σ, the server returns the result c_q $(c_q \subset \sigma)$ to the client

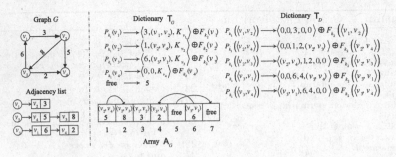

Fig. 3. An example of the encrypted graph construction.

immediately; otherwise, the server executes the Dijkstra's algorithm with the aid of a Fibonacci heap H in a private way. Concretely, the server first reads off the vertices that are adjacent to the source s and inserts to the heap H (line 14 to 22). Subsequently, each iteration of the loop from line 23 to 49 starts by extracting the vertex α with the minimum key. If the vertex α is the requested destination τ_2, the server updates the query history σ based on the newly-obtained path, computes the encrypted result c_q via reverse iteration and returns it to the client. Else, the server recovers the pointer to the head of the adjacency list for the vertex α, and then retrieves nodes in the adjacency list. Specifically, for the node N_i, once an update of $\xi[\alpha_i]$ occurs it indicates that a shorter path to α_i via α has been discovered, the server then updates the path. Next, the server either runs Insert(H, α_i) (if α_i is not in H) or Decrease-Key(H, α_i, $key(\alpha_i)$). It is worth noting that both the conditional statement $\xi[\alpha] \cdot c_i < \xi[\alpha_i]$ and some specific operations on the Fibonacci heap (*e.g.*, Extract-MIN) require performing a comparison on the encrypted data. Hence we build a secure comparison protocol (see Sect. 4.3) based on the garbled circuits and invoke it as a subroutine.

Finally, the client runs Dec(c_q, sk) to obtain the dist$_q$ as follows. Given c_q, the client parses it as a sequence of $\langle c_1, c_2 \rangle$ pairs, and for each pair, the client decrypts c_1 (the path) and c_2 (the distance) by using k_1 and sk_p, respectively.

Remarks. Conceptually, the history σ consists of all previous de-duplicated queried results. For a new query, the server traverses σ and checks whether the new query belongs to a record in σ. For example, let history σ consist of a shortest path from s to t (*i.e.*, $\{s, \ldots, u, \ldots, v, \ldots, t\}$), then for a new query $q = (u, v)$, the corresponding encrypted result $c_q = \{u, \ldots, v\}$ where $c_q \subset \sigma$ can be returned immediately. Note that only lookup operations (of dictionary) are required, thus making the whole process highly efficient.

Secure Comparison Protocol. We now present the secure comparison protocol which is based on the garbled circuits [12,32] for selecting the minimum of two encrypted values. This subroutine is implemented by the circuit shown in Fig. 2, and we use a CMP circuit and two SUB circuits constructed in [17] to realize the desired functionality.

Algorithm 2. DistanceQuery protocol

Input:
 The client $\mathcal{C}$'s input is $sk, q = (s, t)$;
 The server $\mathcal{S}$'s input is Ω_G, σ;
Output:
 The client $\mathcal{C}$'s output is c_q;
 The server $\mathcal{S}$'s output is σ';

1:   $\mathcal{C}$: compute $\tau_q := (P_{k_1}(s), P_{k_1}(t), F_{k_2}(s))$;
2:   $\mathcal{C} \Rightarrow \mathcal{S}$: output τ_q to the server;
3:   $\mathcal{S}$: parse τ_q as (τ_1, τ_2, τ_3);
4:   **if** $T_G[\tau_1] = \perp$ or $T_G[\tau_2] = \perp$ **then**
5:    $\mathcal{S} \Rightarrow \mathcal{C}$: return $\perp$ to the client;
6:   **else if** $\{\tau_1, \tau_2\} \subset \sigma$ **then**
7:    $\mathcal{S} \Rightarrow \mathcal{C}$: return c_q to the client;
8:   **else**
9:    $\mathcal{S}$: initialize a Fibonacci heap $H \leftarrow$ Make-Heap();
10:    $\mathcal{S}$: initialize two dictionaries ξ and path;
11:    $\mathcal{S}$: compute $\langle \mathtt{addr}_1, \mathtt{str}, K_s \rangle := T_G[\tau_1] \oplus \tau_3$;
12:    $\mathcal{S}$: parse $A_G[\mathtt{addr}_1]$ as $\langle \mathtt{N}'_1, r_1 \rangle$;
13:    $\mathcal{S}$: compute $\mathtt{N}_1 := \mathtt{N}'_1 \oplus H(K_s, r_1)$;
14:    **while** $\mathtt{addr}_{i+1} \neq$ NULL **do**
15:     $\mathcal{S}$: parse $\mathtt{N}_i$ as $\langle \alpha_i, \beta_i, c_i, \mathtt{addr}_{i+1} \rangle$;
16:     $\mathcal{S}$: store path$[\alpha_i] := \langle \tau_1, c_i \rangle$
17:     $\mathcal{S}$: set $\xi[\alpha_i] := c_i$ and $key(\alpha_i) := \xi[\alpha_i]$;
18:     $\mathcal{S}$: run Insert(H, α_i) with the $key(\alpha_i)$;
19:     $\mathcal{S}$: parse $A_G[\mathtt{addr}_{i+1}]$ as $\langle \mathtt{N}'_{i+1}, r_{i+1} \rangle$;
20:     $\mathcal{S}$: compute $\mathtt{N}_{i+1} := \mathtt{N}'_{i+1} \oplus H(K_s, r_{i+1})$;
21:     $\mathcal{S}$: increase $i = i + 1$;
22:    **end while**
23:    **repeat**
24:     $\mathcal{S}$: parse Extract-MIN(H) as $\langle \alpha, key(\alpha) \rangle$;
25:     **if** $\alpha = \tau_2$ **then**
26:      $\mathcal{S}$: update σ' based on path;
27:      $\mathcal{S} \Rightarrow \mathcal{C}$: return c_q to the client;
28:      $\mathcal{S}$: break;
29:     **end if**
30:     $\mathcal{S}$: compute $\langle \mathtt{addr}_1, \mathtt{str}, K_u \rangle := T_G[\alpha] \oplus \beta$;
31:     $\mathcal{S}$: parse $A_G[\mathtt{addr}_1]$ as $\langle \mathtt{N}'_1, r_1 \rangle$;
32:     $\mathcal{S}$: compute $\mathtt{N}_1 := \mathtt{N}'_1 \oplus H(K_u, r_1)$;
33:     **while** $\mathtt{addr}_{i+1} \neq$ NULL **do**
34:      $\mathcal{S}$: parse $\mathtt{N}_i$ as $\langle \alpha_i, \beta_i, c_i, \mathtt{addr}_{i+1} \rangle$;
35:      **if** $\xi[\alpha] \cdot c_i < \xi[\alpha_i]$ **then**
36:       $\mathcal{S}$: update $\xi[\alpha_i] := \xi[\alpha] \cdot c_i$;
37:       $\mathcal{S}$: set $key(\alpha_i) := \xi[\alpha_i]$;
38:       $\mathcal{S}$: store path$[\alpha_i] := \langle \alpha, c_i \rangle$;
39:      **end if**
40:      **if** $\alpha_i \notin H$ **then**
41:       $\mathcal{S}$: run Insert(H, α_i) with the $key(\alpha_i)$;
42:      **else**
43:       $\mathcal{S}$: run Decrease-Key(H, $\alpha_i, key(\alpha_i)$);
44:      **end if**
45:      $\mathcal{S}$: parse $A_G[\mathtt{addr}_{i+1}]$ as $\langle \mathtt{N}'_{i+1}, r_{i+1} \rangle$;
46:      $\mathcal{S}$: compute $\mathtt{N}_{i+1} := \mathtt{N}'_{i+1} \oplus H(K_u, r_{i+1})$;
47:      $\mathcal{S}$: increase $i = i + 1$;
48:     **end while**
49:    **until** H is empty
50:   **end if**

At the beginning, the server has two encrypted values $[\![a_1]\!]$ and $[\![a_2]\!]$ and the proxy has the secret key sk_p. W.l.o.g., we assume that the longest shortest distance between any pair of vertices (*i.e.*, diameter [10]) lies in $[2^l]$, namely, a_1 and a_2 are two l-bit integers. Instead of sending $[\![a_1]\!]$ and $[\![a_2]\!]$ to the proxy, the server first masks them with two k-bit random numbers r_1 and r_2 (*e.g.*, $[\![a_1 + r_1]\!] = [\![a_1]\!] \cdot [\![r_1]\!]$) respectively, where k is a security parameter ($k > l$). Then the server's inputs are r_1 and r_2, and the proxy's inputs are $a_1 + r_1$ and $a_2 + r_2$. Finally, the output single bit x implies the comparison result: if $x = 1$, then $a_1 > a_2$; 0 otherwise. Note that masking here is done by performing addition over the integers which is a form of statistical hiding. More precisely, for a l-bit integer a_i and a k-bit integer r_i, releasing $a_i + r_i$ gives statistical security of roughly 2^{l-k} for the potential value a_i. Therefore, by choosing the security parameter k properly, we can make this statistical difference arbitrarily low [12].

Packing Optimization. It is worth noting that the message space of the Paillier cryptosystem is much greater than the space of the blinded values. We can therefore provide a great improvement in both computation time and bandwidth by leveraging the packing technique. The key idea lies in that the server can send one aggregated ciphertext in the form $[\![\langle (a_{i+1} + r_{i+1}), \ldots, (a_{i+p} + r_{i+p}) \rangle]\!]$ instead of p ciphertexts of the form $[\![a_i + r_i]\!]$, where $p = \frac{1024}{k}$ (1024-bit modulus used in Paillier cryptosystem).

Algorithm 3. UpdateQuery protocol

Input:
The client $\mathcal{C}$'s input is sk, u;
The server $\mathcal{S}$'s input is Ω_G;
Output:
The client $\mathcal{C}$'s output is $\perp$;
The server $\mathcal{S}$'s output is Ω'_G, σ;

a) Adding new edges
At the client $\mathcal{C}$:
1) u contains information about newly-added edge (v_1, v_2) with the length $\text{len}(v_1, v_2)$;
2) compute the update token $\tau_u := (P_{k_1}(v_1), F_{k_2}(v_1)^{|\langle \text{addr}, \text{str} \rangle|}, P_{k_1}(\langle v_1, v_2 \rangle), F_{k_2}(\langle v_1, v_2 \rangle), \mathbb{N})$, where $\mathbb{N} = \langle \langle P_{k_1}(v_2), F_{k_2}(v_2), [\![\text{len}]\!], 0 \rangle \oplus H(K_{v_1}, r), r \rangle$;
$\mathcal{C} \Rightarrow \mathcal{S}$: output τ_u to the server;
At the server $\mathcal{S}$:
1) parse τ_u as $(\tau_1, \tau_2, \tau_3, \tau_4, \tau_5)$ and return $\perp$ if τ_1 is not in T_G;
2) compute $\langle \text{addr}_1, 0 \rangle := \mathsf{T}_G[\text{free}]$;
3) parse $\mathsf{A}_G[\text{addr}_1]$ as $\langle 0, \text{addr}_2 \rangle$;
4) update the pointer to the next free node $\mathsf{T}_G[\text{free}] := \langle \text{addr}_2, 0 \rangle$;
5) compute $\langle \text{addr}_3, \text{str} \rangle := \mathsf{T}_G[\tau_1]^{|\langle \text{addr}, \text{str} \rangle|} \oplus \tau_2$;
6) parse τ_5 as $\langle \mathbb{N}', r \rangle$ and set $\mathsf{A}_G[\text{addr}_1] := \langle \mathbb{N}' \oplus \langle 0, \text{addr}_3 \rangle, r \rangle$;
7) update the pointer to the newly-added node $\mathsf{T}_G[\tau_1] := \mathsf{T}_G[\tau_1]^{|\langle \text{addr}, \text{str} \rangle|} \oplus \langle \text{addr}_3, \text{str} \rangle \oplus \langle \text{addr}_1, \tau_3 \rangle$;

8) store $\mathsf{T}_D[\tau_3] := \langle 0, 0, \text{addr}_1, \text{addr}_3, \text{str} \rangle \oplus \tau_4$;
9) update $\mathsf{T}_D[\text{str}] := \mathsf{T}_D[\text{str}]^{|\langle \text{addr}, \text{str} \rangle|} \oplus \langle \tau_3, \text{addr}_1 \rangle$;
10) obtain an updated graph Ω'_G and rebuild σ;

b) Deleting existing edges
At the client $\mathcal{C}$:
1) u contains information about the existing edge (v_1, v_2) to be deleted;
2) compute $\tau_u := (P_{k_1}(\langle v_1, v_2 \rangle), F_{k_2}(\langle v_1, v_2 \rangle))$;
$\mathcal{C} \Rightarrow \mathcal{S}$: outputs τ_u to the server;
At the server $\mathcal{S}$:
1) parse τ_u as (τ_1, τ_2) and return $\perp$ if τ_1 is not in T_D;
2) look up in T_D and computes $\langle \text{str}_1, \text{addr}_1, \text{addr}_2, \text{addr}_3, \text{str}_3 \rangle := \mathsf{T}_D[\tau_1] \oplus \tau_2$;
3) compute $\langle \text{addr}_4, 0 \rangle := \mathsf{T}_G[\text{free}]$;
4) free the node and set $\mathsf{A}_G[\text{addr}_2] := \langle 0, \text{addr}_4 \rangle$;
5) update the pointer $\mathsf{T}_G[\text{free}] := \langle \text{addr}_2, 0 \rangle$;
6) parse $\mathsf{A}_G[\text{addr}_1]$ as $\langle \mathbb{N}'_1, r_1 \rangle$;
7) update node $\mathsf{A}_G[\text{addr}_1] := \langle \mathbb{N}'_1 \oplus \text{addr}_2 \oplus \text{addr}_3, r_1 \rangle$;
8) update the corresponding entry $\mathsf{T}_D[\text{str}_1] := \mathsf{T}_D[\text{str}_1] \oplus \langle \text{addr}_2, \tau_1 \rangle \oplus \langle \text{addr}_3, \text{str}_3 \rangle$;
9) update the corresponding entry $\mathsf{T}_D[\text{str}_3] := \mathsf{T}_D[\text{str}_3] \oplus \langle \text{addr}_2, \tau_1 \rangle \oplus \langle \text{addr}_1, \text{str}_1 \rangle$;
10) obtain an updated graph Ω'_G and rebuild σ;

4.4 Supporting Encrypted Graph Dynamics

We next discuss the support of update operations over the encrypted graph, and the details are given in Algorithm 3. Here, we do not particularly consider the addition and removal of vertices, because the update of the vertex can be viewed as the update of a collection of related edges.

To add new edges, the client generates the corresponding token τ_u for an update object u and sends it to the server. After receiving τ_u, the server locates the first free node addr_1 in the array A_G, and modifies the pointer in T_G to point to the second one. Later, the server retrieves the high-order useful information (without the key K_{v_1}) of the head node N_1, stores N that represents the newly edge at location addr_1 and modifies its pointer to point to the original head node N_1 without decryption. Then, the server updates the pointer in T_G to point to the newly-added node, and finally updates the corresponding entries in the dictionary T_D. To remove the existing edges, the client generates the update token τ_u and submits it to the server. Subsequently, the server looks up in the T_D and recovers the adjacency information of the specified edge. In the following steps, the server frees the node, inserts it into the head of the free list and then homomorphically modifies the pointer of the previous node to point to the next node in A_G. Eventually, the server updates the related entries in the dictionary T_D. Note that modifying a specified edge can be easily achieved by removing the "old" edge first, and adding a "new" edge with the modified length later. After the encrypted graph has been updated, the old query history is deleted and a new empty history will be rebuilt simultaneously.

4.5   Performance Analysis

The time cost of initialization phase is dominated by encrypting all the edges using Paillier cryptosystem and processing all the vertices, thus the time complexity of this part is $O(m + n)$. The generated encrypted graph, which consists of an array and two dictionaries, has the storage complexity $O(m + n)$. In the query phase, we use the Fibonacci heap to speed up the Dijkstra's algorithm, and thus we obtain an $O(n \log n + m)$ time complexity which is optimal among other priority queue optimization techniques (e.g., binary or binomial heap) [7]. During the execution of the secure comparison protocol, the overheads between the server and the proxy are directly related to the number of gates in the comparison circuit. Since many expensive operations of the garbled circuits can be pushed into a pre-computation phase, most of the costs will be relieved from the query phase. By maintaining an auxiliary structure history σ at the server, we can obtain an even better amortization time complexity over multiple queries, i.e., the query time for subsequent queries that can be looked up in the history are (almost) constant. Besides, it is obvious that the time complexity for both addition and removal operations on the encrypted graph are only $O(1)$.

5   Security

We allow reasonable leakage to the server to trade it for efficiency. Now, we provide a formal description of the three leakage functions $\mathcal{L}_1$, $\mathcal{L}_2$ and $\mathcal{L}_3$ considered in our scheme as follows.

- (*Leakage function* $\mathcal{L}_1$). Given a graph G, $\mathcal{L}_1(G) = \{n, m, \#\mathsf{A}_G\}$, where n is the total number of vertices, m is the total number of edges in the graph G and $\#\mathsf{A}_G$ denotes the number of entries (i.e., $m + z$) in the array A_G.
- (*Leakage function* $\mathcal{L}_2$). Given a graph G, a query q, $\mathcal{L}_2(G, q) = \{\mathsf{QP}(G, q), \mathsf{AP}(G, q)\}$, where $\mathsf{QP}(G, q)$ denotes the query pattern and $\mathsf{AP}(G, q)$ denotes the access pattern, both of which are given in the following definitions.
- (*Leakage function* $\mathcal{L}_3$). Given a graph G, an update object u, $\mathcal{L}_3(G, u) = \{\mathsf{id}_v, \mathsf{id}_{new}, \mathsf{next}\}$ is for add updates, and $\mathcal{L}_3(G, u) = \{\mathsf{id}_{del}, \mathsf{next}, \mathsf{prev}\}$ is for delete updates, where id_v denotes the identifier of the start vertex in the newly edge, id_{new} and id_{del} denote the identifiers of the edges to be added and deleted, respectively. prev and next contain the neighboring information (i.e., the identifiers of the neighboring edges) of the edge to be updated. If there are no nodes in A_G before and after the edge to be updated then prev and next are set to $\perp$.

Definition 3 (*Query Pattern*). *For two shortest distance queries* $q = (s, t), q' = (s', t')$, *define* $\mathsf{sim}(q, q') = (s = s', s = t', t = s', t = t')$, *i.e., whether each of the* *vertices in q matches each of the vertices in q'. Let $\mathsf{q} = (q_1, \ldots, q_\delta)$ be a sequence of δ queries, the query pattern $\mathsf{QP}(G, \mathsf{q})$ induced by q is a $\delta \times \delta$ symmetric matrix such that for $1 \leq i, j \leq \delta$, the element in the ith row and j^{th} column equals $\mathsf{sim}(q_i, q_j)$. Namely, the query pattern reveals whether the vertices in the query have appeared before.*

Definition 4 *(Access Pattern). Given a shortest distance query q for the graph G, the access pattern is defined as $\mathsf{AP}(G, q) = \{\mathsf{id}(c_q), \mathsf{id}(c_q)', \mathsf{id}^*(c_q)\}$, where $\mathsf{id}(c_q)$ denotes the identifiers of vertices in the encrypted result c_q, $\mathsf{id}(c_q)'$ denotes the identifiers of vertices contained in the dictionary* path *and it reveals the subgraph consisting of vertices reachable from the source ($\mathsf{id}(c_q) \subset \mathsf{id}(c_q)'$), and $\mathsf{id}^*(c_q)$ denotes the identifiers of the edges with one of its endpoints is the head node of retrieved adjacency lists.*

Discussion. The query pattern implies whether a new query has been issued before, and the access pattern discloses the structural information such as graph connectivity associated with the query. The leakage is not revealed unless its corresponding query has been issued. This is similar to keyword-based SSE schemes, where the leakage (*i.e.*, patterns associated with a keyword query) is revealed only if the corresponding keyword is searched. Fortunately, we can guarantee some level of privacy to the structural information with slightly lower efficiency in our setting, namely, we can add some form of noise (*i.e.*, padding carefully designed fake entries [3,4,15] to each original adjacency list) when generates the encrypted graph. Moreover, in various application scenarios where the data may be abstracted and modeled as sparse graphs (see Table 1), the leakage would not be a big problem. Fully protecting the above two patterns (also forward privacy defined in [30]) without using expensive ORAM techniques remains an open challenging problem, which is our future research focus.

Theorem 1. *If Paillier cryptosystem is CPA-secure and P, F and G are pseudo-random, then the encrypted graph query database system is adaptively $(\mathcal{L}_1, \mathcal{L}_2, \mathcal{L}_3)$-semantically secure in the random oracle model.*

Due to the space limitation, please refer to our technical report for the proof details.

6   Experimental Evaluation

In this section, we present experimental evaluations of our construction on different large-scale graphs. The experiments are performed on separate machines with different configurations: the client runs on a machine with an Intel Core CPU with 4-core operating at 2.90 GHz and equipped with 12 GB RAM, both the server and the proxy run on machines with an Intel Xeon CPU with 24-core operating at 2.10 GHz and equipped with 128 GB RAM. We implemented algorithms described in Sect. 4 in Java, used HMAC for PRF/PRPs and instantiated the random oracle with HMAC-SHA-256. Our secure comparison protocol is built on top of FastGC [11], a Java-based open-source framework.

Table 1. The characteristics of datasets.

Dataset	Type	Vertices	Edges	Storage
Talk	directed	2,394,385	5,021,410	63.3 MB
Youtube	undirected	1,134,890	2,987,624	36.9 MB
EuAll	directed	265,214	420,045	4.76 MB
Gowalla	undirected	196,591	1,900,654	21.1 MB
Vote	directed	7,115	103,689	1.04 MB
Enron	undirected	36,692	367,662	3.86 MB

Table 2. The cost of initialization phase.

Dataset	Time (min.)	Storage (MB)			
		T_G	T_D	A_G	Total
Talk	1042.1	3.6	172.3	1460.5	1636.4
Youtube	460.6	8.93	102	874	984.93
EuAll	76.8	5.37	14.4	122	141.77
Gowalla	307.77	4.69	65.24	556.42	626.35
Vote	17.8	0.14	3.55	30.3	33.99
Enron	69.4	0.88	12.6	107	120.48

Our implementation used the following parameters: we use Paillier cryptosystem with a 1024-bit modulus, the bit length allocated for the diameter l is 16 and the bit length of each random mask is 32. Besides, the FastGC framework provides a 80-bit security level; namely, it uses 80-bit wire labels for garbled circuits and security parameter $c = 80$ for the OT extension.

6.1   Datasets

We used real-world graph datasets publicly available from the Stanford SNAP website (available at https://snap.stanford.edu/data/), and selected the following six representative datasets: *wiki-Talk*, a large network extracted from all user talk pages; *com-Youtube*, a large social network based on the Youtube web site; *email-EuAll*, an email network generated from a European research institution; *loc-Gowalla*, a location-based social network; *wiki-Vote*, a network that contains all the Wikipedia voting data; and *email-Enron*, an email communication network. Table 1 summarizes the main characteristics of these datasets.

6.2   Experimental Results

Table 2 shows the performance of the initialization phase (one-time cost). As can be seen, the time to encrypt a graph ranges from a few minutes to several hours which is practical. For example, it takes only 17.4 h to obtain an encryption of the *wiki-Talk* graph including 2.4 million vertices and 5.1 million edges. Besides, we note that this phase is highly-parallelizable; namely, we bring the setup time down to just over 30 min by utilizing a modest cluster of 32 nodes. Furthermore, the storage cost of an encrypted graph is dominated by A_G with the total size ranging from 33.99 MB for *wiki-Vote* to 1.60 GB for *wiki-Talk*. We also note that our construction has less storage space requirements compared to Meng *et al.* [24] (*e.g.*, 2.07 GB for *com-Youtube* in [24], whereas our scheme takes 984.93 MB).

We first measured the time to query an encrypted graph without query history. To simulate realistic queries that work in a similar manner with [8], we choose the query vertices in a random fashion weighted according to their outdegrees. The average time at the server (taken over 1,000 random queries) is given in Fig. 4(a) for all encrypted graphs. In general, the results show that the query time ranges from 20.4 s for *wiki-Vote* to 46.4 min for *wiki-Talk*. Additionally, we can obtain an order-of-magnitude improvement in both computation time and bandwidth by using the packing optimization presented in Sect. 4.3. The actual time for the client to generate the token and decrypt the encrypted result per each query is always less than 0.1 s which is very fast. In addition, about 1.5 KB communication overhead is required to transfer the token and the encrypted result for each query.

Next, the performance of the query phase with the help of history stored on the server is illustrated in Fig. 4(b) and (c), and a block of 1,000 random executions results in one measurement point in both figures. In Fig. 4(b), the y-axis represents the ratio of the average query time using history to that without using history. Generally, it reflects that the average query time decreases with the increase of the number of queries, because subsequent queries can first be answered by leveraging the history. Furthermore, as can be seen, after 10,000 queries, it obtains about 86% reduction of the query time for *wiki-Vote* compared to that without using history, *i.e.*, it only needs roughly 2.9 s to answer a subsequent query. Figure 4(c) demonstrates the increasing size of history (instantiated by HashMap in our implementation) with the increasing amount of total shortest distance queries.

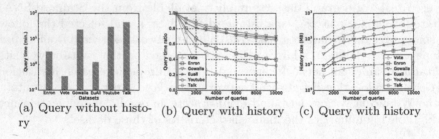

(a) Query without history

(b) Query with history

(c) Query with history

Fig. 4. The cost of distance query phase.

Figure 5 shows the execution time (averaged over 1,000 runs) for adding and deleting an edge over all the encrypted graphs. Obviously, both addition and deletion operations are practically efficient and independent of the scale of the graphs. As shown in Fig. 5(a), the time

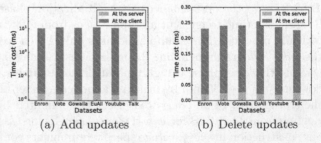

(a) Add updates

(b) Delete updates

Fig. 5. The time cost of dynamic updates.

cost at the client side is dominated by generating an encryption of the length of the edge to be updated (roughly 10 ms), while the server side has a negligible running time. Similar results can be obtained in Fig. 5(b) for the delete updates. It only needs about 0.25 ms to delete a specified edge, and the time to generate the delete token at the client side dominates the time cost of the entire process.

In addition, about 0.3 KB and tens of bytes are consumed when performing adding and deleting operations, respectively.

7   Conclusion

In this paper, we designed a new graph encryption scheme–SecGDB to encrypt graph structures and enforce private graph queries. In our construction, we used additively homomorphic encryption and garbled circuits to support shortest distance queries with optimal time and storage complexities. On top of this, we further proposed an auxiliary data structure called *query history* stored on the remote server to achieve better amortized time complexity over multiple queries. Compared to the state-of-the-art, SecGDB returns the exact distance results and allows efficient graph updates over large-scale encrypted graph database. SecGDB is proven to be adaptively semantically-secure in the random oracle model. We finally evaluated SecGDB on representative real-world datasets, showing its efficiency and practicality for use in real-world applications.

Acknowledgment. Qian and Qi's researches are supported in part by National Natural Science Foundation of China (Grant No. 61373167, U1636219, 61572278), National Basic Research Program of China (973 Program) under Grant No. 2014CB340600, and National High Technology Research and Development Program of China (Grant No. 2015AA016004). Kui's research is supported in part by US National Science Foundation under grant CNS-1262277. Aziz's research is supported in part by the NSF under grant CNS-1643207 and the Global Research Lab (GRL) Program of the National Research Foundation (NRF) funded by Ministry of Science, ICT (Information and Communication Technologies) and Future Planning (NRF-2016K1A1A2912757). Qian Wang is the corresponding author.

References

1. Boneh, D., Gentry, C., Halevi, S., Wang, F., Wu, D.J.: Private database queries using somewhat homomorphic encryption. In: Jacobson, M., Locasto, M., Mohassel, P., Safavi-Naini, R. (eds.) ACNS 2013. LNCS, vol. 7954, pp. 102–118. Springer, Heidelberg (2013). https://doi.org/10.1007/978-3-642-38980-1_7
2. Cash, D., Jarecki, S., Jutla, C., Krawczyk, H., Roşu, M.-C., Steiner, M.: Highly-scalable searchable symmetric encryption with support for boolean queries. In: Canetti, R., Garay, J.A. (eds.) CRYPTO 2013. LNCS, vol. 8042, pp. 353–373. Springer, Heidelberg (2013). https://doi.org/10.1007/978-3-642-40041-4_20
3. Chase, M., Kamara, S.: Structured encryption and controlled disclosure. In: Abe, M. (ed.) ASIACRYPT 2010. LNCS, vol. 6477, pp. 577–594. Springer, Heidelberg (2010). https://doi.org/10.1007/978-3-642-17373-8_33
4. Curtmola, R., Garay, J., Kamara, S., Ostrovsky, R.: Searchable symmetric encryption: improved definitions and efficient constructions. In: Proceedings of CCS 2006, pp. 79–88. ACM (2006)
5. Dijkstra, E.W.: A note on two problems in connexion with graphs. Numer. Math. **1**(1), 269–271 (1959)

6. Elmehdwi, Y., Samanthula, B.K., Jiang, W.: Secure k-nearest neighbor query over encrypted data in outsourced environments. In: Proceedings of ICDE 2014, pp. 664–675. IEEE (2014)
7. Fredman, M.L., Tarjan, R.E.: Fibonacci heaps and their uses in improved network optimization algorithms. JACM **34**(3), 596–615 (1987)
8. Hahn, F., Kerschbaum, F.: Searchable encryption with secure and efficient updates. In: Proceedings of CCS 2014, pp. 310–320. ACM (2014)
9. Han, W.-S., Lee, S., Park, K., Lee, J.-H., Kim, M.-S., Kim, J., Yu, H.: Turbo-Graph: a fast parallel graph engine handling billion-scale graphs in a single PC. In: Proceedings of SIGKDD 2013, pp. 77–85. ACM (2013)
10. Harary, F.: Graph Theory. Westview Press, Boulder (1969)
11. Huang, Y., Evans, D., Katz, J., Malka, L.: Faster secure two-party computation using garbled circuits. In: Proceedings of USENIX Security 2011. USENIX (2011)
12. Huang, Y., Malka, L., Evans, D., Katz, J.: Efficient privacy-preserving biometric identification. In: Proceedings of NDSS 2011, pp. 250–267 (2011)
13. Ishai, Y., Kilian, J., Nissim, K., Petrank, E.: Extending oblivious transfers efficiently. In: Boneh, D. (ed.) CRYPTO 2003. LNCS, vol. 2729, pp. 145–161. Springer, Heidelberg (2003). https://doi.org/10.1007/978-3-540-45146-4_9
14. Kamara, S., Papamanthou, C.: Parallel and dynamic searchable symmetric encryption. In: Sadeghi, A.-R. (ed.) FC 2013. LNCS, vol. 7859, pp. 258–274. Springer, Heidelberg (2013). https://doi.org/10.1007/978-3-642-39884-1_22
15. Kamara, S., Papamanthou, C., Roeder, T.: Dynamic searchable symmetric encryption. In: Proceedings of CCS 2012, pp. 965–976. ACM (2012)
16. Katz, J., Lindell, Y.: Introduction to Modern Cryptography. CRC Press, Boca Raton (2014)
17. Kolesnikov, V., Sadeghi, A.-R., Schneider, T.: Improved garbled circuit building blocks and applications to auctions and computing minima. In: Garay, J.A., Miyaji, A., Otsuka, A. (eds.) CANS 2009. LNCS, vol. 5888, pp. 1–20. Springer, Heidelberg (2009). https://doi.org/10.1007/978-3-642-10433-6_1
18. Kolesnikov, V., Schneider, T.: Improved garbled circuit: free XOR gates and applications. In: Aceto, L., Damgård, I., Goldberg, L.A., Halldórsson, M.M., Ingólfsdóttir, A., Walukiewicz, I. (eds.) ICALP 2008. LNCS, vol. 5126, pp. 486–498. Springer, Heidelberg (2008). https://doi.org/10.1007/978-3-540-70583-3_40
19. Lai, R.W.F., Chow, S.S.M.: Structured encryption with non-interactive updates and parallel traversal. In: Proceedings of ICDCS 2015, pp. 776–777. IEEE (2015)
20. Lai, R.W.F., Chow, S.S.M.: Parallel and dynamic structured encryption. In: Proceedings of SECURECOMM 2016 (2016, to appear)
21. Lai, R.W.F., Chow, S.S.M.: Forward-secure searchable encryption on labeled bipartite graphs. In: Gollmann, D., Miyaji, A., Kikuchi, H. (eds.) ACNS 2017. LNCS, vol. 10355, pp. 478–497. Springer, Cham (2017). https://doi.org/10.1007/978-3-319-61204-1_24
22. Low, Y., Bickson, D., Gonzalez, J., Guestrin, C., Kyrola, A., Hellerstein, J.M.: Distributed graphlab: a framework for machine learning and data mining in the cloud. PVLDB **5**(8), 716–727 (2012)
23. Malkhi, D., Nisan, N., Pinkas, B., Sella, Y., et al.: Fairplay-secure two-party computation system. In: Proceedings of USENIX Security 2004, pp. 287–302. USENIX (2004)
24. Meng, X., Kamara, S., Nissim, K., Kollios, G.: GRECS: graph encryption for approximate shortest distance queries. In: Proceedings of CCS 2015, pp. 504–517. ACM (2015)

25. Naor, M., Pinkas, B.: Efficient oblivious transfer protocols. In: Proceedings of SODA 2001, SIAM, pp. 448–457 (2001)
26. Nikolaenko, V., Weinsberg, U., Ioannidis, S., Joye, M., Boneh, D., Taft, N.: Privacy-preserving ridge regression on hundreds of millions of records. In: Proceedings of S&P 2013, pp. 334–348. IEEE (2013)
27. Paillier, P.: Public-key cryptosystems based on composite degree residuosity classes. In: Stern, J. (ed.) EUROCRYPT 1999. LNCS, vol. 1592, pp. 223–238. Springer, Heidelberg (1999). https://doi.org/10.1007/3-540-48910-X_16
28. Pinkas, B., Schneider, T., Smart, N.P., Williams, S.C.: Secure two-party computation is practical. In: Matsui, M. (ed.) ASIACRYPT 2009. LNCS, vol. 5912, pp. 250–267. Springer, Heidelberg (2009). https://doi.org/10.1007/978-3-642-10366-7_15
29. Sarwat, M., Elnikety, S., He, Y., Kliot, G.: Horton: Online query execution engine for large distributed graphs. In: Proceedings of ICDE 2012, pp. 1289–1292. IEEE (2012)
30. Stefanov, E., Papamanthou, C., Shi, E.: Practical dynamic searchable encryption with small leakage. In: Proceedings of NDSS 2014 (2014)
31. Wang, Q., He, M., Du, M., Chow, S.S., Lai, R.W., Zou, Q.: Searchable encryption over feature-rich data. IEEE Trans. Dependable Secure Comput. **PP**(99), 1 (2016)
32. Yao, A.: Protocols for secure computations. In: Proceedings of FOCS 1982, pp. 160–164. IEEE (1982)

Outsourcing Medical Dataset Analysis: A Possible Solution

Gabriel Kaptchuk[✉], Matthew Green, and Aviel Rubin

John Hopkins University, Baltimore, USA
{gkaptchuk,mgreen,rubin}@cs.jhu.edu

Abstract. We explore the possible ways modern cryptographic methods can be applied to the field of medical data analysis. Current systems require large computational facilities owned by the data owners or excessive trust given to the researchers. We implement one possible solution in which researchers operate directly on homomorphically encrypted data and the data owner decrypts the results. We test our implementation on large datasets and show that it is sufficiently practical that it could be a helpful tool for modern researchers. We also perform a heuristic analysis of the security of our system.

1 Introduction

Modern medical dataset analysis methods take large sets of medical records and attempt to extract truths about the underlying population. Because of the sensitive nature of the data being analysed and regulations requiring strict limitations on the sharing of that data, it is difficult for researchers to share datasets. Today, it can take up to a *year* before a researcher can actually begin the computational process of analyzing a dataset that they did not collect on their own. Data is often shared in sanitized form, with much of the data removed; this sanitization process requires time, labor and statistical expertise. Some data owners have chosen to allow researchers to send their queries to the data owners, who perform the analysis on the researcher's behalf. The process of analyzing medical datasets requires large amounts of computation on the part of the data owner for each question posed by a researcher. To best serve the medical research community, data owners must acquire technical expertise to properly anonymize and maintain datasets or contract a trusted third party to do it for them.

In this work we consider an institutional medical researcher, such as a member of a university or the research division of a company, interested in answering some query but who is without access to the required data. While it may be infeasible to independently gather data, it is likely that there exists a dataset containing sufficient information to answer the researcher's query. The data owner may want to share with the researcher but because the information is related to the medical history of patients, and therefore considered sensitive, sharing that dataset may be a complicated process.

We explore existing cryptographic methods in an effort to tackle the two main problems with the current way of sharing medical data. First, we wish to

© International Financial Cryptography Association 2017
A. Kiayias (Ed.): FC 2017, LNCS 10322, pp. 98–123, 2017.
https://doi.org/10.1007/978-3-319-70972-7_6

move the burden of cost from data owners to the researchers who want access to the data. All modern solutions that properly secure patient data require data owners to make large investments in hardware and technical expertise. While it is possible for a data owner to recoup those costs over time, requiring large startup costs deters the sharing of data and charging for access to the dataset limits the kinds of researchers able to use it. Second, it takes far too long for a researcher to acquire and analyze a dataset that has been properly anonymized and certified. Even after proper permission has been acquired, it may be extremely inconvenient to actually run analysis or to tweak the nature of the researcher's query.

2   Objectives

In order to build something useful to the medical research community, we attempt evaluate the usefulness of Fully Homomorphic Encryption while still ensuring the following six properties. These objectives were derived from conversations with professionals working in the medical research industry. Additionally, the analysis we ran to confirm that our system was practical enough to be used by members of the medical research community were also informed by these conversations.

Authenticity of results - the results obtained by the researcher should be as authentic and accurate as possible without compromising the privacy of individuals.

A rich range of possible analyses - virtually any analytical technique should be possible to the researcher. More formally, the limits on the possible set of operations should depend only on the parameters chosen for the FHE scheme.

Minimal computation on the part of the data owner - the computational responsibility of the data owner should be almost entirely limited to preprocessing the dataset a single time. We propose that a data owner should only have to provide a single server to allow for large numbers of researchers to perform analysis.

Privacy for individuals in the dataset - it should be impossible for a researcher with auxiliary information to learn anything about an individual in the population using legitimate analysis techniques. Specifically, we invoke differential privacy to protect information about individuals.

Security against adversarial researchers - an adversarial researcher attempting to extract information about individuals from the dataset should be caught with very high probability.

Practicality - our system should shorten the time it takes for a researcher to conceive of a researcher question to when their computational analysis has finished. The actual time it takes for a single run of the analysis process may take longer than current methods, providing this overall time shrinks.

While many existing solutions address some subset of these objectives, none accomplish all of them. In particular, existing systems lack practicality, proper cost distribution or a large space of possible computation. Anonymization presents security concerns and lacks practicality due to the long wait times for dataset acquisition. Analysis as a service requires a misappropriation of costs between the researcher and the data owner. Attempts like [19] have managed to be both practical and to outsource computation, but failed to allow for rich space of analytical techniques required by the medical industry. Our construction satisfies all the requirements of researchers in the medical industry.

3   Background

To understand our motivation, it is important to consider the ways in which modern medical dataset analysis is done. The reality of current analysis systems is that they are both extremely expensive for the data owner and take a long time for the query of a researcher to be fully answered. Researchers interested in fields as diverse as drug side effects, public health and genetics all utilize the large amounts of data regularly collected by medical professionals, insurance companies, or governments to make new discoveries or confirm theories. Under ideal circumstances, analysis is done with large sample sizes - discussions with professionals in the field lead us to believe that most studies utilize around 100,000 data points. The analytical models used by researchers vary from simplistic count and average to complex regressions or machine learning. While complex methods are gaining in popularity, measurements like regression, covariance and averages remain the primary tools employed by researchers.

There are various practical constructions employed to allow external researchers access to private data. The obvious, simple, and clearly insecure solution is to naively share the data without any security. While efficient, this makes the assumption that the researcher is a trusted party, which is often invalid.

3.1   Anonymization

Anonymization is a technique in which large amounts of information, hopefully all irrelevant, is purged before a dataset is shared with a researcher. The goal of anonymization is to allow an untrusted third party to confirm results or perform original analysis without revealing any personally identifiable information. The process is computationally expensive because it requires a data owner to reprocess the dataset each time a researcher posits a new query. For example, a researcher may start the process interested in a certain subset of the information about each patient only to later decided that other qualities of each patient are also required to confirm their hypothesis. This method also makes it extremely expensive for a researcher to explore a dataset without a specific hypothesis in mind. Additionally, there have been recent results showing that anonymization is not as secure as previously thought [28]. While a single instance of an anonymized dataset leaks minimal information under most circumstances, combining it with a version of the same dataset anonymized for a different query can certainly allow a malicious researcher to compromise the privacy of individuals.

3.2 Analysis as a Service

This model has becoming increasingly popular recently as the medical community has adopted cloud technologies. Data owners or trusted third parties provide a service through which researchers are able to submit requests for work. The data owners or their surrogates then perform the computation over the dataset stored as plaintext. This requires data owners to acquire the technical expertise to maintain the system. More importantly, this forces data owners to shoulder the cost of providing their data to the medical research community or possibly charge researchers for the use of their data which would discourage collaboration.

3.3 Cost Consideration

While both anonymization and analysis as a service are common models for sharing statistical datasets, cutting-edge systems combine both techniques. The largest data owners maintain massive datasets on expensive computational infrastructure. When a researcher wants to answer some new query, they access the infrastructure itself, either physically or over a secure channel. Then, based on the requirements of their query, they select a certain anonymization of the dataset to use. A certain anonymization of the data may leave more information about income, but may contain little geographical information. Each time a new anonymization of the data is required by a researcher, the data owners must prepare a new subset of the data and get statisticians to certify it.

Once an appropriate version of the dataset has been prepared, the analysis is run on the data owner's systems. Because of inference attacks, allowing researchers to remove even anonymized datasets can be dangerous, especially when the researcher is likely to return to the same data owner to perform a different analysis soon afterwards. The two main concerns addressed in this work are time and cost. It is not uncommon for the time between the conception of a question and the moment when computational analysis begins to be months or even a year.

It is nearly inevitable that research will involve high costs for at least some of the parties involved. While typically one might assume that the burden of cost should be on the researchers themselves, given that they are the ones directly benefiting from computation, it is often the data owners who are forced to acquire expertise and infrastructure to service the researcher community. One company with which we spoke had $1 million in hardware costs to support the needs of researchers. While costs might eventually be recouped by charging researchers for use of the dataset, the costs from purchasing hardware alone may make it infeasible for a data owner to securely share their data. Especially if their dataset becomes desirable to many researchers, the costs of scaling up their operations quickly make it impossible to support widespread interest.

3.4   Existing Cryptographic Options

In order to construct a system that addresses the problems above, we call upon existing cryptographic primitives and systems. Some, like differential privacy, have been widely used in the field and their limitations are well understood. The practicality of others, like FHE and homomorphic signatures, has yet to be fully tested. Because we are attempting to build a practical system that minimizes the amount of time between the medical researcher's initial query and receiving the final answer, we choose our cryptographic primitives carefully. Additionally, various primitives may be helpful in achieving some of the objectives in Sect. 2 but may prohibit the achievement of others. We give a broad summary of the cryptographic methods chose to use in our case study below and include methods we chose not to utilize in Appendix D.

3.5   Fully Homomorphic Encryption

FHE allows for addition and multiplication on encrypted data without the need for decryption. The first construction of FHE was published in [21] but was too inefficient for practical computation. Subsequent efforts, most notably the BGV construction in [9], have attempted to increase the efficiency and modern constructions are teetering on the edge of practicality. To make the schemes more usable, there has been a push towards "leveled" homomorphic encryption schemes which can compute a certain depth of circuit before inherent noise renders the ciphertext useless. For a full background on the intricacies of FHE and a more complete list of citations, refer to [33].

Smart and Vercauteren proposed an addition to the BGV FHE in [31], in which many plaintext values could be encoded into a single ciphertext. To do this, the plaintext values are put into a vector and all additions and multiplications are computed entrywise. This allows for single instruction multiple data operations and significantly increasing the efficiency of the scheme. Our implementation requires that the FHE scheme used supports Smart-Vercauteren plaintext packing and for the rest of this work all homomorphic operations can be considered to be done within this framework.

3.6   HELib

The best available implementation of a modern leveled FHE is the C++ library HELib. While most of the code currently written using HELib implements relatively simple computations, our testing shows that is both robust and reasonably efficient for more complex computations. The FHE scheme it implements encodes integers into BGV ciphertext, supporting addition and multiplication operations. The underlying plaintext values are added and multiplied modulo some prime. The choice of primes, the maximum level of the circuit, and security parameter all influence the size of the ciphertext and the efficiency of the operations. Details about the use of HELib and the FHE scheme it implements can be found at [23].

3.7   Differential Privacy

Differential privacy prevents an attacker from learning anything about individuals while still gleaning meaningful information from aggregated statistics. This is not the only notion of privacy that can be applied to statistical datasets, but it has recently become the most popular. With the rise of laws requiring the protection medical data, ensuring it is impossible to recover the information of any given individual effectively shields data owners from legal action. We give a more detailed background of differential privacy in Appendix C.

4   Construction

We assume a data owner $\mathcal{D}$ with a medical dataset D_{initial} of vectors $\boldsymbol{d} \in \mathbb{R}^n$. $\mathcal{D}$ transforms the dataset into the proper format, encrypts it using fully homomorphic encryption as $D^* = \mathsf{Encrypt}(D_{\text{formatted}})$ and publishes it on the internet. A researcher $\mathcal{R}$ then prepares a program to be run on the dataset, described in the form of a transcript T and performs the computation $T(D^*)$. The result of this computation is a ciphertext c with an embedded integrity check and transmits c to $\mathcal{D}$. Finally $\mathcal{D}$ verifies that T and c match, computes the decryption, adds noise to guarantee differential privacy and sends this final result to $\mathcal{R}$. A protocol diagram can be found in Appendix B.

4.1   Dataset Formatting

We assume that the data owner $\mathcal{D}$ has some set of $D = \{\boldsymbol{d}_1, \boldsymbol{d}_2, \dots, \boldsymbol{d}_{|D|}\}$ s.t. $\boldsymbol{d}_i \in \mathbb{R}^n$ where each dimension of $\boldsymbol{d}_i$ represents part of the medical record for patient i. Each vector $\boldsymbol{d}$ is made up of data entries α and binary entries β. The data entries are real valued and represent information about the patient like age, blood pressure or income. The binary entries represent the qualities of a patient, like the presence of a medication or medical condition.

$$
D_{\text{initial}} = \left\{ \begin{pmatrix} \alpha_1 \\ \vdots \\ \alpha_m \\ \beta_1 \\ \vdots \\ \beta_{n-m} \end{pmatrix} \cdots \begin{pmatrix} \alpha_1 \\ \vdots \\ \alpha_m \\ \beta_1 \\ \vdots \\ \beta_{n-m} \end{pmatrix} \right\}
$$

If $\mathcal{D}$ has a dataset that is formatted differently, it is clear how to transform any dataset into this format. The only intricacy of this transformation is that all values in the vector must be integer valued, while real medical datasets also contain both text and real-number values. For the most part, this problem can be easily solved while only losing a little granularity in the data. Real-number values can be scaled and rounded such that the information is still rich enough to convey meaning. Text data can either be automatically binned, adding a β value for each possible value of that text field, or can be manually translated into a integer scale as appropriate.

4.2   Data Binning

Data binning beings with $\mathcal{D}$ dividing the range of each data entry α_i into continuous disjoint bins $\{\beta_1^{\alpha_i}, \beta_2^{\alpha_i}, \ldots, \beta_{b_i}^{\alpha_i}\}$, where the number of bins b_i is chosen separately for each α_i. $\mathcal{D}$ then inserts a new row into the data set for each $\beta_j^{\alpha_i}$ and sets the $\beta_j^{\alpha_i} = 1$ containing the value for α_i for each α_i. For example, if α_i represents age, $\mathcal{D}$ might create $\beta_j^{\alpha_i}$ as 5 year bins from 0 to 100. A patient of age 37 would have $\beta_8^{\alpha_i} = 1$ and $\beta_j^{\alpha_i} = 0 \; \forall j \neq 8$.

The increased number of bins for each α give researchers greater granularity of possible computations but also increases the size of the dataset. Because this dataset will be prepared only once, the data owner chooses the maximum possible granularity for all researchers at once. Many fields, like age or income, have natural bin sizes while other fields will be completely at the discretion of the data owner.

4.3   Integrity Check Embedding and Encryption

The FHE scheme used in encrypting the dataset should include Smart-Vercauteren plaintext packing. This property allows a vector of plaintext values to be encrypted into a single ciphertext and all operations are computed entry-wise. The length l of the plaintext vectors is determined by the various parameters to the FHE scheme, but in general we will consider vectors of about 1000 values.

Each plaintext vector contains values from a single row of the database (i.e. a specific α or β from multiple patients). Each vector begins $\frac{l}{2}$ values from the dataset, in the order listed in the dataset. Thus, the first ciphertext will be an encryption of the α_1 entry from the first $\frac{l}{2}$ patient record; the second will be the α_1 entries from the next $\frac{l}{2}$ patient records, and so on. For each such vector, $\mathcal{D}$ embeds the tools to allow for rapid verification. $\mathcal{D}$ selects a random value π and a random permutation Φ, both to be used for all vectors in the D. For each entry e in the vector $\boldsymbol{v}$, $\mathcal{D}$ computes $e' = \pi e \mod p$, where p is a prime and a parameter to the FHE scheme, and appends that value to $\boldsymbol{v}$. Next, $\mathcal{D}$ appends a different random value k to the end of each vector and records k for each vector. Finally, $\mathcal{D}$ applies Φ it to all vectors in D.

$$\Phi\left(\alpha_1^1 \; \pi\alpha_1^1 \; \alpha_1^2 \; \pi\alpha_1^2 \; \alpha_1^2 \; \pi\alpha_1^2 \ldots \alpha_1^{\frac{l}{2}} \; \pi\alpha_1^{\frac{l}{2}} \; k\right)$$

To encrypt the dataset, $\mathcal{D}$ runs FHEKeyGen() to generate a public key pk and a secret key sk. Each permuted vector is then encrypted under sk and the entire encrypted data set is released to researchers, along with pk. In the scheme we use, the evaluation key is the same as the public key, but if another scheme with a separate evaluation key were to be substituted, the evaluation key would be released to the researcher instead.

4.4   Researcher Computation

Once the new data set D^* has been published, a researcher $\mathcal{R}$ prepares a transcript T of the steps of some operation they want to perform over D^*. Imagine $\mathcal{R}$ wants to compute the average age of death of patients with a certain disease who are also taking a certain medication. To compute this value, $\mathcal{R}$ uses the β associated with the disease and the β associated with the medication to include only patients with both characteristics when summing age of death.

$$\frac{\sum_{d \in D^*} (\beta_i^1 \times \beta_i^2 \times \alpha_j)}{\sum_{d \in D} \beta_i^1 \times \beta_i^2}$$

While machine learning style analysis has been growing more popular among the research community, computing more simple metrics like counts, correlations, and linear regressions are still the main methods of conducting computational analysis. All of these techniques can clearly be implemented using the same filter and sum method above. For example, a simple linear regression between the variables x_1 and x_2 can be computed as

$$x_2 = ax_1 + b$$

Such that a and b can be calculated as

$$a = \frac{\sum x_2 - b \sum x_1}{n} \quad b = \frac{n \sum x_1 x_2 - \sum x_1 \sum x_2}{n \sum x_1^2 - (\sum x_2)^2}$$

where n is the number of samples in the dataset. Clearly all of these summations are easy to compute. Because of the data binning process, a researcher can also restrict their analysis to certain cohorts, focusing their attention on, for instance, subsets of the socioeconomic ladder or only more urgent hospital admittances.

4.5   Verification

When $\mathcal{D}$ receives the result of $\mathcal{R}$'s computation, he runs the verification algorithm Verify(T, m^*): It is important that the multiplicative depth of the transcript can be easily extracted; we denote the multiplicative depth d.

Verify(T, m^*) takes a transcript T and some encrypted vector c as input. The goal of the verification algorithm is to quickly decide if the steps taken in T would result in the vector c, returning 1 if it is the result vector and 0 if it is not. The verification algorithm is as follows:

1. $m = \mathsf{Decrypt}(c)$
2. Compute $\phi^{-1}(m)$
3. For each plaintext value a in $\phi^{-1}(m)$ make sure the corresponding verification value is $\pi^{d-1}a$, where d can be learned from T
4. Perform the computation described in T over the random tags in each vector and make sure it matches the tag of $\phi^{-1}(v)$
5. Return 1 if steps 3 and 4 both pass, otherwise return 0

While running the verification algorithm is constant in the computation time because the random tags must be computed, it is still much quicker and less memory intensive than running the computation itself. There is a single value for k in each vector, so the runtime will be at least $\frac{1}{l}$, where l is length of each plaintext vector.

If the verification algorithm returns 1, $\mathcal{D}$ strips out all values associated with the verification process before the data is put through the differential privacy process. In this way, the permutation, the random tag, and π all stay secret and the adversarial researcher gains no advantage once they perform a single valid computation. If the algorithm returns a 0, $\mathcal{D}$ must assume $\mathcal{R}$ is attempting to circumvent the encryption on the data. A cheating researcher is banned from further use of the system and their results immediately discarded.

4.6   Additive Noise

One of the goals of our construction is to make it difficult for a malicious researcher to extract information about an individual while performing a legitimate analysis. Because of the verification algorithm, we can show that it is difficult to gain information by cheating on computation. To ensure that it is difficult to gain information from legitimate analysis, we introduce differential privacy as the final step in the process. To this end, $\mathcal{D}$ adds noise sampled from a laplacian distribution with variance equal to the sensitivity of the function computed, where sensitivity is defined in Appendix C. This method has been shown to ensure differential privacy for single queries in previous works [17]. There have been no constructions for imposing differential privacy when an adversary can make any number of queries.

5   Security Analysis

It is clear that an adversarial researcher cannot directly access the plaintext data because the encryption scheme is semantically secure. We must give a heuristic argument that it is impossible for the system to leak unintended information when decrypting queries. This model is odd because it allows for limited decryption queries even though the underlying encryption scheme is not CCA2. The goal of our security analysis is to determine if it is possible for an adversarial researcher to gain information about the contents of the dataset besides the answer to the exact query specified in the transcript. Because it is difficult to characterize every kind of attack that a researcher might mount to learn about an individual in the population, we must ensure that there has been no deviation whatsoever from the supplied transcript.

In order to formalize our argument about the security of our scheme against information leakage, we begin by creating a security game. Unlike traditional games in the cryptographic setting, we do not allow an adversarial researcher to continue accessing the system once they have been caught attempting to cheat the system. In modern systems, it is common for the researcher to sign documents making them liable for large sums of money if they are noticed attempting to recover the private information of a patient. Currently, these agreements are enforced by human log auditors. We borrow this notion and include it in our security game. The goal of the adversary is to cheat undetected; if their cheating is detected they are banned from use of the system and heavily fined (Fig. 1).

1 : $(x, F) \leftarrow$ Client()	1 : $T \leftarrow$ Select($\mathbb{T}$)
2 : $(\pi, r) \leftarrow$ Server(x, F)	2 : $D^* \leftarrow$ Encrypt(D)
3 : $y \leftarrow$ Verify(π, r)	3 : $c \leftarrow \mathcal{A}(T, D^*)$
4 : **if** $y = 1$:	4 : $y \leftarrow$ Verify(T, c)
5 : **return** Decrypt(r)	5 : **if** $y = 1$:
6 : **else** :	6 : **return** Decrypt(r)
7 : **return** $\perp$	7 : **else** :
	8 : **return** $\perp$

Fig. 1. Left: Traditional verifiable computation game. Right: Our updated version of this game

The traditional game for verifiable information is between a client, corresponding to the data owner, and a server, corresponding to the researcher. The client chooses some function F, usually represented in circuit form, and an input x. The server is then charged with computing $F(x)$ and proving that the computation was done honestly. We modify this game slightly to allow an adversary to select their own function, represented as a transcript, from a family of acceptable transcripts $\mathbb{T}$. We put some minimal limitations on $\mathbb{T}$, but additional limitation can be imposed by each individual data owner as needed. Valid transcripts must have the following properties:

1. The first level of computation must be performed within a single patient vector and the same computation must be performed on each patient vector.
2. The results of each such computation must be combined in a way such that the result of T when computed over the dataset is a single value (or a constant number of values with respect to the size of the dataset).
3. Results of the computation, including the processing of the results vector, must be independent of the order of vectors in the dataset.

The first property should ensure that a researcher doesn't combine β's from one patient with α's from another patient. If a researcher somehow learns about the contents of the record for a single patient and learns its location in the dataset, it should be impossible for them to leverage that information to compromise the privacy of another patient. Similarly, we require that all of the results of the computations on individual are combined into a single result. This prevents an adversarial researcher submitting a transcript that simply decrypts patient vectors directly. Finally, the order of the vectors in the dataset should not impact the final results. Because the result of a computation over the ciphertext will yield a result vector instead of a single value, shuffling the order of the patient vectors will likely affect the individual values in the results vector but will have no impact on the sum (or product, as appropriate).

It is known to be hard to impose security policies on queries. In order to impose this specific set of security policies, the researcher is required to state their transcript in two pieces, (1) the computation to be done on each patient vector and (2) the method used to combine the results of each patient vector. Because there are no limitations on the valid kinds of computations that can be done within a single patient vector and we require that the method for combining vector results must be written in a vector independant way, any transcript that can be written in this form is valid.

We show that with our construction, the probability of creating a transcript T and ciphertext m^* that verify but were not generated honestly is bounded by the probability of guessing the random permutation Φ, specifically the location of the random tag k in the permuted vector. We assume the adversary has submitted a transcript-message pair which passes the verification algorithm, specifically recomputation of T over the random tags only. One of two things must be true: (1) the computation was done honestly or (2) some of the vectors used in the computation were altered. In the first case, clearly there is no unintended information leakage; only the answer to the adversaries exact, legitimate query has been decrypted. If some of the vectors were altered, there are two possibilities.

1. In a given vector $j < |v|$ values of the vector were altered. Given that Φ is unknown to the adversary

$$Pr[\text{Successful Edit of } j \text{ elements}] = Pr[\text{Editing } k]$$
$$+ Pr[\text{Not editing } k] \times Pr[\text{Edit results in format}]$$

$$= \frac{j}{|v|} + \frac{|v| - j}{|v|} \left(1 - \frac{\binom{|v|}{j}}{\binom{\frac{|v|}{2}}{\frac{j}{2}}} \right) < Pr[\text{guessing location of } k]$$

2. All values in some vector were edited without editing the tag k. In the worst case, an adversary has all elements of the vector besides k properly formatted (i.e. the contents of another vector in the dataset). The probability of switching out the contents of vector with the contents of another without editing the k is $\frac{1}{|v|}$.

Therefore, in all cases, the probability of an adversarial researcher computing some m without following T properly is bounded by the probability of finding k in the randomly permuted vector. We assume that the length of the vector is roughly around 1000, so $\frac{1}{|v|} \approx \frac{1}{1000}$. If this probability of being caught is too low in the eyes of the data owner, additional k's can be added to the vector. Each additional k must also be avoided when editing an existing vector, so the chance of correcting identifying all k's in the vector goes down by approximately a multiplicative factor of $\frac{1}{1000}$ for each additional k.

6   Implementation

We implemented the above construction to measure its practical feasibility. To ensure that a medical dataset could be meaningfully transformed into the proper format, we processed NY State's public hospital discharge dataset from 2012 [32]. The dataset comprises 2.5 million patient encounters, recording data including facility information, patient demographics, patient complaint, and medical code information. While our system can scale to be used with datasets of this size, discussions with members working in the medical dataset analysis indicated that most researcher do analysis on smaller datasets of around 100,000 patient vectors. In order to test the practicality of our system, we chose to test on this *normal* cohort size.

The NY State dataset contained data in the form of text, integers and real-valued numbers. We transformed the dataset into the format described in Sect. 4.2. Some fields, like *length of stay* and *total charges*, mapped cleanly into the construction; while there were minor choices to be made regarding the granularity of the bins and how we wanted to round the decimal values to integers, the process was very intuitive. Other fields, like *admit day of week* and *APR risk of mortality* were less obvious. We chose to map each day of the week to a separate β value. In the original dataset, *APR risk of mortality* was assigned values like "Minor" and "Major". We chose to create a scale such that the lowest rating was a 0 and then each increasing level of risk was one above the previous level. Additionally we mapped each possible value of this field to its own β value. Through this process, the initial dataset, which was 100,000 vectors of length 39, was transformed into a dataset in which each vector was 912 elements long.

We encrypted large portions of the dataset for testing purposes. We chose not to encrypt the entire dataset because of space concerns, but we did encrypt 50 rows of the dataset for trial purposes. When stored naively, these 50 encrypted rows take a total of 752 GB, consuming approximately 7 MB per ciphertext. The key information and encryption context was stored in a separate file which was 16 GB. We can easily cut the size of the stored data by a factor of 2 using naive compression and there are other possible optimizations to make the storage scheme more efficient (see Appendix E.1).

Encryption was done on consumer grade electronics, specifically a MacBook Pro with a 2.5 GHz Intel i7 Core processor and 16 GB of RAM. The ciphertext was written out to an external storage device over USB 3, so the efficiency of the system was impacted severely by disk IO. We chose to set the maximum circuit depth to 100, which would accommodate most computations. We chose a security parameter of 80 and a prime modulo of 17389. Generating the context and secret key for the scheme took 22.8 min. Once the context was set up, we wrote it out to a file. To encrypt vectors, we read in the context and secret key, which took 19 min and then each plaintext vector took 10.4 s to encrypt. We split the encryption onto two separate threads, the first thread encrypting α values and the second encrypting β values. In total, the encryption time of 50 vectors was 30.04 h and encrypting the entire dataset would have taken 584 h. Note that all the times recorded were when operations are performed linearly and without any optimizations (Fig. 2).

Task	Key Setup	Key Reading	Encryption	Sum per Ciphertext	Sum Total
Time	22.8m	15.2m	10.4s each	33.08s each	1.98hr

Fig. 2. Timing results

We performed a linear regression to test the runtime that a researcher might encounter. A linear regression is a simplistic metric to compute but is a method still often used by researchers today. Regressions and averages are basically the same operations; averages are computed with two sums and linear regressions are computed with four. Reading in the context and key information takes 15.2 min. Processing a single set of ciphertexts take 33.08 s, which includes multiplying an α ciphertext by a β ciphertext and summing it with a ciphertext that is a running sum of all previous vectors. We performed our computation without any parallelization, so a single sum of the linear regression took 1.98 h to compute when done naively. To compute the full linear regression, it took approximately 9.5 h when each sum was computed consecutively.

7   Discussion

In order for this system to be useful, there must be a clear economic incentive for the data owner. Specifically, it must be beneficial to use homomorphic encryption rather than simply performing analysis on local plaintext and returning results to the researcher. We can denote the time it take for the data owner to perform a some computation on behalf of the user as $t_{computation}$.

We consider the various costs associated with doing computation. In addition to the time to perform the computation itself, there is $t_{encryption}$, the total computation time required to encrypt a single ciphertext, and $t_{decryption}$, the time required to decrypt a single ciphertext. Additionally, the time to verify that a researcher has performed their computation honestly is denoted t_{verify}. We can express the cost of using this system for q queries as

$$\text{Cost}_{system} = \frac{|D|}{\frac{\ell}{2}} t_{encryption} + q t_{decryption} + \sum_{i=0}^{q} t_{verify}^{i}$$

whereas the cost of the data owner performing each query on the plaintext is given as

$$\text{Cost}_{naive} = \sum_{i=0}^{q} t^i_{computation}$$

The computational time required to impose differential privacy on the result of the analysis is consistent no matter the manner in which the result is computed so it can be ignored when comparing the costs of the two alternatives. Thus the marginal cost of system over simply performing the plaintext in the clear is given by

$$\text{Marginal Cost} = \text{Cost}_{system} - \text{Cost}_{naive}$$

$$= \frac{2|D|}{\ell} t_{encryption} + qt_{decryption} + \sum_{i=0}^{q} t^i_{verify} - \sum_{i=0}^{q} t^i_{computation}$$

$$= \frac{2|D|}{\ell} t_{encryption} + qt_{decryption} + \sum_{i \neq 0}^{q} t^i_{computation}\left(\frac{2}{\ell} - 1\right)$$

Notice that the encryption time is a one-time cost incurred by the data owner; no additional encryption processing time is required for each new query posed by researchers. While the cost is very high, it can be amortized over many queries. In order for the data owner to be incentivized to use this system, the marginal cost of the system must be negative, that is

$$\frac{2|D|}{\ell} t_{encryption} + qt_{decryption} + \sum_{i=0}^{q} t^i_{computation}\left(\frac{2}{\ell} - 1\right) < 0$$

Intuitively, the computational savings from just doing verification instead of the full computation must outweigh the cost of decrypting the result vector. To give concrete examples for the variables above, we use the same parameters from Sect. 6. $t_{decryption}$ is a constant value no matter the query; as computation gets more complex the advantage of this system increases. With these parameters, decrypting a ciphertext will take approximately 18 min. We note that we measured decryption time using simple consumer grade electronics and a CPU. It may be possible to speed this process up using hardware accelerators [12,13]. In Fig. 3 we graph the marginal cost per query as a function of the decryption time and computation time, ignoring the initial encryption time. Red areas of the surface represent values for which the system is more efficient than the naive strategy. We note that the efficiency of Fully Homomorphic Encryption Schemes is likely to increase in the future, whereas the statistical tests researchers want to perform will only grow in complexity.

Remember that $t_{computation}$ denotes the total time that it would take the data owner to perform analysis, including system overhead like accessing data, which can become logistically complicated. Using this system for simple operations on small numbers of records is actually more computationally intensive for the data owner; the computation required to decrypt the results vector would be more

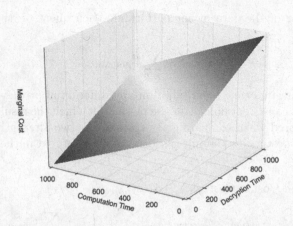

Fig. 3. Marginal cost as a function of computation time and decryption time. Negative values, red, show where this system has advantages over the naive approach (Color figure online)

than the computation itself. More complex regression methods and statistical tests are the best candidate operations for which a data owner would gain an advantage by using this system. Specifically, functionalities that would take more than the approximately 18 min decryption time. One concrete example that fits into this category is computing maximum likelihood estimators (MLE) for large numbers of parameters over a fairly large datasets. While computing simple estimators can be faster than decryption time, computing complicated estimators or estimators when data independence cannot be assumed is far more expensive. Without data independence, computing even a single iteration of MLE can be computationally infeasible on consumer hardware. Extreme examples of these costly functions can be seen in the field of economics, like [10]. While simple functions like linear regression might be the most common tools for medical researchers today, the field is growing increasingly computationally complex and being able to outsource the computation of these costly functions to researchers is a powerful tool.

In Sect. 1, we proposed six properties that would ensure that our system is useful, efficient, and secure. Our system was constructed to specifically address these properties, and we show that each one is satisfied.

Authenticity of Results. Fully homomorphic encryption guarantees addition and multiplication operate as though there were not encryption layer present. Because the researcher is doing the computation on internal systems, they do not have to be worried about some mistake in computation. We assume that the data owner is a trusted entity so there is no worry that the decrypted results do not correspond to the ciphertext delivered by the researcher. Therefore, we can conclude that all results from this system are authentic.

A Rich Range of Possible Analyses. We want to ensure that a researcher can perform any operations required for their analysis. Other solutions that manage to be both practical and cost efficient are lacking this property. The only limitations imposed on computation in our system are the limitations on valid transcripts. With access to addition and multiplication, most analysis techniques can be realized including basic machine learning algorithms.

Minimal Computation on the Part of the Data Owner. In order to maintain a secure system that can be helpful to the medical community, it is impossible not to incur high costs. The construction presented in this work shares that cost burden with researchers. For the purposes of this work, we restrict our interest to researchers with access to large computational infrastructure, like those with affiliations at universities or members of industrial researcher teams. This infrastructure currently cannot be leveraged because of difficulties obtaining data. In our discussions with individuals who work in the industry, they consider it a reasonable assumption that researchers will have access to large computational infrastructure. Most of the work we have done in our system can utilize many cores to speed up computation. No matter the computational requirements, most of the costs associated with computation are placed on the researcher. The verification time is $\frac{1}{1000}$ of the computation itself, so the system offloads $\frac{999}{1000}$ of the computation to the researcher, minus the time required to decrypt the result vector.

Privacy for Individuals in the Dataset. Fully homomorphic encryption allows for exporting the dataset does not compromise the security of any individual in the dataset. Fully homomorphic encryption guarantees semantic security, so no information can leak from ciphertext without access to a decryption oracle. Our limited decryption oracle only decrypts the results of computation that operates over the entire dataset, meaning that it can only disclose meaningful information about individuals if the legitimate query only operates over a very small subset of the dataset population. When this is the case, the noise added by the differential privacy mechanism makes it impossible to glean any information.

The main concern when sharing data is that an individual's privacy is compromised and differential privacy make that impossible for a single query. While differential privacy makes it impossible for a single query to reveal any information about a single individual in the population, it is still theoretically possible for a determined researcher to learn about an individual because we allow for multiple queries. Unfortunately, there are no constructions that we are aware of that allow for both a rich, repeated query space and multiple query differential privacy. The notion of a privacy budget, in which a researcher has a maximum number of queries or an upper bound on the allowable complexity of queries, might be used to protect about this kind of attack. We choose to leave it to each data owner if and how they would like to implement a privacy budget.

Security Against Adversarial Researchers. Because we give researchers access to a decryption oracle, it must be impossible for an adversarial researcher to simply decrypt arbitrary ciphertext. Clearly, an insecure decryption oracle would allow an adversary to trivially learn private information about individuals. The verifiable computation scheme embedded into the system guarantees that only decryption queries that operate over the entire dataset are processed. We have argued in Sect. 5 that it is very unlikely for an adversarial researcher to go unnoticed. Indeed, the data owner can tweak the probability of catching a researcher until they are comfortable with the odds.

In a traditional security model, the probability of catching a cheating adversary in our system is insufficient. Importantly, in our system a cheating adversary is banned from ever using the system again and is heavily fined. Banning an adversary prevents them from searching Φ for the location of k. Charging them for attempting to cheat means it is impractical to run multiple analyses under different identities. If there are two k's in each vector, the probability of a cheating researcher of not being caught is $\frac{1}{10^6}$, which may be insufficient for a theoretical system but is sufficient for a practical one.

Practicality. Current systems suffer from two major time related weaknesses. The first is that it takes a long time to actually begin computation. Second, if a data owner instead chooses to leverage an analysis as a service style solution, it becomes more difficult and time consuming for a researcher to access the data.

While fully homomorphic encryption does make running a single analysis significantly slower, it is important to remember that the vast majority of a researcher's time is not spent running their program. Most of the life of a research project is spent waiting to acquire a dataset or waiting to access a dataset. Our system requires a one-time cost of formatting and encryption and every future researcher will be able to use the same version of the dataset without waiting. Because we construct a system that reduces the wait time required to access a dataset, increasing the time it would take to actually perform the computation is acceptable. Recall that our goal was to make the entire process of doing research quicker, not the computation itself.

Our system also allows a researcher to perform their analysis on their own schedule. While working on this project, we found a researcher who waited months to get permission to use a specific dataset and was only able to run analysis from 2 am until 8 am while the servers storing the data were not in use; these kinds of limitations make research impossible. In our system, computation can begin without ever interacting with the data owner.

8   Conclusion

In this work we have presented a practical system for securely outsourcing medical dataset analysis. The system ensures that the researcher has the freedom to compute a rich range of metrics over the database and get results perturbed by the minimum amount of noise to guarantee differential privacy. Our construction moves the burden of cost onto the beneficiaries of the analysis and also shortens the amount of time it takes for them to acquire and analyze a dataset. Together, these properties provide the alternative the medical research industry needs to properly incentivize data owners to share their datasets.

A   Architecture Diagram

See (Fig. 4).

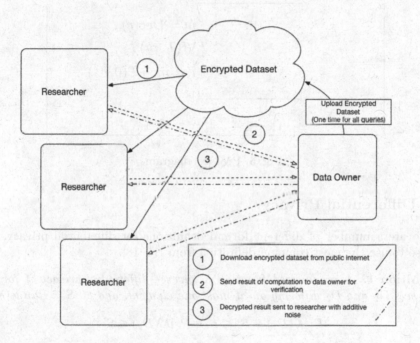

Fig. 4. System overview

B   Protocol Diagram

See (Fig. 5).

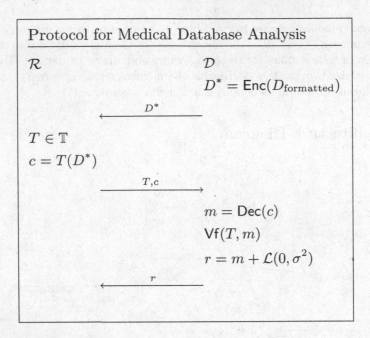

Fig. 5. Protocol diagram

C   Differential Privacy

There are a number of different formal definitions for differential privacy, we choose to use the most common definition from [15–18].

Definition 1. *A randomized function $\mathcal{K}$ gives ϵ-differential privacy if for all data sets D_1 and D_2 differing on at most one element, and all $S \subseteq Range(\mathcal{K})$*

$$Pr[\mathcal{K}(D_1) \in S] \le e^\epsilon \times Pr[\mathcal{K}(D_2) \in S]$$

Intuitively this means that an adversary with access to arbitrary auxiliary information can not use the function $\mathcal{K}$ to distinguish if the dataset in question is D_1 or D_2. Because D_1 or D_2 differ in at most one element, an adversary learns the same information about an individual no matter if they are in the dataset or not. Obviously a dataset without the individual contains no information about that individual, so an adversary can also learn nothing from a dataset with all information about that individual.

The most practical methods for imposing differential privacy on functions without completely destroying the usefulness of their results is introducing noise. A number of attempts have been made to create noiseless differential privacy in [6,14], but neither solution proves robust enough for our purposes. Additionally, a summary of alternative differential privacy methods can be found in [25]; we chose our solution for its elegance and computational simplicity. The most effective way to introduce noise is to add it in once the entire computation has finished; if noise is added to the underlying data before computation, the effects of the noise are harder to predict and control [1]. Because the noise used is additive, this means that any noise-based differential privacy is secure against only single queries. If many queries are allowed, the additive noise can be cancelled out by taking an average over the multiple results. Because it is hard to decide if two queries are equivalent, protecting against these attacks is usually implemented with a privacy budget, in which only a certain number of queries are allowed for each researcher. In our construction, we do not address the issue of a privacy budget and if cancelling out the additive noise is concerning to a data owner, they should implement a privacy budget as appropriate.

C.1   Sensitivity

The method we choose for adding differential privacy to our system is adding noise sampled from a laplacian with variance equal to the sensitivity of the function computed, where sensitivity is defined as

Definition 2. *For $g : S \to R^k$, the sensitivity of g is*

$$\Delta g = \max_{S_1, S_2} \|g(S_1) - g(S_2)\|_1$$

for all datasets S_1, S_2 differing in at most one element.

Because the noise is related directly to the maximum change that changing a single vector could have on the function g, it is intuitive that this method would introduce differential privacy. Computing the sensitivity of a function, at least for the class of functions relevant to this work, can be done in constant time with respect to the function itself.

Because the space of computation is limited by the transcript $\mathcal{T}$, it is easy to compute the sensitivity of any valid function. The limitations on transcripts are formalized in Sect. 5. The data owner stores a patient vector with maximum values in each α entry and a patient vector with minimum values in each α entry. Both of these vectors have all β values set to 1. The main limitation on transcripts is that the same computation is done to each vector. If we denote this computation $g(\cdot)$, the sensitivity can be computed as $|g(v_{\text{maximal}}) - g(v_{\text{minimal}})|$.

D   Related Solutions

D.1   Data Simulation

One current alternative solution to anonymization and analysis as a service is data simulation. While real datasets contain information about real individuals, it is possible to construct synthetic datasets that contain no actual people but contain the same trends as a real data set. These synthetic datasets can then be released to the public without fear of compromising the privacy of any of the original patients. This is a common practice particularly in genetics research [36].

Data simulation provides an interesting solution to the same problem we are attempting to address but ultimately limits the creative abilities of researcher. Because the data is generated using statistical methods and machine learning, it is inherently limited by the foresight of its creators. The data is generated by trends observed by the data owner, but if some trend is missed, the resulting dataset will clearly not contain that trend. For this reason, synthetic data offers a wonderful opportunity to confirm previous findings but is not the best way to allow researchers to find some new information.

D.2   Verifiable Delegation of Computation

Verifiable computation or delegation of computation is a rich field of research in computer science in which a client wants to outsource some computation to an untrusted server. Because the server is an untrusted entity, the client must be able to verify that the server has done the computation honestly. In general, the problem assumes that the client has insufficient computational power to perform the original computation so the verification algorithm must be less computationally intensive than the original computation.

While there are many verifiable computation and delegation of computation constructions that we could use in our system, including [3,5,11,20,24,27], there are many requirements that are different for our problem than the traditional verifiable computation problem. Firstly, in the traditional problem there are no bounds on the computational abilities of the server; constructions prioritize lowering the asymptotical complexity of the verification algorithm at the cost of the running time of the server. Modern methods have found polylogarithmic verification algorithms, but in general the runtime of the server is completely impractical. Because we aim to construct a system that is feasible to use for both researchers and data owners, we attempt to balance the runtime on the two system such that neither is unreasonable.

Traditional Solution. The classic strategy for constructing a solution to the verifiable computation problem involves generating many function inputs, all of which look like they were selected from the same distribution [22]. One of these inputs is the true input and the others are random inputs for which the output is known to the client. The server computes the function over all the inputs and returns them all to client. If all the known outputs match the previously known outputs, the client accepts the unknown output. Otherwise, the client rejects the output and knows that the server is untrustworthy.

The obvious problem with this solution is that it requires the client to know many input - output pairs. Moreover, each time the client wants the server to perform a new computation, a new set of dummy inputs is required. Clearly this is not sustainable for a system that needs to be operational long term. Moreover, we want the server to be able to select their own circuits to compute, as a researcher in this work does. This model does not easily extend to accommodate this stipulation.

PCP and SNARKs. Modern solutions to the verifiable computation problem leverage the PCP theorem to create proofs of computation that can be checked in polylogarithmic time. Probabilistically Checkable Proofs and Probabilistically Checkable Arguments [26] are powerful cryptographic tools that allow a verifier to probabilistically sample small parts of a proof and still be convinced of its reliability. Recently, projects like [29,30,34] make the first steps towards usable PCP constructions but still fall short of being practical tools. While verification of a proof can be done quickly, the process of constructing the proof is prohibitively slow. Because one of our goals was to create a system that could be practically usable, we chose to not use any kind of PCP. As the constructions of these proofs get more efficient, it may become practical to use them instead of the proof embedding and verification methods we use in our construction.

Succinct non-interactive arguments of knowledge, or SNARKs, are an extension of zero-knowledge proofs that do not require interaction [4,7]. SNARKs allow a verifier to be convinced that a challenger possesses a witness to some NP statement without revealing the witness itself. Critically, they allow it to be done without interaction. While the zero-knowledgeness property of a SNARK would not be easily utilized, SNARKS provide another possible way to prove work. Unfortunately, SNARKs suffer from similar weaknesses as PCPs and are not practical enough for use or rely upon non-standard assumptions.

It is worth noting that the computation done by the researcher is assumed to be polynomial in the size of the dataset. If we allow the researcher to be able to compute circuits that are exponential in the size of the dataset, PCPs and SNARKS may be the only viable solutions as our verification algorithm is proportional to the computation time. Additionally, giving the researcher exponential computational power would be problematic given that the security parameter of the FHE scheme is almost certainly going to be smaller than the size of the dataset.

D.3   Systems with Limited Analytics

The work that does the best job addressing the issues with medical research is by Fiore et al. [19]. Their work creates a set of protocols to do verifiable computation on a limited set of functions computed over BGV encrypted data. They use the classic verifiable computation model in which a trusted client supplies both the encrypted data and the function F to be computed. They introduce the notion of a homomorphic, collision resistant, one-way hash function that allows the client to quickly verify if the untrusted party correctly computed F. They are able to guarantee amortized verification time that is either linear or constant in the time of computation. They are able to create protocols for performing a number of helpful functions, including linear combinations and multivariate polynomials of degree two.

While this work provides solutions to the issues of privacy, practicality and allows for the outsourcing of cost, it does not provide the flexibility required by medical researchers. While their scheme is more efficient for linear combinations, the limitations of only being able to compute multivariate polynomials of degree two or univariate polynomials of higher degree renders their construction unsuitable for the needs of researchers. The examples cited in our implementation were already using higher order multiplication than would be supported in their work and our examples are still reasonably simple.

Another similar work is [35], in which the authors investigate the practicality of calculating statistical metrics over encrypted data. Their results of overall positive and similar to our findings. Additionally, the space of operations in their experiments are similar to our experiments. While this work provides a good start towards outsourcing medical analysis, they lack verifiable computation, a critical component given an untrusted researcher.

D.4   Personalized Medicine

Some work has been done utilizing the analysis as a service model for personalized medicine, in which a patient uploads their data to a service provider to learn some metric about their health. In [8] a system for using homomorphically encrypted data to allow the owner of a proprietary algorithm to compute a patient's risk of heart disease without learning about the patient. A similar system is [2], in which medical units can access genomic, clinical, and environmental data to compute risk metrics for a patient. The computational requirements from the FHE scheme for this problem setting are far lower than in our problem setting. The circuits computed are of lower complexity and the number of datapoints are fewer. Most importantly, computation in these system are done only over a single patient's information making the threat vectors different.

E   Optimization and Future Work

E.1   Ciphertext Compression

We utilize the ciphertext I/O in the HELib to write our ciphertexts to file. While HELib provides efficient ciphertext operations, it stores its ciphertexts extremely inefficiently. The coefficients on the polynomials are all written as ascii numbers separated by spaces. To store ciphertext more efficiently, these coefficients can be stored in some binary form and then compressed. We chose to store all ciphertext in a single file for simplicity, but to minimize the size of the file a researcher would have to download, all ciphertexts containing values from a given row of the dataset should be stored in a compressed file. This storage scheme allows a researcher to pick and choose exactly what subset of the data is important to their query.

E.2   Multithreading

Much of the computation done by the researcher can be completely parallelized. Because the same operation must be done on each patient vector before the results of those computations can be combined, each of the vector operations must be completely independent. When illustrating the viability of our system, we did no parallelization whatsoever, so all timing results are worst case. To optimize efficiency, each set of ciphertext can be processed in parallel and then combined pairwise in a tree structure. Additionally, the one-time cost of encrypting the dataset can also benefit from parallelization. Each row in the dataset can be formatted and encrypted independently.

E.3   Future Improvements to FHE

The efficiency of this system is directly tied to the efficiency of the underlying FHE scheme. We have seen tremendous strides in the efficiency of FHE since its initial construction in 2009. While we cannot anticipate the rate at which FHE will improve, it is reasonable to assume that we will see better constructions of FHE in the near future. Although we leverage the Smart-Vercauteren vectors in our construction, if future implementations do not support SIMD ciphertext operations, similar strategies can be used to bind many plaintext values together so verification can be done quickly.

References

1. Adam, N.R., Worthmann, J.C.: Security-control methods for statistical databases: a comparative study. ACM Comput. Surv. 21(4), 515–556 (1989)
2. Ayday, E., Raisaro, J.L., McLaren, P.J., Fellay, J., Hubaux, J.-P.: Privacy-preserving computation of disease risk by using genomic, clinical, and environmental data. Presented as part of the 2013 USENIX workshop on health information technologies, USENIX, Berkeley, CA (2013)
3. Backes, M., Fiore, D., Reischuk, R.M.: Verifiable delegation of computation on outsourced data. Cryptology ePrint Archive, Report 2013/469 (2013). http://eprint.iacr.org/
4. Ben-Sasson, E., Chiesa, A., Genkin, D., Tromer, E., Virza, M.: Snarks for C: verifying program executions succinctly and in zero knowledge. Cryptology ePrint Archive, Report 2013/507 (2013). http://eprint.iacr.org/
5. Benabbas, S., Gennaro, R., Vahlis, Y.: Verifiable delegation of computation over large datasets. Cryptology ePrint Archive, Report 2011/132 (2011). http://eprint.iacr.org/
6. Bhaskar, R., Bhowmick, A., Goyal, V., Laxman, S., Thakurta, A.: Noiseless database privacy. Cryptology ePrint Archive, Report 2011/487 (2011). http://eprint.iacr.org/2011/487
7. Bitansky, N., Canetti, R., Chiesa, A., Tromer, E.: From extractable collision resistance to succinct non-interactive arguments of knowledge, and back again. Cryptology ePrint Archive, Report 2011/443 (2011). http://eprint.iacr.org/
8. Bos, J.W., Lauter, K., Naehrig, M.: Private predictive analysis on encrypted medical data. Technical report MSR-TR-2013-81, September 2013
9. Brakerski, Z., Gentry, C., Vaikuntanathan, V.: (Leveled) fully homomorphic encryption without bootstrapping. In: Goldwasser, S. (ed.) 3rd Innovations in Theoretical Computer Science, ITCS 2012, Cambridge, Massachusetts, USA, 8–10 January 2012, pp. 309–325. Association for Computing Machinery (2012)

10. Christakis, N.A., Fowler, J.H., Imbens, G.W., Kalyanaraman, K.: An empirical model for strategic network formation. Working Paper 16039, National Bureau of Economic Research, May 2010

11. Chung, K.-M., Kalai, Y., Vadhan, S.: Improved delegation of computation using fully homomorphic encryption. Cryptology ePrint Archive, Report 2010/241 (2010). http://eprint.iacr.org/

12. Cousins, D., Rohloff, K., Sumorok, D.: Designing an FPGA-accelerated homomorphic encryption co-processor. IEEE Trans. Emerg. Top. Comput. (2016)

13. Dai, W., Sunar, B.: cuHE: a homomorphic encryption accelerator library. In: Pasalic, E., Knudsen, L.R. (eds.) BalkanCryptSec 2015. LNCS, vol. 9540, pp. 169–186. Springer, Cham (2016). https://doi.org/10.1007/978-3-319-29172-7_11

14. Duan, Y.: Privacy without noise. In: Proceedings of the 18th ACM Conference on Information and Knowledge Management, CIKM 2009, New York, NY, USA, pp. 1517–1520. ACM (2009)

15. Dwork, C.: Differential privacy: a survey of results. In: Agrawal, M., Du, D., Duan, Z., Li, A. (eds.) TAMC 2008. LNCS, vol. 4978, pp. 1–19. Springer, Heidelberg (2008). https://doi.org/10.1007/978-3-540-79228-4_1

16. Dwork, C., Lei, J.: Differential privacy and robust statistics. In: Mitzenmacher, M. (ed.) 41st Annual ACM Symposium on Theory of Computing, Bethesda, Maryland, USA, May 31–June 2, 2009, pp. 371–380. ACM Press (2009)

17. Dwork, C., McSherry, F., Nissim, K., Smith, A.: Calibrating noise to sensitivity in private data analysis. In: Halevi, S., Rabin, T. (eds.) TCC 2006. LNCS, vol. 3876, pp. 265–284. Springer, Heidelberg (2006). https://doi.org/10.1007/11681878_14

18. Dwork, C., Smith, A.: Differential privacy for statistics: what we know and what we want to learn. J. Priv. Confidentiality **1**, 135–154 (2009)

19. Fiore, D., Gennaro, R., Pastro, V.: Efficiently verifiable computation on encrypted data. In: Proceedings of the 2014 ACM SIGSAC Conference on Computer and Communications Security, CCS 2014, New York, NY, USA, pp. 844–855. ACM (2014)

20. Gennaro, R., Gentry, C., Parno, B.: Non-interactive verifiable computing: outsourcing computation to untrusted workers. Cryptology ePrint Archive, Report 2009/547 (2009). http://eprint.iacr.org/

21. Gentry, C.: Fully homomorphic encryption using ideal lattices. In: Mitzenmacher, M. (ed.) 41st Annual ACM Symposium on Theory of Computing, Bethesda, Maryland, USA, May 31–June 2, 2009, pp. 169–178. ACM Press (2009)

22. Golle, P., Mironov, I.: Uncheatable distributed computations. In: Naccache, D. (ed.) CT-RSA 2001. LNCS, vol. 2020, pp. 425–440. Springer, Heidelberg (2001). https://doi.org/10.1007/3-540-45353-9_31

23. Halevi, S., Shoup, V.: Helib. http://shaih.github.io/HElib/

24. Hohenberger, S., Lysyanskaya, A.: How to securely outsource cryptographic computations. In: Kilian, J. (ed.) TCC 2005. LNCS, vol. 3378, pp. 264–282. Springer, Heidelberg (2005). https://doi.org/10.1007/978-3-540-30576-7_15

25. Ji, Z., Lipton, Z.C., Elkan, C.: Differential privacy and machine learning: a survey and review. CoRR, abs/1412.7584 (2014)

26. Kalai, Y.T., Raz, R.: Probabilistically checkable arguments. In: Halevi, S. (ed.) CRYPTO 2009. LNCS, vol. 5677, pp. 143–159. Springer, Heidelberg (2009). https://doi.org/10.1007/978-3-642-03356-8_9

27. Narayan, A., Feldman, A., Papadimitriou, A., Haeberlen, A.: Verifiable differential privacy. In: Proceedings of the Tenth European Conference on Computer Systems, EuroSys 2015, New York, NY, USA, pp. 28:1–28:14. ACM (2015)

28. Narayanan, A., Shmatikov, V.: Robust de-anonymization of large sparse datasets. In: IEEE Symposium on Security and Privacy, SP 2008, pp. 111–125. IEEE (2008)
29. Parno, B., Gentry, C., Howell, J., Raykova, M.: Pinocchio: nearly practical verifiable computation. Cryptology ePrint Archive, Report 2013/279 (2013). http://eprint.iacr.org/
30. Setty, S.T.V., McPherson, R., Blumberg, A.J., Walfish, M.: Making argument systems for outsourced computation practical (sometimes). In: ISOC Network and Distributed System Security Symposium - NDSS 2012, San Diego, California, USA, 5–8 February 2012. The Internet Society (2012)
31. Smart, N., Vercauteren, F.: Fully homomorphic SIMD operations. Cryptology ePrint Archive, Report 2011/133 (2011). http://eprint.iacr.org/2011/133
32. SPARCS: Hospital inpatient discharges (sparcs de-identified) (2012). https://health.data.ny.gov/Health/Hospital-Inpatient-Discharges-SPARCS-De-Identified/u4ud-w55t
33. Vaikuntanathan, V.: Computing blindfolded: new developments in fully homomorphic encryption (tutorial). In: Ostrovsky, R. (ed.) 52nd Annual Symposium on Foundations of Computer Science, Palm Springs, California, USA, 22–25 October 2011, pp. 5–16. IEEE Computer Society Press (2011)
34. Wahby, R.S., Setty, S., Howald, M., Ren, Z., Blumberg, A.J., Walfish, M.: Efficient ram and control flow in verifiable outsourced computation. Cryptology ePrint Archive, Report 2014/674 (2014). http://eprint.iacr.org/
35. Wu, D., Haven, J.: Using homomorphic encryption for large scale statistical analysis (2012)
36. Yuan, X., Miller, D., Zhang, J., Herrington, D., Wang, Y.: An overview of population genetic data simulation. J. Comput. Biol. 19(1), 42–54 (2012)

Homomorphic Proxy Re-Authenticators and Applications to Verifiable Multi-User Data Aggregation

David Derler[1(✉)], Sebastian Ramacher[1], and Daniel Slamanig[2]

[1] IAIK, Graz University of Technology, Graz, Austria
{dderler,sramacher}@iaik.tugraz.at
[2] AIT Austrian Institute of Technology, Vienna, Austria
daniel.slamanig@ait.ac.at

Abstract. We introduce the notion of *homomorphic proxy re-authenticators*, a tool that adds security and verifiability guarantees to multi-user data aggregation scenarios. It allows distinct sources to authenticate their data under their own keys, and a proxy can transform these single signatures or message authentication codes (MACs) to a MAC under a receiver's key without having access to it. In addition, the proxy can evaluate arithmetic circuits (functions) on the inputs so that the resulting MAC corresponds to the evaluation of the respective function. As the messages authenticated by the sources may represent sensitive information, we also consider hiding them from the proxy and other parties in the system, except from the receiver.

We provide a general model and two modular constructions of our novel primitive, supporting the class of linear functions. On our way, we establish various novel building blocks. Most interestingly, we formally define the notion and present a construction of *homomorphic proxy re-encryption*, which may be of independent interest. The latter allows users to encrypt messages under their own public keys, and a proxy can re-encrypt them to a receiver's public key (without knowing any secret key), while also being able to evaluate functions on the ciphertexts. The resulting re-encrypted ciphertext then holds an evaluation of the function on the input messages.

1 Introduction

Proxy re-cryptography [11] is a powerful concept which allows proxies to transform cryptographic objects under one key to cryptographic objects under another

The full version of this paper is available as IACR Cryptology ePrint Archive Report 2017/086. All authors have been supported by EU H2020 project PRISMACLOUD, grant agreement no. 644962. S. Ramacher has additionally been supported by EU H2020 project CREDENTIAL, grant agreement no. 653454.

Work done while Daniel Slamanig was still at IAIK, Graz University of Technology, Graz, Austria.

A. Kiayias (Ed.): FC 2017, LNCS 10322, pp. 124–142, 2017.
https://doi.org/10.1007/978-3-319-70972-7_7

key using a transformation key (a so called re-key). In particular, proxy re-encryption has shown to be of great practical interest in cloud scenarios such as data storage [12,16], data sharing [49], publish-subscribe [15] as well as cloud-based identity management [41,42,47,50]. In contrast, other proxy re-primitives, and in particular proxy re-signatures (or MACs), seem to unleash their full potential not before considering them in combination with homomorphic properties on the message space. Interestingly, however, this direction has received no attention so far. To this end, we introduce the notion of homomorphic proxy re-authenticators (HPRAs), which allows distinct senders to authenticate data under their own keys, and an evaluator (aggregator) can transform these single signatures or message authentication codes (MACs) to a MAC under a receiver's key without knowing it. Most importantly, the aggregator can evaluate arithmetic circuits (functions) on the inputs so that the resulting MAC corresponds to the evaluation of the respective function. Furthermore, we investigate whether we can hide the input messages from the aggregator. On the way to solve this, we formally define the notion of homomorphic proxy re-encryption (HPRE). Data aggregation is the central application of our framework, but it is not limited to this application.

Motivation. Data aggregation is an important task in the Internet of Things (IoT) and cloud computing. We observe a gap in existing work as the important issue of end-to-end authenticity and verifiability of computations on the data (aggregation results) is mostly ignored. We address this issue and propose a versatile non-interactive solution which is tailored to a multi-user setting. The additional authenticity features of our solution add robustness to errors occurring during transmission or aggregation even in the face of a non-trusted aggregator.

Multi-User Data Aggregation. Assume a setting where n senders, e.g., sensor nodes, regularly report data to some entity denoted the aggregator. The aggregator collects the data and then reports computations (evaluations of functions) on these data to a receiver. For example, consider environmental monitoring of hydroelectric plants being located in a mountainous region, where small sensors are used for monitoring purposes. Due to the lack of infrastructure (e.g., very limited cell coverage) sensors are not directly connected to the Internet and collected data is first sent to a gateway running at the premise of some telecommunication provider. This gateway aggregates the data and forwards it to some cloud service operated by the receiver.

Obviously, when the involved parties communicate via public networks, security related issues arise. Apart from achieving security against outsiders, there are also security and privacy related issues with respect to the involved parties.

In general, we identify three main goals. (1) End-to-end authenticity, i.e., protecting data items from unauthorized manipulation and preserving the source authenticity. (2) Concealing the original data from the aggregator and the receiver, and, even further, concealing the result of the computation from the aggregator. Clearly, in (2) we also want to conceal data from any outsider. (3) Establishing independent secret keys for the involved parties so that they do not share a single secret. Latter facilitates a dynamic setting.

Below, we present such an aggregation scenario, discuss why straightforward solutions fall short, and sketch our solution. Then, we discuss the problems popping up when we require stronger privacy guarantees and show how our primitives help to overcome these issues.

Authenticity and Input Privacy. In our first scenario, the n senders each hold their own signing key and within every period sender i reports a signed data item d_i to the aggregator. The aggregator must be able to evaluate functions $f \in \mathcal{F}$ (where $\mathcal{F}$ is some suitable class of functions, e.g., linear functions) on $d_1, \ldots, d_n$ so that a receiver will be convinced of the authenticity of the data and the correctness of the computation without fully trusting the aggregator (recall the end-to-end authenticity requirement). Moreover, although the inputs to the aggregator are not private, we still want them to be hidden relative to the function f, i.e., so that a receiver only learns what is revealed by f and $\hat{d} = f(d_1, \ldots, d_n)$, as a receiver might not need to learn the single input values.

A central goal is that the single data sources have individual keys. Thus, we can not directly employ homomorphic signatures (or MACs). Also the recent concept of multikey-homomorphic signatures [25, 26, 33] does not help: even though they allow homomorphic operations on the key space, they do not consider transformations to some specific target key.[1] With HPRAs we can realize this, as the aggregator (who holds re-keys from the senders to some receiver) can transform all the single signatures or MACs to a MAC under the receiver's key (without having access to it). Moreover, due to the homomorphic property, a MAC which corresponds to the evaluation of a function f on the inputs can be computed. The receiver can then verify the correctness of the computation, i.e., that $\hat{d} = f(d_1, \ldots, d_n)$, and the authenticity of the used inputs (without explicitly learning them) using its independent MAC key.

Adding Output Privacy. In our second scenario, we additionally want data privacy guarantees with respect to the aggregator. This can be crucial if the aggregator is running in some untrusted environment, e.g., the cloud. We achieve this by constructing an output private HPRA. In doing so, one has to answer the question as how to confidentially provide the result of the computation to the receiver and how to guarantee the authenticity (verifiability) of the computation. We tackle this issue by introducing a HPRE where the homomorphism is compatible to the one of the HPRA. The sources then additionally encrypt the data under their own keys and the aggregator re-encrypts the individual ciphertexts to a ciphertext under a receiver's key and evaluates the same function f as on the MACs on the ciphertexts. This enables the receiver to decrypt the result $\hat{d}$ using its *own* decryption key and to verify the MAC on $\hat{d}$ together with a description of the function f. In addition, we use a trick to prevent public verifiability of the signatures from the single data sources, as public verifiability potentially leaks the signed data items which trivially would destroy output privacy.

---

[1] While the homomorphic properties might allow one to define a function mapping to a target key, it is unclear whether handing over the description of such a function to a proxy would maintain the security requirements posed by our application.

Contribution. Our contributions in this paper can be summarized as follows.

- We introduce the notion of homomorphic proxy re-authenticators (HPRA). Our framework tackles multi-user data aggregation in a dynamic setting. For the first time, we thereby consider independent keys of the single parties, the verifiability of the evaluation of general functions on the authenticated inputs by the sources, as well as privacy with respect to the aggregator.
- As a means to achieve the strong privacy requirements imposed by our security model, we formally define the notion of homomorphic proxy re-encryption (HPRE), which may be of independent interest.
- We present two modular constructions of HPRA schemes for the class $\mathcal{F}_{\text{lin}}$ of linear functions, which differ regarding the strength of the provided privacy guarantees. On our way, we establish various novel building blocks. Firstly, we present a linearly homomorphic MAC which is suitable to be used in our construction. Secondly, to achieve the stronger privacy guarantees, we construct a HPRE scheme for linear functions. All our proofs are modular in the sense that we separately prove the security of our building blocks; our overall proofs then build upon the results obtained for the building blocks. Thus, our building blocks may as well easily be used in other constructions.

Related Work. Subsequently, we review related work. As our focus is on non-interactive approaches, we omit interactive approaches where clients download all the data, decrypt them locally, compute a function, and send the results back along with a zero-knowledge proof of correctness (as, e.g., in [24]).

Proxy Re-Cryptography. Proxy re-encryption (PRE) [11] allows a semi-trusted proxy to transform a message encrypted under the key of some party into a ciphertext to the same message under a key of another party, where the proxy performing the re-encryption learns nothing about the message. This primitive has been introduced in [11], further studied in [30] and the first strongly secure constructions have been proposed by Ateniese et al. in [5]. Boneh et al. construct PRE in the symmetric setting [14]. Follow-up work focuses on even stronger (IND-CCA2 secure) schemes (cf. [17,39,43,44]). Since we, however, require certain homomorphic properties, we focus on IND-CPA secure schemes (as IND-CCA2 security does not allow any kind of malleability). In previous work by Ayday et al. [7], a variant of the linearly homomorphic Paillier encryption scheme and proxy encryption in the sense of [30] were combined. Here, the holder of a key splits the key and gives one part to the proxy and one to the sender; with the drawback that the secret key is exposed when both collude. We are looking for proxy re-encryption that is homomorphic, works in a multi-user setting but is collusion-safe and non-interactive, i.e., re-encryption keys can be computed by the sender using only the public key of the receiver without any interaction and a collusion of sender and proxy does not reveal the receiver's key. Also note that, as our focus is on practically efficient constructions, we do not build upon fully homomorphic encryption [27], which allows to build HPRE using the rather expensive bootstrapping technique. In concurrent work Ma et al. [40] follow this approach and propose a construction of a PRE scheme with homomorphic properties which additionally achieves key privacy. They build upon [28] using the bootstrapping techniques in [4] and apply some modifications for key privacy. While their construction can be seen as a HPRE in our sense, they do not formally define a corresponding security model and we are not aware of a suitable formalization for our purposes.

Proxy re-signatures, i.e., the signature analogue to proxy re-encryption, have been introduced in [11] and formally studied in [30]. Later, [6] introduced stronger security definitions, constructions and briefly discussed some applications. However, the schemes in [6] and follow up schemes [38] do not provide a homomorphic property and it is unclear how they could be extended. The concept of *homomorphic proxy re-authenticators*, which we propose, or a related concept, has to the best of our knowledge not been studied before.

Homomorphic Authenticators. General (non-interactive) verifiable computing techniques (cf. [48] for a recent overview) are very expressive, but usually prohibitive regarding proof computation (proof size and verification can, however, be very small and cheap respectively). In addition, the function and/or the data needs to be fixed at setup time and inputs are not authenticated. Using homomorphic authenticators allows evaluations of functions on authenticated inputs under a single key (cf. [19] for a recent overview). They are dynamic with respect to the authenticated data and the evaluated function, and also efficient for interesting classes of functions. Evaluating results is typically not more efficient than computing the function (unless using an amortized setting [8, 21]). Yet, they provide benefits when saving bandwidth is an issue and/or the inputs need to be hidden from evaluators (cf. [22, 32]). Computing on data authenticated under different keys using so called multi-key homomorphic authenticators [25, 26, 33], has only very recently been considered. Even though they are somewhat related, they are no replacement for what we are proposing in this paper.

Aggregator-Oblivious Encryption (AOE). AOE [45, 46] considers data provided by multiple producers, which is aggregated by a semi-honest aggregator. The aggregator does not learn the single inputs but only the final result. Follow-up work [10, 31, 34] improved this approach in various directions. Furthermore, [23] introduced a method to achieve fault tolerance, being applicable to all previous schemes. There are also other lines of work on data aggregation, e.g., [18, 36], [29, 37]. Very recently, [35] combined AOE with homomorphic tags to additionally provide verifiability of the aggregated results. Here, every user has a tag key and the aggregator additionally aggregates the tags. Verification can be done under a pre-distributed combined fixed tag key. Their approach is limited to a single function (the sum) and requires a shared secret key-setting, which can be problematic.

In all previous approaches it is impossible to hide the outputs (i.e., the aggregation results) from the aggregator. In contrast to only hiding the inputs, we additionally want to hide the outputs. In addition, we do not want to assume a trusted distribution of the keys, but every sender should authenticate and encrypt under his own key and the aggregator can then perform re-operations (without any secret key) to the receiver.

2 Preliminaries

Unless stated otherwise, all algorithms run in polynomial time and return a special symbol $\perp$ on error. By $y \leftarrow \mathcal{A}(x)$, we denote that y is assigned the output of the potentially probabilistic algorithm $\mathcal{A}$ on input x and fresh random coins (we may also use sans serif font to denote algorithms). Similarly, $y \xleftarrow{R} S$ means that y is assigned a uniformly random value from a set S. If a and b are strings, $a\|b$ is the concatenated string and $\vec{a}\|b$ means extending the vector $\vec{a}$ with element b. For a sequence of vectors $(\vec{v}_i)_{i\in[n]}$ of length ℓ, we use $f((\vec{v}_i)_{i\in[n]})$ to denote the element-wise application of the function f, i.e., $f((\vec{v}_i)_{i\in[n]}) := (f(v_{i1})_{i\in[n]}, \ldots, f((v_{i\ell})_{i\in[n]}))$. We let $[n] := \{1, \ldots, n\}$ and let $\Pr[\Omega : E]$ denote the probability of an event E over the probability space Ω. A function $\varepsilon(\cdot) : \mathbb{N} \to \mathbb{R}_{\geq 0}$ is called negligible, iff it vanishes faster than every inverse polynomial, i.e., $\forall\, k : \exists\, n_k : \forall\, n > n_k : \varepsilon(n) < n^{-k}$. A polynomial function is denoted by $\mathsf{poly}(\cdot)$.

Let $\mathbb{G}_1 = \langle g \rangle$, $\mathbb{G}_2 = \langle \hat{g} \rangle$, and $\mathbb{G}_T$ be cyclic groups of prime order q. A paring $e : \mathbb{G}_1 \times \mathbb{G}_2 \to \mathbb{G}_T$ is an efficiently computable, bilinear, non-degenerate map. For simplicity we present our results in the (symmetric) Type-1 setting where $\mathbb{G}_1 = \mathbb{G}_2$. We stress that there are tools [1,3] to automatically translate them to the more efficient (asymmetric) Type-3 setting. Henceforth we use BG to denote a description of a bilinear group and use boldface letters to denote elements in $\mathbb{G}_T$. We formally define bilinear group generation and the required computational hardness assumptions in the full version.

Linearly Homomorphic MACs. Our definition is inspired by [2] and covers homomorphic MACs for the family of linear function classes $\{\mathcal{F}_{\mathsf{pp}}^{\mathsf{lin}}\}$, further referred to as HOM-MAC.

Definition 1 (HOM-MAC). *A HOM-MAC is a tuple* $(\mathcal{P}, \mathcal{G}, \mathcal{S}, \mathcal{C}, \mathcal{V})$ *of algorithms defined as:*

$\mathcal{P}(\kappa, \ell)$: *Takes a security parameter* κ *and an upper bound* ℓ *on the vector length as input and outputs public parameters* pp, *determining the message space* $\mathcal{M}^\ell$, *function class* $\mathcal{F}_{\mathsf{pp}}^{\mathsf{lin}}$ *containing functions* $f : (\mathcal{M}^\ell)^n \to \mathcal{M}^\ell$, *as well as a tag space being exponentially large in* κ, *where* $\ell, n \leq \mathsf{poly}(\kappa)$.

$\mathcal{G}(\mathsf{pp})$: *Takes the public parameters* pp *as input and outputs a secret key* sk.

$\mathcal{S}(\mathsf{sk}, \vec{v}, \mathsf{id}, \tau)$: *Takes a MAC key* sk, *a vector* $\vec{v}$, *an identifier* id, *and a tag* τ *as input, and outputs a MAC* μ.

$\mathcal{C}(\mathsf{pp}, f, (\mu_i)_{i\in[n]})$: *Takes public parameters* pp, *a function* $f \in \mathcal{F}_{\mathsf{lin}}$ *and a sequence of valid MACs* $(\mu_i)_{i\in[n]}$ *on vectors* $(\vec{v}_i)_{i\in[n]}$ *as input, and outputs a MAC* μ *on* $\vec{v} = f((\vec{v}_i)_{i\in[n]})$.

$\mathcal{V}(\mathsf{sk}, \vec{v}, \mu, \tau, (\mathsf{id}_i)_{i\in[n]}, f)$: *Takes a MAC key* sk, *a vector* $\vec{v}$, *a MAC* μ, *a tag* τ, *a sequence of identifiers* $(\mathsf{id}_i)_{i\in[n]}$, *and a function* $f \in \mathcal{F}_{\mathsf{lin}}$ *as input, and outputs a bit.*

A linearly homomorphic MAC is required to be correct and unforgeable. Formal definitions are presented in the full version.

Proxy Re-Encryption. A proxy re-encryption (PRE) scheme is an encryption scheme that allows a proxy to transform a message m encrypted under public key rpk_A of party A into a ciphertext to m under rpk_B for another party B, so that the proxy learns nothing about m. A PRE scheme is called *non-interactive* if party A can produce a re-encryption key from A to B locally by having access to its private key and only B's public key, *collusion-safe* if the proxy colluding with either of the parties can not recover the other parties private key, *unidirectional* if a re-encryption key only allows transformations in one direction (e.g., from A to B), and *single-use* if one ciphertext can be transformed only once. For our formal definitions, we largely follow [5].

Definition 2 (PRE). *A PRE is a tuple* $(\mathcal{P}, \mathcal{G}, \vec{\mathcal{E}}, \vec{\mathcal{D}}, \mathcal{RG}, \mathcal{RE})$ *of algorithms, where* $\vec{\mathcal{E}} = (\mathcal{E}^i)_{i \in [2]}$ *and* $\vec{\mathcal{D}} = (\mathcal{D}^i)_{i \in [2]}$, *which are defined as follows:*

$\mathcal{P}(1^\kappa)$: *Takes a security parameter* κ *and outputs parameters* pp.
$\mathcal{G}(\mathsf{pp})$: *Takes parameters* pp *and outputs a key pair* $(\mathsf{rsk}, \mathsf{rpk})$.
$\mathcal{RG}(\mathsf{rsk}_A, \mathsf{rpk}_B)$: *Takes a secret key* rsk_A *and a public key* rpk_B *and outputs a re-encryption key* $\mathsf{rk}_{A \to B}$.
$\mathcal{E}^i(\mathsf{rpk}, m)$: *Takes a public key* rpk *and a message* m *and outputs a ciphertext* c.
$\mathcal{RE}(\mathsf{rk}_{A \to B}, c_A)$: *Takes a re-encryption key* $\mathsf{rk}_{A \to B}$ *and a ciphertext* c_A *under* rpk_A, *and outputs a re-encrypted ciphertext* c_B *for* rpk_B.
$\mathcal{D}^i(\mathsf{rsk}, c)$: *Takes a secret key* rsk *and a ciphertext* c, *and outputs* m.

A PRE scheme needs to be correct. This notion requires that for all security parameters $\kappa \in \mathbb{N}$, all honestly generated parameters $\mathsf{pp} \leftarrow \mathcal{P}(1^\kappa)$, all key pairs $(\mathsf{rsk}_A, \mathsf{rpk}_A) \leftarrow \mathcal{G}(\mathsf{pp})$, $(\mathsf{rsk}_B, \mathsf{rpk}_B) \leftarrow \mathcal{G}(\mathsf{pp})$, all re-encryption keys $\mathsf{rk}_{A \to B} \leftarrow \mathcal{RG}(\mathsf{rsk}_A, \mathsf{rpk}_B)$, all messages m it holds with probability one that

$$\forall\, i \in [2]\ \exists\, j \in [2]\ :\ \mathcal{D}^j(\mathsf{rsk}_A, \mathcal{E}^i(\mathsf{rpk}_A, m)) = m, \text{ and}$$
$$\exists\, i \in [2]\ \exists\, j \in [2]\ :\ \mathcal{D}^j(\mathsf{rsk}_B, \mathcal{RE}(\mathsf{rk}_{A \to B}, \mathcal{E}^i(\mathsf{pk}_A, m))) = m.$$

Thereby i and j determine the level of the ciphertexts. We will henceforth use the following semantics: first-level ciphertexts ($\mathcal{E}^1$) cannot be re-encrypted by a proxy, whereas second-level ciphertexts ($\mathcal{E}^2$) can be re-encrypted.

In addition, a PRE needs to be IND-CPA secure. We, henceforth, only require a relaxed IND-CPA notion which we term IND-CPA⁻. It is clearly implied by the original IND-CPA notion from [5] (some oracles are omitted and the adversary only gets to see a second-level ciphertext).

Definition 3 (IND-CPA⁻). *A PRE is IND-CPA⁻ secure, if for all PPT adversaries* $\mathcal{A}$ *there is a negligible function* $\varepsilon(\cdot)$ *such that*

$$\Pr\left[\begin{array}{l} \mathsf{pp} \leftarrow \mathcal{P}(1^\kappa), b \xleftarrow{R} \{0,1\}, (\mathsf{sk}_t, \mathsf{pk}_t) \leftarrow \mathcal{G}(\mathsf{pp}), \\ (\mathsf{sk}_h, \mathsf{pk}_h) \leftarrow \mathcal{G}(\mathsf{pp}), \mathsf{rk}_{t \to h} \leftarrow \mathcal{RG}(\mathsf{sk}_t, \mathsf{pk}_h), \\ (m_0, m_1, \mathsf{st}) \leftarrow \mathcal{A}(\mathsf{pp}, \mathsf{pk}_t, \mathsf{pk}_h, \mathsf{rk}_{t \to h}), \\ c \leftarrow \mathcal{E}^2(m_b, \mathsf{pk}_t), b^\star \leftarrow \mathcal{A}(\mathsf{st}, c) \end{array} : b = b^\star \right] \leq 1/2 + \varepsilon(\kappa).$$

We remark that $\mathcal{RG}$ as defined in [5] also takes the target secret key to cover interactive schemes. As we only deal with non-interactive ones, we omit it.

3   Homomorphic Proxy Re-Authenticators

We introduce homomorphic proxy re-authenticators (HPRAs) and rigorously formalize a suitable security model. Our goal is to obtain a flexible framework with various possible instantiations. Accordingly, our definitions are rather generic. We stress that both the source and receiver re-key generation, besides the secret key of the executing party, only require public inputs, i.e., are non-interactive.

Definition 4 (HPRA). *A homomorphic proxy re-authenticator* (HPRA) *for a family of function classes* $\{\mathcal{F}_{\mathsf{pp}}\}$ *is a tuple of PPT algorithms* (Gen, SGen, VGen, Sign, Verify, SRGen, VRGen, Agg, AVerify), *where* Verify *is optional. They are defined as follows:*

$\mathsf{Gen}(1^\kappa, \ell)$: *Takes security parameter κ and vector length ℓ and outputs parameters* pp, *determining the message space $\mathcal{M}^\ell$, function class $\mathcal{F}_{\mathsf{pp}}$ containing functions $f : (\mathcal{M}^\ell)^n \to \mathcal{M}^\ell$, as well as a tag space being exponentially large in κ, where $\ell, n \leq \mathsf{poly}(\kappa)$.*

$\mathsf{SGen}(\mathsf{pp})$: *Takes parameters* pp *as input, and outputs a signer key* (id, sk, pk).

$\mathsf{VGen}(\mathsf{pp})$: *Takes parameters* pp, *and outputs a MAC key* mk *and auxiliary information* aux.

$\mathsf{Sign}(\mathsf{sk}, \vec{m}, \tau)$: *Takes a signer secret key* sk, *a message vector $\vec{m}$, and a tag τ as input, and outputs a signature σ.*

$\mathsf{Verify}(\mathsf{pk}, \vec{m}, \tau, \sigma)$: *Takes a signer public key* pk, *a message vector $\vec{m}$, a tag τ, and a signature σ as input, and outputs a bit b.*

$\mathsf{SRGen}(\mathsf{sk}_i, \mathsf{aux})$: *Takes a signer secret key sk_i, some auxiliary information* aux, *and outputs a re-encryption key rk_i.*

$\mathsf{VRGen}(\mathsf{pk}_i, \mathsf{mk}, \mathsf{rk}_i)$: *Takes a signer public key pk_i and a MAC key* mk, *as well as a re-encryption key rk_i as input, and outputs an aggregation key ak_i.*

$\mathsf{Agg}((\mathsf{ak}_i)_{i \in [n]}, (\sigma_i)_{i \in [n]}, \tau, f)$: *Takes n aggregation keys $(\mathsf{ak}_i)_{i \in [n]}$, n signatures $(\sigma_i)_{i \in [n]}$, a tag τ, and a function $f \in \mathcal{F}_{\mathsf{pp}}$ as input, and outputs an aggregate authenticated message vector Λ.*

$\mathsf{AVerify}(\mathsf{mk}, \Lambda, \mathsf{ID}, f)$: *Takes a MAC key* mk, *an aggregate authenticated message vector Λ, n identifiers $\mathsf{ID} = (\mathsf{id}_i)_{i \in [n]}$, and a function $f \in \mathcal{F}_{\mathsf{pp}}$. It outputs a message vector and a tag $(\vec{m}, \tau)$ on success and $(\bot, \bot)$ otherwise.*

Security Properties. Below we define the oracles, where the public parameters and the keys generated in the security games are implicitly available to the oracles. While most oracle definitions are fairly easy to comprehend and therefore not explicitly explained, we note that the RoS oracle is used to model the requirement that signatures do not leak the signed data in a real-or-random style. The environment maintains the initially empty sets HU and CU of honest and corrupted users (CU is only set in the output privacy game). Further, it maintains the initially empty sets S, RK and AK of signer, re-encryption and aggregation keys, and an initially empty set SIG of message-identity pairs.

$\mathsf{SG}(i)$: If $\mathsf{S}[i] \neq \bot$ return $\bot$. Otherwise run $(\mathsf{id}_i, \mathsf{sk}_i, \mathsf{pk}_i) \leftarrow \mathsf{SGen}(\mathsf{pp})$, set $\mathsf{S}[i] \leftarrow (\mathsf{id}_i, \mathsf{sk}_i, \mathsf{pk}_i)$, and, if $i \notin \mathsf{CU}$ set $\mathsf{HU} \leftarrow \mathsf{HU} \cup \{i\}$. Return $(\mathsf{id}_i, \mathsf{pk}_i)$.

SKey(i): If $i \notin$ HU return $\perp$. Otherwise return S$[i]$.

Sig$((j_i)_{i \in [n]}, (\vec{m}_i)_{i \in [n]})$: If S$[j_i] = \perp$ for any $i \in [n]$, or there exists $u, v \in [n], u \neq v$ so that $j_u = j_v$, return $\perp$. Otherwise sample a random tag τ and compute $(\sigma_{j_i} \leftarrow \mathsf{Sign}(\mathsf{S}[j_i][2], \vec{m}_i, \tau))_{i \in [n]}$, set $\mathsf{SIG}[\tau] \leftarrow \mathsf{SIG}[\tau] \cup \{(\vec{m}_i, \mathsf{S}[j_i][1])\}$ for $i \in [n]$, and return $(\sigma_{j_i})_{i \in [n]}$ and τ.

RoS$((j_i)_{i \in [n]}, (\vec{m}_i)_{i \in [n]}, b)$: If S$[j_i] = \perp$ or $j_i \in$ CU for any $i \in [n]$ return $\perp$. Otherwise sample τ uniformly at random and if $b = 0$ compute $(\sigma_{j_i} \leftarrow \mathsf{Sign}(\mathsf{S}[j_i][2], \vec{m}_i, \tau))_{i \in [n]}$. Else choose $(\vec{r}_i)_{i \in [n]} \xleftarrow{R} (\mathcal{M}^\ell)^n$ where $\mathcal{M}$ is the message space and compute $(\sigma_{j_i} \leftarrow \mathsf{Sign}(\mathsf{S}[j_i][2], \vec{r}_i, \tau))_{i \in [n]}$. Finally, return $(\sigma_{j_i})_{i \in [n]}$.

SR(i): If S$[i] = \perp \lor$ RK$[i] \neq \perp$ return $\perp$. Else, set RK$[i] \leftarrow \mathsf{SRGen}(\mathsf{S}[i][2], \mathsf{aux})$ and return RK$[i]$.

VR(i): If S$[i] = \perp \lor$ RK$[i] = \perp \lor$ AK$[i] \neq \perp$ return $\perp$. Else, set AK$[i] \leftarrow \mathsf{VRGen}(\mathsf{S}[i][3], \mathsf{mk}, \mathsf{RK}[i])$.

VRKey(i): Return AK$[i]$.

A$((\sigma_{j_i})_{i \in [n]}, (j_i)_{i \in [n]}, \tau, f)$: Check validity of all σ_{j_i}, whether $f \in \mathcal{F}_{\mathsf{pp}}$, whether $\mathsf{SIG}[\tau] = \perp$, and return $\perp$ if any check fails. Further, check whether there exists $u, v \in [n], u \neq v$ so that $j_u = j_v$ and return $\perp$ if so. Obtain $(\mathsf{ak}_{j_i})_{i \in [n]}$ from AK and return $\perp$ if AK$[j_i] = \perp$ for any $i \in [n]$. Set $\mathsf{SIG}[\tau] \leftarrow \bigcup_{i \in [n]} \{(\vec{m}_{j_i}, \mathsf{S}[j_i][1])\}$ and return $\Lambda \leftarrow \mathsf{Agg}((\mathsf{ak}_{j_i})_{i \in [n]}, (\sigma_{j_i})_{i \in [n]}, \tau, f)$.

We require a HPRA to be correct, signer unforgeable, aggregator unforgeable, and input private. We formally define those notions below. Intuitively, correctness requires that everything works as intended if everyone behaves honestly.

Definition 5 (Correctness). *A HPRA for a family of function classes $\{\mathcal{F}_{\mathsf{pp}}\}$ is correct, if for all κ, for all $\ell \leq \mathsf{poly}(\kappa)$, for all $\mathsf{pp} \leftarrow \mathsf{Gen}(1^\kappa, \ell)$ determining $\mathcal{F}_{\mathsf{pp}}$, for all $n \leq \mathsf{poly}(\kappa)$, for all $((\mathsf{id}_i, \mathsf{sk}_i, \mathsf{pk}_i) \leftarrow \mathsf{SGen}(\mathsf{pp}))_{i \in [n]}$, for all $(\mathsf{mk}, \mathsf{aux}) \leftarrow \mathsf{VGen}(\mathsf{pp})$, for all $(\vec{m}_i)_{i \in [n]}$, for all τ, for all $(\sigma_i \leftarrow \mathsf{Sign}(\mathsf{sk}_i, \vec{m}_i, \tau))_{i \in [n]}$, for all $(\mathsf{ak}_i \leftarrow \mathsf{VRGen}(\mathsf{pk}_i, \mathsf{mk}, \mathsf{SRGen}(\mathsf{sk}_i, \mathsf{aux})))_{i \in [n]}$, for all $f \in \mathcal{F}_{\mathsf{pp}}$, for all $\Lambda^* \leftarrow \mathsf{Agg}((\mathsf{ak}_i)_{i \in [n]}, (\sigma_i)_{i \in [n]}, \tau, f)$ it holds that $(\mathsf{Verify}(\mathsf{pk}_i, \vec{m}_i, \tau, \sigma_i) = 1)_{i \in [n]}$ and that $\mathsf{AVerify}(\mathsf{mk}, \Lambda^*, \mathsf{ID}, f) = 1$, where we sometimes omit to make the domains of the values over which we quantify explicit for brevity.*

Signer unforgeability requires that, as long as the aggregator remains honest, no coalition of dishonest signers can produce a valid aggregate authenticated message vector Λ with respect to function $f \in \mathcal{F}_{\mathsf{pp}}$ so that Λ is outside of the range of f evaluated on arbitrary combinations of actually signed vectors. Aggregator unforgeability is the natural counterpart of signer unforgeability, where the aggregator is dishonest while the signers are honest.[2]

---

[2] It is impossible to consider both, signers and aggregators, to be dishonest at the same time, as such a coalition could essentially authenticate everything. This is in contrast to the setting of proxy re-encryption, where it makes sense to model security in the face of receivers colluding with the proxy.

Definition 6 (T-Unforgeability). *Let* $T \in \{Signer, Aggregator\}$. *A HPRA for family of function classes* $\{\mathcal{F}_{pp}\}$ *is* T-*unforgeable, if for all PPT adversaries* $\mathcal{A}$ *there is a negligible function* $\epsilon(\cdot)$ *such that*

$$
\Pr \left[
\begin{array}{l}
pp \leftarrow Gen(1^\kappa, \ell), \\
(mk, aux) \leftarrow VGen(pp), \\
(\Lambda^*, ID^*, f^*) \leftarrow \mathcal{A}^{\mathcal{O}_T}(pp, aux), \\
(\vec{m}, \tau) \leftarrow AVerify(mk, \Lambda^*, ID^*, f^*)
\end{array}
:
\begin{array}{c}
\vec{m} \neq \bot \wedge f^* \in \mathcal{F}_{pp} \wedge \\
0 < n, \ell \leq poly(\kappa) \wedge \\
(\not\exists (\vec{m}_j)_{j \in [n]} : (\forall j \in [n] : \\
(\vec{m}_j, id_j^*) \in SIG[\tau]) \wedge \\
f^*((\vec{m}_j)_{j \in [n]}) = \vec{m})
\end{array}
\right] \leq \varepsilon(\kappa),
$$

where $\mathcal{O}_T := \{SG(\cdot), SKey(\cdot), SR(\cdot), VR(\cdot), A(\cdot, \cdot, \cdot)\}$ *for* $T = Signer$ *and* $\mathcal{O}_T := \{SG(\cdot), Sig(\,,\,), SR(\cdot), VR(\cdot), VRKey(\cdot)\}$ *for* $T = Aggregator$.

Input privacy captures the requirement that an aggregate authenticated message vector does not leak more about the inputs to f as the evaluation result and the description of f would leak on their own.

Definition 7 (Input Privacy). *A HPRA for a family of function classes* $\{\mathcal{F}_{pp}\}$ *is input private if for all* $\kappa \in \mathbb{N}$, *for all* $\ell \leq poly(\kappa)$, *for all* $pp \leftarrow Gen(1^\kappa, \ell)$ *determining* $\mathcal{F}_{pp}$, *for all* $f \in \mathcal{F}_{pp}$ *implicitly defining* n, *for all tags* τ, *and for all* $(\vec{m}_{11}, \ldots, \vec{m}_{n1})$ *and* $(\vec{m}_{12}, \ldots, \vec{m}_{n2})$ *where* $f(\vec{m}_{11}, \ldots, \vec{m}_{n1}) = f(\vec{m}_{12}, \ldots, \vec{m}_{n2})$, *for all* $(mk, aux) \leftarrow VGen(pp)$, *for all* $((sk_i, pk_i) \leftarrow SGen(pp))_{i \in [n]}$, $(ak_i \leftarrow SRGen(sk_i, aux, VRGen(pk_i, mk)))_{i \in [n]}$, *the following distributions are identical:*

$$\{Agg((ak_i)_{i \in [n]}, (Sign(sk_i, \vec{m}_{i1}, \tau))_{i \in [n]}, \tau, f)\},$$
$$\{Agg((ak_i)_{i \in [n]}, (Sign(sk_i, \vec{m}_{i2}, \tau))_{i \in [n]}, \tau, f)\}.$$

Additionally, a HPRA may provide output privacy. It models that the aggregator neither learns the inputs nor the result of the evaluation of f.

Definition 8 (Output Privacy). *A HPRA for a family of function classes* $\{\mathcal{F}_{pp}\}$ *is output private, if for all PPT adversaries* $\mathcal{A}$ *there is a negligible function* $\epsilon(\cdot)$ *such that:*

$$
\Pr \left[
\begin{array}{l}
pp \leftarrow Gen(1^\kappa, \ell), (CU, st) \leftarrow \mathcal{A}(pp), b \xleftarrow{R} \{0, 1\}, \\
(mk, aux) \leftarrow VGen(pp), \mathcal{O} \leftarrow \{SG(\cdot), SKey(\cdot), \\
RoS(\cdot, \cdot, b), SR(\cdot), VR(\cdot), VRKey(\cdot)\}, \\
b^* \leftarrow \mathcal{A}^{\mathcal{O}}(aux, st)
\end{array}
: b = b^*
\right] \leq 1/2 + \varepsilon(\kappa).
$$

4   An Input Private Scheme for Linear Functions

Now we present our first HPRA for the family of linear function classes $\{\mathcal{F}_{pp}^{lin}\}$. The main challenge we face is to construct a signature scheme with an associated HOM-MAC scheme, where the translation of the signatures under one key to a MAC under some other key works out. Since we believe that our HOM-MAC may as well be useful in other settings we present it as a standalone building block and then proceed with our full construction, where HOM-MAC is used as a

$\mathcal{P}(\kappa, \ell)$: Run $\mathsf{BG} \leftarrow \mathsf{BGGen}(1^\kappa)$, fix $H : \mathbb{Z}_q \rightarrow \mathbb{G}$, choose $(g_i)_{i \in [\ell]} \overset{R}{\leftarrow} (\mathbb{G}^*)^\ell$, and return $\mathsf{pp} \leftarrow (\mathsf{BG}, H, (g_i)_{i \in [\ell]}, \ell)$.

$\mathcal{G}(\mathsf{pp})$: Choose $\alpha \overset{R}{\leftarrow} \mathbb{Z}_p$ and return $\mathsf{sk} \leftarrow (\mathsf{pp}, \alpha)$.

$\mathcal{S}(\mathsf{sk}, \vec{v}, \mathsf{id}, \tau)$: Parse sk as (pp, α) and return $\mu \leftarrow e(H(\tau \| \mathsf{id}) \cdot \prod_{j \in [\ell]} g_j^{v_j}, g^\alpha)$.

$\mathcal{C}(\mathsf{pp}, f, (\mu_i)_{i \in [n]})$: Parse f as $(\omega_i)_{i \in [n]}$ and return $\mu \leftarrow \prod_{i \in [n]} \mu_i^{\omega_i}$.

$\mathcal{V}(\mathsf{sk}, \vec{v}, \mu, \tau, (\mathsf{id}_i)_{i \in [n]}, f)$: Parse sk as (pp, α), f as $(\omega_i)_{i \in [n]}$, and output 1 if the following holds, and 0 otherwise: $\mu = e(\prod_{i \in [n]} H(\tau \| \mathsf{id}_i)^{\omega_i} \prod_{j \in [\ell]} g_j^{v_j}, g^\alpha)$

Scheme 1. Linearly homomorphic MAC based on [13].

submodule. Both build upon the ideas used in the signature scheme presented in [13].

A Suitable Linearly Homomorphic MAC. We present our HOM-MAC in Scheme 1. We can not recycle the security arguments from [13] as we require the ability to submit arbitrary tags τ to the Sig oracle. Thus we directly prove unforgeability.

Lemma 1 (Proven in the full version). *If the bilinear DDH (BDDH) assumption holds, then Scheme 1 is an unforgeable HOM-MAC in the ROM.*

Our Input Private Construction. In Scheme 2 we present our HPRA construction for the family of linear function classes $\{\mathcal{F}_{\mathsf{pp}}^{\mathsf{lin}}\}$. It allows to authenticate vectors of length ℓ, so that the same function can be evaluated per vector component. In our application scenario we have $\ell = 1$. We allow one to parametrize our construction with an algorithm $\mathsf{Eval}(\cdot, \cdot)$, which defines how to compute $f \in \mathcal{F}_{\mathsf{pp}}^{\mathsf{lin}}$ on the message vector. When directly instantiating Scheme 2, Eval is defined as $\mathsf{Eval}(f, (\vec{m}_i)_{i \in [n]}) := f((\vec{m}_i)_{i \in [n]})$.

Theorem 1 (Proven in the full version). *If HOM-MAC in Scheme 1 is unforgeable and the eBCDH assumption holds, then Scheme 2 represents a signer unforgeable, aggregator unforgeable and input private HPRA for the family of linear function classes $\{\mathcal{F}_{\mathsf{pp}}^{\mathsf{lin}}\}$ in the ROM.*

5   Adding Output Privacy

An additional goal is that the aggregator neither learns the input nor the output (output privacy). On our way to achieve this, we formally define the notion of homomorphic proxy-re encryption (HPRE) and develop an instantiation for the family of linear function classes $\{\mathcal{F}_{\mathsf{pp}}^{\mathsf{lin}}\}$. Based on this, we extend Scheme 2 to additionally provide output privacy.

$\underline{\mathsf{Gen}(1^\kappa, \ell)}$: Run $\mathsf{BG} \leftarrow \mathsf{BGGen}(1^\kappa)$, fix $H : \mathbb{Z}_q \rightarrow \mathbb{G}$, choose $(g_i)_{i \in [\ell]} \xleftarrow{R} \mathbb{G}^\ell$, and return $\mathsf{pp} \leftarrow (\mathsf{BG}, H, (g_i)_{i \in [\ell]}, \ell)$.

$\underline{\mathsf{SGen}(\mathsf{pp})}$: Choose $\beta \xleftarrow{R} \mathbb{Z}_q$, set $\mathsf{id} \leftarrow g^\beta$, $\mathsf{pk} \leftarrow (\mathsf{pp}, g^\beta, g^{1/\beta})$, $\mathsf{sk} \leftarrow (\mathsf{pk}, \beta)$, and return $(\mathsf{id}, \mathsf{sk}, \mathsf{pk})$.

$\underline{\mathsf{VGen}(\mathsf{pp})}$: Choose $\alpha \xleftarrow{R} \mathbb{Z}_q$, set $\mathsf{aux} \leftarrow \emptyset$, $\mathsf{mk} \leftarrow (\mathsf{pp}, \alpha)$ and return $(\mathsf{mk}, \mathsf{aux})$.

$\underline{\mathsf{Sign}(\mathsf{sk}, \vec{m}, \tau)}$: Parse sk as $(((\mathsf{BG}, H, (g_i)_{i \in [\ell]}, \ell), g^\beta, \cdot), \beta)$, compute and return $\sigma \leftarrow (\sigma', \vec{m})$, where

$$\sigma' \leftarrow \left(H(\tau \| g^\beta) \cdot \prod_{i=1}^{\ell} g_i^{m_i} \right)^\beta.$$

$\underline{\mathsf{Verify}(\mathsf{pk}, \vec{m}, \tau, \sigma)}$: Parse pk as $((\mathsf{BG}, H, (g_i)_{i \in [\ell]}, \ell), g^\beta,)$, and σ as $(\sigma', \vec{m}')$, and return 1 if the following holds and 0 otherwise:

$$e(H(\tau \| g^\beta) \cdot \prod_{i=1}^{\ell} g_i^{m_i}, g^\beta) = e(\sigma, g) \quad \wedge \quad \vec{m} = \vec{m}'.$$

$\underline{\mathsf{SRGen}(\mathsf{sk}_i, \mathsf{aux})}$: Return $\mathsf{rk}_i \leftarrow \emptyset$.

$\underline{\mathsf{VRGen}(\mathsf{pk}_i, \mathsf{mk}, \mathsf{rk}_i)}$: Parse pk_i as $(\cdot, \cdot, g^{1/\beta_i})$, mk as $(\cdot, \alpha)$, and return $\mathsf{ak}_i \leftarrow (g^{1/\beta_i})^\alpha$.

$\underline{\mathsf{Agg}((\mathsf{ak}_i)_{i \in [n]}, (\sigma_i)_{i \in [n]}, \tau, f)}$: Parse f as $(\omega_i)_{i \in [n]}$, and for $i \in [n]$ parse σ_i as $(\sigma_i', \vec{m}_i)$ and return $\Lambda \leftarrow (\mathsf{Eval}(f, (\vec{m}_i)_{i \in [n]}), \mu, \tau)$, where

$$\mu \leftarrow \prod_{i \in [n]} e(\sigma_i'^{\omega_i}, \mathsf{ak}_i).$$

$\underline{\mathsf{AVerify}(\mathsf{mk}, \Lambda, \mathsf{ID}, f)}$: Parse mk as (pp, α), Λ as $(\vec{m}, \mu, \tau)$, ID as $(g^{\beta_i})_{i \in [n]}$ and f as $(\omega_i)_{i \in [n]}$ and return $(\vec{m}, \tau)$ if the following holds, and $(\bot, \bot)$ otherwise:

$$\mu' = \left(\prod_{i=1}^{n} e(g^{\omega_i}, H(\tau \| g^{\beta_i})) \cdot e(\prod_{i=1}^{\ell} g_i^{m_i}, g) \right)^\alpha$$

Scheme 2. HPRA scheme for the family of linear function families $\{\mathcal{F}_{\mathsf{pp}}^{\mathsf{lin}}\}$ parametrized by Eval.

5.1 Homomorphic Proxy Re-Encryption

A homomorphic proxy re-encryption scheme (HPRE) is a PRE which additionally allows the homomorphic evaluation of functions on the ciphertexts. This functionality firstly allows to aggregate messages encrypted under the same public key, and, secondly, to transform the ciphertext holding the evaluation of a function to a ciphertext for another entity, when given the respective proxy re-encryption key. We stress that if the initial ciphertexts are with respect to different public keys, then one can use the respective re-encryption keys to transform them to a common public key before evaluating the function. More formally:

Definition 9 (HPRE). *A HPRE for the family of function classes $\{\mathcal{F}_{\mathsf{pp}}\}$ is a PRE with an additional evaluation algorithm $\mathcal{EV}$.*

$\mathcal{EV}(\mathsf{pp}, f, \vec{c})$: *This algorithm takes public parameters* pp, *a function* $f \in \mathcal{F}_{\mathsf{pp}}$, *and a vector of ciphertexts* $\vec{c} = (c_i)_{i \in [n]}$ *to messages* $(m_i)_{i \in [n]}$ *all under public key* pk, *and outputs a ciphertext* c *to message* $f((m_i)_{i \in [n]})$ *under* pk.

Additionally, we require the following compactness notion (analogous to [20]).

Definition 10 (Compactness). *A HPRE for the family of function classes* $\{\mathcal{F}_{\mathsf{pp}}\}$ *is called compact if for all* $\mathsf{pp} \leftarrow \mathcal{P}(1^\kappa)$ *and for all* $f \in \mathcal{F}_{\mathsf{pp}}$ *the running time of the algorithms* $\vec{\mathcal{D}}$ *is bounded by a fixed polynomial in the security parameter* κ.

Besides the straightforward adoption of correctness, IND-CPA$^-$ remains identical ($\mathcal{EV}$ is a public algorithm). However, we require an IND-CPA$^-$ variant, where the adversary may adaptively choose the targeted user. To the best of our knowledge, such a notion does not exist for PRE. We introduce such a notion (termed mt-IND-CPA$^-$) and show that it is implied by the conventional IND-CPA notions.

Definition 11 (mt-IND-CPA$^-$). *A (H)PRE is* mt-IND-CPA$^-$ *secure, if for all PPT adversaries* $\mathcal{A}$ *there is a negligible function* $\varepsilon(\cdot)$ *such that*

$$\Pr\left[\begin{array}{l} \mathsf{pp} \leftarrow \mathcal{P}(1^\kappa), b \xleftarrow{R} \{0,1\}, \\ (\mathsf{sk}_h, \mathsf{pk}_h) \leftarrow \mathcal{G}(\mathsf{pp}), \mathcal{O} \leftarrow \{\mathsf{G}(\cdot), \mathsf{RG}(\cdot)\}, \\ (m_0, m_1, i^*, \mathsf{st}) \leftarrow \mathcal{A}^{\mathcal{O}}(\mathsf{pp}, \mathsf{pk}_h), \\ c \leftarrow \mathcal{E}^2(m_b, \mathsf{pk}_{i^*}), b^* \leftarrow \mathcal{A}(\mathsf{st}, c) \end{array} : b = b^*\right] \leq 1/2 + \varepsilon(\kappa),$$

where the environment holds an initially empty list $\mathtt{HU}$. G *and* RG *are defined as:*

$\mathsf{G}(i)$: *If* $\mathtt{HU}[i] \neq \perp$ *return* $\perp$. *Otherwise, run* $(\mathsf{sk}_i, \mathsf{pk}_i) \leftarrow \mathcal{G}(\mathsf{pp})$, *set* $\mathtt{HU}[i] \leftarrow (\mathsf{sk}_i, \mathsf{pk}_i)$, *and return* pk_i.
$\mathsf{RG}(i)$: *If* $\mathtt{HU}[i] = \perp$ *return* $\perp$. *Otherwise, set* $\mathsf{rk}_{i \to h} \leftarrow \mathcal{RG}(\mathtt{HU}[i][1], \mathsf{pk}_h)$ *and return* $\mathsf{rk}_{i \to j}$.

Lemma 2 (proven in the full version). *Every* IND-CPA$^-$ *(and thus every* IND-CPA*) secure PRE also satisfies* mt-IND-CPA$^-$ *security.*

HPREConstruction for the Family of Linear Function Classes. We state our construction in Scheme 3. Essentially, we build upon the PRE scheme in [5, third attempt] and turn it into a HPRE for the family of linear function classes $\{\mathcal{F}_{\mathsf{pp}}^{\mathsf{lin}}\}$, henceforth referred to as HPRE$_{\mathsf{lin}}$. For the desired homomorphism we use a standard trick in the context of ElGamal-like encryption schemes: we encode messages $m \in \mathbb{Z}_q$ into the exponent and encrypt $\mathbf{g}^m$. Decryption then yields $m' = \mathbf{g}^m$ and one additionally needs to compute $m = \log_{\mathbf{g}} m'$ to obtain m. Thus, for the schemes to remain efficient, the size of the message space needs to be polynomial in the security parameter. While this might sound quite restrictive, we stress that in practical settings one deals with numerical values where messages in the order of millions to billions are by far sufficient. Thus, this type of decryption is not a limitation and entirely practical.

As $\mathcal{EV}$ is a public algorithm it does not influence IND-CPA security. Thus, our argumentation is identical to [5] and we can use the following theorem.

$\mathcal{P}(1^\kappa)$: Run $\mathsf{BG} \leftarrow \mathsf{BGGen}(1^\kappa)$, and return $\mathsf{pp} \leftarrow \mathsf{BG}$.

$\mathcal{G}(\mathsf{pp})$: Choose $(a_1, a_2) \overset{R}{\leftarrow} \mathbb{Z}_q^2$, and return $(\mathsf{rsk}_A, \mathsf{rpk}_A) \leftarrow ((a_1, a_2), (\mathbf{g}^{a_1}, g^{a_2}))$.

$\mathcal{RG}(\mathsf{rsk}_A, \mathsf{rpk}_B)$: Parse rsk_A as $(a_{1A}, \cdot)$ and rpk_B as $(\cdot, g^{a_{2B}})$ and return $\mathsf{rk}_{A \to B} \leftarrow (g^{a_{2B}})^{a_{1A}}$.

$\mathcal{E}^1(\mathsf{rpk}, m)$: Parse rpk as $(\mathbf{g}^{a_1}, \cdot)$, choose $k \overset{R}{\leftarrow} \mathbb{Z}_q$, and return $c \leftarrow (\mathbf{g}^k, \mathbf{g}^m \cdot (\mathbf{g}^{a_1})^k, 1)$

$\mathcal{E}^2(\mathsf{rpk}, m)$: Parse rpk as $(\mathbf{g}^{a_1}, \cdot)$, choose $k \overset{R}{\leftarrow} \mathbb{Z}_q$, and return $c \leftarrow (g^k, \mathbf{g}^m \cdot (\mathbf{g}^{a_1})^k, 2)$

$\mathcal{RE}(\mathsf{rk}_{A \to B}, c_A)$: Parse c_A as $(c_1, c_2, 2)$ and return $c \leftarrow (e(c_1, \mathsf{rk}_{A \to B}), c_2, R)$

$\mathcal{D}^1(\mathsf{rsk}, c)$: Parse c as (c_1, c_2, c_3) and rsk as (a_1, a_2), and return $\mathbf{g}^m \leftarrow c_2 \cdot c_1^{-a_1}$ if $c_3 = 1$ and $\mathbf{g}^m \leftarrow c_2 \cdot c_1^{-1/a_2}$ if $c_3 = R$.

$\mathcal{D}^2(\mathsf{rsk}, c)$: Parse c as $(c_1, c_2, 2)$ and rsk as (a_1, a_2), and return $\mathbf{g}^m \leftarrow c_2 \cdot e(g, c_1^{-a_1})$.

$\mathcal{EV}(\mathsf{pp}, f, \vec{c})$: Parse f as $(\omega_1, \ldots, \omega_n)$ and $\vec{c}$ as $(c_i)_{i \in [n]}$, and return $c \leftarrow \prod_{i \in [n]} c_i^{\omega_i}$, where multiplication and exponentiation is component-wise.

Scheme 3. HPRE$_{\mathsf{lin}}$ based on [5, third attempt].

Theorem 2 (cf. [5]). *If the* eDBDH *assumption holds in* $(\mathbb{G}, \mathbb{G}_T)$ *then Scheme 3 is an* IND-CPA *secure* HPRE$_{\mathsf{lin}}$.

We note that compactness of Scheme 3 (Definition 10) is easy to verify.

HPRE$_{\mathsf{lin}}$ **for Vectors.** We extend HPRE$_{\mathsf{lin}}$ to vectors over $\mathbb{Z}_q$, while preserving the support for re-encryption and the homomorphic properties. It turns out that we can employ a communication efficient solution. That is, borrowing the idea of randomness re-use from [9] and applying it to HPRE$_{\mathsf{lin}}$, we can reduce the size of the ciphertexts as long as no re-encryption is performed. Upon setup, we have to fix a maximal length ℓ of the message vectors. The secret and the public keys are then of the form $\mathsf{rsk} \leftarrow (\mathsf{rsk}_i)_{i \in [\ell]} = ((a_{1i}, a_{2i}))_{i \in [\ell]}$, $\mathsf{rpk} \leftarrow (\mathsf{rpk}_i)_{i \in [\ell]} = ((\mathbf{g}^{a_{1i}}, g^{a_{2i}}))_{i \in [\ell]}$, where $(a_{1i}, a_{2i})_{i \in [\ell]} \overset{R}{\leftarrow} (\mathbb{Z}_q^2)^\ell$. First and second level encryption are defined as

$$\mathcal{E}_\ell^1(\mathsf{rpk}, \vec{m}) := (\mathbf{g}^k, (\mathbf{g}^{m_i} \cdot \mathsf{rpk}_i[1]^k)_{i \in [\ell]}, 1), \text{ and}$$

$$\mathcal{E}_\ell^2(\mathsf{rpk}, \vec{m}) := (g^k, (\mathbf{g}^{m_i} \cdot \mathsf{rpk}_i[1]^k)_{i \in [\ell]}, 2), \text{ respectively.}$$

Decryption $\mathcal{D}_\ell^j(\cdot, \cdot)$ of a ciphertext $(c[1], (c[i+1])_{i \in [\ell]}, j)$ is defined as $\mathcal{D}_\ell^1(\mathsf{rsk}, \vec{c}) := (c[i+1] \cdot c[1]^{-\mathsf{rsk}_i[1]})_{i \in [\ell]}$, and $\mathcal{D}_\ell^2(\mathsf{rsk}, \vec{c}) := (c[i+1] \cdot e(c[1], g^{-\mathsf{rsk}_i[1]}))_{i \in [\ell]}$. Re-encryption key generation is $\mathcal{RG}_\ell(\mathsf{rsk}_A, \mathsf{rpk}_B) := (((\mathsf{rpk}_B)_i[2])^{(\mathsf{rsk}_A)_i[1]})_{i \in [\ell]}$. From a second level ciphertext $\vec{c}_A$ for A and a re-encryption key $\mathsf{rk}_{A \to B}$, one can compute a ciphertext $\vec{c}_B$ for B as $\vec{c}_B \leftarrow \mathcal{RE}(\mathsf{rk}_{A \to B}, \vec{c}_A) := ((e(c_A[1], \mathsf{rk}_{A \to B}[i]), c_A[i+1]))_{i \in [\ell]}$. Note that re-encrypted ciphertexts have a different form.

Thus we do not need to add the level as suffix. Decryption $\mathcal{D}^1_\ell(\cdot, \cdot)$ for re-encrypted ciphertexts is $\mathcal{D}^1_\ell(\mathsf{rsk}, (c_i)_{i \in [\ell]}) := (c_i[2] \cdot c_i[1]^{-1/\mathsf{rsk}_i[2]})_{i \in [\ell]}$.

Theorem 3. *If the* eDBDH *assumption holds, then the extension of* $\mathsf{HPRE}_{\mathsf{lin}}$ *as described above, yields an* IND- CPA *secure* $\mathsf{HPRE}_{\mathsf{lin}}$ *for vectors.*

Proof (sketch). IND-CPA security of the original scheme implies Theorem 3 under a polynomial loss: using ℓ hybrids, where in hybrid i $(1 \leq i \leq \ell)$ the i-th ciphertext component is exchanged by random under the original strategy in [5].

Combining the theorem above with Lemma 2 yields:

Corollary 1. *The extension of* $\mathsf{HPRE}_{\mathsf{lin}}$ *as described above yields an* mt-IND-CPA$^-$ *secure* $\mathsf{HPRE}_{\mathsf{lin}}$ *for vectors.*

5.2   Putting the Pieces Together: Output Privacy

Our idea is to combine Scheme 2 with the $\mathsf{HPRE}_{\mathsf{lin}}$ presented above. In doing so, we face some obstacles. First, a naïve combination of those primitives does not suit our needs: one can still verify guesses for signed messages using solely the signatures, since signatures are publicly verifiable. Second, switching to a MAC for the data sources is also no option, as this would require an interactive re-key generation. This is excluded by our model as we explicitly want to avoid it. Thus, we pursue a different direction and turn the signatures used in Scheme 2 into a MAC-like primitive by blinding a signature with a random element g^r. An aggregated MAC holding an evaluation of f is then blinded by $g^{f(\dots, r, \dots)}$, i.e., the receiver needs to evaluate the function f on the all blinding values from the single sources. Now the question arises as how to transmit the blinding values to the receiver. Using our $\mathsf{HPRE}_{\mathsf{lin}}$ for vectors yields an arguably elegant solution: by treating the randomness as an additional vector component, we can use the re-encryption features of the $\mathsf{HPRE}_{\mathsf{lin}}$. More importantly, by executing the $\mathcal{EV}$ algorithm the aggregator simultaneously evaluates the function f on the data and on the randomness so that the receiver can directly obtain the blinding value $f(\dots, r, \dots)$ upon decryption.

Note on the Instantiation. Augmenting Scheme 2 to obtain Scheme 4 using $\mathsf{HPRE}_{\mathsf{lin}}$ requires an alternative decryption strategy for the vector component containing r, as r is uniformly random in $\mathbb{Z}_q$ and can thus not be efficiently recovered. Fortunately, obtaining $r \in \mathbb{Z}_q$ is not required, as g^r (resp. $\mathbf{g}^r$) is sufficient to unblind the signature (resp. MAC). Those values are efficiently recoverable.

Theorem 4 (proven in the full version). *If Scheme 2 is signer and aggregator unforgeable, and* $\mathsf{HPRE}_{\mathsf{lin}}$ *for vectors is* mt-IND-CPA$^-$ *secure, then Scheme 4 is a signer and aggregator unforgeable, input and output private* HPRA *for class* $\mathcal{F}_{\mathsf{lin}}$.

$\mathsf{Gen}(1^\kappa, \ell)$: Fix a homomorphic $\mathsf{PRE} = (\mathcal{P}, \mathcal{G}, \vec{\mathcal{E}}, \vec{\mathcal{D}}, \mathcal{RG}, \mathcal{RE}, \mathcal{EV})$ for class $\mathcal{F}_{\mathsf{lin}}$ and the $\mathsf{HPRA}(\mathcal{EV}) = (\mathbf{Gen}, \mathbf{SGen}, \mathbf{VGen}, \mathbf{Sign}, \mathbf{Verify}, \mathbf{SRGen}, \mathbf{VRGen}, \mathbf{Agg}, \mathbf{AVerify})$ from Scheme 2 such that $\mathcal{M}_{\mathsf{PRA}} \subseteq \mathcal{M}_{\mathsf{PRE}}$, run $\mathsf{pp}_s \leftarrow \mathbf{Gen}(1^\kappa, \ell)$, $\mathsf{pp}_e \leftarrow \mathcal{P}(1^\kappa, \ell + 1)$, and return $\mathsf{pp} \leftarrow (\mathsf{pp}_s, \mathsf{pp}_e)$.

$\mathsf{SGen}(\mathsf{pp})$: Run $(\mathbf{id}, \mathbf{sk}, \mathbf{pk}) \leftarrow \mathbf{SGen}(\mathsf{pp}_s)$, $(\mathsf{rsk}, \mathsf{rpk}) \leftarrow \mathcal{G}(\mathsf{pp}_e)$, and return $(\mathsf{id}, \mathsf{sk}, \mathsf{pk}) \leftarrow (\mathbf{id}, (\mathbf{sk}, \mathsf{rsk}, \mathsf{rpk}), \mathbf{pk})$.

$\mathsf{VGen}(\mathsf{pp})$: Run $(\mathbf{mk}, \mathbf{aux}) \leftarrow \mathbf{VGen}(\mathsf{pp}_s)$, $(\mathsf{rsk}, \mathsf{rpk}) \leftarrow \mathcal{G}(\mathsf{pp}_e)$, and return $(\mathsf{mk}, \mathsf{aux}) \leftarrow ((\mathbf{mk}, \mathsf{rsk}), (\mathbf{aux}, \mathsf{rpk}))$.

$\mathsf{Sign}(\mathsf{sk}, \vec{m}, \tau)$: Parse sk as $(\mathbf{sk}, \cdot, \mathsf{rpk})$, choose $r \xleftarrow{R} \mathbb{Z}_q$, and return $\sigma \leftarrow (\sigma' \cdot g^r, \vec{c})$, where

$$(\sigma', \cdot) \leftarrow \mathbf{Sign}(\mathbf{sk}, \vec{m}, \tau) \text{ and } \vec{c} \leftarrow \mathcal{E}_{\ell+1}^2(\mathsf{rpk}, \vec{m}\|r).$$

$\mathsf{SRGen}(\mathsf{sk}_i, \mathsf{aux})$: Parse sk_i as $(\mathbf{sk}_i, \mathsf{rsk}_i, \mathsf{rpk}_i)$ and aux as $(\mathbf{aux}, \mathsf{rpk})$. Obtain $\mathbf{rk}_i \leftarrow \mathbf{SRGen}(\mathbf{sk}_i, \mathbf{aux})$ and $\mathsf{prk}_i \leftarrow \mathcal{RG}(\mathsf{rsk}_i, \mathsf{rpk})$, and return $\mathsf{rk}_i \leftarrow (\mathbf{rk}_i, \mathsf{prk}_i)$.

$\mathsf{VRGen}(\mathsf{pk}_i, \mathsf{mk}, \mathsf{rk}_i)$: Parse pk_i as $\mathbf{pk}_i$ and mk as $(\mathbf{mk}, \cdot)$, obtain $\mathsf{ak}_i \leftarrow \mathbf{VRGen}(\mathbf{pk}_i, \mathbf{mk})$ and return $\mathsf{ak}_i \leftarrow (\mathbf{ak}_i, \mathsf{rk}_i)$.

$\mathsf{Agg}((\mathsf{ak}_i)_{i \in [n]}, (\sigma_i)_{i \in [n]}, \tau, f)$: For $i \in [n]$ parse ak_i as $(\mathbf{ak}_i, (\mathbf{rk}_i, \mathsf{prk}_i))$, σ_i as $(\sigma'_i, \vec{c}_i)$. Output $\Lambda \leftarrow (\vec{c}', \mu, \tau)$, where

$$(\vec{c}'_i \leftarrow \mathcal{RE}(\mathsf{prk}_i, \vec{c}_i))_{i \in [n]}, \quad (\vec{c}', \mu, \tau) \leftarrow \mathbf{Agg}((\mathbf{ak}_i)_{i \in [n]}, (\sigma'_i, \vec{c}'_i)_{i \in [n]}, f).$$

$\mathsf{AVerify}(\mathsf{mk}, \Lambda, \mathsf{ID}, f)$: Parse mk as $(\mathbf{mk}, \mathsf{rsk})$ and Λ as $(\vec{c}, \mu, \tau)$, obtain $\vec{m}'\|r \leftarrow \mathcal{D}_{\ell+1}^1(\mathsf{rsk}, \vec{c})$ and return $(\vec{m}, \tau)$ if the following holds, and $(\bot, \bot)$ otherwise:

$$\mathbf{AVerify}(\mathbf{mk}, (\vec{m}, \mu \cdot (\mathbf{g}^r)^{-1}, \tau), \mathsf{ID}, f) = 1$$

Scheme 4. Output private HPRA scheme for the family of linear function classes $\{\mathcal{F}_{\mathsf{pp}}^{\mathsf{lin}}\}$ with $\mathcal{F}_{\mathsf{lin}}$ with $\mathsf{Eval}(\cdot, \cdot) := \mathcal{EV}(\mathsf{pp}, \cdot, \cdot)$.

6   Conclusion

In this paper we introduce the notion of homomorphic proxy re-authenticators. This concept covers various important issues in the multi-user data aggregation setting not considered by previous works. We present two provably secure and practically efficient instantiations of our novel concept, which differ regarding the strength of the privacy guarantees. Our schemes are modular in the sense that they are constructed from building blocks which may as well be useful in other settings. One important building block is the concept of homomorphic proxy re-encryption, which we also introduce and construct in this paper.

Acknowledgements. We thank David Nuñez for his valuable comments on a draft of this paper.

References

1. Abe, M., Hoshino, F., Ohkubo, M.: Design in Type-I, run in Type-III: fast and scalable bilinear-type conversion using integer programming. In: CRYPTO 2016 (2016)
2. Agrawal, S., Boneh, D.: Homomorphic MACs: MAC-based integrity for network coding. In: Abdalla, M., Pointcheval, D., Fouque, P.-A., Vergnaud, D. (eds.) ACNS 2009. LNCS, vol. 5536, pp. 292–305. Springer, Heidelberg (2009). https://doi.org/10.1007/978-3-642-01957-9_18
3. Akinyele, J.A., Garman, C., Hohenberger, S.: Automating fast and secure translations from Type-I to Type-III pairing schemes. In: CCS 2015 (2015)
4. Alperin-Sheriff, J., Peikert, C.: Faster bootstrapping with polynomial error. In: Garay, J.A., Gennaro, R. (eds.) CRYPTO 2014. LNCS, vol. 8616, pp. 297–314. Springer, Heidelberg (2014). https://doi.org/10.1007/978-3-662-44371-2_17
5. Ateniese, G., Fu, K., Green, M., Hohenberger, S.: Improved proxy re-encryption schemes with applications to secure distributed storage. ACM Trans. Inf. Syst. Secur. **9**(1), 1–30 (2006)
6. Ateniese, G., Hohenberger, S.: Proxy re-signatures: new definitions, algorithms, and applications. In: CCS 2015 (2005)
7. Ayday, E., Raisaro, J.L., Hubaux, J., Rougemont, J.: Protecting and evaluating genomic privacy in medical tests and personalized medicine. In: WPES 2013 (2013)
8. Backes, M., Fiore, D., Reischuk, R.M.: Verifiable delegation of computation on outsourced data. In: CCS 2013 (2013)
9. Bellare, M., Boldyreva, A., Kurosawa, K., Staddon, J.: Multirecipient encryption schemes: How to save on bandwidth and computation without sacrificing security. IEEE Trans. Inf. Theory **53**(11), 3927–3943 (2007)
10. Benhamouda, F., Joye, M., Libert, B.: A new framework for privacy-preserving aggregation of time-series data. ACM Trans. Inf. Syst. Secur. **18**(3), 21 (2016)
11. Blaze, M., Bleumer, G., Strauss, M.: Divertible protocols and atomic proxy cryptography. In: Nyberg, K. (ed.) EUROCRYPT 1998. LNCS, vol. 1403, pp. 127–144. Springer, Heidelberg (1998). https://doi.org/10.1007/BFb0054122
12. Blazy, O., Bultel, X., Lafourcade, P.: Two secure anonymous proxy-based data storages. In: SECRYPT, pp. 251–258 (2016)
13. Boneh, D., Freeman, D., Katz, J., Waters, B.: Signing a linear subspace: signature schemes for network coding. In: Jarecki, S., Tsudik, G. (eds.) PKC 2009. LNCS, vol. 5443, pp. 68–87. Springer, Heidelberg (2009). https://doi.org/10.1007/978-3-642-00468-1_5
14. Boneh, D., Lewi, K., Montgomery, H., Raghunathan, A.: Key homomorphic PRFs and their applications. In: Canetti, R., Garay, J.A. (eds.) CRYPTO 2013. LNCS, vol. 8042, pp. 410–428. Springer, Heidelberg (2013). https://doi.org/10.1007/978-3-642-40041-4_23
15. Borceaa, C., Guptaa, A.B.D., Polyakova, Y., Rohloffa, K., Ryana, G.: Picador: End-to-end encrypted publish-subscribe information distribution with proxy re-encryption. Future Gener. Comp. Syst. **62**, 119–127 (2016)
16. Canard, S., Devigne, J.: Highly privacy-protecting data sharing in a tree structure. Future Gener. Comp. Syst. **62**, 119–127 (2016)
17. Canetti, R., Hohenberger, S.: Chosen-ciphertext secure proxy re-encryption. In: CCS, pp. 185–194 (2007)
18. Castelluccia, C., Chan, A.C.F., Mykletun, E., Tsudik, G.: Efficient and provably secure aggregation of encrypted data in wireless sensor networks. ACM Trans. Sen. Netw. **5**(3) (2009)

19. Catalano, D.: Homomorphic signatures and message authentication codes. In: Abdalla, M., De Prisco, R. (eds.) SCN 2014. LNCS, vol. 8642, pp. 514–519. Springer, Cham (2014). https://doi.org/10.1007/978-3-319-10879-7_29
20. Catalano, D., Fiore, D.: Using linearly-homomorphic encryption to evaluate degree-2 functions on encrypted data. In: CCS 2015 (2015)
21. Catalano, D., Fiore, D., Warinschi, B.: Homomorphic signatures with efficient verification for polynomial functions. In: Garay, J.A., Gennaro, R. (eds.) CRYPTO 2014. LNCS, vol. 8616, pp. 371–389. Springer, Heidelberg (2014). https://doi.org/10.1007/978-3-662-44371-2_21
22. Catalano, D., Marcedone, A., Puglisi, O.: Authenticating computation on groups: new homomorphic primitives and applications. In: Sarkar, P., Iwata, T. (eds.) ASIACRYPT 2014. LNCS, vol. 8874, pp. 193–212. Springer, Heidelberg (2014). https://doi.org/10.1007/978-3-662-45608-8_11
23. Chan, T.-H.H., Shi, E., Song, D.: Privacy-preserving stream aggregation with fault tolerance. In: Keromytis, A.D. (ed.) FC 2012. LNCS, vol. 7397, pp. 200–214. Springer, Heidelberg (2012). https://doi.org/10.1007/978-3-642-32946-3_15
24. Danezis, G., Livshits, B.: Towards ensuring client-side computational integrity. In: CCSW 2011 (2011)
25. Derler, D., Slamanig, D.: Key-homomorphic signatures and applications to multiparty signatures. Cryptology ePrint Archive **2016**, 792 (2016)
26. Fiore, D., Mitrokotsa, A., Nizzardo, L., Pagnin, E.: Multi-key homomorphic authenticators. In: Cheon, J.H., Takagi, T. (eds.) ASIACRYPT 2016. LNCS, vol. 10032, pp. 499–530. Springer, Heidelberg (2016). https://doi.org/10.1007/978-3-662-53890-6_17
27. Gentry, C.: On Fully homomorphic encryption using ideal lattices. In: STOC 2009 (2009)
28. Gentry, C., Sahai, A., Waters, B.: Homomorphic encryption from learning with errors: conceptually-simpler, asymptotically-faster, attribute-based. In: Canetti, R., Garay, J.A. (eds.) CRYPTO 2013. LNCS, vol. 8042, pp. 75–92. Springer, Heidelberg (2013). https://doi.org/10.1007/978-3-642-40041-4_5
29. Günther, F., Manulis, M., Peter, A.: Privacy-enhanced participatory sensing with collusion resistance and data aggregation. In: Gritzalis, D., Kiayias, A., Askoxylakis, I. (eds.) CANS 2014. LNCS, vol. 8813, pp. 321–336. Springer, Cham (2014). https://doi.org/10.1007/978-3-319-12280-9_21
30. Ivan, A., Dodis, Y.: Proxy cryptography revisited. In: NDSS 2003 (2003)
31. Joye, M., Libert, B.: A scalable scheme for privacy-preserving aggregation of time-series data. In: Sadeghi, A.-R. (ed.) FC 2013. LNCS, vol. 7859, pp. 111–125. Springer, Heidelberg (2013). https://doi.org/10.1007/978-3-642-39884-1_10
32. Lai, J., Deng, R.H., Pang, H., Weng, J.: Verifiable computation on outsourced encrypted data. In: Kutyłowski, M., Vaidya, J. (eds.) ESORICS 2014. LNCS, vol. 8712, pp. 273–291. Springer, Cham (2014). https://doi.org/10.1007/978-3-319-11203-9_16
33. Lai, R.W.F., Tai, R.K.H., Wong, H.W.H., Chow, S.S.M.: A zoo of homomorphic signatures: Multi-key and key-homomorphism. Cryptology ePrint Archive, Report 2016/834 (2016)
34. Leontiadis, I., Elkhiyaoui, K., Molva, R.: Private and dynamic time-series data aggregation with trust relaxation. In: Gritzalis, D., Kiayias, A., Askoxylakis, I. (eds.) CANS 2014. LNCS, vol. 8813, pp. 305–320. Springer, Cham (2014). https://doi.org/10.1007/978-3-319-12280-9_20

35. Leontiadis, I., Elkhiyaoui, K., Önen, M., Molva, R.: PUDA – privacy and unforge-ability for data aggregation. In: Reiter, M., Naccache, D. (eds.) CANS 2015. LNCS, vol. 9476, pp. 3–18. Springer, Cham (2015). https://doi.org/10.1007/978-3-319-26823-1_1

36. Li, Q., Cao, G.: Efficient privacy-preserving stream aggregation in mobile sensing with low aggregation error. In: De Cristofaro, E., Wright, M. (eds.) PETS 2013. LNCS, vol. 7981, pp. 60–81. Springer, Heidelberg (2013). https://doi.org/10.1007/978-3-642-39077-7_4

37. Li, Q., Cao, G., Porta, T.F.L.: Efficient and privacy-aware data aggregation in mobile sensing. IEEE Trans. Dep. Sec. Comput. 11(2), 115–129 (2014)

38. Libert, B., Vergnaud, D.: Multi-use unidirectional proxy re-signatures. In: CCS 2008 (2008)

39. Libert, B., Vergnaud, D.: Unidirectional chosen-ciphertext secure proxy re-encryption. IEEE Trans. Inf. Theory 57(3), 1786–1802 (2011)

40. Ma, C., Li, J., Ouyang, W.: A homomorphic proxy re-encryption from lattices. In: Chen, L., Han, J. (eds.) ProvSec 2016. LNCS, vol. 10005, pp. 353–372. Springer, Cham (2016). https://doi.org/10.1007/978-3-319-47422-9_21

41. Nuñez, D., Agudo, I.: BlindIdM: a privacy-preserving approach for identity man-agement as a service. Int. J. Inf. Sec. 13(2), 199–215 (2014)

42. Nuñez, D., Agudo, I., Lopez, J.: Integrating OpenID with proxy re-encryption to enhance privacy in cloud-based identity services. In: CloudCom, pp. 241–248 (2012)

43. Nuñez, D., Agudo, I., Lopez, J.: A parametric family of attack models for proxy re-encryption. In: CSF, pp. 290–301 (2015)

44. Nuñez, D., Agudo, I., Lopez, J.: On the application of generic CCA-secure transfor-mations to proxy re-encryption. Secur. Commun. Netw. 9(12), 1769–1785 (2016)

45. Rastogi, V., Nath, S.: Differentially private aggregation of distributed time-series with transformation and encryption. In: SIGMOD 2010 (2010)

46. Shi, E., Chan, T.H.H., Rieffel, E.G., Chow, R., Song, D.: Privacy-preserving aggre-gation of time-series data. In: NDSS 2011 (2011)

47. Slamanig, D., Stranacher, K., Zwattendorfer, B.: User-centric identity as a service-architecture for eIDs with selective attribute disclosure. In: SACMAT, pp. 153–164 (2014)

48. Walfish, M., Blumberg, A.J.: Verifying computations without reexecuting them. Commun. ACM 58(2), 74–84 (2015)

49. Xu, P., Xu, J., Wang, W., Jin, H., Susilo, W., Zou, D.: Generally hybrid proxy re-encryption: a secure data sharing among cryptographic clouds. In: AsiaCCS, pp. 913–918 (2016)

50. Zwattendorfer, B., Slamanig, D., Stranacher, K., Hörandner, F.: A federated cloud identity broker-model for enhanced privacy via proxy re-encryption. In: De Decker, B., Zúquete, A. (eds.) CMS 2014. LNCS, vol. 8735, pp. 92–103. Springer, Heidelberg (2014). https://doi.org/10.1007/978-3-662-44885-4_8

Cryptographic Primitives and API's

A Provably Secure PKCS#11 Configuration
Without Authenticated Attributes

Ryan Stanley-Oakes[✉]

University of Bristol, Bristol, UK
ryan.stanley@bristol.ac.uk

Abstract. Cryptographic APIs like PKCS#11 are interfaces to trusted hardware where keys are stored; the secret keys should never leave the trusted hardware in plaintext. In PKCS#11 it is possible to give keys conflicting roles, leading to a number of key-recovery attacks. To prevent these attacks, one can authenticate the attributes of keys when wrapping, but this is not standard in PKCS#11. Alternatively, one can configure PKCS#11 to place additional restrictions on the commands permitted by the API.

Bortolozzo et al. proposed a configuration of PKCS#11, called the Secure Templates Patch (STP), supporting symmetric encryption and key wrapping. However, the security guarantees for STP given by Bortolozzo et al. are with respect to a weak attacker model. STP has been implemented as a set of filtering rules in *Caml Crush*, a software filter for PKCS#11 that rejects certain API calls. The filtering rules in *Caml Crush* extend STP by allowing users to compute and verify MACs and so the previous analysis of STP does not apply to this configuration.

We give a rigorous analysis of STP, including the extension used in *Caml Crush*. Our contribution is as follows:
(i) We show that the extension of STP used in *Caml Crush* is insecure.
(ii) We propose a strong, computational security model for configurations of PKCS#11 where the adversary can adaptively corrupt keys and prove that STP is secure in this model.
(iii) We prove the security of an extension of STP that adds support for public-key encryption and digital signatures.

1 Introduction

In high-risk environments, particularly where financial transactions take place, secret and private keys are often stored inside trusted, tamper-proof hardware such as HSMs and cryptographic tokens. Then ordinary host machines, which could be compromised by malware or malicious users, can issue commands to the trusted hardware via an interface called a cryptographic API. The operations that can be carried out using the API often include key wrapping, which is the encryption of one key under another to enable the secure exchange and storage of

---

R. Stanley-Oakes—The author is supported by an EPSRC Industrial CASE studentship.

© International Financial Cryptography Association 2017
A. Kiayias (Ed.): FC 2017, LNCS 10322, pp. 145–162, 2017.
https://doi.org/10.1007/978-3-319-70972-7_8

keys. The API can also be used to add new keys to the trusted hardware, either by issuing a key generation command or unwrapping a wrapped key. The API refers to each key by a handle, which has attributes used to specify the intended use of the key. By wrapping and unwrapping, it is possible for different handles, each with different attributes, to point to the same key. This could cause a key to have conflicting roles within the API.

The study of cryptographic APIs was initiated by Bond and Anderson in 2001, when they described attacks against ATMs and prepayment utility meters, exploiting weaknesses in the *interfaces* to the trusted hardware, rather than in the cryptographic algorithms performed by the hardware: "The basic idea is that by presenting valid commands to the security processor, but in an unexpected sequence, it is possible to obtain results that break the security policy envisioned by its designer" [3].

While Bond and Anderson identified vulnerabilities in particular devices with bespoke APIs, Clulow then used their approach to find devastating key recovery attacks against a widely-used, generic API [6]. This API, called PKCS#11[1] is independent of the hardware with which it communicates and was designed to enable interoperability between the trusted hardware from different manufacturers [10].

In 2008, Delaune *et al.* presented a formal, Dolev–Yao style model of PKCS#11 and used model-checking tools to find new attacks [7,8]. Bortolozzo *et al.* then developed an automated tool called *Tookan*, built on the model by Delaune *et al.*, that found and executed attacks against real hardware devices using PKCS#11 [4]. As a result of these attacks, an important research question has been to find a *configuration* of PKCS#11, i.e. a set of restrictions on the commands that can be issued to the API, such that the API is secure with these restrictions.

Bortolozzo *et al.* suggested a configuration of PKCS#11, supporting just symmetric encryption and symmetric key wrapping, called the Secure Templates Patch (STP) [4]. In STP, newly-generated keys are separated into encryption/decryption keys and wrapping/unwrapping keys, while keys imported by unwrapping can be used for encryption and unwrapping, but not decryption or wrapping. STP has been implemented as a set of filtering rules in *Caml Crush*, a software filter that rejects certain PKCS#11 calls [1]. However, the filtering rules in *Caml Crush* allow users to compute and verify MACs, which is not captured by the model from Delaune *et al.* [7,8]. Therefore the previous analysis of STP does not apply to what is implemented in *Caml Crush*. Furthermore, while STP is resistant to attack by *Tookan*, there has not yet been a formal proof of security for this configuration, which is the problem we address here.

---

[1] PKCS#11 is actually the name of the cryptographic standards document that describes the API, which is called *Cryptoki*. However, it is conventional to refer to the API itself as PKCS#11.

1.1 Our Contribution

As a first result, we show that the filtering rules in *Caml Crush* are not sufficient to secure PKCS#11. The attacker is assumed to have knowledge of how the filter operates, but can only interact with the API via the filter. Two sets of filtering rules are offered; the first set is trivially broken if the attacker can read the source code of the filter. The second set of rules is designed to emulate STP, but offers MAC functionality that was not modelled by Delaune *et al.* and hence is not exploited by *Tookan*. We show that the filtering does not enforce a separation between encryption and MAC keys. We also show that there exist encryption and MAC schemes that are individually secure, but completely insecure when the same keys are used for both primitives. Therefore STP, as implemented in *Caml Crush*, is only safe to use if one is certain that the encryption and MAC schemes are *jointly* secure.

Our second contribution is a computational security model for configurations of PKCS#11, where certain API calls are rejected according to the *policy* in the configuration. The policy may determine, for example, what attributes newly-generated or newly-imported keys can have. Our model captures the use of both symmetric and asymmetric variants of encryption and signing primitives within the API. We say that an API is secure if, for any cryptographic primitives used by the API, encrypting and signing data using the API is as secure as using the primitives themselves in isolation. This is strictly stronger than the model from Delaune *et al.*, where an API is considered secure if the attacker cannot learn the values of honestly-generated secret keys [7,8]. Moreover, the adversary in our model is allowed to adaptively corrupt certain keys.

Our main result is a PKCS#11 configuration that is provably secure in our model. We first show that STP as proposed by Bortolozzo *et al.* is *not* secure; STP allows the same keys to be used for encryption and unwrapping, so an attacker can *encrypt* (rather than wrap) their own key, import this key by unwrapping and use this key to encrypt or sign data. Since keys used by the API could have been generated by the adversary, there can be no guarantees for data protected by the API, even if the cryptographic primitives are secure. However, we prove that if the policy prevents the encryption (rather than wrapping) of keys, then the configuration is secure. Moreover, our main result holds for an extension of STP that supports public-key encryption and digital signatures.

The proof of our main result is highly non-trivial since we allow the adversary to adaptively corrupt keys. Adaptive corruption captures the realistic threat scenario that certain keys are leaked through side-channel attacks, which, due to the key wrapping operation, can have devastating consequences for the API. Nevertheless, most existing analyses of cryptographic APIs avoid this strong attacker model because traditional proof techniques cannot be used; for a standard cryptographic reduction, one has to know in advance which keys will be corrupted to correctly simulate the environment of the adversary. Instead, our security proof uses techniques from Panjwani's proof that the IND-CPA security of encryption implies its Generalised Selective Decryption (GSD) security [11]. This is a complex hybrid argument where one first guesses a *path*, in the wrapping graph that will be adaptively created by the adversary, from a source node (corresponding to a key that does not appear in a wrap) to a *challenge* node (corresponding to a key used for encryption of data, or signing, etc.). Then the way in which one responds to wrap queries depends on the positions of the corresponding nodes relative to the guessed path. To our knowledge, we are the first to adapt Panjwani's result to the API setting. A detailed discussion of related work is given in the full version of the paper [14].

2   Preliminaries

We use the term *token* to refer to any trusted hardware carrying out cryptographic operations. All keys are stored inside the token and the user has an API used to issue commands to the token.

We assume the API used by the token is compliant with at least v2.20 of the PKCS#11 standard.[2] While the PKCS#11 specification distinguishes between normal users and security officers, we conflate these roles and assume the adversary can perform any operations permitted by the API. Security in this sense automatically implies security against adversaries who can only interact with the API as normal users or security officers.

We assume that tokens store no keys in their initial state. Then keys can be added to the device using one of the following commands: C_GenerateKey or C_GenerateKeyPair, which cause the token to generate a new key or key pair using its own internal randomness; C_UnwrapKey, which causes the token to decrypt the supplied ciphertext and store the plaintext as a new key (without revealing it); C_CreateObject, which we used to model importing public keys from other tokens; or C_TransferKey, which we use to model an out-of-band method for securely transferring long-term secret keys between tokens (this could happen during the manufacturing process, for example).

The API refers to keys using *handles*; these are public identifiers. So, for example, if the user issues the command C_Encrypt(h, m), they expect to receive the encryption of the message m under the key pointed to by the handle h. The *class* of a key is whether it is public, private or secret. For each handle, the token stores the corresponding key, the class of this key and its *template*, which is a set of *attributes* that determine how the key can be used. Attributes are either *set* or *unset*. For example, PKCS#11 mandates that the command C_Encrypt(h, m) must fail if the attribute CKA_ENCRYPT is not set in the template associated to h.

In the language of PKCS#11, the value of a key is also an attribute of its handle, and the API has to prevent the reading of this attribute if the attribute CKA_SENSITIVE is set, i.e. the API should not reveal the values of keys that are supposed to be secret. For simplicity we say that templates do not contain the value of keys. This way all attributes are binary and can be disclosed to the user.

---

[2]   Version 2.20 of the standard was published in 2004, and was the first to introduce the attributes CKA_TRUSTED and CKA_WRAP_WITH_TRUSTED, which we use to prevent key cycles.

Accordingly we have no need for the attribute CKA_SENSITIVE; all public keys will be returned to the user at generation time and other keys can only be revealed by corruption.

PKCS#11 allows an incomplete template to be supplied when a new handle is created, forcing the API to choose whether to set or unset the unspecified attributes; we simply assume that the operation fails if the template is incomplete. For convenience, we also assume that the template of a handle contains the class of the corresponding key.

In PKCS#11, some attributes can be changed by the user (or by the API). For example, perhaps the attribute CKA_ENCRYPT is not initially set in the template of some handle h pointing to the key k, but later the user wishes to use k to encrypt data. We exclude this from our model, preferring to assume that the intended use of all keys is known at generation time. In the language of PKCS#11, all our attributes are *sticky*.

There are nine attributes relevant to our analysis, as follows: CKA_EXTRACTABLE, which we abbreviate by CKA_EXTR, is used to identify those keys that can be wrapped (in the case of private or secret keys), or given out (in the case of public keys). CKA_WRAP_WITH_TRUSTED, which we abbreviate by CKA_WWT, is used to identify those keys that can only be wrapped by keys with CKA_TRUSTED set. CKA_TRUSTED is used to identify those keys that are considered trusted wrapping keys. CKA_WRAP, CKA_UNWRAP, CKA_ENCRYPT, CKA_DECRYPT, CKA_SIGN and CKA_VERIFY are used to identify those keys that can wrap keys, unwrap keys, encrypt data, decrypt data, sign (or MAC) data and verify signatures (or MAC tags), respectively.

PKCS#11 specifies some rules, which we call the *policy*, about how attributes must be used (like how the template of h must have CKA_ENCRYPT set in order for C_Encrypt(h, m) to succeed). But the standard also allows manufacturers, in their own *configurations* of PKCS#11, to impose additional restrictions on how the API operates. For example, the PKCS#11 policy allows a symmetric key to be generated with both CKA_WRAP and CKA_DECRYPT set, leading to the famous wrap/decrypt attack [6]. Manufacturers should therefore disable this command in their configuration. We assume that the policy in the manufacturer's configuration allows a subset of commands allowed by the PKCS#11 policy (so that the configuration is actually compliant with the specification) and therefore we use a single policy algorithm to capture both the standard PKCS#11 policy and any additional restrictions, i.e. any command not rejected by our policy algorithm is automatically allowed within PKCS#11.

3   Vulnerabilities in Caml Crush

In *Caml Crush*, the idea is that the interface to some trusted hardware is a PKCS#11-compliant, but insecure, API [1]. The software is then used to filter out API calls that could lead to attacks. This is rather like having a more restrictive policy *within* the API and so the authors adapt the PKCS#11 configurations suggested by Bortolozzo *et al.* to filtering rules. Bortolozzo *et al.* suggested two configurations of PKCS#11 that are resistant to attack by *Tookan* [4], both of which are implemented in *Caml Crush* as sets of filtering rules [1]:

1. In the *Wrapping Formats Patch (WFP)*, the attributes of a key are transmitted as part of a wrap of the key and authenticated using a MAC.
2. In the *Secure Templates Patch (STP)*, wrapping and encryption keys are separated at generation time and imported symmetric keys can be used for unwrapping and encryption, but not wrapping or decryption.

We remark that the first patch is actually a violation of the PKCS#11 standard: the standard mandates that a wrap of a key is solely the encryption of the value of the key, i.e. the attributes of the key are not included in the output and no MAC tag is added. Tokens whose APIs use WFP are not interoperable with tokens using PKCS#11-compliant APIs.

Moreover, the way WFP is implemented in Caml Crush is trivially insecure. Examining the source code, the MAC used to authenticate the attributes of the wrapped key is computed using a key that is stored in plaintext in the configuration file of the filter [2]. This is a clear violation of Kerckhoffs' principle: the attacker who knows how the filter is constructed (i.e. can read the source code of the filter) can immediately circumvent the additional protection provided by the MAC and use the wrap/decrypt attack to learn the value of any extractable secret key. The authors of *Caml Crush* acknowledge this vulnerability in a comment: "We use the key configured in the filter configuration file ... You might preferably want to use a key secured in a token". We feel this is an understatement of the insecurity of their solution.

We focus our attention on STP, as this is compliant with the PKCS#11 specification. Note that STP, as presented by Bortolozzo *et al.*, only enables the symmetric encryption, decryption, wrapping and unwrapping functions of the API and not, for example, the MAC and verify functions [4]. The implementation in *Caml Crush* adds MAC functionality to STP, but does so in a potentially insecure way. Their filtering rules allow freshly generated symmetric keys to be used for wrapping and unwrapping, encryption and decryption, or signing and verifying (using a MAC scheme). Then keys imported via the unwrap command can either unwrap and encrypt, or unwrap, sign and verify. At first glance, these restrictions appear to maintain a separation between encryption and MAC keys, but this is not the case. One can generate an encryption key, wrap it, and unwrap it as a MAC key. This configuration is only secure if the encryption and MAC schemes are *jointly* secure, i.e. it is safe to use the same key for both primitives. In the full version of the paper, we show that this assumption does not always hold [14].

4   Security Model and Assumptions

PKCS#11 supports both symmetric and asymmetric primitives for encrypting and signing data and for wrapping keys. For simplicity we will assume that all keys and key pairs are generated using the same two algorithms KG and KPG. Moreover, we assume that the key wrap mechanisms use the same encryption schemes as for encrypting data. Therefore our model of a configuration of PKCS#11 is parameterised by four cryptographic primitives: a probabilistic symmetric encryption scheme $\mathcal{E} = (\mathsf{KG}, \mathsf{Enc}, \mathsf{Dec})$, a probabilistic public-key encryption scheme $\mathcal{PKE} = (\mathsf{KPG}, \mathsf{AEnc}, \mathsf{ADec})$, a MAC scheme $\mathcal{M} = (\mathsf{KG}, \mathsf{Mac}, \mathsf{MVrfy})$ and a digital signature scheme $\mathcal{S} = (\mathsf{KPG}, \mathsf{Sign}, \mathsf{SVrfy})$. The syntax of these primitives and the formal definitions of correctness and security are all given in the full version of the paper [14].

The API also has an algorithm NewHandle for generating fresh handles. This will be called when keys are imported via unwrapping or the C_CreateObject command or new keys are generated. This algorithm is assumed to be stateful so that it never returns the same value. For each handle h returned by NewHandle, the API stores a template h.temp and a pointer p to the token memory where the value of the key is stored. By abuse of notation, the contents of the token memory at p will be written h.key (even though this value is not directly accessible to the API). The class of the key, i.e. secret, public or private, is stored in h.class.

The configuration of the API is defined by the *policy*. We model the policy by the algorithm P that takes the name of the API command and the inputs to that command as inputs, then returns 1 if this combination is permitted and 0 otherwise.

Before giving the formal security definition, we introduce a restriction which is necessary for security and considerably simplifies the model:

Remark 1. Asymmetric key wrapping must be disabled.

Even before a formal security definition is given, it should be clear that any mechanism for key wrapping must provide *integrity* as well as secrecy. If it were not the case, then an adversary could generate their own keys, forge wraps of these keys, unwrap them and use them to wrap honestly-generated keys or encrypt and sign data. If this attack is possible, there can be no guarantees for data and keys protected by the API, since any keys used by the API could be adversarially generated. Of course, the notion of integrity of ciphertexts makes no sense in the public key encryption setting without the sender needing a private key as well as a public key to encrypt. Therefore we make the standard assumptions from the literature that all key wrapping is symmetric and, for bootstrapping, there is an out-of-band method for securely exchanging long-term secret keys [4,9,12,13].

4.1 Security Definition

Following [9,12,13], we give a *computational*, rather than symbolic, security definition for a configuration of PKCS#11, where the adversary has access to a number of oracles and plays a game. Winning the game means violating the security of one of the cryptographic primitives used by the token. We say, informally, that a configuration of PKCS#11 is secure if using the API to encrypt and sign data is as secure as encrypting and signing with the separate, individual primitives. This notion of security is similar to the one used by Cachin and Chandran [5].

Formally, for each adversary $\mathcal{A}$ and each $b \in \{0, 1\}$, we define an experiment $\mathsf{API}^b(\mathcal{A}) := \mathsf{API}^b_{\mathcal{E}, \mathcal{M}, \mathcal{PKE}, \mathcal{S}, \mathrm{P}}(\mathcal{A})$ where the adversary has access to a number of oracles capturing the commands one can issue to the API, and some *challenge* oracles whose responses depend on b. The oracles all first check, using the policy P, that the command from the adversary is allowed. If this succeeds, then the oracles perform the cryptographic operations that would be carried out by the token. Note that our formal model conflates the roles of the API and the token, which simplifies notation considerably, but is without loss of generality since we know how PKCS#11-compliant APIs interact with tokens. The only thing we do not know is how the token implements the cryptographic operations, and these details are abstracted away in our model.

After interacting with the API oracles, the adversary returns a guess b'. Provided that certain conditions are met whereby the adversary cannot trivially learn b, the experiment returns b'. Otherwise, the experiment returns 0. The *advantage* of $\mathcal{A}$ against the API is defined to be the following quantity:

$$\mathsf{Adv}^{\mathsf{API}}(\mathcal{A}) := \left| \mathbb{P}[\mathsf{API}^1(\mathcal{A}) = 1] - \mathbb{P}[\mathsf{API}^0(\mathcal{A}) = 1] \right|.$$

The experiment API^b is shown in Fig. 1, with the oracles available to $\mathcal{A}$ shown in Figs. 2 and 3.

Experiment $\mathsf{API}^b_{\mathcal{E}, \mathcal{M}, \mathcal{PKE}, \mathcal{S}, \mathrm{P}}(\mathcal{A})$:

$i \leftarrow 0$
$\mathsf{Chal} \leftarrow \emptyset, \mathsf{Cor} = \{0\}$
$W \leftarrow \emptyset, E \leftarrow \emptyset, V \leftarrow \{0\}$
$P \leftarrow \emptyset, K \leftarrow \emptyset$
for all $j \in [n]$,
$\quad C_1[j], C_1^*[j], C_2[j], C_2^*[j], T[j], T^*[j], S[j], S^*[j] \leftarrow \emptyset$
$b' \leftarrow \mathcal{A}^{\mathcal{O}}$
if $\mathsf{Chal} \cap \mathsf{Comp} \neq \emptyset$ then return 0
if $\exists j \in [n]$ such that:
$\quad C_1[j] \cap C_1^*[j] \neq \emptyset$
$\quad$ or $C_2[j] \cap C_2^*[j] \neq \emptyset$
$\quad$ or $T[j] \cap T^*[j] \neq \emptyset$
$\quad$ or $S[j] \cap S^*[j] \neq \emptyset$:
then return 0
else return b'

Fig. 1. The Security Experiment $\mathsf{API}^b(\mathcal{A})$ for a cryptographic API supporting symmetric and asymmetric encryption, a MAC scheme and a signature scheme. The oracles $\mathcal{O}$ are defined in Figs. 2 and 3.

Oracle $\mathcal{O}^{\texttt{C\_CreateObject}}(pk, t)$:

if P(C_CreateObject, pk, t):
    $h \leftarrow$ NewHandle
    $h.\mathsf{key} \leftarrow pk$
    $h.\mathsf{temp} \leftarrow t$
    $h.\mathsf{class} \leftarrow$ public
    $X \leftarrow \{h' \in P : h'.\mathsf{key} = pk\}$
    if $X \neq \emptyset$:
        $\mathsf{idx}(h) \leftarrow \min_{h' \in X}\mathsf{idx}(h')$
    else $\mathsf{idx}(h) \leftarrow 0$
    return h

Oracle $\mathcal{O}^{\texttt{C\_TransferKey}}(k, t)$:

if P(C_TransferKey, k, t):
    $h \leftarrow$ NewHandle
    $h.\mathsf{key} \leftarrow k$
    $h.\mathsf{temp} \leftarrow t$
    $h.\mathsf{class} \leftarrow$ secret
    $X \leftarrow \left\{ \begin{array}{l} h' \in K : \\ \quad h'.\mathsf{key} = k \wedge h'.\mathsf{temp} = t \end{array} \right\}$
    if $X \neq \emptyset$:
        $\mathsf{idx}(h) \leftarrow \min_{h' \in X}\mathsf{idx}(h')$
    else $\mathsf{idx}(h) \leftarrow 0$
    return h

Oracle $\mathcal{O}^{\texttt{C\_GenerateKey}}(t)$:

if P(C_GenerateKey, t):
    $i\mathrel{+}{+}$
    $h \leftarrow$ NewHandle
    $K = K \cup \{h\}$
    $\mathsf{idx}(h) \leftarrow i$
    $V \leftarrow V \cup \{i\}$
    $h.\mathsf{key} \leftarrow$ KG
    $h.\mathsf{temp} \leftarrow t$
    $h.\mathsf{class} \leftarrow$ secret
    return h

Oracle $\mathcal{O}^{\texttt{C\_GenerateKeyPair}}(t, t')$:

if P(C_GenerateKeyPair, t, t'):
    $i\mathrel{+}{+}$
    $h \leftarrow$ NewHandle
    $h' \leftarrow$ NewHandle
    $P = P \cup \{h\}$
    $\mathsf{idx}(h) \leftarrow i$
    $\mathsf{idx}(h') \leftarrow i$
    $V \leftarrow V \cup \{i\}$
    $(h.\mathsf{key}, h'.\mathsf{key}) \leftarrow$ KPG
    $h.\mathsf{temp} \leftarrow t$
    $h'.\mathsf{temp} \leftarrow t'$
    $h.\mathsf{class} \leftarrow$ public
    $h'.\mathsf{class} \leftarrow$ private
    return $h, h', h.\mathsf{key}$

Oracle $\mathcal{O}^{\texttt{C\_WrapKey}}(h, h')$:

if P(C_WrapKey, h, h'):
    if $h.\mathsf{class} =$ secret:
        if $h'.\mathsf{class} =$ private
    or $h'.\mathsf{class} =$ secret:
        $w \leftarrow$ Enc$(h.\mathsf{key}, h'.\mathsf{key})$
        $W \leftarrow W \cup \{(h, h', w)\}$
        $E \leftarrow E \cup \{(\mathsf{idx}(h), \mathsf{idx}(h'))\}$
        return w

Oracle $\mathcal{O}^{\texttt{C\_UnwrapKey}}(h, w, t)$:

if P(C_UnwrapKey, h, w, t):
    if $h.\mathsf{class} =$ secret:
        $k' \leftarrow$ Dec$(h.\mathsf{key}, w)$
        if $k' \in$ SecretKeys
    or $k' \in$ PrivateKeys:
        $h' \leftarrow$ NewHandle
        $h'.\mathsf{temp} \leftarrow t$
        $h'.\mathsf{key} \leftarrow k'$
        unwrapbookkeeping
        return h'

Macro unwrapbookkeeping:

$X \leftarrow \left\{ \begin{array}{l} h_2 : (h_1, h_2, w) \in W \\ \quad \wedge \mathsf{idx}(h_1) = \mathsf{idx}(h) \end{array} \right\}$
if $X \neq \emptyset$:
    $\mathsf{idx}(h') \leftarrow \min_{h_2 \in X}\mathsf{idx}(h_2)$
else if $\mathsf{idx}(h) \in$ Comp:
    $\mathsf{idx}(h') \leftarrow 0$
else:
    $i\mathrel{+}{+}$
    $\mathsf{idx}(h') \leftarrow i$
    $V \leftarrow V \cup \{i\}$

Oracle $\mathcal{O}^{\texttt{Corrupt}}(h)$:

if $h.\mathsf{class} =$ private
or $h.\mathsf{class} =$ secret:
    Cor $\leftarrow$ Cor $\cup \{\mathsf{idx}(h)\}$
    return $h.\mathsf{key}$

Fig. 2. Oracles Representing PKCS#11 Key Management Commands and Key Corruption

Oracle $\mathcal{O}^{\text{C\_Encrypt}}(h, m)$:
if $P(\text{C\_Encrypt}, h, m)$:
  if $h.\text{class} = \text{secret}$:
    return $\text{Enc}(h.\text{key}, m)$
  if $h.\text{class} = \text{public}$:
    return $\text{AEnc}(h.\text{key}, m)$

Oracle $\mathcal{O}^{\text{C\_Decrypt}}(h, c)$:
if $P(\text{C\_Decrypt}, h, c)$:
  if $h.\text{class} = \text{secret}$:
    $c \leftarrow \text{Dec}(h.\text{key}, c)$
    $C_1[\text{idx}(h)] \leftarrow C_1[\text{idx}(h)] \cup \{c\}$
    return c
  if $h.\text{class} = \text{private}$:
    $c \leftarrow \text{ADec}(h.\text{key}, c)$
    $C_2[\text{idx}(h)] \leftarrow C_2[\text{idx}(h)] \cup \{c\}$
    return c

Oracle $\mathcal{O}^{\text{C\_Sign}}(h, m)$:
if $P(\text{C\_Sign}, h, m)$:
  if $h.\text{class} = \text{secret}$:
    $\tau \leftarrow \text{Mac}(h.\text{key}, m)$
    $T[\text{idx}(h)] \leftarrow T[\text{idx}(h)] \cup \{\tau\}$
    return τ
  if $h.\text{class} = \text{private}$:
    $\sigma \leftarrow \text{Sign}(h.\text{key}, m)$
    $S[\text{idx}(h)] \leftarrow S[\text{idx}(h)] \cup \{\sigma\}$
    return σ

Oracle $\mathcal{O}^{\text{C\_Verify}}(h, m, s)$:
if $P(\text{C\_Verify}, h, m, s)$:
  if $h.\text{class} = \text{secret}$:
    return $\text{MVrfy}(h.\text{key}, m, s)$
  if $h.\text{class} = \text{public}$:
    return $\text{SVrfy}(h.\text{key}, m, s)$

Oracle $\mathcal{O}_b^{\text{Enc-Challenge}}(h, m_0, m_1)$:
if $P(\text{C\_Encrypt}, h, m_0)$:
  if $P(\text{C\_Encrypt}, h, m_1)$:
    if $|m_0| = |m_1|$:
      if $h.\text{class} = \text{secret}$:
        $\text{Chal} \leftarrow \text{Chal} \cup \{\text{idx}(h)\}$
        $c \leftarrow \text{Enc}(h.\text{key}, m_b)$
        $C_1^*[\text{idx}(h)] \leftarrow C_1^*[\text{idx}(h)] \cup \{c\}$
        return c
      if $h.\text{class} = \text{public}$:
        $\text{Chal} \leftarrow \text{Chal} \cup \{\text{idx}(h)\}$
        $c \leftarrow \text{AEnc}(h.\text{key}, m_b)$
        $C_2^*[\text{idx}(h)] \leftarrow C_2^*[\text{idx}(h)] \cup \{c\}$
        return c

Oracle $\mathcal{O}_b^{\text{Sign-Challenge}}(h, m, s)$:
if $P(\text{C\_Verify}, h, m, s)$:
  if $h.\text{class} = \text{secret}$:
    $T^*[\text{idx}(h)] \leftarrow T^*[\text{idx}(h)] \cup \{s\}$
    $\text{Chal} \leftarrow \text{Chal} \cup \{\text{idx}(h)\}$
    if $b = 0$ return $\text{MVrfy}(h.\text{key}, m, s)$
    else return 0
  if $h.\text{class} = \text{public}$:
    $S^*[\text{idx}(h)] \leftarrow S^*[\text{idx}(h)] \cup \{s\}$
    $\text{Chal} \leftarrow \text{Chal} \cup \{\text{idx}(h)\}$
    if $b = 0$ return $\text{SVrfy}(h.\text{key}, m, s)$
    else return 0

Fig. 3. Oracles Representing PKCS#11 Cryptographic Operations and the IND-CCA and EUF-CMA Games

Now we explain some of the rationale behind the security game. We have two challenge oracles $\mathcal{O}_b^{\text{Enc-Challenge}}$ and $\mathcal{O}_b^{\text{Sign-Challenge}}$, corresponding to confidentiality (of public key and symmetric encryption) and authenticity (of signatures and MACs), respectively. These oracles closely resemble the IND-CCA and EUF-CMA games. For encryption, the bit b determines which of the messages m_0 and m_1 is encrypted under the challenge key. As usual, to avoid trivial wins we have to record the ciphertexts output by $\mathcal{O}_b^{\text{Enc-Challenge}}$ and the queries made to the decryption oracle $\mathcal{O}^{\texttt{C\_Decrypt}}$, and check that the two sets corresponding to the same key are disjoint. For signing and MACs, the bit b determines whether the adversary sees the genuine result of the verification algorithm, or always sees the bit 0 (indicating that the verification has failed). To avoid trivial wins here, we record the signatures and tags output by $\mathcal{O}^{\texttt{C\_Sign}}$ and the candidate signatures and tags submitted to $\mathcal{O}_b^{\texttt{Sign-Challenge}}$ and check that the two sets corresponding to the same key are disjoint.

In our model, we include an oracle $\mathcal{O}^{\texttt{Corrupt}}$ that allows the adversary to adaptively corrupt certain keys. This captures the situation where some keys may be leaked, for example through side-channel attacks. Obviously, if such keys are used by the challenge oracles, then $\mathcal{A}$ can trivially recover the bit b. Moreover, if the adversary were to wrap a key under a corrupt key, then the wrapped key must be assumed *compromised*, since it can be trivially recovered by the adversary. Like corrupt keys, compromised keys are not safe for use by the challenge oracles. Therefore we keep track of a set Comp of corrupt and compromised keys and a set Chal of keys used by the challenge oracles, and the experiment only returns the guess b' from $\mathcal{A}$ if Comp and Chal are disjoint.

The situation is complicated by the fact that the adversary queries $\mathcal{O}^{\texttt{Corrupt}}$ with *handles*, not keys, and learns the value of the key pointed to by the handle. But by wrapping and unwrapping a key, the adversary obtains a new handle for the same key and clearly all handles pointing to the same key are compromised by the corruption of just one of them. Therefore we keep track of which handles point to the same key by giving them the same *index* $idx(h)$ and store which *indices* are compromised, rather than which handles. This is based on the security model by Shrimpton *et al.* [13].

We assume that there is an authenticated channel for transmitting public keys using the C_CreateObject command. Therefore we check that any public keys imported via $\mathcal{O}^{\texttt{C\_CreateObject}}$ had at some point been honestly generated by a token. If so, the new handle is given the same index as the handle that was given out when the key was first generated. If not, the new handle is given index 0, which is used to represent automatically compromised keys (and therefore if this new public key is used in the challenge oracles, the guess output by $\mathcal{A}$ will be ignored). Note that we do not check that the template of the imported public key matches the template of the key when it was first generated. This is because we are not assuming that the attributes of keys are always authenticated. Therefore the policy of our configuration will have to restrict the roles of imported public keys.

Similarly, we assume there is a secure out-of-band method for transferring long-term wrapping keys, modelled by the C_TransferKey command, so we check that keys imported via $\mathcal{O}^{\texttt{C\_TransferKey}}$ were previously generated on the token. If this check fails, the new handle is given index 0. Unlike with $\mathcal{O}^{\texttt{C\_CreateObject}}$, we check that the template of the key matches the template it had when it was first generated. This is because the transfer mechanism is designed for keys of the highest privilege, so we must ensure that keys imported this way were always intended to have this role. As a result, the transfer mechanism cannot really benefit the adversary, since they can only import a key with the same value and role as it had previously. We only include this oracle to model a system with multiple tokens.

Finally, when a key is imported via $\mathcal{O}^{\text{C\_UnwrapKey}}$, we check if the wrap had been previously generated by the token. To carry out this check, we maintain a list W of triples (h, h', w) such that the query $\mathcal{O}^{\text{C\_WrapKey}}(h, h')$ received the response w.[3] If the wrap submitted to $\mathcal{O}^{\text{C\_UnwrapKey}}$ was indeed generated by the token, we know the contents of the wrap, so the new handle is given the same index of the originally wrapped handle.[4] If the wrap submitted to $\mathcal{O}^{\text{C\_UnwrapKey}}$ was not generated by the token, then it was forged by the adversary. If the unwrapping key is compromised, then the new handle is assumed compromised and given index 0. This is because it is trivial to forge a wrap under a compromised key and so we do not allow the adversary to win the security game this way. However, if the unwrapping key is not already compromised, then the new handle is given a fresh (non-zero) index, even though there can be no security guarantees for the imported key. This allows the adversary to benefit from creating forged wraps without compromising the wrapping key, which is a realistic attack. It will be necessary for security to prove that this can never happen, using the integrity of the wrapping mechanism.

Now we give the formal definition of the security of a PKCS#11 configuration. Suppose $\mathsf{Adv}^{\text{API}}(\mathcal{A}) \leq \epsilon$ for all adversaries $\mathcal{A}$ running in time at most t, making at most q oracle queries and such that the number of non-zero handle indices used in API^b, i.e. the number of keys generated by the token or imported into the token by forgeing a wrap under an uncompromised key, is at most n. Then we say the API is (t, q, n, ϵ)-secure.

4.2 Security Assumptions

In order for an API to securely support both symmetric and asymmetric cryptographic primitives, we have to assume that the encoding of keys is such that the three key classes cannot be confused.[5] More precisely, algorithms that are supposed to use secret keys will automatically fail if one tries to use a public key or a private key instead, and so on. This is necessary to avoid otherwise secure primitives exhibiting insecure behaviour (such as returning the value of the key) when used with a key of the wrong class. Moreover, when one imports a new key using the C_CreateObject command or the C_UnwrapKey command, the class of the new key will be automatically determined by the input to the command. We capture these assumptions in our formal syntax by having the keyspaces SecretKeys, PublicKeys and PrivateKeys be disjoint sets. These assumptions mean that,

---

[3] A real API does not need to maintain such a list; it is purely for preventing trivial attacks in our model.

[4] Actually it is given the minimal index of all wrapped handles satisfying these conditions, but if the API is secure then all these indices will agree, or they will all be in Comp.

[5] In practice, the length of the bitstring could determine the class of the key.

for example, a secure symmetric encryption scheme and a secure digital signature scheme are automatically jointly secure, but different primitives using the same class of keys, e.g. a symmetric encryption scheme and a MAC scheme, could still interfere with each other.

Furthermore, as explained above, the wrapping mechanism must provide *integrity* (in addition to secrecy) to prevent the adversary from importing their own keys. While we assume the wrapping mechanism authenticates the *values* of keys, we do not assume that the *attributes* of keys are authenticated. We remark that some wrapping mechanisms supported by early versions of PKCS#11, e.g. LYNKS from v2.20, attempted to authenticate the values of keys by adding an encrypted checksum to the ciphertext, which was then checked when unwrapping. On the other hand, even the latest version of PKCS#11 does not explicitly support including and authenticating the attributes of keys when wrapping. While we assume the use of a strong wrapping mechanism, we show how security can be achieved without any changes to the PKCS#11 standard.

5   Secure Templates

Since we do not assume that the PKCS#11 wrapping mechanism authenticates the attributes of keys, we have no way of knowing what the attributes of imported keys were when the keys were first generated. This means the API must impose attributes on imported keys regardless of user input.

Furthermore, it is very difficult to separate the roles of imported keys of the same class without authenticated attributes. This is because forcing the adversary to choose between templates of imported keys (such as unwrap and encrypt or unwrap and sign/verify) does not limit the adversary at all, since the adversary can just unwrap the same wrapped key twice with different roles. Moreover, if one tries to prevent this attack by rejecting unwraps of a ciphertext that has previously been unwrapped on the same token, the adversary can just unwrap the same key on multiple tokens and use them together. The only way to avoid this entirely is with a central log of all the operations performed on any token, as suggested by Cachin and Chandran, which is impractical for more than one token [5]. Since we do not assume that attributes are authenticated or that there is a central log of all operations, our configuration must have exactly one template for all imported keys of the same class. Under our assumption that the three classes of keys cannot be confused, we can have a different template for each class.

Recall that, in STP, imported secret keys can be used for encryption, but not decryption [4]. This is because these keys may be stored under a different handle with the ability to wrap other keys and so we must prevent the wrap/decrypt attack. Similarly, such keys can be used for unwrapping, but not wrapping, since they may be stored under a different handle with the ability to decrypt ciphertexts. However, this does not prevent all the attacks that we consider: STP is actually not secure in our model.

There are two reasons why we will not be able to reduce the security of STP to the confidentiality and integrity of the underlying symmetric encryption scheme. The first is technical: STP allows the creation of key cycles, since any key with CKA_WRAP set can wrap any key with CKA_EXTR set, and key cycles cannot be modelled by standard, computational security notions for encryption. However, one can prevent key cycles using the attributes CKA_TRUSTED and CKA_WWT: we allow the creation of *trusted* wrapping keys that are not extractable and *untrusted* wrapping keys that are extractable but can only be wrapped under trusted wrapping keys. Moreover, all imported secret keys must have CKA_WWT set, since they may be stored under a different handle as an untrusted wrapping key.

The second security flaw is more serious. While *Tookan* found no attacks against STP, this was with respect to a weak security notion that honestly-generated keys cannot be recovered by the adversary. Our stronger security notion requires that all keys on the token that are not trivially compromised are safe to use for encryption and signing. This means the attacker should not be able to import their own keys, which is why we need INT-CTXT security for the wrapping mechanism. However, since STP allows the same keys to be used for encryption and wrapping, the adversary could *encrypt* their own key and then *unwrap* the ciphertext, without violating the integrity property of the wrapping mechanism. The newly-imported key, known to the adversary, can then be used by the encryption challenge oracle, trivially leaking the hidden bit b. To prevent this attack, our policy must not allow the encryption (as opposed to wrapping) of any element of SecretKeys.

Let STP+ be the PKCS#11 configuration obtained by restricting STP as described above, thereby preventing the creation of key cycles and the encryption, rather than wrapping, of secret keys. We will extend STP+ by enabling public-key encryption and signatures and our main result (Theorem 1) is a security reduction for this configuration to the security of the underlying primitives. As an immediate corollary, we see that the security of STP+ is implied by the confidentiality and integrity of the underlying symmetric encryption scheme.

In describing STP, Bortolozzo *et al.* did not consider MAC functionality [4]. As mentioned in Sect. 3, the extension of STP used in *Caml Crush* is such that secret keys can have both MAC and encrypt functionality. We also show in the full version of the paper that a secure MAC scheme and a secure encryption scheme are not always jointly secure [14]. Therefore, if we do not assume the joint security of the encryption and MAC schemes, we cannot prove the security of our configuration of PKCS#11 if it allows unwrapped secret keys to compute or verify MACs. Thus there is no generically secure way to exchange MAC keys between tokens and so we must only use (asymmetric) signatures to provide data authenticity.

Then, since unwrapped private keys need to be used to create signatures, such keys cannot be allowed to decrypt messages (without assuming the joint security of public key encryption and signing). So private decryption keys must be unextractable, meaning there is no way to safely transmit such keys between tokens. However we do not need to disable public-key encryption altogether, since tokens can exchange public encryption keys over an authenticated channel and decrypt ciphertexts using their unextractable, locally-generated private keys.

Since tokens are required to transmit public keys for encryption and verifying signatures, it is quite possible for the adversary to use an encryption key to verify signatures, by generating the key in one role and then re-importing it with a different role. However, this does not affect the joint security of the encryption scheme and the signature scheme. The verification algorithm has no way of knowing that the key it uses was 'intended' as an encryption key and will function as normal. Moreover, as the key is public there is no risk from leaking parts of the key not needed for verification. Similarly there is no risk from encrypting data using keys intended for signature verification. In summary, it is not necessary to authenticate the attributes of public keys, only the *values* of these keys. As a result our configuration of PKCS#11 allows all imported public keys to have both encryption and verification capabilities.

Bringing together this analysis, we obtain a set of attribute templates that, without assuming the joint security of different primitives, is maximal among those with which the API is secure:

1. Generated secret keys must have one of the following templates:
   (a) TRUSTED: trusted wrapping keys that are unextractable and cannot be used for encryption or decryption,
   (b) UNTRUSTED: untrusted wrapping keys that can themselves be wrapped under trusted wrapping keys, but cannot be used for encryption or decryption,
   (c) ENC: keys that can be wrapped and used for encryption and decryption, but cannot wrap other keys.
2. Imported secret keys have the template IMPORTSECRET: they can encrypt data and unwrap keys, but cannot decrypt data or wrap keys. To prevent key cycles, imported secret keys must only be wrapped under trusted wrapping keys.
3. Only trusted wrapping keys, i.e. keys with template TRUSTED, can be transferred using the secure out-of-band mechanism C_TransferKey (for bootstrapping).
4. The templates of generated public and private key pairs must be one of the following:
   (a) AENC, ADEC: the public key can encrypt data and the private key can decrypt data; neither can wrap or unwrap and the private key is *not extractable*.
   (b) VERIFY, SIGN: the public key can verify signatures and the private key can create signatures; neither can wrap or unwrap and both are extractable.
5. Finally, imported public keys must have the template IMPORTPUBLIC: such keys can encrypt data and verify signatures, but cannot wrap or unwrap keys.

In Tables 1 and 2, we define our set of secure templates with respect to the PKCS#11 attributes CKA_EXTR, CKA_WWT, CKA_TRUSTED, CKA_WRAP, CKA_UNWRAP, CKA_ENCRYPT, CKA_DECRYPT, CKA_SIGN, and CKA_VERIFY. Any attributes from this

Table 1. Templates for Secret Keys (note that CKA_SIGN and CKA_VERIFY are always unset). The attribute CKA_TRUSTED, not shown here, is set in the template TRUSTED and unset in all other templates.

Template Name	CKA_EXTR	CKA_WWT	CKA_WRAP	CKA_UNWRAP	CKA_ENCRYPT	CKA_DECRYPT
TRUSTED			✓	✓		
UNTRUSTED	✓	✓	✓	✓		
ENC	✓				✓	✓
IMPORTSECRET	✓	✓		✓	✓	

Table 2. Templates for Public and Private Keys (note that CKA_TRUSTED, CKA_WRAP and CKA_UNWRAP are always unset).

Template Name	CKA_EXTR	CKA_WWT	CKA_ENCRYPT	CKA_DECRYPT	CKA_SIGN	CKA_VERIFY
AENC	✓		✓			
ADEC				✓		
SIGN	✓				✓	
VERIFY	✓					✓
IMPORTPUBLIC	✓		✓			✓

set that are not shown in the tables, or not marked with ✓, are unset. The only exception to this rule is CKA_TRUSTED, which is not shown in any of the tables due to limitations on space, but is set in the template TRUSTED and unset in all other templates.

The policy P used in our configuration is given in Table 3. We remark that $P(C\_UnwrapKey, h, w, t)$ sometimes depends on the value of $\mathsf{Dec}(h.\mathsf{key}, w)$. Since $h.\mathsf{key}$ is not accessible to the API, what this means is that the API makes the relevant decryption call to the token, receives a response, and then determines whether or not to release the response to the user based on its value. Note that this policy could not be achieved by simply using a filter (like *Caml Crush*). For comparison, we also give the default PKCS#11 policy and the STP+ policy in the full version of the paper [14]. One can see that our configuration is indeed PKCS#11 compliant and STP+ is a special case of our configuration.

Let t_{max} be the maximum run time of any of the following operations: Enc, AEnc, ADec, Sign, SVrfy, one call to NewHandle and one call to Dec; one call to NewHandle and two calls to KG; and two calls to NewHandle and two calls to KPG. Then, with the configuration presented here, we obtain our main result, which is proved in the full version of the paper [14]:

Theorem 1. *Suppose P is as defined in Table 3, $\mathcal{E}$ is (t, ϵ_1)-IND-CCA-secure and (t, ϵ_2)-INT-CTXT secure, $\mathcal{PKE}$ is (t, ϵ_3)-IND-CCA-secure and $\mathcal{S}$ is (t, ϵ_4)-EUF-CMA-secure. Then the API is (t', q, n, ϵ')-secure, where:*

$$t' = t - q \cdot t_{max}, \quad \epsilon' = n\left[(8n^2 + 4n + 1)\,\epsilon_1 + 2\epsilon_2 + \epsilon_3 + \epsilon_4\right].$$

Table 3. The policy of our configuration (where $a \in h.\texttt{temp}$ means that the attribute a is set in $h.\texttt{temp}$)

Function	Value
$P(\texttt{C\_CreateObject}, pk, t)$	1 if $t = \texttt{IMPORTPUBLIC}$, 0 otherwise
$P(\texttt{C\_TransferKey}, k, t)$	1 if $t = \texttt{TRUSTED}$, 0 otherwise
$P(\texttt{C\_GenerateKey}, t)$	1 if $t \in \{\texttt{TRUSTED}, \texttt{UNTRUSTED}, \texttt{ENC}\}$, 0 otherwise
$P(\texttt{C\_GenerateKeyPair}, t, t')$	1 if $(t, t') \in \{(\texttt{AENC}, \texttt{ADEC}), (\texttt{VERIFY}, \texttt{SIGN})\}$, 0 otherwise
$P(\texttt{C\_WrapKey}, h, h')$	1 if $\texttt{CKA\_WRAP} \in h.\texttt{temp}, \texttt{CKA\_EXTR} \in h'.\texttt{temp}$ and if $\texttt{CKA\_WWT} \in h'\texttt{temp}$ then $\texttt{CKA\_TRUSTED} \in h.\texttt{temp}$, 0 otherwise
$P(\texttt{C\_UnwrapKey}, h, w, t)$	1 if $\texttt{CKA\_UNWRAP} \in h.\texttt{temp}$ and $\text{Dec}(h.\texttt{key}, w) \in \mathsf{SecretKeys}$ and $t = \texttt{IMPORTSECRET}$ or $\text{Dec}(h.\texttt{key}, w) \in \mathsf{PrivateKeys}$ and $t = \texttt{SIGN}$, 0 otherwise
$P(\texttt{C\_Encrypt}, h, m)$	1 if $\texttt{CKA\_ENCRYPT} \in h.\texttt{temp}$ and $m \notin \mathsf{SecretKeys}$, 0 otherwise
$P(\texttt{C\_Decrypt}, h, c)$	1 if $\texttt{CKA\_DECRYPT} \in h.\texttt{temp}$, 0 otherwise
$P(\texttt{C\_Sign}, h, m)$	1 if $\texttt{CKA\_SIGN} \in h.\texttt{temp}$, 0 otherwise
$P(\texttt{C\_Verify}, h, m, s)$	1 if $\texttt{CKA\_VERIFY} \in h.\texttt{temp}$, 0 otherwise

6   Conclusion and Acknowledgements

We have given a security definition for configurations of PKCS#11, where the adversary can adaptively corrupt keys. We proved the security, in this strong attacker model, of a configuration of PKCS#11 that extends the Secure Templates Patch from Bortolozzo et al. [4]. Unlike most existing analyses of APIs in the literature, we do not assume the attributes of keys are authenticated when wrapping.

Our result holds under the assumption that private, public and secret keys cannot be confused. Moreover, since our configuration does not support asymmetric key wrapping, we have to assume for bootstrapping that there is a secure channel for transmitting long-term secret keys and also an authenticated channel for transmitting public keys. We feel that these assumptions are likely to hold in practice.

Our security proof is far from tight: the advantage of the adversary against the API is potentially n^3 times bigger than the advantage against the underlying symmetric encryption scheme used for wrapping, where n is an upper-bound on the number of distinct keys stored on the token. Whether such losses can ever be avoided is the subject of ongoing research.

The author would like to thank Bogdan Warinschi, Martijn Stam and the anonymous reviewers for their useful feedback on the paper.

References

1. Benadjila, R., Calderon, T., Daubignard, M.: Caml crush: a PKCS#11 filtering proxy. In: Joye, M., Moradi, A. (eds.) CARDIS 2014. LNCS, vol. 8968, pp. 173–192. Springer, Cham (2015). https://doi.org/10.1007/978-3-319-16763-3_11
2. Benadjila, R., Calderon, T., Daubignard, M.: Source code for Caml Crush (2016). https://github.com/ANSSI-FR/caml-crush. Accessed 19 Oct 2016
3. Bond, M., Anderson, R.J.: API-level attacks on embedded systems. IEEE Comput. **34**(10), 67–75 (2001)
4. Bortolozzo, M., Centenaro, M., Focardi, R., Steel, G.: Attacking and fixing PKCS#11 security tokens. In: Proceedings of the 17th ACM Conference on Computer and Communications Security, CCS 2010, Chicago, Illinois, USA, 4–8 October 2010, pp. 260–269 (2010)
5. Cachin, C., Chandran, N.: A secure cryptographic token interface. In: Proceedings of the 22nd IEEE Computer Security Foundations Symposium, CSF 2009, Port Jefferson, New York, USA, 8–10 July 2009, pp. 141–153 (2009)
6. Clulow, J.: On the security of PKCS #11. In: Walter, C.D., Koç, Ç.K., Paar, C. (eds.) CHES 2003. LNCS, vol. 2779, pp. 411–425. Springer, Heidelberg (2003). https://doi.org/10.1007/978-3-540-45238-6_32
7. Delaune, S., Kremer, S., Steel, G.: Formal analysis of PKCS#11. In: Proceedings of the 21st IEEE Computer Security Foundations Symposium, CSF 2008, Pittsburgh, Pennsylvania, 23–25 June 2008, pp. 331–344 (2008)
8. Delaune, S., Kremer, S., Steel, G.: Formal security analysis of PKCS#11 and proprietary extensions. J. Comput. Secur. **18**(6), 1211–1245 (2010)
9. Kremer, S., Steel, G., Warinschi, B.: Security for key management interfaces. In: Proceedings of the 24th IEEE Computer Security Foundations Symposium, CSF 2011, Cernay-la-Ville, France, 27–29 June 2011, pp. 266–280 (2011)
10. PKCS#11 cryptographic token interface base specification version 2.40, April 2015. http://docs.oasis-open.org/pkcs11/pkcs11-base/v2.40/pkcs11-base-v2.40.html
11. Panjwani, S.: Tackling adaptive corruptions in multicast encryption protocols. In: Vadhan, S.P. (ed.) TCC 2007. LNCS, vol. 4392, pp. 21–40. Springer, Heidelberg (2007). https://doi.org/10.1007/978-3-540-70936-7_2
12. Scerri, G., Stanley-Oakes, R.: Analysis of key wrapping APIs: generic policies, computational security. In: IEEE 29th Computer Security Foundations Symposium, CSF 2016, Lisbon, Portugal, 27 June–1 July 2016, pp. 281–295. IEEE (2016)
13. Shrimpton, T., Stam, M., Warinschi, B.: A modular treatment of cryptographic APIs: the symmetric-key case. In: Robshaw, M., Katz, J. (eds.) CRYPTO 2016. LNCS, vol. 9814, pp. 277–307. Springer, Heidelberg (2016). https://doi.org/10.1007/978-3-662-53018-4_11
14. Stanley-Oakes, R.: A provably secure PKCS#11 configuration without authenticated attributes. Cryptology ePrint Archive, Report 2017/158 (2017). http://eprint.iacr.org/2017/134

A Post-quantum Digital Signature Scheme Based on Supersingular Isogenies

Youngho Yoo[1](✉), Reza Azarderakhsh[3](✉), Amir Jalali[3], David Jao[1,2](✉),
and Vladimir Soukharev[4]

[1] University of Waterloo, Waterloo, Canada
{yh2yoo,djao}@uwaterloo.ca
[2] evolutionQ, Inc., Waterloo, Canada
david.jao@evolutionq.com
[3] Florida Atlantic University, Boca Raton, USA
{razarderakhsh,ajalali2016}@fau.edu
[4] InfoSec Global, Inc., North York, Canada
Vladimir.Soukharev@infosecglobal.com

Abstract. We present the first general-purpose digital signature scheme based on supersingular elliptic curve isogenies secure against quantum adversaries in the quantum random oracle model with small key sizes. This scheme is an application of Unruh's construction of non-interactive zero-knowledge proofs to an interactive zero-knowledge proof proposed by De Feo, Jao, and Plût. We implement our proposed scheme on an x86-64 PC platform as well as an ARM-powered device. We exploit the state-of-the-art techniques to speed up the computations for general C and assembly. Finally, we provide timing results for real world applications.

Keywords: Digital signatures · Isogenies
Post-quantum cryptography

1 Introduction

The security of most public-key cryptosystems in use today are based on the intractability of certain mathematical problems, namely integer factorization and discrete logarithms. However, large-scale quantum computers will be able to efficiently solve both of these problems, posing a serious threat to modern cryptography. Post-quantum cryptography is the study of classical cryptosystems that remain secure against quantum adversaries. There are several candidate approaches for building post-quantum cryptographic primitives: lattice-based, code-based, hash-based, and multivariate cryptography. Recently, cryptosystems based on supersingular elliptic curve isogenies were proposed by De Feo, Jao, and Plût [12], who gave protocols for key exchange, zero-knowledge proof of identity, and public key encryption. With small key sizes and efficient implementations [8,17], isogenies provide a strong candidate for post-quantum key establishment.

© International Financial Cryptography Association 2017
A. Kiayias (Ed.): FC 2017, LNCS 10322, pp. 163–181, 2017.
https://doi.org/10.1007/978-3-319-70972-7_9

Various isogeny-based authentication schemes have been proposed as well, such as strong designated verifier signatures [20], undeniable signatures [16], and undeniable blind signatures [19]. However, it was not known whether isogeny-based cryptography could support general authentication. In this paper, we show that this is indeed possible by constructing the first digital signature scheme based on isogenies which is strongly unforgeable under chosen message attack in the quantum random oracle model.

Our signature scheme is obtained by applying a generic transformation to the zero-knowledge proof of identity proposed in [12]. Classically, obtaining a secure digital signature from an interactive zero-knowledge proof can be achieved by applying the Fiat-Shamir transform [13]. However, its classical security proof requires certain techniques such as rewinding and reprogramming the random oracle which do not necessarily apply in the quantum setting. Quantum rewinding is possible in some restricted cases [23,25], but it has been shown to be insecure in general [1]. Further, since random oracles model hash functions which, in a real world implementation, could be evaluated in superposition by a quantum adversary, we require *quantum* random oracles which can be queried in a superposition of possibly exponentially many states. This makes it difficult to observe an adversary's queries as measuring the input disturbs the state.

Unruh [24] recently proposed a transformation which remedies these problems to produce a secure signature in the quantum random oracle model. Its overhead is generally much larger than Fiat-Shamir – in some cases exponentially large, making the scheme impractical. Fortunately, applying it to the isogeny-based zero-knowledge proof incurs only twice as much computation as the Fiat-Shamir transform, producing a workable quantum-safe digital signature scheme with small key sizes.

Our Contributions

- We construct the first general-purpose digital signature scheme based on supersingular elliptic curve isogenies, and prove its security in the quantum random oracle model.
- We analyze implementation aspects of our scheme and compare parameter sizes with various post-quantum signature schemes, showing that our scheme achieves very small key sizes.
- We provide source code[1] as well as performance results on x86-64 platforms and on ARM devices with assembly-optimized arithmetic.

Related Work. Independently of us, Galbraith, Petit, and Silva recently published a preprint containing two isogeny-based digital signature schemes [14]. Their second scheme, based on endomorphism rings, is completely unrelated to our work. Their first scheme, based on the De Feo, Jao, and Plût identification scheme, is conceptually identical to our scheme, but they present significant space optimizations to reduce the signature size down to $12\lambda^2$ bits (or $6\lambda^2$ if

---

[1] Source code is available at https://github.com/yhyoo93/isogenysignature.

non-repudiation is not required), compared to our signature size of $69\lambda^2$ bits. However, we note that their signature size is for classical security level λ and as of this writing their posted preprint contains no signature sizes for post-quantum security, whereas our signature sizes are given in terms of post-quantum security. Moreover, their scheme may be slower, since they use a time-space tradeoff to achieve such small signature sizes. The performance of their scheme is not immediately clear, since they provide no implementation results. In this work, by contrast, we provide a complete implementation of our scheme, as well as performance results on multiple platforms and source code for reference.

Outline. The rest of the paper is organized as follows. In Sect. 2, we give a brief preliminary on isogeny-based cryptography and describe the interactive zero-knowledge proof which will be used to construct our scheme. In Sect. 3, we describe Unruh's construction. We construct our isogeny-based digital signature scheme and analyze its algorithmic aspects and parameter sizes in Sect. 4, and give security proofs in Sect. 5. Performance results are provided in Sect. 6.

2   Isogeny-Based Cryptography

We consider elliptic curves over a finite field $\mathbb{F}_q$. An *isogeny* $\phi\colon E_1 \to E_2$ is a surjective rational map between elliptic curves which preserves the point at infinity $\mathcal{O}$. Isogenies are necessarily group homomorphisms $E_1(\mathbb{F}_q) \to E_2(\mathbb{F}_q)$ and can be identified with their kernels. This gives a one-to-one correspondence between isogenies and subgroups of the curve. Two curves E_1 and E_2 over $\mathbb{F}_q$ are isogenous if and only if $\#E_1(\mathbb{F}_q) = \#E_2(\mathbb{F}_q)$ [22]. The degree of an isogeny is its degree as a rational map. For separable isogenies, as are all isogenies in this paper, the degree is equal to the size of the kernel.

Every isogeny $\phi\colon E_1 \to E_2$ with degree d has a unique dual isogeny $\hat{\phi}\colon E_2 \to E_1$ of the same degree such that $\hat{\phi} \circ \phi\colon E_1 \to E_1$ is the multiplication map $P \mapsto [d]P$. The set of isogenies mapping a curve E to itself forms a ring under pointwise addition and composition, called the endomorphism ring. A curve E is *supersingular* if its endomorphism ring is isomorphic to an order in a quaternion algebra, and *ordinary* otherwise. All supersingular elliptic curves over finite fields of characteristic p are isomorphic to curves defined over $\mathbb{F}_{p^2}$.

The ℓ-torsion group of E is defined as $E[\ell] = \{P \in E(\overline{\mathbb{F}}_{p^2})\colon [\ell]P = \mathcal{O}\}$. If ℓ is coprime to p, then $E[\ell] \cong (\mathbb{Z}/\ell\mathbb{Z})^2$, thus an ℓ-torsion group is generated by two elements of order ℓ.

2.1   Zero-Knowledge Proof of Identity

We use primes of the form $p = \ell_A^{e_A} \ell_B^{e_B} f \pm 1$ where ℓ_A, ℓ_B are small primes (typically 2 and 3) with roughly $\ell_A^{e_A} \approx \ell_B^{e_B}$, and f is a small cofactor to ensure p is prime. The public parameters consist of a prime $p = \ell_A^{e_A} \ell_B^{e_B} f \pm 1$, a supersingular curve $E(\mathbb{F}_{p^2})$ of order $(\ell_A^{e_A} \ell_B^{e_B} f)^2$, and generators P_B, Q_B of the $\ell_B^{e_B}$-torsion subgroup $E[\ell_B^{e_B}]$.

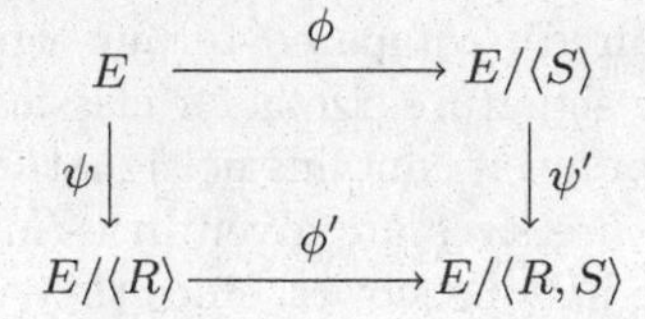

$$E \xrightarrow{\phi} E/\langle S \rangle$$

$$\psi \downarrow \qquad \qquad \downarrow \psi'$$

$$E/\langle R \rangle \xrightarrow{\phi'} E/\langle R, S \rangle$$

Fig. 1. Each arrow is labelled by the isogeny and its kernel.

The zero-knowledge proof takes place over the diagram in Fig. 1. Peggy (the prover) has a secret point S generating the kernel of the isogeny $\phi \colon E \to E/\langle S \rangle$. Her private key is S (or any generator of $\langle S \rangle$) and her public key is the curve $E/\langle S \rangle$ and the images of the public generators $\phi(P_B), \phi(Q_B)$.

In order to prove her knowledge of $\langle S \rangle$ to Vic (the verifier), Peggy chooses a random point R of order $\ell_B^{e_B}$ defining an isogeny $\psi \colon E \to E/\langle R \rangle$. Note that

$$(E/\langle S \rangle)/\langle \phi(R) \rangle = E/\langle R, S \rangle = (E/\langle R \rangle)/\langle \psi(S) \rangle$$

In other words, the diagram in Fig. 1 commutes.

Peggy computes the isogenies in the diagram and sends to Vic the two non-public curves. Vic sends her a challenge bit $b \in \{0, 1\}$, and Peggy reveals some of the isogenies depending on b, which Vic then verifies.

More precisely, Peggy and Vic run the following protocol:

1. – Peggy chooses a random point R of order $\ell_B^{e_B}$.
    – She computes the isogeny $\psi \colon E \to E/\langle R \rangle$.
    – She computes the isogeny $\phi' \colon E/\langle R \rangle \to E/\langle R, S \rangle$ with kernel $\langle \psi(S) \rangle$ (alternatively the isogeny $\psi' \colon E/\langle S \rangle \to E/\langle R, S \rangle$ with kernel $\langle \phi(R) \rangle$).
    – She sends the commitment com $= (E_1, E_2)$ to Vic, where $E_1 = E/\langle R \rangle$ and $E_2 = E/\langle R, S \rangle$.
2. Vic randomly chooses a challenge bit ch $\in \{0, 1\}$ and sends it to Peggy.
3. Peggy sends the response resp where
    – If ch $= 0$, then resp $= (R, \phi(R))$.
    – If ch $= 1$, then resp $= \psi(S)$.
4. – If ch $= 0$, Vic verifies that R and $\phi(R)$ have order $\ell_B^{e_B}$ and generate the kernels for the isogenies $E \to E_1$ and $E/\langle S \rangle \to E_2$ respectively.

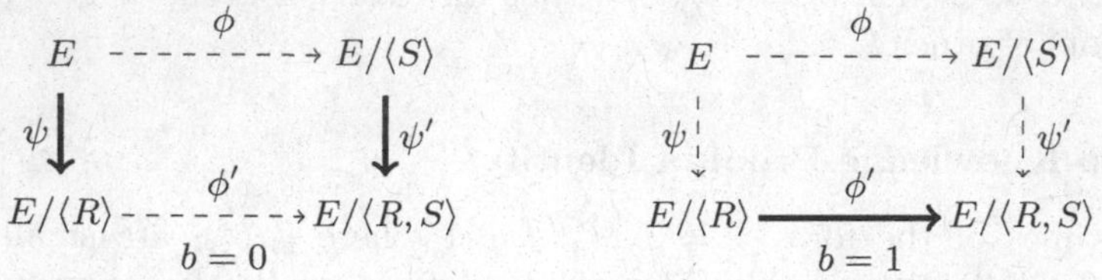

$$E \dashrightarrow^{\phi} E/\langle S \rangle \qquad\qquad E \dashrightarrow^{\phi} E/\langle S \rangle$$

$$\psi \downarrow \qquad \downarrow \psi' \qquad\qquad\qquad \psi \downarrow \qquad \downarrow \psi'$$

$$E/\langle R \rangle \dashrightarrow^{\phi'} E/\langle R, S \rangle \qquad\qquad E/\langle R \rangle \xrightarrow{\phi'} E/\langle R, S \rangle$$

$$b = 0 \qquad\qquad\qquad\qquad\qquad b = 1$$

Fig. 2. Hidden isogenies are indicated by dashed lines. Bolded lines indicate the isogenies revealed by Peggy on challenge b. In either case, the revealed isogenies do not leak information about the secret isogeny ϕ.

- If ch = 1, Vic verifies that $\psi(S)$ has order $\ell_A^{e_A}$ and generates the kernel for the isogeny $E_1 \to E_2$ (Fig. 2).

To achieve λ bits of security, the prime p should be roughly 6λ bits (see Sect. 5) and this protocol should be run λ times. If Vic successfully verifies all λ rounds of the protocol, then Peggy has proved her identity (knowledge of the private key S) to Vic. Otherwise, Vic rejects.

3   Unruh's Construction

Unruh's construction [24] transforms an interactive zero-knowledge proof system into a non-interactive one. The construction satisfies *online extractability* which allows us to extract the witness (private key) from a successful adversary without rewinding. It also avoids the problem of determining the query inputs of the quantum random oracle by including its outputs in the proof (signature) and "inverting" them in the security proof. See [24] for the full security proof.

We fix a binary relation R. A statement x holds if there exists w such that $(x, w) \in R$. In this case, we call w a *witness* to x. In a proof system, a prover P tries to prove a statement x to a verifier V (in other words, to convince V that P knows a witness w to x). We assume that all parties have access to a quantum random oracle H which can be queried in superposition.

3.1   Sigma Protocols

A *sigma protocol* $\Sigma = ((P^1, P^2), V)$ is an interactive proof system consisting of three messages in order: a commitment com $= P^1(x, w)$ made by the prover, a challenge ch chosen uniformly at random by the verifier, and the response resp $= P^2(x, w, \text{com}, \text{ch})$ computed by the prover based on the challenge. Then V outputs $V(x, \text{com}, \text{ch}, \text{resp})$, indicating whether they accept or reject the proof.

Let $\Sigma = (P, V)$ be a sigma protocol where $P = (P^1, P^2)$. We define the following properties of sigma protocols (from [24, Sect. 2.2]):

Completeness: If P knows a witness w to the statement x, then V accepts.

Special soundness: There exists a polynomial time extractor E_Σ such that, given any pair of valid interactions (com, ch, resp) and (com, ch′, resp′) with ch $\neq$ ch′ that V accepts, E_Σ can compute a witness w such that $(x, w) \in R$.

Honest-verifier zero-knowledge (HVZK): There is a polynomial time simulator S_Σ with outputs of the form (com, ch, resp) that are indistinguishable from valid interactions between a prover and an honest verifier by any quantum polynomial time algorithm.

Note that the isogeny-based zero-knowledge proof of identity from the previous section is a sigma protocol. We will show in Sect. 5 that it satisfies all three properties listed above.

3.2 Non-interactive Proof Systems

A *non-interactive proof system* consists of two algorithms: a prover $P(x, w)$ outputting a proof π of the statement x (which has witness w), and a verifier $V(x, \pi)$ outputting whether it accepts or rejects the proof π of x.

For a non-interactive proof system (P, V), we define the following properties (from [24, Sect. 2.1]):

Completeness: If $(x, w) \in R$, then V accepts the proof $\pi = P(x, w)$.

Zero-knowledge (NIZK): There exists a polynomial time simulator S such that, given the ability to program the random oracle, S can output proofs indistinguishable from those produced by P by any quantum polynomial time algorithm.

  The simulator is modeled by two algorithms $S = (S_{\text{init}}, S_P)$, where S_{init} outputs an initial circuit H simulating a quantum random oracle, and S_P is a stateful algorithm which may reprogram H and produce proofs using H.

Simulation-sound online-extractability: (with respect to a simulator $S = (S_{\text{init}}, S_P)$) There exists a polynomial time extractor E such that, if a quantum polynomial time algorithms $\mathcal{A}$ with quantum access to $H \leftarrow S_{\text{init}}$ and classical access to the prover S_P outputs a new valid proof of a statement x, then E can compute (extract) a witness w of x.

Remark 1. Granting $\mathcal{A}$ classical access to the simulated prover S_P is analogous to granting the adversary access to a classical signing oracle in a chosen message attack in the context of signatures. We could allow $\mathcal{A}$ to have *quantum* access to S_P, corresponding to a *quantum* chosen message attack as defined in [6]. We do not know whether Unruh's construction remains secure under this relaxation.

3.3 Unruh's Construction

Unruh's construction transforms a sigma protocol Σ into a non-interactive proof system (P_{OE}, V_{OE}) so that, if Σ satisfies completeness, special soundness, and HVZK, then the result is a complete NIZK proof system with simulation-sound online extractability.

Suppose we have a sigma protocol $\Sigma = (P_\Sigma, V_\Sigma)$ with $P_\Sigma = (P_\Sigma^1, P_\Sigma^2)$, where there are c possible challenges in the challenge domain N_{ch} and the parties want to run the protocol t times, where t depends on the security parameter λ (in our signature scheme we will have $N_{ch} = \{0, 1\}$, $c = 2$, and $t = 2\lambda$). Let G, H be quantum random oracles, where G has the same domain and range. We define a non-interactive proof system (P_{OE}, V_{OE}) where P_{OE} and V_{OE} are given by Algorithms 1 and 2 respectively.

The idea is to simulate the interaction in Σ by setting the challenge $J = J_1 \| \ldots \| J_t$ as the output of the random function H. However, instead of evaluating H on the commitments $(\text{com}_i)_i$ alone as in the Fiat-Shamir transform, we also include the hashes $h_{i,j} = G(\text{resp}_{i,j})$ of the responses $\text{resp}_{i,j}$ to each possible challenge $\text{ch}_{i,j}$, for each commitment com_i. Then the produced proof consists of the commitments, an ordering of all possible challenges, hashed

Algorithm 1. Prover: P_{OE} on input (x, w)

```
// Create t · c proofs and hash each response
```
for $i = 1$ **to** t **do**
   $\text{com}_i \leftarrow P_\Sigma^1(x, w)$
   for $j = 1$ **to** c **do**
      $\text{ch}_{i,j} \leftarrow_R N_{ch} \setminus \{\text{ch}_{i,1}, \ldots, \text{ch}_{i,j-1}\}$
      $\text{resp}_{i,j} \leftarrow P_\Sigma^2(x, w, \text{com}_i, \text{ch}_{i,j})$
      $h_{i,j} \leftarrow G(\text{resp}_{i,j})$
```
// Get challenge by hashing
```
$J_1 \| \ldots \| J_t \leftarrow H(x, (\text{com}_i)_i, (\text{ch}_{i,j})_{i,j}, (h_{i,j})_{i,j})$
```
// Return proof
```
return $\pi \leftarrow ((\text{com}_i)_i, (\text{ch}_{i,j})_{i,j}, (h_{i,j})_{i,j}, (\text{resp}_{i,J_i})_i)$

---

responses to the corresponding challenges, and the responses to the challenges given by $J_1 \| \ldots \| J_t$. The verifier can then take the data to reproduce $J_1 \| \ldots \| J_t$, check that the data was produced properly, and verify the responses $(\text{resp}_{i,J_i})_i$ for each round of Σ.

The main theorem of [24] proves that this construction is secure in the quantum oracle model. Its proof is based on the fact that the random oracle G is indistinguishable from a random permutation, and replaces G with an efficiently invertible function (a random polynomial of high degree) which is unnoticeable by any quantum polynomial time adversary. This allows the hashes to be inverted to obtain the hidden responses in the adversary's forged proof.

Theorem 1. ([24, Corollary 19]). *If Σ satisfies completeness, special soundness, and HVZK, then (P_{OE}, V_{OE}) is a complete non-interactive zero-knowledge proof system with simulation-sound online extractability in the quantum random oracle model.*

Algorithm 2. Verifier: V_{OE} on input (x, π), where
$\pi = ((\text{com}_i)_i, (\text{ch}_{i,j})_{i,j}, (h_{i,j})_{i,j}, (\text{resp}_{i,J_i})_i)$

```
// Compute the challenge hash
```
$J_1 \| \ldots \| J_t \leftarrow H(x, (\text{com}_i)_i, (\text{ch}_{i,j})_{i,j}, (h_{i,j})_{i,j})$

for $i = 1$ **to** t **do**
   check $\text{ch}_{i,1}, \ldots, \text{ch}_{i,m}$ pairwise distinct
   check $h_{i,J_i} = G(\text{resp}_i)$
   check $V_\Sigma(x, \text{com}_i, \text{ch}_{i,J_i}, \text{resp}_i) = 1$
if all checks succeed **then**
   return 1

3.4 Signatures from Non-interactive Zero-Knowledge Proofs

A *digital signature* scheme consists of three algorithms:

- Keygen(λ): takes a security parameter λ and outputs a key pair (pk, sk).
- Sign(sk, m): signs the message m using sk, outputting a signature σ.
- Verify(pk, m, σ): takes the public key of the claimed signer and verifies the signature σ on the message m.

A digital signature scheme is *strongly unforgeable under chosen message attack (SUF-CMA)* if, for any quantum polynomial time adversary $\mathcal{A}$ with classical access to the signing oracle sig: $m \mapsto \mathrm{Sign}(\mathrm{sk}, m)$, $\mathcal{A}$ cannot produce a new valid message-signature pair with non-negligible probability.

Suppose we have a function Keygen generating a public-private key pair (pk, sk) such that no quantum polynomial-time algorithm can recover a valid sk from pk with non-negligible probability. A proof of identity can be viewed as proving the statement $x = $ pk with witness $w = $ sk, where $(x, w) \in R$ if and only if (x, w) is a valid key pair that can be generated by Keygen.

In this sense, a digital signature is basically a non-interactive zero-knowledge proof of identity, except that we need to incorporate a specific message into each proof (signature). This is done by including the message as a part of the statement $x = (\mathrm{pk}, m)$, and the relation R ignores the message m; i.e. $((\mathrm{pk}, m), w) \in R$ if and only if (pk, w) is a valid key pair. Thus, from a NIZK proof of identity (P, V), we obtain a digital signature scheme $\mathcal{DS} = (\mathrm{Keygen}, \mathrm{Sign}, \mathrm{Verify})$ where $\mathrm{Sign}(\mathrm{sk}, m) = P((\mathrm{pk}, m), \mathrm{sk})$ and $\mathrm{Verify}(\mathrm{pk}, m, \sigma) = V((\mathrm{pk}, m), \sigma)$.

Theorem 2. ([24, Theorem 23]). *If (P, V) is a NIZK proof of identity satisfying simulation-sound online-extractability, then the signature scheme $\mathcal{DS}$ above is SUF-CMA in the quantum random oracle model.*

Proof (sketch). Since (P, V) is zero-knowledge, there is a polynomial time simulator that can indistinguishably simulate proofs (signatures) by reprogramming the random oracle. If an adversary can forge a new valid message-signature pair by querying the simulator, then by simulation-sound online-extractability, we can efficiently extract a witness sk. □

4   Isogeny-Based Digital Signature

We propose our isogeny-based digital signature scheme based on the results from previous sections. Let Σ denote the isogeny-based zero-knowledge proof of identity described in Sect. 2.1. Applying Unruh's construction to Σ, we obtain a non-interactive proof of identity (P_{OE}, V_{OE}), from which we get a digital signature scheme:

Public Parameters. We have the same public parameters as in Σ: a prime $p = \ell_A^{e_A} \ell_B^{e_B} f \pm 1$, a supersingular curve E of cardinality $(\ell_A^{e_A} \ell_B^{e_B})^2$ over $\mathbb{F}_{p^2}$, and generators (P_B, Q_B) of the torsion group $E[\ell_B^{e_B}]$.

Key Generation. To generate keys, select a random point S of order $\ell_A^{e_A}$, compute the isogeny $\phi \colon E \to E/\langle S \rangle$, and output the key pair (pk, sk) where $\mathrm{pk} = (E/\langle S \rangle, \phi(P_B), \phi(Q_B))$ and $\mathrm{sk} = S$.

Signing. To sign a message m, set $\text{Sign}(\text{sk}, m) = P_{OE}((\text{pk}, m), \text{sk})$.

Verification. To verify the signature σ of message m, set $\text{Verify}(\text{pk}, m, \sigma) = V_{OE}((\text{pk}, m), \sigma)$.

Algorithms 3, 4, and 5 give explicit descriptions of $(\text{Keygen}, \text{Sign}, \text{Verify})$.

Algorithm 3. Keygen(λ)

Pick a random point S of order $\ell_A^{e_A}$
Compute the isogeny $\phi: E \to E/\langle S \rangle$
$\text{pk} \leftarrow (E/\langle S \rangle, \phi(P_B), \phi(Q_B))$
$\text{sk} \leftarrow S$
return (pk, sk)

Algorithm 4. Sign(sk, m)

---

for $i = 1$ **to** 2λ **do**
  Pick a random point R of order $\ell_B^{e_B}$
  Compute the isogeny $\psi: E \to E/\langle R \rangle$
  Compute either $\phi': E/\langle R \rangle \to E/\langle R, S \rangle$ or $\psi': E/\langle S \rangle \to E/\langle R, S \rangle$
  $(E_1, E_2) \leftarrow (E/\langle R \rangle, E/\langle R, S \rangle)$
  $\text{com}_i \leftarrow (E_1, E_2)$
  $\text{ch}_{i,0} \leftarrow_R \{0, 1\}$
  $(\text{resp}_{i,0}, \text{resp}_{i,1}) \leftarrow ((R, \phi(R)), \psi(S))$
  if $\text{ch}_{i,0} = 1$ **then**
    $\text{swap}(\text{resp}_{i,0}, \text{resp}_{i,1})$
  $h_{i,j} \leftarrow G(\text{resp}_{i,j})$
$J_1 \| \ldots \| J_{2\lambda} \leftarrow H(\text{pk}, m, (\text{com}_i)_i, (\text{ch}_{i,j})_{i,j}, (h_{i,j})_{i,j})$
return $\sigma \leftarrow ((\text{com}_i)_i, (\text{ch}_{i,j})_{i,j}, (h_{i,j})_{i,j}, (\text{resp}_{i,J_i})_i)$

4.1   Algorithmic Aspects

We describe some of the lower-level algorithmic aspects of our signature scheme. Full details can be found in [8,12]. For efficiency in our implementation, we mainly follow [8] for their algorithms and representations of parameters.

Sampling Torsion Points. Let P, Q be fixed generators for the torsion group $E[\ell^e]$. To sample a point R of order ℓ^e, we choose $m, n \in \mathbb{Z}/\ell^e\mathbb{Z}$, not both divisible by ℓ, and compute $R = [m]P + [n]Q$. Since R and $[k]R$ generate the same subgroup $\langle R \rangle = \langle [k]R \rangle$ for any k not divisible by ℓ, we can replace R by $P + [m^{-1}n]Q$ or $[mn^{-1}]P + Q$, depending on which coefficient is coprime to ℓ.

For simplicity, we ignore the coefficient of P as in [8] where it is shown that, for certain pairs of generators P, Q related by distortion maps, each value of $n \in \{1, 2, \ldots, \ell^{e-1} - 1\}$ gives a point $R = P + [\ell n]Q$ of full order ℓ^e generating distinct subgroups. Note that this procedure samples from $\ell^{e-1} - 1$ possible subgroups (Fig. 3).

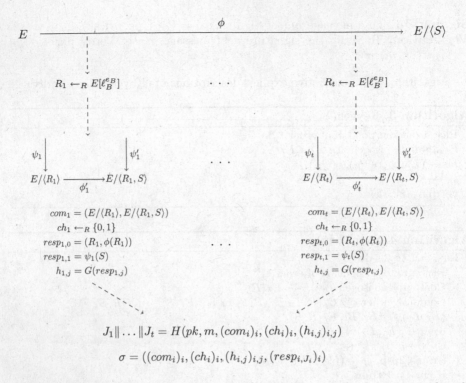

$$J_1 \| \ldots \| J_t = H(pk, m, (com_i)_i, (ch_i)_i, (h_{i,j})_{i,j})$$

$$\sigma = ((com_i)_i, (ch_i)_i, (h_{i,j})_{i,j}, (resp_{i,J_i})_i)$$

Fig. 3. An illustration of the signing algorithm running t rounds of the isogeny-based zero-knowledge proof. For each ZKP round, the signer chooses a random full-order $\ell_B^{e_B}$-torsion point R and computes the relevant data in the ZKP and hashes of the responses (note that these can run in parallel and be precomputed before the message m is known). The collective data is then hashed together with the message to obtain the challenge bits $J_1 \| \ldots \| J_t$. The signature σ contains the data necessary for the verifier to compute $J_1 \| \ldots \| J_t$, and the responses to the challenges.

Computing Isogenies. Isogenies of degree ℓ^e can be computed by composing e isogenies of degree ℓ. Isogeny computation is by far the most expensive process in isogeny-based systems. Detailed analysis on optimizing isogeny computation can be found in [8,12].

Representing of Curves and Points. We use projective coordinates for both points and curve coefficients as in [8] to reduce the number of field inversions. The curves in our system are isomorphic to Montgomery curves which have the form $E_{(A,B)} : By^2 = x^3 + Ax^2 + x$. The Kummer line on a Montgomery curve, which identifies each point $(X : Y : Z)$ with its inverse $(X : -Y : Z)$, has efficient point arithmetic and allows us to disregard the Y coordinate .in our computations. This allows us to represent points by just one field element X/Z in $\mathbb{F}_{p^2}$. However, to compute linear combinations we require an additional x-coordinate of $P - Q$ to perform *differential addition*. We thus include the

---

Algorithm 5. Verify(pk, m, σ)

$J_1 \| \ldots \| J_{2\lambda} \leftarrow H(m, x, (\text{com}_i)_i, (\text{ch}_{i,j})_{i,j}, (h_{i,j})_{i,j})$

for $i = 1$ **to** 2λ **do**
    check $h_{i,J_i} = G(\text{resp}_{i,J_i})$
    if $\text{ch}_{i,J_i} = 0$ **then**
        Parse $(R, \phi(R)) \leftarrow \text{resp}_{i,J_i}$
        check $R, \phi(R)$ have order $\ell_B^{e_B}$
        check R generates the kernel of the isogeny $E \to E_1$
        check $\phi(R)$ generates the kernel of the isogeny $E/\langle S \rangle \to E_2$
    else
        Parse $\psi(S) \leftarrow \text{resp}_{i,J_i}$
        check $\psi(S)$ has order $\ell_A^{e_A}$
        check $\psi(S)$ generates the kernel of the isogeny $E_1 \to E_2$
if all checks succeed **then**
    return 1

---

x-coordinate of $\phi(P_B - Q_B)$ as part of the public key. Isogeny computations are unaffected because a point R and its inverse $-R$ generate the same subgroup.

In the Montgomery form, it turns out that there are only two isomorphism classes of Montgomery curves for a given coefficient value A, and they have the same Kummer line. So the B coefficient also does not affect our computations, and curves can also be represented by one field element for their A-coordinate.

4.2 Parameter Sizes

Recall that our primes have the form $p = \ell_A^{e_A} \ell_B^{e_B} f \pm 1$ with roughly $\ell_A^{e_A} \approx \ell_B^{e_B}$. Note that we require primes of bitlength 6λ in order to achieve λ bits of post-quantum security (see Sect. 5), so we have $\ell_A^{e_A} \approx \ell_B^{e_B} \approx 2^{3\lambda}$.

Since all supersingular curves are defined over $\mathbb{F}_{p^2}$, each field element requires 12λ bits. Our curves are represented in Montgomery form $By^2 = x^3 + Ax^2 + x$ where the A-coefficient suffices for isogeny computations. Similarly, a point on the Kummer line can be represented by their X-coordinate. In both cases, we need one field element, requiring 12λ bits.

Compression. Azarderakhsh et al. [2] showed that torsion points can be compressed by representing them by their coefficients with respect to a deterministically generated basis (computing 2-dimensional discrete log is polynomial-time for smooth curves). Their implementation was however very slow. Recent work by Costello et al. [7] proposed new algorithms accelerating the previous work by more than an order of magnitude and further reduce public key sizes. Their improved compression algorithm runs roughly as fast as a round of the ZKP protocol.

A torsion point used to generate a subgroup can be represented by one coefficient since we can always normalize the coefficient of one generator. Compressing two generators of a torsion group requires three coefficients to keep track of their relation when computing linear combinations. Each coefficient requires roughly 3λ bits.

We can apply the compression to our signature scheme in two ways: first to the public key and second to the responses $\psi(S)$ for the rounds where $ch = 1$. The private key and the other responses $(R, \phi(R))$ are generated using a 3λ-bit coefficient and as such do not require additional computation for compression.

Public Keys. The public key has the form pk $= (a, x(P_B), x(Q_B), x(P_B - Q_B))$, where a denotes the A-coefficient of the public curve $E/\langle S \rangle$. These four field elements require 48λ bits of storage.

We can compress the public key significantly by compressing the torsion basis $(\phi(P_B), \phi(Q_B))$, requiring three 3λ-bit coefficients. Moreover, the X-coordinate of $\phi(P_B - Q_B)$ is no longer required since the full coordinates of $\phi(P_B)$ and $\phi(Q_B)$ can be recovered from their compressed coefficients. Thus the compressed public key requires 12λ bits for the curve and 9λ bits for the generators, for a total of 21λ bits.

Private Keys. The private key S can be stored as a single coefficient n with respect to a $\ell_A^{e_A}$-torsion basis P_A, Q_A (i.e. $S = P_A + [n]Q_A$), requiring 3λ bits.

Signatures. The signature contains $(com_i, ch_{i,j}, h_{i,j}, resp_{i,J_i})$ for each round i of the ZKP protocol. Each commitment contains two curves (E_1, E_2), each requiring one field element. We need one bit to indicate the first challenge bit $ch_{i,0}$. We do not need to send $ch_{i,1}$ since $ch_{i,1} = 1 - ch_{i,0}$. The hash $h_{i,j} = G(resp_{i,j})$ should have bitlength 3λ (this will be justified in Sect. 5.2). Note that we do not need to send h_{i,J_i} since it can be computed from $resp_{i,J_i}$.

The response has a different length depending on the challenge bit J_i. If $J_i = 0$, the response $(R, \phi(R))$ can be represented by their coefficients with respect to the public bases at no additional computational cost, requiring only 3λ bits. If $J_i = 1$, the response $\psi(S)$ requires 12λ bits as a field element. With compression, $\psi(S)$ can be represented in 3λ bits.

In total, each round of the ZKP requires roughly $24\lambda + 1 + 3\lambda + \frac{3\lambda + 12\lambda}{2} \approx 34.5\lambda$ bits on average without compression, and roughly 30λ bits on average with compression. Although λ rounds of the ZKP sufficed for λ bits of post-quantum security, the signature requires 2λ rounds of the ZKP protocol due to the challenge hash being vulnerable to Grover's algorithm [15] (see Sect 5.3). So the entire signature has size roughly $69\lambda^2$ ($60\lambda^2$ compressed) bits on average.

For instance, to achieve 128 bits of post-quantum security, our signature scheme requires $48\lambda = 6144$ bits (768 bytes) for the public key (336 bytes compressed), $3\lambda = 384$ bits (48 bytes) for the private key, and $69\lambda^2 = 1,130,496$ bits (141,312 bytes) for the signature (122,880 bytes compressed) on average.

Comparison. We compare our parameter sizes with various post-quantum signature schemes: the stateless hash-based signature SPHINCS-256 [4], a code-based signature based on Niederreiter's variant of the McEliece cryptosystem

Table 1. Comparison of parameter sizes (in bytes) with various post-quantum signature schemes at the quantum 128-bit security level.

Scheme	Public-key size	Private-key size	Signature size
Hash-based	1,056	1,088	41,000
Code-based	192,192	1,400,288	370
Lattice-based	7,168	2,048	5,120
Ring-LWE-based	7,168	4,608	3,488
Multivariate-based	99,100	74,000	424
Isogeny-based	768	48	141,312
Compressed	336	48	122,880

[5,9], a lattice-based signature BLISS [11], a recent ring-LWE-based signature TESLA# [3], and the multivariate polynomial-based Rainbow signature [10, 18].

It is clear from Table 1 that our isogeny-based signature achieves very small key sizes relative to the other post-quantum signature schemes. We note that the variants of the Merkle signature scheme can achieve smaller (32 byte) key sizes at the same security level, but require state management. We expect future works in isogenies to improve upon signature sizes and performance to produce more practical signatures with still compact keys.

5 Security

The security of isogeny-based cryptosystems are based on the following problems (from [12, Sect. 5]), which are believed to be intractable even for quantum computers.

Computational Supersingular Isogeny (CSSI) problem: Let $\phi_A \colon E_0 \to E_A$ be an isogeny whose kernel is $\langle R_A \rangle$ where R_A is a random point with order $\ell_A^{e_A}$. Given $E_A, \phi_A(P_B), \phi_A(Q_B)$, find a generator of $\langle R_A \rangle$.

Decisional Supersingular Product (DSSP) problem: Let $\phi \colon E_0 \to E_3$ be an isogeny of degree $\ell_A^{e_A}$. Given (E_1, E_2, ϕ') sampled with probability $1/2$ from one or the other of the following distributions, determine which distribution it is from.

   – A random point R of order $\ell_B^{e_B}$ is chosen and $E_1 = E_0/\langle R \rangle$, $E_2 = E_3/\langle \phi(R) \rangle$, and $\phi' \colon E_1 \to E_2$ is an isogeny of degree ℓ_A^e.
   – E_1 is chosen randomly among curves of the same cardinality as E_0, and $\phi' \colon E_1 \to E_2$ is a random isogeny of degree $\ell_A^{e_A}$

The best known attack for the CSSI problem involves claw-finding algorithms using quantum walks [21] and takes $O(p^{1/6})$ time, which is optimal for a black-box claw attack [26]. Therefore it is believed that a prime with bitlength 6λ achieves λ bits of post-quantum security.

5.1   Security of the Zero-Knowledge Proof

It is proven in [12, Sect. 6.2] that our isogeny-based zero-knowledge proof of identity from Sect. 2.1 satisfies completeness, soundness, and honest-verifier zero-knowledge under the assumption that the CSSI and DSSP problems are hard. However, Unruh's construction requires *special soundness*.

Theorem 3 ([12, Theorem 6.3]). *The isogeny-based zero-knowledge proof of identity satisfies completeness, special soundness, and HVZK.*

Proof. We only prove special soundness. Suppose we are given two valid transcripts $(\text{com}, 0, \text{resp}_0)$ and $(\text{com}, 1, \text{resp}_1)$, where com $= (E_1, E_2)$. Then we can use $\text{resp}_0 = (R, \phi(R))$ to compute the isogeny $\psi \colon E \to E/\langle R \rangle$. Since $\text{resp}_1 = \psi(S)$ is a generator of the kernel of ϕ', we can take the dual isogeny $\hat{\psi} \colon E/\langle R \rangle \to E$, and compute $\hat{\psi}(\text{resp}_1)$, a generator for $\langle S \rangle$ (Fig. 4). $\square$

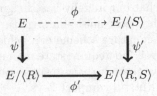

Fig. 4. If ψ and ϕ' are both known, then we can recover the secret subgroup $\langle S \rangle$.

5.2   Security of the Signature

Theorem 2 implies that our isogeny-based signature scheme obtained in Sect. 4 is SUF-CMA. However, one important detail in Unruh's proof is that the quantum random oracle G must have the same domain and range for both response types, so that one can substitute G with a random polynomial and invert hashes in the security proof. In Sect. 4.2, we described compression techniques giving us a few variants of our signature scheme with a space-time tradeoff (we could compress the public key, the responses, or both), and we also took G to be a random oracle outputting hashes of bitlength $k \approx 3\lambda$. While Unruh's proof applies directly to our compressed signatures, it is invalid in our uncompressed signature scheme where the responses can have bitlength k or $4k$. In this case, the only way to apply Unruh's construction directly is to pad the shorter responses to $4k$ bits. G should then output hashes of bitlength $4k$ so that the domain and range of G are both equal to $\{0, 1\}^{4k}$, increasing signature sizes by roughly $18\lambda^2$ bits.

We show by an ad-hoc argument that compression is not necessary—the uncompressed signature scheme remains secure when G outputs hashes of bitlength $k \approx 3\lambda$. Let $\mathcal{DS}_u$ denote the uncompressed signature scheme and $\mathcal{DS}_c$ denote the scheme where the responses $\psi(S)$ are compressed.

Theorem 4. $\mathcal{DS}_c$ *is SUF-CMA in the quantum random oracle model.*

Proof. Since all responses are represented by bitstrings of length k, the security of $\mathcal{DS}_c$ follows from Theorem 2. □

Theorem 5. $\mathcal{DS}_u$ *is SUF-CMA in the quantum random oracle model.*

Proof. Suppose there exists a quantum polynomial-time adversary $\mathcal{A}$ breaking the SUF-CMA security of $\mathcal{DS}_u$. We show that, given a classical signing oracle to an instance of $\mathcal{DS}_c$ with quantum random oracle $G_c\colon \{0,1\}^k \to \{0,1\}^k$, we can forge a new valid message-signature pair for $\mathcal{DS}_c$ using $\mathcal{A}$.

Suppose we are given the public key pk and a signing oracle to an instance of $\mathcal{DS}_c$ with quantum random oracles G_c and H. Let C_0, C_1 denote the set of possible responses to the challenge $ch = 0, 1$ respectively in $\mathcal{DS}_c$. Note that both sets have cardinality roughly 2^k and consist of k bitstrings. We create an instance of $\mathcal{DS}_u$ with the same setup, except the quantum random oracle G_u is to be defined as follows.

Let U_0, U_1 denote the set of possible responses to the challenge $ch = 0, 1$ respectively in $\mathcal{DS}_u$. Then we have $C_0 = U_0$ and $|C_1| = |U_1|$, but the elements of U_1 are $4k$-bitstrings. Let $\mathcal{C}\colon U_1 \to C_1$ denote the compression map taking the field representation of a point $\psi(S)$ in U_1 to its compressed coefficient representation in C_1. Then $\mathcal{C}$ is a bijection that can be computed efficiently both ways since the compression map is injective and its inverse just computes the linear combination. Let $G'_u\colon \{0,1\}^{4k} \to \{0,1\}^k$ be a quantum random oracle such that $G'_u(z\|x) = G_c(x)$ for all $x \in \{0,1\}^k$, where z denotes the all-zeros string of length $3k$. Define $G_u\colon \{0,1\}^{4k} \to \{0,1\}^k$ where

$$G_u(x) = \begin{cases} G'_u(z\|\mathcal{C}(x)) & \text{if } x \in U_1 \\ G'_u(\mathcal{C}^{-1}(y)) & \text{if } x = z\|y \text{ where } y \in C_1 \\ G'_u(x) & \text{otherwise} \end{cases}$$

Since G_u just permutes the inputs according to the bijection $\mathcal{C}$ (with MSB zero-padding) before applying the quantum random oracle G'_u, it follows that G_u is indistinguishable from G'_u. Hence $\mathcal{A}$ can break $\mathcal{DS}_u$ when instantiated with G_u.

We give $\mathcal{A}$ the same public key pk with quantum random oracles G_u and H. When $\mathcal{A}$ makes a signing query on a message m, we relay it to the $\mathcal{DS}_c$ signing oracle to get back a signature

$$\sigma = ((\text{com}_i)_i, (\text{ch}_{i,j})_{i,j}, (h_{i,j})_{i,j}, (\text{resp}_{i,J_i})_i)$$

where $J_1\| \ldots \|J_t = H(\text{pk}, m, (\text{com}_i)_i, (\text{ch}_{i,j})_{i,j}, (h_{i,j})_{i,j})$ and $h_{i,j} = G_c(\text{resp}_{i,j})$. We simply decompress all responses resp_{i,J_i} in σ where $\text{ch}_{i,J_i} = 1$, and give this modified σ to $\mathcal{A}$. Since $G_u(\mathcal{C}^{-1}(y)) = G'_u(z\|y) = G_c(y)$ for all $y \in C_1$, and $G_u(x) = G_c(x)$ for all $x \in C_0$ (with MSB zero-padding of input), it follows that the $h_{i,j}$'s are still valid hashes in $\mathcal{DS}_u$ with G_u. Hence the modified σ is a valid signature for m in $\mathcal{DS}_u$.

Therefore we can answer $\mathcal{A}$'s signing oracle queries so that $\mathcal{A}$ can forge a new valid message-signature pair (m, σ) in $\mathcal{DS}_u$. By similar reasoning, we can then re-compress the new signature without recalculating the hashes to obtain a valid message-signature pair for $\mathcal{DS}_c$, contradicting Theorem 4. □

5.3   Number of Rounds

To achieve λ bits of security, the protocol must be run at least $t = 2\lambda$ times, since a quantum adversary can choose arbitrary bits $J_1 \| \ldots \| J_t$, compute simulated proofs using $J_1 \| \ldots \| J_t$ as challenge, then perform a pre-image search on H using Grover's algorithm [15] to find a message m that will give the required hash. A faster collision attack does not seem to apply since an adversary must know the challenge bits beforehand in order for their simulated proofs to be verifiable with non-negligible probability. Thus to achieve λ bits of security against quantum attacks, our signature scheme runs the zero-knowledge proof $t = 2\lambda$ times.

We have seen that, in the underlying zero-knowledge proof, revealing responses to both challenges $b = 0, 1$ will allow anyone to compute the secret isogeny. Consequently, it is crucial that our signature scheme does not use the same commitment twice. We show that this happens with negligible probability.

Recall that $p = \ell_A^{e_A} \ell_B^{e_B} f \pm 1 \approx 2^{6\lambda}$ with $\ell_A^{e_A} \approx \ell_B^{e_B} \approx 2^{3\lambda}$. There are roughly $\ell_B^{e_B - 1} - 1 \approx 2^{3\lambda}$ distinct cyclic subgroups of $E[\ell_B^{e_B}]$ from which the commitments are chosen randomly. The zero-knowledge protocol is run 2λ times for each signature, so if we sign 2^s messages, we would select $2^{s+1}\lambda$ cyclic subgroups of $E[\ell_B^{e_B}]$ at random. An upper bound on the probability that we will select the same subgroup at least twice is given by the Birthday bound:

$$\frac{2^{s+1}\lambda(2^{s+1}\lambda - 1)}{2 \cdot 2^{3\lambda}} \leq \frac{2^{2s+2}\lambda^2}{2^{3\lambda+1}} \leq \frac{\lambda^2}{2^{\lambda-1}}$$

for $s \leq \lambda$, which is negligible in λ.

6   Implementations

For maximum performance, we implemented the uncompressed signature scheme by modifying the Supersingular Isogeny Diffie-Hellman (SIDH) library published by Costello, Longa, and Naehrig [8]. The SIDH implementation uses fixed public parameters: the prime $p = 2^{372} \cdot 3^{239} - 1$, the curve $E_0 : y^2 = x^3 + x$, and generators P_B, Q_B related by a distortion map. The prime p has bitlength 751, providing 186 bits of classical security and 124 bits of quantum security.

6.1   Performance

Performance tests of the uncompressed signature scheme were run on an Intel Xeon E5-2637 v3 3.5 GHz Haswell processor running CentOS v6.8, compiled with GCC v4.4.7. We also present timing results on the high-performance ARM Cortex-A57 processor in both C and an optimized arithmetic library on ASM [17]. The Juno platform provides a combination of Cortex-A57 and Cortex-A53 cores for ARMv8 big.LITTLE technology. However, our software is only benchmarked on a single high-performance Cortex-A57 core to get the most performance-oriented results. The software is compiled with Linaro GCC v4.9.4 on a single core 1.1 GHz ARM Cortex-A57 running OpenEmbedded Linux v4.5.0.

The signing and verifying algorithms are easily parallelizable with linear speedup, since the computations required for each round of the ZKP protocol is independent. We have implemented parallelization for the PC platform. The timing results are summarized in Table 2.

Table 2. Performance results (in 10^6 clock cycles) on Intel Xeon E5-2637 v3 3.5 GHz.

Platform	Threads	Keygen	Signing	Verifying
	1	63	28,776	19,679
PC	2	-	14,474	10,042
	4	-	7,449	5,536
ARM (C)		1,656	767,928	103,797
ARM (ASM)	-	123	57,092	36,757

As noted before, the computing costs in the signing algorithm are incurred almost entirely in the ZKP rounds which can be precomputed offline. With precomputation, the signing algorithm simply needs to evaluate a hash function on the data and output the appropriate responses for the signature.

7   Conclusion

We present and implement a stateless quantum-resistant digital signature scheme based on supersingular elliptic curve isogenies with very small key sizes, useful for post-quantum applications with strict key size requirements. Combined with previous works, these results show that isogenies can provide the full range of public-key cryptographic primitives including key establishment, encryption, and digital signatures. Though our results are promising, further improvements are still needed to bring isogeny-based signatures truly into the realm of practicality.

Acknowledgments. We thank Steven Galbraith for helpful comments on an earlier version of this paper, and the anonymous reviewers for their constructive feedback. This work was partially supported by NSF grant no. CNS-1464118, NIST award 60NANB16D246, the CryptoWorks21 NSERC CREATE Training Program in Building a Workforce for the Cryptographic Infrastructure of the 21st Century, and InfoSec Global, Inc.

References

1. Ambainis, A., Rosmanis, A., Unruh, D.: Quantum attacks on classical proof systems: the hardness of quantum rewinding. In: 55th IEEE Annual Symposium on Foundations of Computer Science, FOCS 2014, Philadelphia, PA, USA, 18–21 October 2014, pp. 474–483 (2014)
2. Azarderakhsh, R., Jao, D., Kalach, K., Koziel, B., Leonardi, C.: Key compression for isogeny-based cryptosystems. In: Proceedings of the 3rd ACM International Workshop on ASIA Public-Key Cryptography, AsiaPKC 2016, pp. 1–10. ACM, New York (2016)

3. Barreto, P.S.L.M., Longa, P., Naehrig, M., Ricardini, J.E., Zanon, G.: Sharper ring-LWE signatures. Cryptology ePrint Archive, report 2016/1026 (2016)
4. Bernstein, D.J., Hopwood, D., Hülsing, A., Lange, T., Niederhagen, R., Papachristodoulou, L., Schneider, M., Schwabe, P., Wilcox-O'Hearn, Z.: SPHINCS: practical stateless hash-based signatures. In: Oswald, E., Fischlin, M. (eds.) EURO-CRYPT 2015. LNCS, vol. 9056, pp. 368–397. Springer, Heidelberg (2015). https://doi.org/10.1007/978-3-662-46800-5_15
5. Bernstein, D.J., Lange, T., Peters, C.: Attacking and defending the McEliece cryptosystem. In: Buchmann, J., Ding, J. (eds.) PQCrypto 2008. LNCS, vol. 5299, pp. 31–46. Springer, Heidelberg (2008). https://doi.org/10.1007/978-3-540-88403-3_3
6. Boneh, D., Zhandry, M.: Secure signatures and chosen ciphertext security in a quantum computing world. In: Canetti, R., Garay, J.A. (eds.) CRYPTO 2013. LNCS, vol. 8043, pp. 361–379. Springer, Heidelberg (2013). https://doi.org/10.1007/978-3-642-40084-1_21
7. Costello, C., Jao, D., Longa, P., Naehrig, M., Renes, J., Urbanik, D.: Efficient compression of SIDH public keys. Cryptology ePrint Archive, report 2016/963 (2016)
8. Costello, C., Longa, P., Naehrig, M.: Efficient algorithms for supersingular isogeny Diffie-Hellman. In: Robshaw, M., Katz, J. (eds.) CRYPTO 2016. LNCS, vol. 9814, pp. 572–601. Springer, Heidelberg (2016). https://doi.org/10.1007/978-3-662-53018-4_21
9. Courtois, N.T., Finiasz, M., Sendrier, N.: How to achieve a McEliece-based digital signature scheme. In: Boyd, C. (ed.) ASIACRYPT 2001. LNCS, vol. 2248, pp. 157–174. Springer, Heidelberg (2001). https://doi.org/10.1007/3-540-45682-1_10
10. Ding, J., Schmidt, D.: Rainbow, a new multivariable polynomial signature scheme. In: Ioannidis, J., Keromytis, A., Yung, M. (eds.) ACNS 2005. LNCS, vol. 3531, pp. 164–175. Springer, Heidelberg (2005). https://doi.org/10.1007/11496137_12
11. Ducas, L., Durmus, A., Lepoint, T., Lyubashevsky, V.: Lattice signatures and bimodal Gaussians. In: Canetti, R., Garay, J.A. (eds.) CRYPTO 2013. LNCS, vol. 8042, pp. 40–56. Springer, Heidelberg (2013). https://doi.org/10.1007/978-3-642-40041-4_3
12. Feo, L.D., Jao, D., Plût, J.: Towards quantum-resistant cryptosystems from supersingular elliptic curve isogenies. J. Math. Cryptol. 8(3), 209–247 (2014)
13. Fiat, A., Shamir, A.: How to prove yourself: practical solutions to identification and signature problems. In: Odlyzko, A.M. (ed.) CRYPTO 1986. LNCS, vol. 263, pp. 186–194. Springer, Heidelberg (1987). https://doi.org/10.1007/3-540-47721-7_12
14. Galbraith, S.D., Petit, C., Silva, J.: Signature schemes based on supersingular isogeny problems. Cryptology ePrint Archive, report 2016/1154 (2016)
15. Grover, L.K.: A fast quantum mechanical algorithm for database search. In: Proceedings of the Twenty-Eighth Annual ACM Symposium on Theory of Computing, STOC 1996, pp. 212–219. ACM, New York (1996)
16. Jao, D., Soukharev, V.: Isogeny-based quantum-resistant undeniable signatures. In: Mosca, M. (ed.) PQCrypto 2014. LNCS, vol. 8772, pp. 160–179. Springer, Cham (2014). https://doi.org/10.1007/978-3-319-11659-4_10
17. Koziel, B., Jalali, A., Azarderakhsh, R., Jao, D., Kermani, M.M.: NEON-SIDH: Efficient implementation of supersingular isogeny Diffe-Hellman key exchange protocol on ARM. In: Cryptology and Network Security - 15th International Conference, CANS 2016, Milan, Italy, 14–16 November 2016, Proceedings, pp. 88–103 (2016)

18. Petzoldt, A., Bulygin, S., Buchmann, J.: Selecting parameters for the rainbow signature scheme. In: Sendrier, N. (ed.) PQCrypto 2010. LNCS, vol. 6061, pp. 218–240. Springer, Heidelberg (2010). https://doi.org/10.1007/978-3-642-12929-2_16

19. Seshadri, S.M., Chandrasekaran, V.: Isogeny-based quantum-resistant undeniable blind signature scheme. Cryptology ePrint Archive, Report 2016/148 (2016)

20. Sun, X., Tian, H., Wang, Y.: Toward quantum-resistant strong designated verifier signature from isogenies. In: 2012 Fourth International Conference on Intelligent Networking and Collaborative Systems (2012)

21. Tani, S.: Claw finding algorithms using quantum walk. Theor. Comput. Sci. **410**(50), 5285–5297 (2009)

22. Tate, J.: Endomorphisms of Abelian varieties over finite fields. Inventiones Mathematicae **2**(2), 134–144 (1966)

23. Unruh, D.: Quantum proofs of knowledge. In: Pointcheval, D., Johansson, T. (eds.) EUROCRYPT 2012. LNCS, vol. 7237, pp. 135–152. Springer, Heidelberg (2012). https://doi.org/10.1007/978-3-642-29011-4_10

24. Unruh, D.: Non-interactive zero-knowledge proofs in the quantum random Oracle model. In: Oswald, E., Fischlin, M. (eds.) EUROCRYPT 2015. LNCS, vol. 9057, pp. 755–784. Springer, Heidelberg (2015). https://doi.org/10.1007/978-3-662-46803-6_25

25. Watrous, J.: Zero-knowledge against quantum attacks. SIAM J. Comput. **39**(1), 25–58 (2009)

26. Zhang, S.: Promised and distributed quantum search. In: Wang, L. (ed.) COCOON 2005. LNCS, vol. 3595, pp. 430–439. Springer, Heidelberg (2005). https://doi.org/10.1007/11533719_44

Optimally Sound Sigma Protocols Under DCRA

Helger Lipmaa[(⊠)]

University of Tartu, Tartu, Estonia
helger.lipmaa@gmail.com

Abstract. Given a well-chosen additively homomorphic cryptosystem and a Σ protocol with a linear answer, Damgård, Fazio, and Nicolosi proposed a non-interactive designated-verifier zero knowledge argument in the registered public key model that is sound under non-standard complexity-leveraging assumptions. In 2015, Chaidos and Groth showed how to achieve the weaker yet reasonable culpable soundness notion under standard assumptions but only if the plaintext space order is prime. It makes use of Σ protocols that satisfy what we call the *optimal culpable soundness*. Unfortunately, most of the known additively homomorphic cryptosystems (like the Paillier Elgamal cryptosystem that is secure under the standard Decisional Composite Residuosity Assumption) have composite-order plaintext space. We construct optimally culpable sound Σ protocols and thus culpably sound non-interactive designated-verifier zero knowledge protocols for NP under standard assumptions given that the least prime divisor of the plaintext space order is large.

Keywords: Culpable soundness · Designated verifier
Homomorphic encryption · Non-interactive zero knowledge
Optimal soundness · Registered public key model

1 Introduction

Non-interactive zero knowledge (NIZK, [8]) proof system enable the prover to convince the verifier in the truth of a statement without revealing any side information. Unfortunately, it is well known that NIZK proof systems are not secure in the standard model. Usually, this means that one uses the random oracle model [6] or the common reference string (CRS, [8]) model. In particular, Σ protocols [14] can be efficiently transformed into NIZK proof systems in the random oracle model by using the Fiat-Shamir heuristic [21]. However, the random oracle model (and this concrete transformation) is questionable, since there exist protocols secure in the random oracle model that are not instantiable with any function [11,24]. While newer transformations make less use of the random oracle (for example, by relying on non-programmable random oracles [13,32]), it is commonly felt that the random oracle model is at best a heuristic.

On the other hand, using the CRS model results often — though, not always, one notable exception being zk-SNARKs [23,26,33] — in less efficient protocols;

© International Financial Cryptography Association 2017
A. Kiayias (Ed.): FC 2017, LNCS 10322, pp. 182–203, 2017.
https://doi.org/10.1007/978-3-319-70972-7_10

moreover, also the CRS model is quite strong and requires significant amount of trust in the creator of the CRS. See [3] for some of the critique; although one can partially decrease the required trust by using multi-party computation to generate the CRS [7,9] and verify the correctness of the CRS (subversion zero-knowledge, [1,5,22]). Still, it is desirable to construct NIZK proof systems based on a less demanding trust model.

Moreover, NIZK proof systems in the CRS model are not always perfect approximations of interactive zero knowledge proof systems [3,16,30].

First, interactive zero knowledge provides undeniability: since the verifier can simulate the proof, she cannot convince third parties that she received a ZK proof from the specific prover. Undeniability is important in many applications where it provides a certain amount of protection against third parties (for example, coercers, see [30] for more motivation).

To provide undeniability also in the case of NIZK, Jakobsson *et al.* [30] introduced the notion of *designated verifier proof systems*. A designated verifier NIZK (NIDVZK) proof system is of type "either the statement is true or I am the intended verifier (i.e., I know some witness w_V associated with the verifier)". Hence, the designated verifier is convinced that the claim is true, while for everybody else it could look like this proof came from the verifier instead of the prover and thus they will not be convinced in the veracity of the claim. While NIDVZK proofs are verifiable only by (the prover and) the designated verifier, one can argue that an NIDVZK proof system provides a good approximation of interactive zero knowledge proof systems since neither is transferable [30].

Second, one can rewind interactive zero knowledge proofs of knowledge to extract the prover's witness. This guarantees that an accepted prover also knows the witness. Such extraction is impossible, for example, in the case of some Groth-Sahai proof systems [29]. To "emulate" extractability, Groth *et al.* [28] introduced the notion of culpable soundness. In a nutshell, culpable soundness means that it should be difficult to break the soundness of a zero knowledge proof system while knowing a witness w_{guilt} that the input does not belong to the input language. Culpable soundness has been successfully used in applications like shuffling [20,27]; see [28] for other applications. Moreover, culpable soundness is also sometimes the most one can get since there exist no computationally (non-culpably) sound statistical NIZK argument systems for non-trivial languages under standard assumptions [2].

Closer to the current work, Damgård, Fazio, and Nicolosi [16] constructed what we will call the *DFN transformation* from an optimally sound [35][1] and specially honest-verifier zero knowledge Σ-protocol [14] with a linear answer to an NIDVZK argument system (i.e., a computationally sound NIDVZK proof system) under a complexity leveraging assumption. Recall that a Σ protocol for language $\mathcal{L}$ is *optimally sound* if the following holds: if the common input x is not in $\mathcal{L}$, then for every a there exists at most one *good e* for which there exists a z, such that (x, a, e, z) is an accepting view of the Σ protocol. Optimal soundness is a potentially weaker requirement than special soundness.

---

[1] This property is also known under the name of *relaxed special soundness* [16].

Importantly, the DFN transformation results in an NIDVZK argument system that is secure in the registered-public key (RPK, [3]) model that is considered to be significantly weaker than the CRS model. Moreover, the resulting NIDVZK argument systems are almost as efficient as the original Σ-protocols. While the DFN transformation can be only applied to optimally sound Σ-protocols with a linear answer, most of the known Σ-protocols in the discrete-logarithm based setting have those properties. In particular, [16] constructed an NIDVZK argument system in the RPK model for the NP-complete language Circuit-SAT.

As argued before, the designated verifier property of the DFN transformation is very useful in certain applications. Hence, the DFN transformation results in efficient argument systems, secure in a weaker trust model (the RPK model) that better approximate security properties of interactive zero knowledge proof systems than say the Groth-Sahai proof system. However, it also has weaknesses. In particular, the original DFN transform from [16] is only secure under non-standard complexity leveraging assumptions.

Ventre and Visconti [39] modified the DFN transformation to work under standard (non-leveraged) assumptions, but their NIDVZK argument system only achieves weak culpable soundness (called weak co-soundness in [39]).[2] As we argued before, culpable soundness approximates interactive zero knowledge. However, weak culpable soundness seems to be too restrictive, and results in undesirable overhead. We omit discussion due to space limits and refer to [12].

Recently, Chaidos and Groth [12] further modified the DFN transformation so that the resulting NIDVZK argument systems are culpably sound under standard assumptions. However, for this they assumed that the plaintext space of the underlying strongly additively homomorphic cryptosystem (see [12] for the definition of such cryptosystems), about which the Σ-protocols are, has a prime order p. Under this assumption, they showed that several known efficient Σ protocols have the optimal culpable soundness property.

However, the restriction that p is prime can be a problem in many applications, since only some cryptosystems with required properties (like the Okamoto-Uchiyama cryptosystem [36]) are known. Moreover, in the Okamoto-Uchiyama cryptosystem, p must stay secret; this complicates the design of many common protocols where one needs to know the order of the plaintext space. Currently, the fact that one would like to have efficient Σ-protocols excludes known lattice-based cryptosystems with prime-order plaintext space.

Our Contributions. We construct a DFN-transform under standard assumption for additively homomorphic cryptosystems where the plaintext space has a composite order N, such that it is solely required that the least prime factor of N is sufficiently large. While all our examples are about the DCRA-based

---

[2] Briefly, weak culpable soundness means that it is intractable to cheat while knowing a witness assessing the fact that you are cheating, and also know that your cheating succeeds (i.e., know a witness that certifies that the verification equations hold). In the case of culpable soundness [28], the latter is not needed. See [39] for more details.

Paillier Elgamal cryptosystem [10,18], it is clear that they can modified to work with other suitable cryptosystems. The main novelty of our work is proving that several *known* Σ protocols over composite order plaintext spaces are optimally culpably sound. We postpone the construction of culpably sound NIDVZK argument systems to the appendix.

More precisely, an optimally sound Σ protocol is *optimally culpable sound*[3] if the following property holds: a successful cheating prover $\mathcal{A}$ who knows that she cheats (e.g., she knows the secret key of the public key cryptosystem Π) can efficiently recover the good e. That is, there exists an efficient extractor $\mathcal{S}.\mathsf{EX}$ that extracts good e (if it exists), given the common input, the first message of the Σ protocol (e.g., a tuple of ciphertexts) output by $\mathcal{A}$, and the guilt witness (e.g., the secret key of Π). We emphasize that the optimal culpable soundness is a stronger notion of security compared to the optimal soundness.

The main technical contribution of the current paper is the construction of an efficient $\mathcal{S}.\mathsf{EX}$ for several (known) Σ protocols about the plaintexts of the Paillier Elgamal cryptosystem. By using $\mathcal{S}.\mathsf{EX}$, we prove optimal culpable soundness of corresponding Σ protocols without relying on the Strong RSA or any other computational assumption. Importantly, the proofs of optimal culpable soundness are simpler than the special soundness proofs — that we also reproduce for the sake of completeness — for the same Σ protocols.

For the constructed extractors to be successful, it is only required that the least prime factor of N is large enough. This means that one can use essentially any known additively homomorphic public key cryptosystem that has a large plaintext space. On the other hand, Chaidos and Groth [12] constructed $\mathcal{S}.\mathsf{EX}$ only in the case of prime-order plaintext space (with the Okamoto-Uchiyama cryptosystem being the sole mentioned candidate cryptosystem in [12]).

Before we give more details about the new Σ protocols, let us recall that the Paillier Elgamal cryptosystem has several other interesting properties:

1. First, it is double trapdoor [10]: it has two statistically independent trapdoors, the prime factorization sk_{fact} of an RSA modulus N, and an Elgamal-like secret key sk_{dl}. Decryption is possible, given either of the two trapdoors. Hence, given that N is securely generated, many different parties can operate with plaintexts and ciphertexts modulo the same N; this simplifies the design of threshold encryption schemes, [18].
2. Second, many of the standard Σ protocols, see [31], working on top of the Paillier Elgamal cryptosystem satisfy special soundness only under the Strong RSA assumption [4].

In the case of the Paillier Elgamal cryptosystem, $\mathcal{S}.\mathsf{EX}$ only needs to use the second trapdoor sk_{dl}. Hence, if a cheating prover manages to make the verifier to accept, the extractor who knows sk_{dl} can extract the good challenge, given that it exists. On top of it, the extractor may also extract a non-trivial factor of N, which means that he will break the factoring assumption. In practice, this fact is relevant in the case of threshold encryption, where such a factor can be

---

[3] Chaidos and Groth called it soundness with the unique identifiable challenge.

recovered only when a majority of the key generating parties collaborate, while extraction is possible by every single party who knows the key sk_{dl}.

However, the extractor does not need factoring to be hard to be successful, i.e., extraction is unconditionally successful. Thus, while some Σ protocols about the plaintexts of the Paillier Elgamal cryptosystem are specially sound only under the Strong RSA assumption, their optimal culpable soundness (and hence, also optimal soundness) is unconditional. Up to our knowledge, this separation has not been noticed before. We leave it as in interesting question whether such a phenomenon is widespread.

The modified DFN-transform achieves culpable soundness in the sense that soundness is guaranteed against adversaries that return together with the accepting view also the secret key of the prover (but no other secret value). If the verifiers gives to the authority a zero knowledge proof of knowledge of her secret key sk, we can construct an adversary that retrieves sk from the registration process, and thus achieves the standard (not culpable) notion of soundness.

2   Preliminaries

For a predicate P, let $[P(x)]$ be 1 iff $P(x)$ is true, and 0 otherwise. We denote uniform distribution on set S by $U(S)$, and let $a \leftarrow_r S$ to denote choosing a from $U(S)$. The statistical distance between two sets $S_1, S_2 \subseteq \Omega$ is $\mathrm{SD}(U(S_1), U(S_2)) = \frac{1}{2} \sum_{x \in \Omega} |\Pr[x \in S_2] - \Pr[x \in S_1]|$. We will implicitly use the following lemma.

Lemma 1. *Let S_1 and S_2 be two finite sets. If $S_1 \subseteq S_2$, we have $\mathrm{SD}(U(S_1), U(S_2)) = 1 - |S_1|/|S_2|$. In particular, if $|S_2| = (1 + 1/t) \cdot |S_1|$ for some positive integer t, then $\mathrm{SD}(U(S_1), U(S_2)) = 1/(t+1)$.*

Proof. $\mathrm{SD}(U(S_1), U(S_2)) = \frac{1}{2} (|S_2 \setminus S_1|/|S_2| + |S_1| \cdot (1/|S_1| - 1/|S_2|)) = 1 - |S_1|/|S_2|$. □

For a positive integer N, let $\mathrm{lpf}(N)$ be its least prime factor. Let $\varphi(N)$ be the Euler totient function. Given that $\gcd(a, b) = \gamma$, the Extended Euclidean Algorithm returns integers α and β, such that $\alpha a + \beta b = \gamma$.

For any integer a and an odd prime p, the Legendre symbol $\left(\frac{a}{p}\right)$ is defined as $\left(\frac{a}{p}\right) = 0$, if $a \equiv 0 \pmod{p}$, $\left(\frac{a}{p}\right) = +1$, if $a \not\equiv 0 \pmod{p}$ and for some integer x, $a \equiv x^2 \pmod{p}$, and $\left(\frac{a}{p}\right) = -1$, if there is no such x. For any integer a and any positive odd integer N, the Jacobi symbol is defined as the product of the Legendre symbols corresponding to the prime factors of N: $\left(\frac{a}{N}\right) = \prod_{i=1}^{t} \left(\frac{a}{p_i}\right)^{\alpha_i}$, where $N = \prod_{i=1}^{t} p_i^{\alpha_i}$ for different primes p_i. Let $J_N = \{a \in \mathbb{Z}_N : \left(\frac{a}{N}\right) = 1\}$; clearly $J_N \trianglelefteq \mathbb{Z}_N^*$ (i.e., J_N is a subgroup of $\mathbb{Z}_N^*$). Let $Q_N \trianglelefteq J_N$ be the subgroup of quadratic residues in $\mathbb{Z}_N$. The Jacobi symbol can be computed in polynomial time, given only a and N.

2.1 Cryptographic Assumptions

Within this paper, κ is an exponential (e.g., $\kappa \approx 128$) security parameter. We denote $f(\kappa) \approx_\kappa f'(\kappa)$, if $|f(\kappa) - f'(\kappa)| = \kappa^{-\omega(1)}$. A function $f(\kappa)$ is *negligible*, if $f(\kappa) \approx_\kappa 0$. For any κ, we assume that factoring $\tau(\kappa)$-bit integers is intractable.

Strong RSA. We say that the *Strong RSA assumption* [4] holds, if given a product $N = pq$ of two randomly chosen $\tau(\kappa)/2$-bit safe primes $p = 2p' + 1$ and $q = 2q' + 1$, and $y \leftarrow_r \mathbb{Z}_N^*$, it is computationally difficult to output (x, e), such that $e > 1$ and $y \equiv x^e \mod N$.

DCR [15,37]. Let $N = pq$ be a product of two $\tau(\kappa)/2$-bit random safe primes $p = 2p' + 1$ and $q = 2q' + 1$. Let $N' = p'q'$. Let $s \geq 1$. Write $\mathbb{G} := \mathbb{Z}_{N^{s+1}}^* \cong G_{N^s} \oplus G_{N'} \oplus G_2 \oplus T$, where $\cong$ indicates group isomorphism, $\oplus$ is the direct sum or Cartesian product, G_i are cyclic groups of order i, and T is the order-2 cyclic group generated by $-1 \mod N^{s+1}$. Let $\mathbb{X} := \mathbb{P} := J_{N^{s+1}} \cong G_{N^s} \oplus G_{N'} \oplus T$, $\mathbb{X}' := \mathbb{P}' := Q_{N^{s+1}} \cong G_{N^s} \oplus G_{N'}$, and $\mathbb{L} \cong G_{N'}$ be multiplicative groups.

Let g be a random generator of $\mathbb{L}$; g can be thought of as a random $2N^s$-th residue. It can be computed by choosing a random $\mu \leftarrow_r \mathbb{Z}_{N^{s+1}}$ and then setting $g \leftarrow \mu^{2N^s} \mod N^{s+1}$.

A witness $w \in \mathbb{W} := \mathbb{Z}$ for $x \in \mathbb{L}$ is such that $x \equiv g^w \pmod{N^{s+1}}$. Finally, let $g_\perp$ be an arbitrary generator of the cyclic group G_{N^s} (for example $g_\perp = 1 + N \in \mathbb{Z}_{N^{s+1}}$). We set $\Lambda = (N, s, g, g_\perp)$.

The Decisional Composite Residuosity (DCR, [37]) assumption says that it is difficult to distinguish random elements of $\mathbb{L}$ from random elements of $\mathbb{X}$.

We remark that we cannot sample uniform witnesses as $\mathbb{W} = \mathbb{Z}$ is infinite. From a mathematical standpoint, we could have set $\mathbb{W} = \mathbb{Z}_{N'}$, but we cannot do that here, as computing N' from Λ requires to factorize N. Instead, we sample witnesses uniformly from $\mathbb{W}_N^* := \mathbb{Z}_{\lfloor N/4 \rfloor}$. This is statistically close to uniform over $\mathbb{Z}_{N'}$ as: $\mathrm{SD}(U(\mathbb{Z}_{N'}), U(\mathbb{W}_N^*)) = 1 - p'q'/(pq/4) = (2p' + 2q' + 1)/(pq) < 2(p + q)/(pq) < 4/\mathrm{lpf}(N)$. From this distribution over $\mathbb{W}$, we can derive a statistically uniform distribution over $\mathbb{L}$.

2.2 Paillier Elgamal Cryptosystem

We use the following CPA-secure double-trapdoor cryptosystem $\Pi = (\mathsf{K}, \mathsf{VK}, \mathsf{E}, \mathsf{D})$ that is based on a projective hash proof system from [15]. We make it proof-friendly by using ideas from [18] and augment it with the VK procedure needed to get optimal culpable soundness. Following say [34], we call this cryptosystem *Paillier Elgamal*. See, e.g., [10,18] for variants of this cryptosystem.

Let $\Lambda = (N = pq, s, g, g_\perp)$ and $(p = 2p' + 1, q = 2q' + 1)$ be chosen as in Sect. 2.1, with $N' = p'q'$. Set $\mathsf{sk}_{fact} \leftarrow (p, q)$ and $\mathsf{sk}_{dl} \leftarrow_r \mathbb{W}_N^*$. Let $h \leftarrow g^{\mathsf{sk}_{dl}} \mod N^{s+1}$. Hence, $g, h \in \mathbb{P} = J_{N^{s+1}}$. The key generator $\Pi.\mathsf{K}(\Lambda)$ returns the public key $\mathsf{pk} := (\Lambda, h)$ and the secret key $\mathsf{sk} := (\mathsf{sk}_{fact}, \mathsf{sk}_{dl})$. The message space is equal to $\mathcal{M}_{\mathsf{pk}} := \mathbb{Z}_{N^s}$, the ciphertext space is equal to $\mathcal{C}_{\mathsf{pk}} := \mathbb{P}^2$, and the randomizer space is equal to $\mathcal{R}_{\mathsf{pk}} := \mathbb{W}_N^* \times \mathbb{Z}_2 \times \mathbb{Z}_2$.

Define $\mathsf{VK}(\mathsf{sk}_{dl}, \mathsf{pk}) = 1$ iff sk_{dl} is the secret key, corresponding to the public key pk. In the case of the Paillier Elgamal, VK can be evaluated efficiently by checking whether $h \equiv g^{\mathsf{sk}_{dl}} \pmod{N^{s+1}}$. Define

$$\mathsf{E}_{\mathsf{pk}}^s(m; r, t_0, t_1) := ((-1)^{t_0} g^r, (N+1)^m (-1)^{t_1} h^r) \mod N^{s+1}.$$

Here, t_0 and t_1 are only needed for the sake of constructing zero knowledge proofs, to obtain soundness also in the case when $g \notin Q_{N^{s+1}}$ or $h \notin Q_{N^{s+1}}$. By default, one just sets $t_0 = t_1 = 0$.

Given a ciphertext $\boldsymbol{C} = (C_1, C_2)$, the decryption algorithm $\mathsf{D}_{\mathsf{sk}_{dl}}^s(\boldsymbol{C})$ checks that $C_1, C_2 \in \mathbb{P} = J_{N^{s+1}}$ and rejects otherwise. Second, it computes $(N+1)^{2m} = (C_2/C_1^{\mathsf{sk}_{dl}})^2 \mod N^{s+1}$, and then retrieves m from this by using the algorithm described in [17]. Π is IND-CPA secure under the DCR assumption, [15].

The Paillier Elgamal cryptosystem is additively homomorphic, since $\mathsf{E}_{\mathsf{pk}}^s(m_1; r_1, t_{01}, t_{11}) \cdot \mathsf{E}_{\mathsf{pk}}^s(m_2; r_2, t_{02}, t_{12}) = \mathsf{E}_{\mathsf{pk}}^s(m_1 + m_2; r_1 + r_2, t_{01} \oplus t_{11}, t_{02} \oplus t_{12})$. Moreover, it is blindable, since for $r' \leftarrow_r \mathbb{W}_N^*$, $t_{b0} \leftarrow_r \mathbb{Z}_2$ and $t_{b1} \leftarrow_r \mathbb{Z}_2$, $\mathsf{E}_{\mathsf{pk}}^s(m; r, t_0, t_1) \cdot \mathsf{E}_{\mathsf{pk}}^s(0; r'; t_{b0}, t_{b1}) = \mathsf{E}_{\mathsf{pk}}^s(m; r + r', t_0 + t_{b0} \mod 2, t_1 + t_{b1} \mod 2)$ is a (close to uniformly) random encryption of m.

This cryptosystem has two statistically independent trapdoors, $\mathsf{sk}_{fact} = (p, q)$ and sk_{dl}. To decrypt (C_1, C_2), it suffices to have either. However, in some applications N can be generated in a highly secure environment so that its factorization is not known to anybody. Alternatively, one can create a huge N randomly, so that with a high probability it is guaranteed that N has large factors, [38]. Many different parties can then have N as a part of their public key (*without* knowing the factorization), and generate their own trapdoor sk_{dl}. A natural application is threshold encryption, where the factorization of N is only known by a threshold of the parties, while each party has their own trapdoor sk_{dl}; see [18].

2.3 Σ Protocols

Let $\mathcal{R} = \{(x, w)\}$ be a polynomial-time verifiable relation, and let $\mathcal{L}_{\mathcal{R}} = \{x : (\exists w)(x, w) \in \mathcal{R}\}$, where w has polynomial length.

A Σ-*protocol* [14] $\mathcal{S}$ is a three-message protocol between the prover $\mathcal{S}.\mathsf{P}$ and the verifier $\mathcal{S}.\mathsf{V}$, where the first and the third messages are send by the prover, and the second message is a uniformly random message $e \leftarrow_r \mathbb{Z}_{2^\kappa}$ chosen by the verifier. The prover $\mathcal{S}.\mathsf{P}$ and the verifier $\mathcal{S}.\mathsf{V}$ are two efficient algorithms that have a common input x. Additionally, the prover knows a secret witness w. At the end of the Σ protocol, the verifier either accepts ($x \in \mathcal{L}_{\mathcal{R}}$) or rejects ($x \notin \mathcal{L}_{\mathcal{R}}$). We will implicitly assume that the three messages of $\mathcal{S}$ belong to some sets whose memberships can be efficiently tested.

In addition, we require the Σ protocol to have a linear answer [16].

Definition 1. *A Σ protocol with a linear answer for an NP-relation $\mathcal{R}$ that consists of three messages and of the verifier's decision algorithm defined by a pair $(\mathcal{S}.\mathsf{P}, \mathcal{S}.\mathsf{V})$ of efficient algorithms as follows:*

1. $(c_a, z_1, z_2) \leftarrow S.P(x; w)$, where z_1 and z_2 are two m-dimensional vectors for some m. Here, c_a is the first message sent by the prover to the verifier.
2. The second message is $e \leftarrow_r \mathbb{Z}_{2^\kappa}$, chosen by the verifier randomly, and sent to the prover.
3. The third message is $z \leftarrow ez_1 + z_2$, sent by the prover to the verifier.
4. Finally, the verifier outputs $S.V(x; c_a, e, z) \in \{0, 1\}$, that is, the verifier either accepts or rejects.

Here, (x, c_a, e, z) is called the (real) *view* of the Σ protocol. Thus, the verifier either rejects or accepts the view. In the latter case, the view is said to be *accepting* (for S).

A Σ protocol S with a linear answer for relation $\mathcal{R}$ is *perfectly complete*, if for every $(x, w) \in \mathcal{R}$ and every $(c_a, z_1, z_2) \in S.P(x; w)$ and $e \in \{0, 1\}^\kappa$, it holds that $S.V(x; c_a, e, ez_1 + z_2) = 1$.

A Σ protocol S with a linear answer for relation $\mathcal{R}$ is *perfectly (resp., statistically) special honest-verifier zero knowledge* [14], if there exists an efficient simulator $S.\text{sim}$ that inputs x and $e \in \{0, 1\}^\kappa$, and outputs (c_a, z), such that (x, c_a, e, z) is accepting, and moreover, if e is a uniform random element of $\{0, 1\}^\kappa$, then (x, c_a, e, z) has the same (resp., is negligibly different from the) distribution as the real view of S.

A Σ protocol S with a linear answer is *specially sound* [14] for $\mathcal{R}$ if, given two accepting views (x, c_a, e, z) and (x, c_a, e', z') with the same (x, c_a) but with $e \neq e'$, one can efficiently recover a witness w, such that $(x, w) \in \mathcal{R}$. A Σ protocol is *computationally specially sound* for $\mathcal{R}$ if it is specially sound for $\mathcal{R}$ under a computational assumption.

Consider any input x (possibly $x \notin \mathcal{L}_\mathcal{R}$) and any c_a. Then $e \in \{0, 1\}^\kappa$ is a *good challenge* [16] for a Σ protocol S, if there exists a z such that (x, c_a, e, z) is an accepting view for S.

Definition 2 (Optimal Soundness). *A Σ protocol S is* optimally sound *[35] (also known as* relaxed specially sound *[16]) for $\mathcal{R}$, if for any $x \notin \mathcal{L}_\mathcal{R}$ and any purported first message c_a, there exists at most one good $e \in \{0, 1\}^\kappa$ for S.*

We note that in some Σ protocols it will be important not to allow e to fall outside of $\{0, 1\}^\kappa$. For example, it can be the case that if e is good, then also $e + p$ is good, where $p > 2^\kappa$ is a non-trivial factor of N. There will be at most one good $e < 2^\kappa$ under the assumption that $\text{lpf}(N) > 2^\kappa$.

To make the definition of optimal soundness compatible with culpable soundness, Chaidos and Groth [12] modified it as follows. (In [12], this property was called soundness with *uniquely identifiable challenge* using relation $\mathcal{R}^{guilt}$.) We note that differently from [12], we only require the extractor to return e, if it exists; as we will show, there are cases where such e is not available.

Definition 3 (Optimal culpable soundness). *For a relation $\mathcal{R}$, let $\mathcal{R}^{guilt} = \{(x, w)\}$ be a polynomial-time verifiable relation, where it is required that $x \notin \mathcal{L}_\mathcal{R}$ if $(x, w) \in \mathcal{R}^{guilt}$ for some w. A Σ protocol S has* optimal culpable soundness *using relation $\mathcal{R}^{guilt}$ for $\mathcal{R}$, if (i) it is optimally sound for $\mathcal{R}$, and (ii) there exists an* *efficient algorithm* $\mathcal{S}.\mathsf{EX}$, *such that if* $(x, w_{guilt}) \in \mathcal{R}^{guilt}$ *then* $\mathcal{S}.\mathsf{EX}_{w_{guilt}}(x, \boldsymbol{c}_a)$ *returns the unique good* e *where* $\boldsymbol{c}_a$ *is a first message returned by* $\mathcal{S}.\mathsf{P}$.

It is claimed in [16] that every specially sound Σ protocol is optimally sound. As we will show in Sect. 2.3, an even stronger claim holds: there exist cases where the Σ protocol is computationally specially sound (for example, one needs to rely on the Strong RSA assumption [4]) and unconditionally optimally culpably sound and thus also unconditionally optimally sound.

3   New Optimally Culpably Sound Σ-Protocols

Let $\Pi = (\mathsf{K}, \mathsf{VK}, \mathsf{E}, \mathsf{D})$ be the double-trapdoor additively homomorphic cryptosystem from Sect. 2.2. We next describe two simple Σ protocols about the plaintext of a Π ciphertext that both satisfy optimal culpable soundness using a naturally defined relation $\mathcal{R}^{guilt}$ where the witness is just the secret key sk_{dl} of Π. Close variants of these Σ-protocols also work with the DCR-based cryptosystems from [10,17,18]; see, e.g., [31]. Basing the Σ protocols on Π (and not, say, on the cryptosystem from [17]) makes it easier to pinpoint some differences between the special soundness and the optimal culpable soundness.

3.1 Σ-Protocol for Zero

Consider the following Σ protocol, see Fig. 1, with a linear answer for the relation

$$\mathcal{R}_{\mathrm{ZERO}} = \{((\mathsf{pk}, \boldsymbol{C}), (r, b_0, b_1)) : \boldsymbol{C} = \mathsf{E}^s_{\mathsf{pk}}(0; r, b_0, b_1)\}.$$

That is, a honest verifier accepts iff $\boldsymbol{C}$ encrypts to 0.

---

1. $\mathcal{S}.\mathsf{P}(\mathsf{pk}, \boldsymbol{C}; (r \in \mathbb{Z}_{\lfloor N/4 \rfloor}, b_0 \in \mathbb{Z}_2, b_1 \in \mathbb{Z}_2))$ does the following:
   (a) Set $r_a \leftarrow_r \mathbb{Z}_{2^{2\kappa}\lfloor N/4 \rfloor}$, $t_0 \leftarrow_r \mathbb{Z}_2$, $t_1 \leftarrow_r \mathbb{Z}_2$,
   (b) Set $\boldsymbol{c}_a \leftarrow \mathsf{E}^s_{\mathsf{pk}}(0; r_a, t_0, t_1)$,
   (c) Return $(\boldsymbol{c}_a, \boldsymbol{z}_1 \leftarrow (r, b_0, b_1), \boldsymbol{z}_2 \leftarrow (r_a, t_0, t_1))$.
   The prover's first message is $\boldsymbol{c}_a$.
2. The verifier's second message is $e \leftarrow_r \mathbb{Z}_{2^\kappa}$.
3. The prover sets $r_b \leftarrow er + r_a$, $t_{b0} \leftarrow eb_0 + t_0 \mod 2$, $t_{b1} \leftarrow eb_1 + t_1 \mod 2$, and outputs $\boldsymbol{z} \leftarrow (r_b, t_{b0}, t_{b1})$ as the third message.
4. The verifier $\mathcal{S}.\mathsf{V}(\mathsf{pk}, \boldsymbol{C}; \boldsymbol{c}_a, e, \boldsymbol{z})$ checks that
   (a) $\boldsymbol{C}, \boldsymbol{c}_a \in \mathbb{P}^2 = J^2_{N^{s+1}}$,
   (b) $\boldsymbol{z} = (r_b, t_{b0}, t_{b1})$, where $r_b \in \mathbb{Z}_{(2^{2\kappa}+2^\kappa-1)\lfloor N/4 \rfloor - 2^\kappa + 1}$, $t_{b0} \in \mathbb{Z}_2$, $t_{b1} \in \mathbb{Z}_2$,
   (c) the following holds:

$$(\boldsymbol{C}^e \boldsymbol{c}_a \cdot \mathsf{E}^s_{\mathsf{pk}}(0; r_b, 0, 0)^{-1})^2 \equiv 1 \pmod{N^{s+1}}. \tag{1}$$

Fig. 1. Σ protocol for ZERO

Theorem 1. *Let Π be the Paillier Elgamal cryptosystem. The Σ protocol of Fig. 1 has a linear answer, is perfectly complete, and statistically special HVZK. Assume pk is a valid public key. Then this Σ protocol is computationally specially sound for $\mathcal{R}$ under the Strong RSA assumption [4].*

Proof. First, clearly, $r_b \leq (2^{2\kappa} + 2^\kappa - 1)\lfloor N/4 \rfloor - 2^\kappa$.

LINEAR ANSWER: straightforward.

PERFECT COMPLETENESS: straightforward. If the prover is honest, we have $(\boldsymbol{C}^e \boldsymbol{c}_a \cdot \mathsf{E}^s_{\mathsf{pk}}(0; r_b, 0, 0)^{-1})^2 \equiv \mathsf{E}^s_{\mathsf{pk}}(0; er + r_a - (er + r_a), eb_0 + t_0 \mod 2, eb_1 + t_1 \mod 2))^2 \equiv \mathsf{E}^s_{\mathsf{pk}}(0; 0, 0, 0) = \mathbf{1} \pmod{N^{s+1}}$.

STATISTICAL SPECIAL HVZK: the simulator $\mathcal{S}.\mathsf{sim}(x, e)$ first sets $z \leftarrow \mathbb{Z}_{2^{2\kappa}\lfloor N/4\rfloor}$, $t_0 \leftarrow_r \mathbb{Z}_2$, $t_1 \leftarrow_r \mathbb{Z}_2$, and then $\boldsymbol{c}_a \leftarrow \mathsf{E}^s_{\mathsf{pk}}(0; z, t_0, t_1)/\boldsymbol{C}^e$. Clearly, if $e \leftarrow_r \mathbb{Z}_{2^\kappa}$, then due to the choice of r_a, z is statistically close to z in the real protocol. Moreover, in both real and simulated protocols, $\boldsymbol{c}_a$ is defined by $((\mathsf{pk}, \boldsymbol{C}), e, z)$ and the verification equation.

COMPUTATIONAL SPECIAL SOUNDNESS: From two accepting views $(\boldsymbol{c}_a, e, \boldsymbol{z} = (r_b, t_{b0}, t_{b1}))$ and $(\boldsymbol{c}_a, e', \boldsymbol{z}' = (r'_b, t'_{b0}, t'_{b1}))$ with $e \neq e'$ and Eq. (1), we get that

$$\boldsymbol{C}^{2(e-e')} \equiv \mathsf{E}^s_{\mathsf{pk}}(0; 2(r_b - r'_b), 0, 0) \equiv (g^{2(r_b - r'_b)}, h^{2(r_b - r'_b)}) \pmod{N^{s+1}}. \quad (2)$$

To recover from this the witness $r = (r_b - r'_b)/(e - e') \mod \varphi(N)$, we have to compute $(r_b - r'_b)/(e - e')$ modulo $\varphi(N)$, without knowing $\varphi(N)$. We show that one can either recover r, or break the Strong RSA assumption.

First, if $(e - e') \mid (r_b - r'_b)$ over $\mathbb{Z}$, then we set $r \leftarrow (r_b - r'_b)/(e - e')$, and we are done: $\boldsymbol{C}^2 = \mathsf{E}^s_{\mathsf{pk}}(0; 2r, 0, 0)$ and thus $\boldsymbol{C} = \mathsf{E}^s_{\mathsf{pk}}(0; r, b_0, b_1)$ for efficiently recoverable b_0 and b_1.

Second, assume $(e - e') \nmid (r_b - r'_b)$ over $\mathbb{Z}$. In this case, let $\gamma \leftarrow \gcd(2(e - e'), 2(r_b - r'_b))$, $y_e \leftarrow_r 2(e - e')/\gamma$, and $y_b \leftarrow 2(r_b - r'_b)/\gamma$. According to Eq. (2), $C_1^{2(e-e')} \equiv g^{2(r_b - r'_b)} \pmod{N^{s+1}}$, and thus $(-1)^{t_0} C_1^{y_e} \equiv g^{y_b} \pmod{N^{s+1}}$ for efficiently computable $t_0 \in \mathbb{Z}_2$. Since $\gcd(y_b, y_e) = 1$, we can use the extended Euclidean algorithm to compute integers τ_b and τ_e, s.t. $\tau_b y_b + \tau_e y_e = 1$. Thus,

$$g = g^{\tau_b y_b + \tau_e y_e} = g^{\tau_b y_b} g^{\tau_e y_e} \equiv (-1)^{\tau_b t_0} C_1^{\tau_b y_e} g^{\tau_e y_e}$$
$$= (-1)^{\tau_b t_0} (C_1^{\tau_b} g^{\tau_e})^{y_e} \pmod{N^{s+1}}.$$

Since $y_e > 1$, then this means that we have found a non-trivial root $(C_1^{\tau_b} g^{\tau_e} \mod N^{s+1}, y_e)$ of $(-1)^{\tau_b t_0} g$ modulo N^{s+1}, and thus also modulo N, and thus broken the Strong RSA assumption.   □

Next, we will show that the same Σ-protocol from Fig. 1 has optimal culpable soundness using the relation

$$\mathcal{R}^{guilt}_{\text{ZERO}} = \left\{ \begin{array}{c} ((\mathsf{pk}, \boldsymbol{C}), \mathsf{sk}_{dl}) : \boldsymbol{C} \in \mathbb{P}^2 \wedge \mathsf{D}^s_{\mathsf{sk}_{dl}}(\boldsymbol{C}) \neq 0 \wedge \\ \mathsf{VK}(\mathsf{sk}_{dl}, \mathsf{pk}) = 1 \end{array} \right\} \quad (3)$$

without relying on any computational assumptions. Here, w_{guilt} is equal to sk_{dl}; hence, the extractor $\mathcal{S}.\mathsf{EX}$ gets sk_{dl} as the secret input.

Theorem 2. *Let Π be the Paillier Elgamal cryptosystem. Assume that $\mathrm{lpf}(N) > 2^\kappa$. Then the Σ protocol S from Fig. 1 has optimal culpable soundness using $\mathcal{R}_{\mathrm{ZERO}}^{guilt}$.*

Proof. Consider the extractor in Fig. 2 that either returns "reject" (if C is not a valid ciphertext or $\mathsf{VK}(\mathsf{sk}_{dl}, \mathsf{pk})$ does not hold; in such cases $S.\mathsf{V}$ also rejects), "accept" (the prover was honest), or the good challenge (if it exists) together with a non-trivial factor of N.

$S.\mathsf{EX}_{\mathsf{sk}_{dl}}^{s}((\mathsf{pk}, C), c_a)$:

1. If $C \notin \mathbb{P}^2$ or $c_a \notin \mathbb{P}^2$: return "reject";
2. If $\mathsf{VK}(\mathsf{sk}_{dl}, \mathsf{pk}) = 0$: return "reject";
3. Let $m \leftarrow \mathsf{D}_{\mathsf{sk}_{dl}}^{s}(C)$; Let $m_a \leftarrow \mathsf{D}_{\mathsf{sk}_{dl}}^{s}(c_a)$;
4. If $m \equiv 0 \pmod{N^s}$: return "accept"; /* prover was honest */
5. Let $\gamma \leftarrow \gcd(m, N^s)$;
6. Let $\bar{m} \leftarrow m/\gamma$; Let $\bar{m}_a \leftarrow m_a/\gamma$; Let $\bar{N}_s \leftarrow N^s/\gamma$;
7. $e \leftarrow -\bar{m}_a/\bar{m} \bmod \bar{N}_s$;
8. If $e < 2^\kappa$: return e;
9. else: return "no accepted challenges";

Fig. 2. Extractor from Theorem 2 for the Σ protocol from Fig. 1 for $\mathcal{R}_{\mathrm{ZERO}}^{guilt}$

We will now argue that this extractor functions as claimed. First, from the Eq. (1) of the Σ protocol in Fig. 1 it follows that

$$2(em + m_a) \equiv 0 \pmod{N^s}, \tag{4}$$

where m is the plaintext in C and m_a is the plaintext in c_a. Since the verification accepts and N is odd, $em \equiv -m_a \pmod{N^s}$.

If $m \equiv 0 \pmod{N^s}$, then the prover is honest. Otherwise, setting $\gamma \leftarrow \gcd(m, N^s)$, we can retrieve an e that satisfies Eq. (4), given such an e exists. Really, if a good e exists then $2(em + m_a) \equiv 0 \pmod{N^s}$, and thus $em + m_a \equiv 0 \pmod{N^s}$. Hence, $\bar{m}e + \bar{m}_a \equiv 0 \pmod{\bar{N}_s}$, and thus $e \equiv -\bar{m}_a/\bar{m} \pmod{\bar{N}_s}$. Since a good challenge is smaller than 2^κ, it is also smaller than $\bar{N}_s$, and thus computing e modulo $\bar{N}_s = N^s/\gamma$ does not throw away any information. Since $e\bar{m}\gamma + m_a \equiv 0 \pmod{N^s}$ and $\gamma \mid N^s$, we get $m_a \equiv 0 \pmod{\gamma}$ and thus $\gamma \mid m_a$. $\square$

3.2 Σ Protocol for Boolean

Consider the following Σ protocol, see Fig. 3, with a linear answer for the relation

$$\mathcal{R}_{\mathrm{BOOLEAN}} = \{((\mathsf{pk}, C), (m, r)) : C = \mathsf{E}_{\mathsf{pk}}^{s}(m; r, b_0, b_1) \wedge m \in \{0, 1\}\}.$$

I.e., a honest verifier accepts iff C encrypts to either 0 or 1. This Σ protocol is derived from the Σ protocol from [12] where it was stated for prime modulus.

1. $\mathcal{S}.\mathsf{P}(\mathsf{pk}, \boldsymbol{C}; m \in \mathbb{Z}_2, (r \in \mathbb{Z}_{\lfloor N/4 \rfloor}, b_0 \in \mathbb{Z}_2, b_1 \in \mathbb{Z}_2))$ does the following:
   (a) Let $m_a \leftarrow 2^{2\kappa+1} + U(\mathbb{Z}_{2^{2\kappa}})$, $r_a \leftarrow_r \mathbb{Z}_{2^{2\kappa}\lfloor N/4 \rfloor}$, $r_b \leftarrow_r \mathbb{Z}_{2^{3\kappa}\lfloor N/4 \rfloor}$;
   (b) Let $t_{a0}, t_{a1}, t_{b0}, t_{b1}, t_{c0}, t_{c1} \leftarrow_r \mathbb{Z}_2$;
   (c) Let $\boldsymbol{c}_a \leftarrow \mathsf{E}^s_{\mathsf{pk}}(m_a; r_a, t_{a0}, t_{a1})$, $\boldsymbol{c}_b \leftarrow \mathsf{E}^s_{\mathsf{pk}}(-mm_a; r_b, t_{b0}, t_{b1})$;
   (d) Return $((\boldsymbol{c}_a, \boldsymbol{c}_b), \boldsymbol{z}_1 = (m, r, r(m-1), b_0, b_1), \boldsymbol{z}_2 = (m_a, r_a, rm_a + r_b), t_{c0}, t_{c1})$.
   The prover's first message is $(\boldsymbol{c}_a, \boldsymbol{c}_b)$.
2. The verifier's second message is $e \leftarrow_r \mathbb{Z}_{2^\kappa}$,
3. The prover's third message is $\boldsymbol{z} = (z_m, z_a, z_b, t_{d0}, t_{d1})$, where $z_m \leftarrow em + m_a$, $z_a \leftarrow er + r_a$, $z_b \leftarrow er(m-1) + rm_a + r_b$, $t_{d0} \leftarrow eb_0 + t_{c0} \mod 2$, $t_{d1} \leftarrow eb_1 + t_{c1} \mod 2$.
4. The verifier checks that
   (a) $\boldsymbol{C}, \boldsymbol{c}_a, \boldsymbol{c}_b \in \mathbb{P}^2 = J^2_{N^{s+1}}$,
   (b) $z_m \in \mathbb{Z}_{3 \cdot 2^{2\kappa} + 2^\kappa - 1}$, $z_a \in \mathbb{Z}_{(2^{2\kappa} + 2^\kappa - 1)\lfloor N/4 \rfloor - 2^\kappa + 1}$,
   (c) $z_b \in \mathbb{Z}_{(2^{3\kappa} + 3 \cdot 2^{2\kappa} - 1) \cdot \lfloor N/4 \rfloor - 3 \cdot 2^{2\kappa} + 1}$, $t_{d0} \in \mathbb{Z}_2$, $t_{d1} \in \mathbb{Z}_2$,
   (d) the following holds:

$$(\boldsymbol{C}^e \boldsymbol{c}_a \cdot \mathsf{E}^s_{\mathsf{pk}}(z_m; z_a, 0, 0)^{-1})^2 \equiv 1 \pmod{N^{s+1}},$$
$$(\boldsymbol{C}^{z_m - e} \boldsymbol{c}_b \cdot \mathsf{E}^s_{\mathsf{pk}}(0; z_b, 0, 0)^{-1})^2 \equiv 1 \pmod{N^{s+1}}. \tag{5}$$

Fig. 3. Σ protocol for BOOLEAN

Theorem 3. *The Σ protocol (Boolean Proof) of Fig. 3 has a linear answer, and it is perfectly complete and statistically special HVZK. Assume that the Strong RSA assumption [4] holds, pk is a valid public key, and $\mathrm{lpf}(N^s) > 2^\kappa$. Then this Σ protocol is computationally specially sound.*

Proof. Clearly, in the honest case, $z_b = r(z_m - e) + r_b$. The choice of m_a guarantees that $z_b \geq 0$. Now,

$$z_m = em + m_a \leq (2^\kappa - 1) + (2^{2\kappa+1} + 2^{2\kappa} - 1) = 3 \cdot 2^{2\kappa} + 2^\kappa - 2,$$
$$z_a = er + r_a \leq (2^\kappa - 1)(\lfloor N/4 \rfloor - 1) + (2^{2\kappa} \lfloor N/4 \rfloor - 1)$$
$$= (2^{2\kappa} + 2^\kappa - 1) \lfloor N/4 \rfloor - 2^\kappa,$$

and (here we need that $m_a > e$)

$$z_b = er(m-1) + rm_a + r_b$$
$$\leq (2^\kappa - 1)(\lfloor N/4 \rfloor - 1) \cdot 0 + (\lfloor N/4 \rfloor - 1)(2^{2\kappa+1} + 2^{2\kappa} - 1) + (2^{3\kappa} \lfloor N/4 \rfloor - 1)$$
$$= (2^{3\kappa} + 3 \cdot 2^{2\kappa} - 1) \cdot \lfloor N/4 \rfloor - 3 \cdot 2^{2\kappa}.$$

LINEAR ANSWER: straightforward. COMPLETENESS: let $t_{ei} = b_i(m_a + e(m-1)) + t_{bi}$ for $i \in \{0, 1\}$. Equation (5) holds since

$$\boldsymbol{C}^{z_m - e} \boldsymbol{c}_b \equiv \mathsf{E}^s_{\mathsf{pk}}((em + m_a - e)m - mm_a; r(z_m - e) + r_b, t_{e0}, t_{e1})$$
$$\equiv \mathsf{E}^s_{\mathsf{pk}}(e(m-1)m; z_b, t_{e0}, t_{e1}) \equiv \mathsf{E}^s_{\mathsf{pk}}(0; z_b, t_{e0}, t_{e1}),$$

if $m \in \{0, 1\}$. Thus, $\boldsymbol{C}^{2(z_m - e)} \boldsymbol{c}_b^2 \equiv \mathsf{E}^s_{\mathsf{pk}}(0; 2z_b, 0, 0)$ if $m \in \{0, 1\}$. Other verifications are straightforward.

STATISTICAL SPECIAL HVZK: Given $e \in \mathbb{Z}_{2^\kappa}$, the simulator generates $z_m \leftarrow_r 2^{2\kappa+1} + U(\mathbb{Z}_{2^{2\kappa}})$, $z_a \leftarrow_r \mathbb{Z}_{2^{2\kappa}\lfloor N/4 \rfloor}$, $z_b \leftarrow_r \mathbb{Z}_{2^{3\kappa}\lfloor N/4 \rfloor}$, and $t_{a0}, t_{a1}, t_{b0}, t_{b1}, t_{d0}, t_{d1} \leftarrow_r \mathbb{Z}_2$. He sets $z \leftarrow (z_m, z_a, z_b, t_{d0}, t_{d1})$, $c_a \leftarrow \mathsf{E}^s_{\mathsf{pk}}(z_m; z_a, t_{a0}, t_{a1})/C^e \bmod N^{s+1}$ and $c_b \leftarrow \mathsf{E}^s_{\mathsf{pk}}(0; z_b, t_{b0}, t_{b1})/C^{z_m-e} \bmod N^{s+1}$, and returns $(\mathsf{pk}, C; (c_a, c_b), e, z)$ as the view. Clearly, both in the real and simulated proof, c_a and c_b are fixed by $(\mathsf{pk}, C; e, z)$ and the verification equations. Moreover, given that $e \leftarrow_r \mathbb{Z}_{2^\kappa}$, the simulated $z_m, z_a, z_b, t_{d0}, t_{d1}$ are statistically close to the values in the real proof.

SPECIAL SOUNDNESS: Assume that the verifier accepts two views $(\mathsf{pk}, C; c_a, c_b, e, z)$ and $(\mathsf{pk}, C; c_a, c_b, e', z')$ for $e \neq e'$. From the first equality in Eq. (5) we get that

$$C^{2(e-e')} \equiv \mathsf{E}_{\mathsf{pk}}(2(z_m - z'_m); 2(z_a - z'_a), 0, 0). \tag{6}$$

Hence, C encrypts $m := (z_m - z'_m)/(e - e') \bmod N^s$. (Here, we use the fact that $e, e' \in \mathbb{Z}_{2^\kappa} < \mathrm{lpf}(N^s)$, $e \neq e'$, and thus $e - e'$ is invertible.) To recover the randomizer used in encrypting C, we use the same technique as in the proof of Theorem 1: we either obtain that $(e - e') \mid (z_a - z'_a)$ (in this case, we set $r \leftarrow (z_a - z'_a)/(e - e')$), or we break the Strong RSA assumption. Similarly, we obtain the randomizers b_0 and b_1 that were used when computing C.

From the second equality in Eq. (5) holds, we get that

$$C^{2(z_m - z'_m) - 2(e - e')} \equiv \mathsf{E}^s_{\mathsf{pk}}(0; 2(z_b - z'_b), 0, 0) \pmod{N^{s+1}},$$

and thus, when combining it with Eq. (6),

$$\mathsf{E}^s_{\mathsf{pk}}(2(z_m - z'_m)m; 2(z_m - z'_m)r, 0, 0)$$
$$\equiv \mathsf{E}^s_{\mathsf{pk}}(2(z_m - z'_m); 2(z_a - z'_a + z_b - z'_b), 0, 0) \pmod{N^{s+1}},$$

Since $z_m - z'_m \equiv (e - e')m \pmod{N^s}$, we get after decrypting that

$$2(e - e')m^2 \equiv 2(e - e')m \pmod{N^s}.$$

Since $\gcd(e - e', N^s) = 1$, $m \bmod N^s \in \{0, 1\}$.   □

Next, we show that this Σ protocol has optimal culpable soundness using the guilt relation

$$\mathcal{R}^{guilt}_{\mathrm{BOOLEAN}} = \left\{ \begin{array}{c} ((\mathsf{pk}, C), \mathsf{sk}_{dl}) : C \in \mathbb{P}^2 \wedge \mathsf{D}^s_{\mathsf{sk}_{dl}}(C) \notin \{0, 1\} \wedge \\ \mathsf{VK}(\mathsf{sk}_{dl}, \mathsf{pk}) = 1 \end{array} \right\}. \tag{7}$$

Theorem 4. *Let Π be the Paillier Elgamal cryptosystem, and let $\mathrm{lpf}(N) > 2^\kappa$ (thus also $2 \nmid N$). Then the Σ protocol of Fig. 3 has optimal culpable soundness using $\mathcal{R}^{guilt}_{\mathrm{BOOLEAN}}$.*

$\mathcal{S}.\mathsf{EX}_{\mathsf{sk}_{dl}}(\boldsymbol{C}, \boldsymbol{c}_a, \boldsymbol{c}_b)$:
1. If $\boldsymbol{C} \notin \mathbb{P}^2$ or $\boldsymbol{c}_a \notin \mathbb{P}^2$ or $\boldsymbol{c}_b \notin \mathbb{P}^2$: return "reject";
2. If $\mathsf{VK}(\mathsf{sk}_{dl}, \mathsf{pk}) = 0$: return "reject";
3. Let $m \leftarrow \mathsf{D}^s_{\mathsf{sk}_{dl}}(\boldsymbol{C})$;
4. Let $m_a \leftarrow \mathsf{D}^s_{\mathsf{sk}_{dl}}(\boldsymbol{c}_a)$, $m_b \leftarrow \mathsf{D}^s_{\mathsf{sk}_{dl}}(\boldsymbol{c}_b)$;
5. Let $m^* \leftarrow (m-1)m \mod N^s$;
6. If $m^* \equiv 0 \pmod{N^s}$: return "accept";
7. else if $m^* \in \mathbb{Z}^*_{N^s}$: let $e \leftarrow -(mm_a + m_b)/m^* \mod N^s$;
8. else if $\gcd(m, N^s) > 1$:
   (a) Let $\gamma \leftarrow \gcd(m, N^s)$;
   (b) Let $\bar{m} \leftarrow m/\gamma$; $\bar{m}_b \leftarrow m_b/\gamma$, $\bar{m}^* \leftarrow m^*/\gamma$; $\bar{N}_s \leftarrow N^s/\gamma$;
   (c) Let $e \leftarrow_r -(m_a\bar{m} + \bar{m}_b)/\bar{m}^* \mod \bar{N}_s$;
9. else: /* $\gcd(m-1, N^s) > 1$ */
   (a) Let $\gamma \leftarrow \gcd(m-1, N^s)$;
   (b) Let $\bar{m}_1 \leftarrow (m-1)/\gamma$, $\bar{m}_{ab} \leftarrow (m_a + m_b)/\gamma$, $\bar{m}^* \leftarrow m^*/\gamma$, $\bar{N}_s \leftarrow N^s/\gamma$;
   (c) Let $e \leftarrow_r -(m_a\bar{m}_1 + \bar{m}_{ab})/\bar{m}^* \mod \bar{N}_s$;
10. If $e < 2^\kappa$: return e;
11. else: return "no accepted challenges";

Fig. 4. Extractor in Theorem 4 for $\mathcal{R}^{guilt}_{\text{BOOLEAN}}$

Proof. We prove the optimal culpable soundness as in Theorem 2. The main new complication is that there can now be two strategies of cheating: it can be that either $\gcd(m, N^s) > 1$ or $\gcd(m-1, N^s) > 1$, so the extractor has to test for both. We thus construct the following extractor, see Fig. 4.

Let $m^* := (m-1)m \mod N^s$. From the verification equalities in Eq. (5) we get that $z_m \equiv em + m_a \pmod{N^s}$ and $(z_m - e)m + m_b \equiv 0 \pmod{N^s}$, thus $(cm + m_a - e)m + m_b \equiv 0 \pmod{N^s}$, and thus

$$em^* \equiv -(m_a m + m_b) \pmod{N^s}. \tag{8}$$

Clearly, the constructed extractor works correctly. If $m^* \equiv 0 \pmod{N^s}$ or $m^* \equiv 1 \pmod{N^s}$, then the prover was honest. Otherwise, if $m^* \in \mathbb{Z}^*_{N^s}$, then one can recover e from Eq. (8) efficiently. Otherwise, if $\gcd(m^*, N^s) > 1$, we have either $\gcd(m, N^s) > 1$ or $\gcd(m-1, N^s) > 1$. Those two possibilities are mutually exclusive, since $\gcd(m, m-1) = 1$.

In the case $\gamma = \gcd(m, N^s) > 1$, we can divide the left hand side and right hand side of Eq. (8) by γ, and obtain $e \mod (N^s/\gamma)$ as in Fig. 4, line 8c. This is possible since in this case, from Eq. (8) we get that $e(m-1)\bar{m}\gamma \equiv -(m_a\bar{m}\gamma + m_b)$ $\pmod{N^s}$ and hence $m_b \equiv 0 \pmod{\gamma}$ and $\gamma \mid m_b$. Since $e < 2^\kappa < \text{lpf}(N)$, we have obtained e.

In the case $\gamma = \gcd(m-1, N^s) > 1$, we can divide the left hand side and right hand side of Eq. (8) by γ, and obtain $e \mod (N^s/\gamma)$ as in Fig. 4, line 9c. This is possible since in this case, we can rewrite Eq. (8) as $e(m-1)m \equiv -(m_a(m-1) + m_a + m_b) \pmod{N^s}$. Thus, we get that $e\bar{m}_1\gamma m \equiv -(m_a\bar{m}_1\gamma + m_a + m_b)$ $\pmod{N^s}$ and hence $m_a + m_b \equiv 0 \pmod{\gamma}$ and $\gamma \mid (m_a + m_b)$. Since $e < 2^\kappa < \text{lpf}(N)$, we have obtained e.

This finishes the proof. $\qquad\square$

3.3 Σ Protocol for Circuit-SAT

To construct a Σ protocol for the NP-complete language CIRCUIT-SAT, it suffices to construct a Σ protocol for BOOLEAN [12]. Really, each circuit can be represented only by using NAND gates, and a NAND $b = c$ iff $a + b + 2c - 2 \in \{0, 1\}$ [28].

One hence just has to prove that (i) each input and wire value is Boolean, and (ii) each gate is correctly evaluated. According to [19], each test in step ii can be reformulated as a Boolean test. Hence, it is sufficient to run $m + n$ Σ protocols for BOOLEAN in parallel, where m is the summatory number of the inputs and the wires, and n is the number of gates. See [12] for more information.

3.4   General Idea

In both covered cases (ZERO and BOOLEAN), we constructed Σ protocols that were specially sound and HVZK, and then applied the following idea to obtain optimal culpable soundness. We expect the same idea to work also in general.

Let $\mathcal{L} \subset \mathcal{C}_{\mathsf{pk}}^{\mathsf{n}}$ be a language about the ciphertexts of Π that naturally defines a language $\mathcal{L}_M \subset \mathcal{M}_{\mathsf{pk}}^{\mathsf{n}}$ about the plaintexts. For example, in the case $\mathcal{L} = $ ZERO, $\mathcal{L}_M = \{0\}$. Let $\mathcal{R} = \{(x, w) : x \in \mathcal{L}\}$ and, for some n,

$$\mathcal{R}^{guilt} = \left\{ \begin{array}{l} (x = (\mathsf{pk}, \boldsymbol{C}, \mathsf{sk}_{dl}) : \boldsymbol{C} \in \mathcal{C}_{\mathsf{pk}}^{\mathsf{n}} \wedge (\boldsymbol{C}_i)_{i=1}^{\mathsf{n}} \notin \mathcal{L}_{\mathcal{R}} \wedge \\ \mathsf{VK}(\mathsf{sk}_{dl}, \mathsf{pk}) = 1 \end{array} \right\}. \tag{9}$$

The general idea is to construct a Σ-protocol with the following property. If the prover is cheating, then for each first message c_a there is at most one good e. Moreover, this e can be computed as $e = e_1/e_2$, where either e_2 is invertible modulo N^s or e_2/γ is invertible modulo N^s/γ, where γ is the greatest common divisor of N^s and some function $f(m)$ of $m \notin \mathcal{L}_M$ such that $f(m) \neq 0$.

Acknowledgments. We would like to thank Jens Groth, Ivan Visconti and anonymous reviewers for insightful comments. The authors were supported by the European Union's Horizon 2020 research and innovation programme under grant agreement No. 653497 (project PANORAMIX), and by institutional research funding IUT2-1 of the Estonian Ministry of Education and Research.

A   Preliminaries: DFN

A.1   RPK Model

In the registered public key (RPK, [3]) model, we assume that everybody has an access to a key registration functionality F_{kr}. A party (say, Alice) generates her public and secret key pair, and then sends both (together with used random coins) to F_{kr}, who verifies that the keys were created correctly (this means that to register her public key, Alice must know the corresponding private key), and then stores the public key together with Alice's identity in a repository.

Later, Bob (for this, it is not necessary for Bob to register his public key) can query F_{kr} and then retrieve the public key of Alice together with a corresponding certificate. On the other hand, in security proofs, we may give an adversary control over F_{kr}, enabling access not only to the public but also to the secret key of Alice. While every party can use a different F_{kr}, all parties need to trust F_{kr} of other parties in the following sense. F_{kr} guarantees that

(i) the public keys of uncorrupted parties are safe (the corresponding secret key is chosen randomly, and kept secret from the adversary), and
(ii) the public keys of corrupted parties are well-formed (the functionality has seen the corresponding secret key).

Hence, Alice must trust her F_{kr} to do key registration correctly, and Bob must trust that Alice's F_{kr} has verified that Alice knows the corresponding secret key.

As noted in [3,16], one can make this model more realistic by letting Alice to send her public key to F_{kr} and then give an interactive zero knowledge proof that she knows the corresponding private key. In the security proof, we can then construct an adversary who rewinds Alice to extract her private key.

A.2   NIDVZK Argument Systems

In a *non-interactive designated verifier zero knowledge (NIDVZK, [12]) argument system in the RPK model*, the verifier has a public key $\mathcal{Z}$.pk and a corresponding secret key $\mathcal{Z}$.sk specific to this argument system, that she has set up by using a trusted functionality F_{kr}. An NIDVZK argument system $\mathcal{Z}$ consists of the following three efficient algorithms:

$\mathcal{Z}.\mathsf{G}(1^\kappa)$: generates, registers (by using F_{kr}), and then returns a key pair $(\mathcal{Z}.\mathsf{sk}, \mathcal{Z}.\mathsf{pk})$.
$\mathcal{Z}.\mathsf{P}(\mathcal{Z}.\mathsf{pk}, x, w)$: given a public key $\mathcal{Z}$.pk obtained from F_{kr}, an input x and a witness w, returns a proof π.
$\mathcal{Z}.\mathsf{V}(\mathcal{Z}.\mathsf{sk}, x, \pi)$: given a secret key, an input x, and a proof π, returns either 1 (accept) or 0 (reject).

Next, $\mathcal{Z} = (\mathcal{Z}.\mathsf{G}, \mathcal{Z}.\mathsf{P}, \mathcal{Z}.\mathsf{V})$ is an *NIDVZK argument system*[4] *for $\mathcal{R}$ with culpable soundness for $\mathcal{R}^{guilt}$*, if it is perfectly complete, culpably sound [28] for $\mathcal{R}^{guilt}$, and statistically (or computationally) composable zero knowledge, given that the parties have access to the certified public key of the verifier. More precise definitions follow.

Let $\ell_x(\kappa)$ be a polynomial, such that (common) inputs of length $\ell_x(\kappa)$ correspond to security parameter κ. Then let $\mathcal{R}_\kappa = \{(x, w) : bitlength(x) = \ell_x(\kappa)\}$ and $\mathcal{L}_{\mathcal{R},\kappa} = \{x : (\exists w)(x, w) \in \mathcal{R}_\kappa\}$, where again w has polynomial length.

$\mathcal{Z}$ is *perfectly complete*, if for all $\kappa \in \mathbb{N}$, all $(x, w) \in \mathcal{R}_\kappa$, and all $(\mathcal{Z}.\mathsf{sk}, \mathcal{Z}.\mathsf{pk}) \in \mathcal{Z}.\mathsf{G}(1^\kappa)$, $\mathcal{Z}.\mathsf{V}(\mathcal{Z}.\mathsf{sk}, x, \mathcal{Z}.\mathsf{P}(\mathcal{Z}.\mathsf{pk}, x, w)) = 1$.

---

[4] We recall that an argument system is a proof system where soundness only holds against efficient adversaries.

In our constructions we will get zero-knowledge even if the adversary knows the secret verification key. This strong type of zero-knowledge is called composable zero-knowledge in [25] due to it making composition of zero-knowledge arguments easier. More precisely, it is required that even an adversary who knows the secret key (or trapdoor, in the CRS model) cannot distinguish between the real and the simulated argument, [25].

Definition 4. $\mathcal{Z}$ *is* computationally composable zero-knowledge *if there exists an efficient simulator* $\mathcal{Z}$.sim, *such that for all probabilistic polynomial-time stateful adversaries* $\mathcal{A}$,

$$
\Pr\begin{bmatrix} (\mathcal{Z}.\text{sk}, \mathcal{Z}.\text{pk}) \leftarrow \mathcal{Z}.\mathsf{G}(1^\kappa), \\ (x, w) \leftarrow \mathcal{A}(\mathcal{Z}.\text{sk}, \mathcal{Z}.\text{pk}), \\ \pi \leftarrow \mathcal{Z}.\mathsf{P}(\mathcal{Z}.\text{pk}, x, w) : \\ (x, w) \in \mathcal{R} \wedge \mathcal{A}(\pi) = 1 \end{bmatrix} \approx_\kappa \Pr\begin{bmatrix} (\mathcal{Z}.\text{sk}, \mathcal{Z}.\text{pk}) \leftarrow \mathcal{Z}.\mathsf{G}(1^\kappa), \\ (x, w) \leftarrow \mathcal{A}(\mathcal{Z}.\text{sk}, \mathcal{Z}.\text{pk}), \\ \pi \leftarrow \mathcal{Z}.\text{sim}(\mathcal{Z}.\text{sk}, x) : \\ (x, w) \in \mathcal{R} \wedge \mathcal{A}(\pi) = 1 \end{bmatrix}.
$$

$\mathcal{Z}$ *is* statistically composable zero-knowledge *if this holds for all (not necessarily efficient) adversaries* $\mathcal{A}$. *A statistically composable zero-knowledge argument system is* perfectly composable, *if* $\approx_\kappa$ *can be replaced with* = (*i.e., the above two probabilities are in fact equal*).

In the case of culpable soundness [28], we only consider false statements from some language $\mathcal{L}_{guilt} \subseteq \overline{\mathcal{L}}$ characterized by a relation $\mathcal{R}^{guilt}$. We require a successfully cheating prover to output, together with an input x and a successful argument π, also a guilt witness w_{guilt} such that $(x, w_{guilt}) \in \mathcal{R}^{guilt}$. That is, we require a successful cheater to be aware of the fact that she cheated.

Formally, $\mathcal{Z}$ *is (non-adaptively)* culpably sound for $\mathcal{R}^{guilt}$, if for all probabilistic polynomial-time adversaries $\mathcal{A}$,

$$
\Pr\begin{bmatrix} (\mathcal{Z}.\text{sk}, \mathcal{Z}.\text{pk}) \leftarrow \mathcal{Z}.\mathsf{G}(1^\kappa), (x, \pi, w_{guilt}) \leftarrow \mathcal{A}(\mathcal{Z}.\text{pk}) : \\ (x, w_{guilt}) \in \mathcal{R}^{guilt} \wedge \mathcal{Z}.\mathsf{V}(\mathcal{Z}.\text{sk}, x, \pi) = 1 \end{bmatrix} \approx_\kappa 0.
$$

Note that culpable soundness is implicitly computational (defined only w.r.t. to an efficient adversary), thus a culpably sound proof system is always an argument system.

In our applications, w_{guilt} will be the secret key of the cryptosystem, about which the NIDVZK arguments are about. For example, in an NIDVZK argument that the plaintext is 0 (or Boolean), w_{guilt} is equal to the secret key that enables to decrypt the ciphertext. Such culpable soundness is fine in many applications, as we will discuss at the end of the current subsection.

Finally, for some $\varrho = \varrho(\kappa)$, $\mathcal{Z}$ is ϱ-*adaptively* culpably sound for $\mathcal{R}^{guilt}$, if for all probabilistic polynomial-time adversaries $\mathcal{A}$,

$$
\Pr\begin{bmatrix} (\mathcal{Z}.\text{sk}, \mathcal{Z}.\text{pk}) \leftarrow \mathcal{Z}.\mathsf{G}(1^\kappa), (x, \pi, w_{guilt}) \leftarrow \mathcal{A}^{\mathcal{Z}.\mathsf{V}(\mathcal{Z}.\text{sk}, \cdot, \cdot)}(\mathcal{Z}.\text{pk}) : \\ (x, w_{guilt}) \in \mathcal{R}^{guilt} \wedge \mathcal{Z}.\mathsf{V}(\mathcal{Z}.\text{sk}, x, \pi) = 1 \end{bmatrix} \approx_\kappa 0.
$$

Here, the adversary is allowed to make up to ϱ queries to the oracle $\mathcal{Z}.\mathsf{V}$.

As shown in [16], one can handle cases where the adversary has an access to a logarithmic number of queries, simulating their answers by guessing their answers; this still guarantees that her success probability is inverse polynomial.

On Culpable Soundness. We will prove culpable soundness [28] of argument systems about the plaintexts of a cryptosystem by showing that if an adversary outputs an accepting argument and the secret key sk, then she has broken an underlying assumption. This version of culpable soundness is acceptable since in protocols that we are interested in, there always exists a party (namely, the verifier) who knows sk. Hence, the cheating adversary together with the verifier can break the (non-culpable) soundness of the argument system.

Thus, such culpable soundness is very natural the RPK model, especially if we assume that the verifier has provided an interactive zero knowledge proof of knowledge of sk while registering it with the authority. Then, in the soundness proof, we can just construct an adversary who first retrieves sk from the latter zero knowledge proof, and then uses the culpable soundness adversary whom we already have.

A.3   DFN Transform for the Paillier Elgamal Cryptosystem

Consider the DFN [16] transformation, given the Paillier Elgamal cryptosystem $\Pi = (\Pi.\mathsf{K}, \mathsf{VK}, \mathsf{E}, \mathsf{D})$ where the plaintext space is $\mathbb{Z}_{N^s}$ for some reasonably large s. W.l.o.g., we assume that the same cryptosystem is used to encrypt the challenge e and the witness plaintexts and the same value of s, but by using the different secret and public keys where one secret key sk_e is known by the verifier and another secret key sk is (possibly) known by the prover. For the sake of efficiency, one could use different cryptosystems or at least different values of s but we will avoid the general case not to clutter the notation.

This transformation assumes that the original Σ-protocol $\mathcal{S}$ is has a linear answer and optimal culpable soundness using some relation $\mathcal{R}^{guilt}$, see Sect. 2.3. More precisely, we assume that $\mathcal{R}^{guilt}$ is as defined by Eq. (9).

The description of the DFN transform is given in Fig. 5. The following theorem and its proof follows [12,16] in its structure. The part of using the extractor to achieve culpable soundness is from [12] while the idea of letting the constructed adversary $\mathcal{A}_\pi$ answer randomly to oracle queries goes back to [12,16]. The latter means that we only get $O(\log \kappa)$-adaptive soundness.

Theorem 5. *Assume that $\mathcal{S}$ is a complete and computationally (resp., statistically) special HVZK Σ protocol with a linear answer for $\mathcal{R}$ that is optimally culpably sound for $\mathcal{R}^{guilt}$. Let $\Pi = (\mathsf{K}, \mathsf{VK}, \mathsf{E}, \mathsf{D})$ be the Paillier Elgamal cryptosystem. Then the NIDVZK argument system for $\mathcal{R}$ of Fig. 5 is ϱ-adaptively computationally culpably sound for $\mathcal{R}^{guilt}$ of Eq. (9) for $\varrho = O(\log \kappa)$, and computationally (resp., statistically) composable zero knowledge for $\mathcal{R}$.*

Proof. ADAPTIVE CULPABLE SOUNDNESS. We show that if a cheating prover $\mathcal{A}_{zk}$ returns a good challenge e' for the NIDVZK argument system with some

$\mathcal{Z}.\mathsf{G}(1^\kappa)$	$\mathcal{Z}.\mathsf{P}(\mathcal{Z}.\mathsf{pk}; \boldsymbol{C}; \boldsymbol{m}, \boldsymbol{r}, \boldsymbol{b}_0, \boldsymbol{b}_1)$	$\mathcal{Z}.\mathsf{V}(\mathcal{Z}.\mathsf{sk}; \boldsymbol{C}, \pi)$
$(\mathsf{sk}_e, \mathsf{pk}_e) \leftarrow \Pi.\mathsf{K}(1^\kappa)$ $r_e \leftarrow_r U(\mathbb{W}_N^*)$ $e \leftarrow_r \mathbb{Z}_{2^\kappa}$ $c_e \leftarrow_r \mathsf{E}^s_{\mathsf{pk}_e}(e; r_e)$ $\mathcal{Z}.\mathsf{pk} \leftarrow (\mathsf{pk}_e, c_e)$ $\mathcal{Z}.\mathsf{sk} \leftarrow (\mathsf{sk}_e, e)$ Return $(\mathcal{Z}.\mathsf{sk}, \mathcal{Z}.\mathsf{pk})$	// $C_i = \mathsf{E}^s_{\mathsf{pk}}(m_i; r_i, b_{0i}, b_{1i})$ $(c_a, z_1, z_2) \leftarrow$ $\quad\quad \mathcal{S}.\mathsf{P}(\mathsf{pk}, \boldsymbol{C}; \boldsymbol{m}, \boldsymbol{r}, \boldsymbol{b}_0, \boldsymbol{b}_1)$ For $i = 1$ to n: $\quad r_i \leftarrow \mathbb{W}_N^*$ $\quad c_{zi} \leftarrow c_e^{z_{1i}} \cdot \mathsf{E}^s_{\mathsf{pk}_e}(z_{2i}; r_i, b_{0i}, b_{1i})$ Return $\pi \leftarrow (c_a, \boldsymbol{c}_z)$	Parse $\pi = (\boldsymbol{c}_a, \boldsymbol{c}_z)$ For $i = 1$ to n: $\quad z_i \leftarrow \mathsf{D}^s_{\mathsf{sk}_e}(c_{zi})$ Return $\mathcal{S}.\mathsf{V}(\boldsymbol{C}; \boldsymbol{c}_a, e, \boldsymbol{z})$

Fig. 5. The DFN transform for the Paillier Elgamal cryptosystem. Here we assume $s = \max_i \lceil \log_N(z_{2i} + 1) \rceil$ is fixed by the description of $\mathcal{S}.\mathsf{P}$ and thus known to the verifier

probability $\varepsilon = \delta$, then we can break the message recovery security of Π with probability $\varepsilon_\pi = 1/(\varrho 2^\varrho)\delta$.

For this, we note that $\mathcal{A}_{zk}$ gets information about e from two sources, from c_e and from the response of the verifier to different queries. We now construct an adversary $\mathcal{A}_\pi$ that, given access to $\mathcal{A}_{zk}$, breaks the message recovery security of Π (where the public key $\mathcal{Z}.\mathsf{pk}$ includes c_e). It uses the extractor $\mathcal{S}.\mathsf{EX}$, who — given that the prover is dishonest and such a challenge exists — returns the good challenge e'.

First, the challenger uses $\mathcal{Z}.\mathsf{G}(1^\kappa)$ to generate a secret key $\mathcal{Z}.\mathsf{sk} = (\mathsf{sk}_e, e)$ and a public key $\mathcal{Z}.\mathsf{pk} = (\mathsf{pk}_e, c_e)$, and sends $\mathcal{Z}.\mathsf{pk}$ to $\mathcal{A}_\pi$. $\mathcal{A}_\pi$ then runs $\mathcal{A}_{zk}^{\mathcal{Z}.\mathsf{V}(\mathcal{Z}.\mathsf{sk};\cdot,\cdot)}(\mathcal{Z}.\mathsf{pk})$. Assume $\mathcal{A}_{zk}$ replies with a tuple (x_i, π_i, w_i). Since $\mathcal{A}_{zk}$ is successful, $\mathcal{A}_\pi$ emulates the verifier by replying with a random bit b. Once $\mathcal{A}_{zk}$ stops (say after $\varrho = \Theta(\log \kappa)$ steps), $\mathcal{A}_\pi$ chooses uniformly one tuple $(x_{i_0}, \pi_{i_0}, w_{i_0})$, and then runs the extractor with the input (x_{i_0}, w_{i_0}), and obtains either "accept", or a candidate challenge e'. Then, $\mathcal{A}_\pi$ outputs what the extractor outputs.

With probability $2^{-\varrho} = 2^{-\Theta(\log \kappa)} = \kappa^{-\Theta(1)}$, all bits that $\mathcal{A}_\pi$ chose are equal to the bits that the verifier would have sent. Since $\mathcal{A}_{zk}$ is successful, then with a non-negligible probability, one of the input/argument tuples, say $(x_{i_1}, \pi_{i_1}, w_{i_1})$, is such that $(x_{i_1}, w_{i_1}) \in \mathcal{R}^{guilt}$ but the verifier accepts. With probability $1/\varrho = \Theta(1/\log \kappa)$, $i_0 = i_1$. Thus, with probability $\varepsilon_\pi = \frac{\delta}{\varrho 2^\varrho} = \kappa^{-\Theta(1)}$, $\mathcal{A}_\pi$ has given to the extractor an input $(x_{i_0}, w_{i_0}) \in \mathcal{R}^{guilt}$ such that there exists π_{i_0} such that the verifier accepts $(x_{i_0}, \pi_{i_0}, w_{i_0})$. With such inputs, since the verifier accepts, there exists a good challenge e', and the extractor outputs it. In this case, $\mathcal{A}_\pi$ has returned a good e'.

Finally, if the verifier accepts then due to the optimal culpable soundness, the value e' returned by the extractor must be equal to the value e that has been encrypted by c_e. Since the only information that $\mathcal{A}_\pi$ has about e is given in c_e (since $\mathcal{A}_\pi$'s random answers do not reveal anything), this means that $\mathcal{A}_\pi$ has returned the plaintext of c_e with non-negligible probability, and thus break the message recovery security of Π.

COMPOSABLE ZERO KNOWLEDGE. Assume that $(\mathcal{Z}.\mathsf{sk}, \mathcal{Z}.\mathsf{pk}) \leftarrow \mathcal{Z}.\mathsf{G}(1^\kappa)$, and $(x, w) \leftarrow \mathcal{A}(\mathcal{Z}.\mathsf{sk}, \mathcal{Z}.\mathsf{pk})$. The simulator $\mathcal{Z}.\mathsf{sim}(\mathcal{Z}.\mathsf{sk}, x)$ can obtain e from c_e by decrypting it. Given e, he runs $\mathcal{S}.\mathsf{sim}(x, e)$ to obtain an accepting view (c_a, e, z). He then computes $c_z \leftarrow \mathsf{E}_{\mathsf{pk}_e}(z)$ and returns $\pi \leftarrow (c_a, c_z)$.

We now show that the transcript comes from a distribution that is indistinguishable from that of the real view. Consider the following hybrid simulator $\mathcal{Z}.\mathsf{sim}^w$ that gets the witness w as part of the input. $\mathcal{Z}.\mathsf{sim}^w$ does the following:

1. Create $(c_a, z_1, z_2) \leftarrow \mathcal{S}.\mathsf{P}(x, w)$ and the Σ protocol transcript (c_a, e, z), $z \leftarrow ez_1 + z_2$, by following the Σ-protocol.
2. Encrypt z component-wise to get c_z.
3. Return $\pi \leftarrow (c_a, c_z)$

Since the encryption scheme is blindable, such a hybrid argument is perfectly indistinguishable from the real argument. Since the Σ-protocol is specially HVZK, hybrid arguments and simulated arguments are computationally indistinguishable. If the Σ-protocol is statistically specially HVZK, then hybrid arguments and simulated arguments (and thus also real arguments and simulated arguments) are statistically indistinguishable.   □

References

1. Abdolmaleki, B., Baghery, K., Lipmaa, H., Zajac, M.: A Subversion-Resistant SNARK. TR 2017/599, IACR (2017). http://eprint.iacr.org/2017/599
2. Abe, M., Fehr, S.: Perfect NIZK with adaptive soundness. In: Vadhan, S.P. (ed.) TCC 2007. LNCS, vol. 4392, pp. 118–136. Springer, Heidelberg (2007). https://doi.org/10.1007/978-3-540-70936-7_7
3. Barak, B., Canetti, R., Nielsen, J.B., Pass, R.: Universally composable protocols with relaxed set-up assumptions. In: FOCS 2004, pp. 186–195 (2004)
4. Barić, N., Pfitzmann, B.: Collision-free accumulators and fail-stop signature schemes without trees. In: Fumy, W. (ed.) EUROCRYPT 1997. LNCS, vol. 1233, pp. 480–494. Springer, Heidelberg (1997). https://doi.org/10.1007/3-540-69053-0_33
5. Bellare, M., Fuchsbauer, G., Scafuro, A.: NIZKs with an untrusted CRS: security in the face of parameter subversion. In: Cheon, J.H., Takagi, T. (eds.) ASIACRYPT 2016. LNCS, vol. 10032, pp. 777–804. Springer, Heidelberg (2016). https://doi.org/10.1007/978-3-662-53890-6_26
6. Bellare, M., Rogaway, P.: Random oracles are practical: a paradigm for designing efficient protocols. In: ACM CCS 1993, pp. 62–73 (1993)
7. Ben-Sasson, E., Chiesa, A., Green, M., Tromer, E., Virza, M.: Secure sampling of public parameters for succinct zero knowledge proofs. In: IEEE SP 2015, pp. 287–304 (2015)
8. Blum, M., Feldman, P., Micali, S.: Non-interactive zero-knowledge and its applications. In: STOC 1988, pp. 103–112 (1988)
9. Bowe, S., Gabizon, A., Green, M.D.: A multi-party protocol for constructing the public parameters of the Pinocchio zk-SNARK. TR 2017/602, IACR (2017). http://eprint.iacr.org/2017/602

10. Bresson, E., Catalano, D., Pointcheval, D.: A simple public-key cryptosystem with a double trapdoor decryption mechanism and its applications. In: Laih, C.-S. (ed.) ASIACRYPT 2003. LNCS, vol. 2894, pp. 37–54. Springer, Heidelberg (2003). https://doi.org/10.1007/978-3-540-40061-5_3

11. Canetti, R., Goldreich, O., Halevi, S.: The random oracle methodology. In: STOC 1998, pp. 209–218 (1998). Revisited

12. Chaidos, P., Groth, J.: Making sigma-protocols non-interactive without random oracles. In: Katz, J. (ed.) PKC 2015. LNCS, vol. 9020, pp. 650–670. Springer, Heidelberg (2015). https://doi.org/10.1007/978-3-662-46447-2_29

13. Ciampi, M., Persiano, G., Siniscalchi, L., Visconti, I.: A transform for NIZK almost as efficient and general as the Fiat-Shamir transform without programmable random oracles. In: Kushilevitz, E., Malkin, T. (eds.) TCC 2016. LNCS, vol. 9563, pp. 83–111. Springer, Heidelberg (2016). https://doi.org/10.1007/978-3-662-49099-0_4

14. Cramer, R., Damgård, I., Schoenmakers, B.: Proofs of partial knowledge and simplified design of witness hiding protocols. In: Desmedt, Y.G. (ed.) CRYPTO 1994. LNCS, vol. 839, pp. 174–187. Springer, Heidelberg (1994). https://doi.org/10.1007/3-540-48658-5_19

15. Cramer, R., Shoup, V.: Universal hash proofs and a paradigm for adaptive chosen ciphertext secure public-key encryption. In: Knudsen, L.R. (ed.) EUROCRYPT 2002. LNCS, vol. 2332, pp. 45–64. Springer, Heidelberg (2002). https://doi.org/10.1007/3-540-46035-7_4

16. Damgård, I., Fazio, N., Nicolosi, A.: Non-interactive zero-knowledge from homomorphic encryption. In: Halevi, S., Rabin, T. (eds.) TCC 2006. LNCS, vol. 3876, pp. 41–59. Springer, Heidelberg (2006). https://doi.org/10.1007/11681878_3

17. Damgård, I., Jurik, M.: A generalisation, a simpli.cation and some applications of Paillier's probabilistic public-key system. In: Kim, K. (ed.) PKC 2001. LNCS, vol. 1992, pp. 119–136. Springer, Heidelberg (2001). https://doi.org/10.1007/3-540-44586-2_9

18. Damgård, I., Jurik, M.: A length-flexible threshold cryptosystem with applications. In: Safavi-Naini, R., Seberry, J. (eds.) ACISP 2003. LNCS, vol. 2727, pp. 350–364. Springer, Heidelberg (2003). https://doi.org/10.1007/3-540-45067-X_30

19. Danezis, G., Fournet, C., Groth, J., Kohlweiss, M.: Square span programs with applications to succinct NIZK arguments. In: Sarkar, P., Iwata, T. (eds.) ASIACRYPT 2014. LNCS, vol. 8873, pp. 532–550. Springer, Heidelberg (2014). https://doi.org/10.1007/978-3-662-45611-8_28

20. Fauzi, P., Lipmaa, H.: Efficient culpably sound NIZK shuffle argument without random oracles. In: Sako, K. (ed.) CT-RSA 2016. LNCS, vol. 9610, pp. 200–216. Springer, Cham (2016). https://doi.org/10.1007/978-3-319-29485-8_12

21. Fiat, A., Shamir, A.: How to prove yourself: practical solutions to identification and signature problems. In: Odlyzko, A.M. (ed.) CRYPTO 1986. LNCS, vol. 263, pp. 186–194. Springer, Heidelberg (1987). https://doi.org/10.1007/3-540-47721-7_12

22. Fuchsbauer, G.: Subversion-zero-knowledge SNARKs. TR 2017/587, IACR (2017). http://eprint.iacr.org/2017/587

23. Gennaro, R., Gentry, C., Parno, B., Raykova, M.: Quadratic span programs and succinct NIZKs without PCPs. In: Johansson, T., Nguyen, P.Q. (eds.) EUROCRYPT 2013. LNCS, vol. 7881, pp. 626–645. Springer, Heidelberg (2013). https://doi.org/10.1007/978-3-642-38348-9_37

24. Goldwasser, S., Kalai, Y.T.: On the (In)security of the Fiat-Shamir Paradigm. In: FOCS 2003, pp. 102–113 (2003)

25. Groth, J.: Simulation-sound NIZK proofs for a practical language and constant size group signatures. In: Lai, X., Chen, K. (eds.) ASIACRYPT 2006. LNCS, vol. 4284, pp. 444–459. Springer, Heidelberg (2006). https://doi.org/10.1007/11935230_29

26. Groth, J.: Short pairing-based non-interactive zero-knowledge arguments. In: Abe, M. (ed.) ASIACRYPT 2010. LNCS, vol. 6477, pp. 321–340. Springer, Heidelberg (2010). https://doi.org/10.1007/978-3-642-17373-8_19

27. Groth, J., Lu, S.: A non-interactive shuffle with pairing based verifiability. In: Kurosawa, K. (ed.) ASIACRYPT 2007. LNCS, vol. 4833, pp. 51–67. Springer, Heidelberg (2007). https://doi.org/10.1007/978-3-540-76900-2_4

28. Groth, J., Ostrovsky, R., Sahai, A.: New techniques for noninteractive zero-knowledge. J. ACM 59(3), 11:1–11:35 (2012)

29. Groth, J., Sahai, A.: Efficient non-interactive proof systems for bilinear groups. In: Smart, N. (ed.) EUROCRYPT 2008. LNCS, vol. 4965, pp. 415–432. Springer, Heidelberg (2008). https://doi.org/10.1007/978-3-540-78967-3_24

30. Jakobsson, M., Sako, K., Impagliazzo, R.: Designated verifier proofs and their applications. In: Maurer, U. (ed.) EUROCRYPT 1996. LNCS, vol. 1070, pp. 143–154. Springer, Heidelberg (1996). https://doi.org/10.1007/3-540-68339-9_13

31. Jurik, M.J.: Extensions to the Paillier cryptosystem with applications to cryptological protocols. Ph.D. thesis, University of Aarhus, Denmark (2003)

32. Lindell, Y.: An efficient transform from sigma protocols to NIZK with a CRS and non-programmable random oracle. In: Dodis, Y., Nielsen, J.B. (eds.) TCC 2015. LNCS, vol. 9014, pp. 93–109. Springer, Heidelberg (2015). https://doi.org/10.1007/978-3-662-46494-6_5

33. Lipmaa, H.: Progression-free sets and sublinear pairing-based non-interactive zero-knowledge arguments. In: Cramer, R. (ed.) TCC 2012. LNCS, vol. 7194, pp. 169–189. Springer, Heidelberg (2012). https://doi.org/10.1007/978-3-642-28914-9_10

34. Malkin, T., Teranishi, I., Yung, M.: Efficient circuit-size independent public key encryption with KDM security. In: Paterson, K.G. (ed.) EUROCRYPT 2011. LNCS, vol. 6632, pp. 507–526. Springer, Heidelberg (2011). https://doi.org/10.1007/978-3-642-20465-4_28

35. Micciancio, D., Petrank, E.: Simulatable commitments and efficient concurrent zero-knowledge. In: Biham, E. (ed.) EUROCRYPT 2003. LNCS, vol. 2656, pp. 140–159. Springer, Heidelberg (2003). https://doi.org/10.1007/3-540-39200-9_9

36. Okamoto, T., Uchiyama, S.: A new public-key cryptosystem as secure as factoring. In: Nyberg, K. (ed.) EUROCRYPT 1998. LNCS, vol. 1403, pp. 308–318. Springer, Heidelberg (1998). https://doi.org/10.1007/BFb0054135

37. Paillier, P.: Public-key cryptosystems based on composite degree residuosity classes. In: Stern, J. (ed.) EUROCRYPT 1999. LNCS, vol. 1592, pp. 223–238. Springer, Heidelberg (1999). https://doi.org/10.1007/3-540-48910-X_16

38. Sander, T.: Efficient accumulators without trapdoor extended abstract. In: Varadharajan, V., Mu, Y. (eds.) ICICS 1999. LNCS, vol. 1726, pp. 252–262. Springer, Heidelberg (1999). https://doi.org/10.1007/978-3-540-47942-0_21

39. Ventre, C., Visconti, I.: Co-sound zero-knowledge with public keys. In: Preneel, B. (ed.) AFRICACRYPT 2009. LNCS, vol. 5580, pp. 287–304. Springer, Heidelberg (2009). https://doi.org/10.1007/978-3-642-02384-2_18

Economically Optimal Variable Tag Length Message Authentication

Reihaneh Safavi-Naini[1]([⊠]), Viliam Lisý[2,3], and Yvo Desmedt[4,5]

[1] Department of Computer Science, University of Calgary, Calgary, Canada
rei@ucalgary.ca
[2] Department of Computing Science, University of Alberta, Edmonton, Canada
[3] Department of Computing Science, FEE, Czech Technical University in Prague,
Prague, Czech Republic
[4] Department of Computer Science, University College London, London, UK
[5] Department of Computer Science, University of Texas at Dallas, Richardson, USA

Abstract. Cryptographic authentication protects messages against forgeries. In real life, messages carry information of different value and the gain of the adversary in a successful forgery and the corresponding cost of the system designers, depend on the "meaning" of the message. This is easy o see by comparing the successful forgery of a $1,000 transaction with the forgery of a $1 one. Cryptographic protocols require computation and increase communication cost of the system, and an economically optimal system must optimize these costs such that message protection be commensurate to their values. This is especially important for resource limited devices that rely on battery power. A MAC (Message Authentication Code) provides protection by appending a cryptographic tag to the message. For secure MACs, the tag length is the main determinant of the security level: longer tags provide higher protection and at the same time increase the communication cost of the system. Our goal is to find the economically optimal tag lengths when messages carry information of different values.

We propose a novel approach to model the cost and benefit of information authentication as a two-party extensive-form game, show how to find a Nash equilibrium for the game, and determine the optimal tag lengths for messages. We prove that computing an optimal solution for the game is NP-complete, and then show how to find an optimal solution using single Mixed Integer Linear Program (MILP). We apply the approach to the protection of messages in an industrial control system using realistic messages, and give our analysis with numerical results obtained using off-the-shelf IBM CPLEX solver.

Keywords: Message authentication · Economics of authentication
Authentication game · Rational adversary in cryptography
Game complexity

© International Financial Cryptography Association 2017
A. Kiayias (Ed.): FC 2017, LNCS 10322, pp. 204–223, 2017.
https://doi.org/10.1007/978-3-319-70972-7_11

1   Introduction

Information authentication is an indispensable part of today's computer and communication systems. Gilbert et al. [14] considered codes that detect "deception" to provide protection against message tampering. A Message Authentication Code (MAC) is a symmetric key cryptographic primitive that consists of a pair of algorithms: a tag generation algorithm TAG that generates a short string called tag that is appended to the message, and a verification algorithm VER that takes a message and an appended tag, and accepts or rejects the message. Message Authentication Codes (MAC) when the adversary has unlimited computational power, were first modelled and analyzed by Simmons [27] as a two-party zero-sum game. Security of MAC when the adversary is computationally bounded has also been formalized using a two-party zero-sum game that allows the adversary to have a learning phase (by querying authentication and verification oracles), before constructing the forgery. Efficient constructions of MAC with provable security have been proposed using block ciphers [6] and hash functions [5]. In all these works, messages are assumed to have equal values for the adversary and the communicants, and the adversary is considered successful with any forgery that passes the verification test.

In practice however, messages have different values for the adversary and the communicants, and the impact of a successful forgery will depend on the information that they carry: forging a \$1,000 transaction will be much more desirable for the adversary than forging a \$1 one! Similarly, in an industrial control system that uses information communication in the daily operation of the system, a control message that causes the system to shut down is far more *valuable*, than a simple regular status update message.

An authentication system that provides the same protection for all messages, must either choose security parameters of the system for the protection of the most high-valued messages in the system, or accept higher risks for the more important messages.

Cryptographic authentication has two types of cost: the computation cost of generation and verification of MAC, and the extra communication cost of transmitting and receiving the appended tag. These costs could become significant for small devices that must minimize their energy and power consumption, and carefully plan their resources [31]. In the fast growing Internet of Things (IoT), the bulk of messages that are sent between devices are short status update and control messages that must be authenticated, and optimizing the cost becomes highly desirable [26]. In [22], in the context of securing IoT and in particular machine-type communication, the author noted that:

"They generally have low data rate requirements, periodic data traffic arrivals, limited hardware and signal processing capabilities, limited storage memory, compact form factors, and significant energy constraints [20] As an example, a battery life of ten years at a quarter of the cost of wideband LTE-A devices is one of the objectives of the Release 13 LTE-A MTC standardization effort [21]."

Our objective is to optimize the cost of message authentication to be commensurate with the value of information that the message carries.

Our work. We depart from the traditional two-party zero-sum game model of security of MAC, and consider the problem of using an *ideal* MAC for protecting messages that have different values. To adjust the protection level of messages, we will use variable tag lengths for the ideal MAC: the MAC guarantees that when the tag length is τ, the adversary's success chance of a forgery is $2^{-\tau}$. This implicitly assumes that the key length is at least the size of the tag length. Ideal MACs can be closely approximated with existing MAC algorithms in information theoretic and computational security.

We model the problem as a game between two *rational players,* a *system designer* that includes the *sender* and the *receiver*, and an *adversary*. The game is an infinite general-sum extensive form game with perfect information. We consider the following setting: there is a message source with ℓ messages and a publicly known probability distribution; time is divided into intervals; in each interval the source generates a message according to the known distribution. We also allow intervals without any message (empty message). This is similar to the model considered by Simmons [27] and a natural model for many message sources including messages that are generated in an industrial control system.

The cost of a successful forgery for the system designer includes the operational cost of the cryptographic protection that they use, and the loss incurred because of the particular forgery. The adversary's gain will also depend on the particular forgery and the information that the forged message carry. The game proceeds as follows.

There is a publicly known ideal MAC. First, the system designer chooses a vector $T = (\tau_i) \in \mathbb{N}^{\ell+1}$ of authentication tag lengths, one for each message, and makes the vector public. We assume the empty message will also receive a tag. Next, a message $\mathbf{m}_i$ appears in the system (e.g. a message appearing in an industrial plant). The designer computes a tag of length τ_i, appends it to the message, and sends it. Finally, the adversary sees the message and decides how to replace it with another message, including the empty message. The latter is equivalent to removing the message from the channel and had not been considered in traditional MAC systems. We derive expressions that capture the cost and the gain of the designer and the adversary, and by analyzing the strategies of the two, show how to find a Nash equilibrium of the game and determine the optimal tag lengths for messages. Our work makes the following contributions.

(1) It introduces a novel approach to security analysis of cryptographic message authentication that takes into account the value of information that messages carry as well as the cost of using cryptographic protection, and provides an optimal fine-grained protection mechanism using a secure MAC algorithm that supports different tag lengths. The model can realistically capture a variety of costs and rewards for players. The integrity attacks include traditional message forgeries (i.e. message injection and substitution) as well as message deletion (jamming) attack.

(2) We present a sound method of finding optimal (Nash equilibrium) strategies using backward induction argument. The method, however, requires solving

an exponential (in the number of messages) number of non-linear integer optimization problems.

(3) Using a transformation from the vertex cover problem, we show that computing optimal vector of tag lengths, is NP-hard.

(4) We present an equivalent formulation of the problem in the form of a mixed integer linear program (MILP) that proves that the decision version of our problem is NP-complete. The MILP formulation provides an attractive approach which allows us to use an off-the-shelf solver to find a solution to a concrete instance of the problem. We apply our formulation and MILP approach to the analysis of message authentication in an industrial control system for oil pipes.

Paper organization. In Sect. 2 we provide preliminary background and describe the proposed game of message authentication. Section 3 is the analysis of the game and finding a Nash equilibrium using backward induction. Sections 3.2 and 4 give computational complexity of the game and the formulation of finding the Nash equilibrium as a solution to an MILP. In Sect. 5 we discuss related works. Section 6 concludes the paper and suggests directions for future work.

2   An Economic Model for Information Authentication

In the following we recall the security definition of MAC that is relevant to our work, and then describe our game model. Game theoretic definitions and concepts follow [23].

A *Message authentication code* MAC is a symmetric key cryptographic primitive for providing message integrity. A MAC consists of a pair of algorithms (TAG, VER). The TAG algorithm takes two inputs, a shared secret key k, and a message $\mathbf{m}$, and generates a tag $t = TAG_k(\mathbf{m})$ that is appended to the message, resulting in a *tagged message*. The VER algorithm takes a pair of inputs, a key k and a tagged pair $(\mathbf{m}', t')$, and outputs $VER_k(\mathbf{m}', t') = T$ to indicate that the tagged pair is valid and message is accepted as authentic, and $VER_k(\mathbf{m}', t') = F$ to denote detection of a forgery. *Correctness* of the MAC requires that $VER_k(\mathbf{m}, TAG_k(\mathbf{m})) = T$.

A MAC is (ε, u)-*secure* if an adversary who has a learning phase during which they can query u tagged messages from an authentication oracle cannot successfully forge a message with probability better than ε. (One can also allow access to verification oracle.) An u-*time ideal MAC* is a $(2^{-\tau}, u)$-secure MAC, where τ is the length of the tag in bits. A `vlMAC` family in this paper is a family of $(2^{-\tau}, u)$-secure MAC for $\tau \in \mathbb{N}$, where $\mathbb{N} = \{0\} \cup \mathbb{Z}^+$ denotes the set of non-negative integers. We use $u = 1$. This means that the MAC can detect with a high probability, forged messages that are injected into the system, or the substitution of a message with a forged one. Our game theoretic model also considers the cost of dropping a message. To prevent message replay, one needs to consider additional mechanisms such as counters, or ensure that each message includes extra redundancy to make each message unique. This will not affect our analysis.

Game setting. Let $I_\varepsilon = \{\varepsilon, 1, \cdots \ell\}$ denote the set of indexes of possible messages, including the empty message, and let $I = \{1, \cdots \ell\}$, denote the set of indexes of non-empty messages.

- A sender S wants to send messages to a receiver R over a channel that is controlled by an adversary, Eve.Eve can either *inject* a message into the channel, *delete (jam)*, or *modify* the message that is sent by S. S and R together form a *system designer* player.
- Time is divided into intervals. A message source $\mathcal{M} = \{\mathbf{m}_1, \cdots \mathbf{m}_\ell\}$ generates messages independent of the sender and the receiver. In each time interval a message $\mathbf{m}_i, i \in I_\varepsilon$, may appear at the sender terminal that must be sent to the receiver.Let $\mathcal{M}_\varepsilon = \{\mathbf{m}_i, i \in I_\varepsilon\}$ denote the set of messages in the system (e.g. an industrial control system), and $\mathbf{m}_\varepsilon$ be a special message denoting "no-message" appearing in the interval. We assume messages from $\mathcal{M}_\varepsilon$ appear with a publicly known probability distribution $(p_\varepsilon, p_1, \cdots p_\ell)$, and $p_i = \Pr(\mathbf{m}_i)$ is the probability of $\mathbf{m}_i$ appearing in the system, and $p_\varepsilon = \Pr(\mathbf{m}_\varepsilon)$ is the probability that no message appears in a time interval. Messages have different lengths. We will also use m_i to denote the length of the message $\mathbf{m}_i$.
- Messages have different "values" for the system designer and the adversary. If Eve succeeds in changing $\mathbf{m}_i$ to $\mathbf{m}_j$, where $i, j \in I_\varepsilon$, their gain will be $g_{i,j}$. The impact of a successful forgery on the system designer's operation is measured by a cost function $c'_{i,j}$[1] that reflects the economic cost of successful message substitution for the system designer. Note that $i = \varepsilon$ corresponds to message injection and $j = \varepsilon$ is message deletion (jamming, dropping) by the adversary. We also consider the cost d_i of a detected forgery attempt on $\mathbf{m}_i$. This captures the cost of, for example, request for retransmission or using alternative channels for retransmission.
  We assume $g_{i,j}$ and $c'_{i,j}, i, j \in I_\varepsilon$, are non-negative and public.
- The total cost of the system designer when a forgery occurs, includes the economic impact of an undetected forgery, the cost associated with detected forgeries, and the investment to provide the required computation for MAC generation and verification, and the communication cost of sending and receiving messages with the appended tag. We assume that the operational cost of the MAC system is proportional to the length of the authenticated message (i.e. message appended with the tag). This is reasonable for small devices in an IoT setting and can be replaced by other functions to reflect other settings. We use α_t and α_r to denote the (per bit) operational cost of the cryptographic MAC for the sender and the receiver, respectively.
- The system designer uses a v1MAC to provide authentication for messages. Security of MAC guarantees that a tagged message $(\mathbf{m}, t)$ can be forged with probability $2^{-\tau}$, where τ is the length of the tag t. We use $T = (\tau_\varepsilon, \tau_1, \cdots \tau_\ell) \in \mathbb{N}^{\ell+1}$ to denote the vector of tag lengths for messages $\mathbf{m}_\varepsilon, \mathbf{m}_1 \cdots \mathbf{m}_\ell$.

---

[1] For our analysis we define $c_{i,j}$ that includes $c'_{i,j}$.

2.1 Game Structure

We model the interaction between the two players (the system designer and the adversary) in the above scenario when messages are generated by an external source, using a perfect information extensive form game with chance moves. We assume a secure key has been shared between the sender and the receiver.

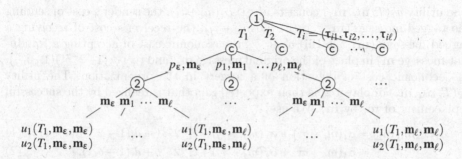

Fig. 1. A sketch of the game tree Θ that represents the message authentication game. The circles labeled by 1, 2 and c, represent the points in the game that the players 1, 2, or the chance player, must take action. The labels on the edges denote the actions taken by the player associated with the circle that is at the higher end of the edge. The leaves of the tree are labelled by the payoffs of the two players.

The game $\Gamma_{auth} = \langle N, H, P, f_c, (u_i) \rangle$ is defined by the set of players N, the set of histories H, a player function P, a fixed distribution for chance moves f_c, and the utility functions $(u_i), i = 1, 2$. A tree representation of the game is given in Fig. 1.

A *history* is a list of actions by players corresponding to a path from the root of the game tree to a node in the tree. The length of a history is the number of elements in the list. The set of histories H is given by:

$$H = \{\emptyset, \{T \in \mathbb{N}^{\ell+1}\}, \{(T, \mathbf{m}_i) \in \mathbb{N}^{\ell+1} \times \mathscr{M}_\varepsilon\}, \{(T, \mathbf{m}_i, \mathbf{m}_j) \in \mathbb{N}^{\ell+1} \times \mathscr{M}_\varepsilon \times \mathscr{M}_\varepsilon\}\}.$$

At a history T of length one, the system designer has chosen a tag length vector $T = (\tau_i)_{i \in I_\varepsilon}$; at a history $(T, \mathbf{m}_i)$ of length 2, the system designer has chosen T and the chance move has selected $\mathbf{m}_i$; finally at a terminal history $(T, \mathbf{m}_i, \mathbf{m}_j)$ of length 3, a length 2 history $(T, \mathbf{m}_i)$ has been followed by player 2's choice of the forged message $\mathbf{m}_j \in \mathscr{M}_\varepsilon$. A *player function* P takes a nonterminal history $h \in H \setminus Z$, and outputs a player in N. The set of actions available to a player at history h is denoted by $A(h) = \{a : (h, a) \in H\}$. For all chance nodes $h = T \in \mathbb{N}^{\ell+1}$, $f_c(\mathbf{m}_i | h) = p(\mathbf{m}_i)$ is an independent probability distribution on possible moves $A(h) = \mathscr{M}_\varepsilon$, at h.

Let *Kronecker delta* $\delta_{i,j}$ be defined as, $\delta_{i,j} = 0$ if $j \neq i$, and $\delta_{i,j} = 1$, otherwise. For a tag length vector $T = (\tau_\varepsilon, \tau_1 \cdots \tau_\ell)$, the chance move $\mathbf{m}_i$, and Eve's move $\mathbf{m}_j$, where $i, j \in I_\varepsilon = \{\varepsilon, 1, \cdots \ell\}$, the players' utilities are,

$$u_1(T, \mathbf{m}_i, \mathbf{m}_j) = \alpha_t(m_i + \tau_i) + \alpha_r(m_j + \tau_j) + c'_{i,j}2^{-\tau_j} + d_i(1 - 2^{-\tau_j})(1 - \delta_{i,j}),$$
$$u_2(T, \mathbf{m}_i, \mathbf{m}_j) = g_{i,j}2^{-\tau_j(1-\delta_{i,j})}.$$

The utility $u_1(T, \mathbf{m}_i, \mathbf{m}_j)$ consists of, (i) $\alpha_t(m_i + \tau_i)$, the sender's cost of sending the tagged message $(\mathbf{m}_i, t_i)$, (ii) $\alpha_r(m_j + \tau_j)$, the receiver's cost of receiving a tagged message $(\mathbf{m}_j, t_j)$, (iii) $c'_{i,j}2^{-\tau_j}$, the economic cost of accepting a fraudulent message $\mathbf{m}_j$ in place of the original message $\mathbf{m}_i$, and (iv) $d_i(1-2^{-\tau_j})(1-\delta_{i,j})$, the economic cost of detection of a forgery in the organization. The utility $u_2(T, \mathbf{m}_i, \mathbf{m}_j)$ of player 2, is their expected gain that is realized by the successful replacement of $\mathbf{m}_i$ by $\mathbf{m}_j$. We use,

$$u_1(T, \mathbf{m}_i, \mathbf{m}_j) = \alpha_t(m_i + \tau_i) + \alpha_r(m_j + \tau_j) + c'_{i,j}2^{-\tau_j} + d_i(1 - 2^{-\tau_j})(1 - \delta_{i,j}) \quad (1)$$
$$= \alpha_t(m_i + \tau_i) + \alpha_r(m_j + \tau_j) + c_{i,j}2^{-\tau_j} + d_i(1 - \delta_{i,j}), \quad (2)$$

where $c_{i,j} = c'_{i,j} - d_i(1 - \delta_{i,j})$, effectively combining the cost of an undetected forgery and a detected forgery.

Assumptions: We assume the cost and gain parameters are known to the system designers. Real world applications of game theory in physical security suggest that these values can be reliably estimated [28]. Although exact values may be hard (or impossible) to find, system designers can use risk analysis methods to categorize messages into types, and attach a value to each type. Small errors in estimates of system designer's costs cannot lead to large errors in the proposed solutions. This might happen due to errors in attacker's gain estimates, however, overestimating attacker's gains for more harmful substitutions increases robustness for the final solution. If the analysis reveals that there is a substantial uncertainty about the motivations of the attackers, the model can be extended to a Bayesian game [20], or a game with interval uncertainly [19]. These are possible future extensions of this work. The case study in the full version of this paper shows how these costs can be meaningfully estimated.

To simplify the analysis of the game, we assume $g_{i,j}$ and $c_{i,j}$ are non-negative. In practice one may use negative values. For example including decoy messages that serve to detect forgeries could result in communicants' cost to be negative. We also assume $c_{i,i} = 0$ and $c'_{i,j} \geq d_i$. The former implies that not changing a message incurs zero cost to the designer, and the latter implies that cost of undetected change of a message to the designer is higher than that of a detected change, resulting in $c_{i,j} = c'_{i,j} - d_i(1 - \delta_{i,j}) \geq 0$. This is a reasonable assumption for all sufficiently valuable messages in the system. We however allow $g_{i,i}$ to be non-zero (we refer to this as no-change substitution), indicating it may be beneficial for the adversary not to change the sent message. These assumptions capture many scenarios in practice and are used in our analysis. Our approach can be used with other assumptions that model specific application scenarios.

2.2   Players' Strategies

A player i's strategy is a tuple that specifies their choices at all histories where $P(h) = i$. Player 1 is associated with $h = \emptyset$ and their strategy $s_1 = T \in \mathbb{N}^{\ell+1}$ specifies the choice of the tag length vector T. The set of player 1 strategies is an infinite set that is denoted by $\mathscr{S}_1$.

The choice nodes of player 2 are at histories of length 2 and are of the form $h = (T, \mathbf{m}_i)$. A player 2 strategy s_2 will choose a substitution message for all such histories. Let $\mathscr{S}_2$ denote the set of player 2's strategies. Histories of length 2 start with the choice node of player 1, and so player 2 at a history of length 2 knows the tag lengths that will be used by player 1. A strategy in $\mathscr{S}_2$ determines the substitution message that will be used for every possible player 1 strategy, and every choice of the chance move. Thus $\mathscr{S}_2$ is also an infinite set. We however introduce *basic strategies* that are from a finite set, and are used to partition $\mathscr{S}_1$ and construct a finite (although very costly) algorithm for finding a Nash equilibrium.

Basic strategies of player 2: A *basic strategy of player 2*, denoted by s_2^b, is a function $s_2^b : \mathscr{M}_\varepsilon \to \mathscr{M}_c$ that specifies the choices (substitution message) of player 2 at all histories $h(T, \mathbf{m}_i), i \in I_\varepsilon$. For each message, player 2 has $\ell + 1$ possible actions, including replacing the message with $\mathbf{m}_\varepsilon$, and keeping the message unchanged. Thus the number of basic strategies is $|\mathscr{S}_2^b| = (\ell + 1)^{\ell+1}$. A basic strategy is represented by a vector $(\mathbf{m}_{j_\varepsilon}, \mathbf{m}_{j_1} \cdots \mathbf{m}_{j_\ell}), \mathbf{m}_{j_i} \in \mathscr{M}_\varepsilon$, or equivalently, by $(j_\varepsilon, j_1 \cdots j_\ell), j_i \in I_\varepsilon$. Note that a basic strategy can be used with any of the player 1's strategies, and does not depend on the tag lengths. The set of player 2's basic strategies is denoted by $\mathscr{S}_2^b$.

A player 2's strategy s_2 is an infinite vector of player 2's actions at all histories of length 2, $(s_2(T, \mathbf{m}_i), T \in \mathbb{N}^{\ell+1}, i \in I_\varepsilon)$, where player 1's action (their strategy) and the chance player's action have been specified. The set of actions $(s_2(T, \mathbf{m}_i), i \in I_\varepsilon)$ for a fixed T, corresponds to a basic strategy of player 2, denoted by $s_2^b(T)$. Thus s_2 can be written as an infinite vector $((T, s_2^b(T)), T \in \mathbb{N}^{\ell+1}, s_2^b(T) \in \mathscr{S}_2^b)$. The set of basic strategies of player 2 is finite. The above discussion is summarized in the following proposition.

Proposition 1. *The sets $\mathscr{S}_1$ and $\mathscr{S}_2$ are infinite. The number of player 2's basic strategies is $(\ell + 1)^{\ell+1}$.*

System designer's cost: The expected cost of player 1 for a strategy profile $(s_1; s_2) = (T = (\tau_1 \cdots \tau_\ell); ((T, (j_\varepsilon, j_1 \cdots j_\ell)), (T', s_2^b(T')) : T' \in \mathscr{S}_1 \setminus \{T\}))$, is given by:

$$C_{s_1,s_2} = \sum_{i \in I_\varepsilon} p_i [\alpha_t(m_i + \tau_i) + \alpha_r(m_{j_i} + \tau_{j_i}) + c_{i,j_i} 2^{-\tau_{j_i}} + d_i(1 - \delta_{i,j})]. \quad (3)$$

That is, the cost of player 1 for strategy $s_1 = T$ will only depend on the basic strategy $s_2^b(T)$ that follows $s_1 = T$.

3 Finding a Nash Equilibrium Using Backward Induction

The authentication game above is an infinite game: both players' strategy sets are infinite and a player 2 strategy is an infinite vector. This prohibits direct use of backward induction and finding a subgame perfect equilibrium. We however show how to use backward induction to partition the infinite strategy set $\mathscr{S}_1$ into finite number of partitions, and find a Nash equilibrium for the game by solving a finite number of constrained non-linear integer optimization problems.

Backward induction: We decompose the tree representation of the game Θ into subtrees, $\Theta(T)$, one for each $T \in \mathbb{N}^{\ell+1}$. The subtree $\Theta(T)$ has the same root as Θ, starts with player 1 strategy T and includes all subsequent actions of chance node and player 2. We can use backward induction for $\Theta(T)$ to determine the expected cost of player 1 for a strategy $s^b(T)$: start from terminal histories of the tree; the first backward step will arrive at a history $h = (T, \mathbf{m}_i)$ which is a choice node for player 2. A tuple of all such choices for all messages $\mathbf{m}_i, i \in I_\varepsilon$, is a basic strategy $s_2^b(T)$. The second backward step reaches the choice node of a chance move. Here the choice is external to the game and is given by a distribution on $\mathscr{M}_\varepsilon$. The third backward step reaches player 1's choice node. At this node, the cost of player 1 for $s_2^b(T)$ that was selected at step 1 of backward induction by player 2, is given by (3). We would like to choose the optimal strategy T for player 1 which minimizes their cost over all choices of player 2. However, there are infinitely many T and the corresponding $\Theta(T)$, and for each one needs to consider $(\ell+1)^{\ell+1}$ basic strategies. We make the following crucial observation that allows us to find a Nash equilibrium of the game in finite number of steps.

The set $\mathscr{S}_1$ can be partitioned into $(\ell+1)^{\ell+1}$ parts, one for each player 2 basic strategy, such that for all player 1 strategies in the partition associated with s_2^b, player 2's best response (maximizing player 2's expected gain), is s_2^b. One can then find the best choice of player 1 (T that minimizes their expected cost) for each partition. The final step is finding the s_2^b that corresponds to the least expected cost for player 1 over all $s_2^b \in \mathscr{S}_1$ More details follow.

Backward induction for $\Theta(T)$: The backward induction steps for $\Theta(T)$ are as follows.

S1: At a terminal history $h = (T, \mathbf{m}_i, \mathbf{m}_j)$, the utilities are,

$$(u_1, u_2) = ([\alpha_t(m_i + \tau_i) + \alpha_r(m_j + \tau_j) + c_{i,j}2^{-\tau_j} + d_i(1 - \delta_{i,j})], [g_{i,j}2^{-\tau_j(1-\delta(i,j))}]).$$

In the first backward step in $\Theta(T)$, the best utilities of player 2 at histories $h = (T, \mathbf{m}_i) \in H_2$, $\mathbf{m}_i \in \mathscr{M}_\varepsilon$, are found by choosing messages $\mathbf{m}_{j_i}$ that maximize player 2 payoffs, where

$$s_2(T, \mathbf{m}_i) = \mathbf{m}_{j_i} \text{ if,} \qquad g_{i,j_i}2^{-\tau_{j_i}(1-\delta_{i,j_i})} \geq g_{i,u}2^{-\tau_u(1-\delta_{i,u})}, \forall u \in I_\varepsilon \setminus \{j_i\}. \quad (4)$$

The inequalities in (4) ensure that choosing $\mathbf{m}_{j_i}$ will have at least the same gain as any other $\mathbf{m}_u$, different from $\mathbf{m}_{j_i}$. The tuple of optimal choices of player 2 for all $\mathbf{m} \in \mathscr{M}_\varepsilon$, determines the (optimal) basic strategy $s_2^{b*}(T)$ of player 2.

S2: At history $h = (T)$, we have $P(h) = c$ and the optimal utility of player 1 is $C_{s_1,s_2^{b*}(T)}$, given by the expression (3), when $s_2^b(T) = s_2^{b*}(T)$, found in step S1.

S3: At history $h = \emptyset$, player 1 has to select the best $s_1 = T$ by minimizing the expected cost $\min_{s_1 \in \mathscr{S}_1} C_{s_1,s_2^{b*}(T)}$ over all choices of s_1.

Let $\mathscr{T}(s_2^b) \subset \mathbb{N}^{\ell+1}$ be the set of player 1 strategies for which s_2^b is player 2's optimal strategy at the first step of backward induction, S1. The following proposition follows from step S1.

Proposition 2. *A basic strategy $s_2^b = (j_\varepsilon, j_1 \cdots j_\ell)$ is optimal for all subtrees $\Theta(T)$ where $T = (\tau_\varepsilon, \tau_1, \cdots \tau_\ell)$, that satisfy the following:*

$$g_{i,j_i} 2^{-\tau_{j_i}(1-\delta_{i,j_i})} \geq g_{i,u} 2^{-\tau_u(1-\delta_{i,u})}, \forall u \in I_\varepsilon \setminus \{j_i\}, i \in I_\varepsilon \quad (5)$$

Moreover, $\bigcup_{s_2^b \in \mathscr{S}_2^b} \mathscr{T}(s_2^b) = \mathscr{S}_1$ and for any two strategies $s_2^b, s_2^{b'} \in \mathscr{S}_2^b$, $T \in \mathscr{T}(s_2^b) \cap \mathscr{T}(s_2^{b'}) \Rightarrow u_2(T, s_2^b) = u_2(T, s_2^{b'})$. Thus, the sets $\mathscr{T}(s_2^b)$ partition the set $\mathscr{S}_1$ with overlaps only due to attacker's indifference.

The proof is in the full version of the paper. Using this lemma we prove the following theorem.

Theorem 1. *A Nash equilibrium for Γ_{auth}, and the associated optimal strategies $(T^*, s_2^{b*}(T^*))$, can be found by solving the following optimization problem,*

$$C^* = \min_{s_2^b \in \mathscr{S}_2^b} C_{s_2^b}^* = \min_{\{s_2^b \subset \mathscr{S}_2^b\}} \min_{[\mathfrak{s}_1 \subset \mathscr{T}(s_2^b)]} C_{s_1,s_2^b}.$$

The tag length vector T^* gives the minimal cost C^* over all strategies $s_1 \in \mathscr{S}_1$.

The proof is in the full version of the paper.

3.1 Tie Breaking of Indifferent Attacker

In general, there may be multiple Nash equilibria in the game. The algorithm above soundly finds the one that optimizes the expected payoff of the defender. When there is equality in (5), that is player 2 has more than one best choice, a player 1 strategy may belong to multiple partitions $\mathscr{T}(s_2^b)$. Since the approach in Theorem 1 select the partition achieving the mimimum cost, if the same strategy is optimal in multiple partitions, it selects the partition which is most favourable for player 1. As a result, it resolves the tie in favour of player 1.

To avoid this unrealistic assumption, we further restrict the sets $\mathscr{T}(s_2^b)$ so that they include only the player 1 strategies for which s_2^b is the worst possible best response of the attacker. In order to do this, we add additional constraints to the definition of $\mathscr{T}(s_2^b)$ in Proposition 2. The constraints request that the system designer's cost be maximized by the substitution of $\mathbf{m}_i$ by $\mathbf{m}_{j_i}$ if there are other alternative messages $\mathbf{m}_u$ that ensure the same gain to the attacker:

$$\text{if} g_{i,j_i} 2^{-\tau_{j_i}(1-\delta_{i,j_i})} = g_{i,u} 2^{-\tau_u(1-\delta_{i,u})} \text{then}$$
$$\alpha_r(m_{j_i} + \tau_{j_i}) + c_{i,j_i} 2^{-\tau_{j_i}(1-\delta_{i,j_i})} + d_i(1 - \delta_{i,j_i}) \geq$$
$$\alpha_r(m_u + \tau_u) + c_{i,u} 2^{-\tau_u(1-\delta_{i,u})} + d_i(1 - \delta_{i,u}), \ \forall u \in I_\varepsilon \setminus \{j_i\}. \quad (6)$$

Denote these further restricted sets by $\mathcal{T}'(s_2^b)$. They still cover the whole strategy space of player 1. Moreover, the overlaps of the sets are formed only by the strategies that make both players indifferent. Computing solution as suggested in Theorem 1 with sets $\mathcal{T}'(s_2^b)$ produces the robust solution that assumes that the attacker breaks ties against the system designer if he is indifferent among multiple substitutions.

3.2 Computational Complexity

The solution to the above game requires solving exponentially many optimization problems. It is not likely that there is a substantially simpler method to solve the game, since we further show that solving the Message Authentication Game is NP-hard.

Theorem 2. *Computing the optimal strategy for the system designer in the Message Authentication Game is NP-hard. This can be shown even if all messages have unit length ($m_i = 1$), occur with uniform probability without empty interval ($p_i = \frac{1}{|\mathcal{M}|}$), detection cost is zero, ($d_i = 0$), and regardless of the tie breaking rule.*

The proof is by reducing the NP-complete Vertex (or Node) Cover problem [17] to the problem of finding an optimal solution to the authentication game Γ_{auth}. Messages correspond to vertices and edges of the graph. Utilities ensure that the optimal solution for Γ_{auth} attaches tags only to messages that correspond to vertices, and a non-zero tag for a message means that the vertex is in subset S. The basic building block of the reduction is an "edge gadget",which ensures high cost if none of its incident vertices is selected (receive a non-zero tag), and lower cost if one or both of its incident vertices are selected (receive a non-zero tag).The complete proof is in the full version of the paper.

4   MILP Formulation of the Game

The solution provided by Theorem 1 is extremely costly. In this section we reformulate the optimization problem in Theorem 1 to improve efficiency of computation and be able to use standard highly optimized solvers. We show a transformation of this optimization problem to a single Mixed Integer Linear Program (MILP) that is polynomial in the size of the problem definition, which in turn is polynomial in the number of messages.

Theorem 1 states that the solution to the game of authentication, is the solution to the following optimization problem:

$$\min_{(j_e \dots j_l) \in S_2^b} \min_{(\tau_e \dots \tau_l) \in \mathbb{N}^{l+1}} \sum_{i \in I_e} p_i \left[\alpha_t(m_i + \tau_i) + \alpha_r(m_{j_i} + \tau_{j_i}) + c_{i,j_i} 2^{-\tau_{j_i}} + d_i(1 - \delta_{i,j}) \right],$$

subject to $g_{i,j_i} 2^{-\tau_{j_i}(1 - \delta_{i,j_i})} \geq g_{i,u} 2^{-\tau_u(1 - \delta_{i,u})} \ \forall i \in I_e, u \in I_e \setminus \{j_i\}.$

The problem is structurally similar to finding strong Stackelberg equilibrium in Bayesian games[2], which is also an NP-hard problem [8]. The proposed game model is a Stackelberg game because first the system designer selects and commits to a vector of tag lengths, and then the attacker observes this commitment and plays their best response. The similarity to the Bayesian games is that there is a set of messages (corresponding to player types) generated with a fixed probability distribution. For each of these messages, the defender performs their actions with a distinct set of payoffs. Using these observations, we derive a MILP for the Authentication Game that is similar to DOBSS [24], the MILP formulation for computing mixed Stackelberg equilibria in Bayesian games. The main differences from the Stackelberg games studied in literature is the discrete combinatorial structure of the commitment and the exponential form of the utility functions. Since our problem is NP-hard, transformation of the problem to a well studied NP-complete problem (such as MILP) and using an existing solver is generally the most efficient solution technique.

MILP is an optimization problem that can be described as the optimization of a linear function, subject to a set of linear constraints, where the variables can have real or integer domains. There are two kinds of issues that need to be resolved to transform the above optimization problem to MILP: (1) The objective function and the constraints are not linear and, (2) the set of basic strategies of player 2, $\mathscr{S}_2^b$, is exponentially large and in the formulation above, a set of constraints for each of these strategies is considered. We start with linearization of the non-linear terms.

4.1   Objective Linearization

The objective function is the minimization of a number of positive terms, some of which are exponential. Since c_{ij_i} is non-negative, we can replace the exponential terms $2^{-\tau_{j_i}}$, with new variables e_{j_i}, and lower bound the new variables by linear constraints so that the approximation is exact for all *meaningful integer values* of τ_{j_i}. Increasing the length of τ_j increases the protection of the system for that message. Increasing the length by one bit from k to $k+1$, reduces the cost of replacing m_i by m_j by $c_{ij}(2^{-k} - 2^{-(k+1)})$. It also has a cost α_t for transmitting, and α_r for receiving. It does not change the cost related to d_i. If the saving in damage incurred by successful forgery is less than the extra cost of sending and receiving, extending the tag length is not meaningful. Denote τ_j^{max} the maximal meaningful value of τ_j. The additional bit in a tag is not worth its cost, if

$$\alpha_t + \alpha_r \geq \max_{i \in I_\epsilon} c_{ij}\left(2^{-\tau_j^{max}} - 2^{-(\tau_j^{max}+1)}\right) \Rightarrow \tau_j^{max} \geq \max_{i \in I_\epsilon} \log\left(\frac{c_{ij}}{\alpha_t + \alpha_r}\right) - 1. \quad (7)$$

A second reason why the defender may want to increase the tag length, is to prevent dropping of some other message that the attacker wants to substitute

---

[2] Players in Bayeasian games receive a randomly selected private type which determines their payoff structure, before they play.

with m_j. This is not worthwhile if the cost of sending and receiving the tags is more than the cost of the dropped message:

$$\tau_j^{max}(\alpha_t + \alpha_r) \geq \max_{i \in I_\epsilon} d_i \Rightarrow \tau_j^{max} \geq \frac{\max_{i \in I_\epsilon} d_i}{(\alpha_t + \alpha_r)}.$$

If we set τ_j^{max} to the maximum of the two values above, the linearized objective will be:

$$\min_{(j_\epsilon \ldots j_l) \in S_2^b} \min_{(\tau_\epsilon \ldots \tau_l) \in \mathbb{N}^l} \sum_{i \in I_\epsilon} p_i \left[\alpha_t(m_i + \tau_i) + \alpha_r(m_{j_i} + \tau_{j_i}) + c_{i,j_i} e_{j_i} + d_i(1 - \delta_{i,j})\right] \quad (8)$$

with the additional constraints:

$$e_j \geq -2^{-(k+1)}(\tau_j - k) + 2^{-k} \quad \forall j \in I;\ k \in 0, 1, \ldots, (\tau_j^{max} + 1).$$

*Note that this linearization does not introduce any error.*Variables τ_j can have only integer values, and the approximation by the linear functions is exact for all meaningful integer values for these variables.

4.2 Best Response Constraints Linearization

The constraints in the original problem also contain exponentials, but they can be linearized by taking the logarithm of both sides. They are equivalent to:

$$log(g_{i,j_i}) - \tau_{j_i}(1 - \delta_{i,j_i}) \geq log(g_{i,u}) - \tau_u(1 - \delta_{i,u}) \forall i \in I_\epsilon, u \in I_\epsilon \setminus \{j_i\}. \quad (9)$$

The only problem with these constraints can occur if g_{i,j_i} or $g_{i,u}$, is zero. In that case, the logarithm is minus infinity. If $g_{i,u}$ is zero and g_{i,j_i} is non-zero, we can omit the constraint since it would always be satisfied. If $g_{i,u}$ is non-zero and g_{i,j_i} is zero, the constraint would never be satisfied. Therefore j_i can be prevented from reaching the value that would cause this situation. Finally, if both values are zero, looking back at the constraint before taking the logarithm reveals the constraint is trivially satisfied and can be omitted.

If an application requires g_{ij} to be negative, it does not change the solution substantially. If for some i, there are both positive and negative g_{ij}, the attacker will never attempt to make the exchange with the negative gain and we can set their gains to 0. If for some message all substitutions cause negative gain, we can reverse the constraint and perform the same linearization.

4.3 Compact Representation of the Attacker's Strategy

After the linearization steps above, we have to find the minimum of exponentially many linear optimization problems, i.e., one for each attacker's basic strategy. We further combine all the optimization problems to a single minimization to allow a solver, such as IBM CPLEX[3], to automatically formulate problem relaxations and prune the space of possible attacker's strategies.

For clarity of exposition, we first describe a more intuitive formulation of the problem with quadratic terms and then further linearize it. In order to represent the attacker's strategies, we define a set of new binary variables $a_{ij} \in \{0,1\}$. The semantics of $a_{ij} = 1$ is that the attacker replaces message m_i with message m_j. To ensure that each message can be replaced by only one other message, we require:

$$\sum_{j \in I_\epsilon} a_{ij} = 1 \ \forall i \in I_\epsilon.$$

We combine all the optimization problems by activating only the best response constraints relevant to specific selection of the attacker's strategy using the standard "big M" notation. The big M method is used to activate or deactivate specific constraints in integer programs, dependent on the value of a binary variable. The quadratic formulation of the original problem is:

$$\min \sum_{i \in I_\epsilon} p_i \left[\alpha_t(m_i + \tau_i) + \sum_{j \in I_\epsilon} a_{ij}(\alpha_r(m_j + \tau_j) + c_{i,j}e_j + d_i(1 - \delta_{i,j})) \right] \quad (10)$$

$$e_j \geq -2^{-(k+1)}(\tau_j - k) + 2^{-k}, \ \forall j \in I; \ k \in 0, \ldots, (\tau_j^{max} + 1) \ (11)$$

$$(1 - a_{ij})M + log(\frac{g_{i,j}}{g_{i,u}}) - \tau_j(1 - \delta_{i,j}) \geq -\tau_u(1 - \delta_{i,u}),$$

$$\forall i, j \in I_\epsilon, u \in I_\epsilon \setminus \{j\} : g_{i,u} > 0 \quad (12)$$

$$\sum_{j \in I_\epsilon} a_{ij} = 1 \ \forall i \in I_\epsilon \quad (13)$$

$$a_{ij} \in \{0,1\}; \tau_j \in \mathbb{N}; e_i \geq 0 \quad (14)$$

The objective function of this optimization problem is the Eq. (8), rewritten using the binary variables a_{ij}. Instead of adding directly the contribution of switching a message i to j_i, it adds the contribution of switching to all alternative messages multiplied by the indicator a_{ij}, which is zero with the exception of a_{ij_i}. Constraints (11) are from the linearization of the exponentials in the objective. Constraints (12) are the linearization of the best response with an additional term $(1 - a_{ij})M$. Here M is a sufficiently large (possibly always different) number, so that with $a_{ij} = 0$ the constraint does not restrict any meaningful assignment of variables in the constraint. As a result, the constraint is effective only in case of $a_{ij} = 1$. Each feasible assignment of variables a_{ij} encodes one of the exponential number of minimization problems that we started with. The indicators in the objective (10) set up the right objective function from Theorem 1 and the indicators in constraints (12) choose the right subset of constraints that is valid for that subproblem.

In order to be able to use any standard MILP solver, we further linearize the quadratic objective function. Since a_{ij} are binary, the quadratic terms can be rewritten using the "big M" notation with the same meaning as above. Instead

---

[3] http://www.ibm.com/software/commerce/optimization/cplex-optimizer/.

of multiplication, they are interpreted more like "if $a_{ij} = 1$ then $a_{ij} \cdot \tau_j = \tau_j$ else $a_{ij} \cdot \tau_j = 0$": For each possible term $a_{ij} \cdot \tau_j$ we define a new variable $a\tau_{ij}$, for each possible term $a_{ij} \cdot e_j$, we define a new variable ae_{ij} and we constrain these new variables to be larger or equal to the original variables only in case of $a_{ij} = 1$. This way the minimization of the objective, in which these variables are present in positive terms, ensures that the new variables will reach their lower bounds.

$$\min \sum_{i \in I_e} p_i \left[\alpha_t(m_i + \tau_i) + \sum_{j \in I_e} (\alpha_r(m_j + a\tau_{ij}) + c_{i,j}ae_{ij} + d_i(1 - \delta_{i,j})a_{ij})) \right]$$

$$\text{constraints}(11) - (14) \quad (15)$$

$$a\tau_{ij} + (1 - a_{ij})M \geq \tau_j \ \forall i,j \in I_e \quad (16)$$

$$ae_{ij} + (1 - a_{ij})M \geq e_j \ \forall i,j \in I_e \quad (17)$$

$$ae_{ij} \geq 0; \ a\tau_{ij} \geq 0 \ \forall i,j \in I_e \quad (18)$$

$$a_{ij} = 0 \ \forall i,j \in I_e : g_{ij} = 0 \ \& \ \exists u \in I_e \ g_{i,u} > 0 \quad (19)$$

The problem formulation in (15–19) is an MILP, which can be solved by any standard solver. If we require the empty message not to have a tag, we can add the constraint $\tau_\epsilon = 0$. The algorithm above computes the optimistic Nash equilibrium assuming that the attacker will break ties in favour of the defender. However, the discrete nature of the defender's commitment allows for a MILP formulation of the pessimistic variant as well. We need to incorporate the constraints (6) in to the program.

4.4   Examples

We apply the above solution method to two cases. First we consider an example of a small message space to show how using differentiated tag lengths reduces the designers' cost, and then model a real life message space to show that the problem can be solved for realistic cases using off-the-shelf software.

A 3-message authentication system. The goal of this example is to show the effectiveness of the proposed variable length tags compared to fixed-length tags. We consider a three message space and use Table 1 to specify the complete set of parameters, m_i (message length), c_{ij}, g_{ij} (cost and gain of substitution of message i with message j), $\alpha_t = \alpha_r = 0.1$ (transmission and reception costs per bit), $p_i = \frac{1}{4}$ (message distribution including empty message), and $d_i = 0$ (detection cost). The system parameters are such that the adversary must break a tie between a number of choices (when $\mathbf{m}_\epsilon$ appears, injecting any of the messages $\mathbf{m}_i, i = 1, 2, 3$ has the same gain 2). We consider two cases: the adversary breaks the tie against the defender, and the case that the adversary is only concerned about their own gain and breaks ties in favour of the defender. The resulting two sets of tags are shown by τ_i^- and τ_i^+, respectively. We also consider the heuristic maximum tag lengths τ_i^{max} defined by expression (6) for each message, that effectively show the highest protection that is "worth" offering to a message. The designers' cost for these cases is given by $u_1(x,y)$ values where

Table 1. (left table) Example with 3 messages, assuming $\alpha_t = \alpha_r = 0.1$, $d_i = 0$ and $p_i = \frac{1}{4}$. Breaking ties in favour of the defender is indicated by $+$ and against the defender by $-$. (right table) Defender's objective values with different tag length vectors. τ without indices indicates constant length tags.

i	m_i	$c_{i\varepsilon}$	c_{i1}	c_{i2}	c_{i3}	$g_{i\varepsilon}$	g_{i1}	g_{i2}	g_{i3}	τ_i^+	τ_i^-	τ_i^{max}	j_i
ε	0	0	0	2	1	0	2	2	2	0	0	3	3
1	10	0	0	2	1	1	0	2	2	1	2	4	ε
2	5	0	1	0	2	1	2	0	2	1	3	4	ε
3	1	1	3	2	0	1	2	2	0	1	2	4	ε

$$u_1(\tau^+, j) = 0.9$$
$$u_1(\tau^-, j) = 0.96$$
$$u_1(\tau^{max}, br^+) = 1.17$$
$$u_1(\tau^{max}, br^-) = 2.14$$

τ	$+$	$-$
0	2.05	3.18
1	1.55	2.35
2	1.38	2.05
3	1.39	2.06

x is the designers' strategy given by the set of tags, and y is the best response strategy for the attacker. The small table on the righthand side of Table 1 gives player 1 utility $u_1(x, y)$, when the tag length is the same (it can be 0,1,2 or 3) for all messages, and tie breaking is in favour or against the designer, as described above. It can be seen that: if the attacker breaks ties against the defender, tags (τ_i^-), they will have expected cost 0.96; if the attacker breaks ties in favour of the defender (indifferent attacker), the optimal tag of all non-empty messages is one bit $(\tau_i^{\,1})$, and the expected cost of the defender is 0.9. In both cases the attacker prefers to replace the empty message with message 3 and drop the other messages (j_i). The defender's cost in these cases are substantially lower than using the best fixed length (leading to costs 1.38 and 2.05), or using the heuristic tag lengths τ_i^{max}.

A case study. In the full version of the paper we also present the case of protecting messages in an industrial control system used for oil pipeline management, using our proposed approach. We consider a system with 23 message types and the empty message, and show how to estimate meaningful values for players' cost, gain and utilities for the forgeries. We compare the proposed game-theoretic solution with a simple heuristic that protects each message with the heuristic tag lengths (τ_j^{max}), as defined in Sect. 4. A single fixed tag length for all messages would lead to higher cost than this heuristic. The analysis shows that when the tags on empty messages are not allowed, the proposed method allows reducing the combined expected cost of the system designer for sending the tagged messages, successful, and unsuccessful attacks by 26% compared to the heuristic. When tags are added to the empty message, the cost is reduced by 33%.

Scalability. Figure 2 presents the runtime of solving games assuming that messages are uniformly distributed, with random game parameters $m_i \in 1 \ldots 20$, $c_{ij} \in [0, 100], g_{ij} \in [0, 100], d_i \in [0, 100], \alpha_r \in [0, 1], \alpha_t \in [0, 1]$, using CPLEX 12.6 on a standard laptop with dual core 2.8 GHz Intel i7 CPU. The solid lines are for the algorithm assuming breaking ties in favour of player 1 and the dashed lines are for the algorithm assuming breaking ties against player 1. Black lines shows the results when the empty message is not tagged, and the gray line shows the results when empty message is tagged. The points represent means of 20 different instances of the given size, the error bars represent the maximum and

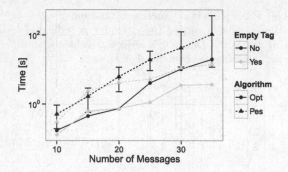

Fig. 2. Computation time required to solve random instances of the games with and without tags on the empty message using for the optimistic and pessimistic equilibrium.

minimum computation time out of the 20 instances for the case with no tag on the empty message and breaking ties against the first player. All problems with 10 messages can be solved in a fraction of second and the most complex problems with 35 messages take on average 100 s.

5   Related Works

In the game-theoretic definition of security [18] for cryptographic protocols, security is defined as a two-party zero-sum game between a challenger and an adversary who can corrupt a subset of parties, and/or (partially) control communication among them.

Rational cryptography is a more recent line of research [1,3,11,15,16,21,25], that assumes protocol participants are "rational" and have well defined preferences, acting in the system in accordance with these preferences.Rational cryptography has resulted in overcoming some impossibility results [3,15] and providing better efficiency [4]. Garay et al. [13] modelled security of a cryptographic protocol as a two-party *zero-sum extensive game with perfect information and observable actions* between the *protocol designer* and the attacker. We also use the same two types of participants in our game definition but use a completely different game. The notion of "cost" in all previous works is in terms of the amount of computation and/or communication. We however consider also the economic cost (and benefit) of using cryptosystems in practice. Game theoretic modelling of*authentication codes* is due to Simmons [27] who used two-party zero-sum games with adversary's action being message injection and substitution. The idea of variable length authentication was first proposed in [10]. Using economics to decide the length of the MAC was proposed in [9].

Using games to model economics of information security and privacy scenarios has been an active area of research [7,12,30].The game FLIPIT is motivated by the Advanced Persistent Threats in computer systems, and models the behaviour of an attacker and a defender who both want to control a resource such as a cryptographic key [29]. Here the "benefit" of a player is defined as "the fraction of time the player controls the resource minus the average move cost", and the goal of each player is to maximize their benefit. A comprehensive resource list is maintained at [2].

6 Concluding Remarks and Future Directions

Game theory provides a powerful framework to model economic cost and benefit of cryptographic systems in real life settings. Our work shows the usefulness of such analysis and insight that can be gained in the case of cryptographic authentication. The example of a three message space in Sect. 4.4 shows how using differentiated tag lengths can reduce the total cost of the designer, comparing the optimal cost to cases that the tag length is constant.

In economic models, one needs estimates of the system parameters and players' gain and cost values. In our model this can be achieved using risk analysis that takes into account probability of attack in a time interval and the impact of the attack. The cost function of the designer combines the cost of the successful forgery, which is the risk of the forgery to the operation of the organization, with the communication cost of one bit. This latter cost must be estimated by taking onto account factors such as frequency of messages, life time of the battery and the operational requirements of the system.

The estimation of system parameters is feasible when the message set is small (e.g. control messages in an IoT setting), or messages are highly structured and can be grouped into well defined classes.

Our work provides a starting point for this line of investigations. We focussed on the basic authentication problem and showed finding Nash equilibrium is NP hard. More complex version of the problem, for example considering forgery after observation of t tagged messages or using other cost functions for communication, could be modelled and analyzed in a similar way. One can also consider confidentiality where different messages, or different parts of messages, require different levels of security, and optimize the cryptographic budget of the system to ensure the best possible protection.

Acknowledgement. First author's work is in part supported by Natural Sciences Research Council of Canada, and Alberta Innovates Technology Futures of the province of Alberta. Third author's work is supported by EPSRC EP/C538285/1 and by BT, as BT Chair of Information Security, and by the State of Texas.

References

1. Abraham, I., Dolev, D., Gonen, R., Halpern, J.: Distributed computing meets game theory: robust mechanisms for rational secret sharing and multiparty computation. In: Proceedings of the Twenty-Fifth Annual ACM Symposium on Principles of Distributed Computing, pp. 53–62. ACM (2006)
2. Anderson, R.: Economics and security resource page. http://www.cl.cam.ac.uk/~rja14/econsec.html. Accessed 19 Feb 2016

3. Asharov, G., Canetti, R., Hazay, C.: Towards a game theoretic view of secure computation. In: Paterson, K.G. (ed.) EUROCRYPT 2011. LNCS, vol. 6632, pp. 426–445. Springer, Heidelberg (2011). https://doi.org/10.1007/978-3-642-20465-4_24
4. Aumann, Y., Lindell, Y.: Security against covert adversaries: efficient protocols for realistic adversaries. In: Vadhan, S.P. (ed.) TCC 2007. LNCS, vol. 4392, pp. 137–156. Springer, Heidelberg (2007). https://doi.org/10.1007/978-3-540-70936-7_8
5. Bellare, M., Canetti, R., Krawczyk, H.: Keying hash functions for message authentication. In: Koblitz, N. (ed.) CRYPTO 1996. LNCS, vol. 1109, pp. 1–15. Springer, Heidelberg (1996). https://doi.org/10.1007/3-540-68697-5_1
6. Bellare, M., Kilian, J., Rogaway, P.: The security of the cipher block chaining message authentication code. J. Comput. Syst. Sci. **61**(3), 362–399 (2000)
7. Bohme, R., Moore, T.: The iterated weakest link - a model of adaptive security investment. In: 8th Workshop on the Economics of Information Security (WEIS) (2009)
8. Conitzer, V., Sandholm, T.: Computing the optimal strategy to commit to. In: Proceedings of the 7th ACM Conference on Electronic Commerce, pp. 82–90. ACM (2006)
9. Desmedt, Y.: Analysis of the Security and New Algorithms for Modern Industrial Cryptography. Ph.D. thesis, K.U. Leuven, Leuven, October 1984
10. Desmedt, Y., Vandewalle, J., Govaerts, R.: The mathematical relation between the economic cryptographic and information theoretical aspects of authentication. In: Proceedings of the 4th Symposium on Information Theory in the Benelux, pp. 63–66. Werkgemeenschap voor Informatie- en Communicatietheorie (1983)
11. Fuchsbauer, G., Katz, J., Naccache, D.: Efficient rational secret sharing in standard communication networks. In: Micciancio, D. (ed.) TCC 2010. LNCS, vol. 5978, pp. 419–436. Springer, Heidelberg (2010). https://doi.org/10.1007/978-3-642-11799-2_25
12. Fultz, N., Grossklags, J.: Blue versus red: towards a model of distributed security attacks. In: Dingledine, R., Golle, P. (eds.) FC 2009. LNCS, vol. 5628, pp. 167–183. Springer, Heidelberg (2009). https://doi.org/10.1007/978-3-642-03549-4_10
13. Garay, J., Katz, J., Maurer, U., Tackmann, B., Zikas, V.: Rational protocol design: cryptography against incentive-driven adversaries. In: 2013 IEEE 54th Annual Symposium on Foundations of Computer Science (FOCS), pp. 648–657. IEEE (2013)
14. Gilbert, E.N., MacWilliams, F.J., Sloane, N.J.: Codes which detect deception. Bell Syst. Tech. J. **53**(3), 405–424 (1974)
15. Groce, A., Katz, J.: Fair computation with rational players. In: Pointcheval, D., Johansson, T. (eds.) EUROCRYPT 2012. LNCS, vol. 7237, pp. 81–98. Springer, Heidelberg (2012). https://doi.org/10.1007/978-3-642-29011-4_7
16. Halpern, J., Teague, V.: Rational secret sharing and multiparty computation. In: Proceedings of the Thirty-Sixth Annual ACM Symposium on Theory of Computing, pp. 623–632. ACM (2004)
17. Karp, R.M.: Reducibility among combinatorial problems. In: Miller, R.E., Thatcher, J.W., Bohlinger, J.D. (eds.) Complexity of Computer Computations. IRSS, pp. 85–103. Springer, Boston (1972)
18. Katz, J., Lindell, Y.: Introduction to Modern Cryptography: Principles and Protocols. CRC Press, Boca Raton (2007)
19. Kiekintveld, C., Islam, T., Kreinovich, V.: Security games with interval uncertainty. In: Proceedings of the 2013 International Conference on Autonomous Agents and Multi-agent Systems, pp. 231–238. International Foundation for Autonomous Agents and Multiagent Systems (2013)

20. Kiekintveld, C., Marecki, J., Tambe, M.: Approximation methods for infinite bayesian stackelberg games: modeling distributional payoff uncertainty. In: The 10th International Conference on Autonomous Agents and Multiagent Systems-Volume 3, pp. 1005–1012. International Foundation for Autonomous Agents and Multiagent Systems (2011)

21. Kol, G., Naor, M.: Cryptography and game theory: designing protocols for exchanging information. In: Canetti, R. (ed.) TCC 2008. LNCS, vol. 4948, pp. 320–339. Springer, Heidelberg (2008). https://doi.org/10.1007/978-3-540-78524-8_18

22. Mukherjee, A.: Physical-layer security in the internet of things: sensing and communication confidentiality under resource constraints. Proc. IEEE 103(10), 1747–1761 (2015)

23. Osborne, M.J., Rubinstein, A.: A Course in Game Theory. MIT Press, Cambridge (1994)

24. Paruchuri, P., Pearce, J.P., Marecki, J., Tambe, M., Ordonez, F., Kraus, S.: Playing games for security: an efficient exact algorithm for solving Bayesian stackelberg games. In: Proceedings of the 7th International Joint Conference on Autonomous Agents and Multiagent Systems-Volume 2, pp. 895–902. International Foundation for Autonomous Agents and Multiagent Systems (2008)

25. Pass, R., Halpern, J.: Game theory with costly computation: formulation and application to protocol security. In: Proceedings of the Behavioral and Quantitative Game Theory: Conference on Future Directions, p. 89. ACM (2010)

26. Rose, K., Eldridge, S., Chapin, L.: The internet of things (IoT): An overview-understanding the issues and challenges of a more connected world. Internet Society (2015)

27. Simmons, G.J.: Authentication theory/coding theory. In: Blakley, G.R., Chaum, D. (eds.) CRYPTO 1984. LNCS, vol. 196, pp. 411–431. Springer, Heidelberg (1985). https://doi.org/10.1007/3-540-39568-7_32

28. Tambe, M.: Security and Game Theory: Algorithms, Deployed Systems, Lessons Learned. Cambridge University Press, Cambridge (2011)

29. Van Dijk, M., Juels, A., Oprea, A., Rivest, R.L.: FLIPIT: the game of stealthy takeover. J. Cryptol. 26(4), 655–713 (2013)

30. Varian, H.: System reliability and free riding. In: Camp, L.J., Lewis, S. (eds.) Economics of Information Security. ADIS, vol. 12, pp. 1–15. Springer, Boston (2004). https://doi.org/10.1007/1-4020-8090-5_1

31. Verbauwhede, I.: VLSI design methods for low power embedded encryption. In: Proceedings of the 26th Edition on Great Lakes Symposium on VLSI, p. 7. ACM (2016)

Vulnerabilities and Exploits

PEEP: Passively Eavesdropping Private Input via Brainwave Signals

Ajaya Neupane[1](✉), Md. Lutfor Rahman[2], and Nitesh Saxena[1]

[1] University of Alabama at Birmingham, Birmingham, USA
{aneupane,saxena}@uab.edu
[2] University of California Riverside, Riverside, USA
mrahm011@ucr.edu

Abstract. New emerging devices open up immense opportunities for everyday users. At the same time, they may raise significant security and privacy threats. One such device, forming the central focus of this work, is an EEG headset, which allows a user to control her computer only using her thoughts.

In this paper, we show how such a malicious EEG device or a malicious application having access to EEG signals recorded by the device can be turned into a new form of a keylogger, called PEEP, that passively eavesdrops over user's sensitive typed input, specifically numeric PINs and textual passwords, by analyzing the corresponding neural signals. PEEP works because user's input is correlated with user's innate visual processing as well as hand, eye, and head muscle movements, all of which are explicitly or implicitly captured by the EEG device.

Our contributions are two-fold. First, we design and develop PEEP against a commodity EEG headset and a higher-end medical-scale EEG device based on machine learning techniques. Second, we conduct the comprehensive evaluation with multiple users to demonstrate the feasibility of PEEP for inferring PINs and passwords as they are typed on a physical keyboard, a virtual keyboard, and an ATM-style numeric keypad. Our results show that PEEP can extract sensitive input with an accuracy significantly higher than a random guessing classifier. Compared to prior work on this subject, PEEP is highly surreptitious as it only requires passive monitoring of brain signals, not deliberate, and active strategies that may trigger suspicion and be detected by the user. Also, PEEP achieves orders of magnitude higher accuracies compared to prior active PIN inferring attacks. Our work serves to raise awareness to a potentially hard-to-address threat arising from EEG devices which may remain attached to the users almost invariably soon.

1 Introduction

Brain-computer interfaces (BCI), which extract physiological signals originated in the human brain to communicate with external devices, were once highly

---

M. L. Rahman—Work done while being a student at UAB.

A. Kiayias (Ed.): FC 2017, LNCS 10322, pp. 227–246, 2017.
https://doi.org/10.1007/978-3-319-70972-7_12

expensive and used only in medical domains. They were mainly used to develop neuroprosthetic applications which helped disabled patients to control prosthetic limbs with their thoughts alone [35]. However, these devices are now commercially available at low-cost and are becoming popular especially in gaming and entertainment industries.

Electroencephalography (EEG) is the most commonly used physiological signal in the BCI devices due to its ease of use, high temporal resolution, and non-invasive setup. EEG measures the task related to electrical activity of the brain, referred to as event-related potentials. In the commercial domain, these EEG-based BCI devices have been used to improve the quality of user experience mainly in gaming and entertainment industries. Currently, EEG-based BCI devices from different vendors are available in the market (e.g., Emotiv [3], Neurosky [7], Neurofocus [5]). These devices also provide software developments kits to build applications, and have application markets (e.g. [2,6]) in which the vendors host the applications developed by their own developers as well as provide a platform for third-party developers to share the applications developed by them. Recently, the BCI devices have been studied for building user authentication models based on user's potentially unique brainwave signals [17].

Given their interesting use cases in a wide variety of settings, the popularity and applicability of these devices is expected to further rise in the future. These devices may become an inevitable part of a users' daily life cycles, including while they use other traditional devices like mobile phones and laptop/desktop computers. In this light, it is important to analyze the potential security and privacy risks associated with these devices, and raise users' awareness to these risks (and possibly come up with viable mitigation strategies).

Our specific goal in this work is to examine how malicious access to EEG signals captured by such devices can be used for potentially offensive proposes. As the use of these devices becomes mainstream, a user may enter passwords or private credentials to their computers or mobile phones, while the BCI device is being worn by the user. To this end, we study the potential of a malicious app to capture the EEG signals when users are typing passwords or PINs in virtual or physical keyboards, and aim to process these signals to infer the sensitive keystrokes. The device to which the sensitive keystrokes are being entered could be the same device with which the BCI headset is "paired" or any other computing terminal. Several previous studies have used EEG signals to infer the types of mental tasks users are performing [36], to infer the objects users are thinking about [21], or to infer the limb movements users are imagining [33]. In line with these works, the premise of our presented vulnerability is that the user's keystroke input to a computer would be correlated with the user's innate visual processing as well as user's hand, eye and head muscle movements, as the user provides the input all of which are explicitly or implicitly captured by the BCI devices.

Based on this premise, we demonstrate the feasibility of inferring user's sensitive keystrokes (PINs and passwords) based on their neural signals captured by the BCI device with accuracies significantly greater than random guessing.

These BCI brain signals may relatively easily get leaked to a malicious app on the mobile device that is paired with the BCI headset since no extra permissions to access such signals is required in current mobile or desktop OSs. An additional avenue of leakage lies with a server, charged with the processing of brain signals in the outsourced computation model, which may get compromised or be malicious on its own.

Our Contributions and Novelty Claims: In this paper, we introduce a new attack vector called PEEP that secretly extracts private information, in particular users' private input such as PINs and passwords, from event-related potentials measured by brain computer interfaces. Our contributions are two-folds:

- We design and develop PEEP, a new type of attack against keystroke inference exploiting BCI devices based on machine learning techniques. We study PEEP against a commodity EEG headset and a higher-end medical-scale EEG device
- We experimentally validate the feasibility of PEEP to infer user's PINs and passwords as they are being typed on a physical or virtual keyboard. We also validate the consistency of results across different BCI headsets.

Related to PEEP, Martinovic et al. [29]) studied the possibility of side-channel attacks using commercial EEG-based BCI to reveal the users' private information like user's familiar banks, ATMs or PIN digits. Their general idea is similar to a guilty knowledge test where items familiar to a user is assumed to evoke the different response as compared to the items unfamiliar to the user. Thus, when a person is shown images of many banks, the brain response to the image of the bank with which user has had more interaction or has opened an account will evoke higher event-related potential. However, their attack setup is intrusive and can be easily detectable as the users may notice the abnormality in the application when it shows the images of banks or ATMs related to her. In contrast, PEEP is highly surreptitious as it only requires passive monitoring of brain signals as users' type their PINs and passwords in regular use, not deliberate, and active strategies that may trigger suspicion and be detected by the user. In addition, PEEP achieves orders of magnitude higher accuracies compared to the active PIN inferring attack of [29].

2   Background and Prior Work

2.1   EEG and BCI Devices Overview

Electroencephalography (EEG) is a non-invasive method of recording electrical activity in the brain, referred to as event-related potentials (ERPs), using electrodes on the surface of the scalp. EEG has higher temporal resolution and can depict changes within milliseconds. The electrical activity can be synchronized with the performed task to study changes in brain activation over time. ERPs are used as a tool in studying human information processing [20].

P300, a positive change in ERPs which appears around 300 ms post-stimuli if the stimuli is a known target, is popularly used ERPs in studies involving EEG. Many devices, both consumer-based and clinical-based devices to measure the ERPs are currently available in market and are used in security studies (see Sect. 2.2).

In this study, we used two different EEG headsets for data collection, namely Emotiv Headset [3] and B-Alert Headset [1]. We use Emotiv as a representative instance of current commercial consumer-grade BCI devices, and B-Alert (a clinical-level Headset) as a representative instance of future devices.

Emotiv Epoch Headset: Emotiv Epoc headset is a wireless and lightweight EEG sensor to acquire and analyze 14 channels of high-quality EEG data. The sensors of this EEG headset follow the 10–20 international system of placement. It uses the AF3, F7, F3, FC5, T7, P7, O1, O2, P8, T8, FC6, F4, F8, AF42 sites to collect EEG data at 128 Hz.

B-Alert Headset: The B-Alert headset is a clinical grade X10-standard wireless and lightweight system, developed by Advanced Brain Monitoring (ABM) [1], to acquire nine channels of high-quality EEG data. The headset also followed the 10–20 international system of electrode placement and used Fz, F3, F4, C3, Cz, C4, P3, POz, P4 sites to collect EEG data at 256 Hz with fixed gain referenced to linked mastoids. The tenth channel was used for measuring electrocardiogram signals. A portable unit is worn on the back of the head which amplifies and sends signals to the computer connected over Bluetooth.

2.2   Related Work

Information Retrieval using Brain Activations: EEG has been explored by researchers to develop user authentication model (for example, [10,17,25,30,37]). Ashby et al. [10] proposed an EEG based authentication system using a consumer grade 14-sensor Emotiv Epoc headset. Thorpe et al. [37] suggested pass-thoughts to authenticate users. Chuang et al. [17] used single-sensor Neurosky headset to develop a user authentication model based on ERPs collected during different mental tasks including pass-thoughts. Bojinov et al. [14] proposed a coercion-resistant authentication based on neuroscience based approach. Most relevant to our work, Martinovic et al. [29] used ERPs as a vector of side-channel attack to snoop into users private information. The authors showed images of numbers, banks, ATMs to the participants when their brain signals were measured. They used the brain signal to decrease entropy of information related to PIN, banks, ATMs by 23–40%. However, our attack is less intrusive and difficult to detect and our malicious app can run in background capturing EEG signals.

The BCI devices are also used to understand users' underlying neural processes when they are performing security tasks. Neupane et al. used fMRI [31] to study brain activations when users were subjected to phishing detection and heeding malware warnings. In another study, Neupane et al. [9] used EEG-based B-Alert Headset to measure mental states and mental workload when users were subject to similar security tasks.

Campbell et al. [16] used P300 ERP, originated when someone shows attention to specific stimuli, for developing neurophone, a brain controlled app for dialing phone number in mobile address book. The authors flashed a number of photos of contact persons in participants' address book, and when P300 potential amplitude for a photo matched the person the user thought of dialing, the app dialed the phone number.

Birbaumer et al. [13] proposed spelling device for paralyzed based on the P300 spikes. The alphanumeric characters were organized in a grid and were flashed to the patient. Whenever the patient focused on the target character, P300 was evoked. Tan et al. [36] asked users to perform different gaming tasks and used ERPs to classify what mental tasks users were performing. Esfahani et al. [21] used 14-channel Emotiv headset to collect neural data from 10 users when they were imagining cube, sphere, cylinder, pyramid or a cone. They were able to discriminate between these five basic primitive objects with an average accuracy of 44.6% using best features in Linear Discriminant Classifier (random guessing would have been $100/5 = 20\%$).

Other Side Channel Attacks: Keystroke inference has received attention due to its potential consequences. Asonov et al. [11], Zhuang et al. [41] and Halevi et al. [22] used sound recorded from physical keyboards when users were typing passwords to infer keystrokes. Vuagnoux et al. [38] used electromagnetic waves emanated on users typing such keyboard. Song et al. [34] used inter-keystroke timing observations to infer keystrokes. Marquardt et al. [28] used accelerometer on a smartphone to record and interpret surface vibrations due to keystrokes to identify the user inputs on a nearby keyboard. All these side channel attacks exploited the physical characteristics of the keyboard, which became infeasible after the advent of smart phone with touch screen. However, new types of attacks to detect users' PINs, passwords and unlock patterns using motion sensors emerged on these smartphones [12,15,32,40].

Unlike these attacks, we propose a new form of keylogger. We show how a malicious EEG device or a malicious application having access to EEG signals recorded by BCI device, can be used to elicit users' private information. We show the feasibility of our attack in both the physical keyboard and virtual keyboards.

3   Threat Model

The attackers' motive in this study is to passively eavesdrop on victim's neural signals, recorded by BCI devices, looking for sensitive information (e.g., PINs or passwords) entered on a virtual or a physical keyboard. The BCI devices provide APIs which allow easy access of raw signals recorded by the BCI devices to app developers. So a third-party developer can develop a malicious app with unfettered access to the ERPs measured by such BCI device. The app developed by attackers first captures the neural patterns of keystrokes to build a classification model (Training Phase) and later utilizes the model to infer the keystrokes only using the neural data (Testing Phase). Such malicious app developers are considered adversary of our system.

Training Phase: We assume the adversary has developed a malicious application to record neural signals and has fooled the victim to install the app on her device. The malicious application can be a gaming application which asks users to press different keys for calibration or enter particular numeric/alphabetical code before playing different levels of the game or resuming the game after a break. The developer can claim such codes will secure the game from being played by other users who has access to the computer. The attacker can then process the numeric/alphabetical code and neural signals corresponding to them to extract features and build a training model. The threat model is similar to the attack model studied in previous work [29]. However, our threat model is less intrusive and weaker as compared to their study as they propose explicitly showing images of ATMs or PINs to users, which users may eventually notice.

It is also possible for attacker to obtain keystroke-neural template may be leaked through servers. For example, a benign application may outsource these signals to some server for computations which may be malicious or can get compromised and can infer sensitive info.

We also assume a different threat model in which attacker does not have access to victims' keystrokes and corresponding brain signals. In this case, we assume the attacker builds a training model using her brain data and keystrokes. The training model is then employed in PEEP.

Testing phase: We assume the attacker has now developed a training model to classify neural signals for each of the numbers and the alphabetic keys using one of the methods described in the previous section. The malicious app with training model is successfully installed in victims device and runs in the background stealthily recording the neural signals whenever victim enters sensitive information in the physical or virtual keyboard. We assume the attacker knows when the victim is entering private credentials in the device (e.g., in mobile devices, the keyboard shows up whenever the user starts to type). These neural signals recorded during the entry of these credentials will then be used by the app to infer the keystrokes which can then be exploited by attackers.

Apart from mobile and desktop apps, these devices also provide web APIs [4] which can be exploited to launch remote attacks. In this case, browser add-ons can be the malicious apps. In our threat model, we assume the victim only uses random numbers or random uppercase character-based passwords. We keep the length of the PIN to 4 and password to 6.

Practicality of Attacks: BCI devices are used by gamers to play games controlled by their mind. The game they are playing is malicious in nature. It asks users to enter predefined set of numbers (like captcha) to restart the game from the last position when they take a break. Doing this, the malicious app can record the ERPs related to each of the entered digits. The app can then be trained with these recorded datasets to predict keystrokes correctly. Now, when the gamers next take a break from the game and enter their login credentials in banking or social media websites, with the headset on, the app can listen to the brain signals and then run the classification model to predict keystrokes.

4 Experimental Design and Data Collection

4.1 Design of the Task

We followed the similar design for all of our experiments, while we varied different parameters, such as users, EEG devices (Emotiv vs. high-end), keypads (virtual vs. real), and data types (4-digit pin vs. 6-character password). Even though the experiments were conducted in controlled lab environment, we tried to simulate real-world PIN/Password entry methodologies. The design of the experiments remained same for both Emotiv and B-Alert headsets.

Virtual Keyboard PIN Entry (VKPE): The goal of this experiment was to assess whether the event-related potentials recorded using consumer-based EEG BCI device or B-Alert headset could be used to infer the numbers entered by the participant. We assume, visual and mental processing of digits, along with the head, hand, and eye movements while entering PIN may tell what key is being processed. For this task, we developed a virtual keyboard similar to the ones employed in login pages of websites (this layout is also similar to the numeric keyboards in smart phones in landscape view) (see Appendix A Fig. 3(a)). We had a text box at the top of this virtual keyboard. The participants were asked to enter 4-digit PIN codes using the mouse in the text box. When the user clicked a key on the virtual keyboard, the key was flashed in its frame for 500 ms or till the next key was clicked, similar to the key press events in touch pads of smart phones. This was done to ensure the user that he had clicked on the right digit. When the user pressed a key, we put a trigger in the recorded event-related potentials to synchronize the neural data with key presses.

Virtual ATM PIN Entry (VAPE): Similar to the design of the virtual numeric keyboard, for this task, we implemented a virtual ATM keyboard with a text box at the top (see Appendix A Fig. 3(b)). The participants were asked to enter 4-digit PIN codes in the text box using the mouse. Like the previous designs, we assumed visual and mental processing of digits might tell what key is being processed. However, this design had the fewer number of keys in the keyboard compared to the virtual keyboard, so we expected the distraction while entering PINs to be lower and results of the prediction model to be higher for this task. This layout is also similar to the numeric keypad in smart phones in portrait view.

Physical Numeric Keypad PIN Entry (PNKPE): For this task, we developed a frame with a text box for entering PIN. Similar to the previous tasks, the participants were provided with random 4-digit numeric PINs and were asked to enter them in the text box. However, the mode of the key input, in this case, was a physical numeric keyboard, unlike virtual keyboard in previous tasks (see Appendix A Fig. 4). In this task we assumed, the mental processing of digits, and the movements of facial muscles, eyes, head, hands, and fingers may create a digit-specific pattern in event-related potentials. These features may be eventually used to develop PEEP.

Physical Keyboard Password Entry (PKPE): In this task, we used a frame with the text box to enter the password. The participants were provided with random upper-case 6-character based passwords and were asked to enter the password in the text box using physical keyboard (e.g., laptop keyboard) (see Appendix A Fig. 5). Like the previous task, in this task, we assumed the finger/hand movement to create a digit-specific pattern in event-related potentials, which may eventually be used to develop PEEP.

4.2 Experimental Set-Up

For all the above mentioned tasks, we collected data in the lab environment using two different headsets, namely Emotiv and B-Alert Headsets. The basic set-up for both the experiments were similar, apart from the computer used for data collection. For Emotiv headset our experimental set-up comprised of a single laptop in which the Emotiv control panel, the virtual keyboards, and the text-input frames were installed. The Emotiv control panel was used to calibrate the headset for better signal-to-noise ratio. An in-house program, developed to record the neural data and the key press logs, was also installed in the stimuli computer (see Fig. 1 left).

Fig. 1. (a) Experimental set up with Emotiv headset (b) Experimental set up with B-Alert headset (face masked for anonymity)

For the B-Alert headset, we used stimuli computer to present experimental tasks and a different data collection computer to record the neural data. The proprietary B-Alert data acquisition software installed in this data collection computer was used to calibrate and record brain data during the task. A signal was sent from stimuli computer to data collection computer using TCP/IP connection to mark the neural data on each key-press to synchronize the brain data and corresponding keystrokes. We could not install the B-Alert data acquisition software in stimuli computer as it was a proprietary software with the license for lab computer only (see Fig. 1 right).

4.3   Study Protocol

Ethical and Safety Considerations: The study was approved by the Institutional Review Board of our university. The participants were recruited using flyers around the campus and on the social media (e.g. Facebook). The participation in our experiment was strictly voluntary, and the participants were provided with an option to withdraw from the research at any point in time. The best standard procedures were applied to ensure the privacy of the participants' data (survey responses, and neural data) acquired during the experiment.

Participant Recruitment and Pre-Experiment Phase: Twelve healthy members of our university (including students, housewives, and workers) were recruited for our study. Informed consent was obtained from these participants and were asked to provide their demographic information (such as age, gender and education level). Our pool was comprised of 66.6% male and 33.3% female, 55% were above the age of 24 and belonged to fairly diverse educational levels (e.g., computer science, civil engineering, business administration, etc.). Ten of these participants performed VKPE task. Rest of the three tasks were performed by two participants each. Some of these participants were among the ten participants who had performed VKPE task.

Task Execution Phase: We used the consumer-based 14-sensors Emotiv headset and 10-sensor B-Alert headset for the experiment. We prepared Emotiv headset and B-Alert headset for proper measurement of the electrical activity in the brain. We then placed the headset on the head of the participant. We calibrated the headset using Emotiv control panel and B-Alert software respectively, where we can validate the signal strength of each electrode, for obtaining better signal-to-noise ratio. Once the headset was properly calibrated and the participants were seated comfortably to perform the task, we provided them with a sheet of paper with randomly generated thirty 4-digit random PINs or randomly generated thirty-six upper-case 6-character random passwords depending on the tasks they were performing.

We instructed participant to enter the PINs or passwords in the text box as if she was logging into her accounts. In case, she realizes to have entered the wrong digit; she was instructed to press the right digit again. The data was collected in four different sessions on the same day for each of the tasks. In every session, users were provided with a new set of randomly generated PINs or passwords. A break of 10-min was given to participant between each session of 4-min length.

5   Data Preprocessing and Feature Extraction

The APIs provided by the Emotiv headset and the B-Alert headset were used to collect the raw ERPs during the experiment. We then used EEGLAB [19] to process the raw data collected from both of these headsets. Before processing the brain data, we first segregated the samples related to each digit from the raw data and created a new file for each one of them. For each keystroke, we considered 235 ms of brain data (30 samples of data) before the key stroke and

468 ms of brain data during the key press (60 samples of data). The reason behind using 235 ms before keypress is to include the ERPs generated when user thinks of the digit before pressing it (Fig. 2).

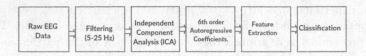

Fig. 2. Data processing flow chart

We processed the raw data using band pass filter in EEGLAB to keep the signals with frequency above 5 Hz and below 25 Hz. The EEG signals measured by the electrodes from the scalp do not represent the electrical potential generated in the sources inside the brain [27]. Rather, they are the aggregation of several neurons' electrical activity in brain. So the filtered data was then processed using independent component analysis (ICA), a technique to separate subcomponents of a linearly mixed signal [24], to segregate the ERPs generated by statistically independent sources inside the brain.

A sample of recorded EEG data can be represented as $x(t) = (x_1(t), x_2(t),..x_m(t))$, where m is the number of electrodes in the headset, and t is the time at which the neuron potential is measured. The ERPs recorded by each electrode at a time is the sum of the ERPs generated from n independent sources inside brain and can be represented as $(x_j(t) = a_{j1}s_1 + a_{j2}s_2 + ... + a_{jn}s_n)$, where n is the number of source components and a is the weight (like distance from the source) applied to the signal from a source. So we used ICA for identifying and localizing the statistically independent electrical sources s from potential patterns recorded on the scalp surface by electrodes in the headset [27]. This process was repeated for the data collected for each of the digits for each session.

The data acquired after ICA was then processed using Autoregressive (AR) model for feature extraction. AR is commonly used algorithm for feature extraction from EEG data (e.g., [23]). An EEG signal recorded at any discrete time point t is given by $s(t) = \sum_{k=1}^{p} a_k x(t-k) + e(t)$, where p is the model order, $s(t)$ is the signal at the timestamps t, a_k are the real-valued AR coefficients and $e(t)$ represents the error term independent of past samples [23]. We computed features from all 14-electrodes using sixth order Auto Regressive (AR) coefficients. Therefore, we had 6 coefficients for each channel giving a total of 84 features (6 * 14 channels) for each data segment for a digit. The feature extraction process was repeated for the brain data collected across different sessions for each of the digit (0–9).

Next, we used these features to build four classification models for predicting key-strokes based on the neural data. Two of the classification models were built using simple Instance Based Learning (IB1) [8] and KStar [18] algorithms. The other two were built using majority voting of two algorithms, *first*, IB1 with Naive Bayes (NB) [26] algorithm, and *second*, KStar and NB algorithm.

We then used 10-fold cross validation for estimation and validation of these classification models on three different sets of data labeled with 10 different classes (0–9 digits).

First, we used instances for each digit from single session for each individual (called as *Individual Model – Single Session*). *Second*, we vertically merged instances of each digit from all sessions of an individual (called as *Individual Model – Merging Sessions*). *Third*, we vertically merged features for each digit from all users for each session (called as *Global Model*). Global Model is a stronger model compared to individual model, where the attacker will train the classification model on the features extracted from her own neural and keystrokes data and use it to infer victims' keystrokes. Even though the brain signals are assumed to be unique among users, we presumed, there might be similarities in ERPs when numbers/alphabets are observed.

We report the average true positive rate (TPR) and the average false positive rate (FPR) for each digit. True positive rate is the ratio of total number of correctly identified instances to the total number of instances present in the classification model $TPR = TP/(TP + FN)$, where TP is True Positive and FN is false negative. False positive rate is the ratio of total number of negative instances incorrectly classified as positive to the total number of actual negative instances $FPR = FP/(FP + TN)$, where FP is false positive and TN is true negative. An ideal classification model has true positive rate of 100% and false positive rate of 0%.

6 Data Analysis and Results

In this section, we describe the results of the classification models built on the features extracted from the event-related potentials to infer the keystrokes.

6.1 Task 1: Virtual Keyboard PIN Entry (VKPE)

To recall, in this task, we had asked participants to enter thirty randomly generated 4-digit PIN in the virtual keyboard using mouse. Table 1(a) lists the results of different classification models on using datasets from individual sessions. We can observe that the best average true positive rate of predicting digits in this model is 43.4% (false positive 6.2%). Likewise, the best average true positive rate of predicting digits is 31.9% (false positive rate is 7.55) when data from all sessions are merged (see Table 1(b)). We can see that the results are relatively lower than the models trained on individual session because the amplitude of ERPs during the first session might have been different than the amplitudes towards the last session. Similarly, The results of global model are listed in Table 1(c). We can observe that the best average true positive rate of predicting digits is 31.3% (false positive rate is 7.6%). Since, in this model, the samples from all individuals are used, the overall prediction rate is lower than the previous models. The results from both models are significantly better than a random guessing classification model (10% for each digit) which verifies the feasibility of PEEP.

Table 1. VKPE Task: Average true positive rate and average false positive rate (a) Individual Model – Single Session (b) Individual Model – Merging Sessions (c) Global Model

Classifiers	Session 1		Session 2		Session 3		Session 4	
	TPR	FPR	TPR	FPR	TPR	FPR	TPR	FPR
IB1	41.1	6.5	39.9	6.6	38.9	6.7	42.2	6.4
KStar	42.4	6.4	40.1	6.6	38.9	6.7	42.8	9.7
IB1+NB	41.5	6.5	39.4	6.6	38.6	6.8	42.1	6.4
KStar+NB	43.4	6.2	42.4	6.4	39.0	6.7	42.4	6.4

Classifier	All Sessions	
	TPR	FPR
IB1	30.1	7.7
KStar	31.7	7.6
IB1+NB	30.0	7.8
KStar+NB	31.9	7.5

Classifier	All Sessions	
	TPR	FPR
IB1	28.4	7.9
KStar	31.3	7.6
IB1+NB	28.4	7.9
KStar+NB	30.7	7.7

6.2 Task 2: Virtual ATM PIN Entry (VAPE)

The participants in this task were asked to enter thirty randomly generated 4-digit PIN in virtual keyboard similar to the ones employed in ATM touch screens. Table 2(a) and (b) have the results of the classification models for individual single session and merged sessions datasets respectively. We can observe that on average the digits can be best predicted at true positive rate of 47.5% (false positive 5.8%) for single session and 32.6% true positive rate (false positive 7.5%) for merged session. Table 2(c) shows the results for these classification models for grouped data and we can notice that on average the digits can be best predicted at 39.1% true positive rate (false positive rate is 6.7%). The results depict that these models are better than the random guessing model (10%) in predicting the keys entered by users.

Table 2. VAPE Task: Average true positive rate and average false positive rate (a) Individual Model – Single Session (b) Individual Model – Merging Sessions (c) Global Model

Classifiers	Session 1		Session 2		Session 3		Session 4	
	TPR	FPR	TPR	FPR	TPR	FPR	TPR	FPR
IB1	47.0	5.9	47.0	5.9	47.5	5.8	44.5	6.1
KStar	42.5	6.4	40.0	6.6	42.5	6.4	39	6.7
IB1+NB	43.5	6.3	41.5	6.5	44.0	6.2	40.5	6.6
KStar+NB	39.5	6.7	42.5	6.4	39.5	6.7	43	6.3

Classifier	All Sessions	
	TPR	FPR
IB1	31.1	7.6
KStar	31.6	7.6
IB1+NB	31.1	7.6
KStar+NB	32.6	7.5

Classifier	All Sessions	
	TPR	FPR
IB1	39.1	6.7
KStar	39.3	6.7
IB1+NB	39.0	6.8
KStar+NB	37.3	6.9

In this task, we see that the overall true positive rate of the digit prediction is higher than the true positive rate in VKPE task (see Sect. 6.1). The virtual keyboard in VKPE task had many keys compared to the virtual keyboard in VAPE task. The higher number of keys might have caused higher distraction in processing of digits, reducing the strength of features representing the keys, resulting in lower prediction rate.

6.3 Task 3: Physical Numeric Keypad PIN Entry (PNKPE)

In this task, the participants had to enter thirty randomly generated 4-digit PIN using physical numeric keyboard. The movement of the fingers measured using

Table 3. PNKPE Task: Average true positive rate and average false positive rate (a) Individual Model – Merging Sessions (b) Global Model

Classifiers	Session 1 TPR	FPR	Session 2 TPR	FPR	Session 3 TPR	FPR	Session 4 TPR	FPR
IB1	46.0	6.0	37.5	6.9	45.0	6.1	36.5	7.0
KStar	40.5	6.6	31.5	7.6	45.0	6.1	38.5	6.8
IB1+NB	46.0	6.0	3	6.9	44.5	6.2	37.0	7.0
KStar+NB	39.0	6.7	34.0	7.3	46.5	5.9	39.0	6.8

Classifier	All Sessions TPR	FPR
IB1	28.4	7.9
KStar	27.5	8.0
IB1+NB	28.4	7.9
KStar+NB	27.6	8.0

Classifier	All Sessions TPR	FPR
IB1	33.1	7.4
KStar	34.0	7.3
IB1+NB	32.7	7.4
KStar+NB	33.6	7.4

smart watch worn on victims' hand while typing password has been previously used to reveal victims' PIN [39]. Researchers have also translated thoughts about moving fingers into action in prosthetic hands [35]. So we assumed that, there might be unique neural signatures of typing the numbers you are thinking about, which might be used to predict the victims' PIN numbers. Table 3(a) and (b) displays the results on individual model – single session, and individual model – merged session respectively. We can observe that on average the digits can be best predicted in individual model – single session at 46.5% true positive rate (false positive rate is 6.0%), and at 28.4% true positive rate (false positive rate is 7.9%) in individual model – merged session datasets. Similarly, Table 3(c) reports that the digits can be best predicted at 33.6% true positive rate (false positive rate is 6.7%) in global model. All these models again have performance better than a random model (10%).

We observe that the results of PNKPE task are lower than the results of VAPE task (see Sect. 6.2). In VAPE task the keys flashing while typing the numbers, which might have triggered neural signals resulting better features in building classification model. However, from the results of this task, we find that the finger movement while typing a number leave a unique trace in the brain which can be used to infer the keystrokes.

6.4   Task 4: Physical Keyboard Password Entry (PKPE)

To recall, in this task we had asked users to enter thirty-six randomly generated uppercase 6-character password in laptop keyboard. Using the brain and key-strokes data recorded during the task, we built classification models to predict the users' keystrokes. Table 4(a) shows the results for the individual model - single session data. We can see that on average the digits can be best predicted at 34.7% true positive rate (false positive rate is 4.7%). Similarly, in this task, the classification models on merged sessions data can best predict the digits at 23.7% true positive rate (false positive rate is 5.4%) (Table 4(b)). Table 4(c) reports that on average the digits can be best predicted at 30.1% true positive rate (false positive rate is 4.8%) in the group model. Like the previous tasks, we observe that the results are better than random model for keystroke detection (random prediction rate of a character is 3.8%). In this task, we see that the overall results for this classification model is lower than the results in previous tasks (see Sects. 6.1, 6.2 and 6.3). This task involved a physical keyboard with many keys on the keyboard.

Table 4. PKPE Task: Average true positive rate and average false positive rate (a) Individual Model – Single Session (b) Individual Model – Merging Sessions (c) Global Model

Classifiers	Session 1 TPR	FPR	Session 2 TPR	FPR	Session 3 TPR	FPR	Session 4 TPR	FPR
IB1	27.1	5.2	28.7	5.1	34.7	4.7	37.3	4.5
KStar	30.7	5.0	31.3	4.9	28.7	5.1	37.3	4.5
NB+IBk	17.3	5.9	10.7	6.4	23.3	5.5	28.7	5.1
NB+kStar	28.7	5.1	28.9	5.1	34.7	4.7	36.7	4.5

Classifier	All Sessions TPR	FPR
IB1	21.15	5.6
KStar	23.7	5.4
IB1+NB	17.75	5.7
KStar+NB	23.5	5.3

Classifier	All Sessions TPR	FPR
IB1	27.8	5.1
KStar	30.1	4.8
IB1+NB	19.8	5.7
KStar+NB	29.0	5.1

The numbers were not flashed on entering them and multiple fingers were used while typing passwords. Because of all these things, the features representing the digits might not have been strong enough for better detection of the keystrokes.

6.5 High-End B-Alert Headset - VKPE Task

We used high-end B-Alert headset to collect data in VKPE task for one participant, to test the feasibility of our attacks on different categories of headsets used for recording the neural signals.

Table 5. B-Alert Headset VKPE Task: Average true positive rate and average false positive rate (a) Individual Model –Single Session (b) Individual Model – Merging Sessions

Classifiers	Session 1 TPR	FPR	Session 2 TPR	FPR	Session 3 TPR	FPR	Session 4 TPR	FPR
IB1	39.0	6.8	31.0	7.7	31.0	7.7	37.3	4.5
KStar	34.0	7.3	23.0	8.6	36.0	7.1	37.3	4.5
IB1 + NB	37.0	7.0	31.0	7.7	24.0	8.4	28.7	5.1
KStar +NB	25.0	8.3	25.0	8.3	38.0	6.9	36.7	4.5

Classifier	All Sessions TPR	FPR
IB1	20.5	8.8
KStar	19.8	8.9
IB1+NB	17.5	9.2
KStar+NB	19.5	8.9

Table 5(a) shows the results of these classification models on single session data. We can see that on average the digits can be predicted at a true positive rate of 39.0% (false positive 6.8). The performance of the classification models on merged sessions data are presented in Table 5(b). We can see that on average the digits can be best predicted at 20.5% true positive rate (false positive is 8.8%). These results are significantly better than a random guessing classification model (10% for each digit) which shows the feasibility of side-channel attacks using BCI devices.

7 Discussion and Future Work

In this section, we summarize and further discuss the main findings from our study. We also outline the strengths and limitations of our study.

7.1 Vulnerability of the Brainwave Signals

In this study, we focused on studying the vulnerability of BCI devices towards revealing the private information to malicious attackers. We designed PEEP to study the feasibility of brainwave side-channel attacks using such devices. PEEP stealthily monitors and records event-related potentials (ERPs) measured by BCI devices when users are typing their PINs or passwords on to physical or virtual keyboards. PEEP can then analyze the ERPs for extracting features representing each of the digit or character. These features are then used to build a training model which is later used to predict the keystrokes made by the users. We experimentally verified the feasibility of PEEP for both individual and global training models.

Closely related to our study is the work done by Martinovic et al. [29]. They also studied the feasibility of side-channel attack with brain-computer interfaces. They showed the images of banks, ATMs, digits, months, etc., to participants to elucidate their private information related to banks, ATMs, PINs, and month of birth. They used the amplitude of P300 ERP, which appears in neuronal electrical activity for known artifacts, to infer such details. The participants in their study were asked to memorize 4-digit PINs and were shown the images of randomly permuted numbers between 0 and 9, one by one. Each number was shown 16 times, and the experiment lasted around 90 seconds. They were able to correctly predict the first digit of the PIN at 20% accuracy. In contrast, PEEP, on average, was able to predict digits at the true positive rate of 46.5% (FPR 6.0%) for PIN entered in the VAPE task (this is the task closely related to PIN study of Martinovic et al.). Also, their attack set-up is intrusive and can be easily detectable as the users may notice the abnormality in the app when it shows the images of banks or ATMs related to the user. In comparison, PEEP is highly surreptitious as it only requires passive monitoring of brain signals as users' type their PINs and passwords in regular use of computing devices, not fraudulent strategies that may trigger suspicion and be detected by the user. By the passive nature of our attack, it can be used to learn private input from any (secondary) computing device, not necessarily the (primary) one to which the BCI device is connected like in [29].

7.2 Password Entropy

PEEP reduces the entropy of the PIN or textual passwords, making it easier to launch dictionary or brute force attacks. In our study, we assumed the passwords and PINs to be random. We used 0–9 digits to create 4-digit PIN and A-Z characters to create six character-based passwords. If brute-force attack is launched, it will take 10^4 guesses to correctly identify the PIN and 26^6 guesses to correctly identify the password. The success of randomly guessing a digit of the PIN is 100/10 (10%) and the success of randomly guessing a character is 100/26 (3.84%). PEEP increases this accuracy of correctly identifying the digits of PIN to 47.5% and passwords to 34.7%. In case of non-random passwords, PEEP can be used in conjunction with dictionary-based password attacks, and further reduce the number of guesses in the brute-force attacks.

7.3 Possible Defensive Mechanisms

One of the possible strategies to mitigate the threat invoked by PEEP is to automatically insert noise in the neural signals when the user starts typing passwords or PINs (or other sensitive input). However, this might affect other benign applications dependent on brain signals during that time frame. Currently, the third-party developers are offered unfettered access to the neural signals captured by such devices. This access can be managed by operating systems to stop apps other than intended apps to listen on to brain signals while entering the private information in desktops or mobiles. The more sophisticated attacks are imminent with the technological advancements in these BCI devices. So it is important to study probable mitigations of such attacks in the future, especially given their potential hideous and powerful nature.

7.4 Study Strengths and Limitations

We believe that our study has several strengths. The study used randomly generated passwords which users knew at the time of the experiment. Despite the lack of pre- familiarity with the passwords/PINs, we were still able to predict them with true positive rate significantly better than random guessing. In real life, the password might remain in the memory for longer time, and the users might only be using certain fixed digits or characters in their PINs or passwords, which might provide better feature space and better prediction true positive rate. Further, we launched our side channel attacks using different categories of headsets (both consumer and clinical EEG headsets) and verified the feasibility of our attacks in a variety of contexts. Similar to any study involving human subjects, our study also had certain limitations. Our study was conducted in a lab environment. Although we tried to simulate the real-world scenarios of entering PINs or passwords, the layouts of the experimental tasks were simplistic. Also, the performance of the users might have been affected by the fact that their brain signal was recorded during the task. The EEG headsets we used in our experiment were quite light-weight, and the duration of the experiment was short (maximum four minutes for each task), however, the participants might have felt some discomfort that may have impacted their brain responses. Future work may be needed to assess the feasibility of our attacks in real-world or field settings. We believe that our work lays the necessary foundation that serves to highlight the vulnerability.

8 Concluding Remarks

The popularity of BCI devices is ever increasing. In not so distant future, these devices are going to be less costly and more sophisticated and will be integrated into many spheres of daily lives of users. In this light, it is important to study the possible security vulnerabilities of such devices and make people aware of such vulnerabilities. In this paper, we examined the possibility of one such side-channel attack for the purpose of inferring users' private information, in particular, their sensitive keystrokes in the form of PINs and passwords. We designed and developed PEEP, which successfully predicts the sensitive keystrokes made by the users just from the event-related potentials passively recorded during those keystrokes. PEEP predicts numbers entered in 4-digit PINs in virtual keyboard with an average TPR of 43.4%, virtual ATM keyboard with an average TPR of 47.5%, physical numeric keyboard with an average TPR of 46.5% and alphabets entered in 6-character passwords with an average TPR of 37.3%, demonstrating the feasibility of such attacks.

A   Design of Experiments

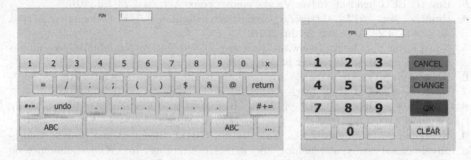

Fig. 3. (a) VKPE task: virtual keyboard (b) VAPE task: virtual ATM keyboard

Fig. 4. PNKPE task: (a) Layout to enter the PIN (b) Physical numeric keyboard used

Fig. 5. PKPE task: (a) Layout to enter 6-digit character based password (b) Physical keyboard used

References

1. B-Alert X-10 Set-Up Manual. http://www.biopac.com/Manuals/b-alert
2. Emotiv app store. https://www.emotiv.com/store/app.php. Accessed 28 Jul 2016
3. Emotiv EEG headset. https://www.emotiv.com. Accessed 28 Jul 2016
4. Emotiv web APIs. https://cpanel.emotivinsight.com/BTLE/document.htm#_Toc396152456. Accessed 28 Jul 2016
5. Neurofocus. http://www.nielsen.com/us/en/solutions/capabilities/consumer-neuroscience.html. Accessed 14 Aug 2016
6. Neurosky app store. https://store.neurosky.com/. Accessed 28 Jul 2016
7. Neurosky EEG headset. https://www.neurosky.com. Accessed 28 Jul 2016
8. Aha, D.W., Kibler, D., Albert, M.K.: Instance-based learning algorithms. Mach. Learn. **6**(1), 37–66 (1991)
9. Neupane, A., Rahman, M.L., Saxena, N., Hirshfield, L.: A multimodal neurophysiological study of phishing and malware warnings. In: ACM Conference on Computer and Communications Security (CCS). ACM, Denver (2015)
10. Ashby, C., Bhatia, A., Tenore, F., Vogelstein, J.: Low-cost electroencephalogram (EEG) based authentication. In: 2011 5th International IEEE/EMBS Conference on Neural Engineering (NER), pp. 442–445. IEEE (2011)
11. Asonov, D., Agrawal, R.: Keyboard acoustic emanations. In: IEEE Symposium on Security and Privacy, vol. 2004, pp. 3–11 (2004)
12. Aviv, A.J., Sapp, B., Blaze, M., Smith, J.M.: Practicality of accelerometer side channels on Smartphones. In: Proceedings of the 28th Annual Computer Security Applications Conference, pp. 41–50. ACM (2012)
13. Birbaumer, N., Ghanayim, N., Hinterberger, T., Iversen, I., Kotchoubey, B., Kübler, A., Perelmouter, J., Taub, E., Flor, H.: A spelling device for the paralysed. Nature **398**(6725), 297–298 (1999)
14. Bojinov, H., Sanchez, D., Reber, P., Boneh, D., Lincoln, P.: Neuroscience meets cryptography: designing crypto primitives secure against rubber hose attacks. In: Presented as part of the 21st USENIX Security Symposium (USENIX Security 12), pp. 129–141 (2012)
15. Cai, L., Chen, H.: TouchLogger: inferring keystrokes on touch screen from Smartphone motion. In: HotSec 2011, p. 9 (2011)
16. Campbell, A., Choudhury, T., Hu, S., Lu, H., Mukerjee, M.K., Rabbi, M., Raizada, R.D.: Neurophone: brain-mobile phone interface using a wireless EEG headset. In: Proceedings of the Second ACM SIGCOMM Workshop on Networking, Systems, and Applications on Mobile Handhelds, pp. 3–8. ACM (2010)

17. Chuang, J., Nguyen, H., Wang, C., Johnson, B.: I think, therefore i am: usability and security of authentication using brainwaves. In: Adams, A.A., Brenner, M., Smith, M. (eds.) FC 2013. LNCS, vol. 7862, pp. 1–16. Springer, Heidelberg (2013). https://doi.org/10.1007/978-3-642-41320-9_1
18. Cleary, J.G., et al.: K*: an instance-based learner using an entropic distance measure
19. Delorme, A., Makeig, S.: EEGLAB: an open source toolbox for analysis of single-trial EEG dynamics including independent component analysis. J. Neurosci. Method. **134**(1), 9–21 (2004)
20. Donchin, E.: Event-related brain potentials: a tool in the study of human information processing. In: Begleiter, H. (ed.) Evoked Brain Potentials and Behavior. The Downstate Series of Research in Psychiatry and Psychology, vol. 2, pp. 13–88. Springer, Boston (1979). https://doi.org/10.1007/978-1-4684-3462-0_2
21. Esfahani, E.T., Sundararajan, V.: Classification of primitive shapes using brain-computer interfaces. Comput.-Aided Des. **44**(10), 1011–1019 (2012)
22. Halevi, T., Saxena, N.: A closer look at keyboard acoustic emanations: random passwords, typing styles and decoding techniques. In: Proceedings of the 7th ACM Symposium on Information, Computer and Communications Security, pp. 89–90. ACM (2012)
23. Huan, N.J., Palaniappan, R.: Neural network classification of autoregressive features from electroencephalogram signals for brain? computer interface design. J. Neural Eng. **1**(3), 142 (2004)
24. Hyvärinen, A., Oja, E.: Independent component analysis: algorithms and applications. Neural Netw. **13**(4), 411–430 (2000)
25. Johnson, D., Maillart, T., Chuang, J.: My thoughts are not your thoughts. In: Proceedings of the 2014 ACM International Joint Conference on Pervasive and Ubiquitous Computing: Adjunct Publication, pp. 1329–1338. ACM (2014)
26. Jordan, A.: On discriminative vs. generative classifiers: A comparison of logistic regression and naive bayes (2002)
27. Makeig, S., et al.: Independent component analysis of electroencephalographic data. In: Advances in Neural Information Processing Systems, pp. 145–151 (1996)
28. Marquardt, P., Verma, A., Carter, H., Traynor, P.: (SP) iPhone: decoding vibrations from nearby keyboards using mobile phone accelerometers. In: Proceedings of the 18th ACM Conference on Computer and Communications Security, pp. 551–562. ACM (2011)
29. Martinovic, I., Davies, D., Frank, M., Perito, D., Ros, T., Song, D.: On the feasibility of side-channel attacks with brain-computer interfaces. In: Presented as part of the 21st USENIX Security Symposium (USENIX Security 12), pp. 143–158 (2012)
30. Monrose, F., Rubin, A.: Authentication via keystroke dynamics. In: Proceedings of the 4th ACM conference on Computer and Communications Security, pp. 48–56. ACM (1997)
31. Neupane, A., Saxena, N., Kuruvilla, K., Georgescu, M., Kana, R.: Neural signatures of user-centered security: an fMRI study of phishing, and malware warnings. In: Proceedings of the Network and Distributed System Security Symposium (NDSS), pp. 1–16 (2014)
32. Owusu, E., Han, J., Das, S., Perrig, A., Zhang, J.: Accessory: password inference using accelerometers on Smartphones. In: Proceedings of the Twelfth Workshop on Mobile Computing Systems and Applications, p. 9. ACM (2012)
33. del R Millan, J., Mouriño, J., Franzé, M., Cincotti, F., Varsta, M., Heikkonen, J., Babiloni, F.: A local neural classifier for the recognition of EEG patterns associated to mental tasks. IEEE Trans. Neural Netw. **13**(3), 678–686 (2002)

34. Song, D.X., Wagner, D., Tian, X.: Timing analysis of keystrokes and timing attacks on SSH. In: Proceedings of the 10th Conference on USENIX Security Symposium, SSYM 2001, vol. 10, USENIX Association, Berkeley, CA, USA (2001). http://dl.acm.org/citation.cfm?id=1251327.1251352
35. Sumon, M.S.P.: First man with two mind-controlled prosthetic limbs. Bangladesh Med. J. **44**(1), 59–60 (2016)
36. Tan, D., Nijholt, A.: Brain-computer interfaces and human-computer interaction. In: Tan, D., Nijholt, A. (eds.) Brain-Computer Interfaces. Human-Computer Interaction Series, pp. 3–19. Springer, London (2010). https://doi.org/10.1007/978-1-84996-272-8_1
37. Thorpe, J., van Oorschot, P.C., Somayaji, A.: Pass-thoughts: authenticating with our minds. In: Proceedings of the 2005 Workshop on New Security Paradigms, pp. 45–56. ACM (2005)
38. Vuagnoux, M., Pasini, S.: Compromising electromagnetic emanations of wired and wireless keyboards. In: Proceedings of the 18th USENIX Security Symposium, pp. 1–16. No. LASEC-CONF-2009-007. USENIX Association (2009)
39. Wang, H., Lai, T.T.T., Roy Choudhury, R.: MoLe: motion leaks through smartwatch sensors. In: Proceedings of the 21st Annual International Conference on Mobile Computing and Networking, pp. 155–166. ACM (2015)
40. Xu, Z., Bai, K., Zhu, S.: TapLogger: inferring user inputs on smartphone touchscreens using on-board motion sensors. In: Proceedings of the Fifth ACM Conference on Security and Privacy in Wireless and Mobile Networks, pp. 113–124. ACM (2012)
41. Zhuang, L., Zhou, F., Tygar, J.D.: Keyboard acoustic emanations revisited. ACM Trans. Inf. Syst. Secur. (TISSEC) **13**(1), 3 (2009)

Fantastic Timers and Where to Find Them: High-Resolution Microarchitectural Attacks in JavaScript

Michael Schwarz[✉], Clémentine Maurice, Daniel Gruss, and Stefan Mangard

Graz University of Technology, Graz, Austria
michael.schwarz@iaik.tugraz.at

Abstract. Research showed that microarchitectural attacks like cache attacks can be performed through websites using JavaScript. These timing attacks allow an adversary to spy on users secrets such as their keystrokes, leveraging fine-grained timers. However, the W3C and browser vendors responded to this significant threat by eliminating fine-grained timers from JavaScript. This renders previous high-resolution microarchitectural attacks non-applicable.

We demonstrate the inefficacy of this mitigation by finding and evaluating a wide range of new sources of timing information. We develop measurement methods that exceed the resolution of official timing sources by 3 to 4 orders of magnitude on all major browsers, and even more on Tor browser. Our timing measurements do not only re-enable previous attacks to their full extent but also allow implementing new attacks. We demonstrate a new DRAM-based covert channel between a website and an unprivileged app in a virtual machine without network hardware. Our results emphasize that quick-fix mitigations can establish a dangerous false sense of security.

1 Introduction

Microarchitectural attacks comprise side-channel attacks and covert channels, entirely implemented in software. Side-channel attacks exploit timing differences to derive secret values used in computations. They have been studied extensively in the past 20 years with a focus on cryptographic algorithms [2,10,16,29–31,48]. Covert channels are special side channels where a sender and a receiver use the side channel actively to transmit data covertly. These attacks require highly accurate timing and thus are typically implemented in native binaries written in C or assembly language to use the best available timing source.

Side channels exist on virtually all systems and software not hardened against side channels. Thus, browsers are an especially easy target for an attacker, because browsers process highly sensitive data and attackers can easily trick a victim to open a malicious website in the browser. Consequently, timing side-channel attacks have been demonstrated and observed in the wild, to recover a user's browser history [8,13,41], but also a user's geolocation [14], whether a user

© International Financial Cryptography Association 2017
A. Kiayias (Ed.): FC 2017, LNCS 10322, pp. 247–267, 2017.
https://doi.org/10.1007/978-3-319-70972-7_13

is logged in to another website [4] and even CSRF tokens [11]. Van Goethem et al. [37] exploited more accurate in-browser timing to obtain information even from within other websites, such as contact lists or previous inputs.

Oren et al. [28] recently demonstrated that cache side-channel attacks can also be performed in browsers. Their attack uses the `performance.now` method to obtain a timestamp whose resolution is in the range of nanoseconds. It allows spying on user activities but also building a covert channel with a process running on the system. Gruss et al. [9] and Bosman et al. [5] demonstrated Rowhammer attacks in JavaScript, leveraging the same timing interface. In response, the W3C [40] and browser vendors [1,3,6] have changed the `performance.now` method to a resolution of $5\,\mu s$. The timestamps in the Tor browser are even more coarse-grained, at $100\,ms$ [25]. In both cases, this successfully stops side-channel attacks by withholding necessary information from an adversary.

In this paper, we demonstrate that reducing the resolution of timing information or even removing these interfaces is completely insufficient as an attack mitigation. We propose several new mechanisms to obtain absolute and relative timestamps. We evaluated 10 different mechanisms on the most recent versions of 4 different browsers: Chrome, Firefox, Edge, as well as the Tor browser, which took even more drastic measures. We show that all browsers leak highly accurate timing information that exceeds the resolution of official timing sources by 3 to 4 orders of magnitude on all browsers, and by 8 on the Tor browser. In all cases, the resolution is sufficient to revive the attacks that were thought mitigated [28].

Based on our novel timing mechanisms, we are the first to exploit DRAM-based timing leaks from JavaScript. There were doubts whether DRAM-based timing leaks can be exploited from JavaScript, as it is not possible to directly reach DRAM [32]. We demonstrate that a DRAM-based covert channel can be used to exfiltrate data from highly restricted, isolated execution environments that are not connected to the network. More specifically, we transmit data from an unprivileged process in a Virtual Machine (VM) without any network hardware to a website, by tunneling the data through the DRAM-based covert channel to the JavaScript running in a web browser on the same host machine.

Our key contributions are:

- We performed a comprehensive evaluation of known and new mechanisms to obtain timestamps. We compared 10 methods on the 3 major browsers on Windows, Linux and Mac OS X, as well as on Tor browser.
- Our new timing methods increase the resolution of official methods by 3 to 4 orders of magnitude on all browsers, and by 8 orders of magnitude on Tor browser. Our evaluation therefore shows that reducing the resolution of timer interfaces does not mitigate any attack.
- We demonstrate the first DRAM-based side channel in JavaScript to exfiltrate data from a highly restricted execution environment inside a VM with no network interfaces.
- Our results underline that quick-fix mitigations are dangerous, as they can establish a false sense of security.

The remainder of this paper is organized as follows. In Sect. 2, we provide background information. In Sect. 3, we comprehensively evaluate new timing measurement methods on all major browsers. In Sect. 4, we demonstrate the revival of cache attacks with our new timing primitives as well as a new DRAM-based covert channel between JavaScript in a website and a process that is strictly isolated inside a VM with no network hardware. Finally, we discuss effective mitigation techniques in Sect. 5 and conclude in Sect. 6.

2   Background

2.1   Microarchitectural Attacks

A large body of recent work has focused on cross-VM covert channels. A first class of work uses the CPU cache for covert communications. Ristenpart et al. [33] are the first to demonstrate a cache-based covert channel between two Amazon EC2 instances, yielding 0.2 bps. Xu et al. [47] optimized this covert channel and assessed the difference in performance between theoretical and practical results. They obtain 215.11 bps with an error rate of 5.12%. Maurice et al. [23] built a cross-VM covert channel, using the last-level cache and a Prime+Probe approach, that achieves a bit rate of 751 bps with an error rate of 5.7%. Liu et al. [21] demonstrated a high-speed cache-based covert channel between two VMs that achieves transmission speeds of up to 600 Kbps and an error rate of less than 1%. In addition to the cache, covert channels have also been demonstrated using memory. Xiao et al. [46] demonstrated a memory-based covert channel using page deduplication. Wu et al. [45] built a covert channel of 746 bps with error correction, using the memory bus. Pessl et al. [32] reverse engineered the DRAM addressing functions that map physical addresses to their physical location inside the DRAM. The mapping allowed them to build a covert channel that relies solely on the DRAM as shared resource. Their cross-core cross-VM covert channel achieves a bandwidth of 309 Kbps. Maurice et al. [24] demonstrated an error-free covert channel between two Amazon EC2 instances of more than 360 Kbps, which allows building an SSH connection through the cache.

2.2   JavaScript and Timing Measurements

JavaScript is a scripting language supported by all modern browsers, which implement just-in-time compilation for performance. Contrary to low-level languages like C, JavaScript is strictly sandboxed and hides the notion of addresses and pointers. The concurrency model of JavaScript is based on a single-threaded *event loop* [26], which consists of a message queue and a call stack. Events are handled in the message queue, moved to the call stack when the stack is empty and processed to completion. As a drawback, if a message takes too long to process, it blocks other messages to be processed, and the browser becomes unresponsive. Browsers received the support for multithreading with the introduction of *web workers*. Each web worker runs in parallel and has its own event loop [26].

For timing measurement, the timestamp counter of Intel CPUs provides the number of CPU cycles since startup and thus a high-resolution timestamp. In native code, the timestamp counter is accessible through the unprivileged `rdtsc` instruction. In JavaScript, we cannot execute arbitrary instructions such as the `rdtsc` instruction. One of the timing primitives provided by JavaScript is the High Resolution Time API [40]. This API provides the `performance.now` method that gives a sub-millisecond timestamp. The W3C standard recommends that the timestamp should be monotonically increasing and accurate to 5 μs. The resolution may be lower if the hardware has no support for such a high resolution.

Remarkably, until Firefox 36 the High Resolution Time API returned timestamps accurate to one nanosecond. This is comparable to the native `rdtsc` instruction which has a resolution of 0.5 ns on a 2 GHz CPU. As a response to the results of Oren et al. [28], the timer resolution was decreased for security reasons [3]. In recent versions of Chrome and WebKit, the timing resolution was also decreased to the suggested 5 μs [1,6]. The Tor project even reduced the resolution to 100 ms [25]. The decreased resolution of the high-resolution timer is supposed to prevent time-based side-channel attacks. In a concurrent work, Kohlbrenner et al. [18] showed that it is possible to recover a high resolution by observing clock edges, as well as to create new implicit clocks using browser features. Additionally, they implemented fuzzy time that aims to degrade the native clock as well as all implicit clocks.

2.3   Timing Attacks in JavaScript

Van Goethem et al. [37] showed different timing attacks in browsers based on the processing time of resources. They aimed to extract private data from users by estimating the size of cross-origin resources. Stone [35] showed that the optimization in SVG filters introduced timing side channels. He showed that this side channel can be used to extract pixel information from iframes.

Microarchitectural side channels have only recently been exploited in JavaScript. Oren et al. [28] showed that it is possible to mount cache attacks in JavaScript. They demonstrated how to generate an eviction set for the last-level cache that can be used to mount a Prime+Probe attack. Based on this attack, they built a covert channel using the last-level cache that is able to transmit data between two browser instances. Furthermore, they showed that the timer resolution is high enough to create a spy application that tracks the user's mouse movements and network activity. As described in Sect. 2.2, this attack caused all major browsers to decrease the resolution of the `performance.now` method.

Gruss et al. [9] demonstrated hardware faults triggered from JavaScript, exploiting the so-called Rowhammer bug. The Rowhammer bug occurs when repeatedly accessing the same DRAM cells with a high frequency [15]. This "hammering" leads to bit flips in neighboring DRAM rows. As memory accesses are usually cached, they also implemented cache eviction in JavaScript.

All these attacks require a different timestamp resolution. The attacks from Goethem et al. [37] and Stone [35] require a timestamp resolution that is on the order of a microsecond, while the attack of Oren et al. [28] relies on the fine-grained timestamps on the order of nanoseconds. More generally, as microarchitectural side channel attacks aim at exploiting timing differences of a few CPU cycles, they depend on the availability of fine-grained timestamps. We note that decreasing the resolution therefore only mitigates microarchitectural attacks on the major browsers that have a resolution of 5 μs, but mitigates more side-channel attacks on the Tor browser which has a resolution of 100 ms.

3   Timing Measurements in the JavaScript Sandbox

This section describes techniques to get accurate measurements with a high-resolution timestamp in the browser. In the first part, we describe methods to recover a high resolution for the provided High Resolution Time API. The second part describes different techniques that allow deriving highly accurate timestamps, with *implicit* timers. These methods are summarized in Table 1.

3.1   Recovering a High Resolution

In both Chrome and Webkit, the timer resolution is decreased by rounding the timestamp down to the nearest multiple of 5 μs. As our measurements fall below this resolution, they are all rounded down to 0. We refer to the underlying clock's resolution as *internal resolution* and to the decreased resolution of the provided timer as *provided resolution*. It has already been observed that it is possible to recover a high resolution by observing the clock edges [18,22,34,38]. The clock edge aligns the timestamp perfectly to its resolution, *i.e.*, we know that the timestamp is an exact multiple of its provided resolution at this time.

Clock Interpolation. As the underlying clock source has a high resolution, the difference between two clock edges varies only as much as the underlying clock. This property gives us a very accurate time base to build upon. As the time between two edges is always constant, we interpolate the time between them. This method has also been used in JavaScript in a concurrent work [18].

Clock interpolation requires a calibration before being able to return accurate timestamps. For this purpose, we repeatedly use a busy-wait loop to increment a counter between two clock edges. This gives us the number of steps we can use for the interpolation. We refer to the average number of increments as *interpolation steps*. The time it takes to increment the counter once equals the resolution we are able to recover. It can be approximated by dividing the time difference of two clock edges by the number of interpolation steps. This makes the timer independent from both the internal and the provided resolution.

The measurement with the improved resolution works as follows. We busy wait until we observe a clock edge. At this point, we start with the operation we want to time. After the timed operation has finished, we again busy wait for the next clock edge while incrementing a counter. We assume that the increment operation is a constant time operation, thus allowing us to linearly interpolate the passed time. From the calibration, we know the time of one interpolation step which will be a fraction of the provided resolution. Multiplying this time by the number of increments results in the interpolated time. Adding the interpolated time to the measured time increases the timer's resolution again.

Using this method, we recover a highly accurate timestamp. Listing A.1 shows the JavaScript implementation. Table 1 shows the recovered resolution for various values of provided resolution. Even for a timer rounded down to a multiple of 100 ms, we recover a resolution of 15 µs.

Edge Thresholding. We do not require an exact timestamp in all cases. For many side-channel attacks it is sufficient to distinguish two operations f_{fast} and f_{slow} based on their execution time. We refer to the execution times of the short-running function and long-running function as t_{fast} and t_{slow} respectively.

We devise a new method that we call edge thresholding. This method again relies on the property that we can execute multiple constant-time operations between two edges of the clock. Edge thresholding works as long as the difference in the execution time is larger than the time it takes to execute one such constant-time operation. Figure 1 illustrates the main idea of edge thresholding. Using multiple constant-time operations, we generate a padding after the function we want to measure. The execution time of the padding $t_{padding}$ is included into the measurement, increasing the total execution time by a constant value. The size of the padding depends on the provided resolution and on the execution time of the functions. We choose the padding in such a way that $t_{slow} + t_{padding}$ crosses one more clock edge than $t_{fast} + t_{padding}$, *i.e.*, both functions take a different amount of clock edges.

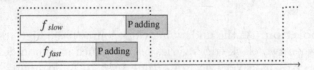

Fig. 1. Edge thresholding: apply padding such that the slow function crosses one more clock edge than the fast function.

To choose the correct padding, we start without padding and increase the padding gradually. We align the function start at a clock edge and measure the number of clock edges it takes to execute the short-running and the long-running function. As soon as the long-running function crosses one more clock edge than the short-running function, we have found a working padding. Subsequently, this padding is used for all execution time measurements. Figure 2 shows the results of classifying two functions with an execution time difference of 0.9 µs and a provided resolution of 10 µs. A normal, unaligned measurement is able to classify the two functions only in the case when one of the measurements crosses a clock edge, whereas the edge thresholding method categorizes over 80% of the function calls correctly by their relative execution time. Moreover, there are no false classifications.

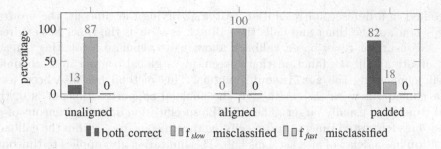

Fig. 2. Results of edge thresholding where the difference between the function's execution time is less then the provided resolution.

3.2 Alternative Timing Primitives

In cases where the High Resolution Time API [40] is not available, e.g., on Tor browser, we have to resort to different timing primitives, as highlighted by Kohlbrenner et al. [18]. As there is no different high-resolution timer available in JavaScript and we cannot access any native timers, we have to create our own timing sources. In most cases, it is sufficient to have a fast-paced monotonically increasing counter as a timing primitive that is not a real representation of time but an approximation of a highly accurate monotonic timer. While this concept was already presented by Wray in 1992 [44], Lipp et al. [20] recently demonstrated a practical high-resolution timing primitive on ARM using a counting thread. As JavaScript is inherently based on a single threaded event loop with no true concurrency, the timing primitive has to be based either on recurring events or non-JavaScript browser features.

We present several novel methods to construct timing primitives in JavaScript. We refer to them as *free-running timers* and *blocking timers*. Free-running timers do not depend on the JavaScript's event loop and run independently from the remaining code. Blocking timers are based on JavaScript events and are either only usable to recover a high resolution or in combination with web workers. If used in combination with web workers, the timers become free-running timers.

At first, it seems that timing primitives blocking the JavaScript event loop might not be useful at all. The higher the resolution of the timing primitive, the more events are added to the event queue and the less time remains for actual code. However, there are still two constructions that are able to use such primitives. First, these primitives can be used for very accurate interpolation steps when applying either clock interpolation or edge thresholding. Second, it is possible to take advantage of the multithreading support with web workers to run the timing primitive in parallel to the method to time.

Timeouts. The first asynchronous feature dating back to the introduction of JavaScript is the WindowTimers API. Specifically the `setTimeout` and `setInterval` functions allow scheduling a timer-based callback. The time is specified in a millisecond resolution. After specifying the timeout, the browser keeps track of the timer and calls the callback as soon as the timer has expired.

A concurrent timer-based callback allows us to simulate a counting thread. We create a callback function that increments a global counter and schedules itself again using the `setTimeout` function. This method has also been used in a concurrent work [18]. Although the minimal supported timeout is 0, the real timeout is usually larger. The HTML5 specification defines a timeout of at least 4 ms for nested timers, *i.e.*, specifying the timeout from within the callback function has a delay of at least 4 ms [42]. This limitation also applies to timeouts specified by the `setInterval` function.

Most browsers comply to the HTML5 specification and treat all timeouts below 4 ms as 4 ms. In Firefox, the minimum timeout is determined by the value of the flag `dom.min_timeout_value` which defaults to 4 ms as well. Note that the timeout only has such a high frequency if it is run in an active tab. Background tasks do not allow such high frequencies.

Microsoft implemented another timeout function in their browsers which is not standardized. The `setImmediate` function behaves similarly to the `setTimeout` function with a timeout of 0. The function is not limited to 4 ms and allows to build a high-resolution counting thread. A counting thread using this function results in a resolution of up to 50 µs which is three orders of magnitude higher than the `setTimeout` method.

Message Passing. By default, the browser enforces a same-origin policy, *i.e.*, scripts are not allowed to access web page data from a page that is served from a different domain. JavaScript provides a secure mechanism to circumvent the same-origin policy and to allow cross-origin communication. Scripts can install message listeners to receive message events from cross-origin scripts. A script from a different origin is allowed to post messages to a listener.

Despite the intended use for cross-origin communication, we can use this mechanism within one script as well. The message listener is not limited to messages sent from cross-origin scripts. Neither is there any limitation for the target of a posted message. Adding checks whether a message should be handled is left to the JavaScript developer. According to the HTML standard, posted messages are added to the event queue, *i.e.*, the message will be handled after any pending event is handled. This behavior leads to a nearly immediate execution of the installed message handler. A counting thread using the `postMessage` functions achieves a resolution of up to 35 µs. An implementation is shown in Listing A.2.

To obtain a free-running timing primitive, we have to move the message posting into separate web workers. This appears to be a straightforward task. However, there are certain limitations for web workers. Web workers cannot post messages to other web workers (including themselves). They can only post messages to the main thread and web workers they spawn, so called sub workers. Posting messages to the main thread again blocks the main thread's event loop, leaving sub web workers as the only viable option. Listing A.3 shows a sample implementation using one worker and one sub worker. The worker can communicate with the main thread and the sub worker. If the worker receives a message from the main thread, it sends back its current counter value. Otherwise, the worker continuously "requests" the current counter value from the sub worker. The sub worker increments the counter on each request and sends the current value back to the worker. The resulting resolution is even higher than with the blocking version of the method. On Tor browser, the achieved resolution is up to 15 μs, which is 4 orders of magnitude higher than the resolution of the native timer.

An alternative to sub workers are broadcast channels. Broadcast channels allow the communication between different sources from the same origin. A broadcast channel is identified by its name. In order to subscribe to a channel, a worker can create a `BroadcastChannel` object with the same name as an existing channel. A message that is posted to the broadcast channel is received by all other clients subscribed to this broadcast channel. We can build a construct that is similar to the sub worker scenario using two web workers. The web workers broadcast a message in their broadcast receiver to send the counter value back and forth. One of the web workers also responds to messages from the main thread to return the current counter value. With a resolution of up to 55 μs, this method is still almost as fast as the worker thread variant.

Message Channel. The Channel Messaging API provides bi-directional pipes to connect two clients. The endpoints of the pipe are called ports, and every port can both send and receive data. A message channel can be used in a similar way as cross-origin message passing. Listing A.4 shows a simple blocking counting thread using a message channel.

As with the cross-origin message passing method, we can also adapt this code to work inside a web worker yielding a free-running timing primitive. Listing A.5 shows the implementation for web workers. The resolution for the free-running message channel method is up to 30 μs, which is lower compared to the cross-origin communication method. However, it is currently the only method that works across browsers and has a resolution in the order of microseconds.

CSS Animations. With CSS version 3, the support for animations [39] was added. These animations are independent of JavaScript and are rendered by the browser. Users can specify keyframes and attributes that will then be animated without any further user interaction.

We demonstrate a new method that uses CSS animations to build a timing primitive. A different method using CSS animations has been used in a concurrent work [18]. We define an animation that changes the width of an element from 0 px to 1 000 000 px within 1 s. Theoretically, if all animation steps are calculated, the current width is incremented every microsecond. However, browsers limit the CSS animations to 60 fps, *i.e.*, the resolution of our timing primitive is 16 ms in the best case. Indeed, most monitors have a maximum refresh rate of 60 Hz, *i.e.*, they cannot display more than 60 fps. Thus, a higher frame rate would only waste resources without any benefit. To get the current timestamp, we retrieve the current width of the element. In JavaScript, we can get the current width of the element using `window.getComputedStyle(elem, null).getPropertyValue("width")`.

SharedArrayBuffer. Web workers do not have access to any shared resource. The communication is only possible via messages. If data is passed using a message, either the data is copied, or the ownership of the data is transferred. This design prevents race conditions and locking problems without having to depend on a correct use of locks. Due to the overhead of message passing for high-bandwidth applications, approaches for sharing data between workers are discussed by the ECMAScript committee [27]. An experimental extension for web workers is the `SharedArrayBuffer`. The ownership of such a buffer can be shared among multiple workers, which can access the buffer simultaneously.

A shared resource provides a way to build a real counting thread with a negligible overhead compared to a message passing approach. This already raised concerns with respect to the creation of a high-resolution clock [19]. In this method, one worker continuously increments the value of the buffer without checking for any events on the event queue. The main thread simply reads the current value from the shared buffer and uses it as a high-resolution timestamp.

We implemented a clock with a parallel counting thread using the `SharedArrayBuffer`. An implementation is shown in Listing A.6. The resulting resolution is close to the resolution of the native timestamp counter. On our Intel Core i5 test machine, we achieve a resolution of up to 2 ns using the shared array buffer. This is equivalent to a resolution of only 4 CPU cycles, which is 3 orders of magnitude better than the timestamp provided by `performance.now`.

3.3   Evaluation

We evaluated all methods on an Intel Core i5-6200U machine using the most popular browsers, up to date at the time of writing: Firefox 51, Chrome 53, Edge 38.14393.0.0, and Tor 6.0.4. All tests were run on Ubuntu 16.10, Windows 10, and Mac OS X 10.11.4. Table 1 shows the timing resolution of every method for every browser and operating system combination. We also evaluated our methods using Fuzzyfox [17], the fork of Firefox hardened against timing attacks [18].

The introduction of multithreading in JavaScript opened several possibilities to build a timing primitive that does not rely on any provided timer. By building a counting thread, we are able to get a timer resolution of several microseconds. This is especially alarming for the Tor browser, where the provided timer only has a resolution of 100 ms. Using the demonstrated methods, we can build a reliable timer with a resolution of up to 15 μs. The lower resolution was implemented as a side channel mitigation and is rendered useless when considering the results of the alternative timing primitives.

The best direct timing source we tested is the experimental `SharedArrayBuffer`. The best measurement method we tested is edge threshold-ing. Both increase the resolution by at least 3 orders of magnitude compared to

Table 1. Timing primitive resolutions on various browsers and operating systems.

	Free-running	Firefox 51	Chrome 53	Edge 38	Tor 6.0.4	Fuzzyfox
performance.now	✓	5 µs	5 µs	1 µs	100 ms	100 ms
CSS animations	✓	16 ms	16 ms	16 ms	16 ms	125 ms
setTimeout		4 ms	4 ms	2 ms	4 ms	100 ms
setImmediate		–	–	50 µs	–	–
postMessage		45 µs	35 µs	40 µs	40 µs	47 ms
Sub worker	✓	20 µs	–[b]	50 µs	15 µs	–
Broadcast Channel	✓	145 µs	–	–	55 µs	760 µs
MessageChannel		12 µs	55 µs	20 µs	20 µs	45 ms
MessageChannel (W)	✓	75 µs	100 µs	20 µs	30 µs	1120 µs
SharedArrayBuffer	✓	2 ns[c]	15 ns[d]	–	–	2 ns
Interpolation[a]		500 ns	500 ns	350 ns	15 µs	–
Edge thresholding[a]		2 ns	15 ns	10 ns	2 ns	–

[a] Uses performance.now for coarse-grained timing information.
[b] Sub workers do not work in Chrome, this is a known issue since 2010 [7].
[c] Currently only available in the nightly version.
[d] It has to be enabled by starting Chrome with —js-flags-—harmony-sharedarraybuffer— enable-blink-feature=SharedArrayBuffer.

performance.now in all browsers. Countermeasures against timing side-channels using fuzzy time have been proposed by Hu et al. [12] and Vattikonda et al. [38]. They suggested to reduce the provided resolution and to randomize the clock edges. However, we can fall back to the constructed timing primitives if this countermeasure is not applied on all implicit clocks.

In a concurrent work, Kohlbrenner et al. [18] proposed Fuzzyfox, a fork of Firefox that uses fuzzy time on both explicit and implicit clocks, and aims to cap all clocks to a resolution of 100 ms. Our evaluation shows that the explicit timer performance.now is reduced to 100 ms, and is fuzzed enough that the interpolation and edge thresholding methods do not work to recover a high resolution. Similarly, some of the implicit timers, such as setTimeout, postMessage, and Message Channel, are also mitigated, with a resolution between 45 ms and 100 ms. However, the Broadcast Channel, Message Channel with web workers, and SharedArrayBuffer still have a fine grained resolution, between 2 ns and 1 ms. It is to be noted that, while these methods stay accurate, the resulting clock is too fuzzy to derive a finer clock with either interpolation or edge thresholding.

4   Reviving and Extending Microarchitectural Attacks

In this section, we demonstrate that with our timing primitives, we are able to revive attacks that were thought mitigated, and build new DRAM-based attacks.

4.1   Reviving Cache Attacks

Oren et al. [28] presented the first microarchitectural side-channel attack running in JavaScript. Their attack was mitigated by decreasing the timer resolution. We verified that the attack indeed does not work anymore on current browser versions. However, we are able to revive cache attacks by using our newly discovered timing sources. Figure 3 shows the timing difference between cache hits and cache misses, measured with the `SharedArrayBuffer` method. The ability to measure this timing difference is the building block of all cache attacks.

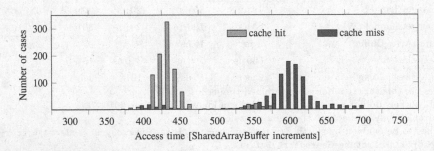

Fig. 3. Histogram for cache hits and cache misses.

4.2   A New DRAM-Based Covert Channel

Pessl et al. [32] established that timing differences in memory accesses can be exploited to build a cross-CPU covert channel. We demonstrate that this attack is also possible using JavaScript. In our scenario, the sender is an unprivileged binary inside a VM without a network connection. The receiver is implemented in sandboxed JavaScript running in a browser outside the VM, on the same host.

Overview. To communicate, the sender and the receiver agree on a certain bank and row of physical memory. This agreement can be done in advance and is not part of the transmission. The receiver continuously measures the access time to a value located inside the agreed row. For continuous accesses, the value will be cached in the row buffer and the access will be fast, resulting in a low access time. The receiver considers this as a 0. If the sender wants to transmit a 1, it accesses a different row inside the same bank. This access triggers a row conflict, resulting in a replacement of the row buffer content. On the receiver's next access, the request cannot be served from the row buffer but has to be fetched from the DRAM, resulting in a high access time.

Challenges. For the sender, we assume that we can run arbitrary unprivileged binary programs inside the VM. We implement the sender in C, which allows us to use the computer's high-resolution timestamp counter. Furthermore, we can flush addresses from the cache using the unprivileged *clflush* instruction. The only limitation on the sender is the absence of physical addresses.

On the receiver side, as the covert channel relies on timing differences that are in the order of tens of nanoseconds, we require a high-resolution timing primitive. We presented in Sect. 3 different methods to build timing primitives if the provided High Resolution Time API is not accurate enough. However, implementing this side channel in JavaScript poses some problems besides high-resolution timers. First, the DRAM mapping function requires the physical address to compute the physical location, *i.e.*, the row and the bank, inside the DRAM. However, JavaScript does not know the concept of pointers. Therefore, we neither have access to virtual nor physical addresses. Second, we have to ensure that memory accesses will always be served from memory and not the cache, *i.e.*, we have to circumvent the cache. Finally, the noise present on the system might lead to corrupt transfers. We have to be able to detect such bit inversions for reliable communication.

Address Selection. The DRAM mapping function reverse engineered by Pessl et al. [32] takes a physical address and calculates the corresponding physical memory location. Due to the absence of addresses in JavaScript, we cannot simply use these functions. We have to rely on another side channel to be able to infer address bits in JavaScript.

We exploit the fact that heap memory in JavaScript is allocated on demand, *i.e.*, the browser acquires additional heap memory from the operating system if this is required. These heap pages are internally backed by 2 MB pages, called Transparent Huge Pages (THP). Due to the way virtual memory works, for THPs, the 21 least-significant bits of a virtual and physical address are the same. On many systems, this is already sufficient as input to the DRAM mapping function. This applies to the sender as well, with the advantage that we know the virtual address which we can use immediately without any further actions.

To get the beginning of a THP in JavaScript, we iterate through an array of multiple megabytes while measuring the time it takes to access the array element, similarly to Gruss et al. [9]. As the physical pages for these THPs are also mapped on-demand, a page fault occurs as soon as an allocated THP is accessed for the first time. Such an access takes significantly longer than an access to an already mapped page. Thus, higher timings for memory accesses with a distance of 2 MB indicate the beginning of a THP. At this array index, the 21 least-significant bits of both the virtual and the physical address are 0.

Cache Circumvention. To measure DRAM access times we have to ensure that all our accesses go to the DRAM and not to the cache. In native code, we can rely on the `clflush` instruction. This unprivileged instruction flushes a virtual address from all cache levels, *i.e.*, the next access to the address is ensured to go to the DRAM.

However, in JavaScript we neither have access to the `clflush` instruction nor does JavaScript provide a function to flush the cache. Thus, we have to resort to cache eviction. Cache eviction is the process of filling the cache with new data until the data we want to flush is evicted from the cache. The straightforward way is to fill a buffer with the size of the last-level cache with data. However, this is not feasible in JavaScript as writing multiple megabytes of data is too slow. Moreover, on modern CPUs, it might not suffice to iteratively write to the buffer as the cache replacement policy is not pseudo-LRU since Ivy Bridge [43].

Gruss et al. [9] demonstrated fast cache eviction strategies for numerous CPUs. They showed that their functions have a success rate of more than 99.75% when implemented in JavaScript. We also rely on these functions to evict the address which we use for measuring the access time.

Transmission. To transmit data from inside the VM to the JavaScript, they have to agree on a common bank. It is not necessary to agree on a bank dynamically, it is sufficient to have the bank hardcoded in both programs. The sender and the receiver both choose a different row from this bank. Again, this can be hardcoded, and there is no requirement for an agreement protocol.

On the sender side, the application inside the VM continuously accesses a memory address in its row if it wants to transmit a binary 1. These accesses cause row conflicts with the receiver's row. To send a binary 0, the sender does nothing to not cause any row conflict. On the receiver side, the JavaScript constantly measures the access time to a memory address from its row and evicts the address afterwards. If the sender has accessed its row, the access to the receiver's row results in a row conflict. As a row conflict takes significantly longer than a row hit, the receiver can determine if the sender has accessed its row.

To synchronize sender and receiver, the receiver measures the access time in a higher frequency than the sender is sending. The receiver maintains a constant-size sliding window that moves over all taken measurements. As soon as the majority of the measurements inside the sliding window is the same, one bit is received. The higher the receiver's sampling frequency is, compared to the sender's sending frequency, the lower the probability of wrongly measured bits. However, a higher sampling frequency also leads to a slower transmission speed due to the increased amount of redundant data.

Due to different noise sources on the system, we encounter transmission errors. Such noise sources are failed evictions, high DRAM activity of other programs or not being scheduled at all. To have a reliable transmission despite those interferences, we encapsulate the data into packets with sequence numbers and protect each packet with an error detection code as shown in Fig. 4. The receiver is then able to detect any transmission error and to discard the packet. The sequence number ensures to keep the data stream synchronized. Thus, transmission errors only result in missing data, but the data stream is still synchronized after transmission errors. To deal with missing data, we can apply high-level error correction as shown by Maurice et al. [24].

Using the `SharedArrayBuffer`, we achieve a transmission rate of 11 bps for a 3 kB file with an error rate of 0% on our Intel Core i5 test machine. The system workload did not influence the transmission, as long as there is at least

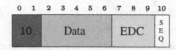

Fig. 4. One packet of the covert channel. It has a 2-bit preamble ''10'', 5 data bits, 3 bits of error detection code and a 1 bit sequence number.

one core fully available to the covert channel. We optimized the covert channel for reliability and not speed. We expect that it is possible to further increase the transmission rate by using multiple banks to transmit data in parallel. However, the current speed is two orders of magnitude higher than the US government's minimum standard for covert channels [36].

5 Countermeasures

Lowering the Timer Resolution. As a reaction to the JavaScript cache attacks published by Oren et al. [28], browsers reduced the resolution of the high-resolution timer. Nevertheless, we are able to recover a higher resolution from the provided timer, as well as to build our own high-resolution timers.

Fuzzy Time. Vattikonda et al. [38] suggested the concept of fuzzy time to get rid of high-resolution timers in hypervisors. Instead of rounding the timestamp to achieve a lower resolution, they move the clock edge randomly within one clock cycle. This method prevents the detection of the underlying clock edge and thus makes it impossible to recover the internal resolution. In a concurrent work, Kohlbrenner et al. [18] implemented the fuzzy time concept in Firefox to show that this method is also applicable in JavaScript. The implementation targets explicit clocks as well as implicit clocks. Nonetheless, we found different implicit clocks exceeding the intended resolution of 100 ms.

Shared Memory and Message Passing. A proposed mitigation is to introduce thread affinity to the same CPU core for threads with shared memory [19]. This prevents true parallelism and should therefore prevent a real asynchronous timing primitive. However, we showed that even without shared memory we can achieve a resolution of up to 15 μs by using message passing. Enforcing the affinity to one core for all communicating threads would lead to a massive performance degradation and would effectively render the use of web workers useless. A compromise is to increase the latency of message passing which should not affect low- to moderate-bandwidth applications. Compared to Fuzzyfox's delay on the main event queue, this has two advantages. First, the overall usability impact is not as severe as only messages are delayed and not every event. Second, it also prevents the high accuracy of the Message Channel and Broadcast Channel method as the delay is not limited to the main event queue.

6   Conclusion and Outlook

High-resolution timers are a key requirement for side-channel attacks in browsers. As more side-channel attacks in JavaScript have been demonstrated against users' privacy, browser vendors decided to reduce the timer resolution.

In this article, we showed that this attempt to close these vulnerabilities was merely a quick-fix and did not address the underlying issue. We investigated different timing sources in JavaScript and found a number of timing sources with a resolution comparable to `performance.now`. This shows that even removing the interface entirely, would not have any effect. Even worse, an adversary can recover a resolution of the former `performance.now` implementation through measurement methods we proposed. We evaluated our new measurement methods on all major browsers as well as the Tor browser that has applied the highest penalty to the timer resolution. Our results are alarming for all browsers, including the privacy-conscious Tor browser, as we are able to recover a resolution in the order of nanoseconds in all cases. In addition to reviving attacks that were now deemed infeasible, we demonstrated the first DRAM-based side channel in JavaScript. In this side-channel attack, we implemented a covert channel between an unprivileged binary in a VM with no network interface and a JavaScript program in a browser outside the VM, on the same host.

While fuzzy timers can lower the resolution of the provided timer interfaces, we show that applying the same mitigation on all implicit clocks, including the one that are not discovered yet, is a complex task. Thus, we conclude that it is likely that an adversary can obtain sufficiently accurate timestamps when running arbitrary JavaScript code. As microarchitectural attacks are not restricted to JavaScript, we recommend to mitigate them at the system- or hardware-level.

Acknowledgments We would like to thank our shepherd Jean Paul Degabriele, Georg Koppen from the Tor Browser project as well as all our anonymous reviewers.

  We would also like to thank the major browser vendors for their quick responses when reporting our findings. This project has received funding from the European Research Council (ERC) under the European Union's Horizon 2020 research and innovation programme (grant agreement No. 681402).

A   JavaScript Code

```
1   function calibrate()
2   {
3       var counter = 0, next;
4       for(var i = 0; i < 10; i++)
5       {
6           next = wait_edge();
7           counter += count_edge();
8       }
9       next = wait_edge();
10      return (wait_edge() - next) /
11          (counter / 10.0);
12  }
13
14  function measure(fnc)
15  {
16      var start = wait_edge();
17      fnc();
18      var count = count_edge();
19      return (performance.now()-start)
20          - count * calibrate();
    }
```

a: Clock interpolation.

```
1   function wait_edge()
2   {
3       var next, last =
            performance.now();
4       while((next =
            performance.now())
            == last) {}
5       return next;
6   }
7
8   function count_edge()
9   {
10      var last = performance.
            now(), count = 0;
11      while(performance.now()
            == last) count++;
12      return count;
13  }
```

b: Helper functions.

Listing A.1: Clock interpolation: calibrate returns the time one increment takes, measure uses interpolation to measure the execution time of fnc

```
1   var count = 0;
2
3   function counter()
4   {
5       count++;
6       window.postMessage(null, window.location);
7   }
8   window.addEventListener("message", counter);
9   window.postMessage(null, window.location);
```

Listing A.2: Abusing cross-origin communication to build a counting thread.

```
1   var ts = new
2     Worker('subworker.js');
3   ts.postMessage(0);
4
5   function counter(event)
6   {
7     timestamp = event.data;
8   }
9   ts.addEventListener("message",
        counter);
10  [...]
11
12  // get timestamp
13  ts.postMessage(0);
```

a: Timing measurement example.

```
1   var count = 0;
2
3   onmessage = function(event)
4   {
5     count++;
6     postMessage(count);
7   }
```

b: subworker2.js

```
1   var sub = new
2     Worker("subworker2.js");
3   sub.postMessage(0);
4
5   var count = 0;
6
7   sub.onmessage = msg;
8   onmessage = msg;
9
10  function msg(event)
11  {
12    if(event.data != 0)
13    {
14      count = event.data;
15      sub.postMessage(0);
16    }
17    else
18      self.postMessage(
            count);
19  }
```

c: subworker.js

Listing A.3: Message passing with web workers to get a free-running timer.

```
1   var count = 0, channel = null;
2   function handleMessage(e)
3   {
4     count++;
5     channel.port2.postMessage(0);
6   }
7
8   channel = new MessageChannel();
9   channel.port1.onmessage = handleMessage;
10  channel.port2.postMessage(0);
```

Listing A.4: A blocking timing primitive using a message channel.

```
1   var worker = new
2     Worker("mcworker.js");
3   var main_channel = new
       / MessageChannel();
4   var side_channel = new
       MessageChannel();
5
6   function handleMessage(e)
7   {
8       timestamp = e.data;
9   }
10
11  main_channel.port2.onmessage =
       handleMessage;
12  worker.postMessage(0,
13    [ main_channel.port1,
          side_channel.port1,
          side_channel.port2 ]);
14  [...]
15
16  // get timestamp
17  main_channel.port2.postMessage
       (0);
```

a: Timing measurement example.

```
1   var main_port, port1, port2,
       count = 0;
2
3   self.onmessage = function(
       event)
4   {
5       main_port = event.ports
          [0];
6       port1 = event.ports[1];
7       port2 = event.ports[2];
8       main_port.onmessage =
9         function()
10        {
11          main_port.postMessage(
              count);
12        };
13      port1.onmessage =
14        function()
15        {
16          count++;
17          port2.postMessage(0);
18        };
19      port2.postMessage(count);
20  };
```

b: mcworker.js

Listing A.5: Message passing with web workers to get a free-running timer.

```
1   var buffer = new
       SharedArrayBuffer(16);
2   var counter = new
3     Worker("counter.js");
4   counter.postMessage([buffer],
5     [buffer]);
6   var arr = new
7     Uint32Array(buffer);
8   [...]
9
10  timestamp = arr[0];
```

a: Timing measurement example.

```
1   self.onmessage = function(
       event)
2   {
3       var [buffer] = event.data;
4       var arr = new
5         Uint32Array(buffer);
6       while(1)
7       {
8           arr[0]++;
9       }
10  }
```

b: counter.js

Listing A.6: Parallel counting thread without additional overhead.

References

1. Christensen, A.: Reduce resolution of performance.now (2015). https://bugs.webkit.org/show_bug.cgi?id=146531
2. Bernstein, D.J.: Cache-Timing Attacks on AES (2004). http://cr.yp.to/antiforgery/cachetiming-20050414.pdf
3. Zbarsky, B.: Reduce resolution of performance.now. https://hg.mozilla.org/integration/mozilla-inbound/rev/48ae8b5e62ab
4. Bortz, A., Boneh, D.: Exposing private information by timing web applications. In: WWW 2007 (2007)
5. Bosman, E., Razavi, K., Bos, H., Giuffrida, C.: Dedup Est Machina: Memory Deduplication as an Advanced Exploitation Vector. In: S&P 2016 (2016)

6. Chromium: window.performance.now does not support sub-millisecond precision on Windows (2015). https://bugs.chromium.org/p/chromium/issues/detail?id=158234#c110
7. Chromium Bug Tracker: HTML5 nested workers are not supported in chromium (2010). https://bugs.chromium.org/p/chromium/issues/detail?id=31666. Accessed 18 Oct 2016
8. Felten, E.W., Schneider, M.A.: Timing attacks on web privacy. In: CCS 2000 (2000)
9. Gruss, D., Maurice, C., Mangard, S.: Rowhammer.js: a remote software-induced fault attack in JavaScript. In: Caballero, J., Zurutuza, U., Rodríguez, R.J. (eds.) DIMVA 2016. LNCS, vol. 9721, pp. 300–321. Springer, Cham (2016). https://doi.org/10.1007/978-3-319-40667-1_15
10. Gullasch, D., Bangerter, E., Krenn, S.: Cache games – bringing access-based cache attacks on AES to practice. In: S&P 2011 (2011)
11. Heiderich, M., Niemietz, M., Schuster, F., Holz, T., Schwenk, J.: Scriptless attacks: stealing the pie without touching the sill. In: Proceedings of the 2012 ACM Conference on Computer and Communications Security, pp. 760–771. ACM (2012)
12. Hu, W.M.: Lattice scheduling and covert channels. In: S&P 1992, pp. 52–61 (1992)
13. Jang, D., Jhala, R., Lerner, S., Shacham, H.: An empirical study of privacy-violating information flows in javascript web applications. In: CCS 2010 (2010)
14. Jia, Y., Dong, X., Liang, Z., Saxena, P.: I know where you've been: geo-inference attacks via the browser cache. IEEE Internet Comput. 19(1), 44–53 (2015)
15. Kim, Y., Daly, R., Kim, J., Fallin, C., Lee, J.H., Lee, D., Wilkerson, C., Lai, K., Mutlu, O.: Flipping bits in memory without accessing them: an experimental study of DRAM disturbance errors. In: ISCA 2014 (2014)
16. Kocher, P.C.: Timing attacks on implementations of Diffie-Hellman, RSA, DSS, and other systems. In: Koblitz, N. (ed.) CRYPTO 1996. LNCS, vol. 1109, pp. 104–113. Springer, Heidelberg (1996). https://doi.org/10.1007/3-540-68697-5_9
17. Kohlbrenner, D., Shacham, H.: Fuzzyfox (2016). https://github.com/dkohlbre/gecko-dev/tree/fuzzyfox. Accessed 23 January 2017
18. Kohlbrenner, D., Shacham, H.: Trusted browsers for uncertain times. In: USENIX Security Symposium (2016)
19. Hansen, L.T.: Shared memory: Side-channel information leaks (2016). https://github.com/tc39/ecmascript_sharedmem/blob/master/issues/TimingAttack.md
20. Lipp, M., Gruss, D., Spreitzer, R., Maurice, C., Mangard, S.: ARMageddon: cache attacks on mobile devices. In: USENIX Security Symposium (2016)
21. Liu, F., Yarom, Y., Ge, Q., Heiser, G., Lee, R.B.: Last-level cache side-channel attacks are practical. In: S&P 2015 (2015)
22. Martin, R., Demme, J., Sethumadhavan, S.: TimeWarp: rethinking timekeeping and performance monitoring mechanisms to mitigate side-channel attacks. In: Proceedings of the 39th International Symposium on Computer Architecture (ISCA 2012) (2012)
23. Maurice, C., Neumann, C., Heen, O., Francillon, A.: C5: cross-cores cache covert channel. In: Almgren, M., Gulisano, V., Maggi, F. (eds.) DIMVA 2015. LNCS, vol. 9148, pp. 46–64. Springer, Cham (2015). https://doi.org/10.1007/978-3-319-20550-2_3
24. Maurice, C., Weber, M., Schwarz, M., Giner, L., Gruss, D., Alberto Boano, C., Mangard, S., Römer, K.: Hello from the other side: SSH over robust cache covert channels in the cloud. In: NDSS 2017 (2017, to appear)
25. Perry, M.: Bug 1517: Reduce precision of time for Javascript (2015). https://gitweb.torproject.org/user/mikeperry/tor-browser.git/commit/?h=bug1517

26. Mozilla Developer Network: Concurrency model and Event Loop (2016). https://developer.mozilla.org/en-US/docs/Web/JavaScript/EventLoop

27. Mozilla Inc.: Ecmascript shared memory and atomics (2016). http://tc39.github.io/ecmascript_sharedmem/shmem.html

28. Oren, Y., Kemerlis, V.P., Sethumadhavan, S., Keromytis, A.D.: The Spy in the sandbox: practical cache attacks in JavaScript and their implications. In: CCS 2015 (2015)

29. Osvik, D.A., Shamir, A., Tromer, E.: Cache attacks and countermeasures: the case of AES. In: Pointcheval, D. (ed.) CT-RSA 2006. LNCS, vol. 3860, pp. 1–20. Springer, Heidelberg (2006). https://doi.org/10.1007/11605805_1

30. Page, D.: Theoretical use of cache memory as a cryptanalytic side-channel. Cryptology ePrint Archive, Report 2002/169 (2002)

31. Percival, C.: Cache missing for fun and profit. In: Proceedings of BSDCan (2005)

32. Pessl, P., Gruss, D., Maurice, C., Schwarz, M., Mangard, S.: DRAMA: exploiting DRAM addressing for cross-CPU attacks. In: USENIX Security Symposium (2016)

33. Ristenpart, T., Tromer, E., Shacham, H., Savage, S.: Hey, You, Get Off of My cloud: exploring information leakage in third-party compute clouds. In: CCS 2009 (2009)

34. Seaborn, M.: Comment on ecmascript shared memory and atomics (2015). https://github.com/tc39/ecmascript_sharedmem/issues/1#issuecomment-144171031

35. Stone, P.: Pixel perfect timing attacks with HTML5. Context Information Security (White Paper) (2013)

36. U.S. Department of Defense: Trusted computing system evaluation "the orange book". Technical report 5200.28-STD (1985)

37. Van Goethem, T., Joosen, W., Nikiforakis, N.: The clock is still ticking: timing attacks in the modern web. In: CCS 2015 (2015)

38. Vattikonda, B.C., Das, S., Shacham, H.: Eliminating fine grained timers in xen. In: CCSW 2011 (2011)

39. W3C: CSS Animations (2016). https://www.w3.org/TR/css3-animations/

40. W3C: High Resolution Time Level 2 (2016). https://www.w3.org/TR/hr-time/

41. Weinberg, Z., Chen, E.Y., Jayaraman, P.R., Jackson, C.: I still know what you visited last summer: leaking browsing history via user interaction and side channel attacks. In: S&P 2011 (2011)

42. WHATWG: HTML Living Standard – Timers (2016). https://html.spec.whatwg.org/multipage/webappapis.html#timers. Accessed 18 Oct 2016

43. Wong, H.: Intel Ivy Bridge Cache Replacement Policy. http://blog.stuffedcow.net/2013/01/ivb-cache-replacement/. Accessed 18 Oct 2016

44. Wray, J.C.: An analysis of covert timing channels. J. Comput. Secur. 1(3–4), 219–232 (1992)

45. Wu, Z., Xu, Z., Wang, H.: Whispers in the hyper-space: high-bandwidth and reliable covert channel attacks inside the cloud. IEEE/ACM Trans. Netw. PP(99), 1 (2014)

46. Xiao, J., Xu, Z., Huang, H., Wang, H.: A covert channel construction in a virtualized environment. In: CCS 2012 (2012)

47. Xu, Y., Bailey, M., Jahanian, F., Joshi, K., Hiltunen, M., Schlichting, R.: An exploration of L2 cache covert channels in virtualized environments. In: CCSW 2011 (2011)

48. Yarom, Y., Falkner, K.: Flush+Reload: a high resolution, low noise, L3 cache side-channel attack. In: USENIX Security Symposium (2014)

Attacks on Secure Logging Schemes

Gunnar Hartung$^{(\boxtimes)}$

Karlsruhe Institute of Technology, Karlsruhe, Germany
gunnar.hartung@kit.edu

Abstract. We present four attacks on three cryptographic schemes intended for securing log files against illicit retroactive modification. Our first two attacks regard the LogFAS scheme by Yavuz et al. (Financial Cryptography 2012), whereas our third and fourth attacks break the BM- and AR-FssAgg schemes by Ma (AsiaCCS 2008).

All schemes have an accompanying security proof, seemingly contradicting the existence of attacks. We point out flaws in these proofs, resolving the contradiction.

Keywords: Log files · LogFAS · FssAgg · Digital signatures
Forward security · Attack · Cryptanalysis

1 Introduction

Log files record user-actions and events in computer systems, providing valuable information for intrusion detection, after-the-fact digital forensics, as well as system maintenance. For all of these objectives, having reliable information is imperative. Therefore, a number of historical and contemporary works on system security (e.g. [8, p. 10], [16, Sects. 18.3, 18.3.1], [7, Sect. 8.6]) recommend or require that log files be protected from unauthorized or retroactive modification.

It is generally desirable to use dedicated hardware (e.g. *write-once read many times drives*, so-called *WORM* drives) for this task, since such hardware can actually *prevent* the modification of log data. However, such special-purpose hardware is not always available. Therefore, cryptographers have devised schemes to provide integrity checks for log files that can purely be implemented in software. Such mechanisms can not prevent the manipulation of log data in the first place, but must be able to discern correct from manipulated information. The cryptographic schemes must retain their functionality *even if* an attacker has broken into the system and obtained the secret key. In order to achieve this, cryptographers have resorted to schemes (e.g. [5,9,11,13,14,17,21,22]) that do not use a single secret key to authenticate information, but use a sequence of

G. Hartung—The research project leading to this report was funded by the German Federal Ministry of Education and Research under grant no. 01|S15035A. The author bears the sole responsibility for the content of this report.

© International Financial Cryptography Association 2017
A. Kiayias (Ed.): FC 2017, LNCS 10322, pp. 268–284, 2017.
https://doi.org/10.1007/978-3-319-70972-7_14

secret keys $sk_1, \ldots, sk_T$ instead.[1] Each key sk_i is used for some time period (called the *i-th epoch*), until it is eventually replaced by its successor. In the following, we will focus on digital signature schemes, though MAC schemes using such a key-chain are used as well.

Informally speaking, a cryptographic signature scheme is called *forward-secure* if no attacker, who is given signatures on messages of his choice as well as a secret key sk_i from the sequence, can forge a signature relating to an epoch *before* the key-compromise. If a forward-secure signature scheme is used to sign log entries, an attacker breaking into the system during some epoch i will not be able to modify log entries from previous epochs $j < i$ without this change being detectable. (The attacker may, however, be able to arbitrarily modify log entries from later epochs. But since the attacker is in control of the *input* to the logging system once he has corrupted the signer, the attacker could control the log file's content even if the cryptographic scheme somehow prevented him from computing a signature).

Since a log file will accumulate log entries over a possibly long period of time, the number of signatures being stored to verify the log messages will grow accordingly. For efficiency reasons, it is therefore desirable to be able to "compress" the signatures. *Aggregate signature schemes* [6] allow the signer to merge signatures on different messages (possibly even originating from different signers) into just one signature, which may be as small as a signature for a single message. Using aggregate signatures for secure logging does not only improve the logging system's efficiency, but also helps preventing so-called truncation attacks [13].

A special, but restricted case of aggregation is *sequential aggregation*. Sequential aggregation demands that aggregation/compression must be done at the time of creating a new signature. Ad-hoc aggregation of signatures that have been created independently needs not be supported. Ma and Tsudik [12] introduced the abbreviation "FssAgg" for forward-secure sequential aggregate signatures.

The LogFAS scheme [22] as well as the BM-FssAgg and AR-FssAgg [11] schemes are modern constructions for securing log files. All three of them try to attain forward-security and aggregation, and were published on notable and peer-reviewed conferences.

Our Contribution. We describe two attacks on LogFAS [22,23], which allow for virtually arbitrary log file forgeries and for the confusion of legitimate signers, respectively, in Sect. 2. Our attacks on LogFAS have been acknowledged in private communication by one of authors of [22].

Furthermore, we present two attacks against the BM-FssAgg and AR-FssAgg schemes [11], which even allow for recovery of the signing key sk_i for specific epochs i. Our findings are given in Sect. 3. We implemented these attacks to verify our findings and to determine the required effort. We found that our first

---

[1] For efficiency reasons, schemes where each secret key can be computed from the previous one, and where there is only single, compact key for verification are desirable. However these properties are not strictly required.

attack on the BM-FssAgg scheme takes (depending on the parameters) between two and fifty minutes of computation, even with an implementation that misses a number of rather obvious optimizations. Our attack on AR-FssAgg required less than 0.05 s in all of our experiments. We present our experimental results in Sect. 3.7.

While LogFAS is a rather recent scheme, the BM- and AR-FssAgg schemes have been proposed several years ago. Nonetheless, the attacks we present have not been brought to public attention.

All three schemes have an accompanying security proof, which should rule out any meaningful attack on the schemes. We analyzed these proofs and identified a flaw in each of them, resolving the contradiction between our findings and the claimed security properties of the schemes. Note that our second attack on LogFAS is outside the security model considered in [22]; it therefore does not contradict the claimed security.

2 LogFAS

LogFAS [22] is a recently proposed forward-secure and aggregate audit log scheme. It offers high computational efficiency and compact public key sizes at the expense of large secret keys and signatures.

Before we describe our attacks, we will briefly introduce LogFAS. The reader is referred to [22, 23] for a more detailed presentation.

2.1 Description of LogFAS

Let G be a subgroup of prime order q of $\mathbb{Z}_p^*$, where p is a prime number such that q divides $p-1$. Let α be a generator of G, and T be the total number of supported epochs. LogFAS assumes a Key Generation Center (KGC) that generates keys for individual signers. Each signer i has an identity ID_i. Signatures consist of several values, some of which can be aggregated. For the remainder of this section, we employ the convention that variables with two indices are aggregated values of several epochs. For instance, $s_{0,l}$ is the aggregation of the values $s_0, \ldots, s_l$.

LogFAS uses three fundamental building blocks: an ordinary signature scheme $\Sigma = (\mathsf{KeyGen}, \mathsf{Sign}, \mathsf{Verify})$, the Schnorr signature scheme [18, 19] (briefly recapped in Appendix A), and an incremental hash function IH based on a collision-resistant hash function H, which is modelled as a random oracle [4].

The key of IH consists of T factors $z_0, \ldots, z_{T-1}$. The hash value of a sequence of $l \in \{0, \ldots, T-1\}$ messages $(m_0, \ldots, m_l)$ is then given by

$$IH(m_0, \ldots, m_l) := \sum_{i=0}^{l} H(m_i) z_i \pmod{q}.$$

The security of this hash function can be shown under subset-sum-style assumptions, see the references in [22, 23] for details.

An individual signer's secret key is derived from a central long-term secret $b \in \mathbb{Z}_q^*$ held by the KGC (which can be compared to a secret key of the Schnorr scheme) and several values chosen uniformly at random. Each signer's secret key includes a set of coefficients $z_0, \ldots, z_{T-1}$ (derived from b) that form the key of IH. The exact relations between the values in the secret key, the public key and the signature are a little complicated, but our attack can be understood without fully comprehending how these values relate to each other.

The algorithms used by LogFAS are given below.

Key Generation. The KGC chooses a random value $b \in \mathbb{Z}_q^*$ and generates a key pair $(\widehat{\mathsf{sk}}, \widehat{\mathsf{pk}})$ using Σ. The long term private and public keys are $(b, \widehat{\mathsf{sk}})$ and $(B := \alpha^{b^{-1} \pmod q}, \widehat{\mathsf{pk}})$, respectively. These values are shared for all signers. Next, for each identity ID_i, the KGC generates temporary keys for each epoch $j \in \{0, \ldots, T-1\}$ based on random values $r_j, a_j, d_j, x_j \leftarrow \mathbb{Z}_q^*$. These values are used to create interdependent variables as follows:

$$
\begin{aligned}
y_j &:= a_j - d_j & \pmod q, \\
z_j &:= (a_j - x_j)b & \pmod q, \\
M_j &:= \alpha^{x_j - d_j} & \pmod p, \quad \text{and} \\
R_j &:= \alpha^{r_j} & \pmod p.
\end{aligned}
$$

Finally, the KGC generates "tokens" $\beta_j \leftarrow \mathsf{Sign}(\widehat{\mathsf{sk}}, H(\mathrm{ID}_i \,\|\, j))$ for each signer ID_i and each epoch number j. These serve as witnesses that signer ID_i has created at least j signatures. Let $\mathsf{sk}_i' := (r_i, y_i, z_i, M_i, R_i, \beta_i)$ for each $i \in \{0, \ldots, T-1\}$. The initial secret key of ID_i is $\mathsf{sk}_0 = \langle \mathsf{sk}_0', \ldots, \mathsf{sk}_{T-1}' \rangle$.

Key Update. A signer updates his key sk_l ($l \in \{0, \ldots, T-2\}$) to the next epoch sk_{l+1} by simply erasing r_l, y_l, M_l, and β_l from sk_l'.

Signature Generation. A LogFAS signature $\sigma_{0,l-1}$ consists of aggregate-so-far values $s_{0,l-1} \in \mathbb{Z}_q$ and $M_{0,l-1}' \in \mathbb{Z}_p^*$, the most recent token β_{l-1}, as well as the random group elements R_j and the elements z_j of IH's key for all $j \in \{0, \ldots, l-1\}$.[2]

Given an aggregate signature $\sigma_{0,l-1}$ for $\langle m_0, \ldots, m_{l-1} \rangle$, a new entry m_l and the temporary secret key $(r_l, y_l, z_l, M_l, R_l, \beta_l)$ for epoch l, first compute the hash value $e_l := H(m_l \,\|\, l \,\|\, z_l \,\|\, R_l)$. Then compute $s_l := r_l - e_l y_l \pmod q$ and aggregate this value into $s_{0,l} := s_{0,l-1} + s_l \pmod q$. Next, set $M_l' := M_l^{e_l} \pmod p$ and aggregate this into $M_{0,l}' := M_{0,l-1}' M_l' \pmod p$. The new aggregate signature is

$$
\sigma_{0,l} := (s_{0,l}, M_{0,l}', \beta_l, \langle (R_j, z_j) \rangle_{j=0}^l).
$$

Verification. To verify an aggregate signature $\sigma_{0,l} = (s_{0,l}, M_{0,l}', \beta_l, \langle (R_j, z_j) \rangle_{j=0}^l)$ over $l+1$ log entries $\langle m_0, \ldots, m_l \rangle$, one first checks the validity

---

[2] The original scheme in [22] includes the value e_j in the signature. We have omitted this, as e_j can be recomputed by the verifier.

of the token β_l. If $\mathsf{Verify}(\widehat{\mathsf{pk}}, H(\mathrm{ID}_i \| l), \beta_l) = 0$, then output 0 and exit. Otherwise, compute $z_{0,l} := IH(m_0 \| 0 \| z_0 \| R_0, \ldots, m_l \| l \| z_l \| R_l)$, and check if

$$\prod_{j=0}^{l} R_j \stackrel{?}{\equiv} M'_{0,l} \cdot B^{z_{0,l}} \cdot \alpha^{s_{0,l}} \pmod{p}. \tag{1}$$

Accept if the equation holds (output 1 and exit). Otherwise, reject the signature (output 0 and exit).

2.2 The Attacks

We report two simple and efficient attacks on LogFAS. The first one allows for virtually arbitrary modification of log entries, but can not change the log file size. It requires only minimal computation and a single signature. This attack contradicts the claimed security of LogFAS. We analyzed the proof of security in [23] and found a flaw, resolving this contradiction.

Our first attack allows an attacker to masquerade a signature created by a signer as originating from another (valid) signer. This attack is outside the formal security model considered in [22], and therefore does not contradict the claimed security. It nonetheless presents a serious threat, as it undermines the signature's authenticity.

Signature Forgery. Our first attack can be used to sign any sequence of log messages $\langle m_0^*, \ldots, m_l^* \rangle$ ($l \in \{0, \ldots, T-1\}$), provided the attacker has a valid signature for some other sequence of log messages $\langle m_0, \ldots, m_l \rangle$ of the same length, and knows the public key pk.

On a high level, our attack exploits the fact that the right hand side of Eq. 1 can be fully determined $M'_{0,l}$. Since $M'_{0,l}$ is part of the signature, an attacker can simply set $M'_{0,l}$ to a value such that the equation holds. Computing the respective value essentially only requires modular multiplication, exponentiation and inversion, which can be implemented quite efficiently.

Concretely, let $\sigma_{0,l} = (s_{0,l}, M'_{0,l}, \beta_l, \langle (R_j, z_j) \rangle_{j=0}^{l})$ be the signature known to the attacker. At first, the adversary computes $R_{0,l} = \prod_{j=0}^{l} R_j$ $\pmod{p}$, and $z_{0,l}^* = IH(m_0^* \| 0 \| z_0 \| R_0, \ldots, m_l^* \| l \| z_l \| R_l)$. (S)he then sets $M_{0,l}^* := R_{0,l} \cdot B^{-z_{0,l}^*} \cdot \alpha^{-s_{0,l}} \pmod{p}$. The forged signature is $\sigma_{0,l}^* = (s_{0,l}, M_{0,l}^*, \beta_l, \langle (R_j, z_j) \rangle_{j=0}^{l})$.

It is easy to see that this signature will be accepted by the verification algorithm. Since β_l is taken from the original signature, it is a valid signature for $H(\mathrm{ID}_i \| l)$ and so $\mathsf{Verify}(\widehat{\mathsf{pk}}, H(\mathrm{ID}_i \| l), \beta_l)$ will return 1, i.e. the first check of the verification algorithm will succeed. Now, by our setup, we have

$$M_{0,l}^* \cdot B^{z_{0,l}^*} \cdot \alpha^{s_{0,l}} \equiv (R_{0,l} \cdot B^{-z_{0,l}^*} \cdot \alpha^{-s_{0,l}}) \cdot B^{z_{0,l}^*} \cdot \alpha^{s_{0,l}} \equiv R_{0,l} \equiv \prod_{j=0}^{l} R_j \pmod{p}.$$

Therefore, the verification algorithm will accept the signature, and the attack is successful. Note that the attack only replaces a single component of the signature, namely $M'_{0,l}$. All other parts of the signature are copied without modification. This simple attack is possible due to the structure of Eq. (1), where the right hand side can be fully determined by $M'_{0,l}$ and this requires only modular multiplication, exponentiation and inversion.

Sender Confusion. If an attacker has two aggregate signatures $\sigma_{0,l}$, $\sigma'_{0,l}$ for two sequences of log messages of the same length $l+1$, created by different signers ID_i, $\mathrm{ID}_{i'}$ the attacker can just exchange the β_l tokens. The receiver will accept $\sigma_{0,l}$ as a signature from $\mathrm{ID}_{i'}$, when the messages were really signed by signer i, and vice versa. This attack is due to the fact that the identity ID_i of the signer is only bound to β_j but not to the other signature components $s_{0,l}, M'_{0,l}, R_j, z_j$.

2.3   Attack Consequences

In this section we present a scenario that shows how our attacks might be used in a real-world attack. Consider a corporate network, where there are multiple servers $S_1, \ldots, S_n$ ($n \in \mathbb{N}$) offering different services. Each server S_i collects information in its log files, and regularly transfers all new log entries together with a signature to some central logging server L. The logging server L checks the signatures, stores the log data, and might examine it automatically for signs of a security breach using an intrusion detection system (IDS). If a server S_i does not transmit any new log entries to L within a certain amount of time, L raises an alarm (as there might be an attacker suppressing the delivery of log messages to L). Assume that LogFAS is used for signing log entries.

An attacker who has broken into a server S_i in the corporate network without raising an alarm might retroactively change the log entries not yet transmitted to L to cover his traces, and then create a new (valid) signature for the modified log file using our first attack. He continues to transmit log entries to L regularly, in order not to raise an alarm, albeit he replaces log entries that might raise suspicion with ones that appear perfectly harmless.

Now, assume that the attacker can bring himself into a man-in-the-middle position between some other server S_j and L. (This might be achieved using techniques such as ARP spoofing.) He may now filter and change log entries sent from S_j to L on-the-fly, while our first attack allows him to create valid signatures. Thus, the attacker may attack S_j without risking detection by the IDS at L.

To illustrate our second attack, suppose that the logging system was fixed to prevent the signature forgery. However, bringing himself into a man-in-the-middle position again, the attacker might still exchange the identities of some servers S_j, S_k included in the signature using our sender confusion attack. He may then try to compromise S_j, while the IDS raises an alarm regarding an attack on S_k. The attacker can thus misdirect the network administrators' efforts to defend their network, giving him an advantage, or at least gaining time until the administrators notice the deception.

2.4   The Proof of Security

In this section we point out the mistake in LogFAS' proof of security that allowed for the false conclusion of LogFAS being secure. The reader is advised to consider [23] while reading this section, or to skip this section entirely.

The security proof for LogFAS follows a simple and mostly standard scheme. One assumes an attacker $\mathcal{A}$ that breaks LogFAS, and constructs an attacker $\mathcal{F}$ against the Schnorr signature scheme, using $\mathcal{A}$ as a subroutine. $\mathcal{F}$ first guesses an index w of a message block that $\mathcal{A}$ will modify. $\mathcal{F}$'s challenge public key (for the Schnorr scheme) is then embedded into the temporary key pair for that message, the remaining key pairs are set up honestly.

When the attacker outputs a forgery, the proof considers three cases. The first case deals with attackers that actually create a new message together with a valid signature (as does our attack). The second case deals with truncation attacks and the third case models a hash collision.

The error is located in the first case, where the authors conclude that a forgery for an entirely new message must imply a forgery of a Schnorr-type signature, i.e. that the values R_w, s_w (when properly extracted from the LogFAS signature) must be a valid signature for the message m_w. We can see that this conclusion is false, since our attack does not modify the values R_w, s_w at all, but only replaces the original message with an arbitrary one. Thus, the verification algorithm of the Schnorr scheme will reject the signature with very high probability, while the authors conclude that the signature will be accepted.

3   The FssAgg Schemes

This section presents the BM-FssAgg scheme, the AR-FssAgg scheme and our attacks on these constructions. Both schemes were presented in [11], and are intended to provide a single signature per epoch. Thus, the respective secret key must be updated every time a message has been signed.

3.1   Description of the BM-FssAgg Scheme

The BM-FssAgg signature scheme [11] is based on a forward-secure signature scheme by Bellare and Miner [3]. Both schemes utilize repeated squaring modulo a Blum integer N. (An integer N is called a *Blum integer* if it is a product of two primes p, q such that $p \equiv q \equiv 3 \pmod 4$). Again, we first describe the BM-FssAgg scheme before we turn to our attack.

Let T be the number of supported epochs and H a hash function that maps arbitrary bit strings to bit strings of some fixed length $l \in \mathbb{N}$.

Intuitively, the scheme is built on $l + 1$ sequences of units modulo N, where in each sequence, each number is obtained by squaring the predecessor. Once the starting points r_0 and $s_{i,0}$ (for $i \in \{1, \ldots, l\}$) have been selected during key generation, the scheme successively computes

$$
\begin{aligned}
r_{j+1} &:= r_j^2 \quad (\text{mod } N) \quad & \text{for } j \in \{0, \ldots, T\} \\
s_{i,j+1} &:= s_{i,j}^2 \quad (\text{mod } N) \quad & \text{for } j \in \{0, \ldots, T\} \text{ and } i \in \{1, \ldots, l\}.
\end{aligned}
\tag{2}
$$

When r_0 and the $s_{i,0}$ are clear from the context, we may thus naturally refer to r_j and $s_{i,j}$ for $j \in \{1, \ldots, T+1\}$ throughout this section. Observe that these sequences form one-way chains: Given any element $s_{i,j}$ of a chain, it is easy to compute the subsequent elements $s_{i,j'}$ with $j' > j$, but it is unknown how to efficiently compute the previous ones without knowing the factors of N. (The same holds analogously for the chain of the r_j-s).

We now describe the BM-FssAgg scheme in more detail.

Key Generation. Pick two random, sufficiently large primes p, q, each congruent to 3 modulo 4, and compute $N = pq$. Next, pick $l + 1$ random integers $r_0, s_{1,0}, \ldots s_{l,0} \leftarrow \mathbb{Z}_N^*$. Compute $y := 1/r_{T+1} \pmod{N}$, and $u_i := 1/s_{i,T+1} \pmod{N}$ for all $i \in \{1, \ldots, l\}$. The public key is then defined as $\mathsf{pk} := (N, T, u_1, \ldots u_l, y)$, whereas the initial secret key is $\mathsf{sk}_1 := (N, j = 1, T, s_{1,1}, \ldots, s_{l,1}, r_1)$.

Key Update. In order to update the secret key, simply replace all $r_j, s_{i,j}$ by the respective $r_{j+1}, s_{i,j+1}$ (i.e., square all these values), and increment the epoch counter j.

Signing. In order to sign a message m_j, first compute the hash value $c := H(j, y, m)$. Let $c_1, \ldots, c_l \in \{0, 1\}$ be the bits of c. The signature for m is $\sigma_j := r_j \prod_{i=1}^{l} s_{i,j}^{c_i}$, i.e., the signature is the product of r_j and all $s_{i,j}$ where $c_i = 1$. An aggregate signature for multiple messages is computed by multiplying the individual signatures. Thus, a signature can be added to an aggregate signature $\sigma_{1,j-1}$ by computing the new aggregate as $\sigma_{1,j} = \sigma_{1,j-1} \cdot \sigma_j \pmod{N}$.

Verification. Given an aggregate signature $\sigma_{1,t}$ for messages $m_1, \ldots, m_t$ signed in epochs 1 through t, the verification algorithm will effectively "strip off" the individual signatures one-by-one, starting with the *last* signature.

More precisely, to verify $\sigma_{1,t}$, act as follows: Recompute the hash value $c_t = c_{1,t} \ldots c_{l,t} := H(t, y, m_t)$ of the last message. (Recall that the signature for m_t is $r_t \prod_{i=1}^{l} s_{i,t}^{c_{i,t}}$.) Square $\sigma_{1,t}$ exactly $T + 1 - t$ times, effectively adding $T + 1 - t$ to the j-indices of all r_j, $s_{i,j}$ contained in $\sigma_{1,t}$. (In particular, this effectively changes the signature for m_t to $r_{T+1} \prod_{i=1}^{l} s_{i,T+1}^{c_{i,T+1}}$). Multiply the result with $y \prod_{i=1}^{l} u_i^{c_{i,t}}$, cancelling out the last signature because y and the u_i are the modular inverses of r_{T+1} and the $s_{i,T+1}$.

For the last-but-one message, square the result another time (projecting the last-but-one signature into the epoch $T + 1$), recompute the hash value $c_{1,t-1} \ldots c_{l,t-1}$, and cancel out the last-but-one signature by multiplication with $y \prod_{i=1}^{l} u_i^{c_{i,t-1}}$.

The scheme continues analogously for the remaining messages $m_{t-2}, \ldots, m_1$. If the procedure terminates at a value of 1, the aggregate signature is accepted as valid, otherwise it is rejected as invalid.

3.2 Attack on the BM-FssAgg Scheme

We show a conceptually simple way to recover the secret key sk_t ($t \geq l + 1$) from t successive aggregate signatures and the public key pk. (Our attack may work with $t = l+1$ signatures, but has a higher success probability if $t > l+1$. In our experiments, $t = l + 11$ signatures have been sufficient for all cases).

Our attack makes use of the fact that the r_j values, which are supposed to randomize the signatures, are not chosen independently at random, but are strongly interdependent.[3] This allows us to set up a set of equations with a limited number of variables (namely, r_t and the $s_{i,t}$), and then solve the equations for these variables, which together make up the secret key sk_t.

We will now describe our attack in more details. Fix arbitrary messages $m_1, \ldots, m_t$ and the respective aggregate signatures $\sigma_{1,j}$, each valid for messages $m_1, \ldots, m_j$. Let $c_{i,j}$ denote the i-th bit of the hash value of message m_j, as computed by the signing algorithm.

First, recover the individual signatures $\sigma_j := \sigma_{1,j}/\sigma_{1,j-1} \pmod{N}$ for all $j \in \{1, \ldots, t\}$, letting $\sigma_{1,0} = 1$. Observe that

$$\sigma_1 = r_1\, s_{1,1}^{c_{1,1}} \cdots s_{l,1}^{c_{l,1}}$$
$$\vdots \quad \vdots \quad \ddots \quad \vdots$$
$$\sigma_t = r_t\, s_{1,t}^{c_{1,t}} \cdots s_{l,t}^{c_{l,t}}.$$

For ease of presentation, we let $s_{0,j} = r_j$ and $c_{0,j} = 1$ for all j. We define $\tau_j := \sigma_j^{(2^{t-j})}$, i.e. we square each signature σ_j for $t - j$ times, effectively adding $t - j$ to the j-index of the $r_j, s_{i,j}$ because of Eq. (2). We thus obtain

$$
\begin{aligned}
\tau_1 &= \sigma_1^{(2^{t-1})} = s_{0,t}^{c_{0,1}}\, s_{1,t}^{c_{1,1}} \cdots s_{l,t}^{c_{l,1}} \\
\tau_2 &= \sigma_2^{(2^{t-2})} = s_{0,t}^{c_{0,2}}\, s_{1,t}^{c_{1,2}} \cdots s_{l,t}^{c_{l,2}} \\
\vdots & \quad\quad \vdots \quad\quad \vdots \quad \vdots \quad \ddots \quad \vdots \\
\tau_{t-1} &= \sigma_{t-1}^{(2^1)} = s_{0,t}^{c_{0,t-1}}\, s_{1,t}^{c_{1,t-1}} \cdots s_{l,t}^{c_{l,t-1}} \\
\tau_t &= \sigma_t^{(2^0)} = s_{0,t}^{c_{0,t}}\, s_{1,t}^{c_{1,t}} \cdots s_{l,t}^{c_{l,t}},
\end{aligned}
\tag{3}
$$

where all $c_{i,j} \in \{0, 1\}$. We thus have $t \geq l + 1$ equations in the $l + 1$ unknown variables $s_{i,t}$. We now want to solve these equations for the $s_{i,t}$, by doing linear algebra "in the exponent". We can later realize addition and subtraction of row vectors $(c_{0,j}, \ldots, c_{l,j})$ by multiplication and division of the τ_j, respectively. Likewise, multiplication of a row vector by a scalar $z \in \mathbb{Z}$ can be realized by raising the respective τ_j to its z-th power.

More concretely, we consider the $c_{i,j}$ as a matrix C over the integers, and try to express each standard basis vector e_i as an integer linear combination of the row vectors $c_j = (c_{0,j}, \ldots, c_{l,j})$.

Note that the Gaussian elimination method is *not* suited for this setting, since it will compute a linear combination of the row-vectors if one exists, but the output may not be an *integer* linear combination. Moreover, a set of $l + 1$

---

[3] For this reason, our attack does not carry over to the underlying forward-secure signature scheme by Bellare and Miner [3]. There, the values r_j are chosen uniformly and independently at random, which prevents our attack.

row vectors $(c_{0,j} \ldots c_{l,j})$ may not form a basis of $\mathbb{Z}^{l+1}$ *even if* they are linearly independent, since $\mathbb{Z}$ is not a field, and thus $\mathbb{Z}^{l+1}$ is not a vector space but only a $\mathbb{Z}$-module. (We will nonetheless continue to refer to elements of $\mathbb{Z}^{l+1}$ as "vectors" for simplicity). We therefore need to employ different algorithms.

Specifically, we compute the *Hermite Normal Form* (HNF) of C. The exact definitions and conventions used for the HNF differ in the literature. The following definition is a special case of Definition 2.8 given by [2, p. 301], applying the preceding Example 2.7 (1) on the same page.

Definition 1. *Let $A \in \mathbb{Z}^{m \times n}$ be an integer matrix. Denote the i-th row of A by a_i, and the j-th entry of the i-th row by $a_{i,j}$ (for $i \in \{1, \ldots, m\}$ and $j \in \{1, \ldots, n\}$). A is in* Hermite Normal Form *iff there is a non-negative integer r with $0 \le r \le m$ such that*

1. $a_i \ne 0$ *for all $1 \le i \le r$ and $a_i = 0$ for all $r + 1 \le i \le m$, and*
2. *there is a sequence of column indices $1 \le n_1 < \ldots < n_r \le n$ such that for all $i \in \{1, \ldots, r\}$ the following three conditions hold:*

$$a_{i,n_i} > 0$$
$$a_{i,j} = 0 \quad \textit{for } j < n_i, \textit{ and}$$
$$0 \le a_{j,n_i} < a_{i,n_i} \quad \textit{for } 1 \le j < i.$$

Intuitively, a matrix is in HNF if only the first r rows are occupied (and the remaining $m - r$ rows are zero), each non-zero row has a positive "pivot" element a_{i,n_i} (which is the first non-zero element in this row), the pivot element of each row is further to the right than the pivot of the preceding row, and all elements *above* a pivot element are between 0 (inclusive) and the pivot (exclusive).

Each integer matrix A can be transformed into a matrix H in HNF by a set of invertible row operations, represented by a unimodular matrix R (i.e. $RA = H$) [2, Theorem 2.9, p. 302], and the HNF H of a given integer matrix A is unique [2, Theorem 2.13, p. 304]. Furthermore, the HNF is known to be computable in polynomial time, see e.g. [10, 15].

Assume for now that the rows of C span $\mathbb{Z}^{l+1}$. (We will show that this is a realistic assumption given enough signatures in Sect. 3.7). If this is the case, then the HNF of C is

$$H = \begin{pmatrix} \mathbf{1}_{l+1} \\ \mathbf{0}_{t-(l+1),l+1} \end{pmatrix} \tag{4}$$

where $\mathbf{1}_{l+1}$ is the $(l+1) \times (l+1)$ identity matrix and $\mathbf{0}_{t-(l+1),l+1}$ is the all-zero matrix with $t - (l + 1)$ rows and $l + 1$ columns. In the following, let $e_i = (e_{i,1}, \ldots, e_{i,l+1}) \in \mathbb{Z}^{l+1}$ be the i-th unit vector. (Thus $e_{i,j} = 1$ if $i = j$, and $e_{i,j} = 0$ otherwise).

Continuing our attack, we compute the matrix $R = (r_{i,j}) \in \mathbb{Z}^{t \times t}$ that transforms C into its Hermite Normal Form H (i.e., $RC = H$). We then fix

$i \in \{0, \ldots, l\}$ and compute

$$\prod_{j=1}^{t}(\tau_j)^{r_{i,j}} = (s_{0,t}^{c_{0,1}} \ldots s_{l,t}^{c_{l,1}})^{r_{i,1}} \cdot \ldots \cdot (s_{0,t}^{c_{0,t}} \ldots s_{l,t}^{c_{l,t}})^{r_{i,t}}$$

$$= s_{0,t}^{r_{i,1}c_{0,1}+\ldots+r_{i,t}c_{0,t}} \cdot \ldots \cdot s_{l,t}^{r_{i,1}c_{l,1}+\ldots+r_{i,t}c_{l,t}}$$

$$= s_{0,t}^{e_{i,0}} \cdot \ldots \cdot s_{l,t}^{e_{i,l}}$$

$$= s_{i,t}$$

where the first equality follows from substituting the τ_j according to Eq. (3) and writing out the product, and the second equality can be obtained by sorting the product by the base terms. To see the third and fourth equality, note that the exponents for the $s_{i,t}$ match the i-th row of the matrix $RC = H$, and that the first $l+1$ rows of H are the unit vectors (see Eq. (4)).

Overall, this gives away $s_{i,t}$. Repeating this step for all $i \in \{0, \ldots, l\}$ allows us to reconstruct all $s_{i,t}$, thus leaking the entire secret key sk_t of the t-th epoch. This concludes the description of our attack against BM-FssAgg.

3.3   Description of the AR-FssAgg Scheme

The AR-FssAgg scheme by Ma [11] is based on a forward-secure digital signature scheme by Abdalla and Reyzin [1], which itself is based on the forward-secure signature scheme by Bellare and Miner [3], but is considerably more efficient.

In the following, we will briefly describe the differences between the AR-FssAgg scheme and the BM-FssAgg scheme. The reader is referred to [11] for a complete description of the AR-FssAgg construction.

The main difference between the AR-FssAgg scheme and the BM-FssAgg scheme is that the former interprets the hash function's output c as an integer in $[0, 2^l - 1]$. Consequently, the $l + 1$ chains of squares $r_j, s_{i,j}$ are replaced by just two chains r_j, s_j of higher powers, namely:

$$r_{j+1} := r_j^{(2^l)} \pmod{N} \quad \text{for } j \in \{0, \ldots, T\}$$
$$s_{j+1} := s_j^{(2^l)} \pmod{N} \quad \text{for } j \in \{0, \ldots, T\}.$$

As for the BM-FssAgg scheme, the starting points r_0 and s_0 are chosen randomly, and N is a Blum integer. The key update procedure is adapted canonically: r_j and s_j are raised to their 2^l-th power instead of being squared. Thus, they are replaced by $r_j^{2^l}$ and $s_j^{2^l}$, respectively. In the signing procedure, the hash value c is computed as before, but the signature for the single message is now $\sigma_j := r_j \cdot s_j^c$ $\pmod{N}$. The aggregate signature is $\sigma_{1,j} := \sigma_{1,j-1} \cdot \sigma_j \pmod{N}$, as before.

3.4   Attack on the AR-FssAgg Scheme

As with the BM-FssAgg scheme, our attack on the AR-FssAgg scheme allows us to reconstruct the secret key of a particular epoch t ($t \geq 3$), requiring only the public key and a few consecutive aggregate signatures $\sigma_{1,1}, \ldots, \sigma_{1,t}$. Our attack again exploits the fact that the supposedly random values r_j are not actually chosen independently at random, but depend on each other.[4]

As before, we first recover the individual signatures as $\sigma_j := \sigma_{1,j}/\sigma_{1,j-1}$ (mod N) for $j \in \{1, \ldots, t\}$, and "project" them into the epoch t, by computing: $\tau_j = \sigma_j^{2^{l(t-j)}}$. We again obtain a system of equations:

$$
\begin{aligned}
\tau_1 &= \sigma_1^{2^{l(t-1)}} = r_t \cdot s_t^{c_1} \\
&\vdots \qquad \vdots \qquad \vdots \qquad \vdots \\
\tau_t &= \sigma_t^{(2^0)} = r_t \cdot s_t^{c_t}
\end{aligned}
\tag{5}
$$

We pick one of the τ_j arbitrarily, say τ_1, and use it to strip the r_t from the other τ_j-s, by computing $\phi_j := \tau_j/\tau_1 = s^{c_j}/s^{c_1} = s^{c_j - c_1}$ for all $j \in \{2, \ldots, t\}$.

For brevity, let $c'_j = c_j - c_1$ for all $j \in \{2, \ldots t\}$. We assume for now that the greatest common divisor of all c'_j is 1. (We will revisit this assumption in Sect. 3.7).

Once we have the ϕ_j, we use the extended Euclidean algorithm to obtain coefficients $f_2, \ldots, f_t$ such that $c'_2 f_2 + c'_3 f_3 + \ldots + c'_t f_t = \gcd(c'_2, c'_3, \ldots c'_t) = 1$. We can then compute $\phi_2^{f_2} \cdot \phi_3^{f_3} \cdots \phi_t^{f_t} = s_t^{c'_2 f_2} \cdot s_t^{c'_3 f_3} \cdots s_t^{c'_t f_t} = s_t^1 = s_t$.

Once we know s_t, r_t can be recovered trivially from (e.g.) τ_1, by computing $r_t := \tau_1/s_t^{c_1}$ (mod N). We have thus recovered the secret key for epoch t.

3.5 Attack Consequences

Reconsider the scenario from Sect. 2.3, but assume that log entries are signed with the BM-FssAgg or AR-FssAgg scheme instead of LogFAS.

Assume again that an attacker has managed to break into a server S_i without raising an alarm. He may then bring himself into a man-in-the-middle position between another server S_j and L again, and first passively observes several transmissions of log entries from S_j to L, storing the respective signatures.

If at least t signatures for individual messages can be recovered from the (aggregate) signatures sent to L, the attacker can launch one of the attacks described above to recover a recent secret key.[5] He may then attack the server S_j, filtering the log messages sent from S_j to L on-the-fly, and create valid signatures using the known secret key.

While it may seem unnatural that the aggregate signatures observed by the attacker are directly consecutive, it is actually a plausible scenario. For example, this might happen when the server S_j is mostly idle, e.g. at night.

---

[4] As with our attack on the BM-FssAgg scheme, our attack does not carry over to the underlying forward-secure signature scheme by Abdalla and Reyzin [1], since the values r_j are chosen independently at random in their signature scheme.

[5] Our attacks can be easily generalized to work with any $t + 1$ consecutive aggregate signatures $\sigma_{1,k}, \ldots, \sigma_{1,k+t+1}$ or even with any t pairs of directly consecutive aggregate signatures $(\sigma_{1,k_1}, \sigma_{1,k_1+1}), \ldots, (\sigma_{1,k_t}, \sigma_{1,k_t+1})$.

3.6   The Proofs of Security

Security proofs for the BM-FssAgg and AR-FssAgg schemes are given in the appendix of [11]. Both proofs give a reduction to the hardness of factoring a Blum integer, assuming an efficient forger $\mathcal{A}$ on the respective scheme, and constructing an attacker $\mathcal{B}$ on the factorization of N. The proofs are incorrect for they assume that not only $\mathcal{A}$ may use a signing oracle, but $\mathcal{B}$ has access to a signing oracle, too.

3.7   Experimental Results

We implemented our attacks on the BM-FssAgg and AR-FssAgg schemes in order to verify them, and to empirically determine the number t of signatures required. (Recall that we assumed that the matrix C spanned $\mathbb{Z}^{l+1}$ for the attack on BM-FssAgg, and that $\gcd(c'_2, \ldots, c'_t) = 1$ for the attack on AR-FssAgg, respectively). We measured the run times of our attacks, and found that they are entirely practical.

Since the attacks require a number of signatures, we also implemented the key generation, key updating and signing procedures of the two schemes.[6] The implementations are written for the computer algebra system Sage [20].

Our attack implementations miss a number of quite obvious optimizations: we did not parallelize independent tasks, and some computations are repeated during the attacks. Our measurements should therefore not be regarded as a precise estimate of the resources required for the respective attacks, but as an upper bound.

Experiment Setup. All experiments used a modulus size of 2048 bit and were conducted on a desktop office PC, equipped with a four-core AMD A10-7850K Radeon R7 processor with a per-core adaptively controlled clock frequency of up to 3.7 GHz, different L1-caches with a total capacity of 256 KiB, two 2 MiB L2-Caches, each shared between two cores, and 14.6 GiB of RAM. The PC was running version 16.04 of the Ubuntu Desktop GNU/Linux operating system, Sage in version 6.7, and Python 2.7.

For our attack on the BM-FssAgg scheme, we used the SHA-224, SHA-256, SHA-384 and SHA-512 hash functions to examine the influence of the hash length l on the runtime of our attack. The BM-FssAgg scheme was instantiated with 512 epochs for the SHA-224, SHA-256 and SHA-384 hash functions, and with 1024 epochs for the SHA-512 hash function. (Recall that the scheme signs exactly one message per epoch, and our attack on the BM-FssAgg scheme requires at least l signatures, where l is the hash length).[7]

---

[6] Our implementation of the schemes is *only* intended to provide a background for our attacks. We did therefore not attempt to harden our implementation against different types of attacks at all.

[7] The number of supported epochs T may be unrealistically low. But since T does not influence the time required for executing our attacks, a small T is sufficient for our demonstration.

Our implementation of the attacks first collects the minimum required number of signatures ($l+1$ for the BM-FssAgg scheme, where l is the output length of the hash function, and 3 for the AR-FssAgg scheme), and then checks if the respective requirement on the hash values is fulfilled. If this is the case, the attack is continued as described above. Otherwise, our implementation gradually requests additional signatures until the requirements are fulfilled.

For both of our schemes, we measured the time that was necessary to collect the total number of signatures. (This includes the time necessary to compute the signatures in the first place, and to update the keys respectively). For our BM-FssAgg implementation, this time also includes the computation of the Hermite Normal Form of the given matrix, along with the transformation matrix. For the AR-FssAgg attack, the time includes the computation of the gcd of the c'_i, as well as the factors f_i. We refer to these times as the *signature collection times*. The remaining time required for the attacks is referred to as *reconstruction time*. A *measurement* corresponds to one execution of an attack.

Our experiments quickly showed that the reconstruction times for BM-FssAgg were quite long. Given the large amount of time required for the reconstruction and the small amount of variation in the reconstruction times, we restricted our examination of the reconstruction times of BM-FssAgg to 50 measurements per hash-function. For the reconstruction time of the attack on the AR-FssAgg scheme, the number of requested signatures (for both schemes), and the signature collection times (for both schemes), we collected 250 measurements per scheme and hash-function.

Results. Our results are summarized in Table 1. All times are given in seconds.

In our experiments regarding the attack on BM-FssAgg, the greatest difference $d = t - (l+1)$ between t (the number of actual required signatures) and $l+1$ (the minimum number of required signatures) was 10. (So, $t = l + 11$ signatures were always sufficient). For AR-FssAgg, $t = 3 + 4$ have been sufficient for all of our 250 tries. The number of signatures actually required in our experiments is shown in the top third of Table 1. The theoretical minimum of signatures required to launch the attacks is given for comparison, denoted as "Theoretical Optimum".

We found that despite the lack of optimizations, our attack on BM-FssAgg took only minutes to recover the respective secret key (in the case of SHA-224) and at most 50 min (in the case of SHA-512). Our attack on the AR-FssAgg scheme took less than 0.05 s in all 250 measurements.

For BM-FssAgg, the reconstruction time turned out to be the major part of the attack time. In retrospect, this is understandable, since the computation of a single $s_{i,t}$ requires t modular exponentiations, so the reconstruction of all $s_{i,t}$ (including $r_t = s_{0,t}$) required $t \cdot (l+1) \geq (l+1)^2$ modular exponentiations.

4   Summary

We have presented four attacks on LogFAS [22], the BM-FssAgg scheme, and the AR-FssAgg scheme [11]. The attacks on LogFAS have been acknowledged by one

Table 1. Experimental results. All times are given in seconds.

Scheme	BM-FssAgg				AR-FssAgg
Hash function	SHA-224	SHA-256	SHA-384	SHA-512	SHA-256
Signatures required					
Theoretical optimum	225	257	385	513	3
Observed minimum	226	258	386	514	3
Average	227.15	259.05	387.27	514.97	3.67
Standard deviation	1.42	1.33	1.73	1.38	0.97
Maximum	234	264	395	522	7
Signature collection times					
Minimum	11.74	17.13	65.46	180.02	9.0e−3
Average	22.18	28.79	118.98	292.33	11e−3
Standard deviation	9.88	12.34	62.34	136.14	3.0e−3
Maximum	67.87	76.59	430.97	1006.61	22e−3
Reconstruction times					
Minimum	104.06	154.14	580.41	1502.37	6.0e−3
Average	121.48	170.81	634.34	1753.68	9.2e−3
Standard deviation	9.09	17.17	48.24	126.57	4.4e−3
Maximum	137.94	207.54	736.52	1935.59	24e−3

of LogFAS' authors, and we have demonstrated the practicality of our attacks on BM-FssAgg and AR-FssAgg experimentally. Our attacks allow for virtually arbitrary forgeries, or even reconstruction of the secret key. We conclude that neither of these schemes should be used in practice. If one of these should already be in use, we suggest immediate replacement.

Acknowledgements. I'd like to thank Alexander Koch for his detailed comments, as well as for questioning the security proof of the BM-FssAgg scheme, which was the starting point for my research presented in Sect. 3.

A   The Schnorr Signature Scheme

The Schnorr Signature Scheme [18,19] is based on the hardness of the discrete logarithm problem in some group G. It uses a prime-order subgroup G of $\mathbb{Z}_p^*$, where p is large a prime, G's order q is also a large prime, and q divides $p - 1$. Let α be a generator of G. A secret key for Schnorr's scheme is $y \leftarrow \mathbb{Z}_q^*$, the corresponding public key is $Y := \alpha^y \pmod{p}$.

In order to sign a message m, choose $r \leftarrow \mathbb{Z}_q^*$, set $R := \alpha^r \pmod{p}$, compute the hash value $e := H(m \parallel R)$ and set $s := r - ey \pmod{q}$. The signature is the tuple (R, s). To verify such a signature, recompute the hash value $e := H(m \parallel R)$

(where R is taken from the signature and m is given as input to the verification algorithm). Then check if $R = Y^e \alpha^s \pmod{p}$ and return 1 if and only if this holds.

The Schnorr signature scheme can be shown to be secure based on the hardness of the discrete logarithm problem in G, if H is modelled as a random oracle [4].

References

1. Abdalla, M., Reyzin, L.: A new forward-secure digital signature scheme. In: Okamoto, T. (ed.) ASIACRYPT 2000. LNCS, vol. 1976, pp. 116–129. Springer, Heidelberg (2000). https://doi.org/10.1007/3-540-44448-3_10
2. Adkins, W.A., Weintraub, S.H.: Algebra: An Approach via Module Theory. Graduate Texts in Mathematics, vol. 136. Springer, New York (1992). https://doi.org/10.1007/978-1-4612-0923-2
3. Bellare, M., Miner, S.K.: A forward-secure digital signature scheme. In: Wiener, M. (ed.) CRYPTO 1999. LNCS, vol. 1666, pp. 431–448. Springer, Heidelberg (1999). https://doi.org/10.1007/3-540-48405-1_28
4. Bellare, M., Rogaway, P.: Random oracles are practical: a paradigm for designing efficient protocols. In: Proceedings of the 1st ACM Conference on Computer and Communications Security, CCS 1993, pp. 62–73. ACM, New York (1993)
5. Bellare, M., Yee, B.S.: Forward integrity for secure audit logs. Technical report, University of California at San Diego (1997)
6. Boneh, D., Gentry, C., Lynn, B., Shacham, H.: Aggregate and verifiably encrypted signatures from bilinear maps. In: Biham, E. (ed.) EUROCRYPT 2003. LNCS, vol. 2656, pp. 416–432. Springer, Heidelberg (2003). https://doi.org/10.1007/3-540-39200-9_26
7. Common Criteria for Information Technology Security Evaluation, version 3.1 r4, part 2, Accessed 19 Nov 2017. https://www.commoncriteriaportal.org/cc/
8. Department of defense trusted computer system evaluation criteria, Accessed 19 Nov 2017. http://csrc.nist.gov/publications/history/dod85.pdf
9. Holt, J.E.: Logcrypt: forward security and public verification for secure audit logs. In: Proceedings of the 2006 Australasian Workshops on Grid Computing and e-Research - Volume 54, ACSW Frontiers 2006, pp. 203–211. Australian Computer Society Inc., Darlinghurst (2006)
10. Kannan, R., Bachem, A.: Polynomial algorithms for computing the smith and hermite normal forms of an integer matrix. SIAM J. Comput. 8(4), 499–507 (1979)
11. Ma, D.: Practical forward secure sequential aggregate signatures. In: Proceedings of the 2008 ACM Symposium on Information, Computer and Communications Security, ASIACCS 2008, pp. 341–352. ACM, New York (2008)
12. Ma, D., Tsudik, G.: Forward-secure sequential aggregate authentication. Cryptology ePrint Archive, Report 2007/052 (2007). http://eprint.iacr.org/
13. Ma, D., Tsudik, G.: A new approach to secure logging. In: Atluri, V. (ed.) DBSec 2008. LNCS, vol. 5094, pp. 48–63. Springer, Heidelberg (2008). https://doi.org/10.1007/978-3-540-70567-3_4
14. Marson, G.A., Poettering, B.: Practical secure logging: seekable sequential key generators. In: Crampton, J., Jajodia, S., Mayes, K. (eds.) ESORICS 2013. LNCS, vol. 8134, pp. 111–128. Springer, Heidelberg (2013). https://doi.org/10.1007/978-3-642-40203-6_7

15. Micciancio, D., Warinschi, B.: A linear space algorithm for computing the hermite normal form. In: Proceedings of the 2001 International Symposium on Symbolic and Algebraic Computation, ISSAC 2001, pp. 231–236. ACM, New York (2001)

16. An Introduction to Computer Security: The NIST Handbook, October 1995. NIST Special Publication 800-12

17. Schneier, B., Kelsey, J.: Cryptographic support for secure logs on untrusted machines. In: The Seventh USENIX Security Symposium Proceedings (1998)

18. Schnorr, C.P.: Efficient identification and signatures for smart cards. In: Quisquater, J.-J., Vandewalle, J. (eds.) EUROCRYPT 1989. LNCS, vol. 434, pp. 688–689. Springer, Heidelberg (1990). https://doi.org/10.1007/3-540-46885-4_68

19. Schnorr, C.-P.: Efficient signature generation by smart cards. J. Cryptol. 4(3), 161–174 (1991)

20. Stein, W.: Sagemath. https://www.sagemath.org/. Accessed 19 Nov 2017

21. Yavuz, A.A., Peng, N.: BAF: an efficient publicly verifiable secure audit logging scheme for distributed systems. In: Annual Computer Security Applications Conference, 2009, ACSAC 2009, pp. 219–228, December 2009

22. Yavuz, A.A., Peng, N., Reiter, M.K.: Efficient, compromise resilient and append-only cryptographic schemes for secure audit logging. In: Keromytis, A.D. (ed.) FC 2012. LNCS, vol. 7397, pp. 148–163. Springer, Heidelberg (2012). https://doi.org/10.1007/978-3-642-32946-3_12

23. Yavuz, A.A., Reiter, M.K.: Efficient, compromise resilient and append-only cryptographic schemes for secure audit logging. Technical Report TR-2011-21, North Carolina State University. Department of Computer Science, September 2011. http://www.lib.ncsu.edu/resolver/1840.4/4284

Economy Class Crypto: Exploring Weak Cipher Usage in Avionic Communications via ACARS

Matthew Smith[1]([✉]), Daniel Moser[2], Martin Strohmeier[1], Vincent Lenders[3], and Ivan Martinovic[1]

[1] Department of Computer Science, University of Oxford, Oxford, UK
{matthew.smith,martin.strohmeier,ivan.martinovic}@cs.ox.ac.uk
[2] Department of Computer Science, ETH Zürich, Zürich, Switzerland
daniel.moser@inf.ethz.ch
[3] armasuisse, Bern, Switzerland
vincent.lenders@armasuisse.ch

Abstract. Recent research has shown that a number of existing wireless avionic systems lack encryption and are thus vulnerable to eavesdropping and message injection attacks. The Aircraft Communications Addressing and Reporting System (ACARS) is no exception to this rule with 99% of the traffic being sent in plaintext. However, a small portion of the traffic coming mainly from privately-owned and government aircraft is encrypted, indicating a stronger requirement for security and privacy by those users. In this paper, we take a closer look at this protected communication and analyze the cryptographic solution being used. Our results show that the cipher used for this encryption is a mono-alphabetic substitution cipher, broken with little effort. We assess the impact on privacy and security to its unassuming users by characterizing months of real-world data, decrypted by breaking the cipher and recovering the keys. Our results show that the decrypted data leaks privacy sensitive information including existence, intent and status of aircraft owners.

1 Introduction

Aviation is undergoing a period of modernization which is expected to last until at least 2030, with the International Civil Aviation Organization (ICAO) aiming to reduce emissions, increase safety and improve efficiency of air transport [11]. This program seeks to replace ageing avionic systems with newer solutions, a significant section of which revolves around avionic data links.

The main data communications system in current use is the Aircraft Communications Addressing and Reporting System (ACARS). A general purpose system, it has become the standard to transfer a wide range of information; for example, it is often used by crews to request permission from air traffic control (ATC) to fly a particular part of their route. Although ACARS will be replaced at some point in the future, this migration is unlikely to be completed within the next 20 years [11]. In the meantime, the vast majority of commercial aircraft and business jets must use ACARS for their data link needs.

© International Financial Cryptography Association 2017
A. Kiayias (Ed.): FC 2017, LNCS 10322, pp. 285–301, 2017.
https://doi.org/10.1007/978-3-319-70972-7_15

Like many current wireless air traffic communication technologies, ACARS was designed several decades ago when security was not considered a main objective. Consequently, it did not include any form of encryption during its original standardization. Due to the technological advantage that aviation held over most potential threat agents, this fact did not raise significant attention over two decades. In recent years, however, cheap software defined radios (SDRs) have changed the threat landscape [21]. Using low-cost hardware and software downloadable from the internet, the capability to eavesdrop on ACARS has become commonplace.

The impact of this changing threat on security and privacy of the data link are manifold: among other possibilities, adversaries can track sensitive flight movements of private, business or government aircraft; confidential information such as financial or health information can be read and compromised; and potentially safety-related data such as engine and maintenance reports can be modified.

As users of ACARS became aware of its practical insecurity and demanded improvements to the confidentiality of their data, several cryptographic solutions were developed to provide a short-term fix but then these became long-term solutions. Only one of these solutions, a proprietary approach, is extensively used. Unfortunately, it has many serious design flaws—the most serious being that it is a mono-alphabetic substitution cipher—which negate any potential security and privacy gain. Indeed, as we argue in this work, this type of solution provides a false sense of security for ACARS users and consequently does more harm for their reasonable expectations of privacy than no solution at all.

Contributions

In this paper, we present our findings on a specific security vulnerability of the aviation data link ACARS. Our contributions are as follows:

- We show that the current most commonly used security solution for ACARS is highly insecure and can be broken on the fly. We analyze the shortcomings of the cipher used in this solution and its implementation.
- We quantify the impact on different aviation stakeholders and users. We analyze the extent of the privacy and security breach to its unassuming users, in particular owners of private and business jets, and government aircraft.
- From this case study, we provide lessons for the development of security solutions for existing legacy technologies, particular in slow-moving, safety-focused critical infrastructure sectors.

The remainder of the paper is structured as follows: We consider privacy aspects in aviation in Sect. 2 and our threat model in Sect. 3. Section 4 describes the workings of ACARS before we illustrate steps taken to break the cipher in question in Sect. 5. The impact of the weakness of the cipher is explained in Sect. 6. In Sect. 7, we discuss the lessons learned from this case and make recommendations for the future. Section 8 covers the related work, Sect. 9 covers legal and ethical considerations, before Sect. 10 concludes.

2 Privacy in Aviation

This section discusses a widely used mechanism with which an aircraft owner can protect their privacy, and the privacy expectations of private aircraft.

2.1 Blocked and Hidden Aircraft

Whilst no provision exists to restrict the sharing of flight information relating to commercial aircraft, it does for smaller, private aircraft. Schemes such as the Federal Aviation Administration's (FAA) Aircraft Situation Display to Industry (ASDI) register allow aircraft owners to restrict the tracking of their aircraft [9]. Some years ago, the scheme changed requiring that for a block to be implemented, a "valid security concern" must be demonstrated [6]. This included a "verifiable threat" against an individual, company or area, illustrating the severe privacy requirements of such entities. Since then, the scheme has been once more relaxed to allow any non-commercial aircraft owner to register a block [8]; even so, we claim that any aircraft owner is making a clear effort to protect their privacy in requesting a block.

ASDI is a data feed produced by the FAA and offered to registrants such as flight tracking websites. The FAA offers two levels of block for this feed—either at the FAA dissemination level, or at the industry level [7]. With the former, information about the aircraft is not included in the ASDI feed at all, whereas for the latter, the requirement to not share the data lies on the registrant. The requesting aircraft owner can choose which level of block to use, however if none is stated, the FAA defaults to the FAA-level block.

In practice, an ASDI blocked aircraft will display either no information at all, or only rudimentary information such as the registration, on flight tracking websites. If an aircraft uses the FAA-level ASDI block then information about it can usually only be sourced from third-party databases such as Airframes.org (see Sect. 4.5 for more details). If an aircraft does not appear even in such third-party sources, we consider them 'unknown'.

Blocking aircraft in this way is particularly relevant as air traffic management is modernized. Most continents are in the process of mandating that new surveillance technologies be fitted to aircraft flying in classified airspace. These will automatically report flight data, thus meaning that schemes such as ASDI blocks will become a key factor in private aircraft user privacy.

2.2 Privacy Expectations

We consider these aircraft which make an effort to hide their activities to be privacy sensitive. More specifically, we consider them sensitive with respect to existence, intention, and status. These three categories are defined as follows:

- **Existence:** Observing an aircraft in the collection range. Simply receiving a message from an aircraft is enough to reveal its existence.

- **Intention:** ACARS messages that reveal what the aircraft will do in the future of its flight; for example, when and where it will land.
- **Status:** Information which describes the current activities of the aircraft. This includes current location, its flight origin, or the flight altitude.

By restricting appearance on flight tracking websites, users of these aircraft make a concerted effort to hide information belonging to each of these categories. Thus, ACARS messages revealing such information can be considered a breach of these privacy expectations.

3   Threat Model

As the basis of our model, we consider an honest-but-curious attacker who is passive with respect to the medium but actively decrypts messages: they collect ACARS messages and aim to break the cipher and decrypt messages that use it.

An attacker of this capability could achieve their aims for a relatively low financial outlay. A low-cost computer such as a Raspberry Pi is sufficient to run the collection, connected to a $10 RTL-SDR stick. Using freely available, open source software and a standard VHF airband antenna available for under $150, an attacker will be able to collect ACARS messages from aircraft. The ease-of-use and availability of SDRs has in turn created an active community which produces a range of free and open-source tools. Avionic communications are no exception, with several tools available to decode ACARS messages, for example. This has brought previously hard-to-access avionic communications into the domain of relatively low-skilled users.

We consider a typical attacker to operate from a single location with the aforementioned equipment, collecting and attempting to decipher messages over a number of months. A more capable attacker would be able to deploy multiple collection units across a larger geographic area in order to increase the message collection rate and the number of unique aircraft observed. As demonstrated below, this will increase the rate at which the analyzed cipher can be broken.

Intention also affects the magnitude of threat—an honest-but-curious attacker is likely to be small scale, while threat agents with specific motives could afford a larger-scale collection. Indeed, tracking aircraft movements as part of insider trading has been used in the past (e.g., [10]), which will require a wider collection network to increase the chance of sightings.

4   Aircraft Communications Addressing and Reporting System

In this section, we describe ACARS, its message structure and methods of transmission, the use cases in aviation, and finally, the existing security mechanisms.

4.1   ACARS at the Physical Level

ACARS is widely utilized around the world as an avionic communications system. Deployed in 1978, it provides support for airlines and ATC to communicate with the vast majority of commercial aircraft [13]. For example, airlines transfer flight plans via ACARS, while ATC issues clearances for particular routes.

ACARS has three delivery methods—High Frequency (HF), satellite (SAT-COM) and Very High Frequency (VHF) [14]. VHF is further subdivided into 'Plain Old' ACARS (POA) and VHF Data Link Mode 2 (VDLm2) ACARS, the latter using a general purpose aviation data link. SATCOM ACARS is offered via the Iridium and Inmarsat satellite constellations, each with slightly different options and service levels. The key properties are summarized in Table 1.

Table 1. Comparison of ACARS delivery sub-networks

Mode	Coverage	Frequency	Link speed
HF	Worldwide	2–30 MHz[a]	Up to 5.4 kbps[b]
'Plain Old' VHF	Continental, over land	~131 MHz	~2.4 kbps
VHF Data Link mode 2	Continental, over land, limited deployment	~136 MHz	~30 kbps
SATCOM	Worldwide, except polar regions	L-Band (1–2 GHz) uplink	Either 10 kbps or up to ~400 kpbs[c]
		C-Band (6–8 GHz) downlink	

[a]Depending on atmospheric conditions, HF frequencies are reassigned regularly.
[b]This depends on the baud rate and keying used.
[c]Exact speeds vary depending on service, here 10 kbps is provided by the Inmarsat ClassicAero service, with the higher rate provided by their SwiftBroadband service.

A high-level diagram of VHF ACARS is shown in Fig. 1(a), with SATCOM ACARS depicted in Fig. 1(b). Messages are transmitted between an aircraft and ground stations managed by service providers. Generally, service providers handle the infrastructure apart from the aircraft and endpoints. For ACARS, endpoints can either be ATC in order to manage air traffic, or airline administration who use ACARS for fleet operational purposes.

4.2   ACARS Messages

All versions of ACARS have the same message structure built around a free text element which forms the largest part of the message (see Fig. 2). Although the system character set is ASCII, Aeronautical Radio Inc. (ARINC) standard 618 notes that most parts of the network are only compatible with a reduced ASCII set [2]. However, to guarantee all parts of the network can handle the message content, the even further reduced Baudot character set would need to be used, effectively limiting the set to A-Z, 0-9, ,-./, and some control characters.

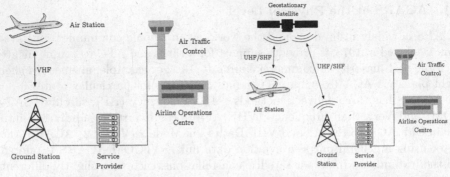

(a) VHF ACARS infrastructure   (b) SATCOM ACARS infrastructure

Fig. 1. High-level diagrams of ACARS modes used in our data collection.

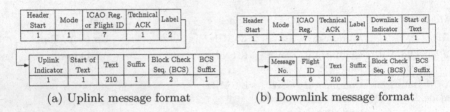

(a) Uplink message format   (b) Downlink message format

Fig. 2. ACARS message structures for uplink (air-to-ground) and downlink (ground-to-air) based on ARINC 618 [2]. Field sizes in ASCII characters/bytes.

Of particular interest is the 'label' field which allows the Communications Management Unit (CMU) to route ACARS messages to the correct endpoint in the aircraft network [14]. Most labels are standardized in ARINC 620, though parts of the label space are user defined, including the labels used by the encrypted messages discussed in this paper [3]. The ICAO registration and flight ID fields are useful for identifying the origin of messages. ICAO registrations are unique to an aircraft, allowing identification across flights. In contrast, flight IDs are tied to a single flight and often only used properly by commercial aircraft.

4.3   Uses of ACARS

As mentioned above, ACARS has gradually developed from being used for a narrow set of tasks to being the most general-purpose data link available in aviation. These tasks can broadly be split into two groups—air traffic control and airline operational/administrative messages.

Air traffic control messages are used to ensure that the aircraft can fly on its route safely. This usually takes the form of clearances and informational data. Clearance is needed for an aircraft to fly a particular route, and is organized by ATC. This usually takes place using voice communications, but in congested or remote regions voice channels are difficult to use. ACARS can be used instead, even when voice cannot. Informational data takes the form of reports on relevant flight data such as weather and aerodromes.

Airline operational and administrative messages form a significant part of ACARS traffic. These messages use the free-text nature of ACARS, with messages ranging from automated, structured reporting to text messaging between crew and ground operators. Lists of passengers transferring to other flights, maintenance issues and requests for aid of disabled passengers are common sights, though exact usage varies between airlines. It is also common for flight plans to be served over ACARS, which a pilot will then input into the flight computer.

4.4 Security in ACARS

Although ACARS has no security system mandated or included in its original standard, fully-featured 'add-on' systems are available. These adhere to the ARINC 823 standard, ACARS Message Security (AMS) [4], an example of which is *Secure ACARS*, from Honeywell Inc. [16]—this offers security through a number of common cryptographic algorithms and tools. Outside of this, ARINC are promoting a common implementation in *Protected ACARS* [19]. AMS provides message authentication, integrity and confidentiality protection mechanisms, using modern cryptographic methods. However, implementations are proprietary and subject to little scrutiny beyond internal testing.

Despite the existence of these security suites, deployment is limited. No official statistics exist and since all implementations are proprietary, performing security analysis on them is difficult. In the course of the analysis carried out in this paper, we could not clearly identify any regular use of AMS-based solutions. Furthermore, these systems typically cost extra on top of the standard ACARS service charge which an aircraft operator will pay—this has slowed uptake and created reluctance from the operators to use it. It has also prompted the use and practical deployment of more temporary security solutions, as explored in this paper. To the best of our knowledge, these schemes have no publicly available documentation with regards to implementation.

4.5 Real World Analysis

We utilized three methods of obtaining real-world air traffic data, in line with the capabilities of an honest-but-curious attacker as defined in our threat model. All data collection was done at sites in Continental Europe, with 1,634,106 messages collected in total.

VHF Collection. VHF collection is possible with low investment using the equipment described in Sect. 3, which can be fed into the ACARSDec decoder.[1] This allows the decoding of 'Plain Old' ACARS signals transmitted around 131 MHz.

---

[1] https://sourceforge.net/projects/acarsdec/.

Satellite Collection. Collection of L-band SATCOM is similarly achievable with minimal equipment and setup. For example, an L-band (1–2 GHz) horn antenna pointed towards the INMARSAT 3F2 satellite can be fed into band-pass filter and low-noise amplifier. Using an RTL-SDR stick and the open-source JAERO decoder[2] the ACARS message data can be then be recovered. To collect C-band uplink messages more costly antenna would be required.

Third Party Data Sources. In order to compare collected data to a publicly available source, flight tracking websites such as Flightradar24[3] allow verification of many aircraft being in the air or the flights they have completed. However, it is susceptible to government-mandated filtering as explained in Sect. 2.1. To get more comprehensive records on aircraft, one can use the Airframes.org database [12]. This provides ICAO registration information and records on aircraft not available on the flight tracker. To the best of our knowledge, this is the most complete and up-to-date publicly available aircraft registration database.

Beyond this, ACARS data has been collected and disseminated on the internet for a number of years. A wide range of ACARS decoders existed in the early 2000s, though most apart from acarsd[4] appear to no longer be maintained. Indeed, the acarsd website lists a range of webservers using the software to produce public ACARS feeds. Some services, such as AvDelphi[5] go further, offering ACARS feeds and tools to understand the messages for a fee.

5   Cryptanalysis of the ACARS Cipher

As our first contribution, we analyze the proprietary cipher used in ACARS communications. Our curiosity was piqued when we noted that some aircraft transmit scrambled ACARS messages, sent primarily with labels '41', '42' and '44' and prefixed by two numbers.[6] In order to decrypt these messages, we follow several classic cryptanalytic steps. We first describe how character substitutions can be recovered before moving to analyze the properties of the cipher.

5.1   Recovering Character Substitutions

Inspecting the available ciphertext, we note that all messages ciphered under this label are prefixed by two digits, from 01 to 09. We refer to this as the *key identifier*. When messages are grouped by these digits, repeating characters in the same position across messages can be seen. From the similar set of characters used between messages of the same key identifier, this implies the use of a substitution cipher as well as an underlying common structure between messages.

---

[2] https://github.com/jontio/JAERO.
[3] https://www.flightradar24.com/.
[4] http://www.acarsd.org/.
[5] https://www.avdelphi.com.
[6] Labels '41' and '42' are primarily used in SATCOM and label '44' is most common in VHF—as such we focus our analysis in this way.

Next, frequency analysis can be used to compare the per-character distribution for each key identifier against all messages in our dataset. Since the encrypted messages are a small portion of our overall message set, we expected the character distribution of the underlying plaintext to be similar to the overall ACARS character distribution. Examples of these frequency distributions are shown in Fig. 3. We can see two clear peaks, which we match to peaks for frequency analysis per key identifier. This provides a starting point for decryption.

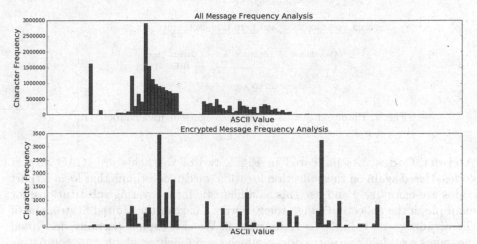

Fig. 3. Character frequency distribution across all received ACARS messages (top) and messages of one key identifier (bottom).

This knowledge can be combined with the fact that some messages sent on the same labels are in plaintext and of similar length. Using the substitutions gained from frequency analysis, we see that the majority of the messages are of a similar structure—later identified as a status update. A labelled plaintext status report message can be seen in Fig. 4, in which we identified the fields based on meta-information and structure. Using this, we recover other substituting characters using domain knowledge as explained in the remainder of this section.

5.2   Character Recovery Heuristics

Since we have a limited set of ciphertexts but now possess knowledge about the underlying structure of one message type and content of the fields, we can use heuristics to recover the remaining characters.

Recovering Coordinates. As the second field in plaintext messages is a coordinate field, we use this to retrieve a number of substitution characters exploiting the position of the receiver. Since the reported coordinates are limited to ±2–4° longitude and latitude from a receiver, the options for the first two digits and direction letter (i.e. N for north) are restricted. This becomes less reliable if the collection location lies on a point of 0° longitude or latitude.

Message Prefixes. For some message types, the first field follows the structure of a three-letter code followed by two digits which we refer to as a message prefix; in the plaintext example of Fig. 4, this is POS02. Looking at all plaintext messages received, one three-letter code is significantly more common. Combined with already known letters, this reveals further substitution characters.

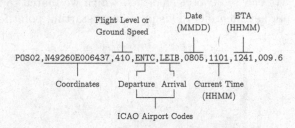

Fig. 4. Plaintext status report message sent under label '44'.

Airport Codes. As indicated in Fig. 4, two of the fields are ICAO airport codes. Based again on the collection location, we can determine that local airport codes are more likely and use this as a heuristic for recovering substitutions; for example, if the collection range solely covers a part of the United States, one of the airport codes is likely to begin with K. We also exploit partially decrypted messages containing airport codes—which are publicly available—by comparing various possible airport codes with a common encrypted character, revealing many further alphabetic characters.

SATCOM Meteorological Messages. Not all character substitutions can be recovered from the reporting messages as used above. However, aircraft receive periodic meteorological data over the SATCOM uplink to inform the pilots about the weather on their destination airport. Such messages take the form of Pilot Weather Reports (PIREP), Notice to Airmen (NOTAM), Meteorological Aerodrome Reports (METAR) and Terminal Aerodrome Forecasts (TAF). Each has a consistent structure and contains regularly occurring phrases, which allows for character recovery when compared with plaintext obtained from other aircraft.

5.3   Key Recovery

Based on our observations, many of these messages use a limited set of ASCII characters, namely digits 0-9, characters A-Z and symbols ,.*-:/? and whitespace which falls between the Baudot and limited ASCII sets defined in ARINC 620 [3]. With this in mind, using 2690 messages, from the Baudot set of 44 characters per key we recovered 377/396 (95.2%) of the substitutions across the nine keys. For limited ASCII, with there being 97 substitutions for each key, we recovered 661/873 (75.7%) substitution characters across the nine keys. However, we can decode and read most received messages, implying the Baudot set is closer to the actual character set. By extending the collection range or period, we will be able to recover the remaining characters.

Theoretically, the ACARS alphabet size of 127 offers a potential space of 127! keys. For reasons unknown to us, only 9 of these 3×10^{213} possibilities are used—and they are clearly marked. Furthermore, these keys are shared across all aircraft using this cipher. This significantly reduces the difficulty of recovery by quickly providing sufficient known plaintext for each key.

6   Impact Analysis

Even without recovering every single substitution, the nature of the cipher enables us to still read practically all message content. Indeed, recovering the full keys is a matter-of-time process, simply requiring more messages. This process could be sped up significantly by having many sensors distributed over a wide geographic area, increasing the collection from unique aircraft. In this section, we demonstrate why the weakness of the cipher is a significant problem: the data it should protect is naturally considered private by many of its users.

6.1   Usage Analysis

Our observations indicate that it is exclusively 'business jet' type aircraft that use this encryption. In Table 2 we provide a breakdown of these aircraft by manufacturers alphabetically for anonymity purposes. Manufacturers A and B make up the vast majority of the aircraft transmitting these kinds of messages. In Table 2 we also give a breakdown of models by manufacturer, in which we see that models A-1, A-2, A-3 and B-1 make up the majority of aircraft using this weak cipher. These models are of varying ages, some of which were built within the last two years. On top of this, aircraft appear to either send encrypted messages or not, with no crossover.

Table 2. Number of unique aircraft using the cipher by manufacturer and model. Names have been removed for anonymity.

Manufacturer	A			B			C	D	E
Model	A-1	A-2	A-3	B-1	B-2	B-3	C-1	D-1	E-1
Avg. Manuf. year	2008	2008	2014	2014	2010	2012	2010	2002	2011
No. per Model	118	56	12	11	3	2	1	1	1
No. per Manuf.	186			16			1	1	1

In looking for a connection, we found that all models use Primus suite avionics equipment from Honeywell, Inc., pointing towards the source of the cipher. As such, we believe that any aircraft choosing this suite will be affected by the weak cipher, should they opt to use it. Given the use of a small set of global keys, users of many different aircraft models might have the illusion of privacy when in fact this security solution is breakable. Furthermore, we have seen no attempts at key distribution or rekeying over the course of several months; the substitution characters recovered from the first collected data work on our most recent data, too.

6.2   Blocked Aircraft

Although the pool of aviation stakeholders affected is relatively small, the privacy impact is significant simply due to the nature of aircraft using the cipher. This is illustrated by the number of aircraft concealing their existence on flight tracking websites as described in Sect. 6.2. In Table 3 we see the distribution of ASDI blocks on flight tracking websites for aircraft using this encryption. For 'not blocked' aircraft we can see location and flight history, whereas 'blocked' are aircraft with some level of ASDI block, i.e. missing flight history or information. We use flight tracking websites for this purpose since they utilize ASDI data; whilst direct ASDI access would be preferable, steps to obtain the feed appear to be outside of the public domain.

Table 3. Absolute and relative distributions of flight tracking website blocks on aircraft transmitting encrypted messages.

Data set	Not blocked	Blocked	Unknown	Total
VHF	5 (10%)	41 (84%)	3 (6%)	49
SATCOM	10 (6%)	93 (60%)	53 (34%)	156

We can see that in the VHF set, 90% of the aircraft seen to be using this encryption are making a concerted effort to hide their existence, whereas in the SATCOM set a similar fraction of 94% do the same. This implies that those aircraft are particularly privacy-conscious and using a weak cipher like the one seen here undermines their desire to protect their sensitive information. For example, we observed several ASDI-blocked military-owned jets (United States and Netherlands) using this encryption.

6.3   Security and Privacy Implications of the Message Content

After establishing that the vast majority of encrypting aircraft have a great interest in hiding existence, intent and status of the aircraft, we now consider the content of the encrypted messages and analyze its sensitivity. We collected a total of 2690 messages from encrypting aircraft.

Status Reports. From the 2690 encrypted messages collected, 29.5% are status reports (as seen in Fig. 4). Although we have no official documentation on these messages, from the message format we can deduce with certainty the fields for coordinates, ICAO airport codes, date, current time and ETA. Decrypting these messages reveals a significant amount of potentially private data. As indicated above, many of the aircraft which we have observed transmitting status reports are at least subject to ASDI blocks. We observed that 63.3% of aircraft sending this type of message use an ASDI block, with an even higher percentage of all status reporting messages (90.3%) coming from these aircraft. As such, the blocked aircraft we observed made more use of encrypted position reports than visible aircraft and are undermined greatly by their insecurity.

Airport Information. As part of status reporting messages, both the departure and arrival airports are provided. This reveals a great deal of information on routing, particularly for blocked aircraft. Using this section of the message, not only can we determine the existence of an aircraft but also its intention. Across all status reporting messages, we identified 151 airport codes over 50 country codes, using 1569 instances. From these, 12.6% of instances were from the countries in which data was collected. We claim that using this data, a threat actor can learn a significant amount of information about the aircraft from a single message. By using sensors deployed to cover as great an area as possible, this could allow the tracking of target aircraft without having to cover their entire flightpath.

Free Text Messages. As with airport information, free text messages—especially those relating to flight plans—have the potential to reveal a significant amount of information about an aircraft from a single message. Through this, we saw some examples of using the cipher to protect this type of message. We received 555 free-text messages, 184 of which were related to flight plan administration, with 150 of these revealing the departure/arrival airports. In two instances, in searching for flight plans, previous flight plan information seemingly used by that aircraft were also transmitted.

Meteorological Reporting. Meteorological reports (METAR) are encrypted by a smaller section of the aircraft, primarily over satellite ACARS. We observed 1395 encrypted METAR messages from 125 aircraft, all of which came from satellite collection. Of these, 21.6% of aircraft were ASDI blocked. Whilst the scope for privacy sensitive information is limited, METAR, can also reveal arrival airports.

7 Discussion

As protocols are in use for many decades and are surpassed by technical progress and new user requirements, the temptation for quick fixes is great. In aviation, data links evolved to serve applications for which they were not initially intended (e.g., ACARS for ATC [13]) and requirements changed to include confidentiality to enable privacy for its users. Unfortunately, the presently deployed attempt to protect ACARS does not meet these requirements as we have shown.

It is thus critical to take away several lessons from this study. We strongly believe similar cases can be found not only in the wider aviation scenario but in many safety-focused critical infrastructures using legacy communication systems.

1. As the discussed solution has been greatly obscured, we could not obtain the exact time when it was first deployed but the age of the aircraft using it points to the mid-2000s. This in turn means this solution has been in use for at least 10 years without proper independent analysis. Integrating the security community early on could have avoided the deployment of inferior solutions.

2. The described attack serves to illustrate the dangers of attempting to produce cryptosystems without due peer-review or use of well-known secure primitives—indeed in this case, without any reasonable primitives at all. This is especially the case in this situation where the nature of ACARS limits the cryptographic solution due to characterset, message size and bit rate. Indeed, proposals such as Secure ACARS use AES, which is standardized and widely tested [16]. To draw parallels outside of the aviation scenario, WEP encryption suffered a similar fate in that an attempt to devise a security solution was critically impaired simply by misusing cryptographic primitives [5]. However in the case of WEP, the primitives themselves were sound—in the system discussed in this paper, even the primitives were not sound.

3. Developing—and deploying—solutions without such expertise can indeed be harmful. A solution that provides no effective protection has two distinct negative effects: First, it undermines the development and use of better solutions. In the case of ACARS, a demonstrably secure solution based on ACARS Message Security would be standardized and use reasonable primitives, but users who want data link confidentiality have opted exclusively for the discussed cipher be it for cost or marketing reasons. Secondly, it provides its users with a false sense of security. Believing in the hardness of the encryption may lead operators to rely on the confidentiality they seek and potentially even modify their behavior.

Based on these lessons, we recommend that this security solution should not be used further. With little cryptographic knowledge or resources, message content can be recovered in real time. At the very least, manufacturers should discontinue the inclusion of it in future systems. Ideally, it would be patched out or replaced with a more secure option on existing aircraft and avionics. For users relying on this cipher and seeking better protection, we propose that they demand an established solution such as Secure ACARS which is a more complete security suite.

8   Related Work

Contrary to large parts of the aviation community, the military is aware of security issues in ACARS, see, e.g., [17] where the clear-text nature of ACARS is considered an important weakness. Furthermore, [15] demonstrates efforts to manage the lack of security through encryption, highlighting the requirement for privacy in the military context. In both, ACARS defaulting to clear-text drives users to require some measure of security. As shown in our work, this led to a weak cipher being used widely.

The role of ACARS security has occasionally been discussed outside of academic research. In [1], the authors note the challenges of deploying Secure ACARS, as well as its development process with the US military. Elsewhere, [22] claims to use ACARS to upload malware onto a flight management computer. From this we can see that ACARS is used across aviation, and given the claims of exploitation, the case for encryption is strong.

In [18,19] issues caused by the lack of security on standard ACARS are discussed. Particularly in the latter, the authors highlight that crews rely on information sent via ACARS, which could have safety implications. In [23], a security solution is presented but it has not seen production or further analysis of its security properties. As demonstrated these steps are crucial for effective, lasting security.

User perceptions are also notable: [20] shows that out of hundreds of pilots, users of general aviation, and air traffic controllers, who were asked about the integrity and authenticity of ACARS, most believed the protocol offered some kind of protection.

9   Legal and Ethical Considerations

Due to the sensitive nature of this work, we have ensured that it has been conducted in a manner which upholds good ethical and legal practice. At the start of the work we obtained ethical approval process to sensitive messages and we followed a responsible disclosure process with Honeywell, Inc. We adhered to all relevant local laws and regulations.

We have further chosen not to name the aircraft manufacturers and models affected, as this could unduly impact the users of the affected aircraft before there is a chance to address the problem. Furthermore, we have outlined the steps taken to break the cipher but decided to omit further details and example messages in order to avoid making such an attack straightforward to replicate. Overall, we believe it is crucial that all aviation users are aware of weak security solutions protecting their communications so that they do not fall prey to a false sense of security but instead can take the necessary steps to protect themselves.

10   Conclusion

In this paper we have demonstrated the shortcomings of a proprietary encryption technique used to protect sensitive information relating to privacy-aware aircraft operators. More specifically, we have shown that it cannot meet any security objective. As such we recommend its users are made fully aware that it does not provide actual protection; thus, users should either seek a more robust security solution or avoid using ACARS for sensitive material.

We demonstrated the privacy issues arising due to this, since the cipher is primarily used to transmit locations and destinations by aviation users attempting to hide their existence and intentions. We show the cipher's weakness consistently undermines the users' efforts to hide their positional reporting, or protect message content which might be valuable to an attacker.

Consequently, we claim that when such solutions are deployed in practice it does more harm than good for users who require confidentiality from their data link. It is crucial that the aviation industry takes the lessons learned from this case study and addresses these problems before they are widely exploited in real-world attacks.

Acknowledgements. This work has been funded by armasuisse under the Cyberspace and Information research program. Matthew Smith has been supported by the Engineering and Physical Sciences Research Council UK (EPSRC UK), as part of the Centre for Doctoral Training for Cyber Security at the University of Oxford. Daniel Moser has been supported by the Zurich Information Security and Privacy Center. It represents the views of the authors.

References

1. Adams, C.: Securing ACARS: Data Link in the Post 9/11 Environment. Avionics Magazine, 24–26 June 2006
2. Aeronautical Radio Inc. (ARINC): 618–7: Air/Ground Character-Oriented Protocol Specification. Technical Standard (2013)
3. Aeronautical Radio Inc. (ARINC): 620–8: Datalink Ground System Standard and Interface Specification. Technical Standard (2014)
4. Aeronautical Radio Inc. (ARINC): 823–P1: DataLink Security, Part 1 - ACARS Message Security. Technical Standard (2007)
5. Borisov, N., Goldberg, I., Wagner, D.: Intercepting mobile communications: the insecurity of 802.11. In: Proceedings of the 7th Annual International Conference on Mobile Computing and Networking (MobiCom) (2001)
6. Federal Aviation Administration: Access to Aircraft Situation Display (ASDI) and National Airspace System Status Information (NASSI) (2011). https://www.federalregister.gov/documents/2011/03/04/2011-4955/access-to-aircraft-situation-display-asdi-and-national-airspace-system-status-information-nassi. Accessed 11 Nov 2016
7. Federal Aviation Administration: Access to Aircraft Situation Display to Industry (ASDI) and National Airspace System Status Information (NASSI) Data (2012). https://www.federalregister.gov/documents/2012/05/09/2012-11251/access-to-aircraft-situation-display-to-industry-asdi-and-national-airspace-system-status. Accessed 11 Nov 2016
8. Federal Aviation Administration: Access to Aircraft Situation Display to Industry (ASDI) and National Airspace System Status Information (NASSI) Data (2013). https://www.federalregister.gov/documents/2013/08/21/2013-20375/access-to-aircraft-situation-display-to-industry-asdi-and-national-airspace-system-status. Accessed 11 Nov 2016

9. Federal Aviation Administration: Limiting Aircraft Data Displayed via Aircraft Situation Display to Industry (ASDI) (Formerly the Block Aircraft Registration Request (BARR) Program) (2016). https://www.fly.faa.gov/ASDI/asdi.html. Accessed 11 Nov 2016

10. Gloven, D., Voreacos, D.: Dream Insider Informant Led FBI From Galleon to SAC (2012). http://www.bloomberg.com/news/articles/2012-12-03/dream-insider-informant-led-fbi-from-galleon-to-sac. Accessed 11 Nov 2016

11. International Civil Aviation Organization: Global Air Navigation Plan, Fourth Edition. Technical rep., International Civil Aviation Organization, Montreal, p. 120 (2013). http://www.icao.int/publications/Documents/97504eden.pdf

12. Kloth, R.D.: Airframes.org (2016). http://www.airframes.org/. Accessed 11 Nov 2016

13. Oishi, R.T., Heinke, A.: Air-ground communication. In: Spitzer, C.R., Ferrell, U., Ferrell, T. (eds.) Digital Avionics Handbook, 3rd edn., pp. 2.1–2.3. CRC Press (2015)

14. Oishi, R.T., Heinke, A.: Data communications. In: Spitzer, C.R., Ferrell, U., Ferrell, T. (eds.) Digital Avionics Handbook, 3rd edn., pp. 2.7–2.13. CRC Press (2015)

15. Risley, C., McMath, J., Payne, B.: Experimental encryption of Aircraft Communications Addressing and Reporting System (ACARS) Aeronautical Operational Control (AOC) Messages. In: 20th Digital Avionic Systems Conference. IEEE, Daytona Beach (2001)

16. Roy, A.: Secure Aircraft Communications Addressing and Reporting System (ACARS). US Patent 6,677,888, January 2004

17. Roy, A.: Security strategy for US Air Force to use commercial data link. In: 19th Digital Avionics Systems Conference. IEEE, Philadelphia (2000)

18. Smith, M., Strohmeier, M., Lenders, V., Martinovic, I.: On the security and privacy of ACARS. In: Integrated Communications Navigation and Surveillance Conference (ICNS), Herndon (2016)

19. Storck, P.E.: Benefits of commercial data link security. In: Integrated Communications, Navigation and Surveillance Conference (ICNS). IEEE, Herndon (2013)

20. Strohmeier, M., Schäfer, M., Pinheiro, R., Lenders, V., Martinovic, I.: On perception and reality in wireless air traffic communication security. IEEE Trans. Intell. Transp. Syst. 18(6), 1338–1357 (2017)

21. Strohmeier, M., Smith, M., Schäfer, M., Lenders, V., Martinovic, I.: Assessing the impact of aviation security on cyber power. In: 8th International Conference on Cyber Conict (CyCon). NATO CCD COE, Tallinn (2016)

22. Teso, H.: Aircraft hacking: practical aero series. Presented at the fourth annual hack in the box security conference in Europe (HITB), Amsterdam, NL, April 2013

23. Yue, M., Wu, X.: The approach of ACARS data encryption and authentication. In: International Conference on Computational Intelligence and Security (CIS). IEEE (2010)

Short Paper: A Longitudinal Study of Financial Apps in the Google Play Store

Vincent F. Taylor$^{(\boxtimes)}$ and Ivan Martinovic

Department of Computer Science, University of Oxford, Oxford, UK
{vincent.taylor,ivan.martinovic}@cs.ox.ac.uk

Abstract. Apps in the FINANCE category constitute approximately 2% of the 2,000,000 apps in the Google Play Store. These apps handle extremely sensitive data, such as online banking credentials, budgets, salaries, investments and the like. Although apps are automatically vetted for malicious activity before being admitted to the Google Play Store, it remains unclear whether app developers themselves check their apps for vulnerabilities before submitting them to be published. Additionally, it is not known how financial apps compare to other apps in terms of dangerous permission usage or how they evolve as they are updated. We analyse 10,400 apps to understand how apps in general and financial apps in particular have evolved over the past two years in terms of dangerous permission usage and the vulnerabilities they contain. Worryingly, we discover that both financial and non-financial apps are getting more vulnerable over time. Moreover, we discover that while financial apps tend to have less vulnerabilities, the rate of increase in vulnerabilities in financial apps is three times as much as that of other apps.

1 Introduction

Android is the dominant mobile operating system with control of 84.7% of the smartphone market as of 2015 Q3, dwarfing its nearest rival, iOS, at 13.1% [10]. Smartphone users use over 26 different apps per month, and spend more than one hour per day using apps on average [14]. In the United Kingdom, banking using a mobile device such as a smartphone or tablet has already overtaken the act of going into a branch or using a PC to bank [4]. Recently, Finance Monthly reported that usage of finance and banking apps rose 17% among "affluent middle class" customers [9]. Along similar lines, Google reports that 75% of users use only one or two finance apps, but that 44% of users use these finance apps on a daily basis [11].

Fraudsters and other adversaries have long been known to exploit victims for the greatest financial gain, and with the rising popularity of financial apps, we expect their attention to turn there. Previous work has analysed apps in the Google Play Store as a whole [6], but it remains unclear whether a one-size-fits-all approach to understanding smartphone apps in general properly encapsulates the idiosyncrasies of financial apps in particular. Indeed, financial apps handle

© International Financial Cryptography Association 2017
A. Kiayias (Ed.): FC 2017, LNCS 10322, pp. 302–309, 2017.
https://doi.org/10.1007/978-3-319-70972-7_16

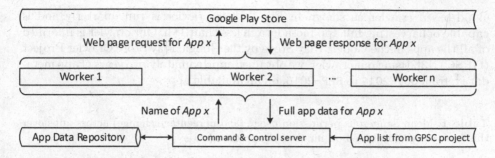

Fig. 1. Highly-scalable cloud-based crawler architecture.

more sensitive information than most typical apps and thus have a requirement for the secure storage, processing and transmission of this data.

To address this gap in the literature, we performed several tasks. We collected snapshots of the entire Google Play Store quarterly over a two-year period to understand how apps in general and financial[1] apps in particular have evolved in terms of dangerous[2] permission usage. Additionally, we used our most recent snapshot of apps to compare and contrast financial apps to the remainder of apps in the Google Play Store. Finally, we used open-source Android app vulnerability scanning tools to understand how financial apps compare to other apps in terms of the vulnerabilities they contain and how this changes as apps are updated by their developers.

Contributions. Specifically, our contributions are as follows:

- We analyse how financial apps have evolved over the past two years when compared to other apps in terms of their dangerous permission usage.
- We perform security analyses on 10,400 apps using static vulnerability analysis tools to understand how financial apps compare to other apps in terms of the vulnerabilities they contain and how they change as apps are updated.

Roadmap. Sect. 2 overviews the evolution of dangerous permission usage; Sect. 3 describes how our dataset was collected and the vulnerabilities examined; Sect. 4 presents our vulnerability scanning results; Sect. 5 discusses our observations and future work; Sect. 6 surveys the most related work; and finally Sect. 7 concludes the paper.

2 Google Play Store Analysis

Our first task was to understand how financial apps have evolved in terms of dangerous permission usage. To capture app metadata, we developed a highly-scalable

---

[1] We consider financial apps to be those apps listed in the Google Play Store under the FINANCE category.

[2] Dangerous permissions guard access to sensitive user data and must be requested by apps and approved by users before the relevant data can be accessed [3].

cloud-based crawler as shown in Fig. 1. This crawler is run quarterly and is capable of harvesting full app metadata in less than 48 h. Our crawler is informed of all the apps in the Google Play Store by the Google Play Store Crawler Project (GPSC) [13]. Using our crawler, we obtained approximately two years of app metadata[3], from OCT-2014 to SEP-2016, on all available apps.

Table 1. Mean dangerous permission usage (and percentage change) across apps over the two-year period based on number of app downloads.

Downloads	ALL apps			FINANCE apps		
	OCT-2014	SEP-2016	Change	OCT-2014	SEP-2016	Change
1-1K	3.13	3.16	+0.96%	2.75	2.85	+3.64%
1K-1M	2.37	2.45	+3.38%	3.20	3.43	+7.19%
1M-5B	3.40	3.58	+5.29%	5.62	6.44	+14.59%

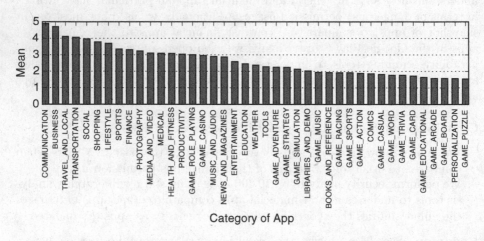

Fig. 2. Mean number of dangerous permissions used per category of app.

Figure 2 shows how the number of dangerous permissions per category of app varied. Apps in the FINANCE category use among the highest number of dangerous permissions at 3.3. Moreover, as shown in Table 1, financial apps had a greater percentage increase in the number of dangerous permissions used over the last two years when compared to all apps. From Fig. 3, we can see that financial apps use permissions typical to that of other apps, except permissions used to access a user's location, camera, and contacts, as notable examples.

---

[3] Our app metadata is available to the research community upon request.

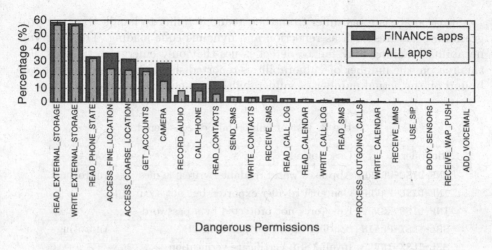

Fig. 3. Permission usage in FINANCE apps compared to ALL apps.

3   Dataset and Tools

The next step was to understand how the vulnerabilities contained within financial apps changed as apps were updated. To construct our app dataset, we randomly chose and downloaded 200 apps in the FINANCE category and 5,000 apps from all OTHER categories. Additionally, we leveraged the PlayDrone [16] dataset to get the corresponding .apk files for these apps from two years ago for a total of 10,400 apps. Our dataset is summarised in Table 2.

Table 2. Dataset of apps used in the analysis.

Category	Dataset name	# of APKs	Source	Date
FINANCE	FIN-OLD	200	PlayDrone	Oct-2014
	FIN-NEW	200	Google Play	Sep-2016
OTHER	OTH-OLD	5,000	PlayDrone	Oct-2014
	OTH-NEW	5,000	Google Play	Sep-2016

3.1   Vulnerabilities Analysed

The vulnerabilities that were analysed are listed in Table 3. Vulnerabilities were synthesised from the OWASP Top 10 [15] which lists common vulnerabilities affecting mobile apps. We used two popular app security analysis frameworks to analyse apps for vulnerabilities: AndroBugs [1] and MobSF [2]. These frameworks leverage static code analysis and are lightweight and scalable, making them suitable for our purpose.

Static analysis tools suffer from their reduced ability to handle dynamic programming features such as reflection and dynamic code loading. Thus our vulnerability scanning may fail to detect issues that only emerge at runtime. For this reason, the number of vulnerabilities reported should be considered a lower bound on the actual number of vulnerabilities present within apps.

Table 3. List of vulnerabilities considered.

Identifier	Description	Tool Used
INF-DISC-WRLRD	App uses world readable/writeable files	AndroBugs
INF-DISC-PRVDR	ContentProvider exported but not secured	
INF-DISC-KSNPW	Keystores not protected by a password	
SSL-TLSX-PLAIN	Sending data over plain HTTP	AndroBugs
SSL-TLSX-INVLD	Invalid SSL certificate verification	
SSL-TLSX-WVIEW	Improper WebView certificate validation	
BRK-CRYP-ECBMD	Use of the ECB cryptographic function	MobSF
BRK-CRYP-RANDG	Use of insecure random number generators	
OTH-MISC-INTNT	Starting services with implicit Intents	AndroBugs
OTH-MISC-DEBUG	App is debuggable	
BIN-ROOT-DTECT	App does not have root detection	MobSF

4   Results

The results of our vulnerability analysis is shown in Table 4. Worryingly, both classes of apps became more vulnerable as they were updated for a majority of the vulnerabilities considered. For financial apps however, the prevalence of vulnerabilities overall was lower when compared to other apps. While this is welcome, we note that the average percentage increase in vulnerabilities in financial apps was approximately three times that of other apps.

Non-financial apps had four types of vulnerabilities that actually improved as apps were updated: SSL-TLSX-VERIF, SSL-TLSX-WVIEW, OTH-MISC-DEBUG and BIN-ROOT-DTECT. The only vulnerability that improved for financial apps was BIN-ROOT-DTECT. The Top 4 vulnerabilities that had the highest increase in prevalence were shared between financial and non-financial apps. These vulnerabilities involved apps creating world readable/writeable files (INF-DISC-WRLRD), using unsecured ContentProviders (INF-DISC-PRVDR), generating random numbers insecurely (BRK-CRYP-RANDG) and using implicit intents to start services (OTH-MISC-INTNT). Unsecured ContentProviders and world-readable files introduce the possibility of malicious apps on a device reading data stored by a vulnerable app. Considering that financial apps handle sensitive data, care should be taken by app developers to ensure that such data is stored securely on the device.

Table 4. Percentage of apps within each dataset containing one or more of each studied vulnerability.

Vulnerability	OTH-OLD (%)	OTH-NEW (%)	FIN-OLD (%)	FIN-NEW (%)
INF-DISC-WRLRD	16.5	24.7	10.5	20.5
INF-DISC-PRVDR	2.22	2.92	2.00	3.00
INF-DISC-KSNPW	2.32	2.34	2.00	2.00
SSL-TLSX-PLAIN	80.1	80.7	75.5	77.0
SSL-TLSX-VERIF	15.4	14.6	15.5	16.0
SSL-TLSX-WVIEW	9.74	9.21	9.50	10.0
BRK-CRYP-ECBMD	12.7	12.7	10.5	11.1
BRK-CRYP-RANDG	59.3	63.8	54.5	61.1
OTH-MISC-INTNT	3.22	5.19	2.50	7.50
OTH-MISC-DEBUG	2.30	2.06	2.00	2.00
BIN-ROOT-DTECT*	95.2	93.4	96.5	92.9

*Root detection may be implemented in many ways, thus false positives may be present in our result, and consequently we consider these numbers an upper bound.

5 Discussion

It is welcome to observe that financial apps on average have a lower prevalence of vulnerabilities. However, it is worrying that these numbers are increasing, and indeed increasing faster than that of other apps. Given that financial apps potentially handle very sensitive information, great care needs to be taken by app developers to safeguard the data that their apps use.

As a first step, app developers should familiarise themselves with the OWASP Top 10 [15] to understand the typical security problems that affect mobile apps. By gaining a better understanding of typical security problems, app developers can avoid common mistakes that make their apps easily exploitable by adversaries. App developers can also leverage any of the myriad open-source static/dynamic vulnerability analysis tools to check their apps for vulnerabilities before publishing them to app stores. In some cases, app developers may not be the primary source of the vulnerabilities contained within their apps. Many app developers unwittingly use vulnerable libraries and introduce vulnerabilities into otherwise secure apps. App developers must take care to ensure that they always use up-to-date versions of libraries whenever they update their apps.

The official Android app store, Google Play, can be a catalyst for improving the quality of apps by performing vulnerability analysis checks on apps at the time when they are submitted to be published. During this research, we observed that scanning apps for vulnerabilities takes less than one minute on average. Publishing an app to the Google Play Store already takes up to several hours, so we expect that lightweight vulnerability scanning will not cause a noticeable delay. Apps containing vulnerabilities can be returned to app developers for fixing, penalised in search results, or flagged as being vulnerable when presented to users.

Static analysis alone does not paint the full picture of what is happening inside apps. For future work, we plan to use dynamic analysis tools to further understand the vulnerabilities contained within apps, as well as explore a wider range of app vulnerabilities.

6   Related Work

Viennot et al. [16] developed a tool called PlayDrone and used it to perform the first indexing of apps in the Google Play Store. We leverage their dataset to obtain old versions of apps to perform our longitudinal analysis of vulnerability evolution. Along similar lines, Book et al. [5] perform a longitudinal analysis of permission usage in ad libraries. The authors discover that not only have ad libraries gained greater sensitive access to devices over time, but they typically get access that risks user privacy and security. We complement this analysis by evaluating how permissions have increased in apps overall and within financial apps specifically.

A number of authors identified different classes of vulnerabilities in Android apps and proposed various tools to detect them. We list a few for brevity. Fahl et al. [8] investigated SSL/TLS related vulnerabilities using a tool called Mallodroid. The authors found that approximately 8% of the apps that were examined were potentially vulnerable to man-in-the-middle attacks. Equally important, Lu et al. [12] investigated Android apps being vulnerable to component hijacking attacks. Subsequently, Egele et al. [7] investigated whether apps were using cryptographic APIs securely. They found that 88% of the apps investigated made at least one mistake when using cryptographic APIs. Complementary to these pieces of work, we use static analysis tools to evaluate the extent to which Android apps currently suffer from these and other vulnerabilities. Additionally, we examine how the prevalence of vulnerabilities has changed as apps have been updated, as well as how financial apps compare to regular apps as it relates to vulnerability evolution.

7   Conclusion

In this paper, we investigated permission usage in Android apps in general and in finance apps in particular. While both classes of apps had increases in the number of permissions used, financial apps typically used more permissions and also had greater percentage increases in permission usage. By doing vulnerability analysis of apps, we observed that apps tend to become more vulnerable as they are updated. While financial apps were less likely to contain vulnerabilities overall, as they were updated their prevalence in containing vulnerabilities increased three times as much as other apps. As users become more comfortable with using smartphone apps for sensitive tasks, it becomes imperative that app developers take appropriate measures to secure sensitive data.

Acknowledgement. Vincent F. Taylor is supported by the UK EPSRC.

References

1. AndroBugs Framework. https://github.com/AndroBugs/AndroBugs_Framework
2. Mobile Security Framework. https://github.com/ajinabraham/Mobile-Security-Framework-MobSF
3. Requesting   Permissions.   https://developer.android.com/guide/topics/permissions/ requesting.html
4. BBA: Mobile phone apps become the UK's number one way to bank, June 2015. https://www.bba.org.uk/news/press-releases/mobile-phone-apps-become-the-uks-number-one-way-to-bank/
5. Book, T., Pridgen, A., Wallach, D.S.: Longitudinal analysis of Android ad library permissions. arXiv preprint arXiv:1303.0857 (2013)
6. Carbunar, B., Potharaju, R.: A longitudinal study of the Google app market. In: 2015 Proceedings of the 2015 IEEE/ACM International Conference on Advances in Social Networks Analysis and Mining, ASONAM 2015, pp. 242–249. ACM, New York (2015)
7. Egele, M., Brumley, D., Fratantonio, Y., Kruegel, C.: An empirical study of cryptographic misuse in android applications. In: Proceedings of the 2013 ACM SIGSAC Conference on Computer and Communications Security, CCS 2013, pp. 73–84. ACM, New York (2013)
8. Fahl, S., Harbach, M., Muders, T., Baumgärtner, L., Freisleben, B., Smith, M.: Why eve and mallory love android: an analysis of android SSL (in)security. In: Proceedings of the 2012 ACM Conference on Computer and Communications Security, CCS 2012, pp. 50–61. ACM, New York (2012)
9. Finance Monthly. Banking and finance app usage rises 17 class customers, July 2016. http://www.finance-monthly.com/2016/07/banking-and-finance-app-usage-rises-17-amongst-affluent-middle-class-customers-sounding-a-warning-shot-for-loyalty-initiatives/
10. Gartner: Gartner Says Emerging Markets Drove Worldwide Smartphone Sales to 15.5 Percent Growth in Third Quarter of 2015, November 2015. http://www.gartner.com/newsroom/id/3169417
11. Google Inc., Apps And Mobile Sites: Consumption Across Finance, Retail And Travel, March 2016. https://www.thinkwithgoogle.com/intl/en-gb/research-studies/apps-and-mobile-sites-consumption-across-finance-retail-and-travel.html
12. Lu, L., Li, Z., Wu, Z., Lee, W., Jiang, G.: CHEX: statically vetting android apps for component hijacking vulnerabilities. In: Proceedings of the 2012 ACM Conference on Computer and Communications Security, pp. 229–240 (2012)
13. Lins, M.: Google Play Apps Crawler. https://github.com/MarcelloLins/ GooglePlayAppsCrawler
14. Nielson: Smartphones: So Many Apps, So Much Time, July 2014. http://www.nielsen.com/us/en/insights/news/2014/smartphones-so-many-apps-so-much-time.html
15. OWASP: Projects/OWASP Mobile Security Project - Top Ten Mobile Risks. https://www.owasp.org/index.php/Projects/OWASP_Mobile_Security_Project_--Top_Ten_Mobile_Risks
16. Viennot, N., Garcia, E., Nieh, J.: A measurement study of Google play. In: The 2014 ACM International Conference on Measurement and Modeling of Computer Systems, SIGMETRICS 2014, pp. 221–233. ACM, New York, NY, USA (2014)

Short Paper: Addressing Sophisticated Email Attacks

Markus Jakobsson[(✉)]

Agari, San Mateo, CA, USA
mjakobsson@agari.com

Abstract. We argue that as email attacks continue to increase in sophistication, error rates and filter processing times are both likely to increase. We address the problem at its root by introducing the notion of *open quarantine*, an approach that avoids tradeoffs between filtering precision and delivery delays. This is achieved using a multi-phase filtering approach, combined with the neutralization of messages with undetermined security posture.

Keywords: Email · Error rate · Nation-state attacks
Social engineering

1 Introduction

Just ten years ago, Internet security abuses were almost synonymous with small-time crime, whether involving poorly spelled email messages used in attempts to steal banking credentials or computer viruses used to send Viagra spam to millions of consumers.

The threat is very different these days, and points in the direction of dramatically increased attacker sophistication. This increase can be tracked and predicted by observing techniques used in nation-state sponsored attacks, such as recent politically motivated attacks, as techniques developed for or perfected in nation-state attacks are commonly re-used to attack enterprise targets and—in some cases—individuals.

While early politically motivated cyberattacks focused on *disruption*—whether related to the Internet [2], the power grid [5] or the operation of uranium centrifuges [14]—a more recent breed of politically motivated attacks have instead aimed at extraction of sensitive information [1,3,6,19]. Another form of attack based on extraction focuses on *funds* instead of *information*; an example of this is the 2016 attacks on banks using Swift, epitomized by the heist on Bangladesh Bank [17]. This attack straddled the fence between politics and profit by transferring massive amounts of funds to a politically ostracized regime.

Interestingly, while the sophistication of attacks has shot through the roof as groups sponsored by nation states have entered the playing field, the principal attack vectors have remained much the same. Namely, most of the attacks described above involved malware, and most used deceptive emails—commonly

© International Financial Cryptography Association 2017
A. Kiayias (Ed.): FC 2017, LNCS 10322, pp. 310–317, 2017.
https://doi.org/10.1007/978-3-319-70972-7_17

for delivering Trojans, sometimes for stealing credentials. This paper focuses on the use of email as an attack vector.

Deceptive emails are used by cyberattackers to carry out three different types of attacks: (1) to coerce the recipient to follow a hyperlink to a website masquerading as a trusted site, where the recipient's login credentials are requested; (2) to compel the recipient to install malware – whether by opening a malicious attachment or visiting a malicious website; and (3) to convince the recipient to surrender sensitive information or willingly transmit money to the attacker. To succeed with their deception, attackers masquerade as parties trusted by their intended victims; use social engineering laden messages; and, occasionally, hyperlinks or attachments that pose danger to users.

In contrast to traditional phishing attacks and typical spam, the detection of deceptive emails cannot be done in ways that leverage large volumes of identical or near-identical unwanted messages, disreputable senders, or keywords indicative of abuse. This is because cyberattacks typically are *targeted*. They use customized messages, senders and hyperlinks without bad reputation, and—to the extent that they contain malware attachments—individually repacked malware instances that avoid triggering signature-based anti-virus filters.

The analysis of messages with the goal of identifying targeted attacks, accordingly, is time consuming. Diligent scrutiny can easily take minutes of computational effort for difficult emails, and the time is expected to increase as more rules are added to address the mushrooming of new attacks and the increased sophistication likely to be seen onwards. Particularly subtle forms of deceit may require human-assisted review to detect, further adding to the worst-case delivery delays. Without meticulous screening, of course, we expect to see either false positives or false negatives to increase—or, potentially, both of these.

The delays caused by filtering—and the associated fears of lost messages— may very well become the greatest liability when it comes to deploying strong security against targeted attacks. This is due to the resistance among decision makers to accept security methods that have the potential of introducing noticeable delivery delays or, worse still, causing false positives. Given the relatively low commonality of targeted attacks and a widespread hubris among end users as it comes to being able to identify threats, this reluctance is understandable.

This paper addresses the intrinsic tradeoffs between false positives, false negatives and delivery delays by introducing a new filtering paradigm that we refer to as *open quarantine*. Open quarantine balances the needs of security and usability using a two-phase filter process. In the first phase, a risk score is computed for each incoming message. Messages with a risk score corresponding to near-certainty *malice* (e.g., those containing known malware attachments) are *blocked*, and messages with a risk score corresponding to a near-certainty *benevolence* (e.g., messages from trusted parties, with no risky contents) are *delivered*. The remainder—which comprises on the order of 1% of the traffic volume for typical organizations—will be subject to careful scrutiny carried out in a second phase. The power of open quarantine is that the undetermined emails will not be kept out of the inbox of the recipient as they are being subjected to additional scrutiny. Instead, they will be neutralized and delivered. The neutralization limits the functionality of the email but allows the recipient to access non-risky components while the second-phase filtering is performed. After the second phase of filtering concludes, the neutralization will be reverted (for safe emails) or a blocking action will be carried out.

Open quarantine enables additional security measures that were not practically meaningful in a world where filtering decisions need to be made within milliseconds. For example, consider an email received from a trusted sender, e.g., a party with whom the recipient has communicated extensively in the past. Under normal circumstances, this would be considered safe. However, if the email contains high-risk content, such as apparent wiring instructions, and the sender does not have a DMARC reject policy, then this poses an uncomfortable risk since the email may have been spoofed. To address this potential threat, the receiver's system can send an automated message to the apparent sender[1], asking this party to confirm having sent the email by clicking on a link or replying to the message. If an affirmative user response is received then this is evidence that the email was not spoofed, as an attacker that spoofs emails would not receive the confirmation request.

Outline. After reviewing the related work (Sect. 2), we describe open quarantine, providing detailed examples of the filters to be used in the two phases (Sect. 3). We then turn to the user experience, describing example neutralization methods (Sect. 4).

2   Related Work

Our focus is on addressing fraudulent email. DMARC [20], which combines DKIM and SPF, has done a terrific job addressing one type of fraudulent mail, namely *spoofed* emails. However, it does not address abuse using look-alike domains, display name attacks or corrupted accounts, nor does it protect an organization against malicious incoming email as much as it protects it against abuse of its brand. This paper considers the threat of fraudulent email from the perspective of the *receiving* organization, as opposed to the *impersonated* organization.

The use of social engineering in cyberattacks is on the rise [7,10], and has long been known that the use of targeting increases an attacker's yield dramatically [9]. Publicly available resources, including social network services, can be used by criminals to improve the success of targeting [8]. In addition to being part of the recipe of many of the attacks described in the introduction, the confluence of email-borne social engineering and Trojans has recently resulted in a rapid rise of ransomware attacks [15].

A problem of growing importance is the attack of personal accounts of users belonging to targeted organizations; this is known to have taken place, for

---

[1] Note, however, that the confirmation request would *not* be sent to a potential reply-to address.

example, in the attacks on the DNC [1,6]. This is made easier as a result of
large-scale breaches (e.g., [18]) and using clustering of identities [4]. One of the
reasons for the increasing prominence of this attack is that it is mounted outside
the security perimeter of the targeted organization, and as such, circumvents traditional detection methods. We show how open quarantine enables the validation
of high-risk messages coming from personal accounts.

Another problem is that, increasingly, sophisticated attacks rely on custom
messages and, to the extent malware is employed, custom-packed Trojans. This
complicates automated analysis, sometimes requiring manual review of contents
to make security determinations. This is an approach that has been started to be
tested in a handful organizations (e.g., [16]). While promising, it is an approach
that causes longer processing times. Consequently, manual review is impractical
for the traditional email delivery paradigm, as it requires quarantine in order to
offer security improvements. The use of open quarantine enables increased use
of manual review without imposing delays.

Traditional wisdom has that there is a tradeoff between false positives and
false negatives where ROC curves are defined in the context of a limited amount
of processing. This means that the maximum tolerable to delivery delay defines
the ROC curve in the context of a particular problem and filter technology.
Our approach shows that these constraints can be escaped by the introduction
of temporary neutralization methods applied to messages of uncertain security
posture, and a user experience designed to convey potential risk.

3   Open Quarantine

The notion of open quarantine depends on being able to perform a tripartite
classification of messages into *good, bad* and *undetermined*, where the two first
categories have a close to negligible probability of containing misclassified messages. For email delivery, this classification can be done *in flow*, i.e., without any
notable delay. One approach uses a scoring, of each incoming email, in terms of
its measured *authenticity* (determining the likelihood that it was not spoofed,
based on the infrastructure that it originated from); *reputation* (a measure of
the past behavior of the sending infrastructure) and *trust* (a measure of previous engagement between the sender and the recipient, and their organizations).
More details can be found in the extended version of this paper [12].

The second phase filtering depends on the outcome of the first phase filtering,
and may involve in-depth database lookups; manual review; automated messaging to the apparent sender; and more. We will provide details around three of
these filtering actions to clarify the approach:

High Risk of Spoofing. While DMARC deployment is on the rise, there is far
from universal deployment of this de-factor standard. As a result, email spoofing
is still a reality organizations have to deal with. Roughly half of all attempts to
pose as somebody else involve spoofing. For emails that the first-phase review
identify as undetermined due to a low authenticity score, more thorough scrutiny
should be performed.

Automated analysis can identify senders that are particularly vulnerable to spoofing attacks, as DMARC records are publicly available. This corresponds to email from senders whose organizations do not have a DMARC reject policy in place. Messages that are at high risk of having been spoofed can be validated by generating an automated message for the apparent sender, requesting a confirmation that he or she sent the message. If an affirmative reaction to this message is observed, the initial message is classified as good; if a negative reaction is received, it is classified as bad. Heuristics can be used how to classify messages resulting in no response after a set time has elapsed; for example, a message with a reply-to address not previously associated with the sender, or containing high-risk content, could be classified as spoofed if there is no affirmative reaction within ten minutes of the transmission of the automated validation request.

High Risk of Impersonation. The first phase filtering may indicate a higher than normal risk for impersonation. Consider, for example, an email is received from a sender that is neither trusted by the recipient or her organization, nor has a good reputation in general, but for which the display name is similar to the display name of a trusted party or a party with high reputation (see, e.g., [10]). This, by itself, is not a guarantee that the email is malicious, of course. Therefore, additional scrutiny of the message is beneficial.

Automated analysis can be used to identify some common benevolent and malicious cases. One common benevolent case involves a sender for which the display name and user name match[2], and where the sender's domain is one for which account creation is controlled[3]. A common malevolent case corresponds to a newly created domain, and especially if the domain is similar to the domain of the trusted user to which the sender's display name is similar. There are additional heuristic rules that are useful to identify likely benevolent and malevolent cases. However, a large portion of display names and user names do not match any of these common cases—whether the message is good or bad—for these, manual review of the message contents can be used to help make a determination.

Another helpful approach is to send an automated request to the trusted party whose name is matches the sender's name, asking to confirm whether the email from the new identity was sent by him or her. For example, the request may say *"Recently, <recipient> received an email from a sender with a similar name to yours. If you just sent that email, please click on the link below and copy in the subject line of the email and click submit. Doing this will cause your email to be immediately delivered, and fast-track the delivery of future emails sent from the account."*

High Risk of Account Take-Over. The first phase filtering may indicate a higher than normal risk for an account take-over of the account of the sender.

---

[2] This does not mean a character-by-character equivalence, but rather, a match according to one of the common user name conventions.

[3] This corresponds to typical enterprise, government and university accounts, for example, but not to typical webmail accounts or domains that may have been created by a potential attacker.

For example, one such indication is an email with high trust, authenticity and risk scores—this is an email likely to be sent from the account of a trusted party, but whose content indicates potential danger.

If the source of potential danger is an attachment then this can be scrutinized, including both an anti-virus scan and processing of potential text contents of the attachment to identify high-risk storylines (see, e.g., [13]). Similarly, a suspect URL can be analyzed by automatically visit the site and determine whether it causes automated software downloads, or has a structure indicative of a phishing webpage. The system can also attempt to identify additional indications of risk; for example, by determining if the sender of the suspect email is associated with a recent traffic anomaly: if the sender has communication relationships with a large number of users protected by the system, and an unusual number of these received emails from the sender in the recent past, then this increases the probability of an ATO having taken place. A second-phase risk score is computed using methods like this. If the cumulative risk score falls below a low-risk threshold, then the message is deemed safe, and the second phase concludes. If the cumulative score exceeds a high-risk threshold, then the message is determined to be dangerous, and a protective filter action is taken. If the score is in between these two thresholds then additional analysis may be performed. For example, the message can be sent for manual review, potentially after being partially redacted to protect the privacy of the communication. An another approach involves automatically contacting the sender using a second channel (such as SMS) to request a confirmation that the sender intended to send the message. Based on the results of the manual review, the potential response of the sender, and other related results, a filtering decision is made.

4   Recipient User Experience

The user experience of the recipient is closely related to the method of neutralization of messages that are classified as *undetermined*. As soon as a message is identified as undetermined, its primary risk(s) are also identified, and one or more neutralization actions are taken accordingly. Generally speaking, the neutralization may involve a *degradation or modification of functionality* and the *inclusion of warnings*. We provide details on the same three cases described in Sect. 3:

High Risk of Spoofing. A message that is identified in the first phase as being at a higher-than-normal risk of being spoofed can be modified by rewriting the the display name associated with the email with a subtle warning—e.g., replacing "Pat Peterson" with "Claims to be Pat Peterson"—and by inclusion of a warning. An example warning may state *"This email has been identified as potentially being forged, and is currently scrutinized in further detail. This will take no more than 30 min. If you need to respond to the message before the scrutiny has completed, please proceed with caution."*. In addition, any potential reply-to address can be rewritten by the system, e.g., by a string that is not an email address but which acts as a warning: *"You cannot respond to this* *email until the scrutiny has completed. If you know that this email is legitimate, please ask the sender to confirm its legitimacy by responding to the automatically generated validation message he/she has received. You will then be able to reply."*

High Risk of Impersonation. Emails appearing to be display name attacks can be modified by removing or rewriting the display name, and by adding warnings. These warnings would be different from those for a high-risk spoof message; an example warning is "This sender has a similar name to somebody you have interacted with in the past, but may not be the same person". Alternatively, the recipient can be challenged to classify the source of the email [11] in order to identify situations in which the recipient believes an email comes from a trusted party, whereas it does not.

High Risk of Account Take-Over. Account Take-Overs (ATOs) are often used by attackers to send requests, instructions and attachments to parties who have a trust relationship with the user whose account was compromised. Accordingly, when an email suspected of being the result of an ATO contains any element of this type, the email recipient needs to be protected. One traditional way to do this is to rewrite any URL to point to a proxy; this allows the system to alert the user of risk and to block access without having to rewrite the message. Attachments can be secured in a similar way—namely, by replacing the attachment with an attachment of a proxy website that, when loaded, provides the recipient with a warning and the attachment. Text that is considered high-risk can be partially redacted or augmented with warnings, such as instructions to verify the validity of the message in person, by phone or SMS before acting on it.

In addition, emails with an undetermined security posture can be augmented by control of access to associated material – whether websites, attachments, or *aspects of* attachments (such as a macro for an excel file). All emails with an undetermined security posture can also be visually modified, e.g., by changing the background color of the text. As soon as the second-phase classification of an email has made a determination—whether identifying an email as good or bad—any modifications can be undone and limitations lifted by a replacement of the modified message with an unmodified version in the inbox of the recipient.

References

1. Alperovitch, D.: Bears in the midst: intrusion into the Democratic National Committee. CrowdStrike Blog, 15 June 2016
2. Anderson, N.: Massive DDoS attacks target Estonia; Russia accused. Arstechnica, 14 May 2007
3. Barrett, D., Yadron, D., Paletta, D.: U.S. suspects hackers in china breached about four (4) million people's records, official say. Wall Street J., 5 June 2015
4. Bird, C., Gourley, A., Devanbu, P., Gertz, M., Swaminathan, A.: Mining email social networks. In: Proceedings of the 2006 International Workshop on Mining Software Repositories, MSR 2006, pp. 137–143. ACM, New York (2006)
5. E-ISAC and SANS. Analysis of the Cyber Attack on the Ukrainian Power Grid Defense, 18 March 2016

6. Franceshi-Bicchierai, L.: How hackers broke into John Podesta and Colin Powell's Gmail accounts. Motherboard, 20 October 2016
7. Hadnagy, C.: Social Engineering: The Art of Human Hacking. Wiley, Indianapolis (2010). ISBN-13: 978–0470639535
8. Irani, D., Balduzzi, M., Balzarotti, D., Kirda, E., Pu, C.: Reverse social engineering attacks in online social networks. In: Holz, T., Bos, H. (eds.) DIMVA 2011. LNCS, vol. 6739, pp. 55–74. Springer, Heidelberg (2011). https://doi.org/10.1007/978-3-642-22424-9_4
9. Jagatic, T.N., Johnson, N.A., Jakobsson, M., Menczer, F.: Social phishing. Commun. ACM **50**(10), 94–100 (2007)
10. Jakobsson, M.: Understanding Social Engineering Based Scams. Springer, New York (2016). ISBN 978-1-4939-6457-4
11. Jakobsson, M.: User trust assessment: a new approach to combat deception. In: STAST (2016)
12. Jakobsson, M.: Addressing sophisticated email attacks. In: Proceedings of Financial Cryptography (2017). Full version of paper at http://www.markus-jakobsson.com/publications
13. Jakobsson, M., Leddy, W.: Fighting today's targeted email scams. IEEE Spectr., April 2016
14. Kushner, D.: The real story of Stuxnet-How Kaspersky Lab tracked down the malware that stymied Iran's nuclear-fuel enrichment program. IEEE Spectr., 26 February 2013
15. Manly, L., Salvador, M., Maglalang, A.: From RAR to JavaScript: ransomware figures in the fluctuations of email attachments. Trendmicro blog, 22 September 2016
16. Olivarez-Giles, N.: To fight trolls, periscope puts users in flash juries. Wall Street J., 31 May 2016
17. Shevchenko, S.: Two Bytes To $951M, BAE Systems Threat Research Blog, 25 April 2016
18. Snider, M., Weise, E.: 500 Million Yahoo accounts breached. USA Today, 22 September 2016
19. Turton, W.: YahooMail is so bad that congress just banned it. Gizmodo, 10 May 2016
20. Zwicky, E., Martin, F., Lear, E., Draegen, T., Andersen, K.: Interoperability issues between DMARC and indirect email flows. Internet-Draft draft-ietf-dmarc-interoperability-18, Internet Engineering Task Force, September 2016. Work in Progress

Blockchain Technology

Escrow Protocols for Cryptocurrencies: How to Buy Physical Goods Using Bitcoin

Steven Goldfeder[1](✉), Joseph Bonneau[2,3], Rosario Gennaro[4], and Arvind Narayanan[1]

[1] Princeton University, Princeton, USA
{stevenag,arvindn}@cs.princeton.edu
[2] Stanford University, Stanford, USA
jbonneau@cs.stanford.edu
[3] EFF, San Francisco, USA
[4] City College, City University of New York, New York, USA
rosario@cs.ccny.cuny.edu

Abstract. We consider the problem of buying physical goods with cryptocurrencies. There is an inherent circular dependency: should be the buyer trust the seller and pay before receiving the goods or should the seller trust the buyer and ship the goods before receiving payment? This dilemma is addressed in practice using a third party escrow service. However, we show that naive escrow protocols introduce both privacy and security issues. We formalize the escrow problem and present a suite of schemes with improved security and privacy properties. Our schemes are compatible with Bitcoin and similar blockchain-based cryptocurrencies.

1 Introduction

While Bitcoin and its many successor cryptocurrencies offer a secure way to transfer ownership of coins, difficulty arises when users wish to exchange digital assets for physical goods. At a high level, parties wish to perform an *atomic exchange* with *guaranteed fairness*—i.e. either both the currency and goods will change ownership or neither will. The same difficulty arises in electronic commerce with traditional payment mechanisms. A buyer doesn't want to pay without assurance that the seller will ship the purchased goods, while a seller doesn't want to ship without assurance that payment will be received

Traditionally, this problem is solved in one of two ways. For large retailers with significant reputation (e.g. Walmart or Overstock) most customers are sufficiently confident that goods will be shipped that they are willing to pay in advance. For smaller sellers without a global reputation, buyers typically pay via a trusted third party, such as eBay or Amazon. If the buyer does not receive the item or the transaction is otherwise disputed, the third party will mediate the dispute and refund the buyer if deemed necessary. In the interim, the funds are in escrow with the intermediary.When users pay with credit cards, credit

© International Financial Cryptography Association 2017
A. Kiayias (Ed.): FC 2017, LNCS 10322, pp. 321–339, 2017.
https://doi.org/10.1007/978-3-319-70972-7_18

card companies often serve a similar role. A buyer can register a complaint with their issuer who will mediate and reverse charges if fraud is suspected.

This model has been adapted for online marketplaces employing cryptocurrencies for payment, including the original Silk Road [22] and many successors. In this model, the buyer transfers the payment to a trusted third party who only transfers it to the seller once it has ascertained that the product was delivered. However, this approach is not optimal for two reasons. First, it requires the third party to be actively involved in every transaction, even when there is no dispute. Second, it is vulnerable to misbehavior by the mediator, which can simply pocket the buyer's payment and never transfer it to the seller. This is considerably more difficult to trace or rectify due to the irreversible and pseudonymous nature of Bitcoin transactions. Furthermore, the history of Bitcoin exchanges [38] and online marketplaces [22] has been plagued by fraud and hacks, making it difficult for buyers or sellers to place high trust in any single service as a trusted third party. While better escrow protocols, which do not allow the mediator to trivially abscond with funds, are known in the literature [19] (and in practice [7]), they still introduce a number of problems.

Fortunately, Bitcoin's scripting language enables better protocols than the ones currently in use. We define a series of desirable properties for escrow protocols to have:

Security. Intuitively, an escrow protocol is secure if the mediator(s) cannot transfer the funds to anyone other than the buyer or the seller.

Passivity. A passive escrow protocol requires no action on the part of the mediator if no dispute arises, making the common case efficient.

Privacy. If implemented naively, escrow transactions can leave a distinct fingerprint visible on the blockchain which can potentially leak sensitive business information. For example, online merchants may not want their competitors to learn the rate at which they enter disputes with customers. We define a series of privacy properties regarding whether observers can determine that an escrow protocol was used, if a dispute occurred, or how that dispute was resolved.

Group escrow. To reduce the risk of trusting any single party to adjudicate disputes honestly, we introduce the notion of *group escrow*, relying on a group of mediators chosen jointly by the buyer and seller. Group escrow schemes should not require communication between the mediators, leaving the buyer and seller free to assemble a new group in an ad-hoc manner. Cheating should only be possible if a majority of the mediators colludes with one of the transacting parties.

Our contributions. To our knowledge, we are the first to formally study the escrow problem for physical goods and define the related properties. We introduce a series schemes with various properties, building up to our group escrow schemes which is secure, private, and passive. We note that our protocol is fully compatible with Bitcoin today as well as most other blockchain-based cryptocurrencies.

2 Background and Tools

2.1 ECDSA

Bitcoin, along with most subsequent cryptocurrencies, employs the Elliptic Curve Digital Signature Algorithm (ECDSA) using NIST's `secp256k1` curve [2–4]. Our protocols in this paper are largely agnostic to the details of the signature algorithm, but we include a summary of ECDSA in the full version of this paper.

2.2 Secret Sharing and Threshold Cryptography

Threshold secret sharing is a way to split a secret value into shares that can be given to different participants, or players, with two properties: (1) any subset of shares can reconstruct the secret, as long as the size of the subset equals or exceeds a specified threshold (2) any subset of shares smaller than this threshold together yields *no information* about the secret. In the most popular scheme, due to Shamir, the secret is encoded as a degree t polynomial, and a random point on this polynomial is given to each of n players, any $t + 1$ of which can be used to precisely reconstruct the polynomial using Lagrange interpolation [40].

Secret sharing schemes are fundamentally one-time use in that once the secret is reconstructed, it is known to those who participated in reconstructing it. A more general approach is *threshold cryptography*, whereby a sufficient quorum of participants can agree to use a secret to execute a cryptographic computation without necessarily reconstructing the secret in the process. A (t, n)-*threshold signature* scheme distributes signing power to n players such that any group of at least $t + 1$ players can generate a signature, whereas a smaller group cannot.

A key property of threshold signatures is that the private key need not ever be reconstructed. Even after repeated signing, nobody learns any information about the private key that would allow them to produce signatures without a threshold sized group. Indeed, threshold cryptography is a specific case which led to the more general development of secure multiparty computation [29].

2.3 ECDSA Threshold Signatures

Gennaro *et al.* presented an ECDSA threshold signature scheme in [26]. While previous threshold DSA signature schemes existed in the literature [27,28,34], the scheme in [26] is the only ECDSA scheme that works for arbitrary n and any $t < n$. All of our constructions that use threshold signatures can be instantiated with the scheme from [26]. The shared key in this scheme can either be distributed by a trusted dealer or generated jointly by the participating parties in a trustless manner.

2.4 Stealth Addresses and Blinded Addresses

Bitcoin stealth addresses [6] are a special address type that solve the following problem: Alice would like to publish a static address to which people can send money. While she can do this, a blockchain observer will be able to trace all incoming payments to Alice. Alice would thus like to publish such an address while ensuring that the incoming payments she receives are neither linkable to her nor to each other. Moreover, the payer and Alice should not need to have any off-blockchain communication.

While stealth addresses are an elegant solution to this problem, these addresses have a unique structure, and as a result, the anonymity set provided by using stealth addresses is limited to the set of Bitcoin users that use them. For the use cases in this paper, we can relax the requirement that all communication must take place on the blockchain. Indeed, when there is a dispute in an escrow transaction, we expect that the parties will communicate offline with the mediator. Thus, we allow offline communication and as a result are able to extend the anonymity set provided by such addresses to all Pay-to-PubkeyHash transactions on the blockchain.

Our basic technique is largely the same as the one used in Bitcoin stealth addresses [6] as well as deterministic wallets [41]. However, to our knowledge, we are the first to prove its security. We present the details here, and refer to these addresses as *blinded addresses*.

An ECDSA key pair is a private key $x \in Z_q$ and a public key $y = g^x$ computed in $\mathcal{G}$. For a given ECDSA key pair, (y, x), we show a blinding algorithm that has the following property: anybody that knows just the public key y can create a new public key y' and an auxiliary secret $\hat{x}$ such that in order to create a signature over a message with the key y', one needs to know both the original key x as well as the auxiliary secret $\hat{x}$. We stress that the input to this algorithm is only the public parameters and the public key y.

On input y:

- choose $\hat{x} \in Z_q$ at random
- compute $\hat{y} = g^{\hat{x}}$ in $\mathcal{G}$
- compute $y' = y \cdot \hat{y}$ in $\mathcal{G}$
- output blinded public key y' and auxiliary secret $\hat{x}$

One who knows both x and $\hat{x}$ can create a signature that will verify with the public key y'. This is clear as the private key corresponding to y' is simply $x' = x + \hat{x}$ in $\mathcal{G}$.

See the full version of this paper for a security and privacy argument for this blinding scheme.

3 Related Work

3.1 Fair Exchange

The problem of fair exchange is how two mutually distrusting parties can jointly exchange digital commodities such that both parties receive the other party's input or neither do. Indeed, fair exchange is a special case of fair two-party computation in which two parties wish to jointly perform a function over private inputs such that either both parties receive the output or neither does.

Fair exchange has been studied extensively in the cryptographic literature [12,16,30]. Blum [18] and later Bahreman *et al.* [14] studied the problem of contract signing and how to send certified electronic mail – that is one party sends a document and the other sends a receipt – in a fair manner. Jakobsson studied fair exchange in the context of electronic checks [30].

The study of fair exchange naturally leads to the desire for *optimistic* (or *passive*) protocols [12] in which the third party only gets involved when there is a dispute. Such protocols are ideal in that they are far easier to use at scale as presumably the majority of transactions will not be disputed. This model is often used in designing fair protocols [13,20,25,32,37].

One approach to building fair two-party protocols uses monetary penalties [32,33]. Intuitively, parties are incentivized to complete the protocol fairly, and if one party receives its output but aborts before the other party does, the cheating party will have to pay a penalty. Recently, several papers have proposed variations of this idea and shown how one could build secure protocols on top of Bitcoin, crafting Bitcoin transactions in such a way that a cheater will be automatically penalized or an honest party rewarded [10,11,17].

3.2 Exchanging Bitcoins for Digital Goods

Exchanging units of a cryptocurrency for a digital good can be thought of as a special case of fair exchange. Elegant protocols exist which facilitate cross-currency exchange in a fair and trustless manner [1,9,19,23].

Zero-knowledge contingent payments (ZKCP) solves the problem of using Bitcoin to purchase a solution to an NP-problem. Maxwell first presented the ZKCP protocol in 2011 [36] and it was publicly demonstrated in 2016 when bitcoins were traded for the solution to a Sudoku puzzle [35]. Banasiki *et al.* formalize and refine Maxwell's ZKCP protocol [15].

Juels *et al.* [31] propose a protocol for purchasing the private key to a specified public key, using a platform with a Turing-complete scripting language such as Ethereum. We limit our focus to the simpler capabilities of Bitcoin, which are sufficient to build protocols for escrowing payment for physical goods.

4 Escrow: Motivation, Definitions, and Model

Existing fair-exchange schemes apply only to the transfer of digital assets and generally fall into one of the following categories:

- Protocols that rely on transferring a digital signature (or "electronic check" [30]). These protocols give a trusted third party the ability to reconstruct the signature, thus assuring fairness.
- Protocols that rely on the fact that the digital asset can be reproduced and re-sent. Broadly, these schemes resolve disputes by enabling the mediator to reconstruct the desired asset. The disputing party in essence deposits a copy of its digital asset with the mediator.

Bitcoin breaks both of these assumptions, so none of the existing fair-exchange techniques work. While Bitcoin transactions are signed with digital signatures, they are fundamentally different from the electronic checks and other electronic forms of payment that are discussed in the existing literature. Under those schemes, the assumption was always that the transfer of the digitally signed transaction was equivalent to being paid. This was either because it relied on an older form of electronic cash in which the signed statement served as a bearer token and anyone bearing it could cash in the money, or it was due to the fact that the signed statement served as a contract, and one could take the contract to a court to receive payment.

With Bitcoin, however, a digitally signed transaction is insufficient since until the transaction is included in the blockchain, the buyer can double spend that transaction. Thus, bitcoins cannot be escrowed in the traditional manner. The buyer can sign a transaction that pays the seller, but this cannot be kept in escrow. If it is in escrow, the buyer can attempt to prevent its inclusion in the blockchain by *frontrunning*. That is, the buyer can quickly broadcast a conflicting transaction if he sees the escrowed transaction broadcast to the network.

The only guaranteed way to know a signed transaction will have value is to include it in the blockchain—but at that point the seller has been paid.

Of course, if the buyer double spends, the seller can use the signed transaction to prove that fraud has occurred. But remember that Bitcoin does not use real-world identities and often parties interact anonymously, so proof of fraud will generally be insufficient to recover lost money.

From the seller's point of view, shipping physical goods is also unlike scenarios considered in the fair exchange literature because it is not possible to cryptographically prove that the seller behaved honestly. We assume our mediator will have to evaluate non-cryptographic evidence, such as package tracking numbers or sign-on-delivery receipts, as online merchants already do today.

The public nature of the Bitcoin blockchain – i.e. the entire transaction history of Bitcoin is public – is also distinct from traditional fair exchange assumptions. In a traditional fair exchange protocol, there is no global ledger so no outsider could learn anything about the exchange or the escrow transactions. With Bitcoin transactions, however, we will need to consider and actively protect against the privacy implications imposed by the public nature of the blockchain.

Thus, unlike existing protocols for fair-exchange, our goal in this paper is *not* to provide a cryptographic way to mediate disputes. Our goal is instead to develop techniques in which the transacting parties can *passively* and *privately* allow a third party to mediate their transaction. To achieve *fairness*, our protocols will make sure that both transacting parties cannot deviate from the semi-trusted third party's ruling.

4.1   Our Scenario

Suppose Alice, an (online) merchant, is selling an item to Bob, a (remote) customer. A natural dilemma arises: when should Bob pay? If Bob pays immediately, he runs the risk of Alice defrauding him and never sending him the item.

Yet if he demands to receive the item before paying, Alice runs the risk of being defrauded by never being paid.

This problem arises in any payment system where the service and the payment cannot be simultaneously exchanged. A trivial solution is to use a payment platform which escrows the payment and can mediate in the event of a dispute. Reversible payment systems (e.g. credit card payments) enable the transaction to go through right away, but we still describe them as escrow services because the intermediary has the ability to undo the payment. Because Bitcoin transactions are irreversible, we must rely on an explicit escrow service if the buyer and seller don't trust each other. Thus, instead of sending money to Alice directly, Bob sends the payment to a special *escrow address* that neither Bob nor Alice is able to withdraw from unilaterally. A *mediator* is a third-party used to mediate a transaction which is capable of deciding which party can withdraw funds from the escrow address.

4.2   Active and Optimistic Protocols

While a mediator must take action in the case of a dispute, we would like to avoid requiring any action by the mediator if no dispute arises. We define the requirements placed on the mediator with the following two properties:

Definition 4.1 (Active on deposit). *An escrow protocol is active on deposit if the mediator must actively participate when transacting parties deposit money into escrow.*

Definition 4.2 (Active on withdrawal). *An escrow protocol is active on withdrawal if the mediator must actively participate when transacting parties withdraw money from escrow even if there is no dispute.*

Of course a protocol may be both *active on deposit* and *active on withdrawal*. Note that the mediator is, by definition, always active in the event of a dispute, so we only consider the dispute-free case in our definition of active on withdrawal. Combining these two definitions, we can define the requirements for a mediator to be purely passive, or optimistic:

Definition 4.3 (Optimistic). *An escrow protocol is optimistic (eq. passive) if it is neither active on deposit nor active on withdrawal.*

4.3   Security of Escrow Protocols

While the essential nature of a mediator is that both parties must trust it to make a fair decision in the event of a dispute, we can consider the consequences if a mediator acts maliciously.

We will consider only an *external* malicious mediator, meaning an adversary that does not also control one of the transacting parties. An *internal* malicious mediator also controls (or perhaps *is*) one of the participating parties. It is clear that security against an internal malicious mediator is unachievable. Recall that when a dispute arises, it is the responsibility of the mediator to award the funds to the correct party even if the losing party objects. Thus, any mediator by definition must have the ability to award the funds to one of the parties when both the mediator and that party cooperate. An internal adversary that controls the mediator as well as one of the transacting parties can create a dispute and have the mediator rule in its favor, guaranteeing that it receives the funds. For this reason, we define security of mediators only using the notion of an external attacker[1]:

Definition 4.4 (Secure). *An escrow protocol is secure if a malicious mediator cannot transfer any of the money held in escrow to an arbitrary address without the cooperation of either the buyer or seller.*

4.4 Privacy

Another concern for escrow protocols is privacy. The Bitcoin blockchain is public and reveals considerable information, including the amounts and addresses of all transactions. For escrow transactions, we consider three notions of privacy. An external observer is a party other than the transacting parties or the mediator.

Definition 4.5 (Dispute-hiding). *An escrow protocol is dispute-hiding if an external observer cannot tell whether there was a dispute that needed to be resolved by the mediator.*

Definition 4.6 (Externally-hiding). *An escrow protocol is externally-hiding if an external observer cannot determine which transactions on the blockchain are components of that escrow protocol.*

Note that our definition of externally hiding inherently relies on what baseline (non-escrow) transactions are occurring on the blockchain. For our purposes, we assume all non-escrow transactions are simple transactions sending money to a specified address (in Bitcoin parlance, a P2PKH transaction).

Definition 4.7 (Internally-hiding). *An escrow protocol is internally-hiding if the mediator itself cannot identify that the protocol has been executed with itself as a mediator in the absence of a dispute.*

We note that internally-hiding and externally-hiding are distinct properties and neither implies the other. Clearly, a scheme could be externally-hiding but not internally-hiding. This will occur if the mediator can tell that money has been put in its escrow, but an outsider looking at the blockchain cannot detect that escrow is being used. More interestingly though, a scheme can be internally-hiding but not externally-hiding. This occurs when it is clear from looking at the blockchain that escrow is being used, but the mediator cannot detect that its service is the one being used.

---

[1] There may be other desirable features that can be categorized as security properties that are out of the scope of this work.

It is clear why a company may want full privacy as they may want to keep all details of their business private. However, it is possible that an online merchant might not need its escrowed payments externally or internally hiding (say, it publicizes on its website that it uses escrow with a specific mediator). The company may however still want the escrow protocol to be dispute-hiding so that competitors cannot determine how often sales are disputed.

Of course, a buyer may take the exact opposite approach and demand transparency – i.e. that any company that it interacts with uses an escrow service that is not dispute-hiding so that the buyer can use this information to determine how often the seller's transactions are disputed.

4.5 Denial of Service

Our definition of security only prevents a directly profitable attack. Namely, the goal of the adversary is to steal some or all of the money being held in escrow by transferring the money elsewhere (e.g. to an address the adversary controls). However, a malicious mediator might instead deny service by refusing to mediate when there is a dispute.

The power of a denial-of-service attack is directly related to the type of mediator. For an active-on-withdrawal protocol, the denial-of-service attack can be launched even when the parties do not dispute, whereas for an optimistic protocol a denial-of-service attack can only be launched when the parties dispute.

Note that a denial-of-service attack may be-profitable if the mediator is able to extort a bribe from the transacting parties in order to resolve a dispute. If the mediator suffers no loss if the dispute is never resolved, then it carries no financial risk from attempting such extortion. Of course, it may face significant risk to its reputation.

We can design schemes that prevent denial of service in Sect. 5.5, but as we will see, running such a service requires the mediator to put its own money into escrow as a surety bond and requires an active-on-deposit protocol.

5   Escrow Protocols

In the previous section, we provided several definitions and security models outlining various types of mediators. We now propose several protocols for mediators and show which properties they fulfill; we refer the reader to the full version of this paper for detailed analysis of each scheme's properties.

5.1 Escrow via Direct Payment (The Silk Road Scheme)

The simplest scheme is one in which the buyer sends money directly to the mediator's address. The mediator will then transfer the funds to the seller or back to the buyer as appropriate. In case of a dispute, the mediator will investigate and send the funds to the party that it deems to be correct. The illicit marketplace Silk Road famously used a variation of this method of escrow.

To improve privacy, rather than sending the funds to the mediator's long term address, the buyer can send funds to a blinded address (Sect. 2.4). This will allow the scheme to remain not-active-on-deposit while also not using the mediator's long term identifiable address. The buyer and seller can jointly generate the randomness and run this algorithm together so that they are both convinced that it was run properly.

To redeem the escrowed funds, the party to be paid will hand over $\hat{x}$ to the mediator. Using $(\hat{x})$ together with its secret key x, the mediator can now sign over the key y', and thus create the pay-out transaction.

Properties. This naive scheme has many drawbacks: it is not secure, not optimistic, and not internally hiding. On the other hand, the scheme is not active-on-deposit and its simplistic nature scheme is somewhat privacy-preserving as it is both dispute hiding and externally hiding.

5.2   Escrow via Multisig

A well-known improvement uses Bitcoin's multisig feature. In this scheme, the money is not sent directly to the escrow service's address, but instead it is sent to a 2-of-3 multisig address with one key controlled by each of the transacting parties and one controlled by the mediator. When there is no dispute, the two transacting parties can together create the pay-out transaction. Only when there is a dispute will the mediator get involved, collaborating with either the buyer or seller (as appropriate) to redeem the funds. This scheme is available today.[2]

As in the Silk Road scheme, for the sake of adding privacy, rather than including a longstanding address that is publicly associated with the mediator, the parties can use a blinded address.

Properties. This protocol is secure as the mediator cannot unilaterally redeem the escrowed funds. It is also optimistic. However it is susceptible to denial-of-service attack as the mediator can refuse to mediate a dispute.

The use of a blinded address for the mediator makes this scheme internally-hiding. The 2-of-3 structure makes the scheme not externally hiding, however, and it is also not dispute-hiding as one may be able to detect a dispute through transaction graph analysis (see the full version of this paper for more details).

If one's goal is an escrow scheme that is transparent, then the non-blinded version of this scheme is a good candidate as it is secure and allows blockchain observers to detect disputed transactions.

5.3   Escrow via Threshold Signatures

Replacing the 2-of-3 multisignature address with a single 2-of-3 threshold address improves the privacy of this scheme. With threshold signatures, the three parties jointly generate *shares* of a regular single key address such that any 2 of them can jointly spend the money in that address. Unlike multisig, this threshold address is indistinguishable from a typical address and to an external observer would

---

[2] See for example https://escrowmybits.com/.

look like the (blinded) Silk Road scheme. Moreover, the signed transaction on the blockchain does not give any indication as to which parties participated in generating the signature.

Properties. This scheme is secure, externally hiding, and dispute hiding. It is not, however, optimistic as it is active-on-deposit – the threshold signature scheme requires an interactive setup in which all 3 parties must participate. It is also susceptible to denial of service. It also generates a new key every time that both parties as well as the mediator must keep track of.

5.4 Escrow via encrypt-and-swap

We now present a new optimistic protocol which meets all of our privacy properties:

1. Alice and Bob generate a $2-of-2$ shared ECDSA key. Note that we do not need a full threshold scheme, but the `Thresh-Key-Gen` protocol of Gennaro *et al.* [26] is suitable to generate the secret shares in a distributed manner. At the end of the protocol, Alice has x_A, Bob has x_B, and the shared public key is $y = g^{x_A + x_B}$. Moreover, as part of the protocol, both parties learn $y_A = g^{x_A}$ and $y_B = g^{x_B}$.
2. Alice sends $c_A = E_M(x_A)$, an encryption of her secret x_A under M's public key, to Bob together with a zero-knowledge proof[3] π_A that $g^{D(c_A)} = y_A$.
3. Bob sends $c_B = E_M(x_B)$ to Alice together with a zero-knowledge proof π_B that $g^{D(c_B)} = y_B$.
4. In the absence of a dispute, Alice sends x_A to Bob and Bob can now transfer the funds to his own account. Conversely, if both parties agree that a refund is in order, Bob sends x_B to Alice.
5. In the event of a dispute, the mediator investigates and chooses the "winner", which we'll denote $W \in \{A, B\}$. The winner sends c_W to M. M decrypts it and sends it back to W, who now has both shares of the key and thus can sign a redeem transaction.

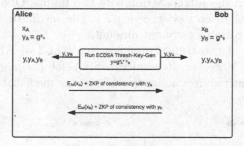

Encrypt-and-swap protocol

---

[3] The zero knowledge proof proves that a ciphertext encrypts the discrete log of a known value for a known base. For details of how to construct this proof see Camenisch *et al.* [21]. Gennaro *et al.* demonstrates that these proofs work with ECDSA and Bitcoin keys [26].

Equivocation. This scheme introduces the risk of an *equivocation* attack in which a malicious mediator tells both parties that they won the dispute. Each party will give their ciphertext to the mediator, at which point the mediator can reconstruct the entire key and steal the escrowed funds.

We can prevent this attack by replacing 2-of-2 shared address with a 3-of-3 address. The third share x_C will be shared by the transacting parties and never given to the mediator. This way, even if the mediator equivocates, it will only receive two shares x_A and x_B and cannot transfer the money.

Properties. This protocol is both secure and optimistic. Moreover it satisfies all of our privacy properties: it is internally-hiding, externally-hiding, and dispute-hiding (on the blockchain, it appears as if funds were sent to an ordinary address). The only con of this scheme is that it is susceptible to a denial-of-service attack.

5.5 Escrow with Bond

We now present a scheme that is resilient to denial-of-service attacks. To do this, we include an incentive system to punish a mediator who fails to release the funds from escrow. At a high level, we require the mediator to deposit a surety bond alongside the transacting parties. The general idea of preventing denial-of-service attacks by having the third party put money in bond has appeared in other contexts [30].

We make use of a feature of the Bitcoin scripting language that requires one to present an x such that SHA-256$(x) = y$ as a condition of spending money. This feature has previously been used, for example, to construct atomic cross-chain swap protocols (see Sect. 3.2) or offline micropayment channels [39].

We use this feature to build a transaction that ensures that the mediator will only be able to take his money out of bond if the escrow transaction is resolved.

1. Alice and Bob agree on a value x that is unknown to the mediator. They compute $y = $ SHA-256(x).
2. Bob, the buyer, creates a transaction with two inputs. One input is the funds that he is putting in escrow; the other is the mediator's bond. The bond should be equal to Bob's payment amount.
3. The first output of the transaction requires 2-of-3 of Alice, Bob, and the mediator to sign. Moreover, it requires a SHA-256 preimage of y (e.g. x).
4. The second output requires a signature from the mediator as well as a SHA-256 preimage of y.

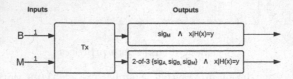

Bond Protocol to prevent denial-of-service attack

In the absence of a dispute, Alice and Bob can redeem the first output themselves). However, in the process, they must reveal x publicly on the blockchain, which the mediator can then use to recover their bond. In case of a dispute, Alice and Bob will refuse to reveal x until the mediator chooses a winner and signs the output transaction, preventing the mediator from recovering the bond until the dispute is resolved.

Properties. This protocol is both secure and resistant to denial of service. However, it is active-on-deposit and not externally-hiding, internally-hiding, nor dispute-hiding.

6   Group Escrow

The escrow protocols we have described so far assume that there is a single mediator. Moreover, only one of these schemes (escrow bond) was resistant to denial-of-service attacks, and this scheme achieved this property at the expense of being active-on-deposit and compromising privacy.

Instead, we propose an entirely different way to deal with denial-of-service attacks (as well as improve resistance to collusion attacks or a mediator simply going offline). By distributing the signing power among n mediators who will resolve disputes by a majority vote (we assume n is odd), we can ensure that no single mediator has the ability to abort and deny service. As long as the majority are willing to complete the protocol, a denial-of-service attack is thwarted.

A recurring lesson in Bitcoin's history is that putting trust in any single party is risky. Bitcoin has been plagued by *exit scams* in which third-party services gain consumer trust and then disappear [5]. In a study of 40 Bitcoin exchanges, Moore and Christin find that approximately 40% of these services went under, often leaving no funds and no recourse for the customers that trusted them [38]. In 2014, the then-largest exchange, Mt. Gox, famously claimed to have lost 850,000 bitcoins, and passed the losses directly to its customers.

6.1   Definitions and Models

Our definitions from single-mediator escrow protocols all remain in place, with the exception that security now requires protection from theft even if *all* of the mediators collude.

Definition 6.1 (Secure group escrow protocol). *A group escrow service is said to be secure if an external adversary that fully controls all of the mediators cannot transfer any of the money being held in escrow.*

We discuss two different models for how such groups of escrow services are assembled. First, we might use an *ad-hoc group* of mediators. In this model, the buyer and seller are free to (jointly) choose anybody with a Bitcoin address to serve as mediators and the mediators need not ever communicate with each other. Note that only one mediator must be jointly chosen (and trusted).

The buyer may choose k mediators and the seller chooses k mediators. They then jointly choose 1 mediator as a "tie-breaker."

We can also leverage *predetermined groups* which have already communicated and agreed to work together. The buyer and the seller merely choose one of these groups to act as their mediator service.

6.2   Group Escrow via Multisig

We can build a scheme using a script specifying that the funds can be redeemed if either (1) the transacting parties both sign or (2) one of the transacting parties together with a majority of the mediators signs. Using A and B to represent signatures by the transacting parties and $M_1, \ldots, M_{2n+1}$ to represent respective signatures by the mediators, the script will check that the following Boolean formula is satisfied:

$$(A \land B) \lor (A \land \text{n+1-of-}\{M_1, \ldots, M_{2n+1}\}) \lor (B \land \text{n+1-of-}\{M_1, \ldots, M_{2n+1}\})$$

For privacy, the mediators' addresses can be blinded as before.

While Bitcoin does limit the number of signature operations that a script can contain, the limits are reasonable in practice. In particular, using Bitcoin's pay to script hash (P2SH) feature, one can create a script that specifies 15 signature operations [8]. The script above requires up to $4 + 2m$ signature operations to validate, where m is the number of moderators. Thus, this script would be acceptable for $m \leq 5$, and in practice 5 mediators will generally be sufficient.

Properties. This scheme is secure and optimistic. Since the mediators' addresses are blinded, it is also internally hiding. However, it is neither dispute hiding nor internally-hiding. It is partially resistant to denial-of-service attacks as in order to launch such an attacks, the majority of the mediators must participate.

6.3   Group Escrow via encrypt-and-swap

We can build a group-analog to our encrypt-and-swap scheme. As before, the transacting parties run the Thresh-Key-Gen protocol of [26] to generate a shared 2-of-2 threshold address. Once they run this protocol, Alice has her key share x_A, and Bob has x_B. Moreover, as a side effect of the Thresh-Key-Gen protocol, both parties learn $y_A = g^{x_A}$ and $y_B = g^{x_B}$.

The parties then create a Shamir secret sharing of x_A and x_B. If there are $n = 2t + 1$ mediators, the transacting parties share their secret on a degree t polynomial, thus ensuring that a majority of the mediators is necessary and sufficient to recover the secret.

Using each mediator's public key M_i, each party encrypts the corresponding share to that mediator and gives all of these ciphertexts to the other party.

If there is no dispute, the party that is paying will give its key share to the other party, who now has both shares and can redeem the money.

In the event of a dispute, the mediators will vote. The winning party will give each mediator the corresponding ciphertext that it received from the other party. The mediators decrypt their shares, and a majority reconstructs the losing party's threshold key share. They then give this reconstructed key share to the winning party who can now create a pay-out transaction to itself.

If all players honestly follow the protocol, it is clear that this protocol is both secure and correct. However, we wish to achieve security against a malicious player that may deviate from the protocol. Intuitively, in order to achieve this, each party needs to prove to the other party that the values that it gives it are indeed Shamir-secret sharings of their threshold secret share.

We implement this proof in two phases: for each mediator, when Alice gives Bob the ciphertext $c_i = E_{M_i}(P_i)$, Alice additionally includes a Feldman VSS [24] (see the full version of this paper for a summary of Feldman VSS) value $w_i = g^{P_i}$ as well as a zero-knowledge proof of consistency between these two values. Using Feldman's scheme, Bob then verifies that w_i is indeed a Shamir secret-share of x_A.

We now present the details of this protocol:

1. Alice and Bob run Thresh-Key-Gen of Gennaro et al. [26] to generate a shared 2-of-2 ECDSA key. Alice has x_A, Bob has x_B, and the shared public key is $y = g^{x_A + x_B}$. As part of the protocol, both parties learn $y_A = g^{x_A}$ and $y_B = g^{x_B}$.

2. Alice shares x_A over a degree t polynomial with coefficients $a_1, \ldots, a_t$.

$$P^{(a)}(w) = x_A + a_1 w + \cdots + a_t w^t$$

3. Alice computes a share $P_i^{(a)} = P^{(a)}(i)$ for each mediator and encrypts that mediator's share under their public key as follows:

$$c_i^{(a)} = E_{M_i}(P_i^{(a)})$$

Alice gives Bob $\{c_1, c_2, \ldots, c_n\}$.

4. For each mediator's share, Alice computes $w_i^{(a)} = g^{P_i^{(a)}}$ and gives Bob $\{w_1^{(a)}, w_2^{(a)}, \ldots, w_n^{(a)}\}$.

5. For each mediator, Alice gives Bob a zero knowledge proof $\Pi_i^{(a)}$ that states

$$g^{D_{M_i}(c_i^{(a)})} = w_i^{(a)}$$

That is Alice proves that the $c_i^{(a)}$ is an encryption of the discrete log with respect to g of $w_i^{(a)}$.

6. Alice creates a Feldman VSS of the shared secret. In particular, she gives Bob $c_1^{(a)} = g^{a_1}, \ldots, c_n^{(a)} = g^{a_n}$. Bob already has $c_0^{(a)} = g^{x_A}$ as this was output in step 1.

7. Bob verifies each of the zero-knowledge proofs $\Pi_i^{(a)}$. Bob also verifies $\forall i$,

$$w_i^{(a)} = c_0^{(a)} \cdot (c_1^{(a)})^i \cdot (c_2^{(a)})^{i^2} \cdots (c_t^{(a)})^{i^t}$$

If any of these checks fail, Bob aborts.

8. Bob and Alice perform steps 2–8 in reverse.
9. Now that each party is convinced that they hold the VSS of the other party's share encrypted to the mediators, Bob (the buyer) deposits the money in the escrow address.

Properties. This protocol is secure, optimistic, internally-hiding, externally-hiding, and dispute-hiding. It supports ad-hoc groups. Moreover, it's group nature means that it has partial denial-of-service resistance as in order to launch such an attack, a majority of the mediators must participate.

7   Conclusion

We have proposed a number of protocols, as summarized and compared in Table 1. Assuming the goal is complete privacy, our recommendation is to use group escrow via encrypt-and-swap as it comes closest to fulfilling all of the properties that we set forth. If, however, the goal is transparency, then one should choose the non-blinded version of the 2-of-3 multisig scheme or the group multisig scheme as they are not dispute-hiding.

Table 1. Comparative evaluation of escrow schemes.

Protocol	Sec.	Activity			Security		Privacy			Groups	
		Not active-on-deposit	Not active-on-withdrawal	Optimistic	Secure	DoS resistant	Dispute-hiding	Externally-hiding	Internally-hiding	Works for predetermined groups	Works for ad-hoc groups
Direct payment	5.1						•	•			
2-of-3 multisig	5.2	•	•	•	•			○	○	•	
2-of-3 threshold signature	5.3			•	•		•	•		•	
Encrypt-and-swap	5.4	•	•	•	•		•	•	•	•	
Escrow with bond	5.5	•			•	•		○			
Group multisig	6.2	•	•	•	•	○			•	•	•
Group encrypt-and-swap	6.3	•	•	•	•	○	•	•	•	•	•

• fully achieves
○ partially achieves

Acknowledgements. We would like to thank Andrew Miler and Washington Sanchez for useful discussions and feedback.

Steven Goldfeder is supported by the NSF Graduate Research Fellowship under grant number DGE 1148900. Rosario Gennaro is supported by NSF Grant 1545759. Arvind Narayanan is supported by NSF Grant CNS-1421689.

References

1. Bitcoin wiki: Atomic cross-chain trading. https://en.bitcoin.it/wiki/Atomic_cross-chain_trading. Accessed 14 Nov 2016
2. Bitcoin wiki: Elliptic Curve Digital Signature Algorithm. https://en.bitcoin.it/wiki/Elliptic_Curve_Digital_Signature_Algorithm. Accessed 11 Feb 2014
3. Bitcoin wiki: Secp265k1. https://en.bitcoin.it/wiki/Secp256k1. Accessed 01 Nov 2016
4. Bitcoin wiki: Transactions. https://en.bitcoin.it/wiki/Transactions. Accessed 01 Nov 2016
5. Monero Loses Darknet Market in Apparent Exit Scam. https://cointelegraph.com/news/monero-loses-darknet-market-in-apparent-exit-scam. Accessed 14 Nov 2016
6. Stealth payments. http://sx.dyne.org/stealth.html. Accessed 14 Nov 2016
7. Open bazaar protocol (2016). https://docs.openbazaar.org/
8. Andresen, G.: Github: Proposal: open up IsStandard for P2SH transactions. https://gist.github.com/gavinandresen/88be40c141bc67acb247. Accessed 16 Feb 2017
9. Andrew, M.: Bitcoin forum post: Alt chains and atomic transfers
10. Andrychowicz, M., Dziembowski, S., Malinowski, D., Mazurek, Ł.: Fair two-party computations via bitcoin deposits. In: Böhme, R., Brenner, M., Moore, T., Smith, M. (eds.) FC 2014. LNCS, vol. 8438, pp. 105–121. Springer, Heidelberg (2014). https://doi.org/10.1007/978-3-662-44774-1_8
11. Andrychowicz, M., Dziembowski, S., Malinowski, D., Mazurek, L.: Secure multi-party computations on bitcoin. In: 2014 IEEE Symposium on Security and Privacy, pp. 443–458. IEEE (2014)
12. Asokan, N., Schunter, M., Waidner, M.: Optimistic protocols for fair exchange. In: Proceedings of the 4th ACM Conference on Computer and Communications Security, pp. 7–17. ACM (1997)
13. Asokan, N., Shoup, V., Waidner, M.: Optimistic fair exchange of digital signatures. In: Nyberg, K. (ed.) EUROCRYPT 1998. LNCS, vol. 1403, pp. 591–606. Springer, Heidelberg (1998). https://doi.org/10.1007/BFb0054156
14. Zhou, J., Gollmann, D.: Certified electronic mail. In: Bertino, E., Kurth, H., Martella, G., Montolivo, E. (eds.) ESORICS 1996. LNCS, vol. 1146, pp. 160–171. Springer, Heidelberg (1996). https://doi.org/10.1007/3-540-61770-1_35
15. Banasik, W., Dziembowski, S., Malinowski, D.: Efficient zero-knowledge contingent payments in cryptocurrencies without scripts. In: Askoxylakis, I., Ioannidis, S., Katsikas, S., Meadows, C. (eds.) ESORICS 2016. LNCS, vol. 9879, pp. 261–280. Springer, Cham (2016). https://doi.org/10.1007/978-3-319-45741-3_14
16. Bao, F., Deng, R.H., Mao, W.: Efficient and practical fair exchange protocols with off-line TTP. In: Proceedings of the 1998 IEEE Symposium on Security and Privacy, pp. 77–85. IEEE (1998)
17. Bentov, I., Kumaresan, R.: How to use bitcoin to design fair protocols. In: Garay, J.A., Gennaro, R. (eds.) CRYPTO 2014. LNCS, vol. 8617, pp. 421–439. Springer, Heidelberg (2014). https://doi.org/10.1007/978-3-662-44381-1_24
18. Blum, M.: Three Applications of the Oblivious Transfer: Part I: Coin Flipping by Telephone; Part II: How to Exchange Secrets; Part III: How to Send Certified Electronic Mail. University of California, Berkeley (1981)
19. Bonneau, J., Miller, A., Clark, J., Narayanan, A., Kroll, J.A., Felten, E.W.: Sok: research perspectives and challenges for bitcoin and cryptocurrencies. In: 2015 IEEE Symposium on Security and Privacy (SP), pp. 104–121. IEEE (2015)

20. Cachin, C., Camenisch, J.: Optimistic fair secure computation. In: Bellare, M. (ed.) CRYPTO 2000. LNCS, vol. 1880, pp. 93–111. Springer, Heidelberg (2000). https://doi.org/10.1007/3-540-44598-6_6

21. Camenisch, J., Shoup, V.: Practical verifiable encryption and decryption of discrete logarithms. In: Boneh, D. (ed.) CRYPTO 2003. LNCS, vol. 2729, pp. 126–144. Springer, Heidelberg (2003). https://doi.org/10.1007/978-3-540-45146-4_8

22. Christin, N.: Traveling the silk road: a measurement analysis of a large anonymous online marketplace. In: Proceedings of the 22nd International Conference on World Wide Web, pp. 213–224. International World Wide Web Conferences Steering Committee (2013)

23. Danezis, G., Meiklejohn, S.: Centrally banked cryptocurrencies. arXiv preprint arXiv:1505.06895 (2015)

24. Feldman, P.: A practical scheme for non-interactive verifiable secret sharing. In: 28th Annual Symposium on Foundations of Computer Science, pp. 427–438. IEEE (1987)

25. Garay, J.A., Jakobsson, M., MacKenzie, P.: Abuse-free optimistic contract signing. In: Wiener, M. (ed.) CRYPTO 1999. LNCS, vol. 1666, pp. 449–466. Springer, Heidelberg (1999). https://doi.org/10.1007/3-540-48405-1_29

26. Gennaro, R., Goldfeder, S., Narayanan, A.: Threshold-optimal DSA/ECDSA signatures and an application to bitcoin wallet security. In: Manulis, M., Sadeghi, A.-R., Schneider, S. (eds.) ACNS 2016. LNCS, vol. 9696, pp. 156–174. Springer, Cham (2016). https://doi.org/10.1007/978-3-319-39555-5_9

27. Gennaro, R., Jarecki, S., Krawczyk, H., Rabin, T.: Robust threshold DSS signatures. In: Maurer, U. (ed.) EUROCRYPT 1996. LNCS, vol. 1070, pp. 354–371. Springer, Heidelberg (1996). https://doi.org/10.1007/3-540-68339-9_31

28. Gennaro, R., Jarecki, S., Krawczyk, H., Rabin, T.: Secure distributed key generation for discrete-log based cryptosystems. In: Stern, J. (ed.) EUROCRYPT 1999. LNCS, vol. 1592, pp. 295–310. Springer, Heidelberg (1999). https://doi.org/10.1007/3-540-48910-X_21

29. Goldreich, O.: Secure multi-party computation. Manuscript. Preliminary version (1998)

30. Jakobsson, M.: Ripping Coins for a Fair Exchange. In: Guillou, L.C., Quisquater, J.-J. (eds.) EUROCRYPT 1995. LNCS, vol. 921, pp. 220–230. Springer, Heidelberg (1995). https://doi.org/10.1007/3-540-49264-X_18

31. Juels, A., Kosba, A., Shi, E.: The ring of gyges: using smart contracts for crime. Aries **40**, 54 (2015)

32. Küpçü, A., Lysyanskaya, A.: Usable optimistic fair exchange. In: Pieprzyk, J. (ed.) CT-RSA 2010. LNCS, vol. 5985, pp. 252–267. Springer, Heidelberg (2010). https://doi.org/10.1007/978-3-642-11925-5_18

33. Lindell, A.Y.: Legally-enforceable fairness in secure two-party computation. In: Malkin, T. (ed.) CT-RSA 2008. LNCS, vol. 4964, pp. 121–137. Springer, Heidelberg (2008). https://doi.org/10.1007/978-3-540-79263-5_8

34. MacKenzie, P., Reiter, M.K.: Two-party generation of DSA signatures. Int. J. Inf. Secur. **2**(3–4), 218–239 (2004)

35. Maxwell, G.: The first successful zero-knowledge contingent payment

36. Maxwell, G.: Zero knowledge contingent payment

37. Micali, S.: Simple and fast optimistic protocols for fair electronic exchange. In: Proceedings of the Twenty-second Annual Symposium on Principles of Distributed Computing, pp. 12–19

38. Moore, T., Christin, N.: Beware the middleman: empirical analysis of bitcoin-exchange risk. In: Sadeghi, A.-R. (ed.) FC 2013. LNCS, vol. 7859, pp. 25–33. Springer, Heidelberg (2013). https://doi.org/10.1007/978-3-642-39884-1_3
39. Poon, J., Dryja, T.: The bitcoin lightning network: scalable off-chain instant payments. Technical report
40. Shamir, A.: How to share a secret. Commun. ACM **22**(11), 612–613 (1979)
41. Wuille, P.: Bip 32: Hierarchical deterministic wallets. https://github.com/bitcoin/bips/blob/master/bip-0032.mediawiki. Accessed 14 Nov 2016

Trust Is Risk: A Decentralized Financial Trust Platform

Orfeas Stefanos Thyfronitis Litos[1](✉) and Dionysis Zindros[2]

[1] National Technical University of Athens, Athens, Greece
olitos@corelab.ntua.gr
[2] National and Kapodistrian University of Athens, Athens, Greece
dionyziz@di.uoa.gr

Abstract. Centralized reputation systems use stars and reviews and thus require algorithm secrecy to avoid manipulation. In autonomous open source decentralized systems this luxury is not available. We create a reputation network for decentralized marketplaces where the trust each user gives to the other users is quantifiable and expressed in monetary terms. We introduce a new model for bitcoin wallets in which user coins are split among trusted associates. Direct trust is defined using shared bitcoin accounts via bitcoin's 1-of-2 multisig. Indirect trust is subsequently defined transitively. This enables formal game theoretic arguments pertaining to risk analysis. We prove that risk and maximum flows are equivalent in our model and that our system is Sybil-resilient. Our system allows for concrete financial decisions on the subjective monetary amount a pseudonymous party can be trusted with. Risk remains invariant under a direct trust redistribution operation followed by a purchase.

1 Introduction

Online marketplaces can be categorized as centralized and decentralized. Two examples of each category are ebay (http://www.ebay.com/) and OpenBazaar (https://www.openbazaar.org/). The common denominator of established online marketplaces is that the reputation of each vendor and client is typically expressed in the form of stars and user-generated reviews that are viewable by the whole network.

The goal of "Trust Is Risk" is to offer a reputation system for decentralized marketplaces where the trust each user gives to the other users is quantifiable in monetary terms. The central assumption used throughout this paper is that trust is equivalent to risk, or the proposition that *Alice*'s *trust* in another user *Charlie* is defined as the *maximum sum of money Alice* can lose when *Charlie* is free to choose any strategy. To flesh out this concept, we will use *lines of credit* as proposed by Sanchez [1]. *Alice* joins the network by explicitly entrusting some money to another user, say her friend, *Bob* (see Figs. 1 and 2). If *Bob* has already entrusted some money to a third user, *Charlie*, then *Alice* indirectly

D. Zindros—Research supported by ERC project CODAMODA, project #259152.

trusts *Charlie* since if the latter wished to play unfairly, he could have already stolen the money entrusted to him by *Bob*. We will later see that *Alice* can now engage in economic interaction with *Charlie*.

To implement lines-of-credit, we use Bitcoin [2], a decentralized cryptocurrency that differs from conventional currencies in that it does not depend on trusted third parties. All transactions are public as they are recorded on a decentralized ledger, the blockchain. Each transaction takes some coins as input and produces some coins as output. If the output of a transaction is not connected to the input of another one, then this output belongs to the UTXO, the set of unspent transaction outputs. Intuitively, the UTXO contains all coins not yet spent.

Fig. 1. A indirectly trusts C 10₿   **Fig. 2.** A indirectly trusts C 5₿

We propose a new kind of wallet where coins are not exclusively owned, but are placed in shared accounts materialized through 1-of-2 multisigs, a bitcoin construct that permits any one of two pre-designated users to spend the coins contained within a shared account [3]. We use the notation $1/\{Alice, Bob\}$ to represent a 1-of-2 multisig that can be spent by either *Alice* or *Bob*. In this notation, the order of names is irrelevant, as either user can spend. However, the user who deposits the money initially into the shared account is relevant – she is the one risking her money.

Our approach changes the user experience in a subtle but drastic way. A user no more has to base her trust towards a store on stars or ratings which are not expressed in financial units. She can simply consult her wallet to decide whether the store is trustworthy and, if so, up to what value, denominated in bitcoin. This system works as follows: Initially *Alice* migrates her funds from her private bitcoin wallet to 1-of-2 multisig addresses shared with friends she comfortably trusts. We call this direct trust. Our system is agnostic to the means players use to determine who is trustworthy for these direct 1-of-2 deposits. Nevertheless, these deposits contain an objective value visible to the network that can be used to deterministically evaluate subjective indirect trust towards other users.

Suppose *Alice* is viewing the listings of vendor *Charlie*. Instead of his stars, *Alice* sees a positive value calculated by her wallet representing the maximum value she can safely pay to purchase from *Charlie*. This value, known as indirect trust, is calculated in Theorem 2 – Trust Flow.

Indirect trust towards a user is not global but subjective; each user views a personalized indirect trust based on the network topology. The indirect trust reported by our system maintains the following desired security property: If *Alice* makes a purchase from *Charlie*, then she is exposed to no more risk than she was already taking willingly. The existing voluntary risk is exactly that which *Alice* was taking by sharing her coins with her trusted friends. We prove this in

Theorem 3 – Risk Invariance. Obviously it is not safe for *Alice* to buy anything from any vendor if she has not directly entrusted any value to other users.

In Trust Is Risk the money is not invested at the time of purchase and directly to the vendor, but at an earlier point in time and only to parties that are trustworthy for out of band reasons. The fact that this system can function in a completely decentralized fashion will become clear in the following sections. We prove this in Theorem 5 – Sybil Resilience.

We make the design choice that an entity can express her trust maximally in terms of her available capital. Thus, an impoverished player cannot allocate much direct trust to her friends, no matter how trustworthy they are. On the other hand, a rich player may entrust a small fraction of her funds to a player that she does not extensively trust and still exhibit more direct trust than the impoverished player. There is no upper limit to trust; each player is only limited by her funds. We thus take advantage of the following remarkable property of money: To normalise subjective human preferences into objective value.

A user has several incentives to join. First, she has access to otherwise inaccessible stores. Moreover, two friends can formalize their mutual trust by directly entrusting the same amount to each other. A company that casually subcontracts others can express its trust towards them. Governments can choose to directly entrust citizens with money and confront them using a corresponding legal arsenal if they make irresponsible use of this trust. Banks can provide loans as outgoing and manage savings as incoming direct trust. Last, the network is an investment and speculation field since it constitutes a new area for financial activity.

Observe that the same physical person can maintain multiple pseudonymous identities in the same trust network and that multiple independent trust networks for different purposes can coexist.

Trust Is Risk is not just a theoretical conception, but can be deployed and applied in existing decentralized markets such as OpenBazaar. All the necessary bitcoin constructs such as multisigs are readily available. Our only concern pertains to the scalability of such an implementation, but we are confident that such difficulties can be overcome.

2   Mechanics

We now trace *Alice*'s steps from joining the network to successfully completing a purchase. Suppose initially all her coins, say 10₿, are under her exclusive control.

Two trustworthy friends, *Bob* and *Charlie*, persuade her to try out Trust Is Risk. She installs the Trust Is Risk wallet and migrates the 10₿ from her regular wallet, entrusting 2₿ to *Bob* and 5₿ to *Charlie*. She now exclusively controls 3₿. She is risking 7₿ to which she has full but not exclusive access in exchange for being part of the network.

A few days later, she discovers an online shoes shop owned by *Dean*, also a member of Trust Is Risk. She finds a nice pair of shoes that costs 1₿ and checks *Dean*'s trustworthiness through her new wallet. Suppose *Dean* is deemed trustworthy up to 5₿. Since 1₿ < 5₿, she confidently proceeds to purchase the shoes with her new wallet.

She can then see in her wallet that her exclusive coins have remained 3₿, the coins entrusted to *Charlie* have been reduced to 4₿ and *Dean* is entrusted 1₿, equal to the value of the shoes. Also, her purchase is marked as pending. If she checks her trust towards *Dean*, it still is 5₿. Under the hood, her wallet redistributed her entrusted coins in a way that ensures *Dean* is directly entrusted with coins equal to the value of the purchased item and that her reported trust towards him has remained invariant.

Eventually all goes well and the shoes reach *Alice*. *Dean* chooses to redeem *Alice*'s entrusted coins, so her wallet does not show any coins entrusted to *Dean*. Through her wallet, she marks the purchase as successful. This lets the system replenish the reduced trust to *Bob* and *Charlie*, setting the entrusted coins to 2₿ and 5₿ respectively once again. *Alice* now exclusively owns 2₿. Thus, she can now use a total of 9₿, which is expected, since she had to pay 1₿ for the shoes.

3   The Trust Graph

We now engage in the formal description of the proposed system, accompanied by helpful examples.

Definition 1 (Graph). *Trust Is Risk is represented by a sequence of directed weighted graphs* $(\mathcal{G}_j)$ *where* $\mathcal{G}_j = (\mathcal{V}_j, \mathcal{E}_j)$, $j \in \mathbb{N}$. *Also, since the graphs are weighted, there exists a sequence of weight functions* (c_j) *with* $c_j : \mathcal{E}_j \to \mathbb{R}^+$.

The nodes represent the players, the edges represent the existing direct trusts and the weights represent the amount of value attached to the corresponding direct trust. As we will see, the game evolves in turns. The subscript of the graph represents the corresponding turn.

Definition 2 (Players). *The set* $\mathcal{V}_j = \mathcal{V}(\mathcal{G}_j)$ *is the set of all players in the network, otherwise understood as the set of all pseudonymous identities.*

Each node has a corresponding non-negative number that represents its capital. A node's capital is the total value that the node possesses exclusively and nobody else can spend.

Definition 3 (Capital). *The capital of A in turn j,* $Cap_{A,j}$, *is defined as the number of coins that belong exclusively to A at the beginning of turn j.*

The capital is the value that exists in the game but is not shared with trusted parties. The capital of A can be reallocated only during her turns, according to her actions. We model the system in a way that no capital can be added in the course of the game through external means. The use of capital will become clear once turns are formally defined.

The formal definition of direct trust follows:

Definition 4 (Direct Trust). *Direct trust from A to B at the end of turn j, $DTr_{A \to B,j}$, is defined as the total finite amount that exists in $1/\{A, B\}$ multisigs in the UTXO in the end of turn j, where the money is deposited by A.*

$$DTr_{A \to B,j} = \begin{cases} c_j(A, B), & if(A, B) \in \mathcal{E}_j \\ 0, & else \end{cases}. \tag{1}$$

The definition of direct trust agrees with the title of this paper and coincides with the intuition and sociological experimental results of Karlan et al. [4] that the trust *Alice* shows to *Bob* in real-world social networks corresponds to the extent of danger in which *Alice* is putting herself into in order to help *Bob*. An example graph with its corresponding transactions in the UTXO can be seen in Fig. 3.

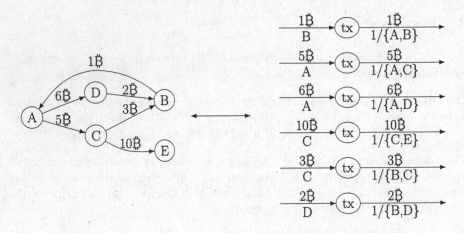

Fig. 3. Trust Is Risk game graph and equivalent bitcoin UTXO

Any algorithm that has access to the graph $\mathcal{G}_j$ has implicitly access to all direct trusts of this graph.

Definition 5 (Neighbourhood). *We use the notation $N^+(A)_j$ to refer to the nodes directly trusted by A at the end of turn j and $N^-(A)_j$ for the nodes that directly trust A at the end of turn j.*

$$N^+(A)_j = \{B \in \mathcal{V}_j : DTr_{A \to B,j} > 0\},$$
$$N^-(A)_j = \{B \in \mathcal{V}_j : DTr_{B \to A,j} > 0\}. \tag{2}$$

These are called out- and in-neighbourhood of A on turn j respectively.

Definition 6 (Total In/Out Direct Trust). *We use* $in_{A,j}, out_{A,j}$ *to refer to the total incoming and outgoing direct trust respectively.*

$$in_{A,j} = \sum_{v \in N^-(A)_j} DTr_{v \to A,j}, \qquad out_{A,j} = \sum_{v \in N^+(A)_j} DTr_{A \to v,j}. \qquad (3)$$

Definition 7 (Assets). *Sum of A's capital and outgoing direct trust.*

$$As_{A,j} = Cap_{A,j} + out_{A,j}. \qquad (4)$$

4 Evolution of Trust

Trust Is Risk is a game that runs indefinitely. In each turn, a player is chosen, decides what to play and, if valid, the chosen turn is executed.

Definition 8 (Turns). *In each turn* j *a player* $A \in \mathcal{V}, A = Player(j)$, *chooses one or more actions from the following two kinds:*

Steal(y_B, B): *Steal value* y_B *from* $B \in N^-(A)_{j-1}$, *where* $0 \leq y_B \leq DTr_{B \to A,j-1}$. *Then set* $DTr_{B \to A,j} = DTr_{B \to A,j-1} - y_B$.

Add(y_B, B): *Add value* y_B *to* $B \in \mathcal{V}$, *where* $-DTr_{A \to B,j-1} \leq y_B$. *Then set* $DTr_{A \to B,j} = DTr_{A \to B,j-1} + y_B$.

$y_B < 0$ *amounts to direct trust reduction, while* $y_B > 0$ *to direct trust increase.*

Let Y_{st}, Y_{add} *be the total value to be stolen and added respectively by* A. *The capital is updated in every turn:* $Cap_{A,j} = Cap_{A,j-1} + Y_{st} - Y_{add}$. *For a turn to be valid we require* $Cap_{A,j} \geq 0$ *and* $DTr_{A \to B,j} \geq 0$ *and* $DTr_{B \to A,j} > 0$. *A player cannot choose two actions of the same kind against the same player in one turn.* $Turn_j$ *denotes the set of actions in turn* j. *The graph that emerges by applying the actions on* $\mathcal{G}_{j-1}$ *is* $\mathcal{G}_j$.

Definition 9 (Prev/Next Turn). *Let* $j \in \mathbb{N}$ *be a turn with* $Player(j) = A$. *Define* $prev(j) / next(j)$ *as the previous/next turn* A *is chosen to play. Formally, let*

$$P = \{k \in \mathbb{N} : k < j \wedge Player(k) = A\} \text{ and}$$
$$N = \{k \in \mathbb{N} : k > j \wedge Player(k) = A\}.$$

Then we define $prev(j), next(j)$ *as follows:*

$$prev(j) = \begin{cases} \max P, & P \neq \emptyset \\ 0, & P = \emptyset \end{cases}, next(j) = \min N.$$

Definition 10 (Damage). *Let* j *be a turn such that* $Player(j) = A$.

$$Dmg_{A,j} = out_{A,prev(j)} - out_{A,j-1}. \qquad (5)$$

We say that A *has been stolen value* $Dmg_{A,j}$ *between* $prev(j)$ *and* j. *We omit turn subscripts if they are implied from the context.*

Definition 11 (History). *We define History, $\mathcal{H} = (\mathcal{H}_j)$, as the sequence of all tuples containing the sets of actions and the corresponding player.*

$$\mathcal{H}_j = (Player\,(j)\,,Turn_j)\,. \tag{6}$$

Knowledge of the initial graph $\mathcal{G}_0$, all players' initial capital and the history amount to full comprehension of the evolution of the game. Building on the example of Fig. 3, we can see the resulting graph when D plays

$$Turn_1 = \{Steal\,(1,A)\,,Add\,(4,C)\,,Add\,(-1,B)\}. \tag{7}$$

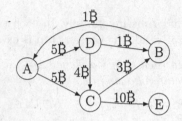

Fig. 4. Game graph after $Turn_1$ (7) on the graph of Fig. 3

We now define the Trust Is Risk Game formally. We assume players are chosen so that, after her turn, a player will eventually play again later (Fig. 4).

```
    Trust Is Risk Game
 1  j = 0
 2  while (True)
 3      j += 1; A ←$ 𝒱_j
 4      Turn = strategy[A](𝒢_0, A, Cap_{A,0}, ℋ_{1...j-1})
 5      (𝒢_j, Cap_{A,j}, ℋ_j) = executeTurn(𝒢_{j-1}, A, Cap_{A,j-1}, Turn)
```

`strategy[A]()` provides player A with full knowledge of the game, except for the capitals of other players. This assumption may not be always realistic. `executeTurn()` checks the validity of `Turn` and substitutes it with an empty turn if invalid. Subsequently, it creates the new graph $\mathcal{G}_j$ and updates the history accordingly.

5   Trust Transitivity

In this section we define some strategies and show the corresponding algorithms. Then we define the Transitive Game, the worst-case scenario for an honest player when another player plays maliciously.

Definition 12 (Idle Strategy). *A player plays the idle strategy if she passes her turn.*

```
  Idle Strategy
  Input : graph G₀, player A, capital Cap_{A,0}, history (H)_{1...j-1}

  Output : Turn_j
1 idleStrategy(G₀, A, Cap_{A,0}, H) :
2   return(∅)
```

The inputs and outputs are identical to those of `idleStrategy()` for the rest of the strategies, thus we avoid repeating them.

Definition 13 (Evil Strategy). *A player plays the evil strategy if she steals all incoming direct trust and nullifies her outgoing direct trust.*

```
1 evilStrategy(G₀, A, Cap_{A,0}, H) :
2   Steals =      ⋃      {Steal(DTr_{v→A,j-1}, v)}
             v∈N⁻(A)_{j-1}
3   Adds =      ⋃      {Add(-DTr_{A→v,j-1}, v)}
           v∈N⁺(A)_{j-1}
4   Turn_j = Steals ⋃ Adds
5   return(Turn_j)
```

Definition 14 (Conservative Strategy). *A player plays conservatively if she replenishes the value she lost since the previous turn by stealing from others who directly trust her as much as she can up to Dmg_A.*

```
1  consStrategy(G₀, A, Cap_{A,0}, H) :
2    Damage = out_{A,prev(j)} - out_{A,j-1}
3    if (Damage > 0)
4      if (Damage >= in_{A,j-1})
5        Turn_j =      ⋃      {Steal(DTr_{v→A,j-1}, v)}
                  v∈N⁻(A)_{j-1}
6      else
7        y = SelectSteal(G_j, A, Damage) #y = {y_v : v ∈ N⁻(A)_{j-1}}

8        Turn_j =      ⋃      {Steal(y_v, v)}
                  v∈N⁻(A)_{j-1}
9    else Turn_j = ∅
10   return(Turn_j)
```

`SelectSteal()` returns y_v with $v \in N^-(A)_{j-1}$ such that

$$\sum_{v\in N^-(A)_{j-1}} y_v = Dmg_{A,j} \wedge \forall v \in N^-(A)_{j-1}, y_v \leq DTr_{v\to A,j-1}. \qquad (8)$$

Player A can arbitrarily define how `SelectSteal()` distributes the $Steal()$ actions each time she calls the function, as long as (8) is respected.

The rationale behind this strategy arises from a real-world common situation. Suppose there are a client, an intermediary and a producer. The client entrusts some value to the intermediary so that the latter can buy the desired product from the producer and deliver it to the client. The intermediary in turn entrusts an equal value to the producer, who needs the value upfront to be able to complete the production process. However the producer eventually does not give the product neither reimburses the value, due to bankruptcy or decision to exit the market with an unfair benefit. The intermediary can choose either to reimburse the client and suffer the loss, or refuse to return the money and lose the client's trust. The latter choice for the intermediary is exactly the conservative strategy. It is used throughout this work as a strategy for all the intermediary players because it models effectively the worst-case scenario that a client can face after an evil player decides to steal everything she can and the rest of the players do not engage in evil activity.

We continue with a possible evolution of the game, the Transitive Game.

```
    Transitive Game
    Input : graph G₀, A ∈ V idle player, B ∈ V evil player
 1  Angry = Sad = ∅ ; Happy = V \ {A, B}
 2  for (v ∈ V \ {B}) Loss_v = 0
 3  j = 0
 4  while (True)
 5      j += 1; v ←$ V \ {A}              # Choose this turn's player
 6      Turn_j = strategy[v](G₀, v, Cap_{v,0}, H_{1...j-1})
 7      executeTurn(G_{j-1}, v, Cap_{v,j-1}, Turn_j)
 8      for (action ∈ Turn_j)
 9          action match do
10              case Steal(y, w) do                  # For each Steal,
11                  exchange = y                     #
12                  Loss_w += exchange               # pass on Loss
13                  if (v != B) Loss_v -= exchange   #
14                  if (w != A)                      # and change the
15                      Happy = Happy \ {w}          # mood of the
16                      if (in_{w,j} == 0) Sad = Sad ∪ {w}   # affected player
17                      else Angry = Angry ∪ {w}
18          if (v != B)
19              Angry = Angry \ {v}                  # Change the mood of
20              if (Loss_v > 0)  Sad = Sad ∪ {v}     # the active player
21              if (Loss_v == 0) Happy = Happy ∪ {v}
```

In turn 0, there is already a network in place. All players apart from A and B follow the conservative strategy. The set of players is not modified throughout the Transitive Game, thus we can refer to V_j as V. Each conservative player can be in one of three states: Happy, Angry or Sad. Happy players have 0 loss, Angry players have positive loss and positive incoming direct trust (line 17), thus are able to replenish their loss at least in part and Sad players have positive loss, but 0 incoming direct trust (line 16), thus they cannot replenish the loss. An example execution can be seen in Fig. 5.

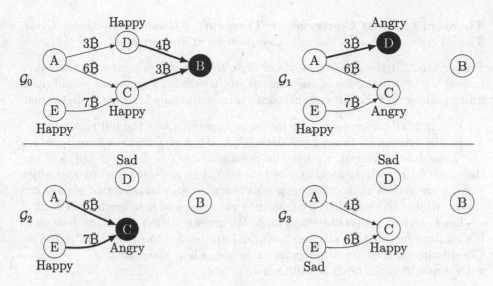

Fig. 5. B steals 7฿, then D steals 3฿ and finally C steals 3฿

Let j_0 be the first turn on which B is chosen to play. Until then, all players will pass their turn since nothing has been stolen yet (see the Conservative World theorem in Appendix A of the full version [5]). Moreover, let $v = Player(j)$. The Transitive Game generates turns:

$$Turn_j = \bigcup_{w \in N^-(v)_{j-1}} \{Steal(y_w, w)\}, \text{ where} \tag{9}$$

$$\sum_{w \in N^-(v)_{j-1}} y_w = \min(in_{v,j-1}, Dmg_{v,j}). \tag{10}$$

We see that if $Dmg_{v,j} = 0$, then $Turn_j = \emptyset$. From the definition of $Dmg_{v,j}$ and knowing that no strategy in this case can increase any direct trust, we see that $Dmg_{v,j} \geq 0$. Also $Loss_{v,j} \geq 0$ because if $Loss_{v,j} < 0$, then v has stolen more value than she has been stolen, thus she would not be following the conservative strategy.

6   Trust Flow

We can now define indirect trust from A to B.

Definition 15 (Indirect Trust). *Indirect trust from A to B after turn j is defined as the maximum possible value that can be stolen from A after turn j in the setting of* `TransitiveGame(`$\mathcal{G}_j$`,A,B)`.

Note that $Tr_{A \to B} \geq DTr_{A \to B}$. The next result shows $Tr_{A \to B}$ is finite.

Theorem 1 (Trust Convergence Theorem). *Consider a Transitive Game. There exists a turn such that all subsequent turns are empty.*

Proof Sketch. If the game didn't converge, the *Steal* () actions would continue forever without reduction of the amount stolen over time, thus they would reach infinity. However this is impossible, since there exists only finite total direct trust.

Proofs of all theorems can be found in Appendix A of the full version [5].

In the setting of `TransitiveGame`$(\mathcal{G}, A, B)$ and j being a turn in which the game has converged, we use the notation $Loss_A = Loss_{A,j}$. $Loss_A$ is not the same for repeated executions of this kind of game, since the order in which players are chosen may differ between executions and conservative players can choose which incoming direct trusts they will steal and how much from each.

Let G be a weighted directed graph. We investigate the maximum flow on it. For an introduction to maximum flows see Introduction to Algorithms, p. 708 [6]. Considering each edge's capacity as its weight, a flow assignment $X = [x_{vw}]_{\mathcal{V} \times \mathcal{V}}$ with source A and sink B is valid when:

$$\forall (v, w) \in \mathcal{E}, x_{vw} \le c_{vw} \text{ and} \tag{11}$$

$$\forall v \in \mathcal{V} \setminus \{A, B\}, \sum_{w \in N^+(v)} x_{wv} = \sum_{w \in N^-(v)} x_{vw}. \tag{12}$$

The flow value is $\sum_{v \in N^+(A)} x_{Av} = \sum_{v \in N^-(B)} x_{vB}$. We do not suppose skew symmetry in X. There exists an algorithm $MaxFlow(A, B)$ that returns the maximum possible flow from A to B. This algorithm needs full knowledge of the graph and runs in $O(|\mathcal{V}||\mathcal{E}|)$ time [7]. We refer to the flow value of $MaxFlow(A, B)$ as $maxFlow(A, B)$.

We will now introduce two lemmas that will be used to prove one of the central results of this work, the Trust Flow theorem.

Lemma 1 (MaxFlows Are Transitive Games). *Let $\mathcal{G}$ be a game graph, let $A, B \in \mathcal{V}$ and $MaxFlow(A, B)$ the maximum flow from A to B executed on $\mathcal{G}$. There exists an execution of `TransitiveGame`$(\mathcal{G}, A, B)$ such that $maxFlow(A, B) \le Loss_A$.*

Proof Sketch. The desired execution of `TransitiveGame`() will contain all flows from the $MaxFlow(A, B)$ as equivalent *Steal* () actions. The players will play in turns, moving from B back to A. Each player will steal from his predecessors as much as was stolen from her. The flows and the conservative strategy share the property that the total input is equal to the total output. □

Lemma 2 (Transitive Games Are Flows). *Let $\mathcal{H} = $`TransitiveGame`$(\mathcal{G}, A, B)$ for some game graph $\mathcal{G}$ and $A, B \in \mathcal{V}$. There exists a valid flow $X = \{x_{wv}\}_{\mathcal{V} \times \mathcal{V}}$ on $\mathcal{G}_0$ such that $\sum_{v \in \mathcal{V}} x_{Av} = Loss_A$.*

Proof Sketch. If we exclude the sad players from the game, the *Steal* () actions that remain constitute a valid flow from A to B. □

Theorem 2 (Trust Flow Theorem). *Let $\mathcal{G}$ be a game graph and $A, B \in \mathcal{V}$. It holds that*

$$Tr_{A \to B} = maxFlow\,(A, B).$$

Proof. From lemma 1 there exists an execution of the Transitive Game such that $Loss_A \geq maxFlow\,(A, B)$. Since $Tr_{A \to B}$ is the maximum loss that A can suffer after the convergence of the Transitive Game, we see that

$$Tr_{A \to B} \geq maxFlow\,(A, B). \tag{13}$$

But some execution of the Transitive Game gives $Tr_{A \to B} = Loss_A$. From lemma 2, this execution corresponds to a flow. Thus

$$Tr_{A \to B} \leq maxFlow\,(A, B). \tag{14}$$

The theorem follows from (13) and (14). $\qquad\square$

Note that the maxFlow is the same in the following two cases: If a player chooses the evil strategy and if that player chooses a variation of the evil strategy where she does not nullify her outgoing direct trust.

Further justification of trust transitivity through the use of $MaxFlow$ can be found in the sociological work by Karlan et al. [4] where a direct correspondence of maximum flows and empirical trust is experimentally validated.

Here we see another important theorem that gives the basis for risk-invariant transactions between different, possibly unknown, parties.

Theorem 3. (Risk Invariance Theorem). *Let $\mathcal{G}$ be a game graph, $A, B \in \mathcal{V}$ and l the desired value to be transferred from A to B, with $l \leq Tr_{A \to B}$. Let also $\mathcal{G}'$ with the same nodes as $\mathcal{G}$ such that*

$$\forall v \in \mathcal{V}' \setminus \{A\}, \forall w \in \mathcal{V}', DTr'_{v \to w} = DTr_{v \to w}.$$

Furthermore, suppose that there exists an assignment for the outgoing direct trust of A, $DTr'_{A \to v}$, such that

$$Tr'_{A \to B} = Tr_{A \to B} - l. \tag{15}$$

Let another game graph, $\mathcal{G}''$, be identical to $\mathcal{G}'$ except for the following change: $DTr''_{A \to B} = DTr'_{A \to B} + l$. It then holds that

$$Tr''_{A \to B} = Tr_{A \to B}.$$

Proof. The two graphs $\mathcal{G}'$ and $\mathcal{G}''$ differ only in the weight of the edge (A, B), which is larger by l in $\mathcal{G}''$. Thus the two $MaxFlows$ will choose the same flow, except for (A, B), where it will be $x''_{AB} = x'_{AB} + l$. $\qquad\square$

A can reduce her outgoing direct trust in a manner that achieves (15), since $maxFlow\,(A, B)$ is continuous with respect to A's outgoing direct trusts.

7 Sybil Resilience

One of our aims is to mitigate Sybil attacks [8] whilst maintaining decentralized autonomy [9]. We begin by extending the definition of indirect trust.

Definition 16 (Indirect Trust to Multiple Players). *Indirect trust from player A to a set of players, $S \subset V$ is defined as the maximum possible value that can be stolen from A if all players in S are evil, A is idle and everyone else ($V \setminus (S \cup \{A\})$) is conservative. Formally, let choices be the different actions between which the conservative players choose, then*

$$Tr_{A \to S, j} = \max_{j' : j' > j, choices} [out_{A,j} - out_{A,j'}]. \tag{16}$$

We now extend the Trust Flow theorem to many players.

Theorem 4 (Multi-player Trust Flow). *Let $S \subset V$ and T be an auxiliary player such that, for the sake of argument, $\forall B \in S, DTr_{B \to T} = \infty$. It holds that*

$$\forall A \in V \setminus S, Tr_{A \to S} = maxFlow\,(A, T).$$

Proof. If T chooses the evil strategy and all players in S play according to the conservative strategy, they will have to steal all their incoming direct trust since they have suffered an infinite loss, thus they will act in a way identical to following the evil strategy as far as $MaxFlow$ is concerned. The theorem follows thus from the Trust Flow theorem.   □

We now define several useful notions to tackle the problem of Sybil attacks. Let Eve be a possible attacker.

Definition 17 (Corrupted Set). *Let G be a game graph and let Eve have a set of players $B \subset V$ corrupted, so that she fully controls their outgoing and incoming direct trusts with any player in V. We call this the corrupted set. The players B are considered legitimate before the corruption, thus they may be directly trusted by any player in V.*

Definition 18 (Sybil Set). *Let G be a game graph. Participation does not require registration, so Eve can create unlimited players. We call the set of these players C, or Sybil set. Moreover, Eve controls their direct and indirect trusts with any player. However, players C can be directly trusted only by players $B \cup C$ but not by players $V \setminus (B \cup C)$, where B is the corrupted set.*

Definition 19 (Collusion). *Let G be a game graph. Let $B \subset V$ be a corrupted set and $C \subset V$ be a Sybil set. The tuple (B, C) is called collusion and is controlled by Eve.*

From a game theoretic point of view, players $V \setminus (B \cup C)$ perceive the collusion as independent players with a distinct strategy each, whereas in reality they are all subject to a single strategy dictated by Eve (Fig. 6).

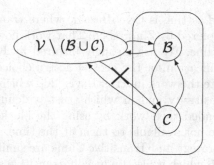

Fig. 6. Collusion

Theorem 5 (Sybil Resilience). *Let $\mathcal{G}$ be a game graph and $(\mathcal{B}, \mathcal{C})$ be a collusion of players on $\mathcal{G}$. It is*

$$Tr_{A \to \mathcal{B} \cup \mathcal{C}} = Tr_{A \to \mathcal{B}}.$$

Proof Sketch. The incoming trust to $\mathcal{B} \cup \mathcal{C}$ cannot be higher than the incoming trust to $\mathcal{B}$ since $\mathcal{C}$ has no incoming trust from $\mathcal{V} \setminus (\mathcal{B} \cup \mathcal{C})$. ☐

We have proven that controlling $|\mathcal{C}|$ is irrelevant for Eve, thus Sybil attacks are meaningless. Note that the theorem does not reassure against deception attacks. Specifically, a malicious player can create several identities, use them legitimately to inspire others to deposit direct trust to these identities and then switch to the evil strategy, thus defrauding everyone that trusted the fabricated identities. These identities correspond to the corrupted set of players and not to the Sybil set because they have direct incoming trust from outside the collusion.

In conclusion, we have delivered on our promise of a Sybil-resilient decentralized financial trust system with invariant risk for purchases.

8   Related Work

Webs-of-trust can be used as a basis for trust as shown by Caronni [10]. PGP [11] implements one and Pathfinder [12] explores its transitive closure. Freenet [13] implements a transitive web-of-trust for fighting spam. Mui et al. [14] and Jøsang et al. [15] propose ways of calculating trust towards distant nodes. Vişan et al. [16] calculate trust in a hierarchical way. CA- and Byzantine-based [17] PKIs [18] and Bazaar [19] require central trusted third parties or at least authenticated membership. FIRE [20], CORE [21], Grünert et al. [22] and Repantis et al. [23] do not prove any Sybil resilience. All these systems define trust in a non-financial manner.

We agree with Gollmann [24] in that the meaning of trust should not be extrapolated. We adopted their advice and urge our readers to adhere to the definitions of *direct* and *indirect* trust as defined here.

Beaver [25] includes a trust model that, to discourage Sybil attacks, relies on fees, something we chose to avoid. Our motivating application for exploring trust in a decentralized setting is OpenBazaar, where transitive financial trust has previously been explored by Zindros [9]. That work however does not define trust as a monetary value. We are strongly inspired by Karlan et al. [4] who give a sociological justification for the central design choice of identifying trust with risk. We appreciate the work in TrustDavis [26], which proposes a financial trust system with transitivity and in which trust is defined as lines-of-credit, similar to us. We extended their work by using the blockchain for automated proofs-of-risk, a feature not available to them at the time.

Our conservative strategy and Transitive Game are similar to the mechanism proposed by Fugger [27] which is also financially transitive and is used by Ripple [28] and Stellar [29]. IOUs in those correspond to reversed edges of trust in our system. The critical difference is that our trust is expressed in a global currency and there is no money-as-debt. Furthermore, we proved that trust and maximum flows are equivalent, a direction not explored in their papers, even though it seems to hold for their systems as well.

9   Further Research

When a purchase is made, outgoing direct trust must be reduced such that (15) holds. Trust redistribution algorithms for this will be discussed in a future paper.

Our game is static. In a future dynamic setting, users should be able to play simultaneously, freely join, depart or disconnect temporarily from the network. An interesting analysis would involve modelling repeated purchases with the respective edge updates on the trust graph and treating trust on the network as part of the utility function. Other types of multisigs, such as 1-of-3, can be explored.

MaxFlow in our case needs complete network knowledge, which can lead to privacy issues [30]. Calculating the flows in zero knowledge remains an open question. SilentWhispers [31] and its centralized predecessor, PrivPay [32], offer insight into how privacy can be achieved.

A wallet implementation of our game on any blockchain is welcome. Experimental results can be harvested by a simulation or implementation of Trust Is Risk. Afterwards, our system can be used in decentralized social networks, such as Synereo [33], and other applications.

References

1. Sanchez, W.: Lines of credit (2016). https://gist.github.com/drwasho/2c40b91e169f55988618#part-3-web-of-credit
2. Nakamoto, S.: Bitcoin: A Peer-to-Peer Electronic Cash System (2008)
3. Antonopoulos, A.M.: Mastering Bitcoin: Unlocking Digital Cryptocurrencies. O'Reilly Media Inc., Sebastopol (2014)
4. Karlan, D., Mobius, M., Rosenblat, T., Szeidl, A.: Trust and social collateral. Q. J. Econ. **124**(3), 1307–1361 (2009)
5. Thyfronitis Litos, O.S., Zindros, D.: Trust is risk: a decentralized financial trust platform. IACR, Cryptology ePrint Archive (2017)

6. Cormen, T.H., Leiserson, C.E., Rivest, R.L., Stein, C.: Introduction to Algorithms, 3rd edn. MIT Press and McGraw-Hill, Cambridge (2009)
7. Orlin, J.B.: Max flows in O(nm) time, or better. In: STOC 2013 Proceedings of the Forty-fifth Annual ACM Symposium on Theory of Computing, pp. 765–774. ACM, New York (2013). http://dx.doi.org/10.1145/2488608.2488705
8. Douceur, J.R.: The Sybil attack. In: International Workshop on Peer-To-Peer Systems (2002)
9. Zindros, D.: Trust in Decentralized Anonymous Marketplaces (2015)
10. Caronni, G.: Walking the web of trust. In: Enabling Technologies: Infrastructure for Collaborative Enterprises, IEEE 9th International Workshops, pp. 153–158 (2000)
11. Zimmermann, P.: PGP Source Code and Internals. The MIT Press, Cambridge (1995)
12. Penning, H.P.: PGP pathfinder. pgp.cs.uu.nl
13. Clarke, I., Sandberg, O., Wiley, B., Hong, T.W.: Freenet: a distributed anonymous information storage and retrieval system. In: Federrath, H. (ed.) Designing Privacy Enhancing Technologies. LNCS, vol. 2009, pp. 46–66. Springer, Heidelberg (2001). https://doi.org/10.1007/3-540-44702-4_4
14. Mui, L., Mohtashemi, M., Halberstadt, A.: A computational model of trust and reputation. In: Proceedings of the 35th Annual Hawaii International Conference on System Sciences, pp. 2431–2439. IEEE (2002)
15. Jøsang, A., Ismail, R.: The beta reputation system. In: Proceedings of the 15th Bled Electronic Commerce Conference (2002)
16. Vişan, A., Pop, F., Cristea, V.: Decentralized trust management in peer-to-peer systems. In: 10th International Symposium on Parallel and Distributed Computing, pp. 232–239 (2011)
17. Lamport, L., Shostak, R., Pease, M.: The Byzantine generals problem. ACM Trans. Progr. Lang. Syst. **4**(3), 382–401 (1982)
18. Adams, C., Lloyd, S.: Understanding PKI: Concepts, Standards, and Deployment. Addison-Wesley Professional, Reading (2003)
19. Post, A., Shah, V., Mislove, A.: Bazaar: strengthening user reputations in online marketplaces. In: Proceedings of NSDI 2011, 8th USENIX Symposium on Networked Systems Design and Implementation, p. 183 (2011)
20. Huynh, T.D., Jennings, N.R., Shadbolt, N.R.: An integrated trust and reputation model for open multi-agent systems. Auton. Agent. Multi-Agent Syst. **13**(2), 119–154 (2006)
21. Michiardi, P., Molva, R.: Core: a collaborative reputation mechanism to enforce node cooperation in mobile Ad Hoc networks. In: Jerman-Blažič, B., Klobučar, T. (eds.) Advanced Communications and Multimedia Security. ITI-FIP, vol. 100, pp. 107–121. Springer, Boston, MA (2002). https://doi.org/10.1007/978-0-387-35612-9_9
22. Grünert, A., Hudert, S., Köning, S., Kaffille, S., Wirtz, G.: Decentralized reputation management for cooperating software agents in open multi-agent systems. In: ITSSA, vol. 1, No. 4, pp. 363–368 (2006)
23. Repantis, T., Kalogeraki, V.: Decentralized trust management for ad-hoc peer-to-peer networks. In: Proceedings of the 4th International Workshop of Middleware for Pervasive and Ad-hoc Computing, MPAC, p. 6. ACM (2006)
24. Gollmann, D.: Why trust is bad for security. Electron. Notes Theor. Comput. Sci. **157**(3), 3–9 (2016)
25. Soska, K., Kwon, A., Christin, N., Devadas, S.: Beaver: A Decentralized Anonymous Marketplace with Secure Reputation (2016)

26. DeFigueiredo, D.D.B., Barr, E.T.: TrustDavis: a non-exploitable online reputation system. In: CEC, vol. 5, pp. 274–283 (2005)
27. Fugger, R.: Money as IOUs in social trust networks & a proposal for a decentralized currency network protocol (2004). http://archive.ripple-project.org/decentralizedcurrency.pdf
28. Schartz, D., Youngs, N., Britto, A.: The Ripple protocol consensus algorithm. White Paper, Ripple Labs Inc., vol. 5 (2014)
29. Mazieres, D.: The stellar consensus protocol: a federated model for internet-level consensus. Stellar Development Foundation (2015)
30. Narayanan, A., Shmatikov, V.: De-anonymizing social networks. In: Proceedings of the 30th Symposium on Security and Privacy, pp. 173–187. IEEE (2009). http://dx.doi.org/10.1109/SP.2009.22
31. Malavolta, G., Moreno-Sanchez, P., Kate, A., Maffei, M.: SilentWhispers: Enforcing Security and Privacy in Decentralized Credit Networks (2016)
32. Moreno-Sanchez, P., Kate, A., Maffei, M., Pecina, K.: Privacy preserving payments in credit networks. In: Network and Distributed Security Symposium (2015)
33. Konforty, D., Adam, Y., Estrada, D., Meredith, L.G.: Synereo: The Decentralized and Distributed Social Network (2015)

A Smart Contract for Boardroom Voting with Maximum Voter Privacy

Patrick McCorry$^{(\boxtimes)}$, Siamak F. Shahandashti, and Feng Hao

School of Computing Science, Newcastle University, Newcastle upon Tyne, UK
{patrick.mccorry,siamak.shahandashti,feng.hao}@ncl.ac.uk

Abstract. We present the first implementation of a decentralised and self-tallying internet voting protocol with maximum voter privacy using the Blockchain. The Open Vote Network is suitable for boardroom elections and is written as a smart contract for Ethereum. Unlike previously proposed Blockchain e-voting protocols, this is the first implementation that does not rely on any trusted authority to compute the tally or to protect the voter's privacy. Instead, the Open Vote Network is a self-tallying protocol, and each voter is in control of the privacy of their own vote such that it can only be breached by a full collusion involving all other voters. The execution of the protocol is enforced using the consensus mechanism that also secures the Ethereum blockchain. We tested the implementation on Ethereum's official test network to demonstrate its feasibility. Also, we provide a financial and computational breakdown of its execution cost.

1 Introduction

Ethereum is the second most popular cryptocurrency with a $870m market capitalisation as of November 2016. It relies on the same innovation behind Bitcoin [28]: namely, the Blockchain which is an append-only ledger. The Blockchain is maintained by a decentralised and open-membership peer-to-peer network. The purpose of the Blockchain was to remove the centralised role of banks for maintaining a financial ledger. Today, researchers are trying to re-use the Blockchain to solve further open problems such as coordinating the Internet of Things [20], carbon dating [6], and healthcare [10].

In this paper, we focus on decentralised internet voting using the Blockchain. E-voting protocols that support verifiability normally assume the existence of a public bulletin board that provides a consistent view to all voters. In practice, an example of implementing the public bulletin board can be seen in the yearly elections of the International Association of Cryptologic Research (IACR) [22]. They use the Helios voting system [1] whose bulletin board is implemented as a single web server. This server is trusted to provide a consistent view to all voters. Instead of such a trust assumption, we explore the feasibility of using the Blockchain as a public bulletin board. Furthermore, we consider a decentralised election setting in which the voters are responsible for coordinating the communication amongst

© International Financial Cryptography Association 2017
A. Kiayias (Ed.): FC 2017, LNCS 10322, pp. 357–375, 2017.
https://doi.org/10.1007/978-3-319-70972-7_20

themselves. Thus, we also examine the suitability of the Blockchain's underlying peer-to-peer network as a potential authenticated broadcast channel.

There already exist proposals to use a Blockchain for e-voting. The Abu Dhabi Stock Exchange is launching a Blockchain voting service [19] and a recent report [3] by the Scientific Foresight Unit of the European Parliamentary Research Service discusses whether Blockchain-enabled e-voting will be a transformative or incremental development. In practice, companies such as The Blockchain Voting Machine [18], FollowMyVote [2] and TIVI [34] propose solutions that use *the Blockchain as a ballot box* to store the voting data.

These solutions achieve *voter privacy* with the involvement of a trusted authority. In FollowMyVote, the authority obfuscates the correspondence between the voter's real world identity and their voting key. Then, the voter casts their vote in plaintext. In TIVI, the authority is required to shuffle the encrypted votes before decrypting and counting the votes. In our work, we show that the voter's privacy does not need to rely on a central authority to decouple the voter's real world identity from their voting key, and the votes can be counted without the cooperation of a central authority. Furthermore, these solutions only use the Blockchain as an append-only and immutable global database to store the voting data. We propose that the network's consensus that secures the Blockchain can also enforce the execution of the voting protocol itself.

To date, both Bitcoin and Ethereum have inherent scalability issues. Bitcoin only supports a maximum of 7 transactions per second [8] and each transaction dedicates 80 bytes for storing arbitrary data. On the other hand, Ethereum explicitly measures computation and storage using a gas metric, and the network limits the gas that can be consumed by its users. As deployed today, these Blockchains cannot readily support storing the data or enforcing the voting protocol's execution for national scale elections. For this reason, we chose to perform **a feasibility study of a boardroom election** over the Blockchain which involves a small group of voters (i.e. 40 participants) whose identities are publicly known before the voting begins. For example, a boardroom election may involve stakeholders voting to appoint a new director.

We chose to implement the boardroom voting protocol as a smart contract on Ethereum. These smart contracts have an expressive programming language and the code is stored directly on the Blockchain. Most importantly, all peers in the underlying peer-to-peer network independently run the contract code to reach consensus on its output. This means that voters can potentially not perform all the computation to verify the correct execution of the protocol. Instead, the voter can trust the *consensus computing* provided by the Ethereum network to enforce the correct execution of the protocol. This enforcement turns *detection* measures seen in publicly verifiable voting protocols into *prevention* measures.

Our contributions. We provide the first implementation of a decentralised and self-tallying internet voting protocol. The Open Vote Network [17] is a board-room scale voting protocol that is implemented as a smart contract in Ethereum. The Open Vote Network provides maximum voter privacy as an individual vote can only be revealed by a full-collusion attack that involves compromising all other voters; all voting data is publicly available; and the protocol allows the tally to be computed without requiring a tallying authority. Most importantly, our implementation demonstrates the feasibility of using the Blockchain for decentralised and secure e-voting.

2 Background

2.1 Self-tallying Voting Protocols

Typically, an e-voting protocol that protects the voter's privacy relies on the role of a trustworthy authority to decrypt and tally the votes in a verifiable manner. E-voting protocols in the literature normally distribute this trust among multiple tallying authorities using threshold cryptography; for example, see Helios [1]. However, voters still need to trust that the tallying authorities do not collude altogether, as in that case, the voter's privacy will be trivially breached.

Remarkably, Kiayias and Yung [24] first introduced a *self-tallying* voting protocol for boardroom voting with subsequent proposals by Groth [16] and Hao et al. [17]. A self-tallying protocol converts tallying into an open procedure that allows any voter or a third-party observer to perform the tally computation once all ballots are cast. This removes the role of a tallying authority in an election as anyone can compute the tally without assistance. These protocols provide *maximum ballot secrecy* as a full collusion of the remaining voters is required to reveal an individual vote and *dispute-freeness* that allows any third party to check whether a voter has followed the voting protocol correctly. Unfortunately, self-tallying protocols have a fairness drawback as the last voter can compute the tally before anyone else[1] which results in both *adaptive* and *abortive* issues.

The adaptive issue is that knowledge of the tally can potentially influence how the last voter casts their vote. Kiayias and Yung [24] and Groth [16] propose that an election authority can cast the final vote which is excluded from the tally. However, while this approach is applicable to our implementation discussed later, it effectively re-introduces an authority that is trusted to co-operate and not to collude with the last voter. Instead, we implement an optional round that requires all voters to hash their encrypted vote and store it in the Blockchain as a commitment. As a result, the final voter can still compute the tally, but is unable to change their vote.

The abortive issue is that if the final voter is dissatisfied with the tally, they can abort without casting their vote. This abortion prevents all other voters and third parties from computing the final tally. Previously, Kiayias and Yung [24] and Khader et al. [23] proposed to correct the effect of abortive voters by engaging the rest of the voters in an additional recovery round. However, the recovery round requires full cooperation of all the remaining voters, and will fail if any member drops out half-way. We highlight that the Blockchain and

---

[1] It is also possible for voters that have not yet cast their vote to collude and compute the partial tally of the cast votes. For simplicity, we discuss a single voter in regards to the fairness issue.

smart contracts can enforce a financial incentive for voter participation using a deposit and refund paradigm [25]. This allows providing a new countermeasure to address the abortive issue: all voters deposit money into a smart contract to register for an election and are refunded upon casting their vote. Any voter who does not vote before the voting deadline simply loses their deposit.

In the next section we present Open Vote Network [17] before discussing its smart contract implementation on Ethereum. We chose to implement this protocol instead of others (e.g., [16,24]) because it is the most efficient boardroom voting protocol in the literature in each of the following aspects: the number of rounds, the computation load per voter and the bandwidth usage [17]. As we will detail in Sect. 3, the efficiency of the voting protocol is critical as even with the choice of the most efficient boardroom voting protocol, its implementation for a small-scale election is already nearing the capacity limit of an *existing* Ethereum block.

2.2   The Open Vote Network Protocol

The Open Vote Network is a decentralized two-round protocol designed for supporting small-scale boardroom voting. In the first round, all voters register their intention to vote in the election, and in the second round, all voters cast their vote. The systems assumes an authenticated broadcast channel is available to all voters. The self-tallying property allows anyone (including non-voters) to compute the tally after observing messages from the other voters. In this paper, we only consider an election with two options, e.g., yes/no. Extending to multiple voting options, and a security proof of the protocol can be found in [17].

A description of the Open Vote Network is as follows. First, all n voters agree on (G, g) where G denotes a finite cyclic group of prime order q in which the Decisional Diffie-Hellman (DDH) problem is intractable, and g is a generator in G. A list of eligible voters $(P_1, P_2, ..., P_n)$ is established and each eligible voter P_i selects a random value $x_i \in_R \mathbb{Z}_q$ as their private voting key.

Round 1. Every voter P_i broadcasts their voting key g^{x_i} and a (non-interactive) zero knowledge proof $ZKP(x_i)$ to prove knowledge of the exponent x_i on the public bulletin board. $ZKP(x_i)$ is implemented as a Schnorr proof [32] made non-interactive using the Fiat-Shamir heuristic [15].

At the end, all voters check the validity of all zero knowledge proofs before computing a list of reconstructed keys:

$$Y_i = \prod_{j=1}^{i-1} g^{x_j} / \prod_{j=i+1}^{n} g^{x_j}$$

Implicitly setting $Y_i = g^{y_i}$, the above calculation ensures that $\sum_i x_i y_i = 0$.

Round 2. Every voter broadcasts $g^{x_i y_i} g^{v_i}$ and a (non-interactive) zero knowledge proof to prove that v_i is either no or yes (with respect to 0 or 1) vote.

This one-out-of-two zero knowledge proof is implemented using the Cramer, Damgård and Schoenmakers (CDS) technique [7].

All zero knowledge proofs must be verified before computing the tally to ensure the encrypted votes are well-formed. Once the final vote has been cast, then anyone (including non-voters) can compute $\prod_i g^{x_i y_i} g^{v_i}$ and calculate $g^{\sum_i v_i}$ since $\prod_i g^{x_i y_i} = 1$ (see [17]). The discrete logarithm of $g^{\sum_i v_i}$ is bounded by the number of voters and is a relatively small value. Hence the tally of yes votes can be calculated subsequently by exhaustive search.

Note that for the election tally to be computable, all the voters who have broadcast their voting key in Round 1 must broadcast their encrypted vote in Round 2. Also note that in Round 2, the last voter to publish their encrypted vote has the ability to compute the tally before broadcasting their encrypted vote (by simulating that he would send a no-vote). Depending on the computed tally, he may change his vote choice. In our implementation, we address this issue by requiring all voters to commit to their votes before revealing them, which adds another round of commitment to the protocol.

The decentralised nature of the Open Vote Network makes it suitable to implement over a Blockchain. Bitcoin's blockchain could be used as the public bulletin board to store the voting data for the Open Vote Network. However, this requires the voting protocol to be externally enforced by the voters. Instead, we propose using Ethereum to enforce the voting protocol's execution. This is possible as conceptually Ethereum can be seen as a global computer that can store and execute programs. These programs are written as smart contracts, and their correct execution is enforced using the same network consensus that secures the Ethereum blockchain. Furthermore, its underlying peer-to-peer network can act as an authenticated broadcast channel.

2.3   Ethereum

In this section, we focus on the types of accounts available, the transaction structure and the Blockchain protocol used in Ethereum.

Ethereum has two account types:

- An **externally owned account (user-controlled)** is a public-private key pair controlled by the user. We denote these accounts by $A, B, \ldots$.
- A **contract account** is a smart contract that is controlled by its code. We denote a smart contract account by λ.

Both account types can store the Ethereum currency 'ether'. Ethereum does not perform computation in a contract without user interaction. As such, a contract account must be activated by a user-controlled account before its code can be executed. Executing code requires the user-controlled account to purchase 'gas' using the ether currency and a gas price set by the user determines the conversion rate of ether to gas. The cost of gas is essentially a transaction fee to encourage miners to include the code execution in the Blockchain. Most importantly, gas is a metric that standardises the cost of executing code on the network and each assembly operation (opcode) has a fixed gas cost based on its expected execution time.

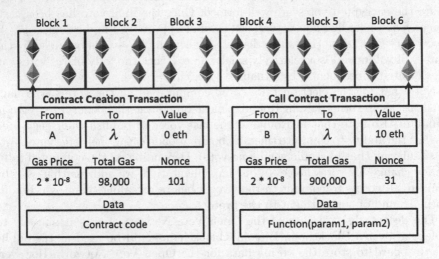

Fig. 1. Alice creates a smart contract on the Blockchain and the contract code is sent in the transaction's 'data' field. The contract is given an address λ. Bob can call a function of the contract using a second transaction sending gas to the address λ.

An **Ethereum Transaction**'s structure can be seen in Fig. 1. Each field of the transaction is described below:

- **From:** A signature from a user-controlled account to authorise the transaction.
- **To:** The receiver of the transaction and can be either a user-controlled or contract address.
- **Data:** Contains the contract code to create a new contract or execution instructions for the contract.
- **Gas Price:** The conversion rate of purchasing gas using the ether currency.
- **Total Gas:** The maximum amount of gas that can be consumed by the transaction.
- **Nonce:** A counter that is incremented for each new transaction from an account.

The Ethereum blockchain is considered an orderly transaction-based state machine. If multiple transactions call the same contract, then the contract's final state is determined by the order of transactions that are stored in the block. Strictly, Ethereum's blockchain is a variation of the GHOST protocol [33] which is a tree-based blockchain. This tree has a main branch of blocks that is represents the 'Blockchain' and transactions in these blocks determine the final state of contracts and account balances. Similar to Bitcoin, the security of the

Blockchain relies upon miners providing a 'proof of work' which authorises the miner to append a new block. This proof of work is a computationally difficult puzzle, and the miner is rewarded 5 ether if the block is successfully appended.

Blocks are created approximately every twelve seconds in Ethereum which is significantly faster than Bitcoin's 10 min interval. As a consequence, it is probabilistically more likely that two or more blocks are created by different miners at the same time. In Bitcoin, only one of the competing blocks can be accepted into the Blockchain, and the remaining blocks are discarded. However, in Ethereum, these discarded blocks are appended to the Blockchain as leaf nodes ('uncle blocks'). It should be noted that the uncle block still rewards the miner a proportion of the 5 ether block reward based on when the block is included in the Blockchain.

Ethereum's blockchain provides a natural platform for the Open Vote Network. It provides a public bulletin board and an authenticated broadcast channel which are necessary in decentralised internet voting protocols to support coordination amongst voters. As well, almost all computations in the Open Vote Network are public computations that can be written as a smart contract. Most importantly, the entire execution of the voting protocol is enforced by the same consensus that secures the Blockchain. In the next section, we discuss our implementation and the feasibility of performing internet voting over the Blockchain.

3   The Open Vote Network over Ethereum

We present an implementation of the Open Vote Network over Ethereum. The code is publicly available[2]. Three HTML5/JavaScript pages are developed to provide a browser interface for all voter interactions. The web browser interacts with an Ethereum daemon running in the background. The protocol is executed in five stages, and requires voter interaction in two (and an optional third) rounds. We give an overview of the implementation in the following.

3.1   Structure of Implementation

There are two smart contracts that are both written in Ethereum's Solidity language. The first contract is called the voting contract. It implements the voting protocol, controls the election process and verifies the two types of zero knowledge proofs we have in the Open Vote Network. The second contract is called the cryptography contract. It distributes the code for creating the two types of zero knowledge proofs[3]. This provides all voters with the same cryptography code that can be used locally without interacting with the Ethereum network. We have also provided three HTML5/JavaScript pages for the users:

---

[2] https://github.com/stonecoldpat/anonymousvoting.
[3] We have included the code to create and verify the two types of zero knowledge proofs in the cryptography contract. The code is independent of the Open Vote Network and can be used by other smart contracts.

- **Election administrator** (`admin.html`) administers the election. This includes establishing the list of eligible voters, setting the election question, and activating a list of timers to ensure the election progresses in a timely manner. The latter includes notifying Ethereum to begin registration, to close registration and begin the election, and to close voting and compute the tally.
- **Voter** (`vote.html`) can register for an election, and once registered must cast their vote.
- **Observer** (`livefeed.html`) can watch the election's progress consisting of the election administrator starting and closing each stage and voters registering and casting votes. The running tally is not computable.

We assume that voters and the election administrator have their own Ethereum accounts. The Web3 framework is provided by the Ethereum Foundation to facilitate communication between a user's web browser and their Ethereum client. The user can unlock their Ethereum account (decrypt their Ethereum's private key using a password) and authorise transactions directly from the web browser. There is no need for the user to interact with an Ethereum wallet, and the Ethereum client can run in the background as a daemon.

3.2   Election Stages

Figure 2 presents the five stages of the election in our implementation. The smart contract has a designated owner that represents the election administrator. This administrator is responsible for authenticating the voters with their user-controlled account and updating the list of eligible voters. A list of timers is enforced by the smart contract to ensure that the election progresses in a timely manner. The contract only allows eligible voters to register for an election, and registered voters to cast a vote. Furthermore, the contract can require each voter to deposit ether upon registration, and automatically refund the ether when their vote is accepted into the Blockchain. Each stage of the election is described in more detail below:

SETUP. The election administrator authenticates each voter with their user-controlled account and updates the voting contract to include a whitelist of accounts as eligible voters. He defines a list of timers to ensure that the election progresses in a timely manner:

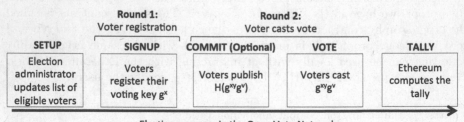

Fig. 2. There are five stages to the election.

- $t_{finishRegistration}$: all voters must register their voting key g^{x_i} before this time.
- $t_{beginElection}$: the election administrator must notify Ethereum to begin the election by this time.
- $t_{finishCommit}$: all voters must commit to their vote $H(g^{x_i y_i} g^{v_i})$ before this time. This is only used if the optional COMMIT stage is enabled.
- $t_{finishVote}$: all voters must cast their vote $g^{x_i y_i} g^{v_i}$ before this time.
- π: a minimum length of time in which the commitment and voting stages must remain active to give voters sufficient time to vote.

The administrator also sets the registration deposit d, the voting question, and if the optional COMMIT stage should be enabled. Finally, the administrator notifies Ethereum to transition from the SETUP to the SIGNUP stage.

SIGNUP. All eligible voters can choose to register for the vote after reviewing the voting question and other parameters set by the election administrator. To register, the voter computes their voting key g^{x_i} and $ZKP(x_i)$. Both the key and proof are sent to Ethereum alongside a deposit of d ether. Ethereum does not accept any registrations after $t_{finishRegistration}$. The election administrator is responsible for notifying Ethereum to transition from the SIGNUP to either the optional COMMIT or the VOTE stage. All voter's reconstructed keys $g^{y_0}, g^{y_1}, ..., g^{y_n}$ are computed by Ethereum during the transition.

COMMIT (Optional). All voters publish a hash of their vote $H(g^{x_i y_i} g^{v_i})$ to the Ethereum blockchain. The contract automatically transitions to the VOTE stage once the final commitment is accepted into the Blockchain.

VOTE. All voters publish their (encrypted) vote $g^{x_i y_i} g^{v_i}$ and a one-out-of-two zero knowledge proof to prove that v_i is either zero or one. The deposit d is refunded to the voter when their vote is accepted by Ethereum. The election administrator notifies Ethereum to compute the tally once the final vote is cast.

TALLY. The election administrator notifies Ethereum to compute the tally. Ethereum computes the product of all votes $\prod_i g^{x_i y_i} g^{v_i} = g^{\sum_i v_i}$ and brute forces the discrete logarithm of the result to find the number of yes votes.

As mentioned before, Open Vote Network requires all the registered voters to cast a vote to enable tally calculation. The deposit d in our implementation provides a financial incentive for registered voters to vote. This deposit is returned to the voter if they follow through with the voting protocol and do not drop out. The list of timestamps defined by the election administrator determines if the voter's deposit d is forfeited or refunded. There are three refund scenarios if a deadline is missed:

- Registered voters can claim their refund if the election does not begin by $t_{beginElection}$.
- Registered voters who have committed can claim their refund if not all registered voters commit to their vote by $t_{finishCommit}$.
- Registered voters can claim their refund if not all registered voters cast their vote by $t_{finishVote}$.

4 Design Choices

In this section, we discuss the design choices we made when developing the implementation. In particular, we elaborate on some attack vectors that are addressed in our smart contract and clarify the trust assumptions that are required for our implementation to be secure.

Individual and public verifiability. We assume that the voter's machine, including their web browser, is not compromised. The voter has an incentive to ensure their machine is secure. If the machine or web browser is compromised, the voter's ether is likely to be stolen. The voter can check that their vote has been *recorded as cast* and *cast as intended* by inspecting the Blockchain and decrypting their vote using the key x_i. Also, the voter, or any observer for that matter, can independently compute the tally to verify that the cast votes have been *tallied as recorded*. Unfortunately, this public verifiability does not provide any coercion resistance as the voting is conducted in a "unsupervised" environment. The voter may vote under the direct duress of a coercer who stands over their shoulder. The voter can also reveal x to prove how their vote was cast to others. As such, in a similar fashion to Helios [1], we note that our implementation is only suitable for low-coercion elections.

Voter authentication. Smart contracts can call other smart contracts. As a result, there exist two methods to identify the caller. The first is `tx.origin` that identifies the user-controlled account that authorised the transaction, and not the immediate caller. The second is `msg.sender` that identifies the immediate caller which can be a contract or a user-controlled address. Initially, a developer might use `tx.origin` as it appears the appropriate choice to identify the voter. Unfortunately, this approach allows a malicious smart contract to impersonate the voter and register for an election.

To illustrate, a voter is given the interface to a smart contract called BettingGame. This lets the voter place a bet using `BettingGame.placeBid()`. Unknowingly to the voter, if this function is called, then BettingGame will call `TheOpenVoteNetwork.register()` and register a voting key on behalf of the voter. To overcome this issue, we recommend using `msg.sender` as it identifies the immediate caller whose address should be in the list of eligible voters.

Defending against replay attacks. All voting keys g^{x_i} and their zero knowledge proofs $ZKP(x_i)$ are publicly sent to the Ethereum blockchain. A potential attack is that another eligible voter can attempt to register the same voting keys by replaying g^{x_i} and $ZKP(x_i)$. This would also let them later copy the targeted voter's vote. We highlight that the commitment (i.e., input arguments to the hash function) in the zero knowledge proof includes `msg.sender` and Ethereum will not accept the zero knowledge proof $ZKP(x_i)$ if `msg.sender` does not match the account that is calling the contract. As such, it is not possible to replay another voter's key g^{x_i} without their co-operation. This also applies to the one-out-of-two zero knowledge proofs.

Blocking re-entrancy. A hacker recently exploited a re-entrancy vulnerability in theDAO to steal over 3.6 million ether. Luu et al. highlight [26] that 186 distinct smart contracts stored on the Blockchain (including theDAO) are also potentially vulnerable. This attack relies on the contract sending ether to the user before deducting their balance. The attacker can recursively call the contract in such a way that the sending of ether is repeated, but the balance is only deducted once. To prevent this attack, we follow the advice of Reitwiessner [30] to first deduct the voter's balance before attempting to send the ether.

The role of timers. The election administrator sets a list of timers to allow Ethereum to enforce that the election progresses in a timely manner. A minimum time interval π (unit in seconds) is set during the SETUP stage to ensure each stage remains active for at least a time interval of length π. In particular, the rules $t_{finishCommit} - t_{beginElection} > \pi$ and $t_{finishVote} - t_{finishCommit} > \pi$ are enforced to provide sufficient time for voters to commit to and cast their vote. Also, it provides a window for the voter's transaction to be accepted into the Blockchain. This is necessary to prevent a cartel of miners ($<51\%$) attempting to censor some transactions. Voters need to check that π is not a small value such as $\pi = 1$. In this case, the voting stage can finish one second after the election begins. As a result, all voters are likely to lose their deposits. Of course, both the COMMIT and VOTE stage can finish early if all voters have participated.

The block's timestamp is used to enforce the above timers. Ethereum has a tight bound on the timestamp which must conform to the following two rules. First, a new block's timestamp must be greater than the previous block. Second, the block's timestamp must be less than the user's local clock. Furthermore, the miner's ability to drift a block's timestamp by 900 s (15 min) as reported in [26] is no longer possible [11].

Ethereum miners. The tip of the Blockchain is uncertain and the state of a contract at the time of signing a transaction is not guaranteed to remain the same. Furthermore, miners control the order of transactions in a block, and can control the order of a contract's execution if there are two or more transactions calling the same contract. Although the order of voting keys or casting a vote does not matter, the order of transactions is important if a timer is about to expire. For example, if the voter attempts to register around the time that $t_{finishRegistration}$ expires, then the miner can prevent the registration in two ways. First, the miner can choose a block timestamp that expires the $t_{finishRegistration}$ timer. Second, if the miner has the voter's registration transaction and the election administrator's begin election transaction, he can order the transactions in the block such that the smart contract begins the election before allowing the voter to register for the election. Unfortunately, in both cases, the voter's registration will fail.

It is important that voters authorise their transactions in good time before the stage is destined to end. We must assume that the majority of miners are not attempting to disrupt the election. A smaller cartel of miners ($<51\%$) can potentially delay transactions being accepted into the Blockchain using techniques such as selfish mining [14,31] or feather forking [29]. This ability of miners to delay a transaction is a fundamental problem for any contract.

The election administrator. An election administrator is required to add voters to the list of eligible voters, set the election's parameters and to begin the registration stage. Unfortunately, smart contracts cannot execute code without the notification of an external user-controlled account. As such, a user is still required to notify the smart contract to begin the election and compute the tally. Deciding who is responsible for notifying Ethereum is an implementation trade-off and we have assumed it is the election administrator's role. If necessary, the contract can be modified to allow any registered voter to perform the notification. However, in that case it is possible that two or more voters attempt to notify Ethereum at the same time and broadcast transactions to the network. If this happens, only one transaction can begin the election or compute the tally. All unsuccessful transactions will still be stored in the Blockchain and all the broadcasting users will still be charged transaction fees.

Removing the COMMIT stage. The COMMIT stage prevents the final voter computing the tally and using this information to decide how to vote. It is possible to remove this stage if we require the election administrator (or a separate external party) to perform some extra tasks. In this case, the administrator is the first voter to register a voting key g^x and deposit of d ether before voter registration begins. Next, he is required to merely reveal his secret x once all voters have cast their vote. Revealing x allows Ethereum to calculate a final dummy vote and compute the tally. The administrator is now trusted not to collude with the last voter. This approach removes the COMMIT phase but requires extra an trust assumption.

Do voters need to use Ethereum? Today, all voters need to download the full Ethereum blockchain to confirm the voting protocol is being executed correctly. In the future, voters will be able to use the Light Ethereum Subprotocol (LES) [12] which is similar to Bitcoin's simplified payment verification (SPV) protocol. In LES, voters will only verify the voting protocol's state and not be required to store the full Blockchain.

Most importantly, it is possible for the voter to participate in the voting protocol without the full Blockchain. In this case, the voter merely broadcasts their transactions and trusts the consensus mechanism of the Ethereum network to enforce the correct execution of the protocol. This would enable voters who have devices with limited resources to vote in our implementation. We have provided `livefeed.html` to allow voters to visit an external website and confirm their registration or vote has been recorded in the Blockchain.

5   Experiment on Ethereum's Test Network

Our implementation was deployed on Ethereum's official test network that mimics the production network. We sent 126 transactions to simulate forty voters participating in the protocol. Each transaction's computational and financial cost is outlined in Table 1. Each transaction by the election administrator (denoted by the prefix 'A:' in the table) is broadcast only once, and each transaction by a voter (denoted by the prefix 'V:' in the table) is broadcast once per voter, i.e., a total of 40 times. Also, we have rounded the cost in US Dollars (denoted by $) to two decimal places.

Table 1. A breakdown of the costs for 40 participants using the Open Vote Network. We have approximated the cost in USD ($) using the conversion rate of 1 ether = $11 and the gas price of 0.00000002 ether which are the real world costs in November 2016. Also, we have identified the cost for the election administrator 'A' and the voter 'V'.

Entity: Transaction	Cost in Gas	Cost in $
A: VoteCon	3,779,963	0.83
A: CryptoCon	2,435,848	0.54
A: Eligible	2,153,461	0.47
A: Begin Signup	234,984	0.05
V: Register	763,118	0.17
A: Begin Election	3,085,449	0.68
V: Commit	70,112	0.02
V: Vote	2,490,412	0.55
A: Tally	746,485	0.16
Administrator total	12,436,190	2.74
Voter total	3,323,642	0.73
Election total	145,381,858	31.98

We had to split the Open Vote Network into two contracts as the code was too large to store in an Ethereum block which has a capacity of approximately 4.7 million gas. The voting contract VoteCon (80% of block capacity, and $0.83 transaction fee) contains the protocol logic. The cryptography contract CryptoCon (52% of block capacity, and $0.54 transaction fee) contains the code to create and verify the two types of zero knowledge proofs we have in the protocol.

CryptoCon can be reused by other contracts requiring similar zero knowledge proofs. It is important to note that the code for computing the zero knowledge proofs is run locally on the voter's machine, and no transactions are sent to the network. CryptoCon's purpose is to ensure that all voters have access to the same cryptography code.

As the figures show, voter registrations and vote casting cost around 16% and 53% of block capacity, respectively. This suggests that the current block sizes in Ethereum support at most six voter registration per block and at most one vote casting per block. Recall that blocks are currently generated in Ethereum at a rate of one block per 12 s.

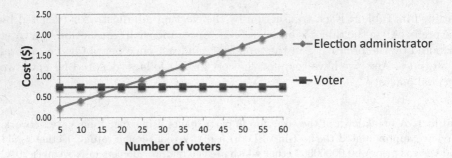

Fig. 3. The average cost for the election administrator and the voter based on the number of voters participating in the election.

Overall, running the election with 40 voters costs the election administrator $2.74. The total election cost including the cost for the administrator and the voters is $31.98 which breaks down to a reasonable cost of $0.73 per voter.

To see how the cost for the election administrator and the voter vary with different number of voters we have carried out experiments with 5, 10, 15,..., 60 voters. Figure 3 highlights the distribution of cost for the election administrator and the voter based on the number of voters participating in the election. This shows that the election administrator's cost increases linearly based on the number of voters, and the voter's cost remains constant.

All testing was performed on the test network due to an ongoing DoS attack, starting from 22 September 2016, on Ethereum's production network [5]. Miners set the block's gas limit to 1,500,000 gas to reduce the impact on the network and a hard fork [4] was deployed on 18 October 2016 to prevent the attack. However, a second DoS attack began on 19 October 2016. Ethereum developers have recommended a temporary gas limit of 2,000,000 until the next scheduled hard fork. As such, the Open Vote Network cannot run on the production network at this time.

5.1   Timing Analysis

Table 2 outlines the timing analysis measurements for tasks in the Open Vote Network. All measurements were performed on a MacBook Pro running OS X 10.10.5 equipped with 4 cores, 2.3 GHz Intel Core i7 and 16 GB DDR3 RAM. All time measurements are rounded up to the next whole millisecond. We use the Web3 framework to facilitate communication between the web browser and the Ethereum daemon. All tasks are executed using .call() that allows us to measure the code's computation time on the local daemon.

The cryptography smart contract is responsible for creating the zero knowledge proofs for the voter. The time required to create the proofs is 81 ms for the Schnorr proof and 461 ms for the one-out-of-two zero knowledge proof. These actions are always executed using .call() as this contract should never receive transactions.

Table 2. A time analysis for actions that run on the Ethereum daemon.

Action	Avg. time (ms)
Create ZKP(x)	81
Register voting key	142
Begin election	277
Create 1-out-of-2 ZKP	461
Cast vote	573
Tally	132

The voting smart contract is responsible for enforcing the election process. Registering a vote involves verifying the Schnorr zero knowledge proof and in total requires 142 ms. To begin the election requires computing the reconstructed public keys which takes 277 ms in total for forty voters. Casting a vote involves verifying the one-out-of-two zero knowledge proof which requires 573 ms. Tallying involves summing all cast votes and brute-forcing the discrete logarithm of the result and on average takes around 132 ms.

We decided to distribute the cryptography code using the Ethereum blockchain to allow all voters to use the same code. Running the code on the voter's local daemon is significantly slower than using a seperate library such as OpenSSL. For example, creating a Schnorr signature using OpenSSL on a comparable machine requires 0.69 ms [27]. This slowness is mostly due to the lack of native support for elliptic curve math in Ethereum smart contracts. The Ethereum Foundation has plans to include native support and we expect this to significantly improve our reported times.

6   Discussion on Technical Difficulties

In this section, we discuss the difficulties faced while implementing the Open Vote Network on Ethereum.

Lack of support for cryptography. Ethereum supports up to 256-bit unsigned integers. For this reason, we chose to implement the protocol over an elliptic curve instead of a finite field. However, Solidity does not currently support Elliptic Curve cryptography, and we had to include an external library to perform the computation. Including the library led to our voting contract becoming too large to store on the Blockchain. As previously discussed, we separated the program into two smart contracts: one voting contract and one cryptography contract. The cryptographic computations are expensive and this results in a block only being able to support six voter registrations, or a single vote.

Call stack issues. The call stack of a program has a hard-coded limit of 1024 stack frames. This limits the amount of local memory available, and the number of function calls allowed. These limitations led to difficulty while implementing the 1-out-of-2 ZKP as the temporary variables typically required exceeded the hard-coded limit of 16 local variables [21]. We had to use variables extremely sparingly to ensure that the 1-out-of-2 ZKP could be implemented.

Lack of debugging tools. The Mix IDE that provides a solidity source code debugger has been discontinued [13] and could not be used for our work. Remix is the replacement for the Mix IDE and it provides a debugger for contracts at the assembly level, but this is too low for debugging Solidity contracts. Instead, we had to create `Events` that log data along with the contract to help with debugging which is incorporated into the contract before deployment.

Mitigate loss of voting key. The voting key is kept secret by the voter and needs to be stored on their local machine. This is important to ensure that if the voter's web browser crashes or is closed, then the voting key is not lost. We provide a standalone Java program `votingcodes.jar` to generate the voting key and store it in `votingcodes.txt`. The voter is required to upload this file to their web browser.

Maximum number of voters. Figure 4 demonstrates the results of our experiment and highlights the breakdown of the election administrator's gas consumption. Except for opening registration, the gas cost for each task increases linearly with the number of voters. The gas limit for a block was set at 4.7 million gas by the miners before the recent DoS attacks. This means that the smart contract reaches the computation and storage limit if it is computing the voter's reconstructed keys for around sixty registered voters. This limit exists as all keys are computed in a single transaction and the gas used must be less than the block's gas limit. To avoid reaching this block limit, we currently recommend a safe upper limit of around 50 voters. However, the contract can be modified to perform the processing in batches and allow multiple transactions to complete the task.

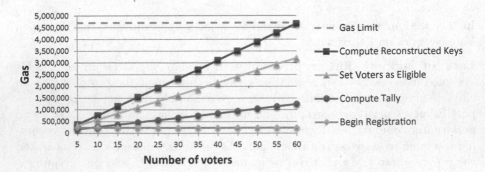

Fig. 4. The gas cost for the election administrator based on the number of voters participating in the election.

7   Conclusion

In this paper, we have presented a smart contract implementation for the Open Vote Network that runs on Ethereum. Our implementation was tested on the official Ethereum test network with forty simulated voters. We have shown that our implementation can be readily used with minimal setup for elections at a cost of $0.73 per voter. The cost can be considered reasonable as this voting protocol provides maximum voter privacy and is publicly verifiable. This is the first implementation of a decentralised internet voting protocol running on a Blockchain. It uses the Ethereum blockchain not just as a public bulletin board, but more importantly, as a platform for *consensus computing* that enforces the correct execution of the voting protocol.

In future work, we will investigate the feasibility of running a national-scale election over the Blockchain. Based on the knowledge gained from this paper, we believe that if such a perspective is ever considered possible, its implementation will almost certainly require a dedicated Blockchain. For example, this can be an Ethereum-like blockchain that only stores the e-voting smart contract. This new blockchain can have a larger block size to store more transactions on-chain and may be maintained in a centralised manner similar to RSCoin [9].

Acknowledgements. The second and third authors are supported by the European Research Council (ERC) Starting Grant (No. 306994). We would like to thank Nick Johnson for taking the time to answer questions about Ethereum, Solidity and the test-framework Dapple. We thank Maryam Mehrnezhad and Ehsan Toreini for their support in this work during the Economist Case Study Challenge, Malte Möser for his comments on an early draft of the paper, and the anonymous reviewers for their constructive feedback.

References

1. Adida, B.: Helios: web-based open-audit voting. In: USENIX Security Symposium, vol. 17, pp. 335–348 (2008)
2. Aradhya, P.: Distributed Ledger Visible to All? Ready for Blockchain? Huffington Post, April 2016
3. Boucher, P.: What if blockchain technology revolutionised voting? Scientific Foresight Unit (STOA), European Parliamentary Research Service, September 2016. http://www.europarl.europa.eu/RegData/etudes/ATAG/2016/581918/EPRS_ATA(2016)581918_EN.pdf
4. Buterin, V.: Long-term gas cost changes for IO-heavy operations to mitigate transaction spam attacks. Ethereum Blog, October 2016. https://github.com/ethereum/EIPs/issues/150. Accessed 01 Nov 2016
5. Buterin, V.: Transaction spam attack: next steps. Ethereum Blog, September 2016. https://blog.ethereum.org/2016/09/22/transaction-spam-attack-next-steps/
6. Clark, J., Essex, A.: CommitCoin: carbon dating commitments with Bitcoin. In: Keromytis, A.D. (ed.) FC 2012. LNCS, vol. 7397, pp. 390–398. Springer, Heidelberg (2012). https://doi.org/10.1007/978-3-642-32946-3_28

7. Cramer, R., Damgård, I., Schoenmakers, B.: Proofs of partial knowledge and simplified design of witness hiding protocols. In: Desmedt, Y.G. (ed.) CRYPTO 1994. LNCS, vol. 839, pp. 174–187. Springer, Heidelberg (1994). https://doi.org/10.1007/3-540-48658-5_19

8. Croman, K., et al.: On scaling decentralized blockchains. In: Clark, J., Meiklejohn, S., Ryan, P.Y.A., Wallach, D., Brenner, M., Rohloff, K. (eds.) FC 2016. LNCS, vol. 9604, pp. 106–125. Springer, Heidelberg (2016). https://doi.org/10.1007/978-3-662-53357-4_8

9. Danezis, G., Meiklejohn, S.: Centrally banked cryptocurrencies. In: 23nd Annual Network and Distributed System Security Symposium, NDSS 2016 (2016)

10. Ekblaw, A., Azaria, A., Halamka, J.D., Lippman, A.: A case study for blockchain in healthcare: MedRec prototype for electronic health records and medical research data (2016). http://dci.mit.edu/assets/papers/eckblaw.pdf. Accessed 26 Oct 2016

11. Eth: How do Ethereum mining nodes maintain a time consistent with the network? Ethereum Wiki, June 2016. https://github.com/ethereum/wiki/wiki/Light-client-protocol. Accessed 6 Feb 2017

12. Ethereum: Light client protocol. Ethereum Wiki, May 2016. https://github.com/ethereum/wiki/wiki/Light-client-protocol

13. Ethereum: The mix Ethereum DApp development tool. GitHub (2016). https://github.com/ethereum/mix. Accessed 10 Oct 2016

14. Eyal, I., Sirer, E.G.: Majority is not enough: Bitcoin mining is vulnerable. In: Christin, N., Safavi-Naini, R. (eds.) FC 2014. LNCS, vol. 8437, pp. 436–454. Springer, Heidelberg (2014). https://doi.org/10.1007/978-3-662-45472-5_28

15. Fiat, A., Shamir, A.: How to prove yourself: practical solutions to identification and signature problems. In: Odlyzko, A.M. (ed.) CRYPTO 1986. LNCS, vol. 263, pp. 186–194. Springer, Heidelberg (1987). https://doi.org/10.1007/3-540-47721-7_12

16. Groth, J.: Efficient maximal privacy in boardroom voting and anonymous broadcast. In: Juels, A. (ed.) FC 2004. LNCS, vol. 3110, pp. 90–104. Springer, Heidelberg (2004). https://doi.org/10.1007/978-3-540-27809-2_10

17. Hao, F., Ryan, P.Y., Zielinski, P.: Anonymous voting by two-round public discussion. IET Inf. Secur. 4(2), 62–67 (2010)

18. Hertig, A.: The first Bitcoin voting machine is on its way. Motherboard Vice, November 2015. http://motherboard.vice.com/read/the-first-bitcoin-voting-machine-is-on-its-way

19. Higgins, S.: Abu Dhabi stock exchange launches blockchain voting. CoinDesk, October 2016. http://www.coindesk.com/abu-dhabi-exchange-blockchain-voting/

20. Higgins, S.: IBM invests $200 million in blockchain-powered IoT. CoinDesk, October 2016. http://www.coindesk.com/ibm-blockchain-iot-office/

21. Horrocks, R.: Error while compiling: stack too deep. Ethereum Stack Exchange, June 2015. http://ethereum.stackexchange.com/a/6065

22. International Association for Cryptologic Research: About the Helios System, October 2016. http://www.iacr.org/elections/eVoting/about-helios.html

23. Khader, D., Smyth, B., Ryan, P.Y., Hao, F.: A fair and robust voting system by broadcast. In: 5th International Conference on Electronic Voting, vol. 205, pp. 285–299. Gesellschaft für Informatik (2012)

24. Kiayias, A., Yung, M.: Self-tallying elections and perfect ballot secrecy. In: Naccache, D., Paillier, P. (eds.) PKC 2002. LNCS, vol. 2274, pp. 141–158. Springer, Heidelberg (2002). https://doi.org/10.1007/3-540-45664-3_10

25. Kumaresan, R., Bentov, I.: How to use Bitcoin to incentivize correct computations. In: Proceedings of the 2014 ACM SIGSAC Conference on Computer and Communications Security, pp. 30–41. ACM (2014)

26. Luu, L., Chu, D.-H., Olickel, H., Saxena, P., Hobor, A.: Making smart contracts smarter. In: Proceedings of the 2016 ACM SIGSAC Conference on Computer and Communications Security, pp. 254–269. ACM (2016)

27. McCorry, P., Shahandashti, S.F., Clarke, D., Hao, F.: Authenticated key exchange over Bitcoin. In: Chen, L., Matsuo, S. (eds.) SSR 2015. LNCS, vol. 9497, pp. 3–20. Springer, Cham (2015). https://doi.org/10.1007/978-3-319-27152-1_1

28. Nakamoto, S.: Bitcoin: a peer-to-peer electronic cash system, November 2008. https://bitcoin.org/bitcoin.pdf. Accessed 01 Jan 2015

29. Narayanan, A., Bonneau, J., Felten, E., Miller, A., Goldfeder, S.: Bitcoin and Cryptocurrency Technologies. Princeton University Press, Princeton (2016)

30. Reitwiessner, C.: Smart contract security, June 2016. https://blog.ethereum.org/2016/06/10/smart-contract-security/

31. Sapirshtein, A., Sompolinsky, Y., Zohar, A.: Optimal selfish mining strategies in Bitcoin. In: Grossklags, J., Preneel, B. (eds.) FC 2016. LNCS, vol. 9603, pp. 515–532. Springer, Heidelberg (2017). https://doi.org/10.1007/978-3-662-54970-4_30

32. Schnorr, C.-P.: Efficient signature generation by smart cards. J. Cryptol. 4(3), 161–174 (1991)

33. Sompolinsky, Y., Zohar, A.: Secure high-rate transaction processing in Bitcoin. In: Böhme, R., Okamoto, T. (eds.) FC 2015. LNCS, vol. 8975, pp. 507–527. Springer, Heidelberg (2015). https://doi.org/10.1007/978-3-662-47854-7_32

34. Business Wire: Now you can vote online with a selfie. Business Wire, October 2016. http://www.businesswire.com/news/home/20161017005354/en/Vote-Online-Selfie

Improving Authenticated Dynamic Dictionaries, with Applications to Cryptocurrencies

Leonid Reyzin[1,3]($\boxtimes$), Dmitry Meshkov[2], Alexander Chepurnoy[2], and Sasha Ivanov[3]

[1] Boston University, Boston, USA
reyzin@bu.edu
[2] IOHK Research, Sestroretsk, Russia
{dmitry.meshkov,alex.chepurnoy}@iohk.io
[3] Waves Platform, Moscow, Russian Federation
sasha@wavesplatform.com

Abstract. We improve the design and implementation of two-party and three-party authenticated dynamic dictionaries and apply these dictionaries to cryptocurrency ledgers.

A public ledger (blockchain) in a cryptocurrency needs to be easily verifiable. However, maintaining a data structure of all account balances, in order to verify whether a transaction is valid, can be quite burdensome: a verifier who does not have the large amount of RAM required for the data structure will perform slowly because of the need to continually access secondary storage. We demonstrate experimentally that authenticated dynamic dictionaries can considerably reduce verifier load. On the other hand, per-transaction proofs generated by authenticated dictionaries increase the size of the blockchain, which motivates us to find a solution with most compact proofs.

Our improvements to the design of authenticated dictionaries reduce proof size and speed up verification by 1.4–2.5 times, making them better suited for the cryptocurrency application. We further show that proofs for multiple transactions in a single block can compressed together, reducing their total length by approximately an additional factor of 2.

We simulate blockchain verification, and show that our verifier can be about 20 times faster than a disk-bound verifier under a realistic transaction load.

1 Introduction

The Motivating Application. A variety of cryptocurrencies, starting with Bitcoin [Nak08], are based on a public ledger of the entire sequence of all transactions that have ever taken place. Transactions are verified and added to this ledger by nodes called *miners*. Multiple transactions are grouped into blocks before being added, and the ledger becomes a chain of such blocks, commonly known as a *blockchain*.

© International Financial Cryptography Association 2017
A. Kiayias (Ed.): FC 2017, LNCS 10322, pp. 376–392, 2017.
https://doi.org/10.1007/978-3-319-70972-7_21

If a miner adds a block of transactions to the blockchain, other miners verify that every transaction is valid and correctly recorded before accepting the new block. (Miners also perform other work to ensure universal agreement on the blockchain, which we do not address here.) However, not only miners participate in a cryptocurrency; others watch the blockchain and/or perform partial verification (e.g., so-called light nodes, such as Bitcoin's SPV nodes [Nak08, Sect. 8]). It is desirable that these other participants are able to check a blockchain with full security guarantees on commodity hardware, both for their own benefit and because maintaining a large number of nodes performing full validation is important for the health of the cryptocurrency [Par15]. To verify each transactions, they need to know the balance of the payer's account.

The simple solution is to have every verifier maintain a dynamic dictionary data structure of (key, value) pairs, where keys are account addresses (typically, public keys) and values are account balances. Unfortunately, as this data structure grows, verifiers need to invest into more RAM (and thus can no longer operate with commodity hardware), or accept significant slowdowns that come with storing data structures in secondary storage. These slowdowns (especially the ones caused by long disk seek times in an adversarially crafted set of transactions) have been exploited by denial of service attacks against Bitcoin [Wik13] and Ethereum [But16].

Authenticated Dictionaries to the Rescue. We propose using cryptographically authenticated data structures to make *verifying* transactions in the blockchain much cheaper than *adding* them to the blockchain. Cheaper verification benefits not only verifiers, but also miners: in a multi-token blockchain system (where tokens may represent, for example, different currencies or commodities), such as Nxt [nxt], miners may choose to process transactions only for some types of tokens, but still need to verify all transactions.

Specifically, we propose storing balance information in a *dynamic authenticated dictionary*. In such a data structure, *provers* (who are, in our case, miners) hold the entire data structure and modify it as transactions are processed, publishing *proofs* that each transaction resulted in the correct modification of the data structure (these proofs will be included with the block that records the transaction). In contrast, *verifiers*, who hold only a short *digest* of the data structure, verify a proof and compute the new digest that corresponds to the new state of the data structure, without ever having to store the structure itself. We emphasize that with authenticated data structures, the verifier can perform these checks and updates without trusting the prover: the verification algorithm will reject any attempt by a malicious prover or man-in-the-middle who tries to fool the verifier into accepting incorrect results or making incorrect modifications. In contrast to the unauthenticated case discussed above, where the verifier must store the entire data structure, here verifier storage is minimal: 32 bytes suffice for a digest (at 128-bit security level), while each proof is only a few hundred bytes long and can be discarded immediately upon verification.

1.1   Our Contributions

A Better Authenticated Dictionary Data Structure. Because reducing block size a central concern for blockchain systems [CDE+16, DW13], we focus on reducing the length of a modification proof, which must be included into the block for each transaction. Moreover, because there is no central arbiter in a blockchain network, we require an authenticated data structure that can work without any assumptions about the existence of a trusted author or setup and without any secret keys (unlike, for example, [PTT16, BGV11, CF13, CLH+15, MWMS16, CLW+16]). And, because miners may have incentives to make verification more time-consuming for others, we prefer data structures whose performance is independent of the choices made by provers.

We design and implement an authenticated dictionary data structure requiring no trusted setup or authorship whose proofs are, on average, 1.4 times shorter than authenticated skip lists of [PT07] and 2.5 times shorter than the red-black trees of [CW11]. Moreover, our prover and verifier times are faster by the same factor than corresponding times for authenticated skip lists, and, unlike the work of [PT07], our data structure is deterministic, not permitting the prover to bias supposedly random choices in order to make performance worse for the verifier. In fact, our data structure's *worst-case* performance is comparable to the *expected-case* performance of [PT07]. Our work was inspired by the dynamic Merkle [Mer89] trees of [NN00, AGT01, CW11, MHKS14] in combination with the classic tree-balancing algorithm of [AVL62].

We further reduce proof length per operation when putting together proofs for multiple operations. For example, when proofs for 1000 operations on a 1 000 000-entry dictionary are put together, our proof length is cut almost by half.

Our setting of authenticated data structures—in which verifiers are able to compute the new digest after modifications—is often called the "two-party" case (because there are only two kinds of parties: provers and verifiers). It should not be confused with the easier "three-party" case addressed in multiple works [Mer89, NN00, GT00, GTS01, AGT01, MND+04, GPT07, CW11], in which verifiers are simply given the new digest after modifications (e.g., by a trusted data owner). While we design primarily for the two-party case, our results can be used also in the three-party case, and can, for example, replace authenticated skip lists of [GTS01] in both two-party and three-party applications that rely on them (e.g., [BP07, GPTT08, HPPT08, EK13] and many others), improving performance and removing the need for randomization.

Application to Blockchains. We consider a multi-token blockchain system (unlike Bitcoin, which has bitcoins as the only tokens) with accounts in which balances can grow or shrink over time (again, unlike Bitcoin, in which a transaction output must be spent all at once). One example of such a system is Nxt [nxt]. For each token type t, there is an authenticated data structure S_t maintaining balances of all accounts, locally stored by miners who are interested in the ability to add transactions for that token type. All miners, regardless of interest, maintain a local copy of the short digest of S_t.

In order to publish a block with a number of transactions, a miner adds to the block the proof of validity of these transactions, including the proofs of correct updates to S_t, and also includes the new digest of S_t into the block header. All miners, as well as verifiers, verify the proof with respect to the digest they know and check that the new digest in the block header is correct. (It is important to note that verification of transactions includes other steps that have nothing to do with the data structure, such as verifying the signature of the payer on the transaction; these steps do not change.) In contrast to simple payment verification nodes [Nak08, Sect. 8] in Bitcoin, who cannot fully verify the validity of a new block because they do not store all unspent outputs, our verifiers can do so without storing any balance information.

While there have been many proposals to use authenticated data structures for blockchains (see, e.g., [Tod16, Mil12] and references therein), not many have suggested publishing proofs for modifications to the data structure. At a high level, our approach is similar to (but considerably more efficient than) the proposal by White [Whi15], who suggests building a trie-based authenticated data structure for Bitcoin (although he does not use those terms).

Because of our improved authenticated data structure, provers[1] and verifiers are more efficient, and proofs are shorter, than they would be with previous solutions. We show that whenever a block includes multiple transactions for a given token, their proofs can be combined, further reducing the amount of space used per transaction, by about a factor of 2 for realistic conditions. We benchmark block generation verification and demonstrate that verifying the authenticated data structure can be about 20 times faster than maintaining a full on-disk unauthenticated data structure, while generating proofs does not add much to a miner's total cost.

Reducing the Cost of a Miner's Initial Setup. A new miner Molly wishing to join the network has to download the entire blockchain and verify the validity of every block starting from the first (so-called "genesis") block. It is not necessary to verify the validity of every transaction, because the presence of the block in the blockchain assures Molly that each transaction was verified by other miners when the block was added. However, without authenticated data structures, Molly still needs to download and replay all the transactions in order to establish the up-to-date amount held in each account and be able to validate future transactions.

Our solution allows Molly to reduce communication, computation, and memory costs of joining the network, by permitting her to download not entire blocks with their long lists of transactions, but only the block headers, which, in addition to demonstrating that the block has been correctly generated and linked to

---

[1] How much efficiency of proof generation matters depends on the cryptocurrency design. In those cryptocurrencies for which every miner attempts to generate a block (such as Bitcoin), it matters a lot, because every miner has to run the proof generation procedure. On the other hand, in those cryptocurrencies for which the miner wins a right to generate a block before the block is produced (such as ones based on proof of stake [BGM16, KKR+16]), only one miner per block will generate proofs.

the chain, contain the digest of all the transactions processed and digests of every authenticated data structure S_t that has changed since the previous block. This information is enough to start validating future transactions. If Molly wants to not only validate, but also process transactions for tokens of type t, she needs to obtain the full S_t; importantly, however, she does not need a trusted source for this data, because she can verify the correctness of S_t against the digest.[2]

2   The Model for Two-Party Authenticated Dictionaries

Given the variety of security models for authenticated data structures, let us briefly explain ours (to the best of our knowledge, it was first implicitly introduced in [BEG+91] and more explicitly in [GSTW03, PT07]; it is commonly called the *two-party* model; see [Pap11] for an overview of the relevant literature).

Each state of the data structure is associated with an efficiently computable *digest*; it is computationally infeasible to find two different states of the data structure that correspond to the same digest. There are two types of parties: *provers* and *verifiers*. The provers possess the data structure, perform operations on it, and send *proofs* of these operations to verifiers, who, possessing only the digest of the current state of the data structure, can use a proof to obtain the result of the operation and update their digests when the data structure is modified. The security goal is to ensure that malicious provers can never fool verifiers into accepting incorrect results or computing incorrect digests. Importantly, neither side generates or possesses any secrets.

A secondary security goal (to prevent denial of service attacks by provers who may have more computing resources than verifiers) is to ensure that a malicious prover cannot create proofs (whether valid or not) that take the verifier more time to process than a prespecified upper bound.

Importantly, the model assumes that the verifiers and the provers agree on which data structure operations need to be performed (in our cryptocurrency application, the operations will come from the transactions, and the verifier will check whether the operations themselves are valid by, for example, checking the signature and account balance of the payer). A verifier is not protected if she performs an operation that is different from the prover's, because she may still compute a valid new digest; she will notice this difference only if she is able to see that her new digest is different from the prover's new digest. The model also assumes that the verifier initially has the correct digest (for example, by

---

[2] Ethereum [Woo14] adds the digest of the current state of the system to each block, but, because it does not implement proofs for data structure modifications, this digest cannot be used unless the miner downloads the entire state of the system—although, importantly, this state may be downloaded from an untrusted source and verified against the digest. Miller et al. [MHKS14, Appendix A] suggested using authenticated data structures to improve memory usage, but not communication or computation time, of Bitcoin's initial setup.

maintaining it continuously starting with the initial empty state of the data structure).

The specific data structure we wish to implement is a dictionary (also known as a map): it allows insertion of (key, value) pairs (for a new key), lookup of a value by key, update of a value for a given key, and deletion by key.

We provide formal security definitions in the full version [RMCI16].

3 Our Construction

Despite a large body of work on authenticated data structures, to the best of our knowledge, only two prior constructions—those of [PT07] (based on skip lists) and [MHKS14] (based on skip lists and red-black trees)—address our exact setting. As mentioned in the introduction, many other works address the three-party setting (which we also improve), in which modifications are performed by a trusted author and only lookups are performed by the provers, who trust the digest. Some works also propose solutions requiring a secret key that remains unknown to the prover.

We will explain our construction from the viewpoint of unifying prior work and applying a number of optimizations to existing ideas. The explanation here is terse for lack of space; a more detailed and accessible explanation is available in the full version of the paper [RMCI16].

Starting Point: Merkle Tree. We start with a Merkle tree [Mer89] (not necessarily perfectly balanced) with leaves storing (key, value) pairs, sorted by key. Each internal node stores the minimum of its right subtree to enable searching like in binary search trees (the same way as in [NN00, AGT01, MHKS14], but not in [CW11], where (key, value) pairs are stored also in internal nodes, which, as we demonstrate below in Sect. 4, results in longer proofs). To ensure every non-leaf has two children, and every insertion creates a new internal node with an existing left leaf and a new right leaf, we start with a $-\infty$ sentinel. To enabling proving nonmembership of a key (in particular, during insertion), each leaf stores the next key in addition to its own.

Updates and Simple Insertions. If the prover updates the value stored at a leaf (for example, subtracting from it money used for a transaction), the authenticating path for the leaf already contains all the information needed to compute the new digest. Thus, the proof for an update is the same as the proof for a lookup. Similarly for insertions: as long as an insertion doesn't require rebalancing the tree, the authenticating path to the leaf where insertion took place already contains the information necessary to compute the new digest.

3.1 Our Improvements

Observation 1: Use Tree-Balancing Operations that Stay on Path. A variety of algorithms for balancing binary search trees exist. Here we focus on AVL trees [AVL62], red-black trees [GS78] (and their left-leaning variant [Sed08]), and treaps [SA96] (and their equivalent randomly-balanced binary search trees [MR98]). They all maintain some extra information in the nodes that enables the insertion and deletion algorithms to make a decision as to whether, and how, to perform tree rotations in order to maintain a reasonably balanced tree. We will add this information to the hash function input for computing the label of each node and to the authenticating path. For insertions, we observe that if the tree balancing operation rotates only ancestors of the newly inserted leaf, and does not use or modify information in any other nodes, then the authenticating path already has sufficient information for the verifier to perform the insertion and the tree-balancing operation. This is the case for AVL trees and treaps, but not for red-black trees.

However, of all the balanced tree options, only red-black trees have been implemented in our setting [MHKS14], and this implementation sometimes must access the color of a node that is not an ancestor of the newly inserted leaf. According to Miller [Mil16], proofs for insertions in the red-black trees of [MHKS14] are therefore approximately three times longer than proofs for lookups. Other balancing approaches enable us to keep insertion proofs short.

Observation 2: Do Not Hash Internal Keys. To verify that a particular leaf is present (which is all we need for both positive and negative answers), the verifier does not need to know how the leaf was found—only that it is connected to the root via an appropriate hash chain. Therefore, like the authors of [PT07] (and many works in the three-party setting), we do not add the keys of internal nodes into the hash input, and do not put them into the proof. This is in contrast to the work of [MHKS14], whose general approach requires the label to depend on the entire contents of a node, and therefore requires keys of internal nodes to be sent to the verifier, so that the verifier can compute the labels. When keys do not take up much space (as in [MHKS14]), the difference between sending the key of an internal node and sending the direction (left or right) that the search path took is small. However, when keys are comparable in length to labels (as in the cryptocurrency application, because they are account identifiers, computed as hash function outputs or public keys), this difference can mean nearly a factor of two in the proof length.

Observation 3: Skip Lists are Just a Variant of Treaps. Dean and Jones [DJ07] observed that skip lists [Pug90] are equivalent to binary search trees. This view enables us to test the performance of skip lists and treaps with essentially the same implementation, which no prior implementation has done. (More details are provided in [RMCI16]).

Observation 4: Deterministic is Better. Treaps and skip lists perform well in expectation when the priorities (for treaps) and levels (for skip lists) are chosen at random, independently of the keys in the data structure. However, if an adversary is able to influence or predict the random choices, performance guarantees no longer hold. In our setting, the problem is that the provers and verifiers need to somehow agree on the randomness used. (This is not a problem for the three-party setting, where the randomness can be supplied by the trusted author).

Prior work in the three-party model suggested choosing priorities and levels by applying hash functions to the keys [CW11, Sect. 3.1.1]. However, since inserted keys may be influenced by the adversary, this method of generating randomness may give an attacker the ability to make the data structure very slow and the proofs very long, effectively enabling a denial of service attack. To eliminate this attack by an external adversary, we could salt the hash function after the transactions are chosen for incorporation into the data structure (for example, including a fresh random salt into each the block header). However, an internal adversary still presents a problem: the prover choosing this salt and transactions would have the power to make the data structure less efficient for everyone by choosing a bad salt, violating our secondary security goal stated in Sect. 2.

Observation 5: AVL Trees Outperform on the Most Relevant Parameters. Regardless of the tree balancing method (as long as it satisfies observations 1 and 2), costs of lookups, updates, and insertions are determined simply by the depth of the relevant leaf, because the amount of nodes traversed, the size of the proof, and the number of hashes performed by both provers and verifiers is directly proportional to this depth.

The average-case distance between the root and a random leaf for both AVL and red-black trees after the insertion of n random keys is very close to the optimal $\log_2 n$ [Knu98, p. 468], [Sed08]. The worst-case distance for red-black trees is twice the optimal [Sed08], while the worst-case distance for AVL trees is 1.44 times the optimal [Knu98, p. 460]. In contrast, the expected (not worst-case!) distance for treaps and skip lists is 1.5 times the optimal [Pug90]. Thus, AVL trees, even the *worst case*, are better than treaps and skip lists *in expectation*.

Observation 6: Proofs for Multiple Operations Can Be Compressed. When multiple operations on the data structure are processed together, their proofs can be compressed. A verifier will not need the label of any node more than once. Moreover, the verifier will not need the label of any node that lies on the path to a leaf in another proof (because it will be computed during the verification of that proof). Nor will the verifier need the label of any node that is created by the verifier (for example, if there is an insertion into the right subtree of the root, then the verifier will replace the right child of the root with a new node and will thus know its label when the label is needed for a proof about some subsequent operation on the left subtree).

Performing this compression is nontrivial (generic compression algorithms, as used in [MHKS14] and reported to us by [Mil16], can take care of repeated labels, but will not perform the other optimizations). Our approach for compressing a batch of operations is described in [RMCI16].

Putting these observations together, we obtain the data structure to implement: an AVL tree with values stored only at the leaves, sometimes known as an AVL+ tree. We implement this data structure and compare it against other options in the next section. We prove its security in [RMCI16].

4   Implementation and Evaluation

We implemented our AVL+ trees, as well as treaps and our tree-based skip lists, in the Scala [sca] programming language using the Blake2b [ANWOW13] hash function with 256-bit (32-byte) outputs. Our implementation is available at [cod][3]. For the AVL+ implementation, we used the textbook description [Wei06] with the same balance computation procedure as in [Pfa02, Chap. 5]. We ran experiments by measuring the cost of 1000 random insertions (with 26-byte keys and 8-byte values), into the data structure that already had size $n = 0, 1000, 2000, \ldots, 999000$ keys in it.

As expected, the length of the path from the root to a random leaf in the n-leaf AVL+ tree was only 2–3% worse than the optimal $\log_2 n$. In contrast, the length of the path in a skip list was typically about 44% worse than optimal, and in a treap about 32% worse than optimal.

Proof length for a single operation. The average length of our proof for inserting a new key into a 1 000 000-node tree with 32-byte hashes, 26-byte keys, and 8-byte values, is 753 bytes. We now explain this number and compare it to prior work.

Note that for a path of length k, the proof consists of:

- k labels (which are hash values),
- $k + 1$ symbols indicating whether the next step is right or left, or we are at a leaf with no next step (these fit into two bits each),
- k pieces of balance or level information (these fit into two bits for an AVL+ tree, but require a byte for skip lists and three or four bytes for treaps),
- the leaf key, the next leaf key, and the value stored in the leaf node (the leaf key is not needed in the proof for lookups and updates of an existing key, although our compression technique of Observation 6 will include it anyway, because it does not keep track of why a leaf was reached)

Thus, the proof length is almost directly proportional to the path length: with the 32-byte hashes, 26-byte keys, and 8-byte values, the proof takes $34k+61$ bytes assuming we don't optimize at bit level, or about k bytes fewer if we do (our implementation currently does not). Note that the value of k for $n = 1\,000\,000$ is about 20 for AVL+ trees and about 29 for skip lists, which means that AVL-tree-based proofs are about 1.4 times

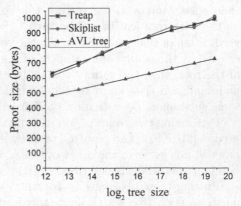

---

[3] Note that the implementation of AVL+ trees with proof compression for a batch of multiple operations is fully featured, while the other implementations (contained in subdirectory "legacy") are sufficient to perform the measurements reported in this paper, but are missing features, such as deletions, error handling, and compression of multiple proofs.

shorter than skip-list-based ones. Treap proofs have slightly smaller k, but this advantage is completely negated in our experiments by the extra bytes needed to write down the level.

Proof length for deletions is more variable (because the deletion operation goes to two neighboring leaves and may also need off-path nodes for rotations), but is on average 50 bytes greater than for insertions, lookups, and updates.

Proof Length Comparison with Existing Work. Our numbers are consistent with those reported by Papamanthou and Tamassia [PT07, Sect. 4], who also report paths of length 30 for skip lists with 1 000 000 entries. (They use a less secure hash function whose output length is half of ours, resulting in shorter proofs; if they transitioned to a more secure hash function, their proofs would be about the same length as our skip-list-based proofs, thus 1.4 times longer than our AVL+-based proofs).

Direct comparison with the work of [MHKS14] is harder, because information on proof length for a single insertion in red-black trees is not provided in [MHKS14] (what is reported in [MHKS14] is the result of off-the-shelf data compression by gzip [GA] of the concatenation of proofs for 100 000 lookup operations). However, because keys of internal nodes are included in the proofs of [MHKS14], the proofs for lookups should be about 1.7 longer than in our AVL+ trees (for our hash and key lengths). According to [Mil16], the proofs for insertions for the red-black trees of [MHKS14] are about 3 times longer than for lookups (and thus about 5 times longer than proofs for insertions in our AVL+ trees). Of course, the work [MHKS14] has the advantage of being generic, allowing implementation of any data structure, including AVL+ trees, which should reduce the cost of insertions to that of lookups; but, being generic, it cannot avoid sending internal keys, so the cost of lookups will remain.

We can also compare our work with work on three-party authenticated data structures, because our data structure also works in the three-party model (but not vice versa: three-party authenticated data structures do not work in our model, because they do not allow the verifier to compute the new digest, though some can be adapted to do so). Work based on skip lists, such as [AGT01, GTS01, GPT07], has proof sizes that are the same as the already-mentioned [PT07], and therefore our improvement is about the same factor of 1.4.

For three-party work based on red-black trees, there are two variants. The variant that stores values only at leaves, like we do, was implemented by Anagnostopoulos et al. [AGT01], who do not report proof length; however, we can deduce it approximately from the number of hashes reported in [AGT01, Fig. 6, "hashes per insertion"] and conclude that it is about 10–20% worse than ours. The variant that uses a standard binary search tree, with keys and values in every node, was implemented by [CW11] and had the shortest proofs among the data structures tested in [CW11]. The average proof length (for a positive answer) in [CW11] is about 1500 bytes when searching for a random key in a tree that starts empty and grows to 10^5 nodes, with 28-byte keys, values, and hashes. In contrast, our average proof size in such a scenario is only 593 bytes (an improvement of 2.5 times), justifying our decision to put all the values in the leaves.

Finally, Ethereum implements a Merkle patricia trie [Woo14, Appendix D] in a model similar to the three-party model (because it does not implement proofs for changes to the trie). In our experiments (which used the code from [Tea16, trie/proof.go] to generate proofs for the same parameter lengths as ours) using for n ranging from 2000 to 1 000 000, Ethereum's proofs for lookups were consistently over 3 times longer than our AVL+-

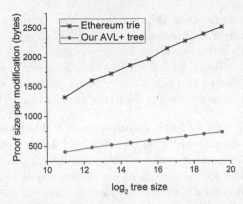

based ones. Tendermint's implementation of Merkle AVL+ trees [Kwo16] has no provisions for proving absence of a key (nor for proving any modifications, because it is in the three-party model), but appears to have roughly the same proof length as ours when we adjust for hash and key lengths.

Proof Length for Multiple Operations. Compressing together proofs for a batch of B operations at once (using Observation 6 in Sect. 3) reduces the proof length per operation by approximately $36 \cdot \log_2 B$ bytes. This improvement is considerably greater than what we could achieve by concatenating individual proofs and then applying gzip [GA], which, experimentally, never exceeded 150 bytes, regardless of the batch size. The improvements reported in this section and in Fig. 1 are for uniformly random keys; biases in key distribution can only help our compression, because they result in more overlaps among tree paths used during the operations.

For example, for $n = 1 000 000$, the combined proof for 1000 updates and 1000 inserts was only 358 bytes per operation. If a transaction in a block modifies two

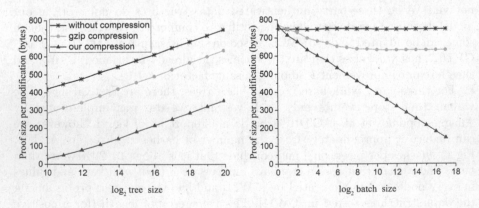

Fig. 1. Left: proof size per modification for $B = 2000$, as a function of starting tree size n. Right: proof size per modification for a tree with $n = 1 000 000$ keys, as a function of batch size B. In both cases, half of the modifications were inserts of new (key, value) pairs and half were changes of values for existing keys.

accounts, and there are 1 000 000 accounts and 1 000 transactions in the block (this number is realistic—see [tbp]), then we can obtain proofs of 716 bytes per transaction remaining at 128-bit security level. If some accounts are more active and participate in more than one transaction, then the per transaction space is even less, because repeated paths get compressed.

We can compare our results with those reported in Miller et al. [MHKS14, Fig. 13d], who report the results of batching together (using a "suspended disbelief" buffer to eliminate some labels and gzip to compress the stream) $B = 100\,000$ proofs for lookup operations on a red-black tree of size n ranging from 2^4 to 2^{21}. For these parameter ranges, our proofs are at least 2.4 times shorter, even though we use 1.6-times longer hashes, as well as longer keys and values. For example, for $n = 2^{21}$, our proofs take up 199 bytes per operation vs. 478 bytes of [MHKS14]. Proofs for insertions are even longer in [MHKS14], while in our work they are the same as for lookups. We emphasize, again, that the work of Miller et al. has the advantage of supporting general data structures.

Prover and Verifier Running times. The benchmarks below were run on an Intel(R) Core(TM) i7-5820K CPU @ 3.30 GHz Linux machine with 8 GB of RAM running in 64-bit mode and using only one core. We used Java 8.0.51 and compiled our Scala code with scalac 2.11.8. The Java implementation of Blake2b hash function was obtained from the official Blake website https://blake2.net/. The average prover (resp, verifier) time for inserting a random key into our AVL+ tree with 1 000 000 random keys was 31 μs (resp., 47 μs).

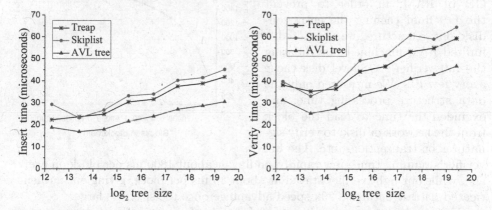

It is difficult to make comparisons of running times across implementations due the variations in hardware environments, programming language used, etc. Note, however, that regardless of those variables, the running times of the prover and verifier are closely correlated with path length k: the prover performs k key comparisons (to find the place to insert) and computes $k + 1$ hash values (to obtain the label of two new nodes and $k - 1$ existing nodes whose labels change), while the verifier performs two comparisons (with the keys of two neighboring leaves) and computes $2k + 1$ hash values (k to verify the proof and $k + 1$ to compute the new digest). Tree rotations do not change these numbers. Therefore, AVL+ trees perform about 1.4 times faster than skip lists.

When we batch multiple transactions together, prover and verifier times improve slightly as the batch size grows, in particular because labels of nodes need not be computed until the entire batch is processed, and thus labels of some nodes (the ones that are created and then replaced) are never computed.

Simulated Blockchain Proving and Verifying. We used a server (Intel(R) Core(TM) i7-5820K CPU @ 3.60 GHz Linux machine with 64 GB of RAM and SSD storage) to simulate two different methods of verifying account balances: simply maintaining a full on-disk (SSD) data structure of (key, value) pairs (similar to the process a traditional "full verifier" would perform) vs. maintaining only a digest of this data structure and verifying proofs for data structure operations, using very little RAM and no on-disk storage (similar to the process a "light verifier" would perform when provers use our AVL+ trees). The data structure was populated with 5 000 000 random 32-byte keys (with 8-byte values) at the start. Our simulated blocks contained 1500 updates of values for randomly chosen existing keys and 500 insertions of new random keys. We ran the simulation for 90 000 blocks (thus ending with a data structure of 50 000 000 keys, similar to Bitcoin UTXO set size [Lop] at the time of writing).

Both the full and the light verifier were limited to 1 GB of RAM. Because the actual machine had 64 GB of RAM, in order to prevent the OS from caching the entire on-disk data structure, we simulated a limited-RAM machine by invalidating the full verifier's OS-level disk cache every few 10 s. We measured only the data structure processing time, and excluded the time to read the block from the network or disk, to verify signatures on transactions, etc. The full

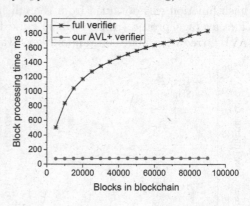

verifier's running time grew rapidly, ending at about 1800 ms per block on average, while our light verifier stayed at about 85 ms per block, giving our authenticated data structures a 20x speed advantage once the size gets large.

To make sure that generating proofs is feasible for a powerful machine, we also ran our prover, but permitted it to use up to 48 GB of RAM. The prover stayed at about 70 ms per block, which is a small fraction of a full node's total cost. For example, the cost to verify 1000 transaction signatures—just one of the many things a full node has to do in order to include transactions into a block—was 280 ms on the same machine (using the Ed25519 [BDL+12] signature scheme). The proofs size varied from 0.8 to 1.0 MB per block (i.e., 423–542 bytes per data structure operation).

5 Conclusion

We demonstrated the first significant performance improvement in two-party authenticated data structures since [PT07] and three-party authenticated data structures since [CW11]. We did so by showing that skip lists are simply a special case of the more general balanced binary search tree approach; finding a better binary search tree to use; and developing an algorithm for putting together proofs for multiple operations. We also demonstrated that our two-party authenticated data structures can be used to greatly improve blockchain verification by light nodes without adding much burden to full nodes—providing the first such demonstration in the context of cryptocurrencies.

Acknowledgements. We thank Andrew Miller for helpful and detailed explanations of his work [MHKS14], for running his code to get us comparison data, and for comments on our draft. We thank Peter Todd and Pieter Wuille for fascinating discussions.

References

[AGT01] Anagnostopoulos, A., Goodrich, M.T., Tamassia, R.: Persistent authenticated dictionaries and their applications. In: Davida, G.I., Frankel, Y. (eds.) ISC 2001. LNCS, vol. 2200, pp. 379–393. Springer, Heidelberg (2001). https://doi.org/10.1007/3-540-45439-X_26

[ANWOW13] Aumasson, J.-P., Neves, S., Wilcox-O'Hearn, Z., Winnerlein, C.: BLAKE2: simpler, smaller, fast as MD5. In: Jacobson, M., Locasto, M., Mohassel, P., Safavi-Naini, R. (eds.) ACNS 2013. LNCS, vol. 7954, pp. 119–135. Springer, Heidelberg (2013). https://doi.org/10.1007/978-3-642-38980-1_8

[AVL62] Adel'son-Vel'skii and Landis. An algorithm for the organization of information. Dokladi Akademia Nauk SSSR, 146(2), : English translation in Soviet Math. Doklady 3(1962), 1259–1263 (1962)

[BDL+12] Bernstein, D.J., Duif, N., Lange, T., Schwabe, P., Yang, B.-Y.: High-speed high-security signatures. J. Cryptographic Eng. 2(2), 77–89 (2012). https://ed25519.cr.yp.to/

[BEG+91] Blum, M., Evans, W.S., Gemmell, P., Kannan, S., Naor, M.: Checking the correctness of memories. In: 32nd Annual Symposium on Foundations of Computer Science, San Juan, Puerto Rico, 1–4 October 1991, pp. 90–99. IEEE Computer Society (1991). Later appears as [?], which is available at http://citeseerx.ist.psu.edu/viewdoc/summary?doi=10.1.1.29.2991

[BGM16] Bentov, I., Gabizon, A., Mizrahi, A.: Cryptocurrencies without proof of work. In: Clark, J., Meiklejohn, S., Ryan, P.Y.A., Wallach, D., Brenner, M., Rohloff, K. (eds.) FC 2016. LNCS, vol. 9604, pp. 142–157. Springer, Heidelberg (2016). https://doi.org/10.1007/978-3-662-53357-4_10

[BGV11] Benabbas, S., Gennaro, R., Vahlis, Y.: Verifiable delegation of computation over large datasets. In: Rogaway, P. (ed.) CRYPTO 2011. LNCS, vol. 6841, pp. 111–131. Springer, Heidelberg (2011). https://doi.org/10.1007/978-3-642-22792-9_7

[BP07] Di Battista, G., Palazzi, B.: Authenticated relational tables and authenticated skip lists. In: Barker, S., Ahn, G.-J. (eds.) DBSec 2007. LNCS, vol. 4602, pp. 31–46. Springer, Heidelberg (2007). https://doi.org/10.1007/978-3-540-73538-0_3

[But16] Buterin, V.: Transaction spam attack: Next steps (2016). https://blog.ethereum.org/2016/09/22/transaction-spam-attack-next-steps/

[CDE+16] Croman, K., Decker, C., Eyal, I., Gencer, A.E., Juels, A., Kosba, A., Miller, A., Saxena, P., Shi, E., Gün, E.: On scaling decentralized blockchains. In: Proceedings of 3rd Workshop on Bitcoin and Blockchain Research (2016)

[CF13] Catalano, D., Fiore, D.: Vector commitments and their applications. In: Kurosawa, K., Hanaoka, G. (eds.) PKC 2013. LNCS, vol. 7778, pp. 55–72. Springer, Heidelberg (2013). https://doi.org/10.1007/978-3-642-36362-7_5

[CLH+15] Chen, X., Li, J., Huang, X., Ma, J., Lou, W.: New publicly verifiable databases with efficient updates. IEEE Trans. Dependable Sec. Comput. 12(5), 546–556 (2015)

[CLW+16] Chen, X., Li, J., Weng, J., Ma, J., Lou, W.: Verifiable computation over large database with incremental updates. IEEE Trans. Comput. 65(10), 3184–3195 (2016)

[cod] Implementation of authenticated data structures within scorex. https://github.com/input-output-hk/scrypto/

[CW11] Crosby, S.A., Wallach, D.S.: Authenticated dictionaries: real-world costs and trade-offs. ACM Trans. Inf. Syst. Secur. 14(2), 17 (2011). http://tamperevident.cs.rice.edu/Storage.html

[DJ07] Dean, B.C., Jones, Z.H.: Exploring the duality between skip lists and binary search trees. In: John, D., Kerr, S.N. (eds.) Proceedings of the 45th Annual Southeast Regional Conference, 2007, Winston-Salem, North Carolina, USA, 23–24 March 2007, pp. 395–399. ACM (2007). https://people.cs.clemson.edu/~bcdean/skip_bst.pdf

[DW13] Decker, C., Wattenhofer, R.: Information propagation in the bitcoin network. In: IEEE P2P 2013 Proceedings, pp. 1–10. IEEE (2013)

[EK13] Etemad, M., Küpçü, A.: Database outsourcing with hierarchical authenticated data structures. In: Lee, H.-S., Han, D.-G. (eds.) ICISC 2013. LNCS, vol. 8565, pp. 381–399. Springer, Cham (2014). https://doi.org/10.1007/978-3-319-12160-4_23

[GA] Gailly, J.-L., Adler, M.: gzip. http://www.gzip.org/

[GPT07] Goodrich, M.T., Papamanthou, C., Tamassia, R.: On the cost of persistence and authentication in skip lists. In: Demetrescu, C. (ed.) WEA 2007. LNCS, vol. 4525, pp. 94–107. Springer, Heidelberg (2007). https://doi.org/10.1007/978-3-540-72845-0_8

[GPTT08] Goodrich, M.T., Papamanthou, C., Tamassia, R., Triandopoulos, N.: Athos: efficient authentication of outsourced file systems. In: Wu, T.-C., Lei, C.-L., Rijmen, V., Lee, D.-T. (eds.) ISC 2008. LNCS, vol. 5222, pp. 80–96. Springer, Heidelberg (2008). https://doi.org/10.1007/978-3-540-85886-7_6

[GS78] Guibas, L.J., Sedgewick, R.: A dichromatic framework for balanced trees. In: 19th Annual Symposium on Foundations of Computer Science, Ann Arbor, Michigan, USA, 16–18 October 1978, pp. 8–21. IEEE Computer Society (1978). http://professor.ufabc.edu.br/~jesus.mena/courses/mc3305-2q-2015/AED2-13-redblack-paper.pdf

[GSTW03] Goodrich, M.T., Shin, M., Tamassia, R., Winsborough, W.H.: Authenticated dictionaries for fresh attribute credentials. In: Nixon, P., Terzis, S. (eds.) iTrust 2003. LNCS, vol. 2692, pp. 332–347. Springer, Heidelberg (2003). https://doi.org/10.1007/3-540-44875-6_24

[GT00] Goodrich, M.T., Tamassia, R.: Efficient authenticated dictionaries with skip lists and commutative hashing. Technical report, Johns Hopkins Information Security Institute (2000). http://cs.brown.edu/cgc/stms/papers/hashskip.pdf

[GTS01] Goodrich, M.T., Tamassia, R., Schwerin, A.: Implementation of an authenticated dictionary with skip lists and commutative hashing. Presented in Proceedings of DARPA Information Survivability Conference and Exposition II (DISCEX II) (2001). http://cs.brown.edu/cgc/stms/papers/discex2001.pdf

[HPPT08] Heitzmann, A., Palazzi, B., Papamanthou, C., Tamassia, R.: Efficient integrity checking of untrusted network storage. In: Kim, Y., Yurcik, W. (eds.) Proceedings of the 2008 ACM Workshop On Storage Security and Survivability, StorageSS 2008, Alexandria, VA, USA, 31 October 2008, pp. 43–54. ACM (2008). http://www.ece.umd.edu/~cpap/published/alex-ber-cpap-rt-08b.pdf

[KKR+16] Kiayias, A., Konstantinou, I., Russell, A., David, B., Oliynykov, R.: A provably secure proof-of-stake blockchain protocol. Cryptology ePrint Archive, Report 2016/889 (2016). http://eprint.iacr.org/2016/889

[Knu98] Knuth, D.: The Art of Computer Programming: Volume 3: Sorting and Searching. Addison-Wesley, 2nd edition (1998)

[Kwo16] Kwon, J.: Tendermint go-merkle (2016). https://github.com/tendermint/go-merkle

[Lop] Lopp, J.: Unspent transactions outputs in Bitcoin. http://statoshi.info/dashboard/db/unspent-transaction-output-set. Accessed 7 Nov 2016

[Mer89] Merkle, R.C.: A certified digital signature. In: Brassard, G. (ed.) CRYPTO 1989. LNCS, vol. 435, pp. 218–238. Springer, New York (1990). https://doi.org/10.1007/0-387-34805-0_21

[MHKS14] Miller, A., Hicks, M., Katz, J., Shi, E.: Authenticated data structures, generically. In: Jagannathan, S., Sewell, P. (eds.) The 41st Annual ACM SIGPLAN-SIGACT Symposium on Principles of Programming Languages, POPL 2014, San Diego, CA, USA, 20–21 January 2014, pp. 411–424. ACM (2014). http://amiller.github.io/lambda-auth/paper.html

[Mil12] Miller, A.: Storing UTXOs in a balanced Merkle tree (zero-trust nodes with O(1)-storage) (2012). https://bitcointalk.org/index.php?topic=101734.msg1117428

[Mil16] Miller, A.: Private communication (2016)

[MND+04] Martel, C.U., Nuckolls, G., Devanbu, P.T., Gertz, M., Kwong, A., Stubblebine, S.G.: A general model for authenticated data structures. Algorithmica 39(1), 21–41 (2004). http://citeseerx.ist.psu.edu/viewdoc/summary?doi=10.1.1.75.3658

[MR98] Martínez, C., Roura, S.: Randomized binary search trees. J. ACM 45(2), 288–323 (1998). http://citeseer.ist.psu.edu/viewdoc/summary?doi=10.1.1.17.243

[MWMS16] Miao, M., Wang, J., Ma, J., Susilo, W.: Publicly verifiable databases with efficient insertion/deletion operations. J. Comput. Syst. Sci. (2016). http://dx.doi.org/10.1016/j.jcss.2016.07.005. To appear in print

[Nak08] Nakamoto, S.: Bitcoin: A peer-to-peer electronic cash system (2008). https://bitcoin.org/bitcoin.pdf

[NN00] Naor, M., Nissim, K.: Certificate revocation and certificate update. IEEE J. Sel. Areas Commun. **18**(4), 561–570 (2000). http://citeseerx.ist.psu.edu/viewdoc/summary?doi=10.1.1.41.7072

[nxt] The Nxt cryptocurrency. https://nxt.org/

[Pap11] Papamanthou, C.: Cryptography for efficiency: new directions in authenticated data structures. Ph.D. thesis, Brown University (2011). http://www.ece.umd.edu/cpap/published/theses/cpap-phd.pdf

[Par15] Parker, L.: The decline in bitcoin full nodes (2015). http://bravenewcoin.com/news/the-decline-in-bitcoins-full-nodes/

[Pfa02] Pfaff, B.: GNU libavl 2.0.2 (2002). http://adtinfo.org/libavl.html/index.html

[PT07] Papamanthou, C., Tamassia, R.: Time and space efficient algorithms for two-party authenticated data structures. In: Qing, S., Imai, H., Wang, G. (eds.) ICICS 2007. LNCS, vol. 4861, pp. 1–15. Springer, Heidelberg (2007). https://doi.org/10.1007/978-3-540-77048-0_1

[PTT16] Papamanthou, C., Tamassia, R., Triandopoulos, N.: Authenticated hash tables based on cryptographic accumulators. Algorithmica **74**(2), 664–712 (2016)

[Pug90] Pugh, W.: Skip lists: a probabilistic alternative to balanced trees. Commun. ACM **33**(6), 668–676 (1990). http://citeseer.ist.psu.edu/viewdoc/summary?doi=10.1.1.15.9072

[RMCI16] Reyzin, L., Meshkov, D., Chepurnoy, A., Ivanov, S.: Improving authenticated dynamic dictionaries, with applications to cryptocurrencies. Technical report 2016/994, IACR Cryptology ePrint Archive (2016). http://eprint.iacr.org/2016/994

[SA96] Seidel, R., Aragon, C.R.: Randomized search trees. Algorithmica **16**(4/5), 464–497 (1996). https://faculty.washington.edu/aragon/pubs/rst96.pdf

[sca] The Scala programming language. http://www.scala-lang.org/

[Sed08] Sedgewick, R.: Left-leaning red-black trees (2008). http://www.cs.princeton.edu/rs/talks/LLRB/LLRB.pdf

[tbp] Transactions per block. https://blockchain.info/charts/n-transactions-per-block

[Tea16] The Go Ethereum Team. Official golang implementation of the ethereum protocol (2016). http://geth.ethereum.org/

[Tod16] Todd, P.: Making UTXO set growth irrelevant with low-latency delayed TXO commitments (2016). https://petertodd.org/2016/delayed-txo-commitments

[Wei06] Weiss, M.A.: Data Structures and Algorithm Analysis in Java, 2nd edn. Prentice Hall, Pearson (2006)

[Whi15] White, B.: A theory for lightweight cryptocurrency ledgers (2015). http://qeditas.org/lightcrypto.pdf. (see also code at https://github.com/bitemyapp/ledgertheory)

[Wik13] Bitcoin Wiki. CVE-2013-2293: New DoS vulnerability by forcing continuous hard disk seek/read activity (2013). https://en.bitcoin.it/wiki/CVE-2013-2293

[Woo14] Wood, G.: Ethereum: A secure decentralised generalised transaction ledger (2014). http://gavwood.com/Paper.pdf

Short Paper: Service-Oriented Sharding for Blockchains

Adem Efe Gencer[✉], Robbert van Renesse, and Emin Gün Sirer

Initiative for CryptoCurrencies and Contracts (IC3),
Computer Science Department, Cornell University, Ithaca, USA
{gencer,rvr,egs}@cs.cornell.edu

Abstract. The rise of blockchain-based cryptocurrencies has led to an explosion of services using distributed ledgers as their underlying infrastructure. However, due to inherently single-service oriented blockchain protocols, such services can bloat the existing ledgers, fail to provide sufficient security, or completely forego the property of trustless auditability. Security concerns, trust restrictions, and scalability limits regarding the resource requirements of users hamper the sustainable development of loosely-coupled services on blockchains.

This paper introduces Aspen, a sharded blockchain protocol designed to securely scale with increasing number of services. Aspen shares the same trust model as Bitcoin in a peer-to-peer network that is prone to extreme churn containing Byzantine participants. It enables introduction of new services without compromising the security, leveraging the trust assumptions, or flooding users with irrelevant messages.

1 Introduction

Blockchains offer many opportunities for facilitating innovation in traditional industries. They have received extensive attention due to the trustless auditability, tamper-resistance, and transparency they provide in networks with Byzantine participants. Not surprisingly, there is much commercial interest in developing specialized blockchain solutions [13]. There have been proposals to use blockchains as an underlying layer for services including managing digital assets [14], issuing securities [12], tracking intellectual property [8,22,28], maintaining land records and deeds [1,30], facilitating online voting [2], registering domain names [24], as well as others. Ongoing projects explore ways to make it easier to build such services using Blockchain-as-a-Service (BaaS) platforms [20,26].

This movement, towards increased adoption of blockchains for specialized purposes, portends a dangerous trend: accommodating all of these diverse uses, either in a single blockchain or in separate blockchains, inherently requires complex tradeoffs. The simplest approach, of layering these additional blockchains on top of an existing, secure blockchain with sufficient mining power to withstand attacks, such as Bitcoin [27], leads to a stream of costly and burdensome transactions. Indeed, we have seen the controversial OP_RETURN opcode adopted for

© International Financial Cryptography Association 2017
A. Kiayias (Ed.): FC 2017, LNCS 10322, pp. 393–401, 2017.
https://doi.org/10.1007/978-3-319-70972-7_22

this purpose, and its use has been increasing rapidly [4], in line with increased usage of layered blockchains. Yet these transactions, which use Bitcoin solely as a timestamping and ordering service, increase the resource requirements for system participation and the time to bootstrap a node. In contrast, creating a dedicated, specialized, standalone blockchain avoids this problem, but suffers from a lack of independent mining power to secure the infrastructure. Duplicating the mining infrastructure used to secure Bitcoin is not only costly and environmentally unfriendly, but it is difficult to bootstrap such a system. Faced with this dilemma, some have turned to permissioned ledgers with closed participants [11,23], forgoing the open architecture, the flexible trust model, and the strong security guarantees of the existing Bitcoin mining ecosystem.

In this paper, we present Aspen, a protocol that securely shards the blockchain to provide high scalability to service users. This protocol employs a sharding approach that comes with the following benefits: (1) preserves the total computational power of miners to secure the whole blockchain, (2) prevents users from double-spending their funds while maintaining the same trustless setup assumptions as Bitcoin, (3) improves scalability by absolving non-miner participants – i.e. service users – from the responsibility of storing, processing, and propagating irrelevant data to confirm the validity of services they are interested in. In this protocol, a coffee shop does not have to worry about the land and deed records in the blockchain to validate the payment system.

Sharding is a well-established technique to improve scalability by distributing contents of a database across nodes in a network. But sharding blockchains is non-trivial. The main difficulty is to preserve the trustless nature while hiding parts of a blockchain from other nodes. It is an open research question whether it is possible to shard blockchains in a way that the output of a transaction in one shard can be spent at another while still satisfying the trustless validation of transaction history. In this work, the key insight behind sharding the blockchain is to distribute transactions to blocks with respect to services they are used for.

This paper outlines *service-oriented sharding*, a technique for sharding blockchains that promises higher scalability and extensibility without modifying Bitcoin's trust model. It instantiates this technique in *Aspen*, a blockchain sharding protocol that expedites user access to relevant services, makes service integration and maintenance easier, and achieves better fairness while demanding only a fraction of resources from users.

2   Service-Oriented Sharding

The core idea behind service-oriented sharding is to partition a blockchain such that users can fully validate the correct functioning of their services (1) without relying on trusted entities and (2) while keeping track of only the subset of the blockchain relevant to their services. This technique shares the same network and trust model as Bitcoin and related cryptocurrencies. Service-oriented sharding is built around a multiblockchain structure, where multiple chains are rooted in the same genesis block and share common checkpoints (See Fig. 1). Building blocks comprising service-oriented sharding can be summarized as follows:

Fig. 1. Multiblockchain structure of service-oriented sharding. Each channel contains the same genesis block (drop) and checkpoints (valves), as well as the exclusive transactions of a specific service (buckets with the same symbol). Generating a checkpoint requires a proof of work. Miners distribute transactions to designated blocks (a subset of dashed rectangles) secured by checkpoints.

Channel. A chain in a blockchain built on a shared genesis block containing (1) all transactions of a specific service, and (2) common checkpoints involving transactions for the overall management of services. For instance, a domain name resolution service would use a dedicated channel to store custom transactions in the form of DNS resource records. Such transactions are kept separate from common checkpoints. Hence, services are loosely coupled and resilient to changes.

Service-oriented sharding handles requests associated with a certain service by annotating each channel and the corresponding transactions with the same unique identifier, called *service number*. Two special channels, *payment* and *registration*, are defined by the system and help bootstrap the network. The default service that enables users to exchange funds runs on the payment channel, and the registration channel is used to add or update services. Users store, process, and propagate transactions on channels only for the relevant services.

Protocol. A set of rules regarding services and their integration. A *service protocol* defines the validity of transactions in a given channel. It describes: (1) the syntax for each transaction type, (2) the relationship between transactions within a channel, (3) the size, frequency, and format constraints for blocks that keep transactions. The *integration protocol* specifies the security, incentive mechanism, valid service numbers, the genesis block, and the inter-channel communication process between the payment channel and the other channels.

Transaction. The smallest unit of data for adding content to a channel. Transactions are grouped into blocks and appended to each channel according to their service number. A block is valid if it (1) embodies valid transactions sharing the same service number and (2) complies with the integration protocol and the relevant service protocol.

Service Integration and Maintenance. The process of introducing services and updating the existing ones. Service-oriented sharding resolves this process completely on the blockchain in three phases. First, users propose protocols to introduce or update services by generating transactions for the registration channel. Each such transaction contains a set of service protocols with distinct service numbers. A service protocol is specified in a platform-independent language such as WebAssembly [5] or Lua [3]. In the second phase, miners conduct an election to choose a registration channel transaction. This transaction specifies the protocols that miners are collectively willing to adopt. Miners indicate their choice using *ballots*. A ballot is a transaction that contains a reference to a particular transaction in the registration channel. Each ballot is part of a checkpoint that requires a proof of work to generate. This provides (1) representation proportional to mining power, and (2) protection against censorship of ballots. Finally, if a particular transaction is referred by more than a certain fraction τ of ballots, its protocols become active. An active service protocol determines the validity of new transactions added to the corresponding channel.

This process enables evolutionary refinement with the confidence of sustainability. Users are involved in the process through their proposals. The election mechanism ensures that the majority of the mining power intends to serialize transactions for the new or updated services.

3   Aspen

While service-oriented sharding can be built on any blockchain protocol [16, 17, 21, 27], we instantiate on Bitcoin-NG [17], a blockchain protocol that improves transaction throughput and consensus latency of Bitcoin under the same trust model. The protocol makes the following changes with service-oriented sharding:

Multiple Microblock Chains. Traditional blockchain protocols strive to agree on a single *main chain* in which all transactions are totally ordered. However, not all transactions are related or even need such an ordering. This leads to a seemingly irreconcilable tradeoff between the scalability of independent blockchains and the security of monolithic ones. The central idea behind Aspen is to resolve this conundrum by having a series of independent microblock chains conjoined at common key blocks. A channel represents the combination of the same genesis block, all key blocks, and the set of microblock chains containing custom transactions annotated with the same service number. Figure 2 illustrates the structure.

Each channel maintains key blocks to enforce the integration protocol. To prevent bloating key blocks, Aspen (1) limits the number of channel references in a key block and (2) omits references to non-payment channels with no transactions on their latest microblock chain – i.e. *inert channels*. Note that users can fully validate an inert channel service using key blocks of the payment channel.

Extensibility. Aspen updates or introduces services at designated growth points, called *buds* (See Fig. 2). A bud is a key block at a protocol-defined height representing the number of key blocks from the genesis block. Aspen adopts proposals based on ballots in key blocks between the current and the preceding bud.

Flow of Funds. Aspen enables users to detect double spends by making each fund spendable only in a specific channel. A special payment channel transaction, *funding pore*, enables users to lock funds to other channels. A funding

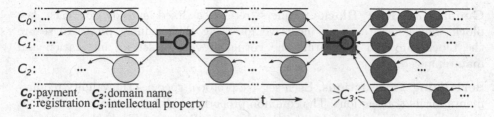

C_0:payment C_2:domain name
C_1:registration C_3:intellectual property

Fig. 2. Structure of the Aspen chain. Upon generating a key block shared by all channels, a miner serializes service-specific transactions only in the corresponding microblock (circles) chains. Shading indicates blocks generated by a specific miner. A bud (dashed key block) introduces the intellectual property service.

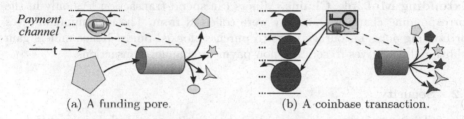

(a) A funding pore.   (b) A coinbase transaction.

Fig. 3. (a) A funding pore (cylinder) makes payment channel outputs (pentagons) spendable at specific channels. (b) Rewards are split between the current and the previous miner for each channel.

pore annotates each output with the service number of an existing destination channel where it can be spent. Note that transfers across channels are allowed only in one way, from the payment channel to others. Figure 3(a) illustrates a funding pore.

Alternatively, users can directly buy locked funds at the target channel to pay for the service running on the corresponding channel. The protocol enforces a high minimum fee for serializing funding pores to (1) discourage users from bloating the payment channel and (2) improve the fungibility of funds in non-payment channels. Contrary to Bitcoin's OP_RETURN transactions, this process does not yield any unspendable outputs.

Following sections detail the incentive and security mechanisms in Aspen.

3.1 Reward Structure

The process of keeping the complete blockchain, serializing transactions, and securing the system consumes miner resources. Aspen uses a Bitcoin-like cryptocurrency to encourage miners to continue facilitating this costly process. A coinbase transaction in a key block provides separate outputs to compensate the current and the previous miner for each service they provision. Each output indicates the source channel of rewards where funds can be spent (See Fig. 3(b)).

Generating Key Blocks. Miners receive a fixed subsidy for each key block they generate as an incentive for using their mining power to secure the blockchain and facilitating the voting process of service integration and maintenance.

Serializing Transactions. Each service protocol specifies the validity requirements for its transactions. The common property of all transactions is a fee that miners collect for adding them to the corresponding microblocks.

Extending the Longest Chains. As an incentive for the next miner to attach her key block to the latest microblock [17], Aspen distributes fees between the current miner and the next one for each microblock chain.

Extending Multiple Chains. Miners can spend transaction fees only in the corresponding channels that they were collected from. The high minimum fees for funding pores encourage users to purchase locked funds. Hence miners gain additional incentives to serialize non-payment channel transactions.

3.2   Security

The following properties are critical to the security of a blockchain protocol.

Authenticity. The property of having an indisputable origin. Transactions require a set of cryptographic signatures to prove the ownership of funds that are used as fees. Hence, provided that it is infeasible to forge signatures, pseudonymous identities cannot deny committing transactions.

Irreversibility. The protection against overwriting or deleting transactions. Double spending is an instance of violating this property. Malicious miners may modify or remove a set of transactions from a blockchain by updating some common prefix with different blocks – i.e. forks. Aspen secures the blockchain against (1) key block forks by picking the chain containing the most proof of work with random tie-breaking and (2) microblock forks using poison transactions [17].

Censorship. The ability of miners to block submission or retrieval of transactions. A key block miner becomes eligible to update the blockchain for a discrete epoch. However, she may ignore certain transactions in particular channels due to benign failures or malicious behavior. The extend of such censorship is limited to the miner's epoch, which can be adjusted by changing the key block frequency.

An adversary can leave a victim unable to retrieve transactions by controlling all of its connections [19] or delaying the delivery of valid transactions to her [18]. Countermeasures to mitigate such attacks apply to this work, as well.

4   Related Work

Federated Chains. Sidechains [7] allow users to transfer funds across blockchains. However, this leads to fragmentation of the hash power. A compromised sidechain makes the main chain and the other sidechains vulnerable.

Transfers across sidechains bloat the main chain. To guarantee that funds will not be pruned from the corresponding chains, such transfers incur high latencies. Drivechain [31] attempts to minimize the impact of sidechains on the main chain regarding the required knowledge and effort to prove validity of transfers. However, this approach does not address inherent limitations regarding the security of sidechains.

Multiple Services in Bitcoin's Blockchain. Bitcoin permits storage of arbitrary data on its blockchain using OP_RETURN transactions [10]. While there is no format requirement for the data, the size limit (currently 80 bytes) usually enforces users to store only a hash of their original content on the blockchain, which they externally validate [14,29]. This limitation imposes a critical tradeoff between data growth management and the diversity of services.

Users download and process the full history to validate the state of the existing blockchain protocols [16,17,27]. Using commodity hardware, this bootstrapping process takes many hours in Bitcoin [15]. Such protocols force users to handle the complexity of irrelevant services. Therefore, a monolithic history is not a viable option for scaling blockchains with multiple services.

Outsourcing the Security. Services with distinct blockchains attempt to improve their security with merged mining [9] and anchoring.

In merged mining, a blockchain with insufficient mining power accepts proof of work submissions from a designated parent chain. This approach raises three issues. First, if a miner is already part of the parent blockchain, she can use her mining power to attack the merged-mined blockchain at no cost. Second, a merged-mined blockchain becomes dependent on its parent chain, making it fragile with respect to changes in the parent's security. Finally, it is non-trivial to maintain the miner coordination across blockchains. Ali et al. [6] show that even the largest merged-mined cryptocurrency, NameCoin [24], suffers from a single merged mining pool whose mining power exceeds the 51% threshold.

Anchoring relies on periodically submitting the cumulative hash of all data, such as the root of a Merkle tree, to a trusted publishing medium, such as the blockchain of Bitcoin. Anchoring bloats the external blockchain and becomes dependent on its security.

Sharding the Same Service. Elastico is a service-agnostic protocol for sharding blockchains [25]. This approach assigns miners to committees for serializing transactions using a classical Byzantine consensus protocol. As in anchoring, a final committee creates a cumulative digest based on all shards and broadcasts it to the network. However, to prevent double spends, Elastico requires splitting up the payment functionality into as many sub-services as the number of shards, which effectively means as many cryptocurrencies.

Treechains [32] is a sharding idea based on restructuring a blockchain into a tree of blocks, where each output has a dedicated branch to spend. However, this proposal is at an early stage with no prototype or a detailed technical analysis.

5   Conclusion

Service-oriented sharding provides a means for improving the scalability and extensibility of blockchains with multiple services. Aspen, the instantiation of this technique, reduces the resource requirements and the bootstrapping time to participate in the system. It provides trustless validation while preserving the same network and trust model as Bitcoin. Finally, it avoids fragmentation of the mining power that secures the blockchain.

Acknowledgements. The authors thank Ittay Eyal, and the anonymous reviewers for their comments and suggestions. This work was supported in part by NSF grants CNS-1422544, CNS-1561209, CNS-1518779, NIST, a Google Faculty Research Award, IC3 sponsorship from Chain, IBM, and Intel, as well as gifts from Infosys and Facebook.

References

1. Benben. http://benben.com.gh/. Accessed Oct 2016
2. Follow my vote. https://followmyvote.com/. Accessed Oct 2016
3. Lua. http://www.lua.org/. Accessed Nov 2016
4. OP_RETURN stats. http://opreturn.org/. Accessed Nov 2016
5. WebAssembly. http://webassembly.org/. Accessed Nov 2016
6. Ali, M., Nelson, J., Shea, R., Freedman, M.J.: Blockstack: a global naming and storage system secured by blockchains. In: USENIX Annual Technical Conference, Denver, CO, USA (2016)
7. Back, A., Corallo, M., Dashjr, L., Friedenbach, M., Maxwell, G., Miller, A., Poelstra, A., Timón, J., Wuille, P.: Enabling blockchain innovations with pegged sidechains (2014). https://blockstream.com/sidechains.pdf
8. BigchainDB GmbH. Ascribe. https://www.ascribe.io/. Accessed Oct 2016
9. Bitcoin Community. Merged mining specification. https://en.bitcoin.it/wiki/Merged_mining_specification. Accessed Oct 2016
10. Bitcoin Community. OP_RETURN. https://en.bitcoin.it/wiki/OP_RETURN. Accessed Oct 2016
11. Brown, R.G., Carlyle, J., Grigg, I., Hearn, M.: Corda: An introduction, August 2016. http://r3cev.com/s/corda-introductory-whitepaper-final.pdf
12. Chain Inc. Chain open standard: A secure blockchain protocol for high-scale financial networks. http://chain.com/os/. Accessed Sep 2016
13. CoinDesk. State of blockchain Q1 2016: Blockchain funding overtakes Bitcoin. http://coindesk.com/state-of-blockchain-q1-2016/. Accessed Oct 2016
14. Colu. Colored Coins. http://coloredcoins.org/. Accessed Sep 2016
15. Croman, K., Decker, C., Eyal, I., Gencer, A.E., Juels, A., Kosba, A., Miller, A., Saxena, P., Shi, E., Sirer, E.G., Song, D., Wattenhofer, R.: On scaling decentralized blockchains (a position paper). In: 3rd Workshop on Bitcoin and Blockchain Research, Barbados (2016)
16. Ethereum Foundation. A next generation smart contract and decentralized application platform. https://github.com/ethereum/wiki/wiki/White-Paper. Accessed Oct 2016
17. Eyal, I., Gencer, A.E., Sirer, E.G., van Renesse, R.: Bitcoin-NG: a scalable blockchain protocol. In: 13th USENIX Symposium on Networked Systems Design and Implementation, Santa Clara, CA, USA, pp. 45–59 (2016)

18. Gervais, A., Ritzdorf, H., Karame, G.O., Capkun, S.: Tampering with the delivery of blocks and transactions in Bitcoin. In: Proceedings of the 22nd ACM SIGSAC Conference on Computer and Communications Security, Denver, CO, USA, pp. 692–705 (2015)
19. Heilman, E., Kendler, A., Zohar, A., Goldberg, S.: Eclipse attacks on Bitcoin's peer-to-peer network. In: 24th USENIX Security Symposium, Washington, D.C., USA, pp. 129–144 (2015)
20. IBM Corporation. IBM Blockchain on Bluemix. http://www.ibm.com/blockchain/bluemix.html. Accessed Oct 2016
21. Kokoris-Kogias, E., Jovanovic, P., Gailly, N., Khoffi, I., Gasser, L., Ford, B.: Enhancing Bitcoin security and performance with strong consistency via collective signing. arXiv preprint arXiv:1602.06997 (2016)
22. Ledger Assets Pty Ltd., Uproov. https://uproov.com/. Accessed Sep 2016
23. Linux Foundation. Hyperledger. https://hyperledger.org/. Accessed Sep 2016
24. Loibl, A.: Namecoin (2014). https://namecoin.info
25. Luu, L., Narayanan, V., Baweja, K., Zheng, C., Gilbert, S., Saxena, P.: A secure sharding protocol for open blockchains. In: Conference on Computer and Communications Security, Vienna, Austria. ACM (2016)
26. Microsoft. Blockchain-as-a-Service. https://azure.microsoft.com/en-us/solutions/blockchain/. Accessed Oct 2016
27. Nakamoto, S.: Bitcoin: A peer-to-peer electronic cash system (2008)
28. OMI. Open music initiative. http://open-music.org/. Accessed Oct 2016
29. Omni Team. Omni layer. http://www.omnilayer.org/. Accessed Oct 2016
30. Shin, L.: Republic of Georgia to pilot land titling on blockchain. Forbes, 21 April 2016
31. Sztorc, P.: Drivechain (2015). http://www.truthcoin.info/blog/drivechain/
32. Todd, P.: [bitcoin-development] Tree-chains preliminary summary (2014). https://lists.linuxfoundation.org/pipermail/bitcoin-dev/2014-March/004797.html

Security of Internet Protocols

The Security of NTP's Datagram Protocol

Aanchal Malhotra[1(✉)], Matthew Van Gundy[2], Mayank Varia[1],
Haydn Kennedy[1], Jonathan Gardner[2], and Sharon Goldberg[1]

[1] Boston University, Boston, USA
aanchal4@bu.edu
[2] Cisco (ASIG), San Jose, USA

Abstract. For decades, the Network Time Protocol (NTP) has been used to synchronize computer clocks over untrusted network paths. This work takes a new look at the security of NTP's datagram protocol. We argue that NTP's datagram protocol in RFC5905 is both underspecified and flawed. The NTP specifications do not sufficiently respect (1) the conflicting security requirements of different NTP modes, and (2) the mechanism NTP uses to prevent off-path attacks. A further problem is that (3) NTP's control-query interface reveals sensitive information that can be exploited in off-path attacks. We exploit these problems in several attacks that remote attackers can use to maliciously alter a target's time. We use network scans to find millions of IPs that are vulnerable to our attacks. Finally, we move beyond identifying attacks by developing a cryptographic model and using it to prove the security of a new backwards-compatible client/server protocol for NTP.

1 Introduction

Millions of hosts [10,19,22,27,31] use the Network Time Protocol (NTP) [25] to synchronize their computer clocks to public Internet timeservers (using NTP's client/server mode), or to neighboring peers (using NTP's symmetric mode). Over the last few years, the security of NTP has come under new scrutiny. Along with significant attention paid to NTP's role in UDP amplification attacks [10,18], there is also a new focus on attacks on the NTP protocol itself, both in order to maliciously alter a target's time (*timeshifting attacks*) or to prevent a target from synchronizing its clock (*denial of service (DoS) attacks*) [19,39]. These attacks matter, because the correctness of time underpins many other basic protocols and services. For instance, cryptographic protocols use timestamps to prevent replay attacks and limit the use of stale or compromised cryptographic material (*e.g.,* TLS [17,34], HSTS [33], DNSSEC, RPKI [19], bitcoin [9], authentication protocols [17,19]), while accurate time synchronization is a basic requirement for various distributed protocols.

© International Financial Cryptography Association 2017
A. Kiayias (Ed.): FC 2017, LNCS 10322, pp. 405–423, 2017.
https://doi.org/10.1007/978-3-319-70972-7_23

1.1   Problems with the NTP Specification

We start by identifying three fundamental problems with the NTP specification in RFC5905, and then exploit these problems in four different off-path attacks on *ntpd*, the "reference implementation" of NTP.

Problem 1: Lack of respect for basic protection measures. The first issue stems from a lack of respect for TEST2, the mechanism that NTP uses to prevent off-path attacks. Off-path attacks are essentially the weakest (and therefore the most scary) threat model that one could consider for a networking protocol. An *off-path attacker* cannot eavesdrop on the NTP traffic of their targets, but can *spoof* IP packets *i.e.*, send packets with a bogus source IP. This threat model captures 'remote attacks' launched by arbitrary IPs that do not occupy a privileged position on the communication path between the parties. (See Fig. 2.)

NTP attempts to prevent off-path attacks much in the same way that TCP and UDP do: every client query includes a nonce, and this nonce is reflected back to the client in the server's response. The client then checks for matching nonces in the query and response, *i.e.*, "TEST2". Because an off-path attacker cannot see the nonce (because it cannot eavesdrop on traffic), it cannot spoof a valid server response. Despite the apparent simplicity of this mechanism, its specification in RFC5905 is flawed and leads to several off-path attacks.

Problem 2: Same code for different modes. NTP operates in several different modes. Apart from the popular *client/server mode* (where the client synchronizes to a time server), NTP also has a *symmetric mode* (where neighboring peers take time from each other), and several other modes. RFC5905 recommends that all of NTP's different modes be processed by the same codepath. However, we find that the security requirements of client/server mode and symmetric mode conflict with each other, and result in some of our off-path attacks.

Problem 3: Leaky control queries. NTP's control-query interface is not specified in RFC5905, but its specification does appear in the obsoleted RFC1305 [23] from 1992 and a new IETF Internet draft [24]. We find that it can be exploited remotely to leak information about NTPs internal timing state variables. While the DDoS amplification potential of NTP's control query interface is well known [10,18], here we show that it is also a risk to the correctness of time (Fig. 1).

We exploit these three problems to find working off-path attacks on ntpd (Sects. 3 and 4), and use IPv4 Internet scans to identify millions of IPs that are vulnerable to our attacks (Sect. 5). The first three attacks maliciously shift time on a client using NTP's client/server mode, and the fourth prevents time synchronization in symmetric mode.

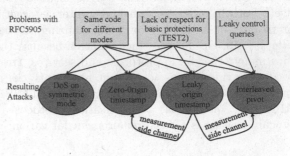

Fig. 1. Paper overview.

Attack 1: Leaky Origin Timestamp Attack (Sect. 4). Our network scans find a staggering 3.8 million IPs that leak the nonce used in TEST2 in response to control queries made from arbitrary IPs (CVE-2015-8139). An off-path attacker can maliciously shift time on a client by continuously querying for this nonce, and using it to spoof packets that pass TEST2.

Attack 2: Zero-Origin Timestamp Attack (Sect. 3.3). This attack (CVE-2015-8138) follows from RFC5905, and is among the strongest timeshifting attacks on NTP that has been identified thus far. The attacker bypasses TEST2 by spoofing server response packets with their nonce set to zero. We use leaky NTP control queries as a side-channel to measure the prevalence of this attack. We find 1.3 million affected IPs. However, we expect that the true attack surface is even larger, since this attack itself does not require the control-query interface, works on clients operating in default mode, and has been part of ntpd for seven years (since ntpd v4.2.6, December 2009).

Attack 3: Interleaved-Pivot Attack (Sect. 4). Our third off-path timeshifting attack (CVE-2016-1548) exploits the fact that NTP's client/server mode shares the same codepath as NTP's interleaved mode. First, the attacker spoofs a single packet that tricks the target into thinking that he is in interleaved mode. The target then rejects all subsequent legitimate client/server mode packets. This is a DoS attack (Sect. 4). We further leverage NTP's leaky control queries to convert this DoS attack to an off-path timeshifting attack. NTP's control-query interface also leaks the nonce used in the special version of TEST2 used in interleaved mode. The attacker spoofs a sequence of interleaved-mode packets, with nonce value revealed by these queries, that maliciously shifts time on the client. Our scans find 1.3 million affected IPs.

Attack 4: Attacks on symmetric mode (full version). We then present security analysis of NTP's symmetric mode, as specified in RFC5905, and present off-path attacks that prevent time synchronization. We discuss why the security requirements of symmetric mode are at odds with that of client/server mode, and may have been the root cause of the zero-Origin timestamp attack.

Disclosure. Our disclosure timeline is in the full version. Our research was done against ntpd v4.2.8p6, the latest version as of April 25, 2016. Since then, three versions have been released: ntpd v4.2.8p7 (April 26, 2016), ntpd v4.2.8p8 (June 2, 2016), ntpd v4.2.8p9 (November 21, 2016). Most of our attacks have been patched in these releases. We provide recommendations for securing the client/server mode in Sect. 7 and symmetric mode in the full version.

1.2 Provably secure protocol design.

Our final contribution is to go beyond attacks and patches, and identify a more robust security solution (Sect. 6) We propose a new backwards-compatible protocol for client/server mode that preserves the semantics of the timestamps in NTP packets (Figs. 6 and 7). We then leverage ideas from the universal composability framework [7] to develop a cryptographic model for attacks on NTP's datagram protocol. We use this model to prove (in the full version) that our protocol *correctly synchronizes time* in the face of both (1) *off-path attackers* when NTP is unauthenticated and (2) *on-path attackers* when NTP packets are authenticated with a MAC. We also use our model to prove similar results about a different protocol that is used by chronyd [2] and openntpd [4] (two alternate implementations of NTP). The chronyd/openntpd protocol is secure, but unlike our protocol, does not preserve the semantics of packet timestamps.

Our cryptographic model models both on-path attackers and off-path attackers. An on-path attacker can eavesdrop, inject, spoof, and replay packets, but *cannot* drop, delay, or tamper with legitimate traffic. An on-path attacker eavesdrops on a copy of the target's traffic, so it need not disrupt live network traffic, or even operate at line rate. For this reason, on-path attacks are commonly seen in the wild, disrupting TCP [40], DNS [12], BitTorrent [40], or censoring web content [8]. Meanwhile, we cannot prove that NTP provides correct time synchronization in the face of the traditional Man-in-The-

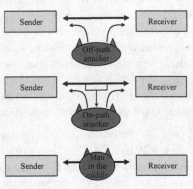

Fig. 2. Threat models.

Middle (MiTM) attacks (*aka.* 'in-path attacks') because an MiTM can always prevent time synchronization by dropping packets. Moreover, an MiTM can also bias time synchronization by delaying packets [28,29].[1]

Taking a step back, our work can be seen as a case study of the security risks that arise when network protocols are underspecified. It also highlights the importance of handling diverse protocol requirements in separate and rigorously tested codepaths. Finally, our network protocol analysis introduces new ways of reasoning about network attacks on time synchronization protocols.

1.3   Related Work

Secure protocols. Our design and analysis of secure client/server protocols complement recent efforts to cryptographically secure NTP and its "cousin" PTP (Precision Time Protocol) [29]. Our interest is in securing the core datagram protocol used by NTP, which was last described in David Mill's book [26]. To the best of our knowledge, the security of the core NTP datagram protocol has never previously been analyzed. Meanwhile, our analysis assumes that parties

---

[1] This follows because time-synchronization protocols use information about the delay on the network path in order to accurately synchronize clocks (Sect. 2). A client cannot distinguish the delay on the forward path (from client to server) from the delay on the reverse path (from server to client). As such, the client simply takes the total round trip time δ (forward path + reverse path), and assumes that delays on each path are symmetric. The MiTM can exploit this by making delays asymmetric (*e.g.*, causing the delay on the forward path to be much longer than delay on the reverse path), thus biasing time synchronization.

correctly distribute cryptographic keys and use a secure MAC. A complementary stream of works propose protocols for distributing keys and performing the MAC, beginning with the Autokey protocol in RFC5906 [15], which was broken by Rottger [32], which was followed by NTS [36], ANTP [11], other works including [16,30], and on-going activity in the IETF [1].

Attacks. Our analysis of the NTP specification is motivated, in part, by discovery of over 30 ntpd CVEs between June 2015 to July 2016 [39]. These implementation flaws allow remote code execution, DoS attacks, and timeshifting attacks. Earlier, Selvi [33,34] demonstrated MiTM timeshifting attacks on 'simple NTP (SNTP)' (rather than full-fledged NTP). Even earlier, work [9,17,26] considered the impact of timeshifting on the correctness of other protocols. The recent academic work [19] also attacks NTP, but our attacks are stronger. [19] presented attacks that are on-path (weaker than our off-path attacks), or off-path DoS attacks (weaker than our timeshifting attacks), or off-path time-shifting attacks that needed special client/server configurations (our Zero-Origin Timestamp attack works in default mode). Also, our measurements find millions of vulnerable clients, while [19] finds thousands. Finally, NTP's broadcast mode is outside our scope; see [20,29,37] instead.

Measurement. Our work is also related to studies measuring the NTP ecosystem (in past decades) [27,31], the use of NTP for DDoS amplification attacks [10], the performance of NIST's timeservers [35], and network latency [13]. Our attack surface measurements are in the same spirit as those in [19,20], but we use a new set of NTP control queries. We also provide updated measurements on the presence of cryptographically-authenticated NTP associations.

2   NTP Background

NTP's default mode of operation is a hierarchical *client/server* mode. In this mode, timing queries are solicited by clients from a set of servers; this set of servers is typically static and configured manually. *Stratum i* systems act as servers that provide time to stratum $i + 1$ systems, for $i = 1, ...15$. Stratum 1 servers are at the root of the NTP hierarchy. Stratum 0 and stratum 16 indicate failure to synchronize. Client/server packets are not authenticated by default, but a Message Authentication Code (MAC) can optionally be appended to the packet. NTP operates in several additional modes. In *broadcast mode*, a set of clients listen to a server that broadcasts timing information. In *symmetric mode*, peers exchange timing information. There is also an *interleaved mode* for more accurate timestamping.

T_1: *Origin timestamp*.	Client's local time when sending query.
T_2: *Receive timestamp*.	Server's local time when receiving query.
T_3: *Transmit timestamp*.	Server's local time when sending response.
T_4: *Destination timestamp*.	Client's local time when receiving response.

Fig. 3. Timestamps induced by the server response packet (mode 4).

NTP's client/server protocol consists of a periodic two-message *exchange*. The client sends the server a query (*mode 3*), and the server sends back a response (*mode 4*). Each exchange provides a *timing sample*, which uses the four timestamps in Fig. 3. All four timestamps are 64 bits long, where the first 32 bits are seconds elapsed since January 1, 1970, and the last 32 bits are fractional seconds. T_1, T_2, and T_3 are fields in the server response packet (mode 4) shown in Fig. 4. The delay δ is an important NTP parameter [25] that measures the round trip time between the client and the server:

$$\delta = (T_4 - T_1) - (T_3 - T_2) \tag{1}$$

If there are symmetric delays on the forward and reverse network paths, then the difference between the server and client clock is $T_2 - (T_1 + \frac{\delta}{2})$ for the client query, and $T_3 - (T_4 - \frac{\delta}{2})$ for the server response. Averaging, we get *offset* θ:

$$\theta = \tfrac{1}{2} \left((T_2 - T_1) + (T_3 - T_4) \right) \tag{2}$$

A client does *not* immediately update its clock with the offset θ upon receipt of a server response packet. Instead, the client collects several timing samples from each server by completing exchanges at infrequent *polling intervals* (on the order of seconds or minutes). The length of the polling interval is determined by an adaptive randomized *poll process* [25, Sect. 13]. The poll p is a field on the NTP packet, where [25] allows $p \in \{4, 5, .., 17\}$, which corresponds to a polling interval of about 2^p (*i.e.*, 16 s to 36 h).

Once the client has enough timing samples from a server, it computes the jitter ψ. First, it finds the offset value θ^* corresponding to the sample of lowest delay δ^* from the eight most recent samples, and then takes jitter ψ as

$$\psi^2 = \tfrac{1}{k-1} \sum_{i=1}^{k} (\theta_i - \theta^*)^2 \tag{3}$$

Typically, $4 \leq k \leq 8$. A client considers updating its clock only if it gets a stream of k timing samples with low delay δ and jitter ψ. This is called TEST11.

After each exchange, the client chooses a *single* server to which it synchronizes its local clock. This decision is made adaptively by a set of *selection*, *cluster*, *combine* and *clock discipline* algorithms [25, Sect. 10–12]. Importantly, these algorithms

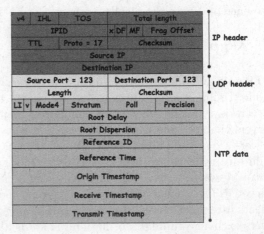

Fig. 4. NTP server response packet (mode 4). (Client queries have the same format, but with mode field set to 3. Symmetric mode uses mode 1 or 2. Broadcast mode uses mode 5).

can also decide *not* to update the client's clock; in this case, the clock runs without input from NTP.

Implementation vs. Specification. RFC5905 [25] specifies NTP version 4, and its "reference implementation" is ntpd [38]. Mills, the inventor of NTP, explains [26] the "relationship between the published standard and the reference implementation" as follows: "It is tempting to construct a standard from first principles, submit it for formal verification, then tell somebody to build it. Of the four generations of NTP, it did not work that way. Both the standard and the reference implementation were evolved from an earlier version... Along the way, many minor tweaks were needed in both the specification and implementation..." For this reason, we consider both ntpd and the specification in RFC5905.

3   The Client/Server Protocol in RFC5905

We now argue that the client/server datagram protocol in RFC5905 is underspecified and flawed. RFC5905 mentions the protocol in two places: in its main body (Sect. 8) and in a pseudo-code listing (Appendix A). Because the two mentions are somewhat contradictory, we begin with an overview of the components of NTP's datagram protocol, and then present its specification in Appendix A of RFC5905, and in the prose of Sect. 8 of RFC5905.

3.1   Components of NTP's Datagram Protocol

NTP uses the *origin timestamp* field of the NTP packet to prevent off- and on-path attacks. (Recall from Fig. 2 that an off-path attacker can spoof IP packets but cannot eavesdrop on its target's NTP traffic, while an on-path attacker can eavesdrop, inject, spoof, and replay packets, but cannot drop, delay, or tamper with legitimate traffic.) Whenever a client queries its server, the client records the query's sending time T_1 in a local state variable [25] named "xmt". The client then sends T_1 in the *transmit timestamp*

```
1   receive()
2       if (pkt.T3 == 0 or    # fail test3
3           pkt.T3 == org): # fail test1
4           return
5
6       synch = True
7       if !broadcast:
8           if pkt.T1 == 0:   # fail test3
9               synch = False
10          elif pkt.T1 != xmt:  # fail test2
11              synch = False
12
13      org = pkt.T3
14      rec = pkt.time_received
15      if (synch):
16          process(pkt)
```

Fig. 5. Pseudocode for the receive function, RFC5905 Appendix A.5.1.

of its client query (Fig. 4). Upon receipt of the query, the server learns T_1 and copies it into the *origin timestamp* field of its server response (Fig. 4). When the client receives the server response, it performs TEST2:

TEST2: The client checks that the origin timestamp T_1 on the server response matches the client's time upon sending the query, as recorded in the client's local state variable xmt.

The origin timestamp is therefore a nonce that the client must check (with TEST2) before it accepts a response.[2] An off-path attacker cannot see the origin timestamp (because it cannot observe the exchange between client and server), and thus has difficulty spoofing a server response containing a valid origin timestamp. Indeed, the origin timestamp looks somewhat random to the off-path attacker. Specifically, its first 32 bits are seconds, and the last 32 bits are subseconds (or fractional seconds). The first 32 bits appear slightly random because the off-path attacker does not know the exact moment that the client sent its query; indeed, Appendix A of RFC5905 has a comment that says "While not shown here, the reference implementation randomizes the poll interval by a small factor" and the current ntpd implementation randomizes the polling interval by 2^{p-4} s when poll $p > 4$. Moreover, the last 32 bits also appear somewhat random because RFC5905 requires a client with a clock of precision ρ randomize the $(32 - \rho)$- lowest-order bits of the origin timestamp.

The origin timestamp thus is analogous to source port randomization in TCP/UDP, sequence number randomization in TCP, *etc.* When NTP packets are cryptographically authenticated with a MAC, this nonce also provides some replay protection: even an on-path attacker cannot replay a packet from an earlier polling interval because its origin timestamp is now stale.

NTP also has mechanisms to prevent replays within the same polling interval. These are needed because an NTP client continuously listens to network traffic, even when it has no outstanding (*i.e.,* unanswered) queries to its servers. Whenever a client receives a server response packet, it records the transmit timestamp field from the packet in its org state variable. The client uses the following test to reject duplicate server response packets:

TEST1: The client checks that the transmit timestamp field T_3 of the server response is *different* from the value in the client's org state variable.
The client deals with the duplicates of the client's query as follows:

Clear xmt: If a server response passes TEST2, the client sets its local xmt state variable to zero.

Suppose the server receives two identical client queries. The server would send responses to both (because NTP servers are stateless [25]). If the client cleared xmt upon receipt of the first server response, the second server response packet will be rejected (by TEST2) because its origin timestamp is non-zero. At this point, one might worry that an off-path attacker could inject a packet with origin timestamp set to zero. But, TEST3 should catch this:

TEST3: Reject any response packet with origin, receive, or transmit timestamp T_1, T_2, T_3 set to zero.

---

[2] Note that ntpd does not randomize the UDP source port to create an additional nonce; instead, all NTP packets have UDP source port 123.

3.2   Query Replay Vulnerability in Appendix A of RFC5905

Pseudocode from Appendix A of RFC5905 (see Fig. 5) handles the processing of received packets of *any* mode, including server mode packets (mode 4), broadcast mode packets (mode 5), and symmetric mode packets (mode 1 or 2). Importantly, this pseudocode requires a host to always listen to and process incoming packets. This is because some NTP modes (*e.g.,* broadcast) process unsolicited packets, and RFC5905 suggest that all modes use the same codepath. We shall see that this single codepath creates various security problems.

On-path query replay vulnerability.   The pseudocode in Fig. 5 is vulnerable to replays of the client's query. Suppose a client query is replayed to the server. Then, the server will send two responses, each with a valid origin timestamp field (passing TEST2) and each with a different transmit timestamp field (passing TEST1). The client will accept both responses. Our experiments show that replays of the client query harm time synchronization; see the full version.

3.3   Zero-Origin Timestamp Vulnerability in RFC5905 Prose

Meanwhile, we find the following in Sect. 8 of RFC5905:

> Before the xmt and org state variables are updated, two sanity checks are performed in order to protect against duplicate, bogus, or replayed packets. In the exchange above, a packet is duplicate or replay if the transmit timestamp t3 in the packet matches the org state variable T3. A packet is bogus if the origin timestamp t1 in the packet does not match the xmt state variable T1. In either of these cases, the state variables are updated, then the packet is discarded. To protect against replay of the last transmitted packet, the xmt state variable is set to zero immediately after a successful bogus check.

This text describes TEST1 and TEST2, but what does it mean to update the state variables? Comparing this to the pseudocode in Appendix A of RFC5905 (Fig. 5 lines 13–14) suggests that this means updating org and rec upon receipt of any packet (including a bogus one failing TEST2), but not the xmt state variable.[3] Next, notice that the quoted text does not mention TEST3, which rejects packets with a zero-0rigin timestamp. Thus, we could realize the quoted text as pseudocode by deleting lines 8–9 of Fig. 5. Finally, notice that the quote suggests clearing xmt if a received packet passes TEST2. Thus, we could add the following after line 11 of Fig. 5 (with lines 8–9 deleted):

```
else: xmt = 0
```

---

[3] Indeed, suppose we did update the xmt variable even after receipt of a bogus packet that fails TEST2, with the bogus origin timestamp in the received packet. In this case, we would be vulnerable to a *chosen-origin-timestamp attack*, where an attacker injects a first packet with an origin timestamp of the their choosing. The injected packet fails TEST2 and is dropped, but its origin timestamp gets written to the target's local xmt variable. Then, the attacker injects another packet with this same origin timestamp, which passes TEST2 and is accepted by the target.

However, if `xmt` is cleared but `TEST3` is not applied, we have:

Zero-Origin Timestamp Attack. The zero-0rigin timestamp vulnerability allows an off-path attacker to hijack an unauthenticated client/server association and shift time on the client.

The attacker sends its target client a spoofed server response packet, spoofed with the source IP address of the target's server.[4] The spoofed server response packet has its origin timestamp T_1 set to zero, and its other timestamps T_2, T_3 set to bogus values designed to convince the client to shift its time. The target will accept the spoofed packet as long is it does not have an outstanding query to its server. Why? If a client has already received a valid server response, the valid response would have cleared the client's `xmt` variable to zero. The spoofed zero-0rigin packet is then subjected to `TEST2`, and its origin timestamp (which is set to zero) will be compared to the `xmt` variable (which is also zero). `TEST3` is never applied, and so the spoofed zero-0rigin packet will be accepted.

Suppose that the attacker wants to convince the client to change its clock by x years. How should the attacker set the timestamps on its spoofed packet? The origin timestamp is set to $T_1 = 0$ and the transmit timestamp T_3 is set to the bogus time now $+ x$. The destination timestamp T_4 (not in the packet) is now $+ d$, where d is the latency between the moment when the attacker sent its spoofed packet and the moment the client received it. Now, the attacker needs to choose the receive timestamp T_2 so that the delay δ is small. (Otherwise, the spoofed packet will be rejected because it fails `TEST11` (Sect. 2).) Per Eq. (1), if the attacker wants delay $\delta = d$, then T_2 should be:

$$T_2 = \delta + T_3 - (T_4 - T_1) = d + \text{now} + x - (\text{now} + d + 0) = x$$

The offset is therefore $\theta = x - \frac{d}{2}$. If the attacker sends the client a stream of spoofed packets with timestamps set as described above, their jitter ϕ is given by the small variance in d (since x is constant) and therefore will be accepted. This vulnerability is actually present in the current version of ntpd. We discuss how we executed it (CVE-2015-8138) against ntpd in the full version.

4   Leaky Control Queries

Thus far, we have implicitly assumed that the timestamps stored in a target's state variables are difficult for an attacker to obtain from off-path. However, we now show how they can be learned from off-path via NTP control queries.

---

[4] As observed by [19], hosts respond to unauthenticated mode 3 queries from arbitrary IP addresses by default. The mode 4 response (Fig. 4) has a *reference ID* field that reveals the IPv4 address of the responding host's time server. Thus, our off-path attacker sends its target a (legitimate) mode 3 query, and receives in response a mode 4 packet, and learns the target's server from its reference ID. Moreover, if the attacker's shenanigans cause the target to synchronize to a different server, the attacker can just learn the IP of the new server by sending the target a new mode 3 query. The attacker can then spoof packets from the new server as well.

UDP-based control queries are notorious as a vector for DDoS amplification attacks [10,18]. These DoS attacks exploit the *length* of the UDP packets sent in response to NTP's mode 7 `monlist` control query, and sometimes also NTP's mode 6 `rv` control query. Here, however, we will exploit their *contents*.

The leaky control queries. We found control queries that reveal the values stored in the `xmt` (which stores T_1 per Fig. 3) and `rec` (which stores T_4) state variables. First, launch the `as` control query to learn the association ID that a target uses for its server(s). (Association ID is a randomly assigned number that the client uses internally to identify each server [23].) Then, the query `rv assocID org` reveals the value stored in `xmt` (*i.e.*, expected origin timestamp T_1 for that server). Moreover, `rv assocID rec` reveals the value in `rec` (*i.e.*, the destination timestamp T_4 for the target's last exchange with its server).

Off-path timeshifting via leaky origin timestamp. If an attacker could continuously query its target for its expected origin timestamp (*i.e.*, the `xmt` state variable), then all bets are off. The off-path attacker could spoof bogus packets that pass TEST2 and shift time on the target. This is CVE-2015-8139.

Off-path timeshifting attack via interleaved pivot. NTP's interleaved mode is designed to provide more accurate time synchronization. Other NTP modes use the 3-bit *mode* field in the NTP packet (Fig. 4) to identify themselves (*e.g.*, client queries use mode 3 and server responses use mode 4). The interleaved mode, however, does not. Instead, a host will *automatically* enter interleaved mode if it receives a packet that passes *Interleaved TEST2*. *Interleaved TEST2* checks that the packet's *origin timestamp* field T_1 matches `rec` state variable, which stores T_4 from the previous exchange. Importantly, there is no codepath that allows the host to exit interleaved mode. The full version shows that this leads to an extremely low-rate DoS attack that works even in the absence of leaky control queries. This is CVE-2016-1548.

Now consider an off-path attacker that uses NTP control queries to continuously query for `rec`. This attacker can shift time on the client by using its knowledge of `rec` to (1) spoof a single packet passing 'interleaved TEST2' that pivots the client into interleaved mode, and then (2) spoof a stream of self-consistent packets that pass 'interleaved TEST2' and contain bogus timing information. We have confirmed that this attack works on ntpd v4.2.8p6.

Recommendation: Block control queries! By default, ntpd allows the client to answer control queries sent by any IP in the Internet. However, in response to `monlist`-based NTP DDoS amplification attacks, best practices recommend configuring ntpd with the `noquery` parameter [38]. While `noquery` should block all control queries, we suspect that `monlist` packets are filtered by middleboxes, rather than by the `noquery` option, and thus many "patched" systems remain vulnerable to our attacks. Indeed, the openNTPproject's IPv4 scan during the week of July 23, 2016 found 705,183 unique IPs responding to `monlist`. Meanwhile, during the same week we found a staggering 3,964,718 IPs responding to the `as` query.[5] The control queries we exploit likely remain out of firewall

---

[5] To avoid being blacklisted, we refrained from sending `monlist` queries.

blacklists because (1) they are undocumented in RFC5905 and (2) are thus far unexploited. As such, we suggest that either (1) `noquery` be used, or (2) firewalls block *all* mode 6 and mode 7 NTP packets from unwanted IPs.

5   Measuring the Attack Surface

We use network measurements to determine the number of IPs in the wild that are vulnerable to our off-path attacks. We start with zmap [14] to scan the entire IPv4 address space (from July 27 – July 29, 2016) using NTP's `as` control query and obtain responses from 3,964,718 unique IPs. The scan was broken up into 254 shards, each completing in 2–3 min and containing 14,575,000 IPs. At the completion of each shard, we run a script that sends each responding IP the sequence of queries shown below.

```
rv 'associd'
rv 'associd' org
rv 'associd' rec
rv
mode 3 NTPv4 query
```

These queries check for leaky origin and destination timestamps, per Sect. 4, and also solicit a regular NTP server response packet (mode 4). Our scan did not modify the internal state of any of the queried systems. We solicit server responses packets using RFC5905-compliant NTP client queries (mode 3), and RFC1305-compliant mode 6 control packets identical to those produced by the standard NTP control query program ntpq. We obtained a response to at least one of the control queries from 3,822,681 (96.4%) of the IPs responding to our `as` scan of IPv4 address space. We obtained server response packets (mode 4) from 3,274,501 (82.6%) of the responding IPs.

5.1   State of Crypto

The general wisdom suggests that NTP client/server communications are typically not cryptographically authenticated; this follows because (1) NTP uses pre-shared symmetric keys for its MAC, which makes key distribution cumbersome [5], and (2) NTP's Autokey [15] protocol for public-key authentication is widely considered to be broken [32]. We can use our scan to validate the general wisdom, since `as` also reveals a host's 'authentication status' with each of its servers or peers. Of 3,964,718 IPs that responded to the `as` command, we find merely 78,828 (2.0%) IPs that have *all* associations authenticated. Meanwhile, 3,870,933 (97.6%) IPs have *all* their associations unauthenticated. We find 93,785 (2.4%) IPs have at least one association authenticated.

5.2   Leaky Origin Timestamps

Of 3,964,718 IPs responding to the `as` query, a staggering 3,759,832 (94.8%) IPs leaked their origin timestamp.

Table 1. Hosts leaking origin timestamp.

Total	Unauthenticated	Stratum 2–15	Good timekeepers
3,759,832	3,681,790	2,974,574	2,484,775

But how many of these leaky hosts are vulnerable to off-path timeshifting attacks described in Sect. 4? Our results are summarized in Table 1. First, we find that only 78,042 (2.1%) of the IPs that leak `org` to us have authenticated *all* associations with their servers, leaving them out of the attackable pool. Next, we note that stratum 1 hosts are not usually vulnerable to this attack, since they sit a the root of the NTP hierarchy (see Sect. 2) and thus don't take time from any server. On the other hand, there are 2,974,574 (80.8%) stratum 2–15 IPs that leak their origin timestamp and synchronize to at least one unauthenticated server. These are all vulnerable to our attack. We do not count 601,043 (16.3%) IPs that have either (1) stratum 0 or 16 (unsynchronized), OR (2) conflicting stratums in `rv` and server responses (mode 4). Finally, we check if these 3M vulnerable IPs are 'functional' or are just misconfigured or broken systems by using data from our mode 3 query scan to determine the quality of their timekeeping. We found that 2,484,775 (83.5%) of these leaky IPs are good timekeepers—their absolute offset values were less than 0.1 s.[6] Of these, we find 490,032 (19.7%) IPs with stratum 2. These are good targets for attack, so that the impact of the attack trickles down the NTP stratum hierarchy.

5.3 Zero-Origin Timestamp Vulnerability

The zero-Origin timestamp vulnerability was introduced seven years ago in ntpd v4.2.6 (Dec 2009),

Table 2. Hosts leaking zero-Origin timestamp.

Total	Unauthenticated	Stratum 2–15	Good timekeepers
1,269,265	1,249,212	892,672	691,902

when a line was added to clear `xmt` after a packet passes `TEST2`.[7] Thus, one way to bound the attack surface for the zero-Origin timestamp vulnerability is to use control queries as measurement side-channel. We consider all our origin-timestamp leaking hosts, and find the ones that leak a timestamp of zero. Of 3,759,832 (94.8%) origin-leaking IPs, we find 1,269,265 (33.8%) IPs that leaked a zero-Origin timestamp. We scrutinize these hosts in Table 2 and find $\approx 700\,K$ interesting targets. Importantly, however, that this is likely an underestimate of the attack surface, since the zero-Origin vulnerability does *not* require the exploitation of leaky control queries.

5.4 Interleaved Pivot Vulnerability

The interleaved pivot DoS vulnerability was introduced in the same version as the zero-Origin timestamp vul-

Table 3. Hosts leaking `rec` and zero-Origin timestamps. (Underestimates hosts vulnerable to the interleaved pivot timeshifting attack.)

Total	Unauthenticated	Stratum 2–15	Good timekeepers
1,267,628	1,247,656	893,979	691,393

nerability. Thus, the IPs described in Sect. 5.3 are also vulnerable to this attack.

---

[6] We compute the offset θ using Eq. (2), with T_1, T_2, T_3 from the packet timestamps and T_4 from the frame arrival time of the mode 4 response packet .

[7] See Line 1094 in `ntp_proto.c` in https://github.com/ntp-project/ntp/commit/fb8fa5f6330a7583ec74fba2dfb7b6bf62bdd246.

Next, we check which IPs are vulnerable to the interleaved pivot *timeshifting attacks* (Sect. 4). These hosts must (1) leak the `rec` state variable and (2) use a version of ntpd later than 4.2.6. Leaks of `rec` are also surprisingly prevalent: 3,724,465 IPs leaked `rec` (93.9% of the 4M that responded to `as`). These could be vulnerable if they are using ntpd versions post v4.2.6. We cannot identify the versions of all of these hosts, but we do know that hosts that also leak zero as their expected origin timestamp are using versions post v4.2.6. We find 1,267,265 (34%) such IPs and scrutinize them in Table 3.

6   Securing the Client/Server Protocol

We now move beyond identifying attacks and *prove security* for modified client/server datagram protocols for NTP. Figures 6 and 7 present a new client/server protocol that provides 32-bits of randomization for the origin timestamp used in TEST2.

Clients use the algorithm in Fig. 6 to process received packets. While the client continues to listen to server response packets (mode 4) even when it does not have an outstanding query, this receive algorithm has several features that differ from RFC5905 (Fig. 5). First, when a packet passes TEST2, we clear `xmt` by setting it to a random 64-bit value, rather than to zero. We also require that, upon reboot, the client initializes its `xmt` values for each server to a random 64-bit value. Second, TEST2 alone provides replay protection and we eliminate TEST1 and TEST3. (TEST3 is not needed because of how `xmt` is cleared. Eliminating TEST3 is also consistent with the implementation in ntpd versions after v4.2.6.)

Clients use the algorithm in Fig. 7 to send packets. Recall that the first 32 bits of the origin timestamp are seconds, and the last 32 bits are subseconds.

```
def client_receive_mode4( pkt ):

    server = find_server(pkt.srcIP)

    if (server.auth == True and
        pkt.MAC is invalid):
        return           # bad MAC

    if pkt.T1 != server.xmt:
        return           # fail test2

    server.xmt = randbits(64)  # clear xmt
    server.org = pkt.T3        # update state variables
    server.rec = pkt.receive_time()
    process(pkt)
return
```

```
def client_transmit_mode3_e32( precision ):

    r = randbits(precision)
    sleep for r*(2**(- precision)) seconds

    # fuzz LSB of xmt
    fuzz = randbits(32 - precision)
    server.xmt = now ^ fuzz

    # form the packet
    pkt.T1 = server.org
    pkt.T2 = server.rec
    pkt.T3 = server.xmt
    ... # fill in other fields

    if server.auth == True:
        MAC(pkt)      #append MAC

    send(pkt)
return
```

Fig. 6. Pseudocode for processing a response. We also require that the xmt variable be initialized as a randomly-chosen 64-bit value, *i.e.*, server.xmt = randbits(64), when ntpd first boots.

Fig. 7. This function is run when the polling algorithm signals that it is time to query server. If server.auth is set, then pkt is authenticated with a MAC.

First, a client with a clock of precision ρ put a $(32 - \rho)$-bit random value in the $(32 - \rho)$ lowest order bits. Next, the client obtains the remaining ρ bits of entropy by randomizing the packet's sending time. When the polling algorithm indicates that a query should be sent, the client sleeps for a random subsecond period in $[0, 2^{-\rho}]$ seconds, and then constructs the mode 3 query packet. We therefore obtain 32 bits of entropy in the expected origin timestamp, while still preserving the semantics of NTP packets—the mode 4 packet's origin timestamp field (Fig. 4) still contains T_1 (where T_1 is as defined in Fig. 3).

The chronyd and openNTPd implementations also use a client/server protocol that differs from the one in RFC5905. This protocol just sets the expected origin timestamp to be a random 64-bit nonce (see Fig. 8).

While this provides 64-bits of randomness in the origin timestamp, it breaks the semantics of the NTP packet timestamps, because the server response packet no longer contains T_1 as defined in Fig. 3. (Instead, the client must additionally retain T_1 in local state variable server.localxmt.) In the full version we explain why this means that the chrony/openNTPd protocol *cannot* be used for NTP's symmetric mode (mode 1/2), but our protocol (which preserves timestamp semantics) can be used for symmetric mode.

Both our protocol (Figs. 6 and 7) and the chronyd/openNTPd protocol (Figs. 6 and 8) can be used to protect client/server mode from off-path

```
def client_transmit_mode3_e64( precision ):

    # store the origin timestamp locally
    server.localxmt = now

    # form the packet
    server.xmt = randbits(64) #64-bit nonce
    pkt.T1 = server.org
    pkt.T2 = server.rec
    pkt.T3 = server.xmt
    ... # fill in other fields

    if server.auth == True:
        MAC(pkt)    #append MAC

    send(pkt)
return
```

Fig. 8. Alternate client/server protocol used by chronyd/openNTPd, that randomizes all 64-bits of the origin timestamp. This function is run when the polling algorithm signals that it is time to query server.

attacks (when NTP packets are unauthenticated) and on-path attacks (when NTP packets are authenticated with a secure message authentication code (MAC)[8].) Security holds as long as (1) all randomization is done with a cryptographic pseudorandom number generator (RNG), rather than the weak ntp_random() function currently used by ntpd [3], (2) the expected origin timestamp is not leaked via control queries, and (3) NTP strictly imposes $k = 4$ or $k = 8$ as the minimum number of consistent timing samples required before the client considers updating its clock. The last requirement is needed because 32-bits of randomness, alone, is not sufficient to thwart a determined attacker. However, by requiring k consistent timing samples in a row, the attacker has to correctly guess about $32k$ random bits (rather than just 32 random bits).

---

[8] RFC5905 specifies MD5(key||message) for authenticating NTP packets, but this is not a secure MAC [6]. We are currently in the processes of standardizing a new secure MAC for NTP [21].

Fortunately, because of TEST11 (see Sect. 2), ntpd already requires $k \geq 4$ *most of the time*.[9]

We obtained these results by developing a cryptographic model for security against off- and on-path NTP attacks. We then used this model prove security for off- and on-path attacks, both for our protocol, and for the chronyd/openNTPd protocol. Details are in the full version.

7   Summary and Recommendations

We have identified several vulnerabilities in the NTP specifications both in RFC5905 [25] and in its control query specification in (obsoleted) RFC1305 [23], leading to several working off-path attacks on NTP's most widely used client/server mode (Sects. 3 and 4). Millions of IPs are vulnerable our these attacks (Sect. 5). In the full version, we also discuss denial-of-service attacks on symmetric mode.

Many of our attacks are possible because RFC5905 recommends that same codepath is used to handle packets from all of NTP's different modes. Our strongest attack, the zero-0rigin timestamp attack (CVE-2015-8139), follows because NTP's client/server mode shares the same codepath as symmetric mode. (In the full version, we explain why the initialization of symmetric mode requires that hosts accept NTP packets with origin timestamp set to zero; this leads to the zero-0rigin timestamp attack on client/server mode, where the attacker convinces a target client to accept a bogus packet because its origin timestamp is set to zero.) Similarly, the fact that interleave mode and client/server mode shares the same codepath gives rise to the interleave pivot attack (CVE-2016-1548). Thus, we recommend that different codepaths be used for different modes. This is feasible, since a packet's mode is trivially determined by its *mode* field (Fig. 4). The one exception is interleaved mode, so we suggest that interleaved mode be assigned a distinguishing value in the NTP packet.

Our attacks also follow because the NTP specification does not properly respect TEST2. We therefore propose a new backwards-compatible client/server protocol that gives TEST2 the respect it deserves (Sect. 6). We developed a framework for evaluating the security of NTP's client/server protocol and used it to prove that our protocol prevents (1) off-path spoofing attacks on unauthenticated NTP and (2) on-path replay attacks when NTP is cryptographically authenticated with a MAC. We have proved the similar results for a different client/server protocol used by chronyd and openNTPD. (The proofs are in the full version.) We recommend that implementations adopt either protocol.

Our final recommendation is aimed at systems administrators. We suggest that firewalls and ntpd clients block *all* incoming NTP control (mode 6, 7) and timing queries (mode 1, 2 or 3) from unwanted IPs (Sect. 4), rather than just the notorious `monlist` control query exploited in DDoS amplification attacks.

---

[9] However, it is not always true that $k \geq 4$. In the full version we present an ntpd bug (CVE-2016-7433) that allows for $k = 1$ upon reboot.

Acknowledgements. We are grateful to Jared Mauch for access to the openNTP-project data. We thank the Network Time Foundation and the maintainers of chrony and NTPsec for patching vulnerabilities described here. We also thank Majdi Abbas, Stephen Gray, Ran Canetti, Ethan Heilman, Yossi Gilad, Leonid Reyzin, and Matt Street for useful discussions. This work was supported by the MACS project under NSF Frontier grant CNS-1414119, by NSF grant 1350733, by a Sloan Research Fellowship, and by gifts from Cisco.

References

1. https://github.com/dfoxfranke/nts
2. https://github.com/mlichvar/chrony/blob/master/ntp_core.c#L908
3. https://github.com/ntp-project/ntp/blob/1a399a03e674da08cfce2cdb847bfb65d 65df237/libntp/ntp_random.c
4. https://github.com/philpennock/openntpd/blob/master/client.c#L174
5. The NIST authenticated NTP service (2010). http://www.nist.gov/pml/div688/ grp40/auth-ntp.cfm. Accessed July 2015
6. Bellare, M., Canetti, R., Krawczyk, H.: Keying hash functions for message authentication. In: Koblitz, N. (ed.) CRYPTO 1996. LNCS, vol. 1109, pp. 1–15. Springer, Heidelberg (1996). https://doi.org/10.1007/3-540-68697-5_1
7. Canetti, R.: Universally composable security: a new paradigm for cryptographic protocols. In: FOCS, pp. 136–145. IEEE (2001)
8. Clayton, R., Murdoch, S.J., Watson, R.N.M.: Ignoring the Great Firewall of China. In: Danezis, G., Golle, P. (eds.) PET 2006. LNCS, vol. 4258, pp. 20–35. Springer, Heidelberg (2006). https://doi.org/10.1007/11957454_2
9. corbixgwelt. Timejacking & bitcoin: The global time agreement puzzle (culubas blog) (2011). http://culubas.blogspot.com/2011/05/timejacking-bitcoin_802.html. Accessed Aug 2015
10. Czyz, J., Kallitsis, M., Gharaibeh, M., Papadopoulos, C., Bailey, M., Karir, M.: Taming the 800 pound gorilla: the rise and decline of NTP DDoS attacks. In: Proceedings of the 2014 Internet Measurement Conference, pp. 435–448. ACM (2014)
11. Dowling, B., Stebila, D., Zaverucha, G.: Authenticated network time synchronization. In: 25th USENIX Security Symposium (USENIX Security 2016), Austin, TX, pp. 823–840. USENIX Association, August 2016
12. Duan, H., Weaver, N., Zhao, Z., Hu, M., Liang, J., Jiang, J., Li, K., Paxson, V.: Hold-on: protecting against on-path DNS poisoning. In: Proceedings of Workshop on Securing and Trusting Internet Names, SATIN (2012)
13. Durairajan, R., Mani, S.K., Sommers, J., Barford, P.: Time's forgotten: using NTP to understand internet latency. In: HotNets 2015, November 2015
14. Durumeric, Z., Wustrow, E., Halderman, J.A.: ZMap: fast internet-wide scanning and its security applications. In: USENIX Security, pp. 605–620. Citeseer (2013)
15. Haberman, B., Mills, D.: RFC 5906: Network Time Protocol Version 4: Autokey Specification. Internet Engineering Task Force (IETF) (2010). https://tools.ietf. org/html/rfc5906
16. Itkin, E., Wool, A.: A security analysis and revised security extension for the precision time protocol. CoRR, abs/1603.00707 (2016)
17. Klein, J.: Becoming a time lord - implications of attacking time sources. Shmoocon Firetalks 2013 (2013). https://youtu.be/XogpQ-iA6Lw

18. Krämer, L., Krupp, J., Makita, D., Nishizoe, T., Koide, T., Yoshioka, K., Rossow, C.: AmpPot: monitoring and defending against amplification DDoS attacks. In: Bos, H., Monrose, F., Blanc, G. (eds.) RAID 2015. LNCS, vol. 9404, pp. 615–636. Springer, Cham (2015). https://doi.org/10.1007/978-3-319-26362-5_28

19. Malhotra, A., Cohen, I.E., Brakke, E., Goldberg, S.: Attacking the network time protocol. In: NDSS 2016, February 2016

20. Malhotra, A., Goldberg, S.: Attacking NTP's authenticated broadcast mode. In: SIGCOMM Computer Communication Review, April 2016

21. Malhotra, A., Goldberg, S.: Message Authentication Codes for the Network Time Protocol. Internet Engineering Task Force (IETF), November 2016. https:// datatracker.ietf.org/doc/draft-ietf-ntp-mac/

22. Mauch, J.: openntpproject: NTP Scanning Project. http://openntpproject.org/

23. Mills, D.: RFC 1305: Network Time Protocol (Version 3) Specification, Implementation and Analysis. Internet Engineering Task Force (IETF) (1992). http://tools. ietf.org/html/rfc1305

24. Mills, D., Haberman, B.: draft-haberman-ntpwg-mode-6-cmds-00: Control Messages Protocol for Use with Network Time Protocol Version 4. Internet Engineering Task Force (IETF), May 2016. https://datatracker.ietf.org/doc/draft-haberman-ntpwg-mode-6-cmds/

25. Mills, D., Martin, J., Burbank, J., Kasch, W.: RFC 5905: Network Time Protocol Version 4: Protocol and Algorithms Specification. Internet Engineering Task Force (IETF) (2010). http://tools.ietf.org/html/rfc5905

26. Mills, D.L.: Computer Network Time Synchronization, 2nd edn. CRC Press, Boca Raton (2011)

27. Minar, N.: A survey of the NTP network (1999)

28. Mizrahi, T.: A game theoretic analysis of delay attacks against time synchronization protocols. In: Precision Clock Synchronization for Measurement Control and Communication (ISPCS), pp. 1–6. IEEE (2012)

29. Mizrahi, T.: RFC 7384 (Informational): Security Requirements of Time Protocols in Packet Switched Networks. Internet Engineering Task Force (IETF) (2012). http://tools.ietf.org/html/rfc7384

30. Moreira, N., Lazaro, J., Jimenez, J., Idirin, M., Astarloa, A.: Security mechanisms to protect IEEE 1588 synchronization: state of the art and trends. In: 2015 IEEE International Symposium on Precision Clock Synchronization for Measurement, Control, and Communication (ISPCS), pp. 115–120. IEEE (2015)

31. Murta, C.D., Torres Jr. P.R., Mohapatra, P.: Characterizing quality of time and topology in a time synchronization network. In: GLOBECOM (2006)

32. Röttger, S.: Analysis of the ntp autokey procedures. Master's thesis, Technische Universitt Braunschweig (2012)

33. Selvi, J.: Bypassing HTTP strict transport security. In: Black Hat Europe (2014)

34. Selvi, J.: Breaking SSL using time synchronisation attacks. In: DEFCON'23 (2015)

35. Sherman, J.A., Levine, J.: Usage analysis of the NIST internet time service. J. Res. Natl. Inst. Stand. Technol. **121**, 33 (2016)

36. Sibold, D., Roettger, S.: draft-ietf-ntp-network-time-security: Network Time Security. Internet Engineering Task Force (IETF) (2015). http://tools.ietf.org/html/ draft-ietf-ntp-network-time-security-08

37. Sibold, D., Roettger, S., Teichel, K.: draft-ietf-ntp-network-time-security-10: Network Time Security. Internet Engineering Task Force (IETF) (2015). https://tools. ietf.org/html/draft-ietf-ntp-network-time-security-10

38. Stenn, H.: Securing the network time protocol. ACM Queue **13**(1), 20–25 (2015). Communications of the ACM

39. Stenn, H.: Security notice, 27 April 2016. http://support.ntp.org/bin/view/Main/SecurityNotice
40. Weaver, N., Sommer, R., Paxson, V.: Detecting forged TCP reset packets. In: NDSS (2009)

Short Paper: On Deployment of DNS-Based Security Enhancements

Pawel Szalachowski$^{(\boxtimes)}$ and Adrian Perrig

ETH Zurich, Zürich, Switzerland
psz@inf.ethz.ch

Abstract. Although the Domain Name System (DNS) was designed as a naming system, its features have made it appealing to repurpose it for the deployment of novel systems. One important class of such systems are security enhancements, and this work sheds light on their deployment. We show the characteristics of these solutions and measure reliability of DNS in these applications. We investigate the compatibility of these solutions with the Tor network, signal necessary changes, and report on surprising drawbacks in Tor's DNS resolution.

1 Introduction

DNS is one of the most successful Internet infrastructures. It is a naming system for resources over the Internet, and its most prominent use is to translate human-readable names to IP addresses. Currently, this hierarchical and distributed system is a core infrastructure of the Internet, and over the years the availability and reliability of standard DNS operations have increased [17]. Although DNS is primarily (and was designed as) a system for name resolution, due to its success and flexibility it is used by various, not initially intended, applications. One family of such applications are various security enhancements. These systems are particularly difficult to deploy [16], as different actors are reluctant to deploy and invest in a security-dedicated infrastructure. Due to low cost, well-understood operations and administration, and its ubiquity, DNS seems like an ideal environment to support deployment of new security enhancements. Thus, it is naturally appealing to protocol designers to repurpose the DNS infrastructure, rather than designing and deploying a new one. For those reasons, DNS is currently being employed by various security enhancements. As a consequence, new systems rely on the infrastructure designed decades ago. Therefore, it is necessary to investigate how robust and applicable the infrastructure is for these use cases. The essence of the new uses is to transport additional information using DNS, however, there exist indications that such a transport can be unreliable.

In this work we make the following contributions: *(1)* investigate the use of DNS-based security enhancements, *(2)* study DNS reliability for these applications, *(3)* check the compatibility of the enhancements if the DNS resolution occurs over Tor.

© International Financial Cryptography Association 2017
A. Kiayias (Ed.): FC 2017, LNCS 10322, pp. 424–433, 2017.
https://doi.org/10.1007/978-3-319-70972-7_24

2 Background

DNS Resolution is a process of translating human-readable domain names to IP addresses. It is conducted through the DNS infrastructure, namely *DNS clients*, *resolvers*, and *servers*. To resolve a domain name, e.g., www.a.com, a client initiates the process by querying its resolver, which in turn contacts one of the *DNS root servers* (root servers' IP addresses are fixed and known to resolvers). The root server returns an address of a *DNS authoritative server* for the com domain. Then, the resolver queries the com authoritative server to find an authoritative server for a.com, which finally is queried about www.a.com. The a.com authoritative server returns the IP address(es) of www.a.com. The lengthy resolution process is usually shortcut by using cached information.

DNS allows to associate various information with domain names. Information is encoded and delivered within *resource records* (RRs) with dedicated types, e.g., A and AAAA RRs map domain names to IPv4 and IPv6 addresses, respectively, NS RRs indicate authoritative servers, while TXT RRs can associate an arbitrary text. DNS responses can contain multiple RRs of the queried type. It is also possible to translate IP addresses into domain names (to this end PTR RRs are used).

DNS deploys UDP as a default transport protocol, however, for responses larger than 512 bytes a *failover* mechanism is introduced. Larger responses are truncated to fit 512 bytes and marked by a truncated flag. Resolvers receiving a truncated response query the server again via TCP to obtain the complete response. (Clients can increase the limit by signaling the maximum UDP response size they can handle [18].)

DNS Resolution (Un)Reliability. Although DNS is reliable for its major application (i.e., translating names to IP addresses), the reliability for other applications is questionable. For instance, many of DNS clients, resolvers, and servers are realized as non-compliant implementations [3]. It was reported [9] that a significant fraction of all clients (2.6%) and a large fraction of resolvers (17%) cannot perform the UDP-to-TCP failover. This behavior limits clients ability to receive responses larger than 512 bytes. Another potential issue [3] is caused by network environments, where devices can handle only unusually small Maximum Transmission Unit (MTU) packets, thus introducing IP fragmentation decreasing the reliability of the DNS resolution. DNS traffic is also a subject to traffic analysis, and some middleboxes manipulate DNS responses [7,19]. It is believed that some non-standard RRs are discriminated by non-compliant implementations or/and network devices. For instance, some experiments [12,19] indicate that A RRs are more reliable than TXT RRs.

3 Security Enhancements Employing DNS

We focus our study on two families of security enhancements that can benefit from a robust DNS infrastructure, namely email and TLS PKI enhancements.

The main reason why DNS infrastructure can be appealing for these technologies is that both email and TLS PKI are domain based. As the DNS lookup usually precedes the email exchange or TLS connection establishment, the client can obtain some relevant information before the connection setup. Additionally, such DNS-based information pre-fetching does not violate the privacy, as no additional third party is contacted (DNS servers are contacted anyways). A security assumption for these schemes is that an adversary cannot control DNS entries of targeted domains.

3.1   Email

SPF [10] enables domains to make assertions (in DNS) about hosts that are authorized to originate email for that domain. When an email is received by an email exchanger, it parses the domain name from the email's `From` address field, and queries the DNS to check whether the sender is authorized to send email. This mitigates spam and phishing emails that abuse the `From` field. SPF mainly uses `TXT` RRs, although a dedicated `SPF` RR was introduced.

Sender ID [1] is an anti-spoofing proposal based on SPF. The main difference is that it aims in verifying the sender address displayed to an email client (the `From` field and the address displayed by email clients can differ). Such an address is introduced as a Purported Responsible Address (PRA) [15]. By setting a special `TXT` or `SPF` record, a domain can specify if only SPF should be verified, or both SPF and PRA, or PRA only.

DKIM [4] is an email authentication protocol based on signatures. A domain publishes RR with its public key. Next, the domain's outbound email server signs sent emails with the corresponding private key. An inbound email server, after receiving a signed email, extracts its origin domain name (via the `From` field) and performs a DNS lookup to obtain the domain's public key used to verify the email. Usually, DKIM is executed by email servers rather than email clients (i.e., authors and recipients). Public keys are stored in `TXT` RRs, and to obtain a key of `a.com`, `_dkim.a.com` is queried. DKIM protects emails from modification, however, the scheme can be bypassed by an active adversary by simply stripping the DKIM headers.

DMARC [11] is a comprehensive system that allows an email-originating organization to express domain-level policies for email management. A policy can specify how emails should be validated and how receivers should handle validation failures. Additionally, DMARC policies can be used to implement a reporting system (i.e., to report on actions performed under a policy). DMARC deploys SPF and DKIM, and domain owners can specify which of those mechanisms (or both) should be used to validate their emails. DMARC uses `TXT` RRs to store policies, and the RRs are associated with domain names prepended with the `_dmarc.` prefix, e.g., `_dmarc.a.com`.

3.2   TLS PKI Enhancement

DANE [8] allows domains to specify their key(s) or key(s) of Certificate Authorities (CAs) they trust. To this end, a domain publishes a special DNS entry with its public key(s) or public key(s) of trusted CA(s). DANE introduces a new `TLSA` RR. The scheme relies on DNSSEC, requiring that the RRs be signed with the domain's DNSSEC key. DANE records are created per service, thus a DANE query encodes a transport protocol, and a port number used. For instance, keys of a HTTPS server running at `www.a.com` can be checked by querying `_443._tcp.www.a.com`. Such a flexible mechanism allows to use DANE for all services that deploy TLS.

CAA [6] aims to provide trust agility and remove a single point of failure from the TLS PKI. Specifically, it allows a domain to specify (in DNS) CA(s) authorized to issue certificates for the domain. This simple procedure can prevent the two following threats: (i) compromised CA: a CA that is not listed by a domain cannot issue a valid certificate for the domain, (ii) identity spoofing: a benign CA can refuse certificate issuance if it is not listed by the domain. CAA introduces new `CAA` RRs, which do not have to be protected via DNSSEC, although it is recommended.

Log-based approaches are recent PKI enhancements that introduce publicly-verifiable logs. The most prominent example is CT [13], whose goal is to make all certificates issued by CAs visible. To this end, every certificate is submitted to a log, which returns a signed *promise* that the certificate will be logged. Then, in every TLS connection a client receives a certificate accompanied with the logging promise. However, it is important to verify whether the promise was met, and to do so the client has to obtain a proof from the log that given certificate indeed was logged. Laurie et al. propose [14] that clients ask a special CT-supported DNS server for such a proof. An advantage of this scheme is that DNS requests are sent via a local resolver, thus the CT DNS server (and the log) cannot identify the client, but only his resolver (usually run by his ISP).

4   Current State of Deployment

First, we investigate deployment characteristics of the enhancements. In particular, we focus on factors that can influence reliability of DNS as a transport (i.e., RRs used and response sizes). To this end, we conduct a measurement of the hundred thousand most popular domains of the Internet (according to the Alexa list: http://www.alexa.com/topsites). For each domain name we queried for RRs that implement a given functionality. We queried for DANE's RRs specific to HTTPS, i.e., `_443._tcp.`, and `_443._tcp.www.` prepended to a queried domain name. We omitted log-based mechanism, as no scheme is combined with DNS yet (up to our knowledge).

Table 1 presents the measured scale of deployment with the response size characteristics, while Fig. 1 presents a CDF of the measured response sizes. As depicted, `TXT` RRs dominate, constituting about 94% of all successful responses. It is mainly due to well-established deployment of the mail enhancements

Table 1. Measured scale of deployment and response sizes.

Mechanism	RR(s) queried	Successful responses	Response size (B)			
			Min	Med	Avg	Max
SPF	TXT	53365 (53.37%)	25	148	185	3138
	SPF	4182 (4.18%)	27	122	144	1606
Sender ID	TXT	1766 (1.77%)	56	303	333	1285
	SPF	98 (0.10%)	79	234	247	538
DKIM	TXT	5049 (5.05%)	49	64	97	1007
DMARC	TXT	7361 (7.36%)	35	133	140	1003
DANE	TLSA	48 (0.05%)	80	88	96	182
CAA	CAA	15 (0.02%)	58	106	106	269

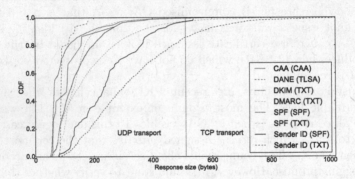

Fig. 1. CDF of the measured response sizes.

(SPF mainly). Although, new RR types (like SPF) were introduced, the operators clearly prefer to rely on older TXT RRs. PKI enhancements do not have significant deployment, which is probably caused by their relative immaturity (e.g., SPF was introduced in 2006, while DANE and CAA in 2012 and 2013, respectively). Another finding is that most of the responses fit the limit of 512 bytes. An exception are responses including Sender ID's data (approximately 15% of them exceed the limit).

5   Reliability of DNS

To investigate how reliable DNS is for the security enhancements, we conducted a series of experiments using RIPE Atlas (https://atlas.ripe.net/), the largest publicly available global testbed for network measurements. RIPE Atlas is a network of hardware devices, called *probes*, used for active Internet measurements. It supports DNS measurements, and provides good geographic coverage [2]. Through the measurements we wanted to answer the two following questions:

1. Are TXT RRs discriminated (dropped or manipulated) by some DNS clients/resolvers or network devices?
2. How reliable is DNS in transporting UDP responses larger than 512 bytes?

The first question is motivated by the importance of TXT RRs (see Sect. 3) and by the common belief that a significant fraction of TXT RRs is not transported correctly (probably due to its non-standard type). We investigate the second question to verify how the 512 bytes limit for UDP DNS responses is enforced by the DNS infrastructure. This question is important as the previous work indicates that the TCP support at DNS resolvers is incomplete [9], thus it is risky to rely on the failover mechanism. (Note, that RIPE Atlas does not expose an option to check whether a probe's DNS client/resolver correctly handles responses with the truncated flag set.)

In order to conduct the measurements, we launched an authoritative DNS server, and prepared it with DNS responses of the following sizes:

494 bytes: the size is below the 512 bytes limit, but it can handle most of the current responses (see Fig. 1). We investigated transport over A and TXT RRs, to verify whether TXT RRs are discriminated (while compared to A RRs).
1005 bytes: responses with this size allow us to investigate how robust the DNS infrastructure is, when the UDP response size limit is exceeded. This size is also below the standard MTUs (i.e., about 1500 bytes).
1997 bytes: by responses with this size, we want to investigate how exceeding the standard MTU influences DNS transport.

Our DNS server was configured not to set the truncated flag, and in the RIPE Atlas setting we set the acceptable response size to 4096 bytes. We scheduled measurements on the RIPE Atlas at the end of August 2016. We assigned all 9270 connected probes to query our DNS server. For response sizes of 1005 and 1997 bytes we investigated only TXT RRs. Depending on the queried target, the following number of probes have responded: 8952 for queried A and TXT RRs sent in 494 bytes responses, 8934 for 1005 bytes responses, and 7990 for 1997 bytes responses. Note, that each probe could respond with multiple DNS responses.

In Table 2 we present the obtained results. As probes can use the same, popular resolvers, beside the absolute number of responses, we also present results for unique resolutions, where a unique resolution is defined as a triple: number of RRs within a response, response size, and resolver's address. The successful results are divided into responses that were received with the exact size served (by the authoritative DNS server), and larger responses (resolvers add other information that is relevant to the query, like addresses of authoritative servers). Failed resolutions are divided into three categories. First, the fraction of resolution errors is presented. These are errors such as a DNS resolver that could not be found, or a failed connection. Then, we present empty DNS responses (i.e., number of answers equals zero). The last category shows the number of truncated responses, i.e., responses with fewer number of RRs than expected or/and shorter payload of the response.

Table 2. Measured reliability of DNS.

	Test	Total	Successful resolutions			Failed resolutions			
			Total	Exact	Larger	Total	Error	Empty	Truncated
All responses	A	16570	15468	15356	112	1102	867	189	46
	494B	100%	93.35%	92.67%	0.68%	6.65%	5.23%	1.14%	0.28%
	TXT	16570	15460	15343	117	1110	892	206	12
	494B	100%	93.30%	92.60%	0.71%	6.70%	5.38%	1.24%	0.07%
	TXT	16553	13480	936	12544	3073	1504	1155	414
	1005B	100%	81.44%	5.65%	75.78%	18.56%	9.09%	6.98%	2.50%
	TXT	13727	7286	29	7257	6441	2360	3617	464
	1997B	100%	53.08%	0.21%	52.87%	46.92%	17.19%	26.35%	3.38%
Unique responses	A	7452	6625	6526	99	827	633	166	28
	494B	100%	88.90%	87.57%	1.33%	11.10%	8.49%	2.23%	0.38%
	TXT	7447	6618	6516	102	829	638	181	10
	494B	100%	88.87%	87.50%	1.37%	11.13%	8.57%	2.43%	0.13%
	TXT	7938	6222	450	5772	1716	922	636	158
	1005B	100%	78.38%	5.67%	72.71%	21.62%	11.62%	8.01%	1.99%
	TXT	6887	3741	19	3722	3146	1252	1652	242
	1997B	100%	54.32%	0.28%	54.04%	45.68%	18.18%	23.99%	3.51%

Our first observation is that for the 494 bytes long responses there is only a negligible difference between reliability of A-only responses versus TXT-only responses. Secondly, the results show that UDP responses with size above the 512 bytes limit increase the failure rate from 6.70% to 18.56% (all responses) and from 11.13% to 21.62% (unique responses). Taking into consideration the results about failing TCP support, it might be more effective to use UDP with increased size instead of TCP. Lastly, the largest responses investigated (1997 bytes) are successfully delivered only in about 50% of all cases. That is probably caused by MTU issues, as common MTUs over the Internet are about 1500 bytes. We also observe, that resolvers enlarge responses usually when they are large already.

Although RIPE Atlas is an ideal open testbed for such tests, it introduces some biases. Probes are plug-and-forget devices, thus an owner may be not aware that DNS resolution at his/her probe does not work properly (this could explain the large fraction of DNS errors even for the smallest responses investigated). Moreover, probes are usually installed by network-savvy users like research institutions, Internet operators, hobbyists, and the probe distribution (based on their ASes) is heavy-tailed [2].

6   Tor and Security Enhancements

Tor [5] is the most popular software and infrastructure for enabling anonymous communication over the Internet. It is an onion routing protocol, where an *encryption circuit* is selected by the Tor client software. DNS querying over Tor is also anonymous and conducted by an *exit node* of the circuit (this node will forward traffic to destinations).

The DNS resolution in Tor is restricted only to A, AAAA, and PTR RRs. This obviously limits the deployment of DNS-supported security enhancements in Tor. It is especially important for the PKI enhancements, as they assume clients to participate in the protocol (the mail enhancements are deployed mainly by the mail infrastructure).

In this section, we investigate whether the supported RRs can be used to implement DNS-supported enhancements (for instance, one could convey information on a series of A or AAAA RRs). We measured DNS resolution over Tor, using our authoritative server, that was also configured as a Tor Linux client (i.e., the server queried itself through the Tor network, as presented in Fig. 2). For every set of queries, a new Tor circuit was selected, and we conducted 15000 such resolutions. We investigated how reliable Tor is in resolving requests for the supported RRs (i.e., A, AAAA, and PTR). We checked PTR queries for both, IPv4 and IPv6 addresses.

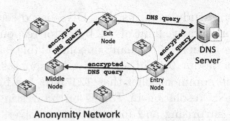

Anonymity Network

Fig. 2. Tor-based measurement scenario.

The first observation is that all asked resolvers limited DNS responses only to a single RR. This limits ways the supported RRs can be used to encode some additional data (e.g., single A query can return only four bytes). Table 3 presents the fraction of successfully resolved requests. As depicted, A queries are resolved slightly more reliably than PTR queries for IPv4 addresses, which in turn are less reliable for IPv6 addresses. The results also show, that although AAAA RRs are supported, they are resolved correctly only for 23% of requests (probably, only nodes supporting IPv6 resolve them).

Table 3. Fraction of successful resolutions (i.e., single RR returned) depending on type.

A	PTR (IPv4)	PTR (IPv6)	AAAA
99.78%	99.22%	98.89%	23.05%

Surprisingly, we observed that some resolvers fail to return any response when the response from the authoritative server is large (but still below 512 bytes). To further investigate this phenomena, we prepared responses with A RRs with different sizes. We then measured when requests are processed successfully (by success we mean a response to the client that contains a single RR, although many were served). The results (see Table 4) show that reliability of DNS

Table 4. Fraction of successful resolutions (i.e., single A RR returned) depending on the response size (from the authoritative server).

61B	110B	158B	254B	366B	398B	430B	462B	478B	494B
1 RRs	4 RRs	7 RRs	13 RRs	20 RRs	22 RRs	24 RRs	26 RRs	27 RRs	28 RRs
99.77%	99.77%	99.77%	99.77%	99.23%	99.16%	98.10%	92.87%	91.27%	38.36%

resolution decreases with the response size. Only 38% of all resolutions succeeded at all with 494 bytes long responses served.

7   Conclusions

Our study confirms that DNS-based security enhancements should respect the conservative limit of 512 bytes for responses, as robustness of DNS transport can be influenced by many uncontrollable factors. Fortunately, the limit is sufficient for about 95% of all received responses. However, our study does not confirm the common belief that TXT RRs are being discriminated. Our work identifies DNS resolution in Tor as an interesting subject for future work, as we found it surprising and inconsistent: resolvers fail to return large responses, slightly differently handle PTR RRs for IPv4 and IPv6 addresses, AAAA RRs are officially supported, but in practice are resolved only by 23% of all resolvers. We also observe that restricting other RRs (especially PKI-related, like TLSA) will actually decrease security of end users. Hence, to fulfill Tor's mission (i.e., *"to allow people to improve their privacy and security on the Internet"*) the developers should consider supporting DNS-based security enhancements.

Acknowledgment. We gratefully acknowledge support from ETH Zurich and from the Zurich Information Security and Privacy Center (ZISC). We thank Brian Trammell and the anonymous reviewers, whose feedback helped to improve the paper.

References

1. Allman, E., Katz, H.: SMTP Service Extension for Indicating the Responsible Submitter of an E-Mail Message. RFC 4405 (2006)
2. Bajpai, V., Eravuchira, S.J., Schönwälder, J.: Lessons learned from using the RIPE Atlas platform for measurement research. In: SIGCOMM CCR (2015)
3. Buddhdev, A.: Testing your Resolver for DNS Reply Size Issues (2009). https://goo.gl/gU7mNu
4. Crocker, D., Hansen, T., Kucherawy, M.: DomainKeys Identified Mail (DKIM) Signatures. RFC 6376 (2011)
5. Dingledine, R., Mathewson, N., Syverson, P.: Tor: the second-generation onion router. Technical report, DTIC Document (2004)
6. Hallam-Baker, P., Stradling, R.: DNS Certification Authority Authorization (CAA) Resource Record. RFC 6844 (2013)
7. Hätönen, S., Nyrhinen, A., Eggert, L., Strowes, S., Sarolahti, P., Kojo, M.: An experimental study of home gateway characteristics. In: ACM IMC (2010)
8. Hoffman, P., Schlyter, J.: The DNS-Based Authentication of Named Entities (DANE) Transport Layer Security (TLS) Protocol: TLSA. RFC 6698 (2012)
9. Huston, G.: A Question of DNS Protocols (2013). https://goo.gl/d8kwCK
10. Kitterman, S.: Sender Policy Framework (SPF) for Authorizing Use of Domains in Email, Version 1. RFC 7208 (2014)
11. Kucherawy, M., Zwicky, E.: Domain-Based Message Authentication, Reporting, and Conformance (DMARC). RFC 7489 (2015)
12. Langley, A.: Why not DANE in browsers (2015). https://goo.gl/0kVppI

13. Laurie, B., Langley, A., Kasper, E.: Certificate Transparency. RFC 6962 (2013)
14. Laurie, B., Phaneuf, P., Eijdenberg, A.: Certificate transparency over DNS (2016). https://goo.gl/PoLkmu
15. Lyon, J.: Purported Responsible Address in E-Mail Messages. RFC 4407 (2006)
16. Nikkhah, M., Dovrolis, C., Guérin, R.: Why didn't my (great!) protocol get adopted? In: HotNets (2015)
17. Pappas, V., Xu, Z., Lu, S., Massey, D., Terzis, A., Zhang, L.: Impact of configuration errors on DNS robustness. In: SIGCOMM CCR (2004)
18. Vixie, P.: Extension Mechanisms for DNS (EDNS0). RFC 2671 (1999)
19. Weaver, N., Kreibich, C., Nechaev, B., Paxson, V.: Implications of Netalyzrs DNS measurements. In: SATIN (2011)

Blind Signatures

A Practical Multivariate Blind Signature Scheme

Albrecht Petzoldt[1,2], Alan Szepieniec[3,4(✉)],
and Mohamed Saied Emam Mohamed[5]

[1] Kyushu University, Fukuoka, Japan
[2] NIST, Gaithersburg, USA
albrecht.petzoldt@nist.gov
[3] KU Leuven, ESAT/COSIC, Heverlee, Belgium
alan.szepieniec@esat.kuleuven.be
[4] imec, Leuven, Belgium
[5] Technische Universität Darmstadt, Darmstadt, Germany
mohamed@cdc.informatik.tu-armstadt.de

Abstract. Multivariate Cryptography is one of the main candidates for creating post-quantum cryptosystems. Especially in the area of digital signatures, there exist many practical and secure multivariate schemes. However, there is a lack of multivariate signature schemes with special properties such as blind, ring and group signatures. In this paper, we propose a generic technique to transform the Rainbow multivariate signature scheme into a blind signature schemes. The resulting scheme satisfies the usual blindness criterion and a one-more-unforgeability criterion adapted to MQ signatures, produces short blind signatures and is very efficient.

Keywords: Multivariate cryptography · Blind signatures
Rainbow signature scheme

1 Introduction

Cryptographic techniques are an essential tool to guarantee the security of communication in modern society. Today, the security of nearly all of the cryptographic schemes used in practice is based on number theoretic problems such as factoring large integers and solving discrete logarithms. The best known schemes in this area are RSA [19], DSA [11] and ECC. However, schemes like these will become insecure as soon as large enough quantum computers are built. The reason for this is Shor's algorithm [23], which solves number theoretic problems like integer factorization and discrete logarithms in polynomial time on a quantum computer. Therefore, one needs alternatives to those classical public key schemes which are based on hard mathematical problems not affected by quantum computer attacks (so called post-quantum cryptosystems).

The increasing importance of research in this area has recently been emphasized by a number of authorities. For example, the american National Security Agency has recommended governmental organizations to change their security

© International Financial Cryptography Association 2017
A. Kiayias (Ed.): FC 2017, LNCS 10322, pp. 437–454, 2017.
https://doi.org/10.1007/978-3-319-70972-7_25

infrastructures from schemes like RSA to post-quantum schemes [13] and the National Institute of Standards and Technologies (NIST) is preparing to standardize these schemes [14]. According to NIST, multivariate cryptography is one of the main candidates for this standardization process. Multivariate schemes are in general very fast and require only modest computational resources, which makes them attractive for the use on low cost devices like smart cards and RFID chips [3,4]. However, while there exist many practical multivariate standard signature schemes such as UOV [12], Rainbow [6] and Gui [18], there is a lack of multivariate signature schemes with special properties such as blind, ring, and group signatures.

Blind signature schemes allow a user, who is not in charge of the private signing key, to obtain a signature for a message d by interacting with the signer. The important point is that this signer, who holds the secret key, receives no information about the message d that is signed nor about the signature s that is created through the interaction. Nevertheless, anyone with access to the public verification key is capable of verifying that signature. Because of these unlinkability and public verifiability properties, blind signature schemes are an indispensable primitive in a host of privacy-preserving applications ranging from electronic cash to anonymous database access, e-voting, and anonymous reputation systems.

In this paper, we present a technique to transform Rainbow, a multivariate quadratic (MQ) signature scheme, into a blind signature scheme. This transformation is accomplished by joining the MQ signature scheme with the zero-knowledge MQ-based identification scheme of Sakumoto *et al.* [22]. The user queries the signer on a blinded version of the message to be signed; the signer's response is then combined with the blinding information in order to produce a non-interactive zero-knowledge proof of knowledge of a pre-image under the public verification key, which is a set of quadratic polynomials that contains the signer's public key in addition to a large random term. The only way the user can produce such a proof is by querying the signer at some point for a partial pre-image; however, because it is zero-knowledge, this proof contains no information on the message that was seen and signed by the signer, thus preventing linkage and ensuring the user's privacy.

We obtain one of the first multivariate signature schemes with special properties and more generally one of the very few candidates for establishing practical and secure post-quantum blind signatures. In terms of security requirements, our scheme satisfies the usual blindness notion, but an adapted one-more-unforgeability one which we call *universal*-one-more-unforgeability. This change is justified by the observation that the usual one-more-unforgeability notion generalizes *existential* unforgeability for regular signatures; however, MQ signatures can only be shown to offer *universal* unforgeability and hence require a universal one-more-unforgeability generalization. We instantiate our scheme with the Rainbow signature scheme and propose parameters targeting various levels of security.

The rest of this paper is organized as follows. Section 2 recalls the basic concepts of blind signatures and discusses the basic security notions. In Sect. 3 we recall the basic concepts of multivariate cryptography and review the Rainbow signature scheme, Sakumoto's multivariate identification scheme [22], and its transformation into a digital signature scheme due to Hülsing [9]. Section 4 presents our technique to extend multivariate signature schemes such as Rainbow to blind signature schemes, while Sect. 5 discusses the security of our construction. In Sect. 6 we give concrete parameter sets and analyze the efficiency of our scheme. Furthermore, in this section, we describe a proof of concept implementation of our scheme and compare it with other existing (classical and post-quantum) blind signature schemes. Finally, Sect. 7 concludes the paper.

2 Blind Signatures

Blind signature schemes as proposed by David Chaum in [2] allow a user, who is not in charge of the private signing key, to obtain a signature for a message d on behalf of the owner of the private key (called the signer). The key point hereby is that the signer gets no information about the content of the message d.

The signature generation process of a blind signature scheme is an interactive process between the user and the signer. In the first step, the user computes from the message d a blinded message $d^\star$ and sends it to the signer. The signer uses his private key to generate a signature $\sigma^\star$ for the message $d^\star$ and sends it back to the signer. Due to certain homomorphic properties in the inner structure of the blind signature scheme, the user is able to compute from $\sigma^\star$ a valid signature σ for the original message d. The receiver of a signed message can check the authenticity of the signature σ in the same way as in the case of a standard signature scheme. Figure 1 shows a graphical illustration of the signature generation process of a blind signature scheme.

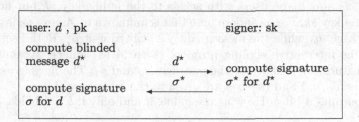

Fig. 1. Signature generation process of a blind signature scheme

Formally, a blind signature scheme $\mathcal{BS}$ is a three-tuple, consisting of two polynomial time algorithms KeyGen and Verify and an interactive signing protocol Sign [10].

– KeyGen(1^κ): The probabilistic algorithm KeyGen takes as input a security parameter κ and outputs a key pair (sk, pk) of the blind signature scheme.

- Sign: The signature generation step is an interactive protocol between the User, who gets as input a message d and a public key pk and the Signer who is given the pair (pk, sk) generated by algorithm KeyGen. At the end of the protocol, the Signer outputs either "completed" or "non-completed", while the user outputs either "failed" or a signature σ.
- Verify$((d, \sigma), pk)$: The deterministic algorithm Verify takes as input a message/signature pair (d, σ) and the public key pk. It outputs **TRUE**, if σ is a valid signature for the message d and **FALSE** otherwise.

In the following, we assume the *correctness* of the blind signature scheme $\mathcal{BS}$: If both the User and the Signer follow the protocol, the Signer outputs always "completed", independently of the message d and the output (sk, pk) of the algorithm KeyGen. Similarly, the User always outputs a signature σ and we have

$$\Pr[\text{Verify}((d, \sigma), pk) = \textbf{TRUE}] = 1.$$

The basic security criteria of a blind signature scheme are Blindness and One-More-Unforgeability.

- **Blindness:** By signing the blinded message $d^\star$, the signer of a message gets no information about the content of the message to be signed nor about the final blind signature σ. More formally, blindness can be defined using the following security game.

Game[Blindness]:
1. The adversary $\mathcal{A}$ uses the algorithm KeyGen to generate a key pair (sk, pk) of the blind signature scheme. The public key pk is made public, while $\mathcal{A}$ keeps sk as his private key.
2. The adversary $\mathcal{A}$ outputs two messages d_0 and d_1, which might depend on sk and pk.
3. Let u_0 and u_1 be users with access to the public key pk but not to the secret key sk. For a random bit b that is unknown to $\mathcal{A}$, user u_0 is given the message d_b, while the message d_{1-b} is sent to user u_1. Both users engage in the interactive signing protocol (with $\mathcal{A}$ as signer), obtaining blind signatures σ_0 and σ_1 for the messages d_0 and d_1. The message/signature pairs (d_0, σ_0) and (d_1, σ_1) are given to the adversary $\mathcal{A}$.
4. $\mathcal{A}$ outputs a bit $\bar{b}$. He wins the game, if and only if $\bar{b} = b$ holds.

The blind signature scheme $\mathcal{BS}$ is said to fulfill the blindness property, if the advantage

$$\text{Adv}_{\mathcal{BS}}^{\text{blindness}}(\mathcal{A}) = |2 \cdot \Pr[b' = b] - 1|$$

for every PPT adversary $\mathcal{A}$ is negligible in the security parameter.

- **One-More-Unforgeability:** Even after having successfully completed L rounds of the interactive signing protocol, an adversary $\mathcal{A}$ not in charge of the private key sk cannot forge another valid blind signatures for a given message. More formally, we can define One-More-Unforgeability using the following game.

Game [Universal-One-More-Unforgeability]

1. The algorithm KeyGen is used to generate a key pair (sk, pk). The public key pk is given to the adversary $\mathcal{A}$, while sk is kept secret by the challenger.
2. The adversary $\mathcal{A}$ engages himself in polynomially many interactive signing protocols with different instances of Signer. Let L be the number of cases in which the Signer outputs *completed*.
3. $\mathcal{A}$ outputs a list $\mathcal{L}$ of L message/signature pairs. The challenger checks if all the message/signature pairs are valid and pairwise distinct.
4. The challenger outputs a message $d^\star$ not contained in the list $\mathcal{L}$. The adversary wins the game, if he is able to generate a valid blind signature σ for the message $d^\star$, i.e. if $\mathtt{Verify}((d^\star, \sigma), pk) = \mathbf{TRUE}$ holds.

The blind signature scheme $\mathcal{BS}$ is said to provide the One-More-Unforgeability property, if the success probability

$$\Pr[\mathcal{A} \text{ wins}]$$

is, for any PPT adversary $\mathcal{A}$, negligible in the security parameter.

We note that this formalism is different from the standard security game for blindness, where the adversary is allowed to choose his own message but is required to forge at least $L + 1$ valid and distinct signatures. We choose to restrict the adversary's choice to accurately reflect the similar lack of choice in the standard security model for MQ signatures: *universal* unforgeability as opposed to *existential* unforgeability.

3   Multivariate Cryptography

The basic objects of multivariate cryptography are systems of multivariate quadratic polynomials. Their security is based on the **MQ Problem:** Given m multivariate quadratic polynomials $p^{(1)}(\mathbf{x}), \ldots, p^{(m)}(\mathbf{x})$ in n variables $x_1, \ldots, x_n$, find a vector $\bar{\mathbf{x}} = (\bar{x}_1, \ldots, \bar{x}_n)$ such that $p^{(1)}(\bar{\mathbf{x}}) = \ldots = p^{(m)}(\bar{\mathbf{x}}) = 0$.

The MQ problem is proven to be NP-hard even for quadratic polynomials over the field GF(2) [8]. Moreover, it is widely assumed as well as experimentally validated that solving *random* instances of the MQ problem (with $m \approx n$) is a hard task, see for example [25].

To build a public key cryptosystem on the basis of the MQ problem, one starts with an easily invertible quadratic map $\mathcal{F} : \mathbb{F}^n \to \mathbb{F}^m$ (central map). To hide the structure of $\mathcal{F}$ in the public key, one composes it with two invertible affine (or linear) maps $\mathcal{S} : \mathbb{F}^m \to \mathbb{F}^m$ and $\mathcal{T} : \mathbb{F}^n \to \mathbb{F}^n$. The *public key* of the scheme is therefore given by $\mathcal{P} = \mathcal{S} \circ \mathcal{F} \circ \mathcal{T} : \mathbb{F}^n \to \mathbb{F}^m$. The *private key* consists of $\mathcal{S}$, $\mathcal{F}$ and $\mathcal{T}$ and therefore allows to invert the public key.

Note: Due to the above construction, the security of multivariate schemes is not only based on the MQ-Problem, but also on the EIP-Problem ("Extended Isomorphism of Polynomials") of finding the decomposition of $\mathcal{P}$.

Signature Generation

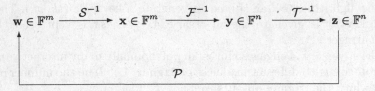

Signature Verification

Fig. 2. Standard workflow of multivariate signature schemes

In this paper we concentrate on multivariate signature schemes. The standard signature generation and verification process of a multivariate signature scheme works as shown in Fig. 2.

Signature generation: To sign a message $\mathbf{w} \in \mathbb{F}^m$, one computes recursively $\mathbf{x} = \mathcal{S}^{-1}(\mathbf{w}) \in \mathbb{F}^m$, $\mathbf{y} = \mathcal{F}^{-1}(\mathbf{x}) \in \mathbb{F}^n$ and $\mathbf{z} = \mathcal{T}^{-1}(\mathbf{y})$. The signature of the message $\mathbf{w}$ is $\mathbf{z} \in \mathbb{F}^n$. Here, $\mathcal{F}^{-1}(\mathbf{x})$ means finding one (of possibly many) pre-image of $\mathbf{x}$ under the central map $\mathcal{F}$.

Verification: To check the authenticity of a signature $\mathbf{z} \in \mathbb{F}^n$, one simply computes $\mathbf{w}' = \mathcal{P}(\mathbf{z}) \in \mathbb{F}^m$. If $\mathbf{w}' = \mathbf{w}$ holds, the signature is accepted, otherwise rejected.

3.1 The Rainbow Signature Scheme

The Rainbow signature scheme [6] is one of the most promising and best studied multivariate signature schemes. The scheme can be described as follows:

Let $\mathbb{F} = \mathbb{F}_q$ be a finite field with q elements, $n \in \mathbb{N}$ and $v_1 < v_2 < \ldots < v_\ell < v_{\ell+1} = n$ be a sequence of integers. We set $m = n - v_1$, $O_i = \{v_i + 1, \ldots, v_{i+1}\}$ and $V_i = \{1, \ldots, v_i\}$ $(i = 1, \ldots, \ell)$.

Key Generation: The *private key* of the scheme consists of two invertible affine maps $\mathcal{S} : \mathbb{F}^m \to \mathbb{F}^m$ and $\mathcal{T} : \mathbb{F}^n \to \mathbb{F}^n$ and a quadratic map $\mathcal{F}(\mathbf{x}) = (f^{(v_1+1)}(\mathbf{x}), \ldots, f^{(n)}(\mathbf{x})) : \mathbb{F}^n \to \mathbb{F}^m$. The polynomials $f^{(i)}$ $(i = v_1 + 1, \ldots, n)$ are of the form

$$f^{(i)} = \sum_{k,l \in V_j} \alpha_{k,l}^{(i)} \cdot x_k \cdot x_l + \sum_{k \in V_j, l \in O_j} \beta_{k,l}^{(i)} \cdot x_k \cdot x_l + \sum_{k \in V_j \cup O_j} \gamma_k^{(i)} \cdot x_k + \eta^{(i)} \quad (1)$$

with coefficients randomly chosen from $\mathbb{F}$. Here, j is the only integer such that $i \in O_j$. The *public key* is the composed map $\mathcal{P} = \mathcal{S} \circ \mathcal{F} \circ \mathcal{T} : \mathbb{F}^n \to \mathbb{F}^m$.

Signature Generation: To generate a signature for a document $\mathbf{w} \in \mathbb{F}^m$, we compute recursively $\mathbf{x} = \mathcal{S}^{-1}(\mathbf{w}) \in \mathbb{F}^m$, $\mathbf{y} = \mathcal{F}^{-1}(\mathbf{x}) \in \mathbb{F}^n$ and $\mathbf{z} = \mathcal{T}^{-1}(\mathbf{y})$. Here, $\mathcal{F}^{-1}(\mathbf{x})$ means finding one (of approximately q^{v_1}) pre-image of $\mathbf{x}$ under the central map $\mathcal{F}$. This is done as shown in Algorithm 1.

Algorithm 1. Inversion of the Rainbow central map

Input: Rainbow central map $\mathcal{F}$, vector $\mathbf{x} \in \mathbb{F}^m$.
Output: vector $\mathbf{y} \in \mathbb{F}^n$ such that $\mathcal{F}(\mathbf{y}) = \mathbf{x}$.
1: Choose random values for the variables $y_1, \ldots, y_{v_1}$ and substitute these values into the polynomials $f^{(i)}$ $(i = v_1 + 1, \ldots, n)$.
2: **for** $k = 1$ to ℓ **do**
3:    Perform Gaussian Elimination on the polynomials $f^{(i)}$ $(i \in O_k)$ to get the values of the variables y_i $(i \in O_k)$.
4:    Substitute the values of y_i $(i \in O_k)$ into the polynomials $f^{(i)}$, $i \in \{v_{k+1} + 1, \ldots, n\}$.
5: **end for**

It might happen that one of the linear systems in step 3 of the algorithm does not have a solution. In this case one has to choose other values for $y_1, \ldots, y_{v_1}$ and start again. The signature of the document $\mathbf{w}$ is $\mathbf{z} \in \mathbb{F}^n$.

Signature Verification: To verify the authenticity of a signature $\mathbf{z} \in \mathbb{F}^n$, one simply computes $\mathbf{w}' = \mathcal{P}(\mathbf{z}) \in \mathbb{F}^m$. If $\mathbf{w}' = \mathbf{w}$ holds, the signature is accepted, otherwise rejected.

3.2   The MQ-based Identification Scheme

In [22] Sakumoto *et al.* proposed an identification scheme based on multivariate polynomials. There exist two versions of the scheme: a 3-pass and a 5-pass variant. In this section we introduce the 5-pass variant.

The scheme uses a system $\mathcal{P}$ of m multivariate quadratic polynomials in n variables as a public parameter. The prover chooses a random vector $\mathbf{s} \in \mathbb{F}^n$ as his secret key and computes the public key $\mathbf{v} \in \mathbb{F}^m$ by $\mathbf{v} = \mathcal{P}(\mathbf{s})$.

To prove his identity to a verifier, the prover performs several rounds of the interactive protocol shown in Fig. 3.

Here,

$$\mathcal{G}(\mathbf{x}, \mathbf{y}) = \mathcal{P}(\mathbf{x} + \mathbf{y}) - \mathcal{P}(\mathbf{x}) - \mathcal{P}(\mathbf{y}) + \mathcal{P}(0) \tag{2}$$

is the polar form of the system $\mathcal{P}$.

The scheme is a zero-knowledge argument of knowledge for a solution of the system $\mathcal{P}(\mathbf{x}) = \mathbf{v}$.

The knowledge error per round is $\frac{1}{2} + \frac{1}{2q}$. To decrease the impersonation probability below $2^{-\eta}$, one therefore needs to perform $r = \lceil \frac{-\eta}{\log_2(1/2 + 1/2q)} \rceil$ rounds of the protocol. For identification purposes, $\eta \approx 30$ may be sufficient, but for signatures we require η to be at least as large as the security level.

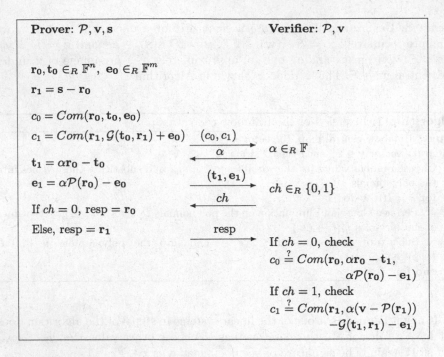

Fig. 3. The 5-pass MQ identification scheme of Sakumoto *et al.* [22].

3.3 The MQDSS Signature Scheme

In [9], Hülsing et al. developed a technique to transform $(2n+1)$ pass identification schemes into signature schemes. The technique can be used to transform the above described 5-pass multivariate identification scheme into an EU-CMA secure signature scheme.

To generate an MQDSS signature for a message d, the signer produces a transcript of the above identification protocol over r rounds. The challenges $\alpha_1, \ldots, \alpha_r$ and $ch_1, \ldots, ch_r$ are hereby computed from the message d and the commitments (using a publicly known hash function $\mathcal{H}$). Therefore, the signature has the form

$$\sigma = (c_{0,1}, c_{1,1}, \ldots, c_{0,r}, c_{1,r}, t_{1,1}, e_{1,1}, \ldots, t_{1,r}, e_{1,r}, \mathrm{resp}_1, \ldots, \mathrm{resp}_r).$$

To check the authenticity of a signature σ, the verifier parses σ into its components, uses the commitments to compute the challenges α_i and ch_i $(i = 1, \ldots, r)$ and checks the correctness of the responses resp_i as shown in Fig. 3 (for $i = 1, \ldots, r$).

4   Our Blind Signature Scheme

In this section we present MBSS, an extension of the Rainbow signature scheme of Sect. 3.1 to a multivariate blind signature scheme. We chose to restrict our discussion to Rainbow due to its short signatures and good performance. Moreover, the key sizes of Rainbow are acceptable and can be further reduced by the technique of Petzoldt *et al.* [17].

Nevertheless, our technique applies to any MQ signature scheme relying on the construction of Fig. 2, *i.e.*, relying on the hiding of a trapdoor to a quadratic map behind linear or affine transforms. As other MQ signature schemes rely on the same construction, our technique applies to those cryptosystems as well. We do not use any property of Rainbow that is not shared by, *e.g.*, $HFEv^-$ [18], pC^* [5], or UOV [12]. The exceptions are the MQ-based signature schemes that do not have the construction of Fig. 2, such as Quartz [15] and MQDSS [9].

4.1   The Basic Idea

The public key of our scheme consists of two multivariate quadratic systems $\mathcal{P} : \mathbb{F}^n \rightarrow \mathbb{F}^m$ and $\mathcal{R} : \mathbb{F}^m \rightarrow \mathbb{F}^m$. Hereby, $\mathcal{P}$ is the Rainbow public key, while $\mathcal{R}$ is a random system. The signer's private key allows him to invert the system $\mathcal{P}$.

In order to obtain a blind signature for a message (hash value) $\mathbf{w} \in \mathbb{F}^m$, the user chooses randomly a vector $\mathbf{z}^\star \in \mathbb{F}^m$, computes $\tilde{\mathbf{w}} = \mathbf{w} - \mathcal{R}(\mathbf{z}^\star)$ and sends $\tilde{\mathbf{w}}$ to the signer. The signer uses his private key to compute a signature $\mathbf{z}$ for the message $\tilde{\mathbf{w}}$ and sends it to the user. Therefore, the user obtains a solution $(\mathbf{z}, \mathbf{z}^\star)$ of the system $\mathcal{P}(\mathbf{x}_1) + \mathcal{R}(\mathbf{x}_2) = \mathbf{w}$. However, the user can not publish $(\mathbf{z}, \mathbf{z}^\star)$ as his signature for the document $\mathbf{w}$ since this would destroy the blindness of the scheme. Instead, the user has to prove knowledge of a solution to the system $\mathcal{P}(\mathbf{x}_1) + \mathcal{R}(\mathbf{x}_2) = \mathbf{w}$ using a zero knowledge protocol. We use the MQDSS technique (see Sect. 3.3) for this proof.

4.2   Description of the Scheme

In this section we give a detailed description of our blind signature scheme. As every blind signature scheme, MBSS consists of three algorithms *KeyGen*, *Sign* and *Verify*, where *Sign* is an interactive protocol between user and signer.

Parameters: Finite field $\mathbb{F}$, integers m, n and r (depending on a security parameter κ). r hereby determines, how many rounds of the identification scheme are performed during the generation of a signature.

Key Generation: The signer chooses randomly a Rainbow private key (consisting of two affine maps $\mathcal{S} : \mathbb{F}^m \rightarrow \mathbb{F}^m$ and $\mathcal{T} : \mathbb{F}^n \rightarrow \mathbb{F}^n$ and a Rainbow central map $\mathcal{F} : \mathbb{F}^n \rightarrow \mathbb{F}^m$). He computes the public key $\mathcal{P}$ as $\mathcal{P} = \mathcal{S} \circ \mathcal{F} \circ \mathcal{T} : \mathbb{F}^n \rightarrow \mathbb{F}^m$ (see Sect. 3.1) and uses a CSPRNG to generate the system $\mathcal{R} = \mathtt{CSPRNG}(\mathcal{P}) : \mathbb{F}^m \rightarrow \mathbb{F}^m$. The *public key* of our blind signature scheme is the pair $(\mathcal{P}, \mathcal{R})$, the signer's *private key* consists of $\mathcal{S}, \mathcal{F}$ and $\mathcal{T}$. However, since $\mathcal{R}$ can be computed from the system $\mathcal{P}$, it is not necessary to publish $\mathcal{R}$ (if the CSPRNG in use is publicly accessible).

Signature Generation: The interactive signature generation process of our blind signature scheme can be described as follows: To get a signature for the message d with hash value $\mathcal{H}(d) = \mathbf{w} \in \mathbb{F}^m$, the user chooses randomly a vector $\mathbf{z}^\star \in \mathbb{F}^m$.

He computes $\mathbf{w}^\star = \mathcal{R}(\mathbf{z}^\star) \in \mathbb{F}^m$ and sends $\tilde{\mathbf{w}} = \mathbf{w} - \mathbf{w}^\star \in \mathbb{F}^m$ to the signer. The signer uses his private key $(\mathcal{S}, \mathcal{F}, \mathcal{T})$ to compute a Rainbow signature $\mathbf{z} \in \mathbb{F}^n$ such that $\mathcal{P}(\mathbf{z}) = \tilde{\mathbf{w}}$ (see Sect. 3.1) and sends $\mathbf{z}$ back to the user, who therefore obtains a solution $(\mathbf{z}, \mathbf{z}^\star)$ of the system $\bar{\mathcal{P}}(\mathbf{x}) = \mathcal{P}(\mathbf{x}_1) + \mathcal{R}(\mathbf{x}_2) = \mathbf{w}$.

To prove this knowledge to the verifier in a zero knowledge way, the user generates an MQDSS signature for the message $\mathbf{w}$. As the public parameter of the scheme he hereby uses the system $\bar{\mathcal{P}}(\mathbf{x}) = \mathcal{P}(\mathbf{x}_1) + \mathcal{R}(\mathbf{x}_2)$, which is a system of m quadratic equations in $n+m$ variables. Furthermore, $\mathcal{G}(\mathbf{x}, \mathbf{y})$ is the polar form of the system $\bar{\mathcal{P}}$, i.e. $\mathcal{G}(\mathbf{x}, \mathbf{y}) = \bar{\mathcal{P}}(\mathbf{x} + \mathbf{y}) - \bar{\mathcal{P}}(\mathbf{x}) - \bar{\mathcal{P}}(\mathbf{y}) + \bar{\mathcal{P}}(\mathbf{0})$. In particular, the user performs the following steps.

1. Use a publicly known hash function $\mathcal{H}$ to compute $\mathcal{C} = \mathcal{H}(\mathcal{P}\|\mathbf{w})$ and $\mathcal{D} = \mathcal{H}(\mathcal{C}\|\mathbf{w})$.
2. Choose random values for $\mathbf{r}_{0,1}, \ldots, \mathbf{r}_{0,r}, \mathbf{t}_{0,1}, \ldots, \mathbf{t}_{0,r} \in \mathbb{F}^{m+n}$, $\mathbf{e}_{0,1}, \ldots, \mathbf{e}_{0,r} \in \mathbb{F}^m$, set $\mathbf{r}_{1,i} = (\mathbf{z}\|\mathbf{z}^\star) - \mathbf{r}_{0,i}$ $(i = 1, \ldots, r)$ and compute the commitments

$$c_{0,i} = Com(\mathbf{r}_{0,i}, \mathbf{t}_{0,i}, \mathbf{e}_{0,i}) \text{ and}$$
$$c_{1,i} = Com(\mathbf{r}_{1,i}, \mathcal{G}(\mathbf{t}_{0,i}, \mathbf{r}_{1,i}) - \mathbf{e}_{0,i}) \quad (i = 1, \ldots, r).$$

Set $\mathrm{COM} = (c_{0,1}, c_{1,1}, c_{0,2}, c_{1,2}, \ldots, c_{0,r}, c_{1,r})$.

3. Derive the challenges $\alpha_1, \ldots, \alpha_r \in \mathbb{F}$ from $(\mathcal{D}, COM)$.
4. Compute $\mathbf{t}_{1,i} = \alpha_i \cdot \mathbf{r}_{0,i} - \mathbf{t}_{0,i} \in \mathbb{F}^{m+n}$ and $\mathbf{e}_{1,i} = \alpha_i \cdot \bar{\mathcal{P}}(\mathbf{r}_{0,i}) - \mathbf{e}_{0,i}$ $(i = 1, \ldots, r)$. Set $Rsp_1 = (\mathbf{t}_{1,1}, \mathbf{e}_{1,1}, \ldots, \mathbf{t}_{1,r}, \mathbf{e}_{1,r})$.
5. Derive the challenges $(ch_1, \ldots, ch_r)$ from $(\mathcal{D}, COM, Rsp_1)$.
6. Set $Rsp_2 = (\mathbf{r}_{ch_1,1}, \ldots, \mathbf{r}_{ch_r,r})$.
7. The blind signature σ for the message $\mathbf{w} \in \mathbb{F}^m$ is given by

$$\sigma = (\mathcal{C}, COM, Rsp_1, Rsp_2).$$

The length of the blind signature σ is given by

$$|\sigma| = 1 \cdot |\text{hash value}| + 2r \cdot |\text{Commitment}| + r \cdot (2n + 3m) \quad \mathbb{F}-\text{elements}.$$

Signature Verification: To check the authenticity of a blind signature σ for a message d with hash value $\mathbf{w} \in \mathbb{F}^m$, the verifier parses σ into its components and computes $\mathcal{D} = \mathcal{H}(\mathcal{C}\|\mathbf{w})$. He derives the challenges $\alpha_i \in \mathbb{F}$ from $(\mathcal{D}, COM)$ and ch_i from $(\mathcal{D}, COM, Rsp_1)$ $(i = 1, \ldots, r)$.

Finally, he parses COM into $(c_{0,1}, c_{1,1}, c_{0,2}, c_{1,2}, \ldots, c_{0,r}, c_{1,r})$, Rsp_1 into $\mathbf{t}_1, \mathbf{e}_1, \ldots, \mathbf{t}_r, \mathbf{e}_r$ and Rsp_2 into $\mathbf{r}_1, \ldots, \mathbf{r}_r$ and checks if, for all $i = 1, \ldots, r$, $\mathbf{r}_i$ is a correct response to ch_i with respect to COM, $\mathbf{t}_i$ and $\mathbf{e}_i$, i.e.

$$c_{0,i} \overset{?}{=} Com(\mathbf{r}_i, \alpha_i \cdot \mathbf{r}_i - \mathbf{t}_i, \alpha_i \cdot \mathcal{P}(\mathbf{r}_i) - \mathbf{e}_i) \quad (\text{for } ch_i = 0)$$
$$c_{1,i} \overset{?}{=} Com(\mathbf{r}_i, \alpha_i \cdot (\mathbf{w} - \mathcal{P}(\mathbf{r}_i)) - \mathcal{G}(\mathbf{t}_i, \mathbf{r}_i) - \mathbf{e}_i) \quad (\text{for } ch_i = 1). \quad (3)$$

If all of these tests are fulfilled, the blind signature σ is accepted, otherwise rejected.

Note: As the resulting blind signature depends on the randomness sampled for generating the zero-knowledge proof, there may be many signatures associated to one tuple $(\mathbf{z}, \mathbf{z}^\star)$. To prevent a malicious user from reusing the same preimage to $\mathcal{P}(\bar{\mathbf{x}}_1) + \mathcal{R}(\bar{\mathbf{x}}_2)$, two signatures to messages d_1, d_2 are considered *essentially* different whenever $\mathbf{w}_1 = \mathcal{H}(d_1) \neq \mathbf{w}_2 = \mathcal{H}(d_2)$. In other words, the zero-knowledge proof is taken into account for validity but not for distinctness.

4.3 Reducing the Signature Length

In this section we present a technique to reduce the length of the blind signature σ, which was already mentioned in [22] and [9].

Instead of including all of the commitments $c_{0,1}, c_{1,1}, \ldots, c_{0,r}, c_{1,r}$ into the signature, we just transmit $COM = \mathcal{H}(c_{0,1}||c_{1,1} \ldots c_{0,r}||c_{1,r})$. However, in this scenario, we have to add $(c_{1-ch_1,1}, \ldots, c_{1-ch_r,r})$ to Rsp_2. In the verification process, the verifier recovers $(c_{ch_1,1}, \ldots, c_{ch_r,r})$ by Eq. (3) and checks if

$$COM \overset{?}{=} \mathcal{H}(c_{0,1}, c_{1,1}, \ldots, c_{0,r}, c_{1,r})$$

is fulfilled. By doing so, we can reduce the length of the blind signature σ to

$$|\sigma| = 2 \cdot |\text{hash value}| + r \cdot (2n + 3m) \ \mathbb{F} \text{ elements} + r \cdot |\text{Commitment}|.$$

4.4 Correctness

At the end of the interactive process, the user obtains a solution $(\mathbf{z}, \mathbf{z}^\star)$ of the system $\mathcal{P}(\mathbf{x}_1) + \mathcal{R}(\mathbf{x}_2) = \mathbf{w}$. This can be seen as follows. In the course of the interactive protocol, the (honest) user chooses randomly a vector $\mathbf{z}^\star$, computes $\mathbf{w}^\star = \mathcal{R}(\mathbf{z}^\star)$ and $\tilde{\mathbf{w}} = \mathbf{w} - \mathbf{w}^\star$ and sends $\tilde{\mathbf{w}}$ to the signer. The (honest) signer uses his private key to compute a vector $\mathbf{z}$ such that $\mathcal{P}(\mathbf{z}) = \tilde{\mathbf{w}}$. Altogether, we get $\mathcal{P}(\mathbf{z}) + \mathcal{R}(\mathbf{z}^\star) = \tilde{\mathbf{w}} + \mathbf{w}^\star = \mathbf{w} - \mathbf{w}^\star + \mathbf{w}^\star = \mathbf{w}$, which means that $(\mathbf{z}, \mathbf{z}^\star)$ is indeed a solution of the public system $\bar{\mathcal{P}}(\mathbf{x}) = \mathcal{P}(\mathbf{x}_1) + \mathcal{R}(\mathbf{x}_2)$.

The correctness proof of the MQDSS [9] shows that an MQDSS signature produced by an honest signer knowing a solution to the public system $\bar{\mathcal{P}}$ is accepted with certainty by an honest verifier.

5 Security

In this section, we analyze the security of our construction. We assume abstractly that the underlying MQ signature scheme is secure. (For a concrete security analysis of the underlying Rainbow scheme we refer to [16]). For this, we have to show the blindness and one-more-unforgeability of the derived scheme.

5.1 Blindness

The adversary has to link $\tilde{\mathbf{w}}$ from one interaction, to the pair (d, σ) from another interaction. Due to the perfect zero-knowledge property of the perfectly hiding commitment scheme, σ contains no information about the solution $(\mathbf{z}, \mathbf{z}^\star)$ and hence no information about $\mathcal{R}(\mathbf{z}^\star)$ or $\mathcal{P}(\mathbf{z})$. Therefore the adversary's task is equivalent linking $\tilde{\mathbf{w}}$ to d, since knowledge of σ gives him no advantage. However, $\mathbf{z}^\star$ is chosen uniformly at random and so $\mathcal{R}(\mathbf{z}^\star)$ is computationally indistinguishable from uniform. As a result, the blinded message $\tilde{\mathbf{w}} = \mathbf{w} - \mathcal{R}(\mathbf{z}^\star)$ is computationally indistinguishable from uniform and no polynomial-time adversary can compute any predicate of $\mathbf{w}$ from $\tilde{\mathbf{w}}$ with more than a negligible success probability. This includes the predicate $\mathcal{H}(d) \overset{?}{=} \mathbf{w}$ or any similar predicate that would allow the adversary to link $\tilde{\mathbf{w}}$ to d.

5.2 (One-More) Unforgeability

The full version of this paper presents a sequence of games argument showing that an adversary who wins the universal-one-more-unforgeability game is capable of finding a solution to the following problem: find a solution $\mathbf{x} = (\mathbf{x}_1, \mathbf{x}_2)$ such that $\bar{\mathcal{P}}(\mathbf{x}) = \mathcal{P}(\mathbf{x}_1) + \mathcal{R}(\mathbf{x}_2) = \mathbf{0}$, which is a system of m quadratic equations in $n + m$ variables. We argue here that this problem is hard. There are two attack strategies known against multivariate systems:

Direct Attacks: In a direct attack, one tries to solve the system $\bar{\mathcal{P}}(\mathbf{x}) = \mathbf{0}$ as an instance of the MQ Problem. Since the system $\bar{\mathcal{P}}$ is underdetermined, there are two possibilities to do this. One can use a special algorithm against underdetermined multivariate systems [24] or, after fixing n of the variables, a Gröbner Basis algorithm such as Faugéres F_4 [7]. For suitably chosen parameters, both approaches are infeasible.

The second possibility to solve a multivariate system such as $\mathcal{P}'$ are the so called **Structural Attacks**. In this type of attack one uses the known structure of the system $\bar{\mathcal{P}}$ in order to find a decomposition $\bar{\mathcal{P}}$ into easily invertible maps. Note that, in our case we can write

$$\begin{aligned}
\bar{\mathcal{P}}(\mathbf{x}) &= \mathcal{P}(\mathbf{x}_1) + \mathcal{R}(\mathbf{x}_2) \\
&= \mathcal{S} \circ \mathcal{F} \circ \mathcal{T}(\mathbf{x}_1) + \mathcal{S} \circ \underbrace{\mathcal{S}^{-1} \circ \mathcal{R}}_{\mathcal{R}'}(\mathbf{x}_2) \\
&= \mathcal{S} \circ \underbrace{(\mathcal{F} + \mathcal{R}')}_{\mathcal{F}'} \circ \mathcal{T}'(\mathbf{x}) \;.
\end{aligned}$$

In order to solve the system $\bar{\mathcal{P}}$ using a structural attack, we have to use the known structure of the map $\mathcal{F}' = \mathcal{F} + \mathcal{S}^{-1} \circ \mathcal{R}$ to recover the linear maps $\mathcal{S}$ and $\mathcal{T}'$ (or rather, its action on the first n components as it leaves the other m intact). However, since the coefficients of both $\mathcal{S}$ and $\mathcal{R}$ are chosen uniformly at random, the map $\mathcal{R}' = \mathcal{S}^{-1} \circ \mathcal{R}$ is a random quadratic map over $\mathbb{F}^m$.

The only structure we can use for a structural attack therefore comes from the map $\mathcal{F}$, which is the central map of the underlying multivariate signature scheme. Therefore, we are in exactly the same situation as if attacking the underlying multivariate scheme using a structural attack. By choosing the parameters of the underlying scheme in an appropriate way, we therefore can prevent this type of attack against our blind signature scheme.

5.3 Quantum Security

The technique proposed in [9] is capable of transforming $(2n + 1)$-pass zero-knowledge proofs into non-interactive zero-knowledge proofs that are secure against classical adversaries in the random oracle model. However, the behaviour of this transform against quantum adversaries is not well understood because the random oracle should be accessible to the quantum adversary and answer queries *in quantum superposition*, and many standard proof techniques do not carry over to this setting. See Boneh et al. [1] for an excellent treatment of proofs that fail in the quantum random oracle model.

Formally proving soundness against quantum adversaries seems to be a rather involved task beyond the scope of this paper. Instead, we are content to conjecture that there exists a commitment scheme such that the technique of [9] results in a non-interactive zero-knowledge proof that is secure against quantum adversaries as well as classical ones. This conjecture is implicit in the works of Sakumoto et al. [22], and Hulsing et al. [9].

6   Discussion

6.1   Parameters

In this section we propose concrete parameter sets for our blind signature scheme. As observed in the previous section, we have to choose the parameters in a way that

(a) solving a random system of m quadratic equations in m variables is infeasible,
(b) inverting an MQ public key with the given parameters is infeasible, and
(c) a direct attack against a system of m quadratic equations in $n+m$ variables is infeasible.

Since condition (a) is implied by (c), we only have to consider (b) and (c). In order to defend our scheme against attacks of type (b), we follow the recommendations of [16]. Regarding (c), we have to consider that the system $\mathcal{P}(\mathbf{x}_1) + \mathcal{R}(\mathbf{x}_2) = \mathbf{w}$ is highly underdetermined (in the case of $\mathcal{P}$ being a Rainbow public key, the number of variables in this system exceeds the number of equations by a factor of about 3). As a result of Thomae et al. shows, such systems can be solved significantly faster than determined systems.

Proposition 1 [24]. *Solving an MQ system of m equations in $n = \omega \cdot m$ variables is only as hard as solving a determined MQ system of $m - \lfloor \omega \rfloor + 1$ equations.*

According to this result, we have to increase the number of equations in our system by 2 (compared to the parameters of a standard Rainbow instance). Table 1 shows the parameters we propose for our scheme for various targeted security levels.

Table 1. Proposed parameters for our blind signature scheme (GF(31)).

Security level (bit)	Parameters $(\mathbb{F}, (v_1, o_1, o_2))$	# rounds	Public key size (kB)	Private key size (kB)	Blind sig. size (kB)
80	(GF(31), (16,18,17))	84	29.4	20.1	11.5
100	(GF(31), (20,22,21))	105	54.6	36.6	17.6
128	(GF(31), (25,27,27))	135	106.8	70.2	28.5
192	(GF(31), (37,35,35))	202	342.8	219.0	63.2
256	(GF(31), (50,53,53))	269	802.4	507.1	111.9

6.2 Efficiency

During the interactive part of the signature generation process, the signer has to generate one Rainbow signature for the message $\tilde{\mathbf{w}} = \mathbf{w} - \mathbf{w}^\star$.

For the user, the most costly part of the signature generation is the repeated evaluation of the system $\bar{\mathcal{P}}(\mathbf{x}) = \mathcal{P}(\mathbf{x}_1) + \mathcal{R}(\mathbf{x}_2)$. During the computation of the commitments $\mathbf{c}_{0,i}$ and $\mathbf{c}_{1,i}$ $(i = 1, \ldots, r)$ (step 2 of the signature generation process) this has to be done $3 \cdot r$ times (one evaluation of $\mathcal{G}$ corresponds to 3 evaluations of $\bar{\mathcal{P}}$). In step 4 of the process (computation of $\mathbf{e}_{1,i}$) we need r evaluations of $\bar{\mathcal{P}}$. Altogether, the user has to evaluate the system $4r$ times.

During verification, the verifier has to compute the commitments $c_{ch_i,i}$ $(i = 1, \ldots, r)$. If $ch_i = 0$, he needs for this 1 evaluation of $\bar{\mathcal{P}}$, in the case of $ch_2 = 1$ he needs 4 evaluations. On average, the verifier needs therefore $\frac{r}{2} \cdot (1 + 4) = 2.5 \cdot r$ evaluations of the system $\bar{\mathcal{P}}$.

While the system $\bar{P}$ consists of m quadratic equations in $m + n$ variables, the inner structure of the system can be used to speed up the evaluation. In fact, the system $\bar{\mathcal{P}}$ is the sum of two smaller systems $\mathcal{P} : \mathbb{F}^n \to \mathbb{F}^m$ and $\mathcal{R} : \mathbb{F}^m \to \mathbb{F}^m$. Therefore, we can evaluate $\bar{\mathcal{P}}$ by evaluating $\mathcal{P}$ and $\mathcal{R}$ separately and adding the results.

6.3 Implementation

We implemented all functionalities in Sage [21] to prove concept validity. Table 2 contains the timing results for the matching parameter sets of Table 1, demonstrating that our scheme is somewhat efficient and practicable even for very

Table 2. Timing results of a Sage implementation of our blind signature scheme. All units are milliseconds, except for the security level.

sec. lvl	Key Gen	Sign (Signer)	Sig. Gen. (User)	Sig. verification
80	4,007	7	2,018	1,424
100	9,392	13	3,649	2,656
128	25,517	19	7,760	5,505
192	87,073	41	23,692	16,040
256	613,968	103	86,540	59,669

poorly-optimized Sage code. These results were obtained on a 3.3 GHz Intel Quadcore with 6,144 kB of cache.

Despite of these relatively large numbers, we are very optimistic about the speed of our blind signatures when implemented in a less abstract and more memory-conscious programming language. For instance, Hülsing et al.'s optimized MQDSS manages to generate (classically) 256-bit-secure signatures in 6.79 ms and verify them in even less time [9]. As the MQDSS represents the bottleneck of our scheme, a similarly optimized implementation could potentially drop signature generation and verification time by several orders of magnitude.

Table 3. Comparison of different blind signature schemes. The security levels are adopted from Rückert [20].

Security lvl. (bit)	Scheme	Comm	Pub. key size (kB)	Sig. size (kB)	Post-quantum?
76	RSA-1229	2	1.2	1.2	×
	Lattice-1024	4	10.2	66.9	✓
	Our scheme (GF(31),16,18,17)	2	29.4	11.5	✓
102	RSA-3313	2	3.3	3.3	×
	Lattice-2048	4	23.6	89.4	✓
	Our scheme (GF(31),20,22,21)	2	54.6	17.6	✓

6.4 Comparison

Table 3 shows a comparison of our scheme to the standard RSA blind signature scheme and the lattice-based blind signature scheme of Rückert [20]. The RSA blind signature scheme does not offer any security against quantum computers. The public keys of Rückert's scheme are smaller than those of our scheme, although ours are still competitive. Like the standard RSA blind signature scheme, our scheme requires 2 steps of communication between the user and the signer in order to produce the blind signature. This is in contrast to Rückert's scheme where this number is 4. More importantly, our scheme outperforms that of Rückert in terms of signature size.

At this point, an apples-to-apples comparison of operational speed is not possible. Nevertheless, regardless of speed, the main selling point of our scheme is its reliance on different computational problems from those used in other branches of cryptography, including lattice-based cryptography.

7 Conclusion

In this paper we proposed the first multivariate based blind signature scheme. Our scheme is very efficient and produces much shorter blind signatures than the lattice based scheme of Rückert [20], making our scheme the most promising candidate for establishing a post-quantum blind signature scheme.

Our construction is notably generic. While we only show that it applies to Rainbow and MQDSS, we use their properties abstractly and it is perfectly conceivable that another combination of trapdoor-based MQ signature scheme with a non-interactive proof of knowledge of the solution to an MQ system will give the same result. Indeed, our design demonstrates that the combination of a dedicated signature scheme with an identification scheme relying on the same hard problem, is a powerful construction — and may apply in other branches of cryptography as well.

Lastly, one major use case of blind signatures is anonymous identification. In this scenario, one may reasonably dispense with the transformed signature scheme and instead directly use the underlying interactive identification scheme, thus sacrificing non-interactivity for less computation and bandwidth. Likewise, other use cases such as anonymous database access require *reusable* anonymous credentials. Our scheme can be adapted to fit this scenario as well, simply by specifying that all users obtain a blind signature on the same public parameter.

Acknowledgements. The authors would like to thank the reviewers and the shepherd in particular for their helpful comments. This work was supported in part by the Research Council KU Leuven: C16/15/058. In addition, this work was supported by the European Commission through the Horizon 2020research and innovation programme under grant agreement No H2020-ICT-2014-644371 WITDOM, H2020-ICT-2014-645622 PQCRYPTO and H2020-DS-2014-653497 PANORAMIX, and through the SECURITY programme under FP7-SEC-2013-1-607049 EKSISTENZ. Alan Szepieniec is being supported by a doctoral grant of the Flemish Agency for Innovation and Entrepreneurship (VLAIO, formerly IWT).

References

1. Boneh, D., Dagdelen, Ö., Fischlin, M., Lehmann, A., Schaffner, C., Zhandry, M.: Random oracles in a quantum world. In: Lee, D.H., Wang, X. (eds.) ASIACRYPT 2011. LNCS, vol. 7073, pp. 41–69. Springer, Heidelberg (2011). https://doi.org/10.1007/978-3-642-25385-0_3
2. Chaum, D.: Blind signatures for untraceable payment. In: Proceedings of CRYPTO 1982, pp. 199–203. Plenum Press (1983)

3. Bogdanov, A., Eisenbarth, T., Rupp, A., Wolf, C.: Time-area optimized public-key engines: $\mathcal{MQ}$-cryptosystems as replacement for elliptic curves? In: Oswald, E., Rohatgi, P. (eds.) CHES 2008. LNCS, vol. 5154, pp. 45–61. Springer, Heidelberg (2008). https://doi.org/10.1007/978-3-540-85053-3_4

4. Chen, A.I.-T., Chen, M.-S., Chen, T.-R., Cheng, C.-M., Ding, J., Kuo, E.L.-H., Lee, F.Y.-S., Yang, B.-Y.: SSE implementation of multivariate PKCs on modern x86 CPUs. In: Clavier, C., Gaj, K. (eds.) CHES 2009. LNCS, vol. 5747, pp. 33–48. Springer, Heidelberg (2009). https://doi.org/10.1007/978-3-642-04138-9_3

5. Ding, J., Dubois, V., Yang, B.-Y., Chen, O.C.-H., Cheng, C.-M.: Could SFLASH be repaired? In: Aceto, L., Damgård, I., Goldberg, L.A., Halldórsson, M.M., Ingólfsdóttir, A., Walukiewicz, I. (eds.) ICALP 2008. LNCS, vol. 5126, pp. 691–701. Springer, Heidelberg (2008). https://doi.org/10.1007/978-3-540-70583-3_56

6. Ding, J., Schmidt, D.: Rainbow, a new multivariable polynomial signature scheme. In: Ioannidis, J., Keromytis, A., Yung, M. (eds.) ACNS 2005. LNCS, vol. 3531, pp. 164–175. Springer, Heidelberg (2005). https://doi.org/10.1007/11496137_12

7. Faugère, J.C.: A new efficient algorithm for computing Gröbner bases (F4). J. Pure Appl. Algebra **139**, 61–88 (1999)

8. Garey, M.R., Johnson, D.S.: Computers and Intractability: A Guide to the Theory of NP-Completeness. W.H. Freeman and Company, New York (1979)

9. Hülsing, A., Rijneveld, J., Samardjiska, S., Schwabe, P.: From 5-pass MQ-based identification to MQ-based signatures. Cryptology ePrint Archive: Report 2016/708

10. Juels, A., Luby, M., Ostrovsky, R.: Security of blind digital signatures. In: Kaliski, B.S. (ed.) CRYPTO 1997. LNCS, vol. 1294, pp. 150–164. Springer, Heidelberg (1997). https://doi.org/10.1007/BFb0052233

11. Kravitz, D.: Digital Signature Algorithm. US patent 5,231,668, July 1991

12. Kipnis, A., Patarin, J., Goubin, L.: Unbalanced oil and vinegar signature schemes. In: Stern, J. (ed.) EUROCRYPT 1999. LNCS, vol. 1592, pp. 206–222. Springer, Heidelberg (1999). https://doi.org/10.1007/3-540-48910-X_15

13. Goodin, D.: NSA preps quantum-resistant algorithms to head off crypto-apocalypse. http://arstechnica.com/security/2015/08/nsa-preps-quantum-resistant-algorithms-to-head-off-crypto-apocolypse/

14. National Institute of Standards and Technology: Report on post-quantum Cryptography. NISTIR draft 8105. http://csrc.nist.gov/publications/drafts/nistir-8105/nistir_8105_draft.pdf

15. Patarin, J., Courtois, N., Goubin, L.: QUARTZ, 128-bit long digital signatures. In: Naccache, D. (ed.) CT-RSA 2001. LNCS, vol. 2020, pp. 282–297. Springer, Heidelberg (2001). https://doi.org/10.1007/3-540-45353-9_21

16. Petzoldt, A., Bulygin, S., Buchmann, J.: Selecting parameters for the rainbow signature scheme. In: Sendrier, N. (ed.) PQCrypto 2010. LNCS, vol. 6061, pp. 218–240. Springer, Heidelberg (2010). https://doi.org/10.1007/978-3-642-12929-2_16

17. Petzoldt, A., Bulygin, S., Buchmann, J.: CyclicRainbow – a multivariate signature scheme with a partially cyclic public key. In: Gong, G., Gupta, K.C. (eds.) INDOCRYPT 2010. LNCS, vol. 6498, pp. 33–48. Springer, Heidelberg (2010). https://doi.org/10.1007/978-3-642-17401-8_4

18. Petzoldt, A., Chen, M.-S., Yang, B.-Y., Tao, C., Ding, J.: Design principles for HFEv- based multivariate signature schemes. In: Iwata, T., Cheon, J.H. (eds.) ASIACRYPT 2015. LNCS, vol. 9452, pp. 311–334. Springer, Heidelberg (2015). https://doi.org/10.1007/978-3-662-48797-6_14

19. Rivest, R.L., Shamir, A., Adleman, L.: A method for obtaining digital signatures and public-key cryptosystems. Commun. ACM **21**(2), 120–126 (1978)

20. Rückert, M.: Lattice-based blind signatures. In: Abe, M. (ed.) ASIACRYPT 2010. LNCS, vol. 6477, pp. 413–430. Springer, Heidelberg (2010). https://doi.org/10. 1007/978-3-642-17373-8_24
21. SageMath, the Sage Mathematics Software System (Version 7.1), The Sage Developers (2016). http://www.sagemath.org
22. Sakumoto, K., Shirai, T., Hiwatari, H.: Public-key identification schemes based on multivariate quadratic polynomials. In: Rogaway, P. (ed.) CRYPTO 2011. LNCS, vol. 6841, pp. 706–723. Springer, Heidelberg (2011). https://doi.org/10. 1007/978-3-642-22792-9_40
23. Shor, P.: Polynomial-time algorithms for prime factorization and discrete logarithms on a quantum computer. SIAM J. Comput. **26**(5), 1484–1509 (1997)
24. Thomae, E., Wolf, C.: Solving underdetermined systems of multivariate quadratic equations revisited. In: Fischlin, M., Buchmann, J., Manulis, M. (eds.) PKC 2012. LNCS, vol. 7293, pp. 156–171. Springer, Heidelberg (2012). https://doi.org/10. 1007/978-3-642-30057-8_10
25. Yasuda, T., Dahan, X., Huang, Y.-J., Takagi, T., Sakurai, K.: MQ challenge: hardness evaluation of solving multivariate quadratic problems. IACR Cryptology ePrint Archive 2015/275 (2015)

Efficient Round-Optimal Blind Signatures in the Standard Model

Essam Ghadafi[✉]

University of the West of England, Bristol, UK
essam.ghadafi@uwe.ac.uk

Abstract. Blind signatures are at the core of e-cash systems and have numerous other applications. In this work we construct efficient blind and partially blind signature schemes over bilinear groups in the standard model. Our schemes yield short signatures consisting of only a couple of elements from the shorter source group and have very short communication overhead consisting of 1 group element on the user side and 3 group elements on the signer side. At 80-bit security, our schemes yield signatures consisting of only 40 bytes which is 67% shorter than the most efficient existing scheme with the same security in the standard model. Verification in our schemes requires only a couple of pairings. Our schemes compare favorably in every efficiency measure to all existing counterparts offering the same security in the standard model. In fact, the efficiency of our signing protocol as well as the signature size compare favorably even to many existing schemes in the random oracle model. For instance, our signatures are shorter than those of Brands' scheme which is at the heart of the U-Prove anonymous credential system used in practice. The unforgeability of our schemes is based on new intractability assumptions of a "one-more" type which we show are intractable in the generic group model, whereas their blindness holds w.r.t. malicious signing keys in the information-theoretic sense. We also give variants of our schemes for a vector of messages.

Keywords: Blind signatures · Round-optimal · Partial blindness E-Cash

1 Introduction

Blind signatures introduced by Chaum [23] are an interactive protocol that allows a user to obtain signatures on messages of her choice without revealing the messages to the signer. Blindness in these schemes ensures that it is infeasible for a malicious signer to link the final signatures to their corresponding signing requests. Blindness can be either proven in the honest-key model where the

The research leading to these results has received funding from the European Research Council under the European Union's Seventh Framework Programme (FP/2007–2013)/ERC Grant Agreement n. 307937 and EPSRC grant EP/J009520/1. The work was done while the author was at University College London.

© International Financial Cryptography Association 2017
A. Kiayias (Ed.): FC 2017, LNCS 10322, pp. 455–473, 2017.
https://doi.org/10.1007/978-3-319-70972-7_26

key pair is produced by the challenger and then revealed to the adversary or in the stronger malicious-key model [1, 49] where the key pair is chosen by the adversary herself and she is not required to reveal the signing key to the challenger. On the other hand, unforgeability ensures that it is infeasible for a malicious user to obtain more valid signatures on distinct messages than the number of completed interactions with the honest signer. Such a primitive is at the core of e-cash systems [23] where the bank acts as the signer; the privacy requirement comes from the non-traceability requirement of cash. It also finds applications in e-voting [34], anonymous credentials [8] and direct anonymous attestation [12, 20]. The primitive is very relevant to practice, besides its prominent role in realizing e-cash systems, blind signatures are the backbone of some anonymous credential systems deployed in practice, which include the U-Prove system [19].

Measures of importance when designing such schemes include their round complexity, i.e. the number of moves between the parties before the user can derive a signature. Round-optimal schemes [27] consisting of only two moves are known to imply security under concurrent executions.

Related Work. After their introduction by Chaum [23], a long line of research on blind signatures has evolved. Constructions of blind signatures relying on random oracles [26] include [2, 8, 11, 15, 18, 23, 52–54]. Most of the early constructions relying on random oracles are essentially Full-Domain-Hash (FDH) style signatures. The user sends a blinded message digest of the message to the signer who in turn returns a signature on such a digest. Upon receiving the signature, thanks to the homomorphic property of the underlying signature scheme, the user is able to transform such a signature to one on the message. This is the underlying idea behind the original (RSA based) scheme in [23] which was proven secure in [52]. The same applies to the (DLog based) scheme in [15].

Constructions dispensing with relying on random oracles but at the expense of assuming a trusted common reference string (CRS) include [6, 21, 40, 46]. Fischlin [27] gave a generic construction of two-move schemes in the CRS model satisfying blindness in the malicious-key model. His construction requires the user to send a commitment to her message which in turn gets signed by the signer. The final signature is then merely a zero-knowledge proof of knowledge of a signature on the (hidden) commitment to the message. Most subsequent constructions in the CRS model are either direct instantiations of Fischlin's construction, e.g. [3, 5], or variations thereof, e.g. [3, 30]. The scheme in [3, 30] adopts a similar approach as Fischlin's but instead of hiding the signed commitment, it exploits a feature of the underlying signature scheme to transform a signature on the commitment to a signature on the message itself. Other round-optimal constructions in the CRS model include [13, 14, 48, 56].

Round-optimal constructions not relying on either of the aforementioned assumptions, i.e. in the standard model, are preferable. However, it is well-known that such schemes are harder to design. Lindell [47] showed that it is impossible to design round-optimal schemes in the standard model conforming to simulation-based (rather than game-based) security definitions. However, Hazay et al. [44] showed that (non-round-optimal) realizations are possible under game-based definitions. Abe and Ohkubo [6] showed that universally composable blind signatures, even non-committing ones, are impossible in the standard model. Okamoto [49] gave a non-round-optimal construction in the standard model which satisfies blindness in the malicious-key model. Fischlin and Schröder [29] proved that it is impossible to reduce the security of a standard-model blind signature scheme in a blackbox manner to the intractability of a non-interactive assumption if the scheme has any of the following properties: (i) the signing protocol has less than 4 moves. (ii) Its blindness holds statistically (iii) the signing transcript allows one to check if a valid signature can be derived from it.

Existing constructions in the standard model [36,37] circumvent the impossibility result by making use of a non-blackbox reduction to the underlying primitive. Garg et al. [37] gave the first round-optimal construction in the standard model solving a long-standing open problem. Their scheme combines fully homomorphic encryption with two-move witness-indistinguishable proofs known otherwise as ZAPs [25]. Their scheme is inefficient and is only considered as a feasibility result. Recently, Garg and Gupta [36] gave a more efficient round-optimal construction which combines structure-preserving signature schemes [3] and Groth-Sahai NIZK proofs [41]. To eliminate the need for a trusted party, they use two CRSs which are part of the signer's public key. The signer is forced to choose those honestly as otherwise she needs to solve an exponential-time problem in order to cheat. The security of their scheme holds w.r.t. non-uniform adversaries and relies on complexity leveraging. Consequently, it suffers from a large communication overhead and a rather large computational cost.

Recently, Fuchsbauer et al. [33] gave a semi-generic construction of round-optimal schemes in the standard model which combines the Pedersen commitment scheme [50] with structure-preserving signatures on equivalence classes [42]. Their construction satisfies blindness against malicious keys. They gave an efficient instantiation whose security relies on a couple of interactive assumptions where they used the optimal construction of signature on equivalence classes from [32]. More recently, Fuchsbauer et al. [31] weakened the assumptions on which the instantiation in [33] is based by eliminating one of the interactive assumptions on which the blindness in [33] was relying. However, the unforgeability of the new variant still relies on an interactive intractability assumption. Hanzlik and Kluczniak [43] gave a construction in the standard model in the honest-key model. The downside of their construction is that it uses an encryption scheme over composite-order groups which requires groups of a large order as well as a strong non-standard "knowledge" assumption [9]. Very recently, Döttling et al. [24] showed that blind signatures in the standard model can be constructed from maliciously circuit-private homomorphic encryption for logarithmic depth circuits.

Baldimtsi and Lysyanskaya [7] showed that existing techniques fall short for proving the security of some existing blind signatures lacking a security proof in the random oracle model. Concerned constructions include Schnorr's [54] and Brands' [18] schemes. The latter is at the core of the U-Prove system.

Abe and Fujisaki [4] put forward the notion of partially blind signatures which extends blind signatures to allow some part of the message to be public. This makes it possible to attach some public attributes, e.g. an expiration date, to the signatures. Recently, Fuchsbauer et al. [31, 33] gave the first efficient round-optimal partially blind schemes in the standard model.

Our Contribution. We construct two efficient blind signature schemes in the standard model satisfying blindness in the malicious-key model. Our schemes yield very short signatures consisting of only a pair of elements from the shorter source group. At 80-bit security, our signatures are only 40 bytes long which means they are 67% shorter than the best existing scheme offering the same security [33]. Verifying signatures in our schemes involves evaluating a couple of pairings. The latter matches the verification overhead of the most efficient existing (non-blind) signature schemes over bilinear groups [16, 17]. Such desirable efficiency means that our schemes can even be deployed on devices with limited computational power if the evaluation of pairings required for verification is outsourced to a third party, e.g. using techniques from [22]. Our schemes have a very low communication overhead on both sides. The blindness of our schemes holds in the information-theoretic sense whereas their unforgeability relies on new intractability assumptions which we show hold in the generic group model [57]. Note that it is well-known that blind signature schemes in the standard model based solely on non-interactive assumptions, e.g. [36, 37], are much less efficient. Furthermore, all existing efficient round-optimal schemes in the standard model offering the same security as ours [31, 33] also rely on interactive intractability assumptions.

We also construct efficient partially blind signature schemes and efficient blind signature schemes for a vector of messages. The techniques underlying our constructions are akin to the blind-unblind paradigm which usually form the basis of the efficient constructions in the random oracle model. However, to obtain the desired efficiency in the standard model, we apply various techniques. Similarly to [31, 33, 40], our constructions do not require expensive zero-knowledge proofs.

Paper Organization. The rest of the paper is organized as follows. In Sect. 2, we give some preliminary definitions. In Sect. 3, we introduce and prove intractability of our new assumptions. In Sect. 4, we recall the syntax and security of blind signatures. In Sect. 5, we give our blind signature constructions. We show in Sect. 6 how to extend our schemes to sign a vector of messages. In Sect. 7, we give our partially blind signature constructions.

Notation. We write $b = \mathsf{Alg}(a; r)$ when algorithm Alg on input a and randomness r outputs b. We write $b \leftarrow \mathsf{Alg}(a)$ for the process of setting $b = \mathsf{Alg}(a; r)$ where r is sampled at random. For an algorithm Alg and an oracle $\mathcal{O}$, $\mathsf{Alg}^{\mathcal{O}^k(\cdot)}$ denotes that Alg can access $\mathcal{O}$ at most k times on inputs of Alg's choice. We write $a \leftarrow \mathcal{S}$ for sampling a uniformly at random from the set $\mathcal{S}$. A function $\nu(.) : \mathbb{N} \to \mathbb{R}^+$ is negligible (in λ) if for every polynomial $\rho(\cdot)$ and all sufficiently large values of λ, it holds that $\nu(\lambda) < \frac{1}{\rho(\lambda)}$. PPT stands for running in probabilistic polynomial time in the relevant security parameter. For $\ell \in \mathbb{N} \setminus \{0\}$, by $[\ell]$ we denote the set $\{1, \ldots, \ell\}$.

2 Preliminaries

In this section we provide some preliminary definitions.

Bilinear Groups. A bilinear group is a tuple $\mathcal{P} := (\mathbb{G}, \hat{\mathbb{G}}, \mathbb{T}, p, G, \hat{G}, e)$ where $\mathbb{G}$, $\hat{\mathbb{G}}$ and $\mathbb{T}$ are groups of a prime order p, and G and $\hat{G}$ generate $\mathbb{G}$ and $\hat{\mathbb{G}}$, respectively. The function e is a non-degenerate bilinear map $e : \mathbb{G} \times \hat{\mathbb{G}} \longrightarrow \mathbb{T}$. To distinguish between elements of $\mathbb{G}$ and $\hat{\mathbb{G}}$, the latter will be accented with $\hat{\ }$. We use multiplicative notation for all the groups. We let $\mathbb{G}^{\times} := \mathbb{G} \setminus \{1_{\mathbb{G}}\}$ and $\hat{\mathbb{G}}^{\times} := \hat{\mathbb{G}} \setminus \{1_{\hat{\mathbb{G}}}\}$. In this paper, we work in the efficient Type-III setting [35], where $\mathbb{G} \neq \hat{\mathbb{G}}$ and there is no efficiently computable isomorphism between the groups in either direction. We assume there is an algorithm $\mathcal{BG}$ that on input a security parameter λ, outputs a description of bilinear groups. Without loss in generality and similarly to e.g. [31,33] in this work we will assume $\mathcal{BG}$ is deterministic, which as argued by [31,33] is the case for instance in the most widely used groups based on BN curves [10].

Pedersen Commitment Scheme. We use a generalized variant of the Pedersen commitment scheme [50] which allows committing to a vector of messages at once. The scheme is information-theoretically hiding and computationally binding under the discrete logarithm assumption. The generalized variant is defined by the following algorithms:

$\mathsf{Setup}(1^{\lambda}, n)$ On input the security parameter λ and the size of the vector n, this algorithm chooses a cyclic group $\mathbb{G}$ of prime order p where $\log p \in \Theta(\lambda)$. It also samples the elements $G_1, \ldots, G_n, H \leftarrow \mathbb{G}$. It returns the commitment key $\mathsf{ck} := (G_1, \ldots, G_n, H)$ which we assume is an implicit input to the rest of the algorithms.

$\mathsf{Commit}(\boldsymbol{m}, r)$ On input a message vector $\boldsymbol{m} = (m_1, \ldots, m_n) \in \mathbb{Z}_p^n$ and a randomness $r \in \mathbb{Z}_p$, this algorithm returns the commitment $\mathsf{Co} := H^r \prod_{i=1}^n G_i^{m_i}$ and the opening information $d := (\boldsymbol{m}, r)$.

$\mathsf{Open}(\mathsf{Co}, d = (\boldsymbol{m}, r))$ On input a commitment Co and its associated opening information d, this algorithm verifies whether such opening information is a valid one by checking that $\mathsf{Co} = H^r \prod_{i=1}^n G_i^{m_i}$ returning 1 or 0 accordingly.

Since the hiding property of the scheme holds in the information-theoretic sense, such a property still holds even if we let the recipient runs the Setup algorithm which is otherwise usually run by a trusted third party. The above argument holds as long as $H \neq 1_{\mathbb{G}}$ which is easy to check.

3 New Intractability Assumptions

In this section we introduce some new assumptions of a "one-more" type where the adversary interacts with an oracle k times and is tasked with outputting $k+1$ valid tuples. They are similar in nature to the E-LRSW assumption introduced by Ghadafi and Smart [40].

3.1 The BSOM Assumption

Our first new assumption which we refer to as the BSOM (short for Blind Signature One More) assumption will form the basis for the unforgeability of our first blind signature construction. It is inspired in part by the assumption underlying the recent signature scheme by Ghadafi [38].

Definition 1 (BSOM Assumption). *Let* $\mathcal{P} = (\mathbb{G}, \hat{\mathbb{G}}, \mathbb{T}, G, \hat{G}, e, p)$ *be the description of Type-III bilinear groups output by* $\mathcal{BG}(1^\lambda)$, *and let* $H := G^h$, $\hat{H} := \hat{G}^h$, $\hat{X} := \hat{G}^x$, $\hat{Y} := \hat{G}^y$ *for some* $h, x, y \leftarrow \mathbb{Z}_p$. *Let* $\mathcal{O}BSOM_{H,\hat{H},\hat{X},\hat{Y}}(\cdot)$ *be an oracle that on input a message* $M = G^m$ *(for some possibly unknown* $m \in \mathbb{Z}_p$*) returns a triple* $\left(A := G^a, B := (G^x M)^{\frac{a}{y}}, C := H^{\frac{a}{y}} \right) \in \mathbb{G}^3$ *for some* $a \leftarrow \mathbb{Z}_p$. *We say the BSOM assumption holds (relative to* $\mathcal{BG}$*) if for all PPT adversaries* $\mathcal{A}$, *the following advantage is negligible (in* λ*):*

$$
\Pr \left[
\begin{array}{l}
\mathcal{P} \leftarrow \mathcal{BG}(1^\lambda);\ h, x, y \leftarrow \mathbb{Z}_p;\ (H, \hat{H}, \hat{X}, \hat{Y}) := (G^h, \hat{G}^h, \hat{G}^x, \hat{G}^y); \\
\{(A_i, B_i, m_i)\}_{i=1}^{k+1} \leftarrow \mathcal{A}^{\mathcal{O}BSOM^k_{H,\hat{H},\hat{X},\hat{Y}}(\cdot)} \left(\mathcal{P}, H, \hat{H}, \hat{X}, \hat{Y} \right) : \\
\left| \{m_i\}_{i=1}^{k+1} \right| = k + 1 \ \wedge\ \forall i \in [k+1]:\ A_i \neq 1_{\mathbb{G}} \wedge e(B_i, \hat{Y}) = e(A_i, \hat{X}\hat{G}^{m_i})
\end{array}
\right]
$$

The proof for the following theorem can be found in the full version [39].

Theorem 1. *For any generic adversary* $\mathcal{A}$ *against the BSOM assumption, if* p *is the (prime) order of the bilinear group and* $\mathcal{A}$ *makes* q_G *group operation queries,* q_P *pairing queries and* q_O *queries to the BSOM oracle* $\mathcal{O}BSOM_{H,\hat{H},\hat{X},\hat{Y}}$, *then the probability of* $\mathcal{A}$ *against the BSOM assumption is* $\mathcal{O}(\frac{q_G^2 q_O + q_P^2 q_O + q_O^3}{p})$.

3.2 The BSOMI Assumption

Our second new assumption which we refer to as the BSOMI assumption will form the basis for the unforgeability of our second blind signature construction. It is inspired in part by the assumption underlying the recent signature scheme by Pointcheval and Sanders [51].

Definition 2 (BSOMI Assumption). *Let* $\mathcal{P} = (\mathbb{G}, \hat{\mathbb{G}}, \mathbb{T}, G, \hat{G}, e, p)$ *be the description of Type-III bilinear groups output by* $\mathcal{BG}(1^\lambda)$, *and let* $H := G^h$, $\hat{H}' := \hat{G}^{\frac{1}{h}}$, $\hat{X} := \hat{G}^x$, $\hat{Y} := \hat{G}^y$ *for some* $h, x, y \leftarrow \mathbb{Z}_p$. *Let* $\mathcal{O}BSOMI_{H,\hat{H}',\hat{X},\hat{Y}}(\cdot)$ *be an oracle that on input a message* $M := G^m$ *(for some possibly unknown* $m \in \mathbb{Z}_p$*) returns a triple* $\left(A := G^a, B := A^x M^{ay}, C := H^{ay} \right) \in \mathbb{G}^3$ *for some* $a \leftarrow \mathbb{Z}_p$. *We say the BSOMI assumption holds (relative to* $\mathcal{BG}$*) if for all PPT adversaries* $\mathcal{A}$, *the following advantage is negligible (in* λ*):*

$$
\Pr \left[
\begin{array}{l}
\mathcal{P} \leftarrow \mathcal{BG}(1^\lambda);\ h, x, y \leftarrow \mathbb{Z}_p;\ (H, \hat{H}', \hat{X}, \hat{Y}) := (G^h, \hat{G}^{\frac{1}{h}}, \hat{G}^x, \hat{G}^y); \\
\{(A_i, B_i, m_i)\}_{i=1}^{k+1} \leftarrow \mathcal{A}^{\mathcal{O}BSOMI^k_{H,\hat{H}',\hat{X},\hat{Y}}(\cdot)} \left(\mathcal{P}, H, \hat{H}', \hat{X}, \hat{Y} \right) : \\
\left| \{m_i\}_{i=1}^{k+1} \right| = k + 1 \ \wedge\ \forall i \in [k+1]:\ A_i \neq 1_{\mathbb{G}} \wedge e(B_i, \hat{G}) = e(A_i, \hat{X}\hat{Y}^{m_i})
\end{array}
\right]
$$

The proof for the following theorem can be found in the full version [39].

Theorem 2. *For any generic adversary $\mathcal{A}$ against the BSOMI assumption, if p is the (prime) order of the bilinear group and $\mathcal{A}$ makes q_G group operation queries, q_P pairing queries and q_O queries to the BSOMI oracle $\mathcal{O}BSOMI_{H,\hat{H}',\hat{X},\hat{Y}}$, then the probability of $\mathcal{A}$ against the BSOMI assumption is $\mathcal{O}(\frac{q_G^2 q_O + q_P^2 q_O + q_O^3}{p})$.*

4 Syntax and Security of Blind Signatures

In this section, we define the syntax and security of blind signatures. Since we are interested in round-optimal schemes, we will specialize our definitions to this case. A blind signature scheme BS (with a two-move signature request) consists of the following polynomial-time algorithms:

KeyGen$_{BS}(1^\lambda)$ On input a security parameter 1^λ, this probabilistic algorithm outputs a pair (vk$_{BS}$, sk$_{BS}$) of public/secret keys for the signer. Without loss of generality we assume the security parameter is an implicit input to the rest of the algorithms.

Request$_{BS}^0$(vk$_{BS}$, m): This algorithm run by the user takes as input a message m in the message space $\mathcal{M}$ and the public key vk$_{BS}$, and produces a signature request ρ, plus some state st (which is assumed to contain m).

Issue$_{BS}$(sk$_{BS}$, ρ): This probabilistic algorithm run by the signer takes as input the secret key sk$_{BS}$ and the signature request ρ, and produces a pre-signature β.

Request$_{BS}^1$(vk$_{BS}$, β, st): On input the public key vk$_{BS}$, the pre-signature β, and the state st, this algorithm produces a blind signature σ on m, or it outputs $\perp$ if it does not accept the transcript.

Verify$_{BS}$(vk$_{BS}$, m, σ): This deterministic algorithm outputs 1 if σ is a valid signature on the message m, or 0 otherwise.

(Perfect) correctness of blind signatures requires that for all $\lambda \in \mathbb{N}$ and all $m \in \mathcal{M}$, we have

$$\Pr\left[\begin{array}{l}(\text{vk}_{BS}, \text{sk}_{BS}) \leftarrow \text{KeyGen}_{BS}(1^\lambda); \; (\rho, \text{st}) \leftarrow \text{Request}_{BS}^0(\text{vk}_{BS}, m); \\ \beta \leftarrow \text{Issue}_{BS}(\text{sk}_{BS}, \rho); \sigma \leftarrow \text{Request}_{BS}^1(\text{vk}_{BS}, \beta, \text{st}) : \text{Verify}_{BS}(\text{vk}_{BS}, m, \sigma) = 1\end{array}\right] = 1.$$

Security of blind signatures [45,52] which was strengthened by [28,55] requires blindness and unforgeability.

Unforgeability. Unforgeability requires that it is infeasible for an adversarial user who interacts with an honest signer on k occasions to output $k+1$ valid signatures on $k+1$ distinct messages.

Definition 3 (Unforgeability). *A blind scheme BS satisfies unforgeability if for all $\lambda \in \mathbb{N}$, for all PPT adversaries $\mathcal{A}$, the advantage $\text{Adv}_{BS,\mathcal{A}}^{Unforge}(\lambda)$ against the game $\text{Exp}_{BS,\mathcal{A}}^{Unforge}$ defined in Fig. 1. is negligible (in λ) where*

$$\text{Adv}_{BS,\mathcal{A}}^{Unforge}(\lambda) = \Pr[\text{Exp}_{BS,\mathcal{A}}^{Unforge}(\lambda) = 1].$$

Experiment: $\mathsf{Exp}_{\mathsf{BS},\mathcal{A}}^{\mathrm{Unforge}}(\lambda)$	Experiment: $\mathsf{Exp}_{\mathsf{BS},\mathcal{A}}^{\mathrm{Blind}}(\lambda)$
- $(\mathsf{vk}_{\mathsf{BS}}, \mathsf{sk}_{\mathsf{BS}}) \leftarrow \mathsf{KeyGen}_{\mathsf{BS}}(1^\lambda)$	- $(\mathsf{vk}_{\mathsf{BS}}, m_0, m_1, \mathsf{st}_{\mathsf{find}}) \leftarrow \mathcal{A}_{\mathsf{find}}(\lambda)$
- $\{(m_i, \sigma_i)\}_{i=1}^{k+1} \leftarrow \mathcal{A}^{\mathsf{Issue}_{\mathsf{BS}}^k(\mathsf{sk}_{\mathsf{BS}}, \cdot)}(\mathsf{vk}_{\mathsf{BS}})$	- $b \leftarrow \{0, 1\}$
- Return 0 if any of the following holds:	- $(\rho_b, \mathsf{st}_b) \leftarrow \mathsf{Request}_{\mathsf{BS}}^0(\mathsf{vk}_{\mathsf{BS}}, m_0)$
- $\exists i, j \in [k+1]$, with $i \neq j$ but $m_i = m_j$	- $(\rho_{1-b}, \mathsf{st}_{1-b}) \leftarrow \mathsf{Request}_{\mathsf{BS}}^0(\mathsf{vk}_{\mathsf{BS}}, m_1)$
- $\exists i \in [k+1]$ s.t. $\mathsf{Verify}_{\mathsf{BS}}(\mathsf{vk}_{\mathsf{BS}}, m_i, \sigma_i) = 0$	- $(\beta_0, \beta_1, \mathsf{st}_{\mathsf{issue}}) \leftarrow \mathcal{A}_{\mathsf{issue}}(\rho_0, \rho_1, \mathsf{st}_{\mathsf{find}})$
- Return 1	- $\sigma_0 \leftarrow \mathsf{Request}_{\mathsf{BS}}^1(\mathsf{vk}_{\mathsf{BS}}, \beta_b, \mathsf{st}_b)$
	- $\sigma_1 \leftarrow \mathsf{Request}_{\mathsf{BS}}^1(\mathsf{vk}_{\mathsf{BS}}, \beta_{1-b}, \mathsf{st}_{1-b})$
	- If $\sigma_0 = \perp$ or $\sigma_1 = \perp$ Then Return 0
	- $b^* \leftarrow \mathcal{A}_{\mathsf{guess}}(\sigma_0, \sigma_1, \mathsf{st}_{\mathsf{issue}})$
	- Return 1 if $b = b^*$ Else Return 0

Fig. 1. The security experiments for unforgeability (left) and blindness w.r.t. malicious keys (right)

Blindness. Blindness (w.r.t. malicious keys [1, 49]) requires that an adversarial signer who freely chooses two messages m_0 and m_1 as well as the keys and then takes part in interactions with an honest user to generate signatures on those messages cannot tell the order in which the messages were signed.

Definition 4 (Blindness w.r.t. malicious keys). *A blind scheme* BS *satisfies blindness w.r.t. malicious keys if for all* $\lambda \in \mathbb{N}$, *for all PPT adversaries* $\mathcal{A}$, *the advantage* $\mathsf{Adv}_{\mathsf{BS},\mathcal{A}}^{Blind}(\lambda)$ *defined as*

$$\mathsf{Adv}_{\mathsf{BS},\mathcal{A}}^{Blind}(\lambda) = \left| \Pr[\mathsf{Exp}_{\mathsf{BS},\mathcal{A}}^{Blind}(\lambda) = 1] - \frac{1}{2} \right|$$

is negligible (in λ) *where* $\mathsf{Exp}_{\mathsf{BS},\mathcal{A}}^{Blind}$ *is defined in Fig. 1.*

5   Blind Signature Constructions

Here we present our two constructions of blind signatures satisfying blindness in the malicious-key model.

5.1   Construction I

Here we present our first construction whose unforgeability is based on the BSOM assumption. The high-level idea is that when requesting a blind signature on the message $m \in \mathbb{Z}_p$, the user uses the Pedersen commitment scheme to commit to m as $\mathsf{Co} := G^m H^r$ and sends the commitment Co to the signer. Unlike many existing constructions, neither the user nor the signer in our construction are required to produce expensive zero-knowledge proofs to prove correctness of their computation. Note that since the Pedersen commitment is perfectly hiding, the commitment Co reveals no information about the committed message. We can think of such a commitment as the message M on which the oracle in the BSOM assumption is queried. Now the signer, playing the role of the oracle in the definition of the BSOM assumption, returns the tuple (A', B', C'). The user can check whether such a tuple corresponds to a valid pre-signature by first verifying that the last element (which is independent of the message) is constructed correctly. This is achieved by verifying that $e(C', \hat{Y}) = e(A', \hat{H})$. If such a check does not pass, the user returns $\perp$. Otherwise, since the user already knows the randomness r she used in constructing the commitment Co, she can now adapt the pre-signature (A', B') on the commitment Co to one on the message m by letting $B' := B'C'^{-r}$ and then randomizing the signature (A', B') into a new one (A, B) so that the two pairs are unlinkable. Similarly to e.g. [31,33], by assuming that the bilinear group generator $\mathcal{BG}$ is deterministic combined with the fact that the Pedersen commitment remains hiding even if the commitment key is generated maliciously, we achieve blindness w.r.t. malicious keys. The construction is detailed in Fig. 2.

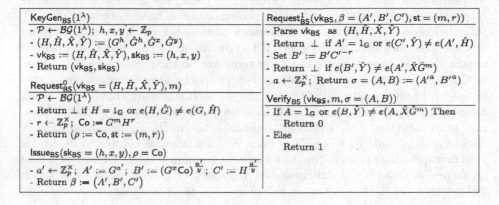

Fig. 2. Our 1st blind signature construction

Note that the checks performed in the $\mathsf{Request}^0_{\mathsf{BS}}$ algorithm to verify well-formedness of the signer's verification key need only be performed once when requesting the first signature and not each time a signature is requested.

Theorem 3. *The construction is a secure blind signature scheme in the malicious-key model.*

Proof. We first show that the scheme is correct. We have that $\mathsf{Co} = G^m H^r$, $B' = (G^x \mathsf{Co})^{\frac{a'}{v}} = G^{\frac{a'x}{v}} \mathsf{Co}^{\frac{a'}{v}} = G^{\frac{a'x}{v}} (G^m H^r)^{\frac{a'}{v}}$ and $C' = H^{\frac{a'}{v}}$. We have that $B' = B'C'^{-r} = G^{\frac{a'x}{v}} (G^m H^r)^{\frac{a'}{v}} H^{\frac{-a'r}{v}} = G^{\frac{a'x}{v}} G^{\frac{ma'}{v}}$. Thus, (A', B') satisfy $e(B', \hat{Y}) = e(A', \hat{X}\hat{G}^m)$.

The following 2 lemmata complete the proof.

Lemma 1 (Unforgeability). *The construction is unforgeable if the BSOM assumption is intractable.*

Proof. Let $\mathcal{A}$ be an adversary against the unforgeability of the scheme. We show how to use $\mathcal{A}$ to construct an adversary $\mathcal{B}$ against the BSOM assumption. Adversary $\mathcal{B}$ gets the tuple $(\mathcal{P}, H, \hat{H}, \hat{X}, \hat{Y})$ from her game and she has access to the oracle $\mathcal{O}\mathrm{BSOM}_{H,\hat{H},\hat{X},\hat{Y}}(\cdot)$ which she can query polynomially many times. $\mathcal{B}$ starts $\mathcal{A}$ on $\mathsf{vk}_{\mathsf{BS}} := (H, \hat{H}, \hat{X}, \hat{Y})$. When queried on Co_i, $\mathcal{B}$ forwards such query to her oracle and returns the answer to $\mathcal{A}$. Eventually, when $\mathcal{A}$ outputs her $k+1$ message-signatures tuples $\{(m_i, A_i, B_i)\}_{i=1}^{k+1}$, $\mathcal{B}$ returns that as the answer in her game. It is clear that $\mathcal{B}$ wins her game with the same advantage as that of $\mathcal{A}$ in her game. Thus, we have $\mathsf{Adv}_{\mathsf{BS},\mathcal{A}}^{\mathsf{Unforge}} = \mathsf{Adv}_{\mathsf{BSOM},\mathcal{B}}$.

Lemma 2. *The construction is perfectly blind in the malicious-key model.*

Proof. Since the Pedersen commitment is perfectly hiding, it is clear that Co sent by the user reveals no information about the committed message. Now the check we perform on the pre-signatures ensures that each pre-signature is valid on its respective commitment. If any of those pre-signatures is invalid, we return $(\bot, \bot)$. It is obvious in the latter case the adversary gains no information about the order in which the messages were signed. If the checks on the pre-signatures pass, it means the first pre-signature is a valid signature on the message m_b committed in Co_b whereas the second signature is valid on the message m_{1-b} committed in Co_{1-b}. From the adversary's point of view each signature could be on either message since the commitment could have been on either message. What remains now is to show that (A', B', C') are unlinkable to (A, B). By definition we have that $A'_0 \neq 1_{\mathbb{G}}$ and $A'_1 \neq 1_{\mathbb{G}}$. Now each final signature is computed by raising the corresponding pre-signature to a random exponent from $\mathbb{Z}_p^{\times}$. Thus, each final signature is uniformly distributed over the space of possible signatures and it follows that the final signature is independent of the pre-signature. $\square$

5.2   Construction II

Here we present our second construction whose unforgeability is based on the BSOMI assumption. The high-level idea is similar to that of the first construction. When requesting a blind signature on the message $m \in \mathbb{Z}_p$, the user uses the Pedersen commitment scheme to commit to m as $\mathsf{Co} := G^m H^r$ and sends the commitment Co to the signer. Here we view the commitment as the message M on which the oracle in the BSOMI assumption is queried. Now the signer, playing the role of the oracle in the definition of the BSOMI assumption, returns the tuple (A', B', C'). The user can check whether such a tuple corresponds to a valid pre-signature by first verifying that the last element (which is independent of the message) is constructed correctly. This is achieved by verifying that $e(C', \hat{H}') = e(A', \hat{Y})$. If such a check does not pass, the user returns $\bot$. Otherwise, since the user already knows the randomness r she used in constructing the commitment Co, she can now adapt the pre-signature (A', B') on the commitment Co to one on the message m by letting $B' := B'C'^{-r}$ and then randomizing the signature (A', B') into a new one (A, B) so that the two pairs are unlinkable.

Again as in our first construction, by assuming that the bilinear group generator $\mathcal{BG}$ is deterministic combined with the fact that the Pedersen commitment remains hiding even if the commitment key is generated maliciously, we achieve blindness w.r.t. malicious keys. The construction is detailed in Fig. 3.

Note that the checks performed in the $\mathsf{Request}^0_{\mathsf{BS}}$ algorithm to verify well-formedness of the signer's verification key need only be performed once when requesting the first signature and not each time a signature is requested.

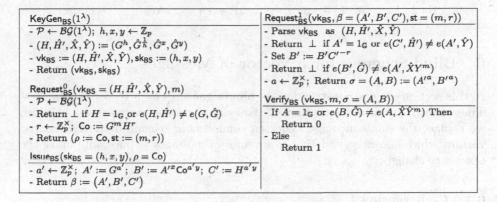

Fig. 3. Our 2nd blind signature construction

The proof for the following theorem can be found in the full version [39].

Theorem 4. *The construction is a secure blind signature scheme in the malicious-key model in the standard model.*

Efficiency Comparison. We compare in Table 1 the efficiency of our blind signature constructions with the most efficient existing schemes offering the same security in the standard model [31,33]. As can be seen from the table, our schemes outperform existing schemes in every efficiency metric. At 80-bit security, the size of our signatures is 40 bytes, i.e. 67% shorter than those of [33]. Also, blindness in our schemes holds in the information-theoretic sense which is another advantage. The security of all schemes in the table including ours rely on interactive intractability assumptions. Note that the most efficient scheme based on non-interactive assumptions in the standard model [36] is much less efficient than the schemes in the table, e.g. the signature size in [36] is 183 group elements in symmetric bilinear groups. In the table, P stands for pairing, A for point addition, and MK Model for the malicious-key model.

Table 1. Efficiency comparison

Scheme	σ		vk		Communication				Verification	MK Model	Blindness
	$\mathbb{G}$	$\hat{\mathbb{G}}$	$\mathbb{G}$	$\hat{\mathbb{G}}$	User		Signer				
					$\mathbb{G}$	$\hat{\mathbb{G}}$	$\mathbb{G}$	$\hat{\mathbb{G}}$			
[33]	4	1	1	4	2	-	2	1	7P	Yes	Computational
[31]	7	3	-	4	4	-	2	1	15P	Yes	Computational
Ours I	2	-	1	3	1	-	3	-	2P + 1A	Yes	Perfect
Ours II	2	-	1	3	1	-	3	-	2P + 1A	Yes	Perfect

6 Blind Schemes for a Vector of Messages

In this section we give constructions of blind signatures for a vector of messages. These constructions are extensions of their single-message counterparts in which we replace the single-message Pedersen commitment scheme by its generalized variant which allows committing to a vector of messages at once, and make the necessary changes.

6.1 Construction I

We show in Fig. 4 that we can without affecting the signature size or the number of pairings involved in the verification extend our scheme from Sect. 5.1 to blindly sign a vector of messages. This variant is unforgeable under the same assumption as the single-message scheme.

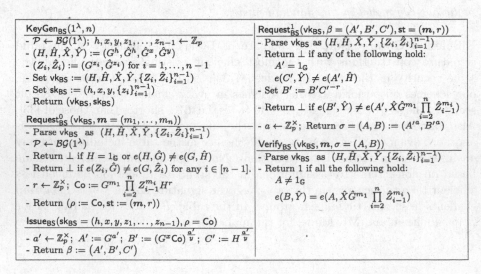

Fig. 4. A blind signature scheme I for a vector of messages $\in \mathbb{Z}_p^n$

All the checks performed in the $\mathsf{Request}^0_{\mathsf{BS}}$ algorithm to verify well-formedness of the signer's verification key need only be performed once when requesting the first signature and not each time a signature is requested.

Theorem 5. *The scheme in Fig. 4 is a secure blind signature.*

Proof. Correctness is straightforward to verify. Perfect blindness in the malicious-key model holds similarly to the perfect blindness of the single-message scheme. The following lemma proves unforgeability of the scheme.

Lemma 3 (Unforgeability). *The scheme is unforgeable if the BSOM assumption is intractable.*

Proof. Let $\mathcal{A}$ be an adversary against the unforgeability of the scheme. We show how to use $\mathcal{A}$ to construct an adversary $\mathcal{B}$ against the BSOM assumption. Adversary $\mathcal{B}$ gets the tuple $(\mathcal{P}, H, \hat{H}, \hat{X}, \hat{Y})$ from her game and she has access to the oracle $\mathcal{O}\mathrm{BSOM}_{H,\hat{H},\hat{X},\hat{Y}}(\cdot)$ which she can query polynomially many times. $\mathcal{B}$ chooses $z_1, \ldots, z_{n-1} \leftarrow \mathbb{Z}_p^\times$ and computes $(Z_i, \hat{Z}_i) := (G^{z_i}, \hat{G}^{z_i})$ for all $i \in [n-1]$. She then starts $\mathcal{A}$ on $\mathsf{vk}_{\mathsf{BS}} := (H, \hat{H}, \hat{X}, \hat{Y}, \{Z_i, \hat{Z}_i\}_{i=1}^{n-1})$. When queried on Co_i, $\mathcal{B}$ forwards such query to her oracle and returns the answer to $\mathcal{A}$. Eventually, when $\mathcal{A}$ outputs her $k+1$ message-signature tuples $\{(\boldsymbol{m}_i = (m_{i,1}, \ldots, m_{i,n}), A_i, B_i)\}_{i=1}^{k+1}$ where the vectors $\boldsymbol{m}_i$ are distinct, $\mathcal{B}$ computes $m'_i = m_{i,1} + \sum_{j=2}^n z_{j-1} m_{i,j}$ for all $i \in [k+1]$ and returns the $k+1$ tuples $\{(m'_i, A_i, B_i)\}_{i=1}^{k+1}$ as the answer in her game. It is clear that $\mathcal{B}$ wins her game with the same advantage as that of $\mathcal{A}$ in her game. Thus, we have $\mathsf{Adv}_{\mathsf{BS},\mathcal{A}}^{\mathrm{Unforge}} = \mathsf{Adv}_{\mathrm{BSOM},\mathcal{B}}$. $\qquad\square$

6.2   Construction II

We extend our scheme from Sect. 5.2 to blindly sign a vector of messages as shown in Fig. 5. This scheme is unforgeable under the same assumption as the single-message scheme.

All the checks performed in the $\mathsf{Request}^0_{\mathsf{BS}}$ algorithm to verify well-formedness of the signer's verification key need only be performed once when requesting the first signature and not each time a signature is requested.

The proof for the following theorem can be found in the full version [39].

Theorem 6. *The scheme in Fig. 5 is a secure blind signature.*

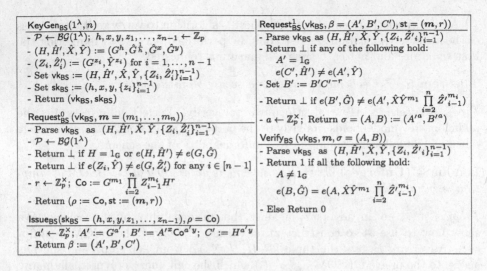

Fig. 5. A blind signature scheme II for a vector of messages $\in \mathbb{Z}_p^n$

7 Partially Blind Signature Schemes

Here we show how to modify our schemes in Sects. 6.1 and 6.2 to obtain partially blind signature schemes. For more generality, we give schemes where the public information is also a vector $\boldsymbol{\tau} = (\tau_1, \ldots, \tau_{n'}) \in \mathbb{Z}_p^{n'}$. This allows to attach multiple attributes to the signature.

7.1 Construction I

To realize our first construction, we modify the blind scheme on vector messages from Sect. 6.1 to attach a vector $\boldsymbol{\tau} = (\tau_1, \ldots, \tau_{n'}) \in \mathbb{Z}_p^{n'}$ of public information to the signature. To do so, we add to the public key of the scheme in Fig. 4 the elements $\hat{W}_i := \hat{G}^{w_i}$ for some randomly chosen elements $w_i \leftarrow \mathbb{Z}_p$ for $i = 1, \ldots, n'$. When asked to sign a commitment Co along with the public information $\boldsymbol{\tau}$, the signer signs the modified commitment $\mathsf{Co}' := \mathsf{Co} G^{\sum_{i=1}^{n'} \tau_i w_i}$. Upon receiving the pre-signature, the user checks that it is valid on the tuple $(\boldsymbol{m}, \boldsymbol{\tau})$. The details of the construction are in Fig. 6. The unforgeability of the scheme relies on a slight extension of the BSOM assumption which we refer to as the E-BSOM assumption. See full version [39] for details.

All the checks performed in the $\mathsf{Request}_{\mathsf{BS}}^0$ algorithm to verify well-formedness of the signer's verification key need only be performed once when requesting the first signature and not each time a signature is requested.

The proof for the following theorem can be found in the full version [39].

Theorem 7. *The scheme in Fig. 6 is a secure partially blind signature.*

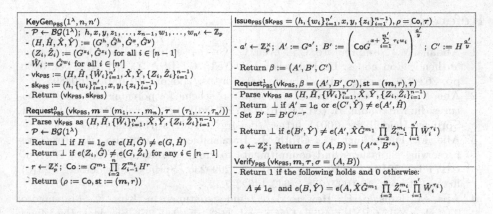

Fig. 6. A partially blind signature scheme I for a vector of messages $\in \mathbb{Z}_p^n$

7.2 Construction II

Our second partially blind signature construction shown in Fig. 7 is an extension of our blind construction from Fig. 5 in a similar manner to the first construction. The unforgeability of the scheme relies on a slight extension of the BSOMI assumption which we refer to as the E-BSOMI assumption. See full version [39] for details.

The proof for the following theorem can be found in the full version [39].

Theorem 8. *The scheme in Fig. 7 is a secure partially blind signature.*

KeyGen$_{\text{PBS}}(1^\lambda, n, n')$
- $\mathcal{P} \leftarrow \mathcal{BG}(1^\lambda); h, w_1, \ldots, w_{n'}, x, y, z_1, \ldots, z_{n-1} \leftarrow \mathbb{Z}_p$
- $(H, \hat{H}, \hat{X}, \hat{Y}) := (G^h, \hat{G}^{\frac{1}{h}}, \hat{G}^x, \hat{G}^y)$
- $(Z_i, \hat{Z}_i) := (G^{z_i}, \hat{Y}^{z_i})$ for all $i \in [n-1]$
- $\hat{W}_i := \hat{G}^{w_i}$ for all $i \in [n']$
- $\text{vk}_{\text{PBS}} := (H, \hat{H}', \{\hat{W}_i\}_{i=1}^{n'}, \hat{X}, \hat{Y}, \{Z_i, \hat{Z}_i\}_{i=1}^{n-1})$
- $\text{sk}_{\text{PBS}} := (h, \{w_i\}_{i=1}^{n'}, x, y, \{z_i\}_{i=1}^{n-1})$
- Return $(\text{vk}_{\text{PBS}}, \text{sk}_{\text{PBS}})$

Request$_{\text{PBS}}^0$($\text{vk}_{\text{PBS}}, \boldsymbol{m} = (m_1, \ldots, m_n), \boldsymbol{\tau} = (\tau_1, \ldots, \tau_{n'})$)
- Parse vk_{PBS} as $(H, \hat{H}', \{\hat{W}_i\}_{i=1}^{n'}, \hat{X}, \hat{Y}, \{Z_i, \hat{Z}_i\}_{i=1}^{n-1})$
- $\mathcal{P} \leftarrow \mathcal{BG}(1^\lambda)$
- Return $\perp$ if $H = 1_G$ or $e(H, \hat{H}') \neq e(G, \hat{G})$
- Return $\perp$ if $e(Z_i, \hat{Y}) \neq e(G, \hat{Z}_i)$ for any $i \in [n-1]$
- $r \leftarrow \mathbb{Z}_p^\times$; $\text{Co} := G^{m_1} \prod_{i=2}^{n} Z_{i-1}^{m_i} H^r$
- Return $(\rho := \text{Co}, \text{st} := (\boldsymbol{m}, r))$

Issue$_{\text{PBS}}$($\text{sk}_{\text{PBS}} = (h, \{w_i\}_{i=1}^{n'}, x, y, \{z_i\}_{i=1}^{n-1}), \rho = \text{Co}, \tau$)
- $a' \leftarrow \mathbb{Z}_p^\times$; $A' := G^{a'}$; $B' := A'^x \text{Co}^{a'} y G^{a' \sum_{i=1}^{n'} \tau_i w_i}$; $C' := H^{a' y}$
- Return $\beta := (A', B', C')$

Request$_{\text{PBS}}^1$($\text{vk}_{\text{PBS}}, \beta = (A', B', C'), \text{st} = (\boldsymbol{m}, r), \tau$)
- Parse vk_{PBS} as $(H, \hat{H}', \{\hat{W}_i\}_{i=1}^{n'}, \hat{X}, \hat{Y}, \{Z_i, \hat{Z}_i\}_{i=1}^{n-1})$
- Return $\perp$ if $A' = 1_G$ or $e(C', \hat{H}') \neq e(A', \hat{Y})$
- Set $B' := B'C'^{-r}$
- Return $\perp$ if $e(B', \hat{G}) \neq e(A', \hat{X}\hat{Y}^{m_1} \prod_{i=2}^{n} \hat{Z}_{i-1}^{m_i} \prod_{i=1}^{n'} \hat{W}_i^{\tau_i})$
- $a \leftarrow \mathbb{Z}_p^\times$; Return $\sigma = (A, B) := (A'^a, B'^a)$

Verify$_{\text{PBS}}$($\text{vk}_{\text{PBS}}, \boldsymbol{m}, \boldsymbol{\tau}, \sigma = (A, B)$)
- Return 1 if the following holds and 0 otherwise:
  $A \neq 1_G$ and $e(B, \hat{G}) = e(A, \hat{X}\hat{Y}^{m_1} \prod_{i=2}^{n} \hat{Z}_{i-1}^{m_i} \prod_{i=1}^{n'} \hat{W}_i^{\tau_i})$

Fig. 7. A partially blind signature scheme II for a vector of messages $\in \mathbb{Z}_p^n$

Acknowledgments. We thank Ian Goldberg for pointing out an issue in the description of the partially blind scheme in an earlier version.

References

1. Abdalla, M., Namprempre, C., Neven, G.: On the (im)possibility of blind message authentication codes. In: Pointcheval, D. (ed.) CT-RSA 2006. LNCS, vol. 3860, pp. 262–279. Springer, Heidelberg (2006). https://doi.org/10.1007/11605805_17
2. Abe, M.: A secure three-move blind signature scheme for polynomially many signatures. In: Pfitzmann, B. (ed.) EUROCRYPT 2001. LNCS, vol. 2045, pp. 136–151. Springer, Heidelberg (2001). https://doi.org/10.1007/3-540-44987-6_9
3. Abe, M., Fuchsbauer, G., Groth, J., Haralambiev, K., Ohkubo, M.: Structure-preserving signatures and commitments to group elements. In: Rabin, T. (ed.) CRYPTO 2010. LNCS, vol. 6223, pp. 209–236. Springer, Heidelberg (2010). https://doi.org/10.1007/978-3-642-14623-7_12
4. Abe, M., Fujisaki, E.: How to date blind signatures. In: Kim, K., Matsumoto, T. (eds.) ASIACRYPT 1996. LNCS, vol. 1163, pp. 244–251. Springer, Heidelberg (1996). https://doi.org/10.1007/BFb0034851
5. Abe, M., Haralambiev, K., Ohkubo, M.: Signing on elements in bilinear groups for modular protocol design. Cryptology ePrint Archive, Report 2010/133. http://eprint.iacr.org/2010/133.pdf
6. Abe, M., Ohkubo, M.: A framework for universally composable non-committing blind signatures. In: Matsui, M. (ed.) ASIACRYPT 2009. LNCS, vol. 5912, pp. 435–450. Springer, Heidelberg (2009). https://doi.org/10.1007/978-3-642-10366-7_26
7. Baldimtsi, F., Lysyanskaya, A.: On the security of one-witness blind signature schemes. In: Sako, K., Sarkar, P. (eds.) ASIACRYPT 2013. LNCS, vol. 8270, pp. 82–99. Springer, Heidelberg (2013). https://doi.org/10.1007/978-3-642-42045-0_5
8. Baldimtsi, F., Lysyanskaya, A.: Anonymous credentials light. In: ACM-CCS 2013, pp. 1087–1098. ACM (2013)
9. Barbosa, M., Farshim, P.: Strong knowledge extractors for public-key encryption schemes. In: Steinfeld, R., Hawkes, P. (eds.) ACISP 2010. LNCS, vol. 6168, pp. 164–181. Springer, Heidelberg (2010). https://doi.org/10.1007/978-3-642-14081-5_11
10. Barreto, P.S.L.M., Naehrig, M.: Pairing-friendly elliptic curves of prime order. In: Preneel, B., Tavares, S. (eds.) SAC 2005. LNCS, vol. 3897, pp. 319–331. Springer, Heidelberg (2006). https://doi.org/10.1007/11693383_22
11. Bellare, M., Namprempre, C., Pointcheval, D., Semanko, M.: The one-more-RSA-inversion problems and the security of Chaum's blind signature scheme. J. Cryptol. **16**(3), 185–215 (2003)
12. Bernhard, D., Fuchsbauer, G., Ghadafi, E., Smart, N.P., Warinschi, B.: Anonymous attestation with user-controlled linkability. Int. J. Inf. Secur. **12**(3), 219–249 (2013)
13. Blazy, O., Fuchsbauer, G., Pointcheval, D., Vergnaud, D.: Signatures on randomizable ciphertexts. In: Catalano, D., Fazio, N., Gennaro, R., Nicolosi, A. (eds.) PKC 2011. LNCS, vol. 6571, pp. 403–422. Springer, Heidelberg (2011). https://doi.org/10.1007/978-3-642-19379-8_25
14. Blazy, O., Pointcheval, D., Vergnaud, D.: Compact round-optimal partially-blind signatures. In: Visconti, I., De Prisco, R. (eds.) SCN 2012. LNCS, vol. 7485, pp. 95–112. Springer, Heidelberg (2012). https://doi.org/10.1007/978-3-642-32928-9_6
15. Boldyreva, A.: Threshold signatures, multisignatures and blind signatures based on the Gap-Diffie-Hellman-Group signature scheme. In: Desmedt, Y.G. (ed.) PKC 2003. LNCS, vol. 2567, pp. 31–46. Springer, Heidelberg (2003). https://doi.org/10.1007/3-540-36288-6_3
16. Boneh, D., Boyen, X.: Short signatures without random oracles and the SDH assumption in bilinear groups. J. Cryptol. **21**(2), 149–177 (2008)

17. Boneh, D., Lynn, B., Shacham, H.: Short signatures from the Weil pairing. J. Cryptol. **17**(4), 297–319 (2004)
18. Brands, S.: Rethinking Public Key Infrastructures and Digital Certificates: Building in Privacy. MIT Press, Cambridge (2000)
19. Brands, S., Paquin, C.: U-Prove Cryptographic Specification v1 (2010)
20. Brickell, E., Camenisch, J., Chen, L.: Direct anonymous attestation. In: CCS 2004, pp. 132–145. ACM (2004)
21. Camenisch, J., Koprowski, M., Warinschi, B.: Efficient blind signatures without random oracles. In: Blundo, C., Cimato, S. (eds.) SCN 2004. LNCS, vol. 3352, pp. 134–148. Springer, Heidelberg (2005). https://doi.org/10.1007/978-3-540-30598-9_10
22. Canard, S., Devigne, J., Sanders, O.: Delegating a pairing can be both secure and efficient. In: Boureanu, I., Owesarski, P., Vaudenay, S. (eds.) ACNS 2014. LNCS, vol. 8479, pp. 549–565. Springer, Cham (2014). https://doi.org/10.1007/978-3-319-07536-5_32
23. Chaum, D.: Blind signatures for untraceable payments. In: Chaum, D., Rivest, R.L., Sherman, A.T. (eds.) CRYPTO 1982, pp. 199–203. Springer, Cham (1983). https://doi.org/10.1007/978-1-4757-0602-4_18
24. Döttling, N., Fleischhacker, N., Krupp, J., Schröder, D.: Two-message, oblivious evaluation of cryptographic functionalities. In: Robshaw, M., Katz, J. (eds.) CRYPTO 2016. LNCS, vol. 9816, pp. 619–648. Springer, Heidelberg (2016). https://doi.org/10.1007/978-3-662-53015-3_22
25. Dwork, C., Naor, M.: Zaps and their applications. In: FOCS 2000, pp. 283–293. IEEE (2000)
26. Fiat, A., Shamir, A.: How to prove yourself: practical solutions to identification and signature problems. In: Odlyzko, A.M. (ed.) CRYPTO 1986. LNCS, vol. 263, pp. 186–194. Springer, Heidelberg (1987). https://doi.org/10.1007/3-540-47721-7_12
27. Fischlin, M.: Round-optimal composable blind signatures in the common reference string model. In: Dwork, C. (ed.) CRYPTO 2006. LNCS, vol. 4117, pp. 60–77. Springer, Heidelberg (2006). https://doi.org/10.1007/11818175_4
28. Fischlin, M., Schröder, D.: Security of blind signatures under aborts. In: Jarecki, S., Tsudik, G. (eds.) PKC 2009. LNCS, vol. 5443, pp. 297–316. Springer, Heidelberg (2009). https://doi.org/10.1007/978-3-642-00468-1_17
29. Fischlin, M., Schröder, D.: On the impossibility of three-move blind signature schemes. In: Gilbert, H. (ed.) EUROCRYPT 2010. LNCS, vol. 6110, pp. 197–215. Springer, Heidelberg (2010). https://doi.org/10.1007/978-3-642-13190-5_10
30. Fuchsbauer, G.: Automorphic signatures in bilinear groups and an application to round-optimal blind signatures. Cryptology ePrint Archive, Report 2009/320. http://eprint.iacr.org/2009/320.pdf
31. Fuchsbauer, G., Hanser, C., Kamath, C., Slamanig, D.: Practical round-optimal blind signatures in the standard model from weaker assumptions. In: Zikas, V., De Prisco, R. (eds.) SCN 2016. LNCS, vol. 9841, pp. 391–408. Springer, Cham (2016). https://doi.org/10.1007/978-3-319-44618-9_21
32. Fuchsbauer, G., Hanser, C., Slamanig, D.: Structure-preserving signatures on equivalence classes and constant-size anonymous credentials. Cryptology ePrint Archive, Report 2014/944. http://eprint.iacr.org/2014/944.pdf
33. Fuchsbauer, G., Hanser, C., Slamanig, D.: Practical round-optimal blind signatures in the standard model. In: Gennaro, R., Robshaw, M. (eds.) CRYPTO 2015. LNCS, vol. 9216, pp. 233–253. Springer, Heidelberg (2015). https://doi.org/10.1007/978-3-662-48000-7_12

34. Fujioka, A., Okamoto, T., Ohta, K.: A practical secret voting scheme for large scale elections. In: Seberry, J., Zheng, Y. (eds.) AUSCRYPT 1992. LNCS, vol. 718, pp. 244–251. Springer, Heidelberg (1993). https://doi.org/10.1007/3-540-57220-1_66
35. Galbraith, S., Paterson, K., Smart, N.P.: Pairings for cryptographers. Discrete Appl. Math. **156**, 3113–3121 (2008)
36. Garg, S., Gupta, D.: Efficient round optimal blind signatures. In: Nguyen, P.Q., Oswald, E. (eds.) EUROCRYPT 2014. LNCS, vol. 8441, pp. 477–495. Springer, Heidelberg (2014). https://doi.org/10.1007/978-3-642-55220-5_27
37. Garg, S., Rao, V., Sahai, A., Schröder, D., Unruh, D.: Round optimal blind signatures. In: Rogaway, P. (ed.) CRYPTO 2011. LNCS, vol. 6841, pp. 630–648. Springer, Heidelberg (2011). https://doi.org/10.1007/978-3-642-22792-9_36
38. Ghadafi, E.: More efficient structure-preserving signatures - or: bypassing the type-III lower bounds. Cryptology ePrint Archive, Report 2016/255. http://eprint.iacr.org/2016/255.pdf
39. Ghadafi, E.: Efficient round-optimal blind signatures in the standard model. Cryptology ePrint Archive, Report 2017/045. http://eprint.iacr.org/2017/045.pdf
40. Ghadafi, E., Smart, N.P.: Efficient two-move blind signatures in the common reference string model. In: Gollmann, D., Freiling, F.C. (eds.) ISC 2012. LNCS, vol. 7483, pp. 274–289. Springer, Heidelberg (2012). https://doi.org/10.1007/978-3-642-33383-5_17
41. Groth, J., Sahai, A.: Efficient non-interactive proof systems for bilinear groups. SIAM J. Comput. **41**(5), 1193–1232 (2012)
42. Hanser, C., Slamanig, D.: Structure-preserving signatures on equivalence classes and their application to anonymous credentials. In: Sarkar, P., Iwata, T. (eds.) ASIACRYPT 2014. LNCS, vol. 8873, pp. 491–511. Springer, Heidelberg (2014). https://doi.org/10.1007/978-3-662-45611-8_26
43. Hanzlik, L., Kluczniak, K.: A short paper on blind signatures from knowledge assumptions. In: Grossklags, J., Preneel, B. (eds.) FC 2016. LNCS, vol. 9603, pp. 535–543. Springer, Heidelberg (2017). https://doi.org/10.1007/978-3-662-54970-4_31
44. Hazay, C., Katz, J., Koo, C.-Y., Lindell, Y.: Concurrently-secure blind signatures without random oracles or setup assumptions. In: Vadhan, S.P. (ed.) TCC 2007. LNCS, vol. 4392, pp. 323–341. Springer, Heidelberg (2007). https://doi.org/10.1007/978-3-540-70936-7_18
45. Juels, A., Luby, M., Ostrovsky, R.: Security of blind digital signatures. In: Kaliski, B.S. (ed.) CRYPTO 1997. LNCS, vol. 1294, pp. 150–164. Springer, Heidelberg (1997). https://doi.org/10.1007/BFb0052233
46. Kiayias, A., Zhou, H.-S.: Concurrent blind signatures without random oracles. In: De Prisco, R., Yung, M. (eds.) SCN 2006. LNCS, vol. 4116, pp. 49–62. Springer, Heidelberg (2006). https://doi.org/10.1007/11832072_4
47. Lindell, Y.: Bounded-concurrent secure two-party computation without setup assumptions. In: STOC 2003, pp. 683–692. ACM (2003)
48. Meiklejohn, S., Shacham, H., Freeman, D.M.: Limitations on transformations from composite-order to prime-order groups: the case of round-optimal blind signatures. In: Abe, M. (ed.) ASIACRYPT 2010. LNCS, vol. 6477, pp. 519–538. Springer, Heidelberg (2010). https://doi.org/10.1007/978-3-642-17373-8_30
49. Okamoto, T.: Efficient blind and partially blind signatures without random oracles. In: Halevi, S., Rabin, T. (eds.) TCC 2006. LNCS, vol. 3876, pp. 80–99. Springer, Heidelberg (2006). https://doi.org/10.1007/11681878_5

50. Pedersen, T.P.: Non-interactive and information-theoretic secure verifiable secret sharing. In: Feigenbaum, J. (ed.) CRYPTO 1991. LNCS, vol. 576, pp. 129–140. Springer, Heidelberg (1992). https://doi.org/10.1007/3-540-46766-1_9

51. Pointcheval, D., Sanders, O.: Short randomizable signatures. In: Sako, K. (ed.) CT-RSA 2016. LNCS, vol. 9610, pp. 111–126. Springer, Cham (2016). https://doi.org/10.1007/978-3-319-29485-8_7

52. Pointcheval, D., Stern, J.: Security arguments for digital signatures and blind signatures. J. Cryptol. **13**(3), 361–396 (2000)

53. Rückert, M.: Lattice-based blind signatures. In: Abe, M. (ed.) ASIACRYPT 2010. LNCS, vol. 6477, pp. 413–430. Springer, Heidelberg (2010). https://doi.org/10.1007/978-3-642-17373-8_24

54. Schnorr, C.P.: Efficient identification and signatures for smart cards. In: Brassard, G. (ed.) CRYPTO 1989. LNCS, vol. 435, pp. 239–252. Springer, New York (1990). https://doi.org/10.1007/0-387-34805-0_22

55. Schröder, D., Unruh, D.: Security of blind signatures revisited. In: Fischlin, M., Buchmann, J., Manulis, M. (eds.) PKC 2012. LNCS, vol. 7293, pp. 662–679. Springer, Heidelberg (2012). https://doi.org/10.1007/978-3-642-30057-8_39

56. Seo, J.H., Cheon, J.H.: Beyond the limitation of prime-order bilinear groups, and round optimal blind signatures. In: Cramer, R. (ed.) TCC 2012. LNCS, vol. 7194, pp. 133–150. Springer, Heidelberg (2012). https://doi.org/10.1007/978-3-642-28914-9_8

57. Shoup, V.: Lower bounds for discrete logarithms and related problems. In: Fumy, W. (ed.) EUROCRYPT 1997. LNCS, vol. 1233, pp. 256–266. Springer, Heidelberg (1997). https://doi.org/10.1007/3-540-69053-0_18

Searching and Processing Private Data

Secure Multiparty Computation from SGX

Raad Bahmani[1]([✉]), Manuel Barbosa[2], Ferdinand Brasser[1], Bernardo Portela[2],
Ahmad-Reza Sadeghi[1], Guillaume Scerri[3], and Bogdan Warinschi[4]

[1] Technische Universität Darmstadt, Darmstadt, Germany
raad.bahmani@trust.tu-darmstadt.de
[2] HASLab – INESC TEC & DCC-FCUP, Porto, Portugal
[3] Laboratoire DAVID – Université de Versailles St-Quentin & INRIA,
Versailles, France
[4] University of Bristol, Bristol, UK

Abstract. In this paper we show how Isolated Execution Environments
(IEE) offered by novel commodity hardware such as Intel's SGX provide a
new path to constructing general secure multiparty computation (MPC)
protocols. Our protocol is intuitive and elegant: it uses code within an
IEE to play the role of a trusted third party (TTP), and the attestation
guarantees of SGX to bootstrap secure communications between participants and the TTP. The load of communications and computations on
participants only depends on the size of each party's inputs and outputs
and is thus small and independent from the intricacies of the functionality
to be computed. The remaining computational load– essentially that of
computing the functionality – is moved to an untrusted party running an
IEE-enabled machine, an attractive feature for Cloud-based scenarios.

Our rigorous modular security analysis relies on the novel notion of
labeled attested computation which we put forth in this paper. This
notion is a convenient abstraction of the kind of attestation guarantees
one can obtain from trusted hardware in multi-user scenarios.

Finally, we present an extensive experimental evaluation of our solution on SGX-enabled hardware. Our implementation is open-source and it
is functionality agnostic: it can be used to securely outsource to the Cloud
arbitrary off-the-shelf collaborative software, such as the one employed on
financial data applications, enabling secure collaborative execution over
private inputs provided by multiple parties.

1 Introduction

Secure multiparty computation (MPC) allows a set of mutually distrusting parties to collaboratively carry out a computation that involves their private inputs.

This work was supported by the European Union's 7th Framework Program
(FP7/2007-2013) under grant agreement no. 609611 (PRACTICE). Manuel Barbosa
and Bernardo Portela were funded by project "NanoSTIMA: Macro-to-Nano Human
Sensing: Towards Integrated Multimodal Health Monitoring and Analytics/NORTE-
01-0145-FEDER-000016", which is financed by the North Portugal Regional Operational Programme (NORTE 2020), under the PORTUGAL 2020 Partnership
Agreement, and through the European Regional Development Fund (ERDF).

© International Financial Cryptography Association 2017
A. Kiayias (Ed.): FC 2017, LNCS 10322, pp. 477–497, 2017.
https://doi.org/10.1007/978-3-319-70972-7_27

The security guarantee that parties get are essentially those provided by carrying out the same computation using a Trusted Third Party (TTP). The computations to be carried out range from simple functionalities, for example where a party commits to a secret value and later on reveals it; or they can be highly complex, for example running sealed bid auctions [9] or bank customer benchmarking [17]. Most of the existent approaches are software only. The trust barrier between parties is overcome using cryptographic techniques that permit computing over encrypted and/or secret-shared data [18,25,31]. Another approach first studied by Katz [28] formalizes a trusted hardware assumption— where users have access to tamper-proof tokens on which they can load arbitrary code—that is sufficient to bootstrap universally composable MPC.

Broadly speaking, this work fits within the same category as that by Katz [13]. However, our starting point is a novel real-world form of trusted hardware that is currently shipped on commodity PCs: Intel's Software Guard Extensions [27]. Our goal is to leverage this hardware to significantly reduce the computational costs of practical secure computation protocols. The main security capability that such hardware offers are Isolated Execution Environments (IEE) – a powerful tool for boosting trust in remote systems under the total or partial control of malicious parties (hijacked boot, corrupt OS, running malicious software, or simply a dishonest service provider). Specifically, code loaded in an IEE is executed in isolation from other software present in the system, and built-in cryptographic attestation mechanisms guarantee the integrity of the code and its I/O behaviour to a remote user.

PROTOCOL OUTLINE. The functionality outlined above suggests a simple and natural design for *general multiparty computation*: load the functionality to be computed into an IEE (which plays the role of a TTP) and have users provide inputs and receive outputs via secure channels to the IEE. Attestation ensures the authenticity of the computed function, inputs and outputs. The resulting protocol is extremely efficient when compared to existing solutions that do not rely on hardware assumptions. Indeed, the load of communications and computations on protocol participants is small and independent of the intricacies of the functionality that is being computed; it depends only on the size of each party's inputs and outputs. The remaining computational load — essentially that of computing the functionality expressed as a transition function in a standard programming language — is moved to an untrusted party running an IEE-enabled machine. This makes the protocol attractive for Cloud scenarios. Furthermore, the protocol is non-interactive in the sense that each user can perform an initial set-up, and then provide its inputs and receive outputs independently of other protocol participants, which means that it provides a solution for "secure computation on the web" [24] with standard MPC security.

Due to its obvious simplicity, variations of the overall idea have been proposed in several practice-oriented works [23,36]. However, currently there is no thorough and rigorous analysis of the security guarantees provided by this solution in the sense of a general approach to MPC. The intuitive appeal of the protocol obscures multiple obstacles in obtaining a formal security proof, including: i. the lack of private channels between the users and the remote machine; ii. the need to authenticate/agree on a computation in a setting where communication between parties is inherently asynchronous and only mediated by the IEE; iii. the need to ensure that the "right" parties are engaged in the computation; iv. dealing with the interaction between different parts of the code that coexist within the same IEE, sharing the same memory space, each potentially corresponding to different users; and v. ensuring that the code running inside an IEE does not leak sensitive information to untrusted code running outside.

In this paper we fill this gap through the following contributions: i. a rigorous specification of the protocol for general MPC computation outlined above; ii. formal security definitions for the security of the overall protocol and that of its components;[1] iii. a modular security analysis of our protocol that relies on a novel notion of labelled attested computation; and iv. an open-source implementation of our protocol and a detailed experimental analysis in SGX-enabled hardware. We give an overview of our results next.

LABELED ATTESTED COMPUTATION. Our protocol relies on ideal functionalities viewed as programs written as transition functions in a programming language compatible with the IEE-enabled machine. We instrument these programs to run inside an IEE and add bootstrapping code that permits protocol participants to establish independent secure channels with the functionality, so that they can provide inputs and receive outputs. The crux of the protocol is a means to provide attestation guarantees which ensures that parties are involved in the "right" run of the protocol (i.e. with the right parties all interacting with the same IEE). We take inspiration from the recent work of Barbosa et al. [4] who provide a formalization for the notion of *attested computation* that can convince a party that its local view of the interaction with a remote IEE matches what actually occurred remotely. This guarantee is close to the one that we need, but it is unfortunately insufficient. The problem is that attested computation a la [4] is concerned with the interaction between a single party and an IEE, and it is non-trivial to extend these guarantees to the interaction of multiple parties with the same IEE when the goal is to reason about *concurrent asynchronous interactions*.

To overcome these problem, we introduce the notion of *labelled attested computation* (LAC), a powerful and clean generalization of the attested computation notion in [4]. In a nutshell, this notion assumes that (parts of) the code loaded in an IEE is marked with labels pertaining to users, and that individual users can get attestation guarantees for those parts of the code that corresponds to specific labels. The gain is that users can now be oblivious of other user's interactions with the IEE, which leads to significantly more simple and efficient protocols. Nonetheless, the user can still derive attestation guarantees about the overall

---

[1] Since our emphasis is on efficiency and analysing SGX-based protocols used in practice, we do not consider Universal Composability, but rather a simulation-based security model akin to those used for other practical secure computation protocols, e.g. [6].

execution of the system, since LAC binds each users' local view to the *same code* running within the IEE, and one can use standard cryptographic techniques to leverage this binding in order to obtain *indirect* attestation guarantees as to the honest executions of the interactions with other users.

We provide syntax and a formal security model for LAC and show how this primitive can be used to deploy arbitrary (labelled) programs to remote IEEs with flexible attestation guarantees. Our provably secure LAC protocol relies on hardware equipped with SGX-like IEEs. Our construction of the MPC protocol then builds on LACs in a modular way. First, we show how to use labelled attested computation schemes[2] to bootstrap an arbitrary number of independent secure channels between local users and an IEE with joint attestation guarantees. We formalize this result as an *utility theorem*. The security of the overall MPC protocol which uses these channels for communication with functionality code inside an IEE is then built on this utility theorem.

IMPLEMENTATION AND EXPERIMENTAL VALIDATION. We conclude the paper with an experimental evaluation of our protocol via a detailed comparison of our solution to state-of-the-art multiparty computation. The experimental results confirm the theoretical performance advantages that we have highlighted above in comparison to non hardware-based solutions. Our implementation of a generic MPC protocol —sgx-mpc— relies on the NaCl[3] cryptographic library [8] and inherits its careful approach to dealing with timing side-channels. We discuss side-channels in SGX-like systems and explain how our *constant-time* code thwarts *all* leaks based on control-flow or memory access patterns that depend on secret data.

Our implementation is functionality agnostic and can be used to outsource to the Cloud arbitrary off-the-shelf collaborative software, enabling multiple parties to jointly execute complex interactive computations without revealing their own inputs. Taking the financial sector as an example, our implementation permits carrying out financial benchmarking [17] using off-the-shelf software, rather than requiring the conversion of the underlying computation into circuit form, as is the case in state-of-the-art secure multiparty computation protocols. One should of course mention that, in order to meet the level of side-channel attack resilience of sgx-mpc, the code that is outsourced to the Cloud should itself be implemented according to the constant-time coding policy. This, however, is a software engineering issue that is outside of the scope of this paper.

RELATED WORK. A relevant line of research leverages trusted hardware to bootstrap entire platforms for secure software execution (e.g. Flicker [32], Trusted Virtual Domains [14], Haven [5]). These are large systems that are currently outside the scope of provable-security techniques. Smaller protocols which solve

---

[2] We use schemes which satisfy the additional notion of *minimal leakage* which ensures that the outsourced instrumented program P^* reveals no information about its internal state beyond what the normal input/output behavior of the original program P would reveal.

[3] https://nacl.cr.yp.to.

specific problems are more susceptible to rigorous analysis. Examples of these are secure disk encryption [33], one-time password authentication [26] outsourced Map-Reduce computations [36], Secure Virtual Disk Images [22], two-party computation [23], secure embedded devices [29,34]. Although some of these protocols (e.g., those of Hoekstra et al. [26] and Gupta et al. [23]) come only with intuition regarding their security, others—most notably those by Schuster et al. [36]— come with a proof of security. The use of attestation in those protocols is akin to our use of attestation in our general MPC protocol. Provable security of realistic protocols that use trusted hardware-based protocols based on the Trusted Platform Module (TPM) have been considered in [10,11,20,21,37]. The weaker capabilities offered by the TPM makes them more suitable for static attestation than for a dynamic setting like the one we consider in this paper.

In recent independent work Pass, Shi and Tramer [35] formalize attestation guarantees offered by trusted hardware in the Universal Composability setting, and consider the feasibility of achieving UC-secure MPC from such assumptions. Interestingly, they show that in the setting that they consider (UC with a Global Setup (GUC) [12]) multiparty computation is impossible to achieve without additional assumptions, unless *all* parties have access to trusted hardware. They bypass this impossibility result by assuming that all parties have access to both trusted hardware as well some additional set-up. The resulting protocols are more intricate and less efficient than ours, so our results can be interpreted as a practice-oriented approach to the security of the most natural MPC protocol that relies on SGX, which trades composability for efficiency while still preserving strong privacy guarantees for the inputs to the computation. Furthermore, contrary to their approach, performing parallel executions of our protocol also entails several initializations, thus increasing performance overhead accordingly.

2   IEEs, Programs, and Machines

The models that we develop in this paper rely on the abstraction for IEEs introduced in [4]. Here we recall the key features of that model. A more in depth description of these formalisms is provided in the full version [3].

An IEE is viewed as an idealised machine running some fixed program P and which exposes an interface through which one can pass inputs and receive outputs to/from P. The I/O behaviour of a process running in an IEE is determined by the program it is running, and the inputs it receives. The interface models the strict isolation between processes running in different IEEs and formalizes that the only information that is revealed about a program running within an IEE is contained in its input-output behaviour.

PROGRAMS. We extend the model for programs from [4] to the setting where inputs/outputs are labeled: programs are transition functions which take a current state st and a label-input pair (l, i), and produce a new output o and an updated state. We write $o \leftarrow P[\mathsf{st}](l, i)$ for each such action and refer to it as an *activation*. Throughout the paper we restrict our attention to programs (even if they are adversarially created) for which the transition function is guaranteed to run in polynomial-time. Programs are assumed to be deterministic modulo of system calls; in particular we assume a system can call rand for providing programs with fresh randomness. Additionally, outputs are assumed to include a flag finished that indicating if the transition function will accept further input. We extend our notation to account for probabilistic programs that invoke the rand system call. We write $o \leftarrow P[\mathsf{st}; r](l, i)$ for the activation of P which when invoked on labeled input (l, i) (with internal state st and random coins r) produced output o. We write a sequence of activations as $(o_1, \ldots, o_n) \leftarrow P[\mathsf{st}; r](l_1, i_1, \ldots, l_n, i_n)$ and denote by $\mathsf{Trace}_{P[\mathsf{st};r]}(l_1, i_1, \ldots, l_n, i_n)$ the corresponding input/output trace $(l_1, i_1, o_1, \ldots, l_n, i_n, o_n)$. For a trace T, we write $\mathsf{filter}[L](T)$ for the projection of the trace that retains only I/O pairs that correspond to labels in L. We use $\mathsf{filter}[l]$ when L is a singleton. We also extend the basic notion of program composition in [4] to consider label-based parallel and sequential program composition. Intuitively, when two labelled programs are composed, the set of labels of the composed program is enriched to encode the precise sub-program that should be activated and the label on which it should be activated.

MACHINES. As in [4] we model machines via a simple external interface, which we see as both the functionality that higher-level cryptographic schemes can rely on when using the machine, and the adversarial interface that will be the basis of our attack models. This interface can be thought of as an abstraction of Intel's SGX [27]. The interface consists of three calls: 1. $\mathsf{Init}(1^\lambda)$ initialises the machine and outputs the global parameters prms. 2. $\mathsf{Load}(P)$ loads the program P in a fresh IEE and returns its handle hdl 3. $\mathsf{Run}(\mathsf{hdl}, l, i)$ passes the label-input pair (l, i) to the IEE with handle hdl We define the I/O trace $\mathsf{Trace}_{\mathcal{M}}(\mathsf{hdl})$ of a process hdl running in a machine $\mathcal{M}$ as the tuple $(l_1, i_1, o_1, \ldots, l_n, i_n, o_n)$ that includes the entire sequence of n inputs/outputs resulting from all invocations of Run on hdl; $\mathsf{Program}_{\mathcal{M}}(\mathsf{hdl})$ is the code (program) running under handle hdl; $\mathsf{Coins}_{\mathcal{M}}(\mathsf{hdl})$ represents the coins given to the program by the rand system call; and $\mathsf{State}_{\mathcal{M}}(\mathsf{hdl})$ is the internal state of the program. Finally, we will write $\mathcal{A}^{\mathcal{M}}$ to indicate that algorithm $\mathcal{A}$ has access to machine $\mathcal{M}$.

3   Labelled Attested Computation

We now formalize a cryptographic primitive that generalizes the notion of Attested Computation proposed in [4], called Labelled Attested Computation. The main difference to the original proposal is that, rather than fixing a particular form of program composition for attestation, Labelled Attested Computation is agnostic of the program's internal structure; on the other hand, it permits controlling data flows and attestation guarantees via the label information included in program inputs.

SYNTAX. A *Labelled Attested Computation* (LAC) scheme is defined by the following algorithms:

– Compile(prms, P, L^*) is the deterministic program compilation algorithm. On input global parameters for some machine $\mathcal{M}$, program P and an attested label set L^*, it outputs program P^*. This algorithm is run locally. P^* is the code to be run as an isolated process in the remote machine, whereas L^* defines which labelled inputs should be subject to attestation guarantees.

– Attest(prms, hdl, l, i) is the stateless attestation algorithm. On input global parameters for $\mathcal{M}$, a process handle hdl and label-input pair (l, i), it uses the interface of $\mathcal{M}$ to obtain attested output o^*. This algorithm is run remotely, but in an unprotected environment: it is responsible for interacting with the isolated process running P^*, providing it with inputs and recovering the attested outputs that should be returned to the local machine.

– Verify(prms, l, i, o^*, st) is the public (stateful) output verification algorithm. On input global parameters for $\mathcal{M}$, a label l, an input i, an attested output o^* and some state st it produces an output value o and an updated state, or the failure symbol $\bot$. This failure symbol is encoded so as to be distinguishable from a valid output of a program, resulting from a successful verification. This algorithm is run locally on claimed outputs from the Attest algorithm. The initial value of the verification state is set to be (prms, P, L^*), the same inputs provided to Compile.

Intuitively, a LAC scheme is correct if, for any given program P and attested label set L^*, assuming an honest execution of all components in the scheme, both locally and remotely, the local user is able to accurately reconstruct a partial view of the I/O sequence that took place in the remote environment, for an arbitrary set of labels L. A formal definition of correctness is provided in the full version [3].

SECURITY. Security of labelled attested computation imposes that an adversary with control of the remote machine cannot convince the local user that some arbitrary remote (partial) execution of a program P has occurred, when it has not. It says nothing about the parts of the execution trace that are hidden from the client *or* are not in the attested label set L^*. Formally, we allow the adversary to freely interact with the remote machine, whilst providing a sequence of (potentially forged) attested outputs for a specific label $l \in L^*$. The adversary wins if the local user reconstructs an execution trace without aborting (i.e., all attested outputs must be accepted by the verification algorithm) and one of two conditions occur: i. there does not exist a remote process hdl* running a compiled version of P where a consistent set of inputs was provided *for label l*; or ii. the outputs recovered by the local user for those inputs are not consistent with the semantics of P.

Technically, these conditions are checked in the definition by retrieving the full sequence of *label-input pairs* and random coins passed to all compiled copies of P running in the remote machine and running P on the same inputs to obtain the expected outputs. One then checks that for at least one of these executions, when the traces are restricted to special label l, that the expected trace matches the locally recovered trace via Verify. Since the adversary is free to interact with the remote machine as it pleases, we cannot hope to prevent it from providing arbitrary inputs to the remote program at arbitrary points in time, while refusing to deliver the resulting (possibly attested) outputs to the local user. This justifies the winning condition referring to a prefix of the execution in the remote machine, rather than imposing trace equality. Indeed, the definition's essence is to impose that, if the adversary delivers attested outputs for a particular label in the attested label set, then the subtrace of verified outputs for that label will be an exact prefix of the projection of the remote trace for that label.

We note that a higher-level protocol relying on LAC can fully control the semantics of labels, as these depend on the semantics of the compiled program. In particular, adopting the specific forms of parallel and sequential composition presented in Sect. 2, it is possible to use labels to get the attested execution of a sub-program that is fully isolated from other programs that it is composed with. This provides a much higher degree of flexibility than that offered by the original notion of Attested Computation.

Definition 1 (Security). *A labelled attested computation scheme is secure if, for all ppt adversaries $\mathcal{A}$, the probability that experiment in Fig. 1 returns T is negligible.*

Game $\mathsf{Att}_{\mathsf{LAC},\mathcal{A}}(1^\lambda)$:

$\mathsf{prms} \leftarrow_\$ \mathcal{M}.\mathsf{Init}(1^\lambda); (P, L^*, l, n, \mathsf{st}_\mathcal{A}) \leftarrow_\$ \mathcal{A}_1(\mathsf{prms}); P^* \leftarrow \mathsf{Compile}(\mathsf{prms}, P, L^*); \mathsf{st}_V \leftarrow (\mathsf{prms}, P, L^*)$
For $k \in [1..n]$:
$\quad (i_k, o_k^*, \mathsf{st}_\mathcal{A}) \leftarrow_\$ \mathcal{A}_2^\mathcal{M}(\mathsf{st}_\mathcal{A}); (o_k, \mathsf{st}_V) \leftarrow \mathsf{Verify}(\mathsf{prms}, l, i_k, o_k^*, \mathsf{st}_V)$
$\quad$ If $o_k = \bot$ Return F
$T \leftarrow (l, i_1, o_1, \ldots, l, i_n, o_n)$
For hdl^* s.t. $\mathsf{Program}_\mathcal{M}(\mathsf{hdl}^*) = P^*$
$\quad (l_1', i_1', o_1', \ldots, l_m', i_m', o_m') \leftarrow \mathsf{Trace}_{\mathcal{M}_R}(\mathsf{hdl}^*); T' \leftarrow \mathsf{filter}[l](\mathsf{Trace}_{P[\mathsf{st};\mathsf{Coins}_\mathcal{M}(\mathsf{hdl}^*)]}(l_1', i_1', \ldots, l_m', i_m'))$
$\quad$ If $T \sqsubseteq T'$ Return F
Return T

Fig. 1. Game defining the security of LAC.

The adversary loses the game if there exists at least one remote process that matches the locally reconstructed trace. This should be interpreted as the guarantee that IEE resources are indeed being allocated in a specific remote machine to run at least one instance of the remote program (note that if the program is deterministic, many instances could exist with exactly the same I/O behaviour, which is *not* seen as a legitimate attack). Furthermore, our definition imposes that the compiled program uses essentially the same randomness as the source program (except of course for randomness that the security module internally uses to provide its cryptographic functionality), as otherwise it is easy for the adversary to make the (idealized) local trace diverge from the remote. This is a consequence of our modelling approach, but it does not limit the applicability of our primitive: it simply spells out that the transformation performed on the code for attestation will typically consist of an instrumentation of the code by applying cryptographic processing to the inputs and outputs it receives.

MINIMAL LEAKAGE. The above discussion shows that a LAC scheme guarantees that the I/O behaviour of the program in the remote machine includes at least the information required to reconstruct an hypothetical local execution of the source program. Next, we require that a compiled program does not reveal any information beyond what the original program would reveal. The following definition imposes that nothing from the internal state of the source programs (in addition to what is public, i.e., the code and I/O sequence) is leaked in the trace of the compiled program.

Definition 2 (Minimal leakage). *A labelled attested computation scheme* LAC *ensures security with minimal leakage if it is secure according to Definition 1 and there exists a ppt simulator S that, for every adversary A, the following distributions are identical:*

$$\{\, \mathsf{Leak\text{-}Real}_{\mathsf{LAC},\mathcal{A}}(1^\lambda) \,\} \approx \{\, \mathsf{Leak\text{-}Ideal}_{\mathsf{LAC},\mathcal{A},\mathcal{S}}(1^\lambda) \,\}$$

where games $\mathsf{Leak\text{-}Real}_{\mathsf{LAC},\mathcal{A}}$ *and* $\mathsf{Leak\text{-}Ideal}_{\mathsf{LAC},\mathcal{A},\mathcal{S}}$ *are shown in Fig. 2.*

Game Leak-Real$_{\mathsf{LAC},\mathcal{A}}(1^\lambda)$:	**Oracle Compile(P, L):**
PrgList ← []	$P^* \leftarrow \mathsf{Compile}(\mathsf{prms}, P, L)$
prms ←\$ $\mathcal{M}.\mathsf{Init}(1^\lambda)$	PrgList ← P^* : PrgList
$b \leftarrow$\$ $\mathcal{A}^O(\mathsf{prms})$	Return P^*
Return b	
Oracle Load(P):	**Oracle Run(hdl, l, i):**
Return $\mathcal{M}.\mathsf{Load}(P)$	Return $\mathcal{M}.\mathsf{Run}(\mathsf{hdl}, l, i)$
Game Leak-Ideal$_{\mathsf{LAC},\mathcal{A},\mathcal{S}}(1^\lambda)$:	**Oracle Compile(P, L):**
PrgList ← []; List ← []	$P^* \leftarrow \mathsf{Compile}(\mathsf{prms}, P, L)$
hdl ← 0	PrgList ← (P^*, L, P) : PrgList
$(\mathsf{prms}, \mathsf{st}_\mathcal{S}) \leftarrow$\$ $\mathcal{S}_1(1^\lambda)$	Return P^*
$b \leftarrow$\$ $\mathcal{A}^O(\mathsf{prms})$	
Return b	**Oracle Run(hdl, l, i):**
	$(P^*, \mathsf{st}) \leftarrow \mathsf{List}[\mathsf{hdl}]$
Oracle Load(P^*):	If $(P^*, L, P) \in$ PrgList :
hdl ← hdl + 1	$\quad o \leftarrow$\$ $P[\mathsf{st}](l, i)$
List[hdl] ← (P^*, ϵ)	$\quad (o^*, \mathsf{st}_\mathcal{S}) \leftarrow$\$ $\mathcal{S}_2(\mathsf{hdl}, P, L, l, i, o, \mathsf{st}_\mathcal{S})$
Return hdl	Else:
	$\quad (o^*, \mathsf{st}_\mathcal{S}) \leftarrow$\$ $\mathcal{S}_3(\mathsf{hdl}, P^*, l, i, \mathsf{st}, \mathsf{st}_\mathcal{S})$
	List[hdl] ← (P^*, st)
	Return o^*

Fig. 2. Games defining minimum leakage of LAC.

Intuitively, this means that one can construct a perfect simulation of the remote trace by simply appending cryptographic material to the local trace. This property is important when claiming that the security of a cryptographic primitive is preserved when it is run within an attested computation scheme.

4   LAC from SGX-like Systems

Our labelled attested computation protocol relies on the capabilities offered by the security module of Secure Guard Extensions (SGX) architecture proposed by Intel [2] (i.e. MACs for authenticated communication between IEEs, and digital signatures for inter-platform attestation of executions). Our security module formalization is the same as the one adopted in [4].

SECURITY MODULE. The security module relies on a signature scheme and a MAC scheme, and operates as follows:

- On initialization, the security module generates a key pair (pk, sk) and a symmetric key key. It also creates a special process running code S^* in an IEE with handle 0. The security module then securely stores the key material, and outputs the public key.
- The operation of IEE with handle 0 is different from all other IEEs in the machine. Program S^* will permanently reside in this IEE, and it will be the only one with direct access to both sk and key. The code of S^* is dedicated to transforming messages authenticated with key into messages signed with sk. On activation, it expects an input (m, t). It obtains key from the security module and verifies the tag. If the previous operation was successful, it obtains sk from the security module, signs the message and outputs the signature.
- The security module exposes a single system call mac(m) to code running in all other IEEs. On such a request from a process running program P, the security module returns a MAC tag t computed using key over both the code of P and the input message m.

LABELLED ATTESTED COMPUTATION SCHEME. We now define a LAC scheme that relies on a remote machine supporting such a security module. Basic replay protection using a sequence number does not suffice to bind a remote process to a subtrace, since the adversary could then run multiple copies of the same process and *mix and match* outputs from various traces. This is similar to the reasoning in [4]. However, in this paper we are interested in validating traces for specific attested labels, independently from each other, rather than the full remote trace. Our LAC scheme works as follows:

- Compile(prms, P, L) generates a new program P^* and outputs it. Program P^* is instrumented as follows:
  - In addition to the internal state st of P, it maintains a list ios_l of all the I/O pairs it has previously received and computed for each label $l \in L$.
  - On input (l, i), P^* computes $o \leftarrow_{\$} P[\text{st}_P](l, i)$ and verifies if $l \in L$. If this is not the case, then P^* simply outputs non-attested output o.
  - Otherwise, it updates the list ios by appending (l, i, o), computes the subset of ios for label l : $\text{ios}_l \leftarrow \text{filter}[l](\text{ios})$ and requests from the security module a MAC of for that list. Due to the operation of the security module, this will correspond to a tag t on the tuple (P^*, ios_l).

- It finally outputs $(o, \mathsf{t}, P^*, \mathsf{ios}_l)$. We note that we include (P^*, ios_l) explicitly in the outputs of P^* for clarity of presentation only. This value would be kept in an insecure environment by a stateful Attest program.

- Attest$(\mathsf{prms}, \mathsf{hdl}, l, i)$ invokes $\mathcal{M}.\mathsf{Run}(\mathsf{hdl}, (l, i))$ using the handle and input value it has received. Attest then checks is the produced output o is to be attested and if so transforms the tag into a signature σ using the IEE with handle 0 and outputs (o', σ). Otherwise it simply outputs o.

- Verify$(\mathsf{prms}, l, i, o^*, \mathsf{st})$ is the stateful verification algorithm. Initially $\mathsf{st} = (\mathsf{prms}, P, L^*)$, on first activation Verify computes and stores P^* and initialises an empty list ios of input-output pairs. Verify returns o^* if $l \notin L$. Otherwise, it first parses o^* into (o, σ), appends (l, i, o) to ios and verifies the digital signature σ using prms and $(P^*, \mathsf{filter}[l](\mathsf{ios}))$. If parsing or verification fails, Verify outputs $\perp$. If not, then Verify outputs o.

Correctness of our LAC scheme is clear – a detailed analysis is in the full version [3].

Theorem 1 (LAC scheme security). *The LAC scheme presented above provides secure attestation if the underlying MAC scheme Π and signature scheme Σ are existentially unforgeable. Furthermore, it unconditionally ensures minimum leakage.*

The proof of this theorem generalizes that of basic attestation schemes in [4] and can be found in the full version [3]. All attested outputs are bound to a partial execution trace that contains the entire I/O sequence associated with the corresponding attested label, so all messages accepted by Verify must exist as a prefix for a remote trace of some instance of P^*. The adversary can only cause an inconsistency in $T \sqsubseteq T'$ if the signature verification performed by Verify accepts a message of label $l \in L^*$ that was never authenticated by an IEE running P^*. However, in this case the adversary either breaks the MAC scheme (and dishonestly executing Attest), or breaks the signature (directly forging attested outputs).

5 Secure Computation with IEEs

FUNCTIONALITIES. We want to securely execute a functionality $\mathcal{F}$ defined by a four-tuple $(n, \mathsf{F}, \mathsf{Lin}, \mathsf{Lout})$, where F is a deterministic stateful transition function that takes inputs of the form (id, i). Here, id is a party identifier, which we assume to be an integer in the range $[1..n]$, and n is the total number of participating parties. On each transition, F produces an output that is intended for party id, as well as an updated state. We associate to F two leakage functions $\mathsf{Lin}(k, i, \mathsf{st})$ and $\mathsf{Lout}(k, o, \mathsf{st})$ which define the public leakage that can be revealed by a protocol about a given input i or output o for party k, respectively; for the sake of generality, both functions may depend on the internal state st of the functionality, although this is not the case in the examples we consider in this paper. Arbitrary reactive functionalities formalized in the Universal Composability framework can be easily recast as a transition function such as this. The upside of our approach is that one obtains a precise code-based definition of what the functionality should do (this is central to our work since these descriptions give rise to concrete programs); the downside is that the code-based definitions may be less clear to a human reader, as one cannot ignore the tedious *book-keeping* parts of the functionality.

EXECUTION MODEL. We assume the existence of a machine $\mathcal{M}$ allowing for the usage of isolated execution environments, as defined in Sect. 2. In secure computation terms, this machine should *not* be seen as an ideal functionality that enables some hybrid model of computation, but rather an additional party that comes with a specific setup assumption, a fixed internal operation, and which cannot be corrupted. Importantly, all interactions with $\mathcal{M}$ and all the code that is run in $\mathcal{M}$ but outside IEEs is considered to be adversarially controlled.

SYNTAX. A protocol π for functionality $\mathcal{F}$ is a seven-tuple of algorithms as follows:

- Setup – This is the party local set-up algorithm. Given the security parameter, the public parameters prms for machine $\mathcal{M}$ and the party's identifier id, it returns the party's initial state st (incluing its secret key material) and its public information pub.
- Compile – This is the (deterministic) code generation algorithm. Given the description of a functionality F, and public parameters (prms, Pub) for both the remote machine and the entire set of public parameters for the participating parties, it generates the instrumented program that will run inside an IEE.
- Remote – This is the untrusted code that will be run in $\mathcal{M}$ and which ensures the correctness of the protocol by controlling its scheduling and input collection order. It has oracle access to $\mathcal{M}$ and is in charge of collecting inputs and delivering outputs. Its initial state describes the order in which inputs of different parties should be provided to the functionality.
- Init – This is the party local protocol initialization algorithm. Given the party's state st produced by Setup and the public information of all participants Pub it outputs an uptated state st. We note that a party can choose to engage in a protocol by checking if the public parameters of all parties are correct and assigned to roles in the protocol that match the corresponding identities.
- AddInput – This is the party local input providing algorithm. Given the party's current state st and an input in, it outputs an uptated state st.
- Process – This is the party local message processing algorithm. Given its internal state st, and an input message m, it runs the next protocol stage, updates the internal state and returns output message m'.
- Output – This is the party local output retrieval algorithm. Given internal state st, it returns the current output o.

Intuitively such a protocol is correct if it can support any execution schedule whilst evaluating the functionality correctly. A precise definition is provided in the full version [3].

SECURITY. As is customary in secure computation models, we take the ideal world versus real world approach to define security of a protocol. Our security model is presented in Fig. 3, and is described as follows. In the real world, the adversary interacts with an IEE-enabled machine $\mathcal{M}$ under adversarial control and oracles SetInput, GetOutput and Send providing it with the locally run part of the protocol. In the ideal world, the adversary is presented with 1. a simulator $\mathcal{S}$ emulating the remote machine, the setup phase, and the Send oracle 2. idealised oracles SetInput, GetOutput. The idealised oracles only do book-keeping of which input should be transmitted next and which output should be retrieved next for each honest party. $\mathcal{S}$ gets given oracle access to a functionality evaluation oracle Fun that consumes the next input of a party (defined in SetInput if the party is honest, passed as input otherwise) and sets the next output for this party, returning the leakage of the input and output if the party is honest, and the full output otherwise. A protocol is deemed secure if there exists a ppt simulator such that no ppt adersary can distinguish the two worlds.

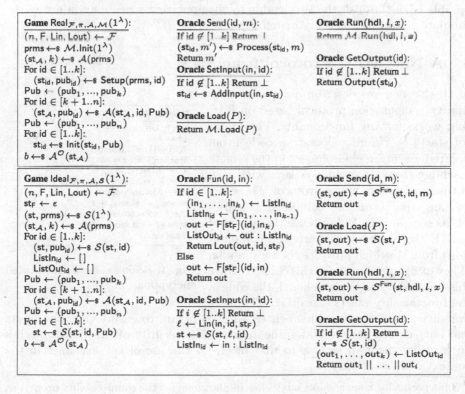

Fig. 3. Real and ideal security games.

Definition 3. *We say π is secure for $\mathcal{F}$ if, for any ppt adversary $\mathcal{A}$, there exists a ppt simulator $\mathcal{S}$ such that the following definition of advantage is a negligible function in the security parameter.*

$$|\Pr[\mathsf{Real}^{\mathcal{F},\pi,\mathcal{A},\mathcal{M}}(1^\lambda) \Rightarrow b = 1] - \Pr[\mathsf{Ideal}^{\mathcal{F},\pi,\mathcal{A},\mathcal{S}}(1^\lambda) \Rightarrow b = 1]|$$

Succinctly, our model is inspired in the UC framework, and can be derived from it when natural restrictions are imposed: PKI, static corruptions, and a distinguished non-corruptible party modeling an SGX-enabled machine.[4] A security proof for a protocol in our model can be interpreted as translation of any attack against the protocol in the real world, as an attack against the ideal functionality in the ideal world. The simulator performs this translation by presenting an execution environment to the adversary that is consistent with what it is expecting in the real world. It does this by simulating the operations of the Load, Run and Send oracles, which represent the operation of honest parties in the protocol. While the adversary is able to provide the inputs and read the outputs for honest parties directly from the functionality, the simulator is only able obtain partial leakage about this values via the Lin and Lout functions. Conversely, it can obtain the functionality outputs for corrupt parties via the Fun oracle and, furthermore, it is also able to control the rate and order in which all inputs are provided to the functionality. Were this not the case, the adversary would be able to distinguish the two worlds by manipulating scheduling in a way the simulator could not possibly match.

6   A New MPC Protocol from SGX

In this section we describe our secure multiparty computation protocol based on LAC that works for any functionality. The protocol starts by running bootstrap code in an isolated execution environment in the remote machine; the code exchanges keys with each of the participants in the protocol. These key exchange programs are composed in parallel, as seen in Sect. 2. We reuse the notion of AttKE (key exchange for attested computation) from [4] which provides the right notion of key exchange security in this context. Once this bootstrap stage is concluded, the code of the functionality starts executing. The func-

```
Program Box⟨F, Λ⟩[st](i*, l):
(n, F, Lin, Lout) ← F
id ← l
If id ∉ [1..n] : Return ⊥
If st.seq_id = ε : st.seq_id ← 0
i ← Λ.Dec(st.key_id, m)
If m ≠ (in, st.seq_id) : Return ⊥
o ← F[st.st_F](id, in)
st.seq_id ← st.seq_id + 1
c ←$ Λ.Enc(st.key_id, (seq, o))
st.seq_id ← st.seq_id + 1
Return c
```

Fig. 4. Boxing using authenticated encryption

tionality uses the secure channels established before to ensure that the inputs and outputs are private and authenticated. The security of this protocol relies on a utility theorem similar to that of [4] for the use of key exchange in the context of attestation.

---

[4] This particular choice in our model has implications for the composability properties of our results, as discussed in the related work section.

Theorem 2. (Local AttKE utility). *If the AttKE is correct and secure, and the LAC protocol is correct, secure and ensures minimal leakage, then for all ppt adversaries in the labelled utility experiment: the probability that the adversary violates the AttKE two-sided entity authentication is negligible; and the key secrecy advantage* $2 \cdot \Pr[\mathsf{guess}] - 1$ *is negligible.*

This theorem shows that, under the specific program composition pattern that we require for our MPC protocol, which guarantees AttKE isolation from other programs, each party obtains a secret key that is indistinguishable from a random string. The detailed labelled utility experiment and the theorem proof can be found in the full version [3]. It follows that the key can be used to construct a secure channel that connects it to code emulating the functionality within an IEE.

BOXING USING AUTHENTICATED ENCRYPTION. As explained above, after the bootstrapping stage of our protocol, we run the ideal functionality within an isolated execution environment. We implement this part of the execution using the *boxing* construction shown in Fig. 4. The name comes by analogy with placing the functionality within a box, which parties can access via secure channels. The labelled program $\mathsf{Box}\langle \mathcal{F}, \Lambda \rangle$ is parametrized by a functionality $\mathcal{F}$ for n parties and a secure authenticated encryption encryption scheme Λ. Its initial state is assumed to contain n symmetric keys compatible with Λ, denoted sk_1 to sk_n (one for each participating party) and the empty initial state for the functionality st_F. The Box expects encrypted inputs i^* under a label l identifying the party providing the input. These are then decrypted using the respective key sk_l and provided to $\mathcal{F}$. The value returned by the functionality is encrypted using the same sk_l and is then returned. To avoid replays of encrypted messages, we keep one sequence number seq_id per communicating party id.

THE PROTOCOL. Building on top of a LAC scheme, an AttKE scheme and our Box construction we define a general secure multiparty computation protocol that works for any (possibly reactive) functionality F. The core of the protocol is the execution of an AttKE for each participant in parallel, followed by the execution of the functionality F on the remote machine, under a secure channel with each participant as specified in the Box construct. More precisely:

- Setup derives the code for a remote key exchange program Rem_KE using the AttKE setup procedure. This code (which intuitively includes cryptographic public key material) is set to be the public information for this party. The algorithm also stores various parameters in the local state for future usage.
- Compile uses the LAC compilation algorithm on a program that results from the parallel composition of all the remote key exchange programs for all parties, which is then sequentially composed with the boxed functionality.
- Init locally reconstructs the program that is intended for remote execution, as this is needed for attestation verification. The set of labels that define the locally recovered trace is set to the pair $((p, (\mathsf{id}, \epsilon)), (q, \mathsf{id}))$, corresponding to the parts of the remote trace that are relevant for this party, namely its key exchange and its inputs/outputs.

- Process is split into two stages. In the first stage it uses LAC with attested labels of the form $(p, (\mathsf{id}, \epsilon))$ to execute AttKE protocol and establish a secure channel with the remote program. In the second stage, it uses non-attested labels of the form (q, id), and it provides inputs to the remote functionality (on request) and recovers the corresponding outputs when they are delivered.
- Output reads the output in the state of the participant and returns it.
- AddInput adds an input to the list of inputs to be transmitted by the participant.

Pseudo code of the protocol as well as formal details of the (untrusted) scheduling algorithm can be found in the full version [3].

For proving security, we restrict the functionalities we consider to a particular leakage function: size of inputs/outputs. We say that a functionality $(n, \mathsf{F}, \mathsf{Lin}, \mathsf{Lout})$ leaks size if it is such that Lin and Lout return the length of the inputs/outputs ($\mathsf{Lin}(k, x, \mathsf{st}) = \mathsf{Lout}(k, x, \mathsf{st}) = |x|$ for every k, x, st).

Theorem 3. *If* LAC *is a correct and secure LAC scheme,* AttKE *is a secure AttKE scheme and* Λ *a secure authenticated encryption scheme, then the protocol described in this Section is correct and secure for any functionality that leaks size.*

PROOF SKETCH. We build the required simulator S as follows. For dishonest parties, the simulator executes the protocol normally while for the honest parties instead of encrypting the inputs/outputs the simulator encrypts dummy messages of the correct length (obtained through the leakage function) under freshly generated keys.

We sketch a proof of indistinguishability between the real and ideal worlds. The full proof can be found in the full version [3]. The proof consists of 3 hops, the first is a hybrid argument over the honest parties. In this hybrid argument one gradually replaces the key derived by each honest party by a random one. In each step, the utility theorem is used to show that this change cannot be noticed by the adversary. In the second hop, we replace the encrypted inputs/outputs for honest parties by encrypted dummy payloads of the correct length. This hop is correct by the indistinguishability of encrypted ciphertexts. After this game hop, the resulting game is *identical until bad* to the ideal world, where the bad event corresponds to the simulator aborting due to an inconsistent message being accepted as the next undelivered input or output. Due to the use of sequence numbers, this bad event can be reduced to the authenticity of the encryption scheme.

7   Implementation

We provide an implementation of our protocol sgx-mpc-nacl relying on NaCl for the cryptographic library and Intel SGX for the IEEs. We use elliptic curves for both the key exchange (Diffie-Hellman) and signatures, and a combination of the Salsa20 and Poly1305 encryption and authentication schemes [8] for authenticated encryption. Our implementation relies on Intel's Software Development

Kit for dealing with the SGX low-level operations. These include loading code into an IEE (our Load abstraction), calling a function within the IEE (our Run abstraction), and constructing an attested message (first getting a MAC'ed message within the IEE, and using the quoting enclave to convert it into a signature). It employs the LAC scheme proposed here, and include wrappers that match our abstractions of signatures and authenticated encryption. These are then used to construct the bootstrapping protocol (AttKE) that enables each party to establish an independent secret key and secure channel to communicate with the Box construction running inside the IEE. Finally, our implementation of the Box is agnostic of the intended functionality, and can be linked to arbitrary functionality implementations, provided that these comply with a simple labelled I/O interface. The top-level interface to our protocol includes the code that runs inside the IEE, the code that runs outside the IEE in the remote machine for book-keeping operations and the client-side code that bootstraps a secure channel and then sends/receives messages from the functionality.

We compare our implementation with measurements we performed using the ABY framework [19]. We chose ABY for comparison, as we could evaluate it on the same platform we used for assessing our protocol, therefore avoiding differences due to performance disparities of heterogeneous evaluation platforms. Although it is specific to the two-party secure computation setting, ABY is representative of state-of-the-art MPC implementations and we expect results for other frameworks such as Sharemind [16] and SPDZ [18] to lead to similar conclusions; indeed, the crux of our performance gains resides in the fact that our solution does not require encoding the computation in circuit form, unlike all the aforementioned protocols.[5]

Like our protocol, the ABY protocol has two phases: a *preparation phase* and an *online phase*. The preparation phase comprises the key exchange between the input parties by means of oblivious transfer (OT), and generation of the garbled circuit (GC) representing the desired function. In the online phase the GC gets evaluated and the result is sent back to the output party. In our protocol, the preparation phase is used to establish a secure channel between the IEE and the input parties. The online phase of our protocol comprises the decryption of inputs in the Box component, the evaluation of the payload function, and the encryption of the results, again by the Box component.

We evaluated the performance of four different secure two-party computation use cases (Table 1): AES, millionaire's problem, private set intersection and hamming distance. In comparison to ABY, the preparation phase and online phase are shorter with sgx-mpc-nacl, and consequently the overall runtime is faster as well. In general, sgx-mpc-nacl is faster for all the testing computations performed. However, the gains are considerably more noticeable when we increase with input size and computation. This has the highest significance on evaluation of the private set intersection with the largest input size (1 mill.), where our implementation is roughly 300 times faster.

---

[5] We also note that ABY assumes a semi-honest adversary, which is weaker than the one we consider; but still our performance gains are significant.

Table 1. Clockwisely, starting from upper left: hamming distance, AES, millionaire's problem and private set intersection

	Phase	Preparation (ms)		Online (ms)		Total (ms)	
	Protocol	ABY	Ours	ABY	Ours	ABY	Ours
Input size (bits)	160	196.3	115.7	0.752	0.050	197.1	117.75
	1,600	196.7	115.7	1.819	0.302	198.5	116.00
	16,000	201.6	115.7	13.14	2.798	214.7	118.50
	160,000	226.2	115.2	144.4	27.77	370.6	142.97

Phase	ABY	Ours
Preparation (ms)	197.9	115.84
Online (ms)	3.249	0.661
Total (ms)	201.1	116.50

	Phase	Preparation		Online		Total	
	Protocol	ABY	Ours	ABY	Ours	ABY	Ours
Set size	100	224.8	115.8	1.084	0.043	225.9	115.84
	1000	368.1	115.8	2.168	0.199	370.3	116.00
	10,000	1442.2	115.8	12.88	1.758	1455.1	117.56
	100,000	10,698.7	115.7	109.5	17.39	10,808.2	133.09
	1,000,000	84,096.6	115.7	1616.0	173.1	85,712.6	288.80

Phase	ABY	Ours
Preparation (ms)	196.3	127.7
Online (ms)	0.404	0.024
Total (ms)	196.7	127.7

SIDE CHANNELS AND SOFTWARE RESILIENT AGAINST TIMING ATTACKS. Recent works [15,38] have pointed out that IEE-enabled systems such as Intel's SGX do not offer more protection against side-channel attacks than traditional microprocessors. This is a relevant concern, since the IEE trust model which we also adopt in this paper admits that the code outside IEEs is potentially malicious and that the machine is under the control of an untrusted party. We believe that there are two aspects to this problem that should be considered separately. The first aspect is the production of the IEE-enabled hardware/firmware itself and the protection of the long-term secrets used by the attestation security module. If the computations performed by the attestation infrastructure itself are vulnerable, then there is nothing that can be done at the protocol design/implementation level. This aspect of trust is within the remit of the manufacturers.

An orthogonal issue is the possibility that software running inside an IEE leaks part of its state or short-term secrets via side channels. One should distinguish between software observations and hardware/physical observations. In the former, software co-located in the machine observes timing channels based on memory access patterns, control flow, branch prediction, cache-based based attacks [15], page-fault side channels [38], etc. Protection against these side-channel attacks has been widely studied in the practical crypto community, where a consensus exists that writing so-called *constant-time* software is the most effective countermeasure [7,30]. As mentioned above, constant-time software has the property that the entire sequence of memory addresses (in both data and code memory) accessed by a program can be predicted in advance from public inputs, e.g., the length of messages. When it comes to hardware/physical side-channel attacks such as those relying on temperature measurements, power analysis, or electromagnetic radiation, the effectiveness of software countermeasures is very limited, and improving hardware defenses again implies obtaining additional guarantees from the equipment manufacturer.

Our implementation sgx-mpc-nacl enforces a strict constant-time policy that is consistent with the IEE trust model. To provide a protocol that is fully constant-time, one must also ensure that the executed functionality is constant-time. Recent work in the formal verification area sheds new light how this can be achieved over low-level code in a fully automatic way [1].

References

1. Almeida, J.B., Barbosa, M., Barthe, G., Dupressoir, F., Emmi, M.: Verifying constant-time implementations. In: USENIX Security Symposium. USENIX Association (2016)
2. Anati, I., Gueron, S., Johnson, S., Scarlata, V.: Innovative technology for CPU based attestation and sealing. In: HASP (2013)
3. Bahmani, R., Barbosa, M., Brasser, F., Portela, B., Sadeghi, A., Scerri, G., Warinschi, B.: Secure multiparty computation from SGX. IACR Cryptology ePrint Archive (2016)
4. Barbosa, M., Portela, B., Scerri, G., Warinschi, B.: Foundations of hardware-based attested computation and application to SGX. In: 2016 IEEE European Symposium on Security and Privacy (EuroS&P). IEEE (2016)
5. Baumann, A., Peinado, M., Hunt, G.C.: Shielding applications from an untrusted cloud with haven. In: OSDI. USENIX Association (2014)
6. Ben-David, A., Nisan, N., Pinkas, B.: Fairplaymp: a system for secure multi-party computation. In: CCS. ACM (2008)
7. Bernstein, D.J.: Cache-timing attacks on AES (2005). http://cr.yp.to/antiforgery/cachetiming-20050414.pdf
8. Bernstein, D.J., Lange, T., Schwabe, P.: The security impact of a new cryptographic library. In: Hevia, A., Neven, G. (eds.) LATINCRYPT 2012. LNCS, vol. 7533, pp. 159–176. Springer, Heidelberg (2012). https://doi.org/10.1007/978-3-642-33481-8_9
9. Bogetoft, P., Damgård, I., Jakobsen, T., Nielsen, K., Pagter, J., Toft, T.: A practical implementation of secure auctions based on multiparty integer computation. In: Di Crescenzo, G., Rubin, A. (eds.) FC 2006. LNCS, vol. 4107, pp. 142–147. Springer, Heidelberg (2006). https://doi.org/10.1007/11889663_10
10. Brickell, E., Chen, L., Li, J.: A new direct anonymous attestation scheme from bilinear maps. In: Lipp, P., Sadeghi, A.-R., Koch, K.-M. (eds.) Trust 2008. LNCS, vol. 4968, pp. 166–178. Springer, Heidelberg (2008). https://doi.org/10.1007/978-3-540-68979-9_13
11. Brickell, E.F., Camenisch, J., Chen, L.: Direct anonymous attestation. In: CCS. ACM (2004)
12. Canetti, R., Dodis, Y., Pass, R., Walfish, S.: Universally composable security with global setup. In: Vadhan, S.P. (ed.) TCC 2007. LNCS, vol. 4392, pp. 61–85. Springer, Heidelberg (2007). https://doi.org/10.1007/978-3-540-70936-7_4
13. Canetti, R., Fischlin, M.: Universally composable commitments. In: Kilian, J. (ed.) CRYPTO 2001. LNCS, vol. 2139, pp. 19–40. Springer, Heidelberg (2001). https://doi.org/10.1007/3-540-44647-8_2
14. Catuogno, L., Dmitrienko, A., Eriksson, K., Kuhlmann, D., Ramunno, G., Sadeghi, A.-R., Schulz, S., Schunter, M., Winandy, M., Zhan, J.: Trusted virtual domains – design, implementation and lessons learned. In: Chen, L., Yung, M. (eds.) INTRUST 2009. LNCS, vol. 6163, pp. 156–179. Springer, Heidelberg (2010). https://doi.org/10.1007/978-3-642-14597-1_10

15. Costan, V., Devadas, S.: Intel SGX explained. IACR Cryptology ePrint Archive (2016)

16. CYBERNETICA. Sharemind. http://sharemind.cyber.ee/

17. Damgård, I., Damgård, K., Nielsen, K., Nordholt, P.S., Toft, T.: Confidential benchmarking based on multiparty computation. IACR Cryptology ePrint Archive (2015)

18. Damgård, I., Pastro, V., Smart, N., Zakarias, S.: Multiparty computation from somewhat homomorphic encryption. In: Safavi-Naini, R., Canetti, R. (eds.) CRYPTO 2012. LNCS, vol. 7417, pp. 643–662. Springer, Heidelberg (2012). https://doi.org/10.1007/978-3-642-32009-5_38

19. Demmler, D., Schneider, T., Zohner, M.: ABY - A framework for efficient mixed-protocol secure two-party computation. In: NDSS. The Internet Society (2015)

20. Francillon, A., Nguyen, Q., Rasmussen, K.B., Tsudik, G.: A minimalist approach to remote attestation. In: Proceedings of the conference on Design, Automation & Test in Europe DATE (2014)

21. Ge, H., Tate, S.R.: A direct anonymous attestation scheme for embedded devices. In: Okamoto, T., Wang, X. (eds.) PKC 2007. LNCS, vol. 4450, pp. 16–30. Springer, Heidelberg (2007). https://doi.org/10.1007/978-3-540-71677-8_2

22. Gebhardt, C., Tomlinson, A.: Secure virtual disk images for grid computing. In: APTC. IEEE (2008)

23. Gupta, D., Mood, B., Feigenbaum, J., Butler, K., Traynor, P.: Using intel software guard extensions for efficient two-party secure function evaluation. In: Clark, J., Meiklejohn, S., Ryan, P.Y.A., Wallach, D., Brenner, M., Rohloff, K. (eds.) FC 2016. LNCS, vol. 9604, pp. 302–318. Springer, Heidelberg (2016). https://doi.org/10.1007/978-3-662-53357-4_20

24. Halevi, S., Lindell, Y., Pinkas, B.: Secure computation on the web: computing without simultaneous interaction. In: Rogaway, P. (ed.) CRYPTO 2011. LNCS, vol. 6841, pp. 132–150. Springer, Heidelberg (2011). https://doi.org/10.1007/978-3-642-22792-9_8

25. Henecka, W., Kögl, S., Sadeghi, A., Schneider, T., Wehrenberg, I.: TASTY: tool for automating secure two-party computations. In: CCS. ACM (2010)

26. Hoekstra, M., Lal, R., Pappachan, P., Phegade, V., del Cuvillo, J.: Using innovative instructions to create trustworthy software solutions. In: HASP@ISCA. ACM (2013)

27. Intel. software guard extensions programming reference (2014). http://software.intel.com/sites/default/files/managed/48/88/329298-002.pdf

28. Katz, J.: Universally composable multi-party computation using tamper-proof hardware. In: Naor, M. (ed.) EUROCRYPT 2007. LNCS, vol. 4515, pp. 115–128. Springer, Heidelberg (2007). https://doi.org/10.1007/978-3-540-72540-4_7

29. Koeberl, P., Schulz, S., Sadeghi, A., Varadharajan, V.: Trustlite: a security architecture for tiny embedded devices. In: EuroSys. ACM (2014)

30. Langley, A.: Lucky thirteen attack on TLS CBC (2013). http://www.imperialviolet.org/2013/02/04/luckythirteen.html

31. Malkhi, D., Nisan, N., Pinkas, B., Sella, Y.: Fairplay - secure two-party computation system. In: USENIX Security Symposium, USENIX (2004)

32. McCune, J.M., Parno, B., Perrig, A., Reiter, M.K., Isozaki, H.: Flicker: an execution infrastructure for tcb minimization. In: EuroSys. ACM (2008)

33. Microsoft. BitLocker drive encryption: data encryption toolkit for mobile PCS: security analysis (2007). http://technet.microsoft.com/en-us/library/cc162804.aspx

34. Noorman, J., Agten, P., Daniels, W., Strackx, R., Herrewege, A.V., Huygens, C., Preneel, B., Verbauwhede, I., Piessens, F.: Sancus: Low-cost trustworthy extensible networked devices with a zero-software trusted computing base. In: USENIX Security Symposium. USENIX Association (2013)
35. Pass, R., Shi, E., Tramèr, F.: Formal abstractions for attested execution secure processors. IACR Cryptology ePrint Archive (2016)
36. Schuster, F., Costa, M., Fournet, C., Gkantsidis, C., Peinado, M., Mainar-Ruiz, G., Russinovich, M.: VC3: trustworthy data analytics in the cloud using SGX. In: 2015 IEEE Symposium on Security and Privacy. IEEE (2015)
37. Smyth, B., Ryan, M., Chen, L.: Direct Anonymous Attestation (DAA): ensuring privacy with corrupt administrators. In: Stajano, F., Meadows, C., Capkun, S., Moore, T. (eds.) ESAS 2007. LNCS, vol. 4572, pp. 218–231. Springer, Heidelberg (2007). https://doi.org/10.1007/978-3-540-73275-4_16
38. Xu, Y., Cui, W., Peinado, M.: Controlled-channel attacks: Deterministic side channels for untrusted operating systems. In: 2015 IEEE Symposium on Security and Privacy. IEEE (2015)

Efficient No-dictionary Verifiable Searchable Symmetric Encryption

Wakaha Ogata[1($\boxtimes$)] and Kaoru Kurosawa[2]

[1] Tokyo Institute of Technology, Tokyo, Japan
ogata.w.aa@m.titech.ac.jp
[2] Ibaraki University, Hitachi, Japan
kaoru.kurosawa.kk@vc.ibaraki.ac.jp

Abstract. In the model of *no-dictionary* verifiable searchable symmetric encryption (SSE) scheme, a client does not need to keep the set of keywords $\mathcal{W}$ in the search phase, where $\mathcal{W}$ is called a dictionary. Still a malicious server cannot cheat the client by saying that "your search word w does not exist in the dictionary $\mathcal{W}$" when it exists. In the previous such schemes, it takes $O(\log m)$ time for the server to prove that $w \notin \mathcal{W}$, where $m = |\mathcal{W}|$ is the number of keywords.

In this paper, we show a generic method to transform any SSE scheme (that is only secure against passive adversaries) to a *no-dictionary* verifiable SSE scheme. In the transformed scheme, it takes only $O(1)$ time for the server to prove that $w \notin \mathcal{W}$.

Keywords: Searchable symmetric encryption · Verifiable · Dictionary

1 Introduction

The notion of searchable symmetric encryption (SSE) schemes was introduced by Song et al. [25]. In the store phase, a client encrypts a set of files and an index table by a symmetric encryption scheme, and then stores them on an untrusted server. In the search phase, he can efficiently retrieve the matching files for a search keyword w keeping the keyword and the files secret.

Since then, single keyword search SSE schemes [10,11,13,18,20], dynamic SSE schemes [8,15,16,19,21,23], multiple keyword search SSE schemes [1,3,7, 14,17,27] and more [9] have been studied extensively by many researchers.

Curtmola et al. [11,12] gave a rigorous definition of privacy against honest but curious servers. Kurosawa and Ohtaki [18,20] showed a definition of reliability against malicious servers who may return incorrect search results to the client, or may delete some encrypted files to save her memory space. Kurosawa and Ohtaki [18,20] also proved a weak equivalence between the UC security and the stand alone security (i.e., the privacy and the reliability), where the UC security is a very strong security notion such that if a protocol Π is UC secure, then its security is preserved under a general protocol composition operation [4].

© International Financial Cryptography Association 2017
A. Kiayias (Ed.): FC 2017, LNCS 10322, pp. 498–516, 2017.
https://doi.org/10.1007/978-3-319-70972-7_28

Now in the model of *no-dictionary* verifiable SSE scheme, a client does not need to keep the set of keywords W in the search phase, where W is called a dictionary. Still a malicious server cannot cheat the client by saying that "your search word w does not exist in the dictionary W" if it exists. This model is really practical, but it is not an easy task to prove that $w \notin W$.

Recently, Taketani and Ogata [26] constructed a *no-dictionary* verifiable SSE scheme. In their scheme, it takes $O(N \log mN)$ time for the server to prove that $w \notin W$, where $m = |W|$ is the number of keywords and N is the number of documents.

Very recently, Bost et al. [2] proposed a generic construction of *no-dictionary* verifiable SSE schemes as an independent work of ours. The idea of their concrete scheme (Algorithm 1 in [2]) is similar to that of Taketani and Ogata [26], and it takes $O(\log m) + time(\mathsf{Search}_0)$ time for the server to prove that $w \notin W$,[1] where $time(\mathsf{Search}_0)$ is the search time in the underlying non-verifiable scheme. They further claim that their generic construction works for dynamic SSE schemes as well. However, they do not show how to instantiate it.

In this paper, we show a generic method to transform any SSE scheme (that is only secure against passive adversaries) to a *no-dictionary* verifiable SSE scheme. In the transformed scheme, it takes only $O(1)$ time for the server to prove that $w \notin W$. The search time for $w \in W$ remains almost the same as that of the original SSE scheme. We also prove that the transformed scheme is UC-secure in Appendix similarly to [18,20].

2   Verifiable Searchable Symmetric Encryption

In this section, we define a no-dictionary (verifiable) SSE scheme and its security. Basically, we follow the notation used in [7,18,20].

- Let $\mathcal{D} = \{D_1, \ldots, D_N\}$ be a set of documents.
- Let $W \subset \{0,1\}^*$ be a set of keywords. We call W a dictionary.
- For $w \in \{0,1\}^*$, define

$$\mathcal{D}(w) = \begin{cases} \text{the set of documents that contain } w & \text{if } w \in W \\ \emptyset & \text{otherwise} \end{cases}$$

- Let $\mathcal{C} = \{C_1, \ldots, C_N\}$, where C_i is a ciphertext of D_i.
- Let

$$\mathcal{C}(w) = \{C_i \mid C_i \text{ is a ciphertext of } D_i \in \mathcal{D}(w)\}. \tag{1}$$

Note that $\mathcal{C}(w) = \emptyset$ if $w \notin W$.

If X is a bit string, $|X|$ denotes the bit length of X. If X is a set, $|X|$ denotes the cardinality of X. "PPT" refers to probabilistic polynomial time, and "PT" refers to polynomial time.

---

[1] This is because the server needs to find $i \in \{1, \ldots, m\}$ such that $key_i < PRF_k(w) < key_{i+1}$, where $PRF_k(w)$ is sent to the server by the client in the search phase, $\{key_1, \ldots, key_m\} = \{PRF_k(w_j) \mid w_j \in W\}$ is stored on the server in the store phase and $key_1 < \ldots < key_m$. PRF_k denotes a pseudo-random function with key k.

2.1   Model

An SSE scheme has two phases, the store phase (which is executed only once) and the search phase (which is executed a polynomial number of times). In the store phase, the client encrypts all documents in $\mathcal{D}$ and stores them on the server. In the search phase, the client sends a ciphertext of a word w, and the server returns $\mathcal{C}(w)$. If there is a mechanism to verify the validity of $\mathcal{C}(w)$, the scheme is called a verifiable SSE (vSSE).

Formally, a vSSE scheme consists of the following six polynomial-time algorithms vSSE = (Gen, Enc, Trpdr, Search, Dec, Verify) such that

- $K \leftarrow \text{Gen}(1^\lambda)$: a PPT algorithm that generates a key K, where λ is a security parameter. This algorithm is run by the client in the store phase.
- $(\mathcal{I}, \mathcal{C}) \leftarrow \text{Enc}(K, \mathcal{D}, \mathcal{W}, \{(w, \mathcal{D}(w)) \mid w \in \mathcal{W}\})$: a PPT algorithm that outputs an encrypted index $\mathcal{I}$ and the set of encrypted documents $\mathcal{C} = \{C_1, \ldots, C_N\}$. This algorithm is run by the client in the store phase. He then stores $(\mathcal{I}, \mathcal{C})$ on the server.
- $t(w) \leftarrow \text{Trpdr}(K, w)$: a PPT algorithm that outputs a trapdoor $t(w)$ for $w \in \{0, 1\}^*$. In *no-dictionary* scheme, w is not necessarily a keyword. This algorithm is run by the client in the search phase. $t(w)$ is sent to the server.
- $(\mathcal{C}(w), \text{Proof}) \leftarrow \text{Search}(\mathcal{I}, \mathcal{C}, t(w))$: a PT algorithm that outputs the search result $\mathcal{C}(w)$ and Proof for the validity check. This algorithm is run by the server in the search phase. She then returns $(\mathcal{C}(w), \text{Proof})$ to the client.
- accept/reject $\leftarrow \text{Verify}(K, t(w), \tilde{\mathcal{C}}, \text{Proof})$: a PT algorithm that verifies the validity of the search result $\tilde{\mathcal{C}}$ based on Proof. This algorithm is run by the client in the search phase.
- $D \leftarrow \text{Dec}(K, C)$: a PT algorithm that decrypts C. The client applies this algorithm to each $C \in \tilde{\mathcal{C}}$ when $\text{Verify}(K, t(w), \tilde{\mathcal{C}}, \text{Proof}) = \text{accept}$ in the search phase.

We say that a no-dictionary vSSE satisfies correctness if the following holds for any $K, \mathcal{D}, \mathcal{W}, \{(w, \mathcal{D}(w)) \mid w \in \mathcal{W}\}$ and any word $w \in \mathcal{W}$.

- If

$$(\mathcal{I}, \mathcal{C}) \leftarrow \text{Enc}(K, \mathcal{D}, \mathcal{W}, \{(w, \mathcal{D}(w)) \mid w \in \mathcal{W}\}),$$
$$t(w) \leftarrow \text{Trpdr}(K, w),$$
$$(\tilde{\mathcal{C}}, \text{Proof}) \leftarrow \text{Search}(\mathcal{I}, \mathcal{C}, t(w)),$$

then

$$\text{Verify}(K, t(w), \tilde{\mathcal{C}}, \text{Proof}) = \text{accept}$$
$$\{D_i \mid D_i \leftarrow \text{Dec}(K, C_i), C_i \in \tilde{\mathcal{C}}\} = \mathcal{D}(w).$$

An (not verifiable) SSE scheme is defined by omitting Proof and Verify.

2.2 Security Definition

We next define the security of no-dictionary vSSE schemes. Note that searched word w does not need to belong to the set $\mathcal{W}$.

Privacy. In a (v)SSE, the server should learn almost no information on $\mathcal{D}, \mathcal{W}$ and the search words w. Let $L_1(\mathcal{D}, \mathcal{W})$ denote the information that the server can learn in the store phase, and let $L_2(\mathcal{D}, \mathcal{W}, \mathbf{w}, w)$ denote that in the search phase, where w is the current search word and $\mathbf{w} = (w_1, w_2, \ldots)$ is the list of the past search words queried so far.

In most existing SSE schemes, $L_1(\mathcal{D}, \mathcal{W}) = (|D_1|, \ldots, |D_N|, |\mathcal{W}|)$, and $L_2(\mathcal{D}, \mathcal{W}, \mathbf{w}, w)$ consists of $\{j \mid D_j \in \mathcal{D}(w)\}$ and the search pattern

$$\texttt{SPattern}((w_1, \ldots, w_{q-1}), w) = (sp_1, \ldots, sp_{q-1}),$$

where

$$sp_j = \begin{cases} 1 & \text{if } w_j = w, \\ 0 & \text{if } w_j \neq w. \end{cases}$$

The search pattern reveals which past queries are the same as w.

Let $L = (L_1, L_2)$. The client's privacy is defined by using two games: a real game **Game**$_{real}$ and a simulation game **Game**$_{sim}^L$, as shown in Figs. 1 and 2,

---

1. Adversary **A** chooses $(\mathcal{D}, \mathcal{W})$ and sends them to challenger **C**.
2. **C** generates $K \leftarrow \texttt{Gen}(1^\lambda)$ and sends $(\mathcal{I}, \mathcal{C}) \leftarrow \texttt{Enc}(K, \mathcal{D}, \mathcal{W}, \{(w, \mathcal{D}(w)) \mid w \in \mathcal{W}\})$ to **A**.
3. For $i = 1, \ldots, q$, do:
   (a) **A** chooses a word $w_i \in \{0, 1\}^*$ and sends it to **C**.
   (b) **C** sends the trapdoor $t(w_i) \leftarrow \texttt{Trpdr}(K, w_i)$ back to **A**.
4. **A** outputs bit b.

Fig. 1. Real game **Game**$_{real}$

---

1. Adversary **A** chooses $(\mathcal{D}, \mathcal{W})$ and sends them to challenger **C**.
2. **C** sends $L_1(\mathcal{D}, \mathcal{W})$ to simulator **S**.
3. **S** computes $(\mathcal{I}, \mathcal{C})$ from $L_1(\mathcal{D}, \mathcal{W})$, and sends them to **C**.
4. **C** relays $(\mathcal{I}, \mathcal{C})$ to **A**.
5. For $i = 1, \ldots, q$, do:
   (a) **A** chooses $w_i \in \{0, 1\}^*$ and sends it to **C**.
   (b) **C** sends $L_2(\mathcal{D}, \mathcal{W}, \mathbf{w}, w_i)$ to **S**, where $\mathbf{w} = (w_1, \ldots, w_{i-1})$.
   (c) **S** computes $t(w_i)$ from $L_2(\mathcal{D}, \mathcal{W}, \mathbf{w}, w_i)$ and sends it to **C**.
   (d) **C** relays $t(w_i)$ to **A**.
6. **A** outputs bit b.

Fig. 2. Simulation game **Game**$_{sim}^L$

respectively. $\mathbf{Game}_{real}$ is played by a challenger $\mathbf{C}$ and an adversary $\mathbf{A}$, and $\mathbf{Game}_{sim}^L$ is played by $\mathbf{C}$, $\mathbf{A}$ and a simulator $\mathbf{S}$.

Definition 1 (L-privacy). *We say that a no-dictionary vSSE scheme has L-privacy, if there exists a PPT simulator $\mathbf{S}$ such that*

$$|\Pr[\mathbf{A} \text{ outputs } b = 1 \text{ in } \mathbf{Game}_{real}] - \Pr[\mathbf{A} \text{ outputs } b = 1 \text{ in } \mathbf{Game}_{sim}^L]| \quad (2)$$

is negligible for any PPT adversary $\mathbf{A}$.

Reliability. In an SSE scheme, a malicious server might cheat a client by returning a false result $\tilde{\mathcal{C}}^*(\neq \mathcal{C}(w))$ during the search phase. (Weak) reliability guarantees that the client can detect such a malicious behavior. Formally, reliability is defined by game $\mathbf{Game}_{reli}$ shown in Fig. 3, which is played by an adversary $\mathbf{B} = (\mathbf{B}_1, \mathbf{B}_2)$ (malicious server) and a challenger $\mathbf{C}$. $\mathbf{B}_1$ and $\mathbf{B}_2$ are assumed to be able to communicate freely.

(Store phase)
1. $\mathbf{B}_1$ chooses $(\mathcal{D}, \mathcal{W})$ and sends them to $\mathbf{C}$.
2. $\mathbf{C}$ generates $K \leftarrow \text{Gen}(1^\lambda)$, and sends $(\mathcal{I}, \mathcal{C}) \leftarrow \text{Enc}(K, \mathcal{D}, \mathcal{W}, \{(w, \mathcal{D}(w)) \mid w \in \mathcal{W}\})$ to $\mathbf{B}_2$.

(Search phase) For $i = 1, \ldots, q$, do
1. $\mathbf{B}_1$ chooses $w_i \in \{0, 1\}^*$ and sends it to $\mathbf{C}$.
2. $\mathbf{C}$ sends the trapdoor $t(w_i) \leftarrow \text{Trpdr}(K, w_i)$ to $\mathbf{B}_2$.
3. $\mathbf{B}_2$ returns $(\tilde{\mathcal{C}}_i^*, \text{Proof}_i^*)$ to $\mathbf{C}$.
4. $\mathbf{C}$ computes

$$\texttt{accept/reject} \leftarrow \text{Verify}(K, t(w_i), \tilde{\mathcal{C}}_i^*, \text{Proof}_i^*)$$

and returns $\mathcal{D}(w_i)^* = \{D_i \mid D_i \leftarrow \text{Dec}(K, C_i), C_i \in \tilde{\mathcal{C}}_i^*\}$ to $\mathbf{B}_1$ if the result is $\texttt{accept}$, otherwise sends $\bot$ to $\mathbf{B}_1$.

Fig. 3. $\mathbf{Game}_{reli}$

Definition 2 (Reliability). *We say that $\mathbf{B}$ wins in $\mathbf{Game}_{reli}$ if $\mathbf{B}_1$ receives $\mathcal{D}(w_i)^*$ such that $\mathcal{D}(w_i)^* \notin \{\mathcal{D}(w_i), \bot\}$ for some i. We say that a no-dictionary vSSE scheme satisfies reliability if for any PPT adversary $\mathbf{B}$,*

$$\Pr[\mathbf{B} \text{ wins in } \mathbf{Game}_{reli}]$$

is negligible.

Strong reliability was also defined in [20]. In strong reliability, the server has to answer a wrong pair $(\tilde{\mathcal{C}}^*, \text{Proof}^*)(\neq (\mathcal{C}(w), \text{Proof}))$ that will be accepted in the search phase to win the game.

Definition 3 (Strong Reliability). *We say that* **B** *strongly wins in* **Game**$_{reli}$ *if there exists* i, *such that both* $\mathtt{Verify}(K, t(w_i), \tilde{\mathcal{C}}_i^*, \mathsf{Proof}_i^*) = \mathtt{accept}$ *and* $(\tilde{\mathcal{C}}_i^*, \mathsf{Proof}_i^*) \neq (\mathcal{C}(w_i), \mathsf{Proof}_i)$ *hold. We say that a no-dictionary vSSE scheme satisfies strong reliability if for any PPT adversary* **B**,

$$\Pr[\mathbf{B} \text{ strongly wins in } \mathbf{Game}_{reli}]$$

is negligible.

3 Building Blocks

3.1 Cuckoo Hashing

Cuckoo Hashing [24] is a hashing algorithm with the advantage that the search time is constant. To store n keys, it uses two tables T_1 and T_2 of size m, and two independent random hash functions h_1 and h_2 with the range $\{1, \ldots, m\}$. Every key x is stored at one of two positions, $T_1(h_1(x))$ or $T_2(h_2(x))$. So we need to inspect at most two positions to search x.

It can happen that both possible places $T_1(h_1(x))$ and $T_2(h_2(x))$ of a given key x are already occupied. This problem is solved by allowing x to throw out the key (say y) occupying the position $T_1(h_1(x))$. Next, we insert y at its alternative position $T_2(h_2(y))$. If it is already occupied, we repeat the above steps until we find an empty position. If we failed after some number of trials, we choose new hash functions and rebuild the data structure.

Let $n = m(1 - \epsilon)$ for some $\epsilon \in (0, 1)$. Then the above algorithm succeeds with probability $1 - c(\epsilon)/m + O(1/m^2)$ for some explicit function $c(\cdot)$ [22]. The expected construction time of (T_1, T_2) is bounded above by [22]

$$2n \frac{1 - e^{\epsilon-1}}{(1 - e^{\epsilon-1}) + \epsilon}. \tag{3}$$

3.2 Pseudo-random Function

Let $\mathcal{R}$ be a family of all functions $f : \{0, 1\}^* \to \{0, 1\}^n$. We say that $F : \{0, 1\}^\ell \times \{0, 1\}^* \to \{0, 1\}^n$ is a pseudo-random function if for any PPT distinguisher **D**,

$$\left| \Pr[k \xleftarrow{\$} \{0, 1\}^\ell : \mathbf{D}^{F(k, \cdot)} = 1] - \Pr[f \xleftarrow{\$} \mathcal{R} : \mathbf{D}^{f(\cdot)} = 1] \right|$$

is negligibly small.

It is well known that a pseudo-random function works as a MAC which is existentially unforgeable against chosen message attack.

4 Generic Transformation from SSE to vSSE

In this section, we show a generic method to transform any SSE (with only privacy) to a no-dictionary verifiable SSE. Namely, in our vSSE scheme, the server can return a proof of the search result even if the search word is not in the dictionary used in the store phase.

4.1 Construction

Let $(\text{Gen}_0, \text{Enc}_0, \text{Trpdr}_0, \text{Search}_0, \text{Dec}_0)$ be an SSE scheme. We construct a no-dictionary verifiable SSE $(\text{Gen}_1, \text{Enc}_1, \text{Trpdr}_1, \text{Search}_1, \text{Verify}_1, \text{Dec}_1)$ as follows. Let F be a pseudo-random function.

- $\text{Gen}_1(1^\lambda)$: Run $\text{Gen}_0(1^\lambda)$ to obtain K_0. Also randomly choose a key k of F. Output (K_0, k). We write $F_k(x)$ instead of $F(k, x)$.
- $\text{Enc}_1((K_0, k), \mathcal{D}, \mathcal{W}, \{(w, \mathcal{D}(w)) \mid w \in \mathcal{W}\})$: Let $\mathcal{W} = \{w_1, w_2, \ldots, w_{|\mathcal{W}|}\}$.
  1. Run $\text{Enc}_0(K_0, \mathcal{D}, \mathcal{W}, \{(w, \mathcal{D}(w)) \mid w \in \mathcal{W}\})$ to obtain $(\mathcal{I}_0, \mathcal{C})$. Note that $C_i \in \mathcal{C}$ is a ciphertext of each document $D_i \in \mathcal{D}$.
  2. Compute $key_j \leftarrow F_k(0\|w_j)$ for all $w_j \in \mathcal{W}$.
  3. Construct cuckoo hash tables (T_1', T_2') of size $|\mathcal{W}| + 1$ which store $\{key_j\}_{j=1}^{|\mathcal{W}|}$. Let (h_1, h_2) be the hash functions which are used to construct (T_1', T_2'). This means that

  $$T_1'(h_1(key_j)) = key_j \text{ or } T_2'(h_2(key_j)) = key_j$$

  for each key_j.
  4. Construct two tables (T_1, T_2) of size $|\mathcal{W}| + 1$ as follows.
     For $a = 1, 2$, do
       For $i = 1, \ldots, |\mathcal{W}| + 1$, do
         If $T_a'(i) = key_j$ for some $key_j = F_k(0\|w_j)$, then
           $$T_a(i) \leftarrow \langle key_j, F_k(a\|i\|key_j), F_k(3\|key_j\|\mathcal{C}(w_j)) \rangle$$
         Else
           $$T_a(i) \leftarrow \langle null, F_k(a\|i\|null), null \rangle$$
  5. Output $(\mathcal{I} = (\mathcal{I}_0, T_1, T_2, h_1, h_2), \mathcal{C})$.

We note that for each $key_j = F_k(0\|w_j)$, it holds that

$$T_1(h_1(key_j)) = \langle key_j, F_k(1\|h_1(key_j)\|key_j), F_k(3\|key_j\|\mathcal{C}(w_j)) \rangle$$

or

$$T_2(h_2(key_j)) = \langle key_j, F_k(2\|h_2(key_j)\|key_j), F_k(3\|key_j\|\mathcal{C}(w_j)) \rangle.$$

- $\text{Trpdr}_1((K_0, k), w)$: Compute $key \leftarrow F_k(0\|w)$ and $t_0(w) \leftarrow \text{Trpdr}_0(K_0, w)$. Output $t(w) = (key, t_0(w))$.
- $\text{Search}_1((\mathcal{I}_0, T_1, T_2, h_1, h_2), \mathcal{C}, t(w) = (key, token))$: Retrieve

$$\langle \alpha_1, \beta_1, \gamma_1 \rangle \leftarrow T_1(h_1(key)),$$
$$\langle \alpha_2, \beta_2, \gamma_2 \rangle \leftarrow T_2(h_2(key)).$$

Let

$$\mathcal{C}^* = \begin{cases} \text{Search}_0(\mathcal{I}_0, \mathcal{C}, token) & \text{if } key \in \{\alpha_1, \alpha_2\} \\ \emptyset & \text{otherwise} \end{cases}$$

$$\text{Proof} = \begin{cases} \gamma_1 & \text{if } key = \alpha_1 \\ \gamma_2 & \text{if } key = \alpha_2 \\ (\alpha_1, \beta_1, \alpha_2, \beta_2) & \text{otherwise} \end{cases}$$

Output $(\mathcal{C}^*, \text{Proof})$.

- $\text{Verify}_1((K_0, k), t(w) = (key, token), C^*, \text{Proof})$:
  (**Case 1**) $\text{Proof} = \gamma$.
  If $\gamma = F_k(3\|key\|C^*)$, then output accept. Otherwise output reject.
  (**Case 2**) $\text{Proof} = (\alpha_1, \beta_1, \alpha_2, \beta_2)$.
  If $C^* \neq \emptyset$ or $key \in \{\alpha_1, \alpha_2\}$ or $\beta_1 \neq F_k(1\|h_1(key)\|\alpha_1)$ or $\beta_2 \neq F_k(2\|h_2(key)\|\alpha_2)$, then output reject. Otherwise output accept.
- $\text{Dec}_1((K_0, k), C_i)$: Output $D_i \leftarrow \text{Dec}_0(K_0, C_i)$.

4.2 Example

Suppose that there are 7 keywords $W = \{w_1, \ldots, w_7\}$ and 8 ciphertexts $C = \{C_1, \ldots, C_8\}$ such that $C(w_j)$ are given in Table 1. In the same table, $h_1(key_j)$ and $h_2(key_j)$ are the hash values which are used to construct the cuckoo hash tables (T_1', T_2') for the set $\{key_j = F_k(0\|w_j) \mid j = 1, \ldots, 7\}$.

Table 1. Example

Keyword w_j	$C(w_j)$	$h_1(key_j)$	$h_2(key_j)$
w_1	C_1, C_4, C_5, C_8	6	1
w_2	C_2	2	4
w_3	C_1, C_4	6	4
w_4	C_1, C_3, C_7	6	3
w_5	C_2, C_6	7	8
w_6	C_5, C_8	7	6
w_7	C_1	2	8

Then T_1 and T_2 are constructed as shown in Table 2.

(**Case 1**) Suppose that a client searches for a keyword $w_3 \in W$.

1. The client sends trapdoor $(key_3, t_0(w_3))$ to the server.
2. Since $h_1(key_3) = 6, h_2(key_3) = 4$, the server retrieves

$$\langle \alpha_1, \beta_1, \gamma_1 \rangle = T_1(6) = \langle key_3, F_k(1\|6\|key_3), F_k(3\|key_3\|C_1, C_4) \rangle,$$
$$\langle \alpha_2, \beta_2, \gamma_2 \rangle = T_2(4) = \langle key_2, F_k(2\|4\|key_2), F_k(3\|key_2\|C_2) \rangle$$

from T_1 and T_2.
Because $\alpha_1 = key_3$, the server obtains the search result

$$C^* = (C_1, C_4) \leftarrow \text{Search}_0(\mathcal{I}_0, C, t_0(w_3))$$
$$\text{Proof} = \gamma_1 = F_k(3\|key_3\|C_1, C_4).$$

and returns (C^*, Proof) to the client.
3. The client verifies if $\gamma_1 = F_k(3\|key_3\|C^*)$.

Table 2. Tables (T_1, T_2)

i	$T_1(i)$
1	$\langle$ null , $F_k(1\|1)$, null $\rangle$
2	$\langle$ key_7, $F_k(1\|2\|key_7)$, $F_k(3\|key_7\|C_1)$ $\rangle$
3	$\langle$ null , $F_k(1\|3)$, null $\rangle$
4	$\langle$ null , $F_k(1\|4)$, null $\rangle$
5	$\langle$ null , $F_k(1\|5)$, null $\rangle$
6	$\langle$ key_3, $F_k(1\|6\|key_3)$, $F_k(3\|key_3\|C_1, C_4)$ $\rangle$
7	$\langle$ key_6, $F_k(1\|7\|key_6)$, $F_k(3\|key_6\|C_5, C_8)$ $\rangle$
8	$\langle$ null , $F_k(1\|8)$, null $\rangle$

i	$T_2(i)$
1	$\langle$ key_1, $F_k(2\|1\|key_1)$, $F_k(3\|key_1\|C_1, C_4, C_5, C_8)$ $\rangle$
2	$\langle$ null , $F_k(2\|2)$, null $\rangle$
3	$\langle$ key_4, $F_k(2\|3\|key_4)$, $F_k(3\|key_4\|C_1, C_3, C_7)$ $\rangle$
4	$\langle$ key_2, $F_k(2\|4\|key_2)$, $F_k(3\|key_2\|C_2)$ $\rangle$
5	$\langle$ null , $F_k(2\|5)$, null $\rangle$
6	$\langle$ null , $F_k(2\|6)$, null $\rangle$
7	$\langle$ null , $F_k(2\|7)$, null $\rangle$
8	$\langle$ key_5, $F_k(2\|8\|key_5)$, $F_k(3\|key_5\|(C_2, C_6))$ $\rangle$

(Case 2) Suppose that the client searches for $w \notin \mathcal{W}$.

1. The client computes $key \leftarrow F_k(0\|w)$ and $t_0(w) \leftarrow \mathtt{Trpdr}_0(K_0, w)$. He sends $t(w) = (key, t_0(w))$ to the server.
2. Suppose that $h_1(key) = 5$ and $h_2(key) = 3$. Then the server retrieves

$$\langle \alpha_1, \beta_1, \gamma_1 \rangle = T_1(5) = \langle null, F_k(1\|5), null \rangle,$$
$$\langle \alpha_2, \beta_2, \gamma_2 \rangle = T_2(3) = \langle key_4, F_k(2\|3\|key_4), F_k(3\|key_4\|C_1, C_3, C_7) \rangle.$$

Because $key \notin \{\alpha_1, \alpha_2\}$, the server returns $\mathcal{C}^* = \emptyset$ and

$$\mathsf{Proof} = (\alpha_1, \beta_1, \alpha_2, \beta_2) = (null, F_k(1\|5), key_4, F_k(2\|3\|key_4)).$$

3. The client verifies if $key \notin \{\alpha_1, \alpha_2\}$, $\beta_1 = F_k(1\|h_1(key)\|\alpha_1)$ and $\beta_2 = F_k(2\|h_2(key)\|\alpha_2)$.

4.3   Efficiency

In our transformed scheme,

- In the store phase, the client takes the expected time $O(|\mathcal{W}|) + time(\mathtt{Enc}_0)$ to run $\mathtt{Enc}_1$ from Eq. (3).
- In the search phase, the search time for $w \in \mathcal{W}$ is almost the same as that of the original scheme.
- The server takes only $O(1)$ time to prove that $w \notin \mathcal{W}$ because the search time is constant in cuckoo hashing.

To prove that $w \notin \mathcal{W}$, in the method of [26], the server takes $O(N \log N |\mathcal{W}|)$ time. In the concrete method (Algorithm 1+2) in [2], it takes $O(\log |\mathcal{W}|) + time(\text{Search}_0)$.

4.4 Security

Theorem 1. *If the SSE scheme has $L = (L_1, L_2)$-privacy and F is a pseudorandom function, then our vSSE scheme has $L' = (L'_1, L'_2)$-privacy such that*

$$L'_1(\mathcal{D}, \mathcal{W}) = L_1(\mathcal{D}, \mathcal{W}) \cup \{|\mathcal{W}|\},$$
$$L'_2(\mathcal{D}, \mathcal{W}, \mathbf{w}, w_i) = L_2(\mathcal{D}, \mathcal{W}, \mathbf{w}, w_i) \cup \{\text{SPattarn}(\mathbf{w}, w_i), [w_i \in \mathcal{W}]\}.$$

In the all existing SSE schemes, $|\mathcal{W}| \in L_1(\mathcal{D}, \mathcal{W})$ and $\{\text{SPattarn}(\mathbf{w}, w_i), [w_i \in \mathcal{W}]\} \subseteq L'_2(\mathcal{D}, \mathcal{W}, \mathbf{w}, w_i)$. (There may be some exceptions which use oblivious RAM. But such SSE schemes are inefficient.) So, the client's privacy in our vSSE scheme has the same level as that of the underlying SSE scheme.

Proof. Let $\mathbf{S}_0$ be a simulator of the underlining SSE scheme which has (L_1, L_2)-privacy. We construct a simulator $\mathbf{S}$ of our vSSE scheme which achieves (L'_1, L'_2)-privacy as follows.

(Store phase). In **Game**$_{sim}$, $\mathbf{S}$ takes $L'_1(\mathcal{D}, \mathcal{W}) = L_1(\mathcal{D}, \mathcal{W}) \cup \{|\mathcal{W}|\}$ as an input. $\mathbf{S}$ runs $\mathbf{S}_0(L_1(\mathcal{D}, \mathcal{W}))$ and gets its output $(\mathcal{I}_0, \mathcal{C})$. Next $\mathbf{S}$ constructs T_1 and T_2 as follows. Note that the size of each T_1, T_2 is $m = |\mathcal{W}| + 1$.

- Choose random strings $key'_1, \ldots, key'_{|\mathcal{W}|}$, and construct the cuckoo hash tables (T'_1, T'_2) which store $(key'_{\pi(1)}, \ldots, key'_{\pi(|\mathcal{W}|)})$, where π is a random permutation. Let h_1, h_2 be the two hash functions which are used to construct (T'_1, T'_2).
- For $a = 1, 2$, do
    For $i = 1, \ldots, |\mathcal{W}| + 1$, do
        If $T'_a(i) = key'_j$ for some j, then
            choose two random strings r, r' and $T_a(i) \leftarrow \langle key'_j, r, r' \rangle$
        Else
            choose a random string r and $T_a(i) \leftarrow \langle null, r, null \rangle$

$\mathbf{S}$ sends $(\mathcal{I}_0, T_1, T_2, h_1, h_2)$ and $\mathcal{C}$ to the challenger. Let $counter \leftarrow 1$.

(Search phase). In the ith search phase, $\mathbf{S}$ takes $L'_2(\mathcal{D}, \mathcal{W}, \mathbf{w}, w^*) = L_2(\mathcal{D}, \mathcal{W}, \mathbf{w}, w^*) \cup \{\text{SPattarn}(\mathbf{w}, w^*), [w^* \in \mathcal{W}]\}$ as an input. $\mathbf{S}$ first obtains $t_0(w^*)$ by running $\mathbf{S}_0(L_2(\mathcal{D}, \mathcal{W}, \mathbf{w}, w^*))$, and sets

$$key_i^* \leftarrow \begin{cases} key'_{counter} & \text{if } sp_j = 0 \text{ for all } j \text{ and } w^* \in \mathcal{W}, \\ key_j^* & \text{if } sp_j = 1 \text{ for some } j, \\ \text{a random string} & \text{otherwise.} \end{cases}$$

$$counter \leftarrow \begin{cases} counter + 1 & \text{if } sp_j = 0 \text{ for all } j \text{ and } w^* \in \mathcal{W}, \\ counter & \text{otherwise.} \end{cases}$$

$\mathbf{S}$ outputs $(key_i^*, t_0(w^*))$ as a simulated trapdoor.

We will prove that there is no adversary $\mathbf{A}$ who can distinguish between $\mathbf{Game}_{real}$ and $\mathbf{Game}_{sim}$. We consider a game sequence ($\mathbf{Game}_{real}$, $\mathbf{Game}_{mid}$, $\mathbf{Game}_{sim}$). $\mathbf{Game}_{mid}$ is the same as $\mathbf{Game}_{real}$ except that all values of $F_k(\cdot)$ are replaced with random strings. For $i \in \{real, mid, sim\}$, define

$$P_i = \Pr[\mathbf{A} \text{ outputs } b = 1 \text{ in } \mathbf{Game}_i].$$

Then $|P_{real} - P_{mid}|$ is negligible because F is a pseudorandom function. We can also see that $|P_{mid} - P_{sim}|$ is negligible from the (L_1, L_2)-privacy of the underlying SSE scheme. Consequently, $|P_{real} - P_{sim}|$ is negligible.   □

Theorem 2. *Our vSSE scheme satisfies strong reliability if F is a pseudorandom function.*

Proof. We look at the pseudorandom function F as a MAC. Suppose that there exists an adversary $\mathbf{B} = (\mathbf{B}_1, \mathbf{B}_2)$ who can break the strong reliability of our vSSE scheme, and $\mathbf{B}$ runs the search phase q times. Let $(\tilde{C}_i^*, \widetilde{\mathsf{Proof}}_i)$ be $\mathbf{B}_2$'s response to $t(w_i) = (key_i, t_0(w_i))$ in the ith search phase, and let

$$(C(w_i), \mathsf{Proof}_i) = \mathtt{Search}_1(\mathcal{I}, \mathcal{C}, t(w_i)).$$

From the definition, $\mathbf{B}$ strongly wins if there exists $i \in \{1, \ldots, q\}$ such that

$$(\tilde{C}_i^*, \widetilde{\mathsf{Proof}}_i) \neq (C(w_i), \mathsf{Proof}_i)$$
$$\text{and} \quad \mathtt{Verify}_1(K, (key_i, t_0(w_i)), \tilde{C}_i^*, \widetilde{\mathsf{Proof}}_i) = \mathtt{accept}. \tag{4}$$

By using $\mathbf{B}$, we will construct a forger $\mathbf{F}$ against the MAC, where $\mathbf{F}$ has oracle access to F_k.

$\mathbf{F}$ at first randomly chooses $J \in \{1, \ldots, q\}$. Then, $\mathbf{F}$ runs $\mathbf{B}$ by playing the role of the challenger $\mathbf{C}$ (see Fig. 3) until the $(J-1)$th search phase. During this simulation, when $\mathbf{C}$ needs to compute $F_k(x)$ for some x, $\mathbf{F}$ queries x to its oracle F_k to obtain $F_k(x)$.

In the Jth search phase, we have the following three cases.

(1) $\widetilde{\mathsf{Proof}}_J = \tilde{\gamma}$.
   In this case, $\mathbf{F}$ outputs $m' = (3\|key_J\|\tilde{C}_J^*)$ and $tag' = \tilde{\gamma}$ as a forgery of the MAC F.
(2) $\mathsf{Proof}_J = \gamma$ and $\widetilde{\mathsf{Proof}}_J = (\tilde{\alpha}_1, \tilde{\beta}_1, \tilde{\alpha}_2, \tilde{\beta}_2)$.
   Since $\mathsf{Proof}_J = \gamma$, there exists $a \in \{1, 2\}$ such that $T_a(h_a(key_J)) = \langle key_J, F_k(a\|h_a(key_J)\|key_J), \ldots \rangle$. For this a, $\mathbf{F}$ outputs $m' = (a\|h_a(key_J)\|\tilde{\alpha}_a)$ and $tag' = \tilde{\beta}_a$ as a forgery.
(3) $\mathsf{Proof}_J = (\alpha_1, \beta_1, \alpha_2, \beta_2)$ and $\widetilde{\mathsf{Proof}}_J = (\tilde{\alpha}_1, \tilde{\beta}_1, \tilde{\alpha}_2, \tilde{\beta}_2)$.
   If there exists $a \in \{1, 2\}$ s.t. $(\alpha_a, \beta_a) \neq (\tilde{\alpha}_a, \tilde{\beta}_a)$, then, $\mathbf{F}$ outputs $m' = (a\|h_a(key_J)\|\tilde{\alpha}_a)$ and $tag' = \tilde{\beta}_a$ as a forgery. Otherwise $\mathbf{F}$ outputs "fail."

Now $\mathbf{F}$ succeeds in forgery if $\mathbf{B}$ strongly wins and $\mathbf{F}$ correctly predicts i which satisfies Eq. (4), i.e., Eq. (4) holds in $i = J$. Since $\mathbf{F}$ predicts J correctly with probability $1/q$, we obtain that

$$\Pr[\mathbf{F} \text{ succeeds in forgery}] \geq \Pr[\mathbf{B} \text{ strongly wins in } \mathbf{Game}_{reli}] \times \frac{1}{q}. \qquad \square$$

We prove the UC-security of the transformed scheme in Appendix.

A   UC-Security for No-Dictionary vSSE

If a protocol is secure in the universally composable (UC) security framework, its security is maintained even if the protocol is combined with other protocols [4–6]. The UC security is defined based on *ideal functionality* $\mathcal{F}$. Kurosawa and Ohtaki introduced an ideal functionality of vSSE [18,20]. Taketani and Ogata [26] generalized it in order to handle the general leakage functions $L = (L_1, L_2)$ as shown in Fig. 4.

Store: Upon receiving the input $(\mathbf{store}, sid, D_1, \ldots, D_N, \mathcal{W})$ from the dummy client, verify that this is the first input from the client with $(\mathbf{store}, sid)$.
If it is, then store $\mathcal{D} = \{D_1, \ldots, D_N\}$, and send $L_1(\mathcal{D}, \mathcal{W})$ to $\mathbf{S}^{uc}$. Otherwise, ignore this input.

Search: Upon receiving $(\mathbf{search}, sid, w)$ from the client, send $L_2(\mathcal{D}, \mathcal{W}, \mathbf{w}, w)$ to $\mathbf{S}^{uc}$. Note that in a no-dictionary vSSE scheme, the client may send $w \notin \mathcal{W}$.
If $\mathbf{S}^{uc}$ returns $\mathbf{accept}$, then send $\mathcal{D}(w)$ to the client. If $\mathbf{S}^{uc}$ returns $\mathbf{reject}$, then send $\bot$ to the client.

Fig. 4. Ideal functionality $\mathcal{F}_{vSSE}^L$

In the no-dictionary verifiable SSE setting, the real world is described as follows. We assume a real adversary, $\mathbf{A}^{uc}$, can control the server arbitrarily, and the client is always honest. For simplicity, we ignore session id.

In the store phase, an environment, $\mathbf{Z}$, chooses $(\mathcal{D}, \mathcal{W})$ and sends them to the client. The client computes $K \leftarrow \mathtt{Gen}(1^\lambda)$ and $(\mathcal{I}, \mathcal{C}) \leftarrow \mathtt{Enc}(K, \mathcal{D}, \mathcal{W}, \{(w, \mathcal{D}(w)) \mid w \in \mathcal{W}\})$, and sends $(\mathcal{I}, \mathcal{C})$ to the server. The client stores K [2] and the server stores $(\mathcal{I}, \mathcal{C})$. In the search phase, $\mathbf{Z}$ chooses a word $w \in \{0,1\}^*$ and sends it to the client. The client computes $t(w) \leftarrow \mathtt{Trpdr}(K, w)$ and sends it to the server. The server, who may be controlled by real adversary $\mathbf{A}^{uc}$, returns $(\tilde{\mathcal{C}}^*, \widetilde{\mathsf{Proof}})$ to the client. If $\mathtt{Verify}(K, t(w), \tilde{\mathcal{C}}^*, \widetilde{\mathsf{Proof}})$ outputs $\mathbf{accept}$, then the client decrypts all $\tilde{C}_i \in \tilde{\mathcal{C}}^*$, and sends the list of plaintexts $\tilde{\mathcal{D}}(w) = (\tilde{D}_1, \tilde{D}_2, \ldots)$ to $\mathbf{Z}$. If $\mathtt{Verify}(K, t(w), \tilde{\mathcal{C}}^*, \widetilde{\mathsf{Proof}})$ outputs $\mathbf{reject}$, then $\bot$ is sent to $\mathbf{Z}$. After the store phase, $\mathbf{Z}$ outputs a bit b.

---

[2]   he may forget $\mathcal{D}, \mathcal{W}, \mathcal{C}, \mathcal{I}$.

On the other hand, the ideal world is described as follows.

In the store phase, $\mathbf{Z}$ sends $(\mathcal{D}, \mathcal{W})$ to the dummy client. The dummy client sends $(\mathbf{store}, \mathcal{D}, \mathcal{W})$ to functionality $\mathcal{F}^L_{vSSE}$ (see Fig. 4). In the search phase, $\mathbf{Z}$ sends w to the dummy client. The dummy client sends $(\mathbf{search}, w)$ to $\mathcal{F}^L_{vSSE}$, and receives $\mathcal{D}(w)$ or $\perp$ (according to ideal adversary $\mathbf{S}^{uc}$'s decision), which is relayed to $\mathbf{Z}$. At last, $\mathbf{Z}$ outputs a bit b

In both worlds, $\mathbf{Z}$ can communicate with $\mathbf{A}^{uc}$ (in the real world) or $\mathbf{S}^{uc}$ (in the ideal world) in an arbitrary way.

UC-security of no-dictionary vSSE scheme is defined as follows.

Definition 4 (UC-security with leakage L). *We say that no-dictionary vSSE scheme has universally composable (UC) security with leakage L against non-adaptive adversaries, if for any PPT real adversary $\mathbf{A}^{uc}$, there exists a PPT ideal adversary (simulator) $\mathbf{S}^{uc}$, and for any PPT environment $\mathbf{Z}$,*

$$| \Pr[\mathbf{Z} \text{ outputs 1 in the real world}] - \Pr[\mathbf{Z} \text{ outputs 1 in the ideal world}]|$$

is negligible.

We can show a weak equivalence of UC security and privacy with reliability.

Theorem 3. *If a no-dictionary vSSE scheme satisfies L-privacy and strong reliability for some L, it has UC security with leakage L against non-adaptive adversaries.*

Proof. Assume that the scheme satisfies L-privacy and strong reliability. We consider four games $\mathbf{Game}_0, \dots, \mathbf{Game}_3$. Let

$$p_i = \Pr[\mathbf{Z} \text{ outputs 1 in } \mathbf{Game}_i]$$

for a fixed $\mathbf{A}^{uc}$. $\mathbf{Game}_0$ is equivalent to the real world in the definition of UC security. So,

$$p_0 = \Pr[\mathbf{Z} \text{ outputs 1 in the real world}].$$

$\mathbf{Game}_1$ is different from $\mathbf{Game}_0$ in the following points.

- In the store phase, the client records $(\mathcal{D}, \mathcal{W}, \mathcal{I})$ as well as the key K.
- In the search phase, if $\mathbf{A}^{uc}$ instructs the server to return $(\tilde{\mathcal{C}}^*, \widetilde{\mathsf{Proof}})$ such that $(\tilde{\mathcal{C}}^*, \widetilde{\mathsf{Proof}}) \neq (\mathcal{C}^*, \mathsf{Proof}) \leftarrow \mathsf{Search}(\mathcal{I}, \mathcal{C}, t(w))$, then the server returns reject to the client. Otherwise the server returns accept.
- If the client receives accept from the server, he sends $\mathcal{D}(w)$ to $\mathbf{Z}$. Otherwise, he sends $\perp$ to $\mathbf{Z}$.

$\mathbf{Game}_1$ is the same as $\mathbf{Game}_0$ until $\mathbf{A}^{uc}$ instructs the server to return $(\tilde{\mathcal{C}}^*, \widetilde{\mathsf{Proof}})$ such that

$$\mathsf{Verify}(K, t(w), \tilde{\mathcal{C}}^*, \widetilde{\mathsf{Proof}}) = \mathtt{accept} \text{ and } (\tilde{\mathcal{C}}^*, \widetilde{\mathsf{Proof}}) \neq (\mathcal{C}^*, \mathsf{Proof}).$$

The above condition is the (strongly) winning condition of $\mathbf{B}$ in $\mathbf{Game}_{reli}$. So, we can obtain

$$|p_0 - p_1| \leq \max_{\mathbf{B}} \Pr[\mathbf{B} \text{ strongly wins in } \mathbf{Game}_{reli}].$$

From the assumption, $|p_0 - p_1|$ is negligibly small.

In $\mathbf{Game}_2$, we split the client into two entities, client1 and client2, as follows. (See Fig. 5(a).)

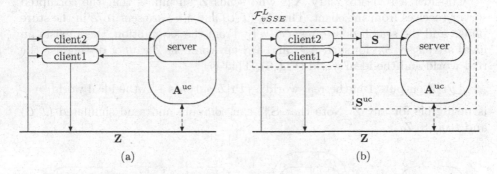

Fig. 5. (a) $\mathbf{Game}_2$, (b) $\mathbf{Game}_3$

- Both client1 and client2 receive all input from $\mathbf{Z}$.
- In the store/search phase, only client2 sends $(\mathcal{I}, \mathcal{C})/t(w)$ to the server.
- In the search phase, only client1 receives $\texttt{accept}/\texttt{reject}$ from the server, and sends $\mathcal{D}(w)/\perp$ to $\mathbf{Z}$.

This change is conceptual only. Therefore $p_2 = p_1$.

Now, we look at $(\mathbf{Z}, \text{client1}, \text{server}, \mathbf{A}^{uc})$ and client2 as an adversary $\mathbf{A}$ and a challenger $\mathbf{C}$ in the real game of privacy, respectively. Then, from the assumption, there exists a simulator $\mathbf{S}$ such that Eq. (2) is negligible.

In $\mathbf{Game}_3$, client2 plays the role of the challenger in the simulation game of privacy; he sends $L_1(\mathcal{D}, \mathcal{W})$ or $L_2(\mathcal{D}, \mathcal{W}, \mathbf{w}, w)$ to the simulator $\mathbf{S}$, and then $\mathbf{S}$ sends its outputs (the simulated message) to the server. (See Fig. 5(b).) Again, we look at $(\mathbf{Z}, \text{client1}, \text{server}, \mathbf{A}^{uc})$ as $\mathbf{A}$. Then $\mathbf{Game}_3$ is the simulation game and $\mathbf{Game}_2$ is the real game. Therefore

$$|p_3 - p_2| \leq |\Pr[\mathbf{A} \text{ outputs } 1 \text{ in } \mathbf{Game}_{real}] - \Pr[\mathbf{A} \text{ outputs } 1 \text{ in } \mathbf{Game}_{sim}^L]|,$$

and it is negligible from the assumption.

In $\mathbf{Game}_3$, (client1, client2) behaves exactly the same way as $\mathcal{F}_{vSSE}^L$ in the ideal world. So, considering $(\mathbf{S}, \text{server}, \mathbf{A}^{uc})$ as a simulator $\mathbf{S}^{uc}$, we obtain

$$p_3 = \Pr[\mathbf{Z} \text{ outputs } 1 \text{ in the ideal world}]$$

for this simulator. Consequently, we can say that for any $\mathbf{A}^{uc}$ there exists $\mathbf{S}^{uc}$ such that $|p_0 - p_3| = |\Pr[\mathbf{Z} \text{ outputs } 1 \text{ in the real world}] - \Pr[\mathbf{Z} \text{ outputs } 1 \text{ in the ideal world}]|$ is negligible. □

Theorem 4. *If a no-dictionary vSSE scheme has UC security with leakage L against non-adaptive adversaries for some L, it has satisfies L-privacy and reliability.*

This theorem is shown by the following lemmas.

Lemma 1. *If vSSE has UC security with leakage L against non-adaptive adversaries for some L, vSSE has satisfies L-privacy.*

Proof. Assume that the scheme has UC security with leakage L.

Consider a real adversary $\mathbf{A}_0^{uc}$ who sends $\mathbf{Z}$ all inputs that the corrupted server receives from the client. That is, $(\mathcal{I}, \mathcal{C})$ and $t(w)$ are sent to $\mathbf{Z}$ in the store phase and the search phase, respectively. From the assumption, there exists an ideal adversary $\mathbf{S}_0^{uc}$ for such $\mathbf{A}_0^{uc}$, and any environment $\mathbf{Z}$ cannot distinguish the real world and the ideal world (Fig. 6). That is,

$$|\Pr[\mathbf{Z} \text{ outputs 1 in the real world}] - \Pr[\mathbf{Z} \text{ outputs 1 in the ideal world}]|$$

is negligible for any $\mathbf{Z}$. Note that $\mathbf{S}_0^{uc}$ can compute and send simulated $(\tilde{\mathcal{I}}, \tilde{\mathcal{C}})$ and $\tilde{t}(w)$ to $\mathbf{Z}$.

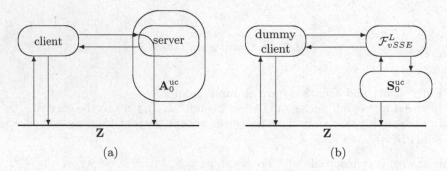

(a)   (b)

Fig. 6. (a) $\mathbf{A}_0^{uc}$, (b) $\mathbf{S}_0^{uc}$

Now we consider restricted environments $\mathbf{Z}_0$ that do not use the answer from the client/dummy client to distinguish the worlds. Namely, in the real world, $\mathbf{Z}_0$ sends $(\mathcal{D}, \mathcal{W})$ and w to the client and receives $(\mathcal{I}, \mathcal{C}) \leftarrow \text{Enc}(K, \mathcal{D}, \mathcal{W}, \{(w, \mathcal{D}(w)) \mid w \in \mathcal{W}\})$ and $t(w) \leftarrow \text{Trpdr}(K, w)$ from $\mathbf{A}_0^{uc}$ in the store phase and the search phase, respectively, and outputs a bit at last. This situation is exactly the same as $\mathbf{A}$ in $\mathbf{Game}_{real}$ (Fig. 7(a)). On the other hand, in the ideal world, $\mathbf{Z}_0$ sends $(\mathcal{D}, \mathcal{W})$ and w to the dummy client and receives $(\tilde{\mathcal{I}}, \tilde{\mathcal{C}})$ and $\tilde{t}(w)$ from $\mathbf{S}_0^{uc}$ in each phase, and outputs a bit. This situation is exactly the same as $\mathbf{A}$ in $\mathbf{Game}_{sim}$ (Fig. 7(b)). Therefore,

$$\max_{\mathbf{A}} |\Pr[\mathbf{A} \text{ outputs 1 in } \mathbf{Game}_{real}] - \Pr[\mathbf{A} \text{ outputs 1 in } \mathbf{Game}_{sim}]|$$

$$= \max_{\mathbf{Z}_0} |\Pr[\mathbf{Z}_0 \text{ outputs 1 in the real world}] - \Pr[\mathbf{Z}_0 \text{ outputs 1 in the ideal world}]|$$

$$\leq \max_{\mathbf{Z}} |\Pr[\mathbf{Z} \text{ outputs 1 in the real world}] - \Pr[\mathbf{Z} \text{ outputs 1 in the ideal world}]|$$

$$= negl.$$

□

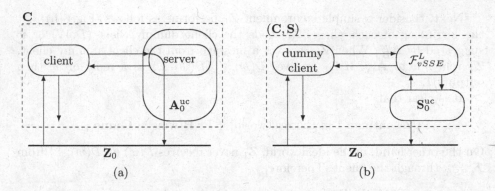

Fig. 7. Z_0 in (a)real and (b)ideal world

Lemma 2. *If vSSE has UC security with leakage L against non-adaptive adversaries for some L, vSSE has satisfies reliability.*

Proof. We fix an arbitrary adversary $\mathbf{B} = (\mathbf{B}_1, \mathbf{B}_2)$ of reliability game. Consider a real adversary $\mathbf{A}_B^{uc}$ such that $\mathbf{A}_B^{uc}$ interacts with the client like $\mathbf{B}_2$ (by controlling the server), while $\mathbf{A}_B^{uc}$ interacts with $\mathbf{Z}$ like $\mathbf{B}_1$ (Fig. 8(a)). More precisely, at the beginning of each phase, $\mathbf{A}_B^{uc}$ suggests which $(\mathcal{D}, \mathcal{W})$ or w the environment should send to the client.

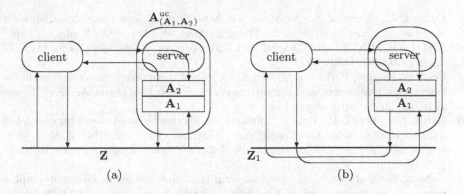

Fig. 8. (a) $\mathbf{A}_B^{uc}$, (b) $\mathbf{Z}_1$

If the scheme has UC security with leakage L, there exists an ideal adversary, $\mathbf{S}_B^{uc}$, and any environment $\mathbf{Z}$ cannot distinguish the real world and the ideal world.

Next, consider a simple environment $\mathbf{Z}_1$ performs as follows (Fig. 8(b)). At the beginning of each phase, $\mathbf{Z}_1$ sends the client/dummy client $(\mathcal{D}, \mathcal{W})$ or w suggested by $\mathbf{A}_{\mathbf{B}}^{uc}$. When $\mathbf{Z}_1$ receives a message from the client/dummy client, $\mathbf{Z}_1$ relays it to $\mathbf{A}_{\mathbf{B}}^{uc}$. If $\mathbf{Z}_1$ receives $\tilde{\mathcal{D}}(w) \notin \{\mathcal{D}(w), \perp\}$ as a reply of w, then outputs 1.

It is clear that

$$\Pr[\mathbf{Z}_1 \text{ outputs 1 in the real world}] = \Pr[\mathbf{B} \text{ wins in } \mathbf{Game}_{reli}].$$

On the other hand, in the ideal world, $\mathbf{Z}_1$ never receives $\tilde{\mathcal{D}}(w) \notin \{\mathcal{D}(w), \perp\}$ from $\mathcal{F}_{vSSE}^L$ through the client. Therefore,

$$\Pr[\mathbf{Z}_1 \text{ outputs 1 in the ideal world}] = 0.$$

Hence

$$\Pr[\mathbf{B} \text{ wins in } \mathbf{Game}_{reli}]$$

$$= |\Pr[\mathbf{Z}_1 \text{ outputs 1 in the real world}] - \Pr[\mathbf{Z}_1 \text{ outputs 1 in the ideal world}]|,$$

which is negligible for any $\mathbf{B}$ from the assumption. $\square$

Corollary 1. *Our transformed scheme is UC-secure with leakage $L' = (L'_1, L'_2)$ if the original SSE scheme has $L = (L_1, L_2)$-privacy, where L and L' are given in Theorem 1.*

References

1. Ballard, L., Kamara, S., Monrose, F.: Achieving efficient conjunctive keyword searches over encrypted data. In: Qing, S., Mao, W., López, J., Wang, G. (eds.) ICICS 2005. LNCS, vol. 3783, pp. 414–426. Springer, Heidelberg (2005). https://doi.org/10.1007/11602897_35
2. Bost, R., Fouque, P.-A., Pointcheval, D.: Verifiable Dynamic Symmetric Searchable Encryption Optimality and Forward Security, Cryptology ePrint Archive, Report 2016/62 (2016). http://eprint.iacr.org/
3. Byun, J.W., Lee, D.H., Lim, J.: Efficient conjunctive keyword search on encrypted data storage system. In: Atzeni, A.S., Lioy, A. (eds.) EuroPKI 2006. LNCS, vol. 4043, pp. 184–196. Springer, Heidelberg (2006). https://doi.org/10.1007/11774716_15
4. Canetti, R.: Universally composable security: a new paradigm for cryptographic protocols. In: Proceedings of 42nd FOCS (2001). https://doi.org/10.1109/SFCS.2001.959888
5. Canetti, R.: Universally Composable Signatures, Certification and Authentication. Cryptology ePrint Archive, Report 2003/239 (2003). http://eprint.iacr.org/
6. Canetti, R.: Universally Composable Security: A New Paradigm for Cryptographic Protocols. Cryptology ePrint Archive, Report 2000/067 (2005). http://eprint.iacr.org/
7. Cash, D., Jarecki, S., Jutla, C., Krawczyk, H., Roşu, M.-C., Steiner, M.: Highly-scalable searchable symmetric encryption with support for boolean queries. In: Canetti, R., Garay, J.A. (eds.) CRYPTO 2013. LNCS, vol. 8042, pp. 353–373. Springer, Heidelberg (2013). https://doi.org/10.1007/978-3-642-40041-4_20

8. Cash, D., Jaeger, J., Jarecki, S., Jutla, C.S., Krawczyk, H., Rosu, M.-C., Steiner, M.: Dynamic searchable encryption in very-large databases: data structures and implementation. In: NDSS (2014). https://eprint.iacr.org/2014/853.pdf
9. Cash, D., Tessaro, S.: The locality of searchable symmetric encryption. In: Nguyen, P.Q., Oswald, E. (eds.) EUROCRYPT 2014. LNCS, vol. 8441, pp. 351–368. Springer, Heidelberg (2014). https://doi.org/10.1007/978-3-642-55220-5_20
10. Chang, Y.-C., Mitzenmacher, M.: Privacy preserving keyword searches on remote encrypted data. In: Ioannidis, J., Keromytis, A., Yung, M. (eds.) ACNS 2005. LNCS, vol. 3531, pp. 442–455. Springer, Heidelberg (2005). https://doi.org/10.1007/11496137_30
11. Curtmola, R., Garay, J.A., Kamara, S., Ostrovsky, R.: Searchable symmetric encryption: improved definitions and efficient constructions. In: ACM Conference on Computer and Communications Security 2006, pp. 79–88 (2006)
12. Full version of [16]: Cryptology ePrint Archive, Report 2006/210 (2006). http://eprint.iacr.org/
13. Goh, E.-J.: Secure Indexes. Cryptology ePrint Archive, Report 2003/216 (2003). http://eprint.iacr.org/
14. Golle, P., Staddon, J., Waters, B.: Secure conjunctive keyword search over encrypted data. In: Jakobsson, M., Yung, M., Zhou, J. (eds.) ACNS 2004. LNCS, vol. 3089, pp. 31–45. Springer, Heidelberg (2004). https://doi.org/10.1007/978-3-540-24852-1_3
15. Kamara, S., Papamanthou, C.: Parallel and dynamic searchable symmetric encryption. In: Sadeghi, A.-R. (ed.) FC 2013. LNCS, vol. 7859, pp. 258–274. Springer, Heidelberg (2013). https://doi.org/10.1007/978-3-642-39884-1_22
16. Kamara, S., Papamanthou, C., Roeder, T.: Dynamic searchable symmetric encryption. In: ACM Conference on Computer and Communications Security, pp. 965–976 (2012). https://doi.org/10.1145/2382196.2382298
17. Kurosawa, K.: Garbled searchable symmetric encryption. In: Christin, N., Safavi-Naini, R. (eds.) FC 2014. LNCS, vol. 8437, pp. 234–251. Springer, Heidelberg (2014). https://doi.org/10.1007/978-3-662-45472-5_15
18. Kurosawa, K., Ohtaki, Y.: UC-secure searchable symmetric encryption. In: Keromytis, A.D. (ed.) FC 2012. LNCS, vol. 7397, pp. 285–298. Springer, Heidelberg (2012). https://doi.org/10.1007/978-3-642-32946-3_21
19. Kurosawa, K., Ohtaki, Y.: How to update documents *Verifiably* in searchable symmetric encryption. In: Abdalla, M., Nita-Rotaru, C., Dahab, R. (eds.) CANS 2013. LNCS, vol. 8257, pp. 309–328. Springer, Cham (2013). https://doi.org/10.1007/978-3-319-02937-5_17
20. The final version of [23]. Cryptology ePrint Archive, Report 2015/251 (2015)
21. Kurosawa, K., Sasaki, K., Ohta, K., Yoneyama, K.: UC-secure dynamic searchable symmetric encryption scheme. In: Ogawa, K., Yoshioka, K. (eds.) IWSEC 2016. LNCS, vol. 9836, pp. 73–90. Springer, Cham (2016). https://doi.org/10.1007/978-3-319-44524-3_5
22. Kutzelnigg, R.: Bipartite random graphs and cuckoo hashing. In: Fourth Colloquium on Mathematics and Computer Science. Discrete Mathematics and Theoretical Computer Science, pp. 403–406 (2006)
23. Naveed, M., Prabhakaran, M., Gunter, C.: Dynamic searchable encryption via blind storage. In: IEEE Security & Privacy (2014). https://doi.org/10.1109/SP.2014.47
24. Pagh, R., Rodler, F.F.: Cuckoo hashing. In: auf der Heide, F.M. (ed.) ESA 2001. LNCS, vol. 2161, pp. 121–133. Springer, Heidelberg (2001). https://doi.org/10.1007/3-540-44676-1_10

25. Song, D., Wagner, D., Perrig, A.: Practical techniques for searches on encrypted data. In: IEEE Symposium on Security and Privacy 2000, pp. 44–55 (2000). https://doi.org/10.1109/SECPRI.2000.848445
26. Taketani, S., Ogata, W.: Improvement of UC secure searchable symmetric encryption scheme. In: Tanaka, K., Suga, Y. (eds.) IWSEC 2015. LNCS, vol. 9241, pp. 135–152. Springer, Cham (2015). https://doi.org/10.1007/978-3-319-22425-1_9
27. Wang, P., Wang, H., Pieprzyk, J.: Keyword field-free conjunctive keyword searches on encrypted data and extension for dynamic groups. In: Franklin, M.K., Hui, L.C.K., Wong, D.S. (eds.) CANS 2008. LNCS, vol. 5339, pp. 178–195. Springer, Heidelberg (2008). https://doi.org/10.1007/978-3-540-89641-8_13

Faster Homomorphic Evaluation of Discrete Fourier Transforms

Anamaria Costache, Nigel P. Smart[✉], and Srinivas Vivek

University of Bristol, Bristol, UK
nigel@cs.bris.ac.uk

Abstract. We present a methodology to achieve low latency homomorphic operations on approximations to complex numbers, by encoding a complex number as an evaluation of a polynomial at a root of unity. We then use this encoding to evaluate a Discrete Fourier Transform (DFT) on data which has been encrypted using a Somewhat Homomorphic Encryption (SHE) scheme, with up to three orders of magnitude improvement in latency over previous methods. We are also able to deal with much larger input sizes than previous methods. Due to the fact that the entire DFT algorithm is an algebraic operation over the underlying ring of the SHE scheme (for a suitably chosen ring), our method for the DFT utilizes exact arithmetic over the complex numbers, as opposed to approximations.

1 Introduction

Since its introduction by Gentry in 2009 [8] most work on Fully (resp. Somewhat) Homomorphic Encryption (FHE/SHE) has focused on evaluating binary or arithmetic circuits. However, for many applications one needs to evaluate functions over more complex data types. In many areas of scientific processing one requires operations on real or complex number, and many applications consist of evaluation of functions of relatively low multiplicative depth. For example, basic statistical calculations are often linear (such as means) or quadratic (such as standard deviations).

This need to process real and complex arithmetic homomorphically has led some authors to propose encoding methods for such numbers [4–6] in the context of encryption schemes based on Ring-LWE. Such schemes are typified by the BGV scheme [3]. The BGV scheme and its extensions [7] are based on a ring

$$R = \mathbb{Z}[X]/\Phi_M(X),$$

where $\Phi_M(X)$ is some cyclotomic polynomial. The ring is considered with respect to two moduli, the plaintext modulus p and the ciphertext modulus q. Writing R_p and R_q for the ring reduced modulo p and q respectively, we have that R_p represents the space of all possible plaintexts and R_q^2 is the ciphertext space.

The first methodology [5,6] to perform homomorphic operations on real numbers (and hence complex numbers) used a fixed point representation based on

© International Financial Cryptography Association 2017
A. Kiayias (Ed.): FC 2017, LNCS 10322, pp. 517–529, 2017.
https://doi.org/10.1007/978-3-319-70972-7_29

the polynomial expansion of the real number with respect to some "base". This polynomial is then embedded into the plaintext space, and homomorphic operations on the polynomials map into homomorphic operations on the underlying fixed point number. During a homomorphic operation the degree of the representing polynomial increases, as does the size of the coefficients. These two increases imply lower bounds on the degree of the ring R and on the plaintext modulus p. It should be noted that we therefore need to track both noise growth (as in all SHE operations) as well as plaintext growth in such an encoding. See [5] where this growth in coefficient sizes of the representing polynomials is considered in depth. This method uses (in most cases) a single ciphertext to represent a single real number, thus no ciphertext "packing", i.e. amortization, is generally supported. On the other hand, once a given approximation is used for an input plaintext, future homomorphic operations are computed exactly; i.e. floating point precision does not decrease.

A second methodology to perform operations on approximations to complex numbers was presented in [4]. In this methodology a set of $\deg(R)$ approximations to complex numbers are encrypted via a single polynomial. In more detail, for each element in the plaintext space $a \in R_p$, we consider the associated polynomial $a(X)$ and then associate this with the $\deg(R)$ complex numbers $a(\theta_i)$, where θ_i are the roots of the polynomial defining R. In other words, the associated complex numbers are precisely the canonical embedding of the plaintext polynomial. This methodology allows one to produce amortized homomorphic operations via packing. A drawback is however that the associated plaintext polynomial, for a given set of input complex numbers, can have relatively large height.

In both [4,5] this ability to homomorphically evaluate on real and complex numbers is demonstrated via a toy example of evaluating a simple image processing pipeline consisting of a DFT, followed by the multiplication of a secret Hadamard transform, followed by an inverse DFT. The results in [4] is particularly interesting, especially when throughput is considered. However, in many applications the main impediment to using homomorphic encryption techniques is low latency; i.e. we are more interested in the time to wait for a single answer than the amortized time over multiple executions.

In this paper, we take this motivating algorithm and show that one can evaluate it over two orders of magnitude faster, by utilizing a completely different representation of the complex numbers. Our method is particularly tailored for DFT operations, however we also show that it can be applied to other more general operations on complex numbers. Note that there are potentially many applications for evaluating DFTs on homomorphic data, as it is widely used in a variety of applications such as signal processing of sound waves and radio signals, or processing of other recurrent data in which determining periodic properties is of interest.

Our techniques make use of the special cyclotomic ring

$$R = \mathbb{Z}[X]/(X^M + 1)$$

where $M = 2^m$ is a power of two. We note that in the ring R the value X corresponds to a formal primitive $2 \cdot M$-th root of unity. Thus by selecting a mapping $X \mapsto \zeta_{2 \cdot M}$ we can interpret a polynomial in R as being an integer linear combination of the powers of the complex number $\zeta = \zeta_{2 \cdot M}$. Thus our method can be seen as associating a polynomial with a single complex number corresponding to a single component of the canonical embedding, as opposed to the set of complex numbers used in [4]. This means our associated input plaintext polynomials can have smaller height; but we will not be able to deal with ciphertext packing. The effect of this is to improve latency, at the expense of throughput.

For example, if we take a complex number α and then approximate it via the sum

$$\alpha \approx \sum_{i=0}^{N-1} a_i \cdot \zeta^{i \cdot 2 \cdot M / N},$$

then we can use this polynomial to encode the complex number. If the coefficients a_i are selected to be relatively small then the methodology in [5] can be applied to estimate the associated coefficient growth of the encoding polynomials as homomorphic operations are performed. Finding suitably small a_i values can be obtained for an arbitrary complex number via the use of the LLL algorithm [11], in a relatively standard way. See Sect. 2 for more details on this general methodology.

For the evaluation of the DFT pipeline our method can also dispense with the associated approximations of complex numbers, and we find we can evaluate the DFT pipeline using exact operations on encodings of exact complex numbers. If N is a power of two which divides M then

$$Y = X^{2 \cdot M / N} \qquad (\text{resp. } \zeta_N = \zeta_{2 \cdot M}^{2 \cdot M / N}) \tag{1}$$

is a primitive N-root of unity lying in R (resp. $\mathbb{C}$). Recall that the DFT operation takes an input vector and applies a linear operation (defined over R) to the input vector. Thus, as long as we encode our input in R, we can perform the DFT using only algebraic operations in R. Thus we can homomorphically evaluate the DFT, as long as the coefficient growth of the underlying polynomials can be supported by our plaintext modulus p. When applying DFT in many applications the input can be scaled to be an integer (e.g. in image processing), therefore the input can easily be encoded in an exact manner as well.

This methodology enables us to achieve a considerable improvement in the ability to homomorphically evaluate a DFT. Notice that despite the DFT being linear, the large number of additions and scalar multiplications means that the often heard mantra of "only multiplications matter" does not apply. We need to be careful not only of the growth of the coefficients of the ring elements which encode our values, but also of the homomorphic noise.

We are able to evaluate a DFT-Hadamard-iDFT pipeline of input size 8192 elements, as opposed to 1024 elements for [4,5]. In terms of latency we were able to evaluate a pipeline for 256 elements in 9.43 s, compared to a latency of 581 min for [5] and 87 min for [4]. Our amortized times are however much worse; since our method does not allow packing our amortized time for the same calculation is still 9.43 s, compared to 89.4 s for [5] and 0.31 s for [4]. So whilst we obtain faster latency (and exact computations), for high throughput calculations the method of [4] is still to be preferred.

2   Encoding Approximations to Arbitrary Complex Numbers

As discussed in the introduction, there are two prior methods used to encode complex numbers. The first encodes the complex number as a pair of real numbers and therefore holds the encrypted complex number as the encryption of two real numbers. The real numbers would then be encrypted using the methods suggested in [5,6] to encode fixed-point numbers. A major downside of this methodology is that to add two encrypted complex numbers requires two homomorphic additions, and to multiply two encrypted complex numbers requires four homomorphic multiplications. The second method suggested in [4] encodes a set of approximations to complex numbers. It looks at these in the canonical embedding of the ring R and then pulls the element back in the canonical embedding to a polynomial. This second method allows multiple complex numbers to be encoded, but the height of the pulled back ring element can be high if only a single complex number is required to be approximated (as would be the case in applications focused on latency).

In this section we present an analogue of the second method where one only wishes to approximate a single complex number. We do this by presenting the folklore method of finding a good approximation to an arbitrary complex number by an element in R. We then can encode the complex number by the associated element in R. As long as we can bound the coefficients of the associated element (in terms of the power basis of R), we can use the method in [5] to bound the growth of the plaintext coefficients as we perform homomorphic operations. Thus we use the method in [5] to bound coefficients of polynomials representing complex numbers, as opposed to polynomials representing fixed-point numbers. The only difference is how we interpret the underlying polynomial/element of R. In comparison to [4] we pull back a single coordinate in the canonical embedding, which allows us a greater degree of freedom in selecting a "small" polynomial to perform the approximation; hence our use of LLL [11] below to find this approximation.

We pick a value n such that n divides $M = 2^m$. This is purely to reduce the size of the associated lattice below from M to the smaller value n, in order to make lattice reduction more manageable. However, a larger value of n will result in an approximation polynomial with smaller coefficients (heuristically, although not provably). We let ζ denote a primitive n-th root of unity, so that ζ is a fixed primitive root of the polynomial $Z^n - 1$, where $Z = X^{M/n}$. Our basic idea for encoding (an approximation to) the complex number α is to write

$$\alpha \approx \overline{\alpha} = \sum_{i=0}^{n-1} z_i \cdot \zeta^i$$

for some "small" integer values z_i, thus we can approximate α by $\overline{\alpha} \in R$.

We first fix a "large" integer C, say $C = 10^{10}$, which encodes how close we want the approximation to be. We then set, for $i = 0, \ldots, n - 1$,

$$a_i = \lceil \mathfrak{Re}(C \cdot \zeta^i) \rfloor \text{ and } b_i = \lceil \mathfrak{Im}(C \cdot \zeta^i) \rfloor,$$

and

$$a = \lceil \mathfrak{Re}(C \cdot \alpha) \rfloor \text{ and } b = \lceil \mathfrak{Im}(C \cdot \alpha) \rfloor.$$

We form the rank $n + 1$ lattice $\mathcal{L}$ in $\mathbb{R}^{n+3}$ generated by the columns of the matrix

$$A = \begin{pmatrix} 1 & & & \\ & \ddots & & \\ & & 1 & \\ & & & T \\ a_0 & \cdots & a_{n-1} & -a \\ b_0 & \cdots & b_{n-1} & -b \end{pmatrix},$$

for some non-zero constant T. The determinant of this lattice $\Delta(\mathcal{L})$ is given by $\sqrt{\det(A^T \cdot A)} \approx n \cdot T \cdot C^2/2$, assuming $|a|, |b| < T \cdot C$. We then apply the LLL [11] algorithm to the lattice generated by the columns of A. We let j denote the index of the shortest LLL basis vector which is non-zero in the n-th position (when the basis is ordered in increasing order of size). For a suitably large (but not too large) choice of T, we expect that the j-th basis vector will have $\pm T$ in its $n + 1$-st position, and hence will be of the form

$$\mathbf{y} = \left(z_0, \ \ldots, \ z_{n-1}, \ \pm T, \ \sum_{i=0}^{n-1} z_i \cdot a_i \mp a, \ \sum_{i=0}^{n-1} z_i \cdot b_i \mp b \right).$$

We then have, by the usual bounds on LLL basis vectors, that the z_i values for $i = 0, \ldots, n - 1$, to be of size bounded by

$$\left(2^{n \cdot (n+1)/4 - 1} \cdot n \cdot T \cdot C^2 \right)^{1/(n+2-j)},$$

resulting in an approximation $\overline{\alpha}$ such that

$$C \cdot |\alpha - \overline{\alpha}| \leq \left| \mathfrak{Re}(C \cdot \alpha) - \sum_{i=0}^{n-1} \mathfrak{Re}(C \cdot z_i \cdot \zeta^i) \right| + \left| \mathfrak{Im}(C \cdot \alpha) - \sum_{i=0}^{n-1} \mathfrak{Im}(C \cdot z_i \cdot \zeta^i) \right|$$

$$\approx \left| \sum_{i=0}^{n-1} z_i \cdot a_i - a \right| + \left| \sum_{i=0}^{n-1} z_i \cdot b_i - b \right|$$

$$\lesssim 2 \cdot \left(2^{n \cdot (n+1)/4 - 1} \cdot n \cdot T \cdot C^2 \right)^{1/(n+2-j)}.$$

In other words, for large enough C, we get a good approximation $\overline{\alpha}$ of α. In addition, since LLL usually behaves much better than the theoretical bounds predict, we expect the actual bound on the approximation and the z_i values to grow roughly as $C^{2/n}$. Thus for fixed C, increasing the rank of the lattice - i.e. increasing n - will result in an approximately linear decrease in the coefficient sizes.

Our estimates of the accuracy of the method above depended on the fact that a and b are not too big. In particular we assumed that $|a|, |b| < T \cdot C$, so that they produce a negligible effect on the determinant of the lattice we are reducing. Thus in practice it helps to scale α down so that $|\alpha|$ is close to one, assuming this is enabled by the application in hand. This may require the appropriate scaling to be tracked through the homomorphic operation; much like was proposed in the method from [5]. A similar scaling is needed in the method from [4].

2.1   Numerical Example

Suppose we are given the complex number

$$\alpha = 0.655981733221013 + 0.923883055400882 \cdot \sqrt{-1} = a + b \cdot \sqrt{-1},$$

and we want to produce an approximation which is correct up to ten decimal digits of accuracy using a lattice of dimension $n = 16$. We apply the above method with $C = 10^{10}$ and $T = 10$, and find that the LLL reduced basis of the above rank $n + 1$ lattice in $\mathbb{R}^{n+3}$ has its first basis vector given by

$$(0, -5, 0, 1, -4, 12, 8, -6, -1, -2, -1, -8, -2, 8, 0, 1, 10, -5, -1).$$

Thus if we form the polynomial

$$P(Z) = Z^{15} + 8 \cdot Z^{13} - 2 \cdot Z^{12} - 8 \cdot Z^{11} - Z^{10} - 2 \cdot Z^9 - Z^8$$
$$- 6 \cdot Z^7 + 8 \cdot Z^6 + 12 \cdot Z^5 - 4 \cdot Z^4 + Z^3 - 5 \cdot Z,$$

then

$$\overline{\alpha} = P\Big(\exp(\pi \cdot \sqrt{-1}/16) \Big)$$
$$\approx 0.65598173270304 + 0.923883055555970 \cdot \sqrt{-1}.$$

3   New Homomorphic DFT Method

The prior method to approximate complex numbers allows us to homomorphically evaluate operations on complex numbers, as long as there is no wrap-around in the plaintext modulus space, i.e. the plaintext modulus p is chosen appropriately large. Suppose we want to evaluate DFT on an input vector

$$v = (v_0, ...v_{N-1}) \tag{2}$$

of N integers in the range $(-B, \dots, B)$. For most of this section, we will restrict ourselves to the integer input case because it suffices for our application to homomorphic image processing that we consider in Sect. 4. However, later in this section, we deal with the case when the DFT inputs are integer polynomials representing elements of the power-of-two cyclotomic rings, i.e. when we want to apply the DFT to the general approximations obtained in the previous section. When the inputs are integers, the nature of the DFT algorithm is such that (as long as the plaintext modulus p is large enough) we obtain an exact computation over the complex numbers. This is because the DFT is an algebraic (in fact linear) operation over the ring R.

For simplicity, let us assume that $N = 2^n$ for some $n \geq 0$. Recall that the ith element $(0 \leq i < N)$ of the DFT output vector is computed as

$$\mathrm{DFT}(\boldsymbol{v})[i] = \sum_{j=0}^{N-1} v_j \cdot \zeta_N^{ij}, \tag{3}$$

where ζ_N is a primitive complex Nth root of unity. We require that ζ_N can be represented by an element in R, and so we must have N dividing $2 \cdot M$. This ensures that the DFT is evaluated exactly.

3.1 Bounding Coefficients

To simulate complex arithmetic in R, the plaintext modulus p must be chosen to be greater than the largest occurring intermediate coefficient in the DFT computation. Hence it is necessary to choose p such that the magnitude of the largest coefficient is less than $p/2$, when we represent the modulo p integers in the interval $(-p/2, \dots, p/2)$. If this is not done then decrypting the result of a homomorphic operation will not result in the correct value; regardless as to whether the homomorphic noise has swamped the computation.

Substituting ζ_N in (3) by Y from (1), we obtain a vector of polynomials in the indeterminate X,
$$(D_0(X), \dots, D_{N-1}(X)),$$
where

$$D_i(X) = \sum_{j=0}^{N-1} \boldsymbol{v}_i \cdot Y^{ij}, \tag{4}$$

for $0 \leq i < N$. This corresponds to the set of polynomials that encodes $\mathrm{DFT}(\boldsymbol{v})$ using our encoding scheme. It is this set of polynomials that we wish to homomorphically compute.

For a polynomial $U(X) = \sum_{k=0}^{d} u_k \cdot X^k \in \mathbb{Z}[X]$ define $\|U(X)\|_\infty := \max_k \{|u_k|\}$ and $\|U(X)\|_1 := \sum_{k=0}^{d} |u_k|$. Recall that

$$\|a \cdot X^k\|_\infty = \|a\|_\infty, \tag{5}$$

$$\|a + b\|_\infty \leq \|a\|_\infty + \|b\|_\infty, \tag{6}$$

where $a, b, k \in \mathbb{Z}$ and $k \geq 0$. The first of the above two properties is crucial to ensure that our encoding scheme leads to much slower growth of coefficients than previous analysis in [5].

From (4) and using the above properties we obtain

$$\|D_i(X)\|_\infty \leq \sum_{j=0}^{N-1} |v_i| = \sum_{j=0}^{N-1} \|v_i\|_\infty < N \cdot B. \tag{7}$$

Invariance. While (7) bounds only the size of the coefficients in the final output, we need to bound the intermediate values as well. But this depends on the method used to compute DFT. In the following, we argue that the bound in (7) also holds for intermediate variables in most of the well-known methods to compute DFT. Two popular methods to compute DFT are:

1. *Naive Fourier Transform* (NFT): the encoded input vector v is multiplied with a matrix A of encoded powers of the primitive Nth root of unity Y, where $A[i, j] = Y^{ij} \pmod{p, X^M + 1}$. This matrix-vector multiplication is usually carried out for small dimensions using either the row approach (scalar product of a column vector and v) or the column approach (as a span of column vectors).
2. *Fast Fourier Transform* (FFT): this is a recursive divide-and-conquer procedure, where the ith element $\mathrm{DFT}(v)[i]$ $(0 \leq i < N)$ is computed as

$$\mathrm{DFT}(v)[i] = \mathrm{DFT}(v[0, \ldots, N/2 - 1])[i] + Y^i \cdot \mathrm{DFT}(v[N/2, \ldots, N-1])[i]).$$

A hybrid of NFT and FFT is particularly interesting in the context of homomorphic evaluation. This is because it provides a trade-off between the number of scalar multiplications and the depth of the circuit. Here, we count scaler multiplications as contributing to homomorphic depth. The resulting so-called Mixed Fourier Transform (MFT) has been investigated in this context [5]. The divide-and-conquer procedure is applied for instances of size greater than some $\mathfrak{B}$ and for instances of size lesser than or equal to $\mathfrak{B}$, the naive matrix-vector multiplication method is applied. However, in our methodology there is no difference between the homomorphic depth required of the naive or the fast Fourier transform. Since all scalar multiplications are by roots of unity in our algorithms, the noise associated to a ciphertext is never increased by a scalar multiplication. In particular, the noise vector is simply rotated by the scalar multiplication. This means that scalar multiplication in our DFT algorithms does not increase homomorphic ciphertext noise, and so does not contribute to the number of levels required of our underlying SHE scheme.

In all the above methods, any intermediate intermediate plaintext polynomial $U(X)$ is of the form

$$U(X) = \sum_{i=0}^{N-1} u_i \cdot v_i \cdot X^{t_i} \pmod{p, X^M + 1},$$

where $u_i = 0$ or $u_i = 1$, depending upon whether the corresponding summand should be present or not. Assuming no wrap around the modulus p, then using properties (5) and (6), we obtain the same bound as in (7). That is,

$$\|U(X)\|_\infty < N \cdot B. \tag{8}$$

Note that our bounds on the plaintext are also invariant of the method used to compute the DFT, this is not the case with the previous method found in [5], since the output is exact no matter which method is used.

3.2 Extending the Analysis to the Ring of Algebraic Integers

Now suppose that the DFT input vector v (cf. (2)) now contains integer polynomials representing elements of R, instead of just elements from $\mathbb{Z}$. Following an analysis similar to that in Sect. 3.1, we obtain that any intermediate variable $U(X)$ in the DFT computation satisfies

$$\|U(X)\|_\infty \le \sum_{i=0}^{N-1} \|v_i(X)\|_\infty \le N \cdot \max_i \|v_i(X)\|_\infty. \tag{9}$$

Note that the above bound is independent of the number of non-zero terms in the input polynomials. This approximation is useful when we discuss a DFT-Hadamard-iDFT pipeline in the next section.

4 Homomorphic Image Processing

In this section, we apply the bounds obtained in Sect. 3 to the case of homomorphic image processing. Previously, homomorphic image processing has been investigated in the works of [1,2,4,5]. The works [1,2] investigate the problem of performing radix-2 DFT in the encrypted domain using additively homomorphic encryption schemes. Because DFT is a linear operation, the authors manage to perform this homomorphically using Paillier encryption scheme [12].

In [5], the authors homomorphically implement a standard image processing pipeline of DFT, followed by Hadamard component-wise multiplication by a fixed but encrypted matrix/vector, and finally inverse DFT to move back from the Fourier domain. The fact that the Hadamard vector is encrypted makes the whole operation non-linear and hence prevents the use of additively homomorphic encryption schemes for this purpose. Yet much smaller parameters size is achieved in [5] compared to [1,2], even for the operation of homomorphically performing a single DFT only. See [5, Sect. A.2] for a detailed comparison of their work with that of [1,2].

In [4] this application is considered again using the packed approximations to complex numbers considered earlier. Here the authors were able to evaluate a degree 256 DFT pipeline in 87 min latency (compared to 581) for the method in [5]. In terms of throughput the authors of [4] obtained an amortized time of 0.31 s, compared to 89.4 s for [5]. Our results below show we can achieve a latency for the same calculation of 9.43 s, but with no improvement possible due to amortization. The largest DFT pipeline reported in previous works was that of a degree 1024 DFT pipeline in [4]. We achieve a pipeline of degree 8192, which we executed with a latency of 1026 s.

4.1   DFT-Hadamard-iDFT Pipeline

Inputs to the (homomorphic evaluation of) a DFT-Hadamard-iDFT pipeline are usually (encrypted) integers in some interval $[0, \ldots, B := 2^{b_1})$ representing, for instance, the colour encoding of a pixel. Assume that there are $N = 2^n$ integer DFT inputs and as many in the Hadamard vector for component-wise multiplication. Using our encoding scheme from Sect. 3, we encode the input integers as themselves in the ring $R = \mathbb{Z}[X]/(p, X^M + 1)$, where as $Y = X^{2M/N}$ encodes a complex primitive Nth root of unity. Because the powers of a primitive root of unity are encoded as monic monomials in R, we do not need to bother to specify the precision for the roots of unity.

From (8), we obtain that during the computation of DFT, the largest occurring ring intermediate coefficient is bounded above by $N \cdot B$. After the Hadamard component-wise multiplication by a vector of (encrypted) integer entries, the new upper bound is $N \cdot B^2$. Finally, using (9), we obtain the following bound for any intermediate polynomial $U(x)$

$$\|U(X)\|_\infty < N^2 \cdot B^2.$$

Hence we need to choose a plaintext modulus p of the ring R such that

$$p \geq 2 \cdot N^2 \cdot B^2.$$

4.2   Comparison of Concrete Parameters

In [5, Sect. A.3], the authors use a computational procedure to compute concrete lower bounds for the sizes of p and $\deg(R)$ chosen to homomorphically evaluate the above DFT-Hadamard-iDFT pipeline. As previously mentioned, this is with the Hadamard vector also encrypted. This computational approach was followed because obtaining sharp closed form bounds seems to be out of reach for their encoding technique. Our technique by contrast enables us to obtain tight bounds on the resulting coefficients relatively easily.

Table 1 compares concrete lower bounds for our method and those from [5]. As in [5], we chose $b_1 = 8$ bits of precision for the magnitude of each input, including the entries of the Hadamard matrix. Unlike our case, in [5], the precision b_2 of the roots of unity had to be adjusted so that the final result has a precision of 32 bits. Since our computation is exact this is not a concern.

Note that, as remarked before, the lower bounds on p are independent of the method used to compute DFT. The parameter $\mathfrak{B}$ corresponds to the depth of the MFT method used (cf. Sect. 3.1). We remark that the size of the plaintext

Table 1. Comparison of the parameters for the DFT-Hadamard-iDFT pipeline.

Method	N	b_2	FFT $\mathfrak{B} = 1$		$\mathfrak{B} = \sqrt{N}$		NFT $\mathfrak{B} = N$	
			$\log_2 p$ $\geq$	$\deg(R)$ $\geq$	$\log_2 p$ $\geq$	$\deg(R)$ $\geq$	$\log_2 p$ $\geq$	$\deg(R)$ $\geq$
[5]	16	29	54	190	37	118	25	46
This paper	16	–	26	8	26	8	26	8
[5]	64	27	74	248	49	146	29	44
This paper	64	–	30	32	30	32	30	32
[5]	256	25	93	298	61	170	33	42
This paper	256	–	34	128	34	128	34	128
[5]	1024	23	112	340	72	190	37	40
This paper	1024	–	38	512	38	512	38	512

modulus in our method is close to that required in the case of NFT for [5]. Recall that we also need to lower bound the degree of R by $\deg(R) = M \geq N/2$, which is a much higher bound than that required in [5] for large values of N. However, in practice the degree will need to be much larger than this lower bound to ensure security of the underlying homomorphic encryption scheme. So this increase in the lower bound on the degree is unlikely to be a problem in practice.

4.3   Comparison of Implementation Timings

As [5], we implemented the full pipeline using the HElib library [10] that implements the BGV Somewhat Homomorphic Encryption scheme [3,9]. Table 2 compares the performance of our method with that of [5]. The experiments were run on a machine with six Intel Xeon E5 2.7 GHz processors with 64 GB RAM. The time, measured in seconds, is that required to evaluate the DFT-Hadamard-iDFT pipeline in the encrypted domain. The parameter $\log_2(q)$ corresponds to the size of the fresh ciphertexts, and "HElib Levels" report the actual number of levels consumed by HElib due to its internal choice of ciphertext moduli. In particular, HElib was allowed to choose by default half-sized primes for the ciphertext modulus chain. Unlike [4,5] we are unable to obtain any form of amortization via SIMD packing.

Since HElib has a restriction of at most 60 bits for the plaintext modulus p, not all instances of the MFT could be run with the method from [5] for our comparison. Thus we compare only against the best possible values for $\mathfrak{B}$ for the method from [5] in the table below. Note that this restriction of HElib does not affect our method at all. We are thus able to cope with a much larger range of parameter choices, as described in Table 3. In this table we report the timing results for our method for select instances of the MFT for the chosen values of N. Indeed the fastest run time for our method always occurred when utilizing the full DFT, i.e. for setting $\mathfrak{B} = 1$ in the MFT algorithm. For $N = 1024, 4096$

Table 2. Comparison of the *best* timing results, for a given N, for homomorphically evaluating a full image processing pipeline.

Method	N	$\mathcal{B}$	deg(R)	$\lceil \log_2(q) \rceil$	HElib levels	CPU time (s)
[5]	16	16	16384	192	9	106
This paper	16	1	8192	150	7	0.46
[5]	64	8	32768	622	30	1500
This paper	64	1	8192	150	7	2.08
[5]	256	256	16384	278	11	34876
This paper	256	1	8192	150	7	9.43

Table 3. Timing results for select instances of MFT for homomorphically evaluating a full image processing pipeline.

N	$\mathcal{B}$	$\lceil \log_2 p \rceil$	deg(R)	$\lceil \log_2 q \rceil$	HElib levels	CPU time (s)
16	1	26	8192	150	7	0.46
16	4	26	8192	150	7	0.51
16	16	26	8192	150	7	0.90
64	1	30	8192	150	7	2.08
64	8	30	8192	150	7	2.75
64	64	30	8192	150	7	11.05
256	1	34	8192	150	7	9.43
256	16	34	8192	150	7	16.48
256	256	34	8192	150	7	165.85
1024	1	38	16384	192	9	104.12
4096	1	42	16384	192	10	464.44
8192	1	44	16384	192	10	1026.1

and 8192, we do not report timings for large values of $\mathcal{B}$ since we did not run the computations until completion as the time taken was too long.

Acknowledgements. This work has been supported in part by ERC Advanced Grant ERC-2015-AdG-IMPaCT and by the European Union's H2020 Programme under grant agreement number ICT-644209 (HEAT). We thank the referee for helpful comments on an earlier version of this paper, and pointing out a few optimizations which we had missed.

References

1. Bianchi, T., Piva, A., Barni, M.: Comparison of different FFT implementations in the encrypted domain. In: 2008 16th European Signal Processing Conference, EUSIPCO 2008, Lausanne, Switzerland, pp. 1–5. IEEE, 25–29 August 2008

2. Bianchi, T., Piva, A., Barni, M.: On the implementation of the discrete fourier transform in the encrypted domain. IEEE Trans. Inf. Forensics Secur. **4**(1), 86–97 (2009)
3. Brakerski, Z., Gentry, C., Vaikuntanathan, V.: (Leveled) fully homomorphic encryption without bootstrapping. In: Goldwasser, S. (ed.) ITCS, pp. 309–325. ACM (2012)
4. Cheon, J.H., Kim, A., Kim, M., Song, Y.S.: Homomorphic encryption for arithmetic of approximate numbers. IACR Cryptology ePrint Archive, 2016:421 (2016)
5. Costache, A., Smart, N.P., Vivek, S., Waller, A.: Fixed-point arithmetic in SHE scheme. In: Selected Areas in Cryptography - SAC (2016). http://eprint.iacr.org/2016/250
6. Dowlin, N., Gilad-Bachrach, R., Laine, K., Lauter, K., Naehrig, M., Wernsing, J.: Manual for using homomorphic encryption for bioinformatics (2015). http://www.microsoft.com/en-us/research/publication/manual-for-using-homomorphic-encryption-for-bioinformatics
7. Fan, J., Vercauteren, F.: Somewhat practical fully homomorphic encryption. IACR Cryptology ePrint Archive, 2012:144 (2012)
8. Gentry, C.: A fully homomorphic encryption scheme. Ph.D. thesis, Stanford University (2009). http://crypto.stanford.edu/craig
9. Gentry, C., Halevi, S., Smart, N.P.: Homomorphic evaluation of the AES circuit. In: Safavi-Naini, R., Canetti, R. (eds.) CRYPTO 2012. LNCS, vol. 7417, pp. 850–867. Springer, Heidelberg (2012). https://doi.org/10.1007/978-3-642-32009-5_49
10. Halevi, S., Shoup, V.: Design and implementation of a homomorphic encryption library. http://people.csail.mit.edu/shaih/pubs/he-library.pdf
11. Lenstra, A.K., Lenstra, H.W., Lovasz, L.: Factoring polynomials with rational coefficients. Math. Ann. **261**, 515–534 (1982)
12. Paillier, P.: Public-key cryptosystems based on composite degree residuosity classes. In: Stern, J. (ed.) EUROCRYPT 1999. LNCS, vol. 1592, pp. 223–238. Springer, Heidelberg (1999). https://doi.org/10.1007/3-540-48910-X_16

Secure Channel Protocols

Short Paper: TLS Ecosystems in Networked Devices vs. Web Servers

Nayanamana Samarasinghe[(✉)] and Mohammad Mannan

Concordia Institute for Information Systems Engineering, Concordia University,
Montreal, Canada
{n_samara,mmannan}@ciise.concordia.ca

Abstract. Recently, high-speed IPv4 scanners, such as ZMap, have
enabled rapid and timely collection of TLS certificates and other security-
sensitive parameters. Such large datasets led to the development of
the Censys search interface, facilitating comprehensive analysis of TLS
deployments in the wild. Several recent studies analyzed TLS certificates
as deployed in web servers. Beyond public web servers, TLS is deployed in
many other Internet-connected devices, at home and enterprise environments, and at network backbones. In this paper, we report the results of
a preliminary analysis using Censys on TLS deployments in such devices
(e.g., routers, modems, NAS, printers, SCADA, and IoT devices in general). We compare certificates and TLS connection parameters from a
security perspective, as found in common devices with Alexa 1M sites.
Our results highlight significant weaknesses, and may serve as a catalyst
to improve TLS security for these devices.

1 Introduction

Beyond user-level computing devices and back-end servers, there are many other
Internet-connected devices that serve important roles in everyday IT operations. Such devices include routers, modems, printers, cameras, SCADA (super-
visory control and data acquisition) controllers, DVR (digital video recorders),
HVAC (heating, ventilating and air conditioning technology), CPS (cyber physical systems), and NAS (network-attached storage) devices. Several past studies
have identified critical security issues in these devices, including authentication
bypass, hard-coded passwords and keys, misconfiguration, serious flaws in their
firmware and web interfaces; example studies include: [7–10,24,26]. The recent
massive DDoS attack on DynDNS as attributed to the Mirai botnet (e.g., [25]),
populated by DVRs, IP cameras and other IoT devices, shows the clear danger
of security flaws and weaknesses in these devices.

Over the years, manufacturers of networked devices have implemented some
security mechanisms, notably, the adoption of SSL/TLS for communication with

---

An extended version of this paper is available as a technical report [27], which additionally includes: analysis of certificate issuers, certificate reuse, DH prime number
reuse, stronger cipher suites, and device type ranking.

© International Financial Cryptography Association 2017
A. Kiayias (Ed.): FC 2017, LNCS 10322, pp. 533–541, 2017.
https://doi.org/10.1007/978-3-319-70972-7_30

other devices. With the help of the ZMap [16] high-speed IPv4 scanner, some recent projects analyzed the TLS ecosystem for web, email and SSH servers, and identified and measured significant security issues in TLS deployments in the wild; see e.g., [1,14,15,21].

Heninger et al. [20] highlighted faulty random number generators in networked devices (see also the recent follow-up work [19]). Chung et al. [6] analyzed over 80 million invalid TLS certificates, and attribute most of them to network devices, including modems/home routers, VPNs, NAS, firewalls, IP cameras and IPTVs. However, we are unaware of any comprehensive study on the overall TLS ecosystem for networked devices. In this paper, we report our results on analyzing certificates and TLS parameters from 299,858 devices (out of 1,018,911), collected from the Censys (censys.io) service on October 8, 2016. Unsurprisingly, many devices still use crypto primitives that are currently being phased out from modern browsers and web servers.

Specifically, we found a significant number of devices use unsafe RSA 512-bit keys (4100 certificates) and 768-bit keys (8919 certificates). The vulnerable/deprecated RC4 stream cipher is still widely used in devices (113,186, 37.7%). A large number of devices (66,540, 22.2%; 19,063) also use (deprecated) SSLv3 and SSLv2, respectively. We also compare TLS security parameters between devices and Alexa Top 1M sites, which clearly highlight the differences in these two domains. In all security aspects that we consider (SSL/TLS version, signature, encryption and hashing algorithms, and RSA key length), all device types are significantly more vulnerable than Alexa 1M sites (see [27]). Our analysis focuses on TLS security weaknesses, but we also summarize the use of stronger security primitives in devices and Alexa 1M sites. We hope our results, albeit preliminary, to serve as a catalyst to quick fixing of TLS issues in devices, so that these devices do not remain less secure than the HTTPS/web ecosystem in the long run.

2   Related Work

We briefly discuss measurement studies on real-world TLS deployments.

To allow researchers to analyze SSL certificates, the EFF SSL Observatory project [17] offered the first large-scale, open certificate repository containing SSL certificates for the IPv4 address space in 2010. Later, in 2013, Durumeric et al. [15] analyzed the ZMap collected data over a period of 14 months to uncover all public certificate authorities (CAs) and the certificates they issued. Censys [13] is a search engine used to query information of hosts and networks stored in daily ZMap scans. As an example application for Censys, the prevalence of the unauthenticated Modbus protocol among SCADA systems has been studied. Numerous such systems have been found across the globe. However, non-SCADA devices, specifically, the TLS ecosystem for those devices have not been studied. We extend existing work to understand the TLS ecosystem for networked devices, mostly used at home, enterprise, and industrial environments, and physical/network infrastructures.

Heninger et al. [20] reported in 2012 that RSA/DSA algorithms as used specifically in embedded network devices are vulnerable due to faulty random number generators. They found that 0.75% of TLS certificates share keys, and RSA private keys can be easily calculated for 0.50% of TLS hosts (also reported similar results for RSA/DSA keys as used in the SSH protocol). However, other TLS/certificate parameters were not analyzed in this study.

Pa et al. [24] propose the IoT honeypot (IoTPOT) to analyze malware attacks against devices such as home routers, smart fridges, and other IoT devices. Their honeypot data also shows significant increase in Telnet-based attacks, including DDoS, against IoT devices. Costin et al. [7] devise a platform to find possible reuse of fingerprints of SSL certificates, public/private keys of devices in ZMap datasets; many devices were found with reused keys.

Shodan.io is a search engine similar to Censys, targeted towards IoT devices (full access requires paid subscriptions). In addition to IPv4 devices, Shodan claimed to have scanned millions of IPv6 addresses, reportedly by exploiting a loophole in the NTP Pool Project [3]. Arnaert et al. [2] highlight challenges in aggregating search results from Shodan and Censys, and propose an ontology to make these engines more usable and effective for finding vulnerable IoT devices.

3   Methodology and Device Info

We rely on the Censys [13] search engine for our analysis. In this section, we provide a brief overview of Censys, and detail our methodology.

Censys enables querying data from the Internet-wide scan repository (`scans.io`), a data repository hosting the periodic scan results as collected by the ZMap scanner [16]. Censys tags the collected data with security-related properties and device types, allowing easy but powerful search queries

Table 1. Type-wise device distribution

Device type	Non-TLS %	Non-TLS count	TLS %	TLS count
Infra. router	23.31	237,540	11.61	118,259
Modem	15.56	158,558	2.53	25,724
Camera	14.11	143,721	0.69	6809
NAS	7.07	71,997	5.45	55,503
Home router	5.04	51,347	2.52	25,667
Network	0.00	3	3.91	39,857
Printer	1.00	10,148	2.19	22,296
Scada	2.45	24,909	0.37	3773
CPS	1.26	12,820	0.09	868
Media	0.79	8000	0.11	1102
Total	70.57	719,043	29.43	299,858

through its online search interface and REST API. Censys also tags TLS and certificate data of Alexa Top 1M web sites. Tagging is done by annotating the raw scan data with additional metadata, e.g., type and manufacturer for devices, and Alexa ranking for sites. The output from the application scanners is used to identify device-specific metadata. The annotation process involves ZTag (paired with ZMap and ZGrab), allowing researchers to add logic to define metadata for currently untagged devices [13]. Apparently, search capabilities in Censys is still evolving (not all device metadata is defined in ZTag, although ZTag can be extended by other researchers); thus, TLS/certificate data and tag information for all device types are still not comprehensively reflected in Censys.

Table 1 lists available device types extracted from Censys, divided by TLS support. We further group some device types from Censys for easier presentation as follows: modem (cable/DSL), printer (all printer models, print servers), network (generic network devices, network analyzers), SCADA (scada controller, router, gateway, server, frontend), media (set-top box, digital video recorders, VoIP, cinema), CPS (PLC, HVAC, industrial control system, water flow controller, light controller, power distribution unit, power monitor, power controller). Certain device types (e.g., CPS) appear to be small in numbers. This may be due to the fact that the tagging process in Censys is still not very comprehensive. We do not consider some devices that are very low in number (e.g., 10 USB devices). The devices appear to come from all around the world (75 countries with >1000 devices); the top 10 countries host about 56% of all devices, including: Germany 17.9%, USA 15.0%, India 4.9%, and China 4.4%.

For comparison, we chose the Alexa Top 1M sites. Data extracted from Censys was transformed to an intermediary format that requires a resource-intensive post-processing phase. Search queries can be executed on Censys in two ways: a RESTful web API or an SQL interface engine. We used the latter option (with the help of a Censys author), as it is more efficient for large-scale search results. After the TLS parameters and certificates are extracted for devices and Alexa 1M sites, we first analyze our selected security parameters and algorithms in devices. We then compare the security parameters from devices with those from Alexa 1M sites, to highlight any important differences between them. Similar to past work (e.g., [15,22]), we choose the following certificate/TLS parameters: cipher suite (algorithms used for hashing, key encryption, key exchange and authentication, signature), SSL/TLS protocol version, and RSA key length.

4   Analysis and Results: Weak Security Practices

On October 8, 2016, we extracted certificates and TLS parameters (contained in a daily dump) from 299,858 TLS-supporting devices (out of a total of 1,018,911 devices), and from 598,888 HTTPS sites in Alexa Top 1M. The client used to extract TLS certificates are ZMap along with ZGrab (i.e., not following any popular browser), which is later queried from Censys. In this section, we provide the results of our analysis and compare the use of TLS/certificate parameters. For each cryptographic primitive in a device certificate and TLS/SSL protocol banner, we compute the percentage to compare the parameters between devices; see Figs. 1, 2, 3, 4 and 5 for a comparison of the weak cryptographic primitives (for exact data, see [27]). We also compare average values from devices with Alexa sites (the last two bars). For brevity, we highlight results for algorithms and parameters that are most vulnerable.

Hash functions in message authentication. The use of SHA1 is prominent in all device types (67.4%), most notably in infrastructure routers (117,550, 99.4%) and network devices (35,918, 90.1%). In contrast, SHA1 usage in Alexa

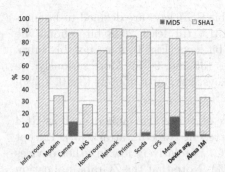

Fig. 1. Hashing algorithms

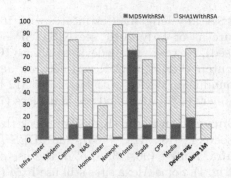

Fig. 2. Signature algorithms

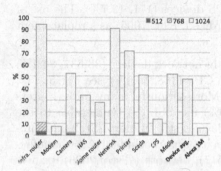

Fig. 3. Key lengths (RSA)

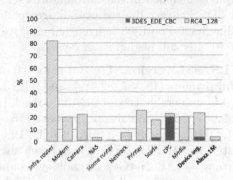

Fig. 4. Encryption algorithms

1M sites is far less (31.2%); see Fig. 1. Some devices still use MD5, e.g., cameras (817, 12%) and media devices (176, 16%). MD5 is broken for more than a decade now [30], and SHA1 is also becoming subject to feasible collision attacks [28] (being phased out as of writing).

Hash functions in signature schemes.
The MD5-RSA signature scheme is predominantly used in devices, notably in printers (16,993, 74.9%) and infra. routers (64,879, 54.9%); see Fig. 2. These devices are vulnerable to certificate collision attacks, where attackers create certificates that collide with arbitrary prefixes/suffixes [29]. SHA1-RSA is also used more in modems (24,025, 93.4%), network (37,836, 94.9%) and CPS (703, 81%). A few devices (102) use "unknown" algorithms; according to a Censys author (email correspondence), these algorithms are not parseable.

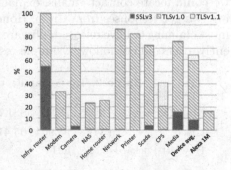

Fig. 5. SSL/TLS protocol versions

RSA key lengths. Certificates with 1024-bit RSA keys are deemed to be insecure as of early 2016; see NIST SP 800-131A (at least 2048 bits should be used). However, many devices still use 1024-bit keys (Fig. 3); most notably infra. routers (98,432, 83.2%) and network devices (35,886, 90%). More seriously, we found many devices with factorable 512-bit keys, e.g., infra. routers (3810, 3.2%), cameras (77, 1.1%) and scada devices (76, 2%).

Encryption algorithms. We check the use of vulnerable ciphers such as RC4 (see e.g., [18], RFC 7465), and 3DES (the recent Sweet32 attack [5]). Except infra. routers (96,433, 81.5%), the use of RC4 is relatively low in other devices (Fig. 4). Some Alexa sites still use RC4 (3.1%). Note that the ZGrab application scanner as used with ZMap includes RC4 as a supported cipher (in addition to ciphers included in the Chrome browser), to support older TLS servers. The use of 3DES is very limited overall, except in CPS devices (171, 19.7%). The use of ChaCha20-Poly1305 (currently being standardized, RFC 7905) as a replacement of RC4 is still negligible in devices.

TLS/SSL version. TLS 1.0 is mostly used in network devices (33,637, 84.4%) and printers (18,367, 82.4%), and TLS 1.1 in CPS (168, 19.4%); see Fig. 5. TLS 1.0 is vulnerable to the BEAST attack [12]. More seriously, many infra. routers (65,061, 55%) and media devices (175, 15.9%) use SSL 3.0 (vulnerable to the POODLE attack [23]). Surprisingly, 19,063 devices still support SSL 2.0 (deprecated in 2011, see RFC 6176). Top-5 such device types include: NAS (manufacturers: QNAP, NetGear, Synology; count: 5517), network (Cisco: 2006), printer (Lexmark, Sharp: 1812), camera (HikVision: 1324), and infra. router (Cisco: 1046). We do not include SSL 2.0 in Fig. 5 or other comparisons, as SSL 2.0 dataset is separately maintained by Censys.

5 Disclosure

The vulnerable devices we found are manufactured by hundreds of different companies; see Table 2. We have contacted the ones with many vulnerable devices, where we could locate contact emails, explaining our findings (Oct. 2016). As of writing, we got responses from Cisco, Honeywell, Hikvision, and Hewlett Packard – most claiming to have released software/firmware upgrades in the past, but apparently, users did not follow. Example responses include: [Honeywell] "This helps a

Table 2. Top 5 manufactures with vulnerable devices

Manufacturer	MD5	RC4	SSLv3	<RSA1024	Device types
Cisco	347	98,904	65,413	12,731	Network, infra. router
Hewlett-Packard	1	5214	1	13	Network, printer, scada, home router
AVM	78	5062	33	2	Modem
Hikvision	664	1085	214	75	Camera
QNAP	383	889	286	51	NAS

lot and as we have looked almost all of the systems you identified are "out of date" systems. Tridium/Honeywell released the patches to address your findings almost three years ago with follow on updates each year. The end users are not updating their systems to make them less vulnerable."

6   Limitations and Future Work

Certain statistics as extracted from Censys appear to be unusual. For example, there is only one infrastructure router from manufacturers, e.g., DrayTek and LinkSys; Hewlett-Packard appears to have only one device with MD5 and SSLv3. We communicated such observations to a Censys author, who attributed them to be possible limitations of the current Censys logic, or device misconfiguration. Also, the SQL engine in Censys is still evolving. Currently, it does not allow querying all device-related information in a flexible structural format from the data available in ZMap. We plan to extend the comparison including all IPv4 web servers, when data hygiene and structure of data improve in Censys.

Some TLS vulnerabilities may have no effect if the services are accessed within a local network (e.g., inside a private home network), or via a modern browser—e.g., no current browser would accept the RC4 cipher or SSL 2.0, even if offered by a server. As these devices are varied (unlike regular web servers), actual exploitation of their weaknesses will depend on how they are used/accessed. These seemingly obsolete attack vectors can also be revived in the presence of a vulnerable TLS proxy between a modern browser and the vulnerable server, such as an anti-virus proxy [11]; simply supporting SSL 2.0 can be exploited as well [4]. We hope our findings to raise awareness of this issue and positively influence the manufactures to push appropriate firmware upgrades (possibly with auto-update).

Acknowledgements. We thank anonymous FC 2017 and IMC 2016 reviewers for their insightful comments and suggestions, and Zakir Durumeric for helping us with Censys. We also appreciate the feedback we received from the members of Concordia's Madiba Security Research Group, especially, Xavier de Carné de Carnavalet. The second author is supported in part by an NSERC Discovery Grant.

References

1. Adrian, D., Bhargavan, K., Durumeric, Z., Gaudry, P., Green, M., Halderman, J.A., Heninger, N., Springall, D., Thomé, E., Valenta, L., VanderSloot, B., Wustrow, E., Zanella-Béguelink, S., Zimmermann, P.: Imperfect forward secrecy: how Diffie-Hellman fails in practice. In: CCS 2015, Denver, USA, October 2015
2. Arnaert, M., Bertrand, Y., Boudaoud, K.: Modeling vulnerable internet of things on SHODAN and CENSYS: an ontology for cyber security. In: SECUREWARE 2016, Nice, France, July 2016
3. ArsTechnica.com. Using IPv6 with Linux? you've likely been visited by Shodan and other scanners. News article, 1 February 2016

4. Aviram, N., Schinzel, S., Somorovsky, J., Heninger, N., Dankel, M., Steube, J., Valenta, L., Adrian, D., Halderman, J.A., Dukhovni, V., Käsper, E., Cohney, S., Engels, S., Paar, C., Shavitt, Y.: DROWN: breaking TLS using SSLv2. In: USENIX Security, Austin, USA, August 2016

5. Bhargavan, K., Leurent, G.: On the practical (in-)security of 64-bit block ciphers: collision attacks on HTTP over TLS and OpenVPN. In: CCS 2016, October 2016

6. Chung, T., Liu, Y., Choffnes, D., Levin, D., Maggs, B.M., Mislove, A., Wilson, C.: Measuring and applying invalid SSL certificates: the silent majority. In: IMC 2016 (2016)

7. Costin, A., Zaddach, J., Francillon, A., Balzarotti, D.: A large-scale analysis of the security of embedded firmwares. In: USENIX Security, August 2014

8. Costin, A., Zarras, A., Francillon, A.: Automated dynamic firmware analysis at scale: a case study on embedded web interfaces. In: ASIACCS 2016 (2016)

9. Cui, A., Costello, M., Stolfo, S.J.: When firmware modifications attack: a case study of embedded exploitation. In: NDSS 2013, San Diego, USA, February 2013

10. Cui, A., Stolfo, S.J.: A quantitative analysis of the insecurity of embedded network devices: results of a wide-area scan. In: ACSAC 2010, December 2010

11. de Carnavalet, X., Mannan, M.: Killed by proxy: analyzing client-end TLS interception software. In: NDSS 2016, San Diego, USA, February 2016

12. Duong, T., Rizzo, J.: Here come the ⊕ ninjas. Technical report, May 2011

13. Durumeric, Z., Adrian, D., Mirian, A., Bailey, M., Halderman, J.: A search engine backed by internet-wide scanning. In: CCS 2015, Denver, USA, October 2015

14. Durumeric, Z., Kasten, J., Adrian, D., Halderman, J.A., Bailey, M., Li, F., Weaver, N., Amann, J., Beekman, J., Payer, M., Paxson, V.: The matter of Heartbleed. In: IMC 2014, Vancouver, Canada, November 2014

15. Durumeric, Z., Kasten, J., Bailey, M.: Analysis of the HTTPS certificate ecosystem. In: IMC 2013, October 2013

16. Durumeric, Z., Wustrow, E., Halderman, J.A.: ZMap: fast internet-wide scanning and its security applications. In: USENIX Security, August 2013

17. Electronic Frontier Foundation. The EFF SSL observatory. https://www.eff.org/observatory

18. Garman, C., Paterson, K.G., Van der Merwe, T.: Attacks only get better: password recovery attacks against RC4 in TLS. In: USENIX Security, August 2015

19. Hastings, M., Fried, J., Heninger, N.: Weak keys remain widespread in network devices. In: IMC 2016, Santa Monica, USA, November 2016

20. Heninger, N., Durumeric, Z., Wustrow, E., Halderman, J.: Mining your Ps and Qs: detection of widespread weak keys in network devices. In: USENIX Security (2012)

21. Holz, R., Amann, J., Mehani, O., Wachs, M., Kaafar, M.A.: TLS in the wild: an internet-wide analysis of TLS-based protocols for electronic communication. In: NDSS 2016, San Diego, USA, February 2016

22. Lee, H., Malkin, T., Nahum, E.: Cryptographic strength of SSL/TLS servers. In: IMC 2007, San Diego, USA, October 2007

23. Möller, B., Duong, T., Kotowicz, K.: This POODLE bites: exploiting the SSL 3.0 fallback. Techical report, September 2014. https://www.openssl.org/bodo/ssl-poodle.pdf

24. Pa, Y.M.P., Suzuki, S., Yoshioka, K., Matsumoto, T., Kasama, T., Rossow, C.: IoTPOT: analysing the rise of IoT compromises. In: USENIX Security (2015)

25. ReadWrite.com. Dyn DDoS attack sheds new light on the growing IoT problem. News article, 24 October 2016

26. Ronen, E., O'Flynn, C., Shamir, A., Weingarten, A.-O.: IoT goes nuclear: creating a ZigBee chain reaction. Cryptology ePrint Archive, Report 2016/1047 (2016)

27. Samarasinghe, N., Mannan,M.: Short paper: TLS ecosystems in networked devices vs. web servers. Technical report 982186, Concordia University, February 2017. http://spectrum.library.concordia.ca/982186/

28. Stevens, M., Karpman, P., Peyrin, T.: Freestart collision for full SHA-1. In: Fischlin, M., Coron, J.-S. (eds.) EUROCRYPT 2016. LNCS, vol. 9665, pp. 459–483. Springer, Heidelberg (2016). https://doi.org/10.1007/978-3-662-49890-3_18

29. Stevens, M., Sotirov, A., Appelbaum, J., Lenstra, A., Molnar, D., Osvik, D.A., de Weger, B.: Short chosen-prefix collisions for MD5 and the creation of a Rogue CA certificate. In: Halevi, S. (ed.) CRYPTO 2009. LNCS, vol. 5677, pp. 55–69. Springer, Heidelberg (2009). https://doi.org/10.1007/978-3-642-03356-8_4

30. Wang, X., Yu, H.: How to break MD5 and other hash functions. In: Cramer, R. (ed.) EUROCRYPT 2005. LNCS, vol. 3494, pp. 19–35. Springer, Heidelberg (2005). https://doi.org/10.1007/11426639_2

Unilaterally-Authenticated Key Exchange

Yevgeniy Dodis[1] and Dario Fiore[2(✉)]

[1] Department of Computer Science, New York University, New York, USA
dodis@cs.nyu.edu
[2] IMDEA Software Institute, Madrid, Spain
dario.fiore@imdea.org

Abstract. Key Exchange (KE), which enables two parties (e.g., a client and a server) to securely establish a common private key while communicating over an insecure channel, is one of the most fundamental cryptographic primitives. In this work, we address the setting of *unilaterally-authenticated key exchange* (UAKE), where an unauthenticated (unkeyed) client establishes a key with an authenticated (keyed) server. This setting is highly motivated by many practical uses of KE on the Internet, but received relatively little attention so far.

Unlike the prior work, defining UAKE by downgrading a relatively complex definition of *mutually authenticated* key exchange (MAKE), our definition follows the opposite approach of upgrading existing definitions of public key encryption (PKE) and signatures towards UAKE. As a result, our new definition is short and easy to understand. Nevertheless, we show that it is *equivalent* to the UAKE definition of Bellare-Rogaway (when downgraded from MAKE), and thus captures a very strong and widely adopted security notion, while looking very similar to the simple "one-oracle" definition of traditional PKE/signature schemes. As a benefit of our intuitive framework, we show two *exactly-as-you-expect* (i.e., having no caveats so abundant in the KE literature!) UAKE protocols from (possibly interactive) signature and encryption. By plugging various one- or two-round signature and encryption schemes, we derive provably-secure variants of various well-known UAKE protocols (such as a unilateral variant of SKEME with and without perfect forward secrecy, and Shoup's A-DHKE-1), as well as new protocols, such as the first 2-round UAKE protocol which is both (passively) forward deniable and forward-secure.

To further clarify the intuitive connections between PKE/Signatures and UAKE, we define and construct stronger forms of (necessarily interactive) PKE/Signature schemes, called *confirmed encryption* and *confidential authentication*, which, respectively, allow the sender to obtain confirmation that the (keyed) receiver output the correct message, or to hide the content of the message being authenticated from anybody but the participating (unkeyed) receiver. Using confirmed PKE/confidential authentication, we obtain two concise UAKE protocols of the form: "send confirmed encryption/confidential authentication of a random key K."

A. Kiayias (Ed.): FC 2017, LNCS 10322, pp. 542–560, 2017.
https://doi.org/10.1007/978-3-319-70972-7_31

1 Introduction

Key exchange (KE) is one of the most fundamental cryptographic primitives. Using a KE protocol, two parties can securely establish a common, private, cryptographic key while communicating over an insecure channel. Although the basic idea of KE dates back to the seminal work of Diffie and Hellman [7], a proper formalization of this notion was proposed only much later by Bellare and Rogaway [2]. In particular, Bellare and Rogaway considered the problem of *mutually authenticated* key exchange where two parties (e.g., a client and a server), each holding a valid long-term key pair, want to agree on a fresh common cryptographic key, while being assured about the identity of their protocol's partner. In [2], Bellare and Rogaway proposed a model for mutually-authenticated KE which allows to formally define security in this context, and in particular formalizes the adversary's capabilities in a proper way.

Building on this remarkable work, many other papers addressed KE in multiple directions, such as efficient and provably-secure realizations [15], or alternative security models [1,5,6]. Notably, the vast majority of papers in this area considered only the mutually authenticated setting where *both* the server and the client have long-term keys. However, it is striking to observe that many practical uses of KE protocols on the Internet work in a restricted setting where only the server has a long-term (certified) public key. A notable example of this setting is perhaps the simple access to web servers using the well known SSL/TLS protocol. This notion of KE has been often called *unilaterally-authenticated* (or, sometimes, anonymous, one-way or server-only) KE. To emphasize the distinction, in our work we will denote unilaterally-authenticated KE as *UAKE*, and mutually-authenticated KE as *MAKE*.

In spite of the practical relevance of unilaterally-authenticated key-exchange, we notice that most prior KE definitions targeted MAKE, and those works that focused on UAKE (e.g., [10,11,17,21]) used definitions that were obtained by slightly "downgrading" definitions of MAKE to the unilateral setting. The problem here is that existing definitions of MAKE are rigorous, but also pretty complex and hard to digest. Therefore, when analyzing the simple notion of UAKE by downgrading existing definitions of MAKE, one ends up with other complex definitions.

One goal of this work is thus to address this state of affairs by taking a different approach. Instead of considering UAKE as a downgraded version of MAKE, we propose a new definition of UAKE obtained by slightly "upgrading" the short and simple definitions of public key encryption and digital signatures. Precisely, we build on the recent work of Dodis and Fiore [8] that proposes a definitional framework for interactive message transmission protocols, and gives new notions of *interactive* public key encryption (PKE) and interactive public key message authentication (PKMA). These two notions naturally extend the classical notions of IND-CCA encryption(resp. strongly unforgeable signatures) to the interactive setting. By building on this framework, we obtain a UAKE definition which is (in our opinion) more intuitive and easier to digest.[1] Nevertheless, we show that our differently-looking UAKE definition is *equivalent* to the one of Bellare-Rogaway (BR) restricted to the single authenticated setting. This shows that we are not providing a new KE notion, but simply suggesting a different, simpler, way to explain the same notion when restricted to the unilateral setting. In fact, the BR UAKE definition "downgraded-from-MAKE" is actually noticeably simpler than the MAKE definition, but still (in our opinion) not as intuitive as our new definition. Hence, by establishing our equivalence, we offer a new path of teaching/understanding MAKE: (1) present our definition of UAKE, and use it to design and prove simple UAKE protocols (see below); (2) point out new subtleties of MAKE, making it hard (impossible?) to have a simple "one-oracle" definition of MAKE; (3) introduce the "downgraded" BR-framework (which has more finer-grain oracles available to the attacker) which is equivalent to our UAKE framework; (4) extend the "downgraded" BR framework to the full setting of MAKE. **We view this philosophy as a major educational contribution of this work.**

In the following, we describe our definitional framework and the remaining results (including simple and intuitive UAKE protocols) in more detail.

1.1   Our Results

DEFINITIONAL FRAMEWORK. The definitional framework proposed by Dodis and Fiore [8] consists of two parts. The first part is *independent* of the particular primitive, and simply introduces the bare minimum of notions/notation to deal with interaction. For example, they define (a) what it means to have *concurrent* oracle access to an *interactive party* under attack; and (b) what it means to 'act as a wire' between two honest parties (this trivial, but unavoidable, attack is called a 'ping-pong' attack). Once the notation is developed, the actual definitions become *as short and simple as in the non-interactive setting* (e.g., see Definitions 5 and 6). So, by building on this framework, we propose a simple notion of UAKE (cf. Definition 8) which we briefly discuss now. The attacker $\mathcal{A}$ has *concurrent* oracle access to the honest secret key owner (the "server"), and simultaneously tries to establish a (wlog single) session key with an honest unauthenticated client (the "challenger"). If the challenger rejects, $\mathcal{A}$ 'lost'.[2] If it accepts and the session is *not* a ping-pong of one of its conversations with the server, then $\mathcal{A}$ 'won', since it 'fooled' the challenger without trivially forwarding messages from the honest server. Otherwise, if $\mathcal{A}$ established a valid key with the

---

[1] We stress, we are not suggesting that we can similarly simplify the more complicated definitions of MAKE. In fact, we believe that UAKE is *inherently easier* than MAKE, which is precisely why we managed to obtain our simpler definition only for UAKE.

[2] Notice, since anybody can establish a key with the server, to succeed $\mathcal{A}$ must establish the key with an honest client.

challenger by a ping-pong attack, $\mathcal{A}$ 'wins' if it can distinguish a (well-defined) 'real' session key from a completely random key.[3]

KEY EXCHANGE PROTOCOLS. As we mentioned, our unilaterally-authenticated key-exchange (UAKE) definition can be seen as a natural extension of the interactive PKE/PKMA definitions in [8]. As a result, we show two simple and very natural constructions of UAKE protocols: from any possibly interactive PKE scheme and a PRF, depicted in Fig. 2, and from any possibly interactive PKMA scheme and CPA-secure key encapsulation mechanism (KEM), depicted in Fig. 3. By plugging various non-interactive or 2-round PKE/PKMA schemes (and KEMs, such as the classical Diffie-Hellman KE), we get a variety of simple and natural UAKE protocols. For example, we re-derive the A-DHKE-1 protocol from [21], the unilateral version of the SKEME protocol [14], and we get (to the best of our knowledge) the first 2-round UAKE, depicted in Fig. 4, which is both forward-deniable and forward-secure.

Hence, the main contribution of our work is not to design new UAKE protocols (which we still do due to the generality of our results!), but rather to have a simple and intuitive UAKE framework where *everything works as expected, without any caveats* (so abundant in the traditional KE literature). Namely, the fact that immediate corollaries of our work easily establish well known and widely used UAKE protocols is a big feature of our approach. Unlike prior work, however, our protocols: (1) work with *interactive* PKE/PKMA; (2) are directly analyzed in the unilateral setting using our simple definition, instead of being "downgraded" from more complex MAKE protocols.

CONFIRMED PKE AND CONFIDENTIAL PKMA. To provide a further smoother transition from basic notions of PKE/PKMA towards KE, another contribution of our work is to define two strengthenings of PKE/PKMA which inherently require interaction. We call these notions *confirmed encryption* and *confidential authentication*, but for lack of space we present them in the full version of this work. In brief, confirmed encryption is an extension of the interactive encryption notion of Dodis and Fiore [8] in which the (unkeyed) sender gets a confirmation that the (keyed) receiver obtained the correct encrypted message, and thus accepts/rejects accordingly. Confidential authentication, instead, adds a privacy property to PKMA protocols [8] in such a way that no information about the message is leakèd to adversaries controlling the communication channel (and, yet, the unkeyed honest receiver gets the message). Clearly, both notions require interaction, and we show both can be realized quite naturally with (optimal) two rounds of interaction. Moreover, these two notions provide two modular and "dual" ways to build secure UAKE protocols. Namely, we further abstract our UAKE constructions in Figs. 2 and 3 by using the notions of confirmed PKE and confidential PKMA, by showing that "confirmed encryption of random K" and "confidential authentication of random K" both yield secure UAKE protocols.

---

[3] Notice, for elegance sake our basic definition does not demand advanced properties, such as forward security or deniability, but (as we show) can be easily extended to do so. Indeed, our goal was not to get the most 'advanced' KE definition, but rather to get a strong and useful definition which is short, intuitive, and easy to digest.

SUMMARY. Although we do not claim a special novelty in showing a connection between PKE/signatures and KE, we believe that the novelty of our contribution is to formally state such connection in a general and intuitive way. In particular, our work shows a path from traditional non-interactive PKE/PKMA schemes, to interactive PKE/PKMA, to (interactive) confirmed PKE/confidential PKMA, to UAKE, to MAKE (where the latter two steps use the equivalence of our simple "one-oracle" definition with the downgraded Bellare-Rogaway definition). Given that unilaterally-authenticated key-exchange, aside from independent interest, already introduces many of the subtleties of mutually-authenticated key-exchange (MAKE), we hope our work can therefore simplify the introduction of MAKE to students. Indeed, we believe all our results can be easily taught in an undergraduate cryptography course.

1.2 Related Work

Following the work of Bellare and Rogaway [2], several works proposed different security definitions for (mutually-authenticated) KE, e.g., [1,3–5,18]. Notably, some of these works focused on achieving secure composition properties [6,21]. Unilaterally-Authenticated Key-Exchange has been previously considered by Shoup [21] (who used the term "anonymous key-exchange"), Goldberg et al. [11] (in the context of Tor), Fiore et al. [10] (in the identity-based setting), and by Jager et al. [12] and Krawczyk et al. [17] (in the context of TLS). All these works arrived at unilaterally-authenticated key-exchange by following essentially the same approach: they started from (some standard definitions of) mutually-authenticated KE, and then they relaxed this notion by introducing one "dummy" user which can run the protocol without any secret (so, the unauthenticated party will run the protocol on behalf of such user), and by slightly changing the party-corruption condition.

Our authentication- (but not encryption-) based UAKE protocols also have conceptual similarities with the authenticator-based design of KE protocols by Bellare et al. [1]. Namely, although [1] concentrate on the mutually-authenticated setting, our UAKE of Fig. 3 is similar to what can be obtained by applying a (unilateral) authenticator to an unauthenticated protocol, such as a one-time KEM. As explained in Sect. 4, however, the derived protocols are not exactly the same. This is because there are noticeable differences between authenticators and interactive PKMA schemes. For example, authenticators already require security against replay attack (and, thus, standard signature schemes *by themselves* are not good authenticators), and also use a very different real/ideal definition than our simple game-based definition of PKMA. In summary, while the concrete protocols obtained are similar (but not identical), the two works use very different definitions and construction paths to arrive at these similar protocols.

In a concurrent and independent work, Maurer, Tackmann and Coretti [20] considers the problem of providing new definitions of unilateral KE, and they do so by building on the constructive cryptography paradigm of Maurer and Renner [19]. Using this approach, they proposed a protocol which is based only on a CPA-secure KEM and an unforgeable digital signature, and is very similar to one of our UAKE protocols.

Finally, we note that a recent paper by Krawczyk [16] considers unilaterally authenticated key exchange and studies the question of building compilers for transforming UAKE protocols into MAKE ones.

2   Background and Definitions

In our paper we use relatively standard notation. Before giving the definitions of message transmission protocols and unilateral key exchange, we discuss two aspects of our definitions.

Session IDs. Throughout this paper, we consider various protocols (e.g., message transmission or key exchange) that may be run concurrently many times between the same two parties. In order to distinguish one execution of a protocol from another, one typically uses session identifiers, denoted sid, of which we can find two main uses in the literature. The first one is to consider purely "administrative" session identifiers, that are used by a user running multiple session to differentiate between them, i.e., to associate what session a message is going to or coming from. This means that the honest parties need some concrete mechanism to ensure the uniqueness of sid's, when honestly running multiple concurrent sessions. E.g., administrative sid can be a simple counter or any other nonce (perhaps together with any information necessary for communication, such as IP addresses or some mutually agreed upon timing information), or could be jointly selected by the parties, by each party providing some part of the sid. However, rather than force some particular choice which will complicate the notation, while simultaneously getting the strongest possible security definition, in our definitions we let the adversary *completely control* all the administrative sid's (as the adversary anyway controls all the protocol scheduling). In order not to clutter the notation with this trivial lower level detail, in our work *we will ignore such administrative* sid*'s from our notation*, but instead implicitly model them as stated above.

The second use of session identifiers in the literature is more technical as sid's are used in security definitions in order to define "benign" adversaries that simply act as a wire in the network. With respect to the use of sid's in security definitions we see three main approaches in the literature. The modern KE approach lets parties define sid's as part of the protocol. While this is more relaxed and allows for more protocols to be proven secure, it also somewhat clutters the notation as the choice of the sid is now part of the protocol specification. The second approach is to let sid be the transcript of a protocol execution, which simplifies the notation and implies the previous approach. In both the first and second approach, benign adversaries are those that cause two sessions have *equal* sid's. The third approach instead does not use explicit sid's, and considers benign adversaries those that cause two sessions have same transcript (seen as a "timed object"). All the approaches have pros and cons. For example, both the second and the third approach rule out some good protocols, but save on syntax and notation. Moreover, the third approach is the strongest one for security: it leaves to protocol implementers the freedom of picking the most convenient "administrative" sid selection mechanism, without worrying about security, since in this model adversaries can arbitrarily control the administrative sid's. For these reasons, in this work we follow the third approach, which also gives us the possibility of making our definitions more in line with those of PKE/signatures, where there are no explicit session identifiers.

Party Identities. Unlike the traditional setting of encryption and authentication, in the KE literature parties usually have external (party) identities in addition to their public/secret keys. This allows the same party to (claim to) have multiple keys, or, conversely, the same key for multiple identities. While generality is quite useful in the mutually authenticated setting, and could be easily added to all our definitions and results in the unilateral setting, we decided to avoid this extra layer of notation. Instead, we implicitly set the identity of the party to be its public key (in case of the server), or null (in case of the client). Aside from simpler notation, this allowed us to make our definitions look very similar to traditional PKE/signatures, which was one of our goals. We remark that this is a trivial and inessential choice which largely follows a historic tradition for PKE/PKMA. Indeed, having party identities is equally meaningful for traditional PKE/PKMA schemes, but is omitted from the syntax, because it can always be trivially achieved by appending the identities of the sender and/or recipient to the message. We stress, we do not assume any key registration authority who checks knowledge of secret keys. In fact, in our definition the attacker pretends to be the owner of the victim's secret key (while having oracle access to the victim), much like in PKE/PKMA the attacker tries to "impersonate" the honest party (signer/decryptor) with only oracle access to this party.

2.1 Message Transmission Protocols

In this section, we recall the definitional framework of *message transmission protocols* as defined in [8], along with suitable security definitions for confidentiality (called iCCA security) and authenticity (called iCMA security).

A message transmission protocol involves two parties, a sender S and a receiver R, such that the goal of S is to send a message m to R while preserving certain security properties on m. Formally, a message transmission protocol Π consists of algorithms (Setup, S, R) defined as follows:

Setup(1^λ): on input the security parameter λ, the setup algorithm generates a pair of keys (sendk, recvk). In particular, these keys contain an implicit description of the message space $\mathcal{M}$.

S(sendk, m): is a possibly interactive Turing machine that is run with the sender key sendk and a message $m \in \mathcal{M}$ as private inputs.

R(recvk): is a possibly interactive Turing machine that takes as private input the receiver key recvk, and whose output is a message $m \in \mathcal{M}$ or an error symbol $\perp$.

We say that Π is an n-round protocol if the number of messages exchanged between S and R during a run of the protocol is n. If Π is 1-round, then we say that Π is *non-interactive*. Since the sender has no output, it is assumed without loss of generality that the S *always speaks last*. This means that in an n-round protocol, R (resp. S) speaks first if n is even (resp. odd). For compact notation, $\langle S(\mathsf{sendk}, m), R(\mathsf{recvk}) \rangle = m'$ denotes the process of running S and R on inputs (sendk, m) and recvk respectively, and assigning R's output to m'. In our notation, we will use $m \in \mathcal{M}$ for messages (aka plaintexts), and capital M for protocol messages.

Definition 1 (Correctness). *A message transmission protocol* $\Pi = ($Setup, S, R$)$ *is correct if for all honestly generated keys* $(\mathsf{sendk}, \mathsf{recvk}) \xleftarrow{\$} \mathsf{Setup}(1^\lambda)$, *and all messages* $m \in \mathcal{M}$, *we have that* $\langle S(\mathsf{sendk}, m), R(\mathsf{recvk}) \rangle = m$ *holds with all but negligible probability.*

Defining Security: Man-in-the-Middle Adversaries. Here we recall the formalism needed to define the security of message transmission protocols. The basic idea is that an adversary with full control of the communication channel has to violate a given security property (say confidentiality or authenticity) in a run of the protocol that is called the *challenge session*. Formally, this session is a protocol execution $\langle S(\mathsf{sendk}, m), \mathcal{A}^{R(\mathsf{recvk})} \rangle$ or $\langle \mathcal{A}^{S(\mathsf{sendk},\cdot)}, R(\mathsf{recvk}) \rangle$ where the adversary runs with an honest party (S or R). $\mathcal{A}^P$ denotes that the adversary has oracle access to *multiple* honest copies of party P (where $P = R$ or $P = S$), i.e., $\mathcal{A}$ can start as many copies of P as it wishes, and it can run the message transmission protocol with each of these copies. In order to differentiate between several copies of P, formally $\mathcal{A}$ calls the oracle providing a session identifier sid. However, as mentioned earlier, to keep notation simple we do not write sid explicitly. The model assumes that whenever $\mathcal{A}$ sends a message to the oracle P, then $\mathcal{A}$ always obtains P's output. In particular, in the case of the receiver oracle, when $\mathcal{A}$ sends the last protocol message to R, $\mathcal{A}$ obtains the (private) output of the receiver, i.e., a message m or $\perp$.

Due to its power, the adversary might entirely replay the challenge session by using its oracle. Since this can constitute a trivial attack to the protocol, in what follows we recall the formalism of [8] to capture replay attacks. The approach is similar to the one introduced by Bellare and Rogaway [2] in the context of key exchange, based on the idea of "matching conversations".

Let t be a global counter which is progressively incremented every time a party (including the adversary) sends a message. Every message sent by a party (S, R or $\mathcal{A}$) is timestamped with the current time t. Using this notion of time,[4] the transcript of a protocol session is defined as follows:

Definition 2 (Protocol Transcript). *The transcript of a protocol session between two parties is the timestamped sequence of messages (including both sent and received messages) viewed by a party during a run of the message*

---

[4] We stress that timestamps are only used in the security definition; in particular they are not used by real-world parties.

transmission protocol Π. *If* Π *is n-round, then a transcript* T *is of the form* $T = \langle (M_1, t_1), \ldots, (M_n, t_n) \rangle$, *where* $M_1, \ldots, M_n$ *are the exchanged messages, and* $t_1, \ldots, t_n$ *are the respective timestamps.*

In a protocol run $\langle \mathsf{S}(\mathsf{sendk}, m), \mathcal{A}^{\mathsf{R}(\mathsf{recvk})} \rangle$ (resp. $\langle \mathcal{A}^{\mathsf{S}(\mathsf{sendk}, \cdot)}, \mathsf{R}(\mathsf{recvk}) \rangle$) we denote by T^* the transcript of the challenge session between S and $\mathcal{A}$ (resp. $\mathcal{A}$ and R), whereas $T_1, \ldots, T_Q$ are the Q transcripts of the sessions established by $\mathcal{A}$ with R (resp. S) via the oracle.

Definition 3 (Matching Transcripts). *Let* $T = \langle (M_1, t_1), \ldots, (M_n, t_n) \rangle$ *and* $T^* = \langle (M_1^*, t_1^*), \ldots, (M_n^*, t_n^*) \rangle$ *be two protocol transcripts. We say that* T *matches* T^* ($T \subseteq T^*$, *for short) if* $\forall i = 1, \ldots, n$, $M_i = M_i^*$ *and the two timestamp sequences are "alternating", i.e.,* $t_1 < t_1^* < t_2^* < t_2 < t_3 < \cdots < t_{n-1} < t_n < t_n^*$ *if* R *speaks first, or* $t_1^* < t_1 < t_2 < t_2^* < t_3^* < \cdots < t_{n-1} < t_n < t_n^*$ *if* S *speaks first. Note that the notion of match is not commutative.*

Using the above definitions, we recall the notion of ping-pong adversary:

Definition 4 (Ping-pong Adversary). *Consider a run of the protocol* Π *involving* $\mathcal{A}$ *and an honest party (it can be either* $\langle \mathsf{S}(\mathsf{sendk}, m), \mathcal{A}^{\mathsf{R}(\mathsf{recvk})} \rangle$ *or* $\langle \mathcal{A}^{\mathsf{S}(\mathsf{sendk}, \cdot)}, \mathsf{R}(\mathsf{recvk}) \rangle$), *and let* T^* *be the transcript of the challenge session, and* $T_1, \ldots, T_Q$ *be the transcripts of all the oracle sessions established by* $\mathcal{A}$. *Then we say that* $\mathcal{A}$ *is a* ping-pong adversary *if there is a transcript* $T \in \{T_1, \ldots, T_Q\}$ *such that* T *matches* T^*, *i.e.,* $T \subseteq T^*$.

Now that we have introduced all the necessary definitions, we recall the two notions of interactive chosen-ciphertext PKE (iCCA) and interactive chosen-message secure PKMA (iCMA) that capture, respectively, confidentiality and authenticity of the messages sent by S to R. Let $\Pi = (\mathsf{Setup}, \mathsf{S}, \mathsf{R})$ be a message transmission protocol, and $\mathcal{A}$ be an adversary. The two notions are defined as follows by considering the experiments in Fig. 1.

Experiment $\mathbf{Exp}_{\Pi, \mathcal{A}}^{\mathsf{iCCA}}(\lambda)$	Experiment $\mathbf{Exp}_{\Pi, \mathcal{A}}^{\mathsf{iCMA}}(\lambda)$
$b \xleftarrow{\$} \{0, 1\}$; $(\mathsf{sendk}, \mathsf{recvk}) \xleftarrow{\$} \mathsf{Setup}(1^\lambda)$	$(\mathsf{sendk}, \mathsf{recvk}) \xleftarrow{\$} \mathsf{Setup}(1^\lambda)$
$(m_0, m_1) \leftarrow \mathcal{A}^{\mathsf{R}(\mathsf{recvk})}(\mathsf{sendk})$	$m^* \leftarrow \langle \mathcal{A}^{\mathsf{S}(\mathsf{sendk}, \cdot)}(\mathsf{recvk}), \mathsf{R}(\mathsf{recvk}) \rangle$
$b' \leftarrow \langle \mathsf{S}(\mathsf{sendk}, m_b), \mathcal{A}^{\mathsf{R}(\mathsf{recvk})}(\mathsf{sendk}) \rangle$	If $m^* \neq \bot$ and $\mathcal{A}$ is not "ping-pong",
If $\mathcal{A}$ is "ping-pong",	then output 1
then output $\tilde{b} \xleftarrow{\$} \{0, 1\}$	Else output 0.
Else if $b' = b$ and $\mathcal{A}$ is not "ping-pong",	
then output 1	
Else output 0.	

Fig. 1. Security experiments of iCCAand iCMAsecurity.

Definition 5 (iCCA security). *For any* $\lambda \in \mathbb{N}$, *we define the advantage of an adversary* $\mathcal{A}$ *in breaking* iCCA *security of a message transmission protocol* Π *as* $\mathbf{Adv}_{\Pi, \mathcal{A}}^{\mathsf{iCCA}}(\lambda) = \Pr[\mathbf{Exp}_{\Pi, \mathcal{A}}^{\mathsf{iCCA}}(\lambda) = 1] - \frac{1}{2}$, *and we say that* Π *is* iCCA-*secure if for any PPT* $\mathcal{A}$, $\mathbf{Adv}_{\Pi, \mathcal{A}}^{\mathsf{iCCA}}(\lambda)$ *is negligible.*

Note that for 1-round protocols, the above notion is the same as the classical IND-CCA security.

Definition 6 (iCMA security). *For any $\lambda \in \mathbb{N}$, the advantage of $\mathcal{A}$ in breaking the iCMA security of a message transmission protocol Π is $\mathbf{Adv}_{\Pi,\mathcal{A}}^{\mathrm{iCMA}}(\lambda) = \Pr[\mathbf{Exp}_{\Pi,\mathcal{A}}^{\mathrm{iCMA}}(\lambda) = 1]$, and we say that Π is iCMA-secure if for any PPT $\mathcal{A}$, $\mathbf{Adv}_{\Pi,\mathcal{A}}^{\mathrm{iCMA}}(\lambda)$ is negligible.*

Note that for 1-round protocols, the above notion is the same as the notion of strong unforgeability for digital signatures.

3 Unilaterally-Authenticated Key-Exchange

In this section we build on the notions of iCCA/iCMA secure message transmission protocols recalled in the previous section in order to obtain a smoother and clean transition from encryption/authentication towards key exchange. In particular, in this work we focus on *unilaterally-authenticated key-exchange* (UAKE, for short). UAKE is a weaker form of mutually-authenticated key-exchange in which only one of the two protocol parties is authenticated.

Following the definitional framework of message transmission protocols [8], we define UAKE as a protocol between two parties—in this case, an un keyed user U and a keyed (aka authenticated) user T—so that, at the end of a successful protocol run, both parties (privately) output a common session key.

Formally, a UAKE protocol Π consists of algorithms (KESetup, U, T) working as follows:

KESetup(1^λ): on input the security parameter λ, the setup algorithm generates a pair of keys (uk, tk). Implicitly, it also defines a session key space $\mathcal{K}$.

U(uk): is a possibly interactive algorithm that takes as input the public key uk of the authenticated user, and outputs a session key or a symbol $\perp$.

T(tk): is a possibly interactive algorithm that takes as input the private key tk, and outputs a session key K or an error symbol $\perp$.

In our security definitions we explicitly include the property that U terminates correctly (i.e., no $\perp$ output) only if U gets confirmation that T can terminate correctly. For this reason, we assume without loss of generality that T *always speaks last*. For compact notation, we denote with $\langle \mathsf{U}(\mathsf{uk}), \mathsf{T}(\mathsf{tk}) \rangle = (\mathsf{K_U}, \mathsf{K_T})$ a run of the protocol in which U and T output session keys $\mathsf{K_U}$ and $\mathsf{K_T}$ respectively.

Definition 7 (Correctness). *An unilaterally-authenticated key-exchange protocol $\Pi = (\mathsf{KESetup}, \mathsf{U}, \mathsf{T})$ is correct if for all honestly generated key pairs (uk, tk) $\xleftarrow{\$}$ KESetup(1^λ), and all session keys $\langle \mathsf{U}(\mathsf{uk}), \mathsf{T}(\mathsf{tk}) \rangle = (\mathsf{K_U}, \mathsf{K_T})$, we have that, when $\mathsf{K_U}, \mathsf{K_T} \neq \perp$, $\mathsf{K_U} = \mathsf{K_T}$ holds with all but negligible probability.*

Security. For UAKE protocols we aim at formalizing two main security properties: *authenticity* and *confidentiality*. Intuitively, authenticity says that the only way for an adversary to make the un-keyed party terminate correctly (no $\perp$ output) is to be ping-pong. Confidentiality aims to capture that, once the un-keyed party U accepted, then the adversary cannot learn any information about the session key (unless it is ping-pong up to learning the key). We formalize these two properties in a single experiment in which $\mathcal{A}$ runs a challenge session with the un-keyed party U while having access to the keyed party T. As for the case for message transmission protocols, the adversary formally refers to the keyed party T oracle by specifying a session id sid. For simplicity of notation, however we do not write explicitly these session identifiers.

Since in UAKE T speaks last, we allow the adversary to make one additional query to T after T generated the last message: in this case T reveals its private output K_T. If $\mathcal{A}$ makes such an additional query in a ping-pong session then we say that $\mathcal{A}$ is *"full-ping-pong"*.

Although the resulting experiment looks a bit more complex compared to the ones of iCCA and iCMA security, we stress that it can be seen as a natural combination of these two security notions. At a high level, the experiment consists in first running $(K_0, \cdot) \leftarrow \langle U(uk), \mathcal{A}^{T(tk)}(uk) \rangle$ and then analyzing U's output K_0 ($\cdot$ means that we do not care about $\mathcal{A}$'s output at this stage). If $K_0 \neq \perp$ and $\mathcal{A}$ is *not* ping-pong, then $\mathcal{A}$ wins (it broke authenticity). Otherwise, we give to $\mathcal{A}$ a real-or-random key K_b and $\mathcal{A}$ wins if it can tell these two cases apart *without*, of course, pushing the ping-pong attack up to getting K_0 revealed from the oracle T. Notice that when $K_0 = \perp$ (i.e., the honest sender did not accept in the challenge session), we also set $K_1 = \perp$. This is meant to capture that if U does not accept, then there is no common session key established by the two parties (essentially, no secure channel will be established). In this case the adversary will have no better chances of winning the game than guessing b.

Experiment $\mathbf{Exp}_{\Pi, \mathcal{A}}^{\mathsf{UAKE-Sec}}(\lambda)$

   $(uk, tk) \xleftarrow{\$} \mathsf{KESetup}(1^\lambda); b \xleftarrow{\$} \{0, 1\}$
   $(K_0, \cdot) \leftarrow \langle U(uk), \mathcal{A}^{T(tk)}(uk) \rangle$
   If $K_0 = \perp$, then $K_1 = \perp$
   Else if $K_0 \neq \perp$ and $\mathcal{A}$ is not "ping-pong", then output 1
   Else $K_1 \xleftarrow{\$} \mathcal{K}$
   $b' \leftarrow \mathcal{A}^{T(tk)}(K_b)$
   If $\mathcal{A}$ is "full-ping-pong", then output $\tilde{b} \xleftarrow{\$} \{0, 1\}$
   Else if $b' = b$ and $\mathcal{A}$ is not "full-ping-pong", then output 1
   Else output 0.

Definition 8 (Security of UAKE). *We define the advantage of an adversary $\mathcal{A}$ in breaking the security of* Π *as* $\mathbf{Adv}_{\Pi, \mathcal{A}}^{\mathsf{UAKE-Sec}}(\lambda) = \left| \Pr[\mathbf{Exp}_{\Pi, \mathcal{A}}^{\mathsf{UAKE-Sec}}(\lambda) = 1] - \frac{1}{2} \right|$, *and we say that a UAKE protocol* Π *is secure if for any PPT $\mathcal{A}$,* $\mathbf{Adv}_{\Pi, \mathcal{A}}^{\mathsf{UAKE-Sec}}(\lambda)$ *is negligible.*

MULTI-USER EXTENSION OF OUR NOTION. While we defined unilaterally-authenticated key-exchange in the single-user setting, we stress that the definition easily extends to the multi-user setting. The reason is that in our notion there is only one keyed user, T. So, when considering the multi-user setting with keyed users $T_1, \ldots, T_n$, we can assume that an adversary attacking a given T_j could simulate the keys of all remaining users $T_i \neq T_j$. In contrast, such an extension is not equally straightforward in MAKE, where, for example, the adversary could choose arbitrary keys for one of the two parties in the challenge session. We also refer the interested reader to [17] for a discussion on the multi-user extension of UAKE.

SINGLE-CHALLENGE VS. MULTIPLE CHALLENGES. Similarly to CCA-secure encryption and other privacy primitives, our attacker has only a single challenge session. Using a standard hybrid argument, this is asymptotically equivalent to the multi-challenge extension of our notion (with all challenge sessions sharing the same challenge bit b). We stress, however, that *single-challenge does not mean single oracle access to* T. Indeed, the attacker $\mathcal{A}^\mathsf{T}$ can start *arbitrarily many interleaved sessions with the keyed user* T, both before and after receiving the (single) challenge K_b. In particular, any UAKE protocol where one can recover the secret key tk given (multiple) oracle access to T will never be secure according to our definition, as then the attacker will trivially win the (single) challenge session by simulating honest T.

RELATION WITH EXISTING DEFINITIONS. As we mentioned earlier in this section, the notion of UAKE has been considered in prior work with different definitions. Notably, two recent works [12,13,17] use a definition (Server only Authenticated and Confidential Channel Establishment – SACCE) which formally captures whether a party accepts or not in a protocol session, and requires that the adversary $\mathcal{A}$ should not let the party accept if $\mathcal{A}$ does not correctly relay messages. If we compare our security definition of UAKE given above and the SACCE notion, we then observe the following main facts. (i) Our notion of ping-pong is stronger than the notion of matching conversations used in SACCE in that ping-pong takes into account the timing of the messages included in the transcripts. (ii) While UAKE and SACCE are very similar w.r.t. capturing the authenticity property, they instead *differ w.r.t. confidentiality*. In particular, our notion aims to capture indistinguishability of the keys, whereas SACCE aims to capture the security of the channel built by using the established session key. As observed in [12], the latter security notion is weaker than mere session key indistinguishability, and might thus be realized from weaker assumptions.

Finally, we formally consider the relation between our security notion of UAKE and the security notion obtained by downgrading the Bellare-Rogaway [2] definition for mutually-authenticated key exchange to the case of a single authenticated party. Although the two definitions use a slightly different formalism, below we show that the notions are essentially the same. The interested reader can see the full version of this work for the Bellare-Rogaway security definition.

The motivation of proving the equivalence to the BR model is to show that our notion does not weaken existing, well studied notions, and can in fact be used in place of them. Indeed, we believe our notion is shorter and more intuitive to work with, as we illustrate in this work. It is worth noting that this is not surprising. Overall, the one-way authenticated setting is simpler than the mutually-authenticated one as there are fewer attacks to be modeled. For example, in UAKE the security definition can involve only one long-term key, and some advanced security properties such as *key-compromise impersonation* no longer apply to the unilateral setting. In other words, this equivalence gives the opportunity of modeling UAKE using our definition, and perhaps using the equivalence to BR as a transition towards the more complex MAKE definition.

Theorem 1. Π *is a secure UAKE protocol if and only if* Π *is secure in the (unilateral version of) Bellare-Rogaway model.*

For lack of space the proof appears in the full version.

UNIQUENESS OF MATCHING TRANSCRIPT. It is interesting to note that our security definition implies that for any secure protocol there can be *at most one* matching transcript. This for instance means that it is hard for an adversary to force two distinct protocol sessions (in which one of the two parties is honest) to have the same session key.[5] Bellare and Rogaway prove in [2] that such property is achieved by any protocol secure according to their (mutually-authenticated) definition. By the equivalence of our UAKE notion to BR security one might be tempted to conclude that this uniqueness property holds for UAKE-secure protocols as well. This is only partially true as the proof in [2] is done for the mutually-authenticated case, and in particular one case of the proof uses the fact mutually-authenticated (BR-secure) protocols require at least 3 rounds. Below we give a separate proof of this statement for UAKE protocols (the proof appears in the full version)

Proposition 1. *Let* MultipleMatch *be the event that in a run of* $\mathbf{Exp}_{\Pi,\mathcal{A}}^{\mathsf{UAKE-Sec}}(\lambda)$ $\mathcal{A}$ *is ping-pong and there are at least two sessions* i *and* j*, with transcripts* T_i *and* T_j*, such that both* $T_i \subseteq T^*$ *and* $T_j \subseteq T^*$*. Then if* Π *is a secure UAKE protocol,* $\Pr[\mathsf{MultipleMatch}]$ *is negligible.*

4 Constructions of UAKE Protocols Based on iCCA and iCMA Security

In this section we show two realizations of unilaterally-authenticated key-exchange based on message transmission protocols. The constructions are simple and they essentially show how to obtain a clean and smooth transition from encryption/authentication towards key exchange. The first construction (described in Fig. 2) uses an iCCA-secure protocol Π' and a pseudorandom function. Our second construction of UAKE (described in Fig. 3) uses an IND-CPA-secure key encapsulation mechanism and an iCMA-secure protocol Π'.

The security of these protocols is proven via the following theorems (whose proofs appear in the full version):

---

[5] We stress that here we mean to force two distinct *oracle* sessions to have the same session key.

Theorem 2. *If Π' is* iCCA-*secure, and F is a pseudo-random function, then the protocol Π in Fig. 2 is a secure UAKE.*

Theorem 3. *If Π' is* iCMA-*secure, and $\mathcal{E}$ is an* IND-CPA-*secure KEM, then the protocol Π in Fig. 3 is a secure UAKE.*

ON THE CONNECTION TO AUTHENTICATORS [1]. We note that, due to the similarity between iCMA-secure message transmission and the notion of authenticators from [1], our design approach of Fig. 3 is similar to what can be obtained by applying a (unilateral) authenticator to an unauthenticated protocol, such as a one-time KEM. However, the derived protocols are not exactly the same. For example, to obtain our same protocols when using the signature-based authenticator one should slightly deviate from the approach of [1] and consider ek' as the nonce of the authenticator.

More conceptually, while the concrete protocols obtained are similar (but not identical), the two works use very different definitions and construction paths to arrive at these similar protocols. Our interactive PKMA notion is game-based and essentially extends the simple notion of signature schemes, whereas authenticators follow the real/ideal paradigm and also require built-in protection against replay attacks. For instance, a regular signature scheme is a 1-round iCMA secure message transmission, whereas it can be considered an authenticator only with certain restrictions, (as per Remark 1 in [1]).

INSTANTIATIONS OF OUR PROTOCOLS. In Sect. 5.1, we discuss four efficient UAKE protocols resulting from instantiating the generic protocols in Figs. 2 and 3 with specific 1- or 2-round iCCA- and iCMA-secure schemes.

ABOUT FRESHNESS OF SESSION KEYS. It is worth noting that both above protocols have the property that the keyed party T generates the session key in a "fresh" way (by sampling a fresh random s in the protocol of Fig. 2, or by running Encap with fresh coins in the protocol of Fig. 3), even if the first part of the protocol is replayed. Such a freshness property is necessary for the security of the protocols in our model. For instance, one might consider a simpler version of

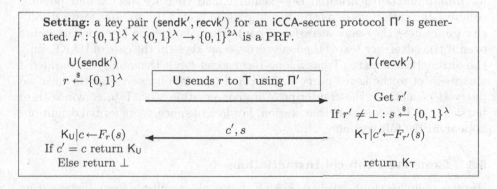

Fig. 2. UAKE from iCCA-secure encryption.

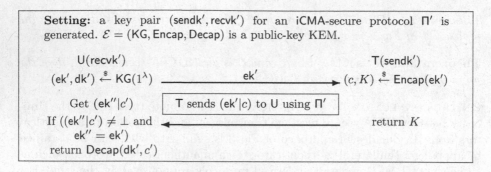

Fig. 3. UAKE from iCMA-secure PKMA and IND-CPA-secure KEM.

the protocol of Fig. 2 in which T generates $K_T|c' \leftarrow G(r)$ using a PRG G. Such a protocol however would not be secure because of the following attack. Consider an instantiation of Π' with a non-interactive CCA encryption scheme. First the adversary plays a ping-pong attack between the challenge session and an oracle session with T: it obtains a real-or-random key K_b. In the second part of the experiment, the adversary starts a new oracle session with T by sending to it the first message of the challenge session. Finally, the adversary makes a last query to T in this second session in order to obtain the corresponding session key. Now, observe that the session key will be the same key as the real key K_0 of the challenge session, and thus the adversary can trivially use it to test whether $K_b = K_0$. To see the legitimacy of the attack note that the second oracle session began *after* the challenge session ended, and thus it does not constitute a full ping-pong. In contrast this attack does not apply to our protocol of Fig. 2: there, even if one replays the first messages, every new session will sample a fresh session key with overwhelming probability.

5 Advanced Security Properties and Concrete Protocols

In this section, we discuss advanced properties of *forward security* and *deniability* for unilaterally-authenticated key-exchange, and then we discuss four possible concrete instantiations of our protocols given in Sect. 4. Informally, forward security guarantees that once a session is completed, the session key remains secure even if the adversary learns the long-term secret keys (in the case of UAKE, only the authenticated party T has a long-term secret key). Deniability is considered with respect to the keyed party T. Informally, deniability says that the unkeyed party U cannot use the transcript of its conversation with T to convince third parties that T took part in that session. For lack of space, more formal definitions appear in the full version.

5.1 Concrete Protocol Instantiations

Here we discuss four efficient UAKE protocols resulting from instantiating the generic protocols in Figs. 2 and 3 with specific 1- or 2-round iCCA- and iCMA-secure schemes. Before proceeding to the analysis, let us briefly recall the instantiations of the iCCA- and iCMA-secure schemes that we consider. First, note that any IND-CCA encryption scheme is a 1-round iCCA protocol, and similarly any strongly unforgeable signature scheme is a 1-round iCMA protocol. Second, Dodis and Fiore [8] show a 2-round iCCA-secure protocol based solely on IND-CPA security and a 2-round iCMA-secure protocol based on IND-CCA encryption and a MAC. Briefly, the iCCA protocol works as follows: the receiver chooses a "fresh" public key ek (of a 1-bounded IND-CCA encryption) and sends this key, signed, to the sender; the sender encrypts the message using ek. The iCMA protocol instead consists in the receiver sending a random MAC key r to the sender using the IND-CCA encryption, while the sender sends the message authenticated using r.

If we plug these concrete schemes in our UAKE protocols of Figs. 2 and 3, we obtain the following four UAKE instantiations that we analyze with a special focus on the properties of forward security vs. deniability:

1. Protocol of Fig. 2 where the iCCA protocol Π' is a non-interactive IND-CCA scheme: we obtain a *2-round* UAKE based on IND-CCA that *is (forward) passive deniable* (a perfectly indistinguishable transcript for an honest U is easily simulatable), but it is *not forwardæsecure* (recovering the long-term key recvk' trivially allows to recover r). This protocol recover the unilateral version of SKEME [14] (without PFS).
2. Protocol of Fig. 2 where the iCCA protocol Π' is the 2-round protocol in [8] based on IND-CPA security: we obtain a *3-round* UAKE based on IND-CPA security that is *not deniable* (as T signs the first message with a digital signature) but it *is passive forward secure* (since so is the 2-round iCCA protocol, as shown in [8]).
3. Protocol of Fig. 3 where the iCMA protocol Π' is a digital signature: we obtain a *2-round* UAKE based on IND-CPA security that is clearly *not deniable* (as T signs c) but it can be shown *passive forward-secure* (as dk' is a short-term key which is deleted once the session is over). It is worth noting that when implementing the KEM with standard DH key-exchange (ek' $= g^x, c = g^y, K = g^{xy}$) we essentially recover protocol A-DHKE-1 in [21]. A very similar protocol based on IND-CPA KEM is also recovered in the recent, independent, work of Maurer et al. [20].
4. Protocol of Fig. 3 where the iCMA protocol Π' is the 2-round PKMA proposed in [8] (called Π_{mac}) which is based on IND-CCA encryption and MACs: we obtain a *2-round* UAKE (as we can piggy-back the first round of Π_{mac} on the first round of the UAKE). Somewhat interestingly, this instantiation achieves *the best possible properties for a 2-round protocol*: it enjoys *both* passive forward deniability (as Π_{mac} is passive forward-deniable) and passive forward security (since dk' is short-term, as in the previous case). The resulting protocol is depicted in Fig. 4, and we note that it essentially recovers the unilateral version of SKEME [14]. Moreover, by using the MAC of [9] and

Setting: $(\mathsf{ek}, \mathsf{dk})$ is a key pair for an IND-CCA-secure PKE $\mathcal{E} = (\mathsf{KG}, \mathsf{Enc}, \mathsf{Dec})$. $\mathcal{E}' = (\mathsf{KG}', \mathsf{Encap}, \mathsf{Decap})$ is an IND-CPA-secure KEM, $(\mathsf{Tag}, \mathsf{Ver})$ a strongly-unforgeable MAC.

$\mathsf{U}(sid, \mathsf{ek})$ $\hspace{6cm}$ $\mathsf{T}(sid, \mathsf{dk})$

$(\mathsf{ek}', \mathsf{dk}') \xleftarrow{\$} \mathsf{KG}'(1^\lambda)$ $\quad\xrightarrow{\hspace{1cm} \mathsf{ek}', c = \mathsf{Enc}(\mathsf{ek}, r) \hspace{1cm}}\quad$ $r' \leftarrow \mathsf{Dec}(\mathsf{dk}, c)$

$\quad r \xleftarrow{\$} \{0, 1\}^\lambda$

If $\mathsf{Ver}(r, \mathsf{ek}'|c', \sigma) = 1$ $\quad\xleftarrow{\hspace{1cm} c', \sigma = \mathsf{Tag}(r', \mathsf{ek}'|c') \hspace{1cm}}\quad$ $(c', K) \xleftarrow{\$} \mathsf{Encap}(\mathsf{ek}')$

return $\mathsf{Decap}(\mathsf{dk}', c')$ $\hspace{6cm}$ return K

Fig. 4. A 2-round forward-deniable and forward-secure UAKE.

Setting: a key pair $(\mathsf{ek}, \mathsf{dk})$ for a labeled IND-CCA-secure PKE $\mathcal{E} = (\mathsf{KG}, \mathsf{Enc}, \mathsf{Dec})$ is generated. $\mathcal{E}' = (\mathsf{KG}', \mathsf{Encap}, \mathsf{Decap})$ is an IND-CPA-secure KEM.

$\mathsf{U}(\mathsf{ek})$ $\hspace{6cm}$ $\mathsf{T}(\mathsf{dk})$

$(\mathsf{ek}', \mathsf{dk}') \xleftarrow{\$} \mathsf{KG}'(1^\lambda)$

$(\mathsf{ek}_M, \mathsf{dk}_M) \xleftarrow{\$} \mathsf{KG}(1^\lambda)$ $\quad\xrightarrow{\hspace{0.5cm} \mathsf{ek}', \mathsf{ek}_M, c = \mathsf{Enc}^{\mathsf{ek}_M}(\mathsf{ek}, r) \hspace{0.5cm}}\quad$ $r' \leftarrow \mathsf{Dec}^{\mathsf{ek}_M}(\mathsf{dk}, c)$

$\quad r \xleftarrow{\$} \{0, 1\}^\lambda$

If $\mathsf{Dec}^{(\mathsf{ek}'|c')}(\mathsf{dk}_M, \sigma) = r$ $\quad\xleftarrow{\hspace{0.3cm} c', \sigma = \mathsf{Enc}^{(\mathsf{ek}'|c')}(\mathsf{ek}_M, r') \hspace{0.3cm}}\quad$ $(c', K) \xleftarrow{\$} \mathsf{Encap}(\mathsf{ek}')$

return $\mathsf{Decap}(\mathsf{dk}', c')$ $\hspace{6cm}$ return K

Fig. 5. A 2-round forward-deniable and forward-secure UAKE based on CCA encryption.

by applying some optimizations[6], we obtain a UAKE protocol based only on CCA security. While for practical efficiency one may use faster MACs, we show this protocol based only on CCA security mostly for elegance. The resulting protocol is depicted in Fig. 5, where we use a "labeled" CCA-secure PKE: $\mathsf{Enc}^L(\mathsf{ek}, m)$ denotes a run of the encryption algorithm to encrypt a message m w.r.t. label L; analogously $\mathsf{Dec}^L(\mathsf{dk}, c)$ denotes decryption w.r.t. label L. We recall that decryption of a ciphertext c w.r.t. L succeeds only if c was created with the same label L.

Acknowledgements. The first author was partially supported by gifts from VMware Labs and Google, and NSF grants 1319051, 1314568, 1065288, 1017471. The second author is partially supported by the European Union's Horizon 2020 Research and Innovation Programme under grant agreement 688722 (NEXTLEAP), the Spanish Ministry of Economy under project references TIN2015-70713-R (DEDETIS), RTC-2016-4930-7 (DataMantium), and under a Juan de la Cierva fellowship to Dario Fiore, and by the Madrid Regional Government under project N-Greens (ref. S2013/ICE-2731).

---

[6] By directly observing the MAC of [9], we notice that the ephemeral secret key dk' (which is part of the MAC key with r) is only used for verification, and there is no need to encrypt it inside c; instead, we can use labels to bind ek' with c.

References

1. Bellare, M., Canetti, R., Krawczyk, H.: A modular approach to the design and analysis of authentication and key exchange protocols (extended abstract). In: 30th ACM STOC, pp. 419–428. ACM Press, May 1998
2. Bellare, M., Rogaway, P.: Entity authentication and key distribution. In: Stinson, D.R. (ed.) CRYPTO 1993. LNCS, vol. 773, pp. 232–249. Springer, Heidelberg (1994). https://doi.org/10.1007/3-540-48329-2_21
3. Blake-Wilson, S., Johnson, D., Menezes, A.: Key agreement protocols and their security analysis. In: Darnell, M. (ed.) Cryptography and Coding 1997. LNCS, vol. 1355, pp. 30–45. Springer, Heidelberg (1997). https://doi.org/10.1007/BFb0024447
4. Blake-Wilson, S., Menezes, A.: Authenticated Diffie-Hellman key agreement protocols. In: Tavares, S., Meijer, H. (eds.) SAC 1998. LNCS, vol. 1556, pp. 339–361. Springer, Heidelberg (1999). https://doi.org/10.1007/3-540-48892-8_26
5. Canetti, R., Krawczyk, H.: Analysis of key-exchange protocols and their use for building secure channels. In: Pfitzmann, B. (ed.) EUROCRYPT 2001. LNCS, vol. 2045, pp. 453–474. Springer, Heidelberg (2001). https://doi.org/10.1007/3-540-44987-6_28
6. Canetti, R., Krawczyk, H.: Universally composable notions of key exchange and secure channels. In: Knudsen, L.R. (ed.) EUROCRYPT 2002. LNCS, vol. 2332, pp. 337–351. Springer, Heidelberg (2002). https://doi.org/10.1007/3-540-46035-7_22
7. Diffie, W., Hellman, M.E.: New directions in cryptography. IEEE Trans. Inf. Theor. 22(6), 644–654 (1976)
8. Dodis, Y., Fiore, D.: Interactive encryption and message authentication. In: Abdalla, M., De Prisco, R. (eds.) SCN 2014. LNCS, vol. 8642, pp. 494–513. Springer, Cham (2014). https://doi.org/10.1007/978-3-319-10879-7_28
9. Dodis, Y., Kiltz, E., Pietrzak, K., Wichs, D.: Message authentication, revisited. In: Pointcheval, D., Johansson, T. (eds.) EUROCRYPT 2012. LNCS, vol. 7237, pp. 355–374. Springer, Heidelberg (2012). https://doi.org/10.1007/978-3-642-29011-4_22
10. Fiore, D., Gennaro, R., Smart, N.P.: Constructing certificateless encryption and ID-based encryption from ID-based key agreement. In: Joye, M., Miyaji, A., Otsuka, A. (eds.) Pairing 2010. LNCS, vol. 6487, pp. 167–186. Springer, Heidelberg (2010). https://doi.org/10.1007/978-3-642-17455-1_11
11. Goldberg, I., Stebila, D., Ustaoglu, B.: Anonymity and one-way authentication in key exchange protocols. Des. Codes Cryptogr. 67(2), 245–269 (2013)
12. Jager, T., Kohlar, F., Schäge, S., Schwenk, J.: On the security of TLS-DHE in the standard model. In: Safavi-Naini, R., Canetti, R. (eds.) CRYPTO 2012. LNCS, vol. 7417, pp. 273–293. Springer, Heidelberg (2012). https://doi.org/10.1007/978-3-642-32009-5_17
13. Kohlar, F., Schge, S., Schwenk, J.: On the security of TLS-DH and TLS-RSA in the standard model. Cryptology ePrint Archive, Report 2013/367 (2013)
14. Krawczyk, H.: SKEME: a versatile secure key exchange mechanism for internet. In: 1996 Proceedings of the Symposium on Network and Distributed System Security, pp. 114–127, February 1996
15. Krawczyk, H.: HMQV: a high-performance secure Diffie-Hellman protocol. In: Shoup, V. (ed.) CRYPTO 2005. LNCS, vol. 3621, pp. 546–566. Springer, Heidelberg (2005). https://doi.org/10.1007/11535218_33

16. Krawczyk, H.: A unilateral-to-mutual authentication compiler for key exchange (with applications to client authentication in TLS 1.3). In: Proceedings of the 2016 ACM SIGSAC Conference on Computer and Communications Security, CCS 2016, pp. 1438–1450. ACM, New York (2016)
17. Krawczyk, H., Paterson, K.G., Wee, H.: On the security of the TLS protocol: a systematic analysis. In: Canetti, R., Garay, J.A. (eds.) CRYPTO 2013. LNCS, vol. 8042, pp. 429–448. Springer, Heidelberg (2013). https://doi.org/10.1007/978-3-642-40041-4_24
18. LaMacchia, B.A., Lauter, K., Mityagin, A.: Stronger security of authenticated key exchange. In: Susilo, W., Liu, J.K., Mu, Y. (eds.) ProvSec 2007. LNCS, vol. 4784, pp. 1–16. Springer, Heidelberg (2007). https://doi.org/10.1007/978-3-540-75670-5_1
19. Maurer, U., Renner, R.: Abstract cryptography. In: Chazelle, B. (ed.) ICS 2011, pp. 1–21. Tsinghua University Press (2011)
20. Maurer, U., Tackmann, B., Coretti, S.: Key exchange with unilateral authentication: Composable security definition and modular protocol design. Cryptology ePrint Archive, Report 2013/555 (2013). http://eprint.iacr.org/
21. Shoup, V.: On formal models for secure key exchange. Cryptology ePrint Archive, Report 1999/012 (1999). http://eprint.iacr.org/

Formal Modeling and Verification for Domain Validation and ACME

Karthikeyan Bhargavan[1](✉), Antoine Delignat-Lavaud[2], and Nadim Kobeissi[1]

[1] INRIA, Paris, France
{karthikeyan.bhargavan,nadim.kobeissi}@inria.fr
[2] Microsoft Research, Cambridge, UK
antdl@microsoft.com

Abstract. Web traffic encryption has shifted from applying only to sensitive websites (such as banks) to a majority of all Web requests. Until recently, one of the main limiting factors for enabling HTTPS was the requirement to obtain a valid certificate from a trusted certification authority. This process traditionally involves steps such as paying a certificate issuance fee, ad-hoc private key and certificate request generation, and domain validation procedures. To remove this barrier of entry, the Internet Security Research Group (ISRG) introduced "Let's Encrypt", a new non-profit certificate authority that uses a new protocol called Automatic Certificate Management Environment (ACME) to automate certificate management at all levels (request, validation, issuance, renewal, and revocation) between clients (website operators) and servers (certificate authority nodes). Let's Encrypt's success is measured by its issuance of over 27 million free certificates since its launch in April 2016. In this paper, we survey the existing process for issuing domain-validated certificates in major certification authorities. Based on our findings, we build a security model of domain-validated certificate issuance. We then model the ACME protocol in the applied pi-calculus and verify its stated security goals against our security model. We compare the effective security of different domain validation methods and show that ACME can be secure under a stronger threat model than that of traditional CAs. We also uncover weaknesses in some flows of ACME 1.0 and propose verified improvements that have been adopted in the latest protocol draft submitted to the IETF.

1 Introduction

Since the dawn of HTTPS, being able to secure a public website with SSL or TLS requires obtaining a signature for the website's public certificate from a certificate authority [1] (CA). All major operating system and browser vendors maintain lists of trusted CAs (represented by their root certificates) that can legitimately attest for a reasonable link between a certificate and the identity of the server or domain it claims to represent.

For example, all major operating systems and browsers include and trust Symantec's root certificates, which allows Alice to ask Symantec to attest that

© International Financial Cryptography Association 2017
A. Kiayias (Ed.): FC 2017, LNCS 10322, pp. 561–578, 2017.
https://doi.org/10.1007/978-3-319-70972-7_32

the certificate she uses on her website AliceShop.com has indeed been issued to her, rather than to an attacker trying to impersonate her website. After Alice pays Symantec some verification fee, Symantec performs some check to verify that Alice and her web server indeed have the authority over AliceShop.com. If successful, Symantec then signs a certificate intended for that domain. Since the aforementioned operating systems already trust Symantec, this trust now extends towards Alice's certificate being representative of AliceShop.com.

The security of this trust model has always relied on the responsibility and trustworthiness of the CAs themselves, since a single malicious CA can issue arbitrary valid certificates for any website on the Internet. Each certificate authority is free to engineer different user sign-up, domain validation, certificate issuance and certificate renewal protocols of its own design. Since these ad-hoc protocols often operate over weak channels such as HTTP and DNS without strong cryptographic authentication of entities, most of them can be considered secure only under relatively weak threat models, reducing user credentials to a web login, and domain validation to an email exchange.

The main guidelines controlling what type of domain validation CAs are allowed to apply are the recommendations in the CA/Browser Forum Baseline Requirements [2]. These requirements, which are adopted by ballot vote between the participating organizations, cover the definition of common notions such as domain common names (CNs), registration authorities (RAs) and differences between regular domain validation (DV) and extended validation (EV).

These guidelines have not proven sufficient for a well-regulated and well specified approach for domain validation: Mozilla was recently forced to remove WoSign [3] (and its subsidiary StartSSL, both major certificate authorities) from the certificate store of Firefox and all other Mozilla products due to a series of documented instances that range from the CA intentionally ignoring security best-practices for certificate issuance, to vulnerabilities allowing attackers to obtain signed certificates for arbitrary unauthorized websites.

The lack of a standardized protocol operating under a well-defined threat model and with clear security goals for certificate issuance has so far prevented a systematic treatment of certificate issuance using well-established formal methods. Instead, academic efforts to improve PKI security focus on measurement studies [4,5] and transparency and public auditability mechanisms [6,7] for already-issued certificates.

In 2015, a consortium of high-profile organizations including Mozilla and the Electronic Frontier Foundation launched "Let's Encrypt" [8], a non-profit effort to specify, standardize and automate certificate issuance between web servers and certificate authorities, and to provide certificate issuance itself as a free-of-charge service. Since its launch in April 2016, Let's Encrypt has issued more than 27 million certificates [9] and has been linked to a general increase in HTTPS adoption across the Internet.

Let's Encrypt also introduces ACME [10], an automated domain validation and certificate issuance protocol that gives us for the first time a protocol that can act as a credible target for formal verification in the context of domain validation. ACME also removes almost entirely the human element from the process of domain validation: the subsequently automated validation and issuance of millions of certificates further increases the necessity of a formal approach to the protocol involved.

In this paper, we formally specify, model and verify ACME using ProVerif, an automated protocol verifier [11] that operates in the symbolic model and accepts protocol representations in the applied-pi calculus. Against a classic symbolic protocol adversary, ACME achieves most of its stated security goals. Notably, we show that ACME's design allows it to resist a substantially stronger threat model than the ad-hoc protocols of traditional CAs that rely on bearer tokens (passwords, cookies, authorization strings) for authentication and domain validation, thanks to its stronger cryptographic credentials and to the binding between the client's identity and the validated domain.

Nevertheless, we still discover issues and weaknesses in ACME's domain validation and account recovery features, potentially amounting to user account compromise. We attempt to address in this paper what seem to be open questions regarding ACME: how does ACME compare to the existing security model of the actual top real-world certificate authorities? How can we most fruitfully illustrate and formally verify its security properties, and what can we prove about them?

Contributions. Our contributions in this paper consist of:

- **A survey of the domain validation practices of current CAs:** In Sect. 2, we survey the issuance process and infrastructure of 10 of the most popular certificate authorities. We observe that traditional CAs support multiple methods for assessing domain control, that rely on different security assumptions.
- **A threat model for domain validation:** In Sect. 3, we specify a high-level threat model for certificate issuance based on domain validation, which applies both to both traditional CAs and ACME. We relate this threat model to the various domain control validation methods surveyed in Sect. 2. In Sect. 4, we demonstrate that ACME resists a stronger threat model than other CAs.
- **Formally specifying and verifying ACME:** In Sect. 4, we formally specify the ACME protocol within a symbolic model in the applied π-calculus that encodes the adversarial capabilities described in Sect. 3. We verify the main security goals of ACME using the ProVerif model checker. Although ACME is shown to be more resistant to attacks than ad-hoc CAs, we also discover weaknesses in ACME's domain validation and account recovery and propose countermeasures.

2   Current State of Domain Validation

A goal of this paper is to establish a relationship between current domain validation practices in the real world and a more formal threat model on which we base our security results. We begin by taking a closer look into the network infrastructure, user authentication and domain validation protocols currently in use by traditional CAs.

Our panel of surveyed CA is selected from the data set of Delignat-Lavaud et al. [5], which uses machine learning to classify certificates issued by domain validation. Our CA panel covers about 85% of the collected domain validated certificates from 2014, which is consistent with the January 2015 market share data from the Netcraft SSL survey[1]. For each CA, we obtain a regular one year, single-domain certificate signature for a domain name that we own.

Section 3.2.2.4 of the CA/Browser Forum's Baseline Requirements allow for domain validation to occur in ten different ways, including over postal mail. Of these methods, only three are in popular use: validation via email, the setting of an arbitrary DNS record, or serving some HTTP value on the target domain.

2.1 Domain Validation Mechanisms

With ad-hoc CAs, user C authenticates its identity C_{pk} to CA A as a simple username/password web login, with an option for account recovery via email. C can then request that A validate some domain $C_w \subset C_w^\star$, where $C_w^\star$ is the set of all domain names that C controls. A's flow with the various domain validation channels proceeds thus:

– *HTTP Identifier.* A sends to C a nonce A_{Nc} via an HTTPS channel that C must then advertise at some agreed-upon location under C_w. A then accesses C_w using an unauthenticated, unencrypted HTTP connection to ensure that it can retrieve A_{Nc}. This identifier depends *both* on honest DNS resolution of the validated domain's A/A6 records and an untampered HTTP connection to the domain.

  In practice, we find that CAs that allow HTTP identifiers require the nonce to be written on a text file with a long random name in the root of the validated domain. An attacker able to respond to HTTP requests for such names may get a certificate without access to the domain's DNS records.

– *DNS identifier.* A sends to C a nonce A_{DNSc} via an HTTPS channel that C must then advertise at some agreed-upon TXT record under the DNS records of C_w. A then queries C_w's name servers using to ensure that it can retrieve A_{DNSc}. This identifier is dependent on honest resolution of the TXT record. None of the CAs we surveyed advertises DNSSEC support to ensure this DNS resolution is indeed authentic. As an experiment, we set up a DNSSEC-enabled domain and configured our nameserver to send an invalid RRSig for the TXT record of the domain validation nonce for Comodo. The validation ultimately completed, indicating that the use of DNSSEC does not currently prevent attacks against DNS-based domain validation by current CAs.

– *Email identifier.* A sends to C a URI A_{URIc} via an email to an address E_C that A presumes to belong to C. Accessing this URI causes A to issue the

[1] https://www.netcraft.com/internet-data-mining/ssl-survey/.

certificate for C_w. This identifier is dependent on the confidential transport of the email (which may be routed through third party SMTP servers that are not guaranteed to use TLS encryption) and honest DNS resolution of the validated domain's MX records.

In practice, we observe that CAs use dangerous heuristics to generate a list of possible E_C that C can pick from: first, they presume that any email addresses that appear in the WHOIS records of C_w is controlled by C. A large majority of registrars provide WHOIS privacy services to defend against spam. Such services can easily obtain certificates for any of their customers' domains as validation email transit through their mail servers. Second, CAs' heuristics include generic names such as `postmaster`, `webmaster`, or `admin`. If the validated domain provides an email service for which users may chose their username, an attacker may register under one of those generic names and obtain a unauthorized certificate. Such attacks have been carried successfully in the past against public email services such as Hotmail.

Once one of the above identifiers succeeds in validating C's ownership of C_w to A, A issues the certificate and the protocol ends.

2.2   User Authentication and Domain Validation

While CAs are required to document their certificate issuance policies in Certificate Practice Statements [12–19], we find that these statements are not always accurate or complete (for instance, they typically provision for validation methods that are not offered in practice; the address heuristics for email-based validation is rarely listed exhaustively). Most ad-hoc CAs in our study favor email-based validation. Unlike HTTP and DNS identifiers, email identifiers effectively rely on a *read* capability challenge instead write access proof for C. In Sect. 3, we discuss how email identifiers are the weakest available form of identification given our threat model. In Sect. 4, we elaborate on a weakness in ACME affecting both account recovery and domain validation. While this weakness is also generalizable to traditional certificate authorities, ACME offers an opportunity for a stronger fix.

None of CAs we surveyed offers a login mechanism that is completely independent of email. An exception almost occurs with StartSSL, which supports browser-generated X.509 client certificates for web login, but this exception is negated by the email-based account recovery in case of a lost certificate private key. Reliance on the security of the email channel can in many cases be even more serious: in many surveyed CAs, simply being able to complete a web login enables user to re-issue certificates for domains they had already validated before, without further validation (Fig. 1).

A scan of the DNS MX and NS records of the web's top 10,000 websites (according to AliceShop.com) [20] showed that roughly 45% of surveyed domain names used only six DNS providers, of which CloudFlare alone had a 18%

CA	Identifiers	Email Recovery	Public Key Auth.	Per-CSR Check
AlphaSSL	Email	✓	✗	N/A
Comodo PositiveSSL	Email	✓	✗	✓
DigiCert	Email	✓	✗	✗
GeoTrust QuickSSL	Email	✓	✗	✗
GlobalSign	HTTP, DNS, Email	✓	✗	✗
GoDaddy SSL	HTTP, DNS	✓	✗	✗
Let's Encrypt (ACME draft-1)	HTTP	✓	✓	✗
Network Solutions	Email	✓	✗	✗
RapidSSL	Email	✓	✗	✓
SSL.com BasicSSL	HTTP, DNS, Email	✓	✗	N/A
StartCom StartSSL	Email	✓	✓	✗

Fig. 1. Popular CAs, their validation methods, whether they permit account recovery via email, whether they allow login via a public-key based approach (such as client certificates) and whether domain validation is carried out once for every certificate request, even for already-validated domain names.

share.[2] A similar centralization of authority exists with email, where the top six providers serve more than 55% of domain names surveyed, with Google alone holding roughly 27% market share (Fig. 2).

These results suggest that the number of actors of which the compromise could affect traditional domain validation is significantly small. This is relevant given how top CAs allow for account recovery, certificate re-issuance and more with simple email-based validation.

3   A Security Model for Domain Validation

The protocols considered in this paper operate between a party C claiming to serve and represent one or more domain names C_w (for which it wants certificates), and it is incumbent upon a certificate issuer A to verify that all domains

---

[2] CloudFlare incidentally also operates Let's Encrypt's infrastructure, rendering it a centralized point of failure for ACME and ad-hoc CAs alike. While ACME is a centralization-agnostic protocol, Let's Encrypt operates with a fully centralized infrastructure.

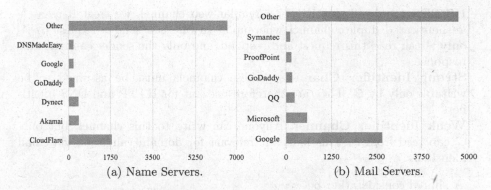

Fig. 2. Provider repartition among the Alexa Top 10,000 global sites, as of October 2016. Notably, CloudFlare and Akamai also provide CDN services to domains under their name servers, allowing them stronger control over HTTP traffic.

in C_w are indeed controlled and managed by C. User C authenticates itself to the certificate authority A using a public key C_{pk} of a private identity C_k. C can then link identifiers under C_k that prove that it manages and controls domains in C_w.

This and following sections are largely based on our full symbolic model[3] of ACME and ad-hoc CA protocol and network flow, which is written in the applied pi calculus and verified using ProVerif. Excerpts of this model are inlined throughout.

3.1 Security Goals and Threat Model

Our security goals are straightforward: for any domain $C_w \in C_w$, A must not sign a certificate asserting C's ownership of C_w for that domain unless C can validate C_{pk} as representing the identity that owns and manages this domain. ACME allows C to validate C_w with respect to C_{pk} by using the secret value C_k in order to demonstrate either read or write capabilities on certain predefined network channels, each with its own security model. A domain name C_w is considered *validated* under C_w if C_k can be used to complete a verification challenge on one of the network channels offered by the ACME protocol between C and A that in consequence asserts a relationship between C_{pk} and C_w.

The network topology, channels and actors are essentially the same for both ACME and ad-hoc CAs. However, the manner in which these actors communicate over the channels is different, and leads to different attempts to establish the same security guarantees (Fig. 3).

Channels. Intuitively, the channels we want encapsulate the following properties:

---

[3] Full model available at https://github.com/Inria-Prosecco/acme-model.

- **HTTPS Channel.** Intuitively a regular web channel, we treat it as a A-authenticated duplex channel whereupon anyone can send a request to A, only A can read this request and respond, and only the sender can read this response.
- **Strong Identifier Channels.** These channels must be assumed to be writable only by C. They are therefore relevant for HTTP and DNS Identifiers.
- **Weak Identifier Channel.** Anyone can write to this channel, but only C can read from it. This makes it relevant for domain validation via email identifiers.

A shared consideration between ACME and ad-hoc CAs involves the critical importance of DNS resolution: if the attacker can simply produce false DNS responses for A resolving a domain request for any domain in C_w, it becomes impossible to safely carry out domain validation under any circumstances. As a sidenote, this allows us to argue that since the DNS channel must be

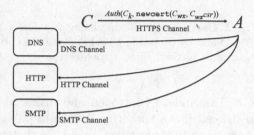

Fig. 3. Channels overview.

trusted, it could also be considered as the safest channel on which to carry out domain validation using DNS Identifiers since that would allow C to avoid needlessly involving other channels.

In formally describing our network model in ProVerif, we simulate simultaneous requests from Alice, Bob and Mallory as independent clients C. Alice and Bob both act as honest clients, while Mallory acts as a compromised participant client. All three follow the same protocol top-level process. We also simulate two independent ACME CAs, which interchangeably assume the role of A. For each C, we specify a triple of distinct channels:

$$(C_{HTTP}, C_{EMAIL}, C_{DNSTXT})$$

Each channel represents access to a different domain validation mechanism. While C is given complete access over these channels, the channels are only handed to C_{EMAIL} is only handed to A after being applied through a "write transformation" which returns a variant of the channel that is effectively write-only:

$$w(channel) \to channel$$

Similarly, a "read transformation" $r(channel) \to channel$ is applied to C_{HTTP} and C_{DNSTXT}.

A routing proxy is then specified in order to model the transportation across these channels by executing the following unbounded processes in parallel[4]:

$$in(w(C_{EMAIL}), x); \ out(r(C_{EMAIL}), x)$$
$$in(pub, x); \ out(r(C_{EMAIL}), x)$$
$$in(w(C_{HTTP}), x); out(pub, x); out(r(C_{HTTP}), x)$$
$$in(w(C_{DNSTXT}), x); out(pub, x); out(r(C_{DNSTXT}), x)$$

Threat Model. We assume that the adversary controls parts of the network and so can intercept, tamper with and inject network messages. As such, an attacker could make requests for domains they do not own, intercept and delay legitimate certificate requests, and so on. Our adversary has full access to pub, $w(C_{EMAIL})$, $r(C_{HTTP})$ and $r(C_{DNSTXT})$. We also publish Mallory's channels and C_k over pub. As such, the attacker controls a set of valid participants (e.g. M) with their own valid identities (e.g. M_k, M_{pk}). The attacker may advertise any identity for its controlled principals, including false identities, and may attempt to obtain a certificate for domains not legitimately under M_w.

The adversary also has at his disposal certain special functions:

- *PoisonDnsARecord*, which takes in a domain C_w and allows the attacker to poison its DNS records to redirect to a server owned by M. Calling this function triggers the $ActiveDnsAttack(C_w)$ event.
- *ManInTheMiddleHttp*, which allows the attacker to write arbitrary HTTP requests as if they were emitting from C_{HTTP} by disclosing C_{HTTP} to the attacker. Calling this function triggers the $ActiveHttpAttack(C_w)$ event.

3.2 ProVerif Events and Queries

Under ProVerif, queries under our symbolic model are constructed from sequences of the following events, each callable by a particular type of actor:

- **Client.** The client is allowed to assert that they own some domain by triggering the event $Owner(C, C_w)$. Once C receives a certificate $C_{w_{cert}}$ for C_w from A, they also trigger $CertReceived(C_w, C_{w_{cert}}, C_{pk}, A_{pk})$
- **Server.** The server (ACME instance or CA) triggers the event $HttpAuth(C_{pk}, C_w)$, $DnsAuth(C_{pk}, C_w)$ and $EmailAuth(C_{pk}, C_w)$ depending on the type of domain validation used. Once A issues a certificate $C_{w_{cert}}$ for C_w to C, they also trigger $CertIssued(C_w, C_{w_{cert}}, C_{pk}, A_{pk})$
- **Adversary.** As noted above, the adversary may trigger the events $ActiveDnsAttack(C_w)$ and $ActiveHttpAttack(C_w)$. In addition, the adversary is allowed to masquerade as M in order assert that they own some domain by triggering the event $Owner(M_{pk}, C_w)$.

---

[4] We also specify a fully public channel named **pub**.

Queries. Queries encode the security properties that we expect our model to satisfy. For example, informally, we expect the a *CertIssued* event may only occur following an *HttpAuth* or *DnsAuth* event for the same domain, expressing the fact that ACME should not issue a certificate for an non-validated domain under any circumstance. Running ProVerif on the query can result in three outcomes: either it diverges (in which case the model or query needs to be simplified), or it proves that the model satisfies the query, or it finds a counter-example and outputs its trace (which can be turned into an attack).

Validation with DNS Identifiers. We assert that if DNS validation succeeded, then A must have been able to successfully carry out DNS validation according to spec, *or* an adversary was able to instantiate an active DNS poisoning attack (with no third possible scenario). In ProVerif, this can be expressed using injective event queries:

$$DnsAuth(C_{pk}, C_w) \implies (Owner(C_k, C_w) \lor DnsAttack(C_w))$$

Validation with HTTP Identifiers. We explicitly show that HTTP authentication is weaker than DNS authentication, since it is possible under both cases of DNS poisoning *and* an HTTP man-in-the-middle attack:

$$HttpAuth(C_{pk}, C_w) \implies Owner(C_k, C_w) \lor (HttpAttack(C_w) \lor DnsAttack(C_w))$$

Predictable Certificate Issuance. We attempt to verify that all received certificates were issued by the expected CA. This query fails to verify, and leads us to the attack we discuss in Sect. 5.2:

$$CertReceived(C_w, C_{w_{cert}}, C_{pk}, A_{pk}) \implies CertIssued(C_w, C_{w_{cert}}, C_{pk}, A_{pk})$$

4   Specifying and Formally Verifying ACME

In this section we provide a formal description of the ACME protocol functionality and identify three issues that affect ACME's security. We also discuss details of how we describe the ACME protocol flow in the applied pi calculus, so that we can verify for certain queries using ProVerif.

4.1   ACME Network Flow

Unlike ad-hoc CAs which are limited to a web login, ACME's authentication depends on C generating a private value C_k and a public signing key C_{pk}, which are used to generate automated client signatures throughout the protocol.

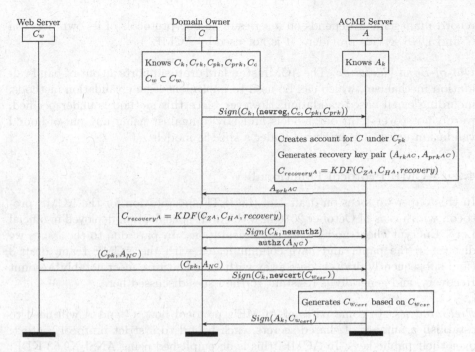

Fig. 4. ACME draft-1 protocol functionality for C account registration, recovery key generation, and validation with certificate issuance for C_w. This chart demonstrates validation via an HTTP identifier. In draft-3 and above, the HTTP challenge (C_{pk}, A_{NC}) is replaced with $Sign(C_k, (C_{pk}, A_{NC}))$.

HTTP Identifier. A sends to C a nonce A_{NC} via the HTTPS channel. C must then advertise, at an agreed-upon location under C_w, the value (C_{pk}, A_{NC}). A then accesses C_w using an unauthenticated, unencrypted HTTP connection to ensure that it can retrieve the intended value.

ACME also supports a very similar validation mode that operates at the level of the TLS handshake rather than at the HTTP level (using the SNI extension and a specially crafted certificate in place of the HTTP request and response). We believe this mode is intended for TLS termination software and hardware, and despite its apparent complexity, it is semantically equivalent to the HTTP identifier method. Since the details of the formatting of payloads is abstracted in our symbolic model we model both TLS-SNI and HTTP validation under the same framework in our model.

DNS Identifier. A sends to C a nonce $A_{nonce}c$ via the HTTPS channel. C advertises this nonce in the form of a DNS record served by C_w's name servers, thereby proving ownership of C_w. A can then query its DNS server to verify that the nonce has been set. While this behavior is specified in ACME, it is not used in any implementation of Let's Encrypt: since ACME is designed to take advantage of domain validation methods that can be automated and since DNS record management depends on a series of ad-hoc protocols of its own between C and DNS service providers, it is not used by ACME.

Out-of-Band Validation. The ACME standard draft supports an out-of-band validation mechanism, which can be used to implement legacy validation methods, including email-based validation. However, since this method is underspecified, we do not cover it in our models and advice against using any out-of-bound validation unless it is analyzed under a specific model.

4.2   ACME Protocol Functionality

In this paper we focus on draft-1 of the IETF specification for the ACME protocol, which is as of October 2016 also the draft specification deployed in official Let's Encrypt client and server implementations. In part due to the issues we discuss in the paper and have communicated with the ACME team, draft-3 (and subsequently draft-4) does away with some features, most notably Account Recovery, and generally is resistant to the issues discussed here.

Preliminaries. In some parts of ACME's protocol flow, C and A will need to establish a number of shared secrets, each bound to a strict protocol context, over their public keys. In ACME, this is accomplished using ANSI-X9.63-KDF:

1. C and A agree on a ECDH shared secret C_{Z^A} using their respective key pairs (C_k, C_{pk}) and (A_k, A_{pk}).
2. A hashing function C_{H^A} is chosen according to the elliptic curve used to calculate C_{Z^A}: $SHA256$ for $P256$, $SHA384$ for $P384$ and $SHA512$ for $P521$.
3. $C_{label^A} = KDF(C_{Z^A}, C_{H^A}, label)$, with $label$ indicating the chosen context for this particular key's usage.

As a protocol, ACME provides the following seven certificate management functionalities (illustrated in Fig. 4) between web server C and certificate management authority A:

– *Account Key Registration.* In this step, C specifies her contact information (email address, phone number, etc.) as C_c and generates a random private signing key C_k with (over a safe elliptic curve) a public key C_{pk}. A POST request is sent to A containing $Sign(C_k, (\texttt{newreg}, C_c, C_{pk}))$. The newreg header indicates to A that this is an account registration request. If A has no prior record of C_{pk} being used for an account, and if the message's signature is valid under C_{pk}, A creates a new account for C using C_{pk} as the identifier and responds with a success message.
– *MAC-Based Account Recovery.* C may choose to identify an account recovery secret with A. In order to do this, C generates an account recovery key pair (C_{rk}, C_{prk}) and simply includes C_{prk} in an optional recoverykey field in its initial newreg message to A. A generates the complementary $(A_{rk^{AC}}, A_{prk^{AC}})$ and both parties calculate $C_{recovery^A}$ using their recovery key pairs. A communicates $A_{prk^{AC}}$ in its response to C. Later, if C loses C_k, she can ask A

to re-assign her account to a new identity $(C_{k'}, C_{pk'})$ by using $C_{recovery^A}$ as a key to generate a MAC of some value chosen by A.

- *Contact-Based Account Recovery.* C can request that A send a verification token to one of the contact methods previously specified in C_c. For example, this could be a URI sent to an email in C_c. If C successfully opens this URI, she becomes free to replace C_{pk} with a $C_{pk'}$ for some arbitrary $C_{k'}$ at A.
- *Identifier Authorization.* C can validate its ownership of a domain C_w in C_w by providing one of the identifiers discussed in Sect. 3 to A. C must first request authorization for C_w by sending a newauthz message. A then responds with the types of identifiers it is willing to accept in a authz message. C is then free to use any one of the permitted identifiers to validate its ownership of C_w and allow A to sign certificates for it issued to C and tied to the identity C_{pk}.
- *Certificate Issuance and Renewal.* After C ties an identifier to C_w under C_{pk}, it may request that a certificate be issued for C_w simply by requesting one from A. Generally, A will send the signed certificate with no further steps required. The renewal procedure is similarly straightforward.
- *Certificate Revocation.* C may ask A to revoke the certificate for C_w by sending a POST message containing the certificate in question, signed under either C_{pk} or the key pair for the certificate itself. C may choose which key to use for this signature. A verifies that the public key of the key pair signing the request matches the public key in the certificate, and that the key pair signing the request is an account key, and the corresponding account is authorized to act for all of the identifier(s) in the certificate.

Given this description of the ACME protocol and the threat model defined in Sect. 3, we modeled ACME using the automated verification tool ProVerif [21]. In our model, we involve three different candidates for C: Alice, Bob and Mallory, and two CA candidates as A.

In our automated verification process, we consider an active attacker over the three channels specified in Sect. 3. As a result, we were able to find the issues discussed in Sect. 5.2. The first two are relatively minor; however, the third could lead to account compromise in the case of contact-based account recovery, and potentially to the issuance of false certificate signatures if email-based domain validation were to be implemented in ACME. Furthermore, this third issue is also generalizable to affect traditional certificate authorities, as described in Sect. 2.

4.3   Model Processes

Using the modeling conventions we established in Sect. 3 which include channels, adversaries, actors and events, we instantiate in our ProVerif model of ACME a top-level process that executes the following processes in parallel:

- *ClientAuth.* Run simultaneously by Alice, Bob and Mallory assuming the role of C (with a compromised Mallory), this process registers a new account with A and sends the queries illustrated in Fig. 4. The events *Owner* and *CertReceived* are triggered as part of this process.

– *ServerAuth.* Run simultaneously by two independent CAs assuming the role of A, this process accepts registrations from C and follows the protocol illustrated in Fig. 4. The events *HttpAuthenticated* and *CertIssued* are triggered as part of this process.

The processes *RoutingProxy*, *PoisonDnsARecord* and *ManInTheMiddleHttp*, all described in Sect. 3, are also run in parallel with the above.

5   Analysis Results

5.1   Weaknesses in Traditional CAs

Traditional CA dependence on weak channels gives us a threat model where real-world attacks can have a small cost and come with severe consequences.

Email Validation. In ad-hoc CAs, C is generally simply sent an email containing a URI to their email inbox, which they're supposed to click in order to validate for their chosen domain. Figure 5 shows an attack rendered possible by this mechanism. A could instead, upon a validation request, redirect C's browser to a secret, nonce-based URI A_{URI^C} served to C over the HTTPS channel, and independently mail C the value $HMAC(A_{hk}, A_{URI^C})$ for some secret A_{hk} held by A. C would need to retrieve this second value and enter it inside the page at A_{URI^C}. This approach would largely negate the weakness discussed in Sect. 5.2, since an attacker-induced validation email would result in an email that does not include a value matching the URI given by A to C at the beginning of the validation process.

Usage of Nonces. Traditional CAs use random nonces with no special cryptographic properties as the values that they then verify over HTTP, email or DNS.

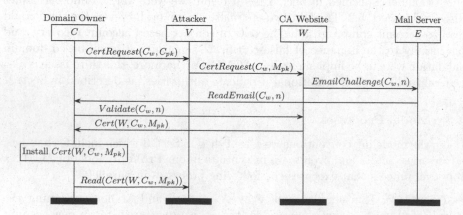

Fig. 5. Attack on email validation: concurrent request by active adversary.

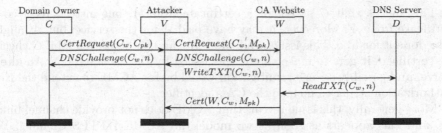

Fig. 6. Active attack on DNS/HTTP/Email validation when using just nonces.

In addition to this helping caused the attack described above, another more general attack on nonces is shown in Fig. 6 in the case of an active attacker. For example, this attack can be used by a compromised CA website to get certificates issued for domain C_w by another (more reputable) CA, hence amplifying the compromise across CAs. None of these attacks would be effective if nonces were tied to some cryptographic properties, such as MACs or even just by deriving them from a hash of the certificate request's public key.

In order to avoid a similar attack, ACME draft-3 and draft-4 require that HTTP identifiers be validated by broadcasting $Sign(C_k, A_{NC})$ via the web server instead of ACME draft-1's (C_{pk}, A_{NC}) (Fig. 7).

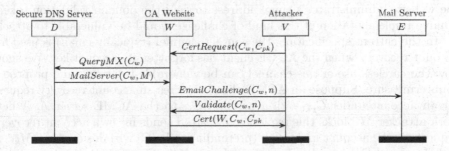

Fig. 7. Attack on email validation: passive adversary on email channel

5.2   Weaknesses in ACME

Cross-CA Attacks on Certificate Issuance. Suppose an ACME client C requests a certificate from A, and but A is malicious or the secure channel between A and C is compromised. Now, an attacker can intercept authorization and certificate requests from C to A, and instead forward them to another ACME server A'. If A' requests domain validation with a token T, the attacker forwards the token to the client, who will dutifully place its account key K and token T on its validation channel. A' will check this token and accept the authorization and issue a certificate that the attacker can forward to C.

This means that C asked for a certificate from A, but instead received a certificate from A'. Moreover, it may have paid A for the service, but A' might have done it for free. This issue, while not critical, can be prevented if C checks the certificate it gets to make sure it was issued by the expected CA. An alternative, and possibly stronger, mitigation would be for ACME to extend the Key Authorization string to include the CA's identifier.

More generally, this issue reveals that ACME does not provide channel binding, and this appears as soon as we model the ACME HTTPS Channel. We would have expected to model this as a mutually-authenticated channel since the client always signs its messages with the account key. However, although the client's signature is tunnelled inside HTTPS, the signature itself is not "bound" to the HTTPS channel. This means that a message from an ACME client C to A can be forwarded by A to a different A' (as long as C supports both A and A'). This kind of "credential forwarding" attack can be easily mitigated by channel binding. For example, ACME could rely on the Token Binding specifications to securely bind the client signature to the underlying channel. Alternatively, ACME could extend the signed request format to always include the server's name or certificate-hash, to ensure that the message cannot be forwarded to other servers.

Contact-Based Recovery Hijacking. While the use of sender-authenticated channels in ACME seems to be relatively secure, more attention needs to be paid to the receiver-authenticated channels. For example, if the ACME server uses the website administrator's email address to send the domain validation token, a naïve implementation of this kind of challenge would be vulnerable to attack.

In the current specification, the contact channel (typically email) is used for account recovery when the ACME client has forgotten its account key. We show how the careless use of this channel can be vulnerable to attack, and propose a countermeasure. Suppose an ACME client C issues an account recovery request for an account under C_{pk} with a new key $C_{k'}$ to the ACME server A. A network attacker M blocks this request and instead sends his own account recovery request for the account under C_{pk} (pretending to be C) with his own key $M_{k'}$. A will then send C an email asking to click on a link. C will think this is a request in response to its own account recovery request and will click on it. Similarly to the (slightly different) flow described in Fig. 5, A will think that C has confirmed account recovery and will transfer the account under C_{pk} to the attacker's key $M_{k'}$. In the above attack, the attacker did not need to compromise the contact channel (or for that matter, the ACME channel).

The key observation here is that on receiver-authenticated channels (e.g. email) the receiver does not get to bind the token provided by A with its own account key. Consequently, we need to add a further check. The email sent from A to C should contain a fresh token in addition to C's new account key. Instead of clicking on the link (out-of-band), C should cut and paste the token into the ACME client which can first check that the account key provided by A matches the one in the ACME client and only then does it send the token back to A, or alternatively that the email recipient at C visually confirms that the account key (thumbprint) provided by A matches the one displayed in the ACME client.

The attack described here is on account recovery, but a similar attack appears if we allow email-based domain validation. A malicious ACME server or man-in-the-middle can then get certificate issued for C's domains with its own public key, without compromising the contact/validation channel. The mitigation for that attack would be very similar to the one proposed above.

6 Conclusion

In this paper, we have provided the results of an empirical case study that allowed us to describe a real-world threat model governing both traditional certificate authorities and ACME in terms of user authentication and domain validation. We formally modeled these protocols and provided the results of security queries under our threat model, using automated verification. As a result of our disclosures to the ACME team, the latest ACME protocol version (draft-4) has been designed to avoid the pitfalls that make these attacks possible.

Given the weak threat model that traditional CAs are assuming for their domain validation process, we are not surprised by the regular occurrences of unauthorized certificate issuance (e.g. StartCom in 2008, Comodo and DigiNotar in 2011, WoSign in 2016). We advocate the CA/Browser forum to eventually mandate the use of ACME (or some other well-defined domain validation protocol that can be formally analyzed) to all certification authorities, as a long-term solution to reduce unauthorized certificate issuance. Until the issuance process for the whole PKI is unified, techniques to improve the validation of certificates such as certificate transparency [6] remain necessary to detect issuance failures, and technologies such as DNSSEC [22], DANE [23], or SMTPS may help strengthen the channels involved in legacy domain validation.

References

1. Chokhani, S., Ford, W., Sabett, R., Merrill, C., Wu, S.: Internet X.509 Public Key Infrastructure: Certificate Policy and Certification Practices Framework, RFC 3647. Internet Engineering Task Force, November 2003
2. CA/Browser Forum: Baseline requirements for the issuance and management of policy-trusted certificates, v. 1.1.5, May 2013
3. Gervase, M., Ryan, S., Richard, B., Kathleen, W.: WoSign and StartCom
4. Levillain, O., Ébalard, A., Morin, B., Debar, H.: One year of SSL internet measurement. In: Proceedings of the 28th Annual Computer Security Applications Conference, ACSAC 2012, pp. 11–20. ACM, New York (2012)
5. Delignat-Lavaud, A., Abadi, M., Birrell, A., Mironov, I., Wobber, T., Xie, Y., Microsoft Research: Web PKI: closing the gap between guidelines and practices. In: NDSS (2014)
6. Google: Certificate transparency

7. Basin, D., Cremers, C., Hyun-Jin, K.T., Perrig, A., Sasse, R., Szalachowski, P.: ARPKI: Attack Resilient Public-Key Infrastructure. In: Proceedings of the 2014 ACM SIGSAC Conference on Computer and Communications Security, CCS 2014, pp. 382–393. ACM, New York (2014)
8. Internet Security Research Group: Let's encrypt overview (2016)
9. Internet Security Research Group: Let's encrypt statistics (2016)
10. Barnes, R., Hoffman-Andrews, J., Kasten, J.: Automatic Certificate Management Environment (ACME), July 2016
11. Blanchet, B., Smyth, B., Cheval, V.: ProVerif 1.90: automatic cryptographic protocol verifier, user manual and tutorial (2014)
12. Comodo CA Ltd.: Comodo certification practice statement. Technical report, Comodo CA Ltd., August 2015
13. DigiCert: DigiCert certification practices statement. Technical report, DigiCert, September 2016
14. GeoTrust Inc.: GeoTrust certification practice statement. Technical report, GeoTrust Inc., September 2016
15. GlobalSign CA: GlobalSign CA certification practice statement. Technical report, GlobalSign CA (2016)
16. Internet Security Research Group: Certification practice statement. Technical report, Internet Security Research Group, October 2016
17. Symantec Corporation: Symantec Trust Network (STN) certification practice statement. Technical report, Symantec Corporation, September 2016
18. StartCom CA Ltd.: StartCom certificate policy and practice statements. Technical report, StartCom CA Ltd., September 2016
19. LLC Network Solutions: Network solutions certification practice statement. Technical report, Network Solutions, LLC, September 2016
20. Alexa Internet Inc.: Top 1,000,000 sites (updated daily) (2013)
21. Küsters, R., Truderung, T.: Using ProVerif to analyze protocols with Diffie-Hellman exponentiation. In: IEEE Computer Security Foundations Symposium (CSF), pp. 157–171 (2009)
22. Ateniese, G., Mangard, S.: A new approach to DNS security (DNSSEC). In: Proceedings of the 8th ACM Conference on Computer and Communications Security, pp. 86–95. ACM (2001)
23. Hoffman, P., Schlyter, J.: The DNS-based Authentication of Named Entities (DANE) Transport Layer Security (TLS) protocol: TLSA. Technical report (2012)

Why Banker Bob (Still) Can't Get TLS Right: A Security Analysis of TLS in Leading UK Banking Apps

Tom Chothia(✉), Flavio D. Garcia, Chris Heppell, and Chris McMahon Stone

School of Computer Science, University of Birmingham, Birmingham, UK
t.p.chothia@cs.bham.ac.uk

Abstract. This paper presents a security review of the mobile apps provided by the UK's leading banks; we focus on the connections the apps make, and the way in which TLS is used. We apply existing TLS testing methods to the apps which only find errors in legacy apps. We then go on to look at extensions of these methods and find five of the apps have serious vulnerabilities. In particular, we find an app that pins a TLS root CA certificate, but do not verify the hostname. In this case, the use of certificate pinning means that all existing test methods would miss detecting the hostname verification flaw. We also find one app that doesn't check the certificate hostname, but bypasses proxy settings, resulting in failed detection by pentesting tools. We find that three apps load adverts over insecure connections, which could be exploited for in-app phishing attacks. Some of the apps used the users' PIN as authentication, for which PCI guidelines require extra security, so these apps use an additional cryptographic protocol; we study the underlying protocol of one banking app in detail and show that it provides little additional protection, meaning that an active man-in-the-middle attacker can retrieve the user's credentials, login to the bank and perform every operation the legitimate user could.

1 Introduction

The use of TLS in smartphone apps has proved challenging for developers to get right. Common mistakes involve accepting self signed certificates, not checking the hostname, accepting weak cipher suites and allowing SSL stripping due to sending HTTPS links over insecure connections [4,9,12]. These issues are all trivial to fix and easy to detect so we would expect that leading international banks would not make such mistakes.

Banking organisations have previously threatened legal action against security researchers [6,18] and the UK courts have granted temporary injunctions against researchers on the grounds that they could not show that they followed proper procedure in their analysis [5]. Therefore, when carrying our work it would be useful to be able to follow all of the terms and conditions of use of

The original version of this chapter was revised: minor error in the author name was corrected. The correction to this chapter is available at
https://doi.org/10.1007/978-3-319-70972-7_36

© International Financial Cryptography Association 2017, corrected publication 2023
A. Kiayias (Ed.): FC 2017, LNCS 10322, pp. 579–597, 2017.
https://doi.org/10.1007/978-3-319-70972-7_33

the apps, failure to do so could lead to legal pressure not to publish the results of the analysis. In particular, the terms and conditions of the banking apps and app store, forbid reverse engineering the code, and accessing app stores outside of your geographical area. We note that our analysis method does not require this and allows analysis without breaking the terms and conditions of the app.

A correctly configured TLS client should check (among other things) that the server it communicates with uses a certificate for the hostname the client is expecting, and that this certificate is signed by someone the client trusts. Additionally, it is good practice for the client to check that the certificate is signed by a single, prearranged Certificate Authority (CA), rather than an arbitrary CA from the list of those trusted by the client's OS. This additional check is known as certificate pinning. There are a number of options as to which certificate in the chain is being pinned to: pinning the server certificate provides the highest security level but it also provides less flexibility, e.g., when this key expires or needs to be revoked. Alternatively, it is possible to pin the intermediate or even the root CA. The higher in the chain you pin, the more flexibility you get at the cost of security.

In this paper we report on the analysis of Android and iOS apps from 15 of the leading retail banks based in the UK (see Table 1). We test all of the apps for the most common TLS flaws, i.e. whether they accept self-signed certificates; correctly check the hostname; permit protocol downgrades or weak cipher suites; allow SSL stripping (by sending secure links over insecure connections); Using available tools and previous defined methods we found no vulnerabilities in any of current versions of the apps.

However, we note that as one of our test devices was an old Apple tablet that did not support the most recent version of iOS. We found that when apps

Table 1. Apps in our test set and vulnerabilities discovered.

App Name	Vulnerabilities			
	Accepts any certificate (self-signed or any hostname)	Pinning or proxy bypass without hostname validation	In-app phishing	Broken second layer protocol
Natwest	Legacy	🤖	✗	✗
Lloyds	✗	✗	✗	✗
RBS	Legacy	✗	✗	✗
Barclays	✗	✗	✗	✗
Co-Op	✗	🤖	✗	🤖
HSBC	✗	✗	✗	✗
Nationwide	✗	✗	✗	✗
Santander UK	✗	✗	🤖	✗
TSB	✗	✗	✗	✗
Halifax	✗	✗	✗	✗
Metro	✗	✗	✗	✗
Tesco	✗	✗	✗	✗
Clydesdale	✗	✗	✗	✗
First Trust	✗	✗	🤖	✗
Allied Irish (GB)	✗	✗	🤖	✗

were downloaded on these older devices, an older legacy version of the app was provided. In fact, two of the legacy apps accepted self-signed certificates, and using this an attacker could steal the initial setup code used to authenticate the app, which is generated during the registration process. It seems likely that this was a flaw in the application that had been previously detected and fixed, but fixing the legacy version of the app had been overlooked.

While checking the up-to-date apps, we found that 7 of the 15 banks we tested used certificate pinning, as we might expect from high security apps. We note that the method of checking that apps are verifying server hostnames used by others [9] is unreliable when certificate pinning is being used. This is because by proxying TLS connections with a trusted certificate for an unrelated hostname, one cannot distinguish whether the app rejects the connection because the hostname is invalid, or because a chain of trust cannot be established due to pinning being in use.

While pinning to the server public key would be secure, to test for apps that pinned to higher up the certificate chain, we obtained a certificates from corresponding root CAs but for our own hostnames. We found two apps that accepted such certificates Co-op and Natwest bank, meaning that these apps could be MITMed and were not secure. While pinning the certificates is good security practice, it seems possible that in the case of Coops app, pinning the certificate hid the more serious problem of having no hostname verification. Natwest on the other hand was not pinning, but implemented proxy bypassing measures. This additional security measure also hid the problem of no hostname verification.

The banks involved all have rigorous security testing regimes, and during the disclosure process they told us that they had also hired leading outside penetration companies to test the apps; however the certificate pinning would have meant that many of the standard penetration tests on apps (such as trying to MITM with a valid certificate for the same hostname) would have failed. While high security apps should certainly continue to pin the certificates, care must be taken to ensure that this does not mean that other vulnerabilities are missed.

When examining the apps we also found that some apps which passed all of the TLS checks, requested some of their data over unencrypted connections. While not a vulnerability in itself, a few of the apps were requesting images with links to be displayed to the user. We found this vulnerability in apps from Allied Irish Bank and Santander UK, among others. We additionally found unencrypted update checks which could be used to make the app tell the user that they needed to upgrade and redirect them to a site of the attacker's choosing, e.g. a phishing website.

When examining apps with failed TLS, we discovered that some apps use an additional layer of security. Requirement 1 of the PCI PIN security regulations [15] states that *PINs must never appear in the clear outside of an SCD*. If this is applied to mobile banking application PINs, it would make a second layer protocol compulsory. Web servers that decrypt TLS traffic from these apps are unlikely to be Secure Cryptographic Devices (SCD). Therefore there is a need to implement a second layer secure protocol so that PIN data can be forwarded to the banks' SCDs for processing. Further to this, new attacks have frequently been discovered against TLS so an additional layer of security is a sensible precaution. We found that some of the apps did use an additional cryptographic protocol on top of TLS, however we show that this protocol is flawed, allowing an adversary to obtain the information needed to log into the victim's online banking. We go on to propose an alternative protocol that would keep mobile banking secure even when the TLS protection failed and we formally verify this protocol.

Summary of Our Contribution:

- Carrying out a manual analysis of the 15 leading UK banking apps and finding that they are not vulnerable to TLS flaws previously reported in the literature.
- Discovering a new vulnerability that can arise when certificate pinning is used incorrectly. We have manually tested for this vulnerability and found it in one of the apps.
- Identifying "in app phishing" as an issue for apps which establish secure TLS connections but request resources, such as images and links, via an insecure connection. We found this vulnerability in three iOS banking apps and their Android counterparts.
- Identifying the existence of vulnerable legacy versions of apps as being an issue for the Apple App Store, and we have found two vulnerable apps from UK banks that were still being made available to customers.
- Studying the cryptographic protocol used by one of the banks as a second layer of security. We found that this protocol is flawed and that an attacker can obtain the credentials needed to take control of a users' Internet banking.
- We propose an improved protocol which addresses this problem and formally verified it using ProVerif.

A summary of the issues found is given in Table 1. For two Android banking apps, we are able to mount a man-in-the-middle attack that is able to retrieve the user's credentials (username and PIN/password), login to the bank and do every operation the legitimate user can i.e., see the balance and past transactions, make and modify bank transfers, etc. For three more iOS and Android banking apps, we could inject our own content and links into the apps, and use this to phish log-in details, and for two legacy iOS apps we found that we could MITM the TLS connection and so eavesdrop on the initial setup process of the app. These attacks are very practical. All an attacker needs to do is to create a "free WiFi" hotspot at a popular coffee shop and run a script that waits for a user to use their banking app, then MITMs the connection and collects the security tokens and user PIN numbers, which the attackers could then use at a later date. Through a lengthy disclosure process we have informed all of the banks involved and all but one have now fixed the problem.

Structure of the Paper

In the next section we discuss related work and then we provide some background, briefly describing the TLS protocol and certificate pinning. Section 3 describes the apps we tested and the approach we took to our security assessment. Section 4 presents a novel vulnerability that arises if certificate pinning is used incorrectly. In Sect. 5 we perform an in depth analysis of an additional protocol used by one of the apps, and show that it provides little extra security. Section 6 looks at banking apps which are vulnerable because they load some of their content over non-TLS connections, and we give examples of in app phishing attacks against banking apps from Santander and Allied Irish Bank. We present our improved secure banking protocol in Sect. 7 and we conclude in Sect. 8.

2   Background and Related Work

2.1   The TLS Protocol

Transport Layer Security (TLS) is a cryptographic protocol designed to provide confidentiality, integrity and server authentication (with optional client authentication) to application layer network traffic. To establish a secure connection between a client and a server, the server must present the client with its public key. This key is usually encapsulated in an X.509 certificate which also contains other information required to provide assurance of the authenticity of the key. A certificate includes a CommonName field and SubjectAltName set, which tie the key to specified hostname(s); a cryptographic signature provided by a CA, usually an RSA encrypted SHA-256 value; and a valid from date and expiry date. Additional meta-data is also present (see RFC 5280).

In order to be sure that a public key belongs to a given server, client applications trust a predefined set of root certificates belonging to trusted certificate authorities. These root CA certificates are carefully selected by the developers of the OS e.g. Android or iOS, and come pre-installed in the OS. This trust store is then updated as required by pushing updates to the OS, but can also modified by the user.

When attempting to set up a TLS connection, the server will provide a chain of certificates so that the user can build up a chain of trust to one of the trusted root CAs. Such chains typically have a length of three: the server or leaf certificate; which is signed by the issuer or intermediate CA which is itself signed by a trusted root CA.

To validate a TLS certificate, the client makes the following default checks:

- Validate that each certificate in the chain is signed by the previous one, starting with the leaf certificate.
- The final certificate in the chain is that of a trusted CA.
- The requested hostname matches the certificate's CommonName value or is contained within the SubjectAltName set.
- The current date is within the certificate's valid date range.

Further verifications should also be carried out such as checking the revocation status of the certificates. However, these are often omitted.

2.2 Certificate Pinning

The trust model that TLS adopts is arguably its biggest weakness. If a single Certificate Authority is compromised, then valid certificates for any hostname can be produced by signing them with the compromised CA root certificate. This would enable an attacker to MITM any TLS connection.

Additionally, an individual user's trust store could be compromised. There is the potential for an attacker to trick a user into adding a custom root certificate to their trust store, for example by suggesting it is a requirement to install a free app. Similarly, but more alarmingly, [19] showed how malicious apps on rooted Android handsets can modify the trust store totally unbeknown to the user. Previous work has also exposed the how bloated trust stores are and identified many root certificates that are unused [16]. Removing these would reduce the attack surface associated with CA compromise, however the risk still remains.

In order to mitigate these risks, Evans et al. proposed a technique named certificate pinning [8]. Applicable in situations where the hostname of the server is known in advance, like connections made by a mobile application, the certificate or public key that the app expects to see can be fixed. This aims at restricting the trust from all valid certificate chains originating from root CAs in the trust store, to a specific public key certificate, or ones derived from a particular fixed certificate. In general there are two ways this can be implemented:

- **Leaf certificate or Public Key** - Pin the servers specific public key certificate which is usually achieved by hard coding it's fingerprint (typically a SHA-256 value). Alternatively, just the server's public key can be pinned. The downside of this type of pinning is reduced flexibility, as the certificate may expire or the use of a static key may violate key rotation policies. If the certificate changes, users will be forced to update the application to continue use.
- **Intermediary or Root certificate** - A specific root CA or intermediary certificate can be pinned. The server can then re-new its leaf certificate whenever needed as long as it is signed by the pinned root or intermediary certificate.

2.3 Related Work

Fahl et al. [9] carried out a large scale analysis of Android apps in 2012 and found widespread misuse of TLS, in particular they found that many apps accepted self-signed certificates, did not check the hostname they connected too and did not encrypt some connections at all. Their testing methods would not find the class of vulnerabilities we are dealing with here, as the use of certificate pinning on its own would have been enough to pass their automated MITM tests. We note that they did not find any flaws in banking apps.

Georgiev et al. [10] carried out a similar analysis for application and library code and find similar issues, some of the same authors go on to develop a testing tool [4] which randomly mutates certificates to look for errors, again this approach would miss the vulnerabilities we present here, as the test would lack the certificate required by the pinning.

Reaves et al. [17] reverse engineered banking apps from developing countries and found a wide range of security issues. We note that while this work did look at banking apps, the banks involved were not large banks that had invested heavily in security, and all of the weaknesses could have been found by a competent penetration testing company. Their analysis involved decompiling the app code to look for vulnerabilities. This approach might find the code which allowed any hostname however it requires considerable time and effort to carry out such an analysis and so does not scale. Such an analysis also breaks the terms and conditions of the app, which as we mention above is something our analysis method does not do.

Oltrogge et al. [14] performed an extensive study on the applicability of certificate pinning in mobile apps. A classification method to establish whether an app would benefit from the use of pinning was applied to over 600,000 Android apps. Developer feedback was collected from a number of respondents and found that only a quarter of them grasped the concept of pinning and yet still found it too complex to use. The pinning vulnerability presented in this paper is therefore perhaps directly a result of the complexity of pinning implementations.

Google has developed a testing tool called "nogotofail"[1] and there are a range of similar online checking tools which carry out tests on TLS configurations[2] but again, none of these can detect the lack of hostname verification if certificate pinning is used.

3   Testing Apps

Test Set. For test cases, this paper focuses on mobile apps from large, leading retail banks. These types of apps have all the necessary ingredients for a good case study:

– They use TLS.
– They are security critical applications, with well motivated attackers, and large user bases.
– They often use techniques to provide additional security such as certificate pinning and two-factor authentication.
– Unlike many other apps, they have been subject to thorough penetration testing, so avoid basic vulnerabilities.

Additionally, customers of high-street banks are increasingly making use of mobile apps to manage their finances. A report by the British Bankers Association [1] found that in 2015 there were 40,000 downloads and 11M logins to UK banking apps per day. These usage statistics and the sensitive nature of the data that is managed by these apps, highlights the need to carry out a thorough review of their security.

We chose the top 15 consumer banks that are based in Great Britain or Northern Ireland. These are all listed in Table 1.

---

[1] https://github.com/google/nogotofail.
[2] see e.g. https://geekflare.com/ssl-test-certificate/.

Approach. The first stage of our investigation was to look for well-known TLS vulnerabilities and misuses that have been brought up in past literature. These included the type of problems that should be detected by penetration tests carried out during the development of the apps. We looked for:

- Sensitive data sent over insecure channels, using BurpSuite.[3]
- Basic invalid certificate verification, using Mallodroid[4] and BurpSuite. Including:
  - Accepting self-signed certificates.
  - Not validating that requested hostname matches CommonName value or contained in SubjectAltName set.
- Secure HTTPS links sent over non-TLS connections. Using SSLStrip,[5] we proxied traffic looking for HTTPS links that we could downgrade to HTTP.
- TLS version downgrade vulnerabilities. Many TLS client implementations do not solely rely on the standard negotiating mechanism. Some will make reconnection attempts using a downgraded version of TLS if initial handshakes fail. We tested for this by proxying TLS handshakes.

We found that none of the up-to-date apps in our test set exhibited any of these vulnerabilites. This led us to explore alternate ways that TLS could be broken or mis-configured.

Vulnerable Legacy iOS Apps. Most of the banking apps we tested required you to have one of the latest iOS versions. However, as one of our testing devices was an old iPad running iOS v5, we found some apps that offered to install of the latest version of the app compatible with your OS. At first glance this sounds reasonable but when considering security critical applications like banking, this deserves more care.

Concretely, we found that the banking apps from NatWest and the Royal Bank of Scotland for iOS v5 would accept self-signed certificates. We established this by using the BurpSuite (without modifying anything on the iOS device) and verified that the apps would accept BurpSuite's certificate and establish the connection as usual, but having BurpSuite as man-in-the-middle. These vulnerabilities have been patched and are no longer present in the latest version of the apps. However, users who have older iOS devices are still exposed.

Legacy apps should either be suitably maintained and patched or removed from the app store in order to avoid compromising user's security and privacy. Experimenting with the apps, we found that both apps first asked for registration codes, which would be delivered to the user out of band. Once entered into the app these codes were sent over the insecure TLS connection, meaning that they could be captured by an attacker. Without accounts at either of these banks we were unable to experiment further.

---

[3] https://portswigger.net/burp/.

[4] https://github.com/sfahl/mallodroid.

[5] https://github.com/moxie0/sslstrip.

Disclosure: We informed the banks concerned in January 2016, and shortly after both apps were updated, to no longer accept self-signed certificates.

4 Certificate Pinning Without Hostname Verification

In addition to checking that the server's certificate has a verifiable chain of trust, it is essential to check that the requested hostname matches the CommonName field or is contained in the SubjectAltName set of the X.509 certificate. This however is an unnecessary step if the leaf certificate or the servers public key is pinned in the application, since the valid hostname is implicit. On the other hand, if the application is pinning to a root or intermediary certificate then hostname verification is still required.

Past work in 2012 [9] has demonstrated that incorrect hostname verification is a mistake that was regularly made by app developers. However, previous analysis of TLS usage in mobile apps has failed to consider the possibility of incorrect hostname verification when certificate pinning is in use.

To detect this form of invalid verification in mobile apps, we manually analysed apps using the following process:

1. Establish if certificate pinning is being used
   (a) We add a custom self-signed root certificate, generated by Burp, to the phone's CA trust store. The phone is also configured to use our machine running Burp as a proxy.
   (b) We start the apps, one by one, and select the log in option to trigger a TLS connection attempt.
   (c) We observe the network traffic and if the app accepts the server certificate signed by the Burp root CA in the handshake, then we know the app is implementing chain of trust verification back to a trust store root certificate. If not, then the app must be pinning a particular certificate or public key.
2. Determine certificate chain in use
   (a) From observations made in the previous test, we analyse the certificate chain provided by the server that the app is communicating with.
   (b) Given this information, we can then obtain a certificate for our own domain from the same intermediary or root CA that the server's certificate is signed by.
   (c) We then install the newly obtained certificate onto our own TLS server.
3. Check if hostname verification is correctly implemented
   (a) The app is then restarted and TLS connection attempts are triggered again.
   (b) The TLS traffic is re-directed to our own TLS server and the handshake is analysed to determine if the hostname is being verified correctly. If so, then it should reject the TLS connection attempt, and if not, we should observe a fully successful TLS handshake with encrypted application data being sent by the app.

For apps that are found to pin a certificate but not check the hostname, an attacker could go to the CA used by the servers certificate and obtain a valid certificate in their own name, as we demonstrate in our testing method. The attacker's certificate can then be used to Man-in-the-Middle TLS traffic and hence break the security of the app.

Results: We followed the process described in Sect. 4 for the iOS and Android apps from the UK banks in our test set. We found apps from two banks in our test set, Co-op and Natwest, passed our initial round of tests, and accepted certificates signed by the same expected root CA but for different hostnames. Co-op pinned to a Comodo root certificate, but didn't check the hostname. Natwest on the other hand, initially appeared to be pinning, but upon further analysis we found it was actually avoiding the phone's proxy settings. Hence, it would also accept a certificate signed by any of the phone's trusted root CAs.

While pinning the certificates is a good security measure, it seems possible that in the case of Co-op, pinning the certificate hid the more serious problem of having no hostname verification. Natwest's flaw was also hidden from the standard tests we carried out due to bypassing the phone's proxy settings, another reasonable security measure to take.

We note that these apps have a collective user-base of up to 5 million people, illustrating the seriousness and potential for this vulnerability to be exploited by an attacker. Additionally, this problem did not occur in any of the iOS apps that we tested which suggests that the iOS API makes it harder for this mistake to be made.

Attack Scenario: This attack could be carried out by an attacker that sets up their own Wi-Fi hotspot, it could also be carried out by any attacker on the route the data takes between the victim and the bank, or an attacker on the same network as the victim, through use of techniques such as ARP or DNS poisoning. Other attacks (e.g. [11]) have shown that it is sometimes possible to access a home network, and when combined with these, an attack could performed against anyone in the vicinity.

Disclosure: Both banks have been given over a year to ship fixes for their apps before we published the issues. We initially contacted Co-op on a Friday, some of their engineers met with us on the following Monday and they shipped a fixed updated app by the end of the week. One month later they removed all support for the vulnerable app and therefore this can no longer be used. A similar process was carried out with Natwest. We note that Co-op said that they had previously hired two penetration testing companies to test their apps, both of which had missed this vulnerability, so they had no reason to believe that their apps were insecure before we contacted them.

5   In-Depth Analysis of a Second Layer Banking Protocol

Breaking the TLS connection of a banking app does not necessarily mean that an attacker can gain access to a victims account. Given the number of vulnerabilities that have been found in the TLS protocol [2,7,13], it would make sense for the apps to implement additional cryptographic protection.

The Co-op app we examined pinned to the Comodo root certificate (instead of the specific bank's certificate or the high security EV intermediate certificate). Since Comodo offers free certificates signed by this root certificate, authenticated only by e-mail, we were able to obtain a certificate for a domain we owned. Equipped with this certificate we were able to get the app to establish a TLS connection with us and take a look at the apps traffic which runs over TLS. We found the app first requested a one-time registration code, sent to the user out of band, after which it used an additional cryptographic protocol when the user logs on.

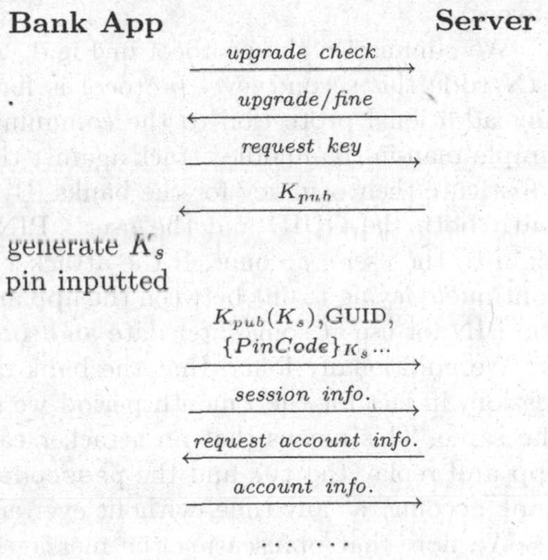

Traffic was sent between the app and the server using HTTP post requests containing JSON encoded data. Much of this included human readable tags. The first message sent by the app, and response from the server checked if the app needed to be updated. Next, the app sent a HTTP post request for an RSAPublicKey. The app then requested the user to enter their banking pin code, and the following two exchanged messages are shown in the appendix.

The forth message includes a JSON encoded modulus and exponent, so it seems logical to conclude this is an RSA key. The 5th message contains a number of fields, of particular interest is the passcode field, which appeared to be encrypted, and the guid which appeared to contain the global unique identifier for the app. The twk field is exactly the right length for a single block of RSA cipher text.

Fig. 1. A 2nd level banking protocol

To investigate this further we tried proxying the traffic, and sending our own RSA public key to the app. Doing so we found that we could then decrypt the twk field with our private key. This decrypted to 112-bits of correctly padded data. This is the correct length for two DES keys, and triple DES is a popular encryption algorithm in the banking community, therefore we tried decrypting the passcode field with these two keys using triple DES and found our banking PIN code, which was entered to access the account. Further investigation found that only the GUID and a correctly encrypted PIN code were needed to access

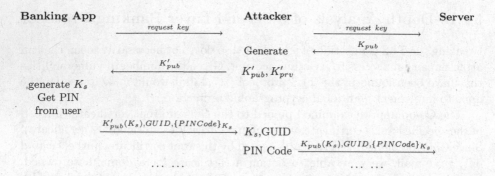

Fig. 2. A simple MITM attack on the banking protocol

the account, and no other cryptographic verification was required after these messages (although confirmation via SMS message was required to add new payees).

We summarise the protocol in Fig. 1. As shown by our ability to learn the PIN code this second level protocol is flawed, and therefore does not provide any additional protection to the communication channel. Figure 2 describes a simple man-in-the-middle attack against this protocol, in which an attacker can substitute their own key for the banks. By running this attack, adversaries can learn both the GUID and the user's PIN number, which is all they need to login to the user's account. If the attacker wants to hide their actions they can continue relaying traffic between the app and the bank, and store the GUID and the PIN for use at some later date and some other location.

We additionally found that the bank did not use a fresh RSA key for each session, in fact for the 2 month period we studied this app, the key was always the same. This means that an attacker can simply record the traffic from the app and replay the `twk` and the `passcode` fields, to gain access to the victims bank account, at any time, without ever actually learning the PIN code.

We note that obfuscating the messages would not have improved security, given the distinct sizes of the cryptography involved, it would have been relatively easy to reverse engineer this protocol without the human readable tags. What would have improved security would have been a correct protocol, which was not vulnerable to MITM and replay attacks, as we propose in Sect. 7.

Disclosure: We described the problems with this protocol to the Co-op at the same time as we disclosed the pinning but no hostname vulnerabilities, and we suggested a secure alternative. The Co-op decided to only fix the TLS vulnerability and leave the underlying protocol as it was. We note that the use of this underlying protocol does not represent a vulnerability, but also does nothing to protect the communications link.

6 In-App Phishing Attacks

While examining the banking apps from our test set, we noticed the First Trust Bank, Santander and Allied Irish Bank apps mixed TLS and non-TLS traffic, requesting some resources over a secure TLS connection and others over an unprotected connection.

Mixing TLS and non-TLS traffic, does not necessarily make an app vulnerable, so we examine the app in more detail and found that it was loading adverts for the banks own products and links to information that may be helpful to its users. In particular, the app loads an image to be displayed to the user and a link to go to, if the user clicked on the image.

Figure 3a gives an example of this. The "Help Centre" box in the middle of the screen on the left was loaded dynamically, and clicking on this takes the user to the screen on the right. At other times adverts for mortgages and savings accounts were loaded.

Downloading images and links over unprotected connections allows an attacker, on the same network as the victim, to replace them with an image and link of their own choice. This could be used to perform a phishing attack. While phishing attacks against banking credentials are common, being able to carry out the phishing attack inside the actual banking app means that the user is far more likely to trust the link.

We give an example of this in Fig. 3b. On the left is a screenshot of the real banking app, which we connected to a wi-fi hotspot we controlled. As no protection is used we where able to replace the "Help centre" image with a "Mobile Banking Log In" image (the real log on option can only be access via the "Banking" icon). We additionally sent our own link to the app that sends the user to the page shown on the right of Fig. 3b: a page with a spoofed URL which steals the users credentials.

In the case of Santander UK, the image was displayed on the bottom portion of the screen, e.g. the mortgage panel in Fig. 3c. Clicking on this takes the user to a Santander website. We show a possible in-app phishing attack against this in Fig. 3d. The real option to view the users accounts is under the menu at the top right of the screen, so a large "My Accounts" button with the same logo as the real one will likely attract many users. Additionally, we found that the information asked for on our phishing page, on the right of Fig. 3d, is all that is needed to install the Santander UK app on another phone. Again, as the app does not use TLS on the site it links to, our site's URL can be spoofed to look like a Santander page to the user.

The Allied Irish Bank app turned out to be very similar to the First Trust Bank, and we found out that the First Trust Bank is in fact a trading name for Allied Irish. We additionally found that Allied Irish Bank performs an unencrypted version check, which, in the case the app needs updating, the server replies to with a link to the Android Marketplace. This can be hijacked to redirect the app's user to any website of the attackers choice.

(a) First Trust Bank Real App

(b) First Trust Bank Phishing Attack

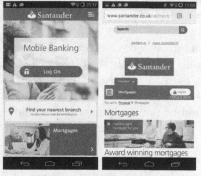

(c) Santander Real App

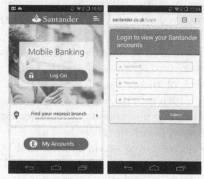

(d) Santander Phishing Attack

Fig. 3. In-App phishing attacks

Attack Scenario: To perform this attack, the attacker must have the same access as required for the previous attack. However, for this attack, they do not need a certificate of their own; as their is no protection on the image and link sent to the app an attacker can substitute their own image and link. Additionally, the attacker can spoof the address of the page to make it seem like it belongs to the bank (none of the apps we found directed users to pages protected with TLS). We emphasise that the attacker does not need to interfere with the victims phone or the banking app in anyway, this attack is carried out purely externally.

Some of the apps we looked at did not have a direct log in button on the opening page of the app. So placing such a button on the first page, with the same look as the other buttons on the app, would attract a lot of users. For systems that didn't require two factor authentication, the users could then be asked for their online banking credentials, or the information needed to install the banking app on another device, so giving the attacker full access to the victims online banking.

Disclosure: These vulnerabilities were disclosed to the banks involved in January 2016 and they were fixed the following month. Shortly following this Allied Irish and First Trust Bank updated their app to a completely new code base, which did not have these errors.

7   A Secure Protocol for Mobile Banking

We have recently seen many attacks against TLS and we are likely to see more in the future. These attacks will compromise the security of TLS used in apps (indeed, when we first approach one of the banks to say we had discovered a vulnerability, their first reaction was to ask if it was the POODLE attack, as they were aware that this had been a problem and had only just fixed it). Additionally, PCI standards on PIN security state that PINs must be encrypted at all times [15], so it should not be sent over TLS in the clear if the host receiving it is just going to send them on to another host to be verified.

In our view this means that TLS should not be the only protection and a lightweight, second level protocol to protect the PIN number and messages should also be used. However, as we have shown in Sect. 5, designing such a protocol appears to be error prone. In this section we work constructively, proposing a protocol which is suitable for this purpose and that can be used, freely, by any system designer. The protocol is a quite straightforward adaptation of an RSA encrypted key transport protocol as depicted in Fig. 4.

This protocol starts off as the protocol in Sect. 5, with an update check. After that the user requests and the server generates a secure random 128-bit nonce. The banking app has the public key of the bank K_{pub} hardcoded, and this can be updated automatically by pushing an app update. This makes use of a second channel (the app update process) to split the public key distribution from the PIN transfer. During authentication, the app will generate a session key K_s and a MAC key K_m uniformly at random, we would recommend AES

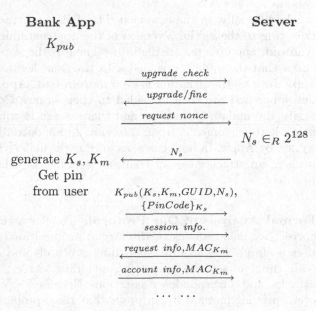

Fig. 4. An improved secure banking protocol

128-bit, but 3-DES may be required for compatibility with backend banking systems. When users input their PIN codes, the app will send an encryption of the session key, a MAC key, app GUID and a nonce from the server encrypted with the banks public key: $K_{pub}(K_s, K_m, GUID, N_s)$, along with an encryption of the *pincode* with the session key K_s (plus potentially any relevant session information as seen in Sect. 5). From this point on the app and the server exchange information in the usual way but authenticating every message with a CBC-MAC using K_m. We pad the PIN and the messages for the CBC-MAC with PKCS5.

Unlike the original protocol, our version includes the GUID in the block that is encrypted with the banks public key. We note that the session key is 128/112 bits therefore, when encrypted in the original protocol it will be padded out to 2048 bits. So in our suggested version of the protocol the GUID and server nonce replaces some of this padding, therefore we require no additional encryption and the message becomes shorter.

We note that this protocol does not keep the session data secret, or prevent message replays in the same session. This should be done by the application layer and (most of the time) by TLS. What it does aim to do is to provide protection for the customer that stops an attacker using their account in the case that the TLS protections fail (which is unfortunately common e.g. [2, 9, 13]), in particular it will keep the data needed for an attacker to log onto the victims account secret, it will prevent replay attacks across different sessions, and it will prevent an attacker from altering messages. Furthermore, it provides this additional protection using a protocol that is slightly shorter and largely compatible with the original broken version.

Additionally, in the case that TLS fails, an attacker is prevented from distributing to the victim a version of the app containing their own public key. In Android, app updates are digitally signed by the app developer and the OS will check that the update is signed with the same key as the current version of the app.[6] In iOS, the situation is even more robust. App updates are signed by the developer and are then uploaded to their iTunes Connect account. Apple the verify the update themselves and then re-sign it with their key before distributing it to customers.[7] Upon receiving app updates, iOS devices will check it is signed by Apple. In both cases, as long as the underlying signature scheme is not broken, an attacker cannot change the public key that is used in our proposed protocol.

Formal Analysis of Our Protocol. To offer assurance that our protocol is correct we analyse it using the formal protocol analysis tool ProVerif [3]. This uses a simple language for modelling protocols and can automatically prove a wide range of security properties, including secrecy, absence of offline guessing attacks, and correspondence assertions. Because ProVerif uses an automated theorem proving method it can prove that these properties hold against an active

---

[6] https://developer.android.com/studio/publish/app-signing.html.

[7] https://developer.apple.com/library/content/documentation/IDEs/Conceptual/
AppDistributionGuide/MaintainingCertificates/MaintainingCertificates.html.

Delov-Yao attacker for an unbounded number of runs of the protocol and protocol participants, however it may sometimes fail to terminate, or report false attacks.

The main part of our model is presented is presented in the appendix of the online version of this paper. In includes an App process to model the smart phone app, and a Server process that defines a bank process and the entire system is defined on the last line using the process key word. The system models an unbounded number of banks that may be using the protocol, each bank has an unbounded number of customers, some of which may be using the same PIN, but each of which has a unique GUID, for each customer we run an arbitrary number of App processes representing the user running the app and Server processes representing the bank handling this particular user.

We use the ProVerif tool to first check that this protocol keeps the session key and the PIN code secret, which ProVerif confirms it does. We next check the authentication properties of this protocol, in particular that every time a server finishes with a particular set of values (a serverFinish(ks,km,guid,pin,bankkey) event is reached) the app has also run the protocol using the same values, i.e., a appInit(ks,km,guid,pin,bankkey) event was reached with the same values as with the serverFinish event. We also check in the other direction confirming that the appFinish is always matched by a corresponding serverInit event with matching values. ProVerif confirms that these correspondences always hold indicating that an attacker cannot impersonate one side of the protocol or interfere with any of the values used, without being detected. Finally, as the PIN code may be a low entropy secret we check if an attacker can perform an offline guessing attack to find it, using ProVerif's weaksecrect test and a second model that uses a fixed PIN code. ProVerif confirms that no such guessing attack exists.

8   Conclusion

In this paper we have carried out an extensive security analysis of TLS implementations in the UK's major banking mobile applications. We have discovered a new vulnerability in one of these banking apps that arises due to a misuse of certificate pinning. To avoid breaking the terms and conditions of high-security apps, such as banking, we have shown to detect this vulnerability dynamically and without reverse engineering the app. We also found one app that fails to verifiy the hostname but hides this flaw from standard tests by bypassing proxy settings. These two cases are examples of how additional security protections have obscured the serious vulnerability of no hostname verification. We have demonstrated how these vulnerabilities could be exploited by an attacker to break the security of the app and eavesdrop sensitive information. We also found apps that are vulnerable to phishing attacks, legacy apps that accept self-signed certificates and a broken application layer banking protocol.

A   Co-Op App Traffic

```
HTTP/1.1 200 OK
Server: webserver
X-response-id: -907159463
Pragma: no-cache
Expires: Thu, 01 Jan 1970 00:00:00 GMT
Cache-control: no-cache no-store
Content-type: application/json;charset=UTF-8
Content-Length: 311


{"modulus":"9C8C54XXXXXXXXXXXXXXXXXXXXXXXXXXXXXXXXXXXXXXXXXXXXXXXXXXXXXXXXX
XXXXXXXXXXXXXXXXXXXXXXXXXXXXXXXXXXXXXXXXXXXXXXXXXXXXXXXXXXXXXXXXXXXXXXXXXXXXXX
XXXXXXXXXXXXXXXXXXXXXXXXXXXXXXXXXXXXXXXXXXXXXXXXXXXXXXXXXXXXXXXXXXXXXXXXXXXXXX
XXXXXXXXXXXXXXXXXXXXXXXXXXXXXXX 4082C1","exponent":"3","keyVersion":"81XXXXXX
C1"}


POST /mrs/3/security/session HTTP/1.1
user-agent: Mozilla/5.0 (Linux; Android 4.4.2; XT1021 Build/KXC20.82-14)
AppleWebKit /537.36 (KHTML, like Gecko) Version/4.0 Chrome/30.0.0.0 Mobile
Safari/537.36
client-version: 4.4.2
X-Request-Id: -907159453
Accept: application/json
Content-Type: application/json;charset=UTF-8
Cookie: JSESSIONID=9f7b4441e12b265fde33d1f0e73b; Path=/mrs; Secure
Cookie: JROUTE=9qIW.9qIW; Path=/mrs; Secure
Content-Length: 577
Connection: Keep-Alive


{"msisdn":"44XXXXXXXXXX","clientType":"|2.2.7||motorola|XT1021|Android|4.4.2|
|","passcode":"93XXXXXXXXXXXX07","twk":"8170b6XXXXXXXXXXXXXXXXXXXXXXXXXXXXXXXX
XXXXXXXXXXXXXXXXXXXXXXXXXXXXXXXXXXXXXXXXXXXXXXXXXXXXXXXXXXXXXXXXXXXXXXXXXXXXXX
XXXXXXXXXXXXXXXXXXXXXXXXXXXXXXXXXXXXXXXXXXXXXXXXXXXXXXXXXXXXXXXXXXXXXXXXXXXXXX
XXXXXXXXXXXXXXXXXXXXXXXXXXXXXXXXXXXXXXXXXXXXXXXXXXXXXXXXXXXXXabf54c",
"pinLength":"6","guid":"d2xxxxxxxxxxxxx83","applicationName":"Coop",
"deviceID":"44XXXXXXXXXX","issuerName":"COOP","authenticationType"
:"passcode","clientVersion":"2.2.7","rootDetection":"NOT_DETECTED"}
```

Fig. 5. Messages sent between the app and bank (with some information blanked out)

References

1. British Bankers' Association. The Way We Bank Now (2016)
2. Beurdouche, B., Bhargavan, K., Delignat-Lavaud, A., Fournet, C., Kohlweiss, M., Pironti, A., Strub, P.-Y., Zinzindohoue, J. K.: A messy state of the union: taming the composite state machines of TLS. In: IEEE Symposium on Security and Privacy (2015)

3. Blanchet, B., Smyth, B., Cheval, V.: Proverif 1.88: Automatic Cryptographic Protocol Verifier, User Manual And Tutorial (2013)
4. Brubaker, C., Jana, S., Ray, B., Khurshid, S., Shmatikov, V.:. Using frankencerts for automated adversarial testing of certificate validation in SSL/TLS implementations. In: IEEE Symposium on Security and Privacy (SP) 2014. IEEE, pp. 114–129 (2014)
5. Carolina, R., Paterson, K.: Megamos Crypto, Responsible Disclosure, and the Chilling Effect of Volkswagen Aktiengesellschaft vs Garcia, et al. (2013)
6. Choudary, O.: The Smart Card Detective: A Hand-held EMV Interceptor (2010)
7. de Ruiter, J., Poll, E.: Protocol state fuzzing of TLS implementations. In: 24th USENIX Security Symposium (USENIX Security 2015), USENIX Association, Washington, D.C., August 2015
8. Evans, C., Palmer, C.: Certificate Pinning Extension for HSTS (2011)
9. Fahl, S., Harbach, M., Muders, T., Baumgärtner, L., Freisleben, B., Smith, M.: Why eve and mallory love android: An analysis of android SSL (in)security. In: Proceedings of the 2012 ACM Conference on Computer and Communications Security, CCS 2012 (2012)
10. Georgiev, M., Iyengar, S., Jana, S., Anubhai, R., Boneh, D., Shmatikov, V.: The most dangerous code in the world: validating SSL certificates in non-browser software. In: Proceedings of the 2012 ACM Conference on Computer and Communications Security, CCS 2012, New York, NY, USA, pp. 38–49 ACM (2012)
11. Lorente, E.N., Meijer, C., Verdult, R.: Scrutinizing WPA2 password generating algorithms in wireless routers. In: 9th USENIX Workshop on Offensive Technologies (WOOT 15), Washington, D.C., USENIX Association, August 2015
12. Marlinspike, M.: New Tricks for Defeating SSL in practice. In Black Hat Europe (2009)
13. Möller, B., Duong, T., Kotowicz, K.: This POODLE Bites: Exploiting the SSL 3.0 Fallback (2014)
14. Oltrogge, M., Acar, Y., Dechand, S., Smith, M., Fahl, S.: To pin or not to pin-helping app developers bullet proof their TLS connections, In: USENIX, Security, pp. 239–254 (2015)
15. PCI. Pin Security Requirements (2014)
16. Perl, H., Fahl, S., Smith, M.: You won't be needing these any more: on removing unused certificates from trust stores. In: Christin, N., Safavi-Naini, R. (eds.) FC 2014. LNCS, vol. 8437, pp. 307–315. Springer, Heidelberg (2014). https://doi.org/10.1007/978-3-662-45472-5_20
17. Reaves, B., Scaife, N., Bates, A., Traynor, P., Butler, K.R.: Mo(bile) money, mo(bile) problems: analysis of branchless banking applications in the developing world. In: 24th USENIX Security Symposium (USENIX Security 2015) (2015)
18. Sample, I.: Bankers fail to censor thesis exposing loophole in bank card security. The Guardian (2010). https://www.theguardian.com/science/2010/dec/30/bankers-thesis-bank-card-security
19. Vallina-Rodriguez, N., Amann, J., Kreibich, C., Weaver, N., Paxson, V.: A tangled mass: The android root certificate stores. In: Proceedings of the 10th ACM International on Conference on emerging Networking Experiments and Technologies, pp. 141–148. ACM (2014)

Privacy in Data Storage and Retrieval

Lavinia: An Audit-Payment Protocol for Censorship-Resistant Storage

Cecylia Bocovich[1]([✉]), John A. Doucette[2], and Ian Goldberg[1]

[1] University of Waterloo, Waterloo, ON, Canada
cbocovic@uwaterloo.ca
[2] New College of Florida, Sarasota, FL, USA

Abstract. As distributed storage systems grow in popularity, there is now a demand for a reliable incentive and payment system to guarantee and reward the pristine storage of documents. However, many existing proof-of-retrieval and micropayment protocols are not secure in a censorship resistance setting, in which powerful adversaries may infiltrate a system or coerce the original publisher to remove content. Additionally, most existing censorship resistance systems lack a rigorous game-theoretic analysis. We propose Lavinia, an audit and payment protocol for censorship-resistant storage. Lavinia incentivizes document availability by providing micropayments to participating servers in exchange for honestly storing and serving content. Our protocol enables the implementation of a digital printing press as described in Anderson's Eternity Service: allowing *the publisher*, as opposed to public interest or an appointed editorial board, to decide whether a document is worth storing, and for how long. In addition to proving the security of our protocol, we provide an in-depth game-theoretic analysis and show that self-interested participants of our system will faithfully implement the desired behaviour and continue to store documents until their expiration date.

Keywords: Censorship resistance · Distributed storage
Economic incentives · Payment contracts

1 Introduction

Throughout history, the spread of information has been assisted by technological advances, but has also faced barriers in the form of censorship. With each new advance in technology that facilitates the spread of knowledge, ideas, and social understanding, there is an increase in the efforts of censors to limit this spread.

A popular example in the history of censorship and its resistance is the advent of the printing press [13]. Not only did the ability to print documents easily and efficiently result in the distribution of previously guarded works, it also led to an increase in the literacy rate of Europe. Despite censorship attempts, printed

---

An extended version of this paper is available as a technical report [6].

© International Financial Cryptography Association 2017
A. Kiayias (Ed.): FC 2017, LNCS 10322, pp. 601–620, 2017.
https://doi.org/10.1007/978-3-319-70972-7_34

documents proved to be resistant to state-level attempts to remove them. Borders were difficult to patrol thoroughly, and the production of many copies of each text made them almost impossible to eradicate completely. The only important impediment to using a printing press was the acquisition of enough capital to purchase the requisite raw materials and labour.

Today, worldwide use of the Internet has enabled an even faster and further spread of ideas than the printing press, and provided the means for near-instantaneous conversations between physically and politically distant groups. However, although the Internet has made the distribution and mirroring of content easier and more cost effective than physical printing, it is also much easier to censor electronic content on a large scale due to the centralized nature of storage and routing services. For example, the Great Firewall of China [31], capable of filtering and inspecting all traffic that enters and leaves the country, is a much more practical and scalable censorship strategy than finding and searching the contents of every physical document that crosses the border. In the United States, the Digital Millennium Copyright Act (DMCA) provides an extremely flexible and versatile tool for commercial interests to target content providers and censor digital content from the web [28].

In an attempt to decrease the centralization of today's Internet services and provide Internet users with the censorship-resistant properties of the printing press, Anderson proposed the Eternity Service [2]. The Eternity Service is a description of an ideal digital printing press and with it Anderson outlines a conceptual framework for building censorship-resistant publishing systems in the context of modern digital communications. However, despite myriad attempts to build systems that fulfill Anderson's goals, many of which *do* provide strong censorship resistance [8,9,26,30], we are still removed from the model of the printing press. Existing systems impose barriers above and beyond the publisher simply paying for raw materials and labour, such as requiring the publisher to stay online, take responsibility for distributing their document, or operate without the guarantee that their document will remain in the system for the desired amount of time.

Censorship-resistant storage relies on a large number of geo-politically diverse participants providing bandwidth and storage space. A significant barrier to the adoption of existing systems has been the lack of incentives to participate honestly in a distributed storage system. Existing incentive models are unfit for censorship resistance because they rely on a centralized audit and payment system or lack a rigorous game-theoretic analysis of possible attempts to subvert the system and thus maximize earnings. Until recently, incentive systems also lacked a candidate electronic payment system with the security and anonymity properties necessary to provide micropayments to participant servers in exchange for their storage space and bandwidth. However, the development of cryptocurrencies has provided a new way to administer electronic payments and enforce *payment contracts*, similar to the original printing press.

In this paper, we propose Lavinia: a distributed audit and payment protocol for censorship-resistant storage in which publishers pay for the storage and bandwidth costs associated with distributing content securely in the presence of powerful censoring adversaries, and receive in return strong guarantees that their content will remain available for the specified amount of time. We give an extensive game-theoretic analysis of our protocol and show that rational, self-interested parties will implement our protocol faithfully, behaving no differently from an honest, altruistic, participant.

In Sect. 2, we discuss related work on distributed audit and payment protocols. We then give the models and definitions for censorship-resistant storage and payment contracts in Sect. 3. In Sect. 4 we describe the Lavinia protocol, and we show that self-interest results in honest participation in the protocol in Sect. 5. We give a security analysis in Sect. 6, and conclude in Sect. 7.

2 Related Work

Anderson first proposed a digital version of the printing press 20 years ago [2]. The Eternity Service is an ideal (yet unrealized) censorship-resistant publishing system that comprises properties such as plausible deniability for participating servers, anonymity for publishing authors, and notably a payment system to mimic the model of the printing press where a publisher pays to have her work replicated and distributed to readers in a way that is difficult for authorities to track and prevent.

Many existing censorship-resistant publishing systems rely on in-kind payments and reputation-management protocols to incentivize *honest* participation and to limit the effects of a storage-based denial-of-service attack, in which an adversary prevents the publication of new documents by filling up all available space. Tangler [30] assigns *storage credits* to participating servers, allowing them to store a set amount of content proportional to their own donated capacity. This gives them the option to "rent out" or donate their storage credits at their own discretion. However, Tangler does not provide a protocol for credit rentals or donations, leaving servers to adopt insecure or biased methods of collecting remuneration for their services. Furthermore, there is no audit process to guarantee that servers continue to store and serve uncorrupted documents over time. While Tangler does use a comparison of messages to inform other participating servers of nearby malicious servers, such a reputation system is not secure against a large number of colluding servers.

Free Haven [11] employs a more complex reputation management system in which servers assign a *reputation* and *credibility* value to all other known servers. Each of these two values is also accompanied by a *confidence rating* that reflects the depth of knowledge about the server in question. Servers broadcast *referrals* that contain suggestions for these values in the event of honest, malicious, or suspicious behaviour. Although such a system can pinpoint malicious servers, it does not defend against more complicated game-theoretic attacks in which an adversary behaves honestly but suspiciously in order to bait other servers into giving false reports.

Vasserman et al.'s one-way indexing scheme [29] solves the complexity of distributed trust assignments by using a centralized editorial board to curate content and defends against denial-of-service attacks by deleting unimportant documents from the system. This centralized design is not ideal for censorship resistance as users cannot store content that the editorial board deems to be uninteresting or offensive, unless it is also popular.

Although the development of an electronic *payment* protocol to incentivize censorship-resistant publishing is novel, it builds on related work in the area of distributed data storage and retrieval. A key problem in distributed storage is that once a document is stored, the server responsible for it may decide to discard the data or leave the storage network. Payment at the time of storage is therefore ineffective, and incremental payments require careful management of server reputations. There is a large body of work that addresses the problem of distributed payment in peer-to-peer systems through the use of micropayments, audits, and escrow services. Most early systems relied on a centralized payment system or suffered from problems in scalability or anonymity [10], which render them unsuitable for censorship resistance. More recent systems tend to rely on escrow payments to incentivize storage, but still require centralized audits [15] or in-kind payments where publishers pay by offering access to unused CPU cycles or bandwidth [22]. These features are undesirable for censorship resistance, where centralized third parties are vulnerable to attack and publishers (e.g., political dissidents) should be allowed to cease interaction with the system after publication.

The proposed storage system most similar to our own [20] is fully distributed and provides micropayments in return for the periodic verification of storage. However, the proof of retrieval technique used to audit document availability allows servers to distinguish between auditors and regular users. This knowledge allows them to maximize profits by refusing to serve content to anyone but an auditor. While this model is appropriate for storing documents that are meant to be accessible by a single user, it does not fit the needs of a censorship-resistant publishing system in which content is meant to be accessed by many users, and *serving content is equally as important as storing it.* For this reason, our proposed solution will make users indistinguishable from auditors, forcing servers to deliver content for *every* access. We utilize a novel micropayment system in our protocol, similar to existing work, but with additional features that ensure suitability for censorship-resistant publication, storage, and retrieval.

3   Models and Definitions

3.1   Censorship-Resistant Storage

The structure of censorship-resistant publishing systems differs from that of traditional storage schemes. Censorship-resistant storage is largely decentralized and dynamic, involving a diverse and constantly changing set of servers. As with traditional printed documents, wide dispersal and redundancy are essential for increasing the likelihood of a document's continued existence over time in a digital setting. The dispersal of sensitive documents across multiple jurisdictions has important advantages: state-sponsored attempts to remove information from the system will not be able to reach a significant subset of servers, and a single entity's attempts to compromise each machine will not scale to physically separate servers.

Our payment and audit protocol will work with a wide variety of storage schemes, including many existing censorship-resistant publishing systems. We base our security and game-theoretic analysis on a general model of storage. Here we briefly describe existing censorship-resistant storage systems and define our general model.

File retrieval: Documents should be encrypted and split into multiple retrievable pieces using a threshold scheme [23]. The act of secret sharing provides honest servers with plausible deniability about what they are hosting, and encryption adds an extra layer of protection, preventing servers that have acquired multiple shares from using existing techniques to reconstruct the document. In some jurisdictions, this may afford them legal protections. We refer to a single document piece as a *file f*.

Many existing systems are built as overlays on top of structured peer-to-peer (P2P) networks such as distributed hash tables (DHTs[1]) [18,21,25]. Each file f is associated with a keyword, and the space of all keywords is partitioned among participant servers to allow for efficient document storage and retrieval. BitTorrent [1] and Freenet [9] are examples of unstructured P2P systems. Rather than deterministically partitioning the keyspace among participant servers, documents are initially stored at one location, and then cached by additional servers when they are retrieved from the system.

In our model, each file f is stored in the system under a lookup key denoted $lookup(f)$. Performing a lookup for this key will return the server that is currently responsible for hosting that file. We assume that a lookup will be routed through, on average, a set of $k > 1$ servers on its way to the correct host. Additionally, we assume that given $lookup(f)$, a user is unable to discover all lookup keys necessary to reconstruct the entire document as in the one-way indexing technique [29]. This will provide servers and auditors with additional plausible deniability.

Redundancy: In the presence of an active censor, a high degree of redundancy ensures that a document does not become lost if some servers leave the system or refuse to serve content. We assume that the underlying storage scheme mirrors each file f on a set of $n \geq 2$ servers $server_{f1}, server_{f2}, \ldots, server_{fn}$. We also assume that the server responsible for the main copy of the file f (i.e., the server that is targeted by performing a lookup on key $lookup(f)$) has a way of contacting the mirroring servers.

Churn: Censorship-resistant storage systems are, by their nature, dynamic. We assume that new servers may join the system and that existing servers will leave.

---

[1] Although many DHTs are vulnerable to Eclipse [7] or Sybil attacks [12], we note that securing DHT join and lookup protocols is an active area of research [4,7,24] and is outside the scope of this paper.

When a server joins the system, she becomes responsible for a subset of the system files. The new server may contact the server(s) that were previously responsible for her files, and any server operator may leave the system at any time, and may contact the server(s) responsible for her files after she leaves.

3.2   Payment System

The main goal of providing compensation to participant servers in a censorship-resistant storage system is to incentivize the storage and availability of a document for an arbitrary amount of time. Anderson originally described an annuity that could accomplish this goal by "following data around", providing incremental payments to any server currently responsible for hosting and serving it [2]. Past precedent indicates that even small operators will go to great lengths to recover valuable missing data [16].

Recent innovations in cryptocurrencies have provided a means to create a travelling annuity. Funds may be transferred from a sending "wallet" to a recipient wallet with knowledge of the sending wallet's private key. This key can be easily transported along with a file or document, thereby following it around the storage system. In this section, we demonstrate the suitability of the Bitcoin cryptocurrency [19] for our protocol. However, our protocol will work with any payment system with the following properties: (1) coercion-resistant through geo-political distribution or anonymization, (2) redeemable with a distributable secret, (3) time-locked where funds can be placed in escrow until a fixed time has passed, and (4) associated with an append-only log.

Bitcoin is coercion resistant through both geo-political distribution and optional anonymous extensions. As long as at least 50% of miners accept Lavinia transactions, there is a high probability that they will not be dropped from the system. Furthermore, Zerocash [5] may be used for anonymization, eliminating the ability to link payments with specific documents and thereby thwarting censorship attempts.

Bitcoins are redeemable with one or more secrets. To redeem (i.e., spend) a coin, a user must be able to sign a transaction with the private key associated with the coin's wallet. It has a time-lock feature, which allows the sender to specify a date before which the coin cannot be redeemed. The payment blockchain doubles as an append-only log, and the Bitcoin scripting language[2] allows the spender to enforce that specific values are added to this log before a payment can be redeemed.

In our system, a publisher Alice constructs a series of *payment contracts* $\mathcal{P}(X, t, S, v)$. Each contract places a set of funds X in temporary wallets with private keys $s_i \in S$. The funds cannot be removed until after the time t has passed, and upon redeeming these funds, the holders of the keys in S must publish the value v to the Bitcoin blockchain. The set of funds, $X = \{s_1 : x_1, \ldots, s_n : x_n\}$,

---

[2] https://bitcoin.org/.

specifies the amount of Bitcoins x_i that belongs to the wallet with private key s_i. The funds may not be redeemed without the cooperation of all recipients.

Each recipient (i.e., holders of the private keys in S) fulfills the contract $\mathcal{P}$ by having all recipients collectively sign and append a transaction to the blockchain that spends the coins to their own personal accounts and posts the now-public value v. We denote this *transaction* as $\mathcal{T}(proof(S), v)$. When the transactions are complete, the funds will be divided amongst the recipients in the amounts specified by X in the payment contract.

We can construct the payment contract

$$\mathcal{P}(\{s_1 : x_1, s_2 : x_2\}, t, \{s_1, s_2\}, v)$$

using the Bitcoin scripting language. When a transaction to spend a coin is processed, its input script is concatenated to the output script of the transaction that created the coin. Alice commits to $\mathcal{P}$ by submitting a transaction spending coins worth a total of $x_1 + x_2$ to the blockchain. This transaction contains the following output script:

```
timelock: t
Output: [
{x1,
    <Pubkey s1> <PubKey s2> 2
    OP_CHECKMULTISIG
    OP_SHA256
    <hash_of_v>
    OP_EQUALVERIFY },
{x2,
    <Pubkey s1> <PubKey s2> 2
    OP_CHECKMULTISIG
    OP_SHA256
    <hash_of_v>
    OP_EQUALVERIFY }]
```

It requires a proof of knowledge of the secrets s_1 and s_2 in the form of signatures on the subsequent spend transaction. It also requires the next spend transaction to include the value v in its input script. It verifies this value by ensuring that it hashes to hash_of_v. The time lock ensures that the next spend transaction will not be submitted to the blockchain until the time t has passed.

The transaction $\mathcal{T}$ that fulfills this contract must have the following input script:

```
<v> <sig s1> <sig s2>
```

Each owner of a secret in the set S must provide a transaction with this input script to redeem their funds. This involves signatures from both parties on each transaction.

4   Lavinia Protocol

4.1   Overview

Lavinia allows a publisher to publish content, submit payments, and then vanish from the system completely—the continued availability of content is not contingent on the actions of the original publisher. This protects against out-of-band coercion tactics such as *rubber-hose cryptanalysis* in the case that the publisher is captured or prosecuted. Additionally, third-party benefactors may fund existing documents to increase the likelihood that they will remain in the system or extend the document's lifetime. This ensures that even popular content with higher bandwidth costs will remain in the system.

Micropayments to participating servers occur during audit periods chosen by the publisher or benefactor during the initial payment step. The publisher chooses a different auditing server for each audit period and places with them the responsibility of checking a file for availability at some time during that period, in exchange for a small remuneration. An auditor lacks sufficient evidence to prove her auditor status and requests the file as a regular user would, forcing the server to respond to both audits and regular requests for content. We place restrictions on the auditor by preventing her from learning which files she will audit until the previous audit period has passed. At that time, she may access the file's lookup key by searching the payment system's append-only log. Finally, we place additional incentives to ensure that all audits and remuneration occur in a timely manner at each audit time.

An important challenge associated with making censorship resistance a possibly profitable endeavor is ensuring that a participant is unable to game the system and receive payments without providing services. We assume that participants in the Lavinia protocol are rational and self-serving entities who will employ any means necessary to receive payments while incurring as few costs as possible in the form of storage space and network bandwidth. The fault tolerance features of our protocol will also defend against a small number of irrational, malicious participants. In Sect. 5, we show that exploiting this self-interest strengthens the censorship-resistant properties of the system and increases the likelihood that a document remains available until its expiration date.

Although Lavinia cannot directly help impoverished users publish documents safely, it does provide a way for third parties to help them more efficiently by allowing them to create payment contracts on behalf of the publisher or to supplement existing documents. For example, concerned free speech advocates could form a fund to store documents they felt were meritorious, and perhaps even participate as servers in the storage system and host content for free.

4.2   Protocol Details

We give the full Lavinia protocol in Fig. 1. During publication (or at any time throughout the life of the document) a publisher or benefactor, Alice, prepares payments for each of their files f stored in the system.

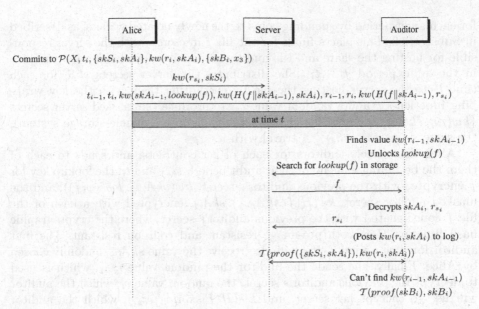

Fig. 1. Protocol for setting up payments and auditing a file f during the period $[t_{i-1}, t_i]$, where $kw(s, K)$ is a function that encrypts a key K with a secret s. The burn procedure is shown in red. (Color figure online)

Alice first determines a set of times $T = \{t_1, \ldots, t_n\}$ that separate the audit periods during which she wishes her document to be checked for availability. (For convenience, let t_0 denote the time of publication of the document.) She creates a payment contract for each time $t_i \in T$. For example, if she wishes her document to be audited approximately once a month for two years, she would then create 24 payment contracts for each file f she uploads to the system. These contracts form an agreement between Alice, the servers hosting her shares, and the auditors responsible for ensuring her document's availability.

For each of Alice's contracts, she randomly generates new wallets with private keys skA and skS for an auditor and server, respectively. She then decides on the payment amounts $X = \{skA : x_a, skS : x_s\}$ for the auditor and server.

The time lock enforces that funds will not be transferred until the audit period ending at time t_i has passed. Let $kw(s, K)$ be a key wrapping function that encrypts a key K with a secret s. We assume that this key wrapping function is secure and that the ciphertext does not leak information about the secret s or the key K. Alice encrypts the auditor's secret with a random value r to produce the masked secret $v = kw(r, skA)$; v becomes the value that must be posted to the append-only log to redeem the contract, as described in Sect. 3.2.

Alice now constructs a contract

$$\mathcal{P}(\{skA_i : x_a, skS_i : x_s\}, t_i, \{skS_i, skA_i\}, kw(r_i, skA_i)).$$

for each audit period by spending coins to the newly created wallets, as described in Subsect. 3.2. This places funds for the file f in escrow with the server responsible for hosting the share and the auditor responsible for assuring its existence in the audit period $[t_{i-1}, t_i]$. She distributes the server secrets skS_i for each time t_i to the server hosting the file by encrypting them with the key wrapping function kw and a random value r_{s_i} to produce the masked server secrets $\{kw(r_{s_i}, skS_i)\}_{i=1}^{n}$. If the file changes hands (as in a dynamic storage system), the secrets $\{kw(r_{s_i}, skS_i)\}_{i=1}^{n}$ travel with it.

Alice then selects auditors for each of her contracts, and sends to each of them the beginning and end of their audit period, t_{i-1} and t_i, the lookup key for f encrypted with the previous auditor's secret, $kw(skA_{i-1}, lookup(f))$, and the masked auditor secret, $kw(H(f\|skA_{i-1}), skA_i)$, encrypted with a hash of the file f concatenated with the previous auditor's secret, where the cryptographic hash function H is both pre-image resistant and collision resistant. The first auditor for time period $[t_0, t_1]$ will also receive the value skA_0, randomly chosen by Alice. Finally, she sends the auditor the random value r_{i-1}, which is used to decrypt the previous auditor's secret, the random value r_i, which the auditor will use to encrypt her secret, and $kw(H(f\|skA_{i-1}), r_{s_i})$, which the auditor will later decrypt and send to the server to unlock skS_i. After this point, the publisher or other benefactor is free to cease all interaction with the system. The construction and distribution of the above payment information can be performed during or after the publication of the document. Note that it is in Alice's interest to construct these values honestly. An incorrect or insecure value that prevents a server or auditor from being paid or allows them to cheat the system will increase the probability that her files will be dropped.

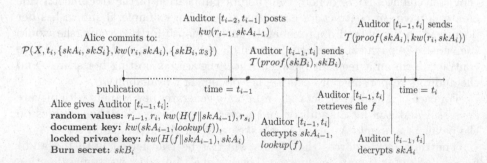

Fig. 2. The timeline of an audit sequence for a file f from the perspective of its auditor for period $[t_{i-1}, t_i]$. If the auditor for period $[t_{i-2}, t_{i-2}]$ fails to complete their audit and post their private key, the next auditor will follow the burn procedure shown in red. (Color figure online)

To ensure that Alice's files will be audited during each time period, the server and auditor should not be paid before their audit period ends and they should not be able to audit the document before their audit period begins. To accomplish this, we use the payment system's time-lock feature and encrypt thelookup keys and secrets for auditor $[t_{i-1}, t_i]$ with the published value v of auditor $[t_{i-2}, t_{i-1}]$. In order for the auditor of period $[t_{i-1}, t_i]$ to unlock her secret skA_i, she must know skA_{i-1}.

This scheme has the advantage of enforcing the time lock with self-interest. The auditor $[t_{i-2}, t_{i-1}]$ cannot redeem her payment until time t_{i-1} has passed. When an auditor moves funds, she must also release her encrypted secret, $kw(r_{i-1}, skA_{i-1})$ to a publicly viewable append-only log. At this time, the auditor for the period $[t_{i-1}, t_i]$, who owns r_{i-1}, is able to compute her own secret and perform the audit of the file. If the previous auditor releases her secret ahead of time, she runs the risk of forfeiting her payment to the next auditor (since her secret will then be visible to that auditor). We note that if a server is temporarily unavailable at the time the auditor attempts to retrieve the file f, the auditor can continue to query for the document until her audit period has passed. We show the timeline for auditing a file f at audit time t_i in Fig. 2.

Alice initializes this sequence by providing the first auditor with a randomly generated initialization key skA_0 and the following values:

$$t_1, lookup(f), kw(H(f\|skA_0), skA_1), r_1, kw(H(f\|skA_0), r_{s_1})$$

Note that this first auditor must still conduct a lookup of the file f to unlock her secret skA_1 and the server's random secret r_{s_1}.

4.3   Burn Contracts

A disadvantage of the method of sequential payments described above is the impact of an auditor leaving the system, even temporarily. If the previous auditor fails to release her information after time t_{i-1}, the auditor during $[t_{i-1}, t_i]$ will not be able to perform her audit or receive remuneration for her efforts. This in turn will prevent subsequent auditors from receiving the information needed to perform their audits, effectively terminating the revenue stream for the file. A malicious party could easily exploit this by posing as an auditor, and simply declining to perform her audit, or coercing an honest auditor into skipping a single payment on some targeted document. To avoid this, we extend the requirements of our payment system to allow an auditor to burn the previous auditor's payment after her time has passed. If an auditor at time t_i becomes aware that the previous audit failed, she will be able to burn the money in both her and her predecessor's accounts and forward the secret to the next auditor in the chain. In order to incentivize burning instead of complete inaction, we allow auditors to keep a small fraction of the profits they would have received if an audit were possible (though not so large that they would prefer burning payments to performing audits).

We define $\mathcal{P}(X, t, S, v, \{skB, x_3\})$ to be an extension of the payment contract in Subsect. 3.2 to allow Alice to specify a burn secret, skB_i and a payment amount x_3 for each time t_i. This will invalidate payments to the secrets in skS_{i-1} and skA_{i-1}, and pay the holder of this secret the amount x_3. The money is burned if and only if an auditor issues a transaction $\mathcal{T}(proof(skB_i), skB_i)$

where she posts skB_i to the log. Alice provides the auditor for period $[t_i, t_{i+1}]$ with the previous auditor's secret locked with their burn secret, $kw(skB_i, skA_i)$ at the initial time of payment. This will allow the auditor at time t_{i+1} to proceed as usual.

Each auditor will then receive the previous auditor's secret locked with the previous burn secret. In addition to preventing deliberate attacks on the chain of audits, this will incentivize auditors to complete their assigned audits before the next time period begins. We now give an implementation of the burn functionality in Bitcoin using the OP_RETURN call. The following Bitcoin script implements the payment contract:

$$\mathcal{P}(\{skS_i : x_1, skA_i : x_2\}, t_i, \{skS_i, skA_i\}, kw(r, skA_i), \{skB_{i+1}, x_3\})$$

```
Output: [
{x1,
    <hash_of_skB> OP_EQUAL
    OP_IF
        OP_RETURN //burns the money
    OP_ELSE
        <Pubkey skS> <Pubkey skA> 2
        OP_CHECKMULTISIG
        OP_SHA256
        <hash_of_kw(r, skA)>
        OP_EQUALVERIFY
    OP_ENDIF
}, {x2, //same as x1 script },
{x3,
    <hash_of_skB> <Pubkey skB>
    OP_CHECKSIG
}]
```

4.4   Choice of Auditors and Audit Times

Auditors can conceivably be any collection of entities willing to participate in the Lavinia protocol. We do not make any assumptions about whether or not they also participate as servers in the system. However, auditors do need to be discoverable by Alice. For maximum security, Alice should choose a different auditor for each audit time and file. This requires a potentially large number of auditors. One way to increase the ease of distribution and discoverability is to make the set of servers and auditors one and the same. This would allow Alice to choose a random lookup key for each payment contract, and probabilistically ensure that no one auditor will be responsible for multiple audit times of a single file.

To reduce the ability of servers to guess future audit times, a publisher can choose times at random intervals, distributed according to a Poisson process. This defends against an attack in which servers only serve content during brief time windows around fixed intervals in an effort to distinguish between auditors and regular users.

We also note that any reader can claim to be an auditor for an audit time t, and servers are unable to verify her identity. Even if the server is certain about the next audit time, there will always be at least some period between the release of the previous secret and the retrieval of the document by the next auditor during which the servers will be forced to serve the document to all users.

5 Game Theory Analysis

In the Lavinia protocol, servers are incentivized to behave correctly by the potential profits they earn from delivering files. While individual operators might have nobler motives, we claim that the harnessing of the profit motive is actually an *advantage* of our system in many respects. Operators who see an opportunity for profit can go to great lengths to ensure the integrity of the system, and to ensure they are able to fulfill their obligations. However, the use of the profit motive also has a distinct disadvantage: profit-seeking operators will not necessarily conform to the desired protocols and behaviours of the system if they can find and implement a more profitable protocol, which may not include desired behaviours [14]. In this section, we show that rational, profit-maximizing server operators will follow the Lavinia protocol faithfully by continuously storing and serving documents to both regular users of the system and auditors.

Game theoretically, we model choices of servers within a censorship-resistant storage system as a *game* played by the set of server operators A, and denote player i by A_i. Each player operates one or more servers, all connected to the same network, and tries to maximize her own profits, but does not try to reduce the profits of other players (unless doing so increases her own profits).[3] We assume there are η servers in total, and denote the set of all servers by S, and server j operated by player i with $S_{i,j}$.

In our model, each player plays several families of games, in which they select a *strategy* in the form of a set of policy decisions (e.g., when to store a file or when to serve a requested file). Strategies are selected to maximize the *profit functions* of each player, potentially based on what the other players do. The set of strategies selected by all players is called a *strategy profile*. A strategy profile forms a *Nash equilibrium* when, even with complete knowledge of what the other players have done, no player could improve her profits by retroactively adopting a different strategy. An equilibrium is a *dominant strategy equilibrium* when no player could improve her profits, *regardless* of what the other players may or may not do. If the dominant strategy equilibrium is not unique (there exists, e.g., two equally good actions for a player to take), we assume that players prefer the strategy that is closest to the Lavinia protocol (a useful assumption in many game theoretic contexts [27]). This is essentially an assumption of sloth: no player should waste resources to change from the default client behaviour to something else, if there is no change in her overall profits.

---

[3] We consider the impact of malicious servers in the next section.

5.1   The Static Game

To begin, we consider a simplified version of the storage system where the network topology is fixed. This environment is unrealistic, but could be a useful approximation of the network in the long run (i.e., after it has operated for a long time, and includes many players). Its study will also provide insights for the model considered in the next subsection, in which servers can both join and leave the network.

In this game operators must pick a strategy for operating their servers. An operator must adopt the following policies:

- A serving policy, Π_{share}, that specifies for each file f held by a server, whether or not to serve the file when it is requested. This policy is expressed as a set of probabilities $0 \leq \Pi_{share}(f) \leq 1$, each of which specifies the probability that the server responds to a request for file f.
- A storage policy Π_{store} that specifies whether or not to continue storing a file f expressed as a set of probabilities $0 \leq \Pi_{store}(f) \leq 1$.
- A routing policy Π_{route}, that specifies how a server s responds to lookup requests that are routed through it. This policy cannot depend on any particular f, but may instead depend on the server or lookup key. This policy can be split into three components: $\Pi_{route}(s, any)$, $\Pi_{route}(s, self)$ and $\Pi_{route}(s, others)$, respectively denoting whether the routing information from server s is sent at all, whether the routing information contains correct information about the keyspace managed by s, and whether the routing information for the keyspace of other servers is correct.

We further model global properties of the network with $\Gamma_{send}(f)$, and $\Gamma_{route}(s)$: the fraction of requests for a file f that are correctly routed (eventually) to the server storing f, and the fraction of routing traffic that passes through s as a fraction of all traffic expected to pass through s (i.e., $\frac{1}{\eta}$ of all traffic is expected to pass through s). Additionally, we denote by Γ_{hop} the average number of routing steps made by a given request. Finally, the function $\lambda_{BR}(f)$ denotes the ratio of lookup requests made by ordinary users to lookup requests made by auditors for a particular file f. The functions $g_{transmit}(f)$ and $c_{transmit}(f)$ denote the profit from sending f to an auditor, and the transmission cost of sending f to anyone, respectively. c_{route} similarly denotes the cost of sending routing information for one lookup key, and T is the total number of lookups into the system. We are now able to state a formal characterization of how rational actors will behave in the important set of static games of this kind (see the extended version of this paper [6] for the proof).

Theorem 1. *If
every server in the network is a starting point for $\frac{1}{\eta}$ lookups, and no lookup
will visit the same server more than once, then provided that for every server s
in the storage system,* $\dfrac{\sum_f \frac{1}{\eta}(g_{transmit}(f) - \lambda_{BR}(f)c_{transmit}(f))}{T} > c_{route},$ *and
for every file f stored at s,* $\frac{1}{\eta}(g_{transmit}(f) - \lambda_{BR}(f)c_{transmit}(f)) > c_{store}(f),$

then there exists a dominant strategy Nash equilibrium where all servers adopt the strategy $\Pi_{store}(f) = 1$ and $\Pi_{send}(f) = 1$, for all f, and $\Pi_{route}(s, all) = R_s$, where R_s is the correct routing information for s.

The interpretation of this result is that, in a static system in which traffic levels for files are relatively constant in the longer term (i.e. $\lambda_{BR}(f)$ does not change much from the server's initial belief), rational servers will conform to the Lavinia protocol even if other servers behave irrationally, subject to some modest, realistic, constraints. Further, when more servers behave rationally, $\Gamma_{send}(f)$ increases, while $\Gamma_{hop}\Gamma_{route}(s)$ decreases, making the cost of irrational behaviour (relative to rational behaviour) increase (see the extended version of this paper [6] for the proof). We conclude that this indicates the system should be quite stable in practice, once established.

We note that, although storage and bandwidth costs will vary by jurisdiction, the price of storage hardware at the moment amounts to approximately \$0.03 per GB in the United States,[4] and the cost of bandwidth is approximately \$10/month per Mbps,[5] which also equals \$0.03 per GB. The profit from hosting a file, $g_{transmit}(f)$, should then be at least $(\eta + \lambda_{BR}) \frac{\$0.03}{\text{GB}} \cdot |f|$.

5.2   Estimating λ_{BR}

Since the strategy adopted by the server is dependent on λ_{BR}, the ratio of unprofitable reader traffic to profitable auditor traffic, we now explain how servers might compute this quantity, and consequently compute their strategies.

If we assume that audit times are Poisson distributed, as mentioned above, then a server A_i still needs to estimate the frequency of non-audit traffic to compute λ_{BR}. In practice, the amount of non-audit traffic may change dramatically over time (e.g., making it an inhomogeneous Poisson process or a Cox process [17]). For example, one might expect a rapid increase in reader traffic if an important file is posted, and then later discovered and reported in the press. If A_i cannot model the change in the process's value over time, then it cannot reasonably decide whether to continue serving the file in response to sudden spikes in traffic (like a denial of service attack). It also cannot decide whether or not to continue storing the file if traffic grows too high (in the hope that traffic rates will decline again in the future), or to discard it (under the assumption that transmitting the file will never again be profitable).

In essence this is a traffic prediction problem, which is an active area of research. We suggest the use of a simple piece-wise linear approximation process [17], to estimate the current rate of requests. Since the auditor's request rates should not change over time, it can be estimated using a conventional maximum likelihood approach, where events take the form of a payment by an auditor. Thus, using the rate of payments for the file, λ_T, and the rate of total requests for the file, λ_f, a server can calculate $\lambda_{BR} = \frac{\lambda_f - \lambda_T}{\lambda_T}$.

---

[4] http://www.mkomo.com/cost-per-gigabyte-update.
[5] https://blog.cloudflare.com/the-relative-cost-of-bandwidth-around-the-world/.

5.3   Dynamic Behaviours

Having established that Lavinia is stable when the set of players is static, we now consider strategic behaviour in scenarios where servers can join and leave the network. In this section, we rely heavily on the presence of *cached* content in the storage system. When Alice publishes a document, she should store copies of each file, *along with its payment keys* at mirroring servers. We will show in this section that servers have strong incentives for continuing to store this information in the long term.

After a server joins the network, it will be present in the routing information of all servers that point to its keyspace[6]. The only needed result is to show that newly joined servers will be able to acquire the content, and vitally, the payment information, associated with their assigned keyspace. We refer to this as the *mirroring subgame*. As stated, we assume that each file f is mirrored by at least two other servers s_{f1} and s_{f2}. The mirroring subgame is then a game played between a new server that wishes to join the network, which we call s_{new}, and three other servers, s_{orig}, s_{f1} and s_{f2}. We denote by $key(s)$ the identity determining the keyspace of a particular server. The other servers are defined as follows: s_{orig} is the server that holds some files that the new server s_{new} would like to take over. s_{f1} and s_{f2} are currently mirroring the file f. We derive the following equilibrium result (see the extended version of this paper [6] for the proof):

Theorem 2. *In the mirroring subgame, there is a Nash equilibrium where the joining server s_{new} offers a one-time payment to either s_{f1} or s_{f2}, selected randomly, and will receive f with certainty. Further, this amount is not more than half the long-run total value of the mirrored file, ensuring a long-run profit for s_{new}.*

We have now established that, under the assumption a joining server s_{new} will receive all income from acquired content, it can still plausibly acquire said content. Having established this, it is straightforward to show that servers are able to come and go from the network at will. To leave the network, a server simply copies the content to the server that will be responsible for the files after she leaves and mirrors the content at the new mirroring servers $server_{f1}, \ldots, server_{fn}$. These mirror servers will accept the extra load if the content is profitable to host in the first place, because it can be sold to future joining servers for a sum that will likely cover its costs, provided that network churn occurs frequently enough *relative to the storage cost of the content*. Since payment times are Poisson distributed, no particular block of time is worth more than any other in expectation, so servers cannot gain value by repeatedly joining and leaving. Note also that although many servers may thus end up with a given file and the associated payment keys, only the server reached by an auditor will receive the r_s value needed to unlock payment for that time period.

---

[6] Note that we assume the presence of a *secure routing protocol*, in which there are protections against servers reporting incorrect routing information [7].

Under our assumptions regarding secure routing, Lavinia incentivizes an equilibrium where servers can join and leave at will, and where content will be stored redundantly. Coupled with the more robust equilibrium for a system with low churn, our results reinforce the idea that Lavinia satisfies the goals of our payment protocol.

6   Security

We claim our audit protocol is secure if an attacker is unable to: (1) compute the value of skA for any audit time t, unless she is the auditor for time t, or time t has passed and the previous auditor has posted to the append-only log, (2) receive a payment for auditing a file f at time t, unless she has retrieved f from the system sometime after the previous audit time has passed, and (3) receive a payment for serving a file f at time t, unless she has served f after the previous audit time has passed. We defend against these attacks through the use of the key wrapping function kw and the cryptographically secure hash function H. For a full proof, see the extended version of this paper [6].

While the security of the protocol itself guarantees that an auditor or server is unable to receive payment without faithfully implementing the protocol, there are a number of attacks that a malicious adversary willing to forego personal gains could employ to drop content from the system. We will now describe these attacks and their defenses.

Denial-of-Service (DoS) Attacks: As mentioned, a document that is frequently accessed will have a higher associated bandwidth cost for the hosting server. An adversary could flood the storage system with lookups in order to make content costly, incentivizing servers to stop serving certain files. There are defenses that servers could deploy individually, such as rate limiting by IP or requiring the performance of a small computational task, to limit the number of lookups by a single user. However, these techniques are useless against distributed attacks. In any case, we argue that a short-lived DoS attack will not result in content being dropped from system, but rather that servers will refuse to serve content only until the number of requests drop back to normal levels. A long-term DoS attack may be discoverable or too costly even for a state-level censor. Even the DDoS attack on Github by the Chinese government [3], which lasted five days, is still short term in the context of a document with a life span of multiple years.

Auditor-Server Collusion: An integral part of our protocol is that an audit must look no different from a regular request, forcing a server to deliver content at every request in return for possible payment. We show that an auditor lacks a sufficient amount of proof to reveal her status to the server without forfeiting her own payment. The only way for an auditor to prove her status before faithfully collecting the file f during the audit is to provide the server with $kw(H(f\|skA_{prev}), r_s)$ and $lookup(f)$, allowing the server to retrieve skS. However, the server cannot validate that this signing key is correct without the other signing key skA, and the only way for the server to validate it without serving the file to *any* auditor or reader that claims to possess skA is for the auditor to give the server $kw(H(f\|skA_{prev}), skA)$, forfeiting her payment.

Join-and-Leave Attacks: In an effort to inherit content from existing servers and drop it from the system entirely, an adversary can employ a join-and-leave attack. By repeatedly joining the network, an adversary will inherit a subset of documents from existing servers in the system. If the adversary leaves the system without replicating or moving these documents, the content will be lost. We argue that the existence of mirrored content and the profit motive will result in multiple redundant copies of each document, and that these copies may be found with minimal investigation.

False Payment Attacks: An adversary can attempt to trick servers or auditors into dropping a document from the system by issuing false payment contracts, forcing the server-auditor pairs to undergo the audit and payment protocol before she realizes that there are no funds associated with the provided payment keys. We argue that a document will still remain in the system as long as the original payments provided by Alice cover the marginal cost of participating in the additional malicious audits, which would be very small. Furthermore, the adversary is required to put some amount of funds in escrow and is unable to receive her funds until the audit time t has passed, allowing an auditor and server pair to race the adversary to complete the protocol and receive the additional payment. An adversary may try to overwhelm Alice's original contract by flooding the system with thousands of worthless ones. Such an attack is quite costly, in both computing resources and capital, as it requires a large amount of transactions in which the adversary must submit real payment contracts.

7   Conclusion

We have proposed Lavinia, a novel audit and payment protocol that incentivizes the continued availability of published content by remunerating server participation in a privacy-preserving manner. Lavinia provides a publisher with the means to specify an arbitrary storage time for her documents. The continued availability of stored documents is ensured by an audit and payment protocol, in which servers and auditors are compensated for ensuring that the document stays in the system until its expiration date. We provide a game-theoretic analysis that shows servers in the storage system acting on behalf of self-interest to maximize profits will participate honestly in the Lavinia protocol. With these requirements met, the Lavinia protocol provides the final pieces for a comprehensive realization of a true digital printing press for the Internet age.

Acknowledgements. We thank the anonymous reviewers for helping us to improve this work. We thank NSERC for grant STPGP-463324.

References

1. BitTorrent. http://www.bittorrent.com/
2. Anderson, R.: The eternity service. In: Pragocrypt 1996, pp. 242–252 (1996)
3. Anthony, S.: GitHub Battles "Largest DDoS" in Site's History, Targeted at Anti-Censorship Tools. Ars Technica, 30 March 2015. http://arstechnica.com/security/2015/03/github-battles-largest-ddos-in-sites-history-targeted-at-anti-censorship-tools/. Accessed June 2016
4. Awerbuch, B., Scheideler, C.: Towards a scalable and robust DHT. In: Proceedings of the Eighteenth Annual ACM Symposium on Parallelism in Algorithms and Architectures, SPAA 2006, pp. 318–327. ACM, New York (2006)
5. Ben Sasson, E., Chiesa, A., Garman, C., Green, M., Miers, I., Tromer, E., Virza, M.: Zerocash: decentralized anonymous payments from Bitcoin. In: 2014 IEEE Symposium on Security and Privacy (SP), pp. 459–474, May 2014
6. Bocovich, C., Doucette, J.A., Goldberg, I.: Lavinia: Censorship-Resistant Publishing with Incentives (2017). http://cacr.uwaterloo.ca/techreports/2015/cacr2015-06.pdf
7. Castro, M., Druschel, P., Ganesh, A., Rowstron, A., Wallach, D.S.: Secure routing for structured peer-to-peer overlay networks. SIGOPS Oper. Syst. Rev. 36(SI), 299–314 (2002)
8. Clarke, I., Sandberg, O., Toseland, M., Verendel, V.: Private Communication Through a Network of Trusted Connections: The Dark Freenet (2010). https://freenetproject.org/papers/freenet-0.7.5-paper.pdf
9. Clarke, I., Sandberg, O., Wiley, B., Hong, T.W.: Freenet: a distributed anonymous information storage and retrieval system. In: Federrath, H. (ed.) Designing Privacy Enhancing Technologies. LNCS, vol. 2009, pp. 46–66. Springer, Heidelberg (2001). https://doi.org/10.1007/3-540-44702-4_4
10. Dai, X., Chaudhary, K., Grundy, J.: Comparing and contrasting micro-payment models for content sharing in P2P networks. In: Third International IEEE Conference on Signal-Image Technologies and Internet-Based System, pp. 347–354. IEEE (2007)
11. Dingledine, R., Freedman, M.J., Molnar, D.: The free haven project: distributed anonymous storage service. In: Federrath, H. (ed.) Designing Privacy Enhancing Technologies. LNCS, vol. 2009, pp. 67–95. Springer, Heidelberg (2001). https://doi.org/10.1007/3-540-44702-4_5
12. Douceur, J.R.: The sybil attack. In: Druschel, P., Kaashoek, F., Rowstron, A. (eds.) IPTPS 2002. LNCS, vol. 2429, pp. 251–260. Springer, Heidelberg (2002). https://doi.org/10.1007/3-540-45748-8_24
13. Eisenstein, E.L.: The Printing Press as an Agent of Change, vol. 1. Cambridge University Press, Cambridge (1980)
14. Eyal, I., Sirer, E.G.: Majority is not enough: bitcoin mining is vulnerable. In: Christin, N., Safavi-Naini, R. (eds.) FC 2014. LNCS, vol. 8437, pp. 436–454. Springer, Heidelberg (2014). https://doi.org/10.1007/978-3-662-45472-5_28
15. Gramaglia, M., Urueña, M., Martinez-Yelmo, I.: Off-line incentive mechanism for long-term P2P backup storage. Comput. Commun. 35(12), 1516–1526 (2012)
16. Hern, A.: Missing: Hard Drive Containing Bitcoins Worth £4m in Newport Landfill Site. The Guardian (2013)
17. Massey, W.A., Parker, G.A., Whitt, W.: Estimating the parameters of a nonhomogeneous poisson process with linear rate. Telecommun. Syst. 5(2), 361–388 (1996)

18. Maymounkov, P., Mazières, D.: Kademlia: a peer-to-peer information system based on the XOR metric. In: Druschel, P., Kaashoek, F., Rowstron, A. (eds.) IPTPS 2002. LNCS, vol. 2429, pp. 53–65. Springer, Heidelberg (2002). https://doi.org/10.1007/3-540-45748-8_5

19. Nakamoto, S.: Bitcoin: A Peer-to-Peer Electronic Cash System (2008). http://bitcoin.org/bitcoin.pdf. Accessed June 2016

20. Oualha, N., Roudier, Y.: Securing P2P storage with a self-organizing payment scheme. In: Garcia-Alfaro, J., Navarro-Arribas, G., Cavalli, A., Leneutre, J. (eds.) DPM/SETOP 2010. LNCS, vol. 6514, pp. 155–169. Springer, Heidelberg (2011). https://doi.org/10.1007/978-3-642-19348-4_12

21. Rowstron, A., Druschel, P.: Pastry: scalable, decentralized object location, and routing for large-scale peer-to-peer systems. In: Guerraoui, R. (ed.) Middleware 2001. LNCS, vol. 2218, pp. 329–350. Springer, Heidelberg (2001). https://doi.org/10.1007/3-540-45518-3_18

22. Seuken, S., Charles, D., Chickering, M., Puri, S.: Market design & analysis for a P2P backup system. In: Proceedings of the 11th ACM Conference on Electronic Commerce, pp. 97–108. ACM (2010)

23. Shamir, A.: How to share a secret. Commun. ACM **22**(11), 612–613 (1979)

24. Singh, A., Ngan, T.-W., Druschel, P., Wallach, D.: Eclipse attacks on overlay networks: threats and defenses. In: Proceedings of the 25th IEEE International Conference on Computer Communications, INFOCOM 2006, pp. 1–12, April 2006

25. Stoica, I., Morris, R., Karger, D., Kaashoek, M.F., Balakrishnan, H.: Chord: a scalable peer-to-peer lookup service for internet applications. In: Proceedings of the 2001 Conference on Applications, Technologies, Architectures, and Protocols for Computer Communications, SIGCOMM 2001, pp. 149–160. ACM, New York (2001)

26. Stubblefield, A., Wallach, D.S.: Dagster: censorship-resistant publishing without replication. Technical report TR01-380, Houston, TX, USA (2001)

27. Thompson, D.R., Lev, O., Leyton-Brown, K., Rosenschein, J.: Empirical analysis of plurality election equilibria. In: Proceedings of the 2013 International Conference on Autonomous Agents and Multi-Agent Systems, pp. 391–398 (2013)

28. Urban, J.M., Quilter, L.: Efficient process or chilling effects—takedown notices under section 512 of the digital millennium copyright act. Santa Clara Comput. High Tech. L J. **22**, 621 (2005)

29. Vasserman, E.Y., Heorhiadi, V., Hopper, N., Kim, Y.: One-way indexing for plausible deniability in censorship resistant storage. In: 2nd USENIX Workshop on Free and Open Communications on the Internet. USENIX (2012)

30. Waldman, M., Mazieres, D.: Tangler: a censorship-resistant publishing system based on document entanglements. In: Proceedings of the 8th ACM Conference on Computer and Communications Security, pp. 126–135. ACM (2001)

31. Winter, P., Lindskog, S.: How the great firewall of China is blocking tor. In: Proceedings of the 2nd USENIX Workshop on Free and Open Communications on the Internet (2012)

A Simpler Rate-Optimal CPIR Protocol

Helger Lipmaa$^{(\boxtimes)}$ and Kateryna Pavlyk

University of Tartu, Tartu, Estonia
helger.lipmaa@gmail.com

Abstract. In PETS 2015, Kiayias, Leonardos, Lipmaa, Pavlyk, and Tang proposed the first $(n, 1)$-CPIR protocol with rate $1 - o(1)$. They use advanced techniques from multivariable calculus (like the Newton-Puiseux algorithm) to establish optimal rate among a large family of different CPIR protocols. It is only natural to ask whether one can achieve similar rate but with a much simpler analysis. We propose parameters to the earlier $(n, 1)$-CPIR protocol of Lipmaa (ISC 2005), obtaining a CPIR protocol that is asymptotically almost as communication-efficient as the protocol of Kiayias et al. However, for many relevant parameter choices, it is slightly more communication-efficient, due to the cumulative rounding errors present in the protocol of Kiayias et al. Moreover, the new CPIR protocol is simpler to understand, implement, and analyze. The new CPIR protocol can be used to implement (computationally inefficient) FHE with rate $1 - o(1)$.

Keywords: Communication complexity
Computationally-private information retrieval
Cryptographic protocols · Optimal rate

1 Introduction

A computationally private information retrieval ($(n, 1)$-CPIR, [11]) protocol enables the receiver to obtain an ℓ-bit element from sender's database of n elements, without the sender getting to know which element was obtained. An efficient CPIR protocol has to be implemented by virtually any two-party privacy-preserving database application, and hence CPIR protocols have received significant attention in the literature.

Since there exists a trivial CPIR protocol with linear communication ℓn where the sender just forwards the whole database to the receiver, a major requirement in the design of new CPIR protocols is their communication efficiency. The first CPIR protocol with sublinear communication was proposed by Kushilevitz and Ostrovsky [11], and slightly optimized by Stern [16]. The first CPIR protocol with polylogarithmic-in-n communication was proposed by Cachin et al. [3]. The first CPIR protocols with *asymptotically* truly efficient communication complexity were proposed by Lipmaa [12,13] and Gentry and Ramzan [6].

All mentioned papers were concerned in the communication complexity as a function of n. However, optimizing the communication complexity of a CPIR

© International Financial Cryptography Association 2017
A. Kiayias (Ed.): FC 2017, LNCS 10322, pp. 621–638, 2017.
https://doi.org/10.1007/978-3-319-70972-7_35

protocol as a function of ℓ is also important, especially in applications where the database elements are very long, e.g., movies. Optimizing the rate—defined as the size of useful information ($\log n + \ell$ in the case of an $(n, 1)$-CPIR protocol) divided by the actual communication complexity of the protocol—is also an interesting theoretical question. Indeed, achieving optimal rate (while still having acceptable computational complexity) is a central question in many areas of computer science and engineering.

The first constant-rate CPIR protocol was proposed by Gentry and Ramzan [6] (ICALP 2005, rate 1/4) and Lipmaa [12] (ISC 2005, rate 1/2). Lipmaa devised another variant of his protocol with optimized results; the resulting CPIR protocol from [13] had rate $1 - 1/a + o(1)$ for some positive constant $a > 1$. However, the drawback of the latter variant (see Sect. 3.3 for its full description) is an additive term $a\kappa \log_2^2 n$ in the communication complexity (here, κ is the security parameter), which means that the optimal value of a is actually quite small unless ℓ is very huge. Moreover, a cannot depend on ℓ (i.e., it has to be constant), and thus this CPIR protocol does not achieve rate $1 - o(1)$.

In a recent paper, Kiayias $et\ al.$ [10] proposed a general parameterized family of so called leveled LBP-homomorphic encryption schemes with rate $1 - o(1)$. Here, LBP denotes the complexity class of functions implementable by polynomial-size (leveled) large-output branching programs, [17]. They then used the fact [8, 13] that such an encryption scheme can be used to efficiently implement CPIR.

However, achieving optimal rate required the authors of [10] to perform extensive technical analysis. More precisely, following earlier papers like [11–13], the $(n, 1)$-CPIR protocol of Kiayias $et\ al.$ is recursive. First, [10] constructs a (leveled) homomorphic encryption scheme that allows to compute an arbitrary function f by constructing a w-ary branching program (for some small $w \ll n$, e.g., $w = 2$) that computes f. Following [8], this homomorphic encryption scheme privately implements the $(w, 1)$ multiplexer function, needed in every internal node of a branching program, by using a simple $(w, 1)$-CPIR protocol that has minimal (i.e., rate $1 - o(1)$) $sender\text{-}side$ communication. However, it has linear client-side (and hence, total) communication.

In addition, at every internal node, the $(n, 1)$-CPIR protocol of [10] applies a precisely defined operation of splitting and concatenating, that guarantees that at the level d of the branching program, the $(w, 1)$-CPIR protocol operates with database elements of length $s_d\kappa$, where s_d is a parameter to be optimized. More precisely, the outputs of the CPIR protocol from level $d - 1$ are cut into some t_d pieces of length $s_d\kappa$. By using this recursive construction, a suitable $(w, 1)$-CPIR protocol can be used to securely implement any function from LBP.

Kiayias $et\ al.$ [10] showed, by using an intricate analysis, that the optimal communication is achieved when $s_1 = \ldots = s_m =: s$, where m is the length of the branching program. In a nutshell, they used multivariable calculus to show that the communication complexity of their CPIR protocol is optimized when s is equal to a root of a certain degree-$(m + 1)$ polynomial f_m. Then, they used Galois theory to show that f_m cannot be solved in radicals. Finally, they used the theory of Newton-Puiseux series to numerically compute an approximation of the optimal s. As the end result, they obtained a CPIR protocol of rate $1 - 1.72\sqrt{\kappa/\ell}\log_2 n + O(\ell^{-1})$.

Hence, the analysis used in [10] is (very) complicated, resulting in (a) a CPIR protocol with a complex description, and (b) an optimal parameter choice that, while it can be done efficiently, seems to be difficult to analyze. For example, the optimal value of s in [10] is given by a series. After that, [10] proves that given the so computed s, the communication complexity will be given by another explicit series. However, in practice one needs to compute an integer approximation of s efficiently. While [10] proposed an efficient algorithm for computing such an approximation, it is unclear how this will influence the precise value of the communication complexity in the general case.

Moreover, one problem of their scheme is due to "rounding errors". First, the claimed rate corresponds to the case when s is a real root while in practice s must be an integer. To deal with this requirement, Kiayias *et al.* presented an $O(\log\log n)$-time algorithm to compute an integer approximation of s. Second, recall that each $(w, 1)$-CPIR protocol at every layer in [10] requires plaintexts of the same length $s\kappa$. However, in the optimal construction of [10], there is no guarantee that the total output length of the previous layer divides by s and hence at every layer one has to round up the length of each plaintext. This means that at every layer, there will be some undue increase in the number of applied $(w, 1)$-CPIR protocols, which increases the actual communication complexity of the resulting $(n, 1)$-CPIR protocol.

The authors of [10] did not compute precise upper bounds on the communication of their CPIR protocol after s is rounded to an integer and one adds up the rounding errors. Instead, [10] provided empirical data (see Sect. 7.1.1 in [10], or Fig. 1 in the current paper) that the increase in communication is insignificant when ℓ is large, at least for some practically relevant values of ℓ and n.

Our Contribution. We show how to achieve *almost* the same communication complexity and rate as in the protocol of Kiayias *et al.* [10]. We provide precise analysis and comparison in Sect. 5, where we show that the difference between the communication of the "ideal" CPIR protocol of [10] (that does not take into account rounding errors) and the new CPIR protocol is $O(\ell^{1/2})$. After taking into account the rounding errors, the new protocol will be *slightly* more communication-efficient for all values of ℓ and n analysed in [10]. (See Fig. 1.) The new CPIR protocol can be used to implement rate $1 - o(1)$ oblivious transfer, strong conditional oblivious transfer, asymmetric fingerprinting protocol, and (computationally inefficient) fully-homomorphic encryption.

We use the CPIR protocol proposed by Lipmaa in ISC 2005 [12] and ICISC 2009 [13] but with parameters that we optimize in the current paper. In particular, we consider general w-ary decision trees instead of just binary contrary to [12,13]. Alternatively, the proposed protocol is an instantiation of the CPIR protocol family of Kiayias *et al.* [10] but with different parameter set, namely, with the values t_d being constant, $t_1 = \cdots = t_m =: t$, and the values s_d being

ℓ/κ	Communication				
	No privacy	Kiayas *et al.* [10]		This work	
		Theoretical	With rounding	Theoretical	With rounding
10^3	2 048 017	4 079 561	4 220 928	4 090 880	4 090 880
10^4	20 480 017	26 439 497	26 759 168	26 443 776	26 443 776
10^5	204 800 017	223 161 724	223 942 656	223 163 148	223 163 343
10^6	2 048 000 017	2 105 572 921	2 107 731 968	2 105 573 376	2 105 573 376
10^7	20 480 000 017	20 661 566 883	20 664 602 624	20 661 567 027	20 661 569 161
10^8	204 800 000 017	205 373 669 331	205 394 259 968	205 373 669 376	205 373 669 376

Fig. 1. Comparison with [10], for $\kappa = 2048$, $w = 5$, $n = 5^7$. The protocol from [10] offers better communication if rounding is not taken into account. However, in all cases, the current work offers better communication in practice (i.e., when parameters have been rounded correctly)

slightly increasing. This means that the new CPIR protocol can be seen as a t-times parallel implementation—each for $\lceil \ell/t \rceil$-bit databases—of the CPIR protocol from [12], for an optimized value of t. The new analysis is significantly simpler than the multi-page analysis of [10] but surprisingly enough delivers almost the same results. (Intuitively, this happens since in [10], in different layers one uses parameters $(s, s, s, \dots)$ while in the new protocol, one uses parameters $(s, s + 1, s + 2, \dots)$. Since ℓ and s both are considered to be large, $s + 1 \approx s$.)

To show that our analysis is really simple, we will very briefly outline it next. The communication function of the w-ary generalization of the CPIR from [12] depends on n (the size of the database), ℓ (the length of database elements), κ (the security parameter), t (the parallelism factor) and w (the arity of the decision tree). Here, t and w are the values to be optimized. First, we use simple univariate analysis to derive the optimal value $t_{opt} = \sqrt{(w - 1)\ell/\kappa}$ of t for any w. Given the value of t_{opt}, we then "near optimize" (see Sect. 4) the value of w. Here, near optimizing means that we write the communication function as a series in ℓ, and then choose the *integer* value of w (namely, $w = 5$) that minimizes the *most significant* coefficients of this series. Since t_{opt} is a function of ℓ, the layout of the series crucially depends on the fact that we first fix t_{opt}.

We show that under these values of t and w, the *asymptotic* communication of the resulting CPIR protocol is practically the same as in the optimal case in [10]. On the other hand, for *interesting*[1] values of ℓ, the proposed variant will have slightly better communication. More precisely, in the new CPIR protocol, the communication complexity function, written down as a series in ℓ coincides with the one of the CPIR from [10] in the first three terms. The communication complexity of the optimal CPIR of [10] has a tailing element $O_\ell(1/\ell)$ that makes

---

[1] Here, by interesting we mean values of ℓ that correspond to the length of an audio or video file; this was also the motivating example given in [10]. If ℓ is much shorter, then optimizing the communication complexity as a function of ℓ is not relevant.

their construction asymptotically slightly more efficient. However, the difference is not big: for example, in a concrete case where the database elements are $10^6 \kappa$ bits long and the database has $n = 5^7$ elements (here, $\kappa = 2048$ is the currently recommended security parameter), the CPIR of [10] is—when ignoring rounding errors—more efficient than the new CPIR by 683 bytes out of more than 3 billion. See Fig. 1 for more examples.

However, this comparison is purely theoretical since it operates with the "ideal" communication function and does not take into account rounding errors. Compared to [10], we do not run into rounding errors at *every* layer of the construction. Intuitively, this is the case since in our construction, each ciphertext of the previous layer is considered to be the plaintext of the next layer and hence the length of the plaintexts increases by κ bits at each layer. On the other hand, in [10], at each layer, the concatenation of t ciphertexts (of total length $(s+1)t_d \kappa$) is divided into new plaintexts, each of length $s\kappa$. The rounding error (at every layer) is caused by the fact that for an s that is chosen optimally by the analysis of [10], $(s + 1)t_d \kappa$ is essentially never divisible by s.

In fact, in the new construction, it is only important that $s \mid \ell$ (or else we get a *one-time* rounding error at the very bottom of the protocol construction). This means, as we show numerically, that in practice, the new CPIR protocol achieves slightly better communication complexity than the CPIR of [10], while being much simpler. See Fig. 1 for a communication efficiency comparison. To demonstrate the (relative) simplicity of the new construction, we will give a full description of the new CPIR protocol on Fig. 3; the only important distinction from the well-known CPIR protocol of [12], as modified by [13], is in the first line (the choice of the paramrters). A comparable full description of the CPIR protocol of [10] is significantly longer, albeit mostly due to the more complicated procedure for selecting optimal parameters. In fact, [10] does *not* give a self-contained description of their CPIR protocol. Figure 3 in [10] describes their new LHE scheme (that then has to be modified to become a CPIR protocol), but the choice of all parameters is described later in that paper, together with the issues rising from rounding the parameters.

Extensions and Applications. Based on the ideas of [8,10] and of the current paper, one can construct a rate $1 - o(1)$ homomorphic encryption scheme that can homomorphically evaluate any function that has a polynomial-size large-output branching program. All known fully homomorphic encryption schemes have a very low rate. (See [7] for insights on why achieving good rate fully homomorphic encryption scheme might be difficult.) Since the generalization from binary decision trees, that are used to construct the new CPIR protocol, to arbitrary branching programs is straightforward yet necessitates introducing a lot of branching program-related terminology, we will omit further discussion and refer to [10].

Similarly, one can build a rate $1 - o(1)$ oblivious transfer, given the new CPIR protocol and known transformations, see [10] for discussion. Finally, based on their CPIR protocol, [10] proposed a new rate $1 - o(1)$ strong conditional oblivious transfer protocol [1], and based on the later, [9] constructed the first optimal rate asymmetric fingerprinting protocol. One can plug in the CPIR protocol of the current paper to those constructions obtaining simpler yet slightly more communication-efficient protocols for (strong conditional) oblivious transfer and asymmetric fingerprinting.

2   Preliminaries

Notation. For a predicate, let $[P(x)] \in \{0, 1\}$ denote the truth value of $P(x)$, e.g., $[x = y]$ is equal to 1 iff $x = y$ and to 0 otherwise. The Lambert's W function is defined by the equation $z = W(z)e^{W(z)}$. Asymptotically, $W(z) \approx \ln z - \ln \ln z$. Let κ be the security parameter; in our case it corresponds to the key length in bits, so $\kappa \geq 2048$.

Public-Key Cryptosystem. A length-flexible cryptosystem (Gen, Enc, Dec) [4,5] consists of three efficient algorithms, Gen for key generation, Enc for encryption, and Dec for decryption. The public key pk fixes the plaintext space, the randomizer space $\mathfrak{R}_{\mathsf{pk}}$, and the ciphertext space. For a public key pk, plaintext m (of bitlength $\ell = |m|$), a positive integer length parameter $s := \lceil \ell / \kappa \rceil$, and a randomizer $r \in \mathfrak{R}_{\mathsf{pk}}$ we have $c = \mathsf{Enc}_{\mathsf{pk}}^s(m; r)$ and $m = \mathsf{Dec}_{\mathsf{sk}}^s(c)$, and it is required that $\mathsf{Dec}_{\mathsf{sk}}^s(\mathsf{Enc}_{\mathsf{pk}}^s(m; r)) = m$.

A length-flexible cryptosystem has to satisfy the usual IND-CPA security requirement [4]. That is, no efficient adversary should be able to distinguish between ciphertexts corresponding to m_0 and m_1 encrypted by using the same integer length parameter, even if m_0 and m_1 were chosen by her.

Let the *rate* of the cryptosystem be $|m|/|c|$, i.e., the ratio between the number of useful bits and the actual transmission length. A length-flexible cryptosystem is *optimal rate* if $|m|/|c| = 1 - o(1)$ when $|m|$ increases.

A cryptosystem is *additively homomorphic* if $\mathsf{Dec}_{\mathsf{sk}}^s(\mathsf{Enc}_{\mathsf{pk}}^s(m_1; r_1) \cdot \mathsf{Enc}_{\mathsf{pk}}^s(m_2; r_2)) = m_1 + m_2$. In [4,5], Damgård and Jurik constructed two IND-CPA secure optimal-rate length-flexible additively homomorphic cryptosystems. See also [2]. An additively homomorphic cryptosystem is also required to be *rerandomizable* in the sense that $\mathsf{Enc}_{\mathsf{pk}}^s(m; r) \cdot \mathsf{Enc}_{\mathsf{pk}}^s(0; r_1')$ is computationally indistinguishable from $\mathsf{Enc}_{\mathsf{pk}}^s(0; r_2')$, for uniformly random $r_1', r_2' \leftarrow_r \mathfrak{R}_{\mathsf{pk}}$.

More precisely, in the cryptosystem of [4], the public key is a well-chosen RSA modulus $N = pq$, the secret key is (p, q), and for a positive integer s, $\mathsf{Enc}_{\mathsf{pk}}^s(m; r) = (1 + N)^m r^{N^s} \mod N^{s+1}$, for $m \in \mathbb{Z}_{N^s}$ and $r \in \mathbb{Z}_N^*$. Hence, if the plaintext is of length $s\kappa$, the cryptosystem of [4] has ciphertext of length $(s + 1)\kappa$. The rate of this cryptosystem is

$$\frac{\ell}{\ell + \kappa} = 1 - \frac{\kappa}{\ell} + \frac{\kappa^2}{\ell^2} + O_\ell(\ell^{-3}) \ .$$

This is intuitively optimal (up to the choice of κ) since κ bits are needed to randomize the ciphertext. The Damgård-Jurik cryptosystem from [4] is IND-CPA secure under the DCR assumption [15].

If pk and r are understood in the context (or if their precise value is not relevant), we will not write them down explicitly.

Computationally-Private Information Retrieval (CPIR). Assume $n > 1$ and ℓ are positive integers, with $n, \ell = poly(\kappa)$. An $(n, 1)$-CPIR protocol [11] for ℓ-bit strings allows the receiver on input $x \in \{0, \ldots, n-1\}$ to obtain $f_x \in \{0, 1\}^{\ell}$ out of the sender's database $\boldsymbol{f} = (f_0, \ldots, f_{n-1})$ without the sender getting any information about x.

In a *two-message CPIR protocol*, the receiver first generates a public and secret key pair $(\mathsf{pk}, \mathsf{sk})$, then sends a query $Q \leftarrow \mathsf{Query}_{\mathsf{pk}}(n, \ell; x)$ and pk to the sender, who answers with a reply $R \leftarrow \mathsf{Reply}_{\mathsf{pk}}(n, \ell; \boldsymbol{f}, Q)$. After that, the receiver uses a function $\mathsf{Answer}_{\mathsf{sk}}(n, \ell; x, R)$ to recover f_x.

The receiver's communication is equal to $|Q|$, the sender's communication is equal to $|R|$, and the *total communication* is equal to $\mathsf{com} := |Q| + |R|$. A non-private CPIR protocol consists of two messages, $Q = x$ (of $\log_2 n$ bits) from the receiver to the sender, and $R = f_x$ (of ℓ bits) from the sender to the receiver. We do not count pk as part of the communication, since (a) it is short, and (b) it can—and will—be reused between many instances of the CPIR protocol. The *rate* of a CPIR protocol is equal to $(\log_2 n + \ell)/\mathsf{com}$.

A two-message CPIR protocol is *IND-CPA secure* if no efficient adversary $\mathcal{A}$ can distinguish between queries corresponding to x_0 and x_1, even if x_0 and x_1 were chosen by her. That is,

$$\Pr \left[\begin{array}{l} (\mathsf{pk}, \mathsf{sk}) \leftarrow \mathsf{Gen}(1^{\kappa}), (x_0, x_1) \leftarrow \mathcal{A}_{\mathsf{pk}}(1^{\kappa}, n, \ell), b \leftarrow_r \{0, 1\}, \\ Q \leftarrow \mathsf{Query}_{\mathsf{pk}}(n, \ell; x_b) : \mathcal{A}_{\mathsf{pk}}(n, \ell; Q) = b \end{array} \right]$$

is negligible in κ, for each probabilistic polynomial-time $\mathcal{A}$ and polynomially large n and ℓ.

3 Related Work

There are very few conceptually different approaches for constructing communication-efficient $(n, 1)$-CPIR protocols. The $(n, 1)$-CPIR protocol by Kiyaias *et al.* [10], following earlier protocols [8,11–13,16], homomorphically executes a branching program, by using a $(w, 1)$-CPIR at every internal node of the branching program. Here, w is a small constant. See [3,6] for a different approach that however results in rate that cannot be better than $1/4$; see [3,6] for a discussion.

3.1 Linear-Communication $(w, 1)$-CPIR Protocol

Recall that s is a positive integer. The concrete underlying $(w, 1)$-CPIR protocol used in [8,10,12,13] is a simple linear-communication CPIR protocol from [12][2].

---

[2] As shown in [14], linear communication is the best one can hope when building a CPIR protocol on top of an additively homomorphic cryptosystem while *not* using recursion.

To transfer one $\ell = s\kappa$-bit database element, the receiver sends to the sender $w-1$ ciphertexts, and the sender responds with one ciphertext, where the length of each ciphertext is $(s+1)\kappa$ bits. More precisely, the receiver sends to the sender $w-1$ ciphertexts C_i encrypting $[x = i]$ for $i \in \{0, \ldots, w-2\}$, $C_i = \mathsf{Enc}^s([x = i]; r_i)$ for a random $r_i \leftarrow_r \mathfrak{R}_{\mathsf{pk}}$. From $\{C_i\}_{i=0}^{w-2}$, by using additive homomorphism, the sender obtains the ciphertext C_{w-1} encrypting $[x = w-1] = 1 - \sum_{i=0}^{w-2}[x = i]$. Hence, $(C_0, \ldots, C_{w-1})$ encrypts the x-th unit vector, $x \in \{0, \ldots, w-1\}$. Then, she uses $\{C_i\}_{i=0}^{w-1}$ to homomorphically compute a randomized ciphertext encrypting $\sum_{i=1}^n [x = i] f_i = f_x$. That is, $Q = \mathsf{Query}_{\mathsf{pk}}(n, \ell; x) = (C_0, \ldots, C_{w-2})$, $C_{w-1} = \mathsf{Enc}^s(1; 0) / \prod_{i=0}^{w-2} C_i$, and $R = \mathsf{Reply}_{\mathsf{pk}}(n, \ell; \boldsymbol{f}, Q) = \prod_{i=0}^{w-1} C_i^{f_i} \cdot \mathsf{Enc}^s(0; r)$ for a random r. The receiver just computes $\mathsf{Answer}_{\mathsf{sk}}(n, \ell; x, R) = \mathsf{Dec}_{\mathsf{sk}}^s(R)$. This CPIR protocol is IND-CPA secure given that the underlying Damgård-Jurik cryptosystem is IND-CPA secure, i.e., under the DCR assumption.

While this $(w, 1)$-CPIR has linear communication, importantly its sender-side communication consists of only one ciphertext and thus has near-optimal rate $(\log_2 n + \ell)/(\ell + \kappa) = 1 - (\kappa - \log_2 n)/\ell + O(\ell^{-2}) = 1 - o(1)$.

3.2   Lipmaa's Recursive $(n, 1)$-CPIR Protocol from [12]

W.l.o.g., assume that n is a power of w, $n = w^m$ for some m, where w is a small positive integer. (In the general case, one can add dummy elements to the database.) The $(n, 1)$-CPIR protocols of [10–13] are built on top of a $(w, 1)$-CPIR, $w \ll n$, in a recursive manner.

Let $(\mathsf{Gen}, \mathsf{Enc}, \mathsf{Dec})$ be an optimal-rate length-flexible additively homomorphic cryptosystem like the one proposed by Damgård and Jurik [4] and $(\mathsf{Query}, \mathsf{Reply}, \mathsf{Answer})$ be the $(w, 1)$-CPIR protocol of Sect. 3.1. In the $(n, 1)$-CPIR protocol of Lipmaa from ISC 2005 [12], a w-ary decision tree of length $m := \log_w n$ is constructed on top of a database of n elements. Then, the internal nodes are assigned labels starting from bottom. Let $x = \sum_{i=0}^{m-1} x_i w^i$, i.e., x_i is the ith w-ary digit of x. For an internal node v that has distance i to the leafs, the label of v is equal to the reply of the $(w, 1)$-CPIR protocol, given a query $\mathsf{Query}(w, s\kappa; x_i)$ and a database $(f_0, \ldots, f_{w-1})$ consisting of the labels of the children of v. (See Fig. 2.) Finally, the sender replies with the label of the root of the binary decision tree, and the receiver applies to it m times the Answer function to recover f_x.

Since we use the $(w, 1)$-CPIR protocol of Sect. 3.1, if the labels of the children of v are say $(f_{v0}, \ldots, f_{v1})$, then the label of v is going to be $\mathsf{Enc}_{\mathsf{pk}}^{s+i-1}(f_{vx_i})$ (as in Fig. 2), and each application of Answer consists of a single decryption.

The receiver's message in the $(n, 1)$-CPIR protocol corresponds to one $(w, 1)$-CPIR receiver's message for each length parameter $s + i$, $i \in \{1, \ldots, \log_w n\}$, while the sender's message corresponds to one $(w, 1)$-CPIR sender's message for the length parameter $s + \log_w n$. The resulting receiver's communication is

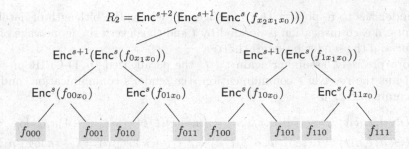

Fig. 2. Using Lipmaa's $(w, 1)$-CPIR from [12] with $w = 2$ and $n = 8$. The receiver sends $\mathsf{Enc}^s(x_0)$, $\mathsf{Enc}^{s+1}(x_1)$, $\mathsf{Enc}^{s+2}(x_2)$ to the sender. The sender computes recursively the values at intermediate nodes, and then replies with R_2.

$$
\begin{aligned}
\mathsf{rec}_1(w, n, \ell, \kappa) &:= \sum_{i=1}^{\log_w n} (w - 1)(\ell/\kappa + i)\kappa \\
&= (w - 1)(\ell/\kappa + (\log_w n + 1)/2)\log_w n \cdot \kappa \\
&= (w - 1)(\ell + (\log_w n + 1)\kappa/2)\log_w n
\end{aligned}
$$

and the sender's communication is

$$
\mathsf{sen}_1(w, n, \ell, \kappa) := (\ell/\kappa + \log_w n)\kappa = \ell + \kappa \log_w n .
$$

(Recall that communication is always measured in bits.) Hence, the total communication $\mathsf{com}_1(w, n, \ell, \kappa) = \mathsf{rec}_1(w, n, \ell, \kappa) + \mathsf{sen}_1(w, n, \ell, \kappa)$ of the CPIR protocol from [12] is equal to

$$
\mathsf{com}_1(w, n, \ell, \kappa) = ((w - 1)\log_w n + 1)\ell + \frac{\kappa \log_w n \cdot ((w - 1)\log_w n + (w + 1))}{2} .
$$

Its rate is $(\log_2 n + \ell)/\mathsf{com}_1(w, n, \ell, \kappa) \approx 1/((w - 1)\log_w n + 1)$. For large ℓ, $\mathsf{com}_1(\cdot, n, \ell, \kappa)$ is clearly minimal when $w = 2$, with

$$
\mathsf{com}_1(2, n, \ell, \kappa) = (\log_2 n + 1)\ell + \frac{\kappa \log_2 n \cdot (\log_2 n + 3)}{2}
$$

and rate $\approx 1/(\log_2 n + 1)$.

3.3   Optimizing the Communication by Data-Parallelization

In [12], Lipmaa additionally noted that one can reduce the communication (assuming $\ell/\kappa \gg \log_2 n$) by executing the protocol from Sect. 3.2 separately and in parallel on every (ℓ/t)-bit chunk of the database elements, where $t \geq 1$, $t \mid \ell$, is a positive integer. This results in optimized total communication since in the $(n, 1)$-CPIR protocol of Sect. 3.2, the receiver's communication is much larger than the sender's communication. If $t > 1$, then the same receiver's message can be used in all t parallel invocations of the protocol from Sect. 3.2, while the sender has to respond with t messages. Crucially, the bitlength of database elements in each invocation is divided by t and thus every single message of the receiver and the sender becomes shorter.

More precisely, assuming again $t \mid \ell$, the parallelized $(n, 1)$-CPIR protocol of [12] has the receiver's communication, the sender's communication, and the total communication

$$\mathsf{rec}_2(w, n, \ell, \kappa, t) := \mathsf{rec}_1(w, n, \ell/t, \kappa) = (w - 1)(\ell/t + (\log_w n + 1)\kappa/2) \log_w n \ ,$$
$$\mathsf{sen}_2(w, n, \ell, \kappa, t) := t \cdot \mathsf{sen}_1(w, n, \ell/t, \kappa) = t(\ell/t + \kappa \log_w n) = \ell + t\kappa \log_w n \ ,$$

$$\mathsf{com}_2(w, n, \ell, \kappa, t) = (w - 1)(\ell/t + (\log_w n + 1)\kappa/2) \log_w n + \ell + t\kappa \log_w n \ . \quad (1)$$

If $t \nmid \ell$, then one has to round ℓ/t upwards.

In ISC 2005 [12], Lipmaa considered parameter settings that resulted in rate $\approx 1/2$. In ICISC 2009 [13], Lipmaa considered the following parameter settings: $w = 2$ and $t = a \log_2 n$ for large a. In this case,

$$\mathsf{com}_2(2, n, \ell, \kappa, a \log_2 n) = \left(\frac{1}{a} + 1\right)\ell + \frac{(2a + 1)\kappa \log_2^2 n}{2} + \frac{\kappa \log_2 n}{2} \ . \quad (2)$$

Thus with such parameters the parallelized $(n, 1)$-CPIR protocol has rate

$$\frac{\log_2 n + \ell}{\mathsf{com}_2(2, n, \ell, \kappa, a \log_2 n)} = \frac{a}{a + 1} + O(\ell^{-2}) \leq 1 - \frac{1}{a} + O(\ell^{-2}) \ .$$

However, for this estimate to hold, it is needed that $a = \Theta_\ell(1)$ does not depend on ℓ. Moreover, due to the additive term $\Theta(a)\kappa \log_2^2 n$ in Eq. (2), the communication complexity will actually increase if a is too large. Hence, by using the parameters proposed in [13], the parallelized $(n, 1)$-CPIR protocol from [12] cannot achieve rate $1 - o(1)$.

3.4   The CPIR Protocol of Kiayias *et al.*

Kiayas *et al.* [10] proposed another twist on top of the CPIR protocol of Lipmaa [12]. In a nutshell, during the recursive procedure, the parallelized CPIR protocol of Sect. 3.3 stores at every childrens' node the concatenation of t plaintexts. The label of the parent node is defined to be equal to the concatenation of t individual ciphertexts. In [10], each childrens' node also stores the concatenation of t plaintexts each being (say) L bits long. However, this concatenation is then redivided into t' equal-length new plaintexts (each of length $\lceil tL/t' \rceil$). The new plaintexts are then encrypted individually and the resulting ciphertexts concatenated as the label of the parent node. The major contribution in [10] is the computation of optimal values t and t' (for each layer of the CPIR tree) and establishing that one can choose those values so as to obtain a CPIR protocol of rate $1 - o(1)$.

4 Simple Optimal-Rate CPIR Protocol

We now propose a different setting of the parameters for the parallelized $(n, 1)$-CPIR protocol from Sect. 3.3, motivated by the approach of [10]. We first continue the analysis of [12,13], and find optimal values of the parameters. After that, for the sake of completeness, we will give a full description of the resulting CPIR protocol together with a security proof.

4.1 Optimization of Parameters

Recall that the communication complexity of Lipmaa's parallelized $(n, 1)$-CPIR protocol is given by Eq. (1). It depends on three variables (κ, ℓ, and n) that are fixed, and two variables (w and t) that can be optimized. We were unable to find the global optimum of com_2, due to the complicated form of $\partial \mathsf{com}_2 / \partial w$,

$$\frac{\partial \mathsf{com}_2}{\partial w} = \frac{\ln n \cdot \ln w \cdot (w \ln w(2\ell + kt) - 2\ell(w-1) - kt(2t + w - 1))}{2tw \ln^3 w}$$
$$+ \frac{\ln^2 n \cdot kt(-2w + w \ln w + 2)}{2tw \ln^3 w} \, .$$

Instead, we will first optimize com_2 as a function of t, and then we will "near optimize" the result as a function of w. By doing so, we obtain a CPIR protocol that has a rate very close to the rate of [10], but with a much simpler analysis.

We will find the optimal value of t by requiring that

$$\frac{\partial \mathsf{com}_2}{\partial t} = \frac{(t^2 \kappa - (w-1)\ell) \log_w n}{t^2} = 0 \, .$$

Since $n \neq 0$, this holds if

$$t = t_{opt} := \sqrt{(w-1)\ell / \kappa} \, .$$

Clearly,

$$\mathsf{com}_2(w, n, \ell, \kappa, t_{opt}) =$$
$$\ell + \frac{2\sqrt{w-1}}{\log_2 w} \cdot \sqrt{\ell \kappa} \cdot \log_2 n + \frac{(w-1)(\log_w n + 1) \log_w n}{2} \cdot \kappa \, . \tag{3}$$

Finding a value of w that optimizes this function seems to be also complicated. Hence, as in [10], we now choose w that just minimizes the most significant term in com_2 that depends on w, i.e., the second term, hoping that the result w will be close to the optimal. The second additive term in the right hand side of Eq. (3) is minimized when

$$\frac{d}{dw} \frac{\sqrt{w-1}}{\log_2 w} = \frac{(w \ln w - 2w + 2) \ln 2}{2\sqrt{w-1} \cdot w \ln^2 w} = 0 \, ,$$

that is, when

$$w = -\frac{2}{W(-2/e^2)} \approx 4.92 \ . \tag{4}$$

Since w has to be an integer, we take $w = 5$, exactly as in [10]. Then, $t_{opt} = 2\sqrt{\ell/\kappa}$. Thus, recalling that $\ell = t \cdot s\kappa$, we get that

$$s = \frac{\ell}{t_{opt}\kappa} = \frac{\ell}{2\sqrt{\ell/\kappa} \cdot \kappa} = \frac{1}{2} \cdot \sqrt{\ell/\kappa} \ .$$

4.2 Full Protocol

Before giving a full efficiency analysis (it will be done in Sect. 5), we now take a step back and give a detailed description of the resulting $(n, 1)$-CPIR protocol. In the description below we do not assume that (say) n is a power of w, hence we will use the $\lceil \cdot \rceil$ function to compute intermediate parameters. See Fig. 3 for a full description. We emphasize that—except the different choice of parameters—this is the same protocol as described in Sect. 3.3 and hence we omit repeating the intuition.

4.3 Security Proof

Lemma 1. *Assume that the underlying public-key cryptosystem is IND-CPA secure. Then, the new CPIR protocol is IND-CPA secure.*

Proof (Sketch). The sender, not having access to the secret key, only sees a vector of ciphertexts $(Q_{00}, \ldots, Q_{m-1,w-2})$. Hence, the security of the CPIR protocol is guaranteed by the IND-CPA security of the cryptosystem via a standard hybrid argument. □

5 Communication Efficiency Analysis

5.1 Asymptotic Analysis

The given parameter choice results in the following theorem.

Theorem 1. *Assume that $s = \sqrt{\ell/\kappa}/2$ and $\log_5 n$ are integers. There exists an $(n, 1)$-CPIR protocol for ℓ-bit strings with communication complexity*

$$\mathsf{com}_2(5, n, \ell, \kappa, 2\sqrt{\ell/\kappa}) = \ell + \frac{4}{\log_2 5} \cdot \sqrt{\ell\kappa} \cdot \log_2 n + 2\left(\log_5^2 n + \log_5 n\right)\kappa \ .$$

Proof. The result follows from preceding discussion. □

Parameters: $\kappa, n, \ell, t = \lceil 2\sqrt{\ell/\kappa} \rceil, s = \lceil \ell/(t\kappa) \rceil, w = 5, m = \lceil \log_w n \rceil$.

Receiver's $\mathsf{Query}^{new}(n, \ell; x)$:

    Generate a new public and secret key pair $(\mathsf{pk}, \mathsf{sk})$ for the Damgård-Jurik cryptosystem.

    Write $x = \sum_{d=0}^{m-1} x_d w^d$ for $x_d \in \{0, \dots, w - 1\}$.

    For $d = 0$ to $m - 1$:

       1. For $j = 0$ to $w - 2$:

          (a) Generate a new randomizer $r_{dj} \leftarrow \Re_{\mathsf{pk}}$

          (b) Let $Q_{dj} \leftarrow \mathsf{Enc}_{\mathsf{pk}}^{s+d-1}([x_d = j]; r_{dj})$

       2. Compute $Q_{d,w-1} \leftarrow \mathsf{Enc}_{\mathsf{pk}}^{s+d-1}(1;1)/\prod_{j=0}^{w-2} Q_{dj}$

    Send pk and $\mathsf{Query}_{\mathsf{pk}}(n, \ell, x) := \boldsymbol{Q} = (Q_{dj})_{d \in [0, m-1], j \in [0, w-2]}$ to the sender

Sender's $\mathsf{Reply}_{\mathsf{pk}}^{new}(n, \ell; \boldsymbol{f}, \boldsymbol{Q})$:

    For $i = 0$ to $n - 1$:

       1. Denote $L_{0,i} = f_i$

       2. Write $L_{0,i} = (L_{0,i,0}, \dots, L_{0,i,t-1})$, with $|L_{0,i,z}| = s\kappa$

    For $d = 0$ to $m - 1$:

       1. Compute $Q_{d,w-1} \leftarrow \mathsf{Enc}_{\mathsf{pk}}^{s+d-1}(1;1)/\prod_{j=0}^{w-2} Q_{dj}$

       2. For $i = 0$ to $n/w^{d+1} - 1$:

          (a) For $z = 0$ to $t - 1$:

             i. $L_{d+1,i,z} = \mathsf{Enc}_{\mathsf{pk}}^{s+d-1}(0; r'_{diz}) \cdot \prod_{j=0}^{w-1} Q_{dj}^{L_{d,iw+j,z}}$ for random $r'_{diz} \leftarrow \Re_{\mathsf{pk}}$

    Let $\boldsymbol{R} = (R_0, \dots, R_{t-1}) := (L_{m,0,0}, \dots, L_{m,0,t-1})$.

    Return $\mathsf{Reply}_{\mathsf{pk}}(n, \ell; \boldsymbol{f}, \boldsymbol{Q}) - \boldsymbol{R}$.

Receiver's $\mathsf{Answer}_{\mathsf{sk}}^{new}(n, \ell; \boldsymbol{R})$:

    For $d = m - 1$ downto 0:

       1. For $z = 0$ to $t - 1$: $R_z \leftarrow \mathsf{Dec}_{\mathsf{sk}}^{s+d}(R_z)$

    Return $f_x = (R_0, \dots, R_{t-1})$

Fig. 3. Full description of the new $(n, 1)$-CPIR protocol

Note that $4/\log_2 5 \approx 1.72$. Note also that

$$\mathsf{rec}_2(5, n, \ell, \kappa, 2\sqrt{\ell/\kappa}) = \frac{2}{\log_2 5} \cdot \sqrt{\ell\kappa} \cdot \log_2 n + 2\left(\log_5^2 n + \log_5 n\right)\kappa \ ,$$

$$\mathsf{sen}_2(5, n, \ell, \kappa, 2\sqrt{\ell/\kappa}) = \ell + \frac{2}{\log_2 5} \cdot \sqrt{\ell\kappa} \cdot \log_2 n \ ,$$

and hence rec_2 is sublinear in ℓ.

To compare, the $(n, 1)$-CPIR protocol of [10] (see Cor. 1 therein) achieves communication complexity

$$\ell + \frac{4}{\log_2 5} \cdot \sqrt{\ell\kappa} \cdot \log_2 n + 2\left(\log_5^2 n + \log_5 n\right)\kappa + O(\ell^{-1/2}) \ .$$

Thus, the $(n, 1)$-CPIR protocol from the current paper has *essentially* the same communication as in [10] (the first three terms of the series expansion of the communication function com are the same as in [10]), but with a much simpler analysis (and construction).

5.2 Optimization w.r.t. n

Consider now the task of optimization com_2 (as in Eq. (1)) as a function of n.

First, finding of the optimal t_{opt} does not depend on whether we optimize as a function of ℓ or n. Hence, we will assume that $t_{opt} = \sqrt{(w-1)\ell/\kappa}$, as before. Writing down the expression for com_2 as a—finite—series in $\log_2 n$, we get

$$
\begin{aligned}
\mathsf{com}_2(w, n, \ell, \kappa, t_{opt}) = & \ell + \frac{(w-1)\kappa}{2\log_2^2 w} \cdot \log_2^2 n \\
& + \frac{4\sqrt{w-1}\sqrt{\ell\kappa} + (w-1)\kappa}{2\log_2 w} \cdot \log_2 n \;.
\end{aligned}
$$

Interestingly enough, the second additive term of this expression is minimized when $w = -\frac{2}{W(-2/e^2)} \approx 4.92 \approx 5$, which seems to hint that this value of w may be close to the global minimum.

5.3 Rate

Assume again that s and $\log_5 n$ are integers. By dividing the length of useful information, $\log_2 n + \ell$, with the communication (3), we get that the new CPIR has rate

$$
\begin{aligned}
R = & \frac{\log_2 n + \ell}{\mathsf{com}_2(w, n, \ell, \kappa, t_{opt})} \\
= & 1 - 2\sqrt{(w-1)\kappa/\ell}\log_w n + \frac{2\log_2 n + (w-1)\kappa\log_w n(7\log_w n - 1)}{2\ell} \quad (5) \\
& + O(\ell^{-3/2}) \;.
\end{aligned}
$$

Indeed, the communication function

$$
\mathsf{com}_2(w, n, \ell, \kappa, t_{opt}) = \sum_{i=0}^{\infty} a_i \ell^{1-i/2}
$$

is given by Eq. (3), where $a_0 = 1$, $a_1 = 2\sqrt{(w-1)\kappa}\log_w n$, $a_2 = ((w-1)\kappa(\log_w n + 1)\log_w n)/2$, $a_i = 0$, where $i \geq 3$. Let

$$
R = \sum_{i=0}^{\infty} b_i \ell^{1-i/2} \;.
$$

We find b_i from the condition $\mathsf{com}_2(w, n, \ell, \kappa, t_{opt}) \cdot R = \log_2 n + \ell$ comparing coefficients of different powers:

$$
\begin{array}{llll}
\ell^2 : & a_0 b_0 = 0 \Rightarrow & b_0 = 0 \ , \\
\ell^{3/2} : & a_0 b_1 + a_1 b_0 = 0 \Rightarrow & b_1 = 0 \ , \\
\ell : & a_0 b_2 + a_1 b_1 + a_2 b_0 = 1 \Rightarrow & b_2 = 1 \ , \\
\ell^{1/2} : & a_0 b_3 + a_1 b_2 + a_2 b_1 = 0 \Rightarrow & b_3 = -a_1 \ , \\
\ell^0 : & a_0 b_4 + a_1 b_3 + a_2 b_2 = \log_2 n \Rightarrow & b_4 = \log_2 n + a_1^2 - a_2 \ , \\
\ell^i \ , i < 0 : & \displaystyle\sum_{i=0}^{n} a_i b_{n-i} = 0 \Rightarrow & b_i \ .
\end{array}
$$

Thus we arrive to Eq. (5).

One can verify that the second term of Eq. (5) is minimized when w is as in Eq. (4). Assuming $w = 5$, the rate is

$$
1 - \frac{4}{\log_2 5} \cdot \sqrt{\kappa/\ell} \cdot \log_2 n + ((14\kappa \log_5 n - 2\kappa + \log_2 5) \log_5 n) \cdot \frac{1}{\ell} + O(\ell^{-3/2}) \ .
$$

See Sect. 5.4 for a figure showing how the rate grows as a function of ℓ/κ for a concrete value of n.

5.4   Concrete Analysis

If the prerequisites of the theorem are not fulfilled (e.g., n is not a power of w), we need to use ceiling function in the computation of the communication function, that is, we are interested in the function $\lceil \mathsf{com}_2(\dots) \rceil := \lceil \mathsf{rec}_2(\dots) \rceil + \lceil \mathsf{sen}_2(\dots) \rceil$.

Kiayias et al. [10] gave a few numerical examples of the efficiency of their CPIR protocol. In Fig. 1, we will give a comparison with the current work; the columns "theoretical" give the value of the function com_2, while the columns "With rounding" give the value of the function $\lceil \mathsf{com}_2 \rceil$. In all cases, $\kappa = 2048$ and $n = w^m = 5^7$. As we can see, due to the rounding errors present in the protocol of [10], the current work achieves always slightly better efficiency.

On Fig. 4, we depict the rate of the $\lceil \mathsf{com}_2 \rceil$ of the new CPIR protocol as a function of $\log_2(\ell/\kappa)$. In particular, the rate of the protocol from the current paper (when rounding included) is 0.917714 for $\ell = 10^5\kappa$ and 0.997207κ for $\ell = 10^8\kappa$. Computing a similar graphic for the CPIR protocol of [10] would be quite time consuming.

If n is arbitrary (not a power of w), then a standard approach is to add to the database a number of dummy elements so as to increase the database size to the next power of w. This will incur similar—very small!—penalties for the protocols of [10] and of the current paper. For example, consider the cases $\kappa = 2048$, $\ell = 10^5\kappa$, and $w = 5$. If $n = 5^7$ is increased to $n = 5^7 + 1$ (the worst case, since one has to add $5^7 - 1$ dummy elements), the rate will decrease from 0.917714 to 0.906919.

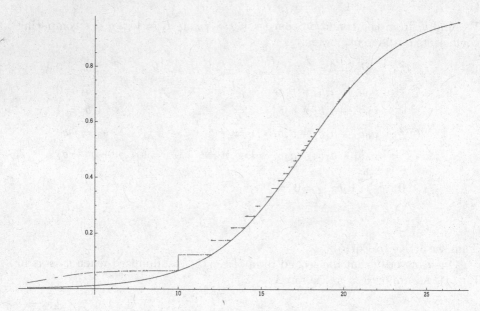

Fig. 4. The rate of the new CPIR protocol as a function of $\log_2(\ell/\kappa)$, i.e., on logarithmic scale, for $w = 5$, $n = 5^7$ and $\kappa = 2048$. The smooth (blue) line corresponds to the case without rounding errors. The jumpy (purple) line corresponds to the case with rounding errors; note that it also rounds up the non-private case, i.e., it uses $\ell + \lceil \log_2 n \rceil$ as the amount of useful information. This explains why the case with rounding errors usually has a better rate than the case without (Color figure online)

Finally, the problem of optimizing the protocol for small values of ℓ is clearly out of scope for the current work since we try to decrease rate for *large* values of ℓ. See, e.g., Sect. 3 of [12] for a discussion of the case of small ℓ.

6   Open Problems

A major open problem left by the current work is to construct a CPIR protocol where the rate function grows faster than Eq. (5), or to show that this is not possible. An impossibility proof might be possible in some restricted model.

The second open problem is to construct a rate-optimal CPIR protocol with the better computational complexity. (See [10] for a detailed discussion about the computational complexity.)

Acknowledgment. The authors were supported by the European Union's Horizon 2020 research and innovation programme under grant agreement No. 653497 (project PANORAMIX). The first (resp., the second) author was supported by institutional research funding IUT2-1 (resp., IUT20-57) of the Estonian Ministry of Education and Research.

References

1. Blake, I.F., Kolesnikov, V.: Strong conditional oblivious transfer and computing on intervals. In: Lee, P.J. (ed.) ASIACRYPT 2004. LNCS, vol. 3329, pp. 515–529. Springer, Heidelberg (2004). https://doi.org/10.1007/978-3-540-30539-2_36
2. Bresson, E., Catalano, D., Pointcheval, D.: A simple public-key cryptosystem with a double trapdoor decryption mechanism and its applications. In: Laih, C.-S. (ed.) ASIACRYPT 2003. LNCS, vol. 2894, pp. 37–54. Springer, Heidelberg (2003). https://doi.org/10.1007/978-3-540-40061-5_3
3. Cachin, C., Micali, S., Stadler, M.: Computationally private information retrieval with polylogarithmic communication. In: Stern, J. (ed.) EUROCRYPT 1999. LNCS, vol. 1592, pp. 402–414. Springer, Heidelberg (1999). https://doi.org/10.1007/3-540-48910-X_28
4. Damgård, I., Jurik, M.: A generalisation, a simplification and some applications of Paillier's probabilistic public-key system. In: Kim, K. (ed.) PKC 2001. LNCS, vol. 1992, pp. 119–136. Springer, Heidelberg (2001). https://doi.org/10.1007/3-540-44586-2_9
5. Damgård, I., Jurik, M.: A length-flexible threshold cryptosystem with applications. In: Safavi-Naini, R., Seberry, J. (eds.) ACISP 2003. LNCS, vol. 2727, pp. 350–364. Springer, Heidelberg (2003). https://doi.org/10.1007/3-540-45067-X_30
6. Gentry, C., Ramzan, Z.: Single-database private information retrieval with constant communication rate. In: Caires, L., Italiano, G.F., Monteiro, L., Palamidessi, C., Yung, M. (eds.) ICALP 2005. LNCS, vol. 3580, pp. 803–815. Springer, Heidelberg (2005). https://doi.org/10.1007/11523468_65
7. Gjøsteen, K., Strand, M.: Can there be efficient and natural FHE schemes? Technical report 2016/105, IACR (2016). http://eprint.iacr.org/2016/105. Accessed June 2016
8. Ishai, Y., Paskin, A.: Evaluating branching programs on encrypted data. In: Vadhan, S.P. (ed.) TCC 2007. LNCS, vol. 4392, pp. 575–594. Springer, Heidelberg (2007). https://doi.org/10.1007/978-3-540-70936-7_31
9. Kiayias, A., Leonardos, N., Lipmaa, H., Pavlyk, K., Tang, Q.: Communication optimal tardos-based asymmetric fingerprinting. In: Nyberg, K. (ed.) CT-RSA 2015. LNCS, vol. 9048, pp. 469–486. Springer, Cham (2015). https://doi.org/10.1007/978-3-319-16715-2_25
10. Kiayias, A., Leonardos, N., Lipmaa, H., Pavlyk, K., Tang, Q.: Optimal rate private information retrieval from homomorphic encryption. Proc. Priv. Enhancing Technol. **2015**(2), 222–243 (2015)
11. Kushilevitz, E., Ostrovsky, R.: Replication is not needed: single database, computationally-private information retrieval. In: FOCS 1997, pp. 364–373 (1997)
12. Lipmaa, H.: An oblivious transfer protocol with log-squared communication. In: Zhou, J., Lopez, J., Deng, R.H., Bao, F. (eds.) ISC 2005. LNCS, vol. 3650, pp. 314–328. Springer, Heidelberg (2005). https://doi.org/10.1007/11556992_23
13. Lipmaa, H.: First CPIR protocol with data-dependent computation. In: Lee, D., Hong, S. (eds.) ICISC 2009. LNCS, vol. 5984, pp. 193–210. Springer, Heidelberg (2010). https://doi.org/10.1007/978-3-642-14423-3_14
14. Ostrovsky, R., Skeith, W.E.: Communication complexity in algebraic two-party protocols. In: Wagner, D. (ed.) CRYPTO 2008. LNCS, vol. 5157, pp. 379–396. Springer, Heidelberg (2008). https://doi.org/10.1007/978-3-540-85174-5_21
15. Paillier, P.: Public-key cryptosystems based on composite degree residuosity classes. In: Stern, J. (ed.) EUROCRYPT 1999. LNCS, vol. 1592, pp. 223–238. Springer, Heidelberg (1999). https://doi.org/10.1007/3-540-48910-X_16

16. Stern, J.P.: A new and efficient all-or-nothing disclosure of secrets protocol. In: Ohta, K., Pei, D. (eds.) ASIACRYPT 1998. LNCS, vol. 1514, pp. 357–371. Springer, Heidelberg (1998). https://doi.org/10.1007/3-540-49649-1_28
17. Wegener, I.: Branching Programs and Binary Decision Diagrams: Theory and Applications. Monographs on Discrete Mathematics and Applications. Society for Industrial Mathematics, Philadelphia (2000)

Correction to: Why Banker Bob (Still) Can't Get TLS Right: A Security Analysis of TLS in Leading UK Banking Apps

Tom Chothia, Flavio D. Garcia, Chris Heppell,
and Chris McMahon Stone

Correction to:
Chapter "Why Banker Bob (Still) Can't Get TLS Right:
A Security Analysis of TLS in Leading UK Banking Apps" in:
A. Kiayias (Ed.): *Financial Cryptography and Data Security*,
LNCS 10322, https://doi.org/10.1007/978-3-319-70972-7_33

In an older version of this paper, there was error in the author name, "Chris Heppel" was incorrect. This has been corrected to "Chris Heppell".

The updated original version of this chapter can be found at
https://doi.org/10.1007/978-3-319-70972-7_33

Poster Papers

Accountability and Integrity for Data Management Using Blockchains (Poster)

Anirban Basu[1](✉), Joshua Jeeson Daniel[2], Sushmita Ruj[3],
Mohammad Shahriar Rahman[1], Theo Dimitrakos[4], and Shinsaku Kiyomoto[1]

[1] KDDI Research, Fujimino, Japan
{basu,mohammad,kiyomoto}@kddi-research.jp
[2] British Telecom, London, UK
joshua.daniel@bt.com
[3] Indian Statistical Institute, Chennai, India
sush@isical.ac.in
[4] University of Kent, Canterbury, UK
t.dimitrakos@kent.ac.uk

Abstract. The proliferation of cloud-hosted Internet-based services has succeeded atop the storage and use of massive amounts of personal data from individual users, who have limited or no control over how data about them are stored, transferred across domain boundaries and used for large-scale data analytics. Regulations (e.g., the EU GDPR 2016/679) are being adopted that, amongst other things, seek accountability in access to such personal data. In order to ensure technical compliance with such data protection regulations, we envisage a permissioned blockchain-supported framework that ensures data integrity, data protection policy uniformity and integrity, and accountability of operations done on the data stored across multiple cloud service providers. This blockchain will be hosted by data service providers, data protection service providers, regulators and other such stakeholders. We assume that every operation on personal data is accounted for by the blockchain. Various proofs can be used, with this framework for accountability, in the form of smart contracts to support integrity and accountability verifications for operations on the data. While the actual data will be stored in one or more cloud environments, the blockchain will store information on any operation on the data as a transaction on that data. Figure 1 is an illustration of the information about a transaction. Implementing this framework over a multi-cloud scenario and running user trials constitute avenues of future work.

Anirban Basu—is also a Visiting Research Fellow at the University of Sussex, UK and Rutgers University, USA.

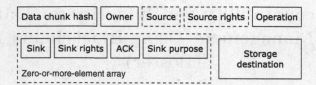

Fig. 1. An operation on data, represented as a 'transaction' is stored in the blockchain for accountability. The source entity, if different from the data owner, is the initiator of the operation while one or more sink entities are its optional beneficiaries. Data storage could involve multi-cloud and cross-border scenarios.

The Amount as a Predictor of Transaction Fraud (Poster)

Niek J. Bouman[1]([envelope]) and Martha E. Nikolaou[2]

[1] ABN AMRO Bank e-Channel Security Research, Amsterdam, The Netherlands
niek.bouman@nl.abnamro.com
[2] IBM Analytics, IBM, Amsterdam, The Netherlands
m.e.nikolaou@nl.ibm.com

Abstract. New European banking legislation (Payment Services Directive 2) gives rise to a payment channel on which a so-called Third Party Payment Service Provider sits in between of the bank and the customer. It is expected that banks will see less customer meta-data (IP addresses, browser cookies, etc.) on this payment channel. In the context of transaction-fraud detection, this motivates research into detection methods that are solely based on the primary features of a transaction, like amount, timestamp, and payor and payee account numbers. In this work we focus on the amount of a transaction as a predictor of fraud. Although we do not claim that the transaction amount alone su ces to distinguish between fraudulent and non-fraudulent transactions with acceptable performance, we demonstrate empirically that the amount does contain valuable information about the likelihood of fraud, which is most useful when combined with other transaction-fraud classifiers based on different features. Our approach is to estimate conditional discrete probability distributions of the amount (with single-cent precision, and up to some maximum amount), conditioned on whether the corresponding transaction is fraudulent or non-fraudulent. The challenging part is to estimate the distribution of the fraudulent amounts: our training data (a set of past transactions) is very skewed towards non-fraudulent transactions, and moreover the number of observations is four orders of magnitude smaller than the size of the support of the distribution that we would like to estimate. To deal with this issue, we model the distribution of fraudulent amounts as a mixture of several components consisting of spikes (Kronecker delta functions) at equispaced points in the support, which we will call combs, for example, capturing multiples of ten euros. Such a "multiples-of-ten comb," will, given an observation of, say, 60 euros, influence the probability of all amounts that are multiples of 10. Hence, the combs establish dependencies between certain amounts, which aid in inferring probabilities of amounts which do not occur in the training set. We infer the mixture weights using Markov-Chain Monte Carlo sampling. The key in making the inference procedure practically feasible is to exploit the sparsity in the histogram of the fraudulent-transaction amounts.

© International Financial Cryptography Association 2017
A. Kiayias (Ed.): FC 2017, LNCS 10322, p. 643, 2017.
https://doi.org/10.1007/978-3-319-70972-7

Σ-State Authentication Language, an Alternative to Bitcoin Script (Poster)

Alexander Chepurnoy[✉]

IOHK Research, Sestroretsk, Russia
alex.chepurnoy@iohk.io

Abstract. Every coin in Bitcoin is protected by a program in stack-based Script language. An interpreter for the language is evaluating the program against a redeeming program (in the same language) as well as a context (few variables containing information about a spending transaction and the blockchain), producing a single boolean value as a result. While Bitcoin Script allows for some contracts to be programmed, its abilities are limited while many instructions were removed after denial-of-service or security issues discovered. To add new cryptographic primitives, for example, ring signatures, a hard-fork is required. Generalizing the Bitcoin Script, we introduce a notion of an authentication language where a verifier is running an interpreter which three inputs are a proposition defined in terms of the language, a context and also a proof (not necessarily defined in the same language) generated by a prover for the proposition against the same context. The interpreter is producing a boolean value and must finish evaluation for any possible inputs within constant time. We propose an alternative authentication language, named Σ-State. It defines guarding proposition for a coin as a logic formula which combines predicates over a context and cryptographic statements provable via Σ-protocols with AND, OR, k-out-of-n connectives. A prover willing to spend the coin first reduces the compound proposition to a compound cryptographic statement by evaluating predicates over known shared context (state of the blockchain system and a spending transaction). Then the prover is turning a corresponding Σ-protocol into a signature with the help of a Fiat-Shamir transformation. A verifier (a full-node in a blockchain setting) checks the proposition against the context and the signature with an interpreter. Language expressiveness is defined by a set of predicates over context and a set of cryptographic statements. We show how the latter could be updated with a soft-fork by using a language like ZKPDL (by Meiklejohn et al. Usenix

© International Financial Cryptography Association 2017
A. Kiayias (Ed.): FC 2017, LNCS 10322, pp. 644–645, 2017.
https://doi.org/10.1007/978-3-319-70972-7

Security, 2010), and how the former could be updated with a soft-fork by using versioning conventions. We propose a set of context predicates for a Bitcoin-like cryptocurrency with a guarantee of constant verification time. We provide several examples: ring and threshold signatures, pre-issued mining rewards, crowdfunding, demurrage currency.

Broker-Mediated Trade Finance
with Blockchains
(Poster)

Mohammad Shahriar Rahman$^{(\boxtimes)}$, Anirban Basu, and Shinsaku Kiyomoto

KDDI Research, Fujimino, Japan
{mohammad,basu,kiyomoto}@kddi-research.jp

Abstract. Processing efficiency and transparency to all parties are the two major factors in trade finance. Geographical distances may hinder parties from verifying each other's credit guarantees without an intermediary or a broker. We propose a blockchain-based trade solution whereby information is shared among a seller, a broker, a buyer and their respective banks on a private distributed ledger that enables them to execute a trade deal automatically through a series of digital smart contracts. Each action in the workflow is captured in a permissioned blockchain, B, giving transparency to authorized participants. The protocol consists of six parties: (1) Buyer, (2) Buyer's bank ($\mathcal{B}_1$), (3) Broker (4) Broker's bank ($\mathcal{B}_2$), (5) Seller, and (6) Seller's bank ($\mathcal{B}_3$). Initially, the buyer, broker and seller register themselves with the system and create their individual ID, password pairs to login to the system for blockchain operations in the later stage. The protocol invloving the blockchain operations consists of the following steps: (1) Buyer creates a MCG (Master Credit Guarantee) document for $\mathcal{B}_1$ to review and stores it in B. (2) $\mathcal{B}_1$ receives notification to review the MCG. It can approve or reject it based on the data provided. Upon approval, access is then provided to $\mathcal{B}_2$ for approval. (3) $\mathcal{B}_2$ approves or rejects the MCG. Once approved, the broker is able to view the MCG requirements and relevant documents. (4) Broker creates a BCG (Back-to-back Credit Guarantee) document for $\mathcal{B}_2$ to review and stores it in B. (5) $\mathcal{B}_2$ receives notification to review the BCG and can then approve or reject it based on the data provided. Upon approval, access is then provided to $\mathcal{B}_3$ automatically for approval. (6) $\mathcal{B}_3$ approves or rejects the BCG. Once approved, the seller is able to view the BCG requirements and relevant documents. (7) Seller completes the shipment, adds invoice and selling application data of required documents. These documents are stored in B. (8) $\mathcal{B}_3$ approves or rejects the application and documents. (9) Broker stores necessary application data and documents in B. (10) $\mathcal{B}_2$ approves or rejects the application and documents. If approved, the BCG goes straight to completed status; otherwise, it is sent to the broker for settlement. (11) $\mathcal{B}_3$ reviews the data and documents against the MCG requirements. If approved, the MCG goes straight to completed status; otherwise, it is sent to the buyer for settlement. (12) If required due to a discrepancy, the buyer can review the export documents and approve or reject them.

Anirban Basu—is also a Visiting Research Fellow at the University of Sussex, UK and Rutgers University, USA.

© International Financial Cryptography Association 2017
A. Kiayias (Ed.): FC 2017, LNCS 10322, p. 646, 2017.
https://doi.org/10.1007/978-3-319-70972-7

OpenTimestamps: Securing Software Updates Using the Bitcoin Blockchain (Poster)

Peter Todd[1] and Harry Halpin[2(✉)]

[1] Toronto, Canada
peter@petertodd.org
[2] Inria, 2 rue Simone Iff, 75012 Paris, France
harry.halpin@inria.fr

Abstract. A timestamp is a statement that a record existed prior to the point in time given by the timestamp. A cryptographically-verified timestamp also proves the integrity of the record using a hash function (and as such is a "proof of existence"). Yet how do we prove the time given by the timestamp is correct? For example, time-stamps are critical in software updates, so a user can verify that they have the latest updates and all users have received the same update. An adversary with insider access can change all the time-stamps or install a backdoor, and could even compel key material to fake signatures (a concern in the Apple vs. FBI case). An powerful adversary could even control and isolate the entire network of a user. The Bitcoin blockchain provides a notary that can prove with reason (due to hashing power already put into Bitcoin) that one is connected to a larger network and that a time-stamp for a particular update is correct. OpenTimestamps adds the ability to add generic cryptographic time stamps for any record to the Bitcoin blockchain by taking advantage of the block header field nTime, so using Bitcoin block headers as attestations for a cryptographic time-stamp, with the hash of the record being a commitment that can be independently verified by any client. Unlike other existing Bitcoin-based timestamp solutions where large numbers of commitments (such as for an entire filesystem) inefficiently require a new transaction for each file to the Bitcoin blockchain, OpenTimestamps instead creates a separate Merkle Tree that contains the hash of each file, and only the timestamp the tip of that tree is recorded in a single transaction. Aggregation servers that allow large sets of files submitted by separate and possibly anonymous users to be aggregated. Although the concept is simple (for links to code and a tutorial see http://opentimestamps.org) the poster will describe OpenTimestamps in more detail, including a graph demonstrating time-to-commit and verification of time-stamps for updates of a real-world large encrypted e-mail system LEAP (built by zriseup.net) as well as the underlying Debian distribution. Since the largest problem OpenTimestamps faces is variation in accuracy of when the timestamps are added to the blockchain (ranging from minutes to up to a few hours), the second graph empirically measures this variation. Currently, this delay is dealt with by public calendering services that record the actual timestamp of an aggregated group of records and then promise to commit them to the Bitcoin blockchain. Lastly, we will discuss next steps including the use of multiple notaries and extensions to permissioned "private" blockchains.

© International Financial Cryptography Association 2017
A. Kiayias (Ed.): FC 2017, LNCS 10322, p. 647, 2017.
https://doi.org/10.1007/978-3-319-70972-7

Author Index

Printed in the United States
by Baker & Taylor Publisher Services